A
GENEVA
SERIES
COMMENTARY

GENESIS

GENESIS

John Calvin

Translated and edited by
John King M.A.

TWO VOLUMES IN ONE

THE BANNER OF TRUTH TRUST

THE BANNER OF TRUTH TRUST
3 *Murrayfield Road, Edinburgh* EH12 6EL
P.O. Box 652, *Carlisle, Pennsylvania* 17013, *U.S.A.*

*

First published in Latin 1554
First English Translation 1578
This edition reprinted from the Calvin
Translation Society edition of 1847
1965
Reprinted 1975

ISBN 0 85151 093 0

*

Printed in Great Britain by offset lithography by
Billing & Sons Limited, Guildford and London

TRANSLATOR'S PREFACE

SEVERAL of the COMMENTARIES OF CALVIN on different portions of the Holy Scripture having been for some time before the public, through the labours of THE CALVIN SOCIETY; it is not improbable that the readers of the following pages will have already become in a great degree familiar with the writings of this celebrated Reformer.

It may, perhaps, therefore be thought an unnecessary, if not a presumptuous undertaking, to preface the present work with any general observations on the character of CALVIN'S EXPOSITORY WRITINGS. But though the Commentary on GENESIS was neither the first which Calvin wrote, nor the first which the Calvin Society has republished; yet since, in the ultimate arrangement of the Commentaries it must take the foremost place, the Editor has determined to offer such preliminary remarks as may seem desirable for a reader who begins to read the Commentaries of Calvin, as he begins to read the Bible itself, at the Book of Genesis. If, in taking such a course, he is charged with repeating some things which have been said by others before him, he will not be extremely anxious either to defend himself from the charge or to meet it with a denial.

It seems to be now generally admitted that though, in the

brilliant constellation formed by the master-spirits of the
REFORMATION, there were those who, in some respects, shone
with brighter lustre than CALVIN, yet, as a Commentator on
Holy Scripture, he far outshines them all.

There is scarcely anything in which the wisdom of God
has been more conspicuous, than in his choice of instruments
for carrying into execution the different parts of that mighty
revolution of sentiment, which affected, more or less, every
portion of Europe during the sixteenth century.

Long before the issue of the movement was seen or apprehended, we behold ERASMUS, the most accomplished scholar
of the age, acting unconsciously as the pioneer of a Reformation, which at length he not only opposed, but apparently
hated. He had been raised up by God to lash the vices of
the Clergy, to expose the ignorance, venality, and sloth of the
Mendicant Orders, and to exhibit the follies of Romanism in
sarcastic invectives rendered imperishable by the elegant La-
tinity in which they were clothed. But he did still more.
The world is indebted to him for the first edition of the entire
New Testament in the Original Greek.[1] He had also the
honour of being the first modern translator of the New Testament into Latin.[2] He published a valuable critical Commentary on the New Testament, which was early translated
into English, and ordered to be placed in the Churches.[3]
Yet, great as the service undoubtedly was which he rendered
to the cause of truth, he never dared to cast the yoke of

---

[1] Horne's Introduction, vol. v. Part I. chap. i. sect. iv. London, 1846.
[2] Ibid. vol. v. Part I. chap. i. sect. vii.
[3] The Editor has now before him "The first tome or volume of the
paraphrase of Erasmus upon the Newe Testamente," printed in 1548,
with a dedication to King Edward VI., and another to Queen Catherine
Parr, by Nicolas Udal. It appears that Udal translated the Gospels
of St Matthew, St Luke, and St John ; and Thomas Key, that of St
Mark.

Rome from his own neck, never stooped to identify himself with the Protestant Reformers; but lived and died, as there is reason to fear, a mean, truckling, time-serving Romanist, panting for preferment in a Church, the unsoundness of which he had so fearfully exposed. It is not, however, to be denied that God employed him as a most important instrument in shaking the foundations of the Papacy, and in preparing the way for the more successful efforts of more sincere and devoted servants of God.

Among these LUTHER and MELANCTHON in one field, CALVIN and ZUINGLIUS in another, occupy posts of the greatest responsibility and usefulness; but Luther and Calvin are manifestly the great leaders in this cause.

In qualifications necessary for the commencing of this great struggle, we readily yield the palm to LUTHER. His indomitable energy, his noble bearing, his contempt for danger, his transparent honesty of purpose, his fiery zeal, his generous frankness—though too often degenerating into peremptory vehemence of spirit and rudeness of manner—eminently fitted him to take the lead in a warfare where so much was to be braved, to be endured, and to be accomplished.

There was still another qualification, which perhaps no man ever possessed in so high a degree as the Saxon Reformer, and that consisted in the prodigious mastery he had over his own mother-tongue. He seized on the rude, yet nervous and copious German of his ancestors, and taught it to speak with a combination of melody and force, which it had never known before. And his vernacular translation of the Holy Scriptures, in opening to the millions of the German empire the Fount of eternal life, also revealed to them the hitherto hidden beauties and powers of their own masculine tongue.

CALVIN, like Luther, was a man of courage; but he wanted Luther's fire, he wanted Luther's ardent frankness of disposition; he wanted, in short, the faculty which Luther possessed in a pre-eminent degree, of laying hold on the affections, and of kindling the enthusiasm of a mighty nation.

CALVIN, like Luther too, was a Translator of the Scriptures, and it is worthy of remark, that he also wrote in a far purer and better style than any of his contemporaries, or than any writers of an age near his own. But he had not the honour, which God conferred on Luther, of sending forth the sacred volume as a whole, through that great nation in which his language was spoken, and of thus pouring, by one single act, a flood of light upon millions of his countrymen.

But whatever advantage may lie on the side of LUTHER in the comparison, so far as it has yet been carried, we shall find it on the side of CALVIN in grasp of intellect, in discriminating power, in calmness, clearness and force of argument, in patience of research, in solid learning, in every quality, in short, which is essential to an Expositor of Holy Writ. We are the better able to institute this comparison, because LUTHER himself wrote a Commentary on the Scriptures; but the slightest inspection of the two Commentaries will convince the Reader of CALVIN's intellectual superiority; and will show, that as a faithful, penetrating, and judicious Expounder of the Holy Spirit's meaning in the Scriptures, he left the great Leader of the Reformation at an immeasurable distance behind.[1]

[1] Nothing is farther from the Editor's intention than to speak slightingly of Luther's Commentaries. That on the Galatians alone has laid the Church of Christ under lasting obligation to its Author. But its excellencies are not of the same order with those which mark the expository writings of Calvin. As a defence of the Gospel of Christ against the prevailing errors of the day—and, alas! of our own day too—it

The doctrinal system of CALVIN is too well known to require explanation in this place. It is however a mistake to suppose that, on those points in which Calvinism is deemed peculiarly to consist, he went a single step farther than LUTHER himself, and the great majority of the Reformers. He states his views with calmness, clearness, and precision ; he reasons on them dispassionately, and never shrinks from any consequences to which he perceives them to lead. But it would be the height of injustice to charge him with obtruding them at every turn upon his reader, or with attempting to force the language of Scripture to bear testimony to his own views.

No writer ever dealt more fairly and honestly by the Word of God. He is scrupulously careful to let it speak for itself, and to guard against every tendency of his own mind to put upon it a questionable meaning for the sake of establishing some doctrine which he feels to be important, or some theory which he is anxious to uphold. This is one of his prime excellencies. He will not maintain any doctrine, however orthodox and essential, by a text of Scripture which to him appears of doubtful application, or of inadequate force. For instance, firmly as he believed the doctrine of the Trinity, he refuses to derive an argument in its favour, from the plural form of the name of God in the first chapter of Genesis. It were easy to multiply examples of this kind, which, whether we agree in his conclusions or not, cannot fail to produce the conviction, that he is, at least, an honest Commentator, and will not make any passage of Scripture speak more or less than, according to his view, its Divine Author intended it to speak. CALVIN has been charged with

stands forth a masterpiece of sound argument and energetic declamation ; and as a balm to wounded consciences, it remains to the present hour without a rival.

ignorance of the language in which the Old Testament was
written. Father Simon says that he scarcely knew more of
Hebrew than the letters! The charge is malicious and ill-
founded. It may, however, be allowed that a critical examination of the text of Holy Scripture was not the end which
CALVIN proposed to himself; nor had he perhaps the materials or the time necessary for that accurate investigation of
words and syllables to which the Scriptures have more
recently been subjected. Still his verbal criticisms are
neither few nor unimportant, though he lays comparatively
little stress upon them himself.[1]

His great strength, however, is seen in the clear, comprehensive view he takes of the subject before him, in the
facility with which he penetrates the meaning of his Author,
in the lucid expression he gives to that meaning, in the variety
of new yet solid and profitable thoughts which he frequently
elicits from what are apparently the least promising portions
of the sacred text, in the admirable precision with which he
unfolds every doctrine of Holy Scripture, whether veiled
under figures and types, or implied in prophetical allusions,
or asserted in the records of the Gospel. As his own mind
was completely imbued with the whole system of divine
truth, and as his capacious memory never seemed to lose anything which it had once apprehended, he was always able to
present a harmonised and consistent view of truth to hi
readers, and to show the relative position in which any given
portion of it stood to all the rest. This has given a completeness and symmetry to his Commentaries which could scarcely

---

[1] The reader is referred, for full information on this subject, to a small
volume entitled, "The Merits of Calvin as an Interpreter of the Holy
Scriptures." By Professor Tholuck of Halle. To which are added,
"Opinions and Testimonies of Foreign and British Divines and Scholars
as to the Importance of the Writings of John Calvin." With a Preface
by the Rev. William Pringle. London, 1845.

have been looked for; as they were not composed in the order in which the Sacred Books stand in the Volume of Inspiration, nor perhaps in any order of which a clear account can now be given. He probably did not, at first, design to expound more than a single Book; and was led onward by the course which his Expository Lectures in public took, to write first on one and then on another, till at length he traversed nearly the whole field of revealed truth.

That, in proceeding with such want of method, his work, instead of degenerating into a congeries of lax and unconnected observations constantly reiterated, should have maintained, to a great degree, the consistency of a regular and consecutive Commentary, is mainly to be imputed to the gigantic intellectual power by which he was distinguished. Through the whole of his writings, this power is everywhere visible, always in action, ingrafting upon every passing incident some forcible remark, which the reader no sooner sees than he wonders that it had not occurred to his own mind. A work so rich in thought is calculated to call into vigorous exercise the intellect of the reader; and, what is the best and highest use of reading, to compel him to think for himself. It is like seed-corn, the parent of the harvest.

It has been objected against CALVIN by Bishop HORSLEY, —no mean authority in Biblical criticism,—that "by his want of taste, and by the poverty of his imagination, he was a most wretched Expositor of the Prophecies,—just as he would have been a wretched expositor of any secular poet." [1]

---

[1] See Horsley's Sermons, vol. i. p. 72.

In opposition to this testimony, it may be well to refer to that of Father Simon, a Roman Catholic, who says, " *Calvinus sublimi ingenio pollebat*," Calvin possessed a sublime genius; and of Scaliger, who exclaims, " *O quam Calvinus bene assequitur mentem prophetarum!—nemo melius*," Oh! how well has Calvin reached the meaning of the prophets —no one better.

It is true, this censure is qualified by the acknowledgment that CALVIN was "a man of great piety, great talents, and great learning." Yet, after all, it would not, perhaps, be difficult to show that, as an expounder of the poetical portions of Holy Scripture,—the Psalms for instance,—Bishop Horsley more frequently errs through an excess of imagination, than Calvin does through the want of it. However this may be, it is not intended here to assert, either that Calvin possessed a high degree of poetical taste, or that he cultivated to any great extent the powers of the imagination. His mind was cast in the more severe mould of chastised, vigorous, and concentrated thought. They who seek for the flowers of poesy must go to some other master; they who would acquire habits of sustained intellectual exercise may spend their days and nights over the pages of Calvin.

But that which gives the greatest charm to these noble compositions is, the genuine spirit of piety which breathes through them. The mind of the writer turns with ease and with obvious delight to the spiritual application of his subject. Hence the heart of the reader is often imperceptibly raised to high and heavenly things. The rare combination of intellect so profound and reasoning so acute, with piety so fervent, inspires the reader with a calm and elevated solemnity, and strengthens his conviction of the excellence and dignity of true religion.

On the mode in which THE EDITOR has executed his task he may be permitted to say, that he has attempted to be faithful as a translator, without binding himself to a servile rendering of word for word, unmindful of the idiomatic differences between one language and another. Yet it has been his determination not to sacrifice sense to sound, nor to depart from the Author's meaning for the sake of giving to any sentence a turn which might seem more agreeable to an English ear. He has occasionally softened an expression which appeared harsh in the original, and would appear harsher still in our own language and in our own times. But in such cases, he has generally placed the Latin expression before the reader in a note. He has done the same, when any sentence appeared capable of a different interpretation from that which is given in the translation. A few passages which justly offend against delicacy are left untranslated; and one it has been thought expedient entirely to omit. Some remarks are, however, made upon it in the proper place.

Clear as the LATIN STYLE OF CALVIN generally is, yet his sententious mode of expressing himself occasionally leaves some ambiguity in his expressions. Such difficulties, however, have generally been overcome by the aid of the valuable FRENCH TRANSLATION, published at Geneva in the year 1564,—the year of CALVIN's death,—of which there is no reason to doubt that CALVIN was the author. Frequent references to this translation in the notes will show to what extent assistance has been derived from it by the Editor.

An ENGLISH TRANSLATION of this Commentary on Genesis, by THOMAS TYMME, in black letter, was printed in the year 1578. It is, upon the whole, fairly executed; but nearly every criticism on Hebrew words is entirely passed over; and where the Translator has not had the sagacity to omit the whole of any such passage, he has betrayed his own ignorance of the language, and obscured the meaning of his author. Tymme claims for Calvin the credit of being the first foreign Protestant Commentator on Genesis who was made to speak in the English language.

The reader will find CALVIN'S LATIN VERSION of the sacred text placed side by side with our own excellent AUTHORISED TRANSLATION.[1] This was thought the best method of meeting the wants of the public. The learned may see Calvin's own words, which they will much prefer to any translation of them, however accurate; the unlearned will have before them that version of the Scriptures which from their youth they have been taught to reverence. Where CALVIN'S version materially differs from our own, and especially where his comments are made on any such different rendering, ample explanation is given in the notes.

The Editor may be expected to say something respecting the notes generally, which he has ventured to append to this Commentary. Some may object that they are too few, others that they are superfluous. It would have been easy to have made them more numerous, had space permitted; and easier still to have omitted them altogether. But the writer of them thought it would hardly be doing justice to CALVIN to leave everything exactly as he found it; for were the distinguished Author of the Commentary now alive to re-edit his own immortal work, there is no doubt that he would reject every error which the increased facilities for criticism would have enabled him to detect, and that he would throw fresh light on many topics which were,

---

[1] The Translator has pleasure in adducing the following testimony to our Authorised version from the pen of that excellent Biblical scholar, Albert Barnes of Philadelphia. "No translation of the Bible was ever made under more happy auspices; and it would now be impossible to furnish another translation in our language under circumstances so propitious. Whether we contemplate the number, the learning, or the piety of the men employed in it; the cool deliberation with which it was executed; the care taken that it should secure the approbation of the most learned men in a country that embosomed a vast amount of literature; the harmony with which they conducted their work; or the comparative perfection of the translation; we see equal cause of gratitude to the great Author of the Bible, that we have so pure a translation of his Word... It has become the standard of our language; and nowhere can the purity and expressive dignity of this language be so fully found as in the Sacred Scriptures."—See *Notes, Explanatory and Practical, on the Gospels*, page 17. London 1846.

in his day, dimly seen, or quite misunderstood. And though it belongs not to an Editor to alter what is erroneous, or to incorporate in his Author's Work any thoughts of his own, or of other men; yet it is not beyond his province,—provided he does it with becoming modesty, and with adequate information,—to point out mistakes, to suggest such considerations as may have led him to conclusions different from those of his Author, and to quote from other Writers passages, sometimes confirmatory of, sometimes adverse to, those advanced in the Work which he presents to the public. Within these limits the Editor has endeavoured to confine himself. How far he has succeeded, it is not for him but for the candid and competent reader to determine.

As it was possible that a doubt might exist whether the version of Scripture used by CALVIN was his own, or whether he had borrowed it from some other source; it was thought worth the labour to investigate the true state of the case, by having recourse to the excellent Library of the British Museum. For this purpose the several versions which CALVIN was most likely to have adopted, had he not made one for himself, were subjected to examination. It was not necessary to refer to any made by Romanists; and those made by Protestants into the Latin language, which there was any probability he should use, were but two. One by SEBASTIAN MUNSTER, printed at Basle with the Hebrew Text, in 1534, from which the version of Calvin varies considerably; the other by LEO JUDA and other learned men, printed at Zurich in 1543, and afterwards reprinted by Robert Stephens in 1545 and 1557. The last of these editions was made use of in comparing the versions of Leo Juda and Calvin; and though there certainly are differences, yet they are so slight as to leave the impression that Calvin took that of Leo Juda as his basis, and only altered it as he saw occasion. To give the reader, however,

the opportunity of judging for himself, a few verses of the
first chapter of Genesis are transcribed from each.

THE VERSION OF LEO JUDA.

1. In principio creavit Deus cœlum et terram.
2. Terra autem erat desolata et
inanis, tenebræque *erant* in superficie voraginis : et Spiritus Dei agitabat sese in superficie aquarum.
3. Dixitque Deus, Sit Lux, et fuit
lux.
4. Viditque Deus lucem quod
esset bona, et divisit Deus lucem à
tenebris.
5. Vocavitque Deus lucem Diem,
et tenebras vocavit Noctem ; fuitque vespera, et fuit mane dies unus.

6. Dixit quoque Deus, Sit expansio, &c.

THE VERSION OF CALVIN.

1. In principio creavit Deus cœlum et terram.
2. Terra autem erat informis et
inanis, tenebræque erant in superficie voraginis : et Spiritus Dei agitabat se in superficie aquarum.
3. Et dixit Deus, Sit Lux, et fuit
lux.
4. Viditque Deus lucem quod bona
esset, et divisit Deus lucem à tenebris.
5. Et vocavit Deus lucem Diem,
et tenebras vocavit Noctem. Fuitque vespera, et fuit mane dies primus.
6. Et dixit Deus, Sit extensio,
&c.

A similar examination was next resorted to, for the purpose
of ascertaining the source of CALVIN'S FRENCH VERSION.
The first printed version of the Scriptures into French was
from the pen of JACQUES LE FEVRE D'ESTAPLES ; or, as he
was more commonly called, Jacobus Faber Stapulensis. It was
printed at Antwerp, by Martin L'Empereur. Though its
Author was in communion with the Church of Rome, yet the
version is " said to be the basis of all subsequent French
Bibles, whether executed by Romanists or Protestants." [1]

The first Protestant French Bible was published by ROBERT
PETER OLIVETAN, with the assistance of his relative, the
illustrious JOHN CALVIN, who corrected the Antwerp edition
wherever it differed from the Hebrew.[2] It might have been
expected that Calvin would have placed this version—made
under his own eye, and perfected by his own assistance—
without alteration at the head of his Commentaries. But it

---

[1] Horne's Introduction, vol. v. p. 116.   [2] *Ibid.* p. 118.

appears that he has not done so, for though he departs but
little from it, he not unfrequently alters a word or two in the
translation.

While on the subject of Versions, it may be added, that in
THE OLD ENGLISH TRANSLATION by Tymme already alluded
to, THE GENEVA VERSION is used. This translation was
made by the learned exiles from England during the Marian
Persecution, and is sometimes distinguished from others by
the name of THE BREECHES BIBLE, on account of the rendering of Gen. iii. 7.[1]

---

[1] Prejudice has existed in some quarters against this version of the
Holy Scriptures, on the ground that its Authors were too deeply imbued
with Calvin's sentiments. Bishop Horsley thus speaks of it :—" This
English translation of the Bible, which is indeed upon the whole a very
good one, and furnished with very edifying notes and illustrations, (except that in many points they savour too much of Calvinism,) was made
and first published at Geneva, by the English Protestants, who fled thither from Mary's persecution. During their residence there, they contracted a veneration for the character of Calvin, which was no more than
was due to his great piety and his great learning: but they unfortunately
contracted also a veneration for his opinions—a veneration more than
was due to the opinions of any uninspired teacher. The bad effects of
this unreasonable partiality, the Church of England feels, in some points,
to the present day." Such language, coming from such a quarter, furnishes strong testimony to the fact, (often very peremptorily and flip-
pantly denied,) that the Church of England has, at least, some leaven
of Calvinism in its composition. More accurate inquiry than Bishop
Horsley's prejudice allowed him to make, would show how largely the
Reformers as a body were indebted to Calvin, how conscious they were
of their obligation, and how deeply their writings were tinctured with
his doctrine. But this is not the place for the discussion of such a
subject. It is more to the purpose to observe, that the version of which
we are now speaking, passed through more editions than any other, in
the early periods of the Reformation ; that it was mainly based upon that
of the martyr Tyndale, that it was the ordinary Family Bible of the nation, and never was superseded till the present Authorised Version was
produced in the reign of James the First.

The version in question has generally been spoken of as the production of the Exiles in Geneva ; but by an accurate investigation of the
subject, Mr Anderson has made it appear highly probable, that the chief,
if not the sole author of this version, was William Whittingham, who
married the sister of John Calvin ; and who, after the Marian persecution had ceased, remained a year and a half in Geneva to finish the work.
On his return to England, he first accompanied the Earl of Warwick on
a mission to the Court of France, and afterwards was made Dean of
Durham. His objection to wear the prescribed habits occasioned him
some trouble.

To give the reader some notion of the order in which CALVIN'S COMMENTARIES succeeded each other, the following List, with the dates appended, taken from Senebier's Literary History of Geneva, is submitted to his consideration:

A *fac-simile* of the title-page of the French Translation of 1563, and of the Dedication to the Duke of Vendome, as a specimen of the French style and spelling of the age, and a further *fac-simile* of the title-page of the English Translation of 1578, as well as of the Dedication to the Earl of Warwick by Thomas Tymme, prefixed to the latter, will be found in this edition. An accurate copy of the Map, roughly sketched

The circulation of this Bible in England was greatly promoted by the zealous exertions of John Bodley, Esq., a native of Exeter, an exile, during Mary's reign, at Geneva, and the father of Sir Thomas Bodley, the munificent founder of the Bodleian Library at Oxford. John Bodley obtained a patent for printing this Bible from Queen Elizabeth, in the year 1560. See "Annals of the English Bible," by Christopher Anderson, vol. ii. pp. 322-324.

[1] Perfect accuracy is, perhaps, not to be expected in all these dates. Beza, in his Life of Calvin, says only that six of St Paul's Epistles were published this year, which were the two to the Corinthians, that to the Galatians, the Ephesians, the Philippians, and the Colossians.

[2] Beza places the Commentary on Joshua in 1563, and says it was the last which Calvin wrote.

[3] Histoire Literaire de Geneve, par Jean Senebier. Tome I. pp. 254-256.

by CALVIN, for the purpose of explaining his hypothesis respecting the situation of the Garden of Eden, and which seems to have been the basis of the most approved theories on the subject, will be found in its proper place. The same Map is given in the French and English translations, and also in the Latin edition of Professor Hengstenberg, published at Berlin in the year 1838. It may be observed, as a coincidence, that the same sketch appears in the Anglo-Geneva Bible, to which reference has been made. A more elaborate Map accompanies the Amsterdam edition of Calvin's Works, published in 1671.

The edition now issuing from the press is also enriched by an engraving, in the first style of art, of *fac-similes* of various medals of Calvin never before submitted to the British public.

HULL, *January* 1, 1847.

PUBLISHERS' NOTE

To reduce size and cost of this one volume edition several items mentioned in the above Preface and included in the Prelims of the Calvin Translation Society edition are omitted. These are : the facsimilies of various medals of Calvin ; the facsimile of the title page of the French translation of 1563 ; the French translation of the Dedication to the Duke of Vendome ; the facsimile of the title page of the English translation of 1578, and the Dedication to the Earl of Warwick by Thomas Tymme prefixed to the English translation of 1578. References to these, however, have not been deleted from the index.

THE AUTHOR'S EPISTLE DEDICATORY

JOHN CALVIN

TO THE

MOST ILLUSTRIOUS PRINCE,

HENRY, DUKE OF VENDOME,

HEIR TO THE KINGDOM OF NAVARRE.[1]

IF many censure my design, most Illustrious Prince, in presuming to dedicate this work to you, that it may go forth to light sanctioned by your name, nothing new or unexpected will have happened to me. For they may object that by such dedication, the hatred of the wicked, who are already more than sufficiently incensed against you, will be still further inflamed. But since, at your tender age, [2] amid various alarms and threatenings, God has inspired you with such magnanimity that you have never swerved from the sincere and ingenuous profession of the faith; I do not see what injury you can sustain by having that profession, which you wish to be openly manifest to all, confirmed by my testimony. Since, therefore, you are not ashamed of the Gospel of Christ,

[1] Afterwards the celebrated Henry IV. of France. A brave and noblespirited Prince, addicted, however, to the frivolities, and enslaved by the licentiousness of the age. He was induced to renounce his Protestant principles for the Crown of France ; and at length fell by the hand of an assassin, on account of his tolerance towards the Hugonots.

[2] He was born in 1553, and therefore in 1563, the date of this dedication, he was ten years old.

this independence of yours has appeared to give me just ground of confidence to congratulate you on such an auspicious commencement, and to exhort you to invincible constancy in future. For that flexibility which belongs to superior natures is the common property of the young, until their character becomes more formed. But however displeasing my labour may be to some, yet if it be approved (as I trust it will) by your most noble mother, THE QUEEN,[1] I can afford to despise both their unjust judgments and their malicious slanders; at least I shall not be diverted by them from my purpose. In one thing I may have acted with too little consideration, namely, in not having consulted her, in order that I might attempt nothing but in accordance with her judgment and her wish; yet for this omission I have an excuse at hand. If, indeed, I had omitted to consult her through negligence, I should condemn myself as guilty not of imprudence only, but of rashness and arrogance. When, however, I had given up all hope of so early a publication, because the Printer would put me off till the next spring-fairs, I thought it unnecessary, for certain reasons, to hasten my work. In the meantime, while others were urging him more vehemently on this point than I had done, I suddenly received a message, that the work might be finished within fifteen days, a thing which had before been pertinaciously refused to myself. Thus beyond my expectation, yet not contrary to my wish, I was deprived of the opportunity of asking her permission. Nevertheless, that most excellent Queen is animated by such zeal for the propagation of the doctrine of

---

[1] Jeanne d'Albret, Queen of Navarre, daughter of Henry d'Albret and of Margaret of Valois, sister to Francis the First, King of France. Henry was her third son, but the two former died in infancy. She and her husband, Antony of Bourbon, were both early favourers of the Reformation; but Antony, remarkable for his inconstancy, deserted the cause of Protestantism in the time of persecution, and at length took arms against its adherents, and perished in the contest. Jeanne remained constant to the faith she had professed, and proceeded to establish it in her dominions. In 1568 she left her capital Bearne, to join the French Protestants; and presented her son Henry to the Prince of Condé at the age of fifteen, together with her jewels, for the purpose of maintaining the war against the persecutors of the Reformed faith. She died in 1572, suddenly, at Paris, whither she had gone to make arrangements for her son's projected marriage with the sister of Charles IX. It was suspected that she died of poison, but no positive proof of the fact has been adduced.

Christ and of pure faith and piety, that I am under no extreme anxiety respecting her willingness to approve of this service of mine, and to defend it with her patronage. She by no means dissembles her own utter estrangement from the superstitions and corruptions with which Religion has been disfigured and polluted. And in the midst of turbulent agitations, [1] it has been rendered evident by convincing proofs, that she carried a more than masculine mind in woman's breast. And I wish that at length even *men* may be put to shame, and that useful emulation may stimulate them to imitate her example. For she conducted herself with such peculiar modesty, that scarcely any one would have supposed her capable of thus enduring the most violent attacks, and, at the same time, of courageously repelling them. Besides, how keenly God exercised her with internal conflicts but few persons are witnesses, of whom, however, I am one.

You truly, most Illustrious Prince, need not seek a better example, for the purpose of moulding your own mind to the perfect pattern of all virtues. Regard yourself as bound in an especial manner to aspire after, to contend, and to labour for the attainment of this object. For, as the heroic disposition which shines forth in you, will leave you the less excusable, if you degenerate from yourself, so education, no common help to an excellent disposition, is like another bond to retain you in your duty. For liberal instruction has been superadded to chaste discipline. Already imbued with the rudiments of literature, you have not cast away (as nearly all are wont to do) these studies in disgust, but still advance with alacrity in the cultivation of your genius. Now, in sending forth this book to the public under your name, my desire is, that it may effectually induce you more freely to profess yourself a disciple of Christ; just as if God, by laying his hand upon you, were claiming you anew to himself. And truly, you can yield no purer gratification to the Queen your mother, who cannot be too highly estimated, than by causing her to hear that you are making continual progress in piety.

Although many things contained in this book are beyond

---

[1] "Et entre les horribles tempestes dont le royaume de France a este agité."—And amid the horrible tempests with which the kingdom of France has been agitated.—*French Tr.*

the capacity of your age, yet I am not acting unreasonably in offering it to your perusal, and even to your attentive and diligent study. For since the knowledge of ancient things is pleasant to the young, you will soon arrive at those years in which the History of the Creation of the World, as well as that of the most Ancient Church, will engage your thoughts with equal profit and delight. And, certainly, if Paul justly condemns the perverse stupidity of men, because with closed eyes they pass by the splendid mirror of God's glory which is constantly presented to them in the fabric of the world, and thus unrighteously suppress the light of truth; not less base and disgraceful has been that ignorance of the origin and creation of the human race which has prevailed almost in every age. It is indeed probable, that shortly after the building of Babel,[1] the memory of those things, which ought to have been discussed and celebrated by being made the subjects of continual discourse, was obliterated. For seeing that to profane men their dispersion would be a kind of emancipation from the pure worship of God, they took no care to carry along with them, to whatever regions of the earth they might visit, what they had heard from their fathers concerning the Creation of the World, or its subsequent restoration. Hence it has happened, that no nation, the posterity of Abraham alone excepted, knew for more than two thousand successive years, either from what fountain itself had sprung, or when the universal race of man began to exist. For Ptolemy, in providing at length that the Books of Moses should be translated into Greek, did a work which was rather laudable than useful, (at least for that period,) since the light which he had attempted to bring out of darkness was nevertheless stifled and hidden through the negligence of men. Whence it may easily be gathered, that they who ought to have stretched every nerve of their mind to attain a knowledge of The Creator of the world, have rather, by a malignant impiety, involved themselves in voluntary blindness. In the meantime, the liberal sciences flourished, men of exalted genius arose, treatises of all kinds were published; but concerning the History of the Creation of the World there was

---

[1] Paulo post conditum Babylonem.

a profound silence. Moreover, the greatest of philosophers,[1] who excelled all the rest in acuteness and erudition, applied whatever skill he possessed to defraud God of his glory, by disputing in favour of the eternity of the world. Although his master, Plato, was a little more religious, and showed himself to be imbued with some taste for richer knowledge, yet he corrupted and mingled with so many figments the slender principles of truth which he received, that this fictitious kind of teaching would be rather injurious than profitable. They, moreover, who devoted themselves to the pursuit of writing history, ingenious and highly-cultivated men though they were, while they ostentatiously boast that they are about to become witnesses to the most remote antiquity, yet, before they reach so high as the times of David, intermix their lucubrations with much turbid feculence;[2] and when they ascend still higher, heap together an immense mass of lies : so far are they from having arrived, by a genuine and clear connection of narrative, at the true origin of the world. The Egyptians also are an evident proof that men were willingly ignorant of things which they had not far to seek, if only they had been disposed to addict their minds to the investigation of truth; for though the lamp of God's word was shining at their very doors, they would yet without shame propagate the rank fables of their achievements, fifteen thousand years before the foundation of the world. Not less puerile and absurd is the fable of the Athenians, who boasted that they were born from their own soil,[3] maintaining for themselves a distinct origin from the rest of mankind, and thus rendering themselves ridiculous even to barbarians. Now, though all nations have been more or less implicated in the same charge of ingratitude, I have nevertheless thought it right to select those whose error is least excusable, because they have deemed themselves wiser than all others.

Now, whether all nations which formerly existed, purposely

---

[1] Aristotle. Mesme Aristotle le principal philosophe.—*French Tr.*

[2] Brouillent leurs escrits de tant des meslinges confus, que ceste lie ont oste toute clarté.—They intersperse their writings with such a confused mixture, that these dregs have deprived them of all clearness.

[3] Qui se ἀυτόχθονας gloriati.

drew a veil over themselves, or whether their own indolence was the sole obstacle to their knowledge, the [First] Book of Moses deserves to be regarded as an incomparable treasure, since it at least gives an indisputable assurance respecting The Creation of the World, without which we should be unworthy of a place on earth. I omit, for the present, The History of the Deluge, which contains a representation of the Divine vengeance in the destruction of mankind, as tremendous, as that which it supplies of Divine mercy in their restoration is admirable. This one consideration stamps an inestimable value on the Book, that it alone reveals those things which are of primary necessity to be known; namely, in what manner God, after the destructive fall of man, adopted to himself a Church; what constituted the true worship of himself, and in what offices of piety the holy fathers exercised themselves; in which way pure religion, having for a time declined through the indolence of men, was restored, as it were, to its integrity; we also learn, when God deposited with a special people his gratuitous covenant of eternal salvation; in what manner a small progeny gradually proceeding from one man, who was both barren and withering, almost half-dead, and (as Isaiah calls him) *solitary*,[1] yet suddenly grew to an immense multitude; by what unexpected means God both exalted and defended a family chosen by himself, although poor, destitute of protection, exposed to every storm, and surrounded on all sides by innumerable hosts of enemies. Let every one, from his own use and experience, form his judgment respecting the necessity of the knowledge of these things. We see how vehemently the Papists alarm the simple by their false claim of the title of The Church. Moses so delineates the genuine features of the Church as to take away this absurd fear, by dissipating these illusions. It is by an ostentatious display of splendour and of pomp that they (the Papists) carry away the less informed to a foolish admiration of themselves, and even render them stupid and infatuated. But if we turn our eyes to those marks by which Moses designates the Church, these vain phantoms will have

---

[1] Isaiah li. 2, "I called him *alone*, and blessed him."

no more power to deceive. We are often disturbed and almost disheartened at the paucity of those who follow the pure doctrine of God; and especially when we see how far and wide superstitions extend their dominion. And, as formerly, the Spirit of God, by the mouth of Isaiah the prophet, commanded the Jews to look to the Rock whence they were hewn,[1] so he recalls us to the same consideration, and admonishes us of the absurdity of measuring the Church by its numbers, as if its dignity consisted in its multitude. If sometimes, in various places, Religion is less flourishing than could be wished, if the body of the pious is scattered, and the state of a well-regulated Church has gone to decay, not only do our minds sink, but entirely melt within us. On the contrary, while we see in this history of Moses, the building of the Church out of ruins, and the gathering of it out of broken fragments, and out of desolation itself, such an instance of the grace of God ought to raise us to firm confidence. But since the propensity, not to say the wanton disposition, of the human mind to frame false systems of worship is so great, nothing can be more useful to us than to seek our rule for the pure and sincere worshipping of God, from those holy Patriarchs, whose piety Moses points out to us chiefly by this mark, that they depended on the Word of God alone. For however great may be the difference between them and us in external ceremonies, yet that which ought to flourish in unchangeable vigour is common to us both, namely, that Religion should take its form from the sole will and pleasure of God.

I am not ignorant of the abundance of materials here supplied, and of the insufficiency of my language to reach the dignity of the subjects on which I briefly touch; but since each of them, on suitable occasions, has been elsewhere more copiously discussed by me, although not with suitable brilliancy and elegance of diction, it is now enough for me briefly to apprize my pious readers how well it would repay their labour, if they would learn prudently to apply to their own use the example of The Ancient Church, as it is described

---

[1] These words are here added in the French Translation—" C'est à dire, à leur pere Abraham, qui n'estoit qu'un, homme seul;"—that is to say, to their father Abraham, who was but one solitary man.

by Moses. And, in fact, God has associated us with the holy Patriarchs in the hope of the same inheritance, in order that we, disregarding the distance of time which separates us from them, may, in the mutual agreement of faith and patience, endure the same conflicts. So much the more detestable, then, are certain turbulent men, who, incited by I know not what rage of furious zeal, are assiduously endeavouring to rend asunder the Church of our own age, which is already more than sufficiently scattered. I do not speak of avowed enemies, who, by open violence, fall upon the pious to destroy them, and utterly to blot out their memory; but of certain morose professors of the Gospel, who not only perpetually supply new materials for fomenting discords, but by their restlessness disturb the peace which holy and learned men gladly cultivate. We see that with the Papists, although in some things they maintain deadly strife among themselves, [1] they yet combine in wicked confederacy against the Gospel. It is not necessary to say how small is the number of those who hold the sincere doctrine of Christ, when compared with the vast multitudes of these opponents. In the meantime, audacious scribblers arise, as from our own bosom, who not only obscure the light of sound doctrine with clouds of error, or infatuate the simple and the less experienced with their wicked ravings, but by a profane license of scepticism, allow themselves to uproot the whole of Religion. For, as if, by their rank ironies and cavils, they could prove themselves genuine disciples of Socrates, they have no axiom more plausible than, that faith must be free and unfettered, so that it may be possible, by reducing everything to a matter of doubt, to render Scripture flexible (so to speak) as a nose of wax. [2] Therefore, they who being captivated by the allure-

---

[1] Combien qu'en tout le reste, ils s'entrebatent comme chiens et chats.— Though in everything else they quarrel together like dogs and cats.—*French Tr.*

[2] Ils n'ont nulle maxime plus agreable que ceste-ci, que la foy doit estre libre, et que les esprits ne doyvent point estre tenus captifs. Et c'est afin qu'il leur soit loisible, en metant tout en doute et en question, tourner et virer l'Escriture a leur poste, et en faire un nez de cire, &c.— They have no maxim more agreeable than this, that faith ought to be free, and that minds ought not to be held captive. And this is in order that they may be permitted, by putting everything into doubt and ques-

ments of this new school, now indulge in doubtful speculations, obtain at length such proficiency, that they are always
learning, yet never come to the knowledge of the truth.

Thus far I have treated briefly, as the occasion required, of
the utility of this History.[1] As for the rest, I have laboured
—how skilfully I know not, but certainly faithfully—that the
doctrine of the Law, the obscurity of which has heretofore
repelled many, may become familiarly known. There will be
readers, I doubt not, who would desire a more ample explica-
tion of particular passages. But I, who naturally avoid prolixity, have confined myself in this Work to narrow limits,
for two reasons. First, whereas these Four Books [of Moses]
already deter some by their length, I have feared lest, if in
unfolding them, I were to indulge in a style too diffuse, I
should but increase their disgust. Secondly, since in my
progress I have often despaired of life, I have preferred giving
a succinct Exposition to leaving a mutilated one behind me.
Yet sincere readers, possessed of sound judgment, will see that
I have taken diligent care, neither through cunning nor negligence, to pass over anything perplexed, ambiguous, or obscure.
Since, therefore, I have endeavoured to discuss all doubtful
points, I do not see why any one should complain of brevity,
unless he wishes to derive his knowledge exclusively from
Commentaries. Now I will gladly allow men of this sort,
whom no amount of verbosity can satiate, to seek for themselves some other master.

But if you, Sire, please to make trial, you will indeed
know, and will believe for yourself, that what I declare is
most true. You are yet a youth; but God, when he commanded Kings to write out the Book of the Law for their
own use, did not exempt the pious Josiah from this class,
but choose rather to present the most noble instance of pious
instruction in a boy, that he might reprove the indolence
of the aged. And your own example teaches the great
importance of having habits formed from tender age.

tion, to turn and twist the Scripture to their purpose, and to make of it
a nose of wax, &c.—*French Tr.*
    [1] Touchant l'utilité de l'histoire contenue au livre de Genese.—Touch-
ing the utility of the history contained in the Book of Genesis.—*French Tr.*

For the germ springing from the root which the principles of
Religion received by you have taken, not only puts forth its
flower, but also savours of a degree of maturity. Therefore
labour, by indefatigable industry, to attain the mark set before
you. And suffer not yourself to be retarded or disturbed by
designing men, to whom it appears unseasonable that boys
should be called to this precocious wisdom, (as they term it.)
For what can be more absurd or intolerable, than that, when
every kind of corruption surrounds you, this remedy should
be prohibited ? Since the pleasures of a Court corrupt even
your servants, how much more dangerous are the snares laid
for great Princes, who so abound in all luxury and delicacies,
that it is a wonder if they are not quite dissolved in lasciviousness ? For it is certainly contrary to nature to possess all
the means of pleasure, and to refrain from enjoying them.
The difficulty, however, of retaining chastity unpolluted
amidst scenes of gaiety, is more than sufficiently evident in
practice. But do you, O most Illustrious Prince, regard
everything as poison which tends to produce a love of pleasures. For if that which stifles continence and temperance
already allures you, what will you not covet when you arrive
at adult age ? The sentiment is perhaps harshly expressed,
that great care for the body is great neglect of virtue, yet
most truly does Cato thus speak. The following paradox also
will scarcely be admitted in common life : " I am greater, and
am born to greater things, than to be a slave to my body ; the
contempt of which is my true liberty." Let us then dismiss
that excessive rigour, by which all enjoyment is taken away
from life ; still there are too many examples to show how
easy is the descent from security and self-indulgence to the
licentiousness of profligacy. Moreover, you will have to contend, not only with luxury, but also with many other vices.
Nothing can be more attractive than your affability and
modesty ; but no disposition is so gentle and well-regulated,
that it may not degenerate into brutality and ferociousness
when intoxicated with flatteries. Now since there are flatterers without number, who will prove so many tempters to
inflame your mind with various lusts, how much more does
it behove you vigilantly to beware of them ? But while I

caution you against the blandishments of a Court, I require nothing more than that, being endued with moderation, you should render yourself invincible. For one has truly said, He is not to be praised who has never seen Asia, but he who has lived modestly and continently in Asia. Seeing, therefore, that to attain this state is most desirable, David prescribes a compendious method of doing so—if you will but imitate his example—when he declares that the precepts of God are his counsellors. And truly, whatever counsel may be suggested from any other quarter will perish, unless you take your commencement of becoming wise from this point. It remains, therefore, most noble Prince, that what is spoken by Isaiah concerning the holy king Hezekiah should perpetually recur to your mind. For the Prophet, in enumerating his excellent qualities, especially honours him with this eulogy, that the fear of God shall be his treasure.

Farewell, most Illustrious Prince, may God preserve you in safety under His protection, may He adorn you more and more with spiritual gifts, and enrich you with every kind of benediction.

GENEVA, *July* 31*st*, 1563.

ARGUMENT

SINCE the infinite wisdom of God is displayed in the admirable structure of heaven and earth, it is absolutely impossible to unfold THE HISTORY OF THE CREATION OF THE WORLD in terms equal to its dignity. For while the measure of our capacity is too contracted to comprehend things of such magnitude, our tongue is equally incapable of giving a full and substantial account of them. As he, however, deserves praise, who, with modesty and reverence, applies himself to the consideration of the works of God, although he attain less than might be wished, so, if in this kind of employment, I endeavour to assist others according to the ability given to me, I trust that my service will be not less approved by pious men than accepted by God. I have chosen to premise this, for the sake not only of excusing myself, but of admonishing my readers, that if they sincerely wish to profit with me in meditating on the works of God, they must bring with them a sober, docile, mild, and humble spirit. We see, indeed, the world with our eyes, we tread the earth with our feet, we touch innumerable kinds of God's works with our hands, we inhale a sweet and pleasant fragrance from herbs and flowers, we enjoy boundless benefits; but in those very things of which we attain some knowledge, there dwells such an immensity of divine power, goodness, and wisdom, as absorbs all our senses. Therefore, let men be satisfied if they obtain only a moderate taste of them, suited to their capacity. And it becomes us so to press towards this mark during our whole life, that (even in extreme old age) we shall not repent of the progress we have made, if only we have advanced ever so little in our course.

The intention of Moses, in beginning his Book with the creation of the world, is, to render God, as it were, visible to us in his works. But here presumptuous men rise up, and scoffingly inquire, whence was this revealed to Moses? They therefore suppose him to be speaking fabulously of things unknown, because he was neither a spectator of the events he records, nor had learned the truth of them by reading. Such is their reasoning; but their dishonesty is easily exposed. For if they can destroy the credit of this history, because it is traced back through a long series of past ages, let them also prove those prophecies to be false in which the same history predicts occurrences which did not take place till many centuries afterwards. Those things, I affirm, are clear and obvious, which Moses testifies concerning the vocation of the Gentiles, the accomplishment of which occurred nearly two thousand years after his death. Was not he, who by the Spirit foresaw an event remotely future, and hidden at the time from the perception of mankind, capable of understanding whether the world was created by God, especially seeing that he was taught by a Divine Master? For he does not here put forward divinations of his own, but is the instrument of the Holy Spirit for the publication of those things which it was of importance for all men to know. They greatly err in deeming it absurd that the order of the creation, which had been previously unknown, should at length have been described and explained by him. For he does not transmit to memory things before unheard of, but for the first time consigns to writing facts which the fathers had delivered as from hand to hand, through a long succession of years, to their children. Can we conceive that man was so placed in the earth as to be ignorant of his own origin, and of the origin of those things which he enjoyed? No sane person doubts that Adam was well-instructed respecting them all. Was he indeed afterwards dumb? Were the holy Patriarchs so ungrateful as to suppress in silence such necessary instruction? Did Noah, warned by a divine judgment so memorable, neglect to transmit it to posterity? Abraham is expressly honoured with this eulogy, that he was the teacher and the master of his family, (Gen. xviii. 19.) And we know that, long before the time of Moses, an acquaintance with the covenant into which God had entered with their fathers was common to the whole people. When he says that the Israelites were sprung from a holy race, which God had chosen for himself, he does not propound it as something new, but only commemorates what all held, what the old men themselves had received from their ancestors, and what, in short, was entirely uncontroverted among them. Therefore, we ought not to doubt that The Creation of the World, as here described, was already known through the ancient and perpetual tradition of the Fathers. Yet, since nothing is more easy than that the truth of God should be so corrupted by men, that, in a long succession of time, it should, as it were, degenerate from itself, it pleased the Lord to commit the history to writing, for the purpose of preserving its purity. Moses, therefore, has established the credibility of that doctrine which is contained in his writings, and which, by the carelessness of men, might otherwise have been lost.

I now return to the design of Moses, or rather of the Holy Spirit, who has spoken by his mouth. We know God, who is himself invisible, only through his works. Therefore, the Apostle elegantly styles the worlds, τὰ μὴ εκ φαινομένων βλεπό-μενα, as if one should say, "the manifestation of things not apparent,"[1] (Heb. xi. 3.) This is the reason why the Lord, that he may invite us to the knowledge of himself, places the fabric of heaven and earth before our eyes, rendering himself, in a certain manner, manifest in them. For his eternal power and Godhead (as Paul says) are there exhibited, (Rom. i. 20.) And that declaration of David is most true, that the heavens, though without a tongue, are yet eloquent heralds of the glory of God, and that this most beautiful order of nature silently proclaims his admirable wisdom,

[1] "Acsi dicas, spectacula rerum non apparentium."—Comme si on disoit, Un regard, ou apparition de ce qui n'apparoist point.—*French Tr.*

(Ps. xix. 1.) This is the more diligently to be observed, because so few pursue the right method of knowing God, while the greater part adhere to the creatures without any consideration of the Creator himself. For men are commonly subject to these two extremes ; namely, that some, forgetful of God, apply the whole force of their mind to the consideration of nature; and others, overlooking the *works* of God, aspire with a foolish and insane curiosity to inquire into his *Essence*. Both labour in vain. To be so occupied in the investigation of the secrets of nature, as never to turn the eyes to its Author, is a most perverted study ; and to enjoy everything in nature without acknowledging the Author of the benefit, is the basest ingratitude. Therefore, they who assume to be philosophers without Religion, and who, by speculating, so act as to remove God and all sense of piety far from them, will one. day feel the force of the expression of Paul, related by Luke, that God has never left himself *without witness*, (Acts xiv. 17.) For they shall not be permitted to escape with impunity because they have been deaf and insensible to testimonies so illustrious. And, in truth, it is the part of culpable ignorance, never to see God, who everywhere gives signs of his presence. But if mockers now escape by their cavils, hereafter their terrible destruction will bear witness that they were ignorant of God, only because they were willingly and maliciously blinded. As for those who proudly soar above the world to seek God in his unveiled essence, it is impossible but that at length they should entangle themselves in a multitude of absurd figments. For God—by other means invisible—(as we have already said) clothes himself, so to speak, with the image of the world, in which he would present himself to our contemplation. They who will not deign to behold him thus magnificently arrayed in the incomparable vesture of the heavens and the earth, afterwards suffer the just punishment of their proud contempt in their own ravings. Therefore, as soon as the name of God sounds in our ears, or the thought of him occurs to our minds, let us also clothe him with this most beautiful ornament; finally, let the world become our school if we desire rightly to know God.

Here also the impiety of those is refuted who cavil against
Moses, for relating that so short a space of time had elapsed
since the Creation of the World. For they inquire why it
had come so suddenly into the mind of God to create the
world; why he had so long remained inactive in heaven:
and thus by sporting with sacred things they exercise their
ingenuity to their own destruction. In the Tripartite History
an answer given by a pious man is recorded, with which I
have always been pleased. For when a certain impure dog
was in this manner pouring ridicule upon God, he retorted,
that God had been at that time by no means inactive,
because he had been preparing hell for the captious. But
by what reasonings can you restrain the arrogance of those
men to whom sobriety is professedly contemptible and odious?
And certainly they who now so freely exult in finding fault
with the inactivity of God will find, to their own great cost,
that his power has been infinite in preparing hell for them.
As for ourselves, it ought not to seem so very absurd that
God, satisfied in himself, did not create a world which he
needed not, sooner than he thought good. Moreover, since
his will is the rule of all wisdom, we ought to be contented
with that alone. For Augustine rightly affirms that injustice is done to God by the Manichæans, because they demand
a cause superior to his will; and he prudently warns his
readers not to push their inquiries respecting the infinity of
duration, any more than respecting the infinity of space.[1]
We indeed are not ignorant, that the circuit of the heavens
is finite, and that the earth, like a little globe, is placed in the
centre.[2] They who take it amiss that the world was not
sooner created, may as well expostulate with God for not

[1] De Genesi contra Manich. lib. xi. De Civit. Dei.
[2] The erroneous system of natural philosophy which had prevailed for
ages was but just giving way to sounder views, at the time when
Calvin wrote. Copernicus, in the close of the preceding century, had
begun to suspect the current opinions on the subject; but the fear of
being misunderstood and ridiculed caused him to withhold for some time
the discoveries he was making; and it was not till 1543, a few hours
before his death, that he himself saw a copy of his own published work.
Up to that period, the earth had been regarded as the centre of the
system, and the whole heavens were supposed to revolve around it.—
See *Maclaurin's Account of Sir Isaac Newton's Discoveries*, Book I.
chap. iii.

having made innumerable worlds. Yea, since they deem it absurd that many ages should have passed away without any world at all, they may as well acknowledge it to be a proof of the great corruption of their own nature, that, in comparison with the boundless waste which remains empty, the heaven and earth occupy but a small space. But since both the eternity of God's existence and the infinity of his glory would prove a twofold labyrinth, let us content ourselves with modestly desiring to proceed no further in our inquiries than the Lord, by the guidance and instruction of his own works, invites us.

Now, in describing the world as a mirror in which we ought to behold God, I would not be understood to assert, either that our eyes are sufficiently clear-sighted to discern what the fabric of heaven and earth represents, or that the knowledge to be hence attained is sufficient for salvation. And whereas the Lord invites us to himself by the means of created things, with no other effect than that of thereby rendering us inexcusable, he has added (as was necessary) a new remedy, or at least by a new aid, he has assisted the ignorance of our mind. For by the Scripture as our guide and teacher, he not only makes those things plain which would otherwise escape our notice, but almost compels us to behold them ; as if he had assisted our dull sight with spectacles.[1] On this point, (as we have already observed,) Moses insists. For if the mute instruction of the heaven and the earth were sufficient, the teaching of Moses would have been superfluous. This herald therefore approaches, who excites our attention, in order that we may perceive ourselves to be placed in this scene, for the purpose of beholding the glory of God ; not indeed to observe them as mere witnesses, but to enjoy all the riches which are here exhibited, as the Lord has ordained and subjected them to our use. And he not only declares generally that God is the architect of the world,

---

[1] " Non secus ac hebetes oculi *specillis* adjuvantur."—Tout ainsi comme si on bailloit des *lunettes* ou miroirs à ceux qui ont la veue debile. Just as if one gave spectacles or mirrors to those who have weak sight.— *French Tr.* This is the translator's authority for rendering *specillis* spectacles.

but through the whole chain of the history he shows how admirable is His power, His wisdom, His goodness, and especially His tender solicitude for the human race. Besides, since the eternal Word of God is the lively and express image of Himself, he recalls us to this point. And thus, the assertion of the Apostle is verified, that through no other means than faith can it be understood that the worlds were made by the word of God, (Heb. xi. 3.) For faith properly proceeds from this, that we being taught by the ministry of Moses, do not now wander in foolish and trifling speculations, but contemplate the true and only God in his genuine image.

It may, however, be objected, that this seems at variance with what Paul declares: "After that, in the wisdom of God, the world through wisdom knew not God, it seemed right to God, through the foolishness of preaching, to save them who believe," (1 Cor. i. 21.) For he thus intimates, that God is sought in vain under the guidance of visible things; and that nothing remains for us but to betake ourselves immediately to Christ; and that we must not therefore commence with the elements of this world, but with the Gospel, which sets Christ alone before us with his cross, and holds us to this one point. I answer, It is in vain for any to reason as philosophers on the workmanship of the world, except those who, having been first humbled by the preaching of the Gospel, have learned to submit the whole of their intellectual wisdom (as Paul expresses it) to the foolishness of the cross, (1 Cor. i. 21.) Nothing shall we find, I say, above or below, which can raise us up to God, until Christ shall have instructed us in his own school. Yet this cannot be done, unless we, having emerged out of the lowest depths, are borne up above all heavens, in the chariot of his cross, that there by faith we may apprehend those things which the eye has never seen, the ear never heard, and which far surpass our hearts and minds.[1] For the earth, with its supply of fruits for our daily nourishment, is not there set before us; but Christ offers himself to us unto life eternal. Nor does heaven,

---

[1] In this, and the following sentences, Calvin shows an intimate experimental acquaintance with the declaration of the Apostle; "And hath made us sit together in heavenly places in Christ Jesus," (Eph. ii. 6.)

by the shining of the sun and stars, enlighten our bodily
eyes, but the same Christ, the Light of the World and the
Sun of Righteousness, shines into our souls; neither does the
air stretch out its empty space for us to breathe in, but
the Spirit of God himself quickens us and causes us to live.
There, in short, the invisible kingdom of Christ fills all
things, and his spiritual grace is diffused through all. Yet
this does not prevent us from applying our senses to the
consideration of heaven and earth, that we may thence seek
confirmation in the true knowledge of God. For Christ is
that image in which God presents to our view, not only his
heart, but also his hands and his feet. I give the name of his
heart to that secret love with which he embraces us in
Christ: by his *hands* and *feet* I understand those works of
his which are displayed before our eyes. As soon as ever
we depart from Christ, there is nothing, be it ever so gross
or insignificant in itself, respecting which we are not necessarily deceived.

And, in fact, though Moses begins, in this Book, with the
Creation of the World, he nevertheless does not confine us
to this subject. For these things ought to be connected
together, that the world was founded by God, and that man,
after he had been endued with the light of intelligence, and
adorned with so many privileges, fell by his own fault, and
was thus deprived of all the benefits he had obtained; afterwards, by the compassion of God, he was restored to the life
he had forfeited, and this through the loving-kindness of
Christ; so that there should always be some assembly on
earth, which being adopted into the hope of the celestial life,
might in this confidence worship God. The end to which
the whole scope of the history tends is to this point, that the
human race has been preserved by God in such a manner as to
manifest his special care for his Church. For this is the argument of the Book: After the world had been created, man was
placed in it as in a theatre, that he, beholding above him and
beneath the wonderful works of God, might reverently adore
their Author. Secondly, that all things were ordained for
the use of man, that he, being under deeper obligation, might
devote and dedicate himself entirely to obedience towards

God. Thirdly, that he was endued with understanding and reason, that being distinguished from brute animals he might meditate on a better life, and might even tend directly towards God, whose image he bore engraven on his own person. Afterwards followed the fall of Adam, whereby he alienated himself from God; whence it came to pass that he was deprived of all rectitude. Thus Moses represents man as devoid of all good, blinded in understanding, perverse in heart, vitiated in every part, and under sentence of eternal death; but he soon adds the history of his restoration, where Christ shines forth with the benefit of redemption. From this point he not only relates continuously the singular Providence of God in governing and preserving the Church, but also commends to us the true worship of God; teaches wherein the salvation of man is placed, and exhorts us, from the example of the Fathers, to constancy in enduring the cross. Whosoever, therefore, desires to make suitable proficiency in this book, let him employ his mind on these main topics. But especially, let him observe, that after Adam had by his own desperate fall ruined himself and all his posterity, this is the basis of our salvation, this the origin of the Church, that we, being rescued out of profound darkness, have obtained a new life by the mere grace of God; that the Fathers (according to the offer made them through the word of God) are by faith made partakers of this life; that this word itself was founded upon Christ; and that all the pious who have since lived were sustained by the very same promise of salvation by which Adam was first raised from the fall.

Therefore, the perpetual succession of the Church has flowed from this fountain, that the holy Fathers, one after another, having by faith embraced the offered promise, were collected together into the family of God, in order that they might have a common life in Christ. This we ought carefully to notice, that we may know what is the society of the true Church, and what the communion of faith among the children of God. Whereas Moses was ordained the Teacher of the Israelites, there is no doubt that he had an especial reference to them, in order that they might acknowledge themselves to be a people elected and chosen by God; and

that they might seek the certainty of this adoption from the
Covenant which the Lord had ratified with their fathers, and
might know that there was no other God, and no other right
faith. But it was also his will to testify to all ages, that
whosoever desired to worship God aright, and to be deemed
members of the Church, must pursue no other course than
that which is here prescribed. But as this is the commencement of faith, to know that there is one only true God whom
we worship, so it is no common confirmation of this faith
that we are companions of the Patriarchs ; for since they
possessed Christ as the pledge of their salvation when he had
not yet appeared, so we retain the God who formerly manifested himself to them. Hence we may infer the difference
between the pure and lawful worship of God, and all those
adulterated services which have since been fabricated by the
fraud of Satan and the perverse audacity of men. Further,
the Government of the Church is to be considered, that the
reader may come to the conclusion that God has been its
perpetual Guard and Ruler, yet in such a way as to exercise it in the warfare of the cross. Here, truly, the peculiar
conflicts of the Church present themselves to view, or rather,
the course is set as in a mirror before our eyes, in which it
behoves us, with the holy Fathers, to press towards the
mark of a happy immortality.

Let us now hearken to MOSES.

COMMENTARY

THE BOOK OF GENESIS

CHAPTER I.

1. In the beginning God created the heaven and the earth.

2. And the earth was without form and void; and darkness *was* upon the face of the deep. And the Spirit of God moved upon the face of the waters.

3. And God said, Let there be light: and there was light.

4. And God saw the light, that *it was* good: and God divided the light from the darkness.

5. And God called the light Day, and the darkness he called Night. And the evening and the morning were the first day.

6. And God said, Let there be a firmament in the midst of the waters, and let it divide the waters from the waters.

7. And God made the firmament, and divided the waters which *were* under the firmament from the waters which *were* above the firmament: and it was so.

8. And God called the firmament Heaven. And the evening and the morning were the second day.

9. And God said, Let the waters under the heaven be gathered together into one place, and let the dry *land* appear: and it was so.

1. In principio creavit Deus cœlum et terram.

2. Terra autem erat informis et inanis; tenebræque erant in superficie voraginis, et Spiritus Dei agitabat se in superficie aquarum.

3. Et dixit Deus, Sit lux. Et fuit lux.

4. Viditque Deus lucem quod bona esset; et divisit Deus lucem a tenebris.

5. Et vocavit Deus lucem, Diem: et tenebras vocavit Noctem. Fuitque vespera, et fuit mane dies primus.

6. Et dixit Deus, Sit extensio in medio aquarum, et dividat aquas ab aquis.

7. Et fecit Deus expansionem: et divisit aquas quæ erant sub expansione, ab aquis quæ erant super expansionem. Et fuit ita.

8. Vocavitque Deus expansionem Cœlum. Et fuit vespera, et fuit mane dies secundus.

9. Postea dixit Deus, Congregentur aquæ quæ sunt sub cœlo, in locum unum, et appareat arida. Et fuit ita.

10. And God called the dry *land* Earth; and the gathering together of the waters called he Seas: and God saw that *it was* good.

11. And God said, Let the earth bring forth grass, the herb yielding seed, *and* the fruit tree yielding fruit after his kind, whose seed *is* in itself, upon the earth: and it was so.

12. And the earth brought forth grass, *and* herb yielding seed after his kind, and the tree yielding fruit, whose seed *was* in itself, after his kind: and God saw that *it was* good.

13. And the evening and the morning were the third day.

14. And God said, Let there be lights in the firmament of the heaven to divide the day from the night; and let them be for signs, and for seasons, and for days, and years:

15. And let them be for lights in the firmament of the heaven to give light upon the earth: and it was so.

16. And God made two great lights; the greater light to rule the day, and the lesser light to rule the night: *he made* the stars also.

17. And God set them in the firmament of the heaven to give light upon the earth,

18. And to rule over the day and over the night, and to divide the light from the darkness: and God saw that *it was* good.

19. And the evening and the morning were the fourth day.

20. And God said, Let the waters bring forth abundantly the moving creature that hath life, and fowl *that* may fly above the earth in the open firmament of heaven.

21. And God created great whales, and every living creature that moveth, which the waters brought forth abundantly, after their kind, and every winged fowl after his kind: and God saw that *it was* good.

22. And God blessed them, saying, Be fruitful, and multiply, and fill the waters in the seas, and let fowl multiply in the earth.

10. Et vocavit Deus aridam, Terram: congregationem vero aquarum appellavit Maria. Et vidit Deus quod esset bonum.

11. Postea dixit Deus, Germinet terra germen, herbam seminificantem semen, arborem fructiferam, facientem fructum juxta speciem suam cui insit semen suum super terram. Et fuit ita.

12. Et protulit terra germen, herbam seminificantem semen juxta speciem suam, et arborem facientem fructum cui semen suum inesset juxta speciem suam. Et vidit Deus quod esset bonum.

13. Et fuit vespera, et fuit mane dies tertius.

14. Tunc dixit Deus, Sint luminaria in firmamentum cœli, ut dividant diem a nocte, et sint in signa, et stata tempora, et dies, et annos:

15. Et sint in luminaria in expansione cœli, ut illuminent terram. Et fuit ita.

16. Et fecit Deus duo luminaria magna: luminare majus in dominium diei, et luminare minus in dominium noctis, & stellas.

17. Posuitque ea Deus in expansione cœli, ut illuminarent terram:

18. Et ut dominarentur diei ac nocti, et dividerent lucem a tenebris: et vidit Deus quod esset bonum.

19. Et fuit vespera, et fuit mane dies quartus.

20. Postea dixit Deus, Repere faciant aquæ reptile animæ viventis, et volatile volet super terram in superficie expansionis cœli.

21. Et creavit Deus cetos magnos, et omnem animum viventem, repentem, quam repere fecerunt aquæ juxta species suas: et omne volatile alatum secundum speciem cujusque. Et vidit Deus quod esset bonum.

22. Benedixitque eis, dicendo, Crescite et multiplicate vos, et replete aquas in maribus; et volatile multiplicet se in terra.

23. And the evening and the morning were the fifth day.

24. And God said, Let the earth bring forth the living creature after his kind, cattle and creeping thing, and beast of the earth after his kind: and it was so.

25. And God made the beast of the earth after his kind, and cattle after their kind, and every thing that creepeth upon the earth after his kind: and God saw that *it was* good.

26. And God said, Let us make man in our image, after our likeness: and let them have dominion over the fish of the sea, and over the fowl of the air, and over the cattle, and over all the earth, and over every creeping thing that creepeth upon the earth.

27. So God created man in his *own* image, in the image of God created he him; male and female created he them.

28. And God blessed them, and God said unto them, Be fruitful, and multiply, and replenish the earth, and subdue it: and have dominion over the fish of the sea, and over the fowl of the air, and over every living thing that moveth upon the earth.

29. And God said, Behold, I have given you every herb bearing seed, which *is* upon the face of all the earth, and every tree, in the which *is* the fruit of a tree yielding seed; to you it shall be for meat.

30. And to every beast of the earth, and to every fowl of the air, and to every thing that creepeth upon the earth, wherein *there is* life, *I have given* every green herb for meat: and it was so.

31. And God saw everything that he had made, and, behold, *it was* very good. And the evening and the morning were the sixth day.

23. Et fuit vespera, et fuit mane dies quintus.

24. Postea dixit Deus, Producat terra animam viventem secundum speciem suam, jumentum et reptile, et bestias terræ secundum speciem suam. Et fuit ita.

25. Fecitque Deus bestiam terræ secundum speciem suam, et jumentum secundum speciem suam, et omne reptile terræ secundum speciem suam: et vidit Deus quod esset bonum.

26. Et dixit Deus, Faciamus hominem in imagine nostra, secundum similitudinem nostram; et dominetur piscibus maris, et volatili cœli, et jumento, et omni terræ, et omni reptili reptanti super terram.

27. Creavit itaque Deus hominem ad imaginem suam, ad imaginem *inquam* Dei creavit illum: masculum et fœminam creavit eos.

28. Et benedixit illis Deus, dixitque ad eos Deus, Crescite, et multiplicate vos, et replete terram, et subjicite eam, et dominemini piscibus maris, et volatili cœli, et omni bestiæ reptanti super terram.

29. Et dixit Deus, Ecce, dedi vobis omnem herbam seminificantem semen, quæ est in superficie universæ terræ, et omnem arborem in qua est fructus arboris seminificans semen: ut vobis sit in escam.

30. Et omni bestiæ terræ, et omni volatili cœli, et omni reptanti super terram in quo est anima vivans, omne olus herbæ *erit* in escam. Et fuit ita.

31. Et vidit Deus omne quod fecerat, et ecce bonum valde. Et fuit vespera, et fuit mane dies sextus.

1. *In the beginning.* To expound the term "beginning," of Christ, is altogether frivolous. For Moses simply intends to assert that the world was not perfected at its very

commencement, in the manner in which it is now seen, but
that it was created an empty chaos of heaven and earth.
His language therefore may be thus explained. When God
in the beginning created the heaven and the earth, the earth
was empty and waste.[1] He moreover teaches by the word
"created," that what before did not exist was now made;
for he has not used the term יָצַר, (*yatsar,*) which signifies to
frame or form, but בָּרָא, (*bara,*) which signifies to create.[2]
Therefore his meaning is, that the world was made out of
nothing. Hence the folly of those is refuted who imagine
that unformed matter existed from eternity; and who gather
nothing else from the narration of Moses than that the world
was furnished with new ornaments, and received a form of
which it was before destitute. This indeed was formerly a
common fable among heathens,[3] who had received only an
obscure report of the creation, and who, according to custom,
adulterated the truth of God with strange figments; but for
Christian men to labour (as Steuchus does[4]) in maintaining
this gross error is absurd and intolerable. Let this, then, be
maintained in the first place,[5] that the world is not eternal,
but was created by God. There is no doubt that Moses
gives the name of heaven and earth to that confused mass
which he, shortly afterwards, (verse 2,) denominates *waters.*
The reason of which is, that this matter was to be the seed
of the whole world. Besides, this is the generally recog-
nized division of the world.[6]

God. Moses has it *Elohim,* a noun of the plural number.
Whence the inference is drawn, that the three Persons of

[1] "La terre estoit vuide, et sans forme, et ne servoit à rien."—"The earth
was empty, and without form, and was of no use."—*French Trans.*

[2] בָּרָא. It has a twofold meaning,—1. *To create out of nothing,* as is
proved from these words, *In the beginning,* because nothing was made
before them. 2. *To produce something excellent out of pre-existent matter;*
as it is said afterwards, *He created whales,* and *man.*—See *Fagius, Drusius,*
and *Estius,* in *Poole's Synopsis.*

[3] Inter profanos homines.

[4] Steuchus Augustinus was the Author of a work, "De Perenni Philo-
sophia," Lugd. 1540, and is most likely the writer referred to by Calvin.
The work, however, is very rare, and probably of little value.

[5] "Sit igitur hæc prima sententia. Que ceci dont soit premierement
resolu."—*French Trans.*

[6] Namely, into heaven and earth.

the Godhead are here noted; but since, as a proof of so great a matter, it appears to me to have little solidity, I will not insist upon the word; but rather caution readers to beware of violent glosses of this kind.[1] They think that they have testimony against the Arians to prove the Deity of the Son and of the Spirit, but in the meantime they involve themselves in the error of Sabellius:[2] because Moses afterwards subjoins that the *Elohim* had spoken, and that the *Spirit of the Elohim* rested upon the waters. If we suppose three persons to be here denoted, there will be no distinction between them. For it will follow, both that the Son is begotten by himself, and that the Spirit is not of the Father,

---

[1] The reasoning of Calvin on this point is a great proof of the candour of his mind, and of his determination to adhere strictly to what he conceives to be the meaning of Holy Scripture, whatever bearing it might have on the doctrines he maintains. It may however be right to direct the reader, who wishes fully to examine the disputed meaning of the plural word אֱלֹהִים, which we translate God, to some sources of information, whence he may be able to form his own judgment respecting the term. *Cocceius* argues that the mystery of the Trinity in Unity is contained in the word; and many other writers of reputation take the same ground. Others contend, that though no clear intimation of the Trinity in Unity is given, yet the notion of *plurality* of Persons is plainly implied in the term. For a full account of all the arguments in favour of this hypothesis, the work of Dr John Pye Smith, on the Scripture testimony of the Messiah—a work full of profound learning, and distinguished by patient industry and calmly courteous criticism—may be consulted. It must however be observed, that this diligent and impartial writer has not met the special objection adduced by Calvin in this place, namely, the danger of gliding into Sabellianism while attempting to confute Arianism.—*Ed.*

[2] The error of Sabellius (according to Theodoret) consisted in his maintaining, " that the Father, Son, and Holy Ghost, are one hypostasis, and one Person under three names;" or, in the language of that eminent ecclesiastical scholar, the late Dr Burton, " Sabellius divided the One Divinity into three, but he supposed the Son and the Holy Ghost to have no distinct personal existence, except when they were put forth for a time by the Father."—See *Burton's Lectures on Ecclesiastical History*, vol. ii. p. 365; and his *Bampton Lectures*, Note 103. This will perhaps assist the reader to understand the nature of Calvin's argument which immediately follows. Supposing the word Elohim to denote the Three Persons of the Godhead in the first verse, it also denotes the same Three Persons in the second verse. But in this second verse Moses says, the Spirit of Elohim, that is, the Spirit of the Three Persons rested on the waters. Hence the distinction of Persons is lost; for the Spirit is himself one of them; consequently the Spirit is sent from himself. The same reasoning would prove that the Son was begotten by himself; because he is one of the Persons of the Elohim by whom the Son is begotten.—*Ed.*

but of himself. For me it is sufficient that the plural number expresses those powers which God exercised in creating the world. Moreover, I acknowledge that the Scripture, although it recites many powers of the Godhead, yet always recalls us to the Father, and his Word, and Spirit, as we shall shortly see. But those absurdities, to which I have alluded, forbid us with subtlety to distort what Moses simply declares concerning God himself, by applying it to the separate Persons of the Godhead. This, however, I regard as beyond controversy, that, from the peculiar circumstance of the passage itself, a title is here ascribed to God, expressive of that power, which was previously in some way included in his eternal essence.[1]

[1] The interpretation above given of the meaning of the word אלהים, (Elohim,) receives confirmation from the profound critical investigations of Dr Hengstenberg, Professor of Theology in the University of Berlin, whose work, cast in a somewhat new form, and entitled " Dissertations on the Genuineness of the Pentateuch," appears in an English dress, under the superintendence of the CONTINENTAL TRANSLATION SOCIETY, while these pages are passing through the press. With other learned critics, he concludes, that the word is derived from the Arabic root *Allah*, which means to *worship*, to *adore*, to be *seized with fear*. He, therefore, regards the title more especially descriptive of the awful aspect of the Divine character.

On the *plural* form of the word he quotes from the Jewish Rabbis the assertion, that it is intended to signify ' Dominus potentiarum omnium,' ' The Lord of all powers.' He refers to *Calvin* and others as having opposed, though without immediate effect, the notion maintained by *Peter Lombard*, that it involved the mystery of the Trinity. He repels the profane intimation of Le Clerc, and his successors of the Noological school, that the name originated in polytheism ; and then proceeds to show that " there is in the Hebrew language a widely extended use of the plural, which expresses the intensity of the idea contained in the singular." After numerous references, which prove this point, he proceeds to argue, that " if, in relation to earthly objects, all that serves to represent a whole order of beings is brought before the mind by means of the plural form, we might anticipate a more extended application of this method of distinguishing in the appellations of God, in whose being and attributes there is everywhere a unity which embraces and comprehends all multiplicity." " The use of the plural," he adds, " answers the same purpose which elsewhere is accomplished by an accumulation of the Divine names; as in Joshua xxii. 22 ; the thrice holy in Isaiah vi. 3 ; and אדני אדנים in Deut. x. 17. It calls the attention to the infinite riches and the inexhaustible fulness contained in the one Divine Being, so that though men may imagine innumerable gods, and invest them with perfections, yet all these are contained in the one אלהים, (Elohim.") See *Dissertations*, pp. 268-273.

It is, perhaps, necessary here to state, that whatever treasures of biblical learning the writings of this celebrated author contains, and they are un-

2. *And the earth was without form and void.* I shall not be very solicitous about the exposition of these two epithets, תֹהוּ, (*tohu,*) and בֹהוּ, (*bohu.*) The Hebrews use them when they designate anything empty and confused, or vain, and nothing worth. Undoubtedly Moses placed them both in opposition to all those created objects which pertain to the form, the ornament and the perfection of the world. Were we now to take away, I say, from the earth all that God added after the time here alluded to, then we should have this rude and unpolished, or rather shapeless chaos.[1] Therefore I regard what he immediately subjoins, that "darkness was upon the face of the abyss,"[2] as a part of that confused emptiness : because the light began to give some external appearance to the world. For the same reason he calls it the *abyss* and *waters,* since in that mass of matter nothing was solid or stable, nothing distinct.

And the Spirit of God. Interpreters have wrested this passage in various ways. The opinion of some that it means the *wind,* is too frigid to require refutation. They who understand by it the Eternal Spirit of God, do rightly ; yet all do not attain the meaning of Moses in the connection of his discourse ; hence arise the various interpretations of the participle מְרַחֶפֶת, (*merachepeth.*) I will, in the first place, state what (in my judgment) Moses intended. We have already heard that before God had perfected the world it was an indigested mass ; he now teaches that the power of the Spirit was necessary in order to sustain it. For this

doubtedly great, the reader will still require to be on his guard in studying them. For, notwithstanding the author's general strenuous opposition to the *anti-supernaturalism* of his own countrymen, he has not altogether escaped the contagion which he is attempting to resist. Occasions may occur in which it will be right to allude to some of his mistakes.—*Ed.*

[1] The words תֹהוּ וּבֹהוּ are rendered in Calvin's text *informis et inanis,* "shapeless and empty." They are, however, substantives, and are translated in Isaiah xxxiv. 11, "confusion" and "emptiness." The two words standing in connection, were used by the Hebrews to describe anything that was most dreary, waste, and desolate. The Septuagint has ἀόρατος καὶ ἀκατασκεύαστος, invisible and unfurnished.—*Ed.*

[2] It is to be remarked, that Calvin does not in his comment always adhere to his own translation. For instance, his version here is, "in superficiem voraginis ;" but in his Commentary he has it, "super faciem abyssi," from the Latin Vulgate.—*Ed.*

doubt might occur to the mind, how such a disorderly heap could stand; seeing that we now behold the world preserved by government, or order.[1] He therefore asserts that this mass, however confused it might be, was rendered stable, for the time, by the secret efficacy of the Spirit. Now there are two significations of the Hebrew word which suit the present place; either that the Spirit moved and agitated itself over the waters, for the sake of putting forth vigour; or that He brooded over them to cherish them.[2] Inasmuch as it makes little difference in the result, whichever of these explanations is preferred, let the reader's judgment be left free. But if that chaos required the secret inspiration of God to prevent its speedy dissolution; how could this order, so fair and distinct, subsist by itself, unless it derived strength elsewhere? Therefore, that Scripture must be fulfilled, ‘ Send forth thy Spirit, and they shall be created, and thou shalt renew the face of the earth,’ (Ps. civ. 30;) so, on the other hand, as soon as the Lord takes away his Spirit, all things return to their dust and vanish away, (ver. 29.)

3. *And God said.* Moses now, for the first time, introduces God in the act of *speaking,* as if he had created the mass of heaven and earth without the Word.[3] Yet John testifies that ‘ without him nothing was made of the things which were made,’ (John i. 3.) And it is certain that the world had been *begun* by the same efficacy of the Word by which it was *completed.* God, however, did not put forth his

---

[1] “ Temperamento servari.” Perhaps we should say, “ preserved by the laws of nature.”—*Ed.*

[2] The participle of the verb רחף is here used instead of the regular tense. “ The Spirit was moving,” instead of “ the Spirit moved.” The word occurs in Deut. xxxii. 11, where the eagle is represented as fluttering over her young. Vatablus, whom Calvin here probably follows, says, the Holy Spirit cherished the earth “ by his secret virtue, that it might remain stable for the time.”—See *Poole's Synopsis.* The word, however, is supposed further to imply a vivifying power ; as that of birds brooding over and hatching their young. Gesenius says that Moses here speaks, “ Von der schaffenden und belebenden Kraft Gottes die über der chaotischen wasserbedeckten Erde schwebt gleichsam brütet ”—“ of the creative and quickening power of God, which hovered over the chaotic and water-covered earth, as if brooding.” The same view is given by P. Martyr on Genesis ; others, however, are opposed to this interpretation. Vide *Johannes Clericus in loco.*—*Ed.*

[3] “ Sans sa Parole”—“ without his Word.”—*French Trans.*

Word until he proceeded to originate light;[1] because in the act of distinguishing[2] his wisdom begins to be conspicuous. Which thing alone is sufficient to confute the blasphemy of Servetus. This impure caviller asserts,[3] that the first beginning of the Word was when God commanded the light to be; as if the cause, truly, were not prior to its effect. Since, however, by the Word of God things which were not came suddenly into being, we ought rather to infer the eternity of His essence. Wherefore the Apostles rightly prove the Deity of Christ from hence, that since he is the Word of God, all things have been created by him. Servetus imagines a new quality in God when he begins to speak. But far otherwise must we think concerning the Word of God, namely, that he is the Wisdom dwelling in God,[4] and without which God could never be ; the effect of which, however, became apparent when the light was created.[5]

[1] " Sed Deus Verbum suum nonnisi in lucis origine, protulit."—"Mais Dieu n'a point mis sa Parole en avant, sinon en la creation de la lumiere." —" But God did not put his Word forward except in the creation of the light."—*French Trans.*

[2] " In distinctione." The French is somewhat different: "Pource que la distinction de sa Sagesse commença lors à apparoir evidemment."— "Because that the distinction of his Wisdom began then to appear evidently." The printing of the word Wisdom with a capital, renders it probable that by it Calvin means the Son of God, who is styled Wisdom in the eighth chapter of Proverbs and elsewhere. Whence it would seem that he intends the whole of what he here says as an argument in favour of the Deity of Christ.—*Ed.*

[3] " Latrat hic obscœnus canis."

[4] " Mais il faut bien autrement sentir de la Parole de Dieu, assavoir que c'est la Sapience residente. en luy."—*French Trans.*

[5] To understand this difficult and obscure passage, it will be necessary to know something of the ground taken by Servetus in his attempt to subvert the doctrine of the Trinity. He maintained that Christ was not the Son of God as to his *divine* nature, but only as to his *human*, and that this title belonged to him solely in consequence of His incarnation. Yet he professed to believe in the Word, as an emanation of some kind from the Deity ; compounded—as he explains it—of the essence of God, of spirit, of flesh, and of three uncreated elements. These three elements appeared, as he supposes, in the *first light of the world*, in the cloud, and in the pillar of fire. (See *Calvin's Institutes*, Book II. c. xiv.) This illustrates what Calvin means when he says, that Servetus imagines a new quality in God when he begins to speak. The distinct personality of the Word being denied, qualities or attributes of Deity are put in his place. Against this Calvin contends. His argument seems to be to the following effect:—The creation of the indigested mass called heaven and earth,

Let there be light. It was proper that the light, by means
of which the world was to be adorned with such excellent
beauty, should be first created; and this also was the commencement of the distinction, [among the creatures.¹] It did
not, however, happen from inconsideration or by accident, that
the light preceded the sun and the moon. To nothing are we
more prone than to tie down the power of God to those instruments, the agency of which he employs. The sun and
moon supply us with light : and, according to our notions, we
so include this power to give light in them, that if they were
taken away from the world, it would seem impossible for any
light to remain. Therefore the Lord, by the very order of
the creation, bears witness that he holds in his hand the light,
which he is able to impart to us without the sun and moon.
Further, it is certain, from the context, that the light was so
created as to be interchanged with darkness. But it may be
asked, whether light and darkness succeeded each other in
turn through the whole circuit of the world ; or whether the

in the first verse, was apparently—though not really—without the Word,
inasmuch as the Word is not mentioned. But when there began to be a
distinction, (such as light developed,) then the Word was *put forward*.
This Word is also the Wisdom of God.

Servetus asserts that the Word had no existence till God said, " Let
there be light." But Calvin argues, that the Word existed before he
acted—the cause was prior to its effect. We ought, therefore, to infer
the eternal existence of the Word, as he contends the Apostles do, from
the fact that all things were created by Him. Whatever quality God
possessed when he began to speak, he must have possessed before. His
Word, or his Wisdom, or his only-begotten Son, dwelt in Him, and was
one with him from eternity ; the same Word, or Wisdom, acted really in
the creation of the chaotic mass, though not apparently. But in the
creation of light, the very commencement of distinguishing, (exordium
distinctionis,) this divine Word or Wisdom was manifest.

Having given, to the best of my judgment, an explanation of Calvin's
reasoning, truth obliges me to add, that it seems to be an involved and
unsatisfactory argument to prove—

1st, That the Second Person of the Trinity is distinctly referred to in
the second verse of this chapter ; and,

2d, That He is *truly* though not *obviously* the Creator of heaven and
earth mentioned in the first verse.

It furnishes occasion rather for regret than for surprise, that the most
powerful minds are sometimes found attempting to sustain a good cause
by inconclusive reasoning.—*Ed.*

¹ " De la distinction des les creatures."—*French Tr*. That is, the beauties
of nature could not be perceived, nor the distinction between different
objects discerned without the light.—*Ed.*

darkness occupied one half of the circle, while light shone in the other.   There is, however, no doubt that the order of their succession was alternate, but whether it was everywhere day at the same time, and everywhere night also, I would rather leave undecided ; nor is it very necessary to be known.[1]

4. *And God saw the light.* Here God is introduced by Moses as surveying his work, that he might take pleasure in it. But he does it for our sake, to teach us that God has made nothing without a certain reason and design. And we ought not so to understand the words of Moses as if God did not know that his work was good, till it was finished. But the meaning of the passage is, that the work, such as we now see it, was approved by God. Therefore nothing remains for us, but to acquiesce in this judgment of God. And this admonition is very useful. For whereas man ought to apply all his senses to the admiring contemplation of the works of God,[2] we see what license he really allows himself in detracting from them.

5. *And God called the light.* That is, God willed that there should be a regular vicissitude of days and nights ; which also followed immediately when the first day was ended. For God removed the light from view, that night might be the commencement of another day. What Moses says, however, admits a double interpretation ; either that this was the evening and morning belonging to the first day, or that the first day consisted of the evening and the morning. Whichever interpretation be chosen, it makes no difference in the sense, for he simply understands the day to have been made up of two parts. Further, he begins the day, according to the custom of his nation, with the evening. It is to no purpose to dispute whether this be the best and the legitimate order or not. We know that darkness preceded time itself ; when God withdrew the light, he closed the day. I do not doubt that

[1] See Note at p. 61.
[2] " L'homme devroit estendere tous ses sens à considerer, et avoir en admiration les œuvres de Dieu."—" Man ought to apply all his senses in considering and having in admiration the works of God."—*French Tr.*

the most ancient fathers, to whom the coming night was the
end of one day and the beginning of another, followed this
mode of reckoning. Although Moses did not intend here to
prescribe a rule which it would be criminal to violate; yet
(as we have now said) he accommodated his discourse to the
received custom. Wherefore, as the Jews foolishly condemn
all the reckonings of other people, as if God had sanctioned
this alone ; so again are they equally foolish who contend that
this mode of reckoning, which Moses approves, is preposterous.

The first day. Here the error of those is manifestly refuted, who maintain that the world was made in a moment.
For it is too violent a cavil to contend that Moses distributes
the work which God perfected at once into six days, for the
mere purpose of conveying instruction. Let us rather conclude that God himself took the space of six days, for the purpose of accommodating his works to the capacity of men.
We slightingly pass over the infinite glory of God, which
here shines forth ; whence arises this but from our excessive
dulness in considering his greatness ?   In the meantime, the
vanity of our minds carries us away elsewhere. For the correction of this fault, God applied the most suitable remedy
when he distributed the creation of the world into successive
portions, that he might fix our attention, and compel us, as
if he had laid his hand upon us, to pause and to reflect. For
the confirmation of the gloss above alluded to, a passage from
Ecclesiasticus is unskilfully cited. ' He who liveth for ever
created all things at once,' (Ecclus. xviii. 1.) For the Greek
adverb κοινῇ, which the writer uses, means no such thing, nor
does it refer to time, but to all things universally. [1]

6. *Let there be a firmament.*[2] The work of the second
day is to provide an empty space around the circumference
of the earth, that heaven and earth may not be mixed together. For since the proverb, 'to mingle heaven and earth,'
denotes the extreme of disorder, this distinction ought to be

[1] So the English translation : " He that liveth for ever made all things
in general."

[2] "Sit extensio" In the next verse he changes the word to "expansio."
" Fecit expansionem."—" He made an expanse."

regarded as of great importance.　Moreover, the word רְקִיעַ,
(*rakia,*) comprehends not only the whole region of the air,
but whatever is open above us : as the word heaven is sometimes understood by the Latins.　Thus the arrangement, as
well of the heavens as of the lower atmosphere, is called רְקִיעַ,
(*rakia,*) without discrimination between them, but sometimes
the word signifies both together, sometimes one part only, as
will appear more plainly in our progress.　I know not why
the Greeks have chosen to render the word στερέωμα, which
the Latins have imitated in the term *firmamentum;* [1] for literally it means *expanse.*　And to this David alludes when he
says that ‘ the heavens are stretched out by God like a cur-
tain,’ (Ps. civ. 2.)　If any one should inquire whether this
vacuity did not previously exist, I answer, however true it
may be that all parts of the earth were not overflowed by the
waters ; yet now, for the first time, a separation was ordained,
whereas a confused admixture had previously existed.　Moses
describes the special use of this expanse, “ to divide the
waters from the waters,” from which words arises a great
difficulty.　For it appears opposed to common sense, and
quite incredible, that there should be waters above the heaven.
Hence some resort to allegory, and philosophize concerning
angels ; but quite beside the purpose.　For, to my mind,
this is a certain principle, that nothing is here treated of but
the visible form of the world.　He who would learn astronomy,[2] and other recondite arts, let him go elsewhere.　Here

---

[1] See the Septuagint and Vulgate, which have both been followed by
our English translators.　Doubtless Calvin is correct in supposing the
true meaning of the Hebrew word to be *expanse ;* but the translators of the Septuagint, the Vulgate, and our own version, were not
without reasons for the manner in which they rendered the word.　The
root, רָקַע, signifies, according to Gesenius, Lee, Cocceius, &c., to stamp
with the foot, to beat or hammer out any malleable substance ; and the
derivative, רָקִיעַ, is the outspreading of the heavens, which, “ according to
ordinary observation, rests like the half of a hollow sphere over the earth.”
To the Hebrews, as Gesenius observes, it presented a crystal or sapphire-
like appearance.　Hence it was thought to be something *firm* as well as
expanded—a roof of crystal or of sapphire.　The reader may also refer
to the note of Johannes Clericus, in his commentary on Genesis, who re ·
tains the word *firmament,* and argues at length in vindication of the term.
—*Ed.*

[2] Astrologia.　This word includes, but is not necessarily confined to
that empyrical and presumptuous science, (falsely so-called,) which we

the Spirit of God would teach all men without exception;
and therefore what Gregory declares falsely and in vain respecting statues and pictures is truly applicable to the history
of the creation, namely, that it is the book of the unlearned.[1]
The things, therefore, which he relates, serve as the garniture of that theatre which he places before our eyes. Whence
I conclude, that the waters here meant are such as the
rude and unlearned may perceive. The assertion of some,
that they embrace by faith what they have read concerning
the waters above the heavens, notwithstanding their ignorance respecting them, is not in accordance with the design
of Moses. And truly a longer inquiry into a matter open and
manifest is superfluous. We see that the clouds suspended
in the air, which threaten to fall upon our heads, yet leave us
space to breathe.[2] They who deny that this is effected by
the wonderful providence of God, are vainly inflated with the
folly of their own minds. We know, indeed, that the rain
is naturally produced; but the deluge sufficiently shows how
speedily we might be overwhelmed by the bursting of the
clouds, unless the cataracts of heaven were closed by the
hand of God. Nor does David rashly recount this among
His miracles, that God "layeth the beams of his chambers
in the waters," (Ps. civ. 31;) and he elsewhere calls upon
the celestial waters to praise God, (Ps. cxlviii. 4.) Since,
therefore, God has created the clouds, and assigned them a
region above us, it ought not to be forgotten that they are

now generally designate by the term *astrology*. As the word originally
means nothing but the science of the stars, so it was among our own earlier
writers applied in the same manner. Consequently, it comprehended the
sublime and useful science of *astronomy*. From the double meaning of the
word, Calvin sometimes speaks of it with approbation, and sometimes
with censure. But attention to his reasoning will show, that what he
commends is *astronomy*, and what he censures is *astrology* in the present
acceptation of the word.—*Ed.*

[1] The following are the words of Pope Gregory I. :—"Idcirco enim pic-
tura in ecclesiis adhibeter, ut hi qui literas nesciunt, saltem in parietibus
videndo legant quæ legere in codicibus non valent."—*Epis.* cix. *ad
Lerenum.*

[2] "Capitibus nostris sic minari, ut spirandi locus nobis relinquant." The
French is more diffuse: "Nous menacent, comme si elles devoyent tomber
sur nos testes; et toutesfois elle nous laissent ici lieu pour respirer."
"They threaten us, as if they would fall upon our heads; and, nevertheless, they leave us here space to breathe."

restrained by the power of God, lest, gushing forth with sudden violence, they should swallow us up: and especially since no other barrier is opposed to them than the liquid and yielding air, which would easily give way unless this word prevailed, 'Let there be an expanse between the waters.' Yet Moses has not affixed to the work of this day the note that "God saw that it was good:" perhaps because there was no advantage from it till the terrestrial waters were gathered into their proper place, which was done on the next day, and therefore it is there twice repeated.[1]

9. *Let the waters . . . . be gathered together.* This also is an illustrious miracle, that the waters by their departure have given a dwelling-place to men. For even philosophers allow that the natural position of the waters was to cover the whole earth, as Moses declares they did in the beginning; first, because, being an element, it must be circular, and because this element is heavier than the air, and lighter than the earth, it ought to cover the latter in its whole circumference.[2] But that the seas, being gathered together as on heaps, should give place for man, is seemingly preternatural; and therefore Scripture often extols the goodness of God in this particular. See Psalm xxxiii. 7, 'He hath gathered the waters together on a heap, and hath laid them up in his treasures.' Also Psalm lxxviii. 13, 'He hath collected the waters as into a bottle.'[3] Jeremiah v. 22, 'Will ye not fear me? will ye not tremble at my presence, who have

---

[1] The Septuagint here inserts the clause, "God saw that it was good;" but, as it is found neither in the Hebrew nor in any other ancient version, it must be abandoned. The Rabbis say that the clause was omitted, because the angels fell on that day; but this is to cut the knot rather than to untie it. There is more probability in the conjecture of Picherellus, who supposes that what follows in the ninth and tenth verses all belonged to the work of the second day, though mentioned after it; and, in the same way, he contends that the formation of the beasts, recorded in the 24th verse, belonged to the fifth day, though mentioned after it. Examples of this kind, of *Hysteron proteron*, are adduced in confirmation of this interpretation. See *Poole's Synopsis in loco.—Ed.*

[2] This reasoning is to be explained by reference to the philosophical theories of the age.—*Ed.*

[3] "Velut in utrem;" from the Vulgate. The English version is, "He made the waters to stand as an heap."

placed the sand as the boundary of the sea?'   Job xxxviii. 8,
' Who hath shut up the sea with doors?   Have not I surrounded it with gates and bars?   I have said, Hitherto shalt
thou proceed; here shall thy swelling waves be broken.'
Let us, therefore, know that we are dwelling on dry ground,
because God, by his command, has removed the waters, that
they should not overflow the whole earth.

11. *Let the earth bring forth grass.*   Hitherto the earth
was naked and barren, now the Lord fructifies it by his
word.   For though it was already destined to bring forth
fruit, yet till new virtue proceeded from the mouth of God,
it must remain dry and empty.   For neither was it naturally
fit to produce anything, nor had it a germinating principle
from any other source, till the mouth of the Lord was opened.
For what David declares concerning the heavens, ought also
to be extended to the earth ; that it was ' made by the word
of the Lord, and was adorned and furnished by the breath
of his mouth,' (Ps. xxxiii. 6.)   Moreover, it did not happen
fortuitously, that herbs and trees were created before the sun
and moon.   We now see, indeed, that the earth is quickened
by the sun to cause it to bring forth its fruits ; nor was God
ignorant of this law of nature, which he has since ordained :
but in order that we might learn to refer all things to him,
he did not then make use of the sun or moon.[1]   He permits
us to perceive the efficacy which he infuses into them, so far
as he uses their instrumentality ; but because we are wont
to regard as part of their nature properties which they
derive elsewhere, it was necessary that the vigour which they
now seem to impart to the earth should be manifest before
they were created.   We acknowledge, it is true, in words,
that the First Cause is self-sufficient, and that intermediate
and secondary causes have only what they borrow from this
First Cause ; but, in reality, we picture God to ourselves
as poor or imperfect, unless he is assisted by second causes.
How few, indeed, are there who ascend higher than the sun
when they treat of the fecundity of the earth?   What there-

---

[1] " Nullas tunc soli et lunæ partes concessit."—" Il ne s'est point servi
en cest endroit du soliel ni de la lune."—*French Trans.*

fore we declare God to have done designedly, was indispensably necessary; that we may learn from the order of the creation itself, that God acts through the creatures, not as if he needed external help, but because it was his pleasure. When he says, ' Let the earth bring forth the herb which may produce seed, the tree whose seed is in itself,' he signifies not only that herbs and trees were then created, but that, at the same time, both were endued with the power of propagation, in order that their several species might be perpetuated. Since, therefore, we daily see the earth pouring forth to us such riches from its lap, since we see the herbs producing seed, and this seed received and cherished in the bosom of the earth till it springs forth, and since we see trees shooting from other trees ; all this flows from the same Word. If therefore we inquire, how it happens that the earth is fruitful, that the germ is produced from the seed, that fruits come to maturity, and their various kinds are annually reproduced ; no other cause will be found, but that God has once spoken, that is, has issued his eternal decree ; and that the earth, and all things proceeding from it, yield obedience to the command of God, which they always hear.

14. *Let there be lights.*[1] Moses passes onward to the fourth day, on which the stars were made. God had before created the light, but he now institutes a new order in nature, that the sun should be the dispenser of diurnal light, and the moon and stars should shine by night. And He assigns them this office, to teach us that all creatures are subject to his will, and execute what he enjoins upon them. For Moses relates nothing else than that God ordained certain instruments to diffuse through the earth, by reciprocal changes, that light which had been previously created. The only difference is this, that the light was before dispersed, but now proceeds from lucid bodies ; which, in serving this purpose, obey the command of God.

To divide the day from the night. He means the arti-

---

[1] " Luminaria"—" Luminaries." Heb. מארות. Instruments of light, from אור, light, in ver. 3. " Lighters ; that is, lightsome bodies, or instruments that show light."—*Ainsworth.*

ficial day, which begins at the rising of the sun and ends at its setting. For the natural day (which he mentions above) includes in itself the night. Hence infer, that the interchange of days and nights shall be continual : because the word of God, who determined that the days should be distinct from the nights, directs the course of the sun to this end.

Let them be for signs. It must be remembered, that Moses does not speak with philosophical acuteness on occult mysteries, but relates those things which are everywhere observed, even by the uncultivated, and which are in common use. A twofold advantage is chiefly perceived from the course of the sun and moon; the one is natural, the other applies to civil institutions.[1] Under the term nature, I also comprise agriculture. For although sowing and reaping require human art and industry ; this, nevertheless, is natural, that the sun, by its nearer approach, warms our earth, that he introduces the vernal season, that he is the cause of summer and autumn. But that, for the sake of assisting their memory, men number among themselves years and months; that of these, they form *lustra* and olympiads; that they keep stated days ; this, I say, is peculiar to civil polity. Of each of these mention is here made. I must, however, in a few words, state the reason why Moses calls them signs ; because certain inquisitive persons abuse this passage, to give colour to their frivolous predictions : I call those men Chaldeans and fanatics, who divine everything from the aspects of the stars.[2] Because Moses declares that the sun and moon were appointed for *signs,* they think themselves entitled to elicit from them anything they please. But confutation is easy : for they are called signs of certain things, not signs to denote whatever is according to our fancy. What indeed does Moses assert to be signified by them, except things belonging to the order of nature ? For the same God who here ordains signs testifies by Isaiah that he 'will dissipate the signs of the diviners,' (Isa. xliv. 25;) and forbids us to be 'dismayed at the signs of heaven,' (Jer. x. 2.) But since it is manifest

[1] " Altera ad ordinem politicum spectat."
[2] " Ex siderum præsagiis nihil non divinant."

that Moses does not depart from the ordinary custom of men, I desist from a longer discussion. The word מוֹעֲדִים, (*moadim*,) which they translate 'certain times,' is variously understood among the Hebrews : for it signifies both time and place, and also assemblies of persons. The Rabbis commonly explain the passage as referring to their festivals. But I extend it further to mean, in the first place, the opportunities of time, which in French are called *saisons*, (seasons;) and then all fairs and forensic assemblies.[1] Finally, Moses commemorates the unbounded goodness of God in causing the sun and moon not only to enlighten us, but to afford us various other advantages for the daily use of life. It remains that we, purely enjoying the multiplied bounties of God, should learn not to profane such excellent gifts by our preposterous abuse of them. In the meantime, let us admire this wonderful Artificer, who has so beautifully arranged all things above and beneath, that they may respond to each other in most harmonious concert.

15. *Let them be for lights.* It is well again to repeat what I have said before, that it is not here philosophically discussed, how great the sun is in the heaven, and how great, or how little, is the moon; but how much light comes to us from them.[2] For Moses here addresses himself to our senses, that the knowledge of the gifts of God which we enjoy may not glide away. Therefore, in order to apprehend the meaning of Moses, it is to no purpose to soar above the heavens; let us only open our eyes to behold this light which God enkindles for us in the earth. By this method (as I have before observed) the dishonesty of those men is sufficiently rebuked, who censure Moses for not speaking with greater exactness. For as it became a theologian, he had

---

[1] See the Lexicons of Schindler, Lee, and Gesenius, and Dathe's Commentary on the Pentateuch. The two latter writers explain the terms " signs and seasons " by the figure Hendiadys, for " signs of seasons." " Zu Zeichen der Zeiten." The word stands—1. For the year. 2. For an assembly. 3. For the place of assembling. 4. For a signal.—*Ed.*

[2] " Great lights ;" " that is, in our eyes, to which the sun and moon are nearer than the fixed stars and the greater planets."—*Johannes Clericus in Genesin*, p. 10.—*Ed.*

respect to *us* rather than to the *stars*. Nor, in truth, was he
ignorant of the fact, that the moon had not sufficient brightness to enlighten the earth, unless it borrowed from the sun ;
but he deemed it enough to declare what we all may plainly
perceive, that the moon is a dispenser of light to us. That
it is, as the astronomers assert, an *opaque* body, I allow to be
true, while I deny it to be a *dark* body. For, first, since it
is placed above the element of fire, it must of necessity be a
fiery body. Hence it follows, that it is also luminous; but
seeing that it has not light sufficient to penetrate to us, it
borrows what is wanting from the sun. He calls it a "lesser
light" by comparison ; because the portion of light which it
emits to us is small compared with the infinite splendour of
the sun.[1]

16. *The greater light.* I have said, that Moses does
not here subtilely descant, as a philosopher, on the secrets of
nature, as may be seen in these words. First, he assigns a
place in the expanse of heaven to the planets and stars ; but
astronomers make a distinction of spheres, and, at the same
time, teach that the fixed stars have their proper place in
the firmament. Moses makes two great luminaries ; but
astronomers prove, by conclusive reasons, that the star of
Saturn, which, on account of its great distance, appears the
least of all, is greater than the moon. Here lies the difference ; Moses wrote in a popular style things which, without
instruction, all ordinary persons, endued with common sense,
are able to understand ; but astronomers investigate with
great labour whatever the sagacity of the human mind can
comprehend. Nevertheless, this study is not to be reprobated,
nor this science to be condemned, because some frantic persons are wont boldly to reject whatever is unknown to them.
For astronomy is not only pleasant, but also very useful to
be known : it cannot be denied that this art unfolds the admirable wisdom of God. Wherefore, as ingenious men are
to be honoured who have expended useful labour on this
subject, so they who have leisure and capacity ought not to

[1] The reader will be in no danger of being misled by the defective
natural philosophy of the age in which this was written.—*Ed.*

neglect this kind of exercise. Nor did Moses truly wish to withdraw us from this pursuit in omitting such things as are peculiar to the art; but because he was ordained a teacher as well of the unlearned and rude as of the learned, he could not otherwise fulfil his office than by descending to this grosser method of instruction. Had he spoken of things generally unknown, the uneducated might have pleaded in excuse that such subjects were beyond their capacity. Lastly, since the Spirit of God here opens a common school for all, it is not surprising that he should chiefly choose those subjects which would be intelligible to all. If the astronomer inquires respecting the actual dimensions of the stars, he will find the moon to be less than Saturn; but this is something abstruse, for to the sight it appears differently. Moses, therefore, rather adapts his discourse to common usage. For since the Lord stretches forth, as it were, his hand to us in causing us to enjoy the brightness of the sun and moon, how great would be our ingratitude were we to close our eyes against our own experience? There is therefore no reason why janglers should deride the unskilfulness of Moses in making the moon the second luminary; for he does not call us up into heaven, he only proposes things which lie open before our eyes. Let the astronomers possess their more exalted knowledge; but, in the meantime, they who perceive by the moon the splendour of night, are convicted by its use of perverse ingratitude unless they acknowledge the beneficence of God.

To rule.[1] He does not ascribe such dominion to the sun and moon as shall, in the least degree, diminish the power of God; but because the sun, in half the circuit of heaven, governs the day, and the moon the night, by turns; he therefore assigns to them a kind of government. Yet let us remember, that it is such a government as implies that the sun is still a servant, and the moon a handmaid. In the meantime, we dismiss the reverie of Plato, who ascribes reason and intelligence to the stars. Let us be content with this simple exposition, that God governs the days and nights

---

[1] " In dominium." For dominion.

by the ministry of the sun and moon, because he has them
as his charioteers to convey light suited to the season.

20. *Let the waters bring forth . . . the moving creature.*[1]
On the fifth day the birds and fishes are created. The
blessing of God is added, that they may of themselves produce offspring. Here is a different kind of propagation from
that in herbs and trees : for there the power of fructifying is
in the plants, and that of germinating is in the seed; but here
generation takes place. It seems, however, but little consonant with reason, that he declares birds to have proceeded
from the waters; and, therefore, this is seized upon by captious men as an occasion of calumny. But although there
should appear no other reason but that it so pleased God,
would it not be becoming in us to acquiesce in his judgment?
Why should it not be lawful for him, who created the world
out of nothing, to bring forth the birds out of water? And
what greater absurdity, I pray, has the origin of birds from
the water, than that of the light from darkness? Therefore,
let those who so arrogantly assail their Creator, look for the
Judge who shall reduce them to nothing. Nevertheless, if
we must use physical reasoning in the contest, we know that the
water has greater affinity with the air than the earth has.
But Moses ought rather to be listened to as our teacher, who
would transport us with admiration of God through the consideration of his works.[2] And, truly, the Lord, although he

---

[1] "Repere faciant aquæ reptile animæ viventis."—"Let the waters cause
to creep forth the reptile, (or creeping thing,) having a living soul."
This is a more literal translation of the original than that of the English
version ; yet it does not express more accurately the sense. The word
שֶׁרֶץ, (*sheretz,*) as a substantive, signifies any worm or reptile, generally
of the smaller kind, either in land or water; and the corresponding verb
rendered " to creep forth" signifies also "to multiply." It is well known
that this class of animals multiply more abundantly than any other.
The expression נֶפֶשׁ חַיָּה, (*nepesh chayah,*) "a living soul," does not
refer (as the word soul in English often does) to the immortal principle,
but to the animal life or breath, and the words might here be rendered
" the breath of life."—*Ed.*

[2] For other opinions respecting the origin of birds, see *Poole's Synopsis.*
Some argue from chap. ii. 19, that fowls were made of the earth ; and
would propose an alteration in the translation of the verse before us to
the following effect,—" and let the fowl fly above the heaven."—See
Notes on Genesis, &c., by Professor Bush, *in loco.* But Calvin's

is the Author of nature, yet by no means has followed nature as his guide in the creation of the world, but has rather chosen to put forth such demonstrations of his power as should constrain us to wonder.

21. *And God created.* A question here arises out of the word *created.* For we have before contended, that because the world was created, it was made out of nothing; but now Moses says that things formed from other matter were created. They who truly and properly assert that the fishes were created because the waters were in no way sufficient or suitable for their production, only resort to a subterfuge: for, in the meantime, the fact would remain, that the material of which they were made existed before; which, in strict propriety, the word [created] does not admit. I therefore do not restrict the creation here spoken of to the work of the fifth day, but rather suppose it to refer to that shapeless and confused mass, which was as the fountain of the whole world.[1] God then, it is said, created *whales* (balænas) and other fishes, not that the beginning of their creation is to be reckoned from the moment in which they receive their form; but because they are comprehended in the universal matter which was made out of nothing. So that, with respect to species, form only was then added to them; but creation is nevertheless a term truly used respecting both the whole and the parts. The word commonly rendered whales (*cetos vel cete*) might, in my judgment, be not improperly translated *thynnus* or *tunny fish,* as corresponding with the Hebrew word *thaninim.*[2]

view is more generally approved. "Natantium et volatilium unam originem ponit Moses. 1. Quia aer, (locus avium,) et aqua, (locus piscium,) elementa cognata sunt," &c.—*Castalio, Lyra, Menochius,* and others, in *Poole.—Ed.*

[1] " Ego vero ad opus diei quinti non restringo creationem; sed potius ex illa infermi et confusa massa pendere dico, quæ fuit veluti scaturigo totius mundi." The passage seems to be obscure ; and if the translation above given is correct, the Old English version by Tymme has not hit the true meaning. The French version is as follows:—" Je ne restrain point la creation a l'ouvrage du cinquieme jour; plustost je di qu'elle depend de cette masse confuse qui a este comme la source de tout le monde."—*Ed.*

[2] תנינם. "Significat omnia ingentia animalia tam terrestria ut dracones, quam aquatica ut balænas." "It signifies all large animals, both terrestrial,

When he says that "the waters brought forth,"[1] he proceeds to commend the efficacy of the word, which the waters hear so promptly, that, though lifeless in themselves, they suddenly teem with a living offspring, yet the language of Moses expresses more; namely, that fishes innumerable are daily produced from the waters, because that word of God, by which he once commanded it, is continually in force.

22. *And God blessed them.* What is the force of this benediction he soon declares. For God does not, after the manner of men, pray that we may be blessed; but, by the bare intimation of his purpose, effects what men seek by earnest entreaty. He therefore blesses his creatures when he commands them to increase and grow; that is, he infuses into them fecundity by his word. But it seems futile for God to address fishes and reptiles. I answer, this mode of speaking was no other than that which might be easily understood. For the experiment itself teaches, that the force of the word which was addressed to the fishes was not transient, but rather, being infused into their nature, has taken root, and constantly bears fruit.

24. *Let the earth bring forth.* He descends to the sixth day, on which the animals were created, and then man. 'Let the earth,' he says, 'bring forth living creatures.' But whence has a dead element life? Therefore, there is in this respect a miracle as great as if God had begun to create out of nothing those things which he commanded to proceed from the earth. And he does not take his material from the earth, because he needed it, but that he might the better combine the separate parts of the world with the universe itself. Yet it may be inquired, why He does not here also add his benediction? I answer, that what Moses before expressed on a similar occasion is here also to be understood, although he

as dragons, and aquatic, as whales."—*Poole's Synopsis.* Sometimes it refers to the crocodile, and seems obviously of kindred signification with the word Leviathan. Schindler gives this meaning among others,—*serpents, dragons, great fishes, whales, thinni.*—See also Patrick's Commentary, who takes it for the crocodile.—*Ed.*

[1] "Aquas fecisse reptare," that "the waters caused to creep forth."—*Ed.*

does not repeat it word for word. I say, moreover, it is sufficient for the purpose of signifying the same thing,[1] that
Moses declares animals were created ' according to their
species :' for this distribution carried with it something stable.
It may even hence be inferred, that the offspring of animals
was included.   For to what purpose do distinct species
exist, unless that individuals, by their several kinds, may be
multiplied ?[2]

Cattle.[3] Some of the Hebrews thus distinguish between
" cattle " and " beasts of the earth," that the cattle feed on
herbage, but that the beasts of the earth are they which eat
flesh.   But the Lord, a little while after, assigns herbs to
both as their common food ; and it may be observed, that in
several parts of Scripture these two words are used indiscriminately.   Indeed, I do not doubt that Moses, after he had
named *Behemoth*, (cattle,) added the other, for the sake of
fuller explanation.   By ' reptiles,'[4] in this place, understand
those which are of an earthly nature.

26. *Let us make man.*[5]   Although the tense here used
is the future, all must acknowledge that this is the language
of one apparently deliberating.   Hitherto God has been introduced simply as *commanding ;* now, when he approaches
the most excellent of all his works, he enters into *consultation.*
God certainly might here command by his bare word what he
wished to be done : but he chose to give this tribute to the
excellency of man, that he would, in a manner, enter into
consultation concerning his creation.   This is the highest
honour with which he has dignified us ; to a due regard

[1] Namely, that God's benediction was virtually added, though not expressed in terms.   See verse 22.—*Ed.*
[2] The reader is referred to Note 1, p. 81, for another mode of interpreting these verses ; and also to Poole's Synopsis on verse 24, where the
opinion of Picherellus is fully stated, namely, that verses 24, 25, contain part of the work of the fifth day.—*Ed.*
[3] Cattle, בהמה, (*Behemah ;*) plural, בהמות, (*Behemoth.*)
[4] " Reptiles."   In the English version, " creeping things," the same
expression which occurs in verse 20.   But the Hebrew word is different.
In the twentieth verse it is שָׁרֶץ, (*sharetz,*) in the twenty-fourth it is
רֶמֶשׂ, (*remes.*) The latter word is generally, (though not always,) as here,
referred to land animals.—*Ed.*
[5] " Faciamus hominem."

for which, Moses, by this mode of speaking, would excite our minds. For God is not now first beginning to consider what form he will give to man, and with what endowments it would be fitting to adorn him, nor is he pausing as over a work of difficulty : but, just as we have before observed, that the creation of the world was distributed over six days, for our sake, to the end that our minds might the more easily be retained in the meditation of God's works : so now, for the purpose of commending to our attention the dignity of our nature, he, in taking counsel concerning the creation of man, testifies that he is about to undertake something great and wonderful. Truly there are many things in this corrupted nature which may induce contempt ; but if you rightly weigh all circumstances, man is, among other creatures, a certain pre-eminent specimen of Divine wisdom, justice, and goodness, so that he is deservedly called by the ancients μιχρόχοσμος, "a world in miniature." But since the Lord needs no other counsellor, there can be no doubt that he consulted with himself. The Jews make themselves altogether ridiculous, in pretending that God held communication with the earth or with angels.[1] The earth, forsooth, was a most excellent adviser ! And to ascribe the least portion of a work so exquisite to angels, is a sacrilege to be held in abhorrence. Where, indeed, will they find that we were created after the image of the earth, or of angels ? Does not Moses directly exclude all creatures in express terms, when he declares that Adam was created after the image of God ? Others, who deem themselves more acute, but are doubly infatuated, say that God spoke of himself in the plural number, according to the custom of princes. As if, in truth, that barbarous style of speaking, which has grown into use within a few past centuries, had, even then, prevailed in the world. But it is well that their canine wickedness has been joined with a stupidity so great, that they betray their folly to children. Christians, therefore, properly contend, from this testimony, that there exists a plurality of Persons in the Godhead. God summons no foreign coun-

---

[1] For the various opinions of Jewish writers on this subject, see *Poole's Synopsis in loco.* See also Bishop Patrick's Commentary on this verse.— *Ed.*

CHAP. I.THE BOOK OF GENESIS.93

sellor; hence we infer that he finds within himself something distinct; as, in truth, his eternal wisdom and power reside within him.[1]

In our image, &c. Interpreters do not agree concerning the meaning of these words. The greater part, and nearly all, conceive that the word *image* is to be distinguished from *likeness*. And the common distinction is, that *image* exists in the substance, *likeness* in the accidents of anything. They who would define the subject briefly, say that in the *image* are contained those endowments which God has conferred on human nature at large, while they expound *likeness* to mean gratuitous gifts.[2] But Augustine, beyond all others, speculates with excessive refinement, for the purpose of fabricating a Trinity in man. For in laying hold of the three faculties of the soul enumerated by Aristotle, the intellect, the memory, and the will, he afterwards out of one Trinity derives many. If any reader, having leisure, wishes to enjoy such speculations, let him read the tenth and fourteenth books on the Trinity, also the eleventh book of the " City of God." I acknowledge, indeed, that there is something in man which refers to the Father, and the Son, and the Spirit: and I have no difficulty in admitting the above distinction of the faculties of the soul: although the simpler division into two parts, which is more used in Scripture, is better adapted to the sound doctrine of piety; but a definition of the image of God ought to rest on a firmer basis than such subtleties. As for myself, before I define the image of God, I would deny that it differs from his likeness. For when Moses afterwards repeats the same thing, he passes over

---

[1] "Ut certe æterna ejus sapientia et virtus in ipso resident." The expression is ambiguous ; but the French translation renders it, " Comme à la verité, sa Sapience eternelle, et Vertu reside en luy;" which translation is here followed. By beginning the words rendered Wisdom and Power with capitals, it would appear that the second and third Persons of the Trinity were in the mind of the writer when the passage was written. And perhaps this is the only view of it which renders the reasoning of Calvin intelligible. See Notes 2 and 5, at page 75.—*Ed.*

[2] Some here distinguish, and say the image is in what is natural, the likeness in what is gratuitous.—*Lyra.* Others blend them together, and say there is an Hendiadys, that is, according to the image most like us —*Tirinus.*—See *Poole's Synopsis.*—*Ed.*

the *likeness*, and contents himself with mentioning the *image*. Should any one take the exception, that he was merely studying brevity; I answer,[1] that where he twice uses the word image, he makes no mention of the likeness. We also know that it was customary with the Hebrews to repeat the same thing in different words. Besides, the phrase itself shows that the second term was added for the sake of explanation, ' Let us make,' he says, ' man in our image, according to our likeness,' that is, that he may be like God, or may represent the image of God. Lastly, in the fifth chapter, without making any mention of *image*, he puts likeness in its place, (verse 1.) Although we have set aside all difference between the two words, we have not yet ascertained what this image or likeness is. The *Anthropomorphites* were too gross in seeking this resemblance in the human body; let that reverie therefore remain entombed. Others proceed with a little more subtlety, who, though they do not imagine God to be corporeal, yet maintain that the image of God is in the body of man, because his admirable workmanship there shines brightly; but this opinion, as we shall see, is by no means consonant with Scripture. The exposition of Chrysostom is not more correct, who refers to the dominion which was given to man in order that he might, in a certain sense, act as God's vicegerent in the government of the world. This truly is some portion, though very small, of the image of God. Since the image of God has been destroyed in us by the fall, we may judge from its restoration what it originally had been. Paul says that we are transformed into the image of God by the gospel. And, according to him, spiritual regeneration is nothing else than the restoration of the same image. (Col. iii. 10, and Eph. iv. 23.) That he made this image to consist in " righteousness and true holiness," is by the figure *synecdoche*;[2] for though this is the chief part, it is not the whole of God's image. Therefore by this word the perfection of our whole nature is designated, as it

[1] " I answer," is not in the original, but is taken from the French translation.—*Ed.*
[2] Synecdoche is the figure which puts a part for the whole, or the whole for a part.—*Ed.*

appeared when Adam was endued with a right judgment,
had affections in harmony with reason, had all his senses
sound and well-regulated, and truly excelled in everything
good. Thus the chief seat of the Divine image was in his
mind and heart, where it was eminent: yet was there no
part of him in which some scintillations of it did not shine
forth. For there was an attempering in the several parts of the
soul, which corresponded with their various offices.[1] In the
mind perfect intelligence flourished and reigned, uprightness
attended as its companion, and all the senses were prepared
and moulded for due obedience to reason; and in the body
there was a suitable correspondence with this internal order.
But now, although some obscure lineaments of that image
are found remaining in us; yet are they so vitiated and
maimed, that they may truly be said to be destroyed. For
besides the deformity which everywhere appears unsightly,
this evil also is added, that no part is free from the infection
of sin.

In our image, after our likeness. I do not scrupulously
insist upon the particles ב, (*beth*,) and כ, (*caph*.[2]) I know
not whether there is anything solid in the opinion of some
who hold that this is said, because the image of God was
only shadowed forth in man till he should arrive at his perfection. The thing indeed is true; but I do not think that
anything of the kind entered the mind of Moses.[3] It is also
truly said that Christ is the only image of the Father, but
yet the words of Moses do not bear the interpretation that
"in the image" means "in Christ." It may also be added,
that even man, though in a different respect, is called the
image of God. In which thing some of the Fathers are deceived who thought that they could defeat the Arians with
this weapon that Christ alone is God's image. This further

[1] " Erat erim in singulis animæ partibus temperatura quæ suis numeris
constabat."
[2] The two prefixes to the Hebrew words signifying *image* and *likeness;*
the former of which is translated *in*, the latter *after*, or still more correctly, *according to*. This sentence is not translated either in the French
or Old English version.—*Ed.*
[3] "Innuit in homine esse *imaginem Dei*, sed *imperfectam* et qualem
umbræ."—*Oleaster in Poli Synopsi.*

difficulty is also to be encountered, namely, why Paul should deny the *woman* to be the image of God, when Moses honours both, indiscriminately, with this title. The solution is short; Paul there alludes only to the domestic relation. He therefore restricts the image of God to *government*, in which the man has superiority over the wife, and certainly he means nothing more than that man is superior in the degree of honour. But here the question is respecting that glory of God which peculiarly shines forth in human nature, where the mind, the will, and all the senses, represent the Divine order.

And let them have dominion. [1] Here he commemorates that part of dignity with which he decreed to honour man, namely, that he should have authority over all living creatures. He appointed man, it is true, lord of the world; but he expressly subjects the animals to him, because they, having an inclination or instinct of their own, [2] seem to be less under authority from without. The use of the plural number intimates that this authority was not given to Adam only, but to all his posterity as well as to him. And hence we infer what was the end for which all things were created; namely, that none of the conveniences and necessaries of life might be wanting to men. In the very order of the creation the paternal solicitude of God for man is conspicuous, because he furnished the world with all things needful, and even with an immense profusion of wealth, before he formed man. Thus man was rich before he was born. But if God had such care for us before we existed, he will by no means leave us destitute of food and of other necessaries of life, now that we are placed in the world. Yet, that he often keeps his hand as if closed is to be imputed to our sins.

27. *So God created man.* The reiterated mention of the image of God is not a vain repetition. For it is a remarkable instance of the Divine goodness which can never be sufficiently proclaimed. And, at the same time, he admonishes us from what excellence we have fallen, that he may

---

[1] "Dominetur."
[2] "Quæ quum habeant proprium nutum."

excite in us the desire of its recovery. When he soon afterwards adds, that God created them "male and female," he commends to us that conjugal bond by which the society of mankind is cherished. For this form of speaking, "God created man, male and female created he them," is of the same force as if he had said, that the man himself was incomplete.[1] Under these circumstances, the woman was added to him as a companion that they both might be one, as he more clearly expresses it in the second chapter. Malachi also means the same thing when he relates, (ii. 15,) that one man was created by God, whilst, nevertheless, he possessed the fulness of the Spirit.[2] For he there treats of conjugal fidelity, which the Jews were violating by their polygamy. For the purpose of correcting this fault, he calls that pair, consisting of man and woman, which God in the beginning had joined together, *one man*, in order that every one might learn to be content with his own wife.

28. *And God blessed them.* This blessing of God may be regarded as the source from which the human race has flowed. And we must so consider it not only with reference to the whole, but also, as they say, in every particular instance. For we are fruitful or barren in respect of offspring, as God imparts his power to some and withholds it from others. But here Moses would simply declare that Adam with his wife was formed for the production of offspring, in order that men might replenish the earth. God could himself indeed have covered the earth with a multitude of men; but it was his will that we should proceed from one fountain, in order that our desire of mutual concord might be the greater, and that each might the more freely embrace the other as his own flesh. Besides, as men were created to occupy the earth, so we ought certainly to conclude that God has marked, as with a boundary, that space of earth which would suffice for the reception of men, and would prove a suitable abode for them. Any inequality which is contrary to this arrangement is nothing else than a

---

[1] "Acsi virum dixisset esse dimidium hominem."

[2] On this difficult passage see Lowth, Archbishop Newcome, and Scott, who confirm in the main the interpretation of Calvin.—*Ed.*

corruption of nature which proceeds from sin. In the meantime, however, the benediction of God so prevails that the earth everywhere lies open that it may have its inhabitants, and that an immense multitude of men may find, in some part of the globe, their home. Now, what I have said concerning marriage must be kept in mind; that God intends the human race to be multiplied by generation indeed, but not, as in brute animals, by promiscuous intercourse. For he has joined the man to his wife, that they might produce a divine, that is, a legitimate seed. Let us then mark whom God here addresses when he commands them to increase, and to whom he limits his benediction. Certainly he does not give the reins to human passions,[1] but, beginning at holy and chaste marriage, he proceeds to speak of the production of offspring. For this is also worthy of notice, that Moses here briefly alludes to a subject which he afterwards means more fully to explain, and that the regular series of the history is inverted, yet in such a way as to make the true succession of events apparent. The question, however, is proposed, whether fornicators and adulterers become fruitful by the power of God; which, if it be true, then whether the blessing of God is in like manner extended to them? I answer, this is a corruption of the Divine institute; and whereas God produces offspring from this muddy pool, as well as from the pure fountain of marriage, this will tend to their greater destruction. Still that pure and lawful method of increase, which God ordained from the beginning, remains firm; this is that law of nature which common sense declares to be inviolable.

Subdue it. He confirms what he had before said respecting dominion. Man had already been created with this condition, that he should subject the earth to himself; but now, at length, he is put in possession of his right, when he hears what has been given to him by the Lord: and this Moses expresses still more fully in the next verse, when he introduces God as granting to him the herbs and the fruits.

---

[1] " Certe frænum viris et muliebris non laxavit, ut in vagas libidines ruierent, absque delectu et pudore : sed a sancto castoque conjugio incipiens, descendit ad generationem."

For it is of great importance that we touch nothing of God's bounty but what we know he has permitted us to do; since we cannot enjoy anything with a good conscience, except we receive it as from the hand of God. And therefore Paul teaches us that, in eating and drinking, we always sin, unless faith be present, (Rom. xiv. 23.) Thus we are instructed to seek from God alone whatever is necessary for us, and in the very use of his gifts, we are to exercise ourselves in meditating on his goodness and paternal care. For the words of God are to this effect: ' Behold, I have prepared food for thee before thou wast formed; acknowledge me, therefore, as thy Father, who have so diligently provided for thee when thou wast not yet created. Moreover, my solicitude for thee has proceeded still further; it was thy business to nurture the things provided for thee, but I have taken even this charge also upon myself. Wherefore, although thou art, in a sense, constituted the father of the earthly family,[1] it is not for thee to be over-anxious about the sustenance of animals.'[2]

Some infer, from this passage, that men were content with herbs and fruits until the deluge, and that it was even unlawful for them to eat flesh. And this seems the more probable, because God confines, in some way, the food of mankind within certain limits. Then, after the deluge, he expressly grants them the use of flesh. These reasons, however, are not sufficiently strong: for it may be adduced on the opposite side, that the first men offered sacrifices from their flocks.[3] This, moreover, is the law of sacrificing rightly, not to offer unto God anything except what he has granted to our use. Lastly, men were clothed in skins; therefore it was lawful for them to kill animals. For these reasons, I think it will be better

[1] "Paterfamilias in mundo."
[2] See verses 29, 30, in which God promises the herbs and fruits of the earth, and every green herb, to the beasts of the earth for food. The reader will perceive that the subsequent observations of Calvin refer more especially to these verses.—*Ed.*
[3] It does not appear that there is much force in Calvin's objections to the opinion, that flesh was not allowed for human food till after the deluge. For if the sacrifices offered were *holocausts*, then the skin only would be left for the use of man. See notes on the offerings of Cain and Abel in the fourth chapter; and, especially, Dr Magee's work on the Atonement, Dissertation LII., *On the date of the permission of animal food to man.*— *Ed.*

for us to assert nothing concerning this matter. Let it suffice for us, that herbs and the fruits of trees were given them as their common food; yet it is not to be doubted that this was abundantly sufficient for their highest gratification. For they judge prudently who maintain that the earth was so marred by the deluge, that we retain scarcely a moderate portion of the original benediction. Even immediately after the fall of man, it had already begun to bring forth degenerate and noxious fruits, but at the deluge, the change became still greater. Yet, however this may be, God certainly did not intend that man should be slenderly and sparingly sustained; but rather, by these words, he promises a liberal abundance, which should leave nothing wanting to a sweet and pleasant life. For Moses relates how beneficent the Lord had been to them, in bestowing on them all things which they could desire, that their ingratitude might have the less excuse.

31. *And God saw everything.* Once more, at the conclusion of the creation, Moses declares that God approved of everything which he had made. In speaking of God as *seeing,* he does it after the manner of men; for the Lord designed this his judgment to be as a rule and example to us; that no one should dare to think or speak otherwise of his works. For it is not lawful for us to dispute whether that ought to be approved or not which God has already approved; but it rather becomes us to acquiesce without controversy. The repetition also denotes how wanton is the temerity of man : otherwise it would have been enough to have said, once for all, that God approved of his works. But God six times inculcates the same thing, that he may restrain, as with so many bridles, our restless audacity. But Moses expresses more than before; for he adds מְאֹד, (*meod,*) that is, *very.* On each of the days, simple approbation was given. But now, after the workmanship of the world was complete in all its parts, and had received, if I may so speak, the last finishing touch, he pronounces it perfectly good; that we may know that there is in the symmetry of God's works the highest perfection, to which nothing can be added.

CHAPTER II.

1. THUS the heavens and the earth were finished, and all the host of them.

2. And on the seventh day God ended his work which he had made; and he rested on the seventh day from all his work which he had made.

3. And God blessed the seventh day, and sanctified it: because that in it he had rested from all his work which God created and made.

4. These *are* the generations of the heavens and of the earth when they were created, in the day that the Lord God made the earth and the heavens,

5. And every plant of the field before it was in the earth, and every herb of the field before it grew; for the Lord God had not caused it to rain upon the earth, and *there was* not a man to till the ground.

6. But there went up a mist from the earth, and watered the whole face of the ground.

7. And the Lord God formed man *of* the dust of the ground, and breathed into his nostrils the breath of life; and man became a living soul.

8. And the Lord God planted a garden eastward in Eden; and there he put the man whom he had formed.

9. And out of the ground made the Lord God to grow every tree that is pleasant to the sight and good for food; the tree of life also in the midst of the garden, and the tree of knowledge of good and evil.

10. And a river went out of Eden to water the garden; and from thence it was parted, and became into four heads.

11. The name of the first *is* Pison: that *is* it which compasseth the whole land of Havilah, where *there is* gold;

12. And the gold of that land *is* good: there *is* bdellium and the onyx stone.

13. And the name of the second river *is* Gihon: the same *is* it that compasseth the whole land of Ethiopia.

1. Perfecti fuerunt igitur cœli et terra, et omnis exercitus eorum.

2. Perfeceratque Deus die septimo opus suum quod fecerat, et quievit die septimo ab omni opere suo quod fecerat.

3. Benedixit autem diei septimo, et sanctificavit illum : quod in illo quievisset ab omni opere suo quod creaverat Deus ut faceret.

4. Istæ sunt generationes cœli et terræ, quando creati sunt, in die qua fecit Jehova Deus terram et cœlos,

5. Et omne virgultum agri antequam esset in terra, et omnem herbam agri antequam germinaret : quia nondum pluere fecerat Jehova Deus super terram, et homo non erat qui coleret terram :

6. Sed vapor ascendebat e terra, et irrigabat universam superficiem terræ.

7. Formaverat autem Jehova Deus hominem e pulvere terræ; et inspiraverat in faciem ejus spiraculum vitæ, et fuit homo in animam viventem.

8. Plantaverat quoque Jehova Deus hortum in Heden ab Oriente : et posuit ibi hominem quem formaverat.

9. Et germinare fecerat Jehova Deus e terra omnem arborem concupiscibilem visu, et bonam ad vescendum; et arborem vitæ in medio horti, et arborem scientiæ boni et mali.

10. Et fluvius egrediebatur ex Heden ad irrigandum hortum; et inde dividebatur, eratque in quatuor capita.

11. Nomen unius, Pison : ipse circuit totam terram Havila, ubi est aurum :

12. Et aurum terræ illius bonum : ibi est bdellium, et lapis onychinus.

13. Nomen vero fluvii secundi Gihon: ipse circuit omnem terram Æthiopiæ.

14. And the name of the third river *is* Hiddekel; that *is* it which goeth toward the east of Assyria. And the fourth river is Euphrates.

15. And the Lord God took the man, and put him into the garden of Eden, to dress it and to keep it.

16. And the Lord God commanded the man, saying, Of every tree in the garden thou mayest freely eat:

17. But of the tree of the knowledge of good and evil, thou shalt not eat of it; for in the day that thou eatest thereof thou shalt surely die.

18. And the Lord God said, *It is* not good that the man should be alone; I will make him an help meet for him.

19. And out of the ground the Lord God formed every beast of the field, and every fowl of the air ; and brought *them* unto Adam to see what he would call them : and whatsoever Adam called every living creature, that *was* the name thereof.

20. And Adam gave names to all cattle, and to the fowl of the air, and to every beast of the field; but for Adam there was not found an help meet for him.

21. And the Lord God caused a deep sleep to fall upon Adam, and he slept : and he took one of his ribs, and closed up the flesh instead thereof;

22. And the rib, which the Lord God had taken from man, made he a woman, and brought her unto the man.

23. And Adam said, This *is* now bone of my bones, and flesh of my flesh : she shall be called Woman, because she was taken out of man.

24. Therefore shall a man leave his father and his mother, and shall cleave unto his wife : and they shall be one flesh.

25. And they were both naked, the man and his wife, and were not ashamed.

14. Et nomen fluvii tertii Hiddekel; ipse tendit ad orientem Assur; et flumen quartum est Perath.

15. Tulit itaque Jehova Deus hominem, et posuit eum in horto Heden, ut coleret eum, et custodiret eum.

16. Præcepitque Jehova Deus homini, dicendo, De omni arbore horti comedendo comedes:

17. At de arbore scientiæ boni et mali ne comedas ex illa : quia in die quo comederis ex ea, moriendo morieris.

18. Et dixit Jehova Deus, Non est bonum esse hominem solum : faciam ei adjutorium quod sit coram ipso.

19. Formaverat autem Jehova Deus e terra omnem bestiam agri, et omne volatile cœli; et adduxerat ad Adam ut videret quomodo vocaret illud : et omne quod vocavit illi, *illi inquum*, animæ viventi, est nomen ejus.

20. Vocavit itaque Adam nomina cuique jumento, et volatili cœli omnique bestiæ agri : Adæ vero non invenerat adjutorium quod esset coram se.

21. Cadere igitur fecit Jehova Deus soporem super Adam, et dormivit : et tulit unam e costis cjus, et clausit carnem pro ea.

22. Et ædificavit Jehova Deus costam quam tulerat ex Adam in mulierem, et adduxit eam ad Adam.

23. Et dixit Adam, Hac vice os *est* ex ossibus meis, et caro ex carne mea : et vocabitur Virissa, quia ex viro sumpta est ista.

24. Idcirco relinquet unusquisque patrem suum et matrem suam, et adhærebit uxori suæ, eruntque in carnem unam.

25. Erant autem ambo nudi, Adam et uxor ejus : et non pudebat eos.

1. *Thus the heavens and the earth were finished.*[1] Moses

---

[1] The three verses at the commencement of this chapter evidently belong to the first, being a summing up of the preceding history of the

summarily repeats that in six days the fabric of the heaven and the earth was completed. The general division of the world is made into these two parts, as has been stated at the commencement of the first chapter. But he now adds, "all the host of them," by which he signifies that the world was furnished with all its garniture. This epilogue, moreover, with sufficient clearness entirely refutes the error of those who imagine that the world was formed in a moment; for it declares that an end was only at length put to the work on the sixth day. Instead of *host* we might not improperly render the term *abundance*;[1] for Moses declares that this world was in every sense completed, as if the whole house were well supplied and filled with its furniture. The heaven, without the sun, and moon, and stars, would be an empty and dismantled palace : if the earth were destitute of animals, trees, and plants, that barren waste would have the appearance of a poor and deserted house. God, therefore, did not cease from the work of the creation of the world till he had completed it in every part, so that nothing should be wanting to its suitable abundance.

2. *And he rested on the seventh day.* The question may not improperly be put, what kind of rest this was. For it is certain that inasmuch as God sustains the world by his power, governs it by his providence, cherishes and even propagates all creatures, he is constantly at work. Therefore that saying of Christ is true, that the Father and he himself had worked from the beginning hitherto,[2] because, if God should but withdraw his hand a little, all things would immediately perish and dissolve into nothing, as is declared in

---

creation, and an account of the sabbatical institution on the seventh day. The remark of Dathe is, "Male capita hoc loco sunt divisa. Tres versus priores ad primum caput sunt referendi."—*Ed.*

[1] "Copiam," a questionable rendering, surely, of the word צבאם. The Septuagint gives the word κόσμος, and the Vulgate, *ornatus;* the meaning of both words is "ornaments," or garniture. The other versions in Walton translate it *exercitus,* host or army. Fagius, in Poli Synopsi, seems the chief maintainer of Calvin's interpretation. The words of Poole are, "Alii, *virtus, copia eorum,* quia eis declarat Deus (sicut rex copiis suis,) potentiam et sapientiam."—*Ed.*

[2] John v. 17. This sentence is omitted in Tymme's English version. —*Ed.*

Psalm civ. 29.[1]   And indeed God is rightly acknowledged as the Creator of heaven and earth only whilst their perpetual preservation is ascribed to him.[2]   The solution of the difficulty is well known, that God ceased from all his work, when he desisted from the creation of new kinds of things.   But to make the sense clearer, understand that the last touch of God had been put, in order that nothing might be wanting to the perfection of the world.   And this is the meaning of the words of Moses, *From all his work which he had made ;* for he points out the actual state of the work as God would have it to be, as if he had said, then was completed what God had proposed to himself.   On the whole, this language is intended merely to express the perfection of the fabric of the world ; and therefore we must not infer that God so ceased from his works as to desert them, since they only flourish and sub-sist in him.   Besides, it is to be observed, that in the works of the six days, those things alone are comprehended which tend to the lawful and genuine adorning of the world.   It is sub-sequently that we shall find God saying, " Let the earth bring forth thorns and briers," by which he intimates that the ap-pearance of the earth should be different from what it had been in the beginning.   But the explanation is at hand; many things which are now seen in the world are rather corruptions of it than any part of its proper furniture.   For ever since man declined from his high original, it became necessary that the world should gradually degenerate from its nature.   We must come to this conclusion respecting the existence of fleas, caterpillars, and other noxious insects.   In all these, I say, there is some deformity of the world, which ought by no means to be regarded as in the order of nature, since it pro-ceeds rather from the sin of man than from the hand of God. Truly these things were created by God, but by God as an avenger.   In this place, however, Moses is not considering God as armed for the punishment of the sins of men ; but as

---

[1] " Thou hidest thy face, they are troubled ; thou takest away their breath, they die, and return to their dust."

[2] The word translated *preservation* is *vegetationem*, which means an *en-livening* or a *quickening motion ;* to explain this the Old English translation here adds, though without authority, " According to this saying of the apostle, In him we live, and move, and have our being."—*Ed.*

the Artificer, the Architect, the bountiful Father of a family, who has omitted nothing essential to the perfection of his edifice. At the present time, when we look upon the world corrupted, and as if degenerated from its original creation, let that expression of Paul recur to our mind, that the creature is liable to vanity, not willingly, but through our fault, (Rom. viii. 20,) and thus let us mourn, being admonished of our just condemnation.

3. *And God blessed the seventh day.* It appears that God is here said to bless according to the manner of men, because they bless him whom they highly extol. Nevertheless, even in this sense, it would not be unsuitable to the character of God; because his blessing sometimes means the favour which he bestows upon his people, as the Hebrews call that man the blessed of God, who, by a certain special favour, has power with God. (See Gen. xxiv. 31.) 'Enter thou blessed of God.' Thus we may be allowed to describe the day as blessed by him which he has embraced with love, to the end that the excellence and dignity of his works may therein be celebrated. Yet I have no doubt that Moses, by adding the word sanctified, wished imme-diately to explain what he had said, and thus all ambi-guity is removed, because the second word is exegetical of the former. For קָדֵשׁ, (*kadesh,*) with the Hebrews, is to separate from the common number. God therefore sanctifies the seventh day, when he renders it illustrious, that by a special law it may be distinguished from the rest. Whence it also appears, that God always had respect to the welfare of men. I have said above, that six days were employed in the formation of the world; not that God, to whom one moment is as a thousand years, had need of this succession of time, but that he might engage us in the con-sideration of his works. He had the same end in view in the appointment of his own *rest,* for he set apart a day selected out of the remainder for this special use. Where-fore, that benediction is nothing else than a solemn consecra-tion, by which God claims for himself the meditations and employments of men on the seventh day. This is, indeed, the

proper business of the whole life, in which men should daily exercise themselves, to consider the infinite goodness, justice, power, and wisdom of God, in this magnificent theatre of heaven and earth. But, lest men should prove less sedulously attentive to it than they ought, every seventh day has been especially selected for the purpose of supplying what was wanting in daily meditation. First, therefore, God rested; then he blessed this rest, that in all ages it might be held sacred among men : or he dedicated every seventh day to rest, that his own example might be a perpetual rule. The design of the institution must be always kept in memory: for God did not command men simply to keep holiday every seventh day, as if he delighted in their indolence; but rather that they, being released from all other business, might the more readily apply their minds to the Creator of the world. Lastly, that is a sacred rest[1] which withdraws men from the impediments of the world, that it may dedicate them entirely to God. But now, since men are so backward to celebrate the justice, wisdom, and power of God, and to consider his benefits, that even when they are most faithfully admonished they still remain torpid, no slight stimulus is given by God's own example, and the very precept itself is thereby rendered amiable. For God cannot either more gently allure, or more effectually incite us to obedience, than by inviting and exhorting us to the imitation of himself. Besides, we must know, that this is to be the common employment not of one age or people only, but of the whole human race. Afterwards, in the Law, a new precept concerning the Sabbath was given, which should be peculiar to the Jews, and but for a season; because it was a legal ceremony shadowing forth a spiritual rest, the truth of which was manifested in Christ. Therefore the Lord the more frequently testifies that he had given, in the Sabbath, a symbol of sanctification to his ancient people.[2] Therefore when we hear that the Sabbath was

[1] Both in the Amsterdam edition of 1761, and Hengstenberg's, the word is *vocatio;* but as the French translation gives *reste*, and the Old English one *rest*, there can be little doubt that the original word was *vacatio*, as the sense of the passage seems to require.—*Ed.*

[2] " Sanctificationis symbolum,"—" A symbol or sign of sanctification ;" that is, a sign that God had set them apart as a holy and peculiar people

abrogated by the coming of Christ, we must distinguish between what belongs to the perpetual government of human life, and what properly belongs to ancient figures, the use of which was abolished when the truth was fulfilled. Spiritual rest is the mortification of the flesh ; so that the sons of God should no longer live unto themselves, or indulge their own inclination. So far as the Sabbath was a figure of this rest, I say, it was but for a season ; but inasmuch as it was commanded to men from the beginning that they might employ themselves in the worship of God, it is right that it should continue to the end of the world.

Which God created and made.[1] Here the Jews, in their usual method, foolishly trifle, saying, that God being anticipated in his work by the last evening, left certain animals imperfect, of which kind are fauns and satyrs, as though he had been one of the ordinary class of artificers who have need of time. Ravings so monstrous prove the authors of them to have been delivered over to a reprobate mind, as a dreadful example of the wrath of God. As to the meaning of Moses, some take it thus: that God created his works in order to *make* them, inasmuch as from the time he gave them being, he did not withdraw his hand from their preservation. But this exposition is harsh. Nor do I more willingly subscribe to the opinion of those who refer the word *make* to man, whom God placed over his works, that he might apply them to use, and in a certain sense perfect them by his industry.

---

to himself. " Moreover, also, I gave them my Sabbaths, to be a sign between me and them, that they might know that I am the Lord that sanctify them," Ezek. xx. 12.—*Ed.*

[1] " Quod creaverat Deus ut faceret."   Heb. אֲשֶׁר בָּרָא אֱלֹהִים לַעֲשׂוֹת.
" Which God created to make." For the various opinions and fancies of learned men on this passage, the reader is referred to *Poole's Synopsis.* The more respectable commentators mainly agree with Calvin. Ainsworth says : " created to make, that is, *to exist and be,* and that perfectly and gloriously, as by divine power of creation. Or rather, created and made perfectly and excellently : for so the Hebrew phrase may be explained." The version of Dathe is " creando perfecerat,"—" he had perfected in creating." See also Professor Bush *in loco.* Le Clerc, whose extraordinary learning and industry render his opinion on merely critical questions of great value, notwithstanding his lamentable scepticism, would rather translate the expression, " which he had begun to make." But the other interpretation is to be preferred. Vide *Johannes Clericus in Genesin.*—*Ed.*

I rather think that the perfect form of God's works is here noted; as if he had said, God so created his works, that nothing should be wanting to their perfection; or the creation has proceeded to such a point, that the work is in all respects perfect.

4. *These are the generations.* [1] The design of Moses was deeply to impress upon our minds the *origin* of the heaven and the earth, which he designates by the word *generation.*

[1] A new section of the history of Moses commences at this point; and, from the repetition which occurs of some facts—such as the creation of man—which had been recorded in the preceding chapter, as well as from certain peculiarities of phraseology, many learned men have inferred, that the early portion of the Mosaic history is older than the time of Moses, and that he, under the infallible direction of the Spirit of God, collected and arranged the several fragments of primeval annals in one consistent narrative. One chief argument on which such a conclusion rests is, that from the commencement of the first chapter to the end of the third verse of the second chapter, God is spoken of only under the name of *Elohim;* from the fourth verse of the second to the end of the third chapter, he is uniformly styled *Jehovah Elohim;* and in the fourth and fifth chapters, the name of Elohim or of Jehovah stands alone. This, it is argued, could scarcely have occurred without some cause; and the inference has been drawn, that different records had different forms of expression, which Moses did not alter, unless truth required him to do so. See *Dathe on the Pentateuch, Professor Bush on Genesis,* and *Robertson's Clavis Pentateuchi,* where reference will be found to Vitringa and others. Against this view, however, Hengstenberg argues with considerable force, in his Dissertation "on the Names of God in the Pentateuch;" and if some of his reasonings in the use of these names seem too refined for the simplicity of the Holy Scriptures, and for the comprehension of those to whom the Scriptures are chiefly addressed, yet we may discover the germ of very important truths, though they may be, in some degree, hidden beneath a variety of fanciful developments.

By a very careful examination of the passages in which the terms אלהים, (*Elohim,*) יהוה, (*Jehovah,*) and יהוה אלהים, (*Jehovah Elohim,*) occur, he thinks he has ascertained a reason for the use of each in its place, so that, with some exceptions, in which he allows one term might have been exchanged for the other, the sense of the passage absolutely requires the introduction of the very appellation, and no other, which is there employed. Believing that a theory so general cannot, with all the author's ingenuity and learning, be applied in every case, we may still admit the importance of the distinction he makes, and may readily allow that these names are intended to present the Divine character under different aspects to our view. For instance, we may suppose that Elohim and Jehovah have different meanings, arising from their derivations; but we are not to infer, that, in reading the Scriptures, we must have this diversity, or any diversity at all, in our view, when we meet with these different names of Deity.

"These are the generations." תולדות, (*toledoth,*) "modo origines ejus rei de qua sermo est, modo posteros eorum de quibus agitur, significat. Priori sensu hoc loco sumitur posteriori, cap. v. 1." "The term

For there have always been ungrateful and malignant men, who, either by feigning that the world was eternal, or by obliterating the memory of the creation, would attempt to obscure the glory of God. Thus the devil, by his guile, turns those away from God who are more ingenious and skilful than others, in order that each may become a god unto himself. Wherefore, it is not a superfluous repetition which inculcates the necessary fact, that the world existed only from the time when it was created, since such knowledge directs us to its Architect and Author. Under the names of heaven and earth, the whole is, by the figure synecdoche, included. Some of the Hebrews think, that the essential name of God is here at length expressed by Moses, because his majesty shines forth more clearly in the completed world.[1]

signifies, sometimes, the *origin* of the thing spoken of, sometimes the posterity of those who are mentioned. It is taken here in the former of these senses ; and in chap. v. 1, in the latter."—*Dathe.*

[1] The word יְהוָה, *Jehovah,* here first occurs,—that most sacred and incommunicable name of Deity, called *tetragrammaton,* because it consisted of four letters, which the Jews, through reverence or superstition, refuse to pronounce. The principal meaning of the term is *self-existence;* which is, in truth, necessary existence, as opposed to that which is derived from, or is dependent upon, another. It has been supposed by some that Moses here introduces this title of Deity by anticipation ; because, in Exodus vi. 3, God declares that he had not been previously known by the name of Jehovah. But this, as Dathe forcibly reasons, is to increase difficulties rather than to remove them ; for the patriarchs, Abraham and Jacob, are represented as using the name ; and God himself, in speaking to them, also makes use of it. The true solution of the passage in Exodus seems to be, that God had not made known to the patriarchs *the full import of his name,* as he was now about to do. An elaborate investigation of the origin and import of the name יְהוָה, *(Jehovah,)* will be found in the work of Hengstenberg, referred to in the preceding note. He begins with putting aside the notion of an Egyptian origin, which has been put forth with much confidence by those who would trace all the religious peculiarities of the Israelites to their connection with Egypt. He then disposes of the fancied Phœnician pedigree of the name, founded upon spurious fragments ascribed to Sanchoniathon ; and concludes the negative part of his argument, by showing that the name was not derived from any heathen source whatever. Consequently, it is to be traced to " a Hebrew etymology." We need not follow him into the discussion on the right pronunciation of the word, and the use of the vowel points belonging to אֲדֹנָ, *(Adonai;)* it may suffice to state, that he deduces the name יְהוָה, *(Jehovah,)* from the future of the verb הוה or היה, *to be.* Hence the meaning of the appellation may be expressed in the words, " *He who is to be (for ever.)*" This derivation of the name Jehovah he regards as being confirmed " by all the passages

5. *And every plant.* This verse is connected with the preceding, and must be read in continuation with it; for he annexes the plants and herbs to the earth, as the garment with which the Lord has adorned it, lest its nakedness should appear as a deformity. The noun שִׂיחַ, (*sicah*,[1]) which we translate plant, sometimes signifies trees, as below, (Gen. xxi. 15.[2]) Therefore, some in this place translate it *shrub,* to which I have no objection. Yet the word *plant* is not unsuitable; because, in the former place, Moses seems to refer to the genus, and here to the species.[3] But although he has before related that the herbs were created on the third day, yet it is not without reason that here again mention is made of them, in order that we may know that they were then produced, preserved, and propagated, in a manner different from that which we perceive at the present day. For herbs and trees are produced from seed; or grafts are taken from another root, or they grow by putting forth shoots : in all this the industry and the hand of man are engaged. But, at that time, the method was different : God clothed the earth, not in the same manner as now, (for there was no seed, no root, no plant, which might germinate,) but each suddenly sprung into existence at the command of God, and by the power of his word.

of Scripture, in which a derivation of the name is either expressly given or simply hinted." And, beginning with the Book of Revelation, at the title ὁ ὤν καὶ ὁ ἦν καὶ ὁ ἐρχόμενος, "who is, and was, and is to come," he goes upward through the sacred volume, quoting the passages which bear upon the question, till he comes to the important passage in Exodus iii. 13-16, in which God declares his name to be, "I am that I am." "Every thing created," he adds, "remains not like itself, but is continually changing under circumstances, God only, because he is THE BEING, is always the same; and because he is always the same, is THE BEING." See *Dissertations*, p. 231-265.

"The Lord God."—*Jehovah Elohim.* The two titles of Deity are here combined. "*Elohim*," says Hengstenberg, "is the more general, and *Jehovah* the deep and more discriminating name of the Godhead." This may well be admitted, without accepting all the inferences which the author deduces.—*Ed.*

[1] שִׂיחַ. *Frutex,* stirps; *a shrub*—"cujus pulluli in summa tellure expatiantur,"—"whose shoots are spread abroad over the surface of the earth."—*Robertson's Clavis Pentateuch.—Ed.*

[2] "And the water was spent in the bottle, and she cast the child under one of the *shrubs.*"—*English version.*

[3] It seems remarkable that Calvin should himself translate the word "virgultum," and then reason, in his commentary, as if he preferred the word "planta."—*Ed.*

They possessed durable vigour, so that they might stand by the force of their own nature, and not by that quickening influence which is now perceived, not by the help of rain, not by the irrigation or culture of man; but by the vapour with which God watered the earth. For he excludes these two things, the rain whence the earth derives moisture, that it may retain its native sap; and human culture, which is the assistant of nature. When he says, that God had 'not yet caused it to rain,' he at the same time intimates that it is God who opens and shuts the cataracts of heaven, and that rain and drought are in his hand.

7. *And the Lord God formed man.* He now explains what he had before omitted in the creation of man, that his body was taken out of the earth. He had said that he was formed after the image of God. This is incomparably the highest nobility; and, lest men should use it as an occasion of pride, their first origin is placed immediately before them; whence they may learn that this advantage was adventitious; for Moses relates that man had been, in the beginning, dust of the earth. Let foolish men now go and boast of the excellency of their nature! Concerning other animals, it had before been said, Let the earth produce every living creature;[1] but, on the other hand, the body of Adam is formed of clay, and destitute of sense; to the end that no one should exult beyond measure in his flesh. He must be excessively stupid who does not hence learn humility. That which is afterwards added from another quarter, lays us under just so much obligation to God. Nevertheless, he, at the same time, designed to distinguish man by some mark of excellence from brute animals: for these arose out of the earth in a moment; but the peculiar dignity of man is shown in this, that he was gradually formed. For why did not God command him immediately to spring alive out of the earth, unless that, by a special privilege, he might outshine all the creatures which the earth produced?

[1] "Omnem animam viventem,"—"every living *soul.*" The word soul is applied here, and frequently in the Holy Scriptures, to describe only the sensitive and animal life, that by which a created being *breathes;* and thus distinguishes the animal from the vegetative life.—*Ed.*

And breathed into his nostrils.[1] Whatever the greater part of the ancients might think, I do not hesitate to subscribe to the opinion of those who explain this passage of the animal life of man; and thus I expound what they call the vital spirit, by the word *breath*. Should any one object, that if so, no distinction would be made between man and other living creatures, since here Moses relates only what is common alike to all: I answer, though here mention is made only of the lower faculty of the soul, which imparts breath to the body, and gives it vigour and motion: this does not prevent the human soul from having its proper rank, and therefore it ought to be distinguished from others.[2] Moses first speaks of the breath; he then adds, that a soul was given to man by which he might live, and be endued with sense and motion. Now we know that the powers of the human mind are many and various. Wherefore, there is nothing absurd in supposing that Moses here alludes only to one of them; but omits the intellectual part, of which mention has been made in the first chapter. Three gradations, indeed, are to be noted in the creation of man; that his dead body was formed out of the dust of the earth; that it was endued with a soul, whence it should receive vital motion; and that on this soul God engraved his own image, to which immortality is annexed.

Man became a living soul.[3] I take נפש, (*nepesh,*) for the very essence of the soul: but the epithet *living* suits only the present place, and does not embrace generally the powers of the soul. For Moses intended nothing more than to explain the animating of the clayey figure, whereby it came to pass that man began to live. Paul makes an antithesis between this living soul and the quickening spirit which Christ confers upon the faithful, (1 Cor. xv. 45,) for no other purpose than to teach us that the state of man was not perfected in the person of Adam; but it is a peculiar benefit conferred by Christ, that we may be renewed to a life which is *celestial,*

[1] " Inspiraverat in faciem."
[2] " Non tamen obstare quin gradum suum obtineat anima, ideoque seorsum poni debuerit."
[3] " Factus est in animam viventem."

whereas before the fall of Adam, man's life was only *earthly*, seeing it had no firm and settled constancy.

8. *And the Lord God planted.*[1] Moses now adds the condition and rule of living which were given to man. And, first, he narrates in what part of the world he was placed, and what a happy and pleasant habitation was allotted to him. Moses says, that God had *planted*, accommodating himself, by a simple and uncultivated style, to the capacity of the vulgar. For since the majesty of God, as it really is, cannot be expressed, the Scripture is wont to describe it according to the manner of men. God, then, had planted Paradise in a place which he had especially embellished with every variety of delights, with abounding fruits, and with all other most excellent gifts. For this reason it is called a garden, on account of the elegance of its situation, and the beauty of its form. The ancient interpreter has not improperly translated it Paradise ;[2] because the Hebrews call the more highly cultivated gardens פרדסים, (*Pardaisim*,[3]) and Xenophon pronounces the word to be Persian, when he treats of the magnificent and sumptuous gardens of kings. That region which the Lord assigned to Adam, as the first-born of mankind, was one selected out of the whole world.

In Eden. That Jerome improperly translates this, from the beginning,[4] is very obvious : because Moses afterwards says, that Cain dwelt in the southern region of this place. Moreover, it is to be observed, that when he describes paradise as in the east, he speaks in reference to the Jews, for he directs his discourse to his own people. Hence we infer, in the first place, that there was a certain region assigned by God to the first man, in which he might have his home. I state this expressly, because there have been authors who

[1] " Plantaverat quoque Dominus."—" The Lord had also planted."
[2] " Paradisum."—*Vulgate.*
[3] פרדס. Baumgarten, Park, &c. " Wahrscheinlich aus der Persischen Sprache, wo es die Lustparks der Könige bezeichnet."—" Orchard, Park, &c.—probably from the Persian, where it signifies the pleasure-parks of kings."—*Gesenius.*
[4] " Plantaverat autem Dominus Deus Paradisum voluptatis à principio."—" But the Lord God had planted a paradise of pleasure from the beginning."—*Vulgate.*

would extend this garden over all regions of the world.
Truly, I confess, that if the earth had not been cursed on
account of the sin of man, the whole—as it had been blessed
from the beginning—would have remained the fairest scene
both of fruitfulness and of delight; that it would have been,
in short, not dissimilar to Paradise, when compared with
that scene of deformity which we now behold. But when
Moses here describes particularly the situation of the region,
they absurdly transfer what Moses said of a certain particular
place to the whole world. It is not indeed doubtful (as I
just now hinted) that God would choose the most fertile and
pleasant place, the first-fruits (so to speak) of the earth, as
his gift to Adam, whom he had dignified with the honour of
primogeniture among men, in token of his special favour.
Again, we infer, that this garden was situated on the earth,
not as some dream in the air; for unless it had been a region
of our world, it would not have been placed opposite to
Judea, towards the east. We must, however, entirely reject
the allegories of Origen, and of others like him, which Satan,
with the deepest subtlety, has endeavoured to introduce into
the Church, for the purpose of rendering the doctrine of
Scripture ambiguous and destitute of all certainty and firmness. It may be, indeed, that some, impelled by a supposed
necessity, have resorted to an allegorical sense, because they
never found in the world such a place as is described by
Moses: but we see that the greater part, through a foolish
affectation of subtleties, have been too much addicted to
allegories. As it concerns the present passage, they speculate
in vain, and to no purpose, by departing from the literal sense.
For Moses has no other design than to teach man that he
was formed by God, with this condition, that he should have
dominion over the earth, from which he might gather fruit,
and thus learn by daily experience that the world was subject
unto him. What advantage is it to fly in the air, and to
leave the earth, where God has given proof of his benevolence towards the human race? But some one may say,
that to interpret this of celestial bliss is more skilful. I
answer, since the eternal inheritance of man is in heaven, it
is truly right that we should tend thither; yet must we fix

our foot on earth long enough to enable us to consider the abode which God requires man to use for a time. For we are now conversant with that history which teaches us that Adam was, by Divine appointment, an inhabitant of the earth, in order that he might, in passing through his earthly life, meditate on heavenly glory; and that he had been bountifully enriched by the Lord with innumerable benefits, from the enjoyment of which he might infer the paternal benevolence of God. Moses, also, will hereafter subjoin that he was commanded to cultivate the fields, and permitted to eat certain fruits : all which things neither suit the circle of the moon, nor the aerial regions. But although we have said, that the situation of Paradise lay between the rising of the sun and Judea, yet something more definite may be required respecting that region. They who contend that it was in the vicinity of Mesopotamia, rely on reasons not to be despised; because it is probable that the sons of Eden were contiguous to the river Tigris. But as the description of it by Moses will immediately follow, it is better to defer the consideration of it to that place. The ancient interpreter has fallen into a mistake in translating the proper name Eden by the word "pleasure."[1] I do not indeed deny that the place was so called from its delights; but it is easy to infer that the name was imposed upon the place to distinguish it from others.

9. *And out of the ground made the Lord God to grow.* The production here spoken of belongs to the third day of the creation. But Moses expressly declares the place to have been richly replenished with every kind of fruitful trees, that there might be a full and happy abundance of all things. This was purposely done by the Lord, to the end that the cupidity of man might have the less excuse if, instead of being contented with such remarkable affluence, sweetness, and variety, it should (as really happened) precipitate itself against the commandment of God. The Holy Spirit also designedly relates by Moses the greatness of Adam's happi-

---

[1] The Hebrew word עֵדֶן signifies pleasure, delight, loveliness.—*Ed.*

ness, in order that his vile intemperance might the more
clearly appear, which such superfluity was unable to restrain
from breaking forth upon the forbidden fruit.   And certainly
it was shameful ingratitude, that he could not rest in a state
so happy and desirable : truly, that was more than brutal lust
which bounty so great was not able to satisfy.   No corner of
the earth was then barren, nor was there even any which was
not exceedingly rich and fertile : but that benediction of
God, which was elsewhere comparatively moderate, had in
this place poured itself wonderfully forth.   For not only was
there an abundant supply of food, but with it was added
sweetness for the gratification of the palate, and beauty to
feast the eyes.   Therefore, from such benignant indulgence,
it is more than sufficiently evident, how inexplicable had
been the cupidity of man.

The tree of life also.   It is uncertain whether he means only
two individual trees, or two kinds of trees.   Either opinion
is probable, but the point is by no means worthy of contention ; since it is of little or no concern to us, which of the
two is maintained.   There is more importance in the epithets,
which were applied to each tree from its effect, and that not
by the will of man but of God.[1]   He gave the tree of life its
name, not because it could confer on man that life with which
he had been previously endued, but in order that it might
be a symbol and memorial of the life which he had received
from God.   For we know it to be by no means unusual that
God should give to us the attestation of his grace by external
symbols.[2]   He does not indeed transfer his power into out-

[1] The above passage is wholly omitted in the Old English translation
by Tymme.—*Ed.*

[2] " Scimus minime esse insolens ut *virtutem* suam Deus externis sym-
bolis testatam nobis reddat."—"Nous savons que ce n'est point chose nou-
velle, que Dieu nous testifie sa *vertu* par signes exterieurs."—*French
Trans.   Virtus* in Latin, and *vertu* in French, may both signify *power,
virtue, efficacy ;* but it seems that the term *grace* more correctly conveys
to an English ear the meaning of the Author.—*Ed.*

On the sacramental character of the tree of life, which Calvin here
maintains, but which Dr Kennicott, in his first Dissertation, endeavours,
with more learning than sound judgment, to set aside, the generality of
commentators seem to be agreed.   See Patrick, Scott, &c.   Patrick says,
—"This garden being a type of heaven, perhaps God intended by this
tree to represent that immortal life which he meant to bestow upon man
with himself, (Rev. xxii. 2.)   And so St Austin, in that famous saying

ward signs; but by them he stretches out his hand to us, because, without assistance, we cannot ascend to him. He intended, therefore, that man, as often as he tasted the fruit of that tree, should remember whence he received his life, in order that he might acknowledge that he lives not by his own power, but by the kindness of God alone; and that life is not (as they commonly speak) an intrinsic good, but proceeds from God. Finally, in that tree there was a visible testimony to the declaration, that 'in God we are, and live, and move.' But if Adam, hitherto innocent, and of an upright nature, had need of monitory signs to lead him to the knowledge of divine grace, how much more necessary are signs now, in this great imbecility of our nature, since we have fallen from the true light? Yet I am not dissatisfied with what has been handed down by some of the fathers, as Augustine and Eucherius, that the tree of life was a figure of Christ, inasmuch as he is the Eternal Word of God : it could not indeed be otherwise a symbol of life, than by representing him in figure. For we must maintain what is declared in the first chapter of John, that the life of all things was included in the Word, but especially the life of men, which is conjoined with reason and intelligence. Wherefore, by this sign, Adam was admonished, that he could claim nothing for himself as if it were his own, in order that he might depend wholly upon the Son of God, and might not seek life anywhere but in him. But if he, at the time when he possessed life in safety, had it only as deposited in the word of God, and could not otherwise retain it, than by acknowledging that it was received from Him, whence may we recover it, after it has been lost? Let us know, therefore, that when we have departed from Christ, nothing remains for us but death.

I know that certain writers restrict the meaning of the expression here used to corporeal life. They suppose such a power of quickening the body to have been in the tree, that it should never languish through age ; but I say, they omit what is the chief

of his, 'Erat ei in cæteris lignis *Alimentum*, in isto autem *Sacramentum*. In other trees there was *nourishment* for man ; but in this also a *sacrament*. For it was both a *symbol* of that life which God had already bestowed upon man, and of that life which he was to hope for in another world, if he proved obedient."—*Ed.*

thing in life, namely, the grace of intelligence; for we must always consider for what end man was formed, and what rule of living was prescribed to him. Certainly, for him to live, was not simply to have a body fresh and lively, but also to excel in the endowments of the soul.

Concerning the tree of knowledge of good and evil, we must hold, that it was prohibited to man, not because God would have him to stray like a sheep, without judgment and without choice; but that he might not seek to be wiser than became him, nor by trusting to his own understanding, cast off the yoke of God, and constitute himself an arbiter and judge of good and evil. His sin proceeded from an evil conscience; whence it follows, that a judgment had been given him, by which he might discriminate between virtues and vices. Nor could what Moses relates be otherwise true, namely, that he was created in the image of God; since the image of God comprises in itself the knowledge of him who is the chief good. Thoroughly insane, therefore, and monsters of men are the libertines, who pretend that we are restored to a state of innocency, when each is carried away by his own lust without judgment. We now understand what is meant by abstaining from the tree of the knowledge of good and evil; namely, that Adam might not, in attempting one thing or another, rely upon his own prudence; but that, cleaving to God alone, he might become wise only by his obedience. Knowledge is here, therefore, taken disparagingly, in a bad sense, for that wretched experience which man, when he departed from the only fountain of perfect wisdom, began to acquire for himself. And this is the origin of free-will, that Adam wished to be independent,[1] and dared to try what he was able to do.

10. *And a river went out.* Moses says that one river flowed to water the garden, which afterwards would divide itself into four heads. It is sufficiently agreed among all, that two of these heads are the Euphrates and the Tigris; for no one disputes that הירקל (*Hiddekel*) is the Tigris. But there is

[1] "Dum Adam per se esse voluit, et quid valeret tentare ausus est." —*Lat.*

a great controversy respecting the other two. Many think, that Pison and Gihon are the Ganges and the Nile; the error, however, of these men is abundantly refuted by the distance of the positions of these rivers. Persons are not wanting who fly across even to the Danube; as if, indeed, the habitation of one man stretched itself from the most remote part of Asia to the extremity of Europe. But since many other celebrated rivers flow by the region of which we are speaking, there is greater probability in the opinion of those who believe that two of these rivers are pointed out, although their names are now obsolete. Be this as it may, the difficulty is not yet solved. For Moses divides the one river which flowed by the garden into four heads. Yet it appears, that the fountains of the Euphrates and the Tigris were far distant from each other. From this difficulty, some would free themselves by saying, that the surface of the globe may have been changed by the deluge; and, therefore, they imagine it might have happened that the courses of the rivers were disturbed and changed, and their springs transferred elsewhere; a solution which appears to me by no means to be accepted. For although I acknowledge that the earth, from the time that it was accursed, became reduced from its native beauty to a state of wretched defilement, and to a garb of mourning, and afterwards was further laid waste in many places by the deluge; still, I assert, it was the same earth which had been created in the beginning. Add to this, that Moses (in my judgment) accommodated his topography to the capacity of his age. Yet nothing is accomplished, unless we find that place where the Tigris and Euphrates proceed from one river. Observe, first, that no mention is made of a spring or fountain, but only that it is said, there was *one* river. But the four heads I understand to mean, both the beginnings from which the rivers are produced, and the mouths [1] by which they discharge themselves into the sea. Now the Euphrates was formerly so joined by confluence with the Tigris, that it might justly be said, one river was divided into four

---

[1] It appears that by the beginnings (*principia*) and the mouths (*ostia*) of the rivers, Calvin simply means the streams above, and the streams below, the site of the garden.—*Ed.*

heads; especially, if what is manifest to all be conceded, that Moses does not speak acutely, nor in a philosophical manner, but popularly, so that every one least informed may understand him. Thus, in the first chapter, he called the sun and moon two great luminaries; not because the moon exceeded other planets in magnitude, but because, to common observation, it seemed greater. Add further, that he seems to remove all doubt when he says, that the river had four heads, because it was divided from that place. What does this mean, except that the channels were divided, out of one confluent stream, either above or below Paradise? I will now submit a plan to view, that the readers may understand where I think Paradise was placed by Moses.[1]

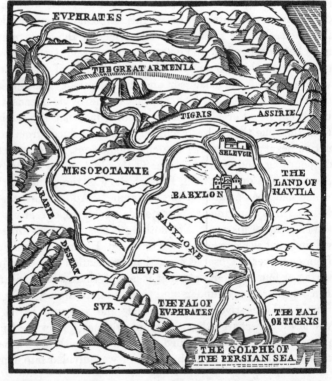

[1] This is a fac-simile from the Old English translation; and the same, with Latin and French names, are introduced in the early editions of each language.—*Ed.*

Pliny indeed relates, in his Sixth Book, that the Euphrates was so stopped in its course by the Orcheni, that it could not flow into the sea, except through the Tigris.[1] And Pomponius Mela, in his Third Book, denies that it flowed by any given outlet, as other rivers, but says that it failed in its course. Nearchus, however, (whom Alexander had made commander of his fleet, and who, under his sanction, had navigated all these regions,) reckons the distance from the mouth of the Euphrates to Babylon, three thousand three hundred stadia.[2] But he places the mouths of the Tigris at the entrance of Susiana; in which region, returning from that long and memorable voyage, he met the king with his fleet, as Arrian relates in his Eighth Book of the Exploits of Alexander. This statement Strabo also confirms by his testimony in his Fifteenth Book. Nevertheless, wherever 'the Euphrates either submerges or mingles its stream, it is certain, that it and the Tigris, below the point of their confluence, are again divided. Arrian, however, in his Seventh Book, writes, that not one channel only of the Euphrates runs into the Tigris, but also many rivers and ditches, because waters naturally descend from higher to lower ground. With respect to the confluence, which I have noted in the plate, the opinion of some was, that it had been effected by the labour of the Præfect Cobaris, lest the Euphrates, by its precipitate course, should injure Babylon. But he speaks of it as of a doubtful matter. It is more credible, that men, by art and industry, followed the guidance of Nature in forming ditches, when they saw the Euphrates any where flowing of its own accord from the higher ground into the Tigris. Moreover, if confidence is placed in Pomponius Mela, Semiramis conducted the Tigris and Euphrates into Mesopotamia, which was previously dry; a thing by no means credible. There is more truth in the statement of Strabo,—a diligent and attentive writer,—in his Eleventh Book, that at Babylon these two rivers unite:

---

[1] "The Orcheni inhabiting a city named Orchoë, caused the diminution of the Euphrates, by deriving it through their lands, which could not otherwise be watered."—D'Anville's Ancient Geography.

[2] About 420 miles.

and then, that each is carried separately, in its own bed, into the Red Sea.[1] He understands that junction to have taken place above Babylon, not far from the town Massica, as we read in the Fifth Book of Pliny. Thence one river flows through Babylon, the other glides by Seleucia, two of the most celebrated and opulent cities. If we admit this confluence, by which the Euphrates was mixed with the Tigris, to have been natural, and to have existed from the beginning, all absurdity is removed. If there is anywhere under heaven a region pre-eminent in beauty, in the abundance of all kinds of fruit, in fertility, in delicacies, and in other gifts, that is the region which writers most celebrate. Wherefore, the eulogies with which Moses commends Paradise are such as properly belong to a tract of this description. And that the region of Eden was situated in those parts is probable from Isaiah xxxvii. 12, and Ezekiel xxvii. 23. Moreover, when Moses declares that a river went forth, I understand him as speaking of the flowing of the stream; as if he had said, that Adam dwelt on the bank of the river, or in that land which was watered on both sides, if you choose to take Paradise for both banks of the river. However, it makes no great difference whether Adam dwelt below the confluent stream towards Babylon and Seleucia, or in the higher part; it is enough that he occupied a well-watered country. How the river was divided into four heads is not difficult to understand. For there are two rivers which flow together into one, and then separate in different directions; thus, it is one at the point of confluence, but there are two heads[2] in its

---

[1] Mare Rubrum. By the Red Sea, in this place, is not meant the Gulf of Suez, which is called by that name in sacred history, and over which the Israelites passed in their journey from Egypt to Canaan; but the Indian Ocean, the Mare Erythræum of the ancients, into which the Tigris and Euphrates flowed, through the Persian Gulf.—Ed.

[2] Or "principal streams." "The river, or single channel, must be looked upon as a highway, crossing over a forest, and which may be said from thence to divide itself into four ways, whether the division be made above or below the forest."—Wells' Geography of the Old and New Test., vol. i. p. 19.

The reader is referred to the first chapter of that useful work, for an account agreeing in many points with Calvin, though differing from it in others. The principal difference in the two accounts lies in this, that Wells places the site of Paradise near the Persian Gulf into which the Tigris

upper channels, and two towards the sea; afterwards, they again begin to be more widely separated.

The question remains concerning the names Pison and Gihon. For it does not seem consonant with reason, to assign a double name to each of the rivers. But it is nothing new for rivers to change their names in their course, especially where there is any special mark of distinction. The Tigris itself (by the authority of Pliny) is called *Diglito* near its source; but after it has formed many channels, and again coalesces, it takes the name of *Pasitigris*. There is, therefore, no absurdity in saying, that after its confluence it had different names. Further, there is some such affinity between Pasin and Pison, as to render it not improbable, that the name Pasitigris is a vestige of the ancient appellation. In the Fifth Book of Quintus Curtius, concerning the Exploits of Alexander, where mention is made of Pasitigris, some copies read, that it was called by the inhabitants Pasin. Nor do the other circumstances, by which Moses describes three of these rivers, ill accord with this supposition. Pison surrounds[1] the land of Havila, where gold is produced. Surrounding is rightly attributed to the Tigris, on account of its winding course below Mesopotamia. The land of Havila, in my judgment, is here taken for a region adjoining Persia. For subsequently, in the twenty-fifth

---

and Euphrates discharge themselves, while Calvin fixes it higher up the streams, in the vicinity of ancient Babylon. Wells derives his account mainly from the celebrated French Bishop, Peter Daniel Huet, who had been the intimate friend of the famous Protestant traveller Bochart. The following extract from a note in the *Clavis Pentateuchi* of Robertson is added for the reader's satisfaction:—" Eden est regio seu in Mesopotamio, seu non procul inde. Observandum est hancce sententiam Calvini, quam parum emendaverat clarissimus Huetius, verissimam omnium videri : Hoc demonstravit clarissimus Vitringa, qui paululum in quibusdam circumstantiis etiam Huetium emendaverat."—" Eden is a region either in Mesopotamia, or near it. It is to be observed, that this opinion of *Calvin*, which the celebrated Huet has slightly amended, seems to be the most true of all. The celebrated Vitringa has demonstrated this ; who also, in some circumstances, has slightly amended Huet."—*Robertson's Clavis*, p. 177.—*Ed.*

[1] Circuit. It is observed, that the word surrounds, or "compasses," conveys, to an English reader, more than is meant by the sacred writer. He only intends to say, that the river sweeps round in that direction, so as to embrace, by its winding, a part of the region of Havila. *Flexuoso cursu alluit.—Johannes Clericus in loco.—Ed.*

chapter, Moses relates, that the Ishmaelites dwelt from Havila unto Shur, which is contiguous to Egypt, and through which the road lies into Assyria. Havila, as one boundary, is opposed to Shur as another, and this boundary Moses places near Egypt, on the side which lies towards Assyria. Whence it follows, that Havila [the other boundary] extends towards Susia and Persia. For it is necessary that it should lie below Assyria towards the Persian Sea; besides, it is placed at a great distance from Egypt; because Moses enumerates many nations which dwelt between these boundaries.[1] Then it appears that the Nabathæans,[2] of whom mention is there made, were neighbours to the Persians. Every thing which Moses asserts respecting gold and precious stones is most applicable to this district.[3]

The river Gihon still remains to be noticed, which, as Moses declares, waters the land of *Chus*. All interpreters translate this word *Ethiopia;* but the country of the Midianites, and the conterminous country of Arabia, are included under the same name by Moses; for which reason, his wife is elsewhere called an Ethiopian woman. Moreover, since the lower course of the Euphrates tends toward that region, I do not see why it should be deemed absurd, that it there receives the name of Gihon. And thus the simple meaning of Moses is, that the garden of which Adam was the possessor was well watered, the channel of a river passing that way, which was afterwards divided into four heads.[4]

---

[1] That is, the nations peopled by the twelve sons of Ishmael. See Gen. xxv. 13-16.—*Ed.*

[2] The descendants of Nebajoth, the eldest son of Ishmael. Yet, as they inhabited the western side of the great desert of Arabia, which lay between them and the Euphrates, they cannot, with much propriety, be called neighbours to the Persians.—*Ed.*

[3] " There is bdellium and the onyx-stone." It is a question among the learned, whether bdellium is an *aromatic gum* of great value, or a *pearl.* The latter opinion seems to prevail. Dathe, however, renders this word " crystal," and the next, " emerald."—*Ed.*

[4] It would be wrong to omit all mention of the work of Adrian Reland on this subject; who devoted to it the most profound learning and diligent investigation. An abstract of his description is given in Dr Adam Clarke's Commentary. He places Eden in Armenia, near the sources of the Euphrates and Tigris, which flow into the Persian Gulf, the Phasis, (Pison,) which empties itself into the Euxine, where *Chabala*, corresponding with Havila, is famous for its gold; and the Araxes, (Gihon,) which

15. *And the Lord God took the man.* Moses now adds, that the earth was given to man, with this condition, that he should occupy himself in its cultivation. Whence it follows, that men were created to employ themselves in some work, and not to lie down in inactivity and idleness. This labour, truly, was pleasant, and full of delight, entirely exempt from all trouble and weariness; since, however, God ordained that man should be exercised in the culture of the ground, he condemned, in his person, all indolent repose. Wherefore, nothing is more contrary to the order of nature, than to consume life in eating, drinking, and sleeping, while in the meantime we propose nothing to ourselves to do. Moses adds, that the custody of the garden was given in charge to Adam, to show that we possess the things which God has committed to our hands, on the condition, that being content with a frugal and moderate use of them, we should take care of what shall remain. Let him who possesses a field, so partake of its yearly fruits, that he may not suffer the ground to be injured by his negligence; but let him endeavour to hand it down to posterity as he received it, or even better cultivated. Let him so feed on its fruits, that he neither dissipates it by luxury, nor permits to be marred or ruined by neglect. Moreover, that this economy, and this diligence, with respect to those good things which God has given us to enjoy, may flourish among us; let every one regard himself as the steward of God in all things which he possesses. Then he will neither conduct himself dissolutely, nor corrupt by abuse those things which God requires to be preserved.

16. *And the Lord God commanded.* Moses now teaches, that man was the governor of the world, with this exception, that he should, nevertheless, be subject to God. A law is imposed upon him in token of his subjection; for it would have made no difference to God, if he had eaten indiscriminately of any fruit he pleased. Therefore, the prohibition of

runs into the Caspian. The objection to this locality is, that these rivers do not actually meet together; so that they cannot be said to divide into four heads, or principal streams in Eden. The learned reader may see *Dathe's Commentary on the Pentateuch*, p. 23, note (k.)—*Ed.*

one tree was a test of obedience. And in this mode, God designed that the whole human race should be accustomed from the beginning to reverence his Deity; as, doubtless, it was necessary that man, adorned and enriched with so many excellent gifts, should be held under restraint, lest he should break forth into licentiousness. There was, indeed, another special reason, to which we have before alluded, lest Adam should desire to be wise above measure; but this is to be kept in mind as God's general design, that he would have men subject to his authority. Therefore, abstinence from the fruit of one tree was a kind of first lesson in obedience, that man might know he had a Director and Lord of his life, on whose will he ought to depend, and in whose commands he ought to acquiesce. And this, truly, is the only rule of living well and rationally, that men should exercise themselves in obeying God. It seems, however, to some as if this did not accord with the judgment of Paul, when he teaches, that "the law was not made for the righteous," (1 Tim. i. 9.) For if it be so, then, when Adam was yet innocent and upright, he had no need of a law. But the solution is ready. For Paul is not there writing controversially; but from the common practice of life, he declares, that they who freely run, do not require to be compelled by the necessity of law; as it is said, in the common proverb, that ' Good laws spring from bad manners.' In the meantime, he does not deny that God, from the beginning, imposed a law upon man, for the purpose of maintaining the right due to himself. Should any one bring, as an objection, another statement of Paul, where he asserts that the "law is the minister of death," (2 Cor. iii. 7,) I answer, it is so accidentally, and from the corruption of our nature. But at the time of which we speak, a precept was given to man, whence he might know that God ruled over him. These minute things, however, I lightly pass over. What I have before said, since it is of far greater moment, is to be frequently recalled to memory, namely, that our life will then be rightly ordered, if we obey God, and if his will be the regulator of all our affections.

Of every tree. To the end that Adam might the more

willingly comply, God commends his own liberality. 'Behold,' he says, 'I deliver into thy hand whatever fruits the earth may produce, whatever fruits every kind of tree may yield: from this immense profusion and variety I except only one tree.' Then, by denouncing punishment, he strikes terror, for the purpose of confirming the authority of the law. So much the greater, then, is the wickedness of man, whom neither that kind commemoration of the gifts of God, nor the dread of punishment, was able to retain in his duty.

But it is asked, what kind of death God means in this place? It appears to me, that the definition of this death is to be sought from its opposite; we must, I say, remember from what kind of life man fell. He was, in every respect, happy; his life, therefore, had alike respect to his body and his soul, since in his soul a right judgment and a proper government of the affections prevailed, there also life reigned; in his body there was no defect, wherefore he was wholly free from death. His earthly life truly would have been temporal; yet he would have passed into heaven without death, and without injury. Death, therefore, is now a terror to us; first, because there is a kind of annihilation, as it respects the body; then, because the soul feels the curse of God. We must also see what is the cause of death, namely, alienation from God. Thence it follows, that under the name of death is comprehended all those miseries in which Adam involved himself by his defection; for as soon as he revolted from God, the fountain of life, he was cast down from his former state, in order that he might perceive the life of man without God to be wretched and lost, and therefore differing nothing from death. Hence the condition of man after his sin is not improperly called both the privation of life, and death. The miseries and evils both of soul and body, with which man is beset so long as he is on earth, are a kind of entrance into death, till death itself entirely absorbs him; for the Scripture everywhere calls those dead, who, being oppressed by the tyranny of sin and Satan, breathe nothing but their own destruction. Wherefore the question is superfluous, how it was that God threatened death to Adam on the day in which he should touch the fruit, when he long deferred the punishment?

For then was Adam consigned to death, and death began its reign in him, until supervening grace should bring a remedy.

18. *It is not good that the man should be alone.*[1] Moses now explains the design of God in creating the woman; namely, that there should be human beings on the earth who might cultivate mutual society between themselves. Yet a doubt may arise whether this design ought to be extended to progeny, for the words simply mean that since it was not expedient for man to be alone, a wife must be created, who might be his helper. I, however, take the meaning to be this, that God begins, indeed, at the first step of human society, yet designs to include others, each in its proper place. The commencement, therefore, involves a general principle, that man was formed to be a social animal. [2] Now, the human race could not exist without the woman; and, therefore, in the conjunction of human beings, that sacred bond is especially conspicuous, by which the husband and the wife are combined in one body, and one soul; as nature itself taught Plato, and others of the sounder class of philosophers, to speak. But although God pronounced, concerning Adam, that it would not be profitable for him to be alone, yet I do not restrict the declaration to his person alone, but rather regard it as a common law of man's vocation, so that every one ought to receive it as said to himself, that solitude is not good, excepting only him whom God exempts as by a special privilege. Many think that celibacy conduces to their advantage,[3] and, therefore, abstain from marriage, lest they should be miserable. Not only have heathen writers defined that to be a happy life which is passed without a wife, but the first book of Jerome, against Jovinian, is stuffed with petulant reproaches, by which he attempts to render hallowed wed-

[1] " Non est bonum ut sit *Adam* solus." This is a variation from Calvin's text, which has man instead of Adam, as the English version has. The word אדם stands for both. As a proper name, it means *Adam;* as an appellation, it belongs to the *human species;* as an adjective, it means *red;* and, with a slight alteration, it signifies *the ground.— Ed.*
[2] " Principium ergo generale est, conditum esse hominem ut sit sociale animal."
[3] "Putant multi suisrationibus conducere cœlibatum."—" Plusieurs estiment que le celibat—leur est plus profitable."—*French Tr.*

lock both hateful and infamous. To these wicked suggestions of Satan let the faithful learn to oppose this declaration of God, by which he ordains the conjugal life for man, not to his destruction, but to his salvation.

I will make him an help. It may be inquired, why this is not said in the plural number, *Let us make,* as before in the creation of man. Some suppose that a distinction between the two sexes is in this manner marked, and that it is thus shown how much the man excels the woman. But I am better satisfied with an interpretation which, though not altogether contrary, is yet different; namely, since in the person of the man the human race had been created, the common dignity of our whole nature was without distinction, honoured with one eulogy, when it was said, " Let us make man ; " nor was it necessary to be repeated in creating the woman, who was nothing else than an accession to the man. Certainly, it cannot be denied, that the woman also, though in the second degree, was created in the image of God ; whence it follows, that what was said in the creation of the man belongs to the female sex. Now, since God assigns the woman as a help to the man, he not only prescribes to wives the rule of their vocation, to instruct them in their duty, but he also pronounces that marriage will really prove to men the best support of life. We may therefore conclude, that the order of nature implies that the woman should be the helper of the man. The vulgar proverb, indeed, is, that she is a necessary evil; but the voice of God is rather to be heard, which declares that woman is given as a companion and an associate to the man, to assist him to live well. I confess, indeed, that in this corrupt state of mankind, the blessing of God, which is here described, is neither perceived nor flourishes; but the cause of the evil must be considered, namely, that the order of nature, which God had appointed, has been inverted by us. For if the integrity of man had remained to this day such as it was from the beginning, that divine institution would be clearly discerned, and the sweetest harmony would reign in marriage ; because the husband would look up with reverence to God ; the woman in this would be a faithful assistant to him ; and both, with one consent, would cultivate a holy, as well as friendly and peaceful intercourse. Now, it has happened by our fault, and by the corruption of nature, that this happiness of marriage has, in a great measure, perished, or, at least, is mixed and infected with many inconveniences. Hence arise strifes, troubles, sorrows, dissensions, and a boundless sea of evils; and hence it follows, that men are often disturbed by their wives, and suffer through them many discouragements. Still, marriage was not capable of being so far vitiated by the depravity of men, that the blessing which God has once sanctioned by his word should be utterly abolished and extinguished. Therefore, amidst many inconveniences of marriage, which are the fruits of degenerate nature, some residue of divine good remains; as in the fire apparently smothered, some sparks still glitter. On this main point hangs another, that women, being instructed in their duty of helping their husbands, should study to keep this divinely appointed order. It is also the part of men to consider what they owe in return to the other half of their kind, for the obligation of both sexes is mutual, and on this condition is the woman assigned as a help to the man, that he may fill the place of her head and leader. One thing more is to be noted, that, when the woman is here called the help of the man, no allusion is made to that necessity to which we are reduced since the fall of Adam; for the woman was ordained to be the man's helper, even although he had stood in his integrity. But now, since the depravity of appetite also requires a remedy, we have from God a double benefit: but the latter is accidental.

Meet for him.[1] In the Hebrew it is כְּנֶגְדּו, (*kenegedo,*) " as if opposite to," or " over against him." כ (*caph*) in that language is a note of similitude. But although some of the Rabbies think it is here put as an affirmative, yet I take it in its general sense, as though it were said that she is a kind of counterpart, [ἀντίστοιχον, or ἀντίστροφον;[2]] for the woman is said to be *opposite to* or *over against* the man, because she responds to him. But the particle of similitude seems to me to be added because it is a form of speech taken from com-

---

[1] " Coram ipso," before him.—" Pour luy assister," to help him.—*Fr. Trans.*

[2] Quod " ex adverso ei" respondet. Lud. de Dieu. His counterpart.

mon usage.[1] The Greek translators have faithfully rendered the sense, Κατ᾽αὐτόν;[2] and Jerome, "Which may be like him,"[3] for Moses intended to note some equality. And hence is refuted the error of some, who think that the woman was formed only for the sake of propagation, and who restrict the word " good," which had been lately mentioned, to the production of offspring. They do not think that a wife was personally necessary for Adam, because he was hitherto free from lust ; as if she had been given to him only for the companion of his chamber, and not rather that she might be the inseparable associate of his life. Wherefore the particle כ (caph) is of importance, as intimating that marriage extends to all parts and usages of life. The explanation given by others, as if it were said, " Let her be ready to obedience," is cold ; for Moses intended to express more, as is manifest from what follows.

19. *And out of the ground the Lord God formed, &c.*[4] This is a more ample exposition of the preceding sentence, for he says that, of all the animals, when they had been placed in order, not one was found which might be conferred upon and adapted to Adam ; nor was there such affinity of nature, that Adam could choose for himself a companion for life out of any one species. Nor did this occur through ignorance, for each species had passed in review before Adam, and he had imposed names upon them, not rashly, but from certain knowledge ; yet there was no just proportion between him and them. Therefore, unless a wife had been given him of the same kind with himself, he would have remained destitute of a suitable and proper help. Moreover, what is here

---

[1] " Quia sit translatitia loquutio."

[2] A help according to him. See Septuagint.

[3] "Adjutorium simile sibi," a help like himself.— *Vulgate. Meet for him.* " In whose company he shall take delight ; so the Hebrew phrase, *as before him,* imports, being as much as answerable to him, every way fitted for him, not only in likeness of body, but of mind, disposition, and affection, which laid the foundation of perpetual familiarity and friendship."— *Patrick.*

[4] " Formaverat autem Deus,"—" God *had* formed," plainly referring to what had already taken place. The Hebrew language has not the same distinction of times in its verbs which is common to more modern tongues.—*Ed.*

said of God's bringing the animals to Adam[1] signifies nothing else than that he endued them with the disposition to obedience, so that they would voluntarily offer themselves to the man, in order that he, having closely inspected them, might distinguish them by appropriate names, agreeing with the nature of each. This gentleness towards man would have remained also in wild beasts, if Adam, by his defection from God, had not lost the authority he had before received. But now, from the time in which he began to be rebellious against God, he experienced the ferocity of brute animals against himself; for some are tamed with difficulty, others always remain unsubdued, and some, even of their own accord, inspire us with terror by their fierceness. Yet some remains of their former subjection continue to the present time, as we shall see in the second verse of the ninth chapter. Besides, it is to be remarked that Moses speaks only of those animals which approach the nearest to man, for the fishes live as in another world. As to the names which Adam imposed, I do not doubt that each of them was founded on the best reason; but their use, with many other good things, has become obsolete.

21. *And the Lord God caused a deep sleep to fall, &c.* Although to profane persons this method of forming woman may seem ridiculous, and some of these may say that Moses is dealing in fables, yet to us the wonderful providence of God here shines forth; for, to the end that the conjunction of the human race might be the more sacred, he purposed that both males and females should spring from one and the same origin. Therefore he created human nature in the person of Adam, and thence formed Eve, that the woman should be only a portion of the whole human race. This is the import of the words of Moses which we have had before, (Chap. i. 28,) " God created man . . . he made them male and female." In this manner Adam was taught to recognise himself in his wife, as in a mirror; and Eve, in her turn, to submit herself willingly to her husband, as being taken out

---

[1] " Porro istud adducere Dei."

of him. But if the two sexes had proceeded from different sources, there would have been occasion either of mutual contempt, or envy, or contentions. And against what do perverse men here object ? 'The narration does not seem credible, since it is at variance with custom.' As if, indeed, such an objection would have more colour than one raised against the usual mode of the production of mankind, if the latter were not known by use and experience.[1] But they object that either the rib which was taken from Adam had been superfluous, or that his body had been mutilated by the absence of the rib. To either of these it may be answered, that they find out a great absurdity. If, however, we should say that the rib out of which he would form another body had been prepared previously by the Creator of the world, I find nothing in this answer which is not in accordance with Divine Providence. Yet I am more in favour of a different conjecture, namely, that something was taken from Adam, in order that he might embrace, with greater benevolence, a part of himself. He lost, therefore, one of his ribs ; but, instead of it, a far richer reward was granted him, since he obtained a faithful associate of life ; for he now saw himself, who had before been imperfect, rendered complete in his wife.[2] And in this we see a true resemblance of our union with the Son of God ; for he became weak that he might have members of his body endued with strength. In the meantime, it is to be noted, that Adam had been plunged in a sleep so profound, that he felt no pain ; and further, that neither had the rupture been violent, nor was any want perceived of the lost rib, because God so filled up the vacuity with flesh, that his strength remained unimpaired ; only the hardness of bone was removed. Moses also designedly used the word *built*,[3] to teach us that in the person of the woman the human race was at length complete, which had before been like a building just begun. Others refer the expression to the domestic economy, as if Moses would say that le-

---

[1] " Ex putrido semine quotidie gigni homines."

[2] " Quum se integrum vidit in uxore, qui prius tantum dimidius erat."

[3] " Et ædificavit Jehova Deus costam quam tulerat ex Adam, in mulierem."—And Jehovah God built the rib which he had taken out of Adam into a woman. ויבן, from בנה, *to build*.

gitimate family order was then instituted, which does not differ widely from the former exposition.

22. *And brought her, &c.*   Moses now relates that marriage was divinely instituted, which is especially useful to be known ; for since Adam did not take a wife to himself at his own will, but received her as offered and appropriated to him by God, the sanctity of marriage hence more clearly appears, because we recognise God as its Author.   The more Satan has endeavoured to dishonour marriage, the more should we vindicate it from all reproach and abuse, that it may receive its due reverence.   Thence it will follow that the children of God may embrace a conjugal life with a good and tranquil conscience, and husbands and wives may live together in chastity and honour.   The artifice of Satan in attempting the defamation of marriage was twofold : first, that by means of the odium attached to it he might introduce the pestilential law of celibacy; and, secondly, that married persons might indulge themselves in whatever license they pleased. Therefore, by showing the dignity of marriage, we must remove superstition, lest it should in the slightest degree hinder the faithful from chastely using the lawful and pure ordinance of God ; and further, we must oppose the lasciviousness of the flesh, in order that men may live modestly with their wives.   But if no other reason influenced us, yet this alone ought to be abundantly sufficient, that unless we think and speak honourably of marriage, reproach is attached to its Author and Patron, for such God is here described as being by Moses.

23. *And Adam said, &c.*   It is demanded whence Adam derived this knowledge, since he was at that time buried in deep sleep.   If we say that his quickness of perception was then such as to enable him by conjecture to form a judgment, the solution would be weak.   But we ought not to doubt that God would make the whole course of the affair manifest to him, either by secret revelation or by his word ; for it was not from any necessity on God's part that He borrowed from man the rib out of which he might form the

woman; but he designed that they should be more closely
joined together by this bond, which could not have been
effected unless he had informed them of the fact. Moses
does not indeed explain by what means God gave them this
information; yet, unless we would make the work of God
superfluous, we must conclude that its Author revealed both
the fact itself and the method and design of its accomplishment. The deep sleep was sent upon Adam, not to hide
from him the origin of his wife, but to exempt him from
pain and trouble, until he should receive a compensation so
excellent for the loss of his rib.

This is now bone of, &c.[1] In using the expression הפעם,
(*hac vice,*) Adam indicates that something had been wanting to him; as if he had said, Now at length I have obtained a suitable companion, who is part of the substance
of my flesh, and in whom I behold, as it were, another self.
And he gives to his wife a name taken from that of man,[2]
that by this testimony and this mark he might transmit a
perpetual memorial of the wisdom of God. A deficiency in the
Latin language has compelled the ancient interpreter to render אשה, (*ishah,*) by the word *virago.* It is, however, to
be remarked, that the Hebrew term means nothing else than
the female of the man.

24. *Therefore shall a man leave.* It is doubted whether
Moses here introduces God as speaking, or continues the

---

[1] " Hac vice os *est* ex ossibus meis." זאת הפעם, (*zot haphaam.*) These
words are rendered in the English version by "This now," which very
feebly and imperfectly expresses the sense of the original; nor does
the version of Calvin, " At this turn," give the true emphasis of the
words. It is perhaps scarcely possible to do so without a paraphrase.
The two words of the original are both intended to be emphatic. " This
living creature (זאת) which at the present time (הפעם, *hâc vice*) passes
before me, is the companion which I need, for it is bone of my bones,
and flesh of my flesh."—Vide *Dathe in loco.*—*Ed.*

[2] " Nomen uxori a viro imponit." אשה, (*ishah,*) from איש, (*ish,*) which
is the Hebrew word *man* with a feminine termination; as if we should
say, " She shall be called *manness,* because she was taken out of the
man." Calvin uses the word *virissa ;* Dathe, after Le Clerc, the word
vira ; and though neither of them are strictly classical, yet are they far
preferable to the term *virago* in the Vulgate, which Calvin justly rejects,
and which means a woman of masculine character. The English word
woman is a contraction of *womb-man.*—*Ed.*

discourse of Adam, or, indeed, has added this, in virtue of his office as teacher, in his own person.[1] The last of these is that which I most approve. Therefore, after he has related historically what God had done, he also demonstrates the end of the divine institution. The sum of the whole is, that among the offices pertaining to human society, this is the principal, and as it were the most sacred, that a man should cleave unto his wife. And he amplifies this by a superadded comparison, that the husband ought to prefer his wife to his father. But the father is said to be *left* not because marriage severs sons from their fathers, or dispenses with other ties of nature, for in this way God would be acting contrary to himself. While, however, the piety of the son towards his father is to be most assiduously cultivated, and ought in itself to be deemed inviolable and sacred, yet Moses so speaks of marriage as to show that it is less lawful to desert a wife than parents. Therefore, they who, for slight causes, rashly allow of divorces, violate, in one single particular, all the laws of nature, and reduce them to nothing. If we should make it a point of conscience not to separate a father from his son, it is a still greater wickedness to dissolve the bond which God has preferred to all others.

They shall be one flesh.[2] Although the ancient Latin interpreter has translated the passage ' in one flesh,' yet the Greek interpreters have expressed it more forcibly : ' They two shall be *into* one flesh,' and thus Christ cites the place in Matthew xix. 5. But though here no mention is made of *two*, yet there is no ambiguity in the sense; for Moses had not said that God has assigned many wives, but only *one* to one man; and in the general direction given, he had put the wife in the singular number. It remains, therefore, that the conjugal bond subsists between two persons only, whence it easily appears, that nothing is less accordant with the divine institution than polygamy. Now, when Christ, in censuring the voluntary divorces of the Jews, adduces as his reason for doing it, that ' it was not so in the beginning,' (Matth. xix. 5;)

---

[1] See Le Clerc on this verse, who takes the same view as Calvin.

[2] " Erunt in carnem unam."—" In carne unâ."—Vulgate. Εἰς σάρκα μίαν.—Sept.

he certainly commands this institution to be observed as a perpetual rule of conduct.   To the same point also Malachi recalls the Jews of his own time : ' Did he not make them one from the beginning? and yet the Spirit was abounding in him.'[1] (Mal. ii. 15.) Wherefore, there is no doubt that polygamy is a corruption of legitimate marriage.

25. *They were both naked.*   That the nakedness of men should be deemed indecorous and unsightly, while that of cattle has nothing disgraceful, seems little to agree with the dignity of human nature.   We cannot behold a naked man without a sense of shame ; yet at the sight of an ass, a dog, or an ox, no such feeling will be produced.   Moreover, every one is ashamed of his own nakedness, even though other witnesses may not be present.   Where then is that dignity in which we excel ? The cause of this sense of shame, to which we are now alluding, Moses will show in the next chapter. He now esteems it enough to say, that in our uncorrupted nature, there was nothing but what was honourable ; whence it follows, that whatsoever is opprobrious in us, must be imputed to our own fault, since our parents had nothing in themselves which was unbecoming until they were defiled with sin.

CHAPTER III.

1. Now the serpent was more subtil than any beast of the field which the Lord God had made. And he said unto the woman, Yea, hath God said, Ye shall not eat of every tree of the garden?
2. And the woman said unto the serpent, We may eat of the fruit of the trees of the garden :
3. But of the fruit of the tree which is in the midst of the garden, God hath said, Ye shall not eat of it, neither shall ye touch it, lest ye die.
4. And the serpent said unto the woman, Ye shall not surely die :
5. For God doth know that in the

1. Porro serpens erat callidior omni bestia agri, quam fecerat Jehova Deus: et dixit ad mulierem, Etiamne dixit Deus, Non comedetis ex omni arbore horti ?

2. Et dixit mulier ad serpentem, De fructu arborum horti vescimur.

3. At de fructu arboris quæ est in medio horti, dixit Deus, Non comedetis ex ea, neque contingetis eam, ne forte moriamini.

4. Tunc dixit serpens ad mulierem, Non moriendo moriemini.

5. Scit enim Deus quod in die

[1] " Spiritus abundans in eo erat." The word *abundans* has in English the force of superabounding.—*Ed.*

day ye eat thereof, then your eyes shall be opened; and ye shall be as gods, knowing good and evil.

6. And when the woman saw that the tree *was* good for food, and that it *was* pleasant to the eyes, and a tree to be desired to make *one* wise, she took of the fruit thereof, and did eat, and gave also unto her husband with her; and he did eat.

7. And the eyes of them both were opened, and they knew that they *were* naked; and they sewed fig leaves together, and made themselves aprons.

8. And they heard the voice of the Lord God walking in the garden in the cool of the day: and Adam and his wife hid themselves from the presence of the Lord God amongst the trees of the garden.

9. And the Lord God called unto Adam, and said unto him, Where *art* thou?

10. And he said, I heard thy voice in the garden, and I was afraid, because I *was* naked; and I hid myself.

11. And he said, Who told thee that thou *wast* naked? Hast thou eaten of the tree, whereof I commanded thee that thou shouldst not eat?

12. And the man said, The woman whom thou gavest *to be* with me, she gave me of the tree, and I did eat.

13. And the Lord God said unto the woman, What *is* this *that* thou hast done? And the woman said, The serpent beguiled me, and I did eat.

14. And the Lord God said unto the serpent, Because thou hast done this, thou *art* cursed above all cattle, and above every beast of the field; upon thy belly shalt thou go, and dust shalt thou eat all the days of thy life.

15. And I will put enmity between thee and the woman, and between thy seed and her seed: it shall bruise thy head, and thou shalt bruise his heel.

16. Unto the woman he said, I will greatly multiply thy sorrow and thy conception: in sorrow thou shalt bring forth children; and thy desire *shall be* to thy husband, and he shall rule over thee.

qua comedetis ex ea, aperientur oculi vestri, et eritis sicut dii, scientes bonum et malum.

6. Et vidit mulier quod bona esset arbor ad vescendum, et quod delectabilis esset oculis, et desiderabilis arbor ad intelligendum : et tulit de fructu ipsius, et comedit : deditque etiam viro suo qui erat cum ea, et ipse comedit.

7. Et aperti sunt oculi amborum ipsorum, et cognoverunt quod nudi essent : et consuerunt folia ficus, feceruntque sibi cingula.

8. Audierunt autem vocem Jehovæ Dei deambulantis per hortum ad auram diei : et abscondit se Adam et uxor ejus a facie Jehovæ Dei, in medio arborum horti.

9. Vocavitque Jehova Deus Adam, et dixit ei, Ubi es tu?

10. Et ait, Vocem tuam audivi in horto, et timui, quia nudus eram, et abscondi me.

11. Tunc dixit, Quis indicavit tibi quod nudus esses? nonne ex ipsa arbore de qua præceperam tibi ne comederes, comedisti?

12. Et ait Adam, Mulier quam dedisti ut esset mecum, ipsa dedit mihi de arbore, et comedi.

13. Dixitque Jehova Deus ad mulierem, Cur hoc fecisti? Et ait mulier, Serpens seduxit me, et comedi.

14. Et dixit Jehova ad serpentem, Quia fecisti hoc, maledictus eris præ omni animali, et præ omni bestia agri : super ventrem tuum gradieris, et pulverem comedes omnibus diebus vitæ tuæ.

15. Et inimicitias ponam inter te et inter mulierem, et inter semen tuum et inter semen ejus : ipsum vulnerabit te in capite, et tu vulnerabis ipsum in calcaneo.

16. Ad mulierem dixit, Multiplicando multiplicabo dolorem tuum, et conceptum tuum : cum dolore paries filios, et ad virum tuum erit desiderium tuum, ipseque dominabitur tibi.

17. And unto Adam he said, Because thou hast hearkened unto the voice of thy wife, and hast eaten of the tree, of which I commanded thee, saying, Thou shalt not eat of it: cursed *is* the ground for thy sake; in sorrow shalt thou eat *of* it all the days of thy life :

18. Thorns also and thistles shall it bring forth to thee; and thou shalt eat the herb of the field.

19. In the sweat of thy face shalt thou eat bread, till thou return unto the ground ; for out of it wast thou taken : for dust thou *art*, and unto dust shalt thou return.

20. And Adam called his wife's name Eve; because she was the mother of all living.

21. Unto Adam also and to his wife did the Lord God make coats of skins, and clothed them.

22. And the Lord God said, Behold, the man is become as one of us, to know good and evil : and now, lest he put forth his hand, and take also of the tree of life, and eat, and live for ever :

23. Therefore the Lord God sent him forth from the garden of Eden, to till the ground from whence he was taken.

24. So he drove out the man ; and he placed at the east of the garden of Eden cherubims, and a flaming sword which turned every way, to keep the way of the tree of life.

17. Adæ vero ait, Quia paruisti voci uxoris tuæ, et comedisti ex arbore de qua præceperam tibi, dicens, Non comedes ex ea : maledicta terra propter te : in labore comedes eam cunctis diebus vitæ tuæ.

18. Et spinam et tribulum germinabit tibi, et comedes herbam agri.

19. In sudore vultus tui vesceris pane, donec revertaris in terram : quia ex ea sumptus es : nam pulvis es, et in pulverem reverteris.

20. Et vocavit Adam nomen uxoris suæ Hava, quia ipsa est mater omnis viventis.

21. Fecitque Jehova Deus Adæ et uxori ejus tunicas pelliceas,. et induit eos.

22. Tunc dixit Jehova Deus, Ecce, Adam factus est tanquam unus ex nobis, sciendo bonum et malum : nunc autem ne forte mittat manum suam, et accipiat etiam de arbore vitæ, et comedat, et vivat in seculum.

23. Et emisit eum Jehova de horto Heden, ad colendum terram ex qua sumptus fuerat.

24. Et ejecit Adam, et collocavit ab Oriente horti Heden cherubim, et laminam gladii versatilis, ad custodiendum viam arboris vitæ.

1. *Now the serpent was more subtil.* In this chapter, Moses explains, that man, after he had been deceived by Satan, revolted from his Maker, became entirely changed, and so degenerate, that the image of God, in which he had been formed, was obliterated. He then declares, that the whole world, which had been created for the sake of man, fell together with him from its primary original; and that, in this way, much of its native excellence was destroyed. But here many and arduous questions arise. For when Moses says that the serpent was crafty beyond all other animals, he seems to intimate, that it had been induced to deceive man,

not by the instigation of Satan, but by its own malignity. I answer, that the innate subtlety of the serpent did not prevent Satan from making use of the animal for the purpose of effecting the destruction of man. For since he required an instrument, he chose from among animals that which he saw would be most suitable for him : finally, he carefully contrived the method by which the ·snares he was preparing might the more easily take the mind of Eve by surprise. Hitherto, he had held no communication with men; he, therefore, clothed himself with the person of an animal, under which he might open for himself the way of access. Yet it is not agreed among interpreters in what sense the serpent is said to be עָרוּם, (*aroom, subtle,*) by which word the Hebrews designate the *prudent* as well as the *crafty.* Some, therefore, would take it in a' good, others in a bad sense. I think, however, Moses does not so much point out a fault as attribute praise to nature, because God had endued this beast with such singular skill, as rendered it acute and quick-sighted beyond all others. But Satan perverted to his own deceitful purposes the gift which had been divinely imparted to the serpent. Some captiously cavil, that more acuteness is now found in many other animals. To whom I answer, that there would be nothing absurd in saying, that the gift which had proved so destructive to the human race has been withdrawn from the serpent : just, as we shall hereafter see, other punishments were also inflicted upon it. Yet, in this description, writers on natural history do not materially differ from Moses, and experience gives the best answer to the objection; for the Lord does not in vain command his own disciples to be ' prudent as serpents,' (Matth. x. 16.) But it appears, perhaps, scarcely consonant with reason, that the serpent only should be here brought forward, all mention of Satan being suppressed. I acknowledge, indeed, that from this place *alone* nothing more can be collected than that men were deceived by the serpent. But the testimonies of Scripture are sufficiently numerous, in which it is plainly asserted that the serpent was only the mouth of the devil; for not the serpent but the devil is declared to be ' the father of lies,' the fabricator of imposture, and the author of death. The question, however, is not yet solved, why Moses has kept back the name of Satan. I willingly subscribe to the opinion of those who maintain that the Holy Spirit then purposely used obscure figures, because it was fitting that full and clear light should be reserved for the kingdom of Christ. In the meantime, the prophets prove that they were well acquainted with the meaning of Moses, when, in different places, they cast the blame of our ruin upon the devil. We have elsewhere said, that Moses, by a homely and uncultivated style, accommodates what he delivers to the capacity of the people; and for the best reason; for not only had he to instruct an untaught race of men, but the existing age of the Church was so puerile, that it was unable to receive any higher instruction. There is, therefore, nothing absurd in the supposition, that they, whom, for the time, we know and confess to have been but as infants, were fed with milk. Or (if another comparison be more acceptable) Moses is by no means to be blamed, if he, considering the office of schoolmaster as imposed upon him, insists on the rudiments suitable to children. They who have an aversion to this simplicity, must of necessity condemn the whole economy of God in governing the Church. This, however, may suffice us, that the Lord, by the secret illumination of his Spirit, supplied whatever was wanting of clearness in outward expressions; as appears plainly from the prophets, who saw Satan to be the real enemy of the human race, the contriver of all evils, furnished with every kind of fraud and villany to injure and destroy. Therefore, though the impious make a noise, there is nothing justly to offend us in this mode of speaking by which Moses describes Satan, the prince of iniquity, under the person of his servant and instrument, at the time when Christ, the Head of the Church, and the Sun of Righteousness, had not yet openly shone forth. Add to this, the baseness of human ingratitude is more clearly hence perceived, that when Adam and Eve knew that all animals were given, by the hand of God, into subjection to them, they yet suffered themselves to be led away by one of their own slaves into rebellion against God. As often as they beheld any one of the animals which were in the world, they ought to have been reminded both of the supreme authority, and of the singular goodness of God; but, on the contrary, when they saw the serpent an apostate from his Creator, not only did they neglect to punish it, but, in violation of all lawful order, they subjected and devoted themselves to it, as participators in the same apostacy. What can be imagined more dishonourable than this extreme depravity? Thus, I understand the name of the serpent, not allegorically, as some foolishly do, but in its genuine sense.

Many persons are surprised that Moses simply, and as if abruptly, relates that men have fallen by the impulse of Satan into eternal destruction, and yet never by a single word explains how the tempter himself had revolted from God. And hence it has arisen, that fanatical men have dreamed that Satan was created evil and wicked as he is here described. But the revolt of Satan is proved by other passages of Scripture; and it is an impious madness to ascribe to God the creation of any evil and corrupt nature; for when he had completed the world, he himself gave this testimony to all his works, that they were "very good." Wherefore, without controversy, we must conclude, that the principle of evil with which Satan was endued was not from nature, but from defection; because he had departed from God, the fountain of justice and of all rectitude. But Moses here passes over Satan's fall, because his object is briefly to narrate the corruption of human nature; to teach us that Adam was not created to those multiplied miseries under which all his posterity suffer, but that he fell into them by his own fault. In reflecting on the number and nature of those evils to which they are obnoxious, men will often be unable to restrain themselves from raging and murmuring against God, whom they rashly censure for the just punishment of their sin. These are their well-known complaints, that God has acted more mercifully to swine and dogs than to them. Whence is this, but that they do not refer the miserable and ruined state, under which we languish, to the sin of Adam as they ought? But what is far worse, they fling back upon God the charge of being the cause of all the inward vices of the mind, (such as its horrible blindness, contumacy against God, wicked desires, and violent propensities to evil;) as if the whole perverseness of our disposition had not been adventitious.[1] The design, therefore, of Moses was to show, in a few words, how greatly our present condition differs from our first original, in order that we may learn, with humble confession of our fault, to bewail our evils. We ought not then to be surprised, that, while intent on the history he purposed to relate, he does not discuss every topic which may be desired by any person whatever.

We must now enter on that question by which vain and inconstant minds are greatly agitated; namely, Why God permitted Adam to be tempted, seeing that the sad result was by no means hidden from him? That He now relaxes Satan's reins, to allow him to tempt us to sin, we ascribe to judgment and to vengeance, in consequence of man's alienation from himself; but there was not the same reason for doing so when human nature was yet pure and upright. God, therefore,[2] permitted Satan to tempt man, who was conformed to His own image, and not yet implicated in any crime, having, moreover, on this occasion, allowed Satan the use of an animal [3] which otherwise would never have obeyed him; and what else was this, than to arm an enemy for the destruction of man? This seems to have been the ground on which the Manichæans maintained the existence of two principles.[4] Therefore, they have imagined that Satan, not being in subjection to God, laid snares for man in opposition to the divine will, and was superior not to man only, but also to God himself. Thus, for

---

[1] "Quasi non *accidentalis* esset." As if it had not been *accidental*, where the word *accidental* is used in the sense of the schoolmen and logicians, as opposed to the word *essential.—Ed.*

[2] The reader will observe that Calvin is here putting forward the argument of an objector.—*Ed.*

[3] "Mesme il luy a preste le serpent."—*French Tr.*

[4] On the intricate subject of Manichæism, and its various cognate heresies, the reader may refer to the Bampton Lectures of the late Dr Burton, who, with incredible erudition and industry, has searched the records of ancient and modern times, and has examined, with the greatest candour, the various conflicting sentiments which have been entertained by learned men in reference to this question. The fundamental error of Manes seems to have been, that, with nearly all the Oriental philosophers of antiquity, he held the necessary and independent existence of matter, which, in his view, was the origin of all evil.—See *Burton's Bampton Lectures*, p. 294 ; and *Lardner's Credibility, &c.* part 2, c. 63.

the sake of avoiding what they dreaded as an absurdity, they have fallen into execrable prodigies of error; such as, that there are two Gods, and not one sole Creator of the world, and that the first God has been overcome by his antagonist. All, however, who think piously and reverently concerning the power of God, acknowledge that the evil did not take place except by his permission. For, in the first place, it must be conceded, that God was not in ignorance of the event which was about to occur; and then, that he could have prevented it, had he seen fit to do so. But in speaking of permission, I understand that he had appointed whatever he wished to be done. Here, indeed, a difference arises on the part of many, who suppose Adam to have been so left to his own free will, that God would not have him fall. They take for granted, what I allow them, that nothing is less probable than that God should be regarded as the cause of sin, which he has avenged with so many and such severe penalties. When I say, however, that Adam did not fall without the ordination and will of God, I do not so take it as if sin had ever been pleasing to Him, or as if he simply wished that the precept which he had given should be violated. So far as the fall of Adam was the subversion of equity, and of well-constituted order, so far as it was contumacy against the Divine Law-giver, and the transgression of righteousness, certainly it was against the will of God; yet none of these things render it impossible that, for a certain cause, although to us unknown, he might will the fall of man. It offends the ears of some, when it is said God *willed* this fall; but what else, I pray, is the *permission* of Him, who has the power of preventing, and in whose hand the whole matter is placed, but his will? I wish that men would rather suffer themselves to be judged by God, than that, with profane temerity, they should pass judgment upon him; but this is the arrogance of the flesh to subject God to its own test. I hold it as a settled axiom, that nothing is more unsuitable to the character of God than for us to say that man was created by Him for the purpose of being placed in a condition of suspense and doubt; wherefore I conclude, that, as it became the Creator, he had before determined with himself what should be man's future condition.   Hence the unskilful rashly infer, that man did not sin by free choice.   For he himself perceives, being convicted by the testimony of his own conscience, that he has been too free in sinning.   Whether he sinned by necessity, or by contingency, is another question; respecting which see the INSTITUTION,[1] and the treatise on PREDESTINATION.

And he said unto the woman.   The impious assail this passage with their sneers, because Moses ascribes eloquence to an animal which only faintly hisses with its forked tongue.   And first they ask, at what time animals began to be mute, if they then had a distinct language, and one common to ourselves and them.   The answer is ready; the serpent was not eloquent by nature, but when Satan, by divine permission, procured it as a fit instrument for his use, he uttered words also by its tongue, which God himself permitted.   Nor do I doubt that Eve perceived it to be extraordinary, and on that account received with the greater avidity what she admired.   Now, if men decide that whatever is unwonted must be fabulous, God could work no miracle.   Here God, by accomplishing a work above the ordinary course of nature, constrains us to admire his power.   If then, under this very pretext, we ridicule the power of God, because it is not familiar to us, are we not excessively preposterous?   Besides, if it seems incredible that beasts should speak at the command of God, how has man the power of speech, but because God has formed his tongue?   The Gospel declares, that voices were uttered in the air, without a tongue, to illustrate the glory of Christ; this is less probable to carnal reason, than that speech should be elicited from the mouth of brute animals.   What then can the petulance of impious men find here deserving of their invective?   In short, whosoever holds that God in heaven is the Ruler of the world, will not deny his power over the creatures, so that he can teach brute animals to speak when he pleases, just as he sometimes renders eloquent men speechless.   Moreover, the craftiness of Satan betrays itself in this, that he does not directly assail the man, but approaches him, as through a mine, in the person of his wife.   This insidious method of

[1] Calvin's Institutes, Book III. c. 1.   Vol. ii. p. 73, of the Calvin Society's edition.

attack is more than sufficiently known to us at the present day, and I wish we might learn prudently to guard ourselves against it. For he warily insinuates himself at that point at which he sees us to be the least fortified, that he may not be perceived till he should have penetrated where he wished. The woman does not flee from converse with the serpent, because hitherto no dissension had existed ; she, therefore, accounted it simply as a domestic animal.

The question occurs, what had impelled Satan to contrive the destruction of man ? Curious sophists have feigned that he burned with envy, when he foresaw that the Son of God was to be clothed in human flesh ; but the speculation is frivolous. For since the Son of God was made man in order to restore us, who were already lost, from our miserable overthrow, how could that be foreseen which would never have happened unless man had sinned ? If there be room for conjectures, it is more probable that he was driven by a kind of fury, (as the desperate are wont to be,) to hurry man away with himself into a participation of eternal ruin. But it becomes us to be content with this single reason, that since he was the adversary of God, he attempted to subvert the order established by Him, and, because he could not drag God from his throne, he assailed man, in whom His image shone. He knew that with the ruin of man the most dreadful confusion would be produced in the whole world, as indeed it happened, and therefore he endeavoured, in the person of man, to obscure the glory of God. [1] Rejecting, therefore, all vain figments, let us hold fast this doctrine, which is both simple and solid.

Yea, hath God said? This sentence is variously expounded and even distorted, partly because it is in itself obscure, and partly because of the ambiguous import of the Hebrew particle. The expression אַף כִּי, (*aph ki,*) sometimes signifies "although" or "indeed," and sometimes, "how much more." [2] David

---

[1] " Being under a final and irreversible doom, he looked on God as an irreconcileable enemy ; and, not being able to injure his *essence*, he struck at his *image*. He singled out *Adam* as the mark of his malice, that by seducing him from his duty, he might defeat God's design, which was to be honoured by man's obedience, and so obscure his glory, as if he had made man in vain."—*Bates' Harmony of the Divine Attributes.*

[2] אַף כִּי, " Hebræis tantundem valet interdum ac Latinis, Etiamsi, vel enimvero ; interdum, quanto magis."

Kimchi takes it in this last sense, and thinks that many words had passed between them on both sides, before the serpent descended to this point; namely, that having calumniated God on other accounts, he at length thus concludes, Hence it *much more* appears how envious and malignant he is towards you, because he has interdicted you from the tree of the knowledge of good and evil. But this exposition is not only forced, it is proved to be false by the reply of Eve. More correct is the explanation of the Chaldean paraphrast, 'Is it true that God has forbidden ? ' &c.[1] Again, to some this appears a *simple*, to others an *ironical* interrogation. It would be a *simple* interrogation, if it injected a doubt in the following manner : ' Can it be, that God should forbid the eating of any tree whatever?' but it would be ironical, if used for the purpose of dissipating vain fear ; as, ' It greatly concerns God, indeed, whether you eat of the tree or not ! It is, therefore, ridiculous that you should think it to be forbidden you !' I subscribe the more freely to the former opinion, because there is greater probability that Satan, in order to deceive more covertly, would gradually proceed with cautious prevarications to lead the woman to a contempt of the divine precept. There are some who suppose that Satan expressly denies the word which our first parents had heard, to have been the word of God. Others think, (with whom I rather agree,) that, under the pretext of inquiring into the cause, he would indirectly weaken their confidence in the word. And certainly the old interpreter has translated the expression, ' Why has God said ? ' [2] which, although I do not altogether approve, yet I have no doubt that the serpent urges the woman to seek out the cause, since otherwise he would not have been able to draw away her mind from God. Very dangerous is the temptation, when it is suggested to us, that God is not to be obeyed, except so far as the reason of his

[1] See the Chaldee paraphrase in Walton's Polyglott. The Latin translation is as follows : " Verumne est quod dixit Deus, non comedatis ex omni arbore horti? Gesenius gives the same explanation : " Sollte denn das wahr seyn, dass Gott gesagt hätte ? " " Can it be true, that God has said ? " &c.—*Ed.*

[2] " Cur præcepit vobis Deus," &c.—*Vulgate.*

command is apparent. The true rule of obedience is, that we being content with a bare command, should persuade ourselves that whatever he enjoins is just and right. But whosoever desires to be wise beyond measure, him will Satan, seeing he has cast off all reverence for God, immediately precipitate into open rebellion. As it respects grammatical construction, I think the expression ought to be translated, ' Hath God even said ? ' or, ' Is it so that God hath said ? ' [1] Yet the artifice of Satan is to be noticed, for he wished to inject into the woman a doubt which might induce her to believe *that* not to be the word of God, for which a plausible reason did not manifestly appear.

Of every tree of the garden. Commentators offer a double interpretation of these words. The former supposes Satan, for the sake of increasing envy, to insinuate that all the trees had been forbidden. " Has God indeed enjoined that you should not dare to touch any tree ?" The other interpretation, however, is, " Have you not then the liberty granted you of eating promiscuously from whatever tree you please ?" The former more accords with the disposition of the devil, who would malignantly amplify the prohibition, and seems to be sanctioned by Eve's reply. For when she says, We do eat of all, one only excepted, she seems to repel the calumny concerning a general prohibition. But because the latter sense of the passage, which suggests the question concerning the simple and bare prohibition of God, was more apt to deceive, it is more credible that Satan, with his accustomed guile, should have begun his temptation from this point, ' Is it possible for God to be unwilling that you should gather the fruit of any tree whatever ?' The answer of the woman, that only one tree was forbidden, she means to be a defence of the command ; as if she would deny that it ought to seem harsh or burdensome, since God had only excepted one single tree out of so great an abundance and variety as he had granted to them. Thus, in these words there will be a concession, that one tree was indeed forbidden ; then, the refutation of a calumny, because it is not

[1] " Vertendum censeo, Etiamne, vel Itane ? "

arduous or difficult to abstain from one tree, when others without number are supplied, of which the use is permitted It was impossible for Eve more prudently or more courageously to repel the assault of Satan, than by objecting against him, that she and her husband had been so bountifully dealt with by the Lord, that the advantages granted to them were abundantly sufficient, for she intimates that they would be most ungrateful if, instead of being content with such affluence, they should desire more than was lawful. When she says, God had forbidden them to eat or to touch, some suppose the second word to be added for the purpose of charging God with too great severity, because he prohibited them even from the *touch*.[1] But I rather understand that she hitherto remained in obedience, and expressed her pious disposition by anxiously observing the precept of God; only, in proclaiming the punishment, she begins to give way, by inserting the adverb "perhaps,"[2] when God has certainly pronounced, "Ye shall die the death."[3] For although with the Hebrews פֶּן (*pen*) does not always imply doubt, yet, since it is generally taken in this sense, I willingly embrace the opinion that the woman was beginning to waver. Certainly, she had not death so immediately before her eyes, should she become disobedient to God, as she ought to have had. She clearly proves that her perception of the true danger of death was distant and cold.

4. *And the serpent said unto the woman.* Satan now springs more boldly forward; and because he sees a breach open before him, he breaks through in a direct assault, for he is never wont to engage in open war until we voluntarily expose ourselves to him, naked and unarmed. He cautiously approaches us at first with blandishments; but when he has stolen in upon us, he dares to exalt himself petulantly and with proud confidence against God; just as he now, seizing upon Eve's doubt, penetrates further, that he may turn it

[1] " Neither shall ye touch it." " The woman herself adds this, which certainly in the divine law we are not permitted to do."—*Peter Martyr's Commentary on Genesis.*

[2] " Ne forte moriamini," lest *perhaps* ye may die.

[3] " Moriendo moriemini." מוֹת תָּמוּת. (Mot tamoot.)

into a direct negative. It behoves us to be instructed, by
such examples, to beware of his snares, and, by making
timely resistance, to keep him far from us, that nearer access
may not be permitted to him. He now, therefore, does not
ask doubtingly, as before, whether or not the command of
God, which he opposes, be true, but openly accuses God of
falsehood, for he asserts that the word by which death was
denounced is false and delusive. Fatal temptation! when,
while God is threatening us with death, we not only securely
sleep, but hold God himself in derision!

5. *For God doth know.* There are those who think that
God is here craftily praised by Satan, as if He never would
prohibit men from the use of wholesome fruit. But they
manifestly contradict themselves, for they at the same time
confess that in the preceding member of the sentence he had
already declared God to be unworthy of confidence, as one
who had lied. Others suppose that he charges God with
malignity and envy, as wishing to deprive man of his highest
perfection; and this opinion is more probable than the other.
Nevertheless, (according to my judgment,) Satan attempts
to prove what he had recently asserted, reasoning, however,
from contraries :[1] God, he says, has interdicted to you the
tree, that he may not be compelled to admit you to the participation of his glory ; therefore, the fear of punishment is
quite needless. In short, he denies that a fruit which is useful and salutary can be injurious. When he says, " God
doth know," he censures God as being moved by jealousy,
and as having given the command concerning the tree, for
the purpose of keeping man in an inferior rank.

Ye shall be as gods. Some translate it, 'Ye shall be like
angels.' It might even be rendered in the singular number,

[1] " Sumpta à contraria ratione."
The meaning of the passage seems to be this : Satan had first said in
plain terms, " Ye shall not surely die ; " and then, to confirm his position,
had argued that, supposing God had forbidden the tree, he must have done
it out of envy, lest he should be compelled to raise them to an equality
with himself, and therefore on no possible supposition had they any ground
to fear ; for they had only to eat in order to be beyond the reach of his
vengeance.—*Ed.*

'Ye shall be as God.' I have no doubt that Satan promises them *divinity;* as if he had said, For no other reason does God defraud you of the tree of knowledge, than because he fears to have you as companions. Moreover, it is not without some show of reason that he makes the Divine glory, or equality with God, to consist in the perfect knowledge of good and evil; but it is a mere pretence, for the purpose of ensnaring the miserable woman. Because the desire of knowledge is naturally inherent in all, happiness is supposed to be placed in it; but Eve erred in not regulating the measure of her knowledge by the will of God. And we all daily suffer under the same disease, because we desire to know more than is right, and more than God allows; whereas the principal point of wisdom is a well-regulated sobriety in obedience to God.

6. *And when the woman saw.* This impure look of Eve, infected with the poison of concupiscence, was both the messenger and the witness of an impure heart. She could previously behold the tree with such sincerity, that no desire to eat of it affected her mind; for the faith she had in the word of God was the best guardian of her heart, and of all her senses. But now, after the heart had declined from faith, and from obedience to the word, she corrupted both herself and all her senses, and depravity was diffused through all parts of her soul as well as her body. It is, therefore, a sign of impious defection, that the woman now judges the tree to be good for food, eagerly delights herself in beholding it, and persuades herself that it is desirable for the sake of acquiring wisdom; whereas before she had passed by it a hundred times with an unmoved and tranquil look. For now, having shaken off the bridle, her mind wanders dissolutely and intemperately, drawing the body with it to the same licentiousness. The word להשכיל, (*lehaskil,*) admits of two explanations: That the tree was desirable either to be *looked upon,* or to *impart prudence.* I prefer the latter sense, as better corresponding with the temptation.

And gave also unto her husband with her. From these words, some conjecture that Adam was present when his wife

was tempted and persuaded by the serpent, which is by no
means credible. Yet it might be that he soon joined her,
and that, even before the woman tasted the fruit of the tree,
she related the conversation held with the serpent, and entangled him with the same fallacies by which she herself had
been deceived. Others refer the particle עִמָּהּ, (immah,)
" with her," to the conjugal bond, which may be received.
But because Moses simply relates that he ate the fruit taken
from the hands of his wife, the opinion has been commonly
received, that he was rather captivated with her allurements
than persuaded by Satan's impostures.[1] For this purpose
the declaration of Paul is adduced, ' Adam was not deceived,
but the woman.' (1 Tim. ii. 14.) But Paul in that place, as he
is teaching that the origin of evil was from the woman, only
speaks comparatively. Indeed, it was not only for the sake
of complying with the wishes of his wife, that he transgressed
the law laid down for him; but being drawn by her into
fatal ambition, he became partaker of the same defection with
her. And truly Paul elsewhere states that sin came not by
the woman, but by Adam himself, (Rom. v. 12.) Then, the
reproof which soon afterwards follows, ' Behold, Adam is as
one of us,' clearly proves that he also foolishly coveted more
than was lawful, and gave greater credit to the flatteries of
the devil than to the sacred word of God.

It is now asked, What was the sin of both of them? The
opinion of some of the ancients, that they were allured by
intemperance of appetite, is puerile. For when there was such
an abundance of the choicest fruits, what daintiness could
there be about one particular kind? Augustine is more correct, who says, that pride was the beginning of all evils, and
that by pride the human race was ruined. Yet a fuller definition of the sin may be drawn from the kind of temptation
which Moses describes. For first the woman is led away
from the word of God by the wiles of Satan, through unbelief.[2]

[1] So our great Poet :—

He scrupled not to eat
Against his better knowledge, not deceived,
But fondly overcome with female charm.
Paradise Lost, Book IX.

[2] " Per infidelitatem."

Wherefore, the commencement of the ruin by which the human race was overthrown was a defection from the command of God. But observe, that men then revolted from God, when, having forsaken his word, they lent their ears to the falsehoods of Satan. Hence we infer, that God will be seen and adored in his word; and, therefore, that all reverence for him is shaken off when his word is despised. A doctrine most useful to be known, for the word of God obtains its due honour only with few, so that they who rush onward with impunity, in contempt of this word, yet arrogate to themselves a chief rank among the worshippers of God. But as God does not manifest himself to men otherwise than through the word, so neither is his majesty maintained, nor does his worship remain secure among us any longer than while we obey his word. Therefore, unbelief was the root of defection; just as faith alone unites us to God. Hence flowed ambition and pride, so that the woman first, and then her husband, desired to exalt themselves against God. For truly they did exalt themselves against God, when, honour having been divinely conferred upon them, they, not contented with such excellence, desired to know more than was lawful, in order that they might become equal with God. Here also monstrous ingratitude betrays itself. They had been made in the *likeness* of God; but this seems a small thing unless *equality* be added. Now, it is not to be endured that designing and wicked men should labour in vain, as well as absurdly, to extenuate the sin of Adam and his wife. For apostacy is no light offence, but a detestable wickedness, by which man withdraws himself from the authority of his Creator, yea, even rejects and denies him. Besides, it was not simple apostacy, but combined with atrocious contumelies and reproaches against God himself. Satan accuses God of falsehood, of envy, and of malignity, and our first parents subscribe to a calumny thus vile and execrable. At length, having despised the command of God, they not only indulge their own lust, but enslave themselves to the devil. If any one prefers a shorter explanation, we may say unbelief has opened the door to ambition, but ambition has proved the parent of rebellion, to the end that men, having cast aside the fear of God, might shake off his yoke. On this account, Paul teaches us, that by the disobedience of Adam sin entered into the world. Let us imagine that there was nothing worse than the transgression of the command; we shall not even thus have succeeded far in extenuating the fault of Adam. God, having both made him free in everything, and appointed him as king of the world, chose to put his obedience to the proof, in requiring abstinence from one tree alone. This condition did not please him. Perverse declaimers may plead in excuse, that the woman was allured by the beauty of the tree, and the man ensnared by the blandishments of Eve. Yet the milder the authority of God, the less excusable was their perverseness in rejecting it. But we must search more deeply for the origin and cause of sin. For never would they have dared to resist God, unless they had first been incredulous of his word. And nothing allured them to covet the fruit but mad ambition. So long as they, firmly believing in God's word, freely suffered themselves to be governed by Him, they had serene and duly regulated affections. For, indeed, their best restraint was the thought, which entirely occupied their minds, that God is just, that nothing is better than to obey his commands, and that to be loved by him is the consummation of a happy life. But after they had given place to Satan's blasphemy, they began, like persons fascinated, to lose reason and judgment; yea, since they were become the slaves of Satan; he held their very senses bound. Still further, we know that sins are not estimated in the sight of God by the external appearance, but by the inward disposition.

Again, it appears to many absurd, that the defection of our first parents is said to have proved the destruction of the whole race; and, on this account, they freely bring an accusation against God. Pelagius, on the other hand, lest, as he falsely feared, the corruption of human nature should be charged upon God, ventured to deny original sin. But an error so gross is plainly refuted, not only by solid testimonies of Scripture, but also by experience itself. The corruption of our nature was unknown to the philosophers, who, in other respects, were sufficiently, and more than sufficiently, acute. Surely this stupor itself was a signal proof of original sin.

For all who are not utterly blind, perceive that no part of us is sound; that the mind is smitten with blindness, and infected with innumerable errors; that all the affections of the heart are full of stubbornness and wickedness; that vile lusts, or other diseases equally fatal, reign there; and that all the senses burst forth [1] with many vices.   Since, however, none but God alone is a proper judge in this cause, we must acquiesce in the sentence which he has pronounced in the Scriptures. In the first place, Scripture clearly teaches us that we are born vicious and perverse. The cavil of Pelagius was frivolous, that sin proceeded from Adam by imitation.   For David, while still enclosed in his mother's womb, could not be an imitator of Adam, yet he confesses that he was conceived in sin, (Psalm li. 5.)   A fuller proof of this matter, and a more ample definition of original sin, may be found in the INSTITUTES; [2] yet here, in a single word, I will attempt to show how far it extends. Whatever in our nature is vicious—since it is not lawful to ascribe it to God—we justly reject as sin.[3] But Paul (Rom. iii. 10) teaches that corruption does not reside in one part only, but pervades the whole soul, and each of its faculties. Whence it follows, that they childishly err who regard original sin as consisting only in lust, and in the inordinate motion of the appetites, whereas it seizes upon the very seat of reason, and upon the whole heart.   To sin is annexed condemnation,[4] or, as Paul speaks, 'By man came sin, and by sin, death,'(Rom. v. 12.) Wherefore he elsewhere pronounces us to be ' the children of wrath; ' as if he would subject us to an eternal curse, (Ephes. ii. 3.)   In short, that we are despoiled of the excellent gifts of the Holy Spirit, of the light of reason, of justice, and of rectitude, and are prone to every evil; that we are also lost and condemned, and subjected to death, is both our hereditary condition, and, at the same time, a just punishment, which God, in the person of Adam, has inflicted on the human race.   Now, if any one should object, that it is unjust for the innocent to bear the punishment of

---

1 " Scatere," send forth as from a fountain.
2 Calvin's Institutes, Book II., chap. 1, 2, 3.
3 " Merito in peccatum rejicimus."
4 " Peccato annexus est reatus."

another's sin, I answer, whatever gifts God had conferred upon us in the person of Adam, he had the best right to take away, when Adam wickedly fell. Nor is it necessary to resort to that ancient figment of certain writers, that souls are derived by descent from our first parents.[1] For the human race has not naturally derived corruption through its descent from Adam; but that result is rather to be traced to the appointment of God, who, as he had adorned the whole nature of mankind with most excellent endowments in one man, so in the same man he again denuded it. But now, from the time in which we were corrupted in Adam, we do not bear the punishment of another's offence, but are guilty by our own fault.

A question is mooted by some, concerning the *time* of this fall, or rather ruin. The opinion has been pretty generally received, that they fell on the day they were created; and, therefore, Augustine writes, that they stood only for six hours. The conjecture of others, that the temptation was delayed by Satan till the Sabbath, in order to profane that sacred day, is but weak. And certainly, by instances like these, all pious persons are admonished sparingly to indulge themselves in doubtful speculations. As for myself, since I have nothing to assert positively respecting the time, so I think it may be gathered from the narration of Moses, that they did not long retain the dignity they had received; for as soon as he has said they were created, he passes, without the mention of any other thing, to their fall. If Adam had lived but a moderate space of time with his wife, the blessing of God would not have been unfruitful in the production of offspring; but Moses intimates that they were deprived of God's benefits before they had become accustomed to use them. I therefore readily subscribe to the exclamation of Augustine, 'O wretched free-will, which, while yet entire, had so little stability!'

---

[1] " Quod animæ ex traduce oriuntur."—" Que les ames procedent de celle d'Adam." That souls proceed from that of Adam.—*French Tr.*

It can be scarcely necessary to inform the reader, that a controversy of some magnitude engaged the attention of the learned, on the subject to which Calvin here alludes; namely, whether the souls of men are, like their bodies, propagated by descent from Adam, or whether they proceed immediately from God. The supposed descent of the soul from Adam was said to be *ex traduce*, by traduction.—*Ed.*

And, to say no more respecting the shortness of the time, the admonition of Bernard is worthy of remembrance: ' Since we read that a fall so dreadful took place in Paradise, what shall we do on the dunghill?' At the same time, we must keep in memory by what pretext they were led into this delusion so fatal to themselves, and to all their posterity. Plausible was the adulation of Satan, ' Ye shall know good and evil;' but that knowledge was therefore accursed, because it was sought in preference to the favour of God. Wherefore, unless we wish, of our own accord, to fasten the same snares upon ourselves, let us learn entirely to depend upon the sole will of God, whom we acknowledge as the Author of all good. And, since the Scripture everywhere admonishes us of our nakedness and poverty, and declares that we may recover in Christ what we have lost in Adam, let us, renouncing all self-confidence, offer ourselves empty to Christ, that he may fill us with his own riches.

7. *And the eyes of them both were opened.* It was necessary that the eyes of Eve should be veiled till her husband also was deceived; but now both, being alike bound by the chain of an unhappy consent, begin to be sensible of their wretchedness, although they are not yet affected with a deep knowledge of their fault. They are ashamed of their nakedness, yet, though convinced, they do not humble themselves before God, nor fear his judgments as they ought; they even do not cease to resort to evasions. Some progress, however, is made; for whereas recently they would, like giants, assault heaven by storm; now, confounded with a sense of their own ignominy, they flee to hiding-places. And truly this opening of the eyes in our first parents to discern their baseness, clearly proves them to have been condemned by their own judgment. They are not yet summoned to the tribunal of God; there is none who accuses them; is not then the sense of shame, which rises spontaneously, a sure token of guilt? The eloquence, therefore, of the whole world will avail nothing to deliver those from condemnation, whose own conscience has become the judge to compel them to confess their fault. It rather becomes us all to open our eyes, that, being con-

founded at our own disgrace, we may give to God the glory which is his due. God created man flexible; and not only permitted, but willed that he should be tempted. For he both adapted the tongue of the serpent beyond the ordinary use of nature, to the devil's purpose, just as if any one should furnish another with a sword and armour; and then, though the unhappy event was foreknown by him, he did not apply the remedy, which he had the power to do. On the other hand, when we come to speak of man, he will be found to have sinned voluntarily, and to have departed from God, his Maker, by a movement of the mind not less free than perverse. Nor ought we to call that a light fault, which, refusing credit to the word of God, exalted itself against him by impious and sacrilegious emulation, which would not be subject to his authority, and which, finally, both proudly and perfidiously revolted from him. Therefore, whatever sin and fault there is in the fall of our first parents remains with themselves; but there is sufficient reason why the eternal counsel of God preceded it, though that reason is concealed from us. We see, indeed, some good fruit daily springing from a ruin so dreadful, inasmuch as God instructs us in humility by our miseries, and then more clearly illustrates his own goodness; for his grace is more abundantly poured forth, through Christ, upon the world, than it was imparted to Adam in the beginning. Now, if the reason why this is so lies beyond our reach, it is not wonderful that the secret counsel of God should be to us like a labyrinth.[1]

And they sewed fig-leaves together. What I lately said, that they had not been brought either by true shame or by serious fear to repentance, is now more manifest. They sew

[1] To the question, 'Why God did not create man without a possibility of sinning,' Peter Martyr replies : ' Because such a state could not be suitable to the nature of any rational creature; since the creature, *as a creature*, remains infirm and feeble; whereas, also, he is not entirely one with the rule by which he is to be directed, (otherwise he would be God, the chief good, and chief rectitude,) it follows, that his nature may diverge from that rule. It was, however, possible for *grace* to confirm him so that he should not sin, which is believed to be the state of angels and of saints in heaven. But that dignity or reward would not be so highly esteemed, if this fallible and inconstant state of man had not preceded it.'—*Peter Martyr, in Gen.*, fol. 14. Tiguri, 1579.—*Ed.*

together for themselves girdles of leaves.[1] For what end? That they may keep God at a distance, as by an invincible barrier! Their sense of evil, therefore, was only confused, and combined with dulness, as is wont to be the case in unquiet sleep. There is none of us who does not smile at their folly, since, certainly, it was ridiculous to place such a covering before the eyes of God. In the meanwhile, we are all infected with the same disease; for, indeed, we tremble, and are covered with shame at the first compunctions of conscience; but self-indulgence soon steals in, and induces us to resort to vain trifles, as if it were an easy thing to delude God. Therefore, unless conscience be more closely pressed, there is no shadow of excuse too faint and fleeting to obtain our acquiescence; and even if there be no pretext whatever, we still make pleasures for ourselves, and, by an oblivion of three days' duration, we imagine that we are well covered.[2] In short, the cold and faint[3] knowledge of sin, which is inherent in the minds of men, is here described by Moses, in order that they may be rendered inexcusable.[4] . . . . . . Then (as we have already said) Adam and his wife were yet ignorant of their cwn vileness, since with a covering so light they attempted to hide themselves from the presence of God.

8. *And they heard the voice of the Lord God.* As soon as the voice of God sounds, Adam and Eve perceive that the leaves by which they thought themselves well protected are of no avail. Moses here relates nothing which does not re-

[1] " Ex foliis perizomata."
[2] " Imo si nullus fucus suppetat, facimus tamen nobis delicias, et tridui oblivione putamus nos bene esse tectos."
[3] " Semimortua."
[4] What immediately follows is here given in the original :—
"Quæri tamen potest, si tota natura peccati sordibus infecta est, cur tantum una in parte corporis deformitas appareat. Neque enim faciem vel pectus operiunt Adam et Heva : sed tantum pudenda quæ vocamus. Hac occasione factum esse arbitror ut vulgo non aliam vitæ corruptelam agnoscerent quam in libidine venerea. Atqui expendere debebant, non minorem fuisse in oculis et auribus verecundiæ causam, quam in parte genitali, quæ peccato nondum fœdata erat : quum aures et oculi inquinassent Adam et Heva, et diabolo quasi arma præbuissent. Sed Deo fuit satis, extare in corpore humano aliquam pudendam notam, quæ nos peccati commonefaciat."

main in human nature, and may be clearly discerned at the
present day. The difference between good and evil is engraven on the hearts of all, as Paul teaches, (Rom. ii. 15;)
but all bury the disgrace of their vices under flimsy leaves,
till God, by his voice, strikes inwardly their consciences.
Hence, after God had shaken them out of their torpor, their
alarmed consciences compelled them to hear his voice. Moreover, what Jerome translates, 'at the breeze after mid-day,'[1]
is, in the Hebrew, 'at the wind of the day;'[2] the Greeks,
omitting the word 'wind,' have put 'at the evening.'[3]
Thus the opinion has prevailed, that Adam, having sinned
about noon, was called to judgment about sunset. But I
rather incline to a different conjecture, namely, that being
covered with their garment, they passed the night in silence
and quiet, the darkness aiding their hypocrisy; then, about
sunrise, being again thoroughly awakened, they recollected
themselves. We know that at the rising of the sun the air
is naturally excited; together, then, with this gentle breeze,
God appeared; but Moses would improperly have called the
evening air that of the *day*. Others take the word as describing the southern part or region; and certainly רוח, (*ruach,*)
sometimes among the Hebrews signifies one or another region of the world.[4] Others think that the time is here specified as one least exposed to terrors, for in the clear light
there is the greater security; and thus, they conceive, is fulfilled what the Scripture declares, that they who have accusing consciences are always anxious and disquieted, even
without any danger. To this point they refer what is added
respecting the wind, as if Adam was terrified at the sound of
a falling leaf. But what I have advanced is more true and
simple, that what was hid under the darkness of the night

---

[1] " Ad auram post meridiem." *Vulgate.*

[2] לרוח היום, (*leruach hayom.*)

[3] Τὸ δειλινόν. *Sept.*

[4] This criticism, it is presumed, cannot be maintained. It seems to
derive no countenance whatever but from some passages of Scripture,
which speak of God as scattering his people to the four winds of heaven.
(See Jer. xlix. 32, and lii. 23.) The common interpretation given in our
version, "the cool of the day," as applied to evening, is supported by the
highest authorities, such as Cocceius, Schindler, Gesenius, and Lee. Le
Clerc, however, adopts the same interpretation as Calvin.—*Ed.*

was detected at the rising of the sun. Yet I do not doubt that some notable symbol of the presence of God was in that gentle breeze; for although (as I have lately said) the rising sun is wont daily to stir up some breath of air, this is not opposed to the supposition that God gave some extraordinary sign of his approach, to arouse the consciences of Adam and his wife. For, since he is in himself incomprehensible, he assumes, when he wishes to manifest himself to men, those marks by which he may be known. David calls the winds the messengers of God, on the wings of which he rides, or rather flies, with incredible velocity. (Psal. civ. 3.) But, as often as he sees good, he uses the winds, as well as other created things, beyond the order of nature, according to his own will. Therefore, Moses, in here mentioning the wind, intimates (according to my judgment) that some unwonted and remarkable symbol of the Divine presence was put forth which should vehemently affect the minds of our first parents. This resource, namely, that of fleeing from God's presence, was nothing better than the former; since God, with his voice alone, soon brings back the fugitives. It is written, ' Whither shall I flee from thy presence? If I traverse the sea, if I take wings and ascend above the clouds, if I descend into the profound abyss, thou, Lord, wilt be everywhere,' (Ps. cxxxix. 7.) This we all confess to be true; yet we do not, in the meantime, cease to snatch at vain subterfuges; and we fancy that shadows of any kind will prove a most excellent defence. Nor is it to be here omitted, that he, who had found a few leaves to be unavailing, fled to whole trees; for so we are accustomed, when shut out from frivolous cavils, to frame new excuses, which may hide us as under a denser shade. When Moses says that Adam and his wife hid themselves ' in the midst of the *tree*[1] of Paradise,' I understand that the singular number is put for the plural; as if he had said, among the *trees.*

---

[1] בְּתוֹךְ עֵץ הַגָּן. (*Betok aitz haggan.*) "In medio ligni Pardisi."—*Vulgate.* Ἐν μέσῳ τοῦ ξύλου τοῦ παραδείσου.—*Sept.* Where the singular number is used in each case. It may be translated, " in the midst of the *wood* of Paradise ;" and wood may be, as in English, used collectively for a number of trees, a forest, or a thicket. Calvin, in his version, translates the clause, " in medio arborum horti."

9. *And the Lord God called unto Adam.* They had been already smitten by the voice of God, but they lay confounded under the trees, until another voice more effectually penetrated their minds. Moses says that Adam was called by the Lord. Had he not been called before? The former, however, was a confused sound, which had no sufficient force to press upon the conscience. Therefore God now approaches nearer, and from the tangled thicket of trees[1] draws him, however unwilling and resisting, forth into the midst. In the same manner we also are alarmed at the voice of God, as soon as his law sounds in our ears; but presently we snatch at shadows, until he, calling upon us more vehemently, compels us to come forward, arraigned at his tribunal. Paul calls this the life of the Law,[2] when it slays us by charging us with our sins. For as long as we are pleased with ourselves, and are inflated with a false notion that we are alive, the law is dead to us, because we blunt its point by our hardness; but when it pierces us more sharply, we are driven into new terrors.

10. *And he said, I heard thy voice.* Although this seems to be the confession of a dejected and humbled man, it will nevertheless soon appear that he was not yet properly subdued, nor led to repentance. He imputes his fear to the voice of God, and to his own nakedness, as if he had never before heard God speaking without being alarmed, and had not been even sweetly exhilarated by his speech. His excessive stupidity appears in this, that he fails to recognise the cause of shame in his sin; he, therefore, shows that he does not yet so feel his punishment, as to confess his fault. In the meantime, he proves what I said before to be true, that original sin does not reside in one part of the body only, but holds its dominion over the whole man, and so occupies every part of the soul, that none remains in its integrity; for, notwithstanding his fig-leaves, he still dreads the presence of God.

11. *Who told thee that thou wast naked?* An indirect re-

---

[1] "Ex multiplici arborum complexu."
[2] "Vitam Legis." The life or power of the law.—See Rom. vii. 6.

primand to reprove the sottishness of Adam in not perceiving
his fault in his punishment, as if it had been said, not simply
that Adam was afraid at the voice of God, but that the voice
of his judge was formidable to him, because he was a sinner.
Also, that not his nakedness, but the turpitude of the vice
by which he had defiled himself, was the cause of fear; and
certainly he was guilty of intolerable impiety against God
in seeking the origin of evil in nature.   Not that he would
accuse God in express terms ; but deploring his own misery,
and dissembling the fact that he was himself the author of it,
he malignantly transfers to God the charge which he ought
to have brought against himself.   What the Vulgate translates, ' Unless it be that thou hast eaten of the tree,' [1] is rather
an interrogation. [2]   God asks, in the language of doubt, not
as if he were searching into some disputable matter, but for
the purpose of piercing more acutely the stupid man, who,
labouring under fatal disease, is yet unconscious of his ma-
lady ; just as a sick man, who complains that he is burning,
yet thinks not of fever.   Let us, however, remember that
we shall profit nothing by any prevarications, but that God
will always bind us by a most just accusation in the sin of
Adam.   The clause, " whereof I commanded thee that thou
shouldest not eat," is added to remove the pretext of ignorance.   For God intimates that Adam was admonished in
time ; and that he fell from no other cause than this, that he
knowingly and voluntarily brought destruction upon himself.   Again, the atrocious nature of sin is marked in this
transgression and rebellion ; for, as nothing is more acceptable to God than obedience, so nothing is more intolerable
than when men, having spurned his commandments, obey
Satan and their own lust.

12. *The woman whom thou gavest to be with me.*   The boldness of Adam now more clearly betrays itself ; for, so far
from being subdued, he breaks forth into coarser blas-

---

[1] " Nisi quod de arbore," are the words which Calvin gives. The
expression of the Vulgate really is—" Nisi quòd ex ligno." There is
no difference in the sense.—*Ed.*

[2] " Nonne ex ipsa arbore . . . comedisti ? " as in our own version.

phemy. He had before been tacitly expostulating with God; now he begins *openly* to contend with him, and triumphs as one who has broken through all barriers. Whence we perceive what a refractory and indomitable creature man began to be when he became alienated from God; for a lively picture of corrupt nature is presented to us in Adam from the moment of his revolt. 'Every one,' says James, 'is tempted by his own concupiscence,' (James i. 14;) and even Adam, not otherwise than knowingly and willingly, had set himself, as a rebel, against God. Yet, just as if conscious of no evil, he puts his wife as the guilty party in his place. 'Therefore I have eaten,' he says, 'because she gave.' And not content with this, he brings, at the same time, an accusation against God; objecting that the wife, who had brought ruin upon him, had been given by God. We also, trained in the same school of original sin, are too ready to resort to subterfuges of the same kind; but to no purpose; for howsoever incitements and instigations from other quarters may impel us, yet the unbelief which seduces us from obedience to God is within us; the pride is within which brings forth contempt.

13. *And the Lord God said unto the woman.* God contends no further with the man, nor was it necessary; for he aggravates rather than diminishes his crime, first by a frivolous defence, then by an impious disparagement of God, in short, though he rages, he is yet held convicted. The Judge now turns to the woman, that the cause of both being heard, he may at length pronounce sentence. The old interpreter thus renders God's address: 'Why hast thou done this?' [1] But the Hebrew phrase has more vehemence; for it is the language of one who wonders as at something prodigious. It ought therefore rather to be rendered, 'How hast thou done this?' [2] as if he had said, 'How was it possible that thou shouldst bring thy mind to be so perverse a counsellor to thy husband?'

The serpent beguiled me. Eve ought to have been confounded at the portentous wickedness concerning which she was admonished. Yet she is not struck dumb, but, after

---

[1] " Quare hoc fecisti ? "— *Vulgate.*

[2] " Quomodo hoc fecisti ? " ‏מה־זאת עשית‎

the example of her husband, transfers the charge to another; by laying the blame on the serpent, she foolishly, indeed, and impiously, thinks herself absolved. For her answer comes at length to this : ' I received from the serpent what thou hadst forbidden; the serpent, therefore, was the impostor.' But who compelled Eve to listen to his fallacies, and even to place confidence in them more readily than in the word of God ? Lastly, how did she admit them, but by throwing open and betraying that door of access which God had sufficiently fortified? But the fruit of original sin everywhere presents itself; being blind in its own hypocrisy, it would gladly render God mute and speechless. And whence arise daily so many murmurs, but because God does not hold his peace whenever we choose to blind ourselves ?

14. *And the Lord God said unto the serpent.* He does not interrogate the serpent as he had done the man and the woman ; because, in the animal itself there was no sense of sin, and because, to the devil he would hold out no hope of pardon. He might truly, by his own authority, have pronounced sentence against Adam and Eve, though unheard. Why then does he call them to undergo examination, except that he has a care for their salvation? This doctrine is to be applied to our benefit. There would be no need of any trial of the cause, or of any solemn form of judgment, in order to condemn us ; wherefore, while God insists upon extorting a confession from us, he acts rather as a physician than as a judge. There is the same reason why the Lord, before he imposes punishment on man, begins with the serpent. For corrective punishments (as we shall see) are of a different kind, and are inflicted with the design of leading us to repentance ; but in this there is nothing of the sort.

It is, however, doubtful to whom the words refer, whether to the serpent or to the devil. Moses, indeed, says that the serpent was a skilful and cunning animal ; yet it is certain, that, when Satan was devising the destruction of man, the serpent was guiltless of his fraud and wickedness. Wherefore, many explain this whole passage allegorically, and plausible are the subtleties which they adduce for this purpose. But when all things are more accurately weighed, readers endued with sound judgment will easily perceive that the language is of a mixed character; for God so addresses the serpent that the last clause belongs to the devil. If it seem to any one absurd, that the punishment of another's fraud should be exacted from a brute animal, the solution is at hand; that, since it had been created for the benefit of man, there was nothing improper in its being accursed from the moment that it was employed for his destruction. And by this act of vengeance, God would prove how highly he estimates the salvation of man; just as if a father should hold the sword in execration by which his son had been slain. And here we must consider, not only the kind of authority which God has over his creatures, but also the end for which he created them, as I have recently said. For the equity of the divine sentence depends on that order of nature which he has sanctioned; it has, therefore, no affinity whatever with blind revenge. In this manner the reprobate will be delivered over into eternal fire with their bodies; which bodies, although they are not self-moved, are yet the instruments of perpetrating evil. So whatever wickedness a man commits is ascribed to his hands, and, therefore, they are deemed polluted; while yet they do not move themselves, except so far as, under the impulse of a depraved affection of the heart, they carry into execution what has been there conceived. According to this method of reasoning, the serpent is said to have done what the devil did by its means. But if God so severely avenged the destruction of man upon a brute animal, much less did he spare Satan, the author of the whole evil, as will appear more clearly in the concluding part of the address.

Thou art cursed above all cattle. This curse of God has such force against the serpent, as to render it despicable, and scarcely tolerable to heaven and earth, leading a life exposed to, and replete with, constant terrors. Besides, it is not only hateful to us, as the chief enemy of the human race, but, being separated also from other animals, carries on a kind of war with nature; for we see it had before been so gentle that the woman did not flee from its familiar approach. But what follows has greater difficulty, because that which God denounces as a punishment seems to be natural; namely, that it should creep upon its belly and eat dust. This objection has induced certain men of learning and ability to say, that the serpent had been accustomed to walk with an erect body before it had been abused by Satan.[1] There will, however, be no absurdity in supposing, that the serpent was again consigned to that former condition, to which he was already naturally subject. For thus he, who had exalted himself against the image of God, was to be thrust back into his proper rank; as if it had been said, ' Thou, a wretched and filthy animal, hast dared to rise up against man, whom I appointed to the dominion of the whole world ; as if, truly, thou, who art fixed to the earth, hadst any right to penetrate into heaven. Therefore, I now throw thee back again to the place whence thou hast attempted to emerge, that thou mayest learn to be contented with thy lot, and no more exalt thyself, to man's reproach and injury.' In the meanwhile, he is recalled from his insolent motions to his accustomed mode of going, in such a way as to be, at the same time, condemned to perpetual infamy. To eat dust is the sign of a vile and sordid nature. This (in my opinion) is the simple meaning of the passage, which the testimony of Isaiah also confirms, (chap. lxv. 25 ;) for while he promises, under the reign of Christ, the complete restoration of a sound and well-constituted nature, he records, among other things, that dust shall be to the serpent for bread. Wherefore, it is not necessary to seek for any fresh change in each particular which Moses here relates.

15. *I will put enmity.* I interpret this simply to mean that there should always be the hostile strife between the human race and serpents, which is now apparent ; for, by a secret feeling of nature, man abhors them. It is regarded, as among prodigies, that some men take pleasure in them ; and as often as the sight of a serpent inspires us with horror, the memory of our fall is renewed. With this I combine in one continued discourse what immediately follows : ' It shall wound thy head, and thou shalt wound its heel.' For he declares that there shall be such hatred that, on both sides, they shall be troublesome to each other ; the serpent shall be

[1] See Bishop Patrick's Commentary.

vexatious towards men, and men shall be intent on the destruction of serpents.   Meanwhile, we see that the Lord acts
mercifully in chastising man, whom he does not suffer Satan
to touch except in the *heel;* while he subjects the *head* of
the serpent to be wounded by him.   For in the terms *head*
and *heel* there is a distinction between the superior and the
inferior.   And thus God leaves some remains of dominion to
man ; because he so places the mutual disposition to injure
each other, that yet their condition should not be equal, but
man should be superior in the conflict.   Jerome, in turning
the first member of the sentence, 'Thou shalt bruise the
head ;'[1] and the second, 'Thou shalt be ensnared in the
heel,'[2] does it without reason, for the same verb is repeated
by Moses ; the difference is to be noted only in the head and
the heel, as I have just now said.   Yet the Hebrew verb,
whether derived from שׁוּף, (*shooph,*) or from שׁפה, (*shapha,*)
some interpret to *bruise* or to *strike*, others to *bite*.[3]   I have,
however, no doubt that Moses wished to allude to the name
of the serpent, which is called in Hebrew שׁפיפון, (*shiphiphon,*)
from שׁפה or שׁוּף.[4]

We must now make a transition from the serpent to the
author of this mischief himself; and that not only in the way
of comparison, for there truly is a literal *anagogy ;*[5] because
God has not so vented his anger upon the outward instrument as to spare the devil, with whom lay all the blame.

[1] "Conteres caput."   The version of the Vulgate is, "conteret caput."
But this does not affect the validity of Calvin's criticism, his object being
to show the impropriety of translating the same Hebrew word by Latin
words of such different meaning as *contero* and *insidior.—Ed.*

[2] "Insidiaberis calcaneo."

[3] See Cocceius, Gesenius, and Professor Lee, *sub voce* שׁוּף.—*Ed.*

[4] There would appear greater force in Calvin's criticism if this had been
the name given to the serpent in the narrative of Moses.   The word here
used, however, is נחש, (*nachash,*) which gives no countenance to the supposed reference ; besides, the word quoted by Calvin only refers to a
particular kind of serpent, not to the whole species.—*Ed.*

[5] Anagogy.   This word is inserted from the original for want of a more
generally intelligible term in our own language to express the author's
meaning.   It is from the Greek 'Αναγωγή,, which signifies " a raising on
high, especially elevation of the mind above earthly things to abstract
speculations, (in ecclesiastical writings,) to the contemplation of the
sublime truths and mysteries of Holy Scripture."   The meaning of Calvin is, that there was an intentional transition from the serpent to the
spiritual being who made use of it.—*Ed.*

That this may the more certainly appear to us, it is worth the while first to observe that the Lord spake not for the sake of the serpent but of the man ; for what end could it answer to thunder against the serpent in unintelligible words? Wherefore respect was had to men ; both that they might be affected with a greater dread of sin, seeing how highly displeasing it is to God, and that hence they might take consolation for their misery, because they would perceive that God is still propitious to them.   But now it is obvious to all, how slender and insignificant would be the argument for a good hope, if mention were here made of a serpent only ; because nothing would be then provided for, except the fading and transient life of the body.   Men would remain, in the meanwhile, the slaves of Satan, who would proudly triumph over them, and trample on their heads.   Wherefore, that God might revive the fainting minds of men, and restore them when oppressed by despair, it became necessary to promise them, in their posterity, victory over Satan, through whose wiles they had been ruined.   This, then, was the only salutary medicine which could recover the lost, and restore life to the dead.   I therefore conclude, that God here chiefly assails Satan under the name of the serpent, and hurls against him the lightning of his judgment.   This he does for a two-fold reason : first, that men may learn to beware of Satan as of a most deadly enemy ; then, that they may contend against him with the assured confidence of victory.

Now, though all do not dissent in their minds from Satan— yea, a great part adhere to him too familiarly—yet, in reality, Satan is their enemy ; nor do even those cease to dread him whom he soothes by his flatteries ; and because he knows that the minds of men are set against him, he craftily insinuates himself by indirect methods, and thus deceives them under a disguised form.[1]   In short, it is ingrafted in us by nature to flee from Satan as our adversary.   And, in order to show that he should be odious not to one generation only, God expressly says, ' between thee and the seed of the woman,' as widely, indeed, as the human race shall be propa-

---

[1] "Et les decoit en se masquant de la personne d'antiuy."—*French Trans.*

gated. He mentions the *woman* on this account, because, as she had yielded to the subtlety of the devil, and being first deceived, had drawn her husband into the participation of her ruin, so she had peculiar need of consolation.

It shall bruise.[1] This passage affords too clear a proof of the great ignorance, dulness, and carelessness, which have prevailed among all the learned men of the Papacy. The feminine gender has crept in instead of the masculine or neuter. There has been none among them who would consult the Hebrew or Greek *codices*, or who would even compare the Latin copies with each other.[2] Therefore, by a common error, this most corrupt reading has been received. Then, a profane exposition of it has been invented, by applying to the mother of Christ what is said concerning her seed.

There is, indeed, no ambiguity in the *words* here used by Moses; but I do not agree with others respecting their *meaning ;* for other interpreters take the seed for *Christ,* without controversy; as if it were said, that some one would arise from the seed of the woman who should wound the serpent's head. Gladly would I give my suffrage in support of their opinion, but that I regard the word *seed* as too violently distorted by them ; for who will concede that a *collective* noun is to be understood of one man *only ?* Further, as the perpetuity of the contest is noted, so victory is promised to the human race through a continual succession of ages. I explain, therefore, the *seed* to mean the posterity of the woman generally. But since experience teaches that not all the sons of Adam by far, arise as conquerors of the devil, we must necessarily come to one head, that we may find to whom the vic-

---

[1] " Ipsum vulnerabit."
[2] See the Vulgate, " *Ipsa* conteret,"—She shall bruise. The following judicious note from Professor Lee's Hebrew Lexicon confirms the criticism of Calvin :—" The attempt that has been made gravely to justify a blunder of the Vulgate, which here reads *ipsa* for *ipse*, is a melancholy proof of the great neglect of the study of Hebrew in this country. Any one acquainted with the first elements of the grammar would see that, to make the Vulgate correct, we must substitute תשופך for ישופך, and תשופנה for תשופנו,"—that is, both the form and the *affixes* of the verb would require alteration, in order to accommodate themselves to the change of gender.—*Ed.*

tory belongs. So Paul, from the seed of Abraham, leads us
to Christ; because many were degenerate sons, and a considerable part adulterous, through infidelity ; whence it follows
that the unity of the body flows from the head. Wherefore,
the sense will be (in my judgment) that the human race,
which Satan was endeavouring to oppress, would at length
be victorious.[1] In the meantime, we must keep in mind that
method of conquering which the Scripture describes. Satan
has, in all ages, led the sons of men " captive at his will,"
and, to this day, retains his lamentable triumph over them,
and for that reason is called the " prince of the world," (John
xii. 31.) But because one stronger than he has descended
from heaven, who will subdue him, hence it comes to pass
that, in the same manner, the whole Church of God, under
its Head, will gloriously exult over him. To this the declaration of Paul refers, " The Lord shall bruise Satan under
your feet shortly," (Rom. xvi. 20.) By which words he signifies that the power of bruising Satan is imparted to faithful men, and thus the blessing is the common property of the
whole Church; but he, at the same time, admonishes us, that
it only has its commencement in this world; because God
crowns none but well-tried wrestlers.

16. *Unto the woman he said.* In order that the majesty of
the judge may shine the more brightly, God uses no long disputation ; whence also we may perceive of what avail are all
our tergiversations with him. In bringing the serpent forward, Eve thought she had herself escaped. God, disregarding her cavils, condemns her. Let the sinner, therefore,
when he comes to the bar of God, cease to contend, lest he
should more severely provoke against himself the anger of
him whom he has already too highly offended. We must
now consider the kind of punishment imposed upon the
woman. When he says, ' I will multiply thy pains,' he
comprises all the trouble women sustain during pregnan-

[1] The judicious reader will hardly acknowledge the reasoning of Calvin
to be valid. The whole subject here referred to is discussed with great
learning and acuteness, as well as with great force of language, by Bishop
Horsley, in his second Sermon on Pet. i. 20, 21.— *Ed.*

cy.[1] . . . It is credible that the woman would have brought forth without pain, or at least without such great suffering, if she had stood in her original condition; but her revolt from God subjected her to inconveniences of this kind. The expression, 'pains and conception,' is to be taken by the figure *hypallage*,[2] for the pains which they endure in consequence of conception. The second punishment which he exacts is *subjection*. For this form of speech, "Thy desire shall be unto thy husband," is of the same force as if he had said that she should not be free and at her own command, but subject to the authority of her husband and dependent upon his will; or as if he had said, 'Thou shalt desire nothing but what thy husband wishes.' As it is declared afterwards, "Unto thee shall be his desire," (chap. iv. 7.) Thus the woman, who had perversely exceeded her proper bounds, is forced back to her own position. She had, indeed, previously been subject to her husband, but that was a liberal and gentle subjection; now, however, she is cast into servitude.

17. *And unto Adam he said.* In the first place, it is to be observed, that punishment was not inflicted upon the first of our race so as to rest on those two alone, but was extended generally to all their posterity, in order that we might know that the human race was cursed in their person; we next observe, that they were subjected only to temporal punishment, that, from the moderation of the divine anger, they might entertain hope of pardon. God, by adducing the reason why he thus punishes the man, cuts off from him the occasion of murmuring. For no excuse was left to him who had obeyed his wife rather than God; yea, had despised God for the sake of his wife, placing so much confidence in the fallacies of Satan, —whose messenger and servant she was,—that he did not hesitate perfidiously to deny his Maker. But, although God deals decisively and briefly with Adam, he yet refutes the pretext

[1] "Quum dicit, *Multiplicabo dolores*, complectitur quicquid molestiæ sustinent mulieres, ex quo gravidæ esse incipiunt, fastidium cibi, deliquia, lassitudines, aliaque innumera, usque dum ventum est ad partum, qui acerbissima tormenta secum affert. Est enim credibile," &c.
[2] The use of one word for another.

by which he had tried to escape, in order the more easily to lead him to repentance. After he has briefly spoken of Adam's sin, he announces that the earth would be cursed for his sake. The ancient interpreter has translated it, ' In thy work ; ' [1] but the reading is to be retained, in which all the Hebrew copies agree, namely, the earth was cursed *on account of Adam*. Now, as the *blessing* of the earth means, in the language of Scripture, that fertility which God infuses by his secret power, so the *curse* is nothing else than the opposite privation, when God withdraws his favour. Nor ought it to seem absurd, that, through the sin of man, punishment should overflow the earth, though innocent. For as the *primum mobile* [2] rolls all the celestial spheres along with it, so the ruin of man drives headlong all those creatures which were formed for his sake, and had been made subject to him. And we see how constantly the condition of the world itself varies with respect to men, according as God is angry with them, or shows them his favour. We may add, that, properly speaking, this whole punishment is exacted, not from the earth itself, but from man alone. For the earth does not bear fruit for itself, but in order that food may be supplied to us out of its bowels. The Lord, however, determined that his anger should, like a deluge, overflow all parts of the earth, that wherever man might look, the atrocity of his sin should meet his eyes. Before the fall, the state of the world was a most fair and delightful mirror of the divine favour and paternal indulgence towards man. Now, in all the elements we perceive that we are cursed. And although (as David says) the earth is still full of the mercy of God, (Psalm xxxiii. 5,) yet, at the same time, appear manifest signs of his dreadful alienation from us, by which, if we are unmoved, we betray our blindness and insensibility. Only, lest sadness and horror should overwhelm us, the Lord

[1] " In opere tuo."—*Vulgate*. The Septuagint makes the same mistake : Εν τοῖς ἔργοις σου.   In thy works.

[2] The *primum mobile* of ancient astronomy was held to be the ninth heaven, which surrounded those of the fixed stars, planets, and the atmosphere, and was regarded as the first mover of all the heavenly bodies. These bodies were at that time supposed to be carried round the earth by this powerful agent, while the earth itself remained as the centre of the system. The Newtonian philosophy put all such theories to flight. —*Ed.*

sprinkles everywhere the tokens of his goodness. Moreover, although the blessing of God is never seen pure and transparent as it appeared to man in innocence, yet, if what remains behind be considered in itself, David truly and properly exclaims, ' The earth is full of the mercy of God.'

Again, by ' eating of the earth,' Moses means ' eating of the *fruits*' which proceed from it. The Hebrew word עצבון, (*itsabon*,) which is rendered *pain*,[1] is also taken for *trouble* and *fatigue*. In this place, it stands in antithesis with the pleasant labour in which Adam previously so employed himself, that in a sense he might be said to play; for he was not formed for idleness, but for action. Therefore the Lord had placed him over a garden which was to be cultivated. But, whereas in that labour there had been sweet delight; now servile work is enjoined upon him, as if he were condemned to the mines. And yet the asperity of this punishment also is mitigated by the clemency of God, because something of enjoyment is blended with the labours of men, lest they should be altogether ungrateful, as I shall again declare under the next verse.

18. *Thorns also and thistles shall it bring forth.* He more largely treats of what he had already alluded to, namely, the participation of the fruits of the earth with labour and trouble. And he assigns as the reason, that the earth will not be the same as it was before, producing perfect fruits; for he declares that the earth would degenerate from its fertility, and bring forth briers and noxious plants. Therefore, we may know, that whatsoever unwholesome things may be produced, are not natural fruits of the earth, but are corruptions which originate from sin. Yet it is not our part to expostulate with the earth for not answering to our wishes, and to the labours of its cultivators, as if it were maliciously frustrating our purpose; but in its sterility let us mark the anger of God, and mourn over our own sins. It has been falsely maintained by some, that the earth is exhausted by the long succession of time, as if constant bringing forth had wearied it. They think more

---

[1] " Quod vertunt dolorem." In Calvin's own text it is, " In labore; " in the Vulgate, " In laboribus." Gesenius renders the word " Saure Arbeit," severe labour.—*Ed.*

correctly who acknowledge that, by the increasing wickedness of men, the remaining blessing of God is gradually diminished and impaired; and certainly there is danger, unless the world repent, that a great part of men should shortly perish through hunger, and other dreadful miseries. The words immediately following, "Thou shalt eat the herb of the field," are expounded too strictly (in my judgment) by those who think that Adam was thereby deprived of all the fruits which he had before been permitted to eat. God intends nothing more than that he should be to such an extent deprived of his former delicacies as to be compelled to use, in addition to them, the herbs which had been designed only for brute animals. For the mode of living at first appointed him, in that happy and delightful abundance, was far more delicate than it afterwards became. God, therefore, describes a part of this poverty by the word *herbs*, just as if a king should send away any one of his attendants from the upper table, to that which was plebeian and mean; or, as if a father should feed a son, who had offended him, with the coarse bread of servants; not that he interdicts man from all other food, but that he abates much of his accustomed liberality. This, however, might be taken as added for the purpose of consolation, as if it had been said, ' Although the earth, which ought to be the mother of good fruits only, be covered with thorns and briers, still it shall yield to thee sustenance whereby thou mayest be fed.'

19. *In the sweat of thy face.* Some, indeed, translate it 'labour;' the translation, however, is forced. But by "sweat" is understood hard labour and full of fatigue and weariness, which, by its difficulty, produces sweat. It is a repetition of the former sentence, where it was said, ' Thou shalt eat it in labour.' Under the cover of this passage, certain ignorant persons would rashly impel all men to manual labour; for God is not here teaching as a master or legislator, but only denouncing punishment as a judge. And, truly, if a *law* had been here prescribed, it would be necessary for all to become husbandmen, nor would any place be given to mechanical arts; we must go out of the world to seek for clothing and other necessary conveniences of life.

What, then, does the passage mean? Truly God pronounces, as from his judgment-seat, that the life of man shall henceforth be miserable, because Adam had proved himself unworthy of that tranquil, happy and joyful state for which he had been created. Should any one object that there are many inactive and indolent persons, this does not prevent the curse from having spread over the whole human race. For I say that no one lies torpid in such a degree of sloth as not to be under the necessity of experiencing that this curse belongs to all. Some flee from troubles, and many more do all they can to grasp at immunity from them; but the Lord subjects all, without exception, to this yoke of imposed servitude. It is, nevertheless, to be, at the same time, maintained that labour is not imposed equally on each, but on some more, on others less. Therefore, the labour common to the whole body is here described; not that which belongs peculiarly to each member, except so far as it pleases the Lord to divide to each a certain measure from the common mass of evils. It is, however, to be observed, that they who meekly submit to their sufferings, present to God an acceptablᴇ obedience, if, indeed, there be joined with this bearing of the cross, that knowledge of sin which may teach them to be humble. Truly it is faith alone which can offer such a sacrifice to God; but the faithful, the more they labour in procuring a livelihood, with the greater advantage are they stimulated to repentance, and accustom themselves to the mortification of the flesh; yet God often remits a portion of this curse to his own children, lest they should sink beneath the burden. To which purpose this passage is appropriate, 'Some will rise early and go late to rest, they will eat the bread of carefulness, but the Lord will give to his beloved sleep,' (Psal. cxxvii. 2.) So far, truly, as those things which had been polluted in Adam are repaired by the grace of Christ, the pious feel more deeply that God is good, and enjoy the sweetness of his paternal indulgence. But because, even in the best, the flesh is to be subdued, it not unfrequently happens that the pious themselves are worn down with hard labours and with hunger. There is, therefore, nothing better for us than that we, being admonished of the

miseries of the present life, should weep over our sins, and
seek that relief from the grace of Christ which may not only
assuage the bitterness of grief, but mingle its own sweetness
with it.[1]   Moreover, Moses does not enumerate all the disadvantages in which man, by sin, has involved himself; for it
appears that all the evils of the present life, which experience
proves to be innumerable, have proceeded from the same
fountain.   The inclemency of the air, frost, thunders, unseasonable rains, drought, hail, and whatever is disorderly in
the world, are the fruits of sin.   Nor is there any other primary cause of diseases.   This has been celebrated in poetical
fables, and was doubtless handed down, by tradition, from
the fathers.   Hence that passage in Horace :—

> " When from Heaven's fane the furtive hand
>   Of man the sacred fire withdrew,
> A countless host—at God's command—
>   To earth of fierce diseases flew ;
> And death—till now kept far away—
>   Hastened his step to seize his prey."[2]

But Moses, who, according to his custom, studies a brevity
adapted to the capacity of the common people, was content
to touch upon what was most apparent, in order that, from
one example, we may learn that the whole order of nature
was subverted by the sin of man.   Should any one again object, that no suffering was imposed on men which did not
also belong to women :   I answer, it was done designedly, to
teach us, that from the sin of Adam, the curse flowed in common to both sexes ; as Paul testifies, that 'all are dead in
Adam,' (Rom. v. 12.)

One question remains to be examined—'When God had

---

[1] " Sed etiam dulci temperamento condiat."
" Laquelle non seulement appaise l'aigreur des douleurs, mais aussi leur
donne saveur, meslant le sucre parmi le vinaigre."—Which not only re-
lieves the sourness of griefs, but also gives them savour, mixing sugar
with the vinegar.—*Fr. Trans.*

[2] " Post ignem ætheria domo
         Subductum, macies et nova febrium
     Terris incubuit cohors ;
         Semotique prius tarda necessitas
     Leti corripuit gradum."—*Hor. Carm.* iii. *Lib.* I.

before shown himself propitious to Adam and his wife,—having given them hope of pardon,—why does he begin anew to exact punishment from them? Certainly in that sentence, 'the seed of the woman shall bruise the head of the serpent,' the remission of sins and the grace of eternal salvation is contained. But it is absurd that God, after he has been reconciled, should actually prosecute his anger.' To untie this knot, some have invented a distinction of a twofold remission, namely, a remission of the *fault* and a remission of the *punishment*, to which the figment of *satisfactions* was afterwards annexed. They have feigned that God, in absolving men from the fault, still retains the punishment; and that, according to the rigour of his justice, he will inflict at least a temporal punishment. But they who imagined that punishments are required as *compensations*, have been preposterous interpreters of the judgments of God. For God does not consider, in chastising the faithful, what they deserve; but what will be useful to them in future; and fulfils the office of a physician rather than of a judge.[1] Therefore, the absolution which he imparts to his children is complete and not by halves. That he, nevertheless, punishes those who are received into favour, is to be regarded as a kind of chastisement which serves as medicine for future time, but ought not properly to be regarded as the vindictive punishment of sin committed. If we duly consider how great is the torpor of the human mind, then, how great its lasciviousness, how great its contumacy, how great its levity, and how quick its forgetfulness, we shall not wonder at God's severity in subduing it. If he admonishes in words, he is not heard; if he adds stripes, it avails but little; when it happens that he is heard, the flesh nevertheless perversely spurns the admonition. That obstinate hardness which, with all its power opposes itself to God, is worse than lasciviousness. If any one is naturally endued with such a gentle disposition that he does not disown the duty of submission to God, yet, having escaped from the hand of God, after one allowed sin, he will soon relapse, unless he

---

[1] "The punishments inflicted by God are the remedies and the restraints of our vitiated nature."—*Peter Martyr, in Gen.* fol. 17.

be drawn back as by force.   Wherefore, this general axiom is
to be maintained, that all the sufferings to which the life of
men is subject and obnoxious, are necessary exercises, by
which God partly invites us to repentance, partly instructs
us in humility, and partly renders us more cautious and more
attentive in guarding against the allurements of sin for the
future.

Till thou return.   He denounces that the termination of a
miserable life shall be death ; as if he would say, that Adam
should at length come, through various and continued kinds of
evil, to the last evil of all.   Thus is fulfilled what we said
before, that the death of Adam had commenced immediately
from the day of his transgression.   For this accursed life of
man could be nothing else than the beginning of death.
'But where then is the victory over the serpent, if death occupies the last place ?   For the words seem to have no other
signification, than that man must be ultimately crushed by
death.   Therefore, since death leaves nothing to Adam, the
promise recently given fails; to which may be added, that
the hope of being restored to a state of salvation was most
slender and obscure.'   Truly I do not doubt that these terrible
words would grievously afflict minds already dejected, from
other causes, by sorrow.   But since, though astonished by their
sudden calamity, they were yet not deeply affected with the
knowledge of sin; it is not wonderful that God persisted the
more in reminding them of their punishment, in order that he
might beat them down, as with reiterated blows.   Although
the consolation offered be in itself obscure and feeble, God
caused it to be sufficient for the support of their hope, lest
the weight of their affliction should entirely overwhelm them.
In the meantime, it was necessary that they should be
weighed down by a mass of manifold evils, until God should
have reduced them to true and serious repentance.   Moreover, whereas death is here put as the final issue,[1] this ought
to be referred to man ; because in Adam himself nothing but
death will be found ; yet, in this way, he is urged to seek a
remedy in Christ.

[1] " Quasi ultima linea."   " Comme le bout."—*Fr. Trans.*

For dust thou art. Since what God here declares belongs to man's *nature*, not to his *crime* or *fault*, it might seem that death was not superadded as adventitious to him. And therefore some understand what was before said, ' Thou shalt die,' in a spiritual sense ; thinking that, even if Adam had not sinned, his body must still have been separated from his soul. But, since the declaration of Paul is clear, that ' all die in Adam, as they shall rise again in Christ,' (1 Cor. xv. 22,) this wound also was inflicted by sin. Nor truly is the solution of the question difficult,—' Why God should pronounce, that he who was taken from the dust should return to it.' For as soon as he had been raised to a dignity so great, that the glory of the Divine Image shone in him, the terrestrial origin of his body was almost obliterated. Now, however, after he had been despoiled of his divine and heavenly excellence, what remains but that by his very departure out of life, he should recognise himself to be earth ? Hence it is that we dread death, because dissolution, which is contrary to nature, cannot naturally be desired. Truly the first man would have passed to a better life, had he remained upright ; but there would have been no separation of the soul from the body, no corruption, no kind of destruction, and, in short, no violent change.

20. *And Adam called,* &c. There are two ways in which this may be read. The former, in the *pluperfect* tense, ' Adam had called.' If we follow this reading, the sense of Moses will be, that Adam had been greatly deceived, in promising *life* to himself and to his posterity, from a wife, whom he afterwards found by experience to be the introducer of *death.* And Moses (as we have seen) is accustomed, without preserving the order of the history, to subjoin afterwards things which had been prior in point of time. If, however, we read the passage in the *preterite* tense, it may be understood either in a good or bad sense. There are those who think that Adam, animated by the hope of a more happy condition, because God had promised that the head of the serpent should be wounded by the seed of the woman,

called her by a name implying life.[1]   This would be a noble
and even heroic fortitude of mind ; since he could not, without an arduous and difficult struggle, deem *her* the mother
of the living, who, before any man could have been born, had
involved all in eternal destruction.   But, because I fear
lest this conjecture should be weak, let the reader consider
whether Moses did not design rather to tax Adam with
thoughtlessness, who being himself immersed in death, yet
gave to his wife so proud a name.   Nevertheless, I do not
doubt that, when he heard the declaration of God concerning
the prolongation of life, he began again to breathe and to
take courage ; and then, as one revived, he gave his wife a
name derived from *life ;* but it does not follow, that by a faith
accordant with the word of God, he triumphed, as he ought
to have done, over death.   I therefore thus expound the
passage ; as soon as he had escaped present death, being
encouraged by a measure of consolation, he celebrated that
divine benefit which, beyond all expectation, he had received,
in the name he gave his wife.[2]

21. *Unto Adam also, and to his wife, did the Lord God make,
&c.* Moses here, in a homely style, declares that the Lord had
undertaken the labour of making garments of skins for Adam
and his wife.   It is not indeed proper so to understand his
words, as if God had been a furrier, or a servant to sew
clothes.   Now, it is not credible that skins should have been
presented to them by chance ; but, since animals had before
been destined for their use, being now impelled by a new
necessity, they put some to death, in order to cover themselves with their skins, having been divinely directed to
adopt this counsel ; therefore Moses calls God the Author of
it.   The reason why the Lord clothed them with garments

---

[1] " Vocasse eam vivificam."
[2] It is probable, however, that more than this is here meant. The
Hebrew word חוה, (*chavah*,) Eve, is in the Septuagint rendered ζωή,
life ; and, as Fagius observes, Adam comforted himself in his wife,
because he should, through Eve, produce a posterity in which (as
parents in their children) they should be permanently victorious.—*Pol.
Syn.—Ed.*

of skin appears to me to be this: because garments formed of this material would have a more degrading appearance than those made of linen or woollen.[1] God therefore designed that our first parents should, in such a dress, behold their own vileness,—just as they had before seen it in their nudity,—and should thus be reminded of their sin.[2] In the meantime, it is not to be denied, that he would propose to us an example, by which he would accustom us to a frugal and unexpensive mode of dress. And I wish those delicate persons would reflect on this, who deem no ornament sufficiently attractive, unless it exceed in magnificence. Not that every kind of ornament is to be expressly condemned; but because when immoderate elegance and splendour is carefully sought after, not only is that Master despised, who intended clothing to be a sign of shame, but war is, in a certain sense, carried on against nature.

22. *Behold, the man is become as one of us.*[3] An ironical reproof, by which God would not only prick the heart of man, but pierce it through and through. He does not, however, cruelly triumph over the miserable and afflicted; but, according to the necessity of the disease, applies a more violent remedy. For, though Adam was confounded and astonished at his calamity, he yet did not so deeply reflect on its cause as to become weary of his pride, that he might learn to embrace true humility. We may add, that God inveighed, by this irony,[4] not more against Adam himself than against his posterity, for the purpose of commending modesty to all ages. The particle, "Behold," denotes that the sen-

---

[1] " Quia [vestes] ex ea materia confectæ, belluinum quiddam magis saperent, quam lineæ vel laneæ."

[2] "As the prisoner, looking on his irons, thinketh on his theft, so we, looking on our garments, should think on our sins."—*Trapp.*

For an ample discussion of the reasons why a more comprehensive view should be taken of this subject than Calvin here adopts, the reader may turn to Dr Magee's learned "Discourses and Dissertations on the Scriptural Doctrines of Atonement and Sacrifice;" where he will see, that the origin of the clothing with skins was most probably connected with a previous appointment of the sacrifice of animals.—See *Magee*, note lii.—*Ed.*

[3] " Adam quasi unus."

[4] " Hac subsannatione."

tence is pronounced upon the cause then in hand. And, truly, it was a sad and horrid spectacle; that he, in whom recently the glory of the Divine image was shining, should lie hidden under fetid skins to cover his own disgrace, and that there should be more comeliness in a dead animal than in a living man! The clause which is immediately added, "To know good and evil," describes the cause of so great misery, namely, that Adam, not content with his condition, had tried to ascend higher than was lawful; as if it had been said, 'See now whither thy ambition and thy perverse appetite for illicit knowledge have precipitated thee.' Yet the Lord does not even deign to hold converse with him, but contemptuously draws him forth, for the sake of exposing him to greater infamy. Thus was it necessary, for his iron pride to be beaten down, that he might at length descend into himself, and become more and more displeased with himself.

One of us. Some refer the plural number here used to the angels, as if God would make a distinction between man, who is an earthly and despised animal, and celestial beings; but this exposition seems far-fetched. The meaning will be more simple if thus resolved, 'After this, Adam will be so like ME, that we shall become companions for each other.' The argument which Christians draw from this passage for the doctrine of the three Persons in the Godhead is, I fear, not sufficiently firm.[1] There is not, indeed, the same reason for it as in the former passage, "Let us make man in our image," since here Adam is included in the word us; but, in the other place, a certain distinction in the essence of God is expressed.

And now, lest, &c. There is a defect in the sentence which I think ought to be thus supplied : 'It now remains that, in future, he be debarred from the fruit of the tree of life ;' for by these words Adam is admonished that the punishment to

[1] Bishop Patrick, who contends for the interpretation here opposed, says, " *Like one of us.* These words plainly insinuate a plurality of Persons in the Godhead, and all other explications of them seem forced and unnatural; that of Mr Calvin's being as disagreeable to the Hebrew phrase as that of Socinus to the excellency of the Divine nature."—*Ed.*

which he is consigned shall not be that of a moment, or of a few days, but that he shall always be an exile from a happy life. They are mistaken who think this also to be an irony; as if God were denying that the tree would prove advantageous to man, even though he might eat of it; for he rather, by depriving him of the symbol, takes also away the thing signified. We know what is the efficacy of sacraments; and it was said above that the tree was given as a pledge of life. Wherefore, that he might understand himself to be deprived of his former life, a solemn excommunication is added; not that the Lord would cut him off from all hope of salvation, but, by taking away what he had given, would cause man to seek new assistance elsewhere. Now, there remained an expiation in sacrifices, which might restore him to the life he had lost. Previously, direct communication with God was the source of life to Adam; but, from the moment in which he became alienated from God, it was necessary that he should recover life by the death of Christ, by whose life he then lived. It is indeed certain, that man would not have been able, had he even devoured the whole tree, to enjoy life against the will of God; but God, out of respect to his own institution, connects life with the external sign, till the promise should be taken away from it; for there never was any intrinsic efficacy in the tree; but God made it life-giving, so far as he had sealed his grace to man in the use of it, as, in truth, he represents nothing to us with false signs, but always speaks to us, as they say, with effect. In short, God resolved to wrest out of the hands of man that which was the occasion or ground of confidence, lest he should form for himself a vain hope of the perpetuity of the life which he had lost.

23. *Therefore the Lord God sent him forth.*[1] Here Moses partly prosecutes what he had said concerning the punishment inflicted on man, and partly celebrates the goodness of God, by which the rigour of his judgment was mitigated. God mercifully softens the exile of Adam, by still providing for him a remaining home on earth, and by assigning to him a

---

[1] גרש, (*gairesh,*) to expel, drive out, or eject by force.

livelihood from the culture—although the laborious culture—
of the ground ; for Adam thence infers that the Lord has
some care for him, which is a proof of paternal love. Moses,
however, again speaks of punishment, when he relates that
man was expelled, and that cherubim were opposed with the
blade of a turning sword,[1] which should prevent his entrance
into the garden. Moses says that the cherubim were placed
in the eastern region, on which side, indeed, access lay open
to man, unless he had been prohibited. It is added, to produce terror, that the sword was turning or sharpened on both
sides. Moses, however, uses a word derived from *whiteness*
or *heat*.[2] Therefore, God having granted life to Adam, and
having supplied him with food, yet restricts the benefit, by
causing some tokens of Divine wrath to be always before his
eyes, in order that he might frequently reflect that he must
pass through innumerable miseries, through temporal exile,
and through death itself, to the life from which he had fallen ;
for what we have said must be remembered, that Adam was
not so dejected as to be left without hope of pardon. He
was banished from that royal palace of which he had been the
lord, but he obtained elsewhere a place in which he might
dwell ; he was bereft of his former delicacies, yet he was still
supplied with some kind of food ; he was excommunicated
from the tree of life, but a new remedy was offered him in
sacrifices. Some expound the ' turning sword ' to mean one
which does not always vibrate with its point directed against
man, but which sometimes shows the side of the blade, for
the purpose of giving place for repentance. But allegory is
unseasonable, when it was the determination of God altogether to exclude man from the garden, that he might seek
life elsewhere. As soon, however, as the happy fertility and
pleasantness of the place was destroyed, the terror of the
sword became superfluous. By cherubim, no doubt, Moses
means angels, and in this accommodates himself to the capacity of his own people. God had commanded two cherubim
to be placed at the ark of the covenant, which should over-

---

[1] " Cum lamina gladii versatilis." להט החרב, *(lahat hachereb.)*
[2] " A candore, vel ardore."

shadow its covering with their wings; therefore he is often said to sit between the cherubim. That he would have angels depicted in this form, was doubtless granted as an indulgence to the rudeness of that ancient people; for that age needed puerile instructions, as Paul teaches, (Gal. iv. 3;) and Moses borrowed thence the name which he ascribed to angels, that he might accustom men to that kind of revelation which he had received from God, and faithfully handed down; for God designed, that what he knew would prove useful to the people, should be revealed in the sanctuary. And certainly this method is to be observed by us, in order that we, conscious of our own infirmity, may not attempt, without assistance, to soar to heaven; for otherwise it will happen that, in the midst of our course, all our senses will fail. The ladders and vehicles, then, were the sanctuary, the ark of the covenant, the altar, the table and its furniture. Moreover, I call them vehicles and ladders, because symbols of this kind were by no means ordained that the faithful might shut up God in a tabernacle as in a prison, or might attach him to earthly elements; but that, being assisted by congruous and apt means, they might themselves rise towards heaven. Thus David and Hezekiah, truly endued with spiritual intelligence, were far from entertaining those gross imaginations, which would fix God in a given place. Still they do not scruple to call upon God, who sitteth or dwelleth between the cherubim, in order that they may retain themselves and others under the authority of the law.

Finally, In this place angels are called cherubim, for the same reason that the name of the *body of Christ* is transferred to the sacred bread of the Lord's Supper. With respect to the etymology, the Hebrews themselves are not agreed. The most generally received opinion is, that the first letter, כ, is a servile letter, and a note of similitude, and, therefore, that the word cherub is of the same force as if it were said, 'like a boy.'[1] But because Ezekiel, who applies the word in com-

---

[1] "כרוב, *(cherub.)* An image like a youth, which the Chaldeans call רבי, *(rabia.")—Schindler.* Other writers give a different derivation, and consequently a different meaning to the word. But Professor Lee says, "It would be idle to offer anything on the etymology; nothing satisfactory having yet been discovered."—See *Lexicon.—Ed.*

mon to different figures, is opposed to this signification ; they think more rightly, in my judgment, who declare it to be a general name. Nevertheless, that it is referred to angels is more than sufficiently known. Whence also Ezekiel (xxviii. 14) signalizes the proud king of Tyre with this title, comparing him to a chief angel.[1]

CHAPTER IV.

1. And Adam knew Eve his wife; and she conceived, and bare Cain, and said, I have gotten a man from the Lord.

2. And she again bare his brother Abel. And Abel was a keeper of sheep, but Cain was a tiller of the ground.

3. And in process of time it came to pass, that Cain brought of the fruit of the ground an offering unto the Lord.

4. And Abel, he also brought of the firstlings of his flock, and of the fat thereof. And the Lord had respect unto Abel, and to his offering :

5. But unto Cain and to his offering he had not respect. And Cain was very wroth, and his countenance fell.

6. And the Lord said unto Cain, Why art thou wroth? and why is thy countenance fallen?

7. If thou doest well, shalt thou not be accepted? and if thou doest not well, sin lieth at the door. And unto thee *shall be* his desire, and thou shalt rule over him.

1. Et Adam cognovit Hava uxorem suam : quæ concepit, et peperit Cain : et dixit, Acquisivi virum a Jehova.

2. Et addidit parere fratrem ejus Ebel : fuit autem Ebel pastor ovium, et Cain fuit cultor terræ :

3. Et fuit, a fine dierum adduxit Cain de fructu terræ oblationem Jehovæ.

4. Et Ebel etiam ipse adduxit de primogenitis pecudum suarum, et de adipe earum : et respexit Jehova ad Ebel, et ad oblationem ejus :

5. Ad Cain vero et ad oblationem ejus non respexit : iratus est itaque Cain valde, et concidit vultus ejus.

6. Et dixit Jehova ad Cain, Utquid excanduisti? et utquid concidit vultus tuus?

7. Annon si recte egeris, erit acceptatio? et si non bene egeris, in foribus peccatum cubat : et ad te erit appetitus ejus, et tu dominaberis ei.

---

[1] *Primario angelo.* It is clear that Ezekiel, in the chapter referred to, has both the garden of Eden and the ark of the covenant in his view, when speaking of the king of Tyre. Thus, in the 17th verse, it is said, "Thou hast been in Eden, the garden of God ;" and, in the next verse, "Thou art the anointed cherub that covereth ; " (namely, that covereth the ark,) " and I have set thee so ; thou wast upon the holy mountain of God."—*Ed.*

8. And Cain talked with Abel his brother: and it came to pass, when they were in the field, that Cain rose up against Abel his brother, and slew him.

9. And the Lord said unto Cain, Where *is* Abel thy brother? And he said, I know not. *Am* I my brother's keeper?

10. And he said, What hast thou done? the voice of thy brother's blood crieth unto me from the ground.

11. And now *art* thou cursed from the earth, which hath opened her mouth to receive thy brother's blood from thy hand.

12. When thou tillest the ground, it shall not henceforth yield unto thee her strength. A fugitive and a vagabond shalt thou be in the earth.

13. And Cain said unto the Lord, My punishment *is* greater than I can bear.

14. Behold, thou hast driven me out this day from the face of the earth; and from thy face shall I be hid; and I shall be a fugitive and a vagabond in the earth: and it shall come to pass, *that* every one that findeth me shall slay me.

15. And the Lord said unto him, Therefore whosoever slayeth Cain, vengeance shall be taken on him sevenfold. And the Lord set a mark upon Cain, lest any finding him should kill him.

16. And Cain went out from the presence of the Lord, and dwelt in the land of Nod, on the east of Eden.

17. And Cain knew his wife; and she conceived, and bare Enoch: and he builded a city, and called the name of the city, after the name of his son, Enoch.

18. And unto Enoch was born Irad: and Irad begat Mehujael: and Mehujael begat Methusael: and Methusael begat Lamech.

19. And Lamech took unto him two wives: the name of the one *was* Adah, and the name of the other Zillah.

20. And Adah bare Jabal: he was the father of such as dwell in tents, and *of such as have* cattle.

21. And his brother's name *was*

8. Et loquutus est Cain ad Ebel fratrem suum: et accidit quum essent in agro, insurrexit Cain contra Ebel fratrem suum, et occidit eum.

9. Et dixit Jehova ad Cain, Ubi est Ebel frater tuus? Et ait, Nescio: nunquid custos fratris mei sum ego?

10. Et dixit, Quid fecisti? vox sanguinis fratris tui clamat ad me è terra.

11. Nunc itaque maledictus eris è terra, quæ aperuit os suum ut exciperet sanguinem fratris tui è manu tua.

12. Quando coles terram, non addet ut det vim suam tibi: vagus et profugus eris in terra.

13. Et dixit Cain ad Jehovam, Major est punitio mea quam ut feram.

14. Ecce, ejecisti me hodie à facie terræ, et à facie tua abscondar, eroque vagus et profugus in terra: et erit, ut quicunque invenerit me, occidat me.

15. Et dixit ei Jehova, Propterea quicunque occiderit Cain, septuplum vindicabitur. Et posuit Jehova signum in Cain, ne percuteret eum ullus qui inveniret eum.

16. Et egressus est Cain à facie Jehovæ, et habitavit in terra Nod ad Orientem Heden.

17. Cognovit autem Cain uxorem suam: quæ concepit, et peperit Hanoch: ædificavitque civitatem, et vocavit nomen civitatis nomine filii sui Hanoch.

18. Porro natus est ipsi Hanoch Hirad, et Hirad genuit Mehujael, et Mehujael genuit Methusael: et Methusael genuit Lemech.

19. Et accepit sibi Lemech duas uxores: nomen unius, Hada, et nomen secundæ, Silla.

20. Et genuit Hada Jabel, ipse fuit pater inhabitantis tentorium, et pecoris.

21. Et nomen fratris ejus,

Jubal : he was the father of all such as handle the harp and organ.

22. And Zillah, she also bare Tubal-cain, an instructor of every artificer in brass and iron : and the sister of Tubal-cain *was* Naamah.

23. And Lamech said unto his wives, Adah and Zillah, Hear my voice ; ye wives of Lamech, hearken unto my speech : for I have slain a man to my wounding, and a young man to my hurt.

24. If Cain shall be avenged seven-fold, truly Lamech seventy and seven-fold.

25. And Adam knew his wife again ; and she bare a son, and called his name Seth : For God, *said she,* hath appointed me another seed instead of Abel, whom Cain slew.

26. And to Seth, to him also there was born a son ; and he called his name Enos : then began men to call upon the name of the Lord.

Jubal : ipse fuit pater omnis contrectantis citharam et organum.

22. Et Silla etiam ipsa peperit Thubal-Cain, polientem omne opificium æreum et ferreum : et soror Thubal-Cain, fuit Nahama.

23. Et dixit Lemech uxoribus suis Hada et Silla, Audite vocem meam uxores Lemech, auscultate sermonem meum, Quoniam virum occidero in vulnere meo, et adolescentem in livore meo.

24. Quia septuplo vindicabitur Cain, et Lemech septuagies septies.

25. Cognovit autem Adam rursum uxorem suam : quæ peperit filium, et vocavit nomen ejus Seth, Quia posuit mihi, *inquit,* Deus semen alterum pro Ebel : quia occidit eum Cain.

26. Et ipsi Seth etiam natus est filius, et vocavit nomen ejus Enos : tunc cœptum est invocari nomen Domini.

1. *And Adam knew his wife Eve.* Moses now begins to describe the propagation of mankind ; in which history it is important to notice that this benediction of God, " Increase and multiply," was not abolished by sin ; and not only so, but that the heart of Adam was divinely confirmed, so that he did not shrink with horror from the production of off-spring. And as Adam recognised, in the very commencement of having offspring, the truly paternal moderation of God's anger, so was he afterwards compelled to taste the bitter fruits of his own sin, when Cain slew Abel. But let us follow the narration of Moses.[1] Although Moses does not state that Cain and Abel were twins, it yet seems to me probable that they were so ; for, after he has said that Eve, by her first conception, brought forth her first-born, he soon after subjoins that she also bore another ; and thus, while commemorating a double birth, he speaks only of one con-

---

[1] The following passage here occurs in the original :—" Cognoscendi verbo congressum viri cum uxore, rem per se pudendam, verecunde insinuat : quanquam coitus fœditas inter peccati fructus numeranda est ; quia nascitur ex libidinis intemperie : porro licet," &c.

ception.[1] Let those who think differently enjoy their own
opinion; to me, however, it appears accordant with reason,
when the world had to be replenished with inhabitants, that
not only Cain and Abel should have been brought forth at
one birth, but many also afterwards, both males and
females.

I have gotten a man. The word which Moses uses signifies
both to *acquire* and to *possess*; and it is of little consequence
to the present context which of the two you adopt. It is
more important to inquire why she says that she has received
אֵת יְהוָֹה, *(eth Yehovah.)* Some expound it, 'with the
Lord;' that is, 'by the kindness, or by the favour, of the
Lord;' as if Eve would refer the accepted blessing of offspring to the Lord, as it is said in Psalm cxxvii. 3, "The
fruit of the womb is the gift of the Lord." A second interpretation comes to the same point, 'I have possessed a man
from the Lord;' and the version of Jerome is of equal force,
'Through the Lord.'[2] These three readings, I say, tend to
this point, that Eve gives thanks to God for having begun
to raise up a posterity through her, though she was deserving
of perpetual barrenness, as well as of utter destruction.
Others, with greater subtlety, expound the words, 'I have
gotten the man of the Lord;' as if Eve understood that she
already possessed that conqueror of the serpent, who had
been divinely promised to her. Hence they celebrate the
faith of Eve, because she embraced, by faith, the promise
concerning the bruising of the head of the devil through her
seed; only they think that she was mistaken in the person or
the individual, seeing that she would restrict to Cain what had
been promised concerning Christ. To me, however, this
seems to be the genuine sense, that while Eve congratulates
herself on the birth of a son, she offers him to God, as the
first-fruits of his race. Therefore, I think it ought to be
translated, 'I have obtained a man from the Lord,' which
approaches more nearly the Hebrew phrase. Moreover, she
calls a new-born infant a man, because she saw the human

---

[1] "Ita duplicem partum commemorans, nonnisi de uno concubitu loquitur."
[2] "Possedi hominem per Deum."—*Vulgate.* "᾽Εκτησάμην ἄνθρωπον
διὰ τοῦ Θεοῦ."—*Sept.*

race renewed, which both she and her husband had ruined by their own fault.[1]

2. *And she again bare his brother Abel.*[2] It is well known whence the name of Cain is deduced, and for what reason it was given to him. For his mother said, קָנִיתִי, (*kaniti*,) I have gotten a man ; and therefore she called his name Cain.[3] The same explanation is not given with respect to Abel.[4] The opinion of some, that he was so called by his mother out of contempt, as if he would prove superfluous and almost useless, is perfectly absurd ; for she remembered the end to which her fruitfulness would lead ; nor had she forgotten the benediction, " Increase and multiply." We should (in my judgment) more correctly infer, that whereas Eve had testified, in the name given to her first-born, the joy which suddenly burst upon her, and celebrated the grace of God ; she afterwards, in her other offspring, returned to the recollection of the miseries of the human race.   And certainly, though the new blessing of God was an occasion for no common joy ; yet, on the other hand, she could not look upon a posterity devoted to so many and great evils, of which she had herself been the cause, without the most bitter grief.   Therefore, she wished that a monument of her sorrow should exist in the name she gave her second son ; and she would, at the same time, hold up a common mirror, by which she might admonish her whole progeny of the *vanity* of man.   That some censure the judg-

---

[1] The reader will find a discussion of this remarkable passage worthy of his attention in Dr J. P. Smith's *Scripture Testimony to the Messiah*, vol. i. p. 228. Third edition. 1837. This learned, indefatigable, and candid writer, argues with considerable force in favour of the translation, ' I have obtained a man, JEHOVAH,' and supposes that Eve really believed her first-born to be the incarnate Jehovah. There is, however, great difficulty in allowing that she could know so much as is here presupposed ; and the remark of Dathe seems fatal to this interpretation : —' Si scivit, Messiam esse debere Jovam, quomodo existimare potuit, Cainam esse Messiam, quem sciebat esse ab Adamo genitum.' If Eve knew that Messiah must be Jehovah, how could she think that Cain was the Messiah, when she knew him to be the offspring of Adam ?—*Ed.*

[2] " Et addidit parere fratrem ejus Ebel ; " and she added to bring forth (or she brought forth in addition) his brother Abel.—*Ed.*

[3] That is, " obtained," or " gotten."

[4] הבל, (*Hebel*,) signifies *vanity*.—*Ed.*

ment of Eve as absurd, because she regarded her just and holy son as worthy to be rejected in comparison with her other wicked and abandoned son, is what I do not approve. For Eve had reason why she should congratulate herself in her first-born; and no blame attaches to her for having proposed, in her second son, a memorial to herself and to all others, of their own vanity, to induce them to exercise themselves in diligent reflection on their own evils.

And Abel was a keeper of sheep. Whether both the brothers had married wives, and each had a separate home, Moses does not relate. This, therefore, remains to us in uncertainty, although it is probable that Cain was married before he slew his brother; since Moses soon after adds, that he knew his wife, and begat children: and no mention is there made of his marriage. Both followed a kind of life in itself holy and laudable. For the cultivation of the earth was commanded by God; and the labour of feeding sheep was not less honourable than useful; in short, the whole of rustic life was innocent and simple, and most of all accommodated to the true order of nature. This, therefore, is to be maintained in the first place, that both exercised themselves in labours approved by God, and necessary to the common use of human life. Whence it is inferred, that they had been well instructed by their father. The rite of sacrificing more fully confirms this; because it proves that they had been accustomed to the worship of God. The life of Cain, therefore, was, in appearance, very well regulated; inasmuch as he cultivated the duties of piety towards God, and sought a maintenance for himself and his, by honest and just labour, as became a provident and sober father of a family. Moreover, it will be here proper to recall to memory what we have before said, that the first men, though they had been deprived of the sacrament of divine love, when they were prohibited from the tree of life, had yet been only so deprived of it, that a hope of salvation was still left to them, of which they had the signs in sacrifices. For we must remember, that the custom of sacrificing was not rashly devised by them, but was divinely delivered to them. For since the Apostle refers the dignity of Abel's accepted sacrifice to *faith*, it follows, first, that he had not offered it without

the command of God, (Heb. xi. 4.) Secondly, it has been
true from the beginning of the world, that obedience is better than any sacrifices, (1 Sam. xv. 22,) and is the parent of all
virtues. Hence it also follows, that man had been taught by
God what was pleasing to Him. Thirdly, since God has been
always like himself, we may not say that he was ever delighted
with mere carnal and external worship. Yet he deemed those
sacrifices of the first age acceptable. It follows, therefore,
further, that they had been spiritually offered to him:
that is, that the holy fathers did not mock him with empty
ceremonies, but comprehended something more sublime and
secret; which they could not have done without divine instruction.[1] For it is interior truth alone[2] which, in the external signs, distinguishes the genuine and rational worship
of God from that which is gross and superstitious. And,
certainly, they could not sincerely devote their mind to the
worship of God, unless they had been assured of his benevolence; because voluntary reverence springs from a sense of,
and confidence in, his goodness; but, on the other hand,
whosoever regards God as hostile to himself, is compelled to
flee from him with very fear and horror. We see then that
God, when he takes away the tree of life, in which he had
first given the pledge of his grace, proves and declares himself
to be propitious to man by other means. Should any one object,
that all nations have had their own sacrifices, and that in these
there was no pure and solid religion, the solution is ready: namely, that mention is here made of such sacrifices as are lawful
and approved by God; of which nothing but an adulterated
imitation afterwards descended to the Gentiles. For although
nothing but the word מִנְחָה, (mincha,[3]) is here placed, which
properly signifies a gift, and therefore is extended generally to
every kind of oblation; yet we may infer, for two reasons, that
the command respecting sacrifice was given to the fathers from
the beginning; first, for the purpose of making the exercise
of piety common to all, seeing they professed themselves to

---

[1] "Absque verbo," literally " without the word."—Ed.
[2] That is, " truth received into the heart."—Ed.
[3] Mincha usually, though not invariably, signifies an " unbloody oblation," in opposition to זֶבַח, (zeba,) a " bloody sacrifice."—See Gesenius,
Lee, &c.—Ed.

be the property of God, and esteemed all they possessed as received from him; and, secondly, for the purpose of admonishing them of the necessity of some expiation in order to their reconciliation with God. When each offers something of his property, there is a solemn giving of thanks, as if he would testify by his present act that he owes to God whatever he possesses. But the sacrifice of cattle and the effusion of blood contains something further, namely, that the offerer should have death before his eyes; and should, nevertheless, believe in God as propitious to him. Concerning the sacrifices of Adam no mention is made.

4. *And the Lord had respect unto Abel, &c.* God is said to have respect unto the man to whom he vouchsafes his favour. We must, however, notice the order here observed by Moses; for he does not simply state that the *worship* which Abel had paid was pleasing to God, but he begins with the *person* of the offerer; by which he signifies, that God will regard no works with favour except those the doer of which is already previously accepted and approved by him. And no wonder; for man sees things which are apparent, but God looks into the heart, (1 Sam. xvi. 7;) therefore, he estimates works no otherwise than as they proceed from the fountain of the heart. Whence also it happens, that he not only rejects but abhors the sacrifices of the wicked, however splendid they may appear in the eyes of men. For if he, who is polluted in his soul, by his mere touch contaminates, with his own impurities, things otherwise pure and clean, how can that but be impure which proceeds from himself? When God repudiates the feigned righteousness in which the Jews were glorying, he objects, through his Prophet, that their hands were " full of blood," (Isaiah i. 15.) For the same reason Haggai contends against the hypocrites. The external appearance, therefore, of works, which may delude our too carnal eyes, vanishes in the presence of God. Nor were even the heathens ignorant of this; whose poets, when they speak with a sober and well-regulated mind of the worship of God, require both a clean heart and pure hands. Hence, even among all nations, is to be traced the solemn rite of washing before sacrifices. Now, seeing that

in another place, the Spirit testifies, by the mouth of Peter, that 'hearts are purified by faith,' (Acts xv. 9;) and seeing, that the purity of the holy patriarchs was of the very same kind, the apostle does not in vain infer, that the offering of Abel was, by faith, more excellent than that of Cain. Therefore, in the first place, we must hold, that all works done before faith, whatever splendour of righteousness may appear in them, were nothing but mere sins, (being defiled from their root,) and were offensive to the Lord, whom nothing can please without inward purity of heart. I wish they who imagine that men, by their own motion of free-will, are rendered meet to receive the grace of God, would reflect on this. Certainly, no controversy would then remain on the question, whether God justifies men gratuitously, and that by faith? For this must be received as a settled point, that, in the judgment of God, no respect is had to works until man is received into favour. Another point appears equally certain; since the whole human race is hateful to God, there is no other way of reconciliation to divine favour than through faith. More-over, since faith is a gratuitous gift of God, and a special illumination of the Spirit, then it is easy to infer, that we are *prevented* [1] by his mere grace, just as if he had raised us from the dead. In which sense also Peter says, that it is God who purifies the hearts by faith. For there would be no agreement of the fact with the statement, unless God had so formed faith in the hearts of men that it might be truly deemed his gift. It may now be seen in what way purity is the effect of faith. It is a vapid and trifling philosophy, to adduce this as the cause of purity, that men are not induced to seek God as their rewarder except by faith. They who speak thus entirely bury the grace of God, which his Spirit chiefly commends. Others also speak coldly, who teach that we are purified by faith, only on account of the gift of regeneration, in order that we may be accepted of God. For not only do they omit half the truth, but build without a foundation; since, on account of the curse on the human race, it became necessary

---

[1] The word *prevented* is here used in the sense now rendered somewhat obsolete, though retained in the Liturgy and Articles of the Church of England. We have, in fact, no other word which so well describes the effect of that *prevenient* grace, which anticipates and goes before every thing that is good in man.—*Ed.*

that gratuitous reconciliation should precede. Again, since God never so regenerates his people in this world, that they can worship him perfectly ; no work of man can possibly be acceptable without expiation. And to this point the ceremony of legal washing belongs, in order that men may learn, that as often as they wish to draw near unto God, purity must be sought elsewhere. Wherefore God will then at length have respect to our obedience, when he looks upon us in Christ.

5. *But unto Cain and to his offering he had not respect.* It is not to be doubted, that Cain conducted himself as hypocrites are accustomed to do ; namely, that he wished to appease God, as one discharging a debt, by external sacrifices, without the least intention of dedicating himself to God. But this is true worship, to offer ourselves as spiritual sacrifices to God. When God sees such hypocrisy, combined with gross and manifest mockery of himself, it is not surprising that he hates it, and is unable to bear it ; whence also it follows, that he rejects with contempt the works of those who withdraw *themselves* from him. For it is his will, first to have us devoted to himself ; he then seeks our works in testimony of our obedience to him, but only in the second place. It is to be remarked, that all the figments by which men mock both God and themselves are the fruits of unbelief. To this is added pride, because unbelievers, despising the Mediator's grace, throw themselves fearlessly into the presence of God. The Jews foolishly imagine that the oblations of Cain were unacceptable, because he defrauded God of the full ears of corn, and meanly offered him only barren or half-filled ears. Deeper and more hidden was the evil ; namely, that impurity of heart of which I have been speaking ; just as, on the other hand, the strong scent of burning fat could not conciliate the divine favour to the sacrifices of Abel ; but, being pervaded by the good odour of faith, they had a sweet-smelling savour.

And Cain was very wroth. In this place it is asked, whence Cain understood that his brother's oblations were preferred to his ? The Hebrews, according to their manner, resort to divination, and imagine that the sacrifice of Abel was consumed by celestial fire; but, since we ought not to allow ourselves so great a license as to invent miracles, for which we have no testimony of Scripture, let Jewish fables be dismissed.[1] It is, indeed, more probable, that Cain formed the judgment which Moses records, from the events which followed. He saw that it was better with his brother than with himself; thence he inferred, that God was pleased with his brother, and displeased with himself. We know also, that to hypocrites nothing seems of greater value, nothing is more to their heart's content, than earthly blessing. Moreover, in the person of Cain is pourtrayed to us the likeness of a wicked man, who yet desires to be esteemed just, and even arrogates to himself the first place among the saints. Such persons truly, by external works, strenuously labour to deserve well at the hands of God; but, retaining a heart inwrapped in deceit, they present to him nothing but a mask; so that, in their laborious and anxious religious worship, there is nothing sincere, nothing but mere pretence. When they afterwards see that they gain no advantage, they betray the venom of their minds; for they not only complain against God, but break forth in manifest fury, so that, if they were able, they would gladly tear him down from his heavenly throne. Such is the innate pride of all hypocrites, that, by the very appearance of obedience, they would hold God as under obligation to them; because they cannot escape from his authority, they try to soothe him with blandishments, as they would a child; in the meantime, while they count much of their fictitious trifles, they think that God does them great wrong if he does not applaud them; but when he pronounces their offerings frivolous and of no value in his sight, they first begin to murmur, and then to rage. Their impiety alone hinders God from being reconciled unto them; but they wish to bargain with

---

[1] It will, perhaps, be admitted that Calvin here deals too hardly with the opinions of the Jews. That God did in some way bear public testimony to his acceptance of Abel's sacrifice, is recorded by St Paul; and there is surely nothing unreasonable in the supposition that he did it, as in several other instances, by fire from heaven. The reader may see several authorities adduced in Poole; he may also consult Ainsworth on the Pentateuch, Dr P. Smith on the Atonement; and especially, Faber's " Treatise on the Origin of Expiatory Sacrifice."—*Ed.*

God on their own terms. When this is denied, they burn with furious indignation, which, though conceived against God, they cast forth upon his children. Thus, when Cain was angry with God, his fury was poured forth on his un-offending brother. When Moses says, " his countenance fell," (the word countenance is in Hebrew put in the plural number for the singular,) he means, that not only was he seized with a sudden vehement anger, but that, from a lingering sadness, he cherished a feeling so malignant that he was wasting with envy.

6. *And the Lord said unto Cain.* God now proceeds against Cain himself, and cites him to His tribunal, that the wretched man may understand that his rage can profit him nothing. He wishes honour to be given him for his sacrifices; but because he does not obtain it, he is furiously angry. Meanwhile, he does not consider that through his own fault he had failed to gain his wish; for had he but been conscious of his inward evil, he would have ceased to expostulate with God, and to rage against his guiltless brother. Moses does not state in what manner God spoke. Whether a vision was presented to him, or he heard an oracle from heaven, or was admonished by secret inspiration, he certainly felt himself bound by a divine judgment. To apply this to the person of Adam, as being the prophet and interpreter of God in censuring his son, is constrained and even frigid. I understand what it is which good men, not less pious than learned, propose, when they sport with such fancies. Their intention is to honour the external ministry of the word, and to cut off the occasion which Satan takes to insinuate his illusions under the colour of revelation.[1] Truly I confess, nothing is more useful than that pious minds should be retained, under the order of preaching, in obedience to the Scripture, that they may not seek the mind of God in erratic speculations. But we may observe, that the word of God was delivered from the begin-ning by oracles, in order that afterwards, when administered by the hands of men, it might receive the greater reve-

---

[1] " Et retrancher les occasions que prend Satan, pour faire illusion aux hommes, en s'insinuant sous couleur des revelations."—*French Tr.*

rence. I also acknowledge that the office of teaching was enjoined upon Adam, and do not doubt that he diligently admonished his children : yet they who think that God only spoke through his ministers, too violently restrict the words of Moses. Let us rather conclude, that, before the heavenly teaching was committed to public records, God often made known his will by extraordinary methods, and that here was the *foundation* which supported reverence for the word ; while the doctrine delivered through the hands of men was like the *edifice* itself. Certainly, though I should be silent, all men would acknowledge how greatly such an imagination as that to which we refer, abates the force of the divine reprimand. Therefore, as the voice of God had previously so sounded in the ears of Adam, that he certainly perceived God to speak; so is it also now directed to Cain.

7. *If thou doest well.* In these words God reproves Cain for having been unjustly angry, inasmuch as the blame of the whole evil lay with himself. For foolish indeed was his complaint and indignation at the rejection of sacrifices, the defects of which he had taken no care to amend. Thus all wicked men, after they have been long and vehemently enraged against God, are at length so convicted by the Divine judgment, that they vainly desire to transfer to others the cause of the evil. The Greek interpreters recede, in this place, far from the genuine meaning of Moses. Since, in that age, there were none of those marks or points which the Hebrews use instead of vowels, it was more easy, in consequence of the affinity of words to each other, to strike into an extraneous sense. However, as any one, moderately versed in the Hebrew language, will easily judge of their error, I will not pause to refute it.[1] Yet even those who are skilled in the Hebrew tongue differ not a little among themselves, although only respecting a single word ; for the

---

[1] The version of the Septuagint is, Οὐκ ἐὰν ὀρθῶς προσενέγκῃς, ὀρθῶς δὲ μὴ διελῃς, ἥμαρτες ; "If thou shouldst rightly offer, but yet not rightly divide, wouldst thou not sin ?" See *Archbishop Magee's Discourses*, &c., No. lxv., where he ingeniously accounts for the manner in which the translators of the Septuagint version may have misunderstood the original.—*Ed.*

Greeks change the whole sentence. Among those who agree
concerning the context and the substance of the address,
there is a difference respecting the word שאת, (seait,) which
is truly in the imperative mood, but ought to be resolved
into a noun substantive. Yet this is not the real difficulty;
but, since the verb נשא, (nasa,[1]) signifies sometimes to *exalt*,
sometimes to *take away* or remit, sometimes to *offer*, and
sometimes to *accept*, interpreters vary among themselves, as
each adopts this or the other meaning. Some of the Hebrew
Doctors refer it to the *countenance* of Cain, as if God promised that he would lift it up though now cast down with
sorrow. Other of the Hebrews apply it to the remission of
sins; as if it had been said, ' Do well, and thou shalt obtain
pardon.' But because they imagine a satisfaction, which
derogates from free pardon, they dissent widely from the
meaning of Moses. A third exposition approaches more
nearly to the truth, that *exaltation* is to be taken for honour,
in this way, ' There is no need to envy thy brother's honour,
because, if thou conductest thyself rightly, God will also raise
thee to the same degree of honour; though he now, offended
by thy sins, has condemned thee to ignominy.' But even
this does not meet my approbation. Others refine more philosophically, and say, that Cain would find God propitious,
and would be assisted by his grace, if he should by faith
bring purity of heart with his outward sacrifices. These I
leave to enjoy their own opinion, but I fear they aim at what
has little solidity. Jerome translates the word, ' Thou shalt
receive;' understanding that God promises a reward to that
pure and lawful worship which he requires. Having recited
the opinions of others, let me now offer what appears to me
more suitable. In the first place, the word שאת means the
same thing as *acceptance*, and stands opposed to *rejection*.
Secondly, since the discourse has respect to the matter in
hand,[2] I explain the saying as referring to sacrifices, namely,
that God will accept them when rightly offered. They who

[1] See Schindler, *sub voce*, No. iii.; and the Discourses before referred
to, No. lxv.
[2] " De re subjecta habitur sermo."

are skilled in the Hebrew language know that here is nothing
forced, or remote from the genuine signification of the word.
Now the very order of things leads us to the same point:
namely, that God pronounces those sacrifices repudiated and
rejected, as being of no value, which are offered improperly;
but that the oblation will be accepted, as pleasant and of
good odour, if it be pure and legitimate. We now perceive
how unjustly Cain was angry that his sacrifices were not
honoured, seeing that God was ready to receive them with
outstretched hands, provided they ceased to be faulty. At
the same time, however, what I before said must be recalled to memory, that the chief point of well-doing is, for
pious persons, relying on Christ the Mediator, and on the
gratuitous reconciliation procured by him, to endeavour to
worship God sincerely and without dissimulation. Therefore,
these two things are joined together by a mutual connection :
that the faithful, as often as they enter into the presence of
God, are commended by the grace of Christ alone, their sins
being blotted out; and yet that they bring thither true purity
of heart.

And if thou doest not well. On the other hand, God pronounces a dreadful sentence against Cain, if he harden his
mind in wickedness and indulge himself in his crime ; for the
address is very emphatical, because God not only repels his
unjust complaint, but shows that Cain could have no greater
adversary than that sin of his which he inwardly cherished.
He so binds the impious man, by a few concise words, that
he can find no refuge, as if he had said, ' Thy obstinacy shall
not profit thee; for, though thou shouldst have nothing
to do with me, thy sin shall give thee no rest, but shall
sharply drive thee on, pursue thee, and urge thee, and never
suffer thee to escape.' Hence it follows, that he not only
raged in vain and to no profit; but was held guilty by his
own inward conviction, even though no one should accuse
him ; for the expression, " sin lieth at the door," relates to
the interior judgment of the conscience, which presses upon
the man convinced of his sin, and besieges him on every side.
Although the impious may imagine that God slumbers in
heaven, and may strive, as far as possible, to repel the fear

of his judgment; yet sin will be perpetually drawing them
back, though reluctant and fugitives, to that tribunal from
which they endeavour to retire. The declarations even of
heathens testify that they were not ignorant of this truth;
for it is not to be doubted that, when they say, ' Conscience
is like a thousand witnesses,' they compare it to a most cruel
executioner. There is no torment more grievous or severe
than that which is hence perceived; moreover, God himself
extorts confessions of this kind. Juvenal says:—

> " Heaven's high revenge on human crimes behold;
> Though earthly verdicts may be bought and sold,
> His judge the sinner in his bosom bears,
> And conscience racks him with tormenting cares."[1]

But the expression of Moses has peculiar energy. Sin is
said to *lie*, but it is at the *door*; for the sinner is not immediately tormented with the fear of judgment; but, gathering
around him whatever delights he is able, in order to deceive
himself, he walks as in free space, and even revels as in pleasant meadows; when, however, he comes to the door, there he
meets with SIN, keeping constant guard; and then conscience,
which before thought itself at liberty, is arrested, and receives
double punishment for the delay.[2]

---

[1] " Prima est ultio quod se
Judice, nemo nocens absolvitur, improba quamvis
Gratia fallacis Prætoris vicerit urnam."
                                        Sat. xiii. *Lib.* v.

[2] The Hebrew word חטאת, (*chatath,*) which primarily means sin, is
also frequently used for sin-offering, and is so translated in various passages of our version. The learned Dr Lightfoot was the first who proposed that it should be so rendered in the present instance. His interpretation has been controverted, especially by Socinians; but not by
them only; the justly celebrated Dr Davison has also attempted to set it
aside, in his *Inquiry into the Origin and Intent of Primitive Sacrifice.*
But the more profound learning of Dr Magee and of Mr Faber has
placed the interpretation of Lightfoot on a basis not easily to be shaken.
The translation of the passage will, on this supposition, be, ' If thou
doest not well, a sin-offering lieth or coucheth at the door;' and the import of the address will be to this effect, ' Thou hast only to offer up a
sacrifice of atonement, and then the defect of thy offering will be supplied,
and the pardon of thy sin granted.'—See *Magee's Second Discourse, and
the Dissertations connected with it;* also *Faber's Treatise on the Origin of
Expiatory Sacrifice.*—*Ed.*

And unto thee shall be his desire.   Nearly all commentators refer this to sin, and think that, by this admonition, those depraved lusts are restrained which solicit and impel the mind of man.   Therefore, according to their view, the meaning will be of this kind, ' If sin rises against thee to subdue thee, why dost thou indulge it, and not rather labour to restrain and control it ? for it is thy part to subdue and bring into obedience those affections in thy flesh which thou perceivest to be opposed to the will of God, and rebellious against him.'   But I suppose that Moses means something entirely different.   I omit to notice that to the Hebrew word for *sin* is affixed the mark of the feminine gender, but that here two masculine relative pronouns are used.   Certainly Moses does not treat particularly of the sin itself which was committed, but of the guilt which is contracted from it, and of the consequent condemnation.   How, then, do these words suit, ' Unto thee shall be his desire ? '[1]   There will, however, be no need for long refutation when I shall produce the genuine meaning of the expression.   It rather seems to me a reproof, by which God charges the impious man with ingratitude, because he held in contempt the honour of primogeniture.   The greater are the divine benefits with which any one of us is adorned, the more does he betray his impiety, unless he endeavours earnestly to serve the Author of grace to whom he is under obligation.   When Abel was regarded as his brother's inferior, he was, nevertheless, a diligent worshipper of God.   But the first-born worshipped God negligently and perfunctorily, though he had, by the Divine kindness, arrived at so high a dignity ; and, therefore, God enlarges upon his sin, because he had not at least imitated his brother, whom he ought to have surpassed as far in piety

---

[1] Faber contends the expression, " Unto thee shall be his (or its) desire," refers to the victim which was to be offered as a sin-offering.—See his *Treatise*, p. 129.   He also gives the following poetical arrangement of God's address to Cain :—

" Why is there hot anger unto thee ;
   And why hath fallen thy countenance ?
   If thou doest well, shall there not be exaltation ?
   And if thou doest not well, at the door a sin-offering is couching.
   And unto thee is its desire,
   And thou shalt rule over it."—*Ed.*

as he did in the degree of honour. Moreover, this form of speech is common among the Hebrews, that the desire of the inferior should be towards him to whose will he is subject; thus Moses speaks of the woman, (iii. 16,) that her desire should be to her husband. They, however, childishly trifle, who distort this passage to prove the freedom of the will; for if we grant that Cain was admonished of his duty in order that he might apply himself to the subjugation of sin, yet no inherent power of man is to be hence inferred; because it is certain that only by the grace of the Holy Spirit can the affections of the flesh be so mortified that they shall not prevail. Nor, truly, must we conclude, that as often as God commands anything we shall have strength to perform it, but rather we must hold fast the saying of Augustine, 'Give what thou commandest, and command what thou wilt.'

8. *And Cain talked with Abel his brother.* Some understand this conversation to have been general; as if Cain, perfidiously dissembling his anger, spoke in a fraternal manner. Jerome relates the language used, 'Come, let us go without.'[1] In my opinion the speech is elliptical, and something is to be understood, yet what it is remains uncertain. Nevertheless, I am not dissatisfied with the explanation, that Moses concisely reprehends the wicked perfidy of the hypocrite, who, by speaking familiarly, presented the appearance of fraternal concord, until the opportunity of perpetrating the horrid murder should be afforded. And by this example we are taught that hypocrites are never to be more dreaded than when they stoop to converse under the pretext of friendship; because when they are not permitted to injure by open violence as much as they please, suddenly they assume a feigned appearance of peace. But it is by no means to be expected that they who are as savage beasts towards God, should sincerely cultivate the confidence of friendship with men. Yet let the reader consider whether Moses did not rather mean, that although Cain was rebuked by God, he, nevertheless, contended with his brother, and thus this saying of his would depend on what had preceded. I certainly rather incline to the opinion that he did not keep his malignant feelings within

---

[1] " Egrediamur foras."—*Vulgate.*

his own breast, but that he broke forth in accusation against his brother, and angrily declared to him the cause of his dejection.

When they were in the field. Hence we gather that although Cain had complained of his brother at home, he had yet so covered the diabolical fury with which he burned, that Abel suspected nothing worse; for he deferred vengeance to a suitable time. Moreover, this single deed of guilt clearly shows whither Satan will hurry men, when they harden their mind in wickedness, so that in the end, their obstinacy is worthy of the utmost extremes of punishment.

9. *Where is Abel?* They who suppose that the *father* made this inquiry of Cain respecting his son Abel, enervate the whole force of the instruction which Moses here intended to deliver; namely, that God, both by secret inspiration, and by some extraordinary method, cited the parricide[1] to his tribunal, as if he had thundered from heaven. For, what I have before said must be firmly maintained: that, as God now speaks with us through the Scriptures, so he formerly manifested himself to the Fathers through oracles; and also in the same manner, revealed his judgments to the reprobate sons of the saints. So the angel spoke to Agar in the wood, after she had fallen away from the Church,[2] as we shall see in the eighth verse of the sixteenth chapter. It is indeed possible that God may have interrogated Cain by the silent examination of his conscience; and that he, in return, may have answered, inwardly fretting and murmuring. We must, however, conclude, that he was examined, not barely by the external voice of man, but by a Divine voice, so as to make him feel that he had to deal directly with God. As often, then, as the secret compunctions of conscience invite us to reflect upon our sins, let us remember that God himself is speaking with us. For that interior sense by which we are convicted of sin is the peculiar judgment-seat of God, where

[1] " Parricidam citaverit." The word parricide is, contrary to its original import, applied to the murderer of any near relative.—*Ed.*
[2] By leaving the family of Abraham, in which alone the true service of God was maintained.—*Ed.*

he exercises his jurisdiction. Let those, therefore, whose consciences accuse them, beware lest, after the example of Cain, they confirm themselves in obstinacy. For this is truly to kick against God, and to resist his Spirit; when we repel those thoughts, which are nothing else than incentives to repentance. But it is a fault too common, to add at length to former sins such perverseness, that he who is compelled, whether he will or not, to feel sin in his mind, shall yet refuse to yield to God. Hence it appears how great is the depravity of the human mind; since, when convicted and condemned by our own conscience, we still do not cease either to mock, or to rage against our Judge. Prodigious was the stupor of Cain, who, having committed a crime so great, ferociously rejected the reproof of God, from whose hand he was nevertheless unable to escape. But the same thing daily happens to all the wicked; every one of whom desires to be deemed ingenious in catching at excuses. For the human heart is so entangled in winding labyrinths, that it is easy for the wicked to add obstinate contempt of God to their crimes; not because their contumacy is sufficiently firm to withstand the judgment of God, (for, although they hide themselves in the deep recesses of which I have spoken, they are, nevertheless, always secretly burned, as with a hot iron,) but because, by a blind obstinacy, they render themselves callous. Hence, the force of the Divine judgment is clearly perceived; for it so pierces into the iron hearts of the wicked, that they are inwardly compelled to be their own judges; nor does it suffer them so to obliterate the sense of guilt which it has extorted, as not to leave the trace or scar of the searing. Cain, in denying that he was the keeper of his brother's life, although, with ferocious rebellion, he attempts violently to repel the judgment of God, yet thinks to escape by this cavil, that he was not required to give an account of his murdered brother, because he had received no express command to take care of him.

10. *What hast thou done? The voice of thy brother's blood.* Moses shows that Cain gained nothing by his tergiversation. God first inquired where his brother was; he now more

closely urges him, in order to extort an unwilling confession
of his guilt; for in no racks or tortures of any kind is there
so much force to constrain evil-doers, as there was efficacy
in the thunder of the Divine voice to cast down Cain in
confusion to the ground.   For God no longer asks whether
he had done it; but, pronouncing in a single word that he
was the doer of it, he aggravates the atrocity of the crime.
We learn, then, in the person of one man, what an unhappy
issue of their cause awaits those, who desire to extricate
themselves by contending against God. For He, the Searcher
of hearts, has no need of a long, circuitous course of investigation; but, with one word, so fulminates against those whom
he accuses, as to be sufficient, and more than sufficient, for
their condemnation.   Advocates place the first kind of defence
in the denial of the fact; where the fact cannot be denied,
they have recourse to the qualifying circumstances of the
case.[1]   Cain is driven from both these defences; for God
both pronounces him guilty of the slaughter, and, at the
same time, declares the heinousness of the crime.   And we
are warned by his example, that pretexts and subterfuges
are heaped together in vain, when sinners are cited to the
tribunal of God.

The voice of thy brother's blood crieth.   God first shows that
he is cognizant of the deeds of men, though no one should
complain of or accuse them; secondly, that he holds the life
of man too dear, to allow innocent blood to be shed with
impunity; thirdly, that he cares for the pious not only while
they live, but even after death.   However earthly judges
may sleep, unless an accuser appeals to them; yet, even when
he who is injured is silent, the injuries themselves are alone
sufficient to arouse God to inflict punishment.   This is a wonderfully sweet consolation to good men, who are unjustly
harassed, when they hear that their own sufferings, which
they silently endure, go into the presence of God of their
own accord, to demand vengeance.   Abel was speechless
when his throat was being cut, or in whatever other manner
he was losing his life; but after death the voice of his blood
was more vehement than any eloquence of the orator.

---

[1] " Ubi negari factum non potest, ad statum qualitatis confugiunt."
—" Ils ont recours aux qualitez et circonstances."—*Fr. Trans.*

Thus oppression and silence do not hinder God from judging the cause which the world supposes to be buried. This consolation affords us most abundant reason for patience when we learn that we shall lose nothing of our right, if we bear injuries with moderation and equanimity ; and that God will be so much the more ready to vindicate us, the more modestly we submit ourselves to endure all things ; because the placid silence of the soul raises effectual cries, which fill heaven and earth. Nor does this doctrine apply merely to the state of the present life, to teach us that among the innumerable dangers by which we are surrounded, we shall be safe under the guardianship of God ; but it elevates us by the hope of a better life ; because we must conclude that those for whom God cares shall survive after death. And, on the other hand, this consideration should strike terror into the wicked and violent, that God declares, that he undertakes the causes deserted by human patronage, not in consequence of any foreign impulse, but from his own nature ; and that he will be the sure avenger of crimes, although the injured make no complaint. Murderers indeed often exult, as if they had evaded punishment ; but at length God will show that innocent blood has not been mute, and that he has not said in vain, ' the death of the saints is precious in his eyes,' (Psalm cxv. 17.) Therefore, as this doctrine brings relief to the faithful, lest they should be too anxious concerning their life, over which they learn that God continually watches ; so does it vehemently thunder against the ungodly, who do not scruple wickedly to injure and to destroy those whom God has undertaken to preserve.

11. *And now art thou cursed from the earth.* Cain, having been convicted of the crime, judgment is now pronounced against him. And first, God constitutes the earth the minister of his vengeance, as having been polluted by the impious and horrible parricide : as if he had said, ' Thou didst just now deny to me the murder which thou hast committed, but the senseless earth itself will demand thy punishment.' He does this, however, to aggravate the enormity of the crime, as if a kind of contagion flowed from it even to the earth, for which the execution of punishment was required. The ima-

gination of some, that cruelty is here ascribed to the earth, as if God compared it to a wild beast, which had drunk up the blood of Abel, is far from the true meaning. Clemency is rather, in my judgment, by personification,[1] imputed to it; because, in abhorrence of the pollution, it had opened its mouth to cover the blood which had been shed by a brother's hand. Most detestable is the cruelty of this man, who does not shrink from pouring forth his neighbour's blood, of which the bosom of the earth becomes the receptacle. Yet we must not here imagine any miracle, as if the blood had been absorbed by any unusual opening of the earth; but the speech is figurative, signifying that there was more humanity in the earth than in man himself. Moreover, they who think that, because Cain is now cursed in stronger words than Adam had previously been, God had dealt more gently with the first man, from a design to spare the human race; have some colour for their opinion. Adam heard the words, " Cursed is the ground for thy sake :" but now the shaft of divine vengeance vibrates against, and transfixes the person of Cain. The opinion of others, that temporal punishment is intended, because it is said, Thou art cursed from the *earth*, rather than from *heaven*, lest the posterity of Cain, being cut off from the hope of salvation, should rush the more boldly on their own damnation, seems to me not sufficiently confirmed. I rather interpret the passage thus: Judgment was committed to the earth, in order that Cain might understand that his judge had not to be summoned from a distance; that there was no need for an angel to descend from heaven, since the earth voluntarily offered itself as the avenger.

12. *When thou tillest the ground.* This verse is the exposition of the former; for it expresses more clearly what is meant by being cursed *from* the earth, namely, that the earth defrauds its cultivators of the fruit of their toil. Should any one object that this punishment had before been alike inflicted on all mortals, in the person of Adam; my answer is, I have no doubt that something of the benediction which had

---

[1] " Κατὰ προσωποποιΐαν."

hitherto remained, was now further withdrawn with respect to the murderer, in order that he might privately feel the very earth to be hostile to him. For although, generally, God causes his sun daily to rise upon the good and the evil, (Matth. v. 45,) yet, in the meantime, (as often as he sees good,) he punishes the sins, sometimes of a whole nation, and sometimes of certain men, with rain and hail, and clouds, so far, at least, as is useful to give determinate proof of future judgment; and also for the purpose of admonishing the world, by such examples, that nothing can succeed when God is angry with and opposed to them. Moreover, in the first murder, God designed to exhibit a singular example of malediction, the memory of which should remain in all ages.

A fugitive and a vagabond shalt thou be.[1] Another punishment is now also inflicted; namely, that he never could be safe, to whatever place he might come. Moses uses two words, little differing from each other, except that the former is derived from נוע, (*noa,*) which is to *wander*, the other from נדד, (*nadad,*) which signifies to *flee.* The distinction which some make, that נע, (*na,*) is he who never has a settled habitation, but נד, (*nad,*) he who knows not which way he ought to turn; as it is defective in proof, is with me of no weight. The genuine sense then of the words is, that wherever Cain might come, he should be *unsettled*, and a *fugitive;* as robbers are wont to be, who have no quiet and secure resting-place; for the face of every man strikes terror into them; and, on the other hand, they have a horror of solitude. But this seems to some by no means a suitable punishment for a murderer, since it is rather the destined condition of the sons of God; for they, more than all others, feel themselves to be strangers in the world. And Paul complains that both he and his companions are without a certain dwelling-place, (1 Cor. iv. 11.[2]) To which I answer, that Cain was not only condemned to personal exile, but was also subjected to still more severe punishment; namely, that he should find no region of the earth where he would not be of a restless and fearful mind; for as a good conscience is pro-

---

[1] " στένων καὶ τρέμων." " Groaning and trembling."—*Sept.*
" Instabiles esse conqueritur."

perly called ' a brazen wall,' so neither a hundred walls, nor as many fortresses, can free the wicked from disquietude.   The faithful are strangers upon the earth, yet, nevertheless, they enjoy a tranquil temporary abode. Often, constrained by necessity, they wander from place to place, but wheresoever the tempest bears them, they carry with them a sedate mind; till finally, by perpetual change of place, they so run their course, and pass through the world, that they are everywhere sustained by the supporting hand of God.   Such security is denied to the wicked, whom all creatures threaten; and should even all creatures favour them, still the mind itself is so turbulent that it does not suffer them to rest.   In this manner, Cain, even if he had not changed his place, could not have shaken off the trepidation which God had fixed in his mind; nor did the fact, that he was the first man who built a city, prevent him from being always restless, even in his own nest.

13. *My punishment is greater, &c.*   Nearly all commentators agree that this is the language of desperation; because Cain, confounded by the judgment of God, had no remaining hope of pardon.   And this, indeed, is true, that the reprobate are never conscious of their evils, till a ruin, from which they cannot escape, overtakes them; yea, truly, when the sinner, obstinate to the last, mocks the patience of God, this is the due reward of his late repentance, that he feels a horrible torment for which there is no remedy,—if, truly, that blind and astonished dread of punishment, which is without any hatred of sin, or any desire to return to God, can be called repentance;—so even Judas confesses his sin, but, overwhelmed with fear, flies as far as possible from the presence of God. And it is certainly true, that the reprobates have no medium ; as long as any relaxation is allowed them, they slumber securely ; but when the anger of God presses upon them, they are broken rather than corrected.   Therefore their fear stuns them, so that they can think of nothing but of hell and eternal destruction.   However, I doubt not, that the words have another meaning.   For I rather take the term עָוֹן, *(aoon,)* in its proper signification ; and the word נָשָׂא, *(nasa,)* I interpret

by the word *to bear*. ' A greater punishment (he says) is imposed upon me than I can bear.' In this manner, Cain, although he does not excuse his sin, having been driven from every shift; yet complains of the intolerable severity of his judgment. So also the devils, although they feel that they are justly tormented, yet do not cease to rage against God their judge, and to charge him with cruelty. And immediately follows the explanation of these words : ' Behold, thou hast driven me from the face of the earth, and I am hidden from thy face.'[1] In which expression he openly expostulates with God, that he is treated more hardly than is just, no clemency or moderation being shown him. For it is precisely as if he had said, ' If a safe habitation is denied me in the world, and thou dost not deign to care for me, what dost thou leave me? would it not be better to die at once than to be constantly exposed to a thousand deaths ? ' Whence we infer, that the reprobate, however clearly they may be convicted, make no end of storming; insomuch that through their impatience and fury, they seize on occasions of contest ; as if they were able to excite enmity against God on account of the severity of their own sufferings. This passage also clearly teaches what was the nature of that wandering condition, or exile, which Moses had just mentioned ; namely, that no corner of the earth should be left him by God, in which he might quietly repose. For, being excluded from the common rights of mankind, so as to be no more reckoned among the legitimate inhabitants of the earth, he declares that he is cast out from the face of the earth, and therefore shall become a fugitive, because the earth will deny him a habitation ; hence it would be necessary, that he should occupy as a robber, what he did not possess by right. To be ' hidden from the face of God,' is to be not regarded by God, or not protected by his guardian care. This confession also, which God extorted from the impious murderer, is a proof that there is no peace for men, unless they acquiesce in the providence of God, and are persuaded that their lives are the object of his care ; it is also a proof, that they can only quietly enjoy any of God's benefits so long as they

[1] " Ecce repulisti me à facie terræ, et à facie tuâ abscondar."

regard themselves as placed in the world, on this condition, that they pass their lives under his government. How
wretched then is the instability of the wicked, who know
that not a foot of earth is granted to them by God !

14. *Every one that findeth me.* Since he is no longer
covered by the protection of God, he concludes that he shall
be exposed to injury and violence from all men. And he
reasons justly ; for the hand of God alone marvellously preserves us amid so many dangers. And they have spoken
prudently who have said, not only that our life hangs on a
thread, but also that we have been received into this fleeting
life, out of the womb, from a hundred deaths. Cain, however,
in this place, not only considers himself as deprived of God's
protection, but also supposes all creatures to be divinely
armed to take vengeance of his impious murder. This is the
reason why he so greatly fears for his life from any one who
may meet him ; for as man is a social animal, and all naturally
desire mutual intercourse, this is certainly to be regarded as
a portentous fact, that the meeting with any man was formidable to the murderer.

15. *Therefore, whosoever slayeth Cain.* They who think that it
was Cain's wish to perish immediately by one death, in order
that he might not be agitated by continual dangers, and that the
prolongation of his life was granted him only as a punishment,
have no reason, that I can see, for thus speaking. But far
more absurd is the manner in which many of the Jews mutilate this sentence. First, they imagine, in this clause, the
use of the figure ἀποσιώπησις, according to which something
not expressed is understood ; then they begin a new sentence,
' He shall be punished sevenfold,' which they refer to Cain.
Still, however, they do not agree together about the sense.
Some trifle respecting Lamech, as we shall soon declare.
Others expound the passage of the deluge, which happened
in the seventh generation. But that is frivolous, since the
latter was not a private punishment of one family only, but a
common punishment of the human race. But this sentence
ought to be read continuously, thus, ' Whosoever killeth Cain,

shall, on this account, be punished sevenfold.' And the causal particle לכן, (lekon,) indicates that God would take care to prevent any one from easily breaking in upon him to destroy him ; not because God would institute a privilege in favour of the murderer, or would hearken to his prayer, but because he would consult for posterity, in order to the preservation of human life. The order of nature had been awfully violated ; what might be expected to happen in future, when the wickedness and audacity of man should increase, unless the fury of others had been restrained by a violent hand ? For we know what pestilent and deadly poison Satan presents to us in evil examples, if a remedy be not speedily applied. Therefore, the Lord declares, if any will imitate Cain, not only shall they have no excuse in his example, but shall be more grievously tormented; because they ought, in his person, to perceive how detestable is their wickedness in the sight of God. Wherefore, they are greatly deceived who suppose that the anger of God is mitigated when men can plead custom as an excuse for sinning ; whereas, it is from that cause the more inflamed.

And the Lord set a mark. I have·lately said, that nothing was granted to Cain for the sake of favouring him; but for the sake of opposing, in future, cruelty and unjust violence. And, therefore, Moses now says, that a mark was set upon Cain, which should strike terror into all; because they might see, as in a mirror, the tremendous judgment of God against bloody men. As Scripture does not describe what kind of mark it was, commentators have conjectured, that his body became tremulous. It may suffice for us, that there was some visible token which should repress in the spectators the desire and the audacity to inflict injury.

16. *And Cain went out from the presence of the Lord.* Cain is said to have departed from the presence of God, because, whereas he had hitherto lived in the earth as in an abode belonging to God, now, like an exile removed far from God's sight, he wanders beyond the limits of His protection. Or certainly, (which is not less probable,) Moses represents him as having stood at the bar of judgment till he was condemned:

but now, when God ceased to speak with him, being freed from the sense of His presence, he hastens elsewhere and seeks a new habitation, where he may escape the eyes of God. The land of Nod[1] without doubt obtained its name from its inhabitant. From its being situated on the eastern side of Paradise, we may infer the truth of what was before stated, that a certain place, distinguished by its pleasantness and rich abundance of fruits, had been given to Adam for a habitation; for, of necessity, that place must be limited, which has opposite aspects towards the various regions of the world.

17. *And Cain knew his wife.* From the context we may gather that Cain, before he slew his brother, had married a wife; otherwise Moses would now have related something respecting his marriage; because it would be a fact worthy to be recorded, that any one of his sisters could be found, who would not shrink with horror from committing herself into the hand of one whom she knew to be defiled with a brother's blood; and while a free choice was still given her, should rather choose spontaneously to follow an exile and a fugitive, than to remain in her father's family. Moreover, he relates it as a prodigy that Cain, having shaken off the terror he had mentioned, should have thought of having children :[2] for it is remarkable, that he who imagined himself to have as many enemies as there were men in the world, did not rather hide himself in some remote solitude. It is also contrary to nature, that he being astounded with fear, and feeling that God was opposed to him, could enjoy any pleasure. Indeed, it seems to me doubtful, whether he had previously had any children; for there would be nothing absurd in saying, that reference is here made especially to those who were born after the crime was committed, as to a detestable seed who would fully participate in the sanguinary disposition, and the savage manners of their father. This, however, is without controversy, that many persons, as well males as females, are omitted in this narrative; it being the design of Moses only

[1] " נוד signifies motion, flight, wandering, exile, and is the name of the region into which Cain was exiled."—*Schindler.*
[2] " Ad sobolem gignendam animum applicuisse."

to follow one line of his progeny, until he should come to Lamech. The house of Cain, therefore, was more populous than Moses states; but because of the memorable history of Lamech, which he is about to subjoin, he only adverts to one line of descendants, and passes over the rest in silence.

He built a city. This, at first sight, seems very contrary, both to the judgment of God, and to the preceding sentence. For Adam and the rest of his family, to whom God had assigned a fixed station, are passing their lives in hovels, or even under the open heaven, and seek their precarious lodging under trees; but the exile Cain, whom God had commanded to rove as a fugitive, not content with a private house, builds himself a city. It is, however, probable, that the man, oppressed by an accusing conscience, and not thinking himself safe within the walls of his own house, had contrived a new kind of defence: for Adam and the rest live dispersed through the fields for no other reason, than that they are less afraid. Wherefore, it is a sign of an agitated and guilty mind, that Cain thought of building a city for the purpose of separating himself from the rest of men; yet, that pride was mixed with his diffidence and anxiety, appears, from his having called the city after his son. Thus different affections often contend with each other in the hearts of the wicked. Fear, the fruit of his iniquity, drives him within the walls of a city, that he may fortify himself in a manner before unknown; and, on the other hand, supercilious vanity breaks forth. Certainly he ought rather to have chosen that his name should be buried for ever; for how could his memory be transmitted, except to be held in execration? Yet, ambition impels him to erect a monument to his race in the name of his city. What shall we here say, but that he had hardened himself against punishment, for the purpose of holding out, in inflated obstinacy, against God? Moreover, although it is lawful to defend our lives by the fortifications of cities and of fortresses, yet the first origin of them is to be noted, because it is always profitable for us to behold our faults in their very remedies. When captious men sneeringly inquire, whence Cain had brought his architects and workmen to build his city, and whence he sent for citizens to inhabit it? I, in return, ask of them, what authority they have for believing that the city was constructed of squared stones, and with great skill, and at much expense, and that the building of it was a work of long continuance? For nothing further can be gathered from the words of Moses, than that Cain surrounded himself and his posterity with walls formed of the rudest materials: and as it respects the inhabitants; that in that commencement of the fecundity of mankind, his offspring would have grown to so great a number when it had reached his children of the fourth generation, that it might easily form the body of one city.

19. *And Lamech took unto him two wives.* We have here the origin of polygamy in a perverse and degenerate race; and the first author of it, a cruel man, destitute of all humanity. Whether he had been impelled by an immoderate desire of augmenting his own family, as proud and ambitious men are wont to be, or by mere lust, it is of little consequence to determine; because, in either way he violated the sacred law of marriage, which had been delivered by God. For God had determined, that " they two should be one flesh," and that is the perpetual order of nature. Lamech, with brutal contempt of God, corrupts nature's laws. The Lord, therefore, willed that the corruption of lawful marriage should proceed from the house of Cain, and from the person of Lamech, in order that polygamists might be ashamed of the example.

20. *Jabal; he was the father of such as dwell in tents.* Moses now relates that, with the evils which proceeded from the family of Cain, some good had been blended. For the invention of arts, and of other things which serve to the common use and convenience of life, is a gift of God by no means to be despised, and a faculty worthy of commendation. It is truly wonderful, that this race, which had most deeply fallen from integrity, should have excelled the rest of the posterity of Adam in rare endowments.[1] I, however, understand Moses to have spoken expressly concerning these arts, as having been invented in the family of Cain, for the purpose of showing that he was not so accursed by

[1] " Non pœnitendis dotibus, præ aliis Adæ posteris excelluisse."

the Lord but that he would still scatter some excellent gifts among his posterity; for it is probable, that the genius of others was in the meantime not inactive; but that there were, among the sons of Adam, industrious and skilful men, who exercised their diligence in the invention and cultivation of arts. Moses, however, expressly celebrates the remaining benediction of God on that race, which otherwise would have been deemed void and barren of all good. Let us then know, that the sons of Cain, though deprived of the Spirit of regeneration, were yet endued with gifts of no despicable kind; just as the experience of all ages teaches us how widely the rays of divine light have shone on unbelieving nations, for the benefit of the present life; and we see, at the present time, that the excellent gifts of the Spirit are diffused through the whole human race. Moreover, the liberal arts and sciences have descended to us from the heathen. We are, indeed, compelled to acknowledge that we have received astronomy, and the other parts of philosophy, medicine, and the order of civil government, from them. Nor is it to be doubted, that God has thus liberally enriched them with excellent favours that their impiety might have the less excuse. But, while we admire the riches of his favour which he has bestowed on them, let us still value far more highly that grace of regeneration with which he peculiarly sanctifies his elect unto himself.

Now, although the invention of the harp, and of similar instruments of music, may minister to our pleasure, rather than to our necessity, still it is not to be thought altogether superfluous; much less does it deserve, in itself, to be condemned. Pleasure is indeed to be condemned, unless it be combined with the fear of God, and with the common benefit of human society. But such is the nature of musi , that it can be adapted to the offices of religion, and made profitable to men; if only it be free from vicious attractions, and from that foolish delight, by which it seduces men from better employments, and occupies them in vanity. If, however, we allow the invention of the harp no praise, it is well known how far and how widely extends the usefulness of the art of the carpenter. Finally, Moses, in my opinion, intends to teach

that that race flourished in various and pre-eminent endowments, which would both render it inexcusable, and would
prove most evident testimonies of the divine goodness.   The
name of " the father of them that dwell in tents," is given to
him who was the first inventor of that convenience, which
others afterwards imitated.

23. *Hear my voice, ye wives of Lamech.*   The intention of
Moses is to describe the ferocity of this man, who was, however, the fifth in descent from the fratricide Cain, in order to
teach us, that, so far from being terrified by the example of
divine judgment which he had seen in his ancestor, he was
only the more hardened.   Such is the obduracy of the impious, that they rage against those chastisements of God,
which ought at least to render them gentle.   The obscurity
of this passage, which has procured for us a variety of interpretations, mainly arises hence; that whereas Moses
speaks abruptly, interpreters have not considered what is the
tendency of his speech.   The Jews have, according to their
manner, invented a foolish fable ; namely, that Lamech was
a hunter and blind, and had a boy to direct his hand; that Cain,
while he was concealed in the woods, was shot through by
his arrow, because the boy, taking him for a wild beast, had
directed his master's hand towards him ; that Lamech then
took revenge on the boy, who, by his imprudence, had been
the cause of the murder.   And ignorance of the true state of
the case has caused every one to allow himself to conjecture what
he pleased.   But to me the opinion of those seems to be true and
simple, who resolve the past tense into the future, and understand its application to be indefinite; as if he had boasted that he
had strength and violence enough to slay any, even the strongest enemy.   I therefore read thus, ' I will slay a man for my
wound, and a young man for my bruise,' or ' in my bruise
and wound.'   But, as I have said, the occasion of his holding
this conversation with his wives is to be noticed.   We know
that sanguinary men, as they are a terror to others, so are
they everywhere hated by all.   The wives, therefore, of Lamech were justly alarmed on account of their husband, whose
violence was intolerable to the whole human race, lest, a con-

spiracy being formed, all should unite to crush him, as one deserving of public odium and execration. Now Moses, to exhibit his desperate barbarity, seeing that the soothing arts of wives are often wont to mitigate cruel and ferocious men, declares that Lamech cast forth the venom of his cruelty into the bosom of his wives. The sum of the whole is this : He boasts that he has sufficient courage and strength to strike down any who should dare to attack him. The repetition occurring in the use of the words 'man' and 'young man' is according to Hebrew phraseology, so that none should think different persons to be denoted by them ; he only amplifies, in the second member of the sentence, his furious audacity, when he glories that young men in the flower of their age would not be equal to contend with him : as if he would say,   Let each mightiest man come forward, there is none whom I will not dispatch.'   So far was he from calming his wives with the hope of his leading a more humane life, that he breaks forth in threats of sheer indiscriminate slaughter against every one, like a furious wild beast. Whence it easily appears, that he was so imbued with ferocity as to have retained nothing human. The nouns *wound* and *bruise* may be variously read. If they be rendered ' for my wound and bruise,' then the sense will be, 'I confidently take upon my own head whatever danger there may be, let what will happen it shall be at my expense ; for I have a means of escape at hand.'   Then what follows must be read in connection with it, " If Cain shall be avenged sevenfold, truly Lamech seventy and seven fold."   If the ablative case be preferred, ' In my wound and bruise,' there will still be a double exposition.   The first is, ' Although I should be wounded, I would still kill the man ; what then will I not do when I am whole ? '   The other, and, in my judgment, the sounder and more consistent exposition, is, ' If any one provoke me by injury, or attempt any act of violence, he shall feel that he has to deal with a strong and valiant man ; nor shall he who injures me escape with impunity.'[1]   This example shows that men ever glide from bad

---

[1] It is clear that Calvin had no perception of the poetical character of this speech, or he would more correctly have interpreted its meaning. There is, however, and will be, much difference of opinion respecting the

to worse. The wickedness of Cain was indeed awful; but the cruelty of Lamech advanced so far that he was unsparing of human blood. Besides, when he saw his wives struck with terror, instead of becoming mild, he only sharpened and confirmed himself the more in cruelty. Thus the brutality of cruel men increases in proportion as they find themselves hated; so that instead of being touched with penitence, they are ready to bury one murder under ten others. Whence it follows that they, having once become imbued with blood, shed it, and drink it, without restraint.

24. *Cain shall be avenged sevenfold.* It is not my intention to relate the ravings or the dreams of every writer, nor would I have the reader to expect this from me; here and there I

real nature of the act spoken of in this obscure poem. Some have thought Lamech guilty of savage cruelty in murdering an innocent person; others have deemed the act to be one of justifiable homicide, done in self-defence. Others, again, have supposed the expression of Lamech to be a mere question, which admitted only of a negative answer, ' Have I slain a man for my wound?' And, lastly, there are those who, with Calvin, take it as the language of bravado, ' I would slay a man for wounding me, if he should attempt to do it.' In Bishop Lowth's fourth Prelection the whole is given in three distiches of Hebrew poetry, of which the following is a translation :—

> " Ada and Zillah, hear my voice :
> Ye wives of Lamech, hearken to my speech ;
> Because I have slain a man for my wound,
> And a boy for my bruise :
> If Cain shall be avenged sevenfold,
> Lamech even seventy times seven."
>
> *De Sacra Poesi Hebræorum.*

See also Dr A. Clarke's Commentary *in loco.*

The following translation from Herder is also worthy of notice :—

> " Ye wives of Lamech, hear my voice,
> And hearken to my speech ;
> I slew a man who wounded me,
> A youth who smote me with a blow.
> If Cain shall be seven times avenged,
> Then Lamech seventy times seven."
>
> *Caunter's Poetry of the Pentateuch,* vol. i. p. 81.

Caunter commends the translation of Bishop Lowth for having got rid of the copulative conjunction in the fourth line. This, however, is a mistake into which he has been led by reading Lowth not in the original, but in Dr Gregory's translation. A remark of Michaelis appears worthy of attention. Speaking of Lamech and his wives, he says, ' It is not to be supposed that he addressed them in verse ; the substance of what he said has been reduced to numbers, for the sake of preserving it easily in the memory.'—*Ed.*

allude to them, though sparingly, especially if there be any colour of deception; that readers, being often admonished, may learn to take heed unto themselves. Therefore, with respect to this passage, which has been variously tortured, I will not record what one or another may have delivered, but will content myself with a true exposition of it. God had intended that Cain should be a horrible example to warn others against the commission of murder; and for this end had marked him with a shameful stigma. Yet lest any one should imitate his crime, He declared whosoever killed him should be punished with sevenfold severity. Lamech, impiously perverting this divine declaration, mocks its severity; for he hence takes greater license to sin, as if God had granted some singular privilege to murderers; not that he seriously thinks so, but being destitute of all sense of piety, he promises himself impunity, and in the meantime jestingly uses the name of God as an excuse: just as Dionysius did, who boasted that the gods favour sacrilegious persons, for the sake of obliterating the infamy which he had contracted. Moreover, as the number seven in Scripture designates a multitude, so *sevenfold* is taken for a very great increase. Such is the meaning of the declaration of Christ, ' I do not say that thou shalt remit the offence seven times, but seventy times seven,' (Matth. xviii. 22.)

Adam knew his wife again. Some hence infer that our first parents were entirely deprived of their offspring when one of their sons had been slain, and the other was cast far away into banishment. But it is utterly incredible that, when the benediction of God in the propagation of mankind was in its greatest force, Adam and Eve should have been through so many years unfruitful. But rather, before Abel was slain, the continual succession of progeny had already rendered the house of Adam populous; for in him and his wife especially the effect of that declaration ought to be conspicuous, " Increase and multiply, and replenish the earth." What, therefore, does Moses mean? Truly, that our first parents, horror-struck at the impious slaughter, abstained for a while from the conjugal bed. Nor could it certainly be otherwise, than that they, in reaping this exceedingly sad and bitter fruit of their apostacy from God, should sink down almost lifeless. The reason why he now passes by others is, that he designed to trace the generation of pious descendants through the line of Seth. In the following chapter, however, where he will say, that " Adam begat sons and daughters," he undoubtedly includes a great number who had been born before Seth; to whom, however, but little regard is paid, since they were separated from that family which worshipped God in purity, and which might truly be deemed the Church of God.

God, saith she, *hath appointed me another seed instead of Abel.* Eve means some peculiar seed; for we have said that others had been born who had also grown up before the death of Abel; but, since the human race is prone to evil, nearly her whole family had, in various ways, corrupted itself; therefore, she entertained slight hope of the remaining multitude, until God should raise up to her a new seed, of which she might expect better things. Wherefore, she regarded herself as bereaved not of one son only, but of her whole offspring, in the person of Abel.

26. *Then began men to call upon the name of the Lord.* In the verb ' to call upon,' there is a *synecdoche,* for it embraces generally the whole worship of God. But religion is here properly designated by that which forms its principal part. For God prefers this service of piety and faith to all sacrifices, (Psalm l. 14.) Yea, this is the spiritual worship of God which faith produces. This is particularly worthy of notice, because Satan contrives nothing with greater care than to adulterate, with every possible corruption, the pure invocation of God, or to draw us away from the only God to the invocation of creatures. Even from the beginning of the world he has not ceased to move this stone, that miserable men might weary themselves in vain in a preposterous worship of God. But let us know, that the entire pomp of adoration is nothing worth, unless this chief point of worshipping God aright be maintained. Although the passage may be more simply explained to mean, that then the name of God was again celebrated; yet I approve the former sense, because it is more

full, contains a useful doctrine, and also agrees with the accustomed phraseology of Scripture. It is a foolish figment, that God then began to be called by other names; since Moses does not here censure depraved superstitions, but commends the piety of one family which worshipped God in purity and holiness, when religion, among other people, was polluted or extinct. And there is no doubt, that Adam and Eve, with a few other of their children, were themselves true worshippers of God; but Moses means, that so great was then the deluge of impiety in the world that religion was rapidly hastening to destruction; because it remained only with a few men, and did not flourish in any one race. We may readily conclude that Seth was an upright and faithful servant of God. And after he begat a son, like himself, and had a rightly constituted family, the face of the Church began distinctly to appear, and that worship of God was set up which might continue to posterity. Such a restoration of religion has been effected also in our time; not that it had been altogether extinct; but there was no certainly defined people who called upon God; and, no sincere profession of faith, no uncorrupted religion could anywhere be discovered. Whence it too evidently appears how great is the propensity of men, either to gross contempt of God, or to superstition; since both evils must then have everywhere prevailed, when Moses relates it as a miracle, that there was at that time a single family in which the worship of God arose.

CHAPTER V.

1. This *is* the book of the generations of Adam. In the day that God created man, in the likeness of God made he him;

2. Male and female created he them; and blessed them, and called their name Adam, in the day when they were created.

1. Iste est liber generationum Adam : in die qua creavit Deus hominem, ad similitudinem Dei fecit illum.

2. Masculum et fœminam creavit eos, et benedixit eis : et vocavit nomen eorum Hominem, in die qua creati sunt.

3. And Adam lived an hundred and thirty years, and begat *a son* in his own likeness, after his image ; and called his name Seth :

4. And the days of Adam after he had begotten Seth were eight hundred years : and he begat sons and daughters :

5. And all the days that Adam lived were nine hundred and thirty years : and he died.

6. And Seth lived an hundred and five years, and begat Enos :

7. And Seth lived after he begat Enos eight hundred and seven years, and begat sons and daughters :

8. And all the days of Seth were nine hundred and twelve years : and he died.

9. And Enos lived ninety years, and begat Cainan :

10. And Enos lived after he begat Cainan eight hundred and fifteen years, and begat sons and daughters :

11. And all the days of Enos were nine hundred and five years : and he died.

12. And Cainan lived seventy years, and begat Mahalaleel :

13. And Cainan lived after he begat Mahalaleel eight hundred and forty years, and begat sons and daughters :

14. And all the days of Cainan were nine hundred and ten years : and he died.

15. And Mahalaleel lived sixty and five years, and begat Jared :

16. And Mahalaleel lived after he begat Jared eight hundred and thirty years, and begat sons and daughters :

17. And all the days of Mahalaleel were eight hundred ninety and five years : and he died.

18. And Jared lived an hundred sixty and two years, and he begat Enoch :

3. Et vixit Adam triginta et centum annos : et genuit ad similitudinem suam, ad imaginem suam *filium*, et vocavit nomen ejus Seth.

4. Et fuerunt dies Adam postquam genuit Seth, octingenti anni : et genuit filios et filias.

5. Fuerunt itaque omnes dies Adam quibus vixit, nongenti anni et triginta anni : et mortuus est.

6. Et vixit Seth quinque annos et centum annos, et genuit Enos.

7. Et vixit Seth postquam genuit Enos, septem annos et octingentos annos : et genuit filios et filias.

8. Fuerunt itaque omnes dies Seth, duodecim anni et nongenti anni : et mortuus est.

9. Et vixit Enos nonaginta annos, et genuit Kenan.

10. Et vixit Enos postquam genuit Kenan, quindecim annos et octingentos annos, et genuit filios et filias.

11. Fuerunt igitur omnes dies Enos, quinque anni et nongenti anni : et mortuus est.

12. Et vixit Kenan septuaginta annos, et genuit Mahalaleel.

13. Et vixit Kenan postquam genuit Mahalaleel, quadraginta annos et octingentos annos : et genuit filios et filias.

14. Fuerunt itaque omnes dies Kenan, decem anni et nongenti anni : et mortuus est.

15. Et vixit Mahalaleel quinque annos et sexaginta annos, et genuit Jered.

16. Et vixit Mahalaleel postquam genuit Jered, triginta annos et octingentos annos : et genuit filios et filias.

17. Fuerunt igitur omnes dies Mahalaleel, quinque anni et octingenti anni : et mortuus est.

18. Et vixit Jered duos et sexaginta annos et centum annos, et genuit Hanoch.

19. And Jared lived after he begat Enoch eight hundred years, and begat sons and daughters:

20. And all the days of Jared were nine hundred sixty and two years: and he died.

21. And Enoch lived sixty and five years, and begat Methuselah:

22. And Enoch walked with God after he begat Methuselah three hundred years, and begat sons and daughters:

23. And all the days of Enoch were three hundred sixty and five years:

24. And Enoch walked with God: and he *was* not; for God took him.

25. And Methuselah lived an hundred eighty and seven years, and begat Lamech:

26. And Methuselah lived after he begat Lamech seven hundred eighty and two years, and begat sons and daughters:

27. And all the days of Methuselah were nine hundred sixty and nine years: and he died.

28. And Lamech lived an hundred eighty and two years, and begat a son:

29. And he called his name Noah, saying, This *same* shall comfort us concerning our work and toil of our hands, because of the ground which the Lord hath cursed.

30. And Lamech lived after he begat Noah five hundred ninety and five years, and begat sons and daughters:

31. And all the days of Lamech were seven hundred seventy and seven years: and he died.

32. And Noah was five hundred years old: and Noah begat Shem, Ham, and Japheth.

19. Et vixit Jered postquam genuit Hanoch octingentos annos: et genuit filios et filias.

20. Fuerunt ergo omnes dies Jered duo et sexaginta anni et nongenti anni: et mortuus est.

21. Et vixit Hanoch quinque et sexaginta annos, et genuit Methuselah.

22. Et ambulavit Hanoch cum Deo, postquam genuit Methuselah, trecentos annos: et genuit filios et filias.

23. Fuerunt itaque omnes dies Hanoch, quinque et sexaginta anni et trecenti anni.

24. Et ambulavit Hanoch cum Deo: et non fuit, quia tulit eum Deus.

25. Et vixit Methuselah septem et octoginta annos et centum annos, et genuit Lemech.

26. Et vixit Methuselah postquam genuit Lemech, duos et octoginta annos et septingentos annos: et genuit filios et filias.

27. Fuerunt igitur omnes dies Methuselah novem et sexaginta anni et nongenti anni: et mortuus est.

28. Et vixit Lemech duos et octoginta annos et centum annos: et genuit filium.

29. Et vocavit nomen ejus Noah, dicendo, Iste consolabitur nos ab opere nostro, et a dolore manuum nostrarum de terra cui maledixit Jehova.

30. Et vixit Lemech postquam genuit ipsum Noah, quinque et nonaginta annos et quingentos annos: et genuit filios et filias.

31. Fuerunt itaque omnes dies Lemech septem et septuaginta anni et septingenti anni: et mortuus est.

32. Et erat Noah quingentorum annorum, et genuit ipse Noah, Sem, Cham, et Jepheth.

1. *This is the book of the generations of Adam.* In this chapter Moses briefly recites the length of time which had

intervened between the creation of the world and the deluge; and also slightly touches on some portion of the history of that period. And although we do not comprehend the design of the Spirit, in leaving unrecorded great and memorable events, it is, nevertheless, our business to reflect on many things which are passed over in silence. I entirely disapprove of those speculations, which every one frames for himself from light conjectures; nor will I furnish readers with the occasion of indulging themselves in this respect; yet it may, in some degree, be gathered from a naked and apparently dry narration, what was the state of those times, as we shall see in the proper places. "The book," according to the Hebrew phrase, is taken for a catalogue. "The generations" signify a continuous succession of a race, or a continuous progeny. Further, the design with which this catalogue was made, was, to inform us, that in the great, or rather, we might say, prodigious multitude of men, there was always a number, though small, who worshipped God; and that this number was wonderfully preserved by celestial guardianship, lest the name of God should be entirely obliterated, and the seed of the Church should fail.

In the day that God created. He does not restrict these "generations" to the day of the creation, but only points out their commencement; and, at the same time, he distinguishes between our first parents and the rest of mankind, because God had brought them into life by a singular method, whereas others had sprung from a previous stock, and had been born of parents.[1] Moreover, Moses again repeats what he had before stated, that Adam was formed according to the image of God, because the excellency and dignity of this favour could not be sufficiently celebrated. It was already a great thing, that the principal place among the creatures was given to man; but it is a nobility far more

---

[1] "Il discerne les premiers hommes d'avec les autres, aus quels Dieu a prolongé la vie en une façon singuliere : combien qu'ils ne fussent de si haute ne si noble race."—*Fr. Trans.* It will be perceived that this translation differs materially in sense from that given above; but, after the fullest consideration, the Editor adheres to his own, as a more literal rendering of the original Latin, and as being more in accordance with the reasoning of the Author.—*Ed.*

exalted, that he should bear resemblance to his Creator, as a son does to his father. It was not indeed possible for God to act more liberally towards man, than by impressing his own glory upon him, thus making him, as it were, a living image of the Divine wisdom and justice. This also is of force in repelling the calumnies of the wicked, who would gladly transfer the blame of their wickedness to their Maker, had it not been expressly declared, that man was formed by nature a different being from that which he has now become, through the fault of his own defection from God.

2. *Male and female created he them.* This clause commends the sacred bond of marriage, and the inseparable union of the husband and the wife. For when Moses has mentioned only *one*, he immediately afterwards includes *both* under *one* name. And he assigns a common name indiscriminately to both, in order that posterity might learn more sacredly to cherish this connection between each other, when they saw that their first parents were denominated as one person. The trifling inference of Jewish writers, that married persons *only* are called Adam, (or man,) is refuted by the history of the creation; nor truly did the Spirit, in this place, mean anything else, than that after the appointment of marriage, the husband and the wife were like one man. Moreover, he records the blessing pronounced upon them, that we may observe in it the wonderful kindness of God in continuing to grant it; yet let us know that by the depravity and wickedness of men it was, in some degree, interrupted.

3. *And begat a son in his own likeness.* We have lately said that Moses traces the offspring of Adam only through the line of Seth, to propose for our consideration the succession of the Church. In saying that Seth begat a son after his own image, he refers in part to the first origin of our nature: at the same time its corruption and pollution is to be noticed, which having been contracted by Adam through the fall, has flowed down to all his posterity. If he had remained upright, he would have transmitted to all his children what he had received: but now we read that Seth, as well as the rest, was

defiled ; because Adam, who had fallen from his original state, could beget none but such as were like himself. If any one should object that Seth with his family had been elected by the special grace of God : the answer is easy and obvious ; namely, that a supernatural remedy does not prevent carnal generation from participating in the corruption of sin. Therefore, according to the flesh, Seth was born a sinner ; but afterwards he was renewed by the grace of the Spirit. This sad instance of the holy patriarch furnishes us with ample occasion to deplore our own wretchedness.

4. *And the days of Adam after he had begotten Seth.* In the number of years here recorded we must especially consider the long period which the patriarchs lived together. For through six successive ages, when the family of Seth had grown into a great people, the voice of Adam might daily resound, in order to renew the memory of the creation, the fall, and the punishment of man ; to testify of the hope of salvation which remained after chastisement, and to recite the judgments of God, by which all might be instructed. After his death his sons might indeed deliver, as from hand to hand, what they had learned, to their descendants ; but far more efficacious would be t' a instruction from the mouth of him, who had been himself the eye-witness of all these things. Yet so wonderful, and even monstrous, was the general obstinacy, that not even the sounder part of the human race could be retained in the obedience and the fear of God.

5. *And he died.* This clause, which records the death of each patriarch, is by no means superfluous. For it warns us that death was not in vain denounced against men ; and that we are now exposed to the curse to which man was doomed, unless we obtain deliverance elsewhere. In the meantime, we must reflect upon our lamentable condition ; namely, that the image of God being destroyed, or, at least, obliterated in us, we scarcely retain the faint shadow of a life, from which we are hastening to death. And it is useful, in a picture of so many ages, to behold, at one glance, the continual course and tenor of divine vengeance ; because, otherwise, we imagine that

God is in some way forgetful; and to nothing are we more prone than to dream of immortality on earth, unless death is frequently brought before our eyes.

22. *And Enoch walked with God.* Undoubtedly Enoch is honoured with peculiar praise among the men of his own age, when it is said that he walked with God. Yet both Seth and Enoch, and Cainan, and Mahalaleel, and Jared, were then living, whose piety was celebrated in the former part of the chapter.[1] As that age could not be rude, or barbarous, which had so many most excellent teachers; we hence infer, that the probity of this holy man, whom the Holy Spirit exempted from the common order, was rare and almost singular. Meanwhile, a method is here pointed out of guarding against being carried away by the perverse manners of those with whom we are conversant. For public custom is as a violent tempest; both because we easily suffer ourselves to be led hither and thither by the multitude, and because every one thinks what is commonly received must be right and lawful; just as swine contract an itching from each other; nor is there any contagion worse, and more loathsome than that of evil examples. Hence we ought the more diligently to notice the brief description of a holy life, contained in the words, "Enoch walked with God." Let those, then, who please, glory in living according to the custom of others; yet the Spirit of God has established a rule of living well and rightly, by which we depart from the examples of men who do not form their life and manners according to the law of God. For he who, pouring contempt upon the word of God, yields himself up to the imitation of the world, must be regarded as living to the devil. Moreover, (as I have just now hinted,) all the rest of the patriarchs are not deprived of the praise of righteousness; but a remarkable example is set before us in the person of one man, who stood firmly in the season of most dreadful dissipation; in order that, if we wish to live rightly and orderly, we may learn to regard God more than men. For the language which Moses uses is of the same force as if he had said, that Enoch, lest he should be drawn aside by the

---

[1] " Superiori capite." Doubtless a mistake.—*Ed.*

corruptions of men, had respect to God alone; so that, with a pure conscience, as under his eyes, he might cultivate uprightness.

24. *And he was not, for God took him.* He must be shamelessly contentious, who will not acknowledge that something extraordinary is here pointed out. All are, indeed, taken out of the world by death; but Moses plainly declares that Enoch was taken out of the world by an unusual mode, and was received by the Lord in a miraculous manner. For לקה, (*lakah,*) among the Hebrews signifies ' to take to one's self,' as well as simply to take. But, without insisting on the *word,* it suffices to hold fast the thing itself; namely, that Enoch, in the middle period of life, suddenly, and in an unexampled method, vanished from the sight of men, because the Lord took him away, as we read was also done with respect to Elijah. Since, in the translation of Enoch, an example of immortality was exhibited; there is no doubt that God designed to elevate the minds of his saints with certain faith before their death; and to mitigate, by this consolation, the dread which they might entertain of death, seeing they would know that a better life was elsewhere laid up for them. It is, however, remarkable that Adam himself was deprived of this support of faith and of comfort. For since that terrible judgment of God, 'Thou shalt die the death,' was constantly sounding in his ears, he very greatly needed some solace, in order that he might in death have something else to reflect upon than curse and destruction. But it was not till about one hundred and fifty years after his death,[1] that the translation of Enoch took place, which was to be as a visible representation of a blessed resurrection; by which, if Adam had been enlightened, he might have girded himself with equanimity for his own departure. Yet, since

[1] Adam died at the age of　　　　930.
Enoch was born when Adam was　　622, } Age of the world,
and was translated when he himself was 365. }　　987.
So that Adam had been dead 57 years when Enoch was translated. Whence it would appear that either the word " centum," a hundred, had slipped by mistake from Calvin's pen; or which is more probable, that, though the two Latin editions before the Editor, have the mistake, the more early ones were free from it. For the French version and the Old English one are correct.—*Ed.*

the Lord, in inflicting punishment, had moderated its rigour, and since Adam himself had heard from his own mouth, what was sufficient to afford him no slight alleviation ; contented with this kind of remedy, it became his duty patiently to bear, both the continual cross in this world, and also the bitter and sorrowful termination of his life. But whereas others were not taught in the same manner, by a manifest oracle to hope for victory over the serpent, there was, in the translation of Enoch, an instruction for all the godly, that they should not keep their hope confined within the boundaries of this mortal life. For Moses shows that this translation was a proof of the Divine love towards Enoch, by connecting it immediately with his pious and upright life. Nevertheless, to be deprived of life is not in itself desirable. It follows, therefore, that he was taken to a better abode ; and that even when he was a sojourner in the world, he was received into a heavenly country; as the Apostle, in the Epistle to the Hebrews, (xi. 5,) plainly teaches. Moreover, if it be inquired, why Enoch was translated, and what is his present condition; I answer, that his transition was by a peculiar privilege, such as that of other men would have been, if they had remained in their first state.[1] For although it was necessary for him to put off what was corruptible; yet was he exempt from that violent separation, from which nature shrinks. In short, his translation was a placid and joyful departure out of the world. Yet he was not received into celestial glory, but only freed from the miseries of the present life, until Christ should come, the first-fruits of those who shall rise again. And since he was one of the members of the Church, it was necessary that he should wait until they all shall go forth together, to meet Christ, that the whole body may be united to its Head. Should any one bring as an objection the saying of the Apostle, ' It is appointed unto all men once to die,' (Heb. ix. 27,) the solution is easy, namely, that death is not always the separation of the soul

---

[1] " S'ils fussent demeurez en leur premier estat." These words, in the French translation, have no corresponding passage in the original, but are so obvious an explanation of Calvin's language, that they are here translated.—Ed.

from the body; but they are said to die, who put off their
corruptible nature: and such will be the death of those who
will be found surviving at the last day.

29. *And he called his name Noah, saying, This same shall
comfort us concerning our work.*   In the Hebrew language, the
etymology of the verb נחם, (*nacham,*) does not correspond
with the noun נוח, (*noach,*) unless we call the letter מ, (*mem,*)
superfluous; as sometimes, in composition, certain letters are
redundant.   נוח signifies to *give rest,* but נחם to *comfort.*
The name Noah is derived from the former verb.   Wherefore, there is either the transmutation of one letter into
another, or only a bare *allusion,* when Lamech says, " This
same shall comfort us concerning our work."[1]   But as to the
point in hand, there is no doubt that he promises to himself
an alleviation, or solace, of his labours.   But it is asked,
whence he had conceived such hope from a son whose disposition he could not yet have discerned.   The Jews do not
judge erroneously in declaring Lamech's expression to be a
prophecy; but they are too gross in restricting to agriculture
what is applicable to all those miseries of human life which
proceed from the curse of God, and are the fruits of sin.   I
come, indeed, to this conclusion; that the holy fathers
anxiously sighed, when, being surrounded with so many evils,
they were continually reminded of the first origin of all evils,
and regarded themselves as under the displeasure of God.
Therefore in the expression, " the toil of our hands," there is
the figure *synecdoche;* because under one kind of toil he comprises the whole miserable state into which mankind had
fallen.   For they undoubtedly remembered what Moses has
related above, concerning the laborious, sad, and anxious life
to which Adam had been doomed: and since the wickedness
of man was daily increasing, no mitigation of the penalty
could be hoped for, unless the Lord should bring unexpected
succour.   It is probable that they were very earnestly look-

[1] See Schindler's Lexicon, *sub voce* נחם, No. III. and also, *sub voce*
נוח, as a proper name, where he derives the latter word from the former,
" litera מ abjecta, aut, quod consolatio sit quies, recreatio."—*Ed.*

ing for the mercy of God; for their faith was strong, and necessity urged them ardently to desire help. But that the name was not rashly given to Noah, we may infer hence, that Moses expressly notes it as a thing worthy to be remembered. Certainly some meaning was couched under the names of other patriarchs; yet he passes by the reason why they were so called, and only insists upon this name of Noah. Therefore the contentious reader is not to be allowed hence to pronounce a judgment, that there was something peculiar in Noah, which did not suit others before him. I have, then, no doubt that Lamech hoped for something rare and unwonted from his son; and that, too, by the inspiration of the Spirit. Some suppose him to have been deceived, inasmuch as he believed that Noah was the Christ; but they adduce no rational conjecture in support of the opinion. It is more probable, that, seeing something great was promised concerning his son, he did not refrain from mixing his own imagination with the oracle; as holy men are also sometimes wont to exceed the measure of revelation, and thus it comes to pass, that they neither touch heaven nor earth.

32. *And Noah was five hundred years old.* Concerning the fathers whom Moses has hitherto enumerated, it is not easy to conjecture whether each of them was the first born of his family or not; for he only wished to follow the continued succession of the Church. But God, to prevent men from being elated by a vain confidence in the flesh, frequently chooses for himself those who are posterior in the order of nature. I am, therefore, uncertain whether Moses has recorded the catalogue of those whom God preferred to others; or of those who, by right of primogeniture, held the chief rank among their brethren; I am also uncertain how many sons each had. With respect to Noah, it plainly appears that he had no more than three sons; and this Moses purposely declares the more frequently, that we may know that the whole of his family was preserved. But they, in my opinion, err, who think that in this place the chastity of Noah is proclaimed, because he led a single life through nearly five centuries. For it is not said that he was unmarried till that time; nor even in what year

of his life he had begun to be a father. But, in simply mentioning the time in which he was warned of the future deluge, Moses also adds, that at the same time, or thereabouts, he was the father of three sons ; not that he already had them, but because they were born not long afterwards. That he had, indeed, survived his five hundredth year before Shem was born, will be evident from the eleventh chapter ; concerning the other two nothing is known with certainty, except that Japheth was the younger.[1] It is wonderful, that, from the time when he had received the dreadful message respecting the destruction of the human race, he was not prevented, by the greatness of his grief, from intercourse with his wife ; but it was necessary that some remains should survive, because this family was destined for the restoration of the second world. Although we do not read at what time his sons took wives, I yet think it was done long before the deluge ; but they were unfruitful by the providence of God, who had determined to preserve only eight souls.

CHAPTER VI.

1. AND it came to pass, when men began to multiply on the face of the earth, and daughters were born unto them,

1. Et fuit, quum cœpissent homines multiplicari in superficie terræ, filiæque natæ essent eis:

[1] This inference, that Japheth was the younger son, Calvin seems to have drawn from a translation of Gen. x. 21, different from our own. In our version Shem is there called "the brother of Japheth the elder." Calvin translates the passage, "the elder" brother of Japheth. But commentators are generally agreed that the English version is right. It not only gives the more natural sense of the original, but is confirmed by collateral testimony. For it is clear that Noah began to have children in his five hundredth year. Shem was one hundred years old two years after the flood, and therefore was born when his father was five hundred and two years old. Some one, then, of Noah's sons must have been born before this. Now we are told that Ham was the younger son, (Gen. ix. 24.) Therefore Japheth must have been his first-born.—See *Patrick's* and *Bush's Commentaries*, and *Wells' Geography of the Old Testament.—Ed.*

2. That the sons of God saw the daughters of men that they *were* fair; and they took them wives of all which they chose.

3. And the Lord said, My Spirit shall not always strive with man, for that he also *is* flesh: yet his days shall be an hundred and twenty years.

4. There were giants in the earth in those days; and also after that, when the sons of God came in unto the daughters of men, and they bare *children* to them, the same *became* mighty men which *were* of old, men of renown.

5. And God saw that the wickedness of man *was* great in the earth, and *that* every imagination of the thoughts of his heart *was* only evil continually.

6. And it repented the Lord that he had made man on the earth, and it grieved him at his heart.

7. And the Lord said, I will destroy man whom I have created from the face of the earth; both man, and beast, and the creeping thing, and the fowls of the air; for it repenteth me that I have made them.

8. But Noah found grace in the eyes of the Lord.

9. These *are* the generations of Noah: Noah was a just man *and* perfect in his generations, *and* Noah walked with God.

10. And Noah begat three sons, Shem, Ham, and Japheth.

11. The earth also was corrupt before God, and the earth was filled with violence.

12. And God looked upon the earth, and, behold, it was corrupt; for all flesh had corrupted his way upon the earth.

13. And God said unto Noah, The end of all flesh is come before me; for the earth is filled with violence through them; and, behold, I will destroy them with the earth.

14. Make thee an ark of gopher wood; rooms shalt thou make in the ark, and shalt pitch it within and without with pitch.

15. And this *is the fashion* which thou shalt make it *of:* The length of

2. Tunc viderunt filii Dei filias hominum quod pulchræ essent: et acceperunt sibi uxores ex omnibus quas elegerant.

3. Et dixit Jehova, Non disceptabit Spiritus meus cum homine in sæculum, eo quod sit etiam ipse caro: et erunt dies ejus centum et viginti anni.

4. Gigantes fuerunt in terra in diebus illis: et etiam postquam ingressi sunt filii Dei ad filias hominum, genuerunt eis: isti sunt potentes, qui a sæculo *fuerunt* viri nominis.

5. Et vidit Jehova quod multa esset malitia hominum in terra, et *quod* omne figmentum cogitationum cordis eorum tantummodo esset malum omni die:

6. Tunc pœnituit Jehovam quod fecisset hominem in terra, et doluit in corde suo.

7. Et dixit Jehova, Delebo hominem quem creavi, a superficie terræ, ab homine usque ad jumentum, usque ad reptile, et usque ad volatile cœli: quia pœnitet me quod fecerim ea.

8. Et Noah invenit gratiam in oculis Jehovæ.

9. Istæ sunt generationes Noah. Noah vir justus, perfectus fuit in generationibus suis: cum Deo ambulavit Noah.

10. Genuit vero Noah tres filios, Sem, Cham, et Jepheth.

11. Et corrupta erat terra coram Deo: repleta erat terra iniquitate.

12. Et vidit Deus terram, et ecce, corrupta erat: nam corruperat omnis caro viam suam super terram.

13. Dixit itaque Deus ad Noah, Finis universæ carnis venit coram me: quia repleta est terra iniquitate a facie eorum: et ecce, ego disperdam eos cum terra.

14. Fac tibi arcam e lignis gopher, mansiunculas facies in arca, et bituminabis eam intrinsecus et extrinsecus bitumine.

15. Et hæc *mensura* qua facies eam: Trecentorum cubitorum

the ark *shall be* three hundred cubits, the breadth of it fifty cubits, and the height of it thirty cubits.

16. A window shalt thou make to the ark, and in a cubit shalt thou finish it above ; and the door of the ark shalt thou set in the side thereof ; *with* lower, second, and third *stories* shalt thou make it.

17. And, behold, I, even I, do bring a flood of waters upon the earth, to destroy all flesh wherein *is* the breath of life, from under heaven ; *and* every thing that *is* in the earth shall die.

18. But with thee will I establish my covenant ; and thou shalt come into the ark, thou, and thy sons, and thy wife, and thy sons' wives with thee.

19. And of every living thing of all flesh, two of every *sort* shalt thou bring into the ark, to keep *them* alive with thee ; they shall be male and female.

20. Of fowls after their kind, and of cattle after their kind, of every creeping thing of the earth after his kind, two of every *sort* shall come unto thee, to keep *them* alive.

21. And take thou unto thee of all food that is eaten, and thou shalt gather *it* to thee ; and it shall be for food for thee, and for them.

22. Thus did Noah ; according to all that God commanded him, so did he.

erit longitudo arcæ, quinquaginta cubitorum latitudo ejus : et triginta cubitorum altitudo ejus.

16. Fenestram facies arcæ, et in cubito consummabis eam superne : ostium vero arcæ in latere ejus pones : inferiora et secunda, et tertia facies in ea.

17. Et ego ecce *ego* adduco diluvium aquarum super terram, ut disperdam omnem carnem in qua est spiritus vitæ sub cœlo : omne quod est in terra morietur.

18. Et statuam pactum meum tecum, et ingredieris arcam tu, et filii tui, et uxor tua, et uxores filiorum tuorum tecum.

19. Et ex omni vivente, ex omni carne, bina ex omnibus introduces in arcam, ut viva serventur tecum, masculus et fœmina erunt.

20. Ex volatili secundum speciem suam, et ex animali secundum speciem suam, ex omni reptili terræ secundum speciem suam, bina ex omnibus ingredientur ad te, ut viva conserventur.

21. Et tu cape tibi ex omni esca quæ comeditur, et congregabis tibi, eritque tibi et illis ad vescendum.

22. Et fecit Noah juxta omnia quæ præceperat ei Deus, sic fecit.

1. *And it came to pass, when men began to multiply.* Moses, having enumerated in order, ten patriarchs, with whom the worship of God remained pure, now relates, that their families also were corrupted. But this narration must be traced to an earlier period than the five hundredth year of Noah. For, in order to make a transition to the history of the deluge, he prefaces it by declaring the whole world to have been so corrupt, that scarcely anything was left to God, out of the widely spread defection. That this may be the more apparent, the principle is to be kept in memory, that the world was then, as if divided into two parts ; because the family of Seth cherished the pure and lawful worship of God, from

which the rest had fallen. Now, although all mankind had been formed for the worship of God, and therefore sincere religion ought everywhere to have reigned; yet since the greater part had prostituted itself, either to an entire contempt of God, or to depraved superstitions; it was fitting that the small portion which God had adopted, by special privilege, to himself, should remain separate from others. It was, therefore, base ingratitude in the posterity of Seth, to mingle themselves with the children of Cain, and with other profane races; because they voluntarily deprived themselves of the inestimable grace of God. For it was an intolerable profanation, to pervert, and to confound, the order appointed by God. It seems at first sight frivolous, that the sons of God should be so severely condemned, for having chosen for themselves beautiful wives from the daughters of men. But we must know first, that it is not a light crime to violate a distinction established by the Lord; secondly, that for the worshippers of God to be separated from profane nations, was a sacred appointment which ought reverently to have been observed, in order that a Church of God might exist upon earth; thirdly, that the disease was desperate, seeing that men rejected the remedy divinely prescribed for them. In short, Moses points it out as the most extreme disorder; when the sons of the pious, whom God had separated to himself from others, as a peculiar and hidden treasure, became degenerate.

That ancient figment, concerning the intercourse of angels with women, is abundantly refuted by its own absurdity; and it is surprising that learned men should formerly have been fascinated by ravings so gross and prodigious. The opinion also of the Chaldean paraphrast is frigid; namely, that promiscuous marriages between the sons of nobles, and the daughters of plebeians, is condemned. Moses, then, does not distinguish the sons of God from the daughters of men, because they were of dissimilar nature, or of different origin; but because they were the sons of God by adoption, whom he had set apart for himself; while the rest remained in their original condition. Should any one object, that they who had shamefully departed from the faith, and the obedience which

God required, were unworthy to be accounted the sons of God;
the answer is easy, that the honour is not ascribed to them,
but to the grace of God, which had hitherto been conspicuous
in their families.   For when Scripture speaks of the sons of
God, sometimes it has respect to eternal election, which extends
only to the lawful heirs ; sometimes to external vocation, according to which many wolves are within the fold; and though,
in fact, they are strangers, yet they obtain the name of
sons, until the Lord shall disown them.   Yea, even by giving
them a title so honourable, Moses reproves their ingratitude,
because, leaving their heavenly Father, they prostituted
themselves as deserters.

2. *That they were fair.*   Moses does not deem it worthy of
condemnation that regard was had to beauty, in the choice of
wives ; but that mere lust reigned.   For marriage is a thing
too sacred to allow that men should be induced to it by the
lust of the eyes.[1]   For this union is inseparable, comprising
all the parts of life ; as we have before seen, that the woman
was created to be a helper of the man.   Therefore our appetite becomes brutal, when we are so ravished with the charms
of beauty, that those things which are chief are not taken
into the account.   Moses more clearly describes the violent
impetuosity of their lust, when he says, that " they took wives
of all that they chose ;" by which he signifies, that the sons of
God did not make their choice from those possessed of necessary endowments, but wandered without discrimination,
rushing onward according to their lust.   We are taught,
however, in these words, that temperance is to be used in
holy wedlock, and that its profanation is no light crime before God.   For it is not fornication which is here condemned
in the sons of the saints, but the too great indulgence of license in choosing themselves wives.   And truly, it is impossible but that, in the succession of time, the sons of God should
degenerate, when they thus bound themselves in the same yoke
with unbelievers.   And this was the extreme policy of Ba-

1 " Est autem res sanctior conjugium quam ut oculis ferri homines
debeant ad voluptatem coitus."

laam; that, when the power of cursing was taken from him, he commanded women to be privily sent by the Midianites, who might seduce the people of God to impious defection. Thus, as in the sons of the patriarchs, of whom Moses now treats, the forgetfulness of that grace which had been divinely imparted to them was, in itself, a grievous evil, inasmuch as they formed illicit marriages after their own lust; a still worse addition was made, when, by mingling themselves with the wicked, they profaned the worship of God, and fell away from the faith; a corruption which is almost always wont to follow the former.

3. *My Spirit shall not always strive.* Although Moses had before shown that the world had proceeded to such a degree of wickedness and impiety, as ought not any longer to be borne; yet in order to prove more certainly, that the vengeance by which the whole world was drowned, was not less just than severe, he introduces God himself as the speaker. For there is greater weight in the declaration when pronounced by God's own mouth, that the wickedness of men was too deplorable to leave any apparent hope of remedy, and that therefore there was no reason why he should spare them. Moreover, since this would be a terrible example of divine anger, at the bare hearing of which we are even now afraid, it was necessary to be declared, that God had not been impelled by the heat of his anger into precipitation, nor had been more severe than was right; but was almost compelled, by necessity, utterly to destroy the whole world, except one single family. For men commonly do not refrain from accusing God of excessive haste; nay, they will even deem him cruel for taking vengeance of the sins of men. Therefore, that no man may murmur, Moses here, in the person of God, pronounces the depravity of the world to have been intolerable, and obstinately incurable by any remedy. This passage, however, is variously expounded. In the first place, some of the Hebrews derive the word which Moses uses from the root נָדָן,[1] (*nadan,*) which signifies a *scabbard.* And hence they

[1] " נָּדֻן. *Vagina,* in qua gladius est reconditus. Per metaphoram *corpus,* cui anima, tanquam gladius vaginæ, inest." "A scabbard in which

elicit the meaning that God was unwilling for his Spirit to be any longer held captive in a human body, as if enclosed like a sword in the scabbard. But because the exposition is distorted, and savours of the delirium of the Manichees, as if the soul of man were a portion of the Divine Spirit, it is by us to be rejected. Even among the Jews, it is a more commonly received opinion, that the word in question is from the root דון, (doon.) But since it often means to judge, and sometimes to litigate, hence also arise different interpretations. For some explain the passage to mean, that God will no longer deign to govern men by his Spirit; because the Spirit of God acts the part of a judge within us, when he so enlightens us with reason that we pursue what is right. Luther, according to his custom, applies the term to the external jurisdiction which God exercises by the ministry of the prophets, as if some one of the patriarchs had said in an assembly, 'We must cease from crying aloud; because it is an unbecoming thing that the Spirit of God, who speaks through us, should any longer weary himself in reproving the world.' This is indeed ingeniously spoken; but because we must not seek the sense of Scripture in uncertain conjectures, I interpret the words simply to mean, that the Lord, as if wearied with the obstinate perverseness of the world, denounces that vengeance as present, which he had hitherto deferred. For as long as the Lord suspends punishment, he, in a certain sense, strives with men, especially if either by threats, or by examples of gentle chastisement, he invites them to repentance. In this way he had striven already, some centuries, with the world, which, nevertheless, was perpetually becoming worse. And now, as if wearied out, he declares that he has no mind to contend any longer.[1] For when God, by inviting the unbelievers to repentance, had long striven with them; the deluge put an end to the controversy. However, I do not entirely reject the opinion of Luther, that God having seen the de-

---

the sword is concealed. Metaphorically, the *body* in which the soul is, as a sword in its scabbard."—*Schindler.*—*Ed.*

[1] " Acsi Gallice quis diceret, c'est trop plaider;" as if any one should say in French, " This is to plead too much."

plorable wickedness of men, would not allow his prophets to
spend their labour in vain. But the general declaration is
not to be restricted to that particular case. When the Lord
says, 'I will not contend for ever,' he utters his censure on
an excessive and incurable obstinacy; and, at the same time,
gives proof of the divine long-suffering: as if he would say,
There will never be an end of contention, unless some unpre-
cedented act of vengeance cuts off the occasion of it. The
Greek interpreters, deceived by the similitude of one letter to
another, have improperly read, 'shall not remain:'[1] which
has commonly been explained, as if men were then deprived
of a sound and correct judgment; but this has nothing to do
with the present passage.

For that he also is flesh. The reason is added why
there is no advantage to be expected from further contention. The Lord here seems to place his Spirit in opposition
to the carnal nature of men. In which method, Paul declares
that the ' animal man does not receive those things which
belong to the Spirit, and that they are foolishness unto him,'
(1 Cor. ii. 14.) The meaning of the passage therefore is,
that it is in vain for the Spirit of God to dispute with the
flesh, which is incapable of reason. God gives the name of
flesh as a mark of ignominy to men, whom he, nevertheless, had
formed in his own image. And this is a mode of speaking
familiar to Scripture. They who restrict this appellation to
the inferior part of the soul are greatly deceived. For since
the soul of man is vitiated in every part, and the reason of
man is not less blind than his affections are perverse, the
whole is properly called carnal. Therefore, let us know, that
the whole man is naturally flesh, until by the grace of regeneration he begins to be spiritual. Now, as it regards the
words of Moses, there is no doubt that they contain a grievous complaint, together with a reproof on the part of God.
Man ought to have excelled all other creatures, on account
of the mind with which he was endued; but now, alienated
from right reason, he is almost like the cattle of the field.

---

[1] "Non permanebit."—*Vulgate.* "Οὐ μὴ καταμείνῃ τὸ πνεῦμά μου."
—*Sept. See on the word* רוח, *Poole's Synopsis in loco,* and *Professor
Lee's Lexicon.*

Therefore God inveighs against the degenerate and corrupt
nature of men; because, by their own fault, they are fallen to
that degree of fatuity, that now they approach more nearly
to beasts than to true men, such as they ought to be, in
consequence of their creation. He intimates, however, this
to be an adventitious fault, that man has a relish only for the
earth, and that, the light of intelligence being extinct, he follows his own desires. I wonder that the emphasis contained
in the particle בְּשַׁגַּם, (beshagam,) has been overlooked by
commentators; for the words mean, ' on this account, because
he also is flesh.'   In which language God complains, that
the order appointed by him has been so greatly disturbed, that
his own image has been transformed into flesh.

Yet his days shall be one hundred and twenty years.   Certain
writers of antiquity, such as Lactantius, and others, have
too grossly blundered, in thinking that the term of human life
was limited within this space of time; whereas, it is evident,
that the language used in this place refers not to the private
life of any one, but to a time of repentance to be granted to
the whole world.   Moreover, here also the admirable benignity of God is apparent, in that he, though wearied with
the wickedness of men, yet postpones the execution of extreme vengeance for more than a century.   But here arises
an apparent discrepancy.   For Noah departed this life when
he had completed nine hundred and fifty years.   It is however
said that he lived from the time of the deluge three hundred
and fifty years.   Therefore, on the day he entered the ark he
was six hundred years old.   Where then will the twenty
years be found? The Jews answer, that these years were cut
off in consequence of the increasing wickedness of men.   But
there is no need of that subterfuge; when the Scripture
speaks of the five hundredth year of his age, it does not affirm,
that he had actually reached that point.   And this mode of
speaking, which takes into account the beginning of a period,
as well as its end, is very common.   Therefore, inasmuch as
the greater part of the fifth century of his life was passed, so
that he was nearly five hundred years old, he is said to have
been of that age.[1]

[1] The whole of this passage might have been more clearly expressed.

4. *There were giants in the earth.* Among the innumerable
kinds of corruptions with which the earth was filled, Moses
especially records one in this place ; namely, that giants practised great violence and tyranny. I do not, however, suppose, that he speaks of all the men of this age ; but of certain
individuals, who, being stronger than the rest, and relying on
their own might and power, exalted themselves unlawfully,
and without measure. As to the Hebrew noun, נפלים,
(nephilim,) its origin is known to be from the verb נפל,
(naphal,) which is *to fall;* but grammarians do not agree concerning its etymology. Some think that they were so called
because they exceeded the common stature ;[1] others, because
the countenance of men fell at the sight of them, on account
of the enormous size of their body; or, because all fell prostrate
through terror of their magnitude. To me there seems more
truth in the opinion of those who say, that a similitude is taken
from a torrent, or an impetuous tempest ; for as a storm and
torrent, violently falling, lays waste and destroys the fields,
so these robbers brought destruction and desolation into the
world.[2] Moses does not indeed say, that they were of extraordinary stature, but only that they were robust. Elsewhere, I acknowledge, the same word denotes vastness of stature, which was formidable to those who explored the land
of Canaan, (Josh. xiii. 34.) But Moses does not distinguish
those of whom he speaks, in this place, from other men, so

At the close of chapter v. it is said, " Noah was five hundred years old :
and Noah begat Shem, Ham, and Japheth." In the verse on which
Calvin here comments, it is stated, that man's days on earth "shall be
one hundred and twenty years ;" but in chapter vii. 11, we are told, that
the deluge came " in the six hundredth year of Noah's life." This would
pare down the one hundred and twenty years to one hundred ; and therefore Calvin asks, " Where are the remaining twenty to be found ?" To
answer this question, he shows that there was something indefinite in the
statement of Noah's age in the first of these passages, and Moses does
not say that the flood began precisely in that year. He therefore concludes that, according to a common mode of speaking among the Hebrews,
Moses states in general terms, that Noah was five hundred years old when
he was in the fifth century of his life ; and therefore he would infer, that
Noah was about four hundred and eighty years of age at the time referred to : if one hundred and twenty years be added, it will make him
six hundred years old at the time of his entering the ark.—*Ed.*

[1] " Quia *excidissent* a communi statura ;" a misprint, undoubtedly, for
excedissent.—*Ed.*

[2] " Vatablus in Poli Synopsi."—*Ed.*

much by the size of their bodies, as by their robberies, and their lust of dominion. In the context, the particle םַגְו, *(vegam,)* which is interposed, is emphatical. Jerome, after whom certain other interpreters have blundered, has rendered this passage in the worst possible manner.[1] For it is literally rendered thus, 'And even after the sons of God had gone in to the daughters of men ;' as if he had said, *Moreover*, or, ' And at this time.' For in the first place, Moses relates that there were giants ; then he subjoins, that there were also others from among that promiscuous offspring, which was produced when the sons of God mingled themselves with the daughters of men. It would not have been wonderful if such outrage had prevailed among the posterity of Cain ; but the universal pollution is more clearly evident from this, that the holy seed was defiled by the same corruption. That a contagion so great should have spread through the few families which ought to have constituted the sanctuary of God, is no slight aggravation of the evil. The giants, then, had a prior origin ; but afterwards those who were born of promiscuous marriages imitated their example.

The same became *mighty men which* were *of old.*[2] The word ' age' is commonly understood to mean *antiquity :* as if Moses had said, that they who first exercised tyranny or power in the world, together with an excessive licentiousness, and an unbridled lust of dominion, had begun from this race. Yet there are those who expound the expression, ' from the age,' to mean, *in the presence of the world :* for the Hebrew word םָלֹעֽ, *(olam,)* has also this signification.[3] Some think that this was spoken proverbially ; because the age immediately posterior to the deluge had produced none like them.

---

[1] " Gigantes autem erant super terram in diebus illis. Postquam enim ingressi sunt," &c. There were giants on the earth in those days. For after the sons of God, &c.—*Vulgate.* The words which the Vulgate translates, ' for after,'—plainly accounting for the birth of the giants from the intercourse alluded to in the next clause,—are translated in the Septuagint, καὶ μετ᾽ ἐκεῖνο, " and after this ;" which favours the interpretation of Calvin, with which also the English version corresponds. —*Ed.*

[2] " Ipsi potentes a sæculo." ' They were mighty men from the age ;' or, from the old time.—*Ed.*

[3] Vide *Schindler's Lexicon, sub voce* םלעֽ.

The first exposition is the more simple; the sum of the whole, however, is, that they were ferocious tyrants, who separated themselves from the common rank. Their first fault was pride; because, relying on their own strength, they arrogated to themselves more than was due. Pride produced contempt of God, because, being inflated by arrogance, they began to shake off every yoke. At the same time, they were also disdainful and cruel towards men; because it is not possible that they, who would not bear to yield obedience to God, should have acted with moderation towards men. Moses adds, they were " men of renown;" by which he intimates that they boasted of their wickedness, and were, what are called, honourable robbers. Nor is it to be doubted, that they had something more excellent than the common people, which procured for them favour and glory in the world. Nevertheless, under the magnificent title of heroes, they cruelly exercised dominion, and acquired power and fame for themselves, by injuring and oppressing their brethren. And this was the first nobility of the world. Lest any one should too greatly delight himself in a long and dingy line of ancestry; this, I repeat, was the nobility, which raised itself on high, by pouring contempt and disgrace on others. Celebrity of name is not in itself condemned; since it is necessary that they whom the Lord has adorned with peculiar gifts should be pre-eminent among others; and it is advantageous that there should be distinction of ranks in the world. But as ambition is always vicious, and more especially so when joined with a tyrannical ferocity, which causes the more powerful to insult the weak, the evil becomes intolerable. It is, however, much worse, when wicked men gain honour by their crimes; and when, the more audacious any one is in doing injury, the more insolently he boasts of the empty smoke of titles. Moreover, as Satan is an ingenious contriver of falsehoods, by which he would corrupt the truth of God, and in this manner render it suspected, the poets have invented many fables concerning the giants; who are called by them the sons of the Earth, for this reason, as it appears to me, because they rushed forward to acquire dominion, without any example of their ancestors.

5. *And God saw that the wickedness of man was great.*
Moses prosecutes the subject to which he had just alluded,
that God was neither too harsh, nor precipitate in exacting
punishment from the wicked men of the world.   And he
introduces God as speaking after the manner of men, by a
figure which ascribes human affections to God ;[1] because he
could not otherwise express what was very important to be
known ; namely, that God was not induced hastily, or for a
slight cause, to destroy the world.   For by the word *saw*, he
indicates long continued patience ; as if he would say, that
God had not proclaimed his sentence to destroy men, until
after having well observed, and long considered, their case,
he saw them to be past recovery.   Also, what follows has
not a little emphasis, that ' their wickedness was great in
the earth.'   He might have pardoned sins of a less aggravated character : if in one part only of the world impiety had
reigned, other regions might have remained free from punishment.   But now, when iniquity has reached its highest point,
and so pervaded the whole earth, that integrity possesses no
longer a single corner ; it follows, that the time for punishment is more than fully arrived.   A prodigious wickedness, then, everywhere reigned, so that the whole earth was
covered with it.   Whence we perceive that it was not
overwhelmed with a deluge of waters till it had first been
immersed in the pollution of wickedness.

Every imagination of the thoughts of his heart.   Moses has
traced the cause of the deluge to external acts of iniquity, he
now ascends higher, and declares that men were not only
perverse by habit, and by the custom of evil living ; but that
wickedness was too deeply seated in their hearts, to leave any
hope of repentance.   He certainly could not have more
forcibly asserted, that the depravity was such as no moderate
remedy might cure.   It may indeed happen, that men will
sometimes plunge themselves into sin, while yet something
of a sound mind will remain ; but Moses teaches us, that the
mind of those, concerning whom he speaks, was so thoroughly
imbued with iniquity, that the whole presented nothing but

[1] Per ἀνθρωποπάθειαν.

what was to be condemned. For the language he employs is very emphatical : it seemed enough to have said, that their heart was corrupt : but not content with this word, he expressly asserts, "every imagination of the thoughts of the heart ;" and adds the word "only," as if he would deny that there was a drop of good mixed with it.

Continually. Some expound this particle to mean, from commencing infancy ; as if he would say, the depravity of men is very great from the time of their birth. But the more correct interpretation is, that the world had then become so hardened in its wickedness, and was so far from any amendment, or from entertaining any feeling of penitence, that it grew worse and worse as time advanced ; and further, that it was not the folly of a few days, but the inveterate depravity which the children, having received, as by hereditary right, transmitted from their parents to their descendants. Nevertheless, though Moses here speaks of the wickedness which at that time prevailed in the world, the general doctrine [1] is properly and consistently hence elicited. Nor do they rashly distort the passage who extend it to the whole human race. So when David says, 'That all have revolted, that they are become unprofitable, that is, none who does good, no not one ; their throat is an open sepulchre ; there is no fear of God before their eyes,' (Ps. v. 10, and xiv. 3 ;) he deplores, truly, the impiety of his own age ; yet Paul (Rom. iii. 12) does not scruple to extend it to all men of every age : and with justice ; for it is not a mere complaint concerning a few men, but a description of the human mind when left to itself, destitute of the Spirit of God. It is therefore very proper that the obstinacy of the men, who had greatly abused the goodness of God, should be condemned in these words ; yet, at the same time, the true nature of man, when deprived of the grace of the Spirit, is clearly exhibited.

6. *And it repented the Lord that he had made man on the earth.* The repentance which is here ascribed to God does not properly belong to him, but has reference to our under-

---

[1] That is, the "general doctrine" of man's total and universal depravity.—*Ed.*

standing of him. For since we cannot comprehend him as he is, it is necessary that, for our sake, he should, in a certain sense, transform himself. That repentance cannot take place in God, easily appears from this single consideration, that nothing happens which is by him unexpected or unforeseen. The same reasoning, and remark, applies to what follows, that God was affected with grief. Certainly God is not sorrowful or sad; but remains for ever like himself in his celestial and happy repose : yet, because it could not otherwise be known how great is God's hatred and detestation of sin, therefore the Spirit accommodates himself to our capacity. Wherefore, there is no need for us to involve ourselves in thorny and difficult questions, when it is obvious to what end these words of repentance and grief are applied; namely, to teach us, that from the time when man was so greatly corrupted, God would not reckon him among his creatures; as if he would say, ' This is not my workmanship; this is not that man who was formed in my image, and whom I had adorned with such excellent gifts : I do not deign now to acknowledge this degenerate and defiled creature as mine.' Similar to this is what he says, in the second place, concerning grief; that God was so offended by the atrocious wickedness of men, as if they had wounded his heart with mortal grief. There is here, therefore, an unexpressed antithesis between that upright nature which had been created by God, and that corruption which sprung from sin. Meanwhile, unless we wish to provoke God, and to put him to grief, let us learn to abhor and to flee from sin. Moreover, this paternal goodness and tenderness ought, in no slight degree, to subdue in us the love of sin; since God, in order more effectually to pierce our hearts, clothes himself with our affections. This figure, which represents God as transferring to himself what is peculiar to human nature, is called ἀνθρωποπάθεια.

7. *And the Lord said, I will destroy man whom I have created from the face of the earth, both man and beast, &c.* He again introduces God as deliberating, in order that we may the better know that the world was not destroyed without mature counsel on the part of God. For the Spirit of the

Lord designed that we should be diligently admonished on this point, in order that he might cut off occasion for those impious complaints, into which we should be otherwise too ready to break forth. The word *said* here means *decreed;* because God utters no voice, without having inwardly determined what he would do. Besides, he had no need of new counsel, according to the manner of men, as if he were forming a judgment concerning something recently discovered. But all this is said in consideration of our infirmity ; that we may never think of the deluge, but it shall immediately occur to us that the vengeance of God was just. Moreover, God, not content with the punishment of man, proceeds even to beasts, and cattle, and fowls, and every kind of living creatures. In which he seems to exceed the bounds of moderation : for although the impiety of men is hateful to him, yet to what purpose is it to be angry with unoffending animals ? But it is not wonderful that those animals, which were created for man's sake, and lived for his use, should participate in his ruin : neither asses, nor oxen, nor any other animals, had done evil; yet being in subjection to man when he fell, they were drawn with him into the same destruction. The earth was like a wealthy house, well supplied with every kind of provision in abundance and variety. Now, since man has defiled the earth itself with his crimes, and has vilely corrupted all the riches with which it was replenished, the Lord also designed that the monument of his punishment should there be placed : just as if a judge, about to punish a most wicked and nefarious criminal, should, for the sake of greater infamy, command his house to be razed to the foundation. And this all tends to inspire us with a dread of sin ; for we may easily infer how great is its atrocity, when the punishment of it is extended even to the brute creation.

8. *But Noah found grace in the eyes of the Lord.* This is a Hebrew phrase, which signifies that God was propitious to him, and favoured him. For so the Hebrews are accustomed to speak :—' If I have found grace in thy sight,' instead of, ' If I am acceptable to thee,' or, ' If thou wilt grant me thy benevolence or favour.' Which phrase requires to be noticed,

because certain unlearned men infer with futile subtlety,
that if men find grace in God's sight, it is because they seek
it by their own industry and merits. I acknowledge, indeed, that here Noah is declared to have been acceptable to
God, because, by living uprightly and holily, he kept himself pure from the common pollutions of the world ; whence,
however, did he attain this integrity, but from the preventing
grace of God ? The commencement, therefore, of this
favour was gratuitous mercy. Afterwards, the Lord, having
once embraced him, retained him under his own hand, lest
he should perish with the rest of the world.

9. *These are the generations of Noah.* The Hebrew word
תּוֹלְדֹת, *(toledoth,)* properly means generation. It has, however, sometimes a more extended sense, and applies to the
whole history of life ; this indeed seems to be its meaning in
the present place.[1] For when Moses had stated that one man
was found whom God,—when he had determined to destroy
the whole world,—would yet preserve, he briefly describes
what kind of person he was. And, in the first place, asserts,
that he was just and upright among the men of his age : for
here is a different Hebrew noun, דּוֹר, *(dor,)* which signifies an
age, or the time of a life.[2] The word תָּמִים, *(tamim,)* which
the ancient interpreter is accustomed to translate *perfect,*[3] is
of the same force as *upright* or *sincere;* and is opposed to
what is deceitful, pretended, and vain. And Moses does not
rashly connect these two things together; for the world,
being always influenced by external splendour, estimates
justice, not by the affection of the heart, but by bare works.
If, however, we desire to be approved by God, and accounted
righteous before him, we must not only regulate our hands,
and eyes, and feet, in obedience to his Law ; but integrity of
heart is above all things required, and holds the chief place
in the true definition of righteousness. Let us, however,
know that they are called just and upright, not who are in

[1] See *Dathe, in loco.*
[2] Though it also means generation.—See *Gesenius, Schindler, &c.,* sub
voce דּוֹר.
[3] " Noe vir justus atque perfectus ferit."—*Vulgate.* " תמים refers
chiefly to moral integrity, *irreproachable, innocent, honest.*"—*Gesenius.*

every respect perfect, and in whom there is no defect; but who cultivate righteousness purely, and from their heart. Because we are assured that God does not act towards his own people with the rigour of justice, as requiring of them a life according to the perfect rule of the Law; for, if only no hypocrisy reigns within them, but the pure love of rectitude flourishes, and fills their hearts, he pronounces them, according to his clemency, to be righteous.

The clause, " in his generations," is emphatical. For he has already often said, and will soon repeat it, that nothing was more corrupt than that age. Therefore, it was a remarkable instance of constancy, that Noah being surrounded on every side with the filth of iniquity, should hence have contracted no contagion. We know how great is the force of custom, so that nothing is more difficult than to live holily among the wicked, and to avoid being led away by their evil examples. Scarcely is there one in a hundred who has not in his mouth that diabolical proverb, ' We must howl when we are among the wolves;' and the greater part,—framing a rule for themselves from the common practice,—judge everything to be lawful which is generally received. As, however, the singular virtue of Noah is here commended; so let us remember that we are instructed what we ought to do, though the whole world were rushing to its own destruction. If, at the present time, the morals of men are so vitiated, and the whole mode of life so confused, that probity has become most rare; still more vile and dreadful was the confusion in the time of Noah, when he had not even one associate in the worship of God, and in the pursuit of holiness. If he could bear up against the corruptions of the whole world, and against such constant and vehement assaults of iniquity; no excuse is left for us, unless, with equal fortitude of mind, we prosecute a right course through innumerable obstacles of vice. It is not improbable that Moses uses the word generations in the plural number, the more fully to declare what a strenuous and invincible combatant Noah was, who, through so many ages, had remained unaltered. Besides, the manner of cultivating righteousness, which he had adopted, is explained in the context; namely, that he had " walked with God," which excellency he had also commended in the holy father Enoch, in the preceding chapter, where we have stated what the expression means. When the corruption of morals was so great in the earth, if Noah had had respect to man, he would have been cast into a profound labyrinth. He sees, therefore, this to be his only remedy ; namely, to disregard men, that he may fix all his thoughts on God, and make Him the sole Arbiter of his life. Whence it appears, how foolishly the Papists clamour that we ought to follow the fathers ; when the Spirit expressly recalls us from the imitation of men, except so far as they lead us to God. Moses again mentions his three sons, for the purpose of showing that, in the greatest sorrow by which he was almost consumed, he was yet able to have offspring, in order that God might have a small remnant of seed for himself.

11. *The earth also was corrupt before God.* In the former clause of this verse Moses describes that impious contempt of God, which had left no longer any religion in the world; but the light of equity being extinct, all men had plunged into sin. In the second clause he declares, that the love of oppression, that frauds, injuries, rapines, and all kinds of injustice, prevailed. And these are the fruits of impiety, that men, when they have revolted from God,—forgetful of mutual equity among themselves,—are carried forward to insane ferocity, to rapines, and to oppressions of all sorts. God again declares that he had *seen* this ; in order that he may commend his long-suffering to us. The earth is here put for its inhabitants ; and the explanation immediately follows, ' that all flesh had corrupted its way.' Yet the word flesh is not here understood as before, in a bad sense ; but is meant for *men*, without any mark of censure : as in other places of Scripture, ' All flesh shall see the glory of the Lord,' (Isaiah xl. 5.) ' Let all flesh be silent before the Lord,' (Zech. ii. 13.)

13. *And God said unto Noah.* Here Moses begins to relate how Noah would be preserved. And first, he says, that the counsel of God respecting the destruction of the world

was revealed to him. Secondly, that the command to build
the ark was given. Thirdly, that safety was promised him,
if, in obedience to God, he would take refuge in the ark.
These chief points are to be distinctly noted; even as the
Apostle, when he proclaims the faith of Noah, joins fear and
obedience with confidence, (Heb. xi. 7.) And it is certain
that Noah was admonished of the dreadful vengeance which
was approaching; not only in order that he might be confirmed
in his holy purpose, but that, being constrained by fear,
he might the more ardently seek for the favour offered
to him. We know that the impunity of the wicked is sometimes the occasion of alluring even the good to sin: the denunciation, therefore, of future punishment ought to be effectual in restraining the mind of a holy man; lest, by gradual
declension, he should at length relax to the same lasciviousness-
ness. Yet God had special reference to the other point;
namely, that by keeping continually in view the terrible destruction of the world, Noah might be more and more excited
to fear and solicitude. For it was necessary, that in utter
despair of help from any other quarter, he should seek his
safety, by faith, in the ark. For so long as life was promised
to him on earth, never would he have been so intent as he
ought, in the building of the ark; but, being alarmed by the
judgment of God, he earnestly embraces the promise of life
given unto him. He no longer relies upon the natural causes
or means of life; but rests exclusively on the covenant of
God, by which he was to be miraculously preserved. No
labour is now troublesome or difficult to him; nor is he broken
down by long fatigue. For the spur of God's anger pierces
him too sharply to allow him to sleep in carnal delights,
or to faint under temptations, or to be delayed in his
course by vain hope: he rather stirs himself up, both to flee
from sin, and to seek a remedy. And the Apostle teaches,
that it was not the least part of his faith, that through the
fear of those things which were not seen he prepared an ark.
When faith is treated of simply, mercy and the gratuitous
promise come into the account; but when we wish to express all its parts, and to canvass its entire force and nature,
it is necessary that fear also should be joined with it. And,

truly, no one will ever seriously resort to the mercy of God, but he who, having been touched with the threatenings of God, shall dread that judgment of eternal death which they denounce, shall abhor himself on account of his own sins, shall not carelessly indulge his vices, nor slumber in his pollution; but shall anxiously sigh for the remedy of his evils. This was, truly, a peculiar privilege of grace, that God warned Noah of the future deluge. Indeed, he frequently commands his threatenings to be proposed to the elect, and reprobate, in common; that by inviting both to repentance, he may humble the former, and render the latter inexcusable. But while the greater part of mankind, with deaf ears, reject whatever is spoken, he especially turns his discourse to his own people, who are still curable, that by the fear of his judgment he may train them to piety. The condition of the wicked might at that time seem desirable, in comparison with the anxiety of holy Noah. They were securely flattering themselves in their own delights; for we know what Christ declares concerning the luxury of that period, (Luke xvii. 26.) Meanwhile, the holy man, as if the world were every moment going to ruin, groaned anxiously and sorrowfully. But if we consider the end; God granted an inestimable benefit to his servant, in denouncing to him a danger, of which he must beware.

The earth is filled with violence through them.[1] God intimates that men were to be taken away, in order that the earth, which had been polluted by the presence of beings so wicked, might be purified. Moreover, in speaking only of the iniquity and violence, of the frauds and rapines, of which they were guilty towards each other; he does it, not as if he were intending to remit his own claims upon them, but because this was a more gross and palpable demonstration of their wickedness.

14. *Make thee an ark of gopher wood.* Here follows the command to build the ark, in which God wonderfully proved the faith and obedience of his servant. Concerning its structure, there is no reason why we should anxiously inquire,

---

[1] " Repleta est terra iniquitate à facie eorum."

except so far as our own edification is concerned. First, the
Jews are not agreed among themselves respecting the kind
of wood of which it was made. Some explain the word gopher
to be the cedar ; others, the fir-tree ; others, the pine. They
differ also respecting the stories; because many think that the
sink was in the fourth place, which might receive the refuse
and other impurities. Others make five chambers in a triple
floor, of which they assign the highest to the birds. There
are those who suppose that it was only three stories in
height; but that these were separated by intermediate divisions. Besides, they do not agree about the window : to
some it appears that there was not one window only, but
many. Some say they were open to receive air; but others
contend that they were only made for the sake of light, and
therefore were covered over with crystal, and lined with pitch.
To me it seems more probable, that there was only one, not
cut out for the sake of giving light ; but to remain shut,
unless occasion required it to be opened, as we shall see afterwards. Further, that there was a triple story, and rooms separated in a manner to us unknown. The question respecting
its magnitude is more difficult. For, formerly, certain profane men ridiculed Moses, as having imagined that so vast
a multitude of animals was shut up in so small a space ; a
third part of which would scarcely contain four elephants.
Origen solves this question, by saying that a geometrical
cubit was referred to by Moses, which is six times greater
than the common one; to whose opinion Augustine assents
in his fifteenth book on the ' City of God,' and his first book
of ' Questions on Genesis.' I grant what they allege, that
Moses, who had been educated in all the science of the
Egyptians, was not ignorant of geometry; but since we
know that Moses everywhere spoke in a homely style, to
suit the capacity of the people, and that he purposely abstained from acute disputations, which might savour of the
schools and of deeper learning ; I can by no means persuade myself, that, in this place, contrary to his ordinary
method, he employed geometrical subtlety. Certainly, in the
first chapter, he did not treat scientifically of the stars, as
a philosopher would do; but he called them, in a popular

manner, according to their appearance to the uneducated, rather than according to truth, "two great lights." Thus we may everywhere perceive that he designates things of every kind by their accustomed names. But what was then the measure of the cubit I know not; it is, however, enough for me, that God (whom, without controversy, I acknowledge to be the chief builder of the ark) well knew what things the place which he described to his servant was capable of holding. If you exclude the extraordinary power of God from this history, you declare that mere fables are related. But, by us, who confess that the remains of the world were preserved by an incredible miracle, it ought not to be regarded as an absurdity, that many wonderful things are here related, in order that hence the secret and incomprehensible power of God, which far surpasses all our senses, may be the more clearly exhibited. Porphyry, or some other caviller,[1] may object, that this is fabulous, because the reason of it does not appear; or because it is unusual; or because it is repugnant to the common order of nature. But I make the rejoinder; that this entire narration of Moses, unless it were replete with miracles, would be cold, and trifling, and ridiculous. He, however, who will reflect aright upon the profound abyss of Divine omnipotence in this history, will rather sink in reverential awe, than indulge in profane mockery. I purposely pass over the allegorical application which Augustine makes of the figure of the ark to the body of Christ, both in his fifteenth book of ' The City of God,' and his twelfth book against Faustus; because I find there scarcely anything solid. Origen still more boldly sports with allegories: but there is nothing more profitable, than to adhere strictly to the natural treatment of things. That the ark was an image of the Church is certain, from the testi-

---

[1] " Hoc Porphyrius, vel quispiam alius canis, fabulosum esse obganniet." Throughout the above passage, Calvin takes for granted, that there was a miracle, when a close examination would have convinced him that there was none. It has only required the use of a little arithmetic, and common sense, to prove that the ark was more than sufficient to contain all the creatures which Noah was commanded to bring into it, as well as provision for the whole time of their residence in it.—See *Wells' Geography of the Old Test.*, chap. ii.— *Ed.*

mony of Peter, (1 Peter iii. 21;) but to accommodate its several parts to the Church, is by no means suitable, as I shall again show, in its proper place.

18. *But with thee will I establish my covenant.* Since the construction of the ark was very difficult, and innumerable obstacles might perpetually arise to break off the work when begun, God confirms his servant by a superadded promise. Thus was Noah encouraged to obey God; seeing that he relied on the Divine promise, and was confident that his labour would not be in vain. For then do we freely embrace the commands of God, when a promise is attached to them, which teaches us that we shall not spend our strength for nought. Whence it appears how foolishly the Papists are deceived, who triflingly argue, that men are led away by the doctrine of faith from the desire of doing well. For what will be the degree of our alacrity in well-doing, unless faith enlighten us? Let us therefore know, that the promises of God alone, are they which quicken us, and inspire each of our members with vigour to yield obedience to God: but that without these promises, we not only lie torpid in indolence, but are almost lifeless, so that neither hands nor feet can do their duty. And hence, as often as we become languid, or more remiss than we ought to be, in good works, let the promises of God recur to us, to correct our tardiness. For thus, according to the testimony of Paul, (Col. i. 5,) love flourishes in the saints, on account of the hope laid up for them in heaven. It is especially necessary that the faithful should be confirmed by the word of God, lest they faint in the midst of their course; to the end that they may certainly be assured that they are not beating the air, as they say; but that, acquiescing in the promise given them, and being sure of success, they follow God who calls them. This connection, then, is to be borne in mind, that when God was instructing his servant Moses what he would have him do, he declares, for the purpose of retaining him in obedience to himself, that he requires nothing of him in vain. Now, the sum of this covenant of which Moses speaks was, that Noah should be safe, although the whole world should perish

in the deluge.   For there is an understood antithesis, that the whole world being rejected, the Lord would establish a peculiar covenant with Noah alone.   Wherefore, it was the duty of Noah to oppose this promise of God, like a wall of iron, against all the terrors of death; just as if it were the purpose of God, by this sole word, to discriminate between life and death.   But the covenant with him is confirmed, with this condition annexed, that his family shall be preserved for his sake ; and also the brute animals, for the replenishing of the new world; concerning which I shall say more in the ninth chapter.

19. *And of every living thing of all flesh.* " All flesh" is the name he gives to animals of whatsoever kind they may be. He says they went in two and two ; not that a single pair of each kind was received into the ark, (for we shall soon see that there were three pairs of the clean kinds, and one animal over, which Noah afterwards offered in sacrifice ;) but whereas here mention is made only of offspring, he does not expressly state the number, but simply couples males with females, that Noah might hence perceive how the world was to be replenished.

22. *Thus did Noah.* In a few words, but with great sublimity, Moses here commends the faith of Noah.   The unskilful wonder that the apostle (Heb. xi. 7) makes him " heir of the righteousness which is by faith."   As if, truly, all the virtues, and whatsoever else was worthy of praise in this holy man, had not sprung from this fountain.   For we ought to consider the assaults of temptation to which his breast was continually exposed.   First, the prodigious size of the ark might have overwhelmed all his senses, so as to prevent him from raising a finger to begin the work. Let the reader reflect on the multitude of trees to be felled, on the great labour of conveying them, and the difficulty of joining them together.   The matter was also long deferred ; for the holy man was required to be engaged more than a hundred years in most troublesome labour.   Nor can we suppose him to have been so stupid, as not to reflect

upon obstacles of this kind. Besides, it was scarcely to be
hoped, that the men of his age would patiently bear with him,
for promising himself an exclusive deliverance, attended with
ignominy to themselves. Their unnatural ferocity has been
before mentioned ; there can therefore be no doubt that they
would daily provoke modest and simple-minded men, even
without cause. But *here* was a plausible occasion for insult ;
since Noah, by felling trees on all sides, was making the earth
bare, and defrauding them of various advantages. It is a
common proverb, that perverse and contentious men will
dispute about an ass's shadow. What, then, might Noah
think, would those fierce Cyclops do for the shadow of so
many trees ; who, being practised in every kind of violence,
would seize with eagerness on all sides an occasion of exercising cruelty ? But this was what chiefly tended to inflame
their rage, that he, by building an asylum for himself, virtually doomed them all to destruction. Certainly, unless
they had been restrained by the mighty hand of God, they
would have stoned the holy man a hundred times ; still it is
probable, that their vehemence was not so far repressed, as
to prevent them from frequently assailing him with scoffs and
derision, from heaping upon him many reproaches, and pursuing him with grievous threats. I even think, that they did
not restrain their hands from disturbing his work. Therefore,
although he may have addressed himself with alacrity to the
work committed to him ; yet his constancy might have failed
more than a thousand times, in so many years, unless it had
been firmly rooted. Moreover, as the work itself appeared im-
practicable, it may be further asked, Whence were provisions
for the year to be obtained ? whence food for so many animals ? He is commanded to lay up what will suffice for food
during ten months, for his whole family, for cattle, and wild
beasts, and even for birds. Truly, it seems absurd, that after
he has been disengaged from agriculture, in order to build the
ark, he should be commanded to collect a two years' store of
provision ; but much more trouble attended the providing
of food for animals. He might therefore have suspected that
God was mocking him. His last work was to gather animals
of all kinds together. As if, indeed, he had all the beasts of

the forest at his command, or was able to tame them; so that, in his keeping, wolves might dwell with lambs, tigers with hares, lions with oxen—as sheep in his fold. But the most grievous temptation of all was, that he was commanded to descend, as into the grave, for the sake of preserving his life, and voluntarily to deprive himself of air and vital spirit; for the smell of dung alone, pent up, as it was, in a closely filled place, might, at the expiration of three days, have stifled all the living creatures in the ark. Let us reflect on these conflicts of the holy man—so severe, and multiplied, and long-continued—in order that we may know how heroic was his courage, in prosecuting, to the utmost, what God had commanded him to do. Moses, indeed, says in a single word that he did it; but we must consider how far beyond all human power was the doing of it: and that it would have been better to die a hundred deaths, than to undertake a work so laborious, unless he had looked to something higher than the present life. A remarkable example, therefore, of obedience is here described to us; because, Noah, committing himself entirely to God, rendered Him due honour. We know, in this corruption of our nature, how ready men are to seek subterfuges, and how ingenious in inventing pretexts for disobedience to God. Wherefore, let us also learn to break through every kind of impediment, and not to give place to evil thoughts, which oppose themselves to the word of God, and with which Satan attempts to entangle our minds, that they may not obey the command of God. For God especially demands this honour to be given to himself, that we should suffer him to judge for us. And this is the true proof of faith, that we, being content with one of his commands, gird ourselves to the work, so that we do not swerve in our course, whatever obstacle Satan may place in our way, but are borne on the wings of faith above the world. Moses also shows, that Noah obeyed God, not in one particular only, but in all. Which is diligently to be observed; because hence, chiefly, arises dreadful confusion in our life, that we are not able, unreservedly, to submit ourselves to God; but when we have discharged some part of our duty, we often blend our own feelings with his word. But the obedience of Noah is celebrated on this account, that it was entire, not partial; so that he omitted none of those things which God had commanded.

CHAPTER VII.

1. And the Lord said unto Noah, Come thou and all thy house into the ark; for thee have I seen righteous before me in this generation.

2. Of every clean beast thou shalt take to thee by sevens, the male and his female: and of beasts that *are* not clean by two, the male and his female.

3. Of fowls also of the air by sevens, the male and the female; to keep seed alive upon the face of all the earth.

4. For yet seven days, and I will cause it to rain upon the earth forty days and forty nights; and every living substance that I have made, will I destroy from off the face of the earth.

5. And Noah did according unto all that the Lord commanded him.

6. And Noah *was* six hundred years old when the flood of waters was upon the earth.

7. And Noah went in, and his sons, and his wife, and his sons' wives with him, into the ark, because of the waters of the flood.

8. Of clean beasts, and of beasts that *are* not clean, and of fowls, and of every thing that creepeth upon the earth,

9. There went in two and two unto Noah into the ark, the male and the female, as God had commanded Noah.

10. And it came to pass after seven days, that the waters of the flood were upon the earth.

11. In the six hundredth year of Noah's life, in the second month, the seventeenth day of the month, the same day were all the fountains of the great deep broken up, and the windows of heaven were opened.

1. Et dixit Jehova ad Noah, Ingredere tu, et omnis domus tua arcam : quia te vidi justum coram me in ætate ista.

2. Ex omni animali mundo capies tibi septena septena, virum et fœmellam ejus: et ex animali quod non mundum est, bina, virum et fœmellam ejus.

3. Etiam ex volatili cœli septena, masculum et fœmellam : ut vivum conservetur semen in superficie omnis terræ.

4. Quia post dies adhuc septem ego pluam super terram quadraginta dies, et quadraginta noctes, et delebo omnem substantiam quam feci, a superficie terræ.

5. Et fecit Noah secundum omnia quæ præceperat ei Jehova.

6. Noah autem erat sexcentorum annorum quando diluvium fuit aquarum super terram.

7. Et ingressus Noah, et filii ejus, et uxor ejus, et uxores filiorum ejus cum eo in arcam, propter aquas diluvii.

8. Ex animali mundo, et ex animali quod non erat mundum, et ex volatili, et ex omni quod reptat super terram,

9. Bina bina ingressa sunt ad Noah in arcam, masculus et fœmella, quemadmodum præceperat Deus ipsi Noah.

10. Et fuit, post septem dies aquæ diluvii fuerunt super terram.

11. In anno sexcentesimo annorum vitæ Noah, in mense secundo, in septimadecima die mensis, die ipsa, rupti sunt omnes fontes voraginis magnæ, et fenestræ cœli apertæ sunt.

12. And the rain was upon the earth forty days and forty nights.

13. In the self-same day entered Noah, and Shem, and Ham, and Japheth, the sons of Noah, and Noah's wife, and the three wives of his sons with them, into the ark:

14. They, and every beast after his kind, and all the cattle after their kind, and every creeping thing that creepeth upon the earth after his kind, and every fowl after his kind, every bird of every sort.

15. And they went in unto Noah into the ark, two and two of all flesh, wherein *is* the breath of life.

16. And they that went in, went in male and female of all flesh, as God had commanded him: and the Lord shut him in.

17. And the flood was forty days upon the earth; and the waters increased, and bare up the ark, and it was lift up above the earth.

18. And the waters prevailed, and were increased greatly upon the earth; and the ark went upon the face of the waters.

19. And the waters prevailed exceedingly upon the earth; and all the high hills, that *were* under the whole heaven, were covered.

20. Fifteen cubits upward did the waters prevail; and the mountains were covered.

21. And all flesh died that moved upon the earth, both of fowl, and of cattle, and of beast, and of every creeping thing that creepeth upon the earth, and every man:

22. All in whose nostrils *was* the breath of life, of all that *was* in the dry *land*, died.

23. And every living substance was destroyed which was upon the face of the ground, both man, and cattle, and the creeping things, and the fowl of the heaven: and they were destroyed from the earth: and Noah only re-

12. Et fuit pluvia super terram quadraginta dies et quadraginta noctes.

13. Ipso eodem die ingressus est Noah, et Sem, et Cham, et Jepheth, filii Noah, et uxor Noah, tresque uxores filiorum ejus cum·illis, in arcam:

14. Ipsi, et omnis bestia juxta speciem suam, et omne animal juxta speciem suam, et omne reptile quod reptat super terram, secundum speciem suam, et omne volatile juxta speciem suam, omnis avis, et omne alatum.

15. Ingressa sunt igitur ad Noah in arcam, bina bina ex omni carne in qua erat spiritus vitæ.

16. Et quæ ingressa sunt, masculus et fœmina ex omni carne ingressa sunt, quemadmodum præceperat ei Deus: et clausit Jehova super eum.

17. Et factum est diluvium quadraginta dies super terram, et multiplicatæ sunt aquæ, elevaveruntque arcam: itaque elevata est a terra.

18. Et prævaluerunt aquæ, et multiplicatæ sunt valde super terram, et fluitabat arca super faciem aquarum.

19. Roboraverunt itaque se aquæ valde super terram, et operti sunt omnes montes excelsi qui erant sub universo cœlo.

20. Quindecim cubitis superne roboraverunt se aquæ, ita ut operti sint montes.

21. Et mortua est omnis caro quæ reptabat super terram, tam de volatili quam de animali et bestia, et omni reptili quod reptat super terram, et omni homine.

22. Omnia in quorum nare erat anhelitus spiritus vitæ, ex omnibus quæ erant in sicco, mortua sunt.

23. Et delevit omnem substantiam vivam, quæ erat super faciem terræ, ab homine usque ad jumentum, usque ad reptile, et usque ad volatile cœli: et deleta sunt e terra, et remansit

mained *alive*, and they that *were* with him in the ark.

24. And the waters prevailed upon the earth an hundred and fifty days.

tantum Noah, et qui cum eo erant in arca.

24. Et roboraverunt se aquæ super terram quinquaginta et centum dies.

1. *And the Lord said unto Noah.* I have no doubt that Noah was confirmed, as he certainly needed to be, by oracles frequently repeated. He had already sustained, during one hundred years, the greatest and most furious assaults; and the invincible combatant had achieved memorable victories; but the most severe contest of all was, to bid farewell to the world, to renounce society, and to bury himself in the ark. The face of the earth was, at that time, lovely; and Moses intimates that it was the season in which the herbs shoot forth and the trees begin to flourish. Winter, which binds the joy of sky and earth in sharp and rugged frost, has now passed away; and the Lord has chosen the moment for destroying the world, in the very season of spring. For Moses states that the commencement of the deluge was in the second month. I know, however, that different opinions prevail on this subject; for there are three who begin the year from the autumnal equinox; but that mode of reckoning the year is more approved, which makes it commence in the month of March. However this might be, it was no light trial for Noah to leave of his own accord, the life to which he had been accustomed during six hundred years, and to seek a new mode of life in the abyss of death. He is commanded to forsake the world, that he may live in a sepulchre which he had been laboriously digging for himself through more than a hundred years. Why was this? because, in a little while, the earth was to be submerged in a deluge of waters. Yet nothing of the kind is apparent: all indulge in feasts, celebrate nuptials, build sumptuous houses; in short, everywhere, daintiness and luxury prevail; as Christ himself testifies, that that age was intoxicated with its own pleasures, (Luke xvii. 26.) Wherefore, it was not without reason, that the Lord encouraged and fortified the mind of his servant afresh, by the renewal of the promise, lest he should faint; as if he would say, ' Hitherto thou hast

laboured with fortitude amid so many causes of offence ; but now the case especially demands that thou shouldst take courage, in order to reap the fruit of thy labour : do not, however, wait till the waters burst forth on every side from the opened veins of the earth, and till the higher waters of heaven, with opposing violence, rush from their opened cataracts ; but while everything is yet tranquil, enter into the ark, and there remain till the seventh day, then suddenly shall the deluge arise.' And although oracles are not now brought down from heaven, let us know that continual meditation on the word is not ineffectual ; for as new difficulties perpetually arise before us, so God, by one and another promise, establishes our faith, so that our strength being renewed, we may at length arrive at the goal. Our duty, indeed, is, attentively to hear God speaking to us ; and neither, through depraved fastidiousness, to reject those exercises, by which He cherishes, or excites, or confirms our faith, according as he knows it to be still tender, or languishing, or weak ; nor yet to reject them as superfluous. " For thee have I seen righteous." When the Lord assigns as his reason for preserving Noah, that he knew him to be righteous, he seems to attribute the praise of salvation to the merit of works ; for if Noah was saved because he was righteous, it follows, that we shall deserve life by good works. But here it behoves us cautiously to weigh the design of God ; which was to place one man in contrast with the whole world, in order that, in his person, he might condemn the unrighteousness of all men. For he again testifies, that the punishment which he was about to inflict on the world was just, seeing that only one man was left who then cultivated righteousness, for whose sake he was propitious to his whole family. Should any one object, that from this passage, God is proved to have respect to works in saving men, the solution is ready ; that this is not repugnant to gratuitous acceptance, since God accepts those gifts which he himself has conferred upon his servants. We must observe, in the first place, that he loves men freely, inasmuch as he finds nothing in them but what is worthy of hatred, since all men are born the children of wrath, and heirs of eternal malediction. In this respect he adopts them to himself in Christ, and justifies them by his mere mercy. After he has, in this manner, reconciled them unto himself, he also regenerates them, by his Spirit, to new life and righteousness. Hence flow good works, which must of necessity be pleasing to God himself. Thus he not only loves the *faithful*, but also their *works*. We must again observe, that since some fault always adheres to our works, it is not possible that they can be approved, except as a matter of indulgence. The grace, therefore, of Christ, and not their own dignity or merit, is that which gives worth to our works. Nevertheless, we do not deny that they come into the account before God : as he here acknowledges, and accepts, the righteousness of Noah which had proceeded from his own grace ; and in this manner (as Augustine speaks) he will crown his own gifts. We may further notice the expression, " I have seen thee righteous before me ;" by which words, he not only annihilates all that hypocritical righteousness which is destitute of interior sanctity of heart, but vindicates his own authority ; as if he would declare, that he alone is a competent judge to estimate righteousness. The clause, " in this generation," is added, as I have said, for the sake of amplification ; for so desperate was the depravity of that age, that it was regarded as a prodigy, that Noah should be free from the common infection.

2. *Of every clean beast.* He again repeats what he had before said concerning animals, and not without occasion. For there was no little difficulty in collecting from woods, mountains, and caves, so great a multitude of wild beasts, many species of which were perhaps altogether unknown ; and there was, in most of them, the same ferocity which we now perceive. Wherefore, God encourages the holy man, lest being alarmed with that difficulty, and having cast aside all hope of success, he should fail. Here, however, at first sight, appears some kind of contradiction, because whereas he before had spoken of *pairs* of animals, he now speaks of *sevens*. But the solution is at hand ; because, previously, Moses does not state the number, but only says that females were added as companions to the males ; as if he had said, Noah himself was commanded not to gather the animals pro-

miscuously together, but to select *pairs* out of them for the propagation of offspring. Now, however, the discourse is concerning the actual number. Moreover, the expression, " by sevens," is to be understood not of seven pairs of each kind, but of three pairs, to which one animal is added for the sake of sacrifice.[1] Besides, the Lord would have a threefold greater number of clean animals than of others preserved, because there would be a greater necessity of them for the use of man. In which appointment, we must consider the paternal goodness of God towards us, by which he is inclined to have regard to us in all things.

3. *To keep seed alive upon the face of all the earth.* That is, that hence offspring might be born. But this is referred to Noah; for although, properly speaking, God alone gives life, yet God here refers to those duties which he had enjoined upon his servant : and it is with respect to his appointed office, that God commands him to collect animals that he may keep seed alive. Nor is this extraordinary, seeing that the ministers of the gospel are said, in a sense, to confer spiritual life. In the clause which next follows, " upon the face of all the earth," there is a twofold consolation : that the waters, after they had covered the earth for a time, would again cease, so that the dry surface of the earth should appear ; and then, that not only should Noah himself survive, but, by the blessing of God, the number of animals should be so increased, as to spread far and wide through the whole world. Thus, in the midst of ruin, future restoration is promised to him. Moses is very earnest in showing that God took care, by every means, to retain Noah in obedience to his word, and that the holy man entirely acquiesced. This doctrine is very useful, especially when God either promises or threatens anything incredible, since men do not willingly receive what seems to them improbable. For nothing was

[1] Le Clerc objects to this interpretation, and supposes that seven of each sex of clean, and two of each sex of unclean animals, were admitted into the ark. Perhaps a sceptical objection to the use of the seventh animal, as a sacrifice, inclined him to adopt this interpretation. Commentators, however, have generally preferred the solution here given.—*Ed.*

less accordant with the judgment of the flesh, than that the
world should be destroyed by its Creator; because this was
to subvert the whole order of nature which he had established.
Wherefore, unless Noah had been well admonished of this
terrible judgment of God, he never would have ventured to
believe it; lest he should conceive of God as acting in contradiction to himself. The word הֵיקִם, (hayekom,) which
Moses here uses, has its origin from a word signifying to
stand; but it properly means whatever lives and flourishes.

5. *And Noah did according to all that the Lord commanded.*
This is not a bare repetition of the former sentence; but
Moses commends Noah's uniform tenor of obedience in
keeping all God's commandments; as if he would say, that
in whatever particular it pleased God to try his obedience,
he always remained constant. And, certainly, it is not becoming to obey one or another commandment of God only,
so that when we have performed a defective obedience, we
should feel at liberty to withdraw; for we must keep in memory the declaration of James, 'He who forbade thee to kill, forbade thee also to steal, and to commit adultery,' (James ii. 11.)

6. *And Noah was six hundred years old.* It is not without
reason that he again mentions the age of Noah. For old age
has this among other evils, that it renders men more indolent
and morose; whence the faith of Noah was the more conspicuous, because it did not fail him in that advanced period of
life. And as it was a great excellence, not to languish through
successive centuries, so his promptitude deserves no little
commendation; because, being commanded to enter the ark,
he immediately obeyed. When Moses shortly afterwards
subjoins, that he had entered on account of the waters of the
deluge, the words ought not to be expounded, as if he were
compelled, by the rushing of the waters, to flee into the ark;
but that he, being moved with fear by the word, perceived by faith the approach of that deluge which all others
ridiculed. Wherefore, his faith is again commended in this
place, because, indeed, he raised his eyes above heaven and
earth.

8. *Of clean beasts.*   Moses now explains,—what had before been doubtful,—in which manner the animals were gathered together into the ark, and says that they came of their own accord.   If this should seem to any one absurd, let him recall to mind what was said before, that in the beginning every kind of animals presented themselves to Adam, that he might give them names.   And, truly, we dread the sight of wild beasts from no other cause than this, that seeing we have shaken off the yoke of God, we have lost that authority over them with which Adam was endued.   Now, it was a kind of restoration of the former state of things, when God brought to Noah those animals which he intended should be preserved through Noah's labour and service.   For Noah retained the untamed animals in his ark, in the very same way in which hens and geese are preserved in a coop.   And it is not superfluously added, that the animals themselves came, as God had instructed Noah; for it shows, that the blessing of God rested on the obedience of Noah, so that his labour should not be in vain.   It was impossible, humanly speaking, that in a moment such an assemblage of all animals should take place; but because Noah, simply trusting the event with God, executed what was enjoined upon him; God, in return, gave power to his own precept, that it might not be without effect.   Properly speaking, this was a promise of God annexed to his commands.   And, therefore, we must conclude, that the faith of Noah availed more, than all snares and nets, for the capture of animals; and that, by the very same gate, lions, and wolves, and tigers, meekly entered, with oxen, and with lambs, into the ark.   And this is the only method by which we may overcome all difficulties; while,—being persuaded, that what is impossible to us is easy to God,—we derive alacrity from hope.   It has before been stated that the animals entered in by pairs.   We have also related the different opinions of interpreters respecting the month in which the deluge took place.   For since the Hebrews begin their year in sacred things from March, but in earthly affairs from September; or,—which is the same thing,—since the two equinoxes form with them a double commencement of the year, some think that the *sacred* year, and some the *political*, is here intended

But because the former method of reckoning the years was Divinely appointed, and is also more agreeable to nature, it seems probable that the deluge began about the time of spring.

11. *The same day were all the fountains of the great deep broken up.* Moses recalls the period of the first creation to our memory ; for the earth was originally covered with water ; and by the singular kindness of God, they were made to recede, that some space should be left clear for living creatures. And this, philosophers are compelled to acknowledge, that it is contrary to the course of nature for the waters to subside, so that some portion of the earth might rise above them. And Scripture records this among the miracles of God, that he restrains the force of the sea, as with barriers, lest it should overwhelm that part of the earth which is granted for a habitation to men. Moses also says, in the first chapter, that some waters were suspended above in the heaven ; and David, in like manner, declares, that they are held enclosed as in a bottle. Lastly, God raised for men a theatre in the habitable region of the earth ; and caused, by his secret power, that the subterraneous waters should not break forth to overwhelm us, and the celestial waters should not conspire with them for that purpose. Now, however, Moses states, that when God resolved to destroy the earth by a deluge, those barriers were torn up. And here we must consider the wonderful counsel of God ; for he might have deposited, in certain channels or veins of the earth, as much water as would have sufficed for all the purposes of human life ; but he has designedly placed us between two graves, lest, in fancied security, we should despise that kindness on which our life depends. For the element of water, which philosophers deem one of the principles of life, threatens us with death from above and from beneath, except so far as it is restrained by the hand of God. In saying that the fountains were broken up, and the cataracts opened, his language is metaphorical, and means, that neither did the waters flow in their accustomed manner, nor did the rain distil from heaven ; but that the distinction, which we see had been

established by God, being now removed, there were no longer
any bars to restrain the violent irruption.

12. *And the rain was upon the earth.* Although the Lord
burst open the flood-gates of the waters, yet he does not
allow them to break forth in a moment, so as immediately to
overwhelm the earth, but causes the rain to continue forty
days; partly, that Noah, by long meditation, might more
deeply fix in his memory what he had previously learned, by
instruction, through the word; partly, that the wicked, even
before their death, might feel that those warnings which they
had held in derision, were not empty threats. For they who
had so long scorned the patience of God, deserved to feel
that they were gradually perishing under that righteous judgment of his, which, during a hundred years, they had treated
as a fable. And the Lord frequently so tempers his judgments, that men may have leisure to consider with more advantage those judgments which, by their sudden eruption,
might overcome them with astonishment. But the wonderful
depravity of our nature shows itself in this, that if the anger of
God is suddenly poured forth, we become stupified and
senseless; but if it advances with measured pace, we become
so accustomed to it as to despise it; because we do not
willingly acknowledge the hand of God without miracles;
and because we are easily hardened, by a kind of superin-
duced insensibility, at the sight of God's works.

13. *In the self-same day entered Noah, and Shem, &c.* A
repetition follows, sufficiently particular, considering the
brevity with which Moses runs through the history of the
deluge, yet by no means superfluous. For it was the design
of the Spirit to retain our minds in the consideration of a
vengeance too terrible to be adequately described by the utmost severity of language. Besides, nothing is here related
but what is difficult to be believed; wherefore Moses the
more frequently inculcates these things, that however remote
they may be from our apprehension, they may still obtain
credit with us. Thus the narration respecting the animals
refers to this point; that by the faith of holy Noah, they were

drawn from their woods and caverns, and were collected in
one place from their wandering courses, as if they had been
led by the hand of God.   We see, therefore, that Moses
does not insist upon this point without an object; but he does
it to teach us that each species of animals was preserved, not
by chance, nor by human industry, but because the Lord
reached out and offered to Noah himself, from hand to hand,
(as they say,) whatever animal he intended to keep alive.

16. *And the Lord shut him in.*   This is not added in vain,
nor ought it to be lightly passed over.   That door must have
been large, which could admit an elephant.   And truly, no
pitch would be sufficiently firm and tenacious, and no joining
sufficiently solid, to prevent the immense force of the water
from penetrating through its many seams, especially in an
irruption so violent, and in a shock so severe.   Therefore,
Moses, to cut off occasion for the vain speculations which our
own curiosity would suggest, declares, in one word, that the
ark was made secure from the deluge, not by human artifice,
but by divine miracle.   It is, indeed, not to be doubted, that
Noah had been endued with new ability and sagacity, that
nothing might be defective in the structure of the ark.   But
lest even this favour should be without success, it was necessary for something greater to be added.   Wherefore, that
we might not measure the mode of preserving the ark, by the
capacity of our own judgment, Moses teaches us, that the
waters were not restrained from breaking in upon the ark,
by pitch or bitumen only, but rather by the secret power of
God, and by the interposition of his hand.

17. *And the flood was forty days, &c.*   Moses copiously insists upon this fact, in order to show that the whole world
was immersed in the waters.   Moreover, it is to be regarded
as the special design of this narration, that we should not
ascribe to fortune, the flood by which the world perished; however customary it may be for men to cast some veil over the
works of God, which may obscure either his goodness or his
judgments manifested in them.   But seeing it is plainly declared,
that whatever was flourishing on the earth was destroyed, we

hence infer, that it was an indisputable and signal judgment of God; especially since Noah alone remained secure, because he had embraced, by faith, the word in which salvation was contained.   He then recalls to memory what we before have said; namely, how desperate had been the impiety, and how enormous the crimes of men, by which God was induced to destroy the whole world; whereas, on account of his great clemency, he would have spared his own workmanship, had he seen that any milder remedy could have been effectually applied. These two things, directly opposed to each other, he connects together; that the whole human race was destroyed, but that Noah and his family safely escaped.   Hence we learn how profitable it was for Noah, disregarding the world, to obey God alone : which Moses states, not so much for the sake of praising the man, as for that of inviting us to imitate his example.   Moreover, lest the multitude of sinners should draw us away from God; we must patiently bear that the ungodly should hold us up to ridicule, and should triumph over us, until the Lord shall show by the final issue, that our obedience has been approved by him.   In this sense, Peter teaches that Noah's deliverance from the universal deluge was a figure of baptism, (1 Pet. iii. 21;) as if he had said, the method of the salvation, which we receive through baptism, agrees with this deliverance of Noah.   Since at this time also, the world is full of unbelievers as it was then; therefore it is necessary for us to separate ourselves from the greater multitude, that the Lord may snatch us from destruction. In the same manner, the Church is fitly, and justly, compared to the ark.   But we must keep in mind the similitude by which they mutually correspond with each other; for that is derived from the word of God alone; because, as Noah believing the promise of God, gathered himself, his wife and his children together, in order that, under a certain appearance of death, he might emerge out of death; so it is fitting that we should renounce the world and die, in order that the Lord may quicken us by his word.   For nowhere else is there any security of salvation.   The Papists, however, act ridiculously, who fabricate for us an ark without the word.

CHAPTER VIII.

1. AND God remembered Noah, and every living thing, and all the cattle that *was* with him in the ark : and God made a wind to pass over the earth, and the waters asswaged ;

2. The fountains also of the deep and the windows of heaven were stopped, and the rain from heaven was restrained ;

3. And the waters returned from off the earth continually : and after the end of the hundred and fifty days the waters were abated.

4. And the ark rested in the seventh month, on the seventeenth day of the month, upon the mountains of Ararat.

5. And the waters decreased continually until the tenth month : in the tenth *month*, on the first *day* of the month, were the tops of the mountains seen.

6. And it came to pass at the end of forty days, that Noah opened the window of the ark which he had made :

7. And he sent forth a raven, which went forth to and fro, until the waters were dried up from off the earth.

8. Also he sent forth a dove from him, to see if the waters were abated from off the face of the ground ;

9. But the dove found no rest for the sole of her foot, and she returned unto him into the ark, for the waters *were* on the face of the whole earth : then he put forth his hand, and took her, and pulled her in unto him into the ark.

10. And he stayed yet other seven days ; and again he sent forth the dove out of the ark ;

11. And the dove came in to him in the evening ; and, lo, in her mouth *was* an olive leaf pluckt off : so Noah knew that the waters were abated from off the earth.

12. And he stayed yet other seven days ; and sent forth the dove ; which returned not again unto him any more.

1. Recordatus est autem Deus Noah, et omnis bestiæ, et omnis animalis quæ erant cum eo in arca : et transire fecit Deus ventum super terram, et quieverunt aquæ.

2. Et clauserunt se fontes abyssi, fenestræque cœli, et prohibita est pluvia e cœlo.

3. Et reversæ sunt aquæ a superficie terræ, eundo et redeundo, et defecerunt aquæ in fine quinquaginta et centum dierum.

4. Et requievit arca mense septimo, septimadecima die mensis super montes Ararath.

5. Et aquæ ibant et deficiebant usque ad mensem decimum : in decimo, in prima mensis visa sunt cacumina montium.

6. Et fuit, in fine quadraginta dierum, aperuit Noah fenestram arcæ quam fecerat.

7. Et misit corvum, et egressus est egrediendo et redeundo, donec siccarentur aquæ quæ erant super terram.

8. Deinde misit columbam a se, ut videret an extenuatæ essent aquæ a superficie terræ.

9. Et non invenit columba requiem plantæ pedis sui, et reversa est ad eum in arcam : quia aquæ erant in superficie omnis terræ : et misit manum suam, et accepit eam, introduxitque eam ad se in arcam.

10. Et expectavit adhuc septem dies alios, et addidit ut mitteret columbam ex arca.

11. Et venit ad eum columba tempore vespertino, et ecce, folium olivæ raptum erat in ore ejus, et cognovit Noah quod extenuatæ essent aquæ a superficie terræ.

12. Et expectavit adhuc septem alios, et misit columbam : et non addidit ut reverteretur ad eum amplius.

13. And it came to pass in the six hundredth and first year, in the first *month*, the first *day* of the month, the waters were dried up from off the earth: and Noah removed the covering of the ark, and looked, and, behold, the face of the ground was dry.

14. And in the second month, on the seven and twentieth day of the month, was the earth dried.

15. And God spake unto Noah, saying,

16. Go forth of the ark, thou, and thy wife, and thy sons, and thy sons' wives with thee.

17. Bring forth with thee every living thing that *is* with thee, of all flesh, *both* of fowl, and of cattle, and of every creeping thing that creepeth upon the earth; that they may breed abundantly in the earth, and be fruitful, and multiply upon the earth.

18. And Noah went forth, and his sons, and his wife, and his sons' wives with him:

19. Every beast, every creeping thing, and every fowl, *and* whatsoever creepeth upon the earth, after their kinds, went forth out of the ark.

20. And Noah builded an altar unto the Lord; and took of every clean beast, and of every clean fowl, and offered burnt-offerings on the altar.

21. And the Lord smelled a sweet savour; and the Lord said in his heart, I will not again curse the ground any more for man's sake; for the imagination of man's heart *is* evil from his youth; neither will I again smite any more every thing living, as I have done.

22. While the earth remaineth, seed-time and harvest, and cold and heat, and summer and winter, and day and night, shall not cease.

13. Et fuit, primo et sexcentesimo anno, primo *mense*, in prima mensis, siccatæ sunt aquæ a superficie terræ: removit autem Noah operimentum arcæ, et vidit, et ecce siccata erat facies terræ.

14. Et in mense secundo, in septima et vicesima die mensis, aruit terra.

15. Loquutus est autem Deus ad Noah, dicendo,

16. Egredere ex arca, tu, et uxor tua, et filii tui, et uxores filiorum tuorum tecum.

17. Omnem bestiam quæ est tecum, ex omni carne, tam de volatili quam de animali, et omni reptili quod reptat super terram educ tecum: ut se moveant in terra, et crescant, multiplicenturque super terram.

18. Et egressus est Noah, et filii ejus, et uxor ejus, et uxores filiorum ejus cum eo.

19. Omnis bestia, omne reptile et omne volatile, omne quod movetur super terram, secundum familias eorum egressa sunt ex arca.

20. Et ædificavit Noah altare Jehovæ, et tulit ex omni animali mundo, et ex omni volatili mundo, et obtulit holocausta in altari.

21. Odoratusque est Jehova odorem quietis. Et dixit Jehova in corde suo, Non addam ut maledicam ultra terræ propter hominem: quia cogitatio cordis hominis mala est a pueritia sua: nec addam ultra ut percutiam omne vivens quemadmodum feci.

22. Posthac omnibus diebus terræ, sementis et messis, et frigus et æstus, et æstas et hyems, et dies et nox non cessabunt.

1. *And God remembered Noah.* Moses now descends more particularly to that other part of the subject, which shows, that Noah was not disappointed in his hope of the salvation

divinely promised to him. The *remembrance* of which Moses
speaks, ought to be referred not only to the external aspect
of things, (so to speak,) but also to the inward feeling of
the holy man. Indeed it is certain, that God, from the time
in which he had once received Noah into his protection, was
never unmindful of him ; for, truly, it was by as great a miracle, that he did not perish through suffocation in the ark, as
if he had lived without breath, submerged in the waters.
And Moses just before has said, that by God's secret closing
up of the ark, the waters were restrained from penetrating it.
But as the ark was floating, even to the fifth month, upon the
waters, the delay by which the Lord suffered his servant to
be anxiously and miserably tortured, might seem to imply a
kind of oblivion. And it is not to be questioned, that his
heart was agitated by various feelings, when he found himself so long held in suspense ; for he might infer, that his life
had been prolonged, in order that he might be more miserable than any of the rest of mankind. For we know that we
are accustomed to imagine God absent, except when we have
some sensible experience of his presence. And although
Noah tenaciously held fast the promise which he had embraced, even to the end, it is yet credible, that he was
grievously assailed by various temptations ; and God, without doubt, purposely thus exercised his faith and patience.
For, why was not the world destroyed in three days ? And
for what purpose did the waters, after they had covered the
highest mountains, rise fifteen cubits higher, unless it was to
accustom Noah, and his family, to meditate the more pro-
fitably on the judgments of God, and when the danger was
past, to acknowledge that they had been rescued from a thousand deaths ? Let us therefore learn, by this example, to
repose on the providence of God, even while he seems to be
most forgetful of us ; for at length, by affording us help, he
will testify that he has been mindful of us. What, if the
flesh persuade us to distrust, yet let us not yield to its restlessness ; but as soon as this thought creeps in, that God has
cast off all care concerning us, or is asleep, or far distant, let
us immediately meet it with this shield, 'The Lord, who has
promised his help to the miserable, will, in due time, be pre-

sent with us, that we may indeed perceive the care he takes of us.' Nor is there less weight in what is added, that God also remembered the animals; for if, on account of the salvation promised to man, his favour is extended to brute cattle, and to wild beasts; what may we suppose will be his favour towards his own children, to whom he has so liberally, and so sacredly, pledged his faithfulness?

And God made a wind to pass over the earth. Here it appears more clearly, that Moses is speaking of the effect of God's remembrance of Noah; namely, that in very deed, and by a sure proof, Noah might know that God cared for his life. For when God, by his secret power, might have dried the earth, he made use of the wind; which method he also employed in drying the Red Sea. And thus he would testify, that as he had the waters at his command, ready to execute his wrath, so now he held the winds in his hand, to afford relief. And although here a remarkable history is recorded by Moses, we are yet taught, that the winds do not arise fortuitously, but by the command of God; as it is said in Psalm civ. verse 4, that ' they are the swift messengers of God;' and again, that God rides upon their wings. Finally, the variety, the contrary motions, and the mutual conflicts of the elements, conspire to yield obedience to God. Moses also adds other inferior means by which the waters were diminished, and caused to return to their former position. The sum of the whole is, that God, for the purpose of restoring the order which he had before appointed, recalled the waters to their prescribed boundaries, so that while the celestial waters, as if congealed, were suspended in the air; others might lie concealed in their gulfs; others flow in separate channels; and the sea also might remain within its barriers.

3. *And after the end of the hundred and fifty days.* Some think that the whole time, from the beginning of the deluge to the abatement of the waters, is here noted; and thus they include the forty days in which Moses relates that there was continued rain. But I make this distinction, that until the fortieth day, the waters rose gradually by fresh additions; then

that they remained nearly in the same state for one hundred and fifty days; for both computations make the period a little more than six months and a half. And Moses says, that about the end of the seventh month, the diminution of the waters appeared to be such that the ark settled upon the highest summit of a mountain, or touched some ground. And by this lengthened space of time, the Lord would show the more plainly, that the dreadful desolation of the world had not fallen upon it accidentally, but was a remarkable proof of his judgment; while the deliverance of Noah was a magnificent work of his grace, and worthy of everlasting remembrance. If, however, we number the seventh month from the beginning of the year, (as some do,) and not from the time that Noah entered the ark, the subsidence of which Moses speaks, took place earlier, namely, as soon as the ark had floated five months. If this second opinion is received, there will be the same reckoning of ten months; for the sense will be, that in the eighth month after the commencement of the deluge, the tops of the mountains appeared. Concerning the name Ararat, I follow the opinion most received. And I do not see why some should deny it to be Armenia, the mountains of which are declared, by ancient authors, almost with one consent, to be the highest.[1] The Chaldean paraphrast also points out the particular part, which he calls mountains of *Cardu*,[2] which others call *Cardueni*. But whether that be true, which Josephus has handed down respecting the fragments of the ark found there in his time; remnants of which, Jerome says, remained to his own age, I leave undecided.

6. *At the end of forty days.* We may hence conjecture

---

[1] " As to the opinion, which takes the mountains of Ararat to be situated within the country of Armenia, the followers of it (some very few excepted) do agree, that the ark of Noah rested in that part of the mountains of Ararat, which in Greek and Latin writers is styled the Gordiæan mountains, (or, with some variation, the mountains of the Cordyæi, Cordueni, Carduchi, Curdi, &c.,) and which lies near the spring of the Tigris."—*Wells' Geography*, vol. i. chap. 2.—*Ed.*

[2] " עַל טוּרֵי קרדו. (Al toorai Kardoo,) Super montes Cardu.—Chaldee paraphrase."—*Walton.*

with what great anxiety the breast of the holy man was oppressed.   After he had perceived the ark to be resting on
solid ground, he yet did not dare to open the window till the
fortieth day; not because he was stunned and torpid, but
because an example, thus formidable, of the vengeance of God,
had affected him with such fear and sorrow combined, that,
being deprived of all judgment, he silently remained in the
chamber of his ark.   At length he sends forth a raven, from
which he might receive a more certain indication of the dryness of the earth.   But the raven perceiving nothing but
muddy marshes, hovers around, and immediately seeks to be
readmitted.   I have no doubt that Noah purposely selected
the raven, which he knew might be allured by the odour of
carcasses, to take a further flight, if the earth, with the animals upon it, were already exposed to view; but the raven,
flying around, did not depart far.   I wonder whence a nega-
tion, which Moses has not in the Hebrew text, has crept into
the Greek and Latin version, since it entirely changes the
sense.[1]   Hence the fable has originated, that the raven, having found carcasses, was kept away from the ark, and forsook
its protector.   Afterwards, futile allegories followed, just as
the curiosity of men is ever desirous of trifling.   But the
dove, in its first egress, imitated the raven, because it flew
back to the ark; afterwards it brought a branch of olive in
its bill; and at the third time, as if emancipated, it enjoyed
the free air, and the free earth.   Some writers exercise their
ingenuity on the olive branch;[2] because among the ancients it
was the emblem of peace, as the laurel was of victory.   But
I rather think, that as the olive tree does not grow upon the
mountains, and is not a very lofty tree, the Lord had given
his servant some token whence he might infer, that pleasant
regions, and productive of good fruits, were now freed from

---

[1] "ויצא יצוא ושוב, Vayetsa yatso vashoob."   "And went out going and
returning."   The Vulgate has it, 'Qui egrediebatur, et *non* revertebatur.
The Septuagint introduces the same negative, so does the Syriac; but
the Chaldee paraphrase, the Samaritan text, and the Arabic version, all
omit the negative.   Our translators, in the text, seem to have followed
the Vulgate, though hesitatingly, but in the margin, they give the rendering of the original.—See *Walton's Polyglott.—Ed.*

[2] "In ramo olivæ quidam philosophantur."

the waters.   Because the version of Jerome says, that it was
a branch with green leaves ; they who have thought, that the
deluge began in the month of September, take this as a confirmation of their opinion.   But the words of Moses have no
such meaning.   And it might be that the Lord, willing to
revive the spirit of Noah, offered some branch to the dove,
which had not yet altogether withered under the waters.

15. *And God spake unto Noah.*   Though Noah was not a
little terrified at the judgment of God, yet his patience is
commended in this respect, that having the earth, which
offered him a home, before his eyes, he yet does not venture
to go forth.   Profane men may ascribe this to timidity, or
even to indolence ; but holy is that timidity which is produced by the obedience of faith.   Let us therefore know,
that Noah was restrained, by a hallowed modesty, from
allowing himself to enjoy the bounty of nature, till he should
hear the voice of God directing him to do so.   Moses winds
this up in a few words, but it is proper that we should attend
to the thing itself.   All ought indeed, spontaneously, to consider how great must have been the fortitude of the man,
who, after the incredible weariness of a whole year, when the
deluge has ceased, and new life has shone forth, does not yet
move a foot out of his sepulchre, without the command of
God.   Thus we see, that, by a continual course of faith, the
holy man was obedient to God ; because, at God's command,
he entered the ark, and there remained until God opened the
way for his egress ; and because he chose rather to lie in a
tainted atmosphere than to breathe the free air, until he
should feel assured that his removal would be pleasing to
God.   Even in minute affairs, Scripture commends to us this
self-government, that we should attempt nothing but with an
approving conscience.   How much less is the rashness of
men to be endured in religious matters, if, without taking
counsel of God, they permit themselves to act as they please.
It is not indeed to be expected that God will every moment
pronounce, by special oracles, what is necessary to be done ;
yet it becomes us to hearken attentively to his voice, in order
to be certainly persuaded that we undertake nothing but

what is in accordance with his word. The spirit of prudence, and of counsel, is also to be sought ; of which he never leaves those destitute, who are docile and obedient to his commands. In this sense, Moses relates that Noah went out of the ark as soon as he, relying on the oracle of God, was aware that a new habitation was given him in the earth.

17. *That they may breed abundantly, &c.* With these words the Lord would cheer the mind of Noah, and inspire him with confidence, that a seed had been preserved in the ark which should increase till it replenished the whole earth. In short, the renovation of the earth is promised to Noah ; to the end that he may know that the world itself was inclosed in the ark, and that the solitude and devastation, at the sight of which his heart might faint, would not be perpetual.

20. *And Noah builded an altar unto the Lord.* As Noah had given many proofs of his obedience, so he now presents an example of gratitude. This passage teaches us that sacrifices were instituted from the beginning for this end, that men should habituate themselves, by such exercises, to celebrate the goodness of God, and to give him thanks. The bare confession of the tongue, yea, even the silent acknowledgment of the heart, might suffice for God ; but we know how many stimulants our indolence requires. Therefore, when the holy fathers, formerly, professed their piety towards God by sacrifices, the use of them was by no means superfluous. Besides, it was right that they should always have before their eyes symbols, by which they would be admonished, that they could have no access to God but through a mediator. Now, however, the manifestation of Christ has taken away these ancient shadows. Wherefore, let us use those helps which the Lord has prescribed.[1] Moreover,

---

[1] " Quare adminiculis utamur," &c. The French translation has it, " Et pourtant usons," &c. " And, nevertheless, let us use," &c. The meaning of the sentence seems to be, that, as the fathers, in obedience to God, used sacrifices, which were afterwards abolished as being of no value, so ought we to avail ourselves of those aids (adminicula) which might seem to be of no importance, had not God enjoined them.—*Ed.*

when I say that sacrifices were made use of, by the holy fathers, to celebrate the benefits of God, I speak only of one kind: for this offering of Noah answers to the peace-offerings, and the first-fruits. But here it may be asked, by what impulse Noah offered a sacrifice to God, seeing he had no command to do so? I answer: although Moses does not expressly declare that God commanded him to do it, yet a certain judgment may be formed from what follows, and even from the whole context, that Noah had rested upon the word of God, and that, in reliance on the divine command, he had rendered this worship, which he knew, indubitably, would be acceptable to God. We have before said, that one animal of every kind was preserved separately; and have stated for what end it was done. But it was useless to set apart animals for sacrifice, unless God had revealed this design to holy Noah, who was to be the priest to offer up the victims. Besides, Moses says that sacrifices were chosen from among clean animals. But it is certain that Noah did not invent this distinction for himself, since it does not depend on human choice. Whence we conclude, that he undertook nothing without divine authority. Also immediately afterwards, Moses subjoins, that the smell of the sacrifice was acceptable to God. This general rule, therefore, is to be observed, that all religious services which are not perfumed with the odour of faith, are of an ill-savour before God. Let us therefore know, that the altar of Noah was founded in the word of God. And the same word was as salt to his sacrifices, that they might not be insipid.

21. *And the Lord smelled a sweet savour.*[1] Moses calls that by which God was appeased, an odour of rest; as if he had said, the sacrifice had been rightly offered. Yet nothing can be more absurd than to suppose that God should have been appeased by the filthy smoke of entrails, and of flesh. But Moses here, according to his manner, invests God with a human character, for the purpose of accommodating himself to the capacity of an ignorant people. For it is not even to

---

[1] " Odorem quietis." " A savour of rest."—*Margin of English Version.*

be supposed, that the rite of sacrifice, in itself, was grateful to God as a meritorious act; but we must regard the end of the work, and not confine ourselves to the external form. For what else did Noah propose to himself than to acknowledge that he had received his own life, and that of the animals, as the gift of God's mercy alone? This piety breathed a good and sweet odour before God; as it is said, (Psalm cxvi. 12,) " What shall I render unto the Lord for all his benefits? I will take the cup of salvation, and will call upon the name of the Lord."

And the Lord said in his heart. The meaning of the passage is, God had decreed that he would not hereafter curse the earth. And this form of expression has great weight: for although God never retracts what he has openly spoken with his mouth, yet we are more deeply affected when we hear, that he has fixed upon something in his own mind; because an inward decree of this kind in no way depends upon creatures. To sum up the whole, God certainly determined that he would never more destroy the world by a deluge. Yet the expression, 'I will not curse,' is to be but generally understood; because we know how much the earth has lost of its fertility since it has been corrupted by man's sin, and we daily feel that it is cursed in various ways. And he explains himself a little afterwards, saying, 'I will not smite any more every thing living.' For in these words he does not allude to every kind of vengeance, but only to that which should destroy the world, and bring ruin both on mankind and the rest of animals: as if he would say, that he restored the earth with this stipulation, that it should not afterwards perish by a deluge. So when the Lord declares, (Isa. liv. 9,) that he will be contented with one captivity of his people, he compares it with the waters of Noah, by which he had resolved that the world should only once be overwhelmed.[1]

For the imagination of man's heart. This reasoning seems incongruous: for if the wickedness of man is so great that it

---

[1] " For this is as the waters of Noah unto me; for as I have sworn that the waters of Noah should no more go over the earth, so have I sworn that I would not be wroth with thee, nor rebuke thee."

does not cease to provoke the anger of God, it must necessarily bring down destruction upon the world. Nay, God seems to contradict himself by having previously declared that the world must be destroyed, because its iniquity was desperate. But here it behoves us more deeply to consider his design; for it was the will of God that there should be some society of men to inhabit the earth. If, however, they were to be dealt with according to their deserts, there would be a necessity for a daily deluge. Wherefore, he declares, that in inflicting punishment upon the second world, he will so do it, as yet to preserve the external appearance of the earth, and not again to sweep away the creatures with which he has adorned it. Indeed, we ourselves may perceive such moderation to have been used, both in the public and special judgments of God, that the world yet stands in its completeness, and nature yet retains its course. Moreover, since God here declares what would be the character of men even to the end of the world, it is evident that the whole human race is under sentence of condemnation, on account of its depravity and wickedness. Nor does the sentence refer only to corrupt morals; but their iniquity is said to be an innate iniquity, from which nothing but evils can spring forth. I wonder, however, whence that false version of this passage has crept in, that the thought is prone to evil;[1] except, as is probable, that the place was thus corrupted, by those who dispute too philosophically concerning the corruption of human nature. It seemed to them hard, that man should be subjected, as a slave of the devil, to sin. Therefore, by way of mitigation, they have said that he had a *propensity* to vices. But when the celestial Judge thunders from heaven, that his thoughts themselves are evil, what avails it to soften down that which, nevertheless, remains unalterable? Let men therefore acknowledge, that inasmuch as they are born of Adam, they are depraved creatures, and therefore can conceive only sinful thoughts, until they become the new workmanship of Christ, and are formed by his Spirit to a new life.

---

[1] " Sensus enim, et cogitatio humani cordis in malum prona sunt."— *Vulgate.*

And it is not to be doubted, that the Lord declares the very mind of man to be depraved, and altogether infected with sin ; so that all the thoughts which proceed thence are evil. If such be the defect in the fountain itself, it follows, that all man's affections are evil, and his works covered with the same pollution, since of necessity they must savour of their original. For God does not merely say that men sometimes think evil ; but the language is unlimited, comprising the tree with its fruits. Nor is it any proof to the contrary, that carnal and profane men often excel in generosity of disposition, undertake designs apparently honourable, and put forth certain evidences of virtue. For since their mind is corrupted with contempt of God, with pride, self-love, ambition, hypocrisy, and fraud ; it cannot be but that all their thoughts are contaminated with the same vices. Again, they cannot tend towards a right end : whence it happens that they are judged to be what they really are, crooked and perverse. For all things in such men, which please us under the colour of virtue, are like wine spoiled by the odour of the cask. For, (as was before said,) the very affections of nature, which in themselves are laudable, are yet vitiated by original sin, and on account of their irregularity, have degenerated from their proper nature ; such are the mutual love of married persons, the love of parents towards their children, and the like. And the clause which is added, " from youth," more fully declares that men are born evil ; in order to show that, as soon as they are of an age to begin to form thoughts, they have radical corruption of mind. Philosophers, by transferring to habit, what God here ascribes to nature, betray their own ignorance. And no wonder ; for we please and flatter ourselves to such an extent, that we do not perceive how fatal is the contagion of sin, and what depravity pervades all our senses. We must, therefore, acquiesce in the judgment of God, which pronounces man to be so enslaved by sin that he can bring forth nothing sound and sincere. Yet, at the same time, we must remember, that no blame is to be cast upon God for that which has its origin in the defection of the first man, whereby the order of the creation was subverted. And further, it must be noted, that men are not exempted from guilt and condemnation, by the pretext of this bondage : because, although all rush to evil, yet they are not impelled by any extrinsic force, but by the direct inclination of their own hearts ; and, lastly, they sin not otherwise than voluntarily.

22. *While the earth remaineth.*[1] By these words the world is again completely restored. For so great was the confusion and disorder which had overspread the earth, that there was a necessity for some renovation. On which account, Peter speaks of the old world as having perished in the deluge, (2 Pet. iii. 6.) Moreover, the deluge had been an interruption of the order of nature. For the revolutions of the sun and moon had ceased: there was no distinction of winter and summer. Wherefore, the Lord here declares it to be his pleasure, that all things should recover their vigour, and be restored to their functions. The Jews erroneously divide their year into six parts; whereas Moses, by placing the summer in opposition to the winter, thus divides the whole year in a popular manner into two parts. And it is not to be doubted, that by *cold* and *heat* he designates the periods already referred to. Under the words, " seed-time," and " harvest," he marks those advantages which flow to men from the moderated temperature of the atmosphere. If it is objected, that this equable temperament is not every year perceived ; the answer is ready, that the order of the world is indeed disturbed by our vices, so that many of its movements are irregular : often the sun withholds its proper heat,—snow or hail follow in the place of dew,—the air is agitated by various tempests; but although the world is not so regulated as to produce perpetual uniformity of seasons, yet we perceive the order of nature so far to prevail, that winter and summer annually recur, that there is a constant succession of days and nights, and that the earth brings forth its fruits in summer and autumn. Moreover, by the expression, ' all the days of the earth,' he means, ' as long as the earth shall last.'

---

[1] " Posthac omnibus diebus terræ."

CHAPTER IX.

1. AND God blessed Noah and his sons, and said unto them, Be fruitful, and multiply, and replenish the earth.

2. And the fear of you and the dread of you shall be upon every beast of the earth, and upon every fowl of the air, upon all that moveth *upon* the earth, and upon all the fishes of the sea; into your hand are they delivered.

3. Every moving thing that liveth shall be meat for you; even as the green herb have I given you all things.

4. But flesh with the life thereof, *which is* the blood thereof, shall ye not eat.

5. And surely your blood of your lives will I require; at the hand of every beast will I require it, and at the hand of man; at the hand of every man's brother will I require the life of man.

6. Whoso sheddeth man's blood, by man shall his blood be shed: for in the image of God made he man.

7. And you, be ye fruitful, and multiply; bring forth abundantly in the earth, and multiply therein.

8. And God spake unto Noah, and to his sons with him, saying,

9. And I, behold, I establish my covenant with you, and with your seed after you;

10. And with every living creature that *is* with you, of the fowl, of the cattle, and of every beast of the earth with you; from all that go out of the ark, to every beast of the earth.

11. And I will establish my covenant with you; neither shall all flesh be cut off any more by the waters of a flood; neither shall there any more be a flood to destroy the earth.

1. Et benedixit Deus Noah, et filiis ejus : et dixit ad eos, Crescite, et multiplicamini, et replete terram.

2. Et timor vester et pavor vester erit super omnem bestiam terræ, et super omne volatile cœli, cum omnibus quæ gradiuntur in terra, et omnibus piscibus maris : *quia* manui vestræ tradita sunt,

3. Omne reptile quod vivit, vobis erit ad vescendum : sicut virentem herbam dedi vobis omnia.

4. Veruntamen carnem cum anima ejus, sanguine ejus, non comedetis.

5. Et profecto sanguinem vestrum, qui vobis est in animas, requiram : de manu omnis bestiæ requiram illum, et de manu hominis, et de manu viri fratris ejus requiram animam hominis.

6. Qui effuderit sanguinem hominis in homine, sanguis ejus effundetur : quia ad imaginem Dei fecit hominem.

7. Et vos crescite, et multiplicamini, et generate in terra, et multiplicemini in ea.

8. Et dixit Deus ad Noah, et ad filios ejus qui cum eo erant, dicendo,

9. Et ego, ecce ego statuo pactum meum vobiscum, et cum semine vestro post vos.

10. Et cum omni anima vivente quæ est vobiscum, tam cum volatili quam cum animali, et omni bestia terræ vobiscum, ab omnibus quæ egressa sunt ex arca : cum omni, *inquam*, bestia terræ.

11. Et statuam pactum meum vobiscum, et non excidetur omnis caro ultra ab aquis diluvii, et non erit ultra diluvium, ut disperdat terram.

12. And God said, This *is* the token of the covenant which I make between me and you, and every living creature that *is* with you, for perpetual generations:

13. I do set my bow in the cloud, and it shall be for a token of a covenant between me and the earth.

14. And it shall come to pass, when I bring a cloud over the earth, that the bow shall be seen in the cloud:

15. And I will remember my covenant, which *is* between me and you and every living creature of all flesh; and the waters shall no more become a flood to destroy all flesh.

16. And the bow shall be in the cloud; and I will look upon it, that I may remember the everlasting covenant between God and every living creature of all flesh that *is* upon the earth.

17. And God said unto Noah, This *is* the token of the covenant, which I have established between me and all flesh that *is* upon the earth.

18. And the sons of Noah, that went forth of the ark, were Shem, and Ham, and Japheth; and Ham *is* the father of Canaan.

19. These *are* the three sons of Noah: and of them was the whole earth overspread.

20. And Noah began *to be* an husbandman, and he planted a vineyard:

21. And he drank of the wine, and was drunken; and he was uncovered within his tent.

22. And Ham, the father of Canaan, saw the nakedness of his father, and told his two brethren without.

23. And Shem and Japheth took a garment, and laid *it* upon both their shoulders, and went backward, and covered the nakedness of their father; and their faces *were* backward, and they saw not their father's nakedness.

24. And Noah awoke from his wine, and knew what his younger son had done unto him.

25. And he said, Cursed *be* Canaan; a servant of servants shall he be unto his brethren.

12. Et dixit Deus, Hoc est signum fœderis quod ego do inter me et vos, et omnem animam viventem quæ est vobiscum in generationes sæculi:

13. Arcum meum ponam in nube, et erit in signum fœderis inter me et terram.

14. Et erit, quum obnubilavero nubem super terram, tunc apparebit arcus in nube.

15. Et recordabor fœderis mei quod est inter me et vos, et omnem animam viventem cum omni carne: et non erit ultra aqua ad diluvium, ut disperdat omnem carnem.

16. Et erit arcus in nube, et videbo illum, ut recorder pacti perpetui inter Deum et omnem animam viventem cum omni carne quæ est super terram.

17. Et dixit Deus ad Noah, Hoc est signum fœderis quod statui inter me et omnem carnem quæ est super terram.

18. Erant autem filii Noah qui egressi sunt de arca, Sem, Cham, et Jepheth: et Cham est pater Chenaan.

19. Tres isti, filii Noah: et ab istis dispersa est universa terra.

20. Cœpit vero Noah colere terram, et plantavit vineam.

21. Et bibit de vino et inebriatus est, et discooperuit se in medio tabernaculi sui.

22. Et vidit Cham pater Chenaan turpitudinem patris sui, et nuntiavit duobus fratribus suis in platea.

23. Et tulerunt Sem et Jepheth vestimentum, et posuerunt super humerum ambo ipsi: et euntes retrorsum, operuerunt turpitudinem patris sui: et facies eorum erant retrorsum, et turpitudinem patris sui non viderunt.

24. Expergefactus autem Noah a vino suo, cognovit quod fecerat sibi filius suus minor.

25. Et dixit, Maledictus Chenaan, servus servorum erit fratribus suis.

26. And he said, Blessed *be* the Lord God of Shem; and Canaan shall be his servant.

26. Et dixit, Benedictus Jehova Deus Sem, et sit Chenaan servus eis.

27. God shall enlarge Japheth, and he shall dwell in the tents of Shem; and Canaan shall be his servant.

27. Dilatet Deus Jepheth, et habitet in tabernaculis Sem: et sit Chenaan servus eis.

28. And Noah lived after the flood three hundred and fifty years.

28. Et vixit Noah post diluvium trecentos annos et quinquaginta annos.

29. And all the days of Noah were nine hundred and fifty years: and he died.

29. Fuerunt autem omnes dies Noah nongenti anni et quinquaginta anni: et mortuus est.

1. *And God blessed Noah.* We hence infer with what great fear Noah had been dejected, because God, so often and at such length, proceeds to encourage him. For when Moses here says, that God blessed Noah and his sons, he does not simply mean that the favour of fruitfulness was restored to them; but that, at the same time, the design of God concerning the new restitution of the world was revealed unto them. For to the blessing itself is added the *voice* of God by which he addresses them. We know that brute animals produce offspring in no other way than by the blessing of God; but Moses here commemorates a privilege which belongs only to men. Therefore, lest those four men and their wives, seized with trepidation, should doubt for what purpose they had been delivered, the Lord prescribes to them their future condition of life: namely, that they shall raise up mankind from death to life. Thus he not only renews the world by the same word by which he before created it; but he directs his word to men, in order that they may recover the lawful use of marriage, may know that the care of producing offspring is pleasing to Himself, and may have confidence that a progeny shall spring from them which shall diffuse itself through all regions of the earth, so as to render it again inhabited; although it had been laid waste and made a desert. Yet he did not permit promiscuous intercourse, but sanctioned anew that law of marriage which he had before ordained. And although the blessing of God is, in some way, extended to illicit connections, so that offspring is thence produced, yet this is an impure fruitfulness; that

which is lawful flows only from the expressly declared benediction of God.

2. *And the fear of you.* This also has chiefly respect to the
restoration of the world, in order that the sovereignty over the
rest of animals might remain with men. And although, after
the fall of man, the beasts were endued with new ferocity, yet
some remains of that dominion over them, which God had conferred on him in the beginning, were still left. He now also
promises that the same dominion shall continue. We see indeed
that wild beasts rush violently upon men, and rend and tear
many of them in pieces; and if God did not wonderfully
restrain their fierceness, the human race would be utterly
destroyed. Therefore, what we have said respecting the
inclemency of the air, and the irregularity of the seasons, is
also here applicable. Savage beasts indeed prevail and rage
against men in various ways, and no wonder; for since we
perversely exalt ourselves against God, why should not the
beasts rise up against us? Nevertheless, the providence of
God is a secret bridle to restrain their violence. For, whence
does it arise that serpents spare us, unless because he represses their virulence? Whence is it that tigers, elephants,
lions, bears, wolves, and other wild beasts without number,
do not rend, tear, and devour everything human, except that
they are withheld by this subjection, as by a barrier? Therefore, it ought to be referred to the special protection and guardianship of God, that we remain in safety. For, were it otherwise, what could we expect; since they seem as if born
for our destruction, and burn with the furious desire to injure
us? Moreover, the bridle with which the Lord restrains the
cruelty of wild beasts, to prevent them falling upon men, is a
certain fear and dread which God has implanted in them, to
the end that they might reverence the presence of men.
Daniel especially declares this respecting kings; namely, that
they are possessed of dominion, because the Lord has put
the fear and the dread of them both on men and beasts. But
as the first use of fear is to defend the society of mankind; so, according to the measure in which God has given
to men a general authority over the beasts, there exists in

the greatest and the least of men, I know not what hidden mark, which does not suffer the cruelty of wild beasts, by its violence, to prevail.   Another advantage, however, and one more widely extended, is here noted ; namely, that men may render animals subservient to their own convenience, and may apply them to various uses, according to their wishes and their necessities.   Therefore, the fact that oxen become accustomed to bear the yoke ; that the wildness of horses is so subdued as to cause them to carry a rider ; that they receive the pack-saddle to bear burdens ; that cows give milk, and suffer themselves to be milked ; that sheep are mute under the hand of the shearer ; all these facts are the result of this dominion, which, although greatly diminished, is nevertheless not entirely abolished.

3. *Every moving thing that liveth shall be meat for you.*   The Lord proceeds further, and grants animals for food to men, that they may eat their flesh.   And because Moses now first relates that this right was given to men, nearly all commentators infer, that it was not lawful for man to eat flesh before the deluge, but that the natural fruits of the earth were his only food.   But the argument is not sufficiently firm.   For I hold to this principle ; that God here does not bestow on men more than he had previously given, but only restores what had been taken away, that they might again enter on the possession of those good things from which they had been excluded.   For since they had before offered sacrifices to God, and were also permitted to kill wild beasts, from the hides and skins of which, they might make for themselves garments and tents, I do not see what obligation should prevent them from the eating of flesh.   But since it is of little consequence what opinion is held, I affirm nothing on the subject.[1]   This ought justly to be deemed by us of greater

[1] The question which Calvin here dismisses as one of little importance, has, in modern controversy, assumed a very different position ; and most commentators have come to a decision, the reverse of that to which he inclines.   His argument appears chargeable with the want of firmness, which he imputes to others.   The inference that the flesh of sacrifices was eaten, since otherwise it must have been wasted, is of no force, if we suppose the first sacrifices to have been all *holocausts*, or whole burnt-

importance, that to eat the flesh of animals is granted to us by the kindness of God; that we do not seize upon what our appetite desires, as robbers do, nor yet tyrannically shed the innocent blood of cattle; but that we only take what is offered to us by the hand of the Lord. We have heard what Paul says, that we are at liberty to eat what we please, only we do it with the assurance of conscience, but that he who imagines anything to be unclean, to him it is unclean, (Rom. xiv. 14.) And whence has this happened to man, that he should eat whatever food he pleased before God, with a tranquil mind, and not with unbridled license, except from his knowing, that it has been divinely delivered into his hand by the right of donation? Wherefore, (the same Paul being witness,) the word of God sanctifies the creatures, that we may purely and lawfully feed on them, (1 Tim. iv. 5.) Let the adage be utterly rejected which says, 'that no one can feed and re-fresh his body with a morsel of bread, without, at the same time, defiling his soul.' Therefore it is not to be doubted, that the Lord designed to confirm our faith, when he ex-pressly declares by Moses, that he gave to man the free use of flesh, so that we might not eat it with a doubtful and trembling conscience. At the same time, however, he in-vites us to thanksgiving. On this account also, Paul adds " prayer" to the " word," in defining the method of sanctifi-cation in the passage recently cited.

And now we must firmly retain the liberty given us by the Lord, which he designed to be recorded as on public tables. For, by this word, he addresses all the posterity of Noah, and renders his gift common to all ages. And why is this done, but that the faithful may boldly assert their right to that which, they know, has proceeded from God as its Author? For it is an insupportable tyranny, when God, the Creator of all things, has laid open to us the earth and the air, in order that we may thence take food as from his storehouse, for

offerings unto the Lord. The garments or tents referred to as made from the skins of animals were, in all probability, those of the very animals which were thus sacrificed; so that there is no reason hence to conclude, that flesh was eaten before the deluge. But let the reader refer to Magee on the Atonement, Dissertation, No. liii.—*Ed.*

these to be shut up from us by mortal man, who is not able to create even a snail or a fly. I do not speak of external prohibition;[1] but I assert, that atrocious injury is done to God, when we give such license to men as to allow them to pronounce that unlawful which God designs to be lawful, and to bind consciences which the word of God sets free, with their fictitious laws. The fact that God prohibited his ancient people from the use of unclean animals, seeing that exception was but temporary, is here passed over by Moses.

4. *But flesh with the life thereof, which is the blood thereof.* Some thus explain this passage, ' Ye may not eat a member cut off from a living animal,' which is too trifling. However, since there is no copulative conjunction between the two words, *blood* and *life,* I do not doubt that Moses, speaking of the *life,* added the word *blood* exegetically,[2] as if he would say, that flesh is in some sense devoured with its life, when it is eaten imbued with its own blood. Wherefore, the life and the blood are not put for different things, but for the same ; not because blood is in itself the life, but inasmuch as the vital spirits chiefly reside in the blood, it is, as far as our feeling is concerned, a token which represents life. And this is expressly declared, in order that men may have the greater horror of eating blood. For if it be a savage and barbarous thing to devour lives, or to swallow down living flesh, men betray their brutality by eating blood. Moreover, the tendency of this prohibition is by no means obscure, namely, that God intends to accustom men to gentleness, by abstinence from the blood of animals ; but, if they should become unrestrained, and daring in eating wild animals, they would at length not be sparing of even human blood. Yet we must remember, that this restriction was part of the old law.[3] Wherefore, what Tertullian relates, that in his time it was

---

[1] By *external prohibition,* is probably meant such as might be enjoined by the magistrate during a time of scarcity, or for any purely civil purpose.—*Ed.*

[2] This is apparent in the English version, where the words, " which is," are added in Italics, showing that in the judgment of the translators, the word following was explanatory of that which preceded.—*Ed.*

[3] " Partem fuisse veteris pædagogiæ."

unlawful among Christians to taste the blood of cattle, savours of superstition. For the apostles, in commanding the Gentiles to observe this rite, for a short time, did not intend to inject a scruple into their consciences, but only to prevent the liberty which was otherwise sacred, from proving an occasion of offence to the ignorant and the weak.

5. *And surely your blood of your lives will I require.* In these words the Lord more explicitly declares that he does not forbid the use of blood out of regard to animals themselves, but because he accounts the life of men precious : and because the sole end of his law is, to promote the exercise of common humanity between them. I therefore think that Jerome, in rendering the particle אַךְ, (*ach*,) *For*, has done better than they who read it as an adversative disjunctive; ' *otherwise* your blood will I require;' yet literally it may best be thus translated, 'And truly your blood.'[1] The whole context is (in my opinion) to be thus read, 'And truly your blood, which is *in* your lives, or which is *as* your lives, that is, which vivifies and quickens you, as it respects your body, will I require : from the hand of all animals will I require it ; from the hand of man, from the hand, I say, of man, his brother, will I require the life of man.' The distinction by which the Jews constitute four kinds of homicide is frivolous ; for I have explained the simple and genuine sense, namely, that God so highly estimates our life, that he will not suffer murder to go unavenged. And he inculcates this in so many words, in order that he may render the cruelty of those the more detestable, who lay violent hands upon their neighbours. And it is no common proof of God's love towards us, that he undertakes the defence of our lives, and declares that he will be the avenger of our death. In saying that he will exact punishment from animals for the violated life of men, he gives us this as an example. For if, on behalf of man, he is angry with brute creatures who are hurried by a blind impulse to feed upon him ; what, do we suppose, will become of

---

[1] Thus agreeing with the English version.

the man who, unjustly, cruelly, and contrary to the sense of nature, falls upon his brother?

6. *Whoso sheddeth man's blood.*[1]   The clause *in man* which is here added, has the force of amplification.   Some expound it, 'Before witnesses.'   Others refer it to what follows, namely, 'that by man his blood should be shed.'[2]   But all these interpretations are forced.   What I have said must be remembered, that this language rather expresses the atrociousness of the crime; because whosoever kills a man, draws down upon himself the blood and life of his brother.   On the whole, they are deceived (in my judgment) who think that a political law, for the punishment of homicides, is here simply intended.   Truly I do not deny that the punishment which the laws ordain, and which the judges execute, are founded on this divine sentence; but I say the words are more comprehensive.   It is written, 'Men of blood shall not live out half their days,' (Ps. lv. 25.)   And we see some die in highways, some in stews, and many in wars.   Therefore, however magistrates may connive at the crime, God sends executioners from other quarters, who shall render unto sanguinary men their reward.   God so threatens and denounces vengeance against the murderer, that he even arms the magistrate with the sword for the avenging of slaughter, in order that the blood of men may not be shed with impunity.

For in the image of God made he man.   For the greater confirmation of the above doctrine, God declares, that he is not thus solicitous respecting human life rashly, and for no purpose.   Men are indeed unworthy of God's care, if respect be had only to themselves: but since they bear the image of God engraven on them, He deems himself violated in their person.   Thus, although they have nothing of their own by which they obtain the favour of God, he looks upon his own gifts in them, and is thereby excited to love and to care for them.   This doctrine, however, is to be carefully observed, that no one can be injurious to his brother without wounding

---

[1] " Qui effuderit sanguinem hominis in homine." He who shall have shed the blood of man in man.

[2] This is the interpretation of the English version.

God himself. Were this doctrine deeply fixed in our minds, we should be much more reluctant than we are to inflict injuries. Should any one object, that this divine image has been obliterated, the solution is easy; first, there yet exists some remnant of it, so that man is possessed of no small dignity; and, secondly, the Celestial Creator himself, however corrupted man may be, still keeps in view the end of his original creation; and according to his example, we ought to consider for what end he created men, and what excellence he has bestowed upon them above the rest of living beings.

7. *And you, be ye fruitful and multiply.* He again turns his discourse to Noah and his sons, exhorting them to the propagation of offspring: as if he would say, ' You see that I am intent upon cherishing and preserving mankind, do you therefore also attend to it.' At the same time, in commending to them the preservation of seed, he deters them from murder, and from unjust acts of violence. Yet his chief end was that to which I have before alluded, that he might encourage their dejected minds. For in these words is contained not a bare precept, but also a promise.

8. *And God spake unto Noah.* That the memory of the deluge might not inspire them with new terrors, as often as the sky were covered with clouds, lest the earth should again be drowned; this source of anxiety is taken away. And certainly, if we consider the great propensity of the human mind to distrust, we shall not deem this testimony to have been unnecessary even for Noah. He was indeed endued with a rare and incomparable faith, even to a miracle; but no strength of constancy could be so great, that this most sad and terrible vengeance of God should not shake it. Therefore, whenever any great and continued shower shall seem to threaten the earth with a deluge, this barrier, on which the holy man may rely, is interposed. Now, although his sons would need this confirmation more than he, yet the Lord speaks especially on his account. And the clause which follows, ' and to his sons who were with him,' is to be referred to this point. For how is it, that God, making his cove-

nant with the sons of Noah, commands them to hope
for the best? Truly, because they are joined with their
father, who is, as it were, the stipulator of the covenant, so
as to be associated with him, in a subordinate place.[1]   Moreover, there is no doubt that it was the design of God to provide for all his posterity.   It was not therefore a private covenant confirmed with one family only, but one which is
common to all people, and which shall flourish in all ages to
the end of the world.   And truly, since at the present time,
impiety overflows not less than in the age of Noah, it is
especially necessary that the waters should be restrained by
this word of God, as by a thousand bolts and bars, lest they
should break forth to destroy us.   Wherefore, relying on
this promise, let us look forward to the last day, in which the
consuming fire shall purify heaven and earth.

10. *And with every living creature.* Although the favour
which the Lord promises extends also to animals, yet it is
not in vain that he addresses himself only to men, who, by
the sense of faith, are able to perceive this benefit.   We enjoy the heaven and the air in common with the beasts, and
draw the same vital breath ; but it is no common privilege,
that God directs his word to us; whence we may learn with
what paternal love he pursues us.   And here three distinct
steps are to be traced.   First, God, as in a matter of present
concern, makes a covenant with Noah and his family, lest
they should be afraid of a deluge for themselves.   Secondly,
he transmits his covenant to posterity, not only that, as by
continual succession, the effect may reach to other ages ; but
that they who should afterwards be born might also apprehend this testimony by faith, and might conclude that the
same thing which had been promised to the sons of Noah,
was promised unto them.   Thirdly, he declares that he will
be propitious also to brute animals, so that the effect of the
covenant towards them, might be the preservation of their
lives only, without imparting to them sense and intelligence.
Hence the ignorance of the Anabaptists may be refuted, who
deny that the covenant of God is common to infants, because

[1] " Ut secundo loco in societatem accedant."

they are destitute of present faith. As if, truly, when God promises salvation to a thousand generations, the fathers were not intermediate parties between God and their children, whose office it is to deliver to their children (so to speak) from hand to hand, the promise received from God. But as many as withdraw their life from this protection of God (since the greater part of men either despise or ridicule this divine covenant) deserve, by this single act of ingratitude, to be immersed in eternal fire. For although this be an earthly promise, yet God designs the faith of his people to be exercised, in order that they may be assured that a certain abode will, by his special goodness, be provided for them on earth, until they shall be gathered together in heaven.

12. *This is the token of the covenant.* A sign is added to the promise, in which is exhibited the wonderful kindness of God; who, for the purpose of confirming our faith in his word, does not disdain to use such helps. And although we have more fully discussed the use of signs in the second chapter, yet we must briefly maintain, from these words of Moses, that it is wrong to sever signs from the word. By the word, I mean not that of which Papists boast; whereby they enchant bread, wine, water, and oil, with their magical whisperings; but that which may strengthen faith : according as the Lord here plainly addresses holy Noah and his sons; he then annexes a seal, for the sake of assurance. Wherefore, if the sacrament be wrested from the word, it ceases to be what it is called. It must, I say, be a vocal sign, in order that it may retain its force, and not degenerate from its nature. And not only is that administration of sacraments in which the word of God is silent, vain and ludicrous; but it draws with it pure satanic delusions. Hence we also infer, that from the beginning, it was the peculiar property of sacraments, to avail for the confirmation of faith. For certainly, in the covenant that promise is included to which faith ought to respond. It appears to some absurd, that faith should be sustained by such helps. But they who speak thus do not, in the first place, reflect on the great ignorance and imbecility of our minds ; nor do they, secondly, ascribe to the work-

ing of the secret power of the Spirit that praise which is due. It is the work of God alone to begin and to perfect faith; but he does it by such instruments as he sees good; the free choice of which is in his own power.

13. *I do set my bow in the cloud.* From these words certain eminent theologians have been induced to deny, that there was any rainbow before the deluge : which is frivolous. For the words of Moses do not signify, that a bow was then formed, which did not previously exist ; but that a mark was engraven upon it, which should give a sign of the divine favour towards men. That this may the more evidently appear, it will be well to recall to memory what we have elsewhere said, that some signs are natural, and some preternatural. And although there are many examples of this second class of signs in the Scriptures ; yet they are peculiar, and do not belong to the common and perpetual use of the Church. For, as it pleases the Lord to employ earthly elements, as vehicles for raising the minds of men on high, so I think the celestial arch which had before existed naturally, is here consecrated into a sign and pledge ; and thus a new office is assigned to it ; whereas, from the nature of the thing itself, it might rather be a sign of the contrary ; for it threatens continued rain. Let this therefore be the meaning of the words, ' As often as the rain shall alarm you, look upon the bow. For although it may seem to cause the rain to overflow the earth, it shall nevertheless be to you a pledge of returning dryness, and thus it will then become you to stand with greater confidence, than under a clear and serene sky.' Hence it is not for us to contend with philosophers respecting the rainbow ; for although its colours are the effect of natural causes, yet they act profanely who attempt to deprive God of the right and authority which he has over his creatures.

15. *And I will remember my covenant.* Moses, by introducing God so often as the speaker, teaches us that the *word* holds the chief place, and that signs are to be estimated by it.[1]

[1] "Precipuas esse verbi partes, et inde æstimanda signa."—"Que le prin-

God, however, speaks after the manner of men, when he
says, that at the sight of the rainbow he will remember his
covenant. But this mode of speaking has reference to the
faith of men, in order that they may reflect, that God, whenever he stretches out his arch over the clouds, is not unmindful of his covenant.

18. *The sons of Noah.* Moses enumerates the sons of
Noah, not only because he is about to pass on to the following history, but for the purpose of more fully illustrating the
force of the promise, " Replenish the earth." For we may
hence better conceive how efficacious the blessing of God
has been, because an immense multitude of men proceeded
in a short time from so small a number ; and because one
family, and that a little one, grew into so many, and such
numerous nations.

20. *And Noah began to be an husbandman.* I do not so
explain the words, as if he then, for the first time, began to
give his attention to the cultivation of the fields ; but, (in
my opinion,) Moses rather intimates, that Noah, with a collected mind, though now an old man, returned to the culture
of the fields, and to his former labours. It is, however, uncertain whether he had been a vine-dresser or not. It is commonly believed that wine was not in use before that time.
And this opinion has been the more willingly received, as
affording an honourable pretext for the excuse of Noah's sin.
But it does not appear to me probable that the fruit of the
vine, which excels all others, should have remained neglected
and unprofitable. Also, Moses does not say that Noah was
drunken on the first day on which he tasted it. Therefore,
leaving this question undetermined, I rather suppose, that we
are to learn from the drunkenness of Noah, what a filthy and
detestable crime drunkenness is. The holy patriarch, though
he had hitherto been a rare example of frugality and temperance, losing all self-possession, did, in a base and shameful

cipal gist en la parole, et que d'icelle il faut estimer les sacramens." That
the principal force is in the word, and that from it we must estimate the
sacraments.—*French Tr.*

manner, prostrate himself naked on the ground, so as to become a laughing-stock to all. Therefore, with what care ought we to cultivate sobriety, lest anything like this, or even worse, should happen to us? Formerly, the heathen philosopher said, that ' Wine is the blood of the earth;' and, therefore, when men intemperately pour it down their throats, they are justly punished by their mother. Let us, however, rather remember, that when men, by shameful abuse, profane this noble and most precious gift of God, He himself becomes the Avenger. And let us know, that Noah, by the judgment of God, has been set forth as a spectacle to be a warning to others, that they should not become intoxicated by excessive drinking. Some excuse might certainly be made for the holy man; who, having completed his labour, and being exhilarated with wine, imagines that he is but taking his just reward. But God brands him with an eternal mark of disgrace. What then, do we suppose, will happen to those idle-bellies and insatiable gluttons, whose sole object of contention is who shall consume the greatest quantity of wine? And although this kind of correction was severe, yet it was profitable to the servant of God; since he was recalled to sobriety, lest by proceeding in the indulgence of a vice to which he had once yielded, he should ruin himself; just as we see drunkards become at length brutalized by continued intemperance.

22. *And Ham, the father of Canaan.* This circumstance is added to augment the sorrow of Noah, that he is mocked by his own son. For we must ever keep in memory, that this punishment was divinely inflicted upon him; partly, because his fault was not a light one; partly, that God in his person might present a lesson of temperance to all ages. Drunkenness in itself deserves as its reward, that they who deface the image of their heavenly Father in themselves, should become a laughing-stock to their own children. For certainly, as far as possible, drunkards subvert their own understanding, and so far deprive themselves of reason as to degenerate into beasts. And let us remember, that if the Lord so grievously avenged the single transgression of the holy man, he will prove an avenger no less severe, against those who are daily intoxicated; and of this we have examples suf-

ficiently numerous before our eyes.   In the meanwhile, Ham, by reproachfully laughing at his father, betrays his own depraved and malignant disposition.   We know that parents, next to God, are most deeply to be reverenced; and if there were neither books nor sermons, nature itself constantly inculcates this lesson upon us.   It is received by common consent, that piety towards parents is the mother of all virtues. This Ham, therefore, must have been of a wicked, perverse, and crooked disposition; since he not only took pleasure in his father's shame, but wished to expose him to his brethren. And this is no slight occasion of offence; first, that Noah, the minister of salvation to men, and the chief restorer of the world, should, in extreme old age, lie intoxicated in his house; and then, that the ungodly and wicked Ham should have proceeded from the sanctuary of God.[1]   God had selected eight souls as a sacred seed, thoroughly purged from all corruption, for the renovation of the Church : but the son of Noah shows, how necessary it is for men to be held as with the bridle of God, however they may be exalted by privilege.   The impiety of Ham proves to us how deep is the root of wickedness in men; and that it continually puts forth its shoots, except where the power of the Spirit prevails over it.   But if, in the hallowed sanctuary of God, among so small a number, one fiend was preserved; let us not wonder if, at this day, in the Church, containing a much greater multitude of men, the wicked are mingled with the good.   Nor is there any doubt that the minds of Shem and Japheth were grievously wounded, when they perceived in their own brother such a prodigy of scorn ; and, on the other hand, their father shamefully lying prostrate on the ground.   Such a debasing alienation of mind in the prince of the new world, and the holy patriarch of the Church, could not less astonish them, than if they had seen the ark itself broken, dashed in pieces, cleft asunder, and destroyed.   Yet this cause of offence they alike overcome by their magnanimity, and conceal by their modesty.   Ham alone eagerly seizes the occasion of ridiculing and inveighing against his father; just as perverse men are wont to catch at occasions of offence in others, which may serve as a pretext for indulgence in sin.

---

[1] Reference is here made to the ark, as the type of the Church.—*Ed.*

And his age renders him the less excusable; for he was not a
lascivious youth, who, by his thoughtless laughter, betrayed his
own folly, seeing that he was already more than one hundred
years old.   Therefore, it is probable, that he thus perversely
insulted his father, for the purpose of acquiring for himself
the license of sinning with impunity.   We see many such at
this day, who most studiously pry into the faults of holy and
pious men, in order that without shame they may precipitate
themselves into all iniquity; they even make the faults of
other men an occasion of hardening themselves into a contempt for God.

23. *And Shem and Japheth took a garment.* Here the piety,
as well as the modesty, of the two brothers is commended;
who, in order that the dignity of their father might not be
lowered in their esteem, but that they might always cherish
and keep entire the reverence which they owed him, turned
away their eyes from the sight of his disgrace. And thus
they gave proof of the regard they paid to their father's
honour, in supposing that their own eyes would be polluted,
if they voluntarily looked upon the nakedness by which he
was disgraced. At the same time they also consulted their own
modesty. For (as it was said in the third chapter) there is
something so unaccountably shameful in the nakedness of
man, that scarcely any one dares to look upon himself, even
when no witness is present. They also censure the impious
rashness of their brother, who had not spared his father.
Hence, then, we may learn how acceptable to God is that
piety, of which the example here recorded receives a
signal encomium of the Spirit. But if piety towards an
earthly father was a virtue so excellent, and so worthy of
praise; with how much greater devotedness of piety ought
the sacred majesty of God to be worshipped? The Papists
make themselves ridiculous by desiring to cover the filthiness
of their idol, yea, the abominations of their whole impure clergy,
with the cloak of Shem and Japheth. I omit to state how
great is the difference between the disgrace of Noah and the
execrable vileness of so many crimes which contaminate heaven
and earth. But it is necessary that Antichrist and his horned

bishops, with all that rabble, should prove themselves to be fathers,[1] if they wish that any honour should be paid them.

24. *And Noah awoke.* It might seem to some that Noah, although he had just cause of anger, still conducted himself with too little modesty and gravity; and that he ought, at least, silently to have mourned over his sin before God; and also, with shame, to have given proof of his repentance to men : but that now, as if he had committed no offence, he fulminates with excessive severity against his son.[2] Moses, however, does not here relate reproaches uttered by Noah, under the excitement of rage and anger, but rather introduces him, speaking in the spirit of prophecy. Wherefore we ought not to doubt, that the holy man was truly humbled (as he ought to be) under a sense of his fault, and honestly reflected on his own deserts; but now, having received the grant of pardon, and his condemnation being removed, he proceeds as the herald of Divine judgment. It is not indeed to be doubted that the holy man, endued with a disposition otherwise gentle, and being one of the best of parents, would pronounce this sentence upon his son with the most bitter grief of mind. For he saw him miraculously preserved amongst a few, and having a place among the very flower of the human race. Now, therefore, when, with his own mouth, he is compelled to separate him from the Church of God, he doubtless would grievously bewail the malediction of his son. But by this example, God would admonish us that the constancy of our faith must be retained, if at any time we see those fail who are most closely united to us, and that our spirits ought not to be broken; nay, that we must so exercise the severity which God enjoins, as not to spare even our own bowels. And whereas, Noah does not pronounce a sentence so harsh, except by Divine inspiration, it behoves us to infer from the severity of the punishment, how abominable in the sight of God is the impious contempt of parents, since it perverts the sacred order of nature, and violates the majesty and

[1] That is, legitimate fathers.
[2] This is an objection, to which the answer immediately follows.

authority of God, in the person of those whom he has commanded to preside in his place.

25. *Cursed be Canaan.*[1] It is asked, in the first place, why Noah, instead of pronouncing the curse upon his son, inflicts the severity of punishment, which that son had deserved, upon his innocent grandson; since it seems not consistent with the justice of God, to visit the crimes of parents upon their children? But the answer is well known; namely, that God, although he pursues his course of judgments upon the sons and the grandchildren of the ungodly, yet, in being angry with them, is not angry with the innocent, because even they themselves are found in fault. Wherefore there is no absurdity in the act of avenging the sins of the fathers upon their reprobate children; since, of necessity, all those whom God has deprived of his Spirit are subject to his wrath. But it is surprising that Noah should curse his grandson; and should pass his son

[1] It has been remarked by Bishop Lowth, that nearly all the indications of future events in the Holy Scriptures are announced in verse and in numbers.—*Præl.* ii. We have here a remarkable instance of this peculiarity. The following is a translation of Bishop Lowth's version of Noah's prediction :—

> Cursed be Canaan!
> A servant of servants he shall be to his brethren.
> Blessed be Jehovah, the God of Shem!
> And let Canaan be their servant.
> May God enlarge Japheth,
> And may he dwell in the tents of Shem;
> And let Canaan be their servant.—*Præl.* iv.

The adoption of some differences of reading has been suggested by later critics. It has been especially observed, that the first hemistich is a broken or short line, and does not correspond with the next in length or rhyme. And on the authority of the Arabic version, (see *Walton's Polyglott,*) many learned men would thus fill up the line—

> " Cursed be Ham, the father of Canaan."

They would also, on the same authority, alter the fourth and sixth lines, by inserting the word "father," thus—

> "And let the father of Canaan be their servant."

Yet such alterations are not lightly to be made in the sacred text; and it seems highly probable, that the addition in the Arabic version was intended for nothing more originally than a paraphrase to explain the translator's view of the passage. The reader is referred to *Caunter on the Poetry of the Pentateuch,* for further information respecting the *poetical* character of these verses; and to *Bishop Newton's Dissertations,* No. I., for its *prophetical* application. Some excellent remarks, of a practical kind, will be found in *Bishop Hall's Contemplations.—Ed.*

Ham, the author of the crime, over in silence. The Jews imagine that the reason of this was to be traced to the special favour of God; and that, since the Lord had bestowed on Ham so great an honour,[1] the curse was transferred from him to his son. But the conjecture is futile. Certainly, to my mind, there is no doubt that the punishment was carried forward even to his posterity, in order that the severity of it might be the more apparent; as if the Lord had openly proclaimed that the punishment of one man would not satisfy him, but that he would attach the curse also to the posterity of the offender, so that it should extend through successive ages. In the meantime, Ham himself is so far from being exempt, that God, by involving his son with him, aggravates his own condemnation.

Another question is also proposed; namely, why among the many sons of Ham, God chooses one to be smitten? But let not our curiosity here indulge itself too freely; let us remember that the judgments of God are, not in vain, called "a great deep," and that it would be a degrading thing for God, before whose tribunal we all must one day stand, to be subjected to our judgments, or rather to our foolish temerity. He chooses whom he sees good, that he may show forth in them an example of his grace and kindness; others he appoints to a different end, that they may be proofs of his anger and severity. Here, although the minds of men are blinded, let every one of us, conscious of his own infirmity, learn rather to ascribe praise to God's justice, than plunge, with insane audacity, into the profound abyss. While God held the whole seed of Ham as obnoxious to the curse, he mentions the Canaanites by name, as those whom he would curse above all others. And hence we infer that this judgment proceeded from God, because it was proved by the event itself. What would certainly be the condition of the Canaanites, Noah could not know by human means. Wherefore in things obscure and hidden, the Spirit directed his tongue.

Another difficulty still remains: for since the Scripture teaches that God avenges the sins of men on the third and

[1] Namely, that of having preserved him in the ark.—*Ed.*

fourth generation, it seems to assign this limit to the wrath
of God; but the vengeance of which mention is now made
extends itself to the tenth generation. I answer, that these
words of Scripture are not intended to prescribe a law to
God, which he may not so far set aside, as to be at liberty to
punish sins beyond four generations. The thing to be here
observed is, the comparison instituted between punishment
and grace; by which we are taught, that God, while he is a
just avenger of crimes, is still more inclined to mercy. In
the meantime, let his liberty remain unquestioned, to extend
his vengeance as far as he pleases.

A servant of servants shall he be. This Hebraism signifies
that Canaan shall be the last, even among servants : as if it
had been said, ' Not only shall his condition be servile, but
worse than that of common servitude.'[1] Yet the thunder of
this severe and dreadful prophecy seems weak and illusory,
since the Canaanites excelled in strength and in riches, and
were possessed of extensive dominion. Where then is this
servitude? In the first place, I answer, that though God, in
threatening men, does not immediately execute what he denounces, yet his threats are never weak and ineffectual.
Secondly, that the judgments of God are not always exhibited before our eyes, nor apprehended by our carnal reason.
The Canaanites, having shaken off the yoke of servitude,
which was divinely imposed upon them, even proceeded to
grasp at empire for themselves. But although they triumph
for a time, yet in the sight of God their condition is not
deemed free. Just as when the faithful are iniquitously oppressed, and tyrannically harassed by the wicked, their spiritual liberty is still not extinct in the sight of God. It behoves us then to be content with this proof of the divine
judgment, that God promised the dominion of the land of
Canaan to his servant Abraham, and at length devoted the
Canaanites to destruction. But because the Pope so earnestly maintains that he sometimes utters prophecies,—as did
even Caiaphas, (John xi. 51,)—lest we should seem to refuse
him everything, I do not deny that the title with which he

---

[1] Vide Ainsworth *in loco*, Bishop Newton's Dissertation i.

adorns himself was dictated by the Spirit of God, ' Let him
be a servant of servants,' in the same sense that Canaan was.

26. *Blessed be the Lord God of Shem.* Noah blesses his
other children, but in a different manner. For he places
Shem in the highest post of honour. And this is the reason
why Noah, in blessing him, breaks forth in the praise of God,
without adhering to the person of man. For the Hebrews,
when they are speaking of any rare and transcendent excellence, raise their thoughts to God. Therefore the holy
man, when he perceived that the most abundant grace of
God was destined for his son Shem, rises to thanksgiving.
Whence we infer, that he spoke, not from carnal reason, but
rather treated of the secret favours of God, the result of
which was to be deferred to a remote period. Finally, by
these words it is declared, that the benediction of Shem
would be divine or heavenly.

27. *God shall enlarge Japheth.* In the Hebrew words יפת
(*Japhthe*) and יפת, (*Japheth*,) there is an elegant allusion.
For the root of the word is פתה, (*pathah*,) which, among the
Hebrews, signifies to entice with smooth words, or to allure
in one direction or another. Here, however, nearly all commentators take it as signifying to enlarge.[1] If this exposition be received, the meaning will be, that the posterity of
Japheth, which for a time would be scattered, and removed
far from the tents of Shem, would at length be increased, so
that it should more nearly approach them, and should dwell
together with them, as in a common home. But I rather approve the other version, ' God shall gently bring back, or
incline Japheth.'[2] Moreover, whichever interpretation we

---

[1] " Dilatet Deus Japheth."—*Vulg.* "πλατύναι ὁ Θεός."—*Sept.*

[2] See marginal reading of English version, " God will persuade Japheth."—See also Schindler's Lexicon, *sub voce* פתה, and Ainsworth *in
loco.* It is however objected, and not without reason, that the word here
rendered *persuade* is rarely, if ever, used in a good sense, that it generally
means to entice, or allure to evil ; and, therefore, the most judicious critics
seem rather inclined to fall back upon the version given in the text of our
translation, than to accept the marginal reading, with which Calvin
agrees. See Professor Bush's note on this place. Dathe gives the preference to the Arabic version, which signifies that God will *prosper* Japheth ; but for this there is no sufficient authority.—*Ed.*

follow, Noah predicts that there will be a temporary dissension between Shem and Japheth, although he retains both in his family, and calls both his lawful heirs; and that afterwards the time will come, in which they shall again coalesce in one body, and have a common home. It is, however, most absolutely certain, that a prophecy is here put forth concerning things unknown to man, of which, as the event, at length, shows, God alone was the Author. Two thousand years, and some centuries more, elapsed before the Gentiles and the Jews were gathered together in one faith. Then the sons of Shem, of whom the greater part had revolted, and cut themselves off from the holy family of God, were collected together, and dwelt under one tabernacle.[1] Also the Gentiles, the progeny of Japheth, who had long been wanderers and fugitives, were received into the same tabernacle. For God, by a new adoption, has formed a people out of those who were separated, and has confirmed a fraternal union between alienated parties. This is done by the sweet and gentle voice of God, which he has uttered in the gospel; and this prophecy is still daily receiving its fulfilment, since God invites the scattered sheep to join his flock, and collects, on every side, those who shall sit down with Abraham, Isaac, and Jacob, in the kingdom of heaven. It is truly no common support of our faith, that the calling of the Gentiles is not only decreed in the eternal counsel of God, but is openly declared by the mouth of the Patriarch; lest we should think it to have happened suddenly, or by chance, that the inheritance of eternal life was offered generally to all. But the form of the expression, ' Japheth shall dwell in the tabernacles of Shem,'[2] commends to us that mutual society, which

[1] Allusion here seems to be made to the words quoted by James from the prophecy of Amos: " I will return, and will build again the tabernacle of David, which is fallen down; and I will build again the ruins thereof, and I will set it up."—Acts xv. 16.—*Ed.*

[2] It is not clear whether the original really means that " Japheth," or that " God," "shall dwell in the tents of Shem." If the former, then this is a plain prediction of events which have been in a remarkable manner fulfilled, by the conversion of the Gentiles, and by the diffusion of a vast European population over those regions which were originally occupied by the descendants of Shem. If the original really means the *latter*, then it has been fulfilled by the manifestation of God's glory among the Israelites, first through the Shechinah which appeared in the taber-

ought to exist, and to be cherished among the faithful.   For whereas God had chosen to himself a Church from the progeny of Shem, he afterwards chose the Gentiles together with them, on this condition, that they should join themselves to that people, who were in possession of the covenant of life.

28. *And Noah lived.*   Although Moses briefly states the age of the holy man, and does not record his annals and the memorable events of his life, yet those things which are certain, and which Scripture elsewhere commemorates, ought to recur to our minds.   Within one hundred and fifty years, the offspring of his three sons became so numerous, that he had sufficient, and even abundant proof of the efficacy of the Divine benediction, "Increase and multiply."   He sees, not one city only, filled with his grandchildren, nor his seed expanded barely to three hundred families; but many nations springing from one of his sons, who should inhabit extensive regions.   This astonishing increase, since it was a visible representation of the divine favour towards him, would doubtless fill him with unbounded joy.   For Abraham was nearly fifty years old when his ancestor Noah died.[1]   In the meantime, he was compelled to behold many things, which would afflict his holy breast with incredible grief.   To omit other things; he saw in the family of Shem, the sanctuary of God,— into which the sons of Japheth were to be received,—destroyed, or, at least, dilapidated and rent.   For whereas the father of Abraham himself, having deserted his proper station, had erected for himself a profane tabernacle; a very small portion indeed remained of those who worshipped God in the harmonious consent of a pure faith.   With what tormenting pains this terrible confusion affected him cannot be sufficiently expressed in words.   Hence we may know, that his eyes of faith must have been exceedingly penetrating, which

nacle and temple, and then more especially through the advent of the Messiah, of whom St John says, "The Word was made flesh, and dwelt among us; and we beheld his glory, the glory as of the only begotten of the Father, full of grace and truth,' (John i. 14.)—*Ed.*

[1] Lightfoot places the death of Noah two years before the birth of Abraham; Dr A. Clarke two years after it. These chronological differences, however, do not materially affect the general conclusions drawn by Calvin.—*Ed.*

did not fail to behold afar off, the grace of God, in preserving the Church, at that time overwhelmed by the wickedness of men.

CHAPTER X.

1. Now these *are* the generations of the sons of Noah, Shem, Ham, and Japheth: and unto them were sons born after the flood.

2. The sons of Japheth; Gomer, and Magog, and Madai, and Javan, and Tubal, and Meshech, and Tiras.

3. And the sons of Gomer; Ashkenaz, and Riphath, and Togarmah.

4. And the sons of Javan; Elishah, and Tarshish, Kittim, and Dodanim.

5. By these were the isles of the Gentiles divided in their lands; every one after his tongue, after their families, in their nations.

6. And the sons of Ham; Cush, and Mizraim, and Phut, and Canaan.

7. And the sons of Cush; Seba, and Havilah, and Sabtah, and Raamah, and Sabtechah: and the sons of Raamah; Sheba, and Dedan.

8. And Cush begat Nimrod: he began to be a mighty one in the earth.

9. He was a mighty hunter before the Lord: wherefore it is said, Even as Nimrod the mighty hunter before the Lord.

10. And the beginning of his kingdom was Babel, and Erech, and Accad, and Calneh, in the land of Shinar.

11. Out of that land went forth Asshur, and builded Nineveh, and the city Rehoboth, and Calah,

12. And Resen between Nineveh and Calah: the same *is* a great city.

13. And Mizraim begat Ludim, and Anamim, and Lehabim, and Naphtuhim,

14. And Pathrusim, and Casluhim, (out of whom came Philistim,) and Caphtorim.

15. And Canaan begat Sidon his firstborn, and Heth,

1. Porro istæ sunt generationes filiorum Noah, Sem, Cham, et Jepheth: quibus nati sunt filii post diluvium.

2. Filii Jepheth, Gomer, et Magog, et Madai, et Javan, et Thubal, et Mesech, et Thiras.

3. Et filii Gomer, Ascenas, et Riphath, et Thogarmah.

4. Et filii Javan, Elisah, et Tharsis, Chitthim, et Dodanim.

5. Ab istis separatæ sunt insulæ Gentium secundum terras suas, singulæ secundum linguam suam, secundum familias suas, in gentibus suis.

6. Et filii Cham, Chus, et Misraim, et Phut, et Chenaan.

7. Et filii Chus, Seba, et Havilah, et Sabthah, et Rahamah, et Sabtecha. Filii autem Rahamah, Seba, et Dedan.

8. Et Chus genuit Nimrod: ipse cœpit esse potens in terra:

9. Ipse fuit potens in venatione coram Jehova: idcirco dicitur, Sicut Nimrod potens venatione coram Jehova.

10. Et fuit principium regni illius Babel, et Erech, et Achad, et Chalneh, in terra Sinhar.

11. E terra illa egressus est Assur, et ædificavit Nineven, et Rehoboth civitatem, et Chelah,

12. Et Resen inter Nineven et inter Chelah; ipsa est civitas magna.

13. Misraim autem genuit Ludim, et Hanamim, et Lehabim, et Naphthuhim,

14. Et Pathrusim, et Casluhim, unde egressi sunt Pelistim, et Chaphthorim.

15. Et Chenaan genuit Sidon primogenitum suum, et Heth,

16. And the Jebusite, and the Amorite, and the Girgasite,

17. And the Hivite, and the Arkite, and the Sinite,

18. And the Arvadite, and the Zemarite, and the Hamathite : and afterward were the families of the Canaanites spread abroad.

19. And the border of the Canaanites was from Sidon, as thou comest to Gerar, unto Gaza ; as thou goest unto Sodom, and Gomorrah, and Admah, and Zeboim, even unto Lasha.

20. These *are* the sons of Ham, after their families, after their tongues, in their countries, *and* in their nations.

21. Unto Shem also, the father of all the children of Eber, the brother of Japheth the elder, even to him were *children* born.

22. The children of Shem ; Elam, and Asshur, and Arphaxad, and Lud, and Aram.

23. And the children of Aram ; Uz, and Hul, and Gether, and Mash.

24. And Arphaxad begat Salah ; and Salah begat Eber.

25. And unto. Eber were born two sons : the name of one *was* Peleg ; for in his days was the earth divided ; and his brother's name *was* Joktan.

26. And Joktan begat Almodad, and Sheleph, and Hazarmaveth, and Jerah,

27. And Hadoram, and Uzal, and Diklah,

28. And Obal, and Abimael, and Sheba,

29. And Ophir, and Havilah, and Jobab : all these were the sons of Joktan.

30. And their dwelling was from Mesha, as thou goest unto Sephar, a mount of the east.

31. These *are* the sons of Shem, after their families, after their tongues, in their lands, after their nations.

32. These *are* the families of the sons of Noah, after their generations, in their nations : and by these were the nations divided in the earth after the flood.

16. Et Jebusi, et Emori, et Girgasi,

17. Et Hivvi, et Arci, et Sini,

18. Et Arvadi, et Semari, et Hamathi : et postea sparsæ sunt familiæ Chenaanæi.

19. Et fuit terminus Chenaanæi a Sidon ingrediente te Gerar usque ad Hazzah, donec ingrediaris Sedom et Hamorah, et Admah, et Seboim, usque ad Lasah.

20. Isti filii Cham per familias suas, per linguas suas, in terris suis, in gentibus suis.

21. Ipsi quoque Sem soboles, etiam ipse *fuit* pater omnium filiorum Eber, frater Jepheth major.

22. Filii Sem, Helam, et Assur, et Arphachsad, et Lud, et Aram.

23. Et filii Aram, Hus, et Hul, et Gether, et Mas.

24. Et Arphachsad genuit Selah, et Selah genuit Eber.

25. Et ipsi Eber nati sunt duo filii : nomen unius Peleg, quia in diebus ejus divisa est terra : et nomen fratris ejus Joctan.

26. Et Joctan genuit Almodad, et Seleph, et Hasarmaveth, et Jarah,

27. Et Hadoram, et Uzal, et Diclah,

28. Et Hobal, et Abimael, et Seba,

29. Et Ophir, et Havilah, et Jobab : omnes isti filii Joctan.

30. Et fuit habitatio eorum a Mesah, donec ingrediaris Sephar, montem Orientis.

31. Isti filii Sem per familias suas, per linguas suas, in terris suis, in gentibus suis.

32. Istæ familiæ filiorum Noah per generationes suas in gentibus suis : et ab istis divisæ sunt gentes in terra post diluvium.

1. *These are the generations.* If any one pleases more accurately to examine the genealogies related by Moses in this

and the following chapter, I do not condemn his industry.[1] And some interpreters have not unsuccessfully applied their diligence and study to this point.   Let them enjoy, as far as I am concerned, the reward of their labours.   It shall, however, suffice for me briefly to allude to those things which I deem more useful to be noticed, and for the sake of which I suppose these genealogies to have been written by Moses. First, in these bare names we have still some fragment of the history of the world; and the next chapter will show how many years intervened between the date of the deluge and the time when God made his covenant with Abraham.   This second commencement of mankind is especially worthy to be known ; and detestable is the ingratitude of those, who, when they had heard, from their fathers and grandfathers, of the wonderful restoration of the world in so short a time, yet voluntarily became forgetful of the grace and the salvation of God. Even the memory of the deluge was by the greater part entirely lost.   Very few cared by what means or for what end they had been preserved.   Many ages afterwards, seeing that the wicked forgetfulness of men had rendered them callous to the judgment and mercy of God, the door was opened to the lies of Satan, by whose artifice it came to pass, that heathen poets scattered abroad futile and even noxious fables, by which the truth respecting God's works was adulterated.   The goodness of God, therefore, wonder-

[1] For ample information on this interesting subject, which the general plan of Calvin's Commentary scarcely allowed him fully to investigate, the reader cannot do better than consult Dr Wells' Geography of the Old Testament, chap. iii.   From certain expressions contained in the Mosaic account here given, of the first settlement of nations after the flood, it is clear that the records of the chapter now before us, have reference to the state of things after the confusion of tongues at the building of the Tower of Babel, though the narration of this event occurs in the chapter following ; for the settlements are said to be made " according to their languages."   But we know that before the attempt to build the tower, the whole earth was of " one language and of one speech ;" and therefore the events here placed first, in the order of narration, were subsequent in the order of time.   It may be proper here to observe, that according to the division of the earth into three great portions, Europe, Asia, and Africa, speaking generally, Japheth was the progenitor of the Europeans, Shem of the Asiatics, and Ham of the Africans.   Yet this line of demarcation is not intended to be accurately drawn.   The whole of Lesser Asia, for instance, falls within the province of the sons of Japheth; and Arabia within that of the sons of Ham.—*Ed.*

fully triumphed over the wickedness of men, in having granted a prolongation of life to beings so ungrateful, brutal, and barbarous. Now, to captious men, (who yet do not think it absurd to refuse to acknowledge a Creator of the world,) such a sudden increase of mankind seems incredible, and therefore they ridicule it as fabulous. I grant, indeed, that if we choose to estimate what Moses relates by our own reason, it may be regarded as a fable; but they act very perversely who do not attend to the design of the Holy Spirit. For what else, I ask, did the Spirit intend, than that the offspring of three men should be increased, not by natural means, or in a common manner, but by the unwonted exercise of the power of God, for the purpose of replenishing the earth far and wide? They who regard this miracle of God as fabulous on account of its magnitude, should much less believe that Noah and his sons, with their wives, breathed in the waters, and that animals lived nearly a whole year without sun and air. This, then, is a gigantic madness,[1] to hold up to ridicule what is said respecting the restoration of the human race: for there the admirable power of God is displayed. How much better would it be, in the history of these events,—which Noah saw with his own eyes, and not without great admiration,—to behold God, to admire his power, to celebrate his goodness, and to acknowledge his hand, not less filled with mysteries in restoring, than in creating the world? We must, however, observe, that in the three catalogues which Moses furnishes,[2] all the heads of the families are not enumerated; but those only, among the grandsons of Noah, are recorded, who were the princes of nations. For as any one excelled among his brethren, in talent, valour, industry, or other endowments, he obtained for himself a name and power, so that others, resting under his shadow, freely conceded to him the priority. Therefore, among the sons of Japheth, of Ham,

---

[1] " Hic ergo Cyclopicus est furor."

[2] The first relating to the sons of Japheth the elder brother, from verse 2 to verse 6; the second, to the sons of Ham, from verse 6 to verse 21; the third, to the sons of Shem, from 21 to the end. Shem, though generally named first as a mark of Divine favour, is here placed last, because the subsequent history of Moses principally concerns this race; as Calvin properly argues.—*Ed.*

and of Shem, Moses enumerates those only who had been celebrated, and by whose names the people were called. Moreover, although no certain cause appears why Moses begins at Japheth, and descends in the second place to Ham, yet it is probable that the first place is given to the sons of Japheth, because they, having wandered over many regions, and having even crossed the sea, had receded farther from their country: and since these nations were less known to the Jews, therefore he alludes to them briefly. He assigns the second place to the sons of Ham, the knowledge of whom, on account of their vicinity, was more familiar to the Jews. But since he had determined to weave the history of the Church in one continuous narrative, he postpones the progeny of Shem, from which the Church flowed, to the last place. Wherefore, the order in which they are mentioned is not that of dignity; since Moses puts those first, whom he wished slightly to pass over, as obscure. Besides, we must observe, that the children of this world are exalted for a time, so that the whole earth seems as if it were made for their benefit, but their glory being transient vanishes away; while the Church, in an ignoble and despised condition, as if creeping on the ground, is yet divinely preserved, until at length, in his own time, God shall lift up her head. I have already declared that I leave to others the scrupulous investigation of the names here mentioned. The reason of certain of them is manifest from the Scripture, such as Cush, Mizraim, Madai, Canaan, and the like: in respect to some others there are probable conjectures; in others, the obscurity is too great to allow of any certain conclusion; and those figments which interpreters adduce are, in part, very much distorted and forced; in part, vapid, and without any fair pretext. Undoubtedly it seems to be the part of a frivolous curiosity to seek for certain and distinct nations in each of these names.[1]

[1] Doubtless there is truth in these remarks of Calvin. Yet he seems to carry his objection too far. For it is one of the strongest possible confirmations of the truth of the Mosaic history, that (notwithstanding some inevitable obscurity) there should be such a mass of undeniable evidence still existing, that the world was really divided in the manner here described. Far more nations than Calvin supposed may, with the highest degree of probability, be traced upward to the progenitors whose

When Moses says, that the islands of the Gentiles were divided by the sons of Japheth, we understand that the regions beyond the sea were parted among them. For Greece and Italy, and other continental lands,—as well as Rhodes and Cyprus,—are called islands by the Hebrews, because the sea interposed. Whence we infer that we are sprung from those nations.

8. *And Cush begat Nimrod.* It is certain that Cush was the prince of the Ethiopians. Moses relates the singular history of his son Nimrod, because he began to be eminent in an unusual degree. Moreover, I thus interpret the passage, that the condition of men was at that time moderate; so that if some excelled others, they yet did not on that account domineer, nor assume to themselves royal power; but being content with a degree of dignity, governed others by civil laws, and had more of authority than power. For Justin, from Trogus Pompeius, declares this to have been the most ancient condition of the world. Now Moses says, that Nimrod, as if forgetting that he was a man, took possession of a higher post of honour. Noah was at that time yet living, and was certainly great and venerable in the eyes of all. There were also other excellent men; but such was their moderation, that they cultivated equality with their inferiors, who yielded them a spontaneous rather than a

---

names are here recorded. See Wells' Geography, Mede's Works, and Bishop Patrick's Commentary. A list of the names, with the supposed corresponding nations, is also given in the Commentary of Professor Bush on this chapter. The following extract from Hengstenberg's 'Egypt, and the Books of Moses,' also bears upon this point :—" It has often been asserted that the genealogical table in Gen. x. cannot be from Moses : since so extended a knowledge of nations lies far beyond the geographical horizon of the Mosaic age. This hypothesis must now be considered as exploded. The new discoveries and investigations in Egypt have shown that they maintained, even from the most ancient times, a vigorous commerce with other nations, and sometimes with very distant nations. .
. . But not merely, in general, do the investigations in Egyptian antiquities favour the belief that Moses was the author of the account in this tenth chapter of Genesis. On the Egyptian monuments, those especially which represent the conquests of the ancient Pharaohs over foreign nations, . . . not a few names have been found which correspond with those contained in the chapter before us." The learned author then proceeds to adduce instances in proof of his position, which the reader may consult with advantage.—See *Hengstenberg's Egypt, and the Books of Moses*, chap. vii. p. 195.—*Ed.*

forced reverence. The ambition of Nimrod disturbed and broke through the boundaries of this reverence. Moreover, since it sufficiently appears that, in this sentence of Moses, the tyrant is branded with an eternal mark of infamy, we may hence conclude, how highly pleasing to God is a mild administration of affairs among men. And truly, whosoever remembers that he is a man, will gladly cultivate the society of others. With respect to the meaning of the terms, ציד, (tsaid,) properly signifies *hunting*, as the Hebrew grammarians state; yet it is often taken for *food*.[1] But whether Moses says that he was robust in hunting, or in violently seizing upon prey; he metaphorically intimates that he was a furious man, and approximated to beasts rather than to men. The expression, " Before the Lord,"[2] seems to me to declare that Nimrod attempted to raise himself above the order of men; just as proud men become transported by a vain self-confidence, that they may look down as from the clouds upon others.

Wherefore it is said.[3] Since the verb is in the future tense, it may be thus explained, Nimrod was so mighty and imperious that it would be proper to say of any powerful tyrant, that he is another Nimrod. Yet the version of Jerome is satisfactory, that thence it became a proverb concerning the powerful and the violent, that they were like Nimrod.[4] Nor do I doubt that God intended the first author of tyranny to be transmitted to odium by every tongue.

10. *And the beginning of his kingdom was Babel.* Moses here designates the seat of Nimrod's empire. He also declares that four cities were subject to him; it is however uncertain whether he was the founder of them, or had thence expelled their rightful lords. And although mention is elsewhere

---

[1] " ציד. Metaphoricè *cibus* venatione partus, aut quovis modo paratus, præter panem."—*Schindler.*—*Ed.*

[2] Some translate it, " Against the Lord;" yet, perhaps, the words will hardly bear this rendering.—*Ed.*

[3] " Qua propter dicetur," &c., " Wherefore it *shall* be said " In Calvin's text it is, " Idcirco dicitur," " Wherefore it is said."

[4] " Ob hoc exivit proverbium, Quasi Nemrod robustus venator eoram Domino."— *Vulgate.*

made of Calneh,[1] yet Babylon was the most celebrated of all. I do not however think that it was of such wide extent, or of such magnificent structure, as the profane historians relate. But since the region was among the first and most fruitful, it is possible that the convenience of the situation would afterwards invite others to enlarge the city. Wherefore Aristotle, in his *Politics*, taking it out of the rank of cities, compares it to a province. Hence it has arisen, that many declare it to have been the work of Semiramis, by whom others say that it was not built, but only adorned and joined together by bridges. The land of Shinar is added as a note of discrimination, because there was also another Babylon in Egypt, which is now called Cairo.[2] But it is asked, how was Nimrod the tyrant of Babylon, when Moses, in the following chapter, subjoins, that a tower was begun there, which obtained this name from the confusion of tongues? Some suppose that a *hysteron proteron*[3] is here employed, and that what Moses is afterwards about to relate concerning the building of the tower was prior in the order of time. Moreover, they add, that because the building of the tower was disasterously obstructed, their design was changed to that of building a city. But I rather think there is a *prolepsis;* and that Moses called the city by the same name, which afterwards was imposed by a more recent event. The reason of the conjecture is, that probably, at this time, the inhabitants of that place, who had engaged in so vast a work, were numerous. It might also happen, that Nimrod, solicitous about his own fame and power, inflamed their insane desire by this pretext, that some famous monument should be erected in which their everlasting memory might remain. Still, since it is the custom of the Hebrews to prosecute more

[1] Amos vi. 2.

[2] " Quam hodie Cairum vocant."—" Babylon was a habitation formed by the Persians, which may with probability be referred to the time of the conquest of Egypt by Cambyses. A quarter retaining the name of Baboul or Babilon, in the city commonly called *Old Cairo*, which overlooks the Nile at some distance above the Delta, shows its true position." —*D'Anville's Ancient Geography*, vol. ii. p. 152.—*Ed.*

[3] ὕστερον πρότερον, is when that which really comes last in the order of time, is for some reason put first in the order of narration.—*Ed.*

diffusely, afterwards, what they had touched upon briefly, I do not entirely reject the former opinion.[1]

11. *Out of that land went forth Asshur.* It is credible that Asshur was one of the posterity of Shem. And the opinion has been commonly received, that he is here mentioned, because, when he was dwelling in the neighbourhood of Nimrod, he was violently expelled thence. In this manner, Moses would mark the barbarous ferocity of Nimrod. And truly these are the accustomed fruits of a greatness which does not keep within bounds; whence has arisen the old proverb, ' Great kingdoms are great robberies.' It is indeed necessary that some should preside over others; but where ambition, and the desire of rising higher than is right, are rampant, they not only draw with them the greatest and most numerous injuries, but also verge closely upon the dissolution of human society. Yet I rather adopt the opinion of those who say that Asshur is not, in this place, the name of a man, but of a country which derived its appellation from him; and thus the sense will be, that Nimrod, not content with his large and opulent kingdom, gave the reins to his cupidity, and pushed the boundaries of his empire even into Assyria, where he also built new cities.[2] The passage in Isaiah (xxiii. 13) is alone opposed to this opinion, where he says, ' Behold the land of the Chaldeans, the people was not, Asshur founded it when they inhabited the deserts, and he reduced it to ruin.'[3] For the prophet seems to say, that cities were built by the Assyrians in Chaldea, whereas pre-

---

[1] A reason why the former of these opinions is to be preferred will be found in a note at page 313, where it is stated that the division of tongues had already taken place, before these nations were settled.—*Ed.*

[2] See the marginal reading of the English version—' He went out into Assyria.'

[3] Bishop Lowth's translation of the passage is as follows :—

  "Behold the land of the Chaldeans ;
  This people was of no account ;
  (The Assyrian founded it for the inhabitants of the desert ;
  They raised the watch-towers, they set up the palaces thereof ;)
  This people hath reduced her to ruin."

See also his note on this passage, which accords with Calvin's supposition, that the prophet referred to some subsequent period of history.—*Ed.*

viously, its inhabitants were wandering and scattered as in a desert. But it may be, that the prophet speaks of other changes of these kingdoms, which occurred afterwards. For, at the time in which the Assyrians maintained the sovereignty, seeing that they flourished in unbounded wealth, it is credible that Chaldea, which they had subjected to themselves, was so adorned and increased by a long peace, that it might seem to have been founded by them. And we know, that when the Chaldeans, in their turn, seized on the empire, Babylon was exalted on the ruins of Nineveh.

21. *Unto Shem also, the father of all the children of Eber.* Moses, being about to speak of the sons of Shem, makes a brief introduction, which he had not done in reference to the others. Nor was it without reason ; for since this was the race chosen by God, he wished to sever it from other nations by some special mark. This also is the reason why he expressly styles him the 'father of the sons of Eber,' and the elder brother of Japheth.[1] For the benediction of Shem does not descend to all his grandchildren indiscriminately, but remains in one family. And although the grandchildren themselves of Eber declined from the true worship of God, so that the Lord might justly have disinherited them ; yet the benediction was not extinguished, but only buried for a season, until Abraham was called, in honour of whom this singular dignity is ascribed to the race and name of Eber. For the same cause, mention is made of Japheth, in order that the promise may be confirmed, ' God shall speak gently unto Japheth, that he may dwell in the tents of Shem.' Shem is not here called the brother of Ham, inasmuch as the latter was cut off from the fraternal order, and was debarred his own right. Fraternity remained only between Shem and Japheth ; because, although they were separated, God had engaged that he would cause them to return from this dissension into union. As it respects the name *Eber,* they who

---

[1] In the English translation it is, 'The brother of Japheth the elder.' The balance of proof seems to lie in favour of the English translation, and gives the seniority to Japheth. Shem is supposed to be placed first, not on account of his age, but because his was the chosen seed.—*Ed.*

deny it to be a proper name, but deduce it from the word which signifies to *pass over*, are more than sufficiently refuted by this passage alone.

CHAPTER XI.

1. AND the whole earth was of one language, and of one speech.

2. And it came to pass, as they journeyed from the east, that they found a plain in the land of Shinar; and they dwelt there.

3. And they said one to another, Go to, let us make brick, and burn them throughly. And they had brick for stone, and slime had they for mortar.

4. And they said, Go to, let us build us a city and a tower, whose top *may reach* unto heaven; and let us make us a name, lest we be scattered abroad upon the face of the whole earth.

5. And the Lord came down to see the city and the tower, which the children of men builded.

6. And the Lord said, Behold, the people *is* one, and they have all one language; and this they begin to do: and now nothing will be restrained from them, which they have imagined to do.

7. Go to, let us go down, and there confound their language, that they may not understand one another's speech.

8. So the Lord scattered them abroad from thence upon the face of all the earth: and they left off to build the city.

9. Therefore is the name of it called Babel; because the Lord did there confound the language of all the earth: and from thence did the Lord scatter them abroad upon the face of all the earth.

10. These *are* the generations of Shem: Shem *was* an hundred years

1. Erat autem universa terra labii unius, et verborum eorundem.

2. Et fuit, quum proficiscerentur ipsi ab Oriente, invenerunt planitiem in terra Sinhar, et habitaverunt ibi.

3. Et dixerunt quisque ad proximum suum, Agite, laterificemus lateres, et coquamus ad coctionem : et fuit eis later pro lapide, et bitumen fuit eis pro cæmento.

4. Et dixerunt, Agite, ædificemus nobis urbem et turrim, cujus caput *pertingat usque* ad cœlum, et faciamus nobis nomen, ne forte dispergamur in superficiem universæ terræ.

5. Et descendit Jehova ut videret urbem et turrim, quam ædificabant filii hominum.

6. Et dixit Jehova, En, populus unus, et labium unum *est* omnibus ipsis : et hoc *est* incipere eorum ut faciant, et nunc non prohibebitur ab eis quod cogitaverunt ut facerent.

7. Agite, descendamus, et confundamus ibi labium eorum, ut non audiant unusquisque labium proximi sui.

8. Et dispersit Jehova eos inde per superficiem omnis terræ, et cessaverunt ædificare civitatem.

9. Propterea vocavit nomen ejus Babel : quia ibi confudit Jehova labium universæ terræ, et inde dispersit eos Jehova in superficiem universæ terræ.

10. Hæ sunt generationes Sem. Sem filius centum an-

old, and begat Arphaxad two years
after the flood:

11. And Shem lived after he begat
Arphaxad five hundred years, and begat
sons and daughters.

12. And Arphaxad lived five and
thirty years, and begat Salah:

13. And Arphaxad lived after he
begat Salah four hundred and three
years, and begat sons and daughters.

14. And Salah lived thirty years, and
begat Eber:

15. And Salah lived after he begat
Eber four hundred and three years, and
begat sons and daughters.

16. And Eber lived four and thirty
years, and begat Peleg:

17. And Eber lived after he begat
Peleg four hundred and thirty years,
and begat sons and daughters.

18. And Peleg lived thirty years, and
begat Reu:

19. And Peleg lived after he begat
Reu two hundred and nine years, and
begat sons and daughters.

20. And Reu lived two and thirty
years, and begat Serug:

21. And Reu lived after he begat
Serug two hundred and seven years,
and begat sons and daughters.

22. And Serug lived thirty years, and
begat Nahor:

23. And Serug lived after he begat
Nahor two hundred years, and begat
sons and daughters.

24. And Nahor lived nine and twenty
years, and begat Terah:

25. And Nahor lived after he begat
Terah an hundred and nineteen years,
and begat sons and daughters.

26. And Terah lived seventy years,
and begat Abram, Nahor, and Haran.

27. Now these *are* the generations
of Terah : Terah begat Abram, Nahor,
and Haran ; and Haran begat Lot.

norum genuit Arphachsad
duobus annis post diluvium.

11. Et vixit Sem, postquam
genuit Arphachsad, quingentos
annos : et genuit filios et filias.

12. Et Arphachsad vixit
quinque et triginta annos, et
genuit Selah.

13. Et vixit Arphachsad,
postquam genuit Selah, tres
annos et quadringentos annos:
et genuit filios et filias.

14. Et Selah vixit triginta
annos, et genuit Eber.

15. Et vixit Selah, post-
quam genuit Eber, tres annos
et quadringentos annos : et
genuit filios et filias.

16. Et vixit Eber quatuor
et triginta annos, et genuit
Peleg.

17. Et vixit Eber, postquam
genuit Peleg, triginta annos et
quadringentos annos : et genuit
filios et filias.

18. Et vixit Peleg triginta
annos, et genuit Rehu.

19. Et vixit Peleg, post-
quam genuit Rehu, novem annos et ducentos annos : et genuit filios et filias.

20. Et vixit Rehu duos et
triginta annos, et genuit Serug.

21. Et vixit Rehu, post-
quam genuit Serug, septem
annos et ducentos annos : et
genuit filios et filias.

22. Et vixit Serug triginta
annos, et genuit Nachor.

23. Et vixit Serug, post-
quam genuit Nachor, ducentos
annos : et genuit filios et filias.

24. Et vixit Nachor novem
et viginti annos, et genuit
Thare.

25. Et vixit Nachor, postquam genuit Thare, novemde-
cim annos et centum annos :
et genuit filios et filias.

26. Et vixit Thare septuaginta annos, et genuit Abram,
Nachor, et Haran.

27. Et istæ sunt genera-
tiones Thare.   Thare genuit
Abram, Nachor, et Haran : et
Haran genuit Lot.

28. And Haran died before his father Terah in the land of his nativity, in Ur of the Chaldees.

28. Et mortuus est Haran coram Thare patre suo in terra nativitatis suæ, in Ur Chaldeæ.

29. And Abram and Nahor took them wives : the name of Abram's wife *was* Sarai ; and the name of Nahor's wife, Milcah, the daughter of Haran, the father of Milcah, and the father of Iscah.

29. Et acceperunt Abram et Nachor uxores : nomen uxoris Abram, Sarai : et nomen uxoris Nachor, Milchah, filia Haran patris Milchah, et patris Ischah.

30. But Sarai was barren ; she *had* no child.

30. At fuit autem Sarai sterilis : nec erat ei filius.

31. And Terah took Abram his son, and Lot the son of Haran his son's son, and Sarai his daughter-in-law, his son Abram's wife ; and they went forth with them from Ur of the Chaldees, to go into the land of Canaan : and they came unto Haran, and dwelt there.

31. Tulit autem Thare Abram filium suum, et Lot filium Haran, filium filii sui, et Sarai nurum suam, uxorem Abram filii sui : et egressi sunt cum eis de Ur Chaldeæ, ut pergerent in terram Chenaan : et venerunt usque ad Charan, et habitaverunt ibi.

32. And the days of Terah were two hundred and five years : and Terah died in Haran.

32. Et fuerunt dies Thare quinque et ducenti anni : et mortuus est Thare in Charan.

1. *And the whole earth was of one language.* Whereas mention had before been made of Babylon in a single word, Moses now more largely explains whence it derived its name. For this is a truly memorable history, in which we may perceive the greatness of men's obstinacy against God, and the little profit they receive from his judgments. And although at first sight the atrocity of the evil does not appear ; yet the punishment which follows it, testifies how highly God was displeased with that which these men attempted. They who conjecture that the tower was built with the intent that it should prove a refuge and protection, if, at any time, God should determine to overwhelm the earth with a deluge, have no other guide, that I can see, but the dream of their own brain. For the words of Moses signify no such thing : nothing, indeed, is here noticed, except their mad ambition, and proud contempt of God. 'Let us build a tower (they say) whose top may reach to heaven, and let us get ourselves a name.' We see the design and the aim of the undertaking. For whatsoever might happen, they wish to have an immortal name on earth ; and thus they build, as if in opposition to the will of God. And doubtless ambition not only does

injury to men, but exalts itself even against God. To erect
a citadel was not in itself so great a crime; but to raise
an eternal monument to themselves, which might endure
throughout all ages, was a proof of headstrong pride, joined
with contempt of God. And hence originated the fable of
the giants, who, as the poets have feigned, heaped mountains
upon mountains, in order to drag down Jove from his
celestial throne. This allegory is not very remote from the
impious counsel to which Moses alludes; for as soon as
mortals, forgetful of themselves, are inflated above measure,
it is certain that, like the giants, they wage war with God.
This they do not openly profess, yet it cannot be otherwise
than that every one who transgresses his prescribed bounds,
makes a direct attack upon God.

With respect to the time in which this event happened, a
fragment of Berosus is extant, (if, indeed, Berosus is to be
accounted the author of such trifles,) where, among other
things, a hundred and thirty years are reckoned from the
deluge to the time when they began to build the tower.
This opinion, though deficient in competent authority, has
been preferred, by some, to that which commonly obtained
among the Jews, and which places about three hundred
and forty years between the deluge and the building of the
tower. Nor is there anything more plausible in what others
relate; namely, that these builders undertook the work, because men were even then dispersed far and wide, and many
colonies were already formed; whence they apprehended
that as their offspring was daily increasing, they must, in a
short time, migrate to a still greater distance. But to this
argument we may oppose the fact, that the peculiar blessing
of God was to be traced in this multiplication of mankind.
Moreover, Moses seems to set aside all controversy. For
after he has mentioned Arphaxad as the third of the sons of
Shem, he then names Peleg, his great-grandson, in whose
days the languages were divided. But from a computation of the years which he sets down, it plainly appears that
one century only intervened. It is, however, to be noted,
that the languages are not said to have been divided immediately after the birth of Peleg, and that no definite time was

ever specified.[1] It must, indeed, have added greatly to the weight of Noah's sufferings, when he heard of this wicked counsel, which had been taken by his posterity. And it is not to be doubted that he was wounded with the deepest grief, when he beheld them, with devoted minds, rushing to their own destruction. But the Lord thus exercised the holy man, even in extreme old age, to teach us not to be discouraged by a continual succession of conflicts. If any one should prefer the opinion commonly received among the Jews; the division of the earth must be referred to the first transmigrations, when men began to be distributed in various regions : but what has been already recorded in the preceding chapter, respecting the monarchy of Nimrod, is repugnant to this interpretation.[2] Still a middle opinion may be entertained; namely, that the confusion of tongues may perhaps have happened in the extreme old age of Peleg. Now he lived nearly two hundred and forty years; nor will it be absurd to suppose that the empire founded by Nimrod endured two or three centuries. I certainly,—as in a doubtful case,—freely admit that a longer space of time might intervene between the deluge and the design of building the tower. Moreover, when Moses says, 'the earth was of one lip,' he commends the peculiar kindness of God, in having willed that the sacred bond of society among men far separated from each other should be retained, by their possessing a common language among themselves. And truly the diversity of tongues is to be regarded as a prodigy. For since language is the impress

[1] Yet as the name פֶּלֶג, (Peleg,) signifies division, the probability is, that the division took place about the date of his birth, and that the name was given him by his parents in consequence of that event. Now it appears that Peleg was born in the hundred and first year after the flood; see verses 11 to 16. This, therefore, seems to set aside Calvin's calculations, doubtingly expressed, respecting the more recent date of the confusion of tongues.—Ed.

[2] There is no repugnance, if it be admitted that the monarchy of Nimrod is mentioned by anticipation in the former chapter, in order that the course of the narrative might not be interrupted by a detail of the particulars of the confusion of Babel. And then, there is no need for the middle opinion which the Author proceeds to state, and which is encumbered with many difficulties. We may easily conceive that the Sacred Writer goes back, in the present chapter, to give a detailed account of events, which had been only slightly referred to, or altogether omitted in the preceding portion of the narrative.—Ed.

of the mind,[1] how does it come to pass, that men, who are partakers of the same reason, and who are born for social life, do not communicate with each other in the same language? This defect, therefore, seeing that it is repugnant to nature, Moses declares to be adventitious; and pronounces the division of tongues to be a punishment, divinely inflicted upon men, because they impiously conspired against God. Community of language ought to have promoted among them consent in religion; but this multitude, of whom Moses speaks, after they had alienated themselves from the pure worship of God, and the sacred assembly of the faithful, coalesce to excite war against God. Therefore, by the just vengeance of God their tongues were divided.

2. *They found a plain in the land of Shinar.* It may be conjectured from these words, that Moses speaks of Nimrod and of the people whom he had collected around him. If, however, we grant that Nimrod was the chief leader in the construction of so great a pile, for the purpose of erecting a formidable monument of his tyranny: yet Moses expressly relates, that the work was undertaken not by the counsel or the will of one man only, but that all conspired together, so that the blame cannot be cast exclusively upon one, nor even upon a few.

3. *And they said one to another.*[2] That is, they mutually exhorted each other; and not only did every man earnestly put his own hand to the work, but impelled others also to the daring attempt.

Let us make brick. Moses intimates that they had not been induced to commence this work, on account of the ease with which it could be accomplished, nor on account of any other advantages which presented themselves; he rather shows that they

[1] "Nam quum mentis character sit lingua." The word *character* means the impression made by a seal upon wax, and the allusion here is a very striking one, though the force of it is not adequately conveyed by the term *impress.* The term in Greek is applied to Christ, and is there translated "express image." See Heb. i. 3.—*Ed.*
[2] "Dixit vir ad proximum suum," as it is in the margin of the English version. "A man said to his neighbour."

had contended with great and arduous difficulties ; by which
means their guilt became the more aggravated. For how is it
that they harass and wear themselves out in vain on a difficult
and laborious enterprise, unless that, like madmen, they rush
impetuously against God? Difficulty often deters us from
necessary works ; but these men, when they had neither stones
nor mortar, yet do not scruple to attempt the raising of an
edifice which may transcend the clouds. We are taught,
therefore, by this example, to what length the lust of men
will hurry them, when they indulge their ambition. Even a
profane poet is not silent on this subject,—

> " Man, rashly daring, full of pride,
> Most covets what is most denied." [1]

And a little afterwards,—

> " Counts nothing arduous, and tries
> Insanely to possess the skies." [2]

4. *Whose top may reach unto heaven.* This is an hyperbolical form of speech, in which they boastingly extol the loftiness of the structure they are attempting to raise. And to
the same point belongs what they immediately subjoin, " Let
us make us a name ;" for they intimate, that the work would
be such as should not only be looked upon by the beholders as
a kind of miracle, but should be celebrated every where to the
utmost limits of the world. This is the perpetual infatuation
of the world ; to neglect heaven, and to seek immortality on
earth, where every thing is fading and transient. Therefore,
their cares and pursuits tend to no other end than that of
acquiring for themselves a name on earth. David, in the forty-
ninth psalm, deservedly holds up to ridicule this blind cupidity ; and the more, because experience (which is the teacher
of the foolish) does not restore posterity to a sound mind,
though instructed by the example of their ancestors ; but

---

[1] " Audax omnia perpeti
Gens humana ruit per vetitum nefas."
Hor. Lib. I. Ode 3.
[2] " Nil mortalibus arduum est
Cœlum ipsum petimus stultitia."
Ibid.

the infatuation creeps on through all succeeding ages. The saying of Juvenal is known,—'Death alone acknowledges how insignificant are the bodies of men.'[1] Yet even death does not correct our pride, nor constrain us seriously to confess our miserable condition : for often more pride is displayed in funerals than in nuptial pomp. By such an example, however, we are admonished how fitting it is that we should live and die humbly. And it is not the least important part of true prudence, to have death before our eyes in the midst of life, for the purpose of accustoming ourselves to moderation. For he who vehemently desires to be great in the world, is first contumelious towards men, and at length, his profane presumption breaks forth against God himself; so that, after the example of the giants, he fights against heaven.

Lest we be scattered abroad. Some interpreters translate the passage thus, ' Before we are scattered :' but the peculiarity of the language will not bear this explanation : for the men are devising means to meet a danger which they believe to be imminent ; as if they would say, ' It cannot be, that when our number increases, this region should always hold all men ; and therefore an edifice must be erected by which their name shall be preserved in perpetuity, although they should themselves be dispersed in different regions.' It is however asked, whence they derived the notion of their future dispersion ? Some conjecture that they were warned of it by Noah ; who, perceiving that the world had relapsed into its former crimes and corruptions, foresaw, at the same time, by the prophetic spirit, some terrible dispersion ; and they think that the Babylonians, seeing they could not directly resist God, endeavoured, by indirect methods, to avert the threatened judgment. Others suppose, that these men, by a secret inspiration of the Spirit, uttered prophecies concerning their own punishment, which they did not themselves understand. But these expositions are constrained ; nor is there any reason which requires us to apply what they here say, to the curse which was inflicted upon them. They knew that

---

[1] " ——— Mors sola fatetur
    Quantula sint hominum corpuscula."
                                        Juv.

the earth was formed to be inhabited, and would every where supply its abundance for the sustenance of men ; and the rapid multiplication of mankind proved to them that it was not possible for them long to remain shut up within their present narrow limits ; wherefore, to whatever other places it would be necessary for them to migrate, they design this tower to remain as a witness of their origin.

5. *And the Lord came down.* The remaining part of the history now follows, in which Moses teaches us with what ease the Lord could overturn their insane attempts, and scatter abroad all their preparations. There is no doubt that they strenuously set about what they had presumptuously devised. But Moses first intimates that God, for a little while, seemed to take no notice of them,[1] in order that, suddenly breaking off their work at its commencement, by the confusion of their tongues, he might give the more decisive evidence of his judgment. For he frequently bears with the wicked, to such an extent, that he not only suffers them to contrive many nefarious things, as if he were unconcerned, or were taking repose; but even furthers their impious and perverse designs with animating success, in order that he may at length cast them down to a lower depth. The *descent* of God, which Moses here records, is spoken of in reference to men rather than to God ; who, as we know, does not move from place to place. But he intimates that God gradually, and as with a tardy step, appeared in the character of an Avenger. The Lord therefore descended that he might see ; that is, he evidently showed that he was not ignorant of the attempt which the Babylonians were making.

6. *Behold, the people is one.* Some thus expound the words, that God complains of a wickedness in men so refractory, that he excites himself by righteous grief to execute vengeance; not that he is swayed by any passions,[2] but to teach us that he is not negligent of human affairs, and that, as he watches

[1] " Sed prius admonet Moses, dissimulasse aliquantisper Deum."
[2] " Non quod in ipsum cadant ulli affectus."

for the salvation of the faithful, so he is intent on observing
the wickedness of the ungodly ; as it is said in Psalm xxxiv.
16, " The face of the Lord is against them that do evil, to
cut off the remembrance of them from the earth." Others
think there is a comparison between the less and the greater,
as if it had been said, ' They are hitherto few, and only use
one language ; what will they not dare, if, on account of their
multitude, they should become separated into various nations?'
But there rather seems to me to be a suppressed irony, as if
God would propose to himself a difficult work in subduing
their audacity : so that the sense may be, ' This people is
compacted together in a firm conspiracy, they communicate
with each other in the same language, by what method
therefore can they be broken?' Nevertheless, he ironically
smiles at their foolish and hasty confidence; because, while
men are calculating upon their own strength, there is nothing
which they do not arrogate to themselves.

This they begin to do. In saying that they *begin*, he intimates that they make a diligent attempt, accompanied with
violent fervour, in carrying on the work. Thus, in the way
of concession, God declares, that supposing matters to be so
arranged, there would be no interruption of the building.

7. *Go to, let us go down.* We have said that Moses has
represented the case to us by the figure *hypotyposis*,[1] that the
judgments of God may be the more clearly illustrated. For
which reason, he now introduces God as the speaker, who
declares that the work which they supposed could not be retarded, shall, without any difficulty, be destroyed. The
meaning of the words is of this kind, ' I will not use many
instruments, I will only blow upon them, and they, through
the confusion of tongues, shall be contemptibly scattered.'
And as they, having collected a numerous band, were contriving how they might reach the clouds; so, on the other
hand, God summons his troops, by whose interposition he may

---

[1] Hypotyposis, in rhetoric, a figure whereby a thing is described, or
painted in such vivid colouring, that it seems to stand before the eyes, and
to be visible or tangible, rather than the subject of writing, or of discourse.—*Ed.*

ward off their fury. It is, however, asked, what troops he
intends? The Jews think that he addresses himself to the
angels. But since no mention is made of the angels, and
God places those to whom he speaks in the same rank with
himself, this exposition is harsh, and deservedly rejected.
This passage rather answers to the former, which occurs in
the account of man's creation, when the Lord said, "Let us
make man after our image." For God aptly and wisely opposes his own eternal wisdom and power to this great multitude; as if he had said, that he had no need of foreign auxi-
liaries, but possessed within himself what would suffice for
their destruction. Wherefore, this passage is not improperly
adduced in proof that Three Persons subsist in One Essence
of Deity. Moreover, this example of Divine vengeance belongs to all ages: for men are always inflamed with the
desire of daring to attempt what is unlawful. And this history shows that God will ever be adverse to such counsels and
designs; so that we here behold, depicted before our eyes,
what Solomon says: ' There is no counsel, nor prudence, nor
strength against the Lord,' (Prov. xxi. 30.) Unless the
blessing of God be present, from which alone we may expect
a prosperous issue, all that we attempt will necessarily perish.
Since, then, God declares that he is at perpetual war with
the unmeasured audacity of men; anything we undertake
without his approval will end miserably, even though all
creatures, above and beneath, should earnestly offer us their
assistance. Now, although the world bears this curse to the
present day; yet, in the midst of punishment, and of the
most dreadful proofs of Divine anger against the pride of
men, the admirable goodness of God is rendered conspicuous,
because the nations hold mutual communication among themselves, though in different languages; but especially because He
has proclaimed one gospel, in all languages, through the whole
world, and has endued the Apostles with the gift of tongues.
Whence it has come to pass, that they who before were
miserably divided, have coalesced in the unity of the faith.
In this sense Isaiah says, that the language of Canaan should
be common to all under the reign of Christ, (Isaiah xix.
18;) because, although their language may differ in sound,

they all speak the same thing, while they cry, Abba, Father.

8. *So the Lord scattered them abroad.* Men had already been spread abroad ; and this ought not to be regarded as a punishment, seeing it rather flowed from the benediction and grace of God. But those whom the Lord had before distributed with honour in various abodes, he now ignominiously scatters, driving them hither and thither like the members of a lacerated body. This, therefore, was not a simple dispersion for the replenishing of the earth, that it might every where have cultivators and inhabitants ; but a violent rout, because the principal bond of conjunction between them was cut asunder.

9. *Therefore is the name of it called Babel.* Behold what they gained by their foolish ambition to acquire a name ! They hoped that an everlasting memorial of their origin would be engraven on the tower ; God not only frustrates their vain expectation, but brands them with eternal disgrace, to render them execrable to all posterity, on account of the great mischief inflicted on the human race, through their fault. They gain, indeed, a name, but not such as they would have chosen : thus does God opprobriously cast down the pride of those who usurp to themselves honours to which they have no title. Here also is refuted the error of those who deduce the origin of Babylon from Jupiter Belus.[1]

10. *These are the generations of Shem.* Concerning the progeny of Shem, Moses had said something in the former chapter : but now he combines with the names of the men, the term of their several lives, that we might not be ignorant of the age of the world. For unless this brief description had been preserved, men at this day would not have known how much time intervened between the deluge and the day

---

[1] בבל, (*Babel,*) is derived from בלל, (*balel,*) which signifies to confound. See *Schindler's Lexicon, sub voce* בלל. The name Babel signifies, as Bishop Patrick says, "*confusion;* so frivolous is their conceit, who make it to have been called by this name, from *Babylon,* the son of *Belus.*"—*Ed.*

in which God made his covenant with Abraham. Moreover, it is to be observed, that God reckons the years of the world from the progeny of Shem, as a mark of honour : just as historians date their annals by the names of kings or consuls. Nevertheless, he has granted this not so much on account of the dignity and merits of the family of Shem, as on account of his own gratuitous adoption ; for (as we shall immediately see) a great part of the posterity of Shem apostatized from the true worship of God. For which reason, they deserved not only that God should expunge them from his calendar, but should entirely take them out of the world. But he too highly esteems that election of his, by which he separated this family from all people, to suffer it to perish on account of the sins of men. And therefore from the many sons of Shem he chooses Arphaxad alone ; and from the sons of Arphaxad, Selah alone ; and from him also, Eber alone ; till he comes to Abram ; the calling of whom ought to be accounted the renovation of the Church. As it concerns the rest, it is probable that before the century was completed, they fell into impious superstitions. For when God brings it as a charge against the Jews, that their fathers Terah and Nahor served strange gods, (Josh. xxiv. 2,) we must still remember, that the house of Shem, in which they were born, was the peculiar sanctuary of God, where pure religion ought most to have flourished ; what then, do we suppose, must have happened to others, who might seem, from the very first, to have been emancipated from this service ? Hence truly appears, not only the prodigious wickedness and depravity, but also the inflexible hardness of the human mind. Noah and his sons, who had been eye-witnesses of the deluge, were yet living : the narration of that history ought to have inspired men with not less terror than the visible appearance of God himself : from infancy they had been embued with those elements of religious instruction, which relate to the manner in which God was to be worshipped, the reverence with which his word was to be obeyed, and the severe vengeance which remains for those who should violate the order prescribed by him : yet they could not be restrained from being so corrupted by their vanity, that they entirely apostatized.

In the meantime, there is no doubt that holy Noah, according to his extraordinary zeal and heroic fortitude, would contend in every way for the maintenance of God's glory: and that he sharply and severely inveighed, yea, fulminated against the perfidious apostacy of his descendants; and whereas all ought to have trembled at his very look, they are yet moved by no chidings, however loud, from proceeding in the course into which their own fury has hurried them. From this mirror, rather than from the senseless flatteries of sophists, let us learn how fruitful is the corruption of our nature. But if Noah and Shem, and other such eminent teachers, could not, by contending most courageously, prevent the prevalence of impiety in the world; let us not wonder, if at this day also, the unbridled lust of the world rushes to impious and perverse modes of worship, against all the obstacles interposed by sound doctrine, admonition, and threats. Here, however, we must observe, in these holy men, how firm was the strength of their faith, how indefatigable their patience, how persevering their cultivation of piety; since they never gave way, on account of the many occasions of offence with which they had to contend. Luther very properly compares the incredible torments, by which they were necessarily afflicted, to many martyrdoms. For such an alienation of their descendants from God did not less affect their minds, than if they had seen their own bowels not only lacerated and torn, but cast into the mire of Satan, and into hell itself. But while the world was thus filled with ungodly men, God wonderfully retained a few under obedience to his word, that he might preserve the Church from destruction. And although we have said that the father and grandfather of Abraham were apostates, and that, probably, the defection did not first begin with them; yet, because the Church, by the election of God, was included in that race, and because God had some who worshipped him in purity, and who survived even to the time of Abraham, Moses deduces a continuous line of descent, and thus enrols them in the catalogue of saints. Whence we infer, (as I have a little before observed,) in what high estimation God holds the Church, which, though so small in number, is yet preferred to the whole world.

Shem was an hundred years old. Since Moses has placed Arphaxad the third in order among the sons of Shem, it is asked how this agrees with his having been born in the second year after the deluge? The answer is easy. It cannot be exactly ascertained, from the catalogues which Moses recites, at what time each was born; because sometimes the priority of place is assigned to one, who yet was posterior in the order of birth. Others answer, that there is nothing absurd in supposing Moses to declare that, after the completion of two years, a third son was born. But the solution I have given is more genuine.

27. *Terah begat Abram.* Here also Abram is placed first among his brethren, not (as I suppose) because he was the first-born; but because Moses, intent on the scope of his history, was not very careful in the arrangement of the sons of Terah. It is also possible that he had other sons. For, the reason why Moses speaks especially of them is obvious; namely, on account of Lot, and of the wives of Isaac and Jacob. I will now briefly state why I think Abram was not the first-born. Moses shortly afterwards says, that Haran died in his own country, before his father left Chaldea, and went to Charran.[1] But Abram was seventy-five years old when he departed from Charran to dwell in the land of Canaan.[2] And this number of seventy-five years is expressly given after the death of Terah. Now, if we suppose that Abram was born in his father's seventieth year, we must also allow that we have lost sixty years of Terah's age; which is most absurd.[3] The conjecture of Luther, that God buried that

[1] There is evidently a mistake in the original, as it appears in the Amsterdam edition of 1671, and in the Berlin edition, by Hengstenberg, of 1838. Terah's name is here put instead of Haran's, thus, ' Thare paulo post dicet Moses in patria mortuum esse,' &c. The Old English translation has kept the name, and made nonsense of the passage; but Calvin's French version is right: ' Moyse dira un peu apres, que Haran mourut en sen pays, devant que Thare son pere s'en allast demeurer en Charran.'—See verse 28.—*Ed.*
[2] See chapter xii. verse 4.
[3] Supposing Terah to be 70 years old at the birth of Abram, and Abram 75 at the death of Terah : it would make Terah 145 years old when he died, instead of 205, which is a loss of 60 years. The in-

time in oblivion, in order to hide from us the end of the
world, in the first place is frivolous, and in the next, may be
refuted by solid and convincing arguments. Others violently
wrest the words to apply them to a former egress ; and think
that he lived together with his father at Charran for sixty years;
which is most improbable. For to what end should they have
protracted their stay so long in the midst of their journey? But
there is no need of laborious discussion. Moses is silent respecting the age of Abraham when he left his own country ; but
says, that in the seventy-fifth year of his age, he came into the
land of Canaan, when his father, having reached the two
hundredth and fifth year of his life, had died. Who will not
hence infer that he was born when his father had attained his
one hundredth and thirtieth year ?[1] But he is named first
among those sons whom Terah is said to have begotten, when
he himself was seventy years old. I grant it ; but this order
of recital does nothing towards proving the order of birth,
as we have already said. Nor, indeed, does Moses declare
in what year of his life Terah begat sons ; but only that he
had passed the above age before he begat the three sons
here mentioned. Therefore, the age of Abraham is to be
ascertained by another mode of computation, namely, from
the fact that Moses assigns to him the age of seventy-five
when his father died, whose life had reached to two hundred
and five years. A firm and valid argument is also deduced

ference, therefore, is, that Abram was not the first-born of the sons mentioned. See also Patrick's Commentary, who says, that Terah " was
seventy years old before he had any children ; and then had three sons,
one after another, who are not set down in the order wherein they were
born. For Abraham's being first named doth not prove him to have
been the eldest son of Terah, no more than Shem's being first named
among Noah's three sons proves him to have been the first-born. For
there are good reasons to prove that Abraham was born sixty years after
Haran, who was the eldest son ; having two daughters married to his
two brothers, Nahor and Abraham ; who seems to have been the youngest
though named first." Le Clerc controverts this view, but it seems the
most free from objections. See, however, his Commentary on Genesis xii.
1 and 4.—*Ed.*

[1] Another palpable numerical mistake in the Amsterdam edition, which
is also perpetuated in that of Hengstenberg, is here corrected as the sense
requires, and under the sanction of the French and Old English versions.
In the Latin text it is : " Quis non inde colliget natum fuisse quum pater
centessimum annum attigisset ? "—*Ed.*

from the age of Sarai. It appears that she was not more than ten years younger than Abraham. If she was the daughter of his younger brother, she would necessarily have equalled her own father in age.[1] They who raise an objection, to the effect that she was the daughter-in-law, or only the adopted daughter of Nahor, produce nothing beyond a sheer cavil.

28. *And Haran died.* Haran is said to have died before the face of his father; because he left his father the survivor. It is also said that he died in his country, that is, in Ur. The Jews turn the proper name into an appellative, and say that he died in the *fire*. For, as they are bold in forging fables, they pretend that he, with his brother Abram, were thrown by the Chaldeans into the fire, because they shunned idolatry; but that Abram escaped by the constancy of his faith. The twenty-fourth chapter of Joshua, however, which I have cited above, openly declares, that this whole family was not less infected with superstitions than the country itself. I confess, indeed, that the name Ur is derived from fire: names, however, are wont to be assigned to cities, either from their situation, or from some particular event. It is possible that they there cherished the sacred fire, or that the splendour of the sun was more conspicuous than in other places. Others will have it, that the city was so named, because it was situated in a valley, for the Hebrews call valleys אָרִים, (*Uraim*.[2]) But there is no reason why we should be very anxious about such a matter: let it suffice, that Moses, speaking of the country of Abram, immediately afterwards declares it to have been Ur of the Chaldeans.

30. *But Sarai was barren.* Not only does he say that Abram was without children, but he states the reason, namely,

---

[1] Or at least nearly so. "Ergo *Haran* (si junior fuisset *Abrahamo*) eam genuisset nondum deceni (imo nec octo) annos natus."—*Lightfoot et alii in Poli Synopsi.* See, however, Lightfoot's *Hebrew and Talmudical Exercitations upon the Acts*, in his Works, vol. ii. p. 666. Fol. London, 1684.—*Ed.*

[2] *Vide* Schindler, *sub voce* אוּר, col. 42, line 54; but it is doubtful whether any clear evidence of such a meaning of the word can be adduced. —*Ed.*

the sterility of his wife; in order to show that it was by
nothing short of an extraordinary miracle that she afterwards
bare Isaac, as we shall declare more fully in its proper place.
Thus was God pleased to humble his servant; and we cannot
doubt that Abram would suffer severe pain through this privation. He sees the wicked springing up everywhere, in great
numbers, to cover the earth; he alone is deprived of children.
And although hitherto he was ignorant of his own future
vocation; yet God designed in his person, as in a mirror, to
make it evident, whence and in what manner his Church should
arise; for at that time it lay hid, as in a dry root under
the earth.

31. *And Terah took Abram his son.* Here the next chapter
ought to commence; because Moses begins to treat of one of
the principal subjects of his book; namely, the calling of
Abram. For he not only relates that Terah changed his
country, but he also explains the design and the end of his
departure, that he left his native soil, and entered on his
journey, in order to come to the land of Canaan. Whence
the inference is easily drawn, that he was not so much the
leader or author of the journey, as the companion of his son.
And it is no obstacle to this inference, that Moses assigns
the priority to Terah, as if Abram had departed under his
auspices and direction, rather than by the command of God:
for this is an honour conferred upon the father's name. Nor
do I doubt that Abram, when he saw his father willingly
obeying the calling of God, became in return the more
obedient to him. Therefore, it is ascribed to the authority
of the father, that he took his son with him. For, that
Abram had been called of God before he moved a foot from
his native soil, will presently appear too plain to be denied.
We do not read that his father had been called. It may
therefore be conjectured, that the oracle of God had been
made known to Terah by the relation of his son. For the divine
command to Abram respecting his departure, did not prohibit
him from informing his father, that his only reason for leaving him was, that he preferred the command of God to all
human obligations. These two things, indeed, without con-

troversy, we gather from the words of Moses; that Abram was divinely called, before Terah left his own country : and that Terah had no other design than that of coming into the land of Canaan; that is, of joining his son as a voluntary companion. Therefore, I conclude, that he had left his country a short time before his death. For it is absurd to suppose, that when he departed from his own country, to go directly to the land of Canaan, he should have remained sixty years a stranger in a foreign land. It is more probable, that being an old man worn out with years, he was carried off by disease and weariness. And yet it may be, that God held them a little while in suspense, because Moses says he dwelt in Charran; but from what follows, it appears that the delay was not long: since, in the seventy-fifth year of his age, Abram departed thence; and he had gone thither already advanced in age, and knowing that his wife was barren. Moreover, the town which by the Hebrews is called Charran, is declared by all writers, with one consent, to be Charran, situated in Mesopotamia; although Lucan, poetically rather than truly, places it in Assyria. The place was celebrated for the destruction of Crassus, and the overthrow of the Roman army.[1]

CHAPTER XII.

1. Now the Lord had said unto Abram, Get thee out of thy country, and from thy kindred, and from thy father's house, unto a land that I will show thee:

2. And I will make of thee a great nation, and I will bless thee, and make thy name great; and thou shalt be a blessing:

3. And I will bless them that bless thee, and curse him that curseth thee: and in thee shall all families of the earth be blessed.

1. Dixerat autem Jehova ad Abram, Abi e terra tua, et e cognatione tua, et e domo patris tui, ad terram quam ostendam tibi.

2. Et faciam te in gentem magnam, et benedicam tibi, et magnificabo nomen tuum, et eris benedictio.

3. Et benedicam benedicentibus tibi : et maledicentibus tibi maledicam : et benedicentur in te omnes familiæ terræ.

[1] See Wells' Geography of the Old Test., chap. vi. *sub fine,* and D'Anville's Compendium, vol. i. 436.—*Ed.*

4. So Abram departed, as the Lord had spoken unto him; and Lot went with him : and Abram *was* seventy and five years old when he departed out of Haran.

5. And Abram took Sarai his wife, and Lot his brother's son, and all their substance that they had gathered, and the souls that they had gotten in Haran; and they went forth to go into the land of Canaan; and into the land of Canaan they came.

6. And Abram passed through the land unto the place of Sichem, unto the plain of Moreh. And the Canaanite *was* then in the land.

7. And the Lord appeared unto Abram, and said, Unto thy seed will I give this land : and there builded he an altar unto the Lord, who appeared unto him.

8. And he removed from thence unto a mountain on the east of Beth-el, and pitched his tent, *having* Beth-el on the west, and Hai on the east : and there he builded an altar unto the Lord, and called upon the name of the Lord.

9. And Abram journeyed, going on still toward the south.

10. And there was a famine in the land: and Abram went down into Egypt to sojourn there; for the famine *was* grievous in the land.

11. And it came to pass, when he was come near to enter into Egypt, that he said unto Sarai his wife, Behold now, I know that thou *art* a fair woman to look upon :

12. Therefore it shall come to pass, when the Egyptians shall see thee, that they shall say, This *is* his wife : and they will kill me, but they will save thee alive.

13. Say, I pray thee, thou *art* my sister : that it may be well with me for thy sake ; and my soul shall live because of thee.

14. And it came to pass, that, when Abram was come into Egypt, the Egyp-

4. Abiit ergo Abram quemadmodum loquutus fuerat ad eum Jehova : et perrexit cum eo Lot: Abram autem erat filius quinque annorum et septuaginta annorum, quando egressus est de Charan.

5. Et cepit Abram Sarai uxorem suam, et Lot filium fratris sui, et omnem substantiam quam acquisierant, et animas quas fecerant in Charan, et egressi sunt ut pergerent in terram Chenaan, et venerunt ad terram Chenaan.

6. Et transivit Abram in terram usque ad locum Sechem, usque ad quercum Moreh: Chenaanæus autem tunc erat in terra.

7. Et visus est Jehova Abræ, et dixit, Semini tuo dabo terram hanc: et ædificavit ibi altare Jehovæ qui apparuerat sibi.

8. Et transtulit se inde ad montem ab Oriente ipsi Bethel, tetenditque tabernaculum suum : Bethel erat ab Occidente, et Hai ab Oriente : et ædificavit ibi altare Jehova, et invocavit nomen Jehovæ.

9. Profectus est et Abram eundo et proficiscendo ad Meridiem.

10. Et fuit fames in terra, et descendit Abram in Ægyptum ut peregrinaretur ibi : quia gravis fames erat in terra.

11. Et fuit, quando appropinquavit ut ingrederetur Ægyptum, dixit ad Sarai uxorem suam, Ecce, nunc novi quod mulier pulchra aspectu sis:

12. Erit itaque, quum viderint te Ægyptii, dicent, Uxor ejus est : et occident me, et te servabunt vivam.

13. Dic nunc quod soror mea sis, ut bene sit mihi propter te, et vivat anima mea propter te.

14. Et fuit quum ingrederetur Abram Ægyptum, vide-

tians beheld the woman, that she *was* very fair.

15. The princes also of Pharaoh saw her, and commended her before Pharaoh : and the woman was taken into Pharaoh's house.

16. And he entreated Abram well for her sake : and he had sheep, and oxen, and he-asses, and men-servants, and maid-servants, and she-asses, and camels.

17. And the Lord plagued Pharaoh and his house with great plagues, because of Sarai, Abram's wife.

18. And Pharaoh called Abram, and said, What *is* this *that* thou hast done unto me? why didst thou not tell me that she *was* thy wife?

19. Why saidst thou, She *is* my sister? so I might have taken her to me to wife : now therefore behold thy wife, take *her*, and go thy way.

20. And Pharaoh commanded *his* men concerning him : and they sent him away, and his wife, and all that he had.

runt Ægyptii mulierem quod pulchra esset valde.

15. Quum igitur vidissent eam principes Pharaonis, laudaverunt eam Pharaoni : et sublata est mulier in domum Pharaonis.

16. Et ipsi Abram benefecit propter eam : fueruntque ei pecudes, et boves, et asini, et servi, et ancillæ, et asinæ, et cameli.

17. Percussit autem Jehova Pharaonem percussionibus magnis et domum ejus, causa Sarai uxoris Abram.

18. Vocavitque Pharao Abram, et dixit, Cur hoc, fecisti mihi? utquid non indicasti mihi quod uxor tua esset?

19. Utquid dixisti, Soror mea est? et tuli eam mihi in uxorem : et nunc ecce uxor tua, cape et vade.

20. Et præcepit super eum Pharao viris, et demiserunt eum et uxorem ejus, et omnia quæ erant ei.

1. *Now the Lord had said unto Abram.* That an absurd division of these chapters may not trouble the readers, let them connect this sentence with the last two verses of the previous chapter. Moses had before said, that Terah and Abram had departed from their country to dwell in the land of Canaan. He now explains that they had not been impelled by levity, as rash and fickle men are wont to be ; nor had been drawn to other regions by disgust with their own country, as morose persons frequently are ; nor were fugitives on account of crime ; nor were led away by any foolish hope, or by any allurements, as many are hurried hither and thither by their own desires ; but that Abram had been divinely commanded to go forth, and had not moved a foot but as he was guided by the word of God. They who explain the passage to mean, that God spoke to Abram after the death of his father, are easily refuted by the very words of Moses : for if Abram was already without a country, and was sojourning as a stranger elsewhere, the command of God would have

been superfluous, ' Depart from thy land, from thy country, and from thy father's house.' The authority of Stephen is also added, who certainly deserves to be accounted a suitable interpreter of this passage: now he plainly testifies, that God appeared to Abraham when he was in Mesopotamia, before he dwelt in Charran; he then recites this oracle which we are now explaining; and at length concludes, that, for this reason, Abraham migrated from Chaldea. Nor is that to be overlooked which God afterwards repeats, (xv. 7,) 'I am the Lord that brought thee out of Ur of the Chaldees;' for we thence infer, that the Divine Hand was not for the first time stretched out to him after he had dwelt in Charran, but while he yet remained at home in Chaldea.[1] Truly this command of God, respecting which doubts are foolishly entertained, ought to be deemed by us sufficient to disprove the contrary error. For God could not have spoken thus, except to a man who had been, up to that time, settled in his nest, having his affairs underanged, and living quietly and tranquilly among his relatives, without any change in his mode of life; otherwise, the answer would have been readily given, ' I *have* left my country, I *am* far removed from my kindred.' In short, Moses records this oracle, in order that we may know that this long journey was undertaken by Abram, and his father Terah, at the command of God. Whence it also appears, that Terah was not so far deluded by superstitions as to be destitute of the fear of God. It was difficult for the old man, already broken and failing in health, to tear himself away from his own country. Some true religion, therefore, although smothered, still remained in his mind. Therefore, when he knew that the place, from which his son was commanded to depart, was accursed, it was his wish not to perish there; but he joined himself as an associate with him whom the Lord was about to deliver. What a witness, I demand, will he prove, in the last day, to condemn our indolence ! Easy and plausible was the excuse

[1] Many learned commentators, Dr A. Clarke among the number, suppose this to have been a second call from God, and to have taken place when he was at Charran. But the objections adduced by Calvin against such an interpretation are of great weight, and cannot be easily set aside. —*Ed.*

which he might have alleged; namely, that he would remain
quietly at home, because he had received no command. But
he, though blind in the darkness of unbelief, yet opened his
eyes to the beam of light which shot across his path ; while
we remain unmoved when the Divine vocation directly shines
upon us. Moreover, this calling of Abram is a signal instance
of the gratuitous mercy of God. Had Abram been beforehand with God by any merit of works ? Had Abram come
to him, or conciliated his favour ? nay, we must ever recall
to mind, (what I have before adduced from the passage in
Joshua,) that he was plunged in the filth of idolatry ; and
now God freely stretches forth his hand to bring back the
wanderer. He deigns to open his sacred mouth, that he may
show to one, deceived by Satan's wiles, the way of salvation.
And it is wonderful, that a man, miserable and lost, should
have the preference given him, over so many holy worshippers
of God ; that the covenant of life should be placed in his
possession ; that the Church should be revived in him, and
he himself constituted the father of all the faithful. But
this is done designedly, in order that the manifestation of the
grace of God might become the more conspicuous in his
person. For he is an example of the vocation of us all ; for
in him we perceive, that, by the mere mercy of God, those
things which are not are raised from nothing, in order that
they may begin to be something.

Get thee out of thy country. This accumulation of words
may seem to be superfluous. To which also may be added,
that Moses, in other places so concise, here expresses a plain
and easy matter in three different forms of speech. But the
case is quite otherwise. For since exile is in itself sorrowful,
and the sweetness of their native soil holds nearly all men
bound to itself, God strenuously persists in his command to
leave the country, for the purpose of thoroughly penetrating
the mind of Abram. If he had said in a single word, Leave
thy country, this indeed would not lightly have pained his
mind ; but Abram is still more deeply affected, when he
hears that he must renounce his kindred and his father's
house. Yet it is not to be supposed, that God takes a cruel
pleasure in the trouble of his servants ; but he thus tries all

their affections, that he may not leave any lurking-places undiscovered in their hearts. We see many persons zealous for a short time, who afterwards become frozen; whence is this, but because they build without a foundation? Therefore God determined, thoroughly to rouse all the senses of Abram, that he might undertake nothing rashly or inconsiderately; lest, repenting soon afterwards, he should veer with the wind, and return. Wherefore, if we desire to follow God with constancy, it behoves us carefully to meditate on all the inconveniences, all the difficulties, all the dangers which await us; that not only a hasty zeal may produce fading flowers, but that from a deep and well-fixed root of piety, we may bring forth fruit in our whole life.

Unto a land that I will show thee. This is another test to prove the faith of Abram. For why does not God immediately point out the land, except for the purpose of keeping his servant in suspense, that he may the better try the truth of his attachment to the word of God? as if he would say, 'I command thee to go forth with closed eyes, and forbid thee to inquire whither I am about to lead thee, until, having renounced thy country, thou shalt have given thyself wholly to me.' And this is the true proof of our obedience, when we are not wise in our own eyes, but commit ourselves entirely unto the Lord. Whensoever, therefore, he requires anything of us, we must not be so solicitous about success, as to allow fear and anxiety to retard our course. For it is better, with closed eyes, to follow God as our guide, than, by relying on our own prudence, to wander through those circuitous paths which it devises for us. Should any one object, that this statement is at variance with the former sentence, in which Moses declared that Terah and Abram departed from their own country, that they might come into the land of Canaan: the solution is easy, if we admit a *prolepsis*[1] in the expression of Moses; such as follows in this very chapter, in the use of the name Bethel; and such as frequently occurs in the Scrip-

[1] Prolepsis is the figure which anticipates in the discourse something still future; as when the word Bethel is used to designate the place which at the time was called Luz, and which did not receive this name till it was given by Jacob.—*Ed.*

tures.   They knew not whither they were going; but because they had resolved to go whithersoever God might call them, Moses, speaking in his own person, mentions the land, which, though hitherto unknown to them both, was afterwards revealed to Abram alone.   It is therefore true, that they departed with the design of coming to the land of Canaan; because, having received the promise concerning a land which was to be shown them, they suffered themselves to be governed by God, until he should actually bestow what he had promised.   Nevertheless it may be, that God, having proved the devotedness of Abram, soon afterwards removed all doubt from his mind.   For we do not know at what precise moment of time, God would intimate to him, what it was his will to conceal only for a season.   It is enough that Abram declared himself to be truly obedient to God, when, having cast all his care on God's providence, and having discharged, as it were, into His bosom, whatever might have impeded him, he did not hesitate to leave his own country, uncertain where, at length, he might plant his foot; for, by this method, the wisdom of the flesh was reduced to order, and all his affections, at the same time, were subdued.   Yet it may be asked, why God sent his servant into the land of Canaan rather than into the East, where he could have lived with some other of the holy fathers?   Some (in order that the change may not seem to have been made for the worse) will have it, that he was led thither, for the purpose of dwelling with his ancestor Shem, whom they imagine to have been Melchizedek. But if such were the counsel of God, it is strange that Abram bent his steps in a different direction; nay, we do not read that he met with Melchizedek, till he was returning from the battle in the plain of Sodom.   But, in its proper place, we shall see how frivolous is the imagination, that Melchizedek was Shem.   As it concerns the subject now in hand, we infer, from the result which at length followed, that God's design was very different from what these men suppose.   The nations of Canaan, on account of their deplorable wickedness, were devoted to destruction.   God required his servant to sojourn among them for a time, that, by faith, he might perceive himself to be the heir of that land, the actual possession of which was reserved for his posterity to a long period after his own death. Wherefore he was commanded to cross over into that country, for this sole reason, that it was to be evacuated by its inhabitants, for the purpose of being given to his seed for a possession. And it was of great importance, that Abram, Isaac, and Jacob, should be strangers in that land, and should by faith embrace the dominion over it, which had been divinely promised them, in order that their posterity might, with the greater courage, gird themselves to take possession of it.

2. *And I will make of thee a great nation.* Hitherto Moses has related what Abram had been commanded to do; now he annexes the promise of God to the command; and that for no light cause. For as we are slothful to obey, the Lord would command in vain, unless we are animated by a super-added confidence in his grace and benediction. Although I have before alluded to this, in the history of Noah, it will not be useless to inculcate it again, for the passage itself requires something to be said; and the repetition of a doctrine of such great moment ought not to seem superfluous. For it is certain that faith cannot stand, unless it be founded on the promises of God. But faith alone produces obedience. Therefore, in order that our minds may be disposed to follow God, it is not sufficient for him simply to command what he pleases, unless he also promises his blessing. We must mark the promise, that Abram, whose wife was still barren, should become a great nation. This promise might have been very efficacious, if God, by the actual state of things, had afforded ground of hope respecting its fulfilment; but now, seeing that the barrenness of his wife threatened him with perpetual privation of offspring, the bare promise itself would have been cold, if Abram had not wholly depended upon the word of God; wherefore, though he perceives the sterility of his wife, he yet apprehends, by hope, that great nation which is promised by the word of God. And Isaiah greatly extols this act of favour, that God, by his blessing, increased his servant Abram, whom he found alone and solitary, to so great a nation, (Isaiah ii. 2.) The noun גּוֹי, (*goi,*) "my

nation," (ver. 4,) though detestable to the Jews,[1] is in this place, as in many others, taken as a term of honour. And it is here used emphatically, to show that he should not only have posterity from his own seed in great number, but a peculiar people, separated from others, who should be called by his own name.

I will bless thee. This is partly added, to explain the preceding sentence. For, lest Abram should despair, God offers his own blessing, which was able to effect more in the way of miracle, than is seen to be effected, in other cases, by natural means. The benediction, however, here pronounced, extends farther than to offspring ; and implies, that he should have a prosperous and joyous issue of all his affairs ; as appears from the succeeding context, " And will make thy name great, and thou shalt be a blessing." For such happiness is promised him, as shall fill all men everywhere with admiration, so that they shall introduce the name of Abram, as an example, into their formularies of pronouncing benediction. Others use the term in the sense of augmentation, 'Thou shalt be a blessing,' that is, 'All shall bless thee.' But the former sense is the more suitable. Some also expound it actively, as if it had been said, 'My grace shall not reside in thee, so that thou alone mayest enjoy it, but it shall flow far unto all nations. I therefore now so deposit it with thee, that it may overflow into all the world.' But God does not yet proceed to that communication, as I shall show presently.

3. *And I will bless them that bless thee.* Here the extraordinary kindness of God manifests itself, in that he familiarly makes a covenant with Abram, as men are wont to do with their companions and equals. For this is the accustomed form of covenants between kings and others, that they mutually promise to have the same enemies and the same friends. This certainly is an inestimable pledge of special love, that

---

[1] The dislike which the Jews have to this word arises from the fact, that they confine its application to heathens, barbarians, and Christians, in short, to all who are not of Israel according to the flesh. They are not, however, warranted by Scripture in so doing, as Calvin rightly argues.—*Ed.*

God should so greatly condescend for our sake. For although he here addresses one man only, he elsewhere declares the same affection towards his faithful people. We may therefore infer this general doctrine, that God so embraces us with his favour, that he will bless our friends, and take vengeance on our enemies. We are, moreover, warned by this passage, that however desirous the sons of God may be of peace, they will never want enemies. Certainly, of all persons who ever conducted themselves so peaceably among men as to deserve the esteem of all, Abram might be reckoned among the chief, yet even he was not without enemies; because he had the devil for his adversary, who holds the wicked in his hand, whom he incessantly impels to molest the good. There is, then, no reason why the ingratitude of the world should dishearten us, even though many hate us without cause, and, when provoked by no injury, study to do us harm; but let us be content with this single consolation, that God engages on our side in the war. Besides, God exhorts his people to cultivate fidelity and humanity with all good men, and, further, to abstain from all injury. For this is no common inducement to excite us to assist the faithful, that if we discharge any duty towards them, God will repay it; nor ought it less to alarm us, that he denounces war against us, if we hurt any one belonging to him.

In thee shall all families of the earth be blessed. Should any one choose to understand this passage in a restricted sense, as if, by a proverbial mode of speech, they who shall bless their children or their friends, shall be called after the name of Abram, let him enjoy his opinion; for the Hebrew phrase will bear the interpretation, that Abram shall be called a signal example of happiness. But I extend the meaning further; because I suppose the same thing to be promised in this place, which God afterwards repeats more clearly, (xxii. 18.) And the authority of Paul brings me to this point; who says, that the promise to the seed of Abraham, that is, to Christ, was given four hundred and thirty years before the law, (Gal. iii. 17.) But the computation of years requires us to understand, that the blessing was promised him in Christ, when he was coming into the land of Canaan. Therefore God (in my judgment) pronounces that all nations should be blessed in his servant Abram, because Christ was included in his loins. In this manner, he not only intimates that Abram would be an *example*, but a *cause* of blessing; so that there should be an understood antithesis between Adam and Christ. For whereas, from the time of the first man's alienation from God, we are all born accursed, here a new remedy is offered unto us. Nor is there any thing contrary to this in the assertion, that we must by no means seek a blessing in Abram himself, inasmuch as the expression is used in reference to Christ. Here the Jews petulantly object, and heap together many testimonies of Scripture, from which it appears, that to bless or curse *in any one*, is nothing else than to wish good or evil to another, according to him as a pattern. But their cavil may be set aside without difficulty. I acknowledge, that what they say is often, but not always true. For when it is said, that the tribe of Levi shall bless in the name of God, in Deut. x. 8; Isa. lxv. 16, and in similar passages, it is sufficiently evident, that God is declared to be the fountain of all good, in order that Israel may not seek any portion of good elsewhere. Seeing, therefore, that the language is ambiguous, let them grant the necessity of choosing this, or the other sense, as may be most suitable to the subject and the occasion. Now Paul assumes it as an axiom which is received among all the pious, and which ought to be taken for granted, that the whole human race is obnoxious to a curse, and therefore that the holy people are blessed only through the grace of the Mediator. Whence he concludes, that the covenant of salvation which God made with Abram, is neither stable nor firm except in Christ. I therefore thus interpret the present place; that God promises to his servant Abram that blessing which shall afterwards flow down to all people. But because this subject will be more amply explained elsewhere, I now only briefly touch upon it.

4. *So Abram departed.* They who suppose that God was now speaking to Abram in Charran, lay hold of these words in support of their error. But the cavil is easily refuted; for after Moses has mentioned the cause of their departure,

namely, that Abram had been constrained by the command of God to leave his native soil, he now returns to the thread of the history. Why Abram for a time should have remained in Charran, we do not know, except that God laid his hand upon him, to prevent him from immediately obtaining a sight of the land, which, although yet unknown, he had nevertheless preferred to his own country. He is now said to have departed from Charran, that he might complete the journey he had begun; which also the next verse confirms, where it is said, that he took Sarai his wife and Lot his nephew with him. As under the conduct and auspices of his father Terah, they had departed from Chaldea; so now, when Abram is become the head of the family, he pursues and completes what his father had begun. Still it is possible, that the Lord again exhorted him to proceed, the death of his father having intervened, and that he confirmed his former call by a second oracle. It is however certain, that in this place the obedience of faith is commended, and not as one act simply, but as a constant and perpetual course of life. For I do not doubt, but Moses intended to say, that Abram remained in Charran, not because he repented, as if he was inclined to swerve from the straight course of his vocation, but as having the command of God always fixed in his mind. And therefore I would rather refer the clause, " As the Lord had spoken to him," to the first oracle; so that Moses should say, ' he stood firmly in his purpose, and his desire to obey God was not broken by the death of his father.' Moreover, we have here in one word, a rule prescribed to us, for the regulation of our whole life, which is to attempt nothing but by Divine authority. For, however men may dispute concerning virtues and duties, no work is worthy of praise, or deserves to be reckoned among virtues, except what is pleasing to God. And he himself testifies, that he makes greater account of obedience than of sacrifice, (1 Sam. xv. 22.) Wherefore, our life will then be rightly constituted, when we depend upon the word of God, and undertake nothing except at his command. And it is to be observed, that the question is not here concerning some one particular work, but concerning

the general principle of living piously and uprightly. For
the subject treated of, is the vocation of Abram, which is a
common pattern of the life of all the faithful. We are not
indeed all indiscriminately commanded to desert our country ;
this point, I grant, is special in the case of Abram ; but generally, it is God's will that all should be in subjection to his
word, and should seek the law, for the regulation of their life,
at his mouth, lest they should be carried away by their own
will, or by the maxims of men. Therefore by the example
of Abram, entire self-renunciation is enjoined, that we may
live and die to God alone.

5. *The souls that they had gotten in Haran.* Souls signify male
and female servants. And this is the first mention of servitude :
whence it appears, that not long after the deluge the wickedness
of man caused liberty which, by nature, was common to all, to
perish with respect to a great part of mankind. Whence servitude originated is not easy to determine, unless according to
the opinion which has commonly prevailed, it arose from wars ;
because the conquerors compelled those whom they took in
battle to serve them ; and hence the name of bondman[1] is
derived. But whether they who were first slaves had
been subjugated by the laws of war, or had been reduced
to this state by want, it is indeed certain, that the order
of nature was violently infringed ; because men were created
for the purpose of cultivating mutual society between each
other. And although it is advantageous that some should
preside over others, yet an equality, as among brethren, ought
to have been retained. However, although slavery is contrary to that right government which is most desirable, and
in its commencement was not without fault ; it does not, on
this account, follow, that the use of it, which was afterwards
received by custom, and excused by necessity, is unlawful.
Abram therefore might possess both servants bought with
money, and slaves born in his house. For that common saying, ' What has not prevailed from the beginning cannot be

[1] " Mancipii. . . A manucapium, quod ab hostibus manu caperetur ;"
because taken by the hand by the enemy.—*Ed.*

rendered valid by length of time,' admits (as is well known) of some exceptions ; and we shall have an example in point in the forty-eighth chapter.

6. *And Abram passed through the land.* Here Moses shows that Abram did not immediately, on his entering into the land, find a habitation in which he might rest. For the expression " passed through," and the position of the place (Sichem) to which he passed, show that the length of his journey had been great. Sichem is not far from Mount Gerizim, which is toward the desert of the Southern region. Wherefore, it is just as Moses had said, that the faith of Abram was again tried, when God suffered him as a wanderer to traverse the whole land, before he gave him any fixed abode. How hard would it seem, when God had promised to be his Protector, that not even a little corner is assigned him on which he may set his foot? But he is compelled to wander in a circuitous route, in order that he may the better exercise self-denial. The word אלון, *(Elon,)* is by some translated an oak forest, by some a valley ;[1] others take it for the proper name of a place. I do not doubt that *Moreh* is the proper name of the place ; but I explain Elon to mean a *plain*, or an *oak*, not that it was a single tree, but the singular is put for the plural number;[2] and this latter interpretation I most approve.

And the Canaanite was then in the land. This clause concerning the Canaanite is not added without reason ; because it was no slight temptation to be cast among that perfidious and wicked nation, destitute of all humanity. What could the holy man then think, but that he was betrayed into the hands of these most abandoned men, by whom he might soon be murdered ; or else that he would have to spend a disturbed and miserable life amid continual injuries and troubles ? But it was profitable for him to be accustomed, by such discipline, to cherish a better hope. For if he had been kindly and courteously received in the land of Canaan, he would have hoped for nothing better than to spend his life there as a

---

[1] By others a plain. *Vide Poli Synopsis in loco.* See our English version, " Abram passed through the land unto the place of Sichem, unto the *plain* of Moreh."—*Ed.*

[2] That is, *an oak* is put for an oak *grove*, or *forest.*—*Ed.*

guest. But now God raises his thoughts higher, in order that he may conclude, that at some future time, the inhabitants being destroyed, he shall be the lord and heir of the land. Besides, he is admonished, by the continual want of repose, to look up towards heaven. For since the inheritance of the land was specially promised to himself, and would only belong to his descendants, for his sake; it follows, that the land, in which he was so ill and inhumanly treated, was not set before him as his ultimate aim, but that heaven itself was proposed to him as his final resting-place.

7. *And the Lord appeared unto Abram.* He now relates that Abram was not left entirely destitute, but that God stretched forth his hand to help him. We must, however, mark, with what kind of assistance God succours him in his temptations. He offers him his bare word, and in such a way, indeed, that Abram might deem himself exposed to ridicule. For God declares he will give the land to his seed: but where is the seed, or where the hope of seed; seeing that he is childless and old, and his wife is barren? This was therefore an insipid consolation to the flesh. But faith has a different taste; the property of which is, to hold all the senses of the pious so bound by reverence to the word, that a single promise of God is quite sufficient. Meanwhile, although God truly alleviates and mitigates the evils which his servants endure, he does it only so far as is expedient for them, without indulging the desire of the flesh. Let us hence learn, that this single remedy ought to be sufficient for us in our sufferings: that God so speaks to us in his word, as to cause our minds to perceive him to be propitious; and let us not give the reins to the importunate desires of our flesh. God himself will not fail on his part; but will, by the manifestation of his favour, raise us when we are cast down.

And there builded he an altar. This altar was a token of gratitude. As soon as God appeared to him he raised an altar: to what end? that he might call upon the name of the Lord. We see, therefore, that he was intent upon giving of thanks; and that an altar was built by him in memory of kindness received. Should any one ask, whether he could not worship God without an altar? I answer, that the inward worship of the heart is not sufficient, unless external profession before men be added. Religion has truly its appropriate seat in the heart; but from this root, public confession afterwards arises, as its fruit. For we are created to this end, that we may offer soul and body unto God. The Canaanites had their religion; they had also altars for sacrifices : but Abram, that he might not involve himself in their superstitions, erects a domestic altar, on which he may offer sacrifice; as if he had resolved to place a royal throne for God within his house. But because the worship of God is spiritual, and all ceremonies which have no right and lawful end, are not only vain and worthless in themselves, but also corrupt the true worship of God by their counterfeited and fallacious appearance ; we must carefully observe what Moses says, that the altar was erected for the purpose of calling upon God. The altar then is the external *form* of divine worship; but *invocation* is its substance and truth. This mark easily distinguishes pure worshippers from hypocrites, who are far too liberal in outward pomp, but wish their religion to terminate in bare ceremonies. Thus all their religion is vague, being directed to no certain end. Their ultimate intention, indeed, is (as they confusedly speak) to worship God : but piety approaches nearer to God; and therefore does not trifle with external figures, but has respect to the truth and the substance of religion. On the whole, ceremonies are no otherwise acceptable to God, than as they have reference to the spiritual worship of God.

To invoke the *name* of God, or to invoke *in his name*, admits of a twofold exposition ; namely, either to pray to God, or to celebrate his name with praises. But because prayer and thanksgiving are things conjoined, I willingly include both. We have before said, in the fourth chapter, that the whole worship of God was not improperly described, by the figure *synecdoche*, under this particular expression; because God esteems no duty of piety more highly, and accounts no sacrifice more acceptable, than the invocation of his name, as is declared in Psalm l. 23, and Psalm li. 19. As often, therefore, as the word *altar* occurs, let the sacrifices also come into our mind; for from the beginning, God would have mankind informed, that there could be no access to himself without sacrifice.   Therefore Abram, from the general doctrine of religion, opened for himself a celestial sanctuary, by sacrifices, that he might rightly worship God.[1]   But we know that God was never appeased by the blood of beasts. Wherefore it follows, that the faith of Abram was directed to the blood of Christ.[2]

It may seem, however, absurd, that Abram built himself an altar, at his own pleasure, though he was neither a priest, nor had any express command from God.   I answer, that Moses removes this scruple in the context: for Abram is not said to have made an altar simply to God, but to God who had *appeared* unto him.   The altar therefore had its foundation in that revelation; and ought not to be separated from that of which it formed but a part and an appendage.   Superstition fabricates for itself such a God as it pleases, and then invents for him various kinds of worship; just as the Papists, at this day, most proudly boast that they worship God, when they are only trifling with their foolish pageantry. But the piety of Abram is commended, because, having erected an altar, he worshipped God who had been manifested to him.   And although Moses declares the design with which Abram built the altar, when he relates that he there called upon God, he yet, at the same time, intimates, that such a service was pleasing to God: for this language implies the approval of the Holy Spirit, who thereby pronounces that he had rightly called upon God.   Others, indeed, confidently boasted that they worshipped God; but God, in praising

---

[1] The sentence seems obscure: " Ergo Abram ex generali pietatis doctrina, sacrificiis cœleste sibi sanctuarium aperuit, ut Deum rite coleret."   The French translation throws little light upon it: ' Abram donc s'est fait ouverture au sanctuaire celeste par une doctrine generale de piete, afin de bien servir Dieu.'   The word sacrifice is here entirely omitted.   Nor does the Old English translator seem to have given himself much trouble to render it accurately: ' Abram, out of a general doctrine of godliness, prepared a heavenly way to himself to offer sacrifices, that he might worship God aright.'—*Ed.*

[2] And consequently that he regarded all his own sacrifices as typical of the great atoning sacrifice of the cross.—*Ed.*

Abram only, rejects all the rites of the heathen as a vile profanation of his name.

8. *And he removed from thence.*   When we hear that Abram
moved from the place where he had built an altar to God,
we ought not to doubt that he was, by some necessity, compelled to do so.   He there found the inhabitants unpropi-
tious ; and therefore transfers his tabernacle elsewhere.   But
if Abram bore his continual wanderings patiently, our fastidiousness is utterly inexcusable, when we murmur against
God, if he does not grant us a quiet nest.   Certainly, when
Christ has opened heaven to us, and daily invites us thither
to dwell with himself ; we should not take it amiss, if he
chooses that we should be strangers in the world.   The sum
of the passage is this, that Abram was without a settled
residence :[1] which title Paul assigns to Christians, (1 Cor.
iv. 11.)   Moreover, there is a manifest *prolepsis* in the word
Bethel ; for Moses gives the place this name, to accommodate
his discourse to the men of his own age.

And there he builded an altar.   Moses commends in Abram
his unwearied devotedness to piety : for by these words, he
intimates, that whatever place he visited, he there exercised
himself in the external worship of God ; both that he might
have no religious rites in common with the wicked, and that
he might retain his family in sincere piety.   And it is probable, that, from this cause, he would be the object of no little
enmity ; because there is nothing which more enrages the
wicked, than a religion different from their own, in which they
conceive themselves to be not only despised, but altogether
condemned as blind.   And we know that the Canaanites were
cruel and proud, and too ready to avenge insults.   This was
perhaps the reason of Abram's frequent removals : that his
neighbours regarded the altars which he built, as a reproach
to themselves.   It ought indeed to be referred to the wonderful favour of God, that he was not often stoned.   Nevertheless, since the holy man knows that he is justly required
to bear testimony that he has a God peculiarly his own,

[1] Ἀστατούμενος.

whom he must not, by dissimulation, virtually deny,[1] he therefore does not hesitate to prefer the glory of God to his own life.

9. *And Abram journeyed.* This was the third removal of the holy man within a short period, after he seemed to have found some kind of abode. It is certain that he did not voluntarily, and for his own gratification, run hither and thither, (as light-minded persons are wont to do:) but there were certain necessities which drove him forth, in order to teach him, by continual habit, that he was not only a stranger, but a wretched wanderer in the land of which he was the lord. Yet no common fruit was the result of so many changes; because he endeavoured, as much as in him lay, to dedicate to God, every part of the land to which he had access, and perfumed it with the odour of his faith.

10. *And there was a famine in the land.* A much more severe temptation is now recorded, by which the faith of Abram is tried to the quick. For he is not only led around through various windings of the country, but is driven into exile, from the land which God had given to him and to his posterity. It is to be observed, that Chaldea was exceedingly fertile; having been, from this cause, accustomed to opulence, he came to Charran, where, it is conjectured, he lived commodiously enough, since it is clear he had an increase of servants and of wealth. But now being expelled by hunger from that land, where, in reliance on the word of God, he had promised himself a happy life, supplied with all abundance of good things, what must have been his thoughts, had he not been well fortified against the devices of Satan? His faith would have been overturned a hundred times. And we know, that whenever our expectation is frustrated, and things do not succeed according to our wishes, our flesh soon harps on this string, ' God has deceived thee.' But Moses shows, in a few words, with what firmness Abram sustained this

---

[1] "Ut testetur se peculiarem habere Deum."—"Qu'il testifie avoir un autre Dieu que celui qui estoit là adoré:" to testify that he has another God than that which was there adored.—*French Tr.*

vehement assault. He does not indeed magnificently proclaim his constancy in verbose eulogies; but, by one little
word, he sufficiently demonstrates, that it was great even to
a miracle, when he says, that he "went down into Egypt to
sojourn there." For he intimates, that Abram, nevertheless,
retained in his mind possession of the land promised unto
him; although, being ejected from it by hunger, he fled
elsewhere, for the sake of obtaining food. And let us be
instructed by this example, that the servants of God must
contend against many obstacles, that they may finish the
course of their vocation. For we must always recall to memory, that Abram is not to be regarded as an individual member
of the body of the faithful, but as the common father of them
all; so that all should form themselves to the imitation of his
example. Therefore, since the condition of the present life
is unstable, and obnoxious to innumerable changes; let us
remember, that, whithersoever we may be driven by famine,
and by the rage of war, and by other vicissitudes which occasionally happen beyond our expectation, we must yet hold
our right course; and that, though our bodies may be carried
hither and thither, our faith ought to stand unshaken. Moreover, it is not surprising, when the Canaanites sustained
life with difficulty, that Abram should be compelled privately
to consult for himself. For he had not a single acre of land;
and he had to deal with a cruel and most wicked people, who
would rather a hundred times have suffered him to perish
with hunger, than they would have brought him assistance
in his difficulty. Such circumstances amplify the praise of
Abram's faith and fortitude: first, because, when destitute of
food for the body, he feeds himself upon the sole promise of
God; and then, because he is not to be torn away by any
violence, except for a short time, from the place where he
was commanded to dwell. In this respect he is very unlike
many, who are hurried away, by every slight occasion, to
desert their proper calling.

11. *He said unto Sarai his wife.* He now relates the counsel
which Abram took for the preservation of his life when he was
approaching Egypt. And, since this place is like a rock, on

which many strike; it is proper that we should soberly and
reverently consider how far Abram was deserving of excuse,
and how he was to be blamed.   First, there seems to be
something of falsehood, mixed with the dissimulation, which
he persuades his wife to practise.   And although afterwards
he makes the excuse, that he had not lied, nor feigned anything that was untrue : in this certainly he was greatly
culpable, that it was not owing to his care that his wife was
not prostituted.   For when he dissembles the fact, that she
was his wife, he deprives her chastity of its legitimate defence.
And hence certain perverse cavillers take occasion to object,[1]
that the holy patriarch was a pander to his own wife; and
that, for the purpose of craftily taking care of himself, he
spared neither her modesty nor his own honour.   But it is
easy to refute this virulent abuse ; because, it may indeed be
inferred, that Abram had far higher ends in view, seeing that,
in other things, he was endued with a magnanimity so great.
Again, how did it happen, that he rather sought to go into
Egypt than to Charran, or into his own country, unless that,
in his journeying, he had God before his eyes, and the divine
promise firmly rooted in his mind ?   Since, therefore, he never
allowed his senses to swerve from the word of God, we may
even thence gather the reason, why he so greatly feared for
his own life, as to attempt the preservation of it from one
danger, by incurring a still greater.   Undoubtedly he would
have chosen to die a hundred times, rather than thus to ruin
the character of his wife, and to be deprived of the society of
her whom alone he loved.   But while he reflected that the
hope of salvation was centred in *himself*, that *he* was the
fountain of the Church of God, that unless *he* lived, the
benediction promised to him, and to his seed, was vain ; he
did not estimate his own life according to the private affection
of the flesh; but inasmuch as he did not wish the effect of the
divine vocation to perish through his death, he was so affected
with concern for the preservation of his own life, that he overlooked every thing besides.   So far, then, he deserves praise,
that, having in view a lawful end of living, he was prepared

---

[1] " Atque hinc latrandi materiam protervi quidam canes arripiunt."

to purchase life at any price. But in devising this indirect method, by which he subjected his wife to the peril of adultery, he seems to be by no means excusable. If he was solicitous about his own life, which he might justly be, yet he ought to have cast his care upon God. The providence of God, I grant, does not indeed preclude the faithful from caring for themselves ; but let them do it in such a way, that they may not overstep their prescribed bounds. Hence it follows, that Abram's end was right, but he erred in the way itself ; for so it often happens to us, that even while we are tending towards God, yet, by our thoughtlessness in catching at unlawful means, we swerve from his word. And this, especially, is wont to take place in affairs of difficulty ; because, while no way of escape appears, we are easily led astray into various circuitous paths. Therefore, although they are rash judges, who entirely condemn this deed of Abram, yet the special fault is not to be denied, namely, that he, trembling at the approach of death, did not commit the issue of the danger to God, instead of sinfully betraying the modesty of his wife. Wherefore, by this example, we are admonished, that, in involved and doubtful matters, we must seek the spirit of counsel and of prudence from the Lord ; and must also cultivate sobriety, that we may not attempt anything rashly, without the authority of his word.

I know that thou art a fair woman to look upon.[1] It is asked,

---

[1] " An aggravation of Abraham's alarm arose from the complexion of his wife,—' Thou art a fair woman.' Though the Egyptian ladies were not so dark as the Nubians and Ethiopians, they were of a browner tinge than the Syrians and Arabians : we also find on the monuments, that ladies of high rank are usually represented in lighter tints than their attendants. . . . There is ample evidence, that a fair complexion was deemed a high recommendation in the age of the Pharaohs. This circumstance, so fully confirmed by the monuments, is recorded in no history but the book of Genesis ; and it is a remarkable confirmation of the veracity of the Pentateuch."—*Gliddon's Ancient Egypt*, quoted in *Hengstenberg's Egypt and the Books of Moses*, p. 200. It may here be proper to remark, that much learned labour has been expended by the Anti-supernaturalist Divines on the Continent, in the fruitless attempt to prove that the Pentateuch could not be the work of Moses, nor of the age in which he lived ; and, consequently, not an inspired production. This has led to a deeper investigation of Egyptian antiquities, the result of which has been to confirm, in every possible way, the authenticity of the Mosaic records. Monuments as ancient as the times of Moses, and

whence had Sarai this beauty, seeing she was an old woman ? For though we grant that she previously had excelled in elegance of form, certainly years had detracted from her gracefulness; and we know how much the wrinkles of old age disfigure the best and most beautiful faces.   In the first place, I answer, there is no doubt that there was then greater vivacity in the human race than there is now ; we also know, that vigour sustains the personal appearance.   Again, her sterility availed to preserve her beauty, and to keep her whole habit of body entire ; for there is nothing which more debilitates females than frequent parturition.   I do not however doubt, that the perfection of her form was the special gift of God ; but why he would not suffer the beauty of the holy woman to be so soon worn down by age, we know not; unless it were, that the loveliness of that form was intended to be the cause of great and severe anxiety to her husband. Common experience also teaches us, that they who are not content with a regular and moderate degree of comeliness, find, to their great loss, at what a cost immoderate beauty is purchased.

12. *Therefore it shall come to pass, that when the Egyptians shall see thee, &c.*   It may seem that Abram was unjust to the Egyptians, in suspecting evil of them, from whom he had yet received no injury.   And, since charity truly is not suspicious ; he may appear to deal unfairly, in not only charging them with lust, but also in suspecting them of murder.   I answer, that the holy man did, not without reason, fear for himself from that nation, concerning which he had heard many unfavourable reports.   And already he had, in other places, experienced so much of the wickedness of men, that he might justly apprehend everything from the profane despisers of God.   He does not however pronounce anything absolutely

bas-reliefs exhibiting different characters, and persons engaged in different occupations, all show, that no writer of comparatively modern times could have composed these books.   We have here an additional proof to many which had been given before, that a slight acquaintance with facts may lead to scepticism ; but that deep investigation of them invariably confirms the testimony of Scripture.— See note at p. 316.—*Ed.*

concerning the Egyptians; but, wishing to bring his wife to his own opinion, he gives her timely warning of what might happen. And God, while he commands us to abstain from malicious and sinister judgments, yet allows to be on our guard against unknown persons; and this may take place without any injury to the brethren. Yet I do not deny that this trepidation of Abram exceeded all bounds, and that an unreasonable anxiety caused him to involve himself in another fault, as we have already stated.

15. *And commended her before Pharaoh.*[1] Although Abram had sinned by fearing too much and too soon, yet the event teaches, that he had not feared without cause: for his wife was taken from him and brought to the king. At first Moses speaks generally of the Egyptians, afterwards he mentions the courtiers; by which course he intimates, that the rumour of Sarai's beauty was everywhere spread abroad; but that it was more eagerly received by the courtiers, who indulge themselves in greater license. Whereas he adds, that they told the king; we hence infer, how ancient is that corruption which now prevails immeasurably in the courts of kings. For as all things there are full of blandishments and flatteries, so the nobles principally apply their minds to introduce, from time to time, what may be gratifying to royalty. Therefore we see, that whosoever among them desires to rise high in favour, is addicted not only to servile flatteries, but also to pandering for their master's lusts.

And the woman was taken into Pharaoh's house. Since she was carried off, and dwelt for some time in the palace, many suppose that she was corrupted by the king. For it is not credible, that a lustful man, when he had her in his power, should have spared her modesty. This, truly, Abram had richly deserved, who had neither relied upon the grace

---

[1] " She must therefore have been unveiled. The monuments show, that, according to Egyptian customs, she could only so appear in public. ' We find from the monuments,' says *Taylor*, 'that the Egyptian women, in the reign of the Pharaohs, exposed their faces, and were permitted to enjoy as much liberty as the ladies of modern Europe. But this custom was changed after the conquest of the country by the Persians.' "—*Hengstenberg's Egypt and the Books of Moses*, p. 199.

of God, nor had committed the chastity of his wife to His faithfulness and care; but the plague which immediately followed, sufficiently proves that the Lord was mindful of her; and hence we may conclude, that she remained uninjured.   And although, in this place, Moses says nothing expressly on the subject, yet, from a comparison with a similar subsequent history, we conjecture, that the guardianship of God was not wanting to Abram at this time also. When he was in similar danger, (Gen. xx. 1,) God did not suffer her to be violated by the king of Gerar; shall we then suppose that she was now exposed to Pharaoh's lust? Would God have thought more about subjecting her, who had been once dishonoured, to a second disgrace, than about preserving her, who had hitherto lived uprightly and chastely? Further, if God showed himself so propitious to Abram, as to rescue his wife, whom he exposed a second time to infamy; how is it possible that He should have failed to obviate the previous danger?   Perhaps, also, greater integrity still flourished in that age; so that the lusts of kings were not so unrestrained as they afterwards became.   Moreover, when Moses adds, that Abram was kindly treated for Sarai's sake; we hence conclude, that she was honourably entertained by Pharaoh, and was not dealt with as a harlot.   When, therefore, Moses says, that she was brought into the king's palace; I do not understand this to have been for any other purpose,[1] than that the king, by a solemn rite, might take her as his wife.

17. *And the Lord plagued Pharaoh.*   If Moses had simply related, that God had punished the king for having committed adultery, it would not so obviously appear that he had taken care of Sarai's chastity; but when he plainly declares, that the house of the king was plagued because of Sarai, Abram's wife, all doubt is, in my judgment, removed; because God, on behalf of his servant, interposed his mighty hand in time, lest Sarai should be violated.   And here we have a remark-

[1] " Non interpretor fuisse factum, ut statim cum rege dormiret, sed ut rex solemni ritu eam duceret uxorem."

able instance of the solicitude with which God protects his servants, by undertaking their cause against the most powerful monarchs; as this and similar histories show, which are referred to in Psalm cv. verse 12-15 :—'When they were but a few men in number ; yea, very few, and strangers in it. When they went from one nation to another, from one kingdom to another people ; he suffered no man to do them wrong ; yea, he reproved kings for their sakes ; saying, Touch not mine anointed, and do my prophets no harm.' From which passage also a confirmation of the opinion just given may be derived. For if God reproved Pharaoh, that he should do Abram no harm ; it follows, that he preserved Sarai's honour uninjured. Instructed by such examples, we may also learn, that however the world may hold us in contempt, on account of the smallness of our number, and our weakness ; we are yet so precious in the sight of God, that he will, for our sake, declare himself an enemy to kings, and even to the whole world. Let us know, that we are covered by his protection, in order that the lust and violence of those who are more powerful, may not oppress us. But it is asked, whether Pharaoh was justly punished, seeing that he neither intended, by guile nor by force, to gain possession of another man's wife ? I answer, that the actions of men are not always to be estimated according to our judgment, but are rather to be weighed in the balances of God ; for it often happens, that the Lord will find in us what he may justly punish, while we seem to ourselves to be free from fault, and while we absolve ourselves from all guilt. Let kings rather learn, from this history, to bridle their own power, and moderately to use their authority ; and, lastly, to impose a voluntary law of moderation upon themselves. For, although no fault openly appears in Pharaoh ; yet, since he has no faithful monitor among men, who dares to repress his licentiousness, the Lord chastises him from heaven. As to his family, it was indeed innocent ; but the Lord has always just causes, though hidden from us, why he should smite with his rod those who seem to merit no such rebuke. That he spared his servant Abram, ought to be ascribed to his paternal indulgence.

18. *And Pharaoh called Abram.*   Pharaoh justly expostulates with Abram, who was chiefly in fault.   No answer on the part of Abram is here recorded; and perhaps he assented to the just and true reprehension.   It is, however, possible that the exculpation was omitted by Moses; whose design was to give an example of the Divine providence in preserving Abram, and vindicating his marriage relation.   But, although Abram knew that he was suffering the due punishment of his folly, or of his unreasonable caution; he, nevertheless, relapsed, as we shall see in its proper place, a second time into the same fault.

20. *And Pharaoh commanded his men.*   In giving commandment that Abram should have a safe-conduct out of the kingdom, Pharaoh might seem to have done it, for the sake of providing against danger; because Abram had stirred up the odium of the nation against himself, as against one who had brought thither the scourge of God along with him; but as this conjecture has little solidity, I give the more simple interpretation, that leave of departure was granted to Abram with the addition of a guard, lest he should be exposed to violence.   For we know how proud and cruel the Egyptians were; and how obnoxious Abram was to envy, because, having there become suddenly rich, he would seem to be carrying spoil away with him.

CHAPTER XIII.

1. AND Abram went up out of Egypt, he, and his wife, and all that he had, and Lot with him, into the south.

2. And Abram *was* very rich in cattle, in silver, and in gold.

3. And he went on his journeys from the south even to Beth-el, unto the place where his tent had been at the beginning, between Beth-el and Hai;

4. Unto the place of the altar, which

1. Et ascendit Abram ex Ægypto, ipse et uxor ejus, et omnia quæ erant ei, et Lot cum eo ad Meridiem.

2. Et Abram dives erat valde pecore, argento et auro.

3. Et perrexit per profectiones suas a Meridie usque ad Bethel, usque ad locum ubi fuerat tabernaculum ejus in principio, inter Bethel et Hai;

4. Ad locum altaris quod

he had made there at the first : and there Abram called on the name of the Lord.

5. And Lot also, which went with Abram, had flocks, and herds, and tents.

6. And the land was not able to bear them, that they might dwell together: for their substance was great, so that they could not dwell together.

7. And there was a strife between the herdmen of Abram's cattle and the herdmen of Lot's cattle: and the Canaanite and the Perizzite dwelled then in the land.

8. And Abram said unto Lot, Let there be no strife, I pray thee, between me and thee, and between my herdmen and thy herdmen; for we *be* brethren.

9. *Is* not the whole land before thee? separate thyself, I pray thee, from me: if *thou wilt take* the left hand, then I will go to the right; or if *thou depart* to the right hand, then I will go to the left.

10. And Lot lifted up his eyes, and beheld all the plain of Jordan, that it *was* well watered every where, before the Lord destroyed Sodom and Gomorrah, *even* as the garden of the Lord, like the land of Egypt, as thou comest unto Zoar.

11. Then Lot chose him all the plain of Jordan; and Lot journeyed east: and they separated themselves the one from the other.

12. Abram dwelled in the land of Canaan, and Lot dwelled in the cities of the plain, and pitched *his* tent towards Sodom.

13. But the men of Sodom *were* wicked and sinners before the Lord exceedingly.

14. And the Lord said unto Abram, after that Lot was separated from him, Lift up now thine eyes, and look from the place where thou art northward, and southward, and eastward, and westward:

15. For all the land which thou seest, to thee will I give it, and to thy seed for ever.

16. And I will make thy seed as the dust of the earth: so that if a man can number the dust of the earth, *then* shall thy seed also be numbered.

feceraat in principio : et invocavit ibi Abram nomen Jehovæ.

5. Et etiam ipsi Lot ambulanti cum Abram erant pecudes, et boves, et tabernacula.

6. Et non ferebat eos terra, ut habitarent pariter: quia erat substantia eorum multa, et non poterant habitare pariter.

7. Et fuit contentio inter pastores pecudum Abram, et pastores pecudum Lot: et Chenaanæus et Pherizæus tunc habitabant in terra.

8. Et dixit Abram ad Lot, Ne nunc sit contentio inter me et te, et inter pastores meos et pastores tuos : quia viri fratres sumus.

9. Numquid non omnis terra est coram te? separa te nunc a me: si ieris ad sinistram, dextram tenebo: et si ad dextram ieris, sinistram tenebo.

10. Et levavit Lot oculos suos, et vidit omnem planitiem Jarden, quod tota esset irrigua, antequam disperderet Jehova Sedom et Hamorah, sicuti hortus Jehovæ, sicut terra Ægypti, ingrediente te in Sohar.

11. Et elegit sibi Lot omnem planitiem Jarden, et profectus est Lot ad Orientem, et separaverunt se alter ab altero.

12. Abram habitavit in terra Chanaan, et Lot habitavit in urbibus planitiei, et tetendit tabernaculum Sedom usque.

13. Viri autem Sedom erant mali, et scelerati coram Jehova valde.

14. Et Jehova dixit ad Abram, postquam separavit se Lot ab eo, Leva nunc oculos tuos, et vide a loco ubi es, ad Aquilonem, Meridiem, Orientem, et Occidentem.

15. Quia omnem terram, quam tu vides, tibi dabo et semini tuo usque in sæculum.

16. Et ponam semen tuum sicut pulverem terræ: quia si poterit quisquam numerare pulverem terræ, etiam semen tuum numerabit.

17. Arise, walk through the land in the length of it and in the breadth of it; for I will give it unto thee.

17. Surge, ambula per terram in longitudinem ejus, et in latitudinem ejus : quia tibi dabo eam.

18. Then Abram removed *his* tent, and came and dwelt in the plain of Mamre, which *is* in Hebron, and built there an altar unto the Lord.

18. Et tetendit tabernaculum Abram, et venit, et habitavit in quercubus Mamre, quæ sunt in Hebron : et ædificavit ibi altare Jehovæ.

1. *And Abram went up out of Egypt.* In the commencement of the chapter, Moses commemorates the goodness of God in protecting Abram ; whence it came to pass, that he not only returned in safety, but took with him great wealth. This circumstance is also to be noticed, that when he was leaving Egypt, abounding in cattle and treasures, he was allowed to pursue his journey in peace ; for it is surprising that the Egyptians would suffer what Abram had acquired among them, to be transferred elsewhere. Moses next shows, that riches proved no sufficient obstacle to prevent Abram from having respect continually to his proposed end, and from moving towards it with unremitting pace. We know how greatly even a moderate share of wealth, hinders many from raising their heads towards heaven ; while they who really possess abundance, not only lie torpid in indolence, but are entirely buried in the earth. Wherefore, Moses places the virtue of Abram in contrast with the common vice of others; when he relates that he was not to be prevented by any impediments, from seeking again the land of Canaan. For he might (like many others) have been able to flatter himself with some fair pretext : such as, that since God, from whom he had received extraordinary blessings, had been favourable and kind to him in Egypt, it was right for him to remain there. But he does not forget what had been divinely commanded him; and, therefore, as one unfettered, he hastens to the place whither he is called. Wherefore, the rich are deprived of all excuse, if they are so rooted in the earth, that they do not attend the call of God. Two extremes, however, are here to be guarded against. Many place angelical perfection in poverty ; as if it were impossible to cultivate piety and to serve God, unless riches are cast

away. Few indeed imitate Crates the Theban, who cast his treasures into the sea; because he did not think that he could be saved unless they were lost. Yet many fanatics repel rich men from the hope of salvation; as if poverty were the only gate of heaven; which yet, sometimes, involves men in more hinderances than riches. But Augustine wisely teaches us, that the rich and poor are collected together in the same inheritance of life; because poor Lazarus was received into the bosom of rich Abraham. On the other hand, we must beware of the opposite evil; lest riches should cast a stumbling-block in our way, or should so burden us, that we should the less readily advance towards the kingdom of heaven.

3. *And he went on his journeys.* In these words Moses teaches us, that Abram did not rest till he had returned to Bethel. For although he pitched his tent in many places, yet he nowhere so fixed his foot, as to make it his permanent abode. He does not speak of the south in reference to Egypt; he merely means that he had come into the southern part of Judea; and that, therefore, he had, by a long and troublesome journey, arrived at the place where he had determined to remain. Moses next subjoins, that an altar had before been there erected by him, and that he then also began anew to call upon the name of the Lord: whereby we may learn, that the holy man was always like himself in worshipping God, and giving evidence of his piety. The explanation given by some, that the inhabitants of the place had been brought to the pure worship of God, is neither probable, nor to be deduced from the words of Moses. And we have stated elsewhere what is the force of the expression, 'To invoke in the name,' or, 'To call upon the name of the Lord;' namely, to profess the true and pure worship of God. For Abram invoked God, not twelve times only, during the whole course of his life; but whenever he publicly celebrated him, and by a solemn rite, made it manifest that he had nothing in common with the superstitions of the heathen, then he is also said to have called upon God. Therefore, although he always worshipped God, and exercised himself in daily prayers; yet, because he did not daily testify his piety by

outward profession before men, this virtue is here especially
commended by Moses. It was therefore proper that invocation should be conjoined with the altar; because, by
the sacrifices offered, he plainly testified what God he worshipped, in order that the Canaanites might know that he
was not addicted to their common idolatries.

5. *And Lot also, which went with Abram.* Next follows the
inconvenience which Abram suffered through his riches :
namely, that he was torn from his nephew, whom he tenderly loved, as if it had been from his own bowels. Certainly, had the option been given him, he would rather have
chosen to cast away his riches, than to be parted from him
whom he had held in the place of an only son : yet he found
no other method of avoiding contentions. Shall we impute
this evil to his own excessive moroseness, or to the forward-
ness of his nephew ? I suppose, however, that we must rather
consider the design of God. There was a danger lest Abram
should be too much gratified with his own success, inasmuch
as prosperity blinds many. Therefore God allays the sweetness of wealth with bitterness; and does not permit the mind
of his servant to be too much enchanted with it. And whenever a fallacious estimate of riches impels us to desire them
inordinately, because we do not perceive the great disadvantages which they bring along with them; let the recollection of this history avail to restrain such immoderate attachment to them. Further, as often as the rich find any trouble
arising from their wealth; let them learn to purify their
minds by this medicine, that they may not become excessively addicted to the good things of the present life. And
truly, unless the Lord were occasionally to put the bridle on
men, to what depths would they not fall, when they overflow
with prosperity ? On the other hand, if we are straitened with
poverty, let us know, that, by this method also, God corrects
the hidden evils of our flesh. Finally, let those who abound
remember, that they are surrounded with thorns, and must
take care lest they be pricked; and let those whose affairs
are contracted and embarrassed know, that God is caring for
them, in order that they may not be involved in evil and

noxious snares.   This separation was sad to Abram's mind;
but it was suitable for the correction of much latent evil,
that wealth might not stifle the ardour of his zeal.   But if
Abram had need of such an antidote, let us not wonder, if
God, by inflicting some stroke, should repress our excesses.
For he does not always wait till the faithful shall have
fallen; but looks forward for them into the future.   So
he does not actually correct the avarice or the pride of
his servant Abram : but, by an anticipated remedy, he
causes that Satan shall not infect his mind with any of his
allurements.

7. *And there was a strife.*   What I hinted respecting
riches, is also true respecting a large retinue of attendants.
We see with what ambition many desire a great crowd of
servants, almost amounting to a whole people.   But since
the family of Abram cost him so dear; let us be well content to have few servants, or even to be entirely without them, if it seem right to the Lord that it should be so.
It was scarcely possible to avoid great confusion, in a house
where there was a considerable number of men.   And experience confirms the truth of the proverb, that a crowd is commonly turbulent.   Now, if repose and tranquillity be an inestimable good; let us know, that we best consult for our real
welfare, when we have a small house, and privately pass our
time, without tumult, in our families.   We are also warned,
by the example before us, to beware lest Satan, by indirect
methods, should lead us into contention.   For when he cannot light up mutual enmities between us, he would involve us
in other men's quarrels.   Lot and Abram were at concord with
each other; but a contention raised between their shepherds,
carried them reluctantly away ; so that they were compelled
to separate from each other.   There is no doubt that Abram
faithfully instructed his own people to cultivate peace; yet he
did not so far succeed in his desire and effort, as to prevent his
witnessing the most destructive fire of discord kindled in his
house.   Wherefore, it is nothing wonderful, if we see tumults
often arising in churches, where there is a still greater number of men.   Abram had about three hundred servants ; it is

probable that the family of Lot was nearly equal to it :[1] what then may be expected to take place between five or six thousand men,—especially free men,—when they contend with each other? As, however, we ought not to be disturbed by such scandals ; so we must, in every way, take care that contentions do not become violent. For unless they be speedily met, they will soon break out into pernicious dissension.

The Canaanite and the Perizzite. Moses adds this for the sake of aggravating the evil. For he declares the heat of the contention to have been so great, that it could neither be extinguished nor assuaged, even by the fear of impending destruction. They were surrounded by as many enemies as they had neighbours. Nothing, therefore, was wanting in order to their destruction, but a suitable occasion; and this they themselves were affording by their quarrels. To such a degree does blind fury infatuate men, when once the vehemence of contention has prevailed, that they carelessly despise death, when placed before their eyes. Now, although we are not continually surrounded by Canaanites, we are yet in the midst of enemies, as long as we sojourn in the world. Wherefore, if we are influenced by any desire for the salvation of ourselves, and of our brethren, let us beware of contentions, which will deliver us over to Satan to be destroyed.

8. *And Abram said unto Lot.* Moses first states, that Abram no sooner perceived the strifes which had arisen, than he fulfilled the duty of a good householder, by attempting to restore peace among his domestics ; and that afterwards, by his moderation, he endeavoured to remedy the evil by removing it. And although the servants alone were contend-

---

[1] " Familiam Lot minime fuisse parem verisimile est." The words are capable of two opposite renderings according to the different sense in which *minime* is taken. It may either mean " by no means," or " at least." The Old English translation renders it in the former method. " It is very likely that the household of Lot was much less." The French version adopts the latter meaning. " Il est bien vraye-semblable que la famille de Lot n'a pas este moindre." Neither of the versions give a very probable meaning. The context seems almost to demand the translation which the Editor has ventured to prefer.—*Ed.*

ing, he yet does not say in vain, " Let there be no strife between me and thee :" because it was scarcely possible but that the contagion of the strife should reach from the domestics to their lords, although they were in other respects perfectly agreed.   He also foresaw that their friendship could not long remain entire, unless he attempted, in time, to heal the insidious evil.   Moreover, he calls to mind the bond of consanguinity between them ; not because this alone ought to avail to promote mutual peace, but that he might more easily bend and mollify the mind of his nephew.   For when the fear of God is less effectual with us than it ought to be ; it is useful to call in other helps also, which may retain us in our duty.   Now, however, since we all are adopted as sons of God, with the condition annexed, that we should be mutually brethren to each other : this sacred bond is less valued by us than it ought to be, if it does not prove sufficient to allay our contentions.

9. *Is not the whole land before thee?*   Here is that moderation of which I have spoken ; namely, that Abram, for the sake of appeasing strife, voluntarily sacrifices his own right. For as ambition and the desire of victory[1] is the mother of all contentions; so when every one meekly and moderately departs, in some degree, from his just claim, the best remedy is found for the removal of all cause of bitterness.   Abram might indeed, with an honourable pretext, have more pertinaciously defended the right which he relinquished, but he shrinks from nothing for the sake of restoring peace : and therefore he leaves the option to his nephew.

10. *And Lot lifted up his eyes.*   As the equity of Abram was worthy of no little praise ; so the inconsideration of Lot, which Moses here describes, is deserving of censure.   He ought rather to have contended with his uncle for the palm of modesty ; and this the very order of nature suggested ; but just as if he had been, in every respect, the superior, he usurps for himself the better portion ; and makes choice of that

---

[1] Φιλονεικία.

region which seemed the more fertile and agreeable. And
indeed it necessarily follows, that whosoever is too eagerly
intent upon his own advantage, is wanting in humanity towards others. There can be no doubt that this injustice
would pierce the mind of Abram; but he silently bore it, lest
by any means, he should give occasion of new offence. And
thus ought we entirely to act, whenever we perceive those
with whom we are connected, to be not sufficiently mindful of their duty: otherwise there will be no end of tumults.
When the neighbouring plain of Sodom is compared to the
paradise of God, many interpreters explain it as simply meaning, that it was excellent, and in the highest degree fertile;
because the Hebrews call anything excellent, *divine*. I however think, that the place where Adam resided at the beginning, is pointed out. For Moses does not propose a general
similitude, but says, ' that region was watered;' just as he
related the same thing respecting the first abode of man;
namely, that a river, divided into four parts, watered it; he
also adds the same thing respecting a part of Egypt.
Whence it more clearly appears, that in one particular only,
this place is compared with two others.

13. *But the men of Sodom.* Lot thought himself happy
that so rich a habitation had fallen to his share : but he learns
at length, that the choice to which he had hastened, with a
rashness equal to his avarice, had been unhappily granted to
him; since he had to deal with proud and perverse neighbours, with whose conduct it was much harder to bear, than it
was to contend with the sterility of the earth. Therefore, seeing that he was led away solely by the pleasantness of the
prospect, he pays the penalty of his foolish cupidity. Let us
then learn by this example, that our eyes are not to be trusted; but that we must rather be on our guard lest we be
ensnared by them, and be encircled, unawares, with many
evils; just as Lot, when he fancied that he was dwelling in
paradise, was nearly plunged into the depths of hell. But it
seems wonderful, that Moses, when he wishes to condemn the
men of Sodom for their extreme wickedness, should say that
they were wicked before the Lord; and not rather before

men ; for when we come to God's tribunal, every mouth
must be stopped, and all the world must be subject to condemnation ; wherefore Moses may be thought to speak thus
by way of extenuation. But the case is otherwise : for he
means that they were not merely under the dominion of those
common vices which everywhere prevail among men, but
were abandoned to most execrable crimes, the cry of which
rose even to heaven, (as we shall afterwards see,) and demanded vengeance from God. That God, however, bore with
them for a time : and not only so, but suffered them to inhabit a most fertile region, though they were utterly unworthy
of light and of life, affords, as we hence learn, no ground to
the wicked of self-congratulation, when God bears also with
them for a time, or when, by treating them kindly, and even
liberally, he, by his indulgence, strives with their ingratitude.
Yet although they exult in their luxury, and even become
outrageous against God, let the sons of God be admonished
not to envy their fortune ; but to wait a little while, till God,
arousing them from their intoxication, shall call them to his
dreadful judgment. Therefore, Ezekiel, speaking of the men
of Sodom, declares it to have been the cause of their destruction, that, being saturated with bread and wine, and filled
with delicacies, they had exercised a proud cruelty against
the poor, (Ezek. xvi. 49.)

14. *And the Lord said unto Abram.* Moses now relates
that after Abram was separated from his nephew, divine consolation was administered for the appeasing of his mind.
There is no doubt that the wound inflicted by that separation
was very severe, since he was obliged to send away one who
was not less dear to him than his own life. When it is said,
therefore, that the Lord spoke, the circumstance of time requires to be noted ; as if he had said, that the medicine of
God's word was now brought to alleviate his pain. And thus he
teaches us, that the best remedy for the mitigation and the
cure of sadness, is placed in the word of God.

Lift up now thine eyes. Seeing that the Lord promises
the land to the seed of Abram, we perceive the admirable
design of God, in the departure of Lot. He had assigned

the land to Abram alone; if Lot had remained with him, the children of both would have been mixed together. The cause of their dissension was indeed culpable; but the Lord, according to his infinite wisdom, turns it to a good issue, that the posterity of Lot should possess no part of the inheritance. This is the reason why he says, 'All the land which is before thee, I assign to thee and to thy seed. Therefore, there is no reason why thou, to whom a reward so excellent is hereafter to be given, shouldst be excessively sorrowful and troubled on account of this solitude and privation.' For although the same thing had been already promised to Abram; yet God now adapts his promise to the relief of the present sorrow. And thus it is to be remembered, that not only was a promise here repeated, which might cherish and confirm Abram's faith; but that a special oracle was given, from which Abram might learn, that the interests of his own seed were to be promoted, by the separation of Lot from him. The speculation of Luther here (as in other places) has no solidity; namely, that God spake through some prophet. In promising the land "for ever," he does not simply denote perpetuity; but that period which was brought to a close by the advent of Christ. Concerning the meaning of the word עוֹלָם, (*olam*,) the Jews ignorantly contend: but whereas it is taken in various senses in Scripture, it comprises in this place (as I have lately hinted) the whole period of the law; just as the covenant which the Lord made with his ancient people is, in many places, called eternal; because it was the office of Christ by his coming to renovate the world. But the change which Christ introduced was not the *abolition* of the old promises, but rather their *confirmation*. Seeing, therefore, that God has not now one peculiar people in the land of Canaan, but a people diffused throughout all regions of the earth; this does not contradict the assertion, that the eternal possession of the land was rightly promised to the seed of Abram, until the future renovation.

16. *And I will make thy seed as the dust.* Omitting those subtleties, by means of which others argue about nothing, I

simply explain the words to signify, that the seed of Abram is compared to the dust, because of its immense multitude; and truly the sense of the term is to be sought for only in Moses' own words. It was, however, necessary to be here added, that God would raise up for him a seed, of which he was hitherto destitute. And we see that God always keeps him under the restraint of his own word; and will have him dependent upon his own lips. Abram is commanded to look at the dust; but when he turns his eyes upon his own family, what similitude is there between his solitariness and the countless particles of dust? This authority the Lord therefore requires us to attribute to his own word, that it alone should be sufficient for us. It may also give occasion to ridicule, that God commands Abram to travel till he should have examined the whole land. To what purpose shall he do this, except that he may more clearly perceive himself to be a stranger; and that, being exhausted by continual and fruitless disquietude, he may despair of any stable and permanent possession? For how shall he persuade himself that he is lord of that land in which he is scarcely permitted to drink water, although he has with great labour dug the wells? But these are the exercises of faith, in order that it may perceive, in the word, those things which are far off, and which are hidden from carnal sense. For faith is the beholding of absent things, (Heb. xi. 1,) and it has the word as a mirror, in which it may discover the hidden grace of God. And the condition of the pious, at this day, is not dissimilar: for since they are hated by all, are exposed to contempt and reproach, wander without a home, are sometimes driven hither and thither, and suffer from nakedness and poverty, it is nevertheless their duty to lay hold on the inheritance which is promised. Let us therefore walk through the world, as persons debarred from all repose, who have no other resource than the mirror of the word.

18. *And Abram removed his tent.*[1] Here Moses relates

---

[1] "Et tetendit Abram tabernaculum." Abram pitched his tent. This seems to be the true meaning of the word ויאהל; yet the term *pitched*

that the holy man, animated by the renewed promise of God, traversed the land with great courage, as if by a look alone, he could subdue it to himself. Thus we see how greatly the oracle had profited him : not that he had heard anything from the mouth of God to which he had been unaccustomed, but because he had obtained a medicine so seasonable and suitable to his present grief, that he rose with collected energy towards heaven. At length Moses records that the holy man, having performed his circuit, returned to the oak, or valley of Mamre, to dwell there. But, again, he commends his piety in raising an altar, and calling upon God. I have already frequently explained what this means : for he himself bore an altar in his heart; but seeing that the land was full of profane altars, on which the Canaanites and other nations polluted the worship of God, Abram publicly professed that he worshipped the true God ; and that, not at random, but according to the method revealed to him by the word. Hence we infer, that the altar of which mention is made, was not built rashly by his hand, but that it was consecrated by the same word of God.

CHAPTER XIV.

1. And it came to pass in the days of Amraphel king of Shinar, Arioch king of Ellasar, Chedorlaomer king of Elam, and Tidal king of nations ;

2. *That these* made war with Bera king of Sodom, and with Birsha king of Gomorrah, Shinab king of Admah, and Shemeber king of Zeboiim, and the king of Bela, which is Zoar.

3. All these were joined together in the vale of Siddim, which is the salt sea.

1. Et fuit in diebus Amraphel regis Sinhar, Arioch rex Elasar, Cedorlaomer rex Helam, et Thidhal rex gentium,

2. Fecerunt bellum cum Berah rege Sedom, et Birsah rege Hamorah, Sinab rege Admah, et Semeber rege Seboim, et rege Belah : ipsa est Sohar.

3. Omnes isti conjuncti sunt in valle Siddim : ipsa est *vallis* Maris salis.

does not so well agree with the context as the term *removed ;* in the use of which word our translators have followed the Septuagint, (ἀποσκηνώσας,) and the Vulgate, (movens igitur tabernaculum.) The Arabic (according to the Latin translation) brings out the same sense, by a periphrasis, " Abram fixed his tent in divers places till he came and dwelt in the land of Mamre." And this is probably the true solution of the difficulty.—*Ed.*

4. Twelve years they served Chedor-laomer, and in the thirteenth year they rebelled.

5. And in the fourteenth year came Chedorlaomer, and the kings that *were* with him, and smote the Rephaims in Ashteroth Karnaim, and the Zuzims in Ham, and the Emims in Shaveh Kiria-thaim,

. 6. And the Horites in their mount Seir, unto El-paran, which *is* by the wilderness.

7. And they returned, and came to En-mishpat, which *is* Kadesh, and smote all the country of the Amalekites, and also the Amorites, that dwelt in Haze-zon-tamar.

8. And there went out the king of Sodom, and the king of Gomorrah, and the king of Admah, and the king of Ze-boiim, and the king of Bela, (the same *is* Zoar;) and they joined battle with them in the vale of Siddim ;

9. With Chedorlaomer the king of Elam, and with Tidal king of nations, and Amraphel king of Shinar, and Arioch king of Ellasar ; four kings with five.

10. And the vale of Siddim *was full of* slime-pits ; and the kings of Sodom and Gomorrah fled, and fell there ; and they that remained fled to the moun-tain.

11. And they took all the goods of Sodom and Gomorrah, and all their victuals, and went their way.

12. And they took Lot, Abram's brother's son, who dwelt in Sodom, and his goods, and departed.

13. And there came one that had escaped, and told Abram the Hebrew ; for he dwelt in the plain of Mamre the Amorite, brother of Eschol, and brother of Aner: and these *were* confederate with Abram.

14. And when Abram heard that his brother was taken captive, he armed his trained *servants*, born in his own house, three hundred and eighteen, and pursued *them* unto Dan.

15. And he divided himself against them, he and his servants, by night, and

4. Duodecim annos servie-rant Cedorlaomer, et decimo-tertio anno defecerant.

5. Decimoquarto autem anno venit Cedorlaomer, et reges qui erant cum eo, et percusserunt Rephaim in Astheroth Carnaim, et Zuzim in Ham, et Emim in Saveh Ciriathaim,

6. Et Hori in monte suo Se-hir, usque ad planitiem Pharan, quæ est juxta desertum.

7. Reversi sunt autem, et venerunt ad Hen-misphat, ipsa est Cades : et percusserunt om-nem agrum Amalecitæ, et etiam Emoræum habitantem in Ha-seson-thamar.

8. Et egressus est rex Sedom, et rex Hamorah, et rex Admah, et rex Seboim, et rex Belah, ipsa est Sohar, et ordinaverunt cum eis prælium in valle Sid-dim,

9. Cum Cedorlaomer rege Hela, et Thidhal rege gentium, et Amraphel rege Sinhar, et Arioch rege Elasar: quatuor reges cum quinque.

10. Vallis autem Siddim plena erat puteis cæmenti : et fugerunt rex Sedom et Hamo-rah, projeceruntque se illuc, et residui in montem fugerunt.

11. Et ceperunt omnem sub-stantiam Sedom et Hamorah, omnemque escam eorum, et abierunt.

12. Ceperunt quoque Lot et substantiam ejus, filium fratris Abram, et abierunt, quia ipse habitabat in Sedom.

13. Et venit quidam qui evaserat, et nuntiavit Abram Ebræo, qui habitabat in quer-cubus Mamre Emori fratris Eschol, fratris Haner, et ipsi erant fœderati cum Abram.

14. Audiens autem Abram quod captivus ductus esset fra-ter suus, armavit a se institutos pueros domus suæ, octodecim et trecentos, et persequutus est usque ad Dan.

15. Et divisit se super eos nocte, ipse et servi ejus, et per-

smote them, and pursued them unto Hobah, which *is* on the left hand of Damascus.

16. And he brought back all the goods, and also brought again his brother Lot, and his goods, and the women also, and the people.

17. And the king of Sodom went out to meet him after his return from the slaughter of Chedorlaomer, and of the kings that *were* with him, at the valley of Shaveh, which *is* the king's dale.

18. And Melchizedek king of Salem brought forth bread and wine : and he *was* the priest of the most high God.

19. And he blessed him, and said, Blessed *be* Abram of the most high God, possessor of heaven and earth :

20. And blessed be the most high God, which hath delivered thine enemies into thy hand. And he gave him tithes of all.

21. And the king of Sodom said unto Abram, Give me the persons, and take the goods to thyself.

22. And Abram said to the king of Sodom, I have lift up mine hand unto the Lord, the most high God, the possessor of heaven and earth,

23. That I will not *take* from a thread even to a shoe-latchet, and that I will not take any thing that *is* thine, lest thou shouldst say, I have made Abram rich :

24. Save only that which the young men have eaten, and the portion of the men which went with me, Aner, Eshcol, and Mamre; let them take their portion.

cussit eos : persequutusque est eos usque ad IIovah, quæ est a læva Dammesec.

16. Et reduxit omnem substantiam, et etiam Lot fratrem suum, et substantiam ejus reduxit, atque etiam mulieres et populum.

17. Et egressus est rex Sedom in occursum ejus, postquam reversus est ipse a cædendo Cedorlaomer, et reges qui erant secum, ad Vallem Saveh : ipsa est Vallis regis.

18. Et Melchisedec rex Salem protulit panem et vinum : et ipse *erat* sacerdos Deo altissimo.

19. Et benedixit ei, et dixit, Benedictus Abram Deo excelso, possessori cœli et terræ.

20. Et benedictus Deus excelsus, qui tradidit hostes tuos in manum tuam : et dedit ei decimam de omnibus.

21. Et dixit rex Sedom ad Abram, Da mihi animas, et substantiam tolle tibi.

22. Et dixit Abram ad regem Sedom, Levavi manum meam ad Jehovam Deum excelsum, possessorem cœli et terræ,

23. Si a filo usque ad corrigiam calceamenti, si accepero ex omnibus quæ sunt tibi : ne dicas, Ego ditavi Abram.

24. Præter ea tantum quæ comederunt pueri, et partem virorum qui profecti sunt mecum, Aner, Eschol, et Mamre : ipsi accipiant partem suam.

1. *And it came to pass in the days of Amraphel.* The history related in this chapter is chiefly worthy of remembrance, for three reasons : first, because Lot, with a gentle reproof, exhorted the men of Sodom to repentance ; they had, however, become altogether unteachable, and desperately perverse in their wickedness. But Lot was beaten with these scourges, because, having been allured and deceived by the richness of the soil, he had mixed himself with unholy and wicked men.

Secondly, because God, out of compassion to him, raised up
Abram as his avenger and liberator, to rescue him, when a
captive, from the hand of the enemy; in which act the incredible goodness and benevolence of God towards his own
people, is rendered conspicuous; since, for the sake of one
man, he preserves, for a time, many who were utterly unworthy. Thirdly, because Abram was divinely honoured with
a signal victory, and was blessed by the mouth of Melchizedek,
in whose person, as appears from other passages of Scripture,
the kingdom and priesthood of Christ was shadowed forth.
As it respects the sum of the history, it is a horrible picture
both of the avarice and pride of man.

The human race had yet their three progenitors, Shem,
Ham, and Japheth, living among them; by the very sight of
whom they were admonished, that they all sprung from one
family, and one ark. Moreover, the memory of their common
origin was a sacred pledge of fraternal connection, which
should have bound them to assist each other, by mutual good
offices. Nevertheless, ambition so prevailed, that they assailed
one another on all sides, with sword and armour, and each
attempted to subdue the rest. Wherefore, while we see,
at the present day, princes raging furiously, and shaking the
earth to the utmost of their power; let us remember that the
evil is of ancient date; since the lust of dominion has, in all
ages, been too prevalent among men. Let us, however, also
remark, that no fault is worse than that loftiness of mind,
which many deem a most heroical disposition. The ambition of Chedorlaomer was the torch of the whole war: for he,
inflamed with the desire of triumphing, drew three others into
a hostile confederacy. And pride compelled the men of Sodom
and their allies to take arms, for the purpose of shaking off
the yoke.

That Moses, however, records the names of so many kings,
while Shem was yet living, (although derided by profane men
as fabulous,) will not appear absurd, if we only reflect that
this great propagation of the human race, was a remarkable
miracle of God. For when the Lord said to Noah himself,
and to his sons, "Increase and multiply," he intended to raise
them to the hope of a far more excellent restoration than

would have taken place, in the ordinary course of nature. This benediction is indeed perpetual, and shall flourish even to the end of the world : but it was necessary that its extraordinary efficacy should then appear; in order that these earliest fathers might know, that a new world had been divinely inclosed within the ark. By the Poets, Deucalion with his wife, is feigned to have sown the race of men after the deluge, by throwing stones behind him.[1] But it followed of necessity, that the miserable minds of men should be deluded with such trifles, when they departed from the pure truth of God; and Satan has made use of this artifice, for the purpose of discrediting the veracity of the miracles of God. For since the memory of the deluge, and the unwonted propagation of a new world, could not be speedily obliterated, he scattered abroad clouds and smoke; introducing puerile conceits, in order that what had before been held for certain truth, might now be regarded as a fable. It is however to be observed, that all are called kings by Moses, who held the priority in any town, or in any considerable assembly of men. It is asked, whether those kings who followed Chedorlaomer dwelt at a great distance; because Tidal is called " the king of nations ?" There are those who imagine that he reigned over different nations far and wide; as if he was a king of kings. The ancient interpreter fetches Arioch from Pontus;[2] which is most absurd. I rather think the true reason of the name was, that he had a band composed of deserters and vagrants, who, having left their own country, had resorted to him. Therefore, since they were not one body—natives of his own country—but gathered together from a promiscuous multitude, he was properly called " king of nations." In saying that the battle was fought in the vale of Siddim, or in the open plain, which, when Moses wrote, had become the Salt Sea, it is not to be doubted that the Dead Sea, or the lake Asphaltites, is meant. For he knew whom he was appointed to instruct, and therefore he always accommodated his words to the rude capacity of the people ; and this is his common cus-

---

[1] See Ovid's Metamorphosis I.
[2] " Arioch rex Ponti."— *Vulgate.*

tom in reference to the names of places, as I have previously intimated. Before, however, the battle was fought, Moses declares that the inhabitants of the region were partially beaten. It is probable that all had been scattered, because they had no leader, under whose auspices they might fight, until five kings advanced to meet them with a disciplined army. Now, though Chedorlaomer had rendered so many people tributary to him by tyranny, rather than by. lawful authority, and on that account his ambition is to be condemned; yet his subjects are justly punished for having rashly rebelled. For although liberty is by no means to be despised, yet the subjection which is once imposed upon us cannot, without implied rebellion against God, be shaken off; because 'every power is ordained by God,' notwithstanding, in its commencement, it may have flowed from the lust of dominion, (Rom. xiii. 1.) Therefore some of the rebels are slaughtered like cattle; and others, though they have clothed themselves in armour, and are prepared to resist, are yet driven to flight; thus, unhappily to all concerned, terminates the contumacious refusal to pay tribute. And such narratives are to be noticed, that we may learn from them, that all who strive to produce anarchy, fight against God.

10. *And the kings of Sodom and Gomorrah fled.* Some expound that they had fallen into pits : but this is not probable, since they were by no means ignorant of the neighbouring places : such an event would rather have happened to foreign enemies. Others say, that they went down into them for the sake of preserving their lives. I, however, understand them to have exchanged one kind of death for another, as is common in the moment of desperation ; as if Moses had said, the swords of the enemy were so formidable to them, that, without hesitation, they threw themselves headlong into the pits. For he immediately afterwards subjoins, that they who escaped fled to the mountains. Whence we infer, that they who had rushed into the pits had perished. Only let us know, that they fell, not so much deceived through ignorance of the place, as disheartened by fear.

12. *And they took Lot.* It is doubtful whether Lot re
mained at home while others went to the battle, and was
there captured by the enemy; or whether he had been
compelled to take arms with the rest of the people. As,
however, Moses does not mention him till he speaks of
the plundering of the city, the conjecture is probable, that at
the conclusion of the battle, he was taken at home, unarmed.
We here see, first, that sufferings are common to the good
and the evil; then, that the more closely we are connected
with the wicked and the ungodly, when God pours down his
vengeance on them, the more quickly does the scourge come
upon us.

13. *And there came one that had escaped.* This is the second
part of the chapter, in which Moses shows, that when God
had respect to his servant Lot, he gave him Abram as his
deliverer, to rescue him from the hands of the enemy. But
here various questions arise; as, whether it was lawful for
Abram, a private person, to arm his family against kings, and
to undertake a public war. I do not, however, doubt, that
as he went to the war endued with the power of the Spirit,
so also he was guarded by a heavenly command, that he did
not transgress the bounds of his vocation. And this ought
not to be regarded as a new thing, but as his special calling;
for he had already been created king of that land. And
although the possession of it was deferred to a future time;
yet God would give some remarkable proof of the power
which he had granted him, and which was hitherto unknown
to men.[1] A similar prelude of what was to follow, we read
in the case of Moses, when he slew the Egyptian, before he
openly presented himself as the avenger and deliverer of his
nation. And for this reason the subject ought to be noticed,
that they who wish to defend themselves by armed force,
whenever any force is used against them, may not, from this
fact, frame a rule for themselves. We shall hereafter see
this same Abram bearing patiently, and with a submissive mind, injuries which had, at least, an equal tendency

---

[1] " Dieu a voulu donner un patron singulier de la puissance qu'il luy
avoit baillee, laquelle estoit encore incognue aux hommes."—*French Tr.*

to provoke his spirit. Moreover, that Abram attempted nothing rashly, but rather, that his design was approved by God, will appear presently, from the commendation of Melchizedek. We may therefore conclude, that this war was undertaken by him, under the special direction of the Spirit. If any one should take exception, that he proceeded further than was lawful, when he spoiled the victors of their prey and captives, and restored them wholly to the men of Sodom, who had, by no means, been committed to his protection; I answer, since it appears that God was his Guide and Ruler in this affair,—as we infer from His approbation,—it is not for us to dispute respecting His secret judgment. God had destined the inhabitants of Sodom, when their neighbours were ruined and destroyed, to a still more severe judgment; because they were themselves the worst of all. He, therefore, raised up his servant Abram, after they had been admonished by a chastisement sufficiently severe, to deliver them, in order that they might be rendered the more inexcusable. Therefore, this peculiar suggestion of the Holy Spirit ought no more to be drawn into a precedent, than the whole war which Abram had carried on. With respect to the messenger who had related to Abram the slaughter at Sodom, I do not accept what some suppose, that he was a pious man. We may rather conjecture that, as a fugitive from home, who had been deprived of all his goods, he came to Abram to elicit something from his humanity. That Abram is called a Hebrew, I do not explain from the fact of his having passed over the river, as is the opinion of some; but from his being of the progeny of *Eber*. For it is a name of descent. And the Holy Spirit here again honourably announces that race as blessed by God.

And these were confederate with Abram. It appears, that in the course of time, Abram was freely permitted to enter into covenant and friendship with the princes of the land: for the heroical virtues of the man, caused them to regard him as one who was not, by any means, to be despised. Nay, as he had so great a family, he might also have been numbered among kings, if he had not been a stranger and a sojourner. But God purposed thus to provide for his peace, by a covenant relating to temporal things, in order that he never might be mingled with those nations. Moreover, that this whole transaction was divinely ordered we may readily conjecture from the fact, that his associates did not hesitate, at great risk, to assail four kings, who (according to the state of the times) were sufficiently strong, and were flushed with the confidence of victory. Surely they would scarcely ever have been thus favourable to a stranger, except by a secret impulse of God.

14. *When Abram heard that his brother was taken captive.* Moses briefly explains the cause of the war which was undertaken; namely, that Abram might rescue his relation from captivity. Meanwhile, what I have before said is to be remembered, that he did not rashly fly to arms; but took them as from the hand of God, who had constituted him lord of that land. With reference to the words themselves, I know not why the ancient interpreter has rendered them, 'Abram numbered his trained servants.' For the word ריק (*rik*) signifies to unsheath, or to draw out.[1] Now Moses calls these servants חניכים, (*chanichim*,) not as having been educated and trained for military service, as many suppose; but rather (in my opinion) as having been brought up under his own authority, and imbued from childhood with his discipline; so that they fought the more courageously, being stimulated by his faith, and going forth under his auspices;[2] and were ready to undergo every kind of danger for his sake. But in this great household troop, we must notice, not only the diligence of the holy patriarch, but the special blessing of God, by which it had been increased beyond the common and usual manner.

15. *And he divided himself against them.* Some explain the words to mean that Abram alone, with his domestic troops, rushed upon the enemy. Others, that he and his three confederates divided their bands, in order to strike greater terror

---

[1] " Comme s'il disoit, Il tira hors de sa maison trois cens dixhuit serviteurs."—" As if he had said, He drew out of his house three hundred and eighteen servants."—*French Tr.*

[2] " Animosius sub fide et auspiciis ejus bellarent."

into the foe. A third class suppose the phrase to be a Hebraism, for making an irruption into the midst of the enemy.
I rather embrace the second exposition; namely, that he invaded the enemy on different sides, and suddenly inspired
them with terror. For the circumstance of time favours this
view, because he attacked them by night. And although
examples of similar bravery occur in profane history; yet it
ought to be ascribed to the faith of Abram, that with a small
band, he dared to assail a numerous army elated with victory.
But that he came off conqueror with little trouble, and with
intrepidity pursued those who far exceeded him in number,
we must ascribe to the favour of God.

17. *And the king of Sodom went out.* Although the king of
Sodom knew that Abram had taken arms only on account of
his nephew, yet he went to meet him with due honour, in order
to show his gratitude. For it is a natural duty to acknowledge benefits conferred upon us, even when not intentionally
rendered, but only from unexpected circumstances and occasions, or (as we say) by accident. Moreover, the whole
affair yields greater glory to God, because the victory of
Abram was celebrated in this manner. He also marks the
place where the king of Sodom met Abram, namely, " the
king's dale," which I think was so called, rather after some
particular king, than because those kings met there for their
pleasure.[1]

18. *And Melchizedek king of Salem brought forth.* This is
the last of the three principal points of this history, that
Melchizedek, the chief father of the Church, having entertained Abram at a feast, blessed him, in virtue of his priesthood, and received tithes from him. There is no doubt that
by the coming of this king to meet him, God also designed
to render the victory of Abram famous and memorable to
posterity. But a more exalted and excellent mystery was,
at the same time, adumbrated: for seeing that the holy
patriarch, whom God had raised to the highest rank of honour,

[1] " Quam quod animi causa reges illuc convenirent."

submitted himself to Melchizedek, it is not to be doubted that God had constituted him the only head of the whole Church ;[1] for, without controversy, the solemn act of benediction, which Melchizedek assumed to himself, was a symbol of pre-eminent dignity. If any one replies, that he did this as a priest; 1 ask, was not Abram also a priest? Therefore God here commends to us something peculiar in Melchizedek, in preferring him before the father of all the faithful. But it will be more satisfactory to examine the passage word by word, in regular order, that we may thence better gather the import of the whole. That he received Abram and his companions as guests belonged to his *royalty ;* but the benediction pertained especially to his *sacerdotal office.* Therefore, the words of Moses ought to be thus con-nected : Melchizedek king of Salem brought forth bread and wine; and seeing he was the priest of God, he blessed Abram ; thus to each character is distinctly attributed what is its own. He refreshed a wearied and famishing army with royal liberality ; but because he was a priest, he blessed, by the rite of solemn prayer, the first-born son of God, and the father of the Church. Moreover, although I do not deny that it was the most ancient custom, for those who were kings to fulfil also the office of the priesthood ; yet this ap-pears to have been, even in that age, extraordinary in Melchizedek. And truly he is honoured with no common eulogy, when the Spirit ratifies his priesthood. We know how, at that time, religion was everywhere corrupted, since Abram himself, who was descended from the sacred race of Shem and Eber, had been plunged in the profound vortex of supersti-tion, with his father and grandfather. Therefore, many ima-gine Melchizedek to have been Shem; to whose opinion I am, for many reasons, hindered from subscribing. For the Lord would not have designated a man, worthy of eternal memory, by a name so new and obscure, that he must remain unknown. Secondly, it is not probable that Shem had migrated from the east into Judea ; and nothing of the kind is to be gathered from Moses. Thirdly, if Shem had

---

[1] " Non dubium est quin illum constituerit unicum totius ecclesiæ caput."—" Il ne faut pas douter que Dieu ne l'ait constituè chef unique de toute l'Eglise."—*French Tr.*

dwelt in the land of Canaan, Abram would not have wandered by such winding courses, as Moses has previously related, before he went to salute his ancestor. But the declaration of the Apostle is of the greatest weight; that this Melchizedek, whoever he was, is presented before us, without any origin, as if he had dropped from the clouds, and that his name is buried without any mention of his death. (Heb. vii. 3.) But the admirable grace of God shines more clearly in a person unknown; because, amid the corruptions of the world, he alone, in that land, was an upright and sincere cultivator and guardian of religion. I omit the absurdities which Jerome, in his Epistle to Evagrius, heaps together; lest, without any advantage, I should become troublesome, and even offensive to the reader. I readily believe that Salem is to be taken for Jerusalem; and this is the generally received interpretation. If, however, any one chooses rather to embrace a contrary opinion, seeing that the town was situated in a plain, I do not oppose it. On this point Jerome thinks differently: nevertheless, what he elsewhere relates, that in his own times some vestiges of the palace of Melchizedek were still extant in the ancient ruins, appears to me improbable.

It now remains to be seen how Melchizedek bore the image of Christ, and became, as it were, his representative, (ἀντίτυπος.[1]) These are the words of David, "The Lord sware, and will not repent, Thou art a priest for ever, after the order of Melchizedek," (Psalm cx. 4.) First, he had placed him on a royal throne, and now he gives him the honour of the priesthood. But under the Law, these two offices were so distinct, that it was unlawful for kings to usurp the office of the priesthood. If, therefore, we concede as true, what Plato declares, and what occasionally occurs in the poets, that it was formerly received, by the common custom of nations, that the same person should be both king and priest; this was by no means the case with David and his posterity, whom the Law peremptorily forbade to intrude on the priestly office. It was therefore right, that what was divinely appointed under the old law, should be abrogated in the person of this priest. And the Apostle does

---

[1] " Il faut voir comment Melchisedech a eu la figure de Christ engravee en soy, et est comme la representation et correspondance."—*French Tr.*

not contend without reason, that a more excellent priesthood than that old and shadowy one, was here pointed out ; which priesthood is confirmed by an oath.   Moreover, we never find that king and priest, who is to be pre-eminent over all, till we come to Christ.   And as no one has arisen except Christ, who equalled Melchizedek in dignity, still less who excelled him ; we hence infer that the image of Christ was presented to the fathers, in his person.   David, indeed, does not propose a similitude framed by himself; but declares the reason for which the kingdom of Christ was divinely ordained, and even confirmed with an oath; and it is not to be doubted that the same truth had previously been traditionally handed down by the fathers.   The sum of the whole is, that Christ would thus be the king next to God, and also that he should be anointed priest, and that for ever; which it is very useful for us to know, in order that we may learn that the royal power of Christ is combined with the office of priest.   The same Person, therefore, who was constituted the only and eternal Priest, in order that he might reconcile us to God, and who, having made expiation, might intercede for us, is also a King of infinite power to secure our salvation, and to protect us by his guardian care.   Hence it follows, that, relying on his advocacy, we may stand boldly in the presence of God, who will, we are assured, be propitious to us ; and that trusting in his invincible arm, we may securely triumph over enemies of every kind.   But they who separate one office from the other, rend Christ asunder, and subvert their own faith, which is deprived of half its support.   It is also to be observed, that Christ is called an eternal King, like Melchizedek.   For since the Scripture, by assigning no end to his life, leaves him as if he were to survive through all ages; it certainly represents or shadows forth to us, in his person, a figure, not of a temporal, but of an eternal kingdom.   But whereas Christ, by his death, has accomplished the office of Priest, it follows that God was, by that one sacrifice, once appeased in such a manner, that now reconciliation is to be sought in Christ alone.   Therefore, they do him grievous wrong, and wrest from him, by abominable sacrilege, the honour divinely conferred upon him by an oath, who either institute other sacrifices for the expiation of sins, or who make other priests.[1] And I wish this had been prudently weighed by the ancient writers of the Church. For then would they not so coolly, and even so ignorantly, have transferred to the bread and wine the similitude between Christ and Melchizedek, which consists in things very different. They have supposed that Melchizedek is the image of Christ, because he offered bread and wine. For they add, that Christ offered his body, which is life-giving bread, and his blood, which is spiritual drink. But the Apostle, while in his Epistle to the Hebrews, he most accurately collects, and specifically prosecutes, every point of similarity between Christ and Melchizedek, says not a word concerning the bread and wine. If the subtleties of Tertullian, and of others like him, were true, it would have been a culpable negligence, not to bestow a single syllable upon the principal point, while discussing the separate parts, which were of comparatively trivial importance. And seeing the Apostle disputes at so great length, and with such minuteness, concerning the priesthood; how gross an instance of forgetfulness would it have been, not to touch upon that memorable sacrifice, in which the whole force of the priesthood was comprehended? He proves the honour of Melchizedek from the benediction given, and tithes received: how much better would it have suited this argument to have said, that he offered not lambs or calves, but the life of the world, (that is, the body and blood of Christ,) in a figure? By these arguments the fictions of the ancients are abundantly refuted. Nevertheless, from the very words of Moses a sufficiently lucid refutation may be taken. For we do not there read that *anything* was offered to God; but in one continued discourse it is stated, ' He offered bread and wine; and seeing he was priest of the Most High God, he blessed him.' Who does not see that the same relative pronoun is common to both verbs; and therefore that Abram was both refreshed

---

[1] " Ceux qui dressent d'autres sacrifices pour nettoyer les pechez, ou forgent d'autres sacrificateurs." Those who prepare other sacrifices to cleanse from sins, or make others sacrificing priests.—*French Tr.*

with the wine, and honoured with the benediction? Utterly ridiculous truly are the Papists, who distort the offering[1] of bread and wine to the sacrifice of their mass. For in order to bring Melchizedek into agreement with themselves, it will be necessary for them to concede that *bread* and *wine* are offered in the mass. Where, then, is transubstantiation, which leaves nothing except the bare *species* of the elements? Then, with what audacity do they declare that the body of Christ is immolated in their sacrifices? Under what pretext, since the Son of God is called the only successor of Melchizedek, do they substitute innumerable successors for him? We see, then, how foolishly they not only deprave this passage, but babble without the colour of reason.

19. *And he blessed him.* Unless these two members of the sentence, ' He was the priest of God,' and ' He blessed,' cohere together, Moses here relates nothing uncommon. For men mutually bless each other; that is, they wish well to each other. But here the priest of God is described, who, according to the right of his office, sanctifies one inferior and subject to himself. For he would never have dared to bless Abram, unless he had known, that in this respect he excelled him. In this manner the Levitical priests are commanded to bless the people; and God promises that the blessing should be efficacious and ratified, (Num. vi. 23.) So Christ, when about to ascend up to heaven, having lifted up his hands, blessed the Apostles, as a minister of the grace of God, (Luke xxiv. 51;) and then was exhibited the truth of this figure. For he testifies that the office of blessing the Church, which had been adumbrated in Melchizedek, was assigned him by his Father.

Blessed be Abram of the most high God. The design of Melchizedek is to confirm and ratify the grace of the Divine vocation to holy Abram; for he points out the honour with which God had peculiarly dignified him, by separating him

---

[1] Oblationem; yet the word ought not to be rendered *oblation*, because this term in English always implies that the offering is made to God; whereas Calvin speaks of the bread and wine simply as being presented by Melchizedek to Abram.—*Ed.*

from all others, and adopting him as his own son. And he calls God, by whom Abram had been chosen, " the Possessor of heaven and earth," to distinguish him from the fictitious idols of the Gentiles. Afterwards, indeed, God invests himself with other titles; that, by some peculiar mark, he may render himself more clearly known to men, who, because of the vanity of their mind, when they simply hear of God as the Framer of heaven and earth, never cease to wander, till at length they are lost in their own speculations. But because God was already known to Abram, and his faith was founded upon many miracles, Melchizedek deems it sufficient to declare that, by the title of Creator,[1] He whom Abram worshipped, is the true and only God. And although Melchizedek himself maintained the sincere worship of the true God, he yet calls Abram blessed of God, in respect of the eternal covenant: as if he would say, that, by a kind of hereditary right, the grace of God resided in one family and nation, because Abram alone had been chosen out of the whole world. Then is added a special congratulation on the victory obtained; not such as is wont to pass between profane men, who puff each other up with inflated encomiums; but Melchizedek gives thanks unto God, and regards the victory which the holy man had gained, as a seal of his gratuitous calling.

20. *And he gave him tithes of all.* There are those who understand that the tithes were given to Abram; but the Apostle speaks otherwise, in declaring that Levi had paid tithes in the loins of Abram, (Heb. vii. 9,) when Abram offered tithes to a more excellent Priest. And truly what the expositors above mentioned mean, would be most absurd; because, if Melchizedek was the priest of God, it behoved him to receive tithes rather than to give them. Nor is it to be doubted but Abram offered the gift to God, in the person of Melchizedek, in order that, by such first-fruits, he might dedicate all his possessions to God. Abram therefore volun-

---

[1] " Creationis elogio testari," &c.—" De donner à Dieu ce titre de Possesseur du ciel et de la terre." To give to God this title of Possesor of heaven and earth.—*French Tr.*

tarily gave tithes to Melchizedek, to do honour to his priesthood. Moreover, since it appears that this was not done wrongfully nor rashly, the Apostle properly infers, that, in this figure, the Levitical priesthood is subordinate to the priesthood of Christ. For other reasons, God afterwards commanded tithes to be given to Levi under the Law; but, in the age of Abram, they were only a holy offering, given as a pledge and proof of gratitude. It is however uncertain whether he offered the tithe of the spoils, or of the goods which he possessed at home. But, since it is improbable that he should have been liberal with other persons' goods, and should have given away a tenth part of the prey, of which he had resolved not to touch even a thread, I rather conjecture, that these tithes were taken out of his own property. I do not, however, admit that they were paid annually, as some imagine, but rather, in my judgment, he dedicated this present to Melchizedek once, for the purpose of acknowledging him as the high priest of God : nor could he, at that time, (as we say,) hand it over;[1] but there was a solemn stipulation, of which the effect shortly after followed.

21. *And the king of Sodom said.* Moses having, by the way, interrupted the course of his narrative concerning the king of Sodom, by the mention of the king of Salem, now returns to it again ; and says that the king of Sodom came to meet Abram, not only for the sake of congratulating him, but of giving him a due reward. He therefore makes over to him the whole prey, except the men ; as if he would say, ' It is a great thing that I recover the men ; let all the rest be given to thee as a reward for this benefit.' And thus to have shown himself grateful to man, would truly have been worthy of commendation; had he not been ungrateful to God, by whose severity and clemency he remained alike unprofited. It was even possible that this man, when poor and deprived of all his goods, might, with a servile affectation of modesty,

---

[1] " Nec tunc potuit de manu (quod aiunt) in manum tradere."—" Ne luy a peu lors builler de main à main, comme on dit." Nor was he then able to commit it to him, from hand to hand, as they say.—*French Tr.*

try to gain the favour of Abram, by asking to have nothing but the captives and the empty city for himself. Certainly we shall afterwards see that the men of Sodom were unmindful of the benefit received, when they proudly and contemptuously vexed righteous Lot.

22. *And Abram said to the king of Sodom, I have lift up mine hand, &c.*[1] This ancient ceremony was very appropriate to give expression to the force and nature of an oath. For by raising the hand towards heaven, we show that we appeal to God as a witness, and also as an avenger, if we fail to keep our oath. Formerly, indeed, they raised their hands in giving votes; whence the Greeks derive the word χειροτονεῖν,[2] which signifies to decree: but in the rite of swearing, the reason for doing so was different. For men hereby declared, that they regarded themselves as in the presence of God, and called upon him to be both the Guardian of truth, and the Avenger of perjury. Yet it may seem strange that Abram should so easily have put himself forward to swear; for he knew that a degree of reverence was due to the name of God, which should constrain us to use it but sparingly, and only from necessity. I answer, there were two reasons for his swearing. First, since inconstant men are wont to measure others by their own standard, they seldom place confidence in bare assertions. The king of Sodom, therefore, would have thought that Abram did not seriously remit his right, unless the name of God had been interposed. And, secondly, it was of great consequence, to make it manifest to all, that he had not carried on a mercenary war. The histories of all times sufficiently declare, that even they who have had just causes of war have, nevertheless, been incited to it by the thirst of private gain. And as men are acute in devising pretexts, they are never at a loss to find plausible reasons for war, even though covetousness may be their only real stimulant. Therefore, unless Abram had

---

[1] A portion of the 22d verse, which is commented upon without being given in the original, is here inserted, in order to make the whole more clear to the reader; it also appears in the French Translation.—*Ed.*

[2] Literally, to stretch forth the hand.

resolutely refused the spoils of war, the rumour would immediately have spread, that, under the pretence of rescuing his
nephew, he had been intent upon grasping the prey. Against
which it was necessary for him carefully to guard, not so
much for his own sake, as for the glory of God, which would
otherwise have received some mark of disparagement. Besides, Abram wished to arm himself with the name of God,
as with a shield, against all the allurements of avarice. For
the king of Sodom would not have desisted from tempting
his mind by various methods, if the occasion for using bland
insinuations had not been promptly cut off.

23. *That I will not take from a thread even to a shoe-latchet.*
The Hebrews have an elliptical form of making oath, in which
the imprecation of punishment is understood. In some places,
the full expression of it occurs in the Scriptures, " The Lord
do so to me and more also," (1 Sam. xiv. 44.) Since, however, it is a dreadful thing to fall into the hands of the living
God ; in order that the obligation of oaths may be the more
binding, this abrupt form of speech admonishes men to reflect
on what they are doing; for it is just as if they should put a
restraint upon themselves, and should stop suddenly in the
midst of their discourse. This indeed is most certain, that
men never rashly swear, but they provoke the vengeance of
God against them, and make Him their adversary.

Lest thou shouldst say. Although these words seem to denote a mind elated, and too much addicted to fame, yet since
Abram is on this point commended by the Spirit, we conclude
that this was a truly holy magnanimity. But an exception is
added, namely, that he will not allow his own liberality to be
injurious to his allies, nor make them subject to his laws.
For this also is not the least part of virtue, to act rightly, yet
in such a manner, that we do not bind others to our example, as to a rule. Let every one therefore regard what
his own vocation demands, and what pertains to his own
duty, in order that men may not prejudge one another according to their own will. For it is a moroseness too imperious, to wish that what we ourselves follow as right, and
consonant with our duty, should be prescribed as a law to
others.

CHAPTER XV.

1. After these things the word of the Lord came unto Abram in a vision, saying, Fear not, Abram: I *am* thy shield, *and* thy exceeding great reward.

2. And Abram said, Lord God, what wilt thou give me, seeing I go childless, and the steward of my house *is* this Eliezer of Damascus?

3. And Abram said, Behold, to me thou hast given no seed: and, lo, one born in my house is mine heir.

4. And, behold, the word of the Lord *came* unto him, saying, This shall not be thine heir; but he that shall come forth out of thine own bowels shall be thine heir.

5. And he brought him forth abroad, and said, Look now toward heaven, and tell the stars, if thou be able to number them: and he said unto him, So shall thy seed be.

6. And he believed in the Lord; and he counted it to him for righteousness.

7. And he said unto him, I *am* the Lord that brought thee out of Ur of the Chaldees, to give thee this land to inherit it.

8. And he said, Lord God, whereby shall I know that I shall inherit it?

9. And he said unto him, Take me an heifer of three years old, and a she-goat of three years old, and a ram of three years old, and a turtle-dove, and a young pigeon.

10. And he took unto him all these, and divided them in the midst, and laid each piece one against another: but the birds divided he not.

11. And when the fowls came down upon the carcases, Abram drove them away.

12 And when the sun was going down, a deep sleep fell upon Abram; and, lo, an horror of great darkness fell upon him.

1. Post hæc fuit verbum Jehovæ ad Abram in visione, dicendo, Ne timeas Abram, ego scutum *ero* tibi, merces tua multa valde.

2. Et dixit Abram, Dominator Jehova, quid dabis mihi? et ego incedo orbus, et filius derelictionis domus meæ erit iste Dammescenus Elihezer.

3. Et dixit Abram, Ecce, mihi non dedisti semen: et ecce, filius domus meæ hæres meus est.

4. Et ecce verbum Jehovæ ad eum, dicendo, Non erit hæres tuus iste, sed qui egredietur de visceribus tuis, ipse hæres tuus erit.

5. Et eduxit eum foras, et dixit, Suspice nunc cœlum, et numera stellas, si poteris numerare eas. Et dixit ei, Sic erit semen tuum.

6. Et credidit Jehovæ, et reputavit illud ei ad justitiam.

7. Et dixit ad eum, Ego Jehova qui eduxi te de Ur Chaldeæ, ut darem tibi terram istam, ut hæredites eam.

8. Et dixit, Dominator Jehova, in quo' cognoscam quod hæreditabo eam?

9. Et dixit ad eum, Tolle mihi vitulam triennem, et capram triennem, et arietem triennem, et turturem, et pullum columbarum.

10. Et tulit sibi omnia ista, et divisit ea per medium, et posuit quamlibet *partem* divisionis suæ e regione sociæ suæ; sed aves non divisit.

11. Et descenderunt aves super cadavera, et abigebat eas Abram.

12. Et fuit, sole occumbente sopor cecidit super Abram: et ecce, terror tenebrosus et magnus cadens super eum.

13. And he said unto Abram, Know of a surety that thy seed shall be a stranger in a land *that is* not theirs, and shall serve them ; and they shall afflict them four hundred years ;

14. And also that nation, whom they shall serve, will I judge : and afterward shall they come out with great substance.

15. And thou shalt go to thy fathers in peace ; thou shalt be buried in a good old age.

16. But in the fourth generation they shall come hither again : for the iniquity of the Amorites *is* not yet full.

17. And it came to pass, that, when the sun went down, and it was dark, behold a smoking furnace, and a burning lamp that passed between those pieces.

18. In the same day the Lord made a covenant with Abram, saying, Unto thy seed have I given this land, from the river of Egypt unto the great river, the river Euphrates:

19. The Kenites, and the Kenizzites, and the Kadmonites,

20. And the Hittites, and the Perizzites, and the Rephaims,

21. And the Amorites, and the Canaanites, and the Girgashites, and the Jebusites.

13. Et dixit ad Abram, Cognoscendo cognosce quod peregrinum erit semen tuum in terra non sua : et servient eis, affligentque eos per quadringentos annos.

14. Sed etiam gentem, cui servierint, ego judicabo, et postea egredientur cum substantia magna.

15. Et tu ingredieris ad patres tuos in pace, sepelieris in canitie bona.

16. Et generatione quarta revertentur huc : quia nondum est completa iniquitas Emoræi.

17. Et fuit, sole occumbente caligo erat, et ecce furnus fumans, et lampas ignis quæ transibat inter divisiones ipsas.

18. In die ipso pepigit, Jehova cum Abram fœdus dicendo, Semini tuo dabo terram hanc, a flumine Ægypti, usque ad flumen magnum, flumen Euphratem :

19. Cenæum, et Cenizæum, et Cadmonæum,

20. Et Hitthæum, et Perizæum, et Rephaim,

21. Et Emoræum, et Chenaanæum, et Girgasæum, et Jebusæum.

1. *The word of the Lord came.* When Abram's affairs were prosperous and were proceeding according to his wish, this vision might seem to be superfluous ; especially since the Lord commands his servant, as one sorrowful and afflicted with fear, to be of good courage. Therefore certain writers conjecture, that Abram, having returned after the deliverance of his nephew, was subjected to some annoyance of which no mention is made by Moses ; just as the Lord often humbles his people, lest they should exult in their prosperity ; and they further suppose that when Abram had been dejected, he was again revived by a new oracle. But since there is no warrant for such conjecture in the words of Moses, I think the cause was different. First, although he was on all sides applauded, it is not to be doubted that various

surmises entered into his own mind. For, notwithstanding Chedorlaomer and his allies had been overcome in battle, yet Abram had so provoked them, that they might with fresh troops, and with renewed strength, again attack the land of Canaan. Nor were the inhabitants of the land free from the fear of this danger. Secondly, as signal success commonly draws its companion envy along with it, Abram began to be exposed to many disadvantageous remarks, after he had dared to enter into conflict with an army which had conquered four kings. An unfavourable suspicion might also arise, that perhaps, by and by, he would turn the strength which he had tried against foreign kings, upon his neighbours, and upon those who had hospitably received him. Therefore, as the victory was an honour to him, so it cannot be doubted, that it rendered him formidable and an object of suspicion to many, while it inflamed the hatred of others; since every one would imagine some danger to himself, from his bravery and good success. It is therefore not strange, that he should have been troubled, and should anxiously have revolved many things, until God animated him anew, by the confident expectation of his assistance. There might be also another end to be answered by the oracle; namely, that God would meet and correct a contrary fault in his servant. For it was possible that Abram might be so elated with victory as to forget his own calling, and to seek the acquisition of dominion for himself, as one who, wearied with a wandering course of life and with perpetual vexations, desired a better fortune, and a quiet state of existence. And we know how liable men are to be ensnared by the blandishments of prosperous and smiling fortune. Therefore God anticipates the danger; and before this vanity takes possession of the mind of the holy man, recalls to his memory the spiritual grace vouchsafed to him, to the end that he, entirely acquiescing therein, may despise all other things. Yet because this expression, "Fear not," sounds as if God would soothe his sorrowing and anxious servant with some consolation; it is probable that he had need of such confirmation, because he perceived that many malignantly stormed against his victory, and that his old age would be exposed to severe annoyances.

It might however be, that God did not forbid him to fear, because he was already afraid; but that he might learn courageously to despise, and to account as nothing, all the favour of the world, and all earthly wealth; as if he had said, 'If only I am propitious to thee, there is no reason why thou shouldst fear; contented with me alone in the world, pursue, as thou hast begun, thy pilgrimage; and rather depend on heaven, than attach thyself to earth.' However this might be, God recalls his servant to himself, showing that far greater blessings were treasured up for him in God; in order that Abram might not rest satisfied with his victory. Moses says that God spake to him " in a vision," by which he intimates that some visible symbol of God's glory was added to the word, in order that greater authority might be given to the oracle. And this was one of two ordinary methods by which the Lord was formerly wont to manifest himself to his prophets, as it is stated in the book of Numbers, (chap. xii. 6.)

Fear not, Abram. Although the promise comes last in the text, it yet has precedence in order; because on it depends the confirmation, by which God frees the heart of Abram from fear. God exhorts Abram to be of a tranquil mind; but what foundation is there for such security, unless by faith we understand that God cares for us, and learn to rest in his providence? The promise, therefore, that God will be Abram's shield and his exceeding great reward, holds the first place; to which is added the exhortation, that, relying upon such a guardian of his safety, and such an author of his felicity, he should not fear. Therefore, to make the sense of the words more clear, the *causal* particle is to be inserted. 'Fear not, Abram, *because* I am thy shield.' Moreover, by the use of the word " shield," he signifies that Abram would always be safe under his protection. In calling himself his " reward," He teaches Abram to be satisfied with Himself alone. And as this was, with respect to Abram, a general instruction, given for the purpose of showing him that victory was not the chief and ultimate good which God had designed him to pursue; so let us know that the same blessing is promised to us all, in the person of this one man. For, by this voice, God daily speaks to his faithful ones; inasmuch as having once undertaken to defend us, he will take care to preserve us in safety under his hand, and to protect us by his power. Now since God ascribes to himself the office and property of a shield, for the purpose of rendering himself the protector of our salvation; we ought to regard this promise as a brazen wall, so that we should not be excessively fearful in any dangers. And since men, surrounded with various and innumerable desires of the flesh, are at times unstable, and are then too much addicted to the love of the present life; the other member of the sentence follows, in which God declares, that he alone is sufficient for the perfection of a happy life to the faithful. For the word " reward " has the force of *inheritance*, or *felicity*. Were it deeply engraven on our minds, that in God alone we have the highest and complete perfection of all good things; we should easily fix bounds to those wicked desires by which we are miserably tormented. The meaning then of the passage is this, that we shall be truly happy when God is propitious to us; for he not only pours upon us the abundance of his kindness, but offers himself to us, that we may enjoy him. Now what is there more, which men can desire, when they really enjoy God? David knew the force of this promise, when he boasted that he had obtained a goodly lot, because the Lord was his inheritance, (Psalm xvi. 6.) But since nothing is more difficult than to curb the depraved appetites of the flesh, and since the ingratitude of man is so vile and impious, that God scarcely ever satisfies them; the Lord calls himself not simply " a reward," but an " exceeding great reward," with which we ought to be more than sufficiently contented. This truly furnishes most abundant material, and most solid support, for confidence. For whosoever shall be fully persuaded that his life is protected by the hand of God, and that he never can be miserable while God is gracious to him; and who consequently resorts to this haven in all his cares and troubles, will find the best remedy for all evils. Not that the faithful can be entirely free from fear and care, as long as they are tossed by the tempests of contentions and of miseries; but because the storm is hushed in their own breast; and whereas the defence of God is greater than all dangers, so faith triumphs over fear.

2. *And Abram said, Lord God.* The Hebrew text has אֲדֹנָי
יְהוִה, *(Adonai Jehovah.)* From which appellation it is inferred that some special mark of divine glory was stamped
upon the vision ; so that Abram, having no doubt respecting
its author, confidently broke out in this expression. For
since Satan is a wonderful adept at deceiving, and deludes
men with so many wiles in the name of God, it was necessary that some sure and notable distinction should appear in
true and heavenly oracles, which would not suffer the faith
and the minds of the holy fathers to waver. Therefore, in the
vision of which mention is made, the majesty of the God of
Abram was manifested, which would suffice for the confirmation of his faith. Not that God appeared as he really is,
but only so far as he might be comprehended by the human
mind. But Abram, in overlooking a promise so glorious, in
complaining that he is childless, and in murmuring against
God, for having hitherto given him no seed, seems to conduct
himself with little modesty. What was more desirable than
to be received under God's protection, and to be happy in
the enjoyment of Him? The objection, therefore, which
Abram raised, when disparaging the incomparable benefit
offered to him, and refusing to rest contented until he receives offspring, appears to be wanting in reverence. Yet
the liberty which he took admits of excuse ; first, because
the Lord permits us to pour into his bosom those cares
by which we are tormented, and those troubles with which
we are oppressed. Secondly, the design of the complaint is
to be considered ; for he does not simply declare that he is
solitary, but, seeing that the effect of all the promises depended upon his seed, he does, not improperly, require that a
pledge so necessary should be given him. For if the benediction and salvation of the world was not to be hoped for
except through his seed ; when that principal point seemed
to fail him, it is not to be wondered at, that other things
should seem to vanish from his sight, or should at least not
appease his mind, nor satisfy his wishes. And this is the very
reason why God not only regards with favour the complaint
of his servant, but immediately gives a propitious answer to
his prayer. Moses, indeed, ascribes to Abram that affection

which is naturally inherent in us all; but this is no proof
that Abram did not look higher, when he so earnestly desired to
be the progenitor of an heir.   And certainly these promises
had not faded from his recollection ; 'To thy seed will I give
this land,' and 'In thy seed shall all nations be blessed;' the
former of which promises is so annexed to all the rest, that if
it be taken away, all confidence in them would perish; while
the latter promise contains in it the whole gratuitous pledge
of salvation.   Therefore, Abram rightly includes in it, every
thing which God had promised.

I go childless.   The language is metaphorical.   We know
that our life is like a race.   Abram, seeing he was of advanced
age, says that he has so far proceeded, that little of his course
still remains. 'Now,' he says, 'I am come near the goal; and
the course of my life being finished, I shall die childless.'
He adds, for the sake of aggravating the indignity, 'that a
foreigner would be his heir.'   For I do not doubt that Damascus is the name of his *country*, and not the proper name of
his *mother*, as some falsely suppose ; as if he had said, 'Not
one of my own relatives will be my heir, but a Syrian from
Damascus.'   For, perhaps, Abram had bought him in Mesopotamia.   He also calls him the son of מֶשֶׁק, (*mesek*,) concerning the meaning of which word grammarians are not agreed.
Some derive it from שָׁקַק, (*shakak*,) which means to run to
and fro, and translate it, *steward* or *superintendent*, because he
who sustains the care of a large house, runs hither and thither
in attending to his business.   Others derive it from שׁוּק,
(*shook*,) and render it *cup-bearer*, which seems to me incongruous.   I rather adopt a different translation, namely, that
he was called the son of the deserted house, (*filius derelictionis*,[1]) because מֶשֶׁק sometimes signifies to *leave*.   Yet I do
not conceive him to be so called, because Abram was about

[1] "Et filius derelictionis domus meæ erit iste Dammescenus Elihezer."
That is, according to the usual interpretation of the Hebrew phrase, the
son or person to whom the house was left in charge by its master;
though Calvin gives it a different turn.   The various ancient versions,
except the Syriac, agree in this interpretation.   Dathe prefers the translation of Schultens, who refers the word to an Arabic root, מסק, which
signifies to *comb*, to *dress*, or *polish*, and which he supposes may be applied
generally to the care which a steward takes of everything in the house.
But this is fanciful.—*Ed.*

to leave all things to him; but because Abram himself had no hope left in any other.   It is therefore (in my judgment) just as if he called him the son of a house destitute of children,[1] because this was a proof of a deserted and barren house, that the inheritance was devolving upon a foreigner who would occupy the empty and deserted place.   He afterwards contemptuously calls him his servant, or his home-born slave, 'the son of my house (he says) will be my heir.'   He thus speaks in contempt, as if he would say, 'My condition is wretched, who shall not have even a freeman for my successor.'   It is however asked, how he could be both a Damascene and a home-born slave of Abram?   There are two solutions of the difficulty, either that he was called the son of the house, not because he was *born*, but only because he was *educated* in it; or, that he sprang from Damascus, because his father was from Syria.

4. *This shall not be thine heir.*   We hence infer that God had approved the wish of Abram.   Whence also follows the other point, that Abram had not been impelled by any carnal affection to offer up this prayer, but by a pious and holy desire of enjoying the benediction promised to him.   For God not only promises him a seed, but a great people, who in number should equal the stars of heaven.   They who expound the passage allegorically; implying that a heavenly seed was promised him which might be compared with the stars, may enjoy their own opinion : but we maintain what is more solid; namely, that the faith of Abram was increased by the sight of the stars.   For the Lord, in order more deeply to affect his own people, and more efficaciously to penetrate their minds, after he has reached their ears by his word, also arrests their eyes by external symbols, that eyes and ears may consent together.   Therefore the sight of the stars was not superfluous; but God intended to strike the mind of Abram with this thought, 'He who by his word alone suddenly produced a host so numerous, by which he might

---

[1] " Acsi vocaret, Filium orbitatis."—"Comme s'il l'appeloit, Fils de la maison, ou il n'y a point d'enfans."—*French Tr.*

adorn the previously vast and desolate heaven; shall not *He* be able to replenish my desolate house with offspring?' It is, however, not necessary to imagine a nocturnal vision, because the stars, which, during the day, escape our sight, would then appear; for since the whole was transacted in vision, Abram had a wonderful scene set before him, which would manifestly reveal hidden things to him. Therefore, though he perhaps might not move a step, it was yet possible for him in vision to be led forth out of his tent. The question now occurs, concerning what seed the promise is to be understood. And it is certain that neither the posterity of Ishmael nor of Esau is to be taken into this account, because the legitimate seed is to be reckoned by the promise, which God determined should remain in Isaac and Jacob; yet the same doubt arises respecting the posterity of Jacob, because many who could trace their descent from him, according to the flesh, cut themselves off, as degenerate sons and aliens, from the faith of their fathers. I answer, that this term seed is, indiscriminately, extended to the whole people whom God has adopted to himself. But since many were alienated by their unbelief, we must come for information to Christ, who alone distinguishes true and genuine sons from such as are illegitimate. By pursuing this method, we find the posterity of Abram reduced to a small number, that afterwards it may be the more increased. For in Christ the Gentiles also are gathered together, and are by faith ingrafted into the body of Abram, so as to have a place among his legitimate sons. Concerning which point more will be said in the seventeenth chapter.

6. *And he believed in the Lord.* None of us would be able to conceive the rich and hidden doctrine which this passage contains, unless Paul had borne his torch before us. (Rom. iv. 3.) But it is strange, and seems like a prodigy, that when the Spirit of God has kindled so great a light, yet the greater part of interpreters wander with closed eyes, as in the darkness of night. I omit the Jews, whose blindness is well known. But it is (as I have said) monstrous, that they who have had Paul as their luminous expositor, should

so foolishly have depraved this place. However, it hence appears, that in all ages, Satan has laboured at nothing more assiduously than to extinguish, or to smother, the gratuitous justification of faith, which is here expressly asserted. The words of Moses are, " He believed in the Lord, and he counted it to him for righteousness." In the first place, the faith of Abram is commended, because by it he embraced the promise of God; it is commended, in the second place, because hence Abram obtained righteousness in the sight of God, and that by imputation. For the word חשב, (chashab,) which Moses uses, is to be understood as relating to the judgment of God, just as in Psalm cvi. 31, where the zeal of Phinehas is said to have been counted to him for righteousness. The meaning of the expression will, however, more fully appear by comparison with its opposites.[1] In Leviticus vii. 18, it is said that when expiation has been made, iniquity ' shall not be imputed' to a man. Again, in chap. xvii. 4, ' Blood shall be imputed unto that man.' So, in 2 Sam. xix. 19, Shimei says, ' Let not the king impute iniquity unto me.' Nearly of the same import is the expression in 2 Kings xii. 15, ' They reckoned not with the man into whose hand they delivered the money for the work;' that is, they required no account of the money, but suffered them to administer it, in perfect confidence. Let us now return to Moses. Just as we understand that they to whom iniquity is imputed are guilty before God; so those to whom he imputes righteousness are approved by him as just persons; wherefore Abram was received into the number and rank of just persons, by the imputation of righteousness. For Paul, in order that he may show us distinctly the force and nature, or quality of this righteousness, leads us to the celestial tribunal of God. Therefore, they foolishly trifle who apply this term to his character as an honest man;[2] as if it meant that Abram was

---

[1] " Melius ex antitheto patebit."—"Toutefois on entendra mieux par l'antithese, c'est a dire, par ce qui est opposite, ce qu' emporte ceci."—*French Tr.*

[2] The French version is strongly expressed. " Et pourtant ceux-la gazouillent bien sottement, qui tirent ceci au bruit et renom de preud'hommie." Especially do they chatter foolishly enough, who draw this aside to the fame and renown of honesty.—*French Tr.*

personally held to be a just and righteous man. They also, no less unskilfully, corrupt the text, who say that Abram is here ascribing to God the glory of righteousness, seeing that he ventures to acquiesce surely in His promises, acknowledging Him to be faithful and true; for although Moses does not expressly mention the name of God, yet the accustomed method of speaking in the Scriptures removes all ambiguity. Lastly, it is not less the part of stupor than of impudence, when this faith is said to have been imputed to him for righteousness, to mingle with it some other meaning, than that the faith of Abram was accepted in the place of righteousness with God.

It seems, however, to be absurd, that Abram should be justified by believing that his seed would be as numerous as the stars of heaven; for this could be nothing but a particular faith, which would by no means suffice for the complete righteousness of man. Besides, what could an earthly and temporal promise avail for eternal salvation? I answer, first, that the *believing* of which Moses speaks, is not to be restricted to a single clause of the promise here referred to, but embraces the whole; secondly, that Abram did not form his estimate of the promised seed from this oracle alone, but also from others, where a special benediction is added. Whence we infer that he did not expect some common or undefined seed, but that in which the world was to be blessed. Should any one pertinaciously insist, that what is said in common of all the children of Abram, is forcibly distorted when applied to Christ; in the first place, it cannot be denied that God now again repeats the promise before made to his servant, for the purpose of answering his complaint. But we have said—and the thing itself clearly proves—that Abram was impelled thus greatly to desire seed, by a regard to the promised benediction. Whence it follows, that this promise was not taken by him separately from others. But to pass all this over; we must, I say, consider what is here treated of, in order to form a judgment of the faith of Abram. God does not promise to his servant this or the other thing only, as he sometimes grants special benefits to unbelievers, who are without the taste of his paternal love; but he declares, that

He will be propitious to him, and confirms him in the confidence of safety, by relying upon His protection and His grace. For he who has God for his inheritance does not exult in fading joy; but, as one already elevated towards heaven, enjoys the solid happiness of eternal life. It is, indeed, to be maintained as an axiom, that all the promises of God, made to the faithful, flow from the free mercy of God, and are evidences of that paternal love, and of that gratuitous adoption, on which their salvation is founded. Therefore, we do not say that Abram was justified because he laid hold on a single word, respecting the offspring to be brought forth, but because he embraced God as his Father. And truly faith does not justify us for any other reason, than that it reconciles us unto God; and that it does so, not by its own merit; but because we receive the grace offered to us in the promises, and have no doubt of eternal life, being fully persuaded that we are loved by God as sons. Therefore, Paul reasons from contraries, that he to whom faith is imputed for righteousness, has not been justified by works. (Rom. iv. 4.) For whosoever obtains righteousness by works, his merits come into the account before God. But we apprehend righteousness by faith, when God freely reconciles us to himself. Whence it follows, that the merit of works ceases when righteousness is sought by faith; for it is necessary that this righteousness should be freely given by God, and offered in his word, in order that any one may possess it by faith. To render this more intelligible, when Moses says that faith was imputed to Abram for righteousness, he does not mean that faith was that first cause of righteousness which is called the *efficient*, but only the *formal* cause; as if he had said, that Abram was therefore justified, because, relying on the paternal loving-kindness of God, he trusted to His mere goodness, and not to himself, nor to his own merits. For it is especially to be observed, that faith borrows a righteousness elsewhere, of which we, in ourselves, are destitute; otherwise it would be in vain for Paul to set faith in opposition to works, when speaking of the mode of obtaining righteousness. Besides, the mutual relation between the free promise and faith, leaves no doubt upon the subject.

We must now notice the circumstance of *time*. Abram
was justified by faith many years after he had been called by
God; after he had left his country a voluntary exile, rendering
himself a remarkable example of patience and of continence ;
after he had entirely dedicated himself to sanctity, and after he
had, by exercising himself in the spiritual and external service
of God, aspired to a life almost angelical.   It therefore follows, that even to the end of life, we are led towards the
eternal kingdom of God by the righteousness of faith.   On
which point many are too grossly deceived. For they grant,
indeed, that the righteousness which is freely bestowed upon
sinners, and offered to the unworthy, is received by faith
alone; but they restrict this to a moment of time, so that he
who at the first obtained justification by faith, may afterwards be justified by good works. By this method, faith is
nothing else than the beginning of righteousness, whereas
righteousness itself consists in a continual course of works.
But they who thus trifle must be altogether insane. For if
the angelical uprightness of Abram, faithfully cultivated
through so many years, in one uniform course, did not prevent him from fleeing to faith, for the sake of obtaining righteousness; where upon earth besides will such perfection be
found, as may stand in God's sight? Therefore, by a consideration of the time in which this was said to Abram,[1] we certainly gather, that the righteousness of works is not to be
substituted for the righteousness of faith, in any such way,
that one should perfect what the other has begun; but that
holy men are only justified by faith, as long as they live in the
world. If any one object, that Abram previously believed
God, when he followed Him at His call, and committed himself to His direction and guardianship, the solution is ready ;
that we are not here told when Abram first began to be justified, or to believe in God; but that in this one place it is
declared, or related, how he had been justified through his
whole life. For if Moses had spoken thus immediately on
Abram's first vocation, the cavil of which I have spoken would

[1] " Ergo ex ratione temporis certo colligimus."—"Nous recueillons donc
pour certain, selon la raison du temps auquel ceci fut dit à Abram."—
French Tr.

have been more specious; namely, that the righteousness of
faith was only *initial* (so to speak) and not perpetual.   But
now, since after such great progress, he is still said to be justified by faith, it thence easily appears that the saints are
justified freely even unto death.   I confess, indeed, that after
the faithful are born again by the Spirit of God, the method
of justifying differs, in some respect, from the former.   For
God reconciles to himself those who are born only of the
flesh, and who are destitute of all good; and since he finds
nothing in them except a dreadful mass of evils, he counts
them just, by imputation.   But those to whom he has imparted the Spirit of holiness and righteousness, he embraces
with his gifts.   Nevertheless, in order that their good works
may please God, it is necessary that these works themselves
should be justified by gratuitous imputation; but some evil
is always inherent in them.   Meanwhile, however, this is a
settled point, that men are justified before God by believing
not by working; while they obtain grace by faith, because
they are unable to deserve a reward by works.   Paul also, in
hence contending, that Abram did not merit by works the
righteousness which he had received before his circumcision,
does not impugn the above doctrine.   The argument of Paul
is of this kind : The circumcision of Abram was posterior to
his justification in the order of time, and therefore could not
be its cause, for of necessity the cause precedes its effect.   I
also grant, that Paul, for this reason, contends that works are
not meritorious, except under the covenant of the law, of
which covenant, circumcision is put as the earnest and the symbol.   But since Paul is not here defining the force and nature
of circumcision, regarded as a pure and genuine institution of
God, but is rather disputing on the sense attached to it, by
those with whom he deals, he therefore does not allude to
the covenant which God before had made with Abram, because the mention of it was unnecessary for the present purpose.   Both arguments are therefore of force; first, that the
righteousness of Abram cannot be ascribed to the covenant
of the law, because it preceded his circumcision; and, secondly,
that the righteousness even of the most perfect characters
perpetually consists in faith; since Abram, with all the excel-

lency of his virtues, after his daily and even remarkable service of God, was, nevertheless, justified by faith. For this also is, in the last place, worthy of observation, that what is here related concerning one man, is applicable to all the sons of God. For since he was called the father of the faithful, not without reason; and since further, there is but one method of obtaining salvation; Paul properly teaches, that a real and not personal righteousness is in this place described.

7. *I am the Lord that brought thee.* Since it greatly concerns us, to have God as the guide of our whole life, in order that we may know that we have not rashly entered on some doubtful way, therefore the Lord confirms Abram in the course of his vocation, and recalls to his memory the original benefit of his deliverance; as if he had said, 'I, after I had stretched out my hand to thee, to lead thee forth from the labyrinth of death, have carried my favour towards thee thus far. Thou, therefore, respond to me in turn, by constantly advancing; and maintain stedfastly thy faith, from the beginning even to the end.' This indeed is said, not with respect to Abram alone, in order that he, gathering together the promises of God, made to him from the very commencement of his life of faith, should form them into one whole;[1] but that all the pious may learn to regard the beginning of their vocation as flowing perpetually from Abram, their common father; and may thus securely boast with Paul, that they know in whom they have believed, (2 Tim. ii. 12,) and that God, who, in the person of Abram, had separated a church unto himself, would be a faithful keeper of the salvation deposited with Him. That, for this very end, the Lord declares himself to have been the deliverer of Abram, appears hence; because he connects the promise which he is now about to give with the prior redemption; as if he were saying, 'I do not now first begin to promise thee this land. For it was on this account that I brought thee out of thy own country, to constitute thee the lord and heir of this land. Now there-

---

[1] "Corpus unum efficeret."—"Et les joindre ensemble comme en un corps." And should join them together, as in one body. —*French Tr.*

fore I covenant with thee in the same form; lest thou shouldst deem thyself to have been deceived, or fed with empty words; and I command thee to be mindful of the first covenant, that the new promise, which after many years I now repeat, may be the more firmly supported.'

8. *Lord God, whereby shall I know.* It may appear absurd, first, that Abram, who before had placed confidence in the simple word of God, without moving any question concerning the promises given to him, should now dispute whether what he hears from the mouth of God be true or not. Secondly, that he ascribes but little honour to God, not merely by murmuring against him, when he speaks, but by requiring some additional pledge to be given him. Further, whence arises the knowledge which belongs to faith, but from the word? Therefore Abram in vain desires to be assured of the future possession of the land, while he ceases to depend upon the word of God. I answer, the Lord sometimes concedes to his children, that they may freely express any objection which comes into their mind. For he does not act so strictly with them, as not to suffer himself to be questioned. Yea, the more certainly Abram was persuaded that God was true, and the more he was attached to His word, so much the more familiarly did he disburden his cares into God's bosom. To this may be added, that the protracted delay was no small obstacle to Abram's faith. For after God had held him in suspense through a great part of his life, now when he was worn down with age, and had nothing before his eyes but death and the grave, God anew declares that he shall be lord of the land. He does not, however, reject, on account of its difficulty, what might have appeared to him incredible, but brings before God the anxiety by which he is inwardly oppressed. And therefore his questioning with God is rather a proof of faith, than a sign of incredulity. The wicked, because their minds are entangled with various conflicting thoughts, do not in any way receive the promises, but the pious, who feel the impediments in their flesh, endeavour to remove them, lest they should obstruct the way to God's word; and they seek a remedy for those evils of which they are conscious.

It is, nevertheless, to be observed, that there were some special impulses in the saints of old, which it would not now be lawful to draw into a precedent. For though Hezekiah and Gideon required certain miracles, this is not a reason why the same thing should be attempted by us in the present day; let it suffice us to seek for such confirmation only as the Lord himself, according to his own pleasure, shall judge most eligible.

9. *Take me an heifer of three years old.* Some, instead of an heifer of three years old, translate the passage, ' three heifers,' and in each species of animals enumerated, would make the number three. Yet the opinion of those who apply the word *three* to the age of the heifer, is more general. Moreover, although God would not deny his servant what he had asked; he yet, by no means, granted what would gratify the desire of the flesh. For, what certainty could be added to the promise, by the slaughter of an heifer, or goat, or ram? For the true design of sacrifice, of which we shall see more presently, was hitherto hidden from Abram. Therefore, by obeying the command of God, of which, however, no advantage was apparent, he hence proves the obedience of his faith; nor did his wish aim at any other end than this; namely, that, the obstacle being removed, he might, as was just, reverently acquiesce in the word of the Lord. Let us, therefore, learn meekly to embrace those helps which God offers for the confirmation of our faith; although they may not accord with our judgment, but rather may seem to be a mockery; until, at length, it shall become plain from the effect, that God was as far as possible from mocking us.

10. *And divided them in the midst.* That no part of this sacrifice may be without mystery, certain interpreters weary themselves in the fabrication of subtleties; but it is our business, as I have often declared, to cultivate sobriety. I confess I do not know why he was commanded to take three kinds of animals besides birds; unless it were, that by this variety itself, it was declared, that all the posterity of Abram, of whatever rank they might be, should be offered up in sacri-

fice, so that the whole people, and each individual, should constitute one sacrifice.   There are also some things, concerning
which, if any one curiously seeks the reason, I shall not be
ashamed to acknowledge my ignorance, because I do not
choose to wander in uncertain speculations.   Moreover, this,
in my opinion, is the sum of the whole : That God, in commanding the animals to be killed, shows what will be the future condition of the Church.   Abram certainly wished to be
assured of the promised inheritance of the land.   Now he is
taught that it would take its commencement from death ;
that is, that he and his children must die before they should
enjoy the dominion over the land.   In commanding the
slaughtered animals to be cut in parts, it is probable that he
followed the ancient rite in forming covenants, whether they
were entering into any alliance, or were mustering an army,
a practice which also passed over to the Gentiles.   Now, the
allies or the soldiers passed between the severed parts, that,
being enclosed together within the sacrifice, they might be
the more sacredly united in one body.   That this method
was practised by the Jews, Jeremiah bears witness, (xxxiv.
18,) where he introduces God as saying, ' They have violated
my covenant, when they cut the calf in two parts, and passed
between the divisions of it, as well the princes of Judah, and
the nobles of Jerusalem, and the whole people of the land.'
Nevertheless, there appears to me to have been this special
reason for the act referred to ; that the Lord would indeed admonish the race of Abram, not only that it should be like a dead
carcase, but even like one torn and dissected.   For the servitude
with which they were oppressed for a time, was more intolerable than simple death ; yet because the sacrifice is offered to
God, death itself is immediately turned into new life.   And
this is the reason why Abram, placing the parts of the sacrifice
opposite to each other, fits them one to the other, because
they were again to be gathered together from their dispersion.   But how difficult is the restoration of the Church, and
what troubles are involved in it, is shown by the horror with
which Abram was seized.   We see, therefore, that two things
were illustrated ; namely, the hard servitude, with which the
sons of Abram were to be pressed almost to laceration and

destruction ; and then their redemption, which was to be the
signal pledge of divine adoption ; and in the same mirror the
general condition of the Church is represented to us, as it is
the peculiar province of God to create it out of nothing, and
to raise it from death.

11. *And when the fowls came down.*   Although the sacrifice
was dedicated to God, yet it was not free from the attack
and the violence of birds.   So neither are the faithful, after
they are received into the protection of God, so covered with
his hand, as not to be assailed on every side ; since Satan and
the world cease not to cause them trouble.   Therefore, in
order that the sacrifice we have once offered to God may not
be violated, but may remain pure and uninjured, contrary
assaults must be repulsed, with whatever inconvenience and
toil.

12. *A deep sleep fell upon Abram.*   The vision is now
mingled with a dream.   Thus the Lord here joins those two
kinds of communication together, which I have before related
from Numbers xii. 6, where it is said, ' When I appear unto my
servants the prophets, I speak to them in a vision or a dream.'
Mention has already been made of a vision : Moses now relates that a dream was superadded.   A horrible darkness intervened, that Abram might know that the dream is not a
common one, but that the whole is divinely conducted ; it
has, nevertheless, a correspondence with the oracle then present, as God immediately afterwards explains in his own
words, " Thou shalt surely know that thy seed shall be a
stranger," &c.   We have elsewhere said, that God was not
wont to dazzle the eyes of his people with bare and empty
spectres ; but that in visions, the principal parts always belonged to the word.   Thus here, not a mute apparition is
presented to the eyes of Abram, but he is taught by an
oracle annexed, what the external and visible symbol meant.
It is, however, to be observed, that before one son is given to
Abram, he hears that his seed shall be, for a long time, in captivity and slavery.   For thus does the Lord deal with his
own people ; he always makes a beginning from death, so

that by quickening the dead, he the more abundantly manifests his power. It was necessary, in part, on Abram's account, that this should have been declared; but the Lord chiefly had regard to his posterity, lest they should faint in their sufferings, of which, however, the Lord had promised a joyful and happy issue; especially since their long continuance would produce great weariness. And three things are, step by step, brought before them; first, that the sons of Abram must wander four hundred years, before they should attain the promised inheritance; secondly, that they should be slaves; thirdly, that they were to be inhumanly and tyrannically treated. Wherefore the faith of Abram was admirable and singular; seeing that he acquiesced in an oracle so sorrowful, and felt assured, that God would be his Deliverer, after his miseries had proceeded to their greatest height.

It is, however, asked, how the number of years here given agrees with the subsequent history? Some begin the computation from the time of his departure out of Charran. But it seems more probable, that the intermediate time only is denoted ;[1] as if he would say, ' It behoves thy posterity to wait patiently; because I have not decreed to grant what I now promise, until the four hundredth year: yea, up to that very time their servitude will continue.' According to this mode of reckoning, Moses says, (Exod. xii. 40,) that the children of Israel dwelt in Egypt four hundred and thirty years: while yet, from the sixth chapter, we may easily gather, that not more than two hundred and thirty years, or thereabouts, elapsed from the time that Jacob went down thither, to their deliverance. Where, then, shall we find the remaining two hundred years, but by referring to the oracle? Of this matter all doubt is removed by Paul, who (Gal. iii. 17) reckons the years from the gratuitous covenant of life, to the promulgation of the Law. In short, God does not indicate how long the servitude of the people should be from its commencement to its close, but how long he intended to suspend, or to defer his promise. As to his omitting the

---

[1] " Sed magis probabile videtur, notari duntaxat tempus intermedium." Calvin evidently means the time which was to intervene between the giving of the oracle and the exodus from Egypt.—*Ed.*

thirty years, it is neither a new nor unfrequent thing, where years are not accurately computed, to mention only the larger sums.   But we see here, that for the sake of brevity, the whole of that period is divided into four centuries.   There-fore, there is no absurdity in omitting the short space of time : this is chiefly to be considered, that the Lord, for the purpose of exercising the patience of his people, suspends his promise more than four centuries.

14. *Also that nation whom they serve.*   A consolation is now subjoined, in which this is the first thing, God testifies that he will be the vindicator of his people.   Whence it follows, that he will take upon himself the care of the salvation of those whom he has embraced, and will not suffer them to be harassed by the ungodly and the wicked with impunity.   And although he here expressly announces that he will take ven-geance on the Egyptians ; yet all the enemies of the Church are exposed to the same judgment : even as Moses in his song extends to all ages and nations the threat that the Lord will exact punishment for unjust persecutions.[1] 'Vengeance is mine, I, saith he, will repay,' (Deut. xxxii. 35.)   Therefore, whenever we happen to be treated with inhumanity by ty-rants, (which is very usual with the Church,) let this be our consolation, that after our faith shall be sufficiently proved by bearing the cross, God, at whose pleasure we are thus humbled, will himself be the Judge, who will repay to our enemies the due reward of the cruelty which they now exer-cise.   Although they now exult with intoxicated joy, it will at length appear by the event itself, that our miseries are happy ones, but their triumphs wretched ; because God, who careth for us, is their adversary.   But let us remember that we must give place unto the wrath of God, as Paul exhorts, in order that we may not be hurried headlong to seek revenge. Place also must be given to hope, that it may sustain us when oppressed and groaning under the burden of evils.   To judge

---

[1] " De *justis* persequutionibus."   Most probably a misprint for *injustis ;* as both the Old French and English translations agree in rendering the word unjust.

the nation, means the same thing as to summon it to judgment, in order that God, when he has long reposed in silence, may openly manifest himself as the Judge.

15. *And thou shalt go to thy fathers in peace.* Hitherto the Lord had respect to the posterity of Abram as well as to himself, that the consolation might be common to all; but now he turns his address to Abram alone, because he had need of peculiar confirmation. And the remedy proposed for alleviating his sorrow was, that he should die in peace, after he had attained the utmost limit of old age. The explanation given by some that he should die a natural death, exempt from violence; or an easy death, in which his vital spirits should spontaneously and naturally fail, and his life itself should fall by its own maturity, without any sense of pain, is, in my opinion, frigid. For Moses wishes to express that Abram should have not only a long, but a placid old age, with a corresponding joyful and peaceful death. The sense therefore is, that although, through his whole life, Abram was to be deprived of the possession of the land, yet he should not be wanting in the essential materials of quiet and joy, so that having happily finished his life, he should cheerfully depart to his fathers. And certainly death makes the great distinction between the reprobate and the sons of God, whose condition in the present life is commonly one and the same, except that the sons of God have by far the worst of it. Wherefore peace in death ought justly to be regarded as a singular benefit, because it is a proof of that distinction to which I have just alluded.[1] Even profane writers, feeling their way in the dark, have perceived this. Plato, in his book on the Republic, (lib. i.) cites a song of Pindar, in which he says, that they who live justly and holily, are attended by a sweet hope, cherishing their hearts and nourishing their old age; which hope chiefly governs the fickle mind of men. Because men, conscious of guilt, must necessarily be miserably harassed by various torments; the Poet, when he asserts that hope is the

---

[1] " Quod nuper *attigit*,"—should doubtless be *attigi;* as the sense requires, and as it is rendered in the French version, with which the Old English Translation corresponds.—*Ed.*

reward of a good conscience, calls it the nurse of old age.[1]
For as young men, while far removed from death, carelessly
take their pleasure;[2] the old are admonished by their own
weakness, seriously to reflect that they must depart.   Now
unless the hope of a better life inspires them, nothing remains
for them but miserable fears.   Finally, as the reprobate indulge themselves during their whole life, and stupidly sleep
in their vices, it is necessary that their death should be full
of trouble ; while the faithful commit their souls into the hand
of God without fear and sadness.   Whence also Balaam was
constrained to break forth in this expression, ' Let my soul
die the death of the righteous,' (Numb. xxiii. 10.)   Moreover,
since men have not such a desirable close of life in their own
power ; the Lord, in promising a placid and quiet death to his
servant Abram, teaches us that it is his own gift.   And we see
that even kings, and others who deem themselves happy in
this world, are yet agitated in death; because they are visited
with secret compunctions for their sins, and look for nothing
in death but destruction.   But Abram willingly and joyfully
went forward to his death, seeing that he had in Isaac a certain pledge of the divine benediction, and knew that a better
life was laid up for him in heaven.

16. *The iniquity of the Amorites is not yet full.*   The reason
here given is deemed absurd, as seeming to imply that the sons
of Abram could not otherwise be saved, than by the destruction
of others.   I answer, that we must with modesty and humility
yield to the secret counsel of God.   Since he had given that
land to the Amorites, to be inhabited by them in perpetuity,
he intimates, that he will not, without just cause, transfer the
possession of it to others; as if he would say, ' I grant the
dominion of this land to thy seed without injury to any one.
The land, at present, is occupied by its lawful possessors, to
whom I delivered it.   Until, therefore, they shall have deserved, by their sins, to be rightfully expelled, the dominion
of it will not come to thy posterity.'   Thus God teaches him

[1] " Eam γηροτρόφον appellat."
[2] " Secure delicientur."—" Prenent leurs plaisirs sans souci ne crainte."
—*French Tr.*

that the land must be evacuated, in order that it may lie open to new inhabitants. And this passage is remarkable, as showing, that the abodes of men are so distributed in the world, that the Lord will preserve quiet people, each in their several stations, till they cast themselves out by their own wickedness. For by polluting the place of their habitation, they in a certain sense tear away the boundaries fixed by the hand of God, which would otherwise have remained immoveable. Moreover, the Lord here commends his own long-suffering. Even then the Amorites had become unworthy to occupy the land, yet the Lord not only bore with them for a short time, but granted them four centuries for repentance. And hence it appears, that he does not, without reason, so frequently declare how slow he is to anger. But the more graciously he waits for men, if, at length, instead of repenting they remain obstinate, the more severely does he avenge such great ingratitude. Therefore Paul says, that they who indulge themselves in sin, while the goodness and clemency of God invite them to repentance, heap up for themselves a treasure of wrath, (Rom. ii. 4 ;) and thus they reap no advantage from delay, seeing that the severity of the punishment is doubled; just as it happened to the Amorites, whom, at length, the Lord commanded to be so entirely cut off, that not even infants were spared. Therefore, when we hear that God out of heaven is silently waiting until iniquities shall fill up their measure; let us know, that this is no time for torpor, but rather let every one of us stir himself up, that we may be beforehand with the celestial judgment. It was formerly said by a heathen, that the anger of God proceeds with a slow step to avenge itself, but that it compensates for its tardiness by the severity of its punishment. Hence there is no reason why reprobates should flatter themselves, when he seems to let them pass unobserved,[1] since he does not so repose in heaven, as to cease to be the Judge of the world; nor will he be unmindful of the execution of his office, in due time.[2] We

---

[1] " Eo dissimulante."
[2] " Nec officii sui in tempore obliviscatur." The sense given in the translation would perhaps scarcely have been elicited from these words,

infer, however, from the words of Moses, that though space
for repentance is given to the reprobate, they are still devoted
to destruction.   Some take the word עון, *(ayon,)* for punishment, as if it had been said that *punishment* was not yet matured for them.   But the former exposition is more suitable;
namely, that they will set no bound to their *wickedness*, until
they bring upon themselves final destruction.

17. *Behold, a smoking furnace.*   Again a new vision was
added, to confirm his faith in the oracle.   At first, Abram
was horror-struck with the thick darkness ; now, in the midst
of a smoking furnace, he sees a burning lamp.   Many suppose
that a sacrifice was consumed with this fire; but I rather
interpret it as a symbol of future deliverance, which would
well agree with the fact itself.   For there are two things
contrary to each other in appearance ; the obscurity of smoke,
and the shining of a lamp.   Hence Abram knew that light
would, at length, emerge out of darkness.   An analogy is
always to be sought for between signs, and the things signified, that there may be a mutual correspondence between
them.   Then, since the symbol, in itself, is but a lifeless
carcase, reference ought always to be made to the word which
is annexed to it.   But here, by the word, liberty was promised to Abram's seed, in the midst of servitude.   Now the
condition of the Church could not be painted more to the
life, than when God causes a burning torch to proceed out of
the smoke, in order that the darkness of afflictions may not
overwhelm us, but that we may cherish a good hope of life
even in death ; because the Lord will, at length, shine upon
us, if only we offer up ourselves in sacrifice to Him.

18. *In the same day the Lord made a covenant.*   I willingly
admit what I have alluded to above, that the covenant was
ratified by a solemn rite, when the animals were divided
into parts.   For there seems to be a repetition, in which he

without the aid of Calvin's own French translation, which thus renders the
passage, ' Et ne s'oublie point de faire son office en temps due.'   The Old
English version, by adhering to a barely literal rendering, deprives the
sentence of all meaning ; " neither doth he in time forget his duty."
—*Ed.*

teaches what was the intent of the sacrifice which he has mentioned. Here, also, we may observe, what I have said, that the word is always to be joined with the symbols, lest our eyes be fed with empty and fruitless ceremonies. God has commanded animals to be offered to him; but he has shown their end and use, by a covenant appended to them. If, then, the Lord feeds us by sacraments, we infer, that they are the evidences of his grace, and the tokens of those spiritual blessings which flow from it.

He then enumerates the nations, whose land God was about to give to the sons of Abram, in order that he may confirm what he before said concerning a numerous offspring. For that was not to be a small band of men, but an immense multitude, for which the Lord assigns a habitation of such vast extent. God had before spoken only of the Amorites, among whom Abram then dwelt; but now, for the sake of amplifying his grace, he recounts all the others by name.

CHAPTER XVI.

1. Now Sarai Abram's wife bare him no children : and she had an handmaid, an Egyptian, whose name *was* Hagar.

2. And Sarai said unto Abram, Behold now, the Lord hath restrained me from bearing : I pray thee, go in unto my maid ; it may be that I may obtain children by her. And Abram hearkened to the voice of Sarai.

3. And Sarai Abram's wife took Hagar, her maid the Egyptian, after Abram had dwelt ten years in the land of Canaan, and gave her to her husband Abram to be his wife.

4. And he went in unto Hagar, and she conceived : and when she saw that she had conceived, her mistress was despised in her eyes.

5. And Sarai said unto Abram, My wrong *be* upon thee : I have given my maid into thy bosom ; and when she saw that she had conceived, I was

1. Porro Sarai uxor Abram non pepererat ei : erat autem ei ancilla Ægyptia, et nomen ejus Hagar.

2. Et dixit Sarai ad Abram, Ecce, nunc conclusit me Jehova, ne parerem : ingredere nunc ad ancillam meam, si forte ædificer ex ea : et paruit Abram voci Sarai.

3. Et tulit Sarai uxor Abram, Hagar Ægyptiam ancillam suam in fine decem annorum, quibus habitavit Abram in terra Chenaan, et dedit **eam** Abram viro suo in uxorem.

4. Et ingressus est ad Hagar, et concepit : et videns quod concepisset, despectui habuit dominam suam in oculis suis.

5. Tunc dixit Sarai ad Abram, Injuria mea super te : ego dedi ancillam meam in sinu tuo, et ubi vidit quod conce-

despised in her eyes : the Lord judge between me and thee.

6. But Abram said unto Sarai, Behold, thy maid *is* in thy hand ; do to her as it pleaseth thee. And when Sarai dealt hardly with her, she fled from her face.

7. And the angel of the Lord found her by a fountain of water in the wilderness, by the fountain in the way to Shur.

8. And he said, Hagar, Sarai's maid, whence camest thou ? and whither wilt thou go ? And she said, I flee from the face of my mistress Sarai.

9. And the angel of the Lord said unto her, Return to thy mistress, and submit thyself under her hands.

10. And the angel of the Lord said unto her, I will multiply thy seed exceedingly, that it shall not be numbered for multitude.

11. And the angel of the Lord said unto her, Behold, thou *art* with child, and shalt bear a son, and shalt call his name Ishmael; because the Lord hath heard thy affliction.

12. And he will be a wild man; his hand *will be* against every man, and every man's hand against him ; and he shall dwell in the presence of all his brethren.

13. And she called the name of the Lord that spake unto her, Thou God seest me : for she said, Have I also here looked after him that seeth me ?

14. Wherefore the well was called Beer-lahai-roi : behold, *it is* between Kadesh and Bered.

15. And Hagar bare Abram a son : and Abram called his son's name, which Hagar bare, Ishmael.

16. And Abram *was* fourscore and six years old when Hagar bare Ishmael to Abram.

pisset, despectui sum in oculis ejus : judicet Jehova inter me et te.

6. Et dixit Abram ad Sarai, Ecce, ancilla tua in manu tua, fac ei quod bonum est in oculis tuis : et afflixit eam Sarai, et fugit a facie ejus.

7. Et invenit eam Angelus Jehovæ juxta fontem aquæ in deserto, juxta fontem in via Sur.

8. Et dixit, Hagar ancilla Sarai, unde venis, et quo vadis ? Et dixit, A facie Sarai dominæ meæ ego fugio.

9. Et dixit ei Angelus Jehovæ, Revertere ad dominam tuam, et humilia te sub manibus ejus.

10. Adhæc dixit ei Angelus Jehovæ, Multiplicando multiplicabo semen tuum, et non numerabitur præ multitudine.

11. Præterea dixit ei Angelus Jehovæ, Ecce, es prægnans, et paries filium, et vocabis nomen ejus Ismael : quia audivit Jehova afflictionem tuam.

12. Et ipse erit ferus homo, manus ejus in omnes : et manus omnium in eum : et co..m omnibus fratribus suis habitabit.

13. Et vocavit nomen Jehovæ qui loquebatur sibi, Tu Deus videns me : quia dixit, Nonne etiam hic vidi post videntem me ?

14. Idcirco vocavit puteum, Puteum viventis videntis me. Ecce, *est* inter Cades et Bared.

15. Et peperit Hagar ipsi Abram filium : et vocavit Abram nomen filii sui, quem peperit Hagar, Ismael.

16. Abram autem erat octoginta annorum et sex annorum, quando peperit Hagar Ismael ipsi Abram.

1. *Now Sarai Abram's wife.* Moses here recites a new history, namely, that Sarai, through the impatience of long delay, resorted to a method of obtaining seed by her husband, at variance with the word of God. She saw that she was

barren, and had passed the age of bearing.　And she inferred
the necessity of a new remedy, in order that Abram might
obtain the promised blessing.　Moses expressly relates, that
the design of marrying a second wife did not originate with
Abram himself, but with Sarai, to teach us that the holy man
was not impelled by lust to these nuptials; but that, when
he was thinking of no such thing, he was induced to engage
in them, by the exhortation of his wife.　It is, however, asked,
whether Sarai substituted her handmaid in her place, through
the mere desire of having offspring?　So it seems to some;
yet to me it is incredible, that the pious matron should not
have been cognizant of those promises, which had been so
often repeated to her husband.　Yea, it ought to be fully
taken for granted, among all pious persons, that the mother
of the people of God, was a participator of the same grace
with her husband.　Sarai, therefore, does not desire offspring
(as is usual) from a merely natural impulse; but she yields
her conjugal rights to another, through a wish to obtain that
benediction, which she knew was divinely promised: not
that she makes a divorce from her husband, but assigns him
another wife, from whom he might receive children.　And
certainly if she had desired offspring in the ordinary manner,
it would rather have come into her mind to do it by the
adoption of a son, than by giving place to a second wife.
For we know the vehemence of female jealousy.　Therefore,
while contemplating the promise, she becomes forgetful of
her own right, and thinks of nothing but the bringing forth
of children to Abram.　A memorable example, from which
no small profit accrues to us.　For however laudable was
Sarai's wish, as regards the end, or the scope to which it
tended; nevertheless, in the pursuit of it, she was guilty of
no light sin, by impatiently departing from the word of God,
for the purpose of enjoying the effect of that word.　While
she reflects upon her own barrenness and old age, she begins
to despair of offspring, unless Abram should have children
from some other quarter; in this there is already some fault.
Yet, however desperate the affair might be, still she ought
not to have attempted anything at variance with the will of
God and the legitimate order of nature.　God designed that

the human race should be propagated by sacred marriage. Sarai perverts the law of marriage, by defiling the conjugal bed, which was appointed only for two persons. Nor is it an available excuse, that she wished Abram to have a concubine and not a wife; since it ought to have been regarded as a settled point, that the woman is joined to the man, 'that they two should be one flesh.' And though polygamy had already prevailed among many; yet it was never left to the will of man, to abrogate that divine law by which two persons were mutually bound together. Nor was even Abram free from fault, in following the foolish and preposterous counsel of his wife. Therefore, as the precipitancy of Sarai was culpable, so the facility with which Abram yielded to her wish was worthy of reprehension. The faith of both of them was defective; not indeed with regard to the substance of the promise, but with regard to the method in which they proceeded;[1] since they hastened to acquire the offspring which was to be expected from God, without observing the legitimate ordinance of God. Whence also we are taught that God does not in vain command his people to be quiet, and to wait with patience, whenever he defers or suspends the accomplishment of their wishes. For they who hasten before the time, not only anticipate the providence of God, but being discontented with his word, precipitate themselves beyond their proper bounds. But it seems that Sarai had something further in view; for she not only wished that Abram should become a father, but would fain acquire to herself maternal rights and honours. I answer, since she knew that all nations were to be blessed in the seed of Abram, it is no wonder that she should be unwilling to be deprived of participation in his honour; lest she should be cut off, as a putrid member, from the body which had received the blessing, and should also become an alien from the promised salvation.

Bare him no children. This seems added as an excuse. And truly Moses intimates that she did not seek help from the womb of her maid, before necessity compelled her to do so. Her own words also show, that she had patiently and

---

[1] "Sed in medio ipso (ut loquuntur) vel agendi ratione."—"Mais au moyen, et en la façon de procéder."—*French Tr.*

modestly waited to see what God would do, until hope was entirely cut off, when she says, that she was restrained from bearing by the Lord. (ver. 2.)   What fault then shall we find in her?   Surely, that she did not, as she ought, cast this care into the bosom of God, without binding his power to the order of nature, or restraining it to her own sense. And then, by neglecting to infer from the past what would take place in future, she did not regard herself as in the hand of God, who could again open the womb which he had closed.

2. *That I may obtain children by her.*[1] This is a Hebrew phrase, which signifies to become a mother. Some, however, expound the word as simply meaning, *to have a son.* And certainly בֵן, (*ben*,) which, among the Hebrews, signifies son, corresponds with the verb here used.[2] But since sons are so called metaphorically, as being the maintainers of the race, and thus building up the family, therefore the primary signification of the word is to be retained. But Sarai claims for herself, by right of dominion, the child which Hagar shall bring forth : because bondmaids do not bring forth for themselves, since they have not power over their own body. By first speaking to her husband, she does not barely *allow* of a concubine, who should be as a harlot ; but *introduces* and *obtrudes* one. And hence it appears, that when persons are wiser in their own eyes than they ought to be, they easily fall into the snare of trying illicit means. The desire of Sarai proceeds from the zeal of faith ; but because it is not so subjected to God as to wait his time, she immediately has recourse to polygamy, which is nothing else than the corruption of lawful marriage. Moreover, since Sarai, that holy woman, yet fanned in her husband the same flame of impatience with which she burned, we may hence learn, how diligently we ought to be on our guard, lest Satan should surprise us by any secret fraud. For not only does he induce

---

[1] " Si forte ædificer ex ea."   " If perhaps I may be built up by her." See margin of English version.
[2] אבנה.

wicked and ungodly men openly to oppose our faith ; but
sometimes, privately and by stealth, he assails us through
the medium of good and simple men, that he may overcome
us unawares.   On every side, therefore, we must be on our
guard against his wiles ; lest by any means he should under-
mine us.

And Abram hearkened to the voice of Sarai.   Truly the
faith of Abram wavers, when he deviates from the word of
God, and suffers himself to be borne away by the persuasion
of his wife, to seek a remedy which was divinely prohibited.
He, however, retains the foundation, because he does not
doubt that he shall, at length, perceive that God is true. By
which example we are taught, that there is no reason why we
should despond, if, at any time, Satan should shake our faith ;
provided that the truth of God be not overthrown in our
hearts.   Meanwhile, when we see Abram, who, through so
many years, had bravely contended like an invincible combatant, and had surmounted so many obstacles, now yielding,
in a single moment, to temptation ; who among us will not
fear for himself in similar danger?   Therefore, although we
may have stood long and firmly in the faith, we must daily
pray, that God would not lead us into temptation.

3. *And gave her to her husband Abram to be his wife.*
Moses states what was the design of Sarai ; for neither did
she intend to make her house a brothel, nor to be the betrayer
of her maid's chastity, nor a pander for her husband.   Yet
Hagar is improperly called a wife ; because she was brought
into another person's bed, against the law of God.   Wherefore, let us know that this connection was so far illicit, as to
be something between fornication and marriage.   The same
thing takes place with all those inventions which are appended to the word of God.   For with whatever fair pretext they
may be covered, there is an inherent corruption, which de-
generates from the purity of the word, and vitiates the
whole.

4. *Her mistress was despised in her eyes.*   Here Moses relates
that the punishment of excessive precipitancy quickly fol-

lowed. The chief blame, indeed, rested with Sarai; yet because Abram had proved himself too credulous, God chastises both, as they deserve. Sarai is grievously and bitterly tried, by the proud contempt of her handmaid; Abram is harassed by unjust complaints; thus we see that both pay the penalty of their levity, and that the contrivance devised by Sarai, and too eagerly embraced by Abram, fails of success. Meanwhile, in Hagar, an instance of ingratitude is set before us; because she, having been treated with singular kindness and honour, begins to hold her mistress in contempt. Since, however, this is an exceedingly common disease of the mind, let the faithful accustom themselves to the endurance of it; if, at any time, a return so unjust be made to them, for their acts of kindness. But especially, let the infirmity of Sarai move us thus to act, since she was unable to bear the contempt of her maid.

5. *My wrong be upon thee.* This also was a part of her punishment, that Sarai was brought so low as to forget herself for a while; and being vehemently excited, conducted herself with so much weakness. Certainly, to the utmost of her power, she had impelled her husband to act rashly; and now she petulantly insults him, although innocent. For she adduces nothing for which Abram was to be blamed. She reproaches him with the fact, that she had given her maid into his bosom; and complains that she is contemned by this maid, without having first ascertained, whether he intended to assist the bad cause, by his countenance, or not. Thus blind is the assault of anger; it rushes impetuously hither and thither; and condemns, without inquiry, those who are entirely free from blame. If ever any woman was of a meek and gentle spirit, Sarai excelled in that virtue. Whereas, therefore, we see that her patience was violently shaken by a single offence, let every one of us be so much the more resolved to govern his own passions.

The Lord judge between me and thee. She makes improper use of the name of God, and almost forgets that due reverence, which is so strongly enforced on those who are godly. She makes her appeal to the judgment of God.

What else is this, than to call down destruction on her own head? for if God had interposed as judge, he must of necessity have executed punishment upon one or other of them. But Abram had done no injury. It remains, therefore, that she must have felt the vengeance of God, whose anger she had so rashly imprecated upon herself, or her husband. Had Moses spoken this of any heathen woman, it might have been passed over as a common thing. But now, the Lord shows us, in the person of the mother of the faithful; first, how vehement is the flame of anger, and to what lengths it will hurry men; then, how greatly they are blinded who, in their own affairs, are too indulgent to themselves; whence we should learn to suspect ourselves, whenever our own concerns are treated of. Another thing also is here chiefly worthy of remark; namely, that the best ordered families are sometimes not free from contentions; nay, that this evil reaches even to the Church of God; for we know that the family of Abram, which was disturbed with strifes, was the living representation of the Church. As to domestic broils, we know that the principal part of social life, which God hallowed among men, is spent in marriage; and yet various inconveniences intervene, which defile that good state, as with spots. It behoves the faithful to prepare themselves to cut off these occasions of trouble. For this end, it is of great importance to reflect on the origin of the evil; for all the troubles men find in marriage, they ought to impute to sin.

6. *Behold, thy maid is in thy hand.* The greatness of Abram's humanity and modesty appears from his answer. He does not quarrel with his wife; and though he has the best cause, yet he does not pertinaciously defend it, but voluntarily dismisses the wife who had been given him. In short, for the sake of restoring peace, he does violence to his feelings, both as a husband, and a father. For, in leaving Hagar to the will of her enraged mistress, he does not treat her as his wife; he also, in a certain way, undervalues that object of his hope which was conceived in her womb. And it is not to be doubted, that he was thus calm and placid in bearing the vehemence of his wife; because, throughout her whole life, he

had found her to be obedient.   Still it was a great excellence, to restrain his temper under an indignity so great.   It may, however, here be asked, how it was that his care for the blessed seed had then vanished from his mind ?   Hagar is great with child ; he hopes that the seed through which the salvation of the world is promised, is about to proceed from her.   Why then does he not set Sarai aside, and turn his love and desire still more to Hagar ?   Truly, we hence infer, that all human contrivances pass away and vanish in smoke, as soon as any grievous temptation is presented.   Having taken a wife against the divine command, he thinks the matter is succeeding well, when he sees her pregnant, and pleases himself in foolish confidence ; but when contention suddenly arises, he is at his wit's end, and rejects all hope, or, at least, forgets it. The same thing must necessarily happen to us, as often as we attempt anything contrary to the word of God.   Our minds will fail at the very first blast of temptation ;[1] since our only ground of stability is, to have the authority of God for what we do.   In the meantime, God purifies the faith of his servant from its rust ; for by mixing his own and his wife's imagination with the word of God, he, in a sense, had stifled his faith ; wherefore, to restore its brightness, that which was superfluous is cut off.   God, by opposing himself in this manner to our sinful designs, recalls us from our stupidity to a sound mind.   A simple promise had been given, ' I will bless thy seed.'   Sarai's gloss supervened,[2] namely, that she could have no seed but a supposititious one by Hagar : this mire of human imagination, with which the promise had been defiled, must be purged away, that Abram might derive his knowledge from no other source, than the pure word of God.

And Sarai dealt hardly with her.[3]   The word עָנָה, *(anah,)* which Moses uses, signifies to afflict and to humble.   I therefore explain it as being put for reducing Hagar to submis-

---

[1] " Ventum trepidationis."—" Wind of trembling."

[2] " Additamentum Sarai supervenerat."—" L'addition ou glose de Sarai estoit survenue."—*French Tr.*

[3] " Et afflixit eam Sarai."   " And Sarah afflicted her."   See margin of English version.

sion. But it was difficult for an angry woman to keep within bounds, in repressing the insolence of her maid. Wherefore, it is possible that she became immoderately enraged against her; not so much considering her own duty, as revolving the means of being avenged for the offences committed. Since Moses brings no heavier charge, I confine myself to what is certain; that Sarai made use of her proper authority in restraining the insolence of her maid. And, doubtless, from the event, we may form a judgment, that Hagar was impelled to flee, not so much by the cruelty of her mistress, as by her own contumacy. Her own conscience accused her; and it is improbable that Sarai should have been so greatly incensed, except by many, and, indeed, atrocious offences. Therefore, the woman being of servile temper, and of indomitable ferocity, chose rather to flee, than to return to favour, through the humble acknowledgment of her fault.

7. *And the angel of the Lord found her.* We are here taught with what clemency the Lord acts towards his own people, although they have deserved severe punishment. As he had previously mitigated the punishment of Abram and Sarai, so now he casts a paternal look upon Hagar, so that his favour is extended to the whole family. He does not indeed altogether spare them, lest he should cherish their vices; but he corrects them with gentle remedies. It is indeed probable, that Hagar, in going to the desert of Sur, meditated a return to her own country. Yet mention seems to be made of the desert and the wilderness, to show that she, being miserably afflicted, wandered from the presence of men, till the angel met her. Although Moses does not describe the form of the vision, yet I do not doubt, that it was clothed in a human body; in which, nevertheless, manifest tokens of celestial glory were conspicuous.

8. *And he said, Hagar, Sarai's maid.* By the use of this epithet, the angel declares, that she still remained a servant, though she had escaped the hands of her mistress; because liberty is not to be obtained by stealth, nor by flight, but by manumission. Moreover, by this expression, God shows that

he approves of civil government, and that the violation of it is inexcusable. The condition of servitude was then hard; and thanks are to be given to the Lord, that this barbarity has been abolished; yet God has declared from heaven his pleasure, that servants should bear the yoke; as also by the mouth of Paul, he does not give servants their freedom, nor deprive their masters of their use; but only commands them to be kindly and liberally treated. (Ephes. vi. 4.) It is to be inferred also, from the circumstance of the time, not only that civil government is to be maintained, as matter of necessity, but that lawful authorities are to be obeyed, for conscience' sake. For although the fugitive Hagar could no longer be compelled to obedience by force, yet her condition was not changed in the sight of God. By the same argument it is proved, that if masters at any time deal too hardly with their servants, or if rulers treat their subjects with unjust asperity, their rigour is still to be endured, nor is there just cause for shaking off the yoke, although they may exercise their power too imperiously. In short, whenever it comes into our mind to defraud any one of his right, or to seek exemption from our proper calling, let the voice of the angel sound in our ears, as if God would draw us back, by putting his own hand upon us. They who have proudly and tyrannically governed shall one day render their account to God; meanwhile, their asperity is to be borne by their subjects, till God, whose prerogative it is to raise the abject and to relieve the oppressed, shall give them succour. If a comparison be made, the power of magistrates is far more tolerable, than that ancient dominion was.[1] The paternal authority is in its very nature amiable, and worthy of regard. If the flight of Hagar was prohibited by the command of God, much less will he bear with the licentiousness of a people, who rebel against their prince; or with the contumacy of children, who withdraw themselves from obedience to their parents.

Whence camest thou? He does not inquire, as concerning a doubtful matter, but knowing that no place for subterfue

---

[1] For this ancient dominion implied slavery. The French translation has it, " Le droit des magistrats est bien plus tolerable, que n'a point este ceste ancienne domination *sur les serfs*."—*Ed.*

is left to Hagar, he peremptorily reproves her for her flight; as if he had said, ' Having deserted thy station, thou shalt profit nothing by thy wandering, since thou canst not escape the hand of God, which had placed thee there.' It might also be, that he censured her departure from that house, which was then the earthly sanctuary of God. For she was not ignorant that God was there worshipped in a peculiar manner. And although she indirectly charges her mistress with cruelty, by saying that she had fled from her presence; still the angel, to cut off all subterfuges, commands her to return and to humble herself. By which words he first intimates, that the bond of subjection is not dissolved either by the too austere, or by the impotent dominion of rulers; he then retorts the blame of the evil upon Hagar herself, because she had obstinately placed herself in opposition to her mistress, and, forgetful of her own condition, had exalted herself more insolently and boldly than became a bondmaid. In short, as she is justly punished for her faults, he commands her to seek a remedy by correcting them. And truly, since nothing is better than, by obedience and patience, to appease the severity of those who are in authority over us; we must more especially labour to bend them to mildness by our humiliation, when we have offended them by our pride.

10. *I will multiply thy seed exceedingly.* For the purpose of mitigating the offence, and of alleviating what was severe in the precept, by some consolation, he promises a blessing in the child which she should bear. God might indeed, by his own authority, have strictly enjoined what was right; but in order that Hagar might the more cheerfully do what she knew to be her duty, he allures her, as by blandishments, to obedience. And to this point those promises tend, by which he invites us to voluntary submission. For he would not draw us by servile methods, so that we should obey his commands by constraint; and therefore he mingles mild and paternal invitations with his commands, dealing with us liberally, as with sons. That the angel here promises to do what is peculiar to God alone, involves no absurdity, for it is sufficiently usual with God to invest his ministers whom he sends with his own character,

that the authority of their word may appear the greater. I do not, however, disapprove the opinion of most of the ancients; that Christ the Mediator was always present in all the oracles, and that this is the cause why the majesty of God is ascribed to angels.[1] On which subject I have already touched, and shall have occasion to say more elsewhere.

11. *And shalt bear a son.* The angel explains what he had briefly said respecting her seed; namely, that it should not be capable of being numbered on account of its multitude; and he commences with Ishmael, who was to be its head and origin. Although we shall afterwards see that he was a reprobate, yet an honourable name is granted to him, to mark the temporal benefit of which Ishmael became a partaker, as being a son of Abram. For I thus explain the passage, God intended that a monument of the paternal kindness, with which he embraced the whole house of Abram, should endure to posterity. For although the covenant of eternal life did not belong to Ishmael; yet, that he might not be entirely without favour, God constituted him the father of a great and famous people. And thus we see that, with respect to this present life, the goodness of God extended itself to the seed of Abram according to the flesh. But if God intended the name of Ishmael [which signifies God will hear] to be a perpetual memorial of his *temporal* benefits; he will by no means bear with our ingratitude, if we do not celebrate his *celestial* and *everlasting* mercies, even unto death.

The Lord hath heard thy affliction. We do not read that Hagar, in her difficulties, had recourse to prayer; and we are rather left to conjecture, from the words of Moses, that when she was stupified by her sufferings, the angel came of his own accord. It is therefore to be observed, that there are two ways in which God looks down upon men, for the purpose of helping them; either when they, as suppliants, implore his aid; or when he, even unasked, succours them in their afflictions. He is indeed especially said to hearken to them who,

[1] See on this subject, Smith's Scripture Testimony to the Messiah, Book II. chap. iv. sect. 33.—*Ed.*

by prayers, invoke him as their Deliverer. Yet, sometimes, when men lie mute, and because of their stupor, do not direct their wishes to him, he is said to listen to their miseries. That this latter mode of hearing was fulfilled towards Hagar, is probable, because God freely met her wandering through the desert. Moreover, because God frequently deprives unbelievers of his help, until they are worn away with slow disease, or else suffers them to be suddenly destroyed; let none of us give indulgence to our own sloth; but being admonished by the sense of our evils, let us seek him without delay. In the meantime, however, it is of no small avail to the confirmation of our faith, that our prayers will never be despised by the Lord, seeing that he anticipates even the slothful and the stupid, with his help; and if he is present to those who seek him not, much more will he be propitious to the pious desires of his own people.

12. *And he will be a wild man.* The angel declares what kind of person Ishmael will be. The simple meaning is, (in my judgment,) that he will be a warlike man, and so formidable to his enemies, that none shall injure him with impunity. Some expound the word פֶרֶא, (*pereh*,) to mean a forester, and one addicted to the hunting of wild beasts. But the explanation must not, it seems, be sought elsewhere than in the context; for it follows immediately after, ' His hand shall be against all men, and the hand of all men against him.' It is however asked, whether this ought to be reckoned among benefits conferred by God, that he is to preserve his rank in life by force of arms; seeing that nothing is, in itself, more desirable than peace. The difficulty may be thus solved; that Ishmael, although all his neighbours should make war upon him, and should, on every side, conspire to destroy him; shall yet, though alone, be endued with sufficient power to repel all their attacks. I think, however, that the angel, by no means, promises Ishmael complete favour, but only that which is limited. Among our chief blessings, we must desire to have peace with all men. Now, since this is denied to Ishmael, that blessing which is next in order is granted to him; namely, that he shall not be overcome by his enemies;

but shall be brave and powerful to resist their force. He does not, however, speak of Ishmael's person, but of his whole progeny; for what follows is not strictly suitable to one man. Should this exposition be approved, no simple or unmixed blessing is here promised; but only a tolerable or moderate condition; so that Ishmael and his posterity might perceive that something was divinely granted to them, for the sake of their father Abram. Therefore, it is, by no means, to be reckoned among the benefits given by God, that he shall have all around him as enemies, and shall resist them all by violence: but this is added as a remedy and an alleviation of the evil; that he, who would have many enemies, should be equal to bear up against them.

And he shall dwell in the presence of all his brethren. As this is properly applicable only to a nation, we hence the more easily perceive, that they are deceived who restrict the passage to the person of Ishmael. Again, others understand, that the posterity of Ishmael was to have a fixed habitation in the presence of their brethren, who would be unwilling to allow it; as if it were said, that they should forcibly occupy the land they inhabit, although their brethren might attempt to resist them. Others adduce a contrary opinion; namely, that the Ishmaelites, though living among a great number of enemies, should yet not be destitute of friends and brethren. I approve, however, of neither opinion: for the angel rather intimates, that this people should be separate from others; as if he would say, ' They shall not form a part or member of any one nation; but shall be a complete body, having a distinct and special name.'

13. *And she called the name of the Lord.* Moses, I have no doubt, implies that Hagar, after she was admonished by the angel, changed her mind: and being thus subdued, betook herself to prayer; unless, perhaps, here the confession of the tongue, rather than change of mind, is denoted. I rather incline, however, to the opinion, that Hagar, who had before been of a wild and intractable temper, begins now at length to acknowledge the providence of God. Moreover, as to that which some suppose; namely, that God is called ' the

God of vision,'[1] because he appears and manifests himself to men, it is a forced interpretation. Rather let us understand that Hagar, who before had appeared to herself to be carried away by chance, through the desert; now perceives and acknowledges that human affairs are under divine government. And whoever is persuaded that he is looked upon by God, must of necessity walk as in his sight.

Have I also here seen after him that seeth me?[2]   Some translate this, ' Have I not seen after the vision?'[3]   But it really is as I have rendered it. Moreover, the obscurity of the sentence has procured for us various interpretations. Some among the Hebrews say that Hagar was astonished at the sight of the angel ; because she thought that God was nowhere *seen* but in the house of Abram. But this is frigid, and in this way the ambition of the Jews often compels them to trifle ; seeing that they apply their whole study to boasting of the glory of their race. Others so understand the passage, 'Have I seen after my vision?' that is, so late, that during the vision I was blind ?[4]   According to these interpreters, the vision of Hagar was twofold : the former erroneous ; since she perceived nothing celestial in the angel ; but the other true, after she had been affected with a sense of the divine

[1] " Deum visionis." Though Calvin regards this interpretation as forced, it must not be denied that it has the sanction of the highest literary authorities. Le Clerc, Peter Martyr, Rosenmüller, Dathe, Gesenius, Lee, Professor Bush, and many others, all regard the word ראי, (*roi*,) as a *substantive*, not as a *participle*,—and consequently God is here spoken of as the God who *reveals himself*, not as the God *who sees*.—*Ed.*

[2] " Nonne etiam hic vidi post videntem me ?"   " Have I *not* also here looked after him who seeth me ?"

[3] " *Annon video*, (h. e. *vivo*,) *post videntem me, i. e.*, post visionem divinam, vel *post* visionem *videntis me ?*"   Do I not see, (that is, live,) after him who seeth me ? that is, after the divine vision, or after the vision of him that seeth me.—Junius, Piscator, &c., in *Poli Syn.*   Ainsworth gives this version, ' Have I also here seen after him that seeth me ?'   Where stress is laid on the word *here*, as is done by Calvin, for the purpose of contrasting the desert with Abram's house. The opinion, also, that the term ' see ' is equivalent to ' live,' is supported by high authority. The meaning of the passage would then be, ' Do I see, that is, live, after having beheld such a vision ?'—*Ed.*

[4] Vatablus in *Poli Syn.* Perhaps the following paraphrase may bring out the sense of this obscure interpretation. We may suppose Hagar to exclaim : ' Have I indeed seen at last ? yet, not till after the vision itself had passed away ; so that when I saw it literally, I was mentally blind, and did not know what I was looking at.'—*Ed.*

nature of the vision. To some it seems that a negative
answer is implied ; as if she would say, I did not see him
departing; and then from his sudden disappearance, she collects that he must have been an angel of God.

Also, on the second member of the sentence, interpreters
disagree. Jerome renders it, ' the back parts of him that
seeth me :'[1] which many refer to an obscure vision, so that
the phrase is deemed metaphorical. For as we do not plainly
perceive men from behind ; so they are said to see the back
parts of God, to whom he does not openly nor clearly manifest himself; and this opinion is commonly received. Others
think that Moses used a different figure ; for they take the
seeing of the back parts of God, for the sense of his anger ;
just as his face is said to shine upon us, when he shows himself propitious and favourable.   Therefore, according to
them, the sense is, ' I thought that I had escaped, so that I
should no more be obnoxious to the rod or chastening of
God ; but here also I perceive that he is angry with me.
So far I have briefly related the opinion of others.[2] And although I have no intention to pause for the purpose of refut-
ing each of these expositions; I yet freely declare, that not
one of these interpreters has apprehended the meaning of
Moses. I willingly accept what some adduce, that Hagar
wondered at the goodness of God, by whom she had been
regarded even in the desert : but this, though something, is
not the whole. In the first place, Hagar chides herself, because, as she had before been too blind, she even now opened
her eyes too slowly and indolently to perceive God. For
she aggravates the guilt of her torpor by the circumstance
both of place and time. She had frequently found, by many
proofs, that she was regarded by the Lord; yet becoming
blind, she had despised his providence, as if, with closed eyes,
she had passed by him, when he presented himself before her.
She now accuses herself for not having more quickly awoke
when the angel appeared. The consideration of place is also

[1] See Vulgate.
[2] These different interpretations, with others, may be seen in Poole's
Synopsis.—*Ed.*

of great weight,[1] because God, who had always testified that
he was present with her in the house of Abram, now pursued
her as a fugitive, even into the desert. It implied, indeed,
a base ingratitude on her part, to be blind to the presence of
God; so that even when she knew he was looking upon her,
she did not, in return, raise her eyes to behold him. But it
was a still more shameful blindness, that she, being regarded
by the Lord, although a wanderer and an exile, paying the just
penalty of her perverseness, still would not even acknowledge him as present. We now see the point to which her
self-reproach tends ; ' Hitherto I have not sought God, nor
had respect to him, except by constraint; whereas, he had
before deigned to look down upon me : even now in the
desert, where being afflicted with evils, I ought immediately
to have roused myself, I have, according to my custom, been
stupified : nor should I ever have raised my eyes towards
heaven, unless I had first been looked upon by the Lord.'

14. *Wherefore the well was called.*[2] I subscribe to the
opinion of those who take the word יִקְרָא, *(yekra,)* indefinitely, which is usual enough in the Hebrew language. In
order that the sense may be the clearer, it is capable of being
resolved into the passive voice, that ' the well was called.'[3]
Yet I think this common appellation originated with Hagar,
who, not content with one simple confession, wished that the
mercy of God should be attested in time to come ; and therefore she transmitted her testimony, as from hand to hand.
Hence we infer how useful it is, that they who do not freely
humble themselves, should be subdued by stripes. Hagar,
who had always been wild and rebellious, and who had, at
length, entirely shaken off the yoke ; now, when the hardness of her heart was broken by afflictions, appears altogether another person. She was not, however, reduced to
order by stripes only ; but a celestial vision was also added,

---

[1] " Loci enim notatio," is in the French translation rendered, " Le
changement du lieu." The change of place, as if it had been mutatio.—*Ed.*
[2] " Idcirco vocavit puteum, Puteum viventis videntis me." "Therefore she called the well, The well of him who liveth and seeth me."
[3] As in the English version.

which thoroughly arrested her.   And the same thing is necessary for us; namely, that God, while chastising us with his hand, should also bring us into a state of submissive meekness by his Spirit.   Some among the Hebrews say that the name of the well was given to it, as being a testimony of a twofold favour, because Ishmael was revived from death, and God had respect to Hagar, his mother.   But they foolishly mutilate things joined together: for Hagar wished to testify that she had been favourably regarded by Him who was the Living God, or the Author of life.

15. *And Abram called.* Hagar had been commanded to give that name to her son; but Moses follows the order of nature; because fathers, by the imposition of the name, declare the power which they have over their sons. We may easily gather, that Hagar, when she returned home, related the events which had occurred.   Therefore, Abram shows himself to be obedient and grateful to God: because he both names his son according to the command of the angel, and celebrates the goodness of God in having hearkened to the miseries of Hagar.

CHAPTER XVII.

1. AND when Abram was ninety years old and nine, the Lord appeared to Abram, and said unto him, I *am* the Almighty God; walk before me, and be thou perfect.

2. And I will make my covenant between me and thee, and will multiply thee exceedingly.

3. And Abram fell on his face: and God talked with him, saying,

4. As for me, behold, my covenant *is* with thee, and thou shalt be a father of many nations.

5. Neither shall thy name any more be called Abram, but thy name shall be

1. Et fuit Abram nonaginta et novem annorum: et visus est Jehova Abram, dixitque ad eum, Ego Deus Omnipotens, ambula coram me, et esto perfectus.

2. Et ponam pactum meum inter me et te, et multiplicabo te vehementissime.

3. Tunc prostravit se Abram super faciem suam, et loquutus est cum eo Deus, dicendo,

4. Ego, ecce pactum meum tecum, et eris in patrem multitudinis gentium.

5. Et non vocabitur ultra nomen tuum Abram, sed erit

Abraham; for a father of many nations have I made thee.

6. And I will make thee exceeding fruitful, and I will make nations of thee, and kings shall come out of thee.

7. And I will establish my covenant between me and thee, and thy seed after thee, in their generations, for an everlasting covenant, to be a God unto thee, and to thy seed after thee.

8. And I will give unto thee, and to thy seed after thee, the land wherein thou art a stranger, all the land of Canaan, for an everlasting possession; and I will be their God.

9. And God said unto Abraham, Thou shalt keep my covenant therefore, thou, and thy seed after thee, in their generations.

10. This *is* my covenant, which ye shall keep, between me and you, and thy seed after thee; Every man-child among you shall be circumcised.

11. And ye shall circumcise the flesh of your foreskin; and it shall be a token of the covenant betwixt me and you.

12. And he that is eight days old shall be circumcised among you, every man-child in your generations, he that is born in the house, or bought with money of any stranger, which *is* not of thy seed.

13. He that is born in thy house, and he that is bought with thy money, must needs be circumcised: and my covenant shall be in your flesh for an everlasting covenant.

14. And the uncircumcised man-child, whose flesh of his foreskin is not circumcised, that soul shall be cut off from his people; he hath broken my covenant.

15. And God said unto Abraham, As for Sarai thy wife, thou shalt not call her name Sarai, but Sarah *shall* her name *be*.

16. And I will bless her, and give thee a son also of her: yea, I will bless her, and she shall be *a mother* of nations; kings of people shall be of her.

17. Then Abraham fell upon his face, and laughed, and said in his heart, Shall *a child* be born unto him that is an hun-

nomen tuum Abraham: quia patrem multitudinis gentium posui te.

6. Et multiplicabo te valde, et ponam te in gentes, et reges ex te egredientur.

7. Et statuam fœdus meum inter me et te, et inter semen tuum post te in generationes suas, in fœdus perpetuum, ut sim tibi in Deum et semini tuo post te.

8. Daboque tibi et semini tuo post te terram peregrinationum tuarum, omnem terram Chenaan in possessionem perpetuam, et ero eis in Deum.

9. Præterea dixit Deus ad Abraham, et tu pactum meum custodies, tu et semen tuum post te in generationibus suis.

10. Hoc pactum meum quod custodietis inter me et vos, et inter semen tuum post te, ut circumcidatur in vobis omnis masculus:

11. Et circumcidetis carnem præputii vestri: et erit in signum fœderis inter me et vos.

12. Et filius octo dierum circumcidetur in vobis: omnis masculus in generationes vestras, verna, et emptus argento ab omni filio alienigenæ, qui non est de semine tuo.

13. Circumcidendo circumcidetur verna tuus, et emptus argento tuo: et erit pactum meum in carne vestra in pactum perpetuum.

14. Et præputiatus masculus, cui non circumcisa fuerit carno præputii sui, exterminabitur anima ipsa de populis suis, quia pactum meum irritum fecit.

15. Et dixit Deus ad Abraham, Sarai uxoris tuæ non vocabis nomen Sarai, sed Sarah est nomen ejus.

16. Et benedicam ei, atque etiam dabo ex ea tibi filium, cui benedicam, et erit in gentes: reges populorum ex ea erunt.

17. Et prostravit se Abraham in faciem suam, et risit, dixitque in corde suo, Numquid

dred years old? and shall Sarah, that is ninety years' old, bear?

18. And Abraham said unto God, O that Ishmael might live before thee!

19. And God said, Sarah thy wife shall bear thee a son indeed; and thou shalt call his name Isaac: and I will establish my covenant with him for an everlasting covenant, *and* with his seed after him.

20. And as for Ishmael, I have heard thee: Behold, I have blessed him, and will make him fruitful, and will multiply him exceedingly; twelve princes shall he beget, and I will make him a great nation.

21. But my covenant will I establish with Isaac, which Sarah shall bear unto thee at this set time in the next year.

22. And he left off talking with him, and God went up from Abraham.

23. And Abraham took Ishmael his son, and all that were born in his house, and all that were bought with his money, every male among the men of Abraham's house; and circumcised the flesh of their foreskin in the self-same day, as God had said unto him.

24. And Abraham *was* ninety years old and nine when he was circumcised in the flesh of his foreskin.

25. And Ishmael his son *was* thirteen years old when he was circumcised in the flesh of his foreskin.

26. In the self-same day was Abraham circumcised, and Ishmael his son.

27. And all the men of his house, born in the house, and bought with money of the stranger, were circumcised with him.

viro centum annorum nascetur proles? et an Sarah mulier nonaginta annorum pariet?

18. Et dixit Abraham ad Deum, Utinam Ismael vivat coram te.

19. Et dixit Deus, Vere Sarah uxor tua pariet tibi filium, et vocabis nomen ejus Isaac: et statuam pactum meum cum eo in pactum perpetuum, et cum semine ejus post eum.

20. Et pro Ismael audivi te: ecce, benedixi ei, et crescere faciam eum, et multiplicare faciam eum supra modum: duodecim principes generabit, et ponam eum in gentem magnam.

21. Et pactum meum statuam cum Isaac, quem pariet tibi Sarah in tempore hoc, anno altero.

22. Et finivit loqui cum eo, et ascendit Deus ab Abraham.

23. Tunc Abraham tulit Ismael filium suum, et omnes vernas domus suæ, et omnem acquisitum argento suo: omnis masculi in viris domus suæ circumcidit carnem præputii eorum in ipsomet die, sicut loquutus fuerat cum eo Deus.

24. Abraham autem vir nonaginta et novem annorum, quando circumcisa fuit carno præputii ipsius.

25. Et Ismael filius ejus erat tredecim annorum, quando circumcisus est ipse in carne præputii sui,

26. In ipsomet die circumcisus est Abraham et Ismael filius ejus.

27. Et omnes viri domus ejus, verna domus, et emptus argento a filio alienigenæ, circumcisi sunt cum ipso.

1. *And when Abram was ninety years old and nine.* Moses passes over thirteen years of Abram's life, not because nothing worthy of remembrance had in the meantime occurred; but because the Spirit of God, according to his own will, selects those things which are most necessary to be known. He

purposely points out the length of time which had elapsed from the birth of Ishmael to the period when Isaac was promised, for the purpose of teaching us that he long remained satisfied with that son who should, at length, be rejected, and that he was as one deluded by a fallacious appearance. Meanwhile, we see in what a circuitous course the Lord led him. It was even possible that he brought this delay upon himself, by his own fault, in having precipitately entered into second nuptials; yet as Moses declares no such thing, I leave it undetermined. Let it suffice to accept what is certain; namely, that Abram being contented with his only son, ceased to desire any other seed. The want of offspring had previously excited him to constant prayers and sighings; for the promise of God was so fixed in his mind, that he was ardently carried forward to seek its fulfilment. And now, falsely supposing that he had obtained his wish, he is led away by the presence of his son according to the flesh, from the expectation of a spiritual seed. Again the wonderful goodness of God shows itself, in that Abram himself is raised, beyond his own expectation and desire, to a new hope, and he suddenly hears, that what it never came into his mind to ask, is granted unto him. If he had been daily offering up importunate prayers for this blessing, we should not so plainly have seen that it was conferred upon him by the free gift of God, as when it is given to him without his either thinking of it or desiring it. Before however we speak of Isaac, it will repay our labour, to notice the order and connection of the words.

First, Moses says that the Lord *appeared* unto him, in order that we may know that the oracle was not pronounced by secret revelation, but that a vision at the same time was added to it. Besides, the vision was not speechless, but had the word annexed, from which word the faith of Abram might receive profit. Now that word summarily contains this declaration, that God enters into covenant with Abram: it then unfolds the nature of the covenant itself, and finally puts to it the seal, with the accompanying attestations.

I am the Almighty God.[1] The Hebrew noun *El*, which is

---

[1] אל שדי, (*El Shaddai*,) a title of Jehovah, apparently of plural form. Gesenius calls it *the plural of majesty*. It seems chiefly intended to con-

derived from power, is here put for God.   The same remark applies to the accompanying word שַׁדַּי, (*shaddai*,) as if God would declare, that he had sufficient power for Abram's protection: because our faith can only stand firmly, while we are certainly persuaded that the defence of God is alone sufficient for us, and can sincerely despise everything in the world which is opposed to our salvation.   God, therefore, does not boast of that power which lies concealed within himself; but of that which he manifests towards his children; and he does so, in order that Abram might hence derive materials for confidence.   Thus, in these words, a promise is included.

Walk before me.   The force of this expression we have elsewhere explained.   In making the covenant, God stipulates for obedience, on the part of his servant.   Yet He does not in vain prefix the declaration that he is ' the Almighty God,' and is furnished with power to help his own people: because it was necessary that Abram should be recalled from all other means of help,[1] that he might entirely devote himself to God alone.   For no one will ever betake himself to God, but he who keeps created things in their proper place, and looks up to God alone.   Where, indeed, the power of God has been once acknowledged, it ought so to transport us with admiration, and our minds ought so to be filled with reverence for him, that nothing should hinder us from worshipping him.   Moreover, because the eyes of God look for faith and truth in the heart, Abram is commanded to aim at integrity. For the Hebrews call him a *man of perfections*, who is not of a deceitful or double mind, but sincerely cultivates rectitude. In short, the integrity here mentioned is opposed, to hypocrisy.   And surely, when we have to deal with God, no place for dissimulation remains.   Now, from these words, we learn for what end God gathers together for himself a church;

---

vey the notion of *Omnipotence*.   Some render the words, ' God all-sufficient ;' but the original root of שַׁדַּי conveys the notion, rather of overwhelming, than of sustaining power.   The word is therefore better rendered, as in our version, *Almighty*.   It corresponds with the Greek παντοκράτωρ, and with the Latin *Omnipotens.—Ed.*

[1] " Ab aliis omnibus."   " De tous autres moyens."   "From all other means."—*French Tr.*

namely, that they whom he has called, may be holy. The foundation, indeed, of the divine calling, is a gratuitous promise; but it follows immediately after, that they whom he has chosen as a peculiar people to himself, should devote themselves to the righteousness of God.[1] For on this condition, he adopts children as his own, that he may, in return, obtain the place and the honour of a Father. And as he himself cannot lie, so he rightly demands mutual fidelity from his own children. Wherefore, let us know, that God manifests himself to the faithful, in order that they may live as in his sight; and may make him the arbiter not only of their works, but of their thoughts. Whence also we infer, that there is no other method of living piously and justly, than that of depending upon God.

2. *And I will make my covenant.* He now begins more fully and abundantly to explain what he had before alluded to briefly. We have said that the covenant of God with Abram had two parts. The first was a declaration of gratuitous love; to which was annexed the promise of a happy life. But the other was an exhortation to the sincere endeavour to cultivate uprightness, since God had given, in a single word only, a slight taste of his grace; and then immediately had descended to the design of his calling; namely, that Abram should be upright. He now subjoins a more ample declaration of his grace, in order that Abram may endeavour more willingly to form his mind and his life, both to reverence towards God, and to the cultivation of uprightness; as if God had said, ' See how kindly I indulge thee : for I do not require integrity from thee simply on account of my authority, which I might justly do; but whereas I owe thee nothing, I condescend graciously to engage in a mutual covenant.' He does not, however, speak of this as of a new thing : but he recalls the memory of the covenant which he had before made, and now fully confirms and establishes its certainty. For God is

---

[1] " Yield yourselves unto God, as those that are alive from the dead, and your members as instruments of righteousness unto God." Rom. vi. 13.—*Ed.*

not wont to utter new oracles, which may destroy the credit, or obscure the light, or weaken the efficacy of those which preceded ; but he continues, as in one perpetual tenor, those promises which he has once given. Therefore, by these words, he intends nothing else than that the covenant, of which Abram had heard before, should be established and ratified : but he expressly introduces that principal point, concerning the multiplication of seed, which he afterwards frequently repeats.

3. *And Abram fell on his face.* We know that this was the ancient rite of adoration. Moreover, Abram testifies, first, that he acknowledges God, in whose presence all flesh ought to keep silence, and to be humbled ; and, secondly, that he reverently receives and cordially embraces whatever God is about to speak. If, however, this was intended as a confession of faith, we must observe, that the faith which relies upon the grace of God cannot be disjoined from a pure conscience. God, in offering his grace to Abram, requires of him a sincere disposition to live justly and holily. Abram, in prostrating himself, declares that he obediently receives both.[1] Let us therefore remember, that in one and the same bond of faith, the gratuitous adoption in which our salvation is placed, is to be combined with newness of life. And although Abram utters not a word, he declares more fully by his silence, than if he had spoken with a loud and sounding voice, that he yields obedience to the word of God.

4. *As for me, behold, my covenant is with thee.*[2] They who translate the passage, ' Behold, I make a covenant with thee,' or, ' Behold, I and my covenant with thee ;' do not seem to me faithfully to represent the meaning of Moses. For, first, God declares that he is the speaker, in order that absolute authority may appear in his words. For since our faith can rest on no other foundation than his eternal veracity, it

---

[1] That is, both the promise of grace, and the command to yield obedience.—*Ed.*

[2] " Ego, ecce pactum meum tecum." " I, behold, my covenant is with thee."

becomes, above all things, necessary for us to be informed that what is proposed to us, has proceeded from his sacred mouth. Therefore, the pronoun I, is to be read separately, as a preface to the rest; in order that Abram might have a composed mind, and might engage, without hesitation, in the proposed covenant. Whence a useful doctrine is deduced, that faith necessarily has reference to God: because, although all angels and men should speak to us, never would their authority appear sufficiently great to confirm our minds. And it cannot but be, that we should at times waver, until that voice sounds from heaven, ' I am.' Whence also it appears what kind of religion is that of the Papacy: where, instead of the word of God, the fictions of men are alone the subject of boast. And they are justly exposed to continual fluctuation, who, depending upon the word of men, act unjustly towards God, by ascribing to them more than is right. But let us have no other foundation of our faith than this word ' I,' not as spoken indifferently by any mouth whatever, but by the mouth of God alone. If, however, myriads of men set themselves in opposition, and proudly exclaim, ' We, we,' let this single word of God suffice to dissipate the empty sound of multitudes.

And thou shalt be a father of many nations.[1] It is asked, what is this multitude of nations? It obviously appears, that different nations had their origin from the holy Patriarch: for Ishmael grew to a great people: the Idumeans, from another branch, were spread far and wide; large families also sprung from other sons, whom he had by Keturah. But Moses looked still further, because, indeed, the Gentiles were to be, by faith, inserted into the stock of Abram, although not descended from him according to the flesh: of which fact Paul is to us a faithful interpreter and witness. For he does not gather together the Arabians, Idumeans, and others, for the purpose of making Abram the father of many nations; but he so extends the name of father, as to make it applicable to the whole world, in order that the Gentiles, in other respects strangers, and separated from each other, might, from all sides,

---

[1] "Multitudinis gentium." "Of a multitude of nations."

combine in one family of Abram. I grant, indeed, that, for a time, the twelve tribes were as so many nations ; but only in order to form a prelude to that immense multitude, which, at length, is collected together as the one family of Abram. And that Moses speaks of those sons, who, being regenerate by faith, acquire the name, and pass over into the stock of Abram, is sufficiently proved by this one consideration. For the carnal race of Abram could not be divided into different nations, without causing those who had departed from the unity, to be immediately accounted strangers. Thus the Church rejected the Ishmaelites, the Idumeans, and others, and regarded them as foreigners. Abram therefore was not called the father of many nations, because his seed was to be divided into many nations ; but rather, because many nations were to be gathered together unto him. . A change also of his name is added as a token. For he begins to be called *Abraham*, in order that the name itself may teach him, that he should not be the father of one family only; but that a progeny should rise up to him from an immense multitude, beyond the common course of nature. For this reason, the Lord so often renews this promise ; because the very repetition of it shows that no common blessing was promised.

7. *And thy seed after thee.* There is no doubt that the Lord distinguishes the race of Abraham from the rest of the world. We must now see what people he intends. Now they are deceived who think that his elect alone are here pointed out; and that all the faithful are indiscriminately comprehended, from whatever people, according to the flesh, they are descended. For, on the contrary, the Scripture declares that the race of Abraham, by lineal descent, had been peculiarly accepted by God. And it is the evident doctrine of Paul concerning the natural descendants of Abraham, that they are holy branches which have proceeded from a holy root, (Rom. xi. 16.) And lest any one should restrict this assertion to the shadows of the law, or should evade it by allegory, he elsewhere expressly declares, that Christ came to be a minister of the circumcision, (Rom. xv. 8.) Wherefore, nothing is more certain, than that God made his covenant

with those sons of Abraham who were naturally to be born
of him. If any one object, that this opinion by no means
agrees with the former, in which we said that they are reckoned the children of Abraham, who being by faith ingrafted
into his body, form one family ; the difference is easily reconciled, by laying down certain distinct degrees of adoption,
which may be collected from various passages of Scripture.
In the beginning, antecedently to this covenant, the condition of the whole world was one and the same. But as soon
as it was said, ' I will be a God to thee and to thy seed after
thee,' the Church was separated from other nations ; just as
in the creation of the world, the light emerged out of the
darkness. Then the people of Israel was received, as the
flock of God, into their own fold : the other nations wandered, like wild beasts, through mountains, woods, and deserts. Since this dignity, in which the sons of Abraham excelled other nations, depended on the word of God alone, the
gratuitous adoption of God belongs to them all in common.
For if Paul deprives the Gentiles of God and of eternal life,
on the ground of their being aliens from the covenant, (Eph.
iv. 18,) it follows that all Israelites were of the household of
the Church, and sons of God, and heirs of eternal life. And
although it was by the grace of God, and not by nature,
that they excelled the Gentiles ; and although the inheritance of the kingdom of God came to them by promise,
and not by carnal descent ; yet they are sometimes said to
differ by nature from the rest of the world. In the Epistle
to the Galatians, chap. ii. ver. 15, and elsewhere, Paul calls
them saints ' by nature,' because God was willing that his
grace should descend,[1] by a continual succession, to the
whole seed. In this sense, they who were unbelievers
among the Jews, are yet called the children of the celestial
kingdom, by Christ. (Matth. viii. 12.) Nor does what St Paul
says contradict this ; namely, that not all who are from Abraham are to be esteemed legitimate children ; because they

[1] " Quia continua serie prosequi *nolebat* Deus, gratiam suam ergo
totum semen." So it is, both in the Amsterdam edition, and in that of
Hengstenberg ; but the word nolebat (was *unwilling*) seems so contrary
to the writer's line of argument, that the French version is followed in
the translation, which is," Pource que Dieu *vouloit* poursuyure," &c.—*Ed.*

are not the children of the promise, but only of the flesh. (Rom. ix. 8.) For there, the promise is not taken generally for that outward word, by which God conferred his favour as well upon the reprobate as upon the elect; but must be restricted to that efficacious calling, which he inwardly seals by his Spirit. And that this is the case, is proved without difficulty; for the promise by which the Lord had adopted them all as children, was common to all: and in that promise, it cannot be denied, that eternal salvation was offered to all. What, therefore, can be the meaning of Paul, when he denies that certain persons have any right to be reckoned among children, except that he is no longer reasoning about the externally offered grace, but about that of which only the elect effectually partake? Here, then, a twofold class of sons presents itself to us, in the Church; for since the whole body of the people is gathered together into the fold of God, by one and the same voice, all without exception, are, in this respect, accounted children; the name of the Church is applicable in common to them all : but in the innermost sanctuary of God, none others are reckoned the sons of God, than they in whom the promise is ratified by faith. And although this difference flows from the fountain of gratuitous election, whence also faith itself springs; yet, since the counsel of God is in itself hidden from us, we therefore distinguish the true from the spurious children, by the respective marks of faith and of unbelief. This method and dispensation continued even to the promulgation of the gospel; but then the middle wall was broken down, (Ephes. ii. 14,) and God made the Gentiles equal to the natural descendants of Abraham. That was the renovation of the world, by which they, who had before been strangers, began to be called sons. Yet whenever a comparison is made between Jews and Gentiles, the inheritance of life is assigned to the former, as lawfully belonging to them; but to the latter, it is said to be adventitious. Meanwhile, the oracle was fulfilled, in which God promises that Abraham should be the father of many nations. For whereas previously, the natural sons of Abraham were succeeded by their descendants in continual succession, and the benediction, which began with him, flowed down to his children; the coming of Christ, by inverting the original order, introduced into his

family those who before were separated from his seed : at
length the Jews were cast out, (except that a hidden seed of
the election remained among them,) in order that the rest
might be saved. It was necessary that these things concerning
the seed of Abraham should once be stated, that they may
open to us an easy introduction to what follows.

In their generations. This succession of generations clearly
proves that the posterity of Abraham were taken into the
Church, in such a manner that sons might be born to them,
who should be heirs of the same grace. In this way the
covenant is called perpetual, as lasting until the renovation of
the world ; which took place at the advent of Christ. I grant,
indeed, that the covenant was without end, and may with
propriety be called eternal, as far as the whole Church is
concerned ; it must, however, always remain as a settled
point, that the regular succession of ages was partly broken,
and partly changed, by the coming of Christ, because the
middle wall being broken down, and the sons by nature being,
at length, disinherited, Abraham began to have a race associated with himself, from all regions of the world.

To be a God unto thee. In this single word we are plainly
taught, that this was a spiritual covenant, not confirmed in
reference to the present life only; but one from which Abraham
might conceive the hope of eternal salvation, so that being
raised even to heaven, he might lay hold of solid and perfect bliss. For those whom God adopts to himself, from
among a people—seeing that he makes them partakers of his
righteousness and of all good things—he also constitutes heirs
of celestial life. Let us then mark this as the principal part
of the covenant, that He who is the God of the living, not
of the dead, promises to be a God to the children of Abraham.
It follows afterwards, in the way of augmentation of the grant,
that he promises to give them the land. I confess, indeed,
that something greater and more excellent than itself was
shadowed forth by the land of Canaan; yet this is not at
variance with the statement, that the promise now made
was an accession to that primary one, 'I will be thy God.'
Now, although God again affirms, as before, that He will
give the land to Abraham himself, we nevertheless know,
that Abraham never possessed dominion over it; but the

holy man was contented with his title to it alone, although
the possession of it was not granted him; and, therefore, he
calmly passed from his earthly pilgrimage into heaven. God
again repeats that He will be a God to the posterity of
Abraham, in order that they may not settle upon earth, but
may regard themselves as trained for higher things.

  9. *Thou shalt keep my covenant.* As formerly, covenants
were not only committed to public records, but were also
wont to be engraven in brass, or sculptured on stones, in
order that the memory of them might be more fully recorded,
and more highly celebrated; so in the present instance,
God inscribes his covenant in the flesh of Abraham. For
circumcision was as a solemn memorial of that adoption, by
which the family of Abraham had been elected to be the
peculiar people of God. The pious had previously possessed
other ceremonies, which confirmed to them the certainty of
the grace of God; but now the Lord attests the new covenant with a new kind of symbol. But the reason why He
suffered the human race to be without this testimony of his
grace, during so many ages, is concealed from us; except that
we see it was instituted at the time when he chose a certain
nation to himself; which thing itself depends on his secret
counsel. Moreover, although it would, perhaps, be more suitable for the purpose of instruction, were we to give a summary of those things which are to be said concerning circumcision; I will yet follow the order of the text, which I
think more appropriate to the office of an interpreter. In the
first place; since circumcision is called, by Moses, the covenant
of God, we thence infer that the promise of grace was included
in it. For had it been only a mark or token of external profession among men, the name of covenant would be by no
means suitable, for a covenant is not otherwise confirmed,
than as faith answers to it. And it is common to all sacraments to have the word of God annexed to them, by which
he testifies that he is propitious to us, and calls us to the hope
of salvation; yea, a sacrament is nothing else than a visible
word, or sculpture and image of that grace of God, which the
word more fully illustrates. If, then, there is a mutual relation

between the word and faith; it follows, that the proposed end and use of sacraments is to help, promote and confirm faith. But they who deny that sacraments are supports to faith, or that they aid the word in strengthening faith, must of necessity expunge the name of covenant; because, either God there offers himself as a Promiser, in mockery and falsely, or else, faith there finds that on which it may support itself, and from which it may confirm its own assurance. And although we must maintain the distinction between the word and the sign; yet let us know, that as soon as the sign itself meets our eyes, the word ought to sound in our ears. Therefore, while, in this place, Abraham is commanded to keep the covenant, God does not enjoin upon him the bare use of the ceremony, but chiefly designs that he should regard the end; and certainly, since the promise is the very soul of the sign, whenever it is torn away from the sign, nothing remains but a lifeless and vain phantom. This is the reason why we say, that sacraments are abolished by the Papists; because, the voice of God having become extinct, nothing remains with them, except the residuum of mute figures. Truly frivolous is their boast, that their magical exorcisms stand in the place of the word. For nothing can be called a covenant, but what is perceived by us to be clearly revealed, so that it may edify our faith; these actors, who by gesture alone, or by a confused murmuring, play as on pipes, have nothing like this.

We now consider how the covenant is rightly kept; namely, when the word precedes, and we embrace the sign as a testimony and pledge of grace; for as God binds himself to keep the promise given to us; so the consent of faith and of obedience is demanded from us. What follows further on this subject is worthy of notice.

Between me and you.[1] Whereby we are taught that a sacrament has not respect only to the external confession, but is an intervening pledge between God and the conscience of man. And, therefore, whosoever is not directed to God through the sacraments, profanes their use. But by the figure meto-

---

[1] 'Inter me et te.' But in the chapter itself it stands, 'Inter me et vos;' as in the English version.—*Ed.*

nymy, the name of covenant is transferred to circumcision, which is so conjoined with the word, that it could not be separated from it.

10. *Every man-child among you shall be circumcised.* Although God promised, alike to males and females, what he afterwards sanctioned by circumcision, he nevertheless consecrated, in one sex, the whole people to himself. For whereas, by this symbol, the promise which was given, indiscriminately, to males and females, is confirmed, and it is certain that females as well as males had need of confirmation, it is hence evident, that the symbol was ordained for the sake of both sexes. Nor is it of any force in opposition to this reasoning, to say that each individual is commanded to communicate in the sacraments, if he would derive any benefit from them, on the ground that no profit is received by those who neglect their use. For the covenant of God was graven on the bodies of the males, with this condition annexed, that the females also should as their associates be partakers of the same sign.

11. *Ye shall circumcise the flesh of your foreskin.* Very strange and unaccountable would this command at first sight appear. The subject treated of, is the sacred covenant, in which righteousness, salvation, and happiness are promised ; whereby the seed of Abraham is distinguished from other nations, in order that it may be holy and blessed; and who can say that it is reasonable for the sign of so great a mystery to consist in circumcision ?[1] But as it was necessary for Abraham to become a fool, in order to prove himself obedient to God; so whosoever is wise, will both soberly and reverently receive what God seems to us foolishly to have commanded. And yet we must inquire, whether any analogy is here apparent between the visible sign, and the thing signified. For the signs which God has appointed to assist our infirmity, should be accommodated to the measure of our capacity, or they would be unprofitable. Moreover, it is probable that the Lord commanded circumcision for two reasons; first, to show that

---

[1] "Tanti mysterii insigne statui in pudendis partibus."

whatever is born of man is polluted; then, that salvation would proceed from the blessed seed of Abraham. In the first place, therefore, whatever men have peculiar to themselves, by generation, God has condemned, in the appointment of circumcision; in order that the corruption of nature being manifest, he might induce them to mortify their flesh. Whence also it follows, that circumcision was a sign of repentance. Yet, at the same time, the blessing which was promised in the seed of Abraham, was thereby marked and attested. If then it seem absurd to any one, that the token of a favour so excellent and so singular, was given in that part of the body, let him become ashamed of his own salvation, which flowed from the loins of Abraham; but it has pleased God thus to confound the wisdom of the world, that he may the more completely abase the pride of the flesh. And hence we now learn, in the second place, how the reconciliation between God and men, which was exhibited in Christ, was testified by this sign. For which reason it is styled by Paul a seal of the righteousness of faith. (Rom. iv. 11.) Let it suffice thus briefly to have touched upon the analogy between the thing signified and the sign.

12. *And he that is eight days old shall be circumcised.*[1] God now prescribes the eighth day for circumcision; whence it appears that this was a part of that discipline, under which he intended to keep his ancient people; for greater liberty is, at this day, permitted in the administration of baptism. Some, however, maintain that we must not contend earnestly about the number of days, because the Lord spared the children on account of their tenderness, since it was not without danger to inflict a wound upon those who were newly born. For although he might have provided that circumcision should produce no harm or injury; yet there would be no absurdity in saying, that He had respect to their tender age, in order to prove to the Jews his paternal love towards their children. To others this seems to be too frigid; therefore they seek a spiritual mystery in the number of days. They think that

---

[1] " Et filius octo dierum circumcidetur."—" And a son of eight days shall be circumcised."

the present life is allegorically signified by the seven days; that God commanded infants to be circumcised on the eighth day, in order to show that though we must give attention to the mortification of the flesh during the whole course of our life, it will not be completed till the end. Augustine also thinks that it had reference to the resurrection of Christ; whereby external circumcision was abolished, and the truth of the figure was set forth. It is probable and consonant with reason, that the number seven designated the course of the present life. Therefore the eighth day might seem to be fixed upon by the Lord, to prefigure the beginning of a new life. But because such a reason is never given in Scripture, I dare affirm nothing. Wherefore, let it suffice to maintain what is certain and solid; namely, that God, in this symbol, has so represented the destruction of the old man, as yet to show that he restores men to life.

He that is born in the house, or bought with money. When God commands Abraham to circumcise all whom he has under his power, his special love towards holy Abraham is conspicuous in this, that He embraces his whole family in His grace. We know that formerly slaves were scarcely reckoned among the number of men. But God, out of regard to his servant Abraham, adopts them as his own sons: to this mercy nothing whatever can be added. The pride also of the flesh is cast down; because God, without respect of persons, gathers together both freemen and slaves. But in the person of Abraham, he has prescribed it as a law to all his servants, that they should endeavour to bring all who are subject to them, into the same society of faith with themselves. For every family of the pious ought to be a church. Therefore, if we desire to prove our piety, we must labour that every one of us may have his house ordered in obedience to God. And Abraham is not only commanded to dedicate and to offer unto God those born in his house, but whomsoever he might afterwards obtain.

13. *For an everlasting covenant.* The meaning of this expression may be twofold: either that God promises that his grace, of which circumcision was a sign and pledge, should

be eternal; or that he intended the sign itself to be perpetually observed. Indeed, I have no doubt that this perpetuity
ought to be referred to the visible sign. But they who hence
infer, that the use of it ought to flourish among the Jews even
of the present time, are (in my opinion) deceived. For they
swerve from that axiom which we ought to regard as fixed;
that since Christ is the end of the law, the perpetuity which
is ascribed to the ceremonies of the law, was terminated as
soon as Christ appeared. The temple was the perpetual
habitation of God, according to that declaration, "This is
my rest for ever, here will I dwell," (Ps. cxxxii. 14.) The
Sabbath indicated not a temporal but a perpetual sanctification of the people. Nevertheless, it is not to be denied, that
Christ brought them both to an end. In the same way must
we also think of circumcision. If the Jews object, that in
this manner, the law was violated by Christ; the answer is
easy; that the external use of the law was so abrogated, as
to establish its truth. For, at length, by the coming of
Christ, circumcision was substantially confirmed, so that it
should endure for ever, and that the covenant which God
had before made, should be ratified. Moreover, lest the
changing of the visible sign should perplex any one, let that
renovation of the world, of which I have spoken, be kept in
mind; which renovation—notwithstanding some interposed
variety—has perpetuated those things which would otherwise
have been fading. Therefore, although the use of circumcision
has ceased; yet it does not cease to be an everlasting, or perpetual covenant, if only Christ be regarded as the Mediator;
who, though the sign be changed, has confirmed the truth.
And that, by the coming of Christ, external circumcision
ceased, is plain from the words of Paul; who not only teaches
that we are circumcised by the death of Christ, spiritually,
and not through the carnal sign: but who expressly substitutes
baptism for circumcision; (Col. ii. 11;) and truly baptism
could not succeed circumcision, without taking it away.
Therefore in the next chapter he denies that there is any
difference between circumcision and uncircumcision; because,
at that time, the thing was indifferent, and of no importance.
Whence we refute the error of those, who think that circum-

cision is still in force among the Jews, as if it were a peculiar symbol of the nation, which never ought to be abrogated.   I acknowledge, indeed, that it was permitted to them for a time, until the liberty obtained by Christ should be better known; but though permitted, it by no means retained its original force.   For it would be absurd to be initiated into the Church by two different signs; of which the one should testify and affirm that Christ was come, and the other should shadow him forth as absent.

14. *And the uncircumcised man-child.*   In order that circumcision might be the more attended to, God denounces a severe punishment on any one who should neglect it.   And as this shows God's great care for the salvation of men; so, on the other hand, it rebukes their negligence.   For since God thus benignantly offers a pledge of his love, and of eternal life, for what purpose does he add threatenings but to rouse the sluggishness of those whose duty it is to run with diligence?   Therefore, this denunciation of punishment virtually charges men with foul ingratitude, because they either reject or despise the grace of God.   The passage however teaches, that such contempt shall not pass unpunished. And since God threatens punishment only to despisers, we infer that the uncircumcision of children would do them no harm, if they died before the eighth day.   For the bare promise of God was effectual to their salvation.   He did not so attest this salvation by external signs, as to restrict his own effectual working to those signs.   Moses, indeed, sets aside all controversy on this subject, by adducing as a reason, that they would make void the covenant of God: for we know, that the covenant was not violated, when the power of keeping it was taken away.   Let us then consider, that the salvation of the race of Abraham was included in that expression, 'I will be a God to thy seed.'   And although circumcision was added as a confirmation, it nevertheless did not deprive the word of its force and efficacy.   But because it is not in the power of man to sever what God has joined together; no one could despise or neglect the sign, without both rejecting the word itself, and depriving himself of the

benefit therein offered. And therefore the Lord punished bare neglect with such severity. But if any infants were deprived by death of the tokens of salvation, he spared them, because they had done nothing derogatory to the covenant of God. The same reasoning is at this day in force respecting baptism. Whoever, having neglected baptism, feigns himself to be contented with the bare promise, tramples, as much as in him lies, upon the blood of Christ, or at least does not suffer it to flow for the washing of his own children. Therefore, just punishment follows the contempt of the sign, in the privation of grace; because, by an impious severance of the sign and the word, or rather by a laceration of them, the covenant of God is violated. To consign to destruction those infants, whom a sudden death has not allowed to be presented for baptism, before any neglect of parents could intervene, is a cruelty originating in superstition. But that the promise belongs to such children, is not in the least doubtful. For what can be more absurd than that the symbol, which is added for the sake of confirming the promise, should really enervate its force? Wherefore, the common opinion, by which baptism is supposed to be necessary to salvation, ought to be so moderated, that it should not bind the grace of God, or the power of the Spirit, to external symbols, and bring against God a charge of falsehood.

He hath broken my covenant. For the covenant of God is ratified, when by faith we embrace what he promises. Should any one object, that infants were guiltless of this fault, because they hitherto were destitute of reason: I answer, we ought not to press this divine declaration too closely, as if God held the infants as chargeable with a fault of their own: but we must observe the antithesis, that as God adopts the infant son in the person of his father, so when the father repudiates such a benefit, the infant is said to cut himself off from the Church. For the meaning of the expression is this, ' He shall be blotted out from the people whom God had chosen to himself.' The explanation of some, that they who remained in uncircumcision would not be Jews, and would have no place in the census of that people, is too frigid. We must go farther, and say, that God, indeed, will not acknowledge those as among his people, who will not bear the mark and token of adoption.

15. *As for Sarai thy wife.* God now promises to Abraham a legitimate seed by Sarai. She had been (as I have said) too precipitate, when she substituted, without any command from God, her handmaid in her own place: Abraham also had been too pliant in following his wife, who foolishly and rashly wished to anticipate the design of God; nevertheless, their united fault did not prevent God from making it known to them that he was about to give them that seed, from the expectation of which, they had, in a manner, cut themselves off. Whence the gratuitous kindness of God shines the more clearly, because, although men impede the course of it by obstacles of their own, it nevertheless comes to them. Moreover, God changes the name of Sarai, in order that he may extend her pre-eminence far and wide, which in her former name had been more restricted. For the letter ' (*yod*) has the force among the Hebrews of the possessive pronoun: this being now taken away, God designs that Sarah should every where, and without exception, be celebrated as a sovereign and princess.[1] And this is expressed in the context, when God promises that he will give her a son, from whom at length nations and kings should be born. And although at first sight this benediction appears most ample, it is still far richer than it seems to be, in the words here used, as we shall see in a little time.

17. *And Abraham fell upon his face.* This was in token, not only of his reverence, but also of his faith. For Abraham not only adores God, but in giving him thanks, testifies that he receives and embraces what was promised concerning a son. Hence also we infer that he laughed, not because he

---

[1] *Sarah shall her name be.* Heb., שרה, Sarah. Sarai properly signifies " my princess," as if sustaining that relation to a single individual or to a family. The restriction implied in the possessive " my " is now to be done away: her limited pre-eminence is to be unspeakably enlarged. Thus, instead of " my princess," she is henceforth to bear an appellation importing " princess of a multitude," and corresponding with the magnificent promise made to her, ver. 16.—*Bush, Notes on Genesis.*

either despised, or regarded as fabulous, or rejected, the promise of God ; but, as is commonly wont to happen in things which are least expected, partly exulting with joy, and partly being carried beyond himself in admiration, he breaks forth into laughter. For I do not assent to the opinion of those who suppose, that this laughter flowed solely from joy ; but I rather think that Abraham was as one astonished ; which his next interrogation also confirms, " Shall a child be born to him that is an hundred years old ?" For although he does not reject as vain what had been said by the angel, he yet shows that he was no otherwise affected, than as if he had received some incredible tidings. The novelty of the thing so strikes him, that for a short time he is confounded ; yet he humbles himself before God, and with confused mind, prostrating himself on the earth, he, by faith, adores the power of God. For, that this was not the language of one who doubts, Paul, in his Epistle to the Romans, is a witness, (iv. 19,) who denies that Abraham considered his body now dead, or the barren womb of Sarah, or that he staggered through unbelief; but declares that he believed in hope against hope. And that which Moses relates, " that Abraham said in his heart," I do not so explain as if he had distinctly conceived this in his mind : but as many things steal upon us contrary to our purpose, the perplexing thought suddenly rushed upon his mind, ' What a strange thing is this, that a son should be born to one a hundred years old !' This, however, seems to some, to be a kind of contest between carnal reason and faith ; for although Abraham, reverently prostrating himself before God, submits his own mind to the divine word, he is still disturbed by the novelty of the affair. I answer, that this admiration, which did not obstruct the course of God's power, was not contrary to faith ; nay, the strength of faith shone the more brightly, in having surmounted an obstacle so arduous. And therefore he is not reprehended for laughing, as Sarah is in the next chapter.

18. *And Abraham said unto God.* Abraham does not now wonder silently within himself, but pours forth his wish and prayer. His language, however, is that of a mind still

perturbed and vacillating, " O that (or I wish that) Ishmael might live !" For, as if he did not dare to hope for all that God promises, he fixes his mind upon the son already born ; not because he would reject the promise of fresh offspring, but because he was contented with the favour already received, provided the liberality of God should not extend further. He does not, then, reject what the Lord offers ; but while he is prepared to embrace it, the expression, " O that Ishmael !" yet flows from him, through the weakness of his flesh. Some think that Abraham spoke thus, because he was afraid for his first-born. But there is no reason why we should suppose that Abraham was smitten with any such fear, as that God, in giving him another son, would take away the former, or as if the latter favour should absorb that which had preceded. The answer of God, which follows shortly after, refutes this interpretation. What I have said is more certain ; namely, that Abraham prayed that the grace of God, in which he acquiesced, might be ratified and confirmed to him. Moreover, without reflection, he breaks forth into this wish, when, for very joy, he could scarcely believe what he had heard from the mouth of God. ' To live before Jehovah' is as much as, to be preserved in safety under his protection, or to be blessed by Him. Abraham therefore desires of the Lord, that he will preserve the life which he has given to Ishmael.

19. *Sarah thy wife shall bear thee a son indeed.* Some take the adverb אֲבָל, *abal*, to mean ' Truly.' Others, however, more rightly suppose it to be used for increasing the force of the expression. For God rouses the slumbering mind of his servant ; as if he would say, ' The sight of one favour prevents thee from raising thyself higher ; and thus it happens that thou dost confine thy thoughts within too narrow limits. Now, therefore, enlarge thy mind, to receive also what I promise concerning Sarah. For the door of hope ought to be sufficiently open to admit the word in its full magnitude.'

And I will establish my covenant with him. He confines the spiritual covenant to one family, in order that Abraham may hence learn to hope for the blessing before promised ;

for since he had framed for himself a false hope, not founded on the word of God, it was necessary that this false hope should first be dislodged from his heart, in order that he might now the more fully rely upon the heavenly oracles, and might fix the anchor of his faith, which before had wavered in a fallacious imagination, on the firm truth of God. He calls the covenant everlasting, in the sense which we have previously explained. He then declares that it shall not be bound to one person only, but shall be common to his whole race, that it may, by continual succession, descend to his posterity. Yet it may seem absurd, that God should command Ishmael, whom he deprives of his grace, to be circumcised. I answer; although the Lord constitutes Isaac the first-born and the head, from whom he intends the covenant of salvation to flow, he still does not entirely exclude Ishmael; but rather, in adopting the whole family of Abraham, joins Ishmael to his brother Isaac as an inferior member, until Ishmael cut himself off from his father's house, and his brother's society. Therefore his circumcision was not useless, until he apostatized from the covenant: for although it was not deposited with him, he might, nevertheless, participate in it, with his brother Isaac. In short, the Lord intends nothing else, by these words, than that Isaac should be the legitimate heir of the promised benediction.

20. *And as for Ishmael.* He here more clearly discriminates between the two sons of Abraham. For in promising to the one wealth, dignity, and other things pertaining to the present life, he proves him to be a son according to the flesh. But he makes a special covenant with Isaac, which rises above the world and this frail life : not for the sake of cutting Ishmael off from the hope of eternal life, but in order to teach him that salvation is to be sought from the race of Isaac, where it really dwells. We infer, however, from this passage, that the holy fathers were by no means kept down to earth, by the promises of God, but rather were borne upwards to heaven. For God liberally and profusely promises to Ishmael whatever is desirable with respect to this earthly life : and yet He accounts as nothing all the gifts He confers on him,

in comparison with the covenant which was to be established
in Isaac.   It therefore follows, that neither wealth, nor power,
nor any other temporal gift, is promised to the sons of the
Spirit, but an eternal blessing, which is possessed only by
hope, in this world.   Therefore, however we may now abound
in delights, and in all good things, our happiness is still transient, unless by faith we penetrate into the celestial kingdom
of God, where a greater and higher blessing is laid up for us.

It is however asked, whether Abraham had respect only
to this earthly life when he prayed for his son?   For this the
Lord seems to intimate, when he declares that he had granted
what Abraham asked, and yet only mentions the things we
have recorded.   But it was not God's design to fulfil the
whole wish of Abraham on this point; only he makes it plain
that he would have some respect to Ishmael, for whom Abraham had entreated; so as to show that the father's prayer
had not been in vain.   For he meant to testify that he
embraced Abraham with such love, that, for his sake, he
had respect to his whole race, and dignified it with peculiar
benefits.

22. *God went up from Abraham.*   This expression contains
a profitable doctrine, namely, that Abraham certainly knew
this vision to be from God; for the ascent here spoken implies as much.   And it is necessary for the pious to be fully
assured that what they hear proceeds from God, in order
that they may not be carried hither and thither, but may
depend alone upon heaven.   And whereas God now, when
he has spoken to us, does not openly ascend to heaven before
our eyes; this ought to diminish nothing from the certainty
of our faith; because a full manifestation of Him has been
made in Christ, with which it is right that we should be
satisfied.   Besides, although God does not daily ascend upwards in a visible form, yet, in this his majesty is not less
resplendent, that he raises us upwards by transforming us into
his own image.   Further, he gives sufficient authority to his
word, when he seals it upon our hearts by his Spirit.

23. *And Abraham took Ishmael.*   Moses now commends

the obedience of Abraham, because he circumcised the whole of his family as he had been commanded. For he must, of necessity, have been entirely devoted to God, since he did not hesitate to inflict upon himself a wound attended with acute pain, and not without danger of life. To this may be added the circumstance of the time; namely, that he does not defer the work to another day, but immediately obeys the Divine mandate. There is, however, no doubt, that he had to contend with various perplexing thoughts. Not to mention innumerable others, this might come into his mind, 'As for me, who have been so long harassed with many adverse affairs, and tossed about in different exiles, and yet have never swerved from the word of God; if, by this symbol, he would consecrate me to himself as a servant, why has he put me off to extreme old age? What does this mean, that I cannot be saved unless I, with one foot almost in the grave, thus mutilate myself?' But this was an illustrious proof of obedience, that having overcome all difficulties, he quickly, and without delay, followed where God called him. And he gave, in so doing, an example of faith not less excellent; because, unless he had certainly embraced the promises of God, he would by no means have become so prompt to obey. Hence, therefore, arose his great alacrity, because he set the word of God in opposition to the various temptations which might disturb his mind, and draw him in contrary directions.

Two things also here are worthy of observation. First, that Abraham was not deterred by the difficulty of the work from yielding to God the duty which he owed him. We know that he had a great multitude in his house, nearly equal to a people. It was scarcely credible that so many men would have suffered themselves to be wounded, apparently to be made a laughing-stock. Therefore it was justly to be feared, that he would excite a great tumult in his tranquil family; yea, that, by a common impulse, the major part of his servants would rise up against him; nevertheless, relying upon the word of God, he strenuously attempts what seemed impossible.

We next see, how faithfully his family was instructed; because not only his home-born slaves, but foreigners, and men bought with money, meekly receive the wound, which was both troublesome, and the occasion of shame to carnal sense. It appears, then, that Abraham diligently took care to have them prepared for due obedience.   And since he held them under holy discipline, he received the reward of his own diligence, in finding them so tractable in a most arduous affair. So, at this day, God seems to enjoin a thing impossible to be done, when he requires his gospel to be preached every where in the whole world, for the purpose of restoring it from death to life.   For we see how great is the obstinacy of nearly all men, and what numerous and powerful methods of resistance Satan employs ; so that, in short, all the ways of access to these principles are obstructed.   Yet it behoves individuals to do their duty, and not to yield to impediments ; and, finally, our endeavours and our labours shall by no means fail of that success, which is not yet apparent.

CHAPTER XVIII.

1. AND the Lord appeared unto him in the plains of Mamre : and he sat in the tent-door in the heat of the day ;

2. And he lift up his eyes and looked, and, lo, three men stood by him : and when he saw *them*, he ran to meet them from the tent-door, and bowed himself toward the ground,

3. And said, My Lord, if now I have found favour in thy sight, pass not away, I pray thee, from thy servant.

4. Let a little water, I pray you, be fetched, and wash your feet, and rest yourselves under the tree :

5. And I will fetch a morsel of bread, and comfort ye your hearts ; after that ye shall pass on : for therefore are ye come to your servant.   And they said, So do as thou hast said.

6. And Abraham hastened into the tent unto Sarah, and said, Make ready quickly three measures of fine meal, knead *it*, and make cakes upon the hearth.

1. Deinde visus est illi Jehova in Querceto Mamre, quum ipse sederet in ostio tabernaculi, quando incalescebat dies.

2. Et elevavit oculos suos, et vidit, et ecce tres viri stabant juxta eum : et vidit, et cucurrit in occursum eorum ab ostio tabernaculi, et incurvavit se super terram.

3. Et dixit, Domine mi, si nunc inveni gratiam in oculis tuis, ne nunc transeas a servo tuo.

4. Tollatur nunc parum aquæ, et lavate pedes vestros, et considite sub arbore.

5. Et capiam buccellam panis, et fulcite cor vestrum, postea transibitis : quia idcirco transiistis ad servum vestrum. Et dixerunt, Sic facias quemadmodum loquutus es.

6. Itaque festinavit Abraham ad tabernaculum ad Sarah, et dixit, Festina, tria sata farinæ similæ consperge, et fac subcinericios panes.

7. And Abraham ran unto the herd, and fetched a calf tender and good, and gave *it* unto a young man ; and he hasted to dress it.

8. And he took butter, and milk, and the calf which he had dressed, and set *it* before them ; and he stood by them under the tree, and they did eat.

9. And they said unto him, Where *is* Sarah thy wife? And he said, Behold, in the tent.

10. And he said, I will certainly return unto thee according to the time of life ; and, lo, Sarah thy wife shall have a son. And Sarah heard *it* in the tent-door, which *was* behind him.

11. Now Abraham and Sarah *were* old, *and* well stricken in age ; *and* it ceased to be with Sarah after the manner of women.

12. Therefore Sarah laughed within herself, saying, After I am waxed old shall I have pleasure, my lord being old also?

13. And the Lord said unto Abraham, Wherefore did Sarah laugh, saying, Shall I of a surety bear a child, which am old?

14. Is any thing too hard for the Lord? At the time appointed I will return unto thee, according to the time of life, and Sarah shall have a son.

15. Then Sarah denied, saying, I laughed not ; for she was afraid. And he said, Nay ; but thou didst laugh.

16. And the men rose up from thence, and looked towards Sodom : and Abraham went with them, to bring them on the way.

17. And the Lord said, Shall I hide from Abraham that thing which I do ;

18. Seeing that Abraham shall surely become a great and mighty nation, and all the nations of the earth shall be blessed in him?

19. For I know him, that he will command his children and his household after him, and they shall keep the way of the Lord, to do justice and judgment ; that the Lord may bring upon Abraham that which he hath spoken of him.

20. And the Lord said, Because the

7. Et ad boves cucurrit Abraham, et tulit vitulum tenerum et bonum, et dedit puero, et festinavit ut pararet eum.

8. Et tulit butyrum, et lac, et vitulum quem paraverat, et posuit ante eos : et ipse stabat juxta eos sub arbore, et comederunt.

9. Et dixerunt ad eum, Ubi est Sarah uxor tua? Et dixit, Ecce, in tabernaculo.

10. Et dixit, Revertendo revertar ad te secundum tempus vitæ, et ecce, filius *erit* Sarah uxori tuæ. Sarah autem audiebat in ostio tabernaculi, quod erat post eum.

11. Et Abraham et Sarah erant senes et provectæ ætatis, desieratque esse ipsi Sarah via secundum mulieres.

12. Risit ergo, Sarah intra sesse, dicendo, Postquam senui, erit mihi voluptas? et dominus meus senuit.

13. Et dixit Jehova ad Abraham, Utquid risit Sarah dicendo, Num etiam vere pariam, et ego senui?

14. Numquid abscondetur a Jehova quicquam? ad tempus revertar ad te secundum tempus vitæ, et ipsi Sarah erit filius.

15. Et negavit Sarah, dicendo, Non risi : quia timuit. Et dixit, Nequaquam, quia risisti.

16. Et surrexerunt inde viri, et respexerunt contra faciem Sedom : et Abraham ibat cum eis, ut deduceret eos.

17. Tunc Jehova dixit, An ego celabo Abraham quod ego facio?

18. Et Abraham erit in gentem magnum et fortem, et benedicent sibi in eo omnes gentes terræ.

19. Quia novi eum : propterea præcipiet filiis suis, et domui suæ post se, et custodient viam Jehovæ, ut faciant justitiam et judicium, ut venire faciat Jehova super Abraham, quod loquutus est super eum.

20. Itaque dixit Jehova,

cry of Sodom and Gomorrah is great, and because their sin is very grievous ;

21. I will go down now, and see whether they have done altogether according to the cry of it, which is come unto me ; and if not, I will know.

22. And the men turned their faces from thence, and went toward Sodom ; but Abraham stood yet before the Lord.

23. And Abraham drew near, and said, Wilt thou also destroy the righteous with the wicked?

24. Peradventure there be fifty righteous within the city : wilt thou also destroy and not spare the place for the fifty righteous that *are* therein ?

25. That be far from thee to do after this manner, to slay the righteous with the wicked : and that the righteous should be as the wicked, that be far from thee. Shall not the Judge of all the earth do right ?

26. And the Lord said, If I find in Sodom fifty righteous within the city, then I will spare all the place for their sakes.

27. And Abraham answered and said, Behold now, I have taken upon me to speak unto the Lord, which *am but* dust and ashes :

28. Peradventure there shall lack five of the fifty righteous : wilt thou destroy all the city for *lack of* five ? And he said, If I find there forty and five, I will not destroy *it*.

29. And he spake unto him yet again, and said, Peradventure there shall be forty found there. And he said, I will not do *it* for forty's sake.

30. And he said *unto him*, Oh let not the Lord be angry, and I will speak : Peradventure there shall thirty be found there. And he said, I will not do *it*, if I find thirty there.

31. And he said, Behold now, I have taken upon me to speak unto the Lord : Peradventure there shall be twenty

Clamor Sedom et Hamorah certe multiplicatus est, et peccatum eorum utique aggravatum est valde.

21. Descendam nunc, et videbo an secundum clamorem ejus, qui venit ad me, fecerint consummationem : et si non, sciam.

22. Et verterunt se inde viri, et perrexerunt in Sedom : ipse vero Abraham adhuc stabat coram Jehova.

23. Et accessit Abraham, et dixit, Numquid etiam disperdes justum cum impio ?

24. Si forte fuerint quinquaginta justi intra civitatem numquid etiam disperdes, et non parces loco propter quinquaginta justos, qui sunt intra eam ?

25. Absit tibi ut facias secundum rem hanc, ut mori facias justum cum impio, et sit justus sicut impius : absit tibi, an qui judex est omnis terræ, non faciet judicium ?

26. Et dixit Jehova, Si invenero in Sedom quinquaginta justos intra civitatem, parcam toti loco propter eos.

27. Et respondit Abraham, et dixit, Ecce, nunc cœpi loqui ad Jehovam, et sum pulvis et cinis :

28. Si forsitan defuerint de quinquaginta justis quinque, numquid disperdes propter quinque totam civitatem ? Et dixit, Non disperdam, si invenero ibi quadraginta et quinque.

29. Et addidit adhuc ut loqueretur ad eum, et dixit, Si forte inventi fuerint ibi quadraginta. Et dixit, Non faciam propter quadraginta.

30. Et dixit, Ne nunc sit ira Domino meo, et loquar, Si forte inventi fuerint ibi triginta ? Et dixit, Non faciam, si invenero ibi triginta.

31. Et dixit, Ecce, nunc cœpi loqui ad Jehovam, Si forsitan inventi fuerint ibi

found there. And he said, I will not destroy *it* for twenty's sake.

32. And he said, Oh let not the Lord be angry, and I will speak yet but this once: Peradventure ten shall be found there. And he said, I will not destroy *it* for ten's sake.

33. And the Lord went his way, as soon as he had left communing with Abraham: and Abraham returned unto his place.

viginti? Et dixit, Non disperdam propter viginti.

32. Et dixit, Ne nunc sit ira Domino meo, et loquar tantummodo semel, Si forsitan inventi fuerint ibi decem? Et dixit, Non disperdam propter decem.

33. Et perrexit Jehova, quando finivit loqui ad Abraham, et Abraham reversus est ad locum suum.

1. *And the Lord appeared unto him.* It is uncertain whether Moses says, that God afterwards appeared again unto Abraham; or whether, reverting to the previous history, he here introduces other circumstances, which he had not before mentioned. I prefer, however, the former of these interpretations; namely, that God confirmed the mind of his servant with a new vision; just as the faith of the saints requires, at intervals, renewed assistance. It is also possible that the promise was repeated for the sake of Sarah. What shall we say, if in this manner, he chose to do honour to the greatness of his grace? For the promise concerning Isaac, from whom, at length, redemption and salvation should shine forth to the world, cannot be extolled in terms adequate to its dignity. Whichever of these views be taken, we perceive that there was sufficient reason why Isaac was again promised. Concerning the word Mamre we have spoken in the thirteenth chapter. Probably a grove of oaks was in that place, and Abraham dwelt there, on account of the convenience of the situation.

2. *And, lo, three men stood by him.* Before Moses proceeds to his principal subject, he describes to us, the hospitality of the holy man; and he calls the angels men, because, being clothed with human bodies, they appeared to be nothing else than men. And this was done designedly, in order that he, receiving them as men, might give proof of his charity. For angels do not need those services of ours, which are the true evidences of charity. Moreover, hospitality holds the chief place among these services; because it is no common virtue to assist strangers, from whom there is no hope of reward.

For men in general are wont, when they do favours to others, to look for a return; but he who is kind to unknown guests and persons, proves himself to be disinterestedly liberal. Wherefore the humanity of Abraham deserves no slight praise; because he freely invites men who were to him unknown, through whom he had received no advantage, and from whom he had no hope of mutual favours. What, therefore, was Abraham's object? Truly, that he might relieve the necessity of his guests. He sees them wearied with their journey, and has no doubt that they are overcome by heat; he considers that the time of day was becoming dangerous to travellers; and therefore he wishes both to comfort, and to relieve persons thus oppressed. And certainly, the sense of nature itself dictates, that strangers are to be especially assisted; unless blind self-love rather impels us to mercenary services. For none are more deserving of compassion and help than those whom we see deprived of friends, and of domestic comforts. And therefore the right of hospitality has been held most sacred among all people, and no disgrace was ever more detestable than to be called inhospitable. For it is a brutal cruelty, proudly to despise those who, being destitute of ordinary protection, have recourse to our assistance. It is however asked, whether Abraham was wont thus to receive indiscriminately all kinds of guests? I answer, that, according to his accustomed prudence, he made a distinction between his guests. And truly the invitation, which Moses here relates, has something uncommon. Undoubtedly, the angels bore, in their countenance and manner, marks of extraordinary dignity; so that Abraham would conclude them to be worthy not only of meat and drink, but also of honour. They who think that he was thus attentive to this office, because he had been taught, by his fathers, that angels often appeared in the world in human form, reason too philosophically. Even the authority of the Apostle is contrary to this; for he denies that they were, at first, known to be angels either by Abraham, or by Lot, since they thought they were entertaining men. (Heb. xiii. 2.) This, then, is to be maintained; that when he saw men of reverend aspect, and having marks of singular excellence, advancing on their journey, he saluted them with honour,

and invited them to repose. But, at that time, there was
greater honesty than is, at present, to be found amid the prevailing perfidy of mankind ; so that the right of hospitality
might be exercised with less danger. Therefore, the great
number of inns are evidence of our depravity, and prove it
to have arisen from our own fault, that the principal duty of
humanity has become obsolete among us.

And bowed himself toward the ground. This token of reverence was in common use with oriental nations. The mystery
which some of the ancient writers have endeavoured to elicit
from this act ; namely, that Abraham adored one out of the
three, whom he saw, and, therefore, perceived by faith, that
there are three persons in one God, since it is frivolous, and
obnoxious to ridicule and calumny, I am more than content
to omit. For we have before said, that the angels were so
received by the holy man, as by one who intended to discharge a duty towards men. But the fact that God honoured
his benignity, and granted it to him as a reward, that angels
should be presented to him for guests, was what he was not
aware of, till they had made themselves known at the conclusion of the meal. It was therefore a merely human and civil
honour, which he paid them. As to his having saluted one
in particular, it was probably done because he excelled the
other two. For we know that angels often appeared with
Christ their Head ; here, therefore, among the three angels,
Moses points out one, as the Chief of the embassy.

3. *Pass not away, I pray thee, from thy servant.* In asking
thus meekly, and even suppliantly, there is no doubt that
Abraham does it, moved by the reason which I have stated.
For if he had slaughtered calves for all kinds of travellers,
his house would soon have been emptied by his profuse ex-
penditure. He, therefore, did honour to their virtue and
their excellent endowments, lest he should pour contempt
upon God. Thus, neither was he so liberal as to invite wanderers, or other men of all kinds, who herd together ; nor did
ambition induce him to deal thus bountifully with these three
persons, but rather his love and affection for those gifts of
God, and those virtues which appeared in them. As to his

offering them simply a morsel of bread, he makes light of an act of kindness which he was about to do, not only for the sake of avoiding all boasting, but in order that they might the more easily yield to his counsel and his entreaties, when they were persuaded that they should not prove too burdensome and troublesome to him. For modest persons do not willingly put others to expense or trouble. The washing of feet, in that age, and in that region of the world, was very common ; perhaps, because persons travelled with naked feet, under burning suns : and it was the great remedy for the alleviation of weariness, to wash the feet parched with heat.

5. *For therefore are ye come to your servant.* He does not mean that they had come designedly, or for the express purpose of seeking to be entertained, as his guests ; but he intimates that their coming had occurred opportunely, as if he would say, ' You have not slipped into this place by chance ; but have been led hither by the design and the direction of God.' He, therefore, refers it to the providence of God, that they had come, so conveniently, to a place where they might refresh themselves a little while, till the heat of the sun should abate. Moreover, as it is certain that Abraham spoke thus in sincerity of mind ; let us, after his example, conclude that, whenever our brethren, who need our help, meet us, they are sent unto us by God.

6. *And Abraham hastened into the tent.* Abraham's care in entertaining his guests is here recorded ; and Moses, at the same time, shows what a well-ordered house he had. In short, he presents us, in a few words, with a beautiful picture of domestic government. Abraham runs, partly, to command what he would have done ; and partly, to execute his own duty, as the master of the house. Sarah keeps within the tent ; not to indulge in sloth, but rather to take her own part also, in the labour. The servants are all prompt to obey. Here is the sweet concord of a well-conducted family ; which could not have thus suddenly arisen, unless each had, by long practice, been accustomed to right discipline. A question, however, arises out of the assertion of Moses, that

the angels " did eat." Some expound it, that they only appeared as persons eating ; which fancy enters their minds through the medium of another error; since they imagine them to have been mere spectres, and not endued with real bodies. But, in my judgment, the thing is far otherwise. In the first place, this was no prophetical vision, in which the images of absent things are brought before the eyes; but the angels really came into the house of Abraham. Wherefore, I do not doubt that God,—who created the whole world out of nothing, and who daily proves himself to be a wonderful Artificer in forming creatures,—gave them bodies, for a time, in which they might fulfil the office enjoined them. And as they truly walked, spoke, and discharged other functions ; so I conclude, they did truly eat ; not because they were hungry, but in order to conceal themselves, until the proper time for making themselves known. Yet as God speedily annihilated those bodies, which had been created for a temporary use ; so there will be no absurdity in saying, that the food itself was destroyed, together with their bodies. But, as it is profitable briefly to touch upon such questions ; and, as religion in no way forbids us to do so; there is, on the other hand, nothing better than that we should content ourselves with a sober solution of them.

9. *Where is Sarah?* Hitherto God permitted Abraham to discharge an obvious duty. But, having given him the opportunity of exercising charity, God now begins to manifest himself in his angels. The reason why Moses introduces, at one time, three speakers, while, at another, he ascribes speech to one only, is, that the three together represent the person of one God. We must also remember what I have lately adduced, that the principal place is given to one ; because Christ, who is the living image of the Father, often appeared to the fathers under the form of an angel, while, at the same time, he yet had angels, of whom he was the Head, for his attendants. And as to their making inquiry respecting Sarah ; we may hence infer, that a son is again here promised to Abraham, because she had not been present at the former oracle.

10. *I will certainly return unto thee.* Jerome translates it, 'I will return, life attending me :'[1] as if God, speaking in the manner of men, had said, 'I will return if I live.' But it would be absurd, that God, who here so magnificently proclaims his power, should borrow from man a form of speech which would suppose him to be mortal. What majesty, I pray, would this remarkable oracle possess, which treats of the eternal salvation of the world? That interpretation, therefore, can by no means be approved, which entirely enervates the force and authority of the promise. Literally it is, "according to the time of life." Which some expound of Sarah; as if the angel had said, Sarah shall survive to that period. But it is more properly explained of the child ; for God promises that He will come, at the just and proper time of bringing forth, that Sarah might become the mother of a living child.

11. *Were old, and well stricken in age.* Moses inserts this verse to inform us that what the angel was saying, justly appeared improbable to Sarah. For it is contrary to nature that children should be promised to decrepit old men. A doubt, however, may be entertained on this point, respecting Abraham : because men are sometimes endued with strength to have children, even in extreme old age : and especially in that period, such an occurrence was not uncommon. But Moses here speaks comparatively : for since Abraham, during the vigour of his life, had remained with his wife, childless; it was scarcely possible for him, now that his body was half-dead, to have children ; he had indeed begotten Ishmael in his old age, which was contrary to expectation. But that now, twelve years afterwards, it should be possible to become a father, through his aged wife,[2] was scarcely credible. Moses, however, chiefly insists upon the case of Sarah ; because the greatest impediment was with her. "It ceased," he says, "to be with Sarah after the manner of women."[3]

---

[1] "Vita comite revertar." See Vulgate, where the expression is, "Revertens veniam ad te tempore illo, vitâ comite."

[2] "Patrem ex vetula effœtaque muliere fieri posse."

[3] The following passage is not translated :— "Quo genere loquendi verecunde menses notat qui mulieribus fluunt. Una autem cum fluxu menstruo desinit concipiendi facultas."

12. *Therefore Sarah laughed within herself.* Abraham had laughed before, as appears in the preceding chapter: but the laughter of both was, by no means, similar. For Sarah is not transported with admiration and joy, on receiving the promise of God; but foolishly sets her own age and that of her husband in opposition to the word of God; that she may withhold confidence from God, when he speaks. Yet she does not, avowedly, charge God with falsehood or vanity; but because, having her mind fixed on the contemplation of the thing proposed, she only weighs what might be accomplished by natural means, without raising her thoughts to the consideration of the power of God, and thus rashly casts discredit on God who speaks to her. Thus, as often as we measure the promises and the works of God, by our own reason, and by the laws of nature, we act reproachfully towards him, though we may intend nothing of the sort. For we do not pay him his due honour, except we regard every obstacle which presents itself in heaven and on earth, as placed under subjection to his word. But although the incredulity of Sarah is not to be excused; she, nevertheless, does not directly reject the favour of God; but is only so kept back by shame and modesty, that she does not altogether believe what she hears. Even her very words declare the greatest modesty; ' After we are grown old, shall we give ourselves up to lust?' Wherefore, let us observe, that nothing was less in Sarah's mind, than to make God a liar. But her sin consisted in this alone, that, having fixed her thoughts too much on the accustomed order of nature, she did not give glory to God, by expecting from him a miracle which she was unable to conceive in her mind. We must here notice the admonition which the Apostle gathers from this passage, because Sarah here calls Abraham her *lord*. (1 Peter iii. 6.) For he exhorts women, after her example, to be obedient and well-behaved towards their own husbands. Many women, indeed, without difficulty, give their husbands this title, when yet they do not scruple to bring them under rule, by their imperious pride: but the Apostle takes it for granted that Sarah testifies, from her heart, what she feels, respecting her husband: nor is it doubtful that she gave proof, by actual services, of the modesty which she had professed in words.

13. *And the Lord said.* Because the majesty of God had
now been manifested in the angels, Moses expressly mentions
his Name. We have before declared, in what sense the name
of God is transferred to the angel; it is not, therefore, now
necessary to repeat it: except, as it is always important to
remark, that the word of the Lord is so precious to himself,
that he would be regarded by us as present, whenever he
speaks through his ministers. Again, whenever he manifested himself to the fathers, Christ was the Mediator between
him and them; who not only personates God in proclaiming
his word, but is also truly and essentially God. And because
the laughter of Sarah had not been detected by the eye of
man, therefore Moses expressly declares that she was reprehended by God. And to this point belong the following
circumstances, that the angel had his back turned to the
tent, and that Sarah laughed within herself, and not before
others. The censure also shows that the laughter of Sarah
was joined with incredulity. For there is no little weight
in this sentence, ' Can anything be wonderful with God?'
But the angel chides Sarah, because she limited the power of
God within the bounds of her own sense. An antithesis is
therefore implied between the immense power of God, and the
contracted measure which Sarah imagined to herself, through
her carnal reason. Some translate the word פלא, (pala,)
hidden, as if the angel meant that nothing was hidden from
God: but the sense is different; namely, that the power of God
ought not to be estimated by human reason.[1] It is not surprising, that in arduous affairs *we* fail, or that *we* succumb to
difficulties: but God's way is far otherwise, for he looks down
with contempt, from above, upon those things which alarm us
by their lofty elevation. We now see what was the sin of
Sarah; namely, that she did wrong to God, by not acknowledging the greatness of his power. And truly, we also
attempt to rob God of his power, whenever we distrust his
word. At the first sight, Paul seems to give cold praise to
the faith of Abraham, in saying, that he did not consider his
body, now dead, but gave glory to God, because he was per-

[1] Does not the English version fully express this meaning? " Is anything too hard for the Lord?"—*Ed.*

suaded that he could fulfil what he had promised. (Rom. iv. 19.) But if we thoroughly investigate the source of distrust, we shall find that the reason why we doubt of God's promises is, because we sinfully detract from his power. For as soon as any extraordinary difficulty occurs, then, whatever God has promised, seems to us fabulous ; yea, the moment he speaks, the perverse thought insinuates itself, How will he fulfil what he promises ? Being bound down, and pre-occupied by such narrow thoughts, we exclude his power, the knowledge of which is better to us than a thousand worlds. In short, he who does not expect more from God than he is able to comprehend in the scanty measure of his own reason, does him grievous wrong. Meanwhile, the *word* of the Lord ought to be inseparably joined with his power; for nothing is more preposterous, than to inquire what God *can* do, to the setting aside of his *declared will.* In this way the Papists plunge themselves into a profound labyrinth, when they dispute concerning the absolute power of God. Therefore, unless we are willing to be involved in absurd dotings, it is necessary that the word should precede us like a lamp; so that his power and his will may be conjoined by an inseparable bond. This rule the Apostle prescribes to us, when he says, ' Being certainly persuaded, that what he has promised, he is able to perform,' (Rom. iv. 21.) The angel again repeats the promise that he would come ' according to the time of life,' that is, in the revolving of the year, when the full time of bringing forth should have arrived.

15. *Then Sarah denied.* Another sin of Sarah's was, that she endeavoured to cover and hide her laughter by a falsehood. Yet this excuse did not proceed from obstinate wickedness, according to the manner in which hypocrites are wont to snatch at subterfuges, so that they remain like themselves, even to the end. Sarah's feelings were of a different kind ; for while she repents of her own folly, she is yet so terrified, as to deny that she had done, what she now perceives to be displeasing to God. Whence we infer, how great is the corruption of our nature, which causes even the fear of God,— the highest of all virtues,—to degenerate into a fault. More-

over, we must observe whence that fear, of which Moses makes mention, suddenly entered the mind of Sarah ; namely, from the consideration that God had detected her secret sin.   We see, therefore, how the majesty of God, when it is seriously felt by us, shakes us out of our insensibility.   We are more especially constrained to feel thus, when God ascends his tribunal, and brings our sins to light.

Nay ; but thou didst laugh.   The angel does not contend in a multiplicity of words, but directly refutes her false denial of the fact.   We may hence learn, that we gain no advantage by tergiversation, when the Lord reproves us, because he will immediately despatch our case with a single word.   Therefore, we must beware lest we imitate the petulance of those who mock God with false pretences, and at length rush into gross contempt of Him.   However he may seem to leave us unnoticed for a time, yet he will fulminate against us with that terrible voice, ' It is not as you pretend.'   In short, it is not enough that the judgment of God should be reverenced, unless we also confess our sins ingenuously, and without shifts or evasions.   For a double condemnation awaits those who, from a desire to escape the judgment of God, betake themselves to the refuge of dissimulation.   We must, therefore, bring a sincere confession, that, as persons openly condemned, we may obtain pardon.   But seeing that God was contented with giving a friendly reprehension, and that he did not more severely punish the double offence of Sarah; we hence perceive with what tender indulgence he sometimes regards his own people.   Zacharias was more severely treated, who was struck dumb for nine months. (Luke i. 9.)   But it is not for us to prescribe a perpetual law to God ; who, as he generally binds his own people to repentance by punishments, often sees it good to humble them sufficiently, without inflicting any chastisement.   In Sarah, truly, he gives a singular instance of his compassion ; because he freely forgives her all, and still chooses that she should remain the mother of the Church.   In the meantime, we must observe, how much better it is that we should be brought before him as guilty, and that like convicted persons we should be silent, than that we should delight ourselves in sin, as a great part of the world is accustomed to do.

16. *And the men rose up from thence.* Moses again calls those *men*, whom he had openly declared to be *angels.* But he gives them the name from the form which they had assumed. We are not, however, to suppose that they were surrounded with human bodies, in the same manner in which Christ clothed himself in our nature, together with our flesh; but God invested them with temporary bodies, in which they might be visible to Abraham, and might speak familiarly with him. Abraham is said to have brought them on the way; not for the sake of performing an office of humanity, as when he had received them at first, but in order to render due honour to the angels. For frivolous is the opinion of some, who imagine that they were believed to be prophets, who had been banished, on account of the word. He well knew that they were angels, as we shall soon see more clearly. But he follows those in the way, whom he did not dare to detain.

17. *Shall I hide from Abraham?* Seeing that God here takes counsel, as if concerning a doubtful matter, he does it for the sake of men; for he had already determined what he would do. But he designed, in this manner, to render Abraham more intent upon the consideration of the causes of Sodom's destruction. He adduces two reasons why He wished to manifest his design to Abraham, before he carried it into execution. The former is, that he had already granted him a singularly honourable privilege; the second, that it would be useful and fruitful in the instruction of posterity. Therefore, in this expression, the scope and use of revelation is briefly noted.

18. *Seeing that Abraham shall surely become a great and mighty nation.* In Hebrew it is, 'And being, he shall be,' &c. But the copulative ought to be resolved into the causal adverb.[1] For this is the reason, to which we have already alluded, why God chose to inform his servant of the terrible

[1] " Copulativa in causalem resolvenda est."—*Vatablus in Poli Syn.* The meaning of the expression is, that the word " and," at the beginning of the verse, should be translated "for." The ו *(vau)* not being intended as a copulative, simply to connect this sentence with the former, but as a *causal* conjunction, or one which states the reason for the course before

vengeance He was about to take upon the men of Sodom; namely, that He had adorned him, above all others, with peculiar gifts. For, in this way, God continues his acts of kindness towards the faithful, yea, even increases them, and gradually heaps new favours upon those before granted. And he daily deals with us in the same manner. For what is the reason why he pours innumerable benefits upon us, in constant succession, unless that, having once embraced us with paternal love, he cannot deny himself? And, therefore, in a certain way, he honours himself and his gifts in us. For what does he here commemorate, except his own gratuitous gifts? Therefore, he traces the cause of his beneficence to himself, and not to the merits of Abraham; for the blessing of Abraham flowed from no other source than the Divine Fountain. And we learn from the passage, what experience also teaches, that it is the peculiar privilege of the Church, to know what the Divine judgments mean, and what is their tendency. When God inflicts punishment upon the wicked, he openly proves that he is indeed the Judge of the world; but because all things seem to happen by chance, the Lord illuminates his own children by his word, lest they should become blind, with the unbelievers. So formerly, when he stretched forth his hand over all regions of the world, he yet confined his sacred word within Judea; that is, when he smote all nations with slaughter and with adversity, he yet taught his only elect people, by his word through the prophets, that he was the Author of these punishments; yea, he predicted beforehand that they would take place; as it is written in Amos, (iii. 7,) 'Shall there be anything which the Lord will hide from his servants the prophets?' Let us therefore remember, that from the time when God begins to be kind towards us, he is never weary, until, by adding one favour to another, he completes our salvation. Then, after he has once adopted us, and has shone into our minds by his word, he holds the torch of the same word burning before our eyes, that we may, by faith, consider those judgments and punishments of ini-

determined upon. In calling the conjunction an adverb, Calvin follows the practice of many writers, who give this as a common title to prepositions, conjunctions, and interjections.—*Ed.*

quity which the impious carelessly neglect. Thus it becomes the faithful to be employed in reflecting on the histories of all times, that they may always form their judgment from the Scripture, of the various destructions which, privately and publicly, have befallen the ungodly. But it is asked; was it necessary that the destruction of Sodom should be explained to Abraham, before it happened? I answer, since we are so dull in considering the works of God, this revelation was by no means superfluous. Although the Lord proclaims aloud, that adversity is the rod of his anger; scarcely any one hearkens to it, because, through the depraved imaginations of our flesh, we ascribe the suffering to some other cause. But the admonition, which precedes the event, does not suffer us to be thus torpid, nor to imagine that fortune, or any thing else which we may fancy, stands in the place of God's word. Thus it necessarily happened, in former times, that the people, although iron-hearted, were more affected by these predictions than they would have been, had they been admonished by the prophets, after they had received punishment. Wherefore, from them, it will be proper for us to assume a general rule, in order that the judgments of God, which we daily perceive, may not be unprofitable to us.

The Lord declares to his servant Abraham, that Sodom was about to perish, while it was yet entire, and in the full enjoyment of its pleasures. Hence no doubt remains, that it did not perish by chance, but was subjected to divine punishment. Hence also, when the cause of the punishment is thus declared before-hand, it will necessarily far more effectually pierce and stimulate the minds of men. We must afterwards come to the same conclusion, concerning other things; for although God does not declare to us, what he is about to do, yet he intends us to be eye-witnesses of his works, and prudently to weigh their causes, and not to be dazzled by a confused beholding of them, like unbelievers, ' who seeing, see not,' and who pervert their true design.

19. *For I know him, that he will command his children.* The second reason why God chooses to make Abraham a partaker of his counsel is, because he foresees that this would not be

done in vain, and without profit.   And the simple meaning of the passage is, that Abraham is admitted to the counsel of God, because he would faithfully fulfil the office of a good householder, in instructing his own family.   Hence we infer, that Abraham was informed of the destruction of Sodom, not for his own sake alone, but for the benefit of his race.   Which is carefully to be observed ; for this sentence is to the same effect, as if God, in the person of Abraham, addressed all his posterity.   And truly, God does not make known his will to us, that the knowledge of it may perish with us ; but that we may be his witnesses to posterity, and that they may deliver the knowledge received through us, from hand to hand, (as we say,) to their descendants.   Wherefore, it is the duty of parents to apply themselves diligently to the work of communicating what they have learned from the Lord to their children.   In this manner the truth of God is to be propagated by us, so that no one may retain his knowledge for his own private use ; but that each may edify others, according to his own calling, and to the measure of his faith.   There is however no doubt, that the gross ignorance which reigns in the world, is the just punishment of men's idleness.   For whereas the greater part close their eyes to the offered light of heavenly doctrine ; yet there are those who stifle it, by not taking care to transmit it to their children.   The Lord therefore righteously takes away the precious treasure of his word, to punish the world for its sloth.   The expression "after him" is also to be noticed ; by which we are taught that we must not only take care of our families, to govern them duly, while we live ; but that we must give diligence, in order that the truth of God, which is eternal, may live and flourish after our death; and that thus, when we are dead, a holy course of living may survive and remain.   Moreover, we hence infer, that those narratives which serve to inspire terror, are useful to be known.   For our carnal security requires sharp stimulants, whereby we may be urged to the fear of God.   And lest any one should suppose that this kind of doctrine belongs only to strangers, the Lord specially appoints it for the sons of Abraham, that is, for the household of the Church.   For those interpreters are infatuated and perverse, who contend that faith is overturned, if consciences are alarmed. For whereas nothing is more contrary to faith than contempt and torpor; that doctrine best accords with the preaching of grace, which so subdues men to the fear of God, that they, being afflicted and famishing, may hasten unto Christ.

And they shall keep the way of the Lord. Moses intimates, in these words, that the judgment of God is proposed, not only in order that they who, by negligence, please themselves in their vices, may be taught to fear, and that being thus constrained, they may sigh for the grace of Christ; but also to the end that the faithful themselves, who are already endued with the fear of God, may advance more and more in the pursuit of piety. For he wills that the destruction of Sodom should be recorded, both that the wicked may be drawn to God, by the fear of the same vengeance, and that they who have already begun to worship God, may be better formed to true obedience. Thus the Law avails, not only for the beginning of repentance, but also for our continual progress. When Moses adds, "to do justice and judgment," he briefly shows the nature of the way of the Lord, which he had before mentioned. This, however, is not a complete definition; but from the duties of the Second Table, he briefly shows, by the figure *synecdoche,* what God chiefly requires of us. And it is not unusual in Scripture, to seek a description of a pious and holy life, from the Second Table of the Law; not because charity is of more account than the worship of God, but because they who live uprightly and innocently with their neighbours, give evidence of their piety towards God. In the names of justice and judgment he comprehends that equity, by which to every one is given what is his own. If we would make a distinction, *justice* is the name given to the rectitude and humanity which we cultivate with our brethren, when we endeavour to do good to all, and when we abstain from all wrong, fraud, and violence. But *judgment* is to stretch forth the hand to the miserable and the oppressed, to vindicate righteous causes, and to guard the weak from being unjustly injured. These are the lawful exercises in which the Lord commands his people to be employed.

That the Lord may bring upon Abraham that which he hath spoken of him. Moses intimates that Abraham should become possessed of the grace promised to him, if he instructed his children in the fear of the Lord, and governed his household well. But under the person of one man, a rule common to all the pious is delivered : for they who are negligent in this part of their duty, cast off or suppress, as much as in them lies, the grace of God. Therefore, that the perpetual possession of the gifts of God may remain to us, and survive to posterity, we must beware lest they be lost through our neglect. Yet it would be false for any one hence to infer, that the faithful could either cause or deserve, by their own diligence, that God should fulfil those things which he has promised. For it is an accustomed method of speaking in Scripture, to denote by the word *that* the consequence rather than the cause. For although the grace of God alone begins and completes our salvation ; yet, since by obeying the call of God, we fulfil our course, we are said, also in this manner, to obtain the salvation promised by God.

20. *The cry of Sodom.* The Lord here begins more clearly to explain to Abraham his counsel concerning the destruction of the five cities ; although he only names Sodom and Gomorrah, which were much more famous than the rest. But before he makes mention of punishment, he brings forward their iniquities, to teach Abraham that they justly deserved to be destroyed : otherwise the history would not tend to instruction. But when we perceive that the anger of God is provoked by the sin of man, we are inspired with a dread of sinning. In saying that the " cry was great,"[1] he indicates the grievousness of their crimes, because, although the wicked may promise themselves impunity, by concealing their evils, and although these evils may be silently and quietly borne by men ; yet their sin will necessarily sound aloud in the ears of God. Therefore this phrase signifies, that all our deeds, even those of which we think the memory to be buried,

---

[1] " Clamorem pro scelerum gravitate multiplicatum fuisse."

are presented before the bar of God, and that they, even of themselves, demand vengeance, although there should be none to accuse.

21. *I will go down now.* Since this was a signal example of the wrath of God, which He intends to be celebrated through all ages, and to which he frequently refers in the Scripture; therefore Moses diligently records those things which are especially to be considered in divine judgments; just as, in this place, he commends the moderation of God, who does not immediately fulminate against the ungodly, and pour out his vengeance upon them; but who, when affairs were utterly desperate, at length executes the punishment which had been long held suspended over them. And the Lord does not testify in vain, that he proceeds to inflict punishment in a suitable and rightly attempered order; because, whenever he chastises us, we are apt to think that he acts towards us more severely than is just. Even when, with astonishing forbearance, he waits for us, until we have come to the utmost limit of impiety, and our wickedness has become too obstinate to be spared any longer; still we complain of the excessive haste of his rigour. Therefore he presents, as in a conspicuous picture, his equity in bearing with us, in order that we may know, that he never breaks forth to inflict punishment, except on those who are mature in crime. Now, if, on the other hand, we look at Sodom; there a horrible example of stupor meets our eyes. For the men of Sodom go on, as if they had nothing to do with God; their sense of good and evil being extinguished, they wallow like cattle in every kind of filth; and just as if they should never have to render an account of their conduct, they flatter themselves in their vices. Since this disease too much prevails in all ages, and is at present far too common, it is important to mark this circumstance, that at the very time when the men of Sodom, having dismissed all fear of God, were indulging themselves, and were promising themselves impunity, however they might sin, God was taking counsel to destroy them, and was moved, by the tumultuous cry of their iniquities, to descend to earth, while they were buried in profound sleep.

Wherefore, if God, at any time, defers his judgments ; let us not, therefore, think ourselves in a better condition ; but before the cry of our wickedness shall have wearied his ears, may we, aroused by His threats, quickly hasten to appease Him.   Since, however, such forbearance of God cannot be comprehended by us, Moses introduces Him as speaking according to the manner of men.

Whether they have done altogether according to the cry of it.[1] The Hebrew noun כָּלָה, (*cala,*) which Moses here uses, means the perfection, or the end of a thing, and also its destruction. Therefore, Jerome turns it, 'If they shall have completed it in act.' I have, indeed, no doubt but Moses intimates, that God came down, in order to inquire whether or not their sins had risen to the highest point : just as he before said, that the iniquities of the Amorites were not yet full.   The sum of the whole then is ; the Lord was about to see whether they were altogether desperate, as having precipitated themselves into the lowest depths of evil ; or whether they were still in the midst of a course, from which it was possible for them to be recalled to a sound mind ; forasmuch as he was unwilling utterly to destroy those cities, if, by any method, their wickedness was curable.   Others translate the passage, 'If they have done this, their final destruction is at hand : but if not, I will see how far they are to be punished.'   But the former sense is most accordant with the context.

22. *But Abraham stood yet before the Lord.*   Moses first declares that the men proceeded onwards, conveying the impression, that having finished their discourse, they took leave of Abraham, in order that he might return home.   He then adds, that Abraham stood before the Lord, as persons are wont to do, who, though dismissed, do not immediately depart, because something still remains to be said or done. Moses, when he makes mention of the journey, with propriety attributes the name of men to the angels ; but he does not, however, say, that Abraham stood before *men,* but before

---

[1] " Fecerint consummationem." If they have brought it to a consummation.   " Assavoir s'ils ont accompli."   If indeed they have accomplished, &c.—*French Tr.*

the face of God; because, although, with his eyes, he beheld the appearance of men, he yet, by faith, looked upon God. And his words sufficiently show, that he did not speak as he would have done with a mortal man. Whence we infer, that we act preposterously, if we allow the external symbols, by which God represents himself, to retard or hinder us from going directly to Him. By nature, truly, we are prone to this fault; but so much the more must we strive, that, by the sense of faith, we may be borne upward to God himself, lest the external signs should keep us down to this world. Moreover, Abraham approaches God, for the sake of showing reverence. For he does not, in a contentious spirit, oppose God, as if he had a right to intercede; he only suppliantly entreats: and every word shows the great humility and modesty of the holy man. I confess, indeed, that at times, holy men, carried away by carnal sense, have no self-government, but that, indirectly at least, they murmur against God. Here, however, Abraham addresses God with nothing but reverence, nor does anything fall from him worthy of censure; yet we must notice the affection of mind by which Abraham had been impelled to interpose his prayers on behalf of the inhabitants of Sodom. Some suppose, that he was more anxious concerning the safety of his nephew alone, than for Sodom and the rest of the cities; but that, being withheld by modesty, he would not request one man expressly to be given to him, while he entirely neglected a great people. But it is, by no means, probable that he made use of such dissimulation. I certainly do not doubt, that he was so touched with a common compassion towards the five cities, that he drew near to God as their intercessor. And if we weigh all things attentively, he had great reasons for doing so. He had lately rescued them from the hand of their enemies; he now suddenly hears that they are to be destroyed. He might imagine that he had rashly engaged in that war; that his victory was under a divine curse, as if he had taken arms against the will of God, for unworthy and wicked men; and it was possible that he would be not a little tormented by such thoughts. Besides, it was difficult to believe them all to have been so ungrateful, that no remembrance of their recent deliverance remained

among them. But it was not lawful for him, by a single
word, to dispute with God, after having heard what He had
determined to do. For God alone best knows what men
deserve, and with what severity they ought to be treated.
Why then does not Abraham acquiesce? Why does he imagine to himself, that there are some just persons in Sodom,
whom God has overlooked, and whom he hastens to overwhelm in a common destruction with the rest? I answer,
that the sense of humanity by which Abraham was moved,
was pleasing to God. First, because, as was becoming, he
leaves the entire cognizance of the fact with God. Secondly,
because he asks with sobriety and submission, for the sole
cause of obtaining consolation. There is no wonder that
he is terrified at the destruction of so great a multitude. He sees men created after the image of God; he
persuades himself that, in that immense crowd, there were,
at least, a few who were upright, or not altogether unjust, and abandoned to wickedness. He therefore alleges
before God, what he thinks available to procure their
forgiveness. He may, however, be thought to have acted
rashly, in requesting impunity to the evil, for the sake
of the good; for he desired God to spare the place, if he
should find fifty good men there. I answer, that the prayers
of Abraham did not extend so far as to ask God not to
scourge those cities, but only not to destroy them utterly; as
if he had said, 'O Lord, whatever punishment thou mayest inflict upon the guilty, wilt thou not yet leave some dwelling-
place for the righteous? Why should that region utterly
perish, as long as a people shall remain, by whom it may be
inhabited?' Abraham, therefore, does not desire that the
wicked, being mixed with the righteous, should escape the
hand of God: but only that God, in inflicting public punishment on a whole nation, should nevertheless exempt the
good who remained from destruction.

23. *Wilt thou also destroy the righteous with the wicked?* It
is certain that when God chastises the body of a people, he
often involves the good and the reprobate in the same punishment. So Daniel, Ezekiel, Ezra, and others like them,
who worshipped God in purity in their own country, were

suddenly hurried away into exile, as by a violent tempest : notwithstanding it had been said, ' The land vomiteth out her inhabitants, because of their iniquities,' (Lev. xviii. 25.) But when God thus seems to be angry with all in common, it behoves us to fix our eyes on the end, which shall evidently discriminate the one from the other. For if the husbandman knows how to separate the grains of wheat in his barn, which with the chaff are trodden under the feet of the oxen, or are struck out with the flail ; much better does God know how to gather together his faithful people,—when he has chastised them for a time,—from among the wicked, (who are like worthless refuse,) that they may not perish together; yea, by the very event, he will, at length, prove that he would not permit those whom he was healing by his chastisements to perish. For, so far is he from hastening to destroy his people, when he subjects them to temporal punishments, that he is rather administering to them a medicine which shall procure their salvation. I do not however doubt, that God had denounced the final destruction of Sodom; and in this sense Abraham now takes exception, that it was by no means consistent, that the same ruin should alike fall on the righteous and the ungodly. There will, however, be no absurdity in saying, that Abraham, having good hope of the repentance of the wicked, asked God to spare them ; because it often happens that God, out of regard to a few, deals gently with a whole people. For we know, that public punishments are mitigated, because the Lord looks upon his own with a benignant and paternal eye. In the same sense the answer of God himself ought to be understood, ' If in the midst of Sodom I find fifty righteous, I will spare the whole place for their sake.' Yet God does not here bind himself by a perpetual rule, so that it shall not be lawful for him, as often as he sees good, to bring the wicked and the just together to punishment. And, in order to show that he has free power of judging, he does not always adhere to the same equable moderation in this respect. He who would have spared Sodom on account of ten righteous persons, refused to grant the same terms of pardon to Jerusalem. (Matth. xi. 24.) Let us know, therefore, that God does not here lay himself under any necessity ; but that he speaks thus, in order to make it better known, that he does not, on light grounds, proceed to the destruction of a city, of which no portion remained unpolluted.

25. *Shall not the Judge of all the earth do right?* He does not here teach God His duty, as if any one should say to a judge, ' See what thy office requires, what is worthy of this place, what suits thy character; ' but he reasons from the nature of God, that it is impossible for Him to intend anything unjust. I grant that, in using the same form of speaking, the impious often murmur against God, but Abraham does far otherwise. For although he wonders how God should think of destroying Sodom, in which he was persuaded there was a number of good men; he yet retains this principle, that it was impossible for God, who is the Judge of the world, and by nature loves equity, yea, whose will is the law of justice and rectitude, should in the least degree swerve from righteousness. He desires, however, to be relieved from this difficulty with which he is perplexed. So, whenever different temptations contend within our minds, and some appearance of contradiction presents itself in the works of God, only let our persuasion of His justice remain fixed, and we shall be permitted to pour into His bosom the difficulties which torment us, in order that He may loosen the knots which we cannot untie. Paul seems to have taken from this place the answer with which he represses the blasphemy of those who charge God with unrighteousness. ' Is God unrighteous? Far from it, for how should there be unrighteousness with Him who judges the world?' (Rom. iii. 5, 6.) This method of appeal would not always avail among earthly judges; who are sometimes deceived by error, or perverted by favour, or inflamed with hatred, or corrupted by gifts, or misled by other means, to acts of injustice. But since God, to whom it naturally belongs to judge the world, is liable to none of these evils, it follows, that He can no more be drawn aside from equity, than he can deny himself to be God.

27. *Which am but dust and ashes.* Abraham speaks thus, for the sake of obtaining pardon. For what is mortal man

when compared with God? He therefore confesses that he is too bold, in thus familiarly interrogating God; yet he desires that this favour may be granted unto him, by the Divine indulgence. It is to be noted, that the nearer Abraham approaches to God, the more fully sensible does he become of the miserable and abject condition of men. For it is only the brightness of the glory of God which covers with shame and thoroughly humbles men, when stripped of their foolish and intoxicated self-confidence. Whosoever, therefore, seems to himself to be something, let him turn his eyes to God, and immediately he will acknowledge himself to be nothing. Abraham, indeed, was not forgetful that he possessed a living soul; but he selects what was most contemptible, in order to empty himself of all dignity. It may seem, however, that Abraham does but sophistically trifle with God, when, diminishing gradually from the number first asked, he proceeds to his sixth interrogation. I answer, that this was rather to be considered as the language of a perturbed mind. At first he anxiously labours for the men of Sodom, wherefore he omits nothing which may serve to mitigate his solicitude. And as the Lord repeatedly answers him so mildly, we know that he had not been deemed importunate, nor troublesome. But if he was kindly heard, when pleading for the inhabitants of Sodom, even to his sixth petition; much more will the Lord hearken to the prayers which any one may pour out for the Church and household of faith. Moreover, the humanity of Abraham appears also in this, that although he knows Sodom to be filled with vilest corruptions, he cannot bring his mind to think that all are infected with the contagion of wickedness; but he rather inclines to the equitable supposition, that, in so great a multitude, some just persons may be concealed. For this is a horrible prodigy, that the filth of iniquity should so pervade the whole body, as to allow no member to remain pure. We are, however, taught by this example, how tyrannically Satan proceeds when once the dominion of sin is established. And certainly, seeing the propensity of men to sin, and the facility for sinning are so great, it is not surprising that one should be corrupted by another, till the contagion reached every individual. For nothing is more dangerous than to live where the public license of crime prevails ; yea, there is no pestilence so destructive, as that corruption of morals, which is opposed neither by laws nor judgments, nor any other remedies. And although Moses, in the next chapter, explains the most filthy crime which reigned in Sodom, we must nevertheless remember what Ezekiel teaches, (xvi. 48, 49,) that the men of Sodom did not fall at once into such execrable wickedness; but that, in the beginning, luxury from the fulness of bread prevailed, and that, afterwards, pride and cruelty followed. At length, when they were given up to a reprobate mind, they were also driven headlong into brutal lusts. Therefore, if we dread this extreme of inordinate passion, let us cultivate temperance and frugality ; and let us always fear, lest a superfluity of food should impel us to luxury ; lest our minds should be infected with pride on account of our wealth, and lest delicacies should tempt us to give the reins to our lusts.

CHAPTER XIX.

1. AND there came two angels to Sodom at even ; and Lot sat in the gate of Sodom : and Lot seeing *them* rose up to meet them ; and he bowed himself with his face toward the ground ;

1. Et venerunt duo angeli in Sedom vesperi, Lot autem sedebat in porta Sedom : et vidit Lot et surrexit in occursum eorum, et incurvavit se facie super terram.

2. And he said, Behold now, my lords, turn in, I pray you, into your servant's house, and tarry all night, and wash your feet, and ye shall rise up early, and go on your ways. And they said, Nay ; but we will abide in the street all night.

2. Et dixit, Ecce, nunc domini mei, declinate obsecro ad domum servi vestri, et pernoctate, et lavate pedes vestros : et mane surgetis, et pergetis in viam vestram. Et dixerunt, Nequaquam, sed in platea pernoctabimus.

3. And he pressed upon them greatly ; and they turned in unto him, and entered into his house ; and he made them a feast, and did bake unleavened bread, and they did eat.

3. Et vehementer compulit eos, et declinaverunt ad eum, veneruntque ad domum ejus : et fecit eis convivium, et infermentata coxit, et comederunt.

4. But before they lay down, the men of the city, *even* the men of Sodom, compassed the house round, both old and young, all the people from every quarter :

4. Antequam dormirent, viri civitatis, viri Sedom gyro cinxerunt domum a puero usque ad senem, omnis populus ab extremo.

5. And they called unto Lot, and said unto him, Where *are* the men which came in to thee this night? bring them out unto us, that we may know them.

6. And Lot went out at the door unto them, and shut the door after him,

7. And said, I pray you, brethren, do not so wickedly.

8. Behold now, I have two daughters which have not known man; let me, I pray you, bring them out unto you, and do ye to them as *is* good in your eyes: only unto these men do nothing; for therefore came they under the shadow of my roof.

9. And they said, Stand back. And they said *again*, This one *fellow* came in to sojourn, and he will needs be a judge: now will we deal worse with thee than with them. And they pressed sore upon the man, *even* Lot, and came near to break the door.

10. But the men put forth their hand, and pulled Lot into the house to them, and shut to the door.

11. And they smote the men that *were* at the door of the house with blindness, both small and great: so that they wearied themselves to find the door.

12. And the men said unto Lot, Hast thou here any besides? son-in-law, and thy sons, and thy daughters, and whatsoever thou hast in the city, bring *them* out of this place:

13. For we will destroy this place, because the cry of them is waxen great before the face of the Lord; and the Lord hath sent us to destroy it.

14. And Lot went out, and spake unto his sons-in-law, which married his daughters, and said, Up, get you out of this place; for the Lord will destroy this city. But he seemed as one that mocked unto his sons-in-law.

15. And when the morning arose, then the angels hastened Lot, saying, Arise, take thy wife, and thy two daugh-

5. Et vocaverunt Lot, et dixerunt ei, Ubi *sunt* viri qui venerunt ad te nocte? educ eos ad nos, et cognoscemus eos.

6. Et egressus est ad eos Lot ad ostium, et ostium clausit post se.

7. Et dixit, Ne quæso, fratres mei, malefaciatis.

8. Ecce, nunc mihi sunt duæ filiæ, quæ non cognoverunt virum, educam nunc eas ad vos, et facite eis sicut bonum erit in oculis vestris: tantum viris istis ne faciatis quicquam, eo quod venerunt in umbram tigni mei.

9. Verum dixerunt, Accede huc. Dixerunt præterea, Unus venit ad perigrinandum, et judicabit judicando? nunc magis malefaciemus tibi quam ipsis. Et vim fecerunt in virum ipsum Lot valde: et appropinquaverunt ut frangerent ostium.

10. At miserunt viri manum suam, et introduxerunt Lot ad se in domum, et ostium clauserunt.

11. Viros autem, qui erant ad ostium domus, percusserunt cæcitate, a minimo usque ad maximum, et laboraverunt ut invenirent ostium.

12. Et dixerunt viri ad Lot, Adhuc est aliquis tibi hic? generum, et filios tuos, et filias tuas, et omnia, quæ sunt tibi in civitate, educ de loco:

13. Quia disperdimus nos locum hunc, eo quod crevit clamor eorum coram Jehova: et misit nos Jehova ad perdendum eum.

14. Et egressus est Lot, et loquutus est ad generos suos, qui acceperant filias ejus, et dixit, Surgite, egredimini de loco isto, quia disperdit Jehova civitatem: et fuit sicut ludens in oculis generorum suorum.

15. Quum vero aurora ascendisset, instabant angeli ipsi Lot, dicendo, Surge, cape ux-

ters, which are here; lest thou be consumed in the iniquity of the city.

16. And while he lingered, the men laid hold upon his hand, and upon the hand of his wife, and upon the hand of his two daughters; the Lord being merciful unto him: and they brought him forth, and set him without the city.

17. And it came to pass, when they had brought them forth abroad, that he said, Escape for thy life; look not behind thee, neither stay thou in all the plain; escape to the mountain, lest thou be consumed.

18. And Lot said unto them, Oh! not so, my lord:

19. Behold now, thy servant hath found grace in thy sight, and thou hast magnified thy mercy, which thou hast showed unto me in saving my life; and I cannot escape to the mountain, lest some evil take me, and I die:

20. Behold now, this city *is* near to flee unto, and it *is* a little one: Oh! let me escape thither, (*is* it not a little one?) and my soul shall live.

21. And he said unto him, See, I have accepted thee concerning this thing also, that I will not overthrow this city, for the which thou hast spoken.

22. Haste thee, escape thither; for I cannot do any thing till thou be come thither. Therefore the name of the city was called Zoar.

23. The sun was risen upon the earth when Lot entered into Zoar.

24. Then the Lord rained upon Sodom and upon Gomorrah brimstone and fire from the Lord out of heaven;

25. And he overthrew those cities, and all the plain, and all the inhabitants of the cities, and that which grew upon the ground.

26. But his wife looked back from behind him, and she became a pillar of salt.

27. And Abraham gat up early in the

orem tuam, et duas filias tuas, quæ adsunt, ne forte pereas in punitione civitatis.

16. Et tardabat: et apprehenderunt viri manum ejui, et manum uxoris ejus, et manum duarum filiarum ejus, eo quod parceret Jehova ei: et eduxerunt eum, et posuerunt eum extra urbem.

17. Et fuit, quum eduxissent ipsi eos foras, dixit, Evade pro anima tua, ne respicias post te, nec stes in tota planitie: in monte serva te, ne forte pereas.

18. Et dixit Lot ad eos, Ne quæso domini mei:

19. Ecce, nunc invenit servus tuus gratiam in oculis tuis, et magnificasti misericordiam tuam, quam fecisti mecum, ut vivificares animam meam: et ego non potero servare me in monte, ne forte hæreat mihi malum, et moriar:

20. Ecce, nunc civitas ista propinqua, ut fugiam illuc, et est parva: evadam nunc illuc: numquid non parva est, et vivet anima mea?

21. Et dixit ad eum, Ecce, suscepi faciem tuam etiam in hoc, ut non subvertam civitatem, ut loquutus es.

22. Festina, serva te illuc: quia non potero facere quicquam, donec ingrediaris illuc: idcirco vocavit nomen civitatis Sohar.

23. Sol egressus est super terram, et Lot ingressus est Sohar.

24. Et Jehova pluit super Sedom et super Hamorah sulphur et ignem a Jehova e cœlis.

25. Et subvertit civitates istas, et omnem planitiem, et omnes habitatores urbium, et germen terræ.

26. Et respexit uxor ejus post eum, et effecta est statua salis.

27. Et surrexit Abraham

morning to the place where he stood before the Lord:

28. And he looked toward Sodom and Gomorrah, and toward all the land of the plain, and beheld, and, lo, the smoke of the country went up as the smoke of a furnace.

29. And it came to pass, when God destroyed the cities of the plain, that God remembered Abraham, and sent Lot out of the midst of the overthrow, when he overthrew the cities in the which Lot dwelt.

30. And Lot went up out of Zoar, and dwelt in the mountain, and his two daughters with him; for he feared to dwell in Zoar: and he dwelt in a cave, he and his two daughters.

31. And the first-born said unto the younger, Our father *is* old, and *there is* not a man in the earth to come in unto us after the manner of all the earth:

32. Come, let us make our father drink wine, and we will lie with him, that we may preserve seed of our father.

33. And they made their father drink wine that night: and the first-born went in, and lay with her father; and he perceived not when she lay down, nor when she arose.

34. And it came to pass on the morrow, that the first-born said unto the younger, Behold, I lay yesternight with my father: let us make him drink wine this night also; and go thou in, *and* lie with him, that we may preserve seed of our father.

35. And they made their father drink wine that night also: and the younger arose, and lay with him; and he perceived not when she lay down, nor when she arose.

36. Thus were both the daughters of Lot with child by their father.

37. And the first-born bare a son, and called his name Moab: the same *is* the father of the Moabites unto this day.

38. And the younger she also bare a

mane ad locum, ubi steterat coram Jehova.

28. Et respexit super faciem Sedom et Hamorah, et super omnem faciem terræ planitiei: et videt, et ecce, ascendebat fumus terræ sicut fumus fornacis.

29. Et fuit, quum disperderet Deus urbes planitiei, recordatus est Deus Abraham, et emisit Lot e medio subversionis, quando subvertit civitates, in quarum una habitabat Lot.

30. Et ascendit Lot de Sohar, et habitavit in monte, et duæ filiæ ejus cum eo: quia timuit habitare in Sohar, et habitavit in spelunca, ipse et duæ filiæ ejus.

31. Et dixit primogenita ad minorem, Pater noster senex est, et vir non est in terra, ut ingrediatur ad nos secundum morem universæ terræ.

32. Veni, potum demus patri nostro vinum, et dormiamus cum eo, et vivificemus de patre nostro semen.

33. Et potum dederunt patri suo vinum, nocte ipsa: et ingressa est primogenita, et dormivit cum patre suo, qui non cognovit, quando dormivit ipsa, nec quando surrexit ipsa.

34. Et fuit postridie, dixit primogenita ad minorem, Ecce, dormivi heri sero cum patre meo: potum demus ei vinum etiam hac nocte, et ingredere, dormi cum eo, et vivificemus de patre nostro semen.

35. Et potum dederunt etiam nocte ipsa patri suo vinum: et surrexit minor, et dormivit cum eo: nec cognovit quando dormivit ipsa, nec quando surrexit ipsa.

36. Et conceperunt duæ filiæ Lot de patre suo.

37. Et peperit primogenita filium, et vocavit nomen ejus Moab: ipse est pater Moab usque ad diem hanc.

38. Et minor etiam ipsa pe-

son, and called his name Ben-ammi :   perit filium, et vocavit nomen
the same *is* the father of the children of   ejus Ben-Hammi: ipse est pater
Ammon unto this day.   filiorum Hammon usque ad
   diem hanc.

1. *And there came two angels to Sodom.* The question
occurs, why one of the three angels has suddenly disappeared,
and two only are come to Sodom ? The Jews (with their
wonted audacity in introducing fables) pretend that one came
to destroy Sodom, the other to preserve Lot. But from the
discourse of Moses, this appears to be frivolous : because we
shall see that they both assisted in the liberation of Lot.
What I have before adduced is more simple ; namely, that it
was granted to Abraham, as a peculiar favour, that God would
not only send him two messengers from the angelic host, but
that, in a more familiar manner, he would manifest himself
to him, in his own Son. For (as we have seen) one of the
messengers held the principal place, as being superior to the
others in dignity. Now, although Christ was always the
Mediator, yet, because he manifested himself more obscurely
to Lot than he did to Abraham, the two angels only came
to Sodom. Since Moses relates, that Lot sat in the gate of
the city about evening, many contend that he did so, according
to daily custom, for the purpose of receiving guests into his
house ; yet, as Moses is silent respecting the cause, it would
be rash to affirm this as certain. I grant, indeed, that he
did not sit as idle persons are wont to do ; but the conjecture
is not less probable, that he had come forth to meet his shepherds, in order to be present when his sheep were folded.
That he was hospitable, the courteous invitation which is
mentioned by Moses clearly demonstrates ; yet, why he
then remained in the gate of the city is uncertain ; unless it
were, that he was unwilling to omit any opportunity of doing
an act of kindness, when strangers presented themselves, on
whom he might bestow his services. What remains, on this
point, may be found in the preceding chapter.

2. *Nay, but we will abide in the street.* The angels do not
immediately assent, in order that they may the more fully
investigate the disposition of the holy man. For he was

about to bring them to his own house, not merely for the sake of supplying them with a supper, but for the purpose of defending them from the force and injury of the citizens. Therefore the angels act, as if it were safe to sleep on the highway; and thus conceal their knowledge of the abandoned wickedness of the whole people. For if the gates of cities are shut, to prevent the incursions of wild beasts and of enemies; how wrong and absurd it is that they who are within should be exposed to still more grievous dangers ? Therefore the angels thus speak, in order to make the wickedness of the people appear the greater. And Lot, in urging the angels to come unto him, for the purpose of protecting them from the common violence of the people, the more clearly shows, how careful he was of his guests, lest they should suffer any dishonour or injury.

3. *And he made them a feast.* By these words, and others following, Moses shows that the angels were more sumptuously entertained than was customary : for Lot did not act thus, indiscriminately, with all. But, when he conceived, from the dignity of their mien and dress, that they were not common men, he baked cakes, and prepared a plentiful feast. Again, Moses says that the angels did eat : not that they had any need to do so ; but because the time was not yet come, for the manifestation of their celestial nature.

4. *Before they lay down.* Here, in a single crime, Moses sets before our eyes a lively picture of Sodom. For it is hence obvious, how diabolical was their consent in all wickedness, since they all so readily conspired to perpetrate the most abominable crime. The greatness of their iniquity and wantonness, is apparent from the fact, that, in a collected troop, they approach, as enemies, to lay siege to the house of Lot. How blind and impetuous is their lust; since, without shame, they rush together like brute animals ! how great their ferocity and cruelty ; since they reproachfully threaten the holy man, and proceed to all extremities ! Hence also we infer, that they were not contaminated with one vice only, but were given up to all audacity in crime, so that no

sense of shame was left them.   And Ezekiel (as we have
above related) accurately describes from what beginnings of
evil they had proceeded to this extreme turpitude, (Ezekiel
xvi. 49.)   What Paul says, also refers to the same point:
that God punished the impiety of men, when he cast them
into such a state of blindness, that they gave themselves up
to abominable lusts, and dishonoured their own bodies. (Rom.
i. 18.)   But when the sense of shame is overcome, and the
reins are given to lust, a vile and outrageous barbarism
necessarily succeeds, and many kinds of sin are blended
together, so that a most confused chaos is the result.   But
if this severe vengeance of God so fell upon the men of
Sodom, that they became blind with rage, and prostituted
themselves to all kinds of crime, certainly we shall scarcely
be more mildly treated, whose iniquity is the less excusable,
because the truth of God has been more clearly revealed
unto us.

Both old and young.   Moses passes over many things in
silence which may come unsought into the reader's mind:
for instance, he does not mention by whom the multitude had
been stirred up.   Yet it is probable that there were some
who fanned the flame: nevertheless, we hence perceive how
freely they were disposed to commit iniquity; since, as at a
given signal, they immediately assemble.   It also shows how
completely destitute they were of all remaining shame; for,
neither did any gravity restrain the old, nor any modesty,
suitable to their age, restrain the young: finally, he intimates,
that all regard to honour was gone, and that the order of
nature was perverted, when he says, that young and old flew
together from the extreme parts of the city.

5. *Where are the men?*   Although it was their intention
shamefully to abuse the strangers to their outrageous appetite,
yet, in words, they pretend that their object is different.   For,
as if Lot had been guilty of a fault in admitting unknown men
into the city, wherein he himself was a stranger, they command these men to be brought out before them.   Some
expound the word *know* in a carnal sense; and thus the Greek

interpreters have translated it.[1]   But I think the word has here a different meaning; as if the men had said, We wish to know whom thou bringest, as guests, into our city.   The Scripture truly is accustomed modestly to describe an act of shame by the word *know;* and therefore we may infer that the men of Sodom would have spoken, in coarser language, of such an act : but, for the sake of concealing their wicked design, they here imperiously expostulate with the holy man, for having dared to receive unknown persons into his house. Here, however, a question arises ; for if the men of Sodom were in the habit of vexing strangers, of all kinds, in this manner, how shall we suppose they had acted towards others ? For Lot was not now for the first time beginning to be hospitable ; and they, too, had always been addicted to lust. Lot was prepared to expose his own daughters to dishonour, in order to save his guests ; how often, then, might it have been necessary to prostitute them before, if the fury of men of such character could not be otherwise assuaged ?[2] Now, truly, if Lot had known that such danger was impending ; he ought rather to have exhorted his guests to withdraw in time.   In my opinion, however, although Lot knew the manners of the city; he had, nevertheless, no suspicion of what really happened, that they would make an assault upon his house ; this, indeed, seems to have been quite a new thing.   It was, however, fitting, when the angels were sent to investigate the true state of the people, that they should all break out into this detestable crime.   So the wicked, after they have long securely exulted in their iniquity, at length, by furiously rushing onward, accelerate their destruction in a moment. God therefore designed, in calling the men of Sodom to judgment, to exhibit, as it were, the extreme act of their wicked life ; and he impelled them, by the spirit of deep infatuation, to a crime, the atrocity of which would not suffer the destruction of the place to be any longer deferred. For as the hospitality of the holy man, Lot, was honoured

---

[1] " Ἵνα συγγενώμεθα αὐτοῖς."—*Sept.*

[2] " Si non alio remedio placari poterat eorum rabies, qui viros ad stuprum flagitabant."

with a signal reward; because he, unawares, received angels instead of men, and had them as guests in his house; so God avenged, with more severe punishment, the shameful lust of the others; who, while endeavouring to do violence to angels, were not only injurious towards men; but, to the utmost of their power, dishonoured the celestial glory of God, by their sacrilegious fury.

6. *And Lot went out at the door unto them.* It appears from the fact that Lot went out and exposed himself to danger, how faithfully he observed the sacred right of hospitality. It was truly a rare virtue, that he preferred the safety and honour of the guests whom he had once undertaken to protect, to his own life: yet this degree of magnanimity is required from the children of God, that where duty and fidelity are concerned, they should not spare themselves. And although he was already grievously injured by the besieging of his house; he yet endeavours, by gentle words, to soothe ferocious minds, while he suppliantly entreats them to lay aside their wickedness, and addresses them by the title of brethren. Now it appears, how savage was their cruelty, and how violent the rage of their lust, when they were in no degree moved by such extraordinary mildness. But the description of a rage so brutal, tends to teach us that punishment was not inflicted upon them, until they had proceeded to the last stage of wickedness. And let us remember, that the reprobate, when they have been blinded by the just judgment of God, rush, as with devoted minds, through every kind of crime, and leave nothing undone, until they render themselves altogether hateful and detestable to God and men.

8. *I have two daughters.* As the constancy of Lot, in risking his own life for the defence of his guests, deserves no common praise; so now Moses relates that a defect was mixed with this great virtue, which sprinkled it with some imperfection. For, being destitute of advice, he devises (as is usual in intricate affairs) an unlawful remedy. He does not hesitate to prostitute his own daughters, that he may restrain the indo-

mitable fury of the people.   But he should rather have
endured a thousand deaths, than have resorted to such a
measure.   Yet such are commonly the works of holy men :
since nothing proceeds from them so excellent, as not to be
in some respect defective.   Lot, indeed, is urged by extreme
necessity ; and it is no wonder that he offers his daughters to
be polluted, when he sees that he has to deal with wild beasts ;
yet he inconsiderately seeks to remedy one evil by means of
another.   I can easily excuse some for extenuating his fault;
yet he is not free from blame, because he would ward off
evil with evil.   But we are warned, by this example, that
when the Lord has furnished us with the spirit of invincible
fortitude, we must also pray that he may govern us by the
spirit of prudence ; and that he will never suffer us to be
deprived of a sound judgment, and a well-regulated reason.   For then only shall we rightly proceed in our course of
duty, when, in complicated affairs, we perceive, with a composed mind, what is necessary, what is lawful, and what is
expedient to be done ; then shall we be prepared promptly to
meet any danger whatever.   For, that our minds should be
carried hither and thither by hastily catching at wicked counsels, is not less perilous than that they should be agitated by
fear.   But when reduced to the last straits, let us learn to
pray, that the Lord would open to us some way of escape.
Others would excuse Lot by a different pretext, namely, that
he knew his daughters would not be desired.   But I have no
doubt that, being willing to avail himself of the first subterfuge which occurred to him, he turned aside from the
right way.   This, however, is indisputable ; although the men
of Sodom had not yet, in express terms, avowed the base
desire with which they were inflamed, yet Lot, from their daily
crimes, had formed his judgment respecting it.   If any one
should raise the objection that such a supposition is absurd ;[1]
I answer, that, since by custom they had imagined the crime
to be lawful, the crowd was easily excited by a few instiga-
tors, as it commonly happens, where no distinction is maintained between right and wrong.   When Lot says, " There-

[1] " Siquis absurdum esse objiciat, totum populum duos viros ad stuprum captasse," &c.

fore came they under the shadow of my roof;" his meaning is, that they had been committed to him by the Lord, and that he should be guilty of perfidy, unless he endeavoured to protect them.[1]

9. *And they said, Stand back.* That Lot, with all his entreaties, than which nothing could be adduced more likely to soothe their rage, was thus harshly repelled, shows the indomitable haughtiness of this people. And, in the first place, they threaten that, if he persists in interceding, they will deal worse with him than with those whom he defends. Then they reproach him with the fact, that he, a foreigner, assumes the province of a judge. Every word proves the pride with which they swell. They place one man in opposition to a multitude, as if they would say, 'By what right dost thou alone challenge to thyself authority over the whole city?' They next boast that, while they are natives, he is but a stranger. Such is, at the present time, the boasting of the Papists against the pious ministers of God's word : they allege against us, as a disgrace, the paucity of our numbers, in contrast with their own great multitude.[2] Then they pride themselves upon their long succession, and contend that it is intolerable for them to be reproved by *new* men.[3] But however contumaciously the wicked may strive, rather than submit to reason, let us know that they are exalted only to their own ruin.

10. *But the men put forth their hand.* Moses again gives the name of men to those who were not so, but who had appeared as such ; for although they begin to exert their celestial force, they do not yet declare that they are angels

---

[1] It will be thought that Calvin has said enough, and more than enough, in excuse of this strange conduct of Lot. It serves to show the low tone of morals, not only in the world at large, but among those who had enjoyed the advantages of a religious education. At the same time, it affords evidence of the kind of chivalrous regard which was paid to strangers, and of which so much is read in profane writers.—*Ed.*

[2] " Car ils objectent comme pour reproche, que nous ne sommes que une pongnee de gens, et qu'eux sont bien en plus grand nombre."—*French Tr.*

[3] As the Reformation was styled the *new religion*, so the reformers were stigmatized as *new men.—Ed.*

divinely sent from heaven. But here Moses teaches, that the Lord, although he may for a time seem regardless, while the faithful are engaged in conflict, yet never deserts his own, but stretches out his hand, (so to speak,) at the critical moment. Thus, in preserving Lot, he defers his aid until the last extremity. Let us, therefore, with tranquil minds, wait on his providence; and let us intrepidly follow what belongs to our calling, and what he commands; for although he may suffer us to be exposed to danger, he will still show, that he has never been unmindful of us. For we see, that as Lot had shut the door of his house for the protection of his guests, so he is repaid, when the angels not only receive him again, through the opened door, but by opposing the barriers of divine power, prevent the impious men from approaching it. For, (as I have before intimated,) they afford him not merely human help, but they come to bring him assistance, armed with divine power. Whereas, Moses says, that the men were smitten with blindness, we are not so to understand it, as if they had been deprived of eye-sight; but that their vision was rendered so dull, that they could distinguish nothing. This miracle was more illustrious, than if their eyes had been thrust out, or entirely blinded; because with their eyes open, they feel about, just like blind men, and seeing, yet do not see. At the same time, Moses wishes to describe their iron obstinacy: they do not find Lot's door; it follows then, that they had laboured in seeking it; but, in this manner, they furiously wage war with God. This, however, has happened, not once only, and not with the men of Sodom alone; but is daily fulfilled in the reprobate, whom Satan fascinates with such madness, that when stricken by the mighty hand of God, they proceed with stupid obstinacy to advance against him. And we need not seek far, for an instance of such conduct; we see with what tremendous punishments God visits wandering lusts; and yet the world ceases not, with desperate audacity, to rush into the certain destruction which is set before their eyes.

12. *Hast thou here any besides?* At length the angels de-

clare for what purpose they came, and what they were about to do. For so great was the indignity of the last act of this people, that Lot must now see how impossible it was for God to bear with them any longer. And, in the first place, they declare, that they are come to destroy the city, because " the cry of it was waxen great." By which words they mean, that God was provoked, not by one act of wickedness only, but that, after he had long spared them, he was now, at last, almost compelled, by their immense mass of crimes, to come down to inflict punishment. For we must maintain, that the more sins men heap together, the higher will their wickedness rise, and the nearer will it approach to God, to cry aloud for vengeance. Wherefore, as the angels testify, that God had been hitherto long-suffering, and of great forbearance; so they declare, on the other hand, what issue awaits all those, who, having gathered together mountains of guilt, exalt themselves with daily increasing audacity, as if, like the giants, they were about to assail heaven. They, however, explain the cause of this destruction, not only that Lot may ascribe praise to the divine righteousness and equity, but that he, being impressed with fear, may the more quickly hasten his departure. For, such is the indolence of our flesh, that we slowly and coldly set ourselves to escape the judgment of God, unless we are deeply stirred by the dread of it : thus Noah, alarmed by the terror of the deluge, applied his industry to the framing of the ark. Meanwhile, the angels inspire the mind of the holy man with hope; lest he should tremble, or should be so possessed by fear, and so desponding respecting his deliverance, as to be too slow to depart. For they not only promise that he shall be safe, but also grant, unasked, the life of his family. And truly, he ought not to have doubted respecting his own life, when he saw others freely given him, as by a superabundance of favour. It is however asked, ' Why was God willing to offer his kindness to ungrateful men, by whom he knew it would be rejected ?' The same question may be put respecting the preaching of the gospel; for God was not ignorant that few would become partakers of that salvation, which, nevertheless, he commands to be offered indiscriminately to all.

In this way, unbelievers are rendered more inexcusable, when they reject the message of salvation. The chief reason, however, why Lot is commanded to set before his own family the hope of deliverance, is, that he may embrace, with greater confidence, the offered favour of God, and may strenuously and quickly prepare himself to depart, not doubting of his own preservation. It is, with probability, inferred from this place, that he had, then, no sons in that city; for, in consequence of the exhortation of the angels, he would immediately have attempted to draw them out of it. We have before seen, that he had an ample and numerous band of servants; but no mention is made of them, since the freemen are here only reckoned. It is, nevertheless, probable, that some servants went forth with him, to carry provisions and some portion of furniture. For, whence did his daughters obtain in the desert mountain, the wine which they gave their father, unless some things, which Moses does not mention, had been conveyed by asses, or camels, or waggons? It was however possible, that, in so great a number, many chose rather to perish with the men of Sodom, than to become associates and companions of their lord, in seeking safety. But it is better to leave as we find them, those things which the Spirit of God has not revealed.

13. *The Lord hath sent us to destroy it.* This place teaches us, that the angels are the ministers of God's wrath, as well as of his grace. Nor does it form any objection to this statement, that elsewhere the latter service is peculiarly ascribed to holy angels : as when the Apostle says, they were appointed for the salvation of those whom God had adopted as sons. (Heb. i. 14.) And the Scripture, in various places, testifies, that the guardianship of the pious is committed to them, (Ps. xci. 11;) while, on the other hand, it declares that God executes his judgments by reprobate angels. (Ps. lxxviii. 49.) For it must be maintained, that God causes his elect angels to preside over those judgments which he executes by means of the reprobate. For it would be absurd to attribute to devils, the honour of presiding over the judgments of God, since they do not yield him voluntary obedience; but rather, while raging contumaciously against him, are yet reluctantly com-

pelled to become his executioners. Let us therefore know,
that it is not foreign to the office of elect angels, to descend
armed for the purpose of executing Divine vengeance, and of
inflicting punishment. As the angel of the Lord destroyed,
in one night, the army of Sennacherib which besieged Jerusalem, (2 Kings xix. 35;) so also the angel of the Lord
appeared to David with his drawn sword, when the pestilence
was raging against the people. (2 Sam. xxiv. 16.)   But, as I
have before said, the angels repeat what they had previously
said to Abraham, concerning the *cry* of Sodom, that they may
the more urgently impel Lot, by a detestation of the place,
to take his flight, and may induce him, by the fear of the
wrath of God, to seek for safety.

14. *And Lot went out.* The faith of the holy man, Lot,
appeared first in this, that he was completely awed and
humbled at the threatenings of God; secondly, that in the
midst of destruction, he yet laid hold of the salvation promised
to him.   In inviting his sons-in-law to join him, he manifests
such diligence as becomes the sons of God; who ought to
labour, by all means, to rescue their own families from destruction.   But when Moses says, ' he appeared as one who
mocked;' the meaning is, that the pious old man was despised
and derided, and that what he said was accounted a fable;
because his sons-in-law supposed him to be seized with delirium, and to be vainly framing imaginary dangers.   Lot,
therefore, did not seem to them to mock purposely, or to have
come for the sake of trifling with them; but they deemed his
language fabulous; because, where there is no religion, and no
fear of God, whatever is said concerning the punishment of
the wicked, vanishes as a vain and illusory thing.   And hence
we perceive how fatal an evil security is, which so inebriates,
yea, fascinates, the minds of the wicked, that they no longer
think God sits as Judge in heaven; and thus they stupidly
sleep in sin, till, while they are saying, "Peace and safety," they
are overwhelmed in sudden ruin.   And especially, the nearer
the vengeance of God approaches, the more does their obstinacy increase and become desperate.   There is nothing more
full of fear, and even of terror, than wicked men are, when

the hand of God presses closely on them ; but until, constrained by force, they perceive their destruction to be imminent, they either reject all threats with proud scorn, or contemptuously pass them by.   But their indolence ought to
awaken us to the fear of God, so that we may be always careful ; but more especially when some token of the wrath of
God presents itself before us.

15. *The angels hastened Lot.*   Having praised the faith
and piety of Lot, Moses shows that something human still
adhered to him ; because the angels hastened him, when he
was lingering.   The cause of his tardiness might be, that he
thought he was going into exile : thus a multiplicity of cares
and fears disturb his anxious mind.   For he doubts what
would happen to him, as a fugitive, when, having left his house
and furniture, naked and in want, he should betake himself
to some desert place.   In the meantime, he does not consider
that he must act like persons shipwrecked, who, in order that
they may come safe into port, cast into the sea their cargo,
and every thing they have.   He does not indeed doubt, that
God is speaking the truth ; nor does he refuse to remove
elsewhere, as he is commanded ; but, as if sinking under his
own infirmity, and entangled with many cares, he, who ought
to have run forth hastily, and without delay, moves with slow
and halting pace.   In his person, however, the Spirit of God
presents to us, as in a mirror, our own tardiness ; in order
that we, shaking off all sloth, may learn to prepare ourselves
for prompt obedience, as soon as the heavenly voice sounds
in our ears ; otherwise, in addition to that indolence which,
by nature, dwells within us, Satan will interpose many delays.
The angels, in order the more effectually to urge Lot forward,
infuse the fear, lest he should be destroyed in the *iniquity*,
or the *punishment* of the city.   For the word עָוֺן *(ayon)*
signifies both.   Not that the Lord rashly casts the innocent
on the same heap with the wicked, but because the man, who
will not consult for his own safety, and who, even being
warned to beware, yet exposes himself, by his sloth, to ruin,
deserves to perish.

16. *And while he lingered, the men laid hold upon his hand.*
The angels first urged him by words; now, seizing him by
the hand, and indeed with apparent violence, they compel
him to depart.   His tardiness is truly wonderful, since,
though he was certainly persuaded that the angels did not
threaten in vain, he could yet be moved, by no force of words,
until he is dragged by their hands out of the city.   Christ
says, 'Though the spirit is willing, the flesh is weak,' (Matth.
xxvi. 41 :) here a worse fault is pointed out ; because the flesh,
by its sluggishness, so represses the alacrity of the spirit, that,
with slow halting, it can scarcely creep along.   And, indeed,
as every man's own experience bears him witness of this evil,
the faithful ought to endeavour, with the greater earnestness,
to prepare themselves to follow God ; and to beware lest, as
with deaf ears, they disregard his threats.   And truly, they
will never so studiously and forcibly press forward as not still
to be retarded, more than enough, in the discharge of their
duty.   For what Moses says is worthy of attention, that the
Lord was merciful to his servant, when, having laid hold of
his hand by the angels, He hurried him out of the city.   For
so it is often necessary for us to be forcibly drawn away from
scenes which we do not willingly leave.   If riches, or honours,
or any other things of that kind, prove an obstacle to any
one, to render him less free and disengaged for the service of
God, when it happens that he is abridged of his fortune, or
reduced to a lower rank, let him know that the Lord has laid
hold of his hand ; because words and exhortations had not
sufficiently profited him.   We ought not, therefore, to deem
it hard, that those diseases, which instruction did not suffice
effectually to correct, should be healed by more violent remedies.   Moses even seems to point to something greater ;
namely, that the mercy of God strove with the sluggishness
of Lot; for, if left to himself, he would, by lingering, have
brought down upon his own head the destruction which was
already near.   Yet the Lord not only pardons him, but, being
resolved to save him, seizes him by the hand, and draws him
away, although making resistance.

17. *Escape for thy life.*   This was added by Moses, to

teach us, that the Lord not only stretches out his hand to us for a moment, in order to begin our salvation ; but that without leaving his work imperfect, he will carry it on even to the end. It certainly was no common act of grace, that the ruin of Sodom was predicted to Lot himself, lest it should crush him unawares ; next, that a certain hope of salvation was given him by the angels ; and, finally, that he was led by the hand out of the danger. Yet the Lord, not satisfied with having granted him so many favours, informs him of what was afterwards to be done, and thus proves himself to be the Director of his course, till he should arrive at the haven of safety.[1] Lot is forbidden to look behind him, in order that he may know, that he is leaving a pestilential habitation. This was done, first, that he might indulge no desire after it, and then, that he might the better reflect on the singular kindness of God, by which he had escaped hell. Moses had before related, how fertile and rich was that plain ; Lot is now commanded to depart thence, that he may perceive himself to have been delivered, as out of the midst of a shipwreck. And although, while dwelling in Sodom, his heart was continually vexed ; it was still scarcely possible that he should avoid contracting some defilement from a sink of wickedness so profound : being now, therefore, about to be purified by the Lord, he is deprived of those delights in which he had taken too much pleasure. Let us also hence learn, that God best provides for our salvation, when he cuts off those superfluities, which serve to the pampering of the flesh ; and when, for the purpose of correcting excessive self-indulgence, he banishes us from a sweet and pleasant plain, to a desert mountain.

18. *And Lot said unto them.* Here another fault of Lot is censured, because he does not simply obey God, nor suffer himself to be preserved according to His will, but contrives some new method of his own. God assigns him a mountain as his future place of refuge, he rather chooses for himself a city. They are therefore under a mistake, who so highly extol his faith, as to deem this a perfect example of

---

[1] " Ad salutis metam."—" Au port de salut."—*French Tr.*

suitable prayer; for the design of Moses is rather to teach,
that the faith of Lot was not entirely pure, and free from all
defects. For it is to be held as an axiom, that our prayers
are faulty, so far as they are not founded on the word. Lot,
however, not only departs from the word, but preposterously
indulges himself in opposition to the word; such importunity
has, certainly, no affinity with faith. Afterwards, a sudden
change of mind was the punishment of his foolish cupidity.
For thus do all necessarily vacillate, who do not submit themselves to God. As soon as they attain one wish, immediately
a new disquietude is produced, which compels them to change
their opinion. It must then, in short, be maintained, that
Lot is by no means free from blame, in wishing for a city as
his residence; for he both sets himself in opposition to the
command of God, which it was his duty to obey; and desires
to remain among those pleasures, from which it was profitable for him to be removed. He, therefore, acts just as a
sick person would do, who should decline an operation, or a
bitter draught, which his physician had prescribed. Nevertheless, I do not suppose, that the prayer of Lot was altogether destitute of faith; I rather think, that though he
declined from the right way, he not only did not depart far
from it, but was even fully purposed in his mind to keep it.
For he always depended upon the word of God; but in one
particular he fell from it, by entreating that a place should be
given to him, which had been denied. Thus, with the pious
desires of holy men, some defiled and turbid admixture is often
found. I am not however ignorant, that sometimes they are
constrained, by a remarkable impulse of the Spirit, to depart
in appearance from the word, yet without really transgressing
its limits. But the immoderate carnal affection of Lot
betrays itself, in that he is held entangled by those very
delights which he ought to have shunned. Moreover, his
inconstancy is a proof of his rashness, because he is soon
displeased with himself for what he has done.

19. *Behold now, thy servant hath found grace in thy sight.*
Though Lot saw two persons, he yet directs his discourse to
one. Whence we infer, that he did not rely upon the

angels; because he was well convinced, that they had no
authority of their own, and that his salvation was not placed
in their hands. He uses therefore their presence in no other
way than as a mirror, in which the face of God may be con-
templated. Besides, Lot commemorates the kindness of God,
not so much for the sake of testifying his gratitude, as of
acquiring thence greater confidence in asking for more. For
since the goodness of God is neither exhausted, nor wearied,
by bestowing; the more ready we find him to give, the
more confident does it become us to be, in hoping for what is
good.   And this truly is the property of faith, to take
encouragement[1] for the future, from the experience of past
favour. And Lot does not err on this point; but he acts
rashly in going beyond the word for the sake of self-gratifica-
tion. Therefore I have said, that his prayer, though it flowed
from the fountain of faith, yet drew something turbid from
the mire of carnal affection. Let us then, relying upon the
mercy of God, not hesitate to expect all things from him ;
especially those which he himself has promised, and which he
permits us to choose.

I cannot escape to the mountain. He does not indeed rage
against God, with determined malice, as the wicked are wont
to do; yet, because he rests not upon the word of God, he
slides, and almost falls away. For why does he fear destruction in the mountain, where he was to be protected by the
hand of God, and yet expect to find a safe abode in that
place, which is both near to Sodom, and obnoxious to similar
vengeance, on account of its impure and wicked inhabitants ?
But this verily is the nature of men, that they choose to seek
their safety in hell itself, rather than in heaven, whenever
they follow their own reason. We see, then, how greatly Lot
errs, in fleeing from, and entertaining suspicions of, a mountain
infected with no contagion of iniquity, and choosing a city
which, overflowing with crimes, could not but be hateful to
God. He pretends that it is a little one, in order that he
may the more easily obtain his request. As if he had said,
that he only wanted a corner where he might be safely shel-

---

[1] " Confirmationem patere."   Quære, *capere.*   " Elle prene confirmation."—*French Tr.—Ed.*

tered. This would have been right, if he had not declined the asylum divinely granted to him, and rashly contrived another for himself.

21. *See, I have accepted thee concerning this thing also.* Some ignorantly argue from this expression, that Lot's prayer was pleasing to God, because he assented to his request, and gave him what he sought. For it is no new thing for the Lord sometimes to grant, as an indulgence, what he, nevertheless, does not approve. And he now indulges Lot, but in such a way, that he soon afterwards corrects his folly. Meanwhile, however, since God so kindly and gently bears with the evil wishes of his own people, what will he not do for us if our prayers are regulated according to the pure direction of his Spirit, and are drawn from his word? But after the angel has granted him his wish respecting the place, he again reproves his indolence, by exhorting him to make haste.

22. *I cannot do any thing.* Since the angel had not only been sent as an avenger to destroy Sodom, but also had received a command for the preservation of Lot; he therefore declares, that he will not do the former act, unless this latter be joined with it; because it is not at the option of the servant to divide those things which God has joined together. I am not, however, dissatisfied with the explanation of some, who suppose the angel to speak in the person of God. For although in appearance the language is harsh, yet there is no absurdity in saying, that God is unable to destroy the reprobate without saving his elect. Nor must we, therefore, deem his power to be limited, when he lays himself under any such necessity;[1] or that anything of his liberty and authority is diminished, when he willingly and freely binds himself. And let us especially remember, that his power is connected by a sacred bond with his grace, and with faith in his promises. Hence it may be truly and properly said, that he can do nothing but what he wills and promises. This is a true and profitable doctrine. There will, however, be less ground of

---

[1] "Dum sibi ipse est necessitas." Literally, "When he is his own necessity."

scruple if we refer the passage to the angels ; who had a positive commandment, from which it was not lawful for them to abate the smallest portion.

24. *Then the Lord rained.* Moses here succinctly relates, in very unostentatious language, the destruction of Sodom and of the other cities. The atrocity of the case might well demand a much more copious narration, expressed in tragic terms ; but Moses, according to his manner, simply recites the judgment of God, which no words would be sufficiently vehement to describe, and then leaves the subject to the meditation of his readers. It is therefore our duty to concentrate all our thoughts on that terrible vengeance, the bare mention of which, as it did not take place without a mighty concussion of heaven and earth, ought justly to make us tremble ; and therefore it is so frequently mentioned in the Scriptures. And it was not the will of God that those cities should be simply swallowed up by an earthquake ; but in order to render the example of his judgment the ore conspicuous, he hurled fire and brimstone upon them out of heaven. To this point belongs what Moses says, " that the Lord rained fire from the Lord." The repetition is emphatical, because the Lord did not then cause it to rain, in the ordinary course of nature ; but, as if with a stretched out hand, he openly fulminated in a manner to which he was not accustomed, for the purpose of making it sufficiently plain, that this rain of fire and brimstone was produced by no natural causes. It is indeed true, that the air is never agitated by chance ; and that God is to be acknowledged as the Author of even the least shower of rain ; and it is impossible to excuse the profane subtlety of Aristotle, who, when he disputes so acutely concerning second causes, in his Book on Meteors, buries God himself in profound silence. Moses, however, here expressly commends to us the extraordinary work of God ; in order that we may know that Sodom was not destroyed without a manifest miracle. The proof which the ancients have endeavoured to derive, from this testimony, for the Deity of Christ, is by no means conclusive : and they are angry, in my judgment, without cause, who severely censure the Jews, because they

do not admit this kind of evidence.   I confess, indeed, that
God always acts by the hand of his Son, and have no doubt
that the Son presided over an example of vengeance so
memorable; but I say, they reason inconclusively, who hence
elicit a plurality of Persons, whereas the design of Moses was
to raise the minds of the readers to a more lively contemplation of the hand of God.   And as it is often asked, from
this passage, ' What had infants done, to deserve to be
swallowed up in the same destruction with their parents?'
the solution of the question is easy; namely, that the human
race is in the hand of God, so that he may devote whom he
will to destruction, and may follow whom he will with his
mercy.   Again, whatever we are not able to comprehend by
the limited measure of our understanding, ought to be submitted to his secret judgment.   Lastly, the whole of that
seed was accursed and execrable, so that God could not justly
have spared, even the least.

26. *But his wife looked back.*   Moses here records
the wonderful judgment of God, by which the wife of
Lot was transformed into a statue of salt.   But under the
pretext of this narrative, captious and perverse men ridicule Moses; for since this metamorphosis has no more
appearance of truth, than those which Ovid has feigned,
they boast that it is undeserving of credit.   But I rather
suppose it to have happened through the artifice of Satan,
that Ovid, by fabulously trifling, has indirectly thrown discredit on this most signal proof of Divine vengeance.   But
whatever heathens might please to fabricate, is no concern of
ours.   It is only of importance to consider, whether the narrative of Moses contains anything absurd or incredible.   And,
first, I ask; Since God created men out of nothing, why may
he not, if he sees fit, reduce them again to nothing?   If this
is granted, as it must be; why, if he should please, may he
not turn them into stones?   Yea, those excellent philosophers,
who display their own acuteness, in derogating from the
power of God, daily see miracles as great in the course of
nature.   For how does the crystal acquire its hardness?
and—not to refer to rare examples—how is the living animal

generated from lifeless seed? how are birds produced from eggs? Why then does a miracle appear ridiculous to them, in this one instance, when they are obliged to acknowledge innumerable examples of a similar kind? and how can they, who deem it inconsistent, that the body of a woman should be changed into a mass of salt, believe that the resurrection will restore to life, a carcase reduced to putrefaction? When, however, it is said, that Lot's wife was changed into a statue of salt, let us not imagine that her soul passed into the nature of salt; for it is not to be doubted, that she lives to be a partaker of the same resurrection with us, though she was subjected to an unusual kind of death, that she might be made an example to all. However, I do not suppose Moses to mean, that the statue had the taste of salt; but that it had something remarkable, to admonish those who passed by. It was therefore necessary, that some marks should be impressed upon it, whereby all might know it to be a memorable prodigy. Others interpret the statue of salt to have been an incorruptible one, which should endure for ever; but the former exposition is the more genuine. It may now be asked, why the Lord so severely punished the imprudence of the unhappy woman; seeing that she did not look back, from a desire to return to Sodom? Perhaps, being yet doubtful, she wished to have more certain evidence before her eyes; or, it might be, that, in pity to the perishing people, she turned her eyes in that direction. Moses, certainly, does not assert that she purposely struggled against the will of God; but, forasmuch as the deliverance of her, and her husband, was an incomparable instance of Divine compassion, it was right that her ingratitude should be thus punished. Now, if we weigh all the circumstances, it is clear that her fault was not light. First, the desire of looking back proceeded from incredulity; and no greater injury can be done to God, than when credit is denied to his word. Secondly, we infer from the words of Christ, that she was moved by some evil desire; (Luke xvii. 32;) and that she did not cheerfully leave Sodom, to hasten to the place whither God called her; for we know that he commands us to remember Lot's wife, lest, indeed, the allurements of the world should draw us aside from the meditation of the heavenly life. It is therefore probable, that she, being discontented with the favour God had granted her, glided into unholy desires, of which thing also her tardiness was a sign ; for Moses intimates, that she was following after her husband, when he says, that she looked back *from behind* him ; for she did not look back *towards* him ; but because, by the slowness of her pace, she was less advanced, she, therefore, was behind him. And although it is not lawful to affirm any thing respecting her eternal salvation ; it is nevertheless probable, that God, having inflicted temporal punishment, spared her soul ; inasmuch as he often chastises his own people in the flesh, that their soul may be saved from eternal destruction. Since, however, the knowledge of this is not very profitable, and we may without danger remain in ignorance, let us rather attend to the example which God designs for the common benefit of all ages. If the severity of the punishment terrifies us ; let us remember, that they sin, at this day, not less grievously, who, being delivered, not from Sodom, but from hell, fix their eyes on some other object than the proposed prize of their high calling.

27. *And Abraham gat up early in the morning.* Moses now reverts to Abraham, and shows that he, by no means, neglected what he had heard from the mouth of the angel ; for he relates that Abraham came to a place where he might see the judgment of God. For we must not suspect that (as we have lately said respecting Lot's wife) he trusted more to his own eyes than to the word of God ; and that he came to explore, because he was in doubt. But we rather infer, from the text, that he, being already persuaded that the angel had not spoken in vain, sought confirmation, by the actual beholding of the event ; which confirmation would be useful both to himself and to posterity. And it is not to be doubted, that during the whole night, he suffered severe anguish respecting the safety of his nephew Lot. Whether he became satisfied on this point or not, we do not know ; yet I rather incline to the conjecture, that he remained anxious about him. And it is possible that, hesitating between hope and fear, he went forward to meet him, in order

that he might see whether he was delivered or not. And although he beholds nothing but the smoke, which generally remains after a great fire ; yet this sign is given him from the Lord, for a testimony to posterity, of a punishment so memorable. God indeed designed that, in the very appearance of the place, a monument of his wrath should exist for ever : but because, through the readiness of the world to cast a doubt upon the judgments of God, it might be easily believed, that such had been the nature of the place from the beginning ; or that the change had occurred accidentally ; the Lord was pleased to exhibit his act of vengeance before the eyes of Abraham, in order that he might discharge the office of a herald to posterity.

29. *God remembered Abraham.* Although Moses does not assert that the deliverance of Abraham's nephew was made known to him ; yet since he says, that Lot was saved from destruction for Abraham's sake, it is probable that he was not deprived of that consolation which he most needed ; and that he was conscious of the benefit, for which it became him to give thanks. If it seems to any one absurd, that the holy man Lot should be granted for the sake of another ; as if the Lord had not respect to his own piety : I answer, these two things well agree with each other ; that the Lord, since he is wont to aid his own people, cared for Lot, whom he had chosen, and whom he governed by his Spirit ; and yet that, at the same time, he would show, in the preservation of his life, how greatly he loved Abraham, to whom he not only granted personal protection, but also the deliverance of others. It is however right to observe, that what the Lord does gratuitously,—induced by no other cause than his own goodness,—is ascribed to the piety or the prayers of men, for this reason ; that we may be stirred up to worship God, and to pray to him. We have seen, a little while before, how merciful God proved himself to be, in preserving Lot ; and truly, he would not have perished, even if he had not been the nephew of Abraham. Yet Moses says, it was a favour granted to Abraham, that Lot was not consumed in the same destruction with Sodom. But if the Lord extended the favour which

he had vouchsafed to his servant, to the nephew also, who now was as a stranger from his family ; how much more confidently ought every one of the faithful to expect, that the same grace shall, by no means, be wanting to his own household ?   And, if the Lord, when he favours us, embraces others also who are connected with us, for our sake, how much more will he have respect to ourselves ? In saying that Lot dwelt in those cities, the figure *synecdoche*, which puts the whole for a part, is used, but it is expressly employed to make the miracle more illustrious ; because it happened, only by the singular providence of God, that when five cities were destroyed, a single person should escape.

30. *And Lot went up out of Zoar.*   This narration proves what I have before alluded to, that those things which men contrive for themselves, by rash counsels, drawn from carnal reason, never prosper : especially when men, deluded by vain hope, or impelled by depraved wishes, depart from the word of God.   For although temerity commonly seems to be successful at the beginning ; and they who are carried away by their lusts, exult over the joyful issue of affairs ; yet the Lord, at length, curses whatever is not undertaken with his approval ; and the declaration of Isaiah is fulfilled, ' Woe to them who begin a work and not by the Spirit of the Lord ; who take counsel, but do not ask at his mouth,' (Isaiah xxx. 1.)   Lot, when commanded to betake himself to the mountain, chose rather to dwell in Zoar.   After this habitation was granted to him, according to his own wish, he soon repents and is sorry, for he trembles at the thought that destruction is every moment hastening on a place so near to Sodom, in which perhaps the same impiety and wickedness was reigning.   But let the readers recall to memory what I have said, that it was only through the wonderful kindness of God, that he did not receive either immediate, or very severe punishment. For the Lord, by pardoning him at the time, caused him finally to become judge of his own sin. For he was neither expelled from Zoar by force nor by the hand of man ; but a blind anxiety of mind drove him and hurried him into a cavern, because he had followed the lust

of his flesh rather than the command of God. And thus in chastising the faithful, God mitigates their punishment, so as to render it their best medicine. For if he were to deal strictly with their folly, they would fall down in utter confusion. He therefore gives them space for repentance, that they may willingly acknowledge their fault.

31. *And the first-born said.*[1]

CHAPTER XX.

1. AND Abraham journeyed from thence toward the south country, and dwelled between Kadesh and Shur, and sojourned in Gerar.

2. And Abraham said of Sarah his wife, She *is* my sister : and Abimelech king of Gerar sent, and took Sarah.

3. But God came to Abimelech in a dream by night, and said to him, Behold, thou *art but* a dead man, for the woman which thou hast taken ; for she *is* a man's wife.

4. But Abimelech had not come near her : and he said, Lord, wilt thou slay also a righteous nation ?

5. Said he not unto me, She *is* my sister ? and she, even she herself said, He *is* my brother : in the integrity of my heart and innocency of my hands have I done this.

1. Postea profectus est inde Abraham ad terram Meridianam, et habitavit inter Cades et Sur, peregrinatusque est in Gerar.

2. Et dixit Abraham de Sarah uxore sua, Soror mea est. Et misit Abimelech rex Gerar, et accepit Sarah.

3. Et venit Jehova ad Abimelech in somnio noctis, et dixit ei, Ecce es mortuus, propter uxorem quam accepisti : quum ipsa maritata sit marito.

4. Abimelech autem non appropinquaverat ad eam : itaque dixit, Jehova, num gentem etiam justam occides ?

5. Numquid non ipse dixit mihi, Soror mea est : et ipsa etiam dixit, Frater meus est? in integritate cordis mei, et in munditia manuum mearum feci hoc.

---

[1] 31. "Et dixit primogenita."—"Hic prodigium narratur a Mose, quod lectores merito obstupefacere debet," &c. The lengthened comment on this and the following verses, it has been deemed necessary entirely to omit. Perhaps the only points worthy of notice in it, are the following : 1. Calvin supposes Lot to have been under judicial infatuation in consequence of his intemperance on this occasion. " Ego quidem ita omnino statuo non tam vino fuisse obrutum, quam propter suam intemperiem divinitus percussum spiritu stuporis." 2. He explains, as other commentators do, the names of the children of Lot's daughters ; the first מוֹאָב, (*Moab,*) which signifies " from a father;" the other בֶן-עַמִּי, (*Ben-ammi,*) which signifies " the son of my people." These were the progenitors of the *Moabites* and *Ammonites.*—*Ed.*

6. And God said unto him in a dream, Yea, I know that thou didst this in the integrity of thy heart; for I also withheld thee from sinning against me: therefore suffered I thee not to touch her.

7. Now therefore restore the man *his* wife; for he *is* a prophet, and he shall pray for thee, and thou shalt live: and if thou restore *her* not, know thou that thou shalt surely die, thou, and all that *are* thine.

8. Therefore Abimelech rose early in the morning, and called all his servants, and told all these things in their ears: and the men were sore afraid.

9. Then Abimelech called Abraham, and said unto him, What hast thou done unto us? and what have I offended thee, that thou hast brought on me and on my kingdom a great sin? thou hast done deeds unto me that ought not to be done.

10. And Abimelech said unto Abraham, What sawest thou, that thou hast done this thing?

11. And Abraham said, Because I thought, Surely the fear of God *is* not in this place; and they will slay me for my wife's sake.

12. And yet indeed *she is* my sister; she *is* the daughter of my father, but not the daughter of my mother; and she became my wife.

13. And it came to pass, when God caused me to wander from my father's house, that I said unto her, This *is* thy kindness which thou shalt show unto me; at every place whither we shall come, say of me, He *is* my brother.

14. And Abimelech took sheep, and oxen, and men-servants, and women-servants, and gave *them* unto Abraham, and restored him Sarah his wife.

15. And Abimelech said, Behold, my land *is* before thee: dwell where it pleaseth thee.

16. And unto Sarah he said, Behold, I have given thy brother a thousand *pieces* of silver: behold, he *is* to thee a covering of the eyes, unto all that *are* with thee, and with all *other:* thus she was reproved.

17. So Abraham prayed unto God:

6. Et dixit ad eum Deus in somnio, Etiam ego novi quod in integritate cordis tui fecisti hoc, et prohibui etiam ego te, ne peccares mihi: idcirco non permisi tibi, ut tangeres eam.

7. Et nunc redde uxorem viro, quia propheta est, et orabit pro te, et vives: quodsi tu non reddideris, scito quod moriendo morieris tu et omne quod est tibi.

8. Et surrexit Abimelech mane, et vocavit omnes servos suos, et loquutus est omnia verba ista in auribus eorum, et timuerunt viri valde.

9. Et vocavit Abimelech Abraham, et dixit ei, Quid fecisti nobis? et quid peccavi tibi, quia induxisti super me et super regnum meum peccatum grande? opera quæ non debent fieri, fecisti mecum.

10. Et dixit Abimelech ad Abraham, Quid vidisti quia fecisti rem hanc?

11. Et dixit Abraham, Quia dixi, Vere non est timor Dei in loco isto: et occident me propter uxorem meam.

12. Et etiam vere soror mea filia patris mei est, veruntamen non filia matris meæ: et fuit mihi in uxorem meam.

13. Et fuit, quando circumduxerunt me Angeli de domo patris mei, dixi ei, Hæc est misericordia 'tua quam facies mecum, in omni loco ad quem veniemus, dic de me, Frater meus est.

14. Et cepit Abimelech pecudes, et boves, et servos, et ancillas, et dedit Abraham: et restituit ei Sarah, uxorem ejus.

15. Et dixit Abimelech, Ecce, terra mea coram te, in *loco* bono coram oculis tuis habita.

16. Et ad Sarah dixit, Ecce, dedi mille argenteos fratri tuo: ecce, est tibi operimentum oculorum, omnibus qui sunt tecum: et in omnibus correcta fuit.

17. Et oravit Abraham ad

and God healed Abimelech, and his wife, and his maid-servants ; and they bare *children.*

18. For the Lord had fast closed up all the wombs of the house of Abimelech, because of Sarah Abraham's wife.

Deum, et sanavit Deus Abimelech et uxorem ejus, et ancillas ejus, et pepererunt :

18. Quia claudendo clauserat Jehova super omnem vulvam domus Abimelech propter Sarah uxorem Abraham.

1. *And Abraham journeyed from thence.* What Moses related respecting the destruction of Sodom, was a digression. He now returns to the continuation of his history, and proceeds to show what happened to Abraham ; how he conducted himself, and how the Lord protected him ; till the promised seed, the future source of the Church, should be born unto him. He also says, that Abraham came into the South country ; not that he travelled beyond the limits of the inheritance given to him, but left his former abode, and went towards the South. Moreover, the region which he points out fell chiefly, afterwards, to the lot of the tribe of Judah. It is, however, unknown what was his intention in removing, or what necessity impelled him to change his place : we ought, however, to be persuaded, that he had not transferred his abode to another place for any insufficient cause ; especially since a son, whom he had not even dared to wish for, had been lately promised him, through Sarah. Some imagine that he fled from the sad spectacle which was continually presented before his eyes ; for he saw the plain, which had lately appeared so pleasant to the view, and so replenished with varied abundance of fruits, transformed into a misshapen chaos. And certainly, it was possible that the whole neighbourhood might be affected with the smell of sulphur, as well as tainted with other corruptions, in order that men might the more clearly perceive this memorable judgment of God. Therefore, there is nothing discordant with facts, in the supposition, that Abraham, seeing the place was under the curse of the Lord, was, by his detestation of it, drawn elsewhere. It is also credible, that (as it happened to him in another place) he was driven away by the malice and injuries of those among whom he dwelt. For the more abundantly the Lord had manifested his grace towards him, the more necessary was it, in return, for his patience to be exercised, in order that

he might reflect upon his condition, as a pilgrim upon earth. Moses also expressly declares, that he dwelt as a stranger in the land of Gerar. Thus we see, that this holy family was driven hither and thither as refuse, while a fixed abode was granted to the wicked. But it is profitable to the pious to be thus unsettled on earth; lest, by setting their minds on a commodious and quiet habitation, they should lose the inheritance of heaven.

2. *And Abraham said of Sarah his wife.* In this history, the Holy Spirit presents to us a remarkable instance, both of the infirmity of man, and of the grace of God. It is a common proverb, that even fools become wise by suffering evil. But Abraham, forgetful of the great danger which had befallen him in Egypt, once more strikes his foot against the same stone; although the Lord had purposely chastised him, in order that the warning might be useful to him, throughout his whole life. Therefore we perceive, in the example of the holy patriarch, how easily the oblivion, both of the chastisements and the favours of God, steals over us. For it is impossible to excuse his gross negligence, in not calling to mind, that he had once tempted God; and that he would have had himself alone to blame, if his wife had become the property of another man. But if we thoroughly examine ourselves, scarcely any one will be found who will not acknowledge, that he has often offended in the same way. It may be added, that Abraham was not free from the charge of ingratitude; because, if he had reflected that his wife had been wonderfully preserved to him by the Lord, he would never again, knowingly and willingly, have cast himself into similar danger. For he makes the former favour divinely offered unto him, so far as he is able, of none effect. We must, however, notice the nature of the sin, on which we have touched before. For Abraham did not, for the sake of providing for his own safety, prostitute his wife, (as impious men cavil.) But, as he had before been anxious to preserve his life, till he should receive the seed divinely promised to him; so now, seeing his wife with child, in the hope of enjoying so great a blessing, he thought nothing of

his wife's danger.[1] Therefore, if we thoroughly weigh all things, he sinned through unbelief, by attributing less than he ought to the providence of God. Whence also, we are admonished, how dangerous a thing it is, to trust our own counsels. For Abraham's disposition is right, while fixing his attention on the promise of God; but inasmuch as he does not patiently wait for God's help, but turns aside to the use of unlawful means, he is, in this respect, worthy of censure.

And Abimelech sent. There is no doubt that the Lord purposed to punish his servant, for the counsel he had so rashly taken. And such fruits of distrust do all receive, who rely not, as they ought, on the providence of God. Some perverse men quarrel with this passage; because nothing seems to them more improbable than that a decrepit old woman should be desired by the king, and taken from the bosom of her husband. But we answer, first, that it is not known what her appearance was, except that Moses before declared her to be a person of singular beauty. And it is possible that she was not much worn with age. For we often see some women in their fortieth year more wrinkled than others in their seventieth. But here another thing is to be considered, that, by the unwonted favour of God, her comeliness was pre-eminent among her other endowments. It might also be, that king Abimelech was less attracted by the elegance of her form, than by the rare virtues with which he saw her, as a matron, to be endued. Lastly, we must remember, that this whole affair was directed by the hand of God, in order that Abraham might receive the due reward of his folly. And as we find that they who are exceedingly acute in discerning the natural causes of things, are yet most blind in reference to the divine judgments; let this single fact suffice us, that Abimelech, being a minister to execute the divine chastisement, acted under a secret impulse.

3. *But God came to Abimelech in a dream by night.* Here Moses shows that the Lord acted with such gentleness, that

---

[1] There seems too much of special pleading in the reasoning of Calvin, both on this occasion, and on that referred to, of a similar kind, in the twelfth chapter.—*Ed.*

in punishing his servant, he yet, as a father, forgave him : just as he deals with us, so that, while chastising us with his rod, his mercy and his goodness far exceed his severity. Hence also we infer, that he takes greater care of the pious than carnal sense can understand; since he watches over them while they sleep.   This also is to be carefully noticed ; that however we may be despised by the world, we are yet precious to him, since for our sake he reproves even kings, as it is written in Psalm cv. 14.   But as this subject was more fully discussed in the twelfth chapter, let the readers there seek what I now purposely omit.   Whereas, God is said to have *come*, this is to be applied to the perception of the king, to whom undoubtedly the majesty of God was manifested; so that he might clearly perceive himself to be divinely reproved, and not deluded with a vain spectre.

Behold, thou art but a dead man.   Although God reproved king Abimelech, for the sake of Abraham, whom he covered with his special protection; he yet intends to show, generally, his high displeasure against adultery.   And, in truth, here is no express mention of Abraham; but rather a general announcement is made, for the purpose of maintaining conjugal fidelity.   ‘ Thou shalt die, because thou hast seized upon a woman who was joined to a husband.’   Let us therefore learn, that a precept was given, in these words, to mankind, which forbids any one to touch his neighbour’s wife.   And, truly, since nothing in the life of man is more sacred than marriage, it is not to be wondered at, that the Lord should require mutual fidelity to be cherished between husbands and wives, and should declare that he will be the Avenger of it, as often as it is violated.   He now addresses himself, indeed, only to one man ; but the warning ought to sound in the ears of all, that adulterers—although they may exult with impunity for a time—shall yet feel that God, who presides over marriage, will take vengeance on them.   (Heb. xiii. 3.)

4. *But Abimelech had not come near her.*   Though Abraham had deprived himself of his wife, the Lord interposed in time to preserve her uninjured.   When Moses previously relates, that she was taken away by Pharaoh, he does not say whether

her chastity was assailed or not; but since the Lord then also declared himself the vindicator of her whom he now saved from dishonour, we ought not to doubt that her integrity was preserved both times. For why did he now forbid the king of Gerar to touch her, if he had previously suffered her to be corrupted in Egypt? We see, however, that when the Lord so defers his aid as not to stretch out his hand to the faithful, till they are in extreme peril, he shows the more clearly how admirable is his Providence.

Wilt thou slay also a righteous nation? The explanation given by some, that Abimelech here compares himself with the men of Sodom, is perhaps too refined. The following meaning appears to me more simple; namely, ' O Lord, although thou dost severely punish adultery, shall thy wrath pour itself out on unoffending men, who have rather fallen into error, than sinned knowingly and willingly?' Moreover, Abimelech seems so to clear himself, as if he were entirely free from blame: and yet the Lord both admits and approves his excuse. We must, however, mark in what way, and to what extent, he boasts that his heart and hands are guiltless. For he does not arrogate to himself a purity which is altogether spotless; but only denies that he was led by lust, either tyrannically or purposely, to abuse another man's wife. We know how great is the difference between a *crime* and a *fault;*[1] thus Abimelech does not exempt himself from every kind of charge, but only shows that he had been conscious of no such wickedness as required this severe punishment. The ' simplicity of heart,' of which he speaks, is nothing else than that ignorance which stands opposed to consciousness of guilt; and 'the righteousness of his hands,' is nothing but that self-government, by which men abstain from force and acts of injustice. Besides, the interrogation which Abimelech used, proceeded from a common feeling of religion. For nature itself dictates, that God preserves a just discrimination in inflicting punishments.

6. *Yea, I know that thou didst this in the integrity of thy heart.*

[1] " Inter scelus et delictum."—"Between an act of abandoned wickedness and a mere fault."—*Ed.*

We infer from this answer of God, (as I have lately remarked,) that Abimelech did not testify falsely concerning his own integrity. Yet, while God allows that his excuse is true, He nevertheless chastises him. Let us hence learn, that even they who are pure, according to human judgment, are not entirely free from blame. For no error may be deemed so excusable, as to be without some deteriorating admixture. Wherefore, it is not for any one to absolve himself by his own judgment; rather let us learn to bring all our conduct to the standard of God. For Solomon does not say in vain, that ' the ways of men seem right to themselves, but the Lord pondereth the hearts,' (Prov. xxi. 2.) But if even they who are unconscious to themselves of any evil, do not escape censure; what will be our condition, if we are held inwardly bound by our own conscience ?

I also withheld thee. This declaration implies that God had respect, not only to Abraham, but also to the king. For because he had no intention of defiling another man's wife, God had compassion on him. And it frequently happens, that the Spirit restrains, by his bridle, those who are gliding into error; just as, on the other hand, he drives those headlong, by infatuation, and a spirit of stupor, who, with depraved affections and lusts, knowingly transgress. And as God brought to the heathen king, who had not been guilty of deliberate wickedness, a timely remedy, in order that his guilt should not be increased; so He proves himself daily to be the faithful guardian of his own people, to prevent them from rushing forward, from lighter faults to desperate crimes.

7. *Now therefore, restore the man his wife.* God does not now speak of Abraham as of a common man, but as of one who is so peculiarly dear unto himself, that He undertakes the defence of his conjugal bed, by a kind of privilege. He calls Abraham a prophet, for the sake of honour; as if he were charging Abimelech with having injured a man of great and singular excellence; that he might not wonder at the greatness of the punishment inflicted upon him. And although the word prophet is properly the name of an office; yet I think it has here a more comprehensive import, and that it is put for a chosen man, and one who is familiar with

God.   For since, at that time, no Scripture was in existence,
God not only made himself known by dreams and visions,
but chose also to himself rare and excellent men, to scatter
abroad the seed of piety, by which the world would become
more inexcusable.   But since Abraham is a prophet, he is
constituted, as it were, a mediator between God and
Abimelech.   Christ, even then, was the only Mediator; but
this was no reason why some men should not pray for
others ; especially they who excelled in holiness, and were
accepted by God; as the Apostle teaches, that ' the fervent
prayers of a righteous man avail much.' (James v. 16.) And
we ought not, at this day, to neglect such intercession, provided it does not obscure the grace of Christ, nor lead us
away from Him.   But that, under this pretext, the Papists
resort to the patronage of the dead, is absurd.   For as the
Lord does not here send the king of Gerar to Noah, or to
any one of the dead fathers, but into the presence of the living Abraham; so the only precept we have on this subject
is, that, by mutually praying for each other, we should cultivate charity among ourselves.

   And if thou restore her not.   Hence we are to learn, the
intention of those threats and denunciations, with which
God terrifies men; namely, forcibly to impel those to repentance, who are too backward.   In the beginning of this
discourse, it had been absolutely declared, ' Thou art a dead
man ;' now the condition is added, 'Unless thou restore her.'
Yet the meaning of both expressions is the same; though at
first God speaks more sharply, that he may inspire the
offender with the greater terror.   But now, when he is subdued, God expresses his intention more clearly, and leaves him
the hope of pardon and salvation.   Thus is the knot untied,
with which many entangle themselves, when they perceive
that God does not always, or instantly, execute the punishments which he has denounced; because they deem it a sign,
either that God has changed his purpose, or that he pretends
a different thing by his word, from that which he has secretly
decreed.   He threatened destruction to the Ninevites, by
Jonah, and afterwards spared them. (Jonah iii. 4.)   The unskilful do not perceive how they can escape from one of two
absurdities ; namely, that God has retracted his sentence ; or

that he had feigned himself to be about to do what he really did not intend.   But if we hold fast this principle, that the inculcation of repentance is included in all threats, the difficulty will be solved.   For although God, in the first instance, addresses men as lost; and, therefore, penetrates them with the present fear of death, still the end is to be regarded.   For if he invites them to repentance, it follows, that the hope of pardon is left them, provided they repent.

8. *Therefore Abimelech rose early in the morning.*   Moses teaches how efficacious the oracle had been.   For Abimelech, alarmed at the voice of God, arose in the morning, not only that he himself might quickly obey the command enjoined upon him, but that he might also exhort his own people to do the same.   An example of such ready obedience is shown us in a heathen king, that we may no more make excuses for our torpor, when we are so little profited by the Divine remonstrances.   God appeared to *him* in a dream; but since he daily cries aloud in *our* ears, by Moses, by the prophets, and by the apostles, and finally, by his only-begotten Son, it were absurd to suppose that so many testimonies should avail less than the vision of a single dream.

9. *Then Abimelech called Abraham.*   There are those who suppose that the king of Gerar did not make a complaint against Abraham; but rather declared his own repentance. If, however, we fairly weigh his words, we find confession mixed with expostulation.   Although he complains that Abraham had acted unjustly, he yet does not so transfer the blame to him, as to free himself from all fault.   And he may, with justice, impute part of the blame to Abraham, as he does; provided he also acknowledges his own sin.   Let us therefore know, that this king did not act as hypocrites are in the habit of doing.   For, as soon as ever a pretext is furnished for inculpating others, they confidently absolve themselves: they even esteem it a lawful purgation for themselves, if they can draw others into a participation of their crime. But Abimelech, while he complains that he had been deceived, and had fallen through imprudence, yet does not, mean-

while, scruple to condemn himself as guilty of a great sin, 'It is not,' he says, 'through thee, that I and my whole kingdom have been prevented from falling into the greatest wickedness.' No one therefore may exonerate himself from blame, under the pretence that he had been induced by others to sin. It is, however, to be noted, that adultery is here called a great sin; because it binds not one man only, but a whole people, as in a common crime. The king of Gerar could not indeed have spoken thus, had he not acknowledged the sacred right of marriage. But, at the present time, Christians—at least they who boast of the name—are not ashamed jocularly to extenuate so great a crime, from which even a heathen shrinks with the greatest horror. Let us however know, that Abimelech was a true herald of that divine judgment, which miserable men in vain endeavour to elude by their cavils. And let that expression of Paul ever recur to our memory, 'Be not deceived; because of those things cometh the wrath of God upon the disobedient.' (1 Cor. v. 9; Eph. v. 6.) It is not without reason, that he makes this sin common to the whole nation; for when crimes are committed with impunity, a whole region is, in a certain sense, polluted. And it is especially notorious, that the anger of God is provoked against the whole body of the people, in the person of the king. Hence, with so much the greater earnestness and care, must we beseech God to govern, by his Spirit, those whom he has placed in authority over us; and then, to preserve the country, in which he has granted us a dwelling-place, exempt and pure from all iniquity.

10. *What sawest thou that thou hast done this thing?* By this question the king provides against the future. He thinks that Abraham had not practised this dissimulation inconsiderately; and, since God was grievously offended, he fears to fall again into the same danger. He therefore testifies, by an inquiry so earnest, that he wishes to remedy the evil. Now, it is no common sign of a just and meek disposition in Abimelech, that he allows Abraham a free defence. We know how sharply, and fiercely, they expostulate, who think themselves aggrieved: so much the greater praise, then, was due

to the moderation of this king, towards an unknown foreigner. Meanwhile, let us learn, by his example, whenever we expostulate with our brethren, who may have done us any wrong, to permit them freely to answer us.

11. *And Abraham said.* There are two points contained in this answer. For, first, he confesses that he had been induced by fear to conceal his marriage. He then denies that he had lied for the purpose of excusing himself. Now, although Abraham declares with truth, that he had not concealed his marriage with any fraudulent intention, nor for the purpose of injuring any one; yet he was worthy of censure, because, through fear, he had submitted, so far as he was concerned, to the prostitution of his wife. Wherefore, much cannot be said in his excuse: since he ought to have been more courageous and resolute in fulfilling the duty of a husband, by vindicating the honour of his wife, whatever danger might threaten him. Besides, it was a sign of distrust, to resort to an unlawful subtlety. With regard to his suspicion; although he had everywhere perceived that a monstrous licentiousness prevailed; it was, nevertheless, unjust to form a judgment so unfavourable of a people whom he had not yet known; for he supposes them all to be homicides. But as I have treated, at some length, on these subjects, in the tenth chapter; it may now suffice to have alluded to them, by the way. Meanwhile, we come to the conclusion, that Abraham does not contend for the justice of his cause before God; but only shows his earnestness to appease Abimelech. His particular form of expression is, however, to be noticed; for wherever the fear of God does not reign, men easily rush onward to every kind of wickedness; so that they neither spare human blood, nor restrain themselves from rapine, violence, and contumelies. And doubtless it is the fear of God alone, which unites us together in the bonds of our common humanity, which keeps us within the bounds of moderation, and represses cruelty; otherwise we should devour each other like wild beasts. It will, indeed, sometimes happen, that they who are destitute of the fear of God, may cultivate the appearance of equity. For God, in

order that he may preserve mankind from destruction, holds in check, with his secret rein, the lusts of the ungodly. It must, however, be always taken into the account, that the door is opened to all kinds of wickedness, when piety and the fear of God have vanished. Of this, at the present day, too clear a proof is manifest, in the horrible deluge of crime, which almost covers the whole earth. For, from what other cause than this arise such a variety of deceptions and frauds, such perfidy and cruelty, that all sense of justice is extinguished by the contempt of God? Now, whenever we have a difficult contest with the corruptions of our own age, let us reflect on the times of Abraham, which, although they were filled with impiety and other crimes, yet did not divert the holy man from the course of duty.

12. *And yet indeed she is my sister.* Some suppose Sarah to have been Abraham's own sister, yet not by the same mother, but born from a second wife. As, however, the name sister has a wider signification among the Hebrews, I willingly adopt a different conjecture; namely, that she was his sister in the second degree; thus it will be true that they had a common father, that is, a grandfather, from whom they had descended by brothers. Moreover, Abraham extenuates his offence, and draws a distinction between his silence and a direct falsehood; and certainly he professed with truth, that he was the brother of Sarah. Indeed, it appears that he feigned nothing in words which differed from the facts themselves; yet when all things have been sifted, his defence proves to be either frivolous, or, at least, too feeble. For since he had purposely used the name of sister as a pretext, lest men should have some suspicion of his marriage; he sophistically afforded them an occasion of falling into error. Wherefore, although he did not lie in words, yet with respect to the matter of fact, his dissimulation was a lie, by implication. He had, however, no other intention than to declare that he had not dealt fraudulently with Abimelech; but that, in an affair of great anxiety, he had caught at an indirect method of escape from death, by the pretext of his previous relationship to his wife.

13. *When God caused me to wander.*[1] Because the verb is here put in the plural number, I freely expound the passage as referring to the angels, who led Abraham through his various wanderings. Some, with too much subtlety, infer from it a Trinity of Persons : as if it had been written, The gods caused me to wander. I grant, indeed, that the *noun* אלהים, (*Elohim,*) is frequently taken for God in the Scripture : but then the *verb* with which it is connected is always singular. Wherever a plural verb is added, then it signifies angels or princes.[2] There are those who think that Abraham, because he was speaking with one who was not rightly instructed, spoke thus in conformity with the common custom of the heathen ; but, in my opinion, most erroneously. For to what purpose did he, by erecting altars, make it manifest that he was devoted to the service of the only true God, if it were lawful for him afterwards to deny, in words, the very God whom he had worshipped? On which subject we have before spoken, as the case required. Abraham, however, does not complain respecting the angels, that he had been led astray by their fallacious guidance : but he points out what his own condition formerly was ; namely, that having left his own country, he had not only migrated into a distant land, but had been constantly compelled to change his abode. Wherefore there is no wonder, that necessity drove him into new designs. Should any one inquire, why he makes angels the guides of his pilgrimage ? the answer is ready ; Although Abraham knew that he was wandering by the will and providence of God alone, he yet refers to angels, who, as he elsewhere acknowledges, were given him to be the guides of his journey. The sum of the address is of this tendency ; to teach Abimelech, that Abra-

---

[1] " Quando circumduxerunt me angeli."—" When the angels led me about.'

[2] The reasoning of Calvin is not conclusive. There are cases, though but few, in which Elohim, as here, when joined to a verb plural, signifies, not angels nor princes, but the true God. See Gen. xxxv. 7. Calvin, however, in this passage also, translates the word, " angels." Still there seems no sufficient reason for departing from our own received version. Dathe agrees with it. " Deinde cum Deus me ex patria mea migrare juberet." It is also confirmed by the Septuagint version.—See the Commentary of Professor Bush, *in loco.*—*Ed.*

ham was alike free from malicious cunning, and from falsehood : and then, that because he was passing a wandering
and unquiet life; Sarah, by agreement, had always said the
same thing which she had done in Gerar. This wretched
anxiety of the holy man might so move Abimelech to compassion, as to cause his anger to cease.

14. *And Abimelech took sheep.* Abraham had before received
possessions and gifts in Egypt; but with this difference, that
whereas Pharaoh had commanded him to depart elsewhere ;
Abimelech offers him a home in his kingdom. It therefore
appears that both kings were stricken with no common degree
of fear. For when they perceived that they were reproved
by the Lord, because they had been troublesome to Abraham;
they found no method of appeasing God, except that of
compensating, by acts of kindness, for the injury they had
brought on the holy man. The latter difference alluded to
flowed hence; that Pharaoh, being more severely censured, was
so terrified, that he could scarcely bear the sight of Abraham :
whereas Abimelech, although alarmed, was yet soon composed, by an added word of consolation, when the Lord said
to him, " He is a prophet, and he shall pray for thee." For
there is no other remedy for the removal of fear, than the
Lord's declaration that he will be propitious. It is indeed of
little advantage for the sinner to present to God only what
fear extorts. But it is a true sign of penitence, when, with
a composed mind and quiet conscience, he yields himself, as
obedient and docile, to God. And seeing that Abimelech
allowed Abraham a habitation in his realm, a blessing of no
trivial kind followed this act of humanity; because Isaac was
born there, as we shall see in the next chapter.

16. *He is to thee a covering of the eyes.* Because there is,
in these words, some obscurity, the passage is variously
explained. The beginning of the verse is free from difficulty.
For when Abimelech had given a thousand pieces of silver;
in order that his liberality might not be suspected, he declares
that he had given them to *Abraham ;* and that since Abraham
had been honourably received, his wife was not to be regarded
as a harlot. But what follows is more obscure, ' He shall be a

veil to thee.' Many interpreters refer this to the gift; in which they seem to me to be wrong. The Hebrews, having no neuter gender, use the feminine instead of it. But Moses, in this place, rather points to the husband ; and this best suits the sense. For Sarah is taught that the husband to whom she is joined was as a veil, with which she ought to be covered, lest she should be exposed to others. Paul says, that the veil which the woman carries on her head, is the symbol of subjection. (1 Cor. xi. 10.) This also belongs to unmarried persons, as referring to the end for which the sex is ordained ; but it applies more aptly to married women ; because they are veiled, as by the very ordinance of marriage. I therefore thus explain the words, ' Thou, if thou hadst no husband, wouldst be exposed to many dangers ; but now, since God has appointed for thee a guardian of thy modesty, it behoves thee to conceal thyself under that veil. Why then hast thou, of thine own accord, thrown off this covering?' This was a just censure ; because Sarah, pretending that she was in the power of her husband, had deprived herself of the divine protection.

Thus she was reproved. Interpreters distort this clause also. The natural exposition seems to me to be, that the Lord had suffered Sarah to be reproved by a heathen king, that he might the more deeply affect her with a sense of shame. For Moses draws especial attention to the person of the speaker ; because it seemed a disgrace that the mother of the faithful should be reprehended by such a master. Others suppose that Moses speaks of the profit which she had received; seeing that she, instructed by such a lesson, would henceforth learn to act differently. But Moses seems rather to point out that kind of correction of which I have spoken ; namely, that Sarah was humbled, by being delivered over to the discipline of a heathen man.

17. *So Abraham prayed.* In two respects the wonderful favour of God towards Abraham was apparent ; first, that, with outstretched hand, He avenged the injury done to him ; and, secondly, that, through Abraham's prayer, He became pacified towards the house of Abimelech. It was necessary

to declare, that the house of Abimelech had been healed in answer to Abraham's prayers; in order that, by such a benefit, the inhabitants might be the more closely bound to him. A question, however, may be agitated respecting the kind of punishment described in the expression, the whole house was barren. For if Abraham had gone into the land of Gerar, after Sarah had conceived, and if the whole of what Moses has here related was fulfilled before Isaac was born, how was it possible that, in so short a time, this sterility should be manifest? If we should say, that the judgment of God was then made plain, in a manner to us unknown, the answer would not be inappropriate. Yet I am not certain, that the series of the history has not been inverted. The more probable supposition may seem to be, that Abraham had already been resident in Gerar, when Isaac was promised to him; but that the part, which had before been omitted, is now inserted by Moses. Should any one object, that Abraham dwelt in Mamre till the destruction of Sodom, there would be nothing absurd in the belief, that what Moses here relates had taken place previously. Yet, since the correct notation of time does little for the confirmation of our faith, I leave both opinions undecided.

CHAPTER XXI.

1. AND the Lord visited Sarah as he had said, and the Lord did unto Sarah as he had spoken.

2. For Sarah conceived, and bare Abraham a son in his old age, at the set time of which God had spoken to him.

3. And Abraham called the name of his son that was born unto him, whom Sarah bare to him, Isaac.

4. And Abraham circumcised his son Isaac being eight days old, as God had commanded him.

5. And Abraham was an hundred years old, when his son Isaac was born unto him.

6. And Sarah said, God hath made

1. Porro Jehova visitavit Sarah, quemadmodum dixit: et fecit Jehova ipsi Sarah, quemadmodum loquutus erat.

2. Itaque concepit et peperit Sarah ipsi Abraham filium in senectute ejus, in tempore quod illi dixerat Deus.

3. Et vocavit Abraham nomen filii sui, qui natus erat ei, quem peperit ei Sarah, Ishac.

4. Et circumcidit Abraham Ishac filium suum, filium octo dierum, quemadmodum præceperat ei Deus.

5. Abraham autem erat centum annorum, quando natus est ei Ishac filius suus.

6. Et dixit Sarah, Risum

me to laugh, so *that* all that hear will laugh with me.

7. And she said, Who would have said unto Abraham, that Sarah should have given children suck? for I have born *him* a son in his old age.

8. And the child grew, and was weaned: and Abraham made a great feast the *same* day that Isaac was weaned.

9. And Sarah saw the son of Hagar the Egyptian, which she had born unto Abraham, mocking.

10. Wherefore she said unto Abraham, Cast out this bondwoman and her son: for the son of this bondwoman shall not be heir with my son, *even* with Isaac.

11. And the thing was very grievous in Abraham's sight because of his son.

12. And God said unto Abraham, Let it not be grievous in thy sight because of the lad, and because of thy bondwoman; in all that Sarah hath said unto thee, hearken unto her voice; for in Isaac shall thy seed be called.

13. And also of the son of the bondwoman will I make a nation, because he *is* thy seed.

14. And Abraham rose up early in the morning, and took bread, and a bottle of water, and gave *it* unto Hagar, putting *it* on her shoulder, and the child, and sent her away: and she departed, and wandered in the wilderness of Beersheba.

15. And the water was spent in the bottle, and she cast the child under one of the shrubs.

16. And she went, and sat her down over against *him* a good way off, as it were a bowshot: for she said, Let me not see the death of the child. And she sat over against *him*, and lift up her voice, and wept.

17. And God heard the voice of the lad; and the angel of God called to Hagar out of heaven, and said unto her, What aileth thee, Hagar? fear not; for God hath heard the voice of the lad where he *is*.

18. Arise, lift up the lad, and hold him in thine hand; for I will make him a great nation.

.fecit mihi Deus: omnis qui audierit, ridebit mihi.

7. Et dixit, Quis nuntiasset Abrahæ lactare filios Sarah? quia peperi filium in senectute ejus.

8. Et crevit puer, et ablactatus est: et fecit Abraham convivium magnum in die qua ablactatus est Ishac.

9. Et vidit Sarah filium Hagar Ægyptiæ, quem peperit ipsi Abraham, ridentem.

10. Et dixit ad Abraham, Ejice ancillam hanc et filium ejus: quia non hæreditabit filius ancillæ hujus cum filio meo, cum Ishac.

11. Et displicuit res valde in oculis Abraham, propter filium suum.

12. Et dixit Deus ad Abraham, Ne displiceat in oculis tuis super puero, et super ancilla tua: in omnibus quæ dixerit tibi Sarah, audi vocem ejus: quia in Ishac vocabitur tibi semen.

13. Et etiam filium ancillæ in gentem ponam, quia semen tuum est.

14. Diluculo igitur surrexit Abraham, et tulit panem, et utrem aquæ, et dedit Hagar, et posuit super humerum ejus, et puerum: et dimisit eam, et perrexit, et erravit in deserto Beer-sebah.

15. Et defecerunt aquæ de utre, et projecit puerum subter unam arborum.

16. Et abiit, et sedit e regione, elongando se quantum est jactus arcus: quia dixit, Non videbo quando morietur puer: et sedit e regione, et elevavit vocem suam, et flevit.

17. Et audivit Deus vocem pueri, et clamavit angelus Dei ad Hagar de cœlis, et dixit ei, Quid tibi Hagar? ne timeas: quia audivit Deus vocem pueri ex *loco* ubi est.

18. Surge, tolle puerum, et tene manu tua eum: quia in gentem magnam ponam cum.

19. And God opened her eyes, and she saw a well of water ; and she went, and filled the bottle with water, and gave the lad drink.

20. And God was with the lad ; and he grew, and dwelt in the wilderness, and became an archer.

21. And he dwelt in the wilderness of Paran : and his mother took him a wife out of the land of Egypt.

22. And it came to pass at that time, that Abimelech, and Phichol the chief captain of his host, spake unto Abraham, saying, God *is* with thee in all that thou doest:

23. Now therefore swear unto me here by God, that thou wilt not deal falsely with me, nor with my son, nor with my son's son : *but* according to the kindness that I have done unto thee, thou shalt do unto me, and to the land wherein thou hast sojourned.

24. And Abraham said, I will swear.

25. And Abraham reproved Abimelech because of a well of water, which Abimelech's servants had violently taken away.

26. And Abimelech said, I wot not who hath done this thing : neither didst thou tell me, neither yet heard I *of it*, but to-day.

27. And Abraham took sheep and oxen, and gave them unto Abimelech ; and both of them made a covenant.

28. And Abraham set seven ewe-lambs of the flock by themselves.

29. And Abimelech said unto Abraham, What *mean* these seven ewe-lambs which thou hast set by themselves?

30. And he said, For *these* seven ewe-lambs shalt thou take of my hand, that they may be a witness unto me, that I have digged this well.

31. Wherefore he called that place Beer-sheba ; because there they sware both of them.

32. Thus they made a covenant at Beer-sheba : then Abimelech rose up, and Phichol the chief captain of his host, and they returned into the land of the Philistines.

19. Tunc aperuit Deus oculos ejus, et vidit puteum aquæ, et perrexit et implevit utrem aqua, et potum dedit puero.

20. Et fuit Deus cum puero, et crevit, habitavitque in deserto, et fuit jaculator sagittarius.

21. Et habitavit in deserto Param, et accepit ei mater ejus uxorem de terra Ægypti.

22. Deinde fuit tempore illo, dixit Abimelech et Phicol princeps exercitus ejus ad Abraham, dicendo, Deus tecum est in omnibus quæ tu facis :

23. Nunc itaque jura mihi per Deum hic, si mentitus fueris mihi,[1] et filio meo, et nepoti meo : secundum misericordiam, quam feci tecum, facies mecum, et cum terra, in qua peregrinatus es.

24. Et dixit Abraham, Ego jurabo.

25. Et increpavit Abraham ipsum Abimelech propter puteum aquæ, quem rapuerant servi Abimelech.

26. Et dixit Abimelech, Non novi quis fecerit hoc, neque etiam tu indicasti mihi, neque etiam ego audivi præterquam hodie.

27. Et accepit Abraham pecudes et boves, et dedit ipsi Abimelech, et percusserunt ambo fœdus.

28. Et statuit Abraham septem agnas pecorum seorsum.

29. Et dixit Abimelech ad Abraham, Quid sunt septem agnæ istæ, quos statuisti seorsum?

30. Et dixit, Quia septem agnas capies e manu mea : ut sit mihi in testimonium, quod foderim puteum hunc.

31. Idcirco vocatus est locus ipse Beer-sebah : quia ibi juraverant ambo.

32. Percusserunt ergo fœdus in Beer-sebah : et surrexit Abimelech, et Phicol princeps exercitus ejus, et reversi sunt in terram Pelisthim.

[1] Vel, si fefelleris, aut infideliter egeris.

33. And *Abraham* planted a grove in Beer-sheba, and called there on the name of the Lord, the everlasting God.	33. Et plantavit nemus in Beer-sebah, et invocavit ibi nomen Jehovæ Dei sæculi.
34. And Abraham sojourned in the Philistines' land many days.	34. Et habitavit Abraham in terra Pelisthim dies multos.

1. *And the Lord visited Sarah.*   In this chapter, not only is the nativity of Isaac related, but because, in his very birth, God has set before us a lively picture of his Church, Moses also gives a particular account of this matter.   And, first, he says that God visited Sarah, as he had promised.   Because all offspring flows from the kindness of God, as it is in the psalm, ' The fruit of the womb is the gift of God ;' (Psalm cxxvii. 3 ;) therefore the Lord is said, not without reason, to visit those, to whom he gives children.   For although the fœtus seems to be produced naturally, each from its own kind ; there is yet no fecundity in animals, except so far as the Lord puts forth his own power, to fulfil what he has said, " Increase and multiply."   But in the propagation of the human race, his special benediction is conspicuous ; and, therefore, the birth of every child is rightly deemed the effect of divine visitation.   But Moses, in this place, looks higher, forasmuch as Isaac was born out of the accustomed course of nature.[1]   Therefore Moses here commends that secret and unwonted power of God, which is superior to the law of nature ; and not improperly, since it is of great consequence for us to know that the gratuitous kindness of God reigned, as well in the origin, as in the progress of the Church ; and that the sons of God were not otherwise born, than from his mere mercy.   And this is the reason why he did not make Abraham a father, till his body was nearly withered.   It is also to be noticed, that Moses declares the visitation which he mentions, to be founded upon promise ; ' Jehovah visited Sarah, as he had promised.'   In these words he annexes the effect to its cause, in order that the special grace of God, of which an example is given in the birth of Isaac, might be the more perceptible.   If he had barely said, that the Lord had respect unto Sarah, when she brought forth a son ; some other cause might have been sought for.   None, however,

---

[1] Calvin here adds, " Nam communis gignendi ratio, et vis illa quam Dominus hominibus indidit, in Abraham et ejus uxore cessaverat."

can doubt, that the promise, by which Isaac had been granted
to his father Abraham, was gratuitous; since the child was
the fruit of that adoption, which can be ascribed to nothing
but the mere grace of God.   Therefore, whoever wishes
rightly and prudently to reflect upon the work of God, in the
birth of Isaac, must necessarily begin with the promise.
There is also great emphasis in the repetition, "The Lord
did unto Sarah as he had spoken."   For he thus retains his
readers, as by laying his hand upon them, that they may
pause in the consideration of so great a miracle.   Meanwhile,
Moses commends the faithfulness of God; as if he had said,
he never feeds men with empty promises, nor is he less true
in granting what he has promised, than he is liberal, and
willing, in making the promise.

2. *She bare Abraham a son.*   This is said according to the
accustomed manner of speaking; because the woman is
neither the head of a family, nor brings forth, properly for
herself, but for her husband.   What follows, however, is
more worthy of notice, "In his old age, at the set time,"
which God had predicted: for the old age of Abraham does,
not a little, illustrate the glory of the miracle.   And now
Moses, for the third time, recalls us to the word of God, that
the constancy of his truth may always be present to our
minds.   And though the time had been predicted, alike to
Abraham and to his wife, yet this honour is expressly attributed to the holy man; because the promise had been especially given on his account.   Both, however, are distinctly
mentioned in the context.

3. *And Abraham called the name.*   Moses does not mean
that Abraham was the inventor of the name; but that he
adhered to the name which before had been given by the
angel.   This act of obedience, however, was worthy of commendation, since he not only ratified the word of God, but
also executed his office as God's minister.   For, as a herald,
he proclaimed to all, that which the angel had committed to
his trust.

4. *And Abraham circumcised his son.*   Abraham pursued

his uniform tenor of obedience, in not sparing his own son. For, although it would be painful for him to wound the tender body of the infant; yet, setting aside all human affection, he obeys the word of God. And Moses records that he did as the Lord had commanded him; because there is nothing of greater importance, than to take the pure word of God for our rule, and not to be wise above what is lawful. This submissive spirit is especially required, in reference to sacraments; lest men should either invent any thing for themselves, or should transfer those things which are commanded by the Lord, to any use they please. We see, indeed, how inordinately the humours of men here prevail; inasmuch as they have dared to devise innumerable sacraments. And to go no further for an example, whereas God has delivered only two sacraments to the Christian Church, the Papists boast that they have seven. As if, truly, it were in their power to forge promises of salvation, which they might sanction with signs imagined by themselves. But it were superfluous to relate with how many figments the sacraments have been polluted by them. This certainly is manifest, that there is nothing about which they are less careful, than to observe what the Lord has commanded.

5. *And Abraham was an hundred years old.* Moses again records the age of Abraham, the better to excite the minds of his readers to a consideration of the miracle. And although mention is made only of Abraham, let us yet remember that he is, in this place, set before us, not as a man of lust, but as the husband of Sarah, who has obtained, through her, a lawful seed, in extreme old age, when the strength of both had failed. For the power of God was chiefly conspicuous in this, that when their marriage had been fruitless more than sixty years, suddenly they obtain offspring.[1] Sarah, truly, in order to make amends for the doubt to which she had given way, now exultingly proclaims the kindness of God, with becoming praises. And first, she says, that God had given her occasion of joy; not of common joy, but of such as should cause all

---

[1] " Quod quum ultra sexaginta annos sterile illis fuisset conjugium, effœtis jam et semimortuis, subito nata est prolis."

men to congratulate her.   Secondly, for the purpose of amplification, she assumes the character of an astonished inquirer,
' Who would have told this to Abraham ?'   Some explain
the clause in question, ' will laugh at me,' as if Sarah had said,
with shame, that she should be a proverb to the common
people.   But the former sense is more suitable ; namely,
' Whosoever shall hear it, will laugh with me ;' that is, for the
sake of congratulating me.

7. *Who would have said unto Abraham, that Sarah should
have given children suck?*   I understand the future tense to
be here put for the subjunctive mood.   And the meaning is,
that such a thing would never have entered into the mind of
any one.   Whence she concludes, that God alone was the
Author of it ; and she now condemns herself for ingratitude,
because she had been so slow in giving credit to the angel
who had told her of it.   Now, since she speaks of children
in the plural number, the Jews, according to their custom,
invent the fable, that whereas a rumour was spread, that the
child was supposititious, a great number of infants were brought
by the neighbours, in order that Sarah, by suckling them,
might prove herself a mother.   As if, truly, this might not
easily be known, when they saw Isaac hanging on her breast.[1]
But the Jews are doubly foolish and infatuated, as not perceiving, that this form of expression is of exactly the same
import, as if Sarah had called herself a nurse.   Meanwhile,
it is to be observed, that Sarah joins the office of nurse with
that of mother ; for the Lord does not in vain prepare nutriment for children, in their mothers' bosoms, before they are
born.   But those on whom he confers the honour of mothers,
he, in this way, constitutes nurses ; and they who deem it a
hardship to nourish their own offspring, break, as far as they
are able, the sacred bond of nature.   If disease, or anything
of that kind, is the hinderance, they have a just excuse ; but
for mothers voluntarily, and for their own pleasure, to avoid
the trouble of nursing, and thus to make themselves only
half-mothers, is a shameful corruption.

[1] It is here added, " Ac non clarior, et in promptu fuerit demonstratio,
si lac digitis expressum ante oculos fluxisset."

8. *And the child grew, and was weaned.* Moses now begins to relate the manner in which Ishmael was rejected from the family of Abraham, in order that Isaac alone might hold the place of the lawful son and heir. It seems, indeed, at first sight, something frivolous, that Sarah, being angry about a mere nothing, should have stirred up strife in the family. But Paul teaches, that a sublime mystery is here proposed to us, concerning the perpetual state of the Church. (Gal. iv. 21.) And, truly, if we attentively consider the persons mentioned, we shall regard it as no trivial affair, that the father of all the faithful is divinely commanded to eject his first-born son ; that Ishmael, although a partaker of the same circumcision, becomes so transformed into a strange nation, as to be no more reckoned among the blessed seed; that, in appearance, the body of the Church is so rent asunder, that only one-half of it remains ; that Sarah, in expelling the son of her bondmaid from the house, claims the entire inheritance for Isaac alone. Wherefore, if due attention be applied in the reading of this history, the very mystery of which Paul treats, spontaneously presents itself.

And Abraham made a great feast. It is asked, why he did not rather make it on the day of Isaac's birth, or circumcision ? The subtile reasoning of Augustine, that the day of Isaac's weaning was celebrated, in order that we may learn, from his example, no more to be children in understanding, is too constrained. What others say, has no greater consistency; namely, that Abraham took a day which was not then in common use, in order that he might not imitate the manners of the Gentiles. Indeed, it is very possible, that he may also have celebrated the birth-day of his son, with honour and joy. But special mention is made of this feast, for another reason ; namely, that then, the mocking of Ishmael was discovered. For I do not assent to the conjecture of those who think that a new history is here begun ; and that Sarah daily contended with this annoyance, until, at length, she purged the house by the ejection of the impious mocker. It is indeed probable, that, on other days also, Ishmael had been elated by similar petulance ; yet I do not doubt but Moses expressly declares, that his contempt was manifested toward Sarah,

at that solemn assembly, and that from that time, it was publicly proclaimed. Now Moses does not speak disparagingly of
the pleasures of that feast, but rather takes their lawfulness
for granted. For it is not his design to prohibit holy men
from inviting their friends, to a common participation of enjoyment, so that they, jointly giving thanks to God, may
feast with greater hilarity than usual. Temperance and
sobriety are indeed always to be observed ; and care must be
taken, both that the provision itself be frugal, and the guests
moderate. I would only say, that God does not deal so aus-
terely with us, as not to allow us, sometimes, to entertain our
friends liberally ; as when nuptials are to be celebrated, or
when children are born to us. Abraham, therefore, made a
great feast, that is, an extraordinary one ; because he was
not accustomed thus sumptuously to furnish his table every
day ; yet this was an abundance which by no means degenerated into luxury. Besides, while he was thus liberal in
entertaining his friends according to his power, he also had
sufficient for unknown guests, as we have seen before.

9. *And Sarah saw the son of Hagar.* As the verb " to
laugh " has a twofold signification among the Latins, so also
the Hebrews use, both in a good and evil sense, the verb from
which the participle מְצַחֵק (*metsachaik*) is derived. That it
was not a childish and innoxious laughter, appears from the
indignation of Sarah. It was, therefore, a malignant expression of scorn, by which the forward youth manifested his
contempt for his infant brother. And it is to be observed,
that the *epithet* which is here applied to Ishmael, and the
name *Isaac*, are both derived from the same root. Isaac was,
to his father and others, the occasion of holy and lawful
laughter ; whence also, the name was divinely imposed upon
him. Ishmael turns the blessing of God, from which such
joy flowed, into ridicule. Therefore, as an impious mocker,
he stands opposed to his brother Isaac. Both (so to speak)
are the sons of laughter : but in a very different sense. Isaac
brought laughter with him from his mother's womb, since he
bore,—engraven upon him,—the certain token of God's
grace. He therefore so exhilarates his father's house, that

joy breaks forth in thanksgiving; but Ishmael, with canine and profane laughter, attempts to destroy that holy joy of faith. And there is no doubt that his manifest impiety against God, betrayed itself under this ridicule. He had reached an age at which he could not, by any means, be ignorant of the promised favour, on account of which his father Abraham was transported with so great joy: and yet—proudly confident in himself—he insults, in the person of his brother, both God and his word, as well as the faith of Abraham. Wherefore it was not without cause that Sarah was so vehemently angry with him, that she commanded him to be driven into exile. For nothing is more grievous to a holy mind, than to see the grace of God exposed to ridicule. And this is the reason why Paul calls his laughter persecution; saying, ' He who was after the flesh persecuted the spiritual seed.' (Gal. iv. 29.) Was it with sword or violence? Nay, but with the scorn of the virulent tongue, which does not injure the body, but pierces into the very soul. Moses might indeed have aggravated his crime by a multiplicity of words; but I think that he designedly spake thus concisely, in order to render the petulance with which Ishmael ridicules the word of God the more detestable.

10. *Cast out this bondwoman.* Not only is Sarah exasperated against the transgressor, but she seems to act more imperiously towards her husband than was becoming in a modest wife. Peter shows, that when, on a previous occasion, she called Abraham lord, she did not do so feignedly; since he proposes her, as an example of voluntary subjection, to pious and chaste matrons. (1 Pet. iii. 6.) But now, she not only usurps the government of the house, by calling her husband to order, but commands him whom she ought to reverence, to be obedient to her will. Here, although I do not deny that Sarah, being moved by womanly feelings, exceeded the bounds of moderation, I yet do not doubt, both that her tongue and mind were governed by a secret impulse of the Spirit, and that this whole affair was directed by the providence of God. Without controversy, she was the minister of great and tremendous judgment. And Paul adduces this

expression, not as a futile reproach, which an enraged woman had poured forth, but as a celestial oracle. But although she sustains a higher character than that of a private woman, yet she does not take from her husband his power; but makes him the lawful director of the ejection.

11. *And the thing was very grievous in Abraham's sight.* Although Abraham had been already assured, by many oracles, that the blessed seed should proceed from Isaac only; yet, under the influence of paternal affection, he could not bear that Ishmael should be cut off, for the purpose of causing the inheritance to remain entire to him, to whom it had been divinely granted; and thus, by mingling two races, he endeavoured, as far as he was able, to confound the distinction which God had made. It may truly seem absurd, that the servant of God should thus be carried away by a blind impulse: but God thus deprives him of judgment, not only to humble him, but also to testify to all ages, that the dispensing of his grace depends upon his own will alone. Moreover, in order that the holy man may bear, with greater equanimity, the departure of his son, a double consolation is promised him. For, first, God recalls to his memory, the promise made concerning Isaac; as if he would say, it is enough, and more than enough, that Isaac, in whom the spiritual benediction remains entire, is left. He then promises, that he will take care of Ishmael, though exiled from his paternal home; and that a posterity shall arise from him which shall constitute a whole nation. But I have explained above, on the seventeenth chapter, what is the meaning of the expression, ' The seed shall be called in Isaac.' And Paul, (Rom. ix. 8,) by way of interpretation, uses the word reckoned, or imputed.[1] And it is certain that, by this method, the other son was cut off from the family of Abraham; so that he should no more have a name among his posterity. For God, having severed Ishmael, shows that the whole progeny of Abraham should flow from one head. He promises also to Ishmael, that he shall be a nation, but estranged from the Church; so that

---

[1] " Ponit verbum λογίζεσθαι, hoc est, censeri vel reputari."

the condition of the brothers shall, in this respect, be different; that one is constituted the father of a spiritual people, to the other is given a carnal seed. Whence Paul justly infers, that not all who are the seed of Abraham are true and genuine sons; but they only who are born of the Spirit. For as Isaac himself became the legitimate son by a gratuitous promise, so the same grace of God makes a difference among his descendants. But because we have sufficiently treated of the various sons of Abraham, on the seventeenth chapter, the subject is now more sparingly alluded to.

12. *In all that Sarah hath said unto thee.* I have just said, that although God used the ministry of Sarah in so great a matter, it was yet possible that she might fail in her method of acting. He now commands Abraham to hearken unto his wife, not because he approves her disposition, but because he will have the work, of which he is Himself the Author, accomplished. And he thus shows that his designs are not to be subjected to any common rule, especially when the salvation of the Church is concerned. For he purposely inverts the accustomed order of nature, in order that he may prove himself to be the Author and the Perfecter of Isaac's vocation. But because I have before declared, that this history is more profoundly considered by Paul, the sum of it is here briefly to be collected. In the first place, he says, that what is here read, was written allegorically : not that he wishes all histories, indiscriminately, to be tortured to an allegorical sense, as Origen does; who, by hunting every where for allegories, corrupts the whole Scripture ; and others, too eagerly emulating his example, have extracted smoke out of light. And not only has the simplicity of Scripture been vitiated, but the faith has been almost subverted, and the door opened to many foolish dotings. The design of Paul was, to raise the minds of the pious to consider the secret work of God, in this history; as if he had said, What Moses relates concerning the house of Abraham, belongs to the spiritual kingdom of Christ; since, certainly, that house was a lively image of the Church. This, however, is the allegorical similitude which Paul commends. Whereas two sons were born

to Abraham, the one by a bondmaid, the other by a free
woman; he infers, that there are two kinds of persons born
in the Church; the faithful, whom God endues with the
Spirit of adoption, that they may enjoy the inheritance; and
hypocritical disciples, who feign themselves to be what they
are not, and usurp, for a time, a name and place among the
sons of God. He therefore teaches, that there are certain
who are conceived and born in a servile manner; but others,
as from a free-born mother. He then proceeds to say, that
the sons of Hagar are they who are generated by the servile
doctrine of the Law; but that they who, having embraced,
by faith, gratuitous adoption, are born through the doctrine
of the Gospel, are the sons of the free woman. At length he
descends to another similitude, in which he compares Hagar
with mount Sinai, but Sarah with the heavenly Jerusalem.
And although I here allude in few words to those things,
which my readers will find copiously expounded by me, in the
fourth chapter to the Galatians; yet, in this short explanation,
it is made perfectly clear what Paul designs to teach. We
know that the true sons of God are born of the incorruptible
seed of the word: but when the Spirit, which gives life to
the doctrine of the Law and the Prophets, is taken away,
and the dead letter alone remains, then that seed is so corrupted, that only adulterous sons are born in a state of slavery; yet because they are apparently born of the word of
God, though corrupted, they are, in a sense, the sons of God.
Meanwhile, none are lawful heirs, except those whom the
Church brings forth into liberty, being conceived by the incorruptible seed of the gospel. I have said, however, that in
these two persons is represented the perpetual condition of
the Church. For hypocrites not only mingle with the sons of
God in the Church, but despise them, and proudly appropriate
to themselves all the rights and honours of the Church. And
as Ishmael, inflated with the vain title of primogeniture, harassed his brother Isaac with his taunts; so these men, relying on
their own splendour, reproachfully assail and ridicule the true
faith of the simple: because, by arrogating all things to themselves, they leave nothing to the grace of God. Hence we are
admonished, that none have a well-grounded confidence of sal-

vation, but they who, being called freely, regard the mercy of God as their whole dignity. Again, the Spirit furnishes the consciences of the pious with strong and effective weapons against the ferociousness of those who, under a false pretext, boast that they are the Church. We see that it is no new thing, for persons who are nothing but hypocrites, to occupy the chief place in the Church of God. Wherefore, while at this day, the Papists proudly exult, there is no reason why we should be disturbed by their empty and inflated boasts. As to their glorying in their long succession, it just means as much as if Ishmael were proclaiming himself the first-born. It is, therefore, necessary to discriminate between the true and the hypocritical Church. Paul describes a mark, which they are never able, with their cavils, to obliterate. For as large bottles are broken with a slight blast; so by this single word, all their glory is extinguished, ' the sons of the hand-maid shall not be eternal inheritors.' In the meantime, their insolence is to be patiently borne, so long as God shall loosen the rein to their tyranny. For the Apostles, formerly, were oppressed by the Jewish hypocrites of their age, with the same reproaches which these men now cast upon us. In the same way, Ishmael triumphed over Isaac, as if he had obtained the victory. Wherefore, we must not wonder, if our own age also has its Ishmaelites. But lest such indignity should break our spirits, let this consolation perpetually occur to us, that they who hold the pre-eminence in the Church, will not always remain within it.

14. *And Abraham rose up early.* How painful was the wound, which the ejection of his first-born son inflicted upon the mind of the holy man, we may gather from the double consolation with which God mitigated his grief. He sends his son into banishment, just as if he were tearing out his own bowels. But being accustomed to obey God, he brings into subjection the paternal love, which he is not able wholly to cast aside. This is the true test of faith and piety, when the faithful are so far compelled to deny themselves, that they even resign the very affections of their original nature, which are neither evil nor vicious in them-

selves, to the will of God. There is no doubt that, during the whole night, he had been tossed with various cares; that he had a variety of internal conflicts, and endured severe torments; yet he arose early in the morning, to hasten his separation from his child; since he knew that it was the will of God.

And took bread, and a bottle of water. Moses intimates, not only that Abraham committed his son to the care of his mother, but that he relinquished his own paternal right over him; for it was necessary for this son to be alienated, that he might not afterwards be accounted the seed of Abraham. But with what a slender provision does he endow his wife and her son? He places a flagon of water and bread upon her shoulder. Why does he not, at least, load an ass with a moderate supply of food? Why does he not add one of his servants, of which his house contained plenty, as a companion? Truly either God shut his eyes, that, what he would gladly have done, might not come into his mind; or Abraham limited her provision, in order that she might not go far from his house. For doubtless he would prefer to have them near himself, for the purpose of rendering them such assistance as they would need. Meanwhile, God designed that the banishment of Ishmael should be thus severe and sorrowful; in order that, by his example, he might strike terror into the proud, who, being intoxicated with present gifts, trample under foot, in their haughtiness, the very grace to which they are indebted for all things. Therefore he brought the mother and child to a distressing issue. For after they have wandered into the desert, the water fails; and the mother departs from her son; which was a token of despair. Such was the reward of the pride, by which they had been vainly inflated. It had been their duty humbly to embrace the grace of God offered to all people, in the person of Isaac: but they impiously spurned him whom God had exalted to the highest honour. The knowledge of God's gifts ought to have formed their minds to modesty. And because nothing was more desirable for them, than to retain some corner in Abraham's house, they ought not to have shrunk from any kind of subjection, for the sake of so great a benefit: God now exacts from them the punishment, which they had deserved, by their ingratitude.

17. *God heard the voice of the lad.* Moses had said before that Hagar wept : how is it then, that, disregarding *her* tears, God only hears the voice of the *lad ?* If we should say, that the mother did not deserve to receive a favourable answer to her prayers; her son, certainly, was in no degree more worthy. For, as to the supposition of some, that they both were brought to repentance by this chastisement, it is but an uncertain conjecture. I leave their repentance, of which I can see no sign, to the judgment of God. The cry of the boy was heard, as I understand it, not because he had prayed in faith; but because God, mindful of his own promise, was inclined to have compassion upon them. For Moses does not say, that their vows and sighs were directed towards heaven ; it is rather to be believed, that, in bewailing their miseries, they did not resort to divine help. But God, in assisting them, had respect, not to what *they desired* of him, but to what *he had promised* to Abraham, concerning Ishmael. In this sense Moses seems to say that the voice of the boy was heard ; namely, because he was the son of Abraham.

What aileth thee, Hagar ?[1] The angel reproves the ingratitude of Hagar ; because, when reduced to the greatest straits, she does not reflect on God's former kindness toward her, in similar danger ; so that, as one who had found him to be a deliverer, she might again cast herself upon his faithfulness. Nevertheless, the angel assures her that a remedy is prepared for her sorrows, if only she will seek it. Therefore in the clause, " What aileth thee ?"[2] is a reproof for having tormented herself in vain, by confused lamentation. When he afterwards says, " Fear not," he invites and exhorts her to hope for mercy. But what, we may ask, is the meaning of the expression, which he adds, " where he is ?"[3] It may seem

---

[1] " Quid tibi est Agar?"
[2] " Ergo in particula, ' Quid agis ?' objurgatio est." The expression, " *Quid agis,*" does not occur in the text, but is only another form in which Calvin puts " Quid tibi est ?"—*Ed.*
[3] " God hath heard the voice of the lad where he is." English version. Calvin has it, " ex loco ubi est."

that there is a suppressed antithesis between the place where he now was, and the house of Abraham; so that Hagar might conclude, that although she was wandering in the desert as an exile from the sanctuary of God, yet she was not entirely forsaken by God; since she had him for a Leader in her exile. Or else, the phrase is emphatical; implying, that, though the boy is cast into solitude, and counted as one forsaken, he nevertheless has God nigh unto him. And thus the angel, to relieve the despair of the anxious mother, commands her to return to the place where she had laid down her son. For (as is usual in desperate circumstances) she had become stupified through grief; and would have lain as one lifeless, unless she had been roused by the voice of the angel. We perceive, moreover, in this example, how truly it is said, that when father and mother forsake us, the Lord will take us up.

18. *Arise, lift up the lad.* In order that she might have more courage to bring up her son, God confirms to her what he had before often promised to Abraham. Indeed, nature itself prescribes to mothers what they owe to their children; but, as I have lately hinted, all the natural feelings of Hagar would have been destroyed, unless God had revived her, by inspiring new confidence, to address herself with fresh vigour to the fulfilment of her maternal office. With respect to the fountain or "well,"[1] some think it suddenly sprung up. But since Moses says, that the *eyes* of Hagar were opened, and not that the *earth* was opened or dug up; I rather incline to the opinion, that, having been previously astonished with grief, she did not discern what was plainly before her eyes; but now, at length, after God has restored her vision, she begins to see it. And it is worthy of especial notice, that when God leaves us destitute of his superintendence, and takes away his grace from us, we are as much deprived of all the aids which are close at hand, as if they were removed to the greatest distance. Therefore we must ask, not only that he would bestow upon

---

[1] Ver. 19. " God opened her eyes, and she saw a well of water." " Quod ad *fontem* pertinet," are Calvin's words; but in his version it stands, " puteum aquæ," a well of water.—*Ed.*

us such things as will be useful to us, but that he will also impart prudence, to enable us to use them ; otherwise, it will be our lot to faint, with closed eyes, in the midst of fountains.

20. *And God was with the lad.* There are many ways in which God is said to be present with men. He is present with his elect, whom he governs by the special grace of his Spirit ; he is present also, sometimes, as it respects external life, not only with his elect, but also with strangers, in granting them some signal benediction : as Moses, in this place, commends the extraordinary grace by which the Lord declares that his promise is not void, since he pursues Ishmael with favour, because he was the son of Abraham. Hence, however, this general doctrine is inferred ; that it is to be entirely ascribed to God that men grow up, that they enjoy the light and common breath of heaven, and that the earth supplies them with food. Only it must be remembered, the prosperity of Ishmael flowed from this cause, that an earthly blessing was promised him, for the sake of his father Abraham. In saying, that Hagar took a wife for Ishmael, Moses has respect to civil order ; for since marriage forms a principal part of human life, it is right that, in contracting it, children should be subject to their parents, and should obey their counsel. This order, which nature prescribes and dictates, was, as we see, observed by Ishmael, a wild man in the barbarism of the desert ; for he was subject to his mother in marrying a wife. Whence we perceive, what a prodigious monster was the Pope, when he dared to overthrow this sacred right of nature. To this is also added the impudent boast of authorising a wicked contempt of parents, in honour of holy wedlock. Moreover, the Egyptian wife was a kind of prelude to the future dissension between the Israelites and the Ishmaelites.

22. *And it came to pass at that time.* Moses relates, that this covenant was entered into between Abraham and Abimelech, for the purpose of showing, that after various agitations, some repose was, at length, granted to the holy man. He had been constrained, as a wanderer, and without a fixed abode, to move his tent from place to place, during sixty

years. But although God would have him to be a sojourner even unto death, yet, under king Abimelech, he granted him a quiet habitation. And it is the design of Moses to show, how it happened, that he occupied one place longer than he was wont. The circumstance of time is to be noted; namely, soon after he had dismissed his son. For it seems that his great trouble was immediately followed by this consolation, not only that he might have some relaxation from continued inconveniences, but that he might be the more cheerful, and might the more quietly occupy himself in the education of his little son Isaac. It is however certain, that the covenant was not, in every respect, an occasion of joy to him; for he perceived that he was tried by indirect methods, and that there were many persons in that region, to whom he was disagreeable and hateful. The king, indeed, openly avowed his own suspicions of him: it was, however, the highest honour, that the king of the place should go, of his own accord, to a stranger, to enter into a covenant with him. Yet it may be asked, whether this covenant was made on just and equal conditions, as is the custom among allies? I certainly do not doubt, that Abraham freely paid due honour to the king; nor is it probable that the king intended to detract anything from his own dignity, in order to confer it upon Abraham. What, then, did he do? Truly, while he allowed Abraham a free dwelling-place, he would yet hold him bound to himself by an oath.

God is with thee in all that thou doest. He commences in friendly and bland terms; he does not accuse Abraham, nor complain that he had neglected any duty towards himself, but declares that he earnestly desires his friendship; still the conclusion is, that he wishes to be on his guard against him. It may then be asked, Whence had he this suspicion, or fear, first of a stranger, and, secondly, of an honest and moderate man? In the first place, we know that the heathen are often anxious without cause, and are alarmed even in seasons of quiet. Next, Abraham was a man deserving of reverence; the number of servants in his house seemed like a little nation; and there is no doubt, that his virtues would acquire for him great dignity; hence it was, that Abimelech suspected his

power. But whereas Abimelech had a private consideration
for himself in this matter ; the Lord, who best knows how
to direct events, provided, in this way, for the repose of his
servant. We may, however, learn, from the example of
Abraham, if, at any time, the gifts of God excite the
enmity of the men of this world against us, to conduct ourselves with such moderation, that they may find nothing
amiss in us.

23. *That thou wilt not deal falsely with me.*[1] Literally it is,
' If thou shalt lie ;' for, among the Hebrews, a defective form
of speech is common in taking oaths, which is to be thus explained : 'If thou shouldst break the promise given to me, we
call upon God to sit as Judge between us, and to show himself the avenger of perjury.' But ' to lie,' some here take for
dealing unjustly and fraudulently; others for failing in the conditions of the covenant. I simply understand it as if it were
said, ' Thou shalt do nothing perfidiously with me or with
my descendants.' Abimelech also enumerates his own acts of
kindness, the more effectually to exhort Abraham to exercise
good faith ; for, seeing he had been humanely treated, Abimelech declares it would be an act of base ingratitude if he did
not, in return, endeavour to repay the benefits he had received.
The Hebrew word חֶסֶד, (*chesed,*) signifies to deal gently or
kindly with any one.[2] For Abimelech did not come to implore compassion of Abraham, but rather to assert his own
royal authority, as will appear from the context.

24. *And Abraham said, I will swear.* Although he had the
stronger claim of right, he yet refuses nothing which belonged
to the duty of a good and moderate man. And truly, since
it is becoming in the sons of God to be freely ready for every
duty ; nothing is more absurd, than for them to appear re-

---

[1] " Si mentitus fueris mihi."—" If thou shalt have lied unto me." In
the margin Calvin gives, " Si fefelleris, aut infideliter egeris."—" If thou
shalt have deceived, or have acted unfaithfully." See margin of English
version.—*Ed.*

[2] " Secundum misericordiam quam feci tecum facies mecum," is Calvin's version ; and the comment is, " Misericordiam facere cum aliquo
Hebræis significat clementer et benigne eum tractare."—*Ed.*

luctant and morose, when what is just is required of them. He did not refuse to swear, because he knew it to be lawful, that covenants should be ratified between men, in the sacred name of God.   In short, we see Abraham willingly submitting himself to the laws of his vocation.

25. *And Abraham reproved Abimelech.*   This complaint seems to be unjust; for, if he had been injured, why did he not resort to the ordinary remedy ? He knew the king to be humane, to have some seed of piety, and to have treated himself courteously and honourably ; why then does he doubt that he will prove the equitable defender of his right ? If, indeed, he had chosen rather to smother the injury received, than to be troublesome to the king, why does he now impute the fault to him, as if he had been guilty ? Possibly, however, Abraham might know that the injury had been done, through the excessive forbearance of the king. We may assuredly infer, both from his manners and his disposition, that he did not expostulate without cause ; and hence the moderation of the holy man is evident ; because, when deprived of the use of water, found by his own industry and labour, he does not contend, as the greatness of the injury would have justified him in doing ; for this was just as if the inhabitants of the place had made an attempt upon his life. But though he patiently bore so severe an injury, yet when, beyond expectation, the occasion of taking security is offered, he guards himself from future aggression. We also see how severely the Lord exercised Abraham, as soon as he appeared to be somewhat more at ease, and had obtained a little alleviation. Certainly, it was not a light trial, to be compelled to contend for water ; and not for water which was public property, but for that of a well, which he himself had digged.

27. *And Abraham took sheep.*   Hence it appears that the covenant made, was not such as is usually entered into between equals : for Abraham considers his own position, and in token of subjection, offers a gift, from his flocks, to king Gerar; for, what the Latins call paying tax or tribute, and what we

call doing homage, the Hebrews call offering gifts.[1] And
truly Abraham does not wait till something is forcibly, and
with authority, extorted from him by the king; but, by a
voluntary giving of honour, anticipates him, whom he knows
to have dominion over the place. It is too well known, how
great a desire of exercising authority prevails among men.
Hence, the greater praise is due to the modesty of Abraham,
who not only abstains from what belongs to another man ;
but even offers, uncommanded, what, in his own mind,
he regards as due to another, in virtue of his office. A
further question however arises ; since Abraham knew that
the dominion over the land had been divinely committed
to him, whether it was lawful for him to profess a subjection by which he acknowledged another as lord ? But
the solution is easy, because the time of entering into
possession had not yet arrived ; for he was lord, only
in expectation, while, in fact, he was a pilgrim. Wherefore, he acted rightly in purchasing a habitation, till the
time should come, when what had been promised to him,
should be given to his posterity. Thus, soon afterwards, as
we shall see, he paid a price for his wife's sepulchre. In
short, until he should be placed, by the hand of God, in
legitimate authority over the land, he did not scruple to treat
with the inhabitants of the place, that he might dwell among
them by permission, or by the payment of a price.

28. *And Abraham set seven ewe-lambs of the flock by themselves.* Moses recites another chief point of the covenant;
namely, that Abraham made express provision for himself
respecting the well, that he should have free use of its water.
And he placed in the midst seven lambs, that the king being
presented with the honorary gift, might approve and ratify
the digging of the well. For the inhabitants might provoke
a controversy, on the ground that it was not lawful for a
private man, and a stranger, to dig a well; but now, when
the public authority of the king intervened, Abraham's peace
was consulted, that no one might disturb him. Many under-

---

[1] " Num pro eo quod dicunt Latini, Pendere vectigal vel tributum, et
Gallice dicimus, *Faire hommage*, Hebræi dicunt Munera offerre."

stand *lambs* here to mean pieces of money coined in the form of lambs, but since mention has previously been made of sheep and oxen, and Moses now immediately subjoins that seven lambs are placed apart, it is absurd, in this connection, to speak of money.

31. *Wherefore he called that place Beer-sheba.* Moses has once already called the place by this name, but proleptically. Now, however, he declares when, and for what reason, the name was given; namely, because there both he and Abimelech had sworn; therefore I translate the term ' the well of swearing.' Others translate it ' the well of seven.' But Moses plainly derives the word from swearing; nor is it of any consequence that the pronunciation slightly varies from grammatical correctness, which in proper names is not very nicely observed. In fact, Moses does not restrict the etymology to the *well*, but comprises the whole covenant. I do not, however, deny that Moses might allude to the number *seven*.[1]

33. *And Abraham planted a grove.* It hence appears that more rest was granted to Abraham, after the covenant was entered into, than he had hitherto enjoyed ; for now he begins to plant trees, which is a sign of a tranquil and fixed habitation ; for we never before read that he planted a single shrub. Wherefore, we see how far his condition was improved, because he was permitted to lead (as I may say) a settled life. The assertion, that he " called on the name of the Lord," I thus interpret; he instituted anew the solemn worship of God, in order to testify his gratitude. Therefore God, after he had led his servant through continually winding paths, gave to him some relaxation in his extreme old age. And he sometimes so deals with his faithful people, that when they have been tossed by various storms, he at length permits them to breathe freely. As it respects calling upon God, we know

---

[1] As the word שׁבע means both an *oath* and the number *seven*, room is left for this difference of interpretation. Calvin seems, however, to allude to a notion not uncommon among learned men, that as oaths were often made before seven witnesses, which perhaps the seven lambs represented, Abraham might have this number as well as the oath in his mind, when he called the well Beer-sheba.—*Ed.*

that Abraham, wherever he went, never neglected this religious duty. Nor was he deterred by dangers from professing himself a worshipper of the true God; although, on this account, he was hateful to his neighbours. But as his conveniences for dwelling in the land increased, he became the more courageous in professing the worship of God. And because he now lived more securely under the protection of the king, he perhaps wished to bear open testimony, that he received even this as from God. For the same reason, the title of " the everlasting God" seems to be given, as if Abraham would say, that he had not placed his confidence in an earthly king, and was not engaging in any new covenant, by which he would be departing from the everlasting God. The reason why Moses, by the figure *synecdoche*, gives to the worship of God the name of *invocation*, I have elsewhere explained. Lastly, Abraham is here said to have sojourned in that land in which he, nevertheless, had a settled abode; whence we learn, that his mind was not so fixed upon this state of repose, as to prevent him from considering what he had before heard from the mouth of God, that he with his posterity should be strangers till the expiration of four hundred years.

CHAPTER XXII.

1. And it came to pass after these things, that God did tempt Abraham, and said unto him, Abraham : and he said, Behold, *here* I *am.*

2. And he said, Take now thy son, thine only *son* Isaac, whom thou lovest, and get thee into the land of Moriah ; and offer him there for a burnt-offering upon one of the mountains which I will tell thee of.

3. And Abraham rose up early in the morning, and saddled his ass, and took two of his young men with him, and Isaac his son, and clave the wood for the burnt-offering, and rose up, and went unto the place of which God had told him.

4. Then on the third day Abraham

1. Et fuit, posthæc Deus tentavit Abraham, et dixit ad eum, Abraham : qui dixit, Ecce ego.

2. Et dixit, Tolle nunc filium tuum, unicum tuum, quem dilexisti Ishac, et vade ad terram Moriah, et offer eum ibi in holocaustum super unum e montibus, quem dixero tibi.

3. Et surrexit Abraham mane, et stravit asinum suum, et cepit duos pueros suos secum, et Ishac filium suum : et scidit ligna holocausti : et surrexit, perrexitque ad locum, quem dixerat ei Deus.

4. Die tertia levavit Abra-

lifted up his eyes, and saw the place afar off.

5. And Abraham said unto his young men, Abide ye here with the ass ; and I and the lad will go yonder and worship, and come again to you.

6. And Abraham took the wood of the burnt-offering, and laid *it* upon Isaac his son ; and he took the fire in his hand, and a knife ; and they went both of them together.

7. And Isaac spake unto Abraham his father, and said, My father : and he said, Here *am* I, my son. And he said, Behold the fire and the wood : but where *is* the lamb for a burnt-offering ?

8. And Abraham said, My son, God will provide himself a lamb for a burnt-offering : so they went both of them together.

9. And they came to the place which God had told him of ; and Abraham built an altar there, and laid the wood in order, and bound Isaac his son, and laid him on the altar upon the wood.

10. And Abraham stretched forth his hand, and took the knife to slay his son.

11. And the angel of the Lord called unto him out of heaven, and said, Abraham, Abraham : and he said, Here *am* I.

12. And he said, Lay not thine hand upon the lad, neither do thou any thing unto him : for now I know that thou fearest God, seeing thou hast not withheld thy son, thine only *son*, from me.

13. And Abraham lifted up his eyes, and looked, and, behold, behind *him* a ram caught in a thicket by his horns : and Abraham went and took the ram, and offered him up for a burnt-offering in the stead of his son.

14. And Abraham called the name of that place Jehovah-jireh : as it is said *to* this day, In the mount of the Lord it shall be seen.

15. And the angel of the Lord called unto Abraham out of heaven the second time,

16. And said, By myself have I sworn, saith the Lord ; for because thou hast

ham oculos suos, et vidit locum procul.

5. Et dixit Abraham ad pueros suos, Manete hic cum asino : et ego et puer pergemus usque illuc, et adorabimus, revertemurque ad vos.

6. Et accepit Abraham ligna holocausti, et posuit super Ishac filium suum, et accepit in manu sua ignem et gladium, et perrexerunt ambo pariter.

7. Dixit autem Ishac ad Abraham patrem suum, dixit, inquam, Pater mi. Et dixit, Ecce ego fili mi. Et dixit, Ecce ignis et ligna, et ubi pecus in holocaustum ?

8. Et dixit Abraham, Deus prospiciet sibi pecudem in holocaustum, fili mi. Itaque perrexerunt ambo pariter.

9. Et venerunt ad locum, quem dixerat ei Deus : et ædificavit ibi Abraham altare, et ordinavit ligna, et ligavit Ishac filium suum, et posuit eum super altare super ligna.

10. Et misit Abraham manum suam, et accepit gladium ut jugularet filium suum.

11. Et clamavit ad eum angelus Jehovæ de cœlo, et dixit, Abraham, Abraham. Et dixit, Ecce ego.

12. Et dixit, Ne extendas manum tuam in puerum, et ne facias ei quicquam : quia nunc cognovi quod times Deum, nec prohibuisti filium tuum unicum a me.

13. Tunc levavit Abraham oculos suos, et vidit, et ecce aries post *eum* detentus in perplexitate *spinarum* cornibus suis : et perrexit Abraham, et accepit arietem, obtulitque eum in holocaustum pro filio suo.

14. Et vocavit Abraham nomen loci ipsius, Jehova videbit : idcirco dicitur hodie, In monte Jehova videbit.

15. Et clamavit angelus Jehovæ ad Abraham secundo e cœlo,

16. Et dixit, Per me juravi, dixit Jehova, certe pro eo quod

done this thing, and hast not withheld thy son, thine only *son;*

17. That in blessing I will bless thee, and in multiplying I will multiply thy seed as the stars of the heaven, and as the sand which *is* upon the sea-shore; and thy seed shall possess the gate of his enemies :

18. And in thy seed shall all the nations of the earth be blessed; because thou hast obeyed my voice.

19. So Abraham returned unto his young men, and they rose up, and went together to Beer-sheba; and Abraham dwelt at Beer-sheba.

20. And it came to pass after these things, that it was told Abraham, saying, Behold, Milcah, she hath also born children unto thy brother Nahor;

21. Huz his first-born, and Buz his brother, and Kemuel the father of Aram,

22. And Chesed, and Hazo, and Pildash, and Jidlaph, and Bethuel.

23. And Bethuel begat Rebekah : these eight Milcah did bear to Nahor, Abraham's brother.

24. And his concubine, whose name *was* Reumah, she bare also Tebah, and Gaham, and Thahash, and Maachah.

fecisti rem hanc, et non prohibuisti filium tuum unicum tuum :

17. Quod benedicendo benedicam tibi, et multiplicando multiplicabo semen tuum sicut stellas cœli, et sicut arenam, quæ est juxta litus maris : et hæreditabit semen tuum portam inimicorum suorum.

18. Et benedicentur in semine tuo omnes gentes terræ, eo quod obedivisti voci meæ.

19. Postea reversus est Abraham ad pueros suos, et surrexerunt, perrexeruntque pariter in Beer-sebah, et habitavit Abraham in Beer-sebah.

20. Et fuit, posthæc nuntiatum fuit ipsi Abraham, dicendo, Ecce, peperit Milchah etiam ipsa filios Nachor fratri tuo.

21. Hus primogenitum suum, et Buz fratrem ejus, et Cemuel patrem Aram,

22. Et Chesed, et Hazo, et Pildas, et Idlaph, et Bethuel :

23. Et Bethuel genuit Ribcah : octo istos peperit Milchah ipsi Nachor fratri Abraham.

24. Et concubina ejus, cujus nomen Reumah, peperit etiam ipsa Tebah, et Gaham, et Thahas, et Mahachah.

1. *And it came to pass.* This chapter contains a most memorable narrative. For although Abraham, through the whole course of his life, gave astonishing proofs of faith and obedience, yet none more excellent can be imagined than the immolation of his son. For other temptations with which the Lord had exercised him, tended, indeed, to his mortification; but this inflicted a wound far more grievous than death itself. Here, however, we must consider something greater and higher than the paternal grief and anguish, which, being produced by the death of an only son, pierced through the breast of the holy man. It was sad for him to be deprived of his only son, sadder still that this son should be torn away by a violent death, but by far the most grievous that he him-

self should be appointed as the executioner to slay him with his own hand. Other circumstances, which will be noted in their proper place, I now omit. But all these things, if we compare them with the spiritual conflict of conscience which he endured, will appear like the mere play, or shadows of conflicts. For the great source of grief to him was not his own bereavement, not that he was commanded to slay his only heir, the hope of future memorial and of name, the glory and support of his family; but that, in the person of this son, the whole salvation of the world seemed to be extinguished and to perish. His contest, too, was not with his carnal passions, but, seeing that he wished to devote himself wholly to God, his very piety and religion filled him with distracting thoughts. For God, as if engaging in personal contest with him, requires the death of the boy, to whose person He himself had annexed the hope of eternal salvation. So that this latter command was, in a certain sense, the destruction of faith. This foretaste of the story before us, it was deemed useful to give to the readers, that they may reflect how deserving it is of diligent and constant meditation.

After these things God did tempt Abraham. The expression, "after these things," is not to be restricted to his last vision; Moses rather intended to comprise in one word the various events by which Abraham had been tossed up and down; and again, the somewhat more quiet state of life which, in his old age, he had lately begun to obtain. He had passed an unsettled life in continued exile up to his eightieth year; having been harassed with many contumelies and injuries, he had endured with difficulty a miserable and anxious existence, in continual trepidation; famine had driven him out of the land whither he had gone, by the command and under the auspices of God, into Egypt. Twice his wife had been torn from his bosom; he had been separated from his nephew; he had delivered this nephew, when captured in war, at the peril of his own life. He had lived childless with his wife, when yet all his hopes were suspended upon his having offspring. Having at length obtained a son, he was compelled to disinherit him, and to drive him far from home.

Isaac alone remained, his special but only consolation ; he was
enjoying peace at home, but now God suddenly thundered
out of heaven, denouncing the sentence of death upon this
son.   The meaning, therefore, of the passage is, that by this
temptation, as if by the last act, the faith of Abraham was
far more severely tried than before.

God did tempt Abraham.   James, in denying that any one
is tempted by God, (James i. 13,) refutes the profane calumnies of those who, to exonerate themselves from the blame of
their sins, attempt to fix the charge of them upon God.
Wherefore, James truly contends, that those sins, of which
we have the root in our own concupiscence, ought not to be
charged upon another.   For though Satan instils his poison,
and fans the flame of our corrupt desires within us, we are
yet not carried by any external force to the commission of sin ;
but our own flesh entices us, and we willingly yield to its
allurements.   This, however, is no reason why God may not be
said to tempt us in his own way, just as he tempted Abraham,—that is, brought him to a severe test,—that he might
make full trial of the faith of his servant.

And said unto him.   Moses points out the kind of temptation ; namely, that God would shake the faith which the holy
man had placed in His *word*, by a counter assault of the word
itself.   He therefore addresses him by name, that there may
be no doubt respecting the Author of the command.   For
unless Abraham had been fully persuaded that it was the voice
of God which commanded him to slay his son Isaac, he would
have been easily released from anxiety ; for, relying on the
certain promise of God, he would have rejected the suggestion
as the fallacy of Satan ; and thus, without any difficulty, the
temptation would have been shaken off.   But now all occasion
of doubt is removed ; so that, without controversy, he acknowledges the oracle, which he hears, to be from God.
Meanwhile, God, in a certain sense, assumes a double character, that, by the appearance of disagreement and repugnance
in which He presents Himself in his word, he may distract
and wound the breast of the holy man.   For the only method
of cherishing constancy of faith, is to apply all our senses to
the word of God.   But so great was then the discrepancy of
the word, that it would wound and lacerate the faith of

Abraham. Wherefore, there is great emphasis in the word, "said,"[1] because God indeed made trial of Abraham's faith, not in the usual manner, but by drawing him into a contest with his own word.[2] Whatever temptations assail us, let us know that the victory is in our own hands, so long as we are endued with a firm faith; otherwise, we shall be, by no means, able to resist. If, when we are deprived of the sword of the Spirit, we are overcome, what would be our condition were God himself to attack us with the very sword, with which he had been wont to arm us? This, however, happened to Abraham. The manner in which Abraham, by faith, wrestled with this temptation, we shall afterwards see, in the proper place.

And he said, Behold, here I am. It hence appears, that the holy man was, in no degree, afraid of the wiles of Satan. For the faithful are not in such haste to obey God, as to allow a foolish credulity to carry them away, in whatever direction the breath of a doubtful vision may blow. But when it was once clear to Abraham, that he was called by God, he testified, by this answer, his prompt desire to yield obedience. For the expression before us is as much as if he said, Whatever God may have been pleased to command, I am perfectly ready to carry into effect. And, truly, he does not wait till God should expressly enjoin this or the other thing; but promises that he will be simply, and without exception, obedient in all things. This, certainly, is true subjection, when we are prepared to act, before the will of God is known to us. We find, indeed, all men ready to boast that they will do as Abraham did; but when it comes to the trial, they shrink from the yoke of God. But the holy man, soon afterwards, proves, by his very act, how truly and seriously he had professed, that he, without delay, and without disputation, would subject himself to the hand of God.

---

[1] " Quare magna subest emphasis verbo loquendi."
[2] God's usual manner of trying the faith of his people is, by causing the dispensations of his providence apparently to contradict his word, and requiring them still to rely upon that word, notwithstanding the apparent inconsistency. But in Abraham's trial, He proposed a test far more severe. For His own command, or word, was in direct contradiction to what he had before spoken; His injunction respecting the slaying of Isaac could, by no human method of reasoning, be reconciled to his promises respecting the future destinies of Abraham's family, of the Church, and of the world.—*Ed.*

2. *Take now thy son.*   Abraham is commanded to immolate
his son.   If God had said nothing more than that his son
should die, even this message would have most grievously
wounded his mind; because, whatever favour he could hope
for from God, was included in this single promise, " In Isaac
shall thy seed be called."   Whence he necessarily inferred,
that his own salvation, and that of the whole human race,
would perish, unless Isaac remained in safety.   For he was
taught, by that word, that God would not be propitious to
man without a Mediator.   For although the declaration of
Paul, that ' all the promises of God in Christ are yea and
Amen,' was not yet written, (2 Cor. i. 20,) it was nevertheless
engraven on the heart of Abraham.   Whence, however, could
he have had this hope, but from Isaac ?   The matter had come
to this; that God would appear to have done nothing but mock
him.   Yet not only is the death of his son announced to him,
but he is commanded with his own hand to slay him ; as if he
were required, not only to throw aside, but to cut in pieces,
or cast into the fire, the charter of his salvation, and to have
nothing left for himself, but death and hell.   But it may be
asked, how, under the guidance of faith, he could be brought
to sacrifice his son, seeing that what was proposed to him,
was in opposition to that word of God, on which it is necessary for faith to rely ?   To this question the Apostle answers,
that his confidence in the word of God remained unshaken ;
because he hoped that God would be able to cause the promised benediction to spring up, even out of the dead ashes of
his son. (Heb. xi. 19.)   His mind, however, must of necessity
have been severely crushed, and violently agitated, when the
command and the *promise* of God were conflicting within him.
But when he had come to the conclusion, that the God with
whom he knew he had to do, could not be his adversary;
although he did not immediately discover how the contradiction might be removed, he nevertheless, by hope, reconciled
the command with the promise; because, being indubitably
persuaded that God was faithful, he left the unknown issue
to Divine Providence.   Meanwhile, as with closed eyes, he
goes whither he is directed.   The truth of God deserves this
honour ; not only that it should far transcend all human

means, or that it alone, even without means, should suffice us, but also that it should surmount all obstacles.   Here, then, we perceive, more clearly, the nature of the temptation which Moses has pointed out.   It was difficult and painful to Abraham to forget that he was a father and a husband ; to cast off all human affections ; and to endure, before the world, the disgrace of shameful cruelty, by becoming the executioner of his son.   But the other was a far more severe and horrible thing ; namely, that he conceives God to con- tradict Himself and His own word ; and then, that he sup- poses the hope of the promised blessing to be cut off from him, when Isaac is torn away from his embrace.   For what more could he have to do with God, when the only pledge of grace is taken away ?   But as before, when he expected seed from his own dead body, he, by hope, rose above what it seemed possible to hope for; so now, when, in the death of his son, he apprehends the quickening power of God, in such a manner, as to promise himself a blessing out of the ashes of his son, he emerges from the labyrinth of temptation ; for, in order that he might obey God, it was necessary that he should tenaciously hold the promise, which, had it failed, faith must have perished.   But with him the promise always flourished ; because he both firmly retained the love with which God had once embraced him, and subjected to the power of God everything which Satan raised up to disturb his mind.   But he was unwilling to measure, by his own understanding, the method of fulfilling the promise, which he knew depended on the incomprehensible power of God.   It remains for every one of us to apply this example to himself. The Lord, indeed, is so indulgent to our infirmity, that he does not thus severely and sharply try our faith : yet he in- tended, in the father of all the faithful, to propose an example by which he might call us to a general trial of faith.   For the faith, which is more precious than gold and silver, ought not to lie idle, without trial ; and experience teaches, that each will be tried by God, according to the measure of his faith.   At the same time, also, we may observe, that God tempts his servants, not only when he subdues the affections of the flesh, but when he reduces all their senses to nothing, that he may lead them to a complete renunciation of themselves.

Thine only son Isaac, whom thou lovest. As if it were not
enough to command in one word the sacrifice of his son, he
pierces, as with fresh strokes, the mind of the holy man. By
calling him his *only* son, he again irritates the wound recently
inflicted, by the banishment of the other son ; he then looks
forward into futurity, because no hope of offspring would remain. If the death of a first-born son is wont to be grievous,
what must the mourning of Abraham be ? Each word which
follows is emphatical, and serves to aggravate his grief.
'Slay' (he says) 'him whom alone thou lovest.' And he
does not here refer merely to his paternal love, but to that
which sprung from faith. Abraham loved his son, not only
as nature dictates, and as parents commonly do, who take delight in their children, but as beholding the paternal love of
God in him : lastly, Isaac was the mirror of eternal life, and
the pledge of all good things. Wherefore God seems not so
much to assail the paternal love of Abraham, as to trample
upon His own benevolence. There is equal emphasis in the
name *Isaac,* by which Abraham was taught, that nowhere
besides did any joy remain for him. Certainly, when he who
had been given as the occasion of joy, was taken away, it was
just as if God should condemn Abraham to eternal torment.
We must always remember that Isaac was not a son of the
common order, but one in whose person the Mediator was
promised.

Get thee into the land of Moriah. The bitterness of grief is
not a little increased by this circumstance. For God does
not require him to put his son immediately to death, but
compels him to revolve this execution in his mind during
three whole days, that in preparing himself to sacrifice his
son, he may still more severely torture all his own senses.
Besides, he does not even name the place where he requires
that dire sacrifice to be offered, "Upon one of the mountains,"
(he says,) "that I will tell thee of." So before, when he
commanded him to leave his country, he held his mind in
suspense. But in this affair, the delay which most cruelly
tormented the holy man, as if he had been stretched upon the
rack, was still less tolerable. There was, however, a twofold
use of this suspense. For there is nothing to which we are
more prone than to be wise beyond our measure. Therefore,

in order that we may become docile and obedient to God, it
is profitable for us that we should be deprived of our own
wisdom, and that nothing should be left us, but to resign ourselves to be led according to his will.   Secondly, this tended
also to make him persevere, so that he should not obey God by
a merely sudden impulse.   For, as he does not turn back in
his journey, nor revolve conflicting counsels; it hence appears,
that his love to God was confirmed by such constancy, that
it could not be affected by any change of circumstances.
Jerome explains "the land of Moriah" to be 'the land of
vision,' as if the name had been derived from רָאָה, *(raha.)*
But all who are skilled in the Hebrew language condemn
this opinion.   Nor am I better satisfied with those who interpret it the *myrrh* of God.[1]   It is certainly acknowledged,
by the consent of the greater part, that it is derived from
the word יָרָה, *(yarah,)* which signifies to *teach*, or from
יָדֵא, *(yarai,)* which signifies to *fear*.   There is, however, even
at this time, a difference among interpreters, some thinking
that the doctrine of God is here specially inculcated.   Let us
follow the most probable opinion; namely, that it is called
the land of divine worship, either because God had appointed
it for the offering of the sacrifice, in order that Abraham might
not dispute whether some other place should not rather be
chosen; or because the place for the temple was already
fixed there; and I rather adopt this second explanation;
that God there required a present worship from his servant
Abraham, because already, in his secret counsel, he had
determined in that place to fix his ordinary worship.   And
sacrifices properly receive their name from the word which
signifies *fear*, because they give proof of reverence to God.
Moreover, it is by no means doubtful that this is the place
where the temple was afterwards built.[2]

[1] This extraordinary interpretation is supposed to be sanctioned by
Canticles iv. 6, " I will get me to the mountain of myrrh, and to the hill
of frankincense."—Vide *Poli Syn. in loc.—Ed.*
[2] It may be doubted whether the interpretation of Jerome, which Calvin rejects, is not preferable to that which he adopts.   From the subsequent explanation in verse 14, it seems highly probable, that ' the land of
vision' is the true explanation of the term in question.   But even this
admits of a double construction.   The Septuagint calls it ' the high land,'
as if it were merely conspicuous on account of its elevation—the land that
might be seen afar off.   But a more suitable interpretation seems to be,

3. *And Abraham rose up early in the morning.* This promptitude shows the greatness of Abraham's faith. Innumerable thoughts might come into the mind of the holy man; each of which would have overwhelmed his spirit, unless he had fortified it by faith. And there is no doubt that Satan, during the darkness of the night, would heap upon him a vast mass of cares. Gradually to overcome them, by contending with them, was the part of heroical courage. But when they were overcome, then immediately to gird himself to the fulfilment of the command of God, and even to rise early in the morning to do it, was a remarkable effort. Other men, prostrated by a message so dire and terrible, would have fainted, and have lain torpid, as if deprived of life; but the first dawn of morning was scarcely early enough for Abraham's haste. Therefore, in a few words, Moses highly extols his faith, when he declares that it surmounted, in so short a space of time, the very temptation which was attended with many labyrinths.

4. *And saw the place.* He saw, indeed, with his eyes, the place which before had been shown him in secret vision. But when it is said, that he lifted up his eyes, Moses doubtless signifies, that he had been very anxious during the whole of the three days. In commanding his servants to remain behind, he does it that they may not lay their hands upon him, as upon a delirious and insane old man. And herein his magnanimity appears, that he has his thoughts so well composed and tranquil, as to do nothing in an agitated manner. When, however, he says, that he will return with the boy, he seems not to be free from dissimulation and falsehood. Some think that he uttered this declaration prophetically; but since it is certain that he never lost sight of what had been promised concerning the raising up of seed in Isaac, it may be, that he, trusting in the providence of God, figured to himself his son as surviving even in death itself. And seeing that he went, as with closed eyes, to the slaughter of his son, there is nothing improbable in the supposition, that he spoke confusedly, in a matter so obscure.

that it was the land favoured by the vision of divine glory, the spot on which the angel of Jehovah appeared to David, and on which the temple was built by Solomon.—*Ed.*

7. *My father.* God produces here a new instrument of torture, by which he may, more and more, torment the breast of Abraham, already pierced with so many wounds. And it is not to be doubted, that God designedly both framed the tongue of Isaac to this tender appellation, and directed it to this question, in order that nothing might be wanting to the extreme severity of Abraham's grief. Yet the holy man sustains even this attack with invincible courage; and is so far from being disturbed in his proposed course, that he shows himself to be entirely devoted to God, hearkening to nothing which should either shake his confidence, or hinder his obedience. But it is important to notice the manner in which he unties this inextricable knot; namely, by taking refuge in Divine Providence, " God will provide himself a lamb." This example is proposed for our imitation. Whenever the Lord gives a command, many things are perpetually occurring to enfeeble our purpose : means fail, we are destitute of counsel, all avenues seem closed. In such straits, the only remedy against despondency is, to leave the event to God, in order that he may open a way for us where there is none. For as we act unjustly towards God, when we hope for nothing from him but what our senses can perceive, so we pay Him the highest honour, when, in affairs of perplexity, we nevertheless entirely acquiesce in his providence.

8. *So they went both of them together.* Here we perceive both the constancy of Abraham, and the modesty of his son. For Abraham is not rendered more remiss by this obstacle, and the son does not persist in replying to his father's answer. For he might easily have objected, Wherefore have we brought wood and the knife without a lamb, if God has commanded sacrifices to be made to him ? But because he supposes that the victim has been omitted, for some valid reason, and not through his father's forgetfulness, he acquiesces, and is silent.

9. *And they came to the place.* Moses purposely passes over many things, which, nevertheless, the reader ought to consider. When he has mentioned the building of the altar, he immediately afterwards adds, that Isaac was bound. But

we know that he was then of middle age, so that he might either be more powerful than his father, or, at least, equal to resist him, if they had to contend by force ; wherefore, I do not think that force was employed against the youth, as against one struggling and unwilling to die : but rather, that he voluntarily surrendered himself. It was, however, scarcely possible that he would offer himself to death, unless he had been already made acquainted with the divine oracle : but Moses, passing by this, only recites that he was bound. Should any one object, that there was no necessity to bind one who willingly offered himself to death ; I answer, that the holy man anticipated, in this way, a possible danger; lest any thing might happen in the midst of the act to interrupt it. The simplicity of the narrative of Moses is wonderful; but it has greater force than the most exaggerated tragical description. The sum of the whole turns on this point ; that Abraham, when he had to slay his son, remained always like himself; and that the fortitude of his mind was such as to render his aged hand equal to the task of offering a sacrifice, the very sight of which was enough to dissolve and to destroy his whole body.

11. *And the angel of the Lord called unto him.* The inward temptation had been already overcome, when Abraham intrepidly raised his hand to slay his son ; and it was by the special grace of God that he obtained so signal a victory. But now Moses subjoins, that suddenly, beyond all hope, his sorrow was changed into joy. Poets, in their fables, when affairs are desperate, introduce some god who, unexpectedly, appears at the critical juncture. It is possible that Satan, by figments of this kind, has endeavoured to obscure the wonderful and stupendous interpositions of God, when he has unexpectedly appeared for the purpose of bringing assistance to his servants. This history ought certainly to be known and celebrated among all people ; yet, by the subtlety of Satan, not only has the truth of God been adulterated and turned into a lie, but also distorted into materials for fable, in order to render it the more ridiculous. But it is our business, with earnest minds to consider how wonderfully God, in the very article of death, both recalled Isaac from death to life, and

restored to Abraham his son, as one who had risen from the tomb.   Moses also describes the voice of the angel, as having sounded out of heaven, to give assurance to Abraham that he had come from God, in order that he might withdraw his hand, under the direction of the same faith by which he had stretched it out.   For, in a cause of such magnitude, it was not lawful for him either to undertake or to relinquish anything, except under the authority of God.   Let us, therefore, learn from his example, by no means, to pursue what our carnal sense may declare to be, probably, our right course ; but let God, by his sole will, prescribe to us our manner of acting and of ceasing to act.   And truly Abraham does not charge God with inconstancy, because he considers that there had been just cause for the exercising of his faith.

12. *Now I know that thou fearest God.*   The exposition of Augustine, ' I have caused thee to know,' is forced.   But how can any thing become known to God, to whom all things have always been present?   Truly, by condescending to the manner of men, God here says that what he has proved by experiment, is now made known to himself.   And he speaks thus with us, not according to his own infinite wisdom, but according to our infirmity.   Moses, however, simply means that Abraham, by this very act, testified how reverently he feared God.   It is however asked, whether he had not already, on former occasions, given many proofs of his piety ?   I answer, that when God had willed him to proceed thus far, he had, at length, completed his true trial ; in other persons a much lighter trial might have been sufficient.[1]   And as Abraham showed that he feared God, by not sparing his own, and only begotten son ; so a common testimony of the same fear is required from all the pious, in acts of self-denial. Now, since God enjoins upon us a continual warfare, we must take care that none desires his release before the time.

13. *And, behold, behind him a ram.*   What the Jews feign

[1] " Respondeo, quando hucusque eum progredi volebat Deus, tunc vera demum probatione, quæ in aliis multo levior sufficeret, defunctum esse."—" Je respond que Dieu vouloit qu'il poursuyvist jusques là ; et que lors finalement, il s'est acquitté de son espreuve, laquelle eust este beaucoup legere en d'auctres, et eust bien suffi."—*French Tr.*

respecting this ram, as having been created on the sixth day of the world, is like the rest of their fictions. We need not doubt that it was presented there by miracle, whether it was then first created, or whether it was brought from some other place; for God intended to give that to his servant which would enable him, with joy and cheerfulness, to offer up a pleasant sacrifice : and at the same time he admonishes him to return thanks. Moreover, since a ram is substituted in the place of Isaac, God shows us, as in a glass, what is the design of our mortification; namely, that by the Spirit of God dwelling within us, we, though dead, may yet be living sacrifices. I am not ignorant that more subtle allegories may be elicited; but I do not see on what foundation they rest.

14. *And Abraham called the name of that place.* He not only, by the act of thanksgiving, acknowledges, at the time, that God has, in a remarkable manner, provided for him; but also leaves a monument of his gratitude to posterity. In most extreme anxiety, he had fled for refuge to the providence of God; and he testifies that he had not done so in vain. He also acknowledges that not even the ram had wandered thither accidentally, but had been placed there by God. Whereas, in process of time, the name of the place was changed, this was done purposely, and not by mistake. For they who have translated the active verb, ' He will see,' *passively*, have wished, in this manner, to teach that God not only looks upon those who are his, but also makes his help manifest to them; so that, in turn, he may be seen by them. The former has precedence in order; namely, that God, by his secret providence, determines and ordains what is best for us; but on this the latter is suspended; namely, that he stretches out his hand to us, and renders himself visible by true experimental tokens.

15. *And the angel of the Lord called unto Abraham.* What God had promised to Abraham before Isaac was born, he now again confirms and ratifies, after Isaac was restored to life, and arose from the altar,—as if it had been from the sepulchre,—to achieve a more complete triumph. The angel speaks in the person of God; in order that, as we have before

said, the embassy of those who bear his name, may have the greater authority, by their being clothed with His majesty. These two things, however, are thought to be hardly consistent with each other; that what before was gratuitously promised, should here be deemed a reward. For we know that grace and reward are incompatible. Now, however, since the benediction which is promised in the seed, contains the hope of salvation, it may seem to follow that eternal life is given in return for good works. And the Papists boldly seize upon this, and similar passages, in order to prove that works are deserving of all the good things which God confers upon us. But I most readily retort this subtle argument upon those who bring it. For if that promise was before gratuitous, which is now ascribed to a reward; it appears that whatever God grants to good works, ought to be received as from grace. Certainly, before Isaac was born, this same promise had been already given; and now it receives nothing more than confirmation. If Abraham deserved a compensation so great, on account of his own virtue, the grace of God, which anticipated him, will be of none effect. Therefore, in order that the truth of God, founded upon his gratuitous kindness, may stand firm, we must of necessity conclude, that what is freely given, is yet called the reward of works. Not that God would obscure the glory of his goodness, or in any way diminish it; but only that he may excite his own people to the love of well-doing, when they perceive that their acts of duty are so far pleasing to him, as to obtain a reward; while yet he pays nothing as a debt, but gives to his own benefits the title of a reward. And in this there is no inconsistency. For the Lord here shows himself doubly liberal; in that he, wishing to stimulate us to holy living, transfers to our works what properly belongs to his pure beneficence. The Papists, therefore, wrongfully distort those benignant invitations of God, by which he would correct our torpor, to a different purpose, in order that man may arrogate to his own merits, what is the mere gift of divine liberality.

17. *Thy seed shall possess the gate of his enemies.* He means, that the offspring of Abraham should be victorious over their enemies; for in the gates were their bulwarks, and in them

they administered judgment. Now, although God often suffered the enemies of the Jews tyrannically to rule over them; yet he so moderated their revenge, that this promise always prevailed in the end. Moreover, we must remember what has before been stated from Paul, concerning the unity of the seed; for we hence infer, that the victory is promised, not to the sons of Abraham promiscuously, but to Christ, and to his members, so far as they adhere together under one Head. For unless we retain some mark which may distinguish between the legitimate and the degenerate sons of Abraham, this promise will indiscriminately comprehend, as well the Ishmaelites and Idumeans, as the people of Israel: but the unity of a people depends on its head. Therefore the prophets, whenever they wish to confirm this promise of God, assume the principle, that they who have hitherto been divided, shall be united, under David, in one body. What further pertains to this subject may be found in the twelfth chapter.

19. *And they rose up, and went together to Beer-sheba.* Moses repeats, that Abraham, after having passed through this severe and incredible temptation, had a quiet abode in Beer-sheba. This narration is inserted, together with what follows concerning the increase of Abraham's kindred, for the purpose of showing that the holy man, when he had been brought up again from the abyss of death, was made happy, in more ways than one. For God would so revive him, that he should be like a new man. Moses also records the progeny of Nahor, but for another reason; namely, because Isaac was to take his wife from it. For the mention of women in Scripture is rare; and it is credible that many daughters were born to Nahor, of whom one only, Rebekah, is here introduced. He distinguishes the sons of the concubine from the others; because they occupied a less honourable place. Not that the concubine was regarded as a harlot; but because she was an inferior wife, and not the mistress of the house, who had community of goods with her husband. The fact, however, that it entered into Nahor's mind to take a second wife, does not render polygamy lawful; it only shows, that, from

the custom of other men, he supposed that to be lawful for him, which had really sprung from the worst corruption.

CHAPTER XXIII.

1. AND Sarah was an hundred and seven and twenty years old ; *these were* the years of the life of Sarah.

2. And Sarah died in Kirjath-arba ; the same *is* Hebron in the land of Canaan : and Abraham came to mourn for Sarah, and to weep for her.

3. And Abraham stood up from before his dead, and spake unto the sons of Heth, saying,

4. I *am* a stranger and a sojourner with you : give me a possession of a burying-place with you, that I may bury my dead out of my sight.

5. And the children of Heth answered Abraham, saying unto him,

6. Hear us, my lord : thou *art* a mighty prince among us : in the choice of our sepulchres bury thy dead ; none of us shall withhold from thee his sepulchre, but that thou mayest bury thy dead.

7. And Abraham stood up, and bowed himself to the people of the land, *even* to the children of Heth.

8. And he communed with them, saying, If it be your mind that I should bury my dead out of my sight, hear me, and entreat for me to Ephron the son of Zohar,

9. That he may give me the cave of Machpelah, which he hath, which *is* in the end of his field ; for as much money as it is worth he shall give it me for a possession of a burying-place amongst you.

10. And Ephron dwelt among the children of Heth : and Ephron the Hittite answered Abraham in the audience of the children of Heth, *even* of all that went in at the gate of his city, saying,

11. Nay, my lord, hear me : The field give I thee, and the cave that *is* therein,

1. Fuit autem vita Sarah centum anni et viginti anni et septem anni : anni vitæ Sarah.

2. Et mortua Sarah in Cirjath-arbah : ipsa est Hebron in terra Chenaan. Et venit Abraham ad plangendum super Sarah, et ad lugendam eam.

3. Deinde surrexit Abraham a facie mortui sui, et loquutus est ad filios Heth, dicendo,

4. Peregrinus et advena sum vobiscum : date mihi hæreditatem sepulchri vobiscum : et sepeliam mortuum meum a facie mea.

5. Et responderunt filii Heth ad Abraham, dicendo ei,

6. Audi nos, domine mi, Princeps Dei es in medio nostri : in electis sepulchris nostris sepeli mortuum tuum : nemo e nobis sepulchrum suum prohibebit a te, ne sepelias mortuum tuum.

7. Tunc surrexit Abraham, et incurvavit se populo terræ, filiis Heth.

8. Et loquutus est cum eis, dicendo, Si est in animis vestris, ut sepeliam mortuum meum a facie mea, audite me, et intercedite pro me apud Ephron filium Sohar :

9. Ut det mihi speluncam duplicem quæ *est* ei in fine agri sui : argento pleno det eam mihi in medio vestri in hæreditatem sepulchri.

10. Et Ephron habitabat in medio filiorum Heth : et respondit Ephron Hitthæus ad Abraham in auribus Heth, in *auribus* omnium ingredientum portam civitatis suæ, dicendo,

11. Non, domine mi, audi me, Agrum dedi tibi, et spe-

I give it thee ; in the presence of the sons of my people give I it thee : bury thy dead.

12. And Abraham bowed down himself before the people of the land.

13. And he spake unto Ephron, in the audience of the people of the land, saying, But if thou *wilt give it*, I pray thee, hear me : I will give thee money for the field ; take *it* of me, and I will bury my dead there.

14. And Ephron answered Abraham, saying unto him,

15. My lord, hearken unto me : the land *is worth* four hundred shekels of silver ; what *is* that betwixt me and thee? bury therefore thy dead.

16. And Abraham hearkened unto Ephron; and Abraham weighed to Ephron the silver, which he had named in the audience of the sons of Heth, four hundred shekels of silver, current *money* with the merchant.

17. And the field of Ephron, which *was* in Machpelah, which *was* before Mamre, the field, and the cave which *was* therein, and all the trees that *were* in the field, that *were* in all the borders round about, were made sure

18. Unto Abraham for a possession, in the presence of the children of Heth, before all that went in at the gate of his city.

19. And after this, Abraham buried Sarah his wife in the cave of the field of Machpelah, before Mamre : the same *is* Hebron in the land of Canaan.

20. And the field, and the cave that *is* therein, were made sure unto Abraham, for a possession of a burying-place, by the sons of Heth.

luncam, quæ est in eo, tibi dedi eam in oculis filiorum populi mei, dedi tibi : sepeli mortuum tuum.

12. Et incurvavit se Abraham coram populi terræ :

13. Et loquutus est ad Ephron in auribus populi terræ, dicendo, Veruntamen si tu : utinam audias me : dabo argentum agri, cape a me, et sepeliam mortuum meum ibi.

14. Et respondit Ephron ad Abraham, dicendo ei,

15. Domine mi, audi me, terra quadringentorum siclorum argenteorum *est* inter me et te, quid est ? et mortuum tuum sepeli.

16. Et obedivit Abraham ipsi Ephron, et appendit Abraham ipsi Ephron argentum quod loquutus fuerat in auribus filiorum Heth, quadringentos siclos argenteos transeuntes per mercatores.

17. Et confirmatus est ager Ephron, qui erat in spelunca duplici, qui *erat* coram Mamre : ager et spelunca, quæ erat in eo, et omnis arbor, quæ erat in agro, quæ *erat* in omni termino ejus per circuitum :

18. Ipsi Abraham in possessionem, in *oculis* filiorum Heth, omnium ingredientum portam civitatis ejus.

19. Et postea sepelivit Abraham Sarah uxorem suam in spelunca agri duplici coram Mamre : hæc est Hebron in terra Chenaan.

20. Et confirmatus est ager, et spelunca que erat in eo, ipsi Abraham in hæreditatem sepulchri a filiis Heth.

1. *And Sarah was an hundred and seven and twenty years old.*[1] It is remarkable that Moses, who relates the death of Sarah in a single word, uses so many in describing her burial : but we shall soon see that the latter record is not superfluous. Why he so briefly alludes to her death, I know not, except that he leaves more to be reflected upon by his

[1] Literally, "The lives of Sarah were a hundred years, and twenty years, and seven years."

readers than he expresses.   The holy fathers saw that they,
in common with reprobates, were subject to death.   Nevertheless, they were not deterred, while painfully leading a life
full of suffering, from advancing with intrepidity towards the
goal.   Whence it follows, that they, being animated by the
hope of a better life, did not give way to fatigue.   Moses says
that Sarah lived a hundred and twenty-seven years, and
since he repeats the word *years* after each of the numbers, the
Jews feign that this was done, because she had been as
beautiful in her hundredth, as in her twentieth year, and as
modest in the flower of her age, as when she was seven years
old.   This is their custom; while they wish to prove themselves skilful in doing honour to their nation, they invent
frivolous trifles, which betray a shameful ignorance : as, for
instance, in this place, who would not say that they were
entirely ignorant of their own language, in which this kind
of repetition is most usual ?   The discussion of others also,
on the word חיים, (*lives*,) is without solidity.   The reason why
the Hebrews use the word *lives*, in the plural number, for *life*,
cannot be better explained, as it appears to me, than the
reason why the Latins express some things which are singular
in plural forms.[1]   I know that the life of men is manifold,
because, beyond merely vegetative life, and beyond the sense
which they have in common with brute animals, they are also
endued with mind and intelligence.   This reasoning, therefore,
is plausible, without being solid.   There is more colour of
truth in the opinion of those who think that the various
events of human life are signified; which life, since it has
nothing stable, but is agitated by perpetual vicissitudes, is
rightly divided into many lives.   I am, however, contented
to refer simply to the idiom of the language; the reason of
which is not always to be curiously investigated.

2. *And Sarah died in Kirjath-arba.*   It appears from Josh.
xv. 54, that this was the more ancient name of the city, which
afterwards began to be called Hebron.   But there is a difference of opinion respecting the etymology.   Some think
the name is derived from the fact, that the city consisted of

---

[1] " Quam quod Latini quadrigas dicant non quadrigam.

four parts; as the Greeks call the city divided into three orders, *Tripoli*, and a given region, *Decapolis*, from the ten cities it contained.   Others suppose that *Arba* is the name of a giant, whom they believe to have been the king or the founder of the city.   Others again prefer the notion, that the name was given to the place from *four*[1] of the Fathers, Adam, Abraham, Isaac, and Jacob, who were buried there with their wives.   I willingly suspend my judgment on a matter of uncertainty, and not very necessary to be known.   It more concerns the present history to inquire, how it happened that Sarah died in a different place from that in which Abraham dwelt.   If any one should reply, that they had both changed their abode, the words of Moses are opposed to that, for he says that Abraham came to bury his dead.   It is hence easily inferred, that he was not present at her death; nor is it probable that they were separated, merely by being in different tents; so that he might walk ten or twenty paces for the sake of mourning, while a more important duty had been neglected.   For this reason, some suspect that he was on a journey at the time.   But to me it seems more likely that their abode was then at Hebron, or at least in the vale of Mamre, which adjoins the city.   For, after a little breathing time had been granted him, he was soon compelled to return to his accustomed wanderings.   And although Moses does not say, that Abraham had paid to his wife, while yet alive, the due attentions of a husband; I think that he omits it, as a thing indubitably certain, and that he speaks particularly of the mourning, as a matter connected with the care of sepulture.   That they dwelt separately we shall afterwards see : not as being in different regions, but because each inhabited separate, though contiguous, tents.   And this was no sign of dissension or of strife, but is rather to be ascribed to the size of the family.   For as Abraham had much trouble in governing so large a herd of servants ; so his wife would have equal difficulty to retain her maids under chaste and honest custody.   Therefore the great number of domestics, which it was not safe to mingle together, compelled them to divide the family.

But it may be asked, what end could it answer to approach

---

[1] The word ארבע (*arba*) signifies *four*.

the body for the sake of mourning over it? was not the death
of his wife sufficiently sad and bitter to call forth his grief,
without this additional means of excitement? It would have
been better to seek the alleviation of his sorrow, than to
cherish, and even augment it, by indulgence. I answer, if
Abraham came to his dead wife, in order to produce excessive
weeping, and to pierce his heart afresh with new wounds, his
example is not to be approved. But if he both privately
wept over the death of his wife, so far as humanity prescribed,
exercising self-government in doing it; and also voluntarily
mourned over the common curse of mankind; there is no fault
in either of these. For to feel no sadness at the contemplation of death, is rather barbarism and stupor than fortitude of
mind. Nevertheless, as Abraham was a man, it might be, that
his grief was excessive. And yet, what Moses soon after
subjoins, that he rose up from his dead, is spoken in praise of
his moderation; whence Ambrose prudently infers, that we
are taught by this example, how perversely they act, who
occupy themselves too much in mourning for the dead. Now,
if Abraham, at that time, assigned a limit to his grief, and put
a restraint on his feelings, when the doctrine of the resurrection was yet obscure; they are without excuse, who, at this
day, give the reins to impatience, since the most abundant
consolation is supplied to us in the resurrection of Christ.

3. *And spake unto the sons of Heth.* Moses is silent respecting the rite used by Abraham in the burial of the body
of his wife: but he proceeds, at great length, to recite the
purchasing of the sepulchre. For what reason he did this,
we shall see presently, when I shall briefly allude to the custom of burial. How religiously this has been observed in all
ages, and among all people, is well known. Ceremonies have
indeed been different, and men have endeavoured to outdo
each other in various superstitions; meanwhile, to bury the
dead has been common to all. And this practice has not
arisen either from foolish curiosity, or from the desire of fruitless consolation, or from superstition, but from the natural
sense with which God has imbued the minds of men; a sense
he has never suffered to perish, in order that men might be
witnesses to themselves of a future life. It is also incredible

that they, who have disseminated certain outrageous expressions in contempt of sepulture, could have spoken from
the heart.   Truly it behoves us, with magnanimity, so far to
disregard the rites of sepulture,—as we would riches and
honours, and the other conveniences of life,—that we should
bear with equanimity to be deprived of them; yet it cannot
be denied that religion carries along with it the care of burial.
And certainly (as I have said) it has been divinely engraven
on the minds of all people, from the beginning, that they
should bury the dead ; whence also they have ever regarded
sepulchres as sacred.   It has not, I confess, always entered
into the minds of heathens that *souls* survived death, and that
the hope of a resurrection remained even for their *bodies ;* nor
have they been accustomed to exercise themselves in a pious
meditation of this kind, whenever they had laid their dead
in the grave ; but this inconsideration of theirs does not disprove the fact; that they had such a representation of a
future life placed before their eyes, as left them inexcusable.
Abraham, however, seeing he had the hope of a resurrection
deeply fixed in his heart, sedulously cherished, as was meet,
its visible symbol.   The importance he attached to it appears
hence, that he thought he should be guilty of pollution, if he
mingled the body of his wife with strangers after death.   For
he bought a cave, in order that he might possess for himself
and his family, a holy and pure sepulchre.   He did not desire
to have a foot of earth whereon to fix his tent ; he only took
care about his grave : and he especially wished to have his
own domestic tomb in that land, which had been promised
him for an inheritance, for the purpose of bearing testimony
to posterity, that the promise of God was not extinguished,
either by his own death, or by that of his family ; but that
it then rather began to flourish ; and that they who were deprived of the light of the sun, and of the vital air, yet always
remained joint-partakers of the promised inheritance.   For
while they themselves were silent and speechless, the sepulchre cried aloud, that death formed no obstacle to their
entering on the possession of it.   A thought like this could
have had no place, unless Abraham by faith had looked up to
heaven.   And when he calls the corpse of his wife, *his dead ;*
he intimates that death is a divorce of that kind, which still

leaves some remaining conjunction. Moreover, nothing but a future restoration cherishes and preserves the law of mutual connection between the living and the dead. But it is better briefly to examine each particular, in its order.

4. *I am a stranger and a sojourner with you.* This introductory sentence tends to one or other of these points; either that he may more easily gain what he desires by suppliantly asking for it; or that he may remove all suspicion of cupidity on his part. He therefore confesses, that since he had only a precarious abode among them, he could possess no sepulchre, unless by their permission. And because, during life, they had permitted him to dwell within their territory, it was the part of humanity, not to deny him a sepulchre for his dead. If this sense be approved, then Abraham both conciliates their favour to himself, by his humility, and in declaring that the children of Heth had dealt kindly with him, he stimulates them, by this praise, to proceed in the exercise of the same liberality with which they had begun. The other sense, however, is not incongruous; namely, that Abraham, to avert the odium which might attach to him as a purchaser, declares that he desires the possession, not for the advantage of the present life, not from ambition or avarice, but only in order that his dead may not lie unburied; as if he had said, I do not refuse to continue to live a stranger among you, as I have hitherto done; I do not desire your possessions, in order that I may have something of my own, which may enable me hereafter to contend for equality with you; it is enough for me to have a place where we may be buried.

6. *Thou art a mighty prince among us.*[1] The Hittites gratuitously offer a burying-place to Abraham wherever he might please to choose one. They testify that they do this, as a tribute to his virtues. We have before seen, that the Hebrews give a divine title to anything which excels. Therefore we are to understand by the expression, 'a prince of God,' a person of great and singular excellency. And they properly signalize him whom they reverence for his virtues,

[1] " Princeps es Dei." See margin of English version. Heb., a prince of God.—*Ed.*

with this eulogium ; thereby testifying, that they ascribe to God alone, whatever virtues in men are deserving of praise and reverence. Now some seed of piety manifests itself in the Hittites, by thus doing honour to Abraham, whom they acknowledge to be adorned with rare gifts of the Spirit of God. For profane and brutal men tread under foot, with barbarous contempt, every excellent gift of God, as swine do pearls. And yet we know with how many vices those nations were defiled ; how much greater then, and more disgraceful, is our ingratitude, if we give no honour to the image of God, when it shines before our eyes ? Abraham's sanctity of manners procures him such favour with the Hittites, that they do not envy his pre-eminence among them ; what excuse then is there for us, if we hold in less esteem those virtues in which the majesty of God is conspicuous ? Truly their madness is diabolical, who not only despise the favours of God, but even ferociously oppose them.

7. *And Abraham stood up.* He declines the favour offered by the Hittites, as some suppose, with this design, that he might not lay himself under obligation to them in so small a matter. But he rather wished to show, in this way, that he would receive no gratuitous possession from those inhabitants who were to be ejected by the hand of God, in order that he might succeed in their place : for he always kept all his thoughts fixed on God, so that he far preferred His bare pro-mise, to present dominion over the land. Moses also com-mends the modesty of the holy man, when he says that he ' rose up to do reverence to the people of the land.' [1] As to the use of the word signifying ' to adore,' it is simply taken for the reverence, which any one declares, either by bowing the knee, or any other gesture of the body. This may be paid to men, as well as to God, but for a different end ; men mutually either bend the knee, or bow the head, before each other, for the sake of civil honour ; but if the same thing be done to them, for the sake of religion, it is profanation. For religion allows of no other worship than that of the true God.

---

[1] " Ut adoraret populum terræ." This is not a correct quotation from his own version of the chapter, which is, " Incurvavit se populo terræ," as in our version, "Bowed himself to the people of the land."—*Ed.*

And they childishly trifle who make a pretext for their idolatry, in the words *dulia* and *latria*,[1] since the Scripture, in general terms, forbids adoration to be transferred to men. But lest any one should be surprised that Abraham acted so suppliantly, and so submissively, we must be aware that it was done from common custom and use. For it is well known that the Orientals were immoderate in their use of ceremonies. If we compare the Greeks or Italians with ourselves, we are more sparing in the use of them than they. But Aristotle, in speaking of the Asiatics and other barbarians, notes this fault, that they abound too much in adorations. Wherefore we must not measure the honour which Abraham paid to the princes of the land by our customs.

8. *If it be in your mind.* Abraham constitutes them his advocates with Ephron, to persuade him to sell the double cave.[2] Some suppose the cave to have been so formed, that one part was above, and the other below. Let every one be at liberty to adopt what opinion he pleases; I, however, rather suppose, that there was one entrance, but that within, the cave was divided by a middle partition. It is more pertinent to remark, that Abraham, by offering a full price, cultivated and maintained equity. Where is there one to be found, who, in buying, and in other business, does not eagerly pursue his own advantage at another's cost? For while the seller sets the price at twice the worth of a thing, that he may extort as much as possible from the buyer, and the buyer, in return, by shuffling, attempts to reduce it to a low price, there is no end of bargaining. And although avarice has specious pretexts, it yet causes those who make contracts with each other, to forget the claims of equity and justice. This also, finally, deserves to be noticed; that Abraham often declares, that he was buying the field for a place of sepulture. And Moses is the more minute in this matter, that we may learn, with our father Abraham, to raise our minds to the hope

---

[1] " Ac pueriliter nugantur qui in vocibus duliæ et latriæ fucum faciunt."—" Qui pensent farder leur idolatrie par ces mots de Dulie et Latrie."—*French Tr.*

[2] Heb. מערת המכפלה, *(mearath hummakpelah,)* ' the double cave.' See Septuagint. Our translators have preferred rendering the word Machpelah as a proper name.—*Ed.*

of the resurrection. He saw the half of himself taken away; but because he was certain that his wife was not exiled from the kingdom of God, he hides her dead body in the tomb, until he and she should be gathered together.

11. *Hear me.* Although Ephron earnestly insisted upon giving the field freely to Abraham, the holy man adheres to his purpose, and at length compels him, by his entreaties, to sell the field. Ephron, in excusing himself, says that the price was too small for Abraham to insist upon giving; yet he estimates it at four hundred shekels. Now, since Josephus says that the shekel of the sanctuary was worth four Attic drachms, if he is speaking of these, we gather from the computation of Budæus that the price of the field was about two hundred and fifty pounds of French money; if we understand the common shekel, it will be half that amount. Abraham was not so scrupulous but that he would have received a greater gift, if there had not been a sufficient reason to prevent him. He had been presented with considerable gifts both by the king of Egypt and the king of Gerar, but he observed this rule; that he would neither receive all *things*, nor in all *places*, nor from all *persons*. And I have lately explained, that he bought the field, in order that he might not possess a foot of land, by the gift of any man.

16. *And Abraham weighed to Ephron the silver.* I know not what had come into Jerome's mind, when he says, that one letter was abstracted from Ephron's name, after he had been persuaded, by Abraham's entreaties, to receive money for the field; because, by the sale of the sepulchre, his virtue was maimed or diminished: for, in fact, the name of Ephron is found written in the very same manner, after that event, as before. Nor ought it to be imputed to Ephron as a fault, that, being pressed, he took the lawful price for his estate; when he had been prepared liberally to give it. If there was any sin in the case, Abraham must bear the whole blame. But who shall dare to condemn a just sale, in which, on both sides, religion, good faith, and equity, are maintained? Abraham, it is argued, bought the field for the sake of having a sepulchre. But ought Ephron on that account to give it

freely, and under the pretext of a sepulchre, to be defrauded of his right? We see here, then, nothing but mere trifling. The Canonists, however,—preposterous and infatuated as they are,—rashly laying hold of the expression of Jerome, have determined that it is a prodigious sacrilege to sell sepulchres. Yet, in the meantime, all the Papal sacrificers securely exercise this traffic : and while they acknowledge the cemetery to be a common sepulchre, they suffer no grave to be dug, unless the price be paid.

Current money with the merchant. Moses speaks thus, because money is a medium of mutual communication between men. It is principally employed in buying and selling merchandise. Whereas Moses says, in the close of the chapter, that the field was confirmed by the Hittites to Abraham for a possession ; the sense is, that the purchase was publicly attested ; for although a private person sold it, yet the people were present, and ratified the contract between the two parties.

A
GENEVA
SERIES
COMMENTARY

GENESIS

VOLUME 2

COMMENTARY

ON

THE BOOK OF GENESIS

CHAPTER XXIV.

1. AND Abraham was old, *and* well stricken in age : and the Lord had blessed Abraham in all things.

2. And Abraham said unto his eldest servant of his house, that ruled over all that he had, Put, I pray thee, thy hand under my thigh;

3. And I will make thee swear by the Lord, the God of heaven, and the God of the earth, that thou shalt not take a wife unto my son of the daughters of the Canaanites, among whom I dwell:

4. But thou shalt go unto my country, and to my kindred, and take a wife unto my son Isaac.

5. And the servant said unto him, Peradventure the woman will not be willing to follow me unto this land: must I needs bring thy son again unto the land from whence thou camest?

6. And Abraham said unto him, Beware thou that thou bring not my son thither again.

7. The Lord God of heaven, which took me from my father's house, and from the land of my kindred, and which spake unto me, and that sware unto me, saying, Unto thy seed will

1. ABRAHAM autem senex venit in dies, et Iehova benedixerat Abraham in omnibus.

2. Et dixit Abraham ad servum suum seniorem domus suæ, qui præerat omnibus qui erant ei, Pone nunc manum tuam sub femore meo:

3. Et adjurabo te per Iehovam Deum cœli, et Deum terræ, quod non capies uxorem filio meo de filiabus Chenaanæi, in cujus medio ego habito:

4. Sed ad terram meam, et ad cognationem meam perges, et capies uxorem filio meo Ishac.

5. Et dixit ad eum servus, Si forsitan noluerit mulier venire post me ad terram hanc, numquid reducendo reducam filium tuum ad terram unde egressus es?

6. Et dixit ad eum Abraham Cave tibi ne forte reducas filium meum illuc.

7. Iehova Deus cœli, qui tulit me e domo patris mei, et e terra cognationis meæ, et qui loquutus est mihi, et qui juravit mihi, dicendo, Semini tuo dabo terram

I give this land; he shall send his angel before thee, and thou shalt take a wife unto my son from thence.

8. And if the woman will not be willing to follow thee, then thou shalt be clear from this my oath: only bring not my son thither again.

9. And the servant put his hand under the thigh of Abraham his master, and sware to him concerning that matter.

10. And the servant took ten camels, of the camels of his master, and departed; for all the goods of his master *were* in his hand; and he arose, and went to Mesopotamia, unto the city of Nahor.

11. And he made his camels to kneel down without the city by a well of water at the time of the evening, *even* at the time that women go out to draw *water*.

12. And he said, O Lord God of my master Abraham, I pray thee, send me good speed this day, and shew kindness unto my master Abraham.

13. Behold, I stand *here* by the well of water; and the daughters of the men of the city come out to draw water:

14. And let it come to pass, that the damsel to whom I shall say, Let down thy pitcher, I pray thee, that I may drink; and she shall say, Drink; and I will give thy camels drink also: *let the same be* she *that* thou hast appointed for thy servant Isaac; and thereby shall I know that thou hast shewed kindness unto my master.

15. And it came to pass, before he had done speaking, that, behold, Rebekah came out, who was born to Bethuel, son of Milcah, the wife of Nahor, Abraham's brother, with her pitcher upon her shoulder.

16. And the damsel *was* very fair to look upon, a virgin; neither had any man known her: and she went down to the well, and filled her pitcher, and came up.

17. And the servant ran to meet

hanc: ipse mittet Angelum suum ante te, et capies uxorem filio meo inde.

8. Quodsi noluerit mulier pergere post te, mundus eris ab adjuratione mea ista: duntaxat filium meum ne reducas illuc.

9. Et posuit servus manum suam sub femore Abraham domini sui, et juravit ei super re hac.

10. Et accepit servus decem camelos e camelis domini sui, et perrexit: quia omne bonum domini sui erat in manu ejus: et surrexit, et profectus est in Aram-naharaim, ad civitatem Nachor.

11. Et genu flectere fecit camelos extra civitatem ad puteum aquæ, tempore vespertino, tempore quo egrediuntur *mulieres*, quæ hauriunt.

12. Et dixit, Iehova Deus domini mei Abraham, occurrere fac nunc coram me hodie, et fac misericordiam cum domino meo Abraham.

13. Ecce, ego sto juxta fontem aquæ, et filiæ virorum civitatis egrediuntur ad hauriendam aquam.

14. Sit ergo, puella ad quam dixero, Inclina nunc hydriam tuam, et bibam: et dixerit, Bibe, et etiam camelis tuis potum dabo: ipsam præparaveris servo tuo Ishac: et per hoc sciam quod feceris misericordiam cum domino meo.

15. Et fuit, antequam ipse complevisset loqui, ecce, Ribca egrediebatur, quæ nata erat Bethuel filio Milchah uxoris Nachor fratris Abraham, et hydria ejus erat super humerum ejus.

16. Puella autem erat pulchra aspectu valde, virgo, et vir non cognoverat eam: quæ descendit ad fontem, et implevit hydriam suam, et ascendit.

17. Itaque cucurrit servus in oc-

her, and said, Let me, I pray thee, drink a little water of thy pitcher.

18. And she said, Drink, my lord: and she hasted, and let down her pitcher upon her hand, and gave him drink.

19. And when she had done giving him drink, she said, I will draw *water* for thy camels also, until they have done drinking.

20. And she hasted, and emptied her pitcher into the trough, and ran again into the well to draw *water*, and drew for all his camels.

21. And the man, wondering at her, held his peace, to wit whether the Lord had made his journey prosperous or not.

22. And it came to pass, as the camels had done drinking, that the man took a golden ear-ring of half a shekel weight, and two bracelets for her hands of ten *shekels* weight of gold,

23. And said, Whose daughter *art* thou? tell me, I pray thee. Is there room *in* thy father's house for us to lodge in?

24. And she said unto him, I *am* the daughter of Bethuel the son of Milcah, which she bare unto Nahor.

25. She said, moreover, unto him, We have both straw and provender enough, and room to lodge in.

26. And the man bowed down his head, and worshipped the Lord.

27. And he said, Blessed *be* the Lord God of my master Abraham, who hath not left destitute my master of his mercy and his truth: I *being* in the way, the Lord led me to the house of my master's brethren.

28. And the damsel ran, and told *them of* her mother's house these things.

29. And Rebekah had a brother, and his name *was* Laban: and Laban ran out unto the man unto the well.

30. And it came to pass, when he saw the ear-ring, and bracelets upon his sister's hands, and when he heard the words of Rebekah his sister, saying, Thus spake the man unto me,

cursum ejus, et dixit, Potum da mihi nunc parum aquæ ex hydria tua.

18. Et dixit, Bibe, domine mi: et festinavit, et demisit hydriam suam super manum suam, et potum dedit ei.

19. Ubi complevit potum dare ei: tunc dixit, Etiam camelis tuis hauriam, donec compleverint bibere.

20. Et festinavit, et effudit hydriam suam in canale, et cucurrit adhuc ad puteum ut hauriret: et hausit omnibus camelis ejus.

21. Porro vir stupebat super ea tacens, ut sciret utrum secundasset Iehova viam suam, an non.

22. Et fuit, quum complevissent cameli bibere, protulit vir inaurem auream, semissis pondus ejus: et duas armillas, et *posuit* super manus ejus: decem aurei pondus earum.

23. Et jam dixerat, Filia, cujus es? indica nunc mihi, numquid est in domo patris tui locus nobis ad pernoctandum?

24. Et dixerat ad eum, Filia Bethuel sum, filii Milchah, quem peperit ipsa Nachor.

25. Et dixit ad eum, Etiam palea, etiam pabulum multum est apud nos, etiam locus ad pernoctandum.

26. Et inclinavit se vir, et incurvavit se Iehovæ.

27. Et dixit, Benedictus Iehova Deus domini mei Abraham, qui non dereliquit misericordiam suam et veritatem suam a domino meo. Ego in via, duxit me Iehova ad domum fratrum domini mei.

28. Et cucurrit puella, et nuntiavit domui matris suæ secundum verba hæc.

29. Et ipsi Ribca erat frater, et nomen ejus Laban: et cucurrit Laban ad virum foras ad fontem.

30. Fuit autem, quum vidisset inaurem et armillas in manibus sororis suæ, et quum audisset ipse verba Ribca sororis suæ, dicendo, Sic loquutus est ad me vir: venit a

that he came unto the man; and, behold, he stood by the camels at the well.

31. And he said, Come in, thou blessed of the Lord; wherefore standest thou without? for I have prepared the house, and room for the camels.

32. And the man came into the house: and he ungirded his camels, and gave straw and provender for the camels, and water to wash his feet, and the men's feet that *were* with him.

33. And there was set *meat* before him to eat: but he said, I will not eat, until I have told mine errand. And he said, Speak on.

34. And he said, I *am* Abraham's servant.

35. And the Lord hath blessed my master greatly, and he is become great; and he hath given him flocks, and herds, and silver, and gold, and men-servants, and maid-servants, and camels, and asses.

36. And Sarah, my master's wife, bare a son to my master when she was old; and unto him hath he given all that he hath.

37. And my master made me swear, saying, Thou shalt not take a wife to my son of the daughters of the Canaanites, in whose land I dwell:

38. But thou shalt go unto my father's house, and to my kindred, and take a wife unto my son.

39. And I said unto my master, Peradventure the woman will not follow me.

40. And he said unto me, The Lord, before whom I walk, will send his angel with thee, and prosper thy way; and thou shalt take a wife for my son of my kindred, and of my father's house.

41. Then shalt thou be clear from *this* my oath, when thou comest to my kindred; and if they give not thee *one*, thou shalt be clear from my oath.

42. And I came this day unto the well, and said, O Lord God of my

virum, et ecce, stabat juxta camelos, juxta fontem.

31. Et dixit, Ingredere benedicte Iehovæ, ut quid manes foris? et ego paravi domum, et locum camelis.

32. Et venit vir ad domum, et solvit camelos, et dedit paleam et pabulum camelis, et aquam ad lavandum pedes ejus, et pedes virorum qui erant cum eo.

33. Et positum est coram eo, ut comederet: et dixit, Non comedam, donec loquutus fuero verba mea. Et dixit, Loquere.

34. Dixit igitur, Servus Abraham sum.

35. Iehova autem benedixit domino meo valde, et magnificatus est, et dedit ei pecudes et boves, et argentum, et aurum, et servos, et ancillas, et camelos, et asinos.

36. Et peperit Sarah uxor domini mei filium domino meo post senectutem suam, et dedit ei omnia quæ sunt ei.

37. Et jurare fecit me dominus meus, dicendo, Non capies uxorem filio meo de filiabus Chenaanæi, in cujus terra ego habito:

38. Sed ad domum patris mei perges, et ad familiam meam, et capies uxorem filio meo.

39. Et dixi domino meo, Forsitan non perget mulier post me.

40. Et dixit ad me, Iehova, in cujus conspectu ambulavi, mittet Angelum suum tecum, et secundabit viam tuam: et capies uxorem filio meo de familia mea, et de domo patris mei.

41. Tunc mundus eris ab adjuratione mea, si veneris ad familiam meam: et si non dederint tibi, eris mundus ab adjuratione mea.

42. Veni igitur hodie ad fontem, et dixi, Iehova Deus domini mei

master Abraham, if now thou do prosper my way which I go:

43. Behold, I stand by the well of water; and it shall come to pass, that when the virgin cometh forth to draw *water*, and I say to her, Give me, I pray thee, a little water of thy pitcher to drink;

44. And she say to me, Both drink thou, and I will also draw for thy camels: *let* the same *be* the woman whom the Lord hàth appointed out for my master's son.

45. And before I had done speaking in mine heart, behold, Rebekah came forth with her pitcher on her shoulder; and she went down unto the well, and drew *water:* and I said unto her, Let me drink, I pray thee.

46. And she made haste, and let down her pitcher from her *shoulder*, and said, Drink; and I will give thy camels drink also: so I drank, and she made the camels drink also.

47. And I asked her, and said, Whose daughter *art* thou? And she said, The daughter of Bethuel, Nahor's son, whom Milcah bare unto him: and I put the ear-ring upon her face, and the bracelets upon her hands.

48. And I bowed down my head, and worshipped the Lord, and blessed the Lord God of my master Abraham, which had led me in the right way, to take my master's brother's daughter unto his son.

49. And now, if ye will deal kindly and truly with my master, tell me: and if not, tell me; that I may turn to the right hand, or to the left.

50. Then Laban and Bethuel answered and said, The thing proceedeth from the Lord: we cannot speak unto thee bad or good.

51. Behold, Rebekah *is* before thee, take *her*, and go, and let her be thy master's son's wife, as the Lord hath spoken.

52. And it came to pass, that, when Abraham's servant heard their words, he worshipped the Lord, *bowing himself* to the earth.

Abraham, si tu nunc secundas viam meam, per quam ego ambulo:

43. Ecce, ego sto juxta fontem aquæ: itaque sit, virgo quæ egredietur ad hauriendum, et dixero ei, Da mihi potum nunc parum aquæ ex hydria tua:

44. Et dixerit mihi, Etiam tu bibe, et etiam camelis tuis hauriam: ipsa *sit* uxor, quam præparavit Iehova filio domini mei.

45. Ego antequam complerem loqui in corde meo, ecce, Ribca egrediebatur, et hydria ejus erat super humerum ejus, et descendit ad fontem, et hausit: et dixi ad eam, Da mihi potum nunc.

46. Et festinavit, et demisit hydriam suam desuper se, et dixit, Bibe, et etiam camelis tuis potum dabo. Et bibi, et etiam camelis dedit potum.

47. Et interrogavi eam, et dixi, Filia cujus es? Et dixit, Filia Bethuel filii Nachor, quem peperit ei Milchah. Et posui inaurem super nares ejus, et armillas super manus ejus.

48. Et inclinavi me, incurvavique me Iehovæ, et benedixi Iehovæ Deo domini mei Abraham, qui duxit me per viam veritatis, (*vel certam fidem,*) ut acciperem filiam fratris domini mei filio ejus.

49. Et nunc si facitis misericordiam et veritatem cum domino meo, indicate mihi: et si non, indicate mihi, et vertam me ad dexteram vel ad sinistram.

50. Et responderunt Laban et Bethuel, et dixerunt, A Iehova egressa est res: non possumus loqui ad te malum vel bonum.

51. Ecce, Ribca coram te, accipe, et vade: et sit uxor filio domini tui, quemadmodum loquutus est Iehova.

52. Et fuit, quando audivit servus Abraham verba eorum, incurvavit se super terram Iehovæ.

53. And the servant brought forth jewels of silver, and jewels of gold, and raiment, and gave *them* to Rebekah : he gave also to her brother and to her mother precious things.

54. And they did eat and drink, he and the men that *were* with him, and tarried all night : and they rose up in the morning; and he said, Send me away unto my master.

55. And her brother and her mother said, Let the damsel abide with us *a few* days, at the least ten; after that she shall go.

56. And he said unto them, Hinder me not, seeing the Lord hath prospered my way; send me away, that I may go to my master.

57. And they said, We will call the damsel, and enquire at her mouth.

58. And they called Rebekah, and said unto her, Wilt thou go with this man? And she said, I will go.

59. And they sent away Rebekah their sister, and her nurse, and Abraham's servant, and his men.

60. And they blessed Rebekah, and said unto her, Thou *art* our sister, be thou *the mother* of thousands of millions, and let thy seed possess the gate of those which hate them.

61. And Rebekah arose, and her damsels, and they rode upon the camels, and followed the man; and the servant took Rebekah, and went his way.

62. And Isaac came from the way of the well Lahai-roi: for he dwelt in the south country.

63. And Isaac went out to meditate in the field at the even-tide; and he lifted up his eyes, and saw, and, behold, the camels *were* coming.

64. And Rebekah lifted up her eyes; and when she saw Isaac, she lighted off the camel.

65. For she *had* said unto the servant, What man *is* this that walketh in the field to meet us? And the servant *had* said, It *is* my master: therefore she took a vail, and covered herself.

66. And the servant told Isaac all things that he had done.

53. Et protulit servus vasa argentea, et vasa aurea, et vestes, et dedit ipsi Ribcæ, et pretiosa dedit fratri ejus, et matri ejus.

54. Et comederunt, et biberunt, ipse et viri qui erant cum eo, et pernoctaverunt: et surrexerunt mane: et dixit, Dimitte me, *ut vadam* ad dominum meum.

55. Et dixit frater ejus et mater ejus, Maneat puella nobiscum per dies, vel decem: postea ibis, (*vel ibit.*)

56. Et dixit ad eos, Ne retardetis me, quando Iehova secundavit viam meam : dimittite me, et ibo ad dominum meum.

57. Et dixerunt, Vocemus puellam, et interrogemus os ejus.

58. Et vocaverunt Ribcam, et dixerunt ad eam, Numquid ibis cum viro isto? Et dixit, Ibo.

59. Et dimiserunt Ribcam sororem suam, et nutricem ejus, et servum Abraham, et viros ejus.

60. Et benedixerunt Ribcæ, et dixerunt ei, Soror nostra es, sis in millia decem millium, et hæreditet semen tuum portam odio habentium illud.

61. Et surrexit Ribca et puellæ ejus, et ascenderunt super camelos, et perrexerunt post virum: et tulit servus Ribcah, et abiit.

62. Ishac autem veniebat, qua venitur a Puteo viventis videntis me: et ipse habitabat in terra Meridiana.

63. Et egressus erat Ishac ad orandum in agro, dum declinaret vespera: et elevavit oculos suos, et vidit, et ecce, cameli veniebant.

64. Tunc elevavit Ribcah oculos suos, et vidit Ishac, et projecit se de camelo.

65. Iam autem dixerat ad servum, Quis est vir iste, qui ambulat per agrum in occursum nostrum? Et dixit servus, Ipse est dominus meus: et accepit velum, et operuit se.

66. Et narravit servus ipsi Ishac omnia quæ fecerat.

67. And Isaac brought her into his mother Sarah's tent, and took Rebekah, and she became his wife; and he loved her: and Isaac was comforted after his mother's *death*.

67. Et introduxit **eam** Ishac in tabernaculum Sarah matris suæ, et accepit Ribcah, fuitque ei in uxorem, et dilexit eam: et consolatus est se Ishac post matrem suam.

1. *And Abraham was old.*[1] Moses passes onward to the relation of Isaac's marriage, because indeed Abraham, perceiving himself to be worn down by old age, would take care that his son should not marry a wife in the land of Canaan. In this place Moses expressly describes Abraham as an old man, in order that we may learn that he had been admonished, by his very age, to seek a wife for his son: for old age itself, which, at the most, is not far distant from death, ought to induce us so to order the affairs of our family, that when we die, peace may be preserved among our posterity, the fear of the Lord may flourish, and rightly-constituted order may prevail. The old age of Abraham was indeed yet green, as we shall see hereafter; but when he reckoned up his own years he deemed it time to consult for the welfare of his son. Irreligious men, partly because they do not hold marriage sufficiently in honour, partly because they do not consider the importance attached especially to the marriage of Isaac, wonder that Moses, or rather the Spirit of God, should be employed in affairs so minute; but if we have that reverence which is due in reading the Sacred Scriptures, we shall easily understand that here is nothing superfluous: for inasmuch as men can scarcely persuade themselves that the Providence of God extends to marriages, so much the more does Moses insist on this point. He chiefly, however, wishes to teach that God honoured the family of Abraham with especial regard, because the Church was to spring from it. But it will be better to treat of everything in its proper order.

2. *And Abraham said unto his eldest servant.* Abraham here fulfils the common duty of parents, in labouring for and being solicitous about the choice of a wife for his son: but he looks somewhat further; for since God had separated

[1] Abraham was a hundred years old when Isaac was born, (xxi. 5,) and Isaac was forty years old when he was married, (xxv. 20.) This makes Abraham's age a hundred and forty years.—*Ed*.

him from the Canaanites by a sacred covenant, he justly fears lest Isaac, by joining himself in affinity with them, should shake off the yoke of God. Some suppose that the depraved morals of those nations were so displeasing to him, that he conceived the marriage of his son must prove unhappy if he should take a wife from among them. But the special reason was, as I have stated, that he would not allow his own race to be mingled with that of the Canaanites, whom he knew to be already divinely appointed to destruction ; yea, since upon their overthrow he was to be put into possession of the land, he was commanded to treat them with distrust as perpetual enemies. And although he had dwelt in tranquillity among them for a time, yet he could not have a community of offspring with them without confounding things which, by the command of God, were to be kept distinct. Hence he wished both himself and his family to maintain this separation entire.

Put, I pray thee, thy hand. It is sufficiently obvious that this was a solemn form of swearing ; but whether Abraham had first introduced it, or whether he had received it from his fathers, is unknown. The greater part of Jewish writers declare that Abraham was the author of it ; because, in their opinion, this ceremony is of the same force as if his servant had sworn by the sanctity of the divine covenant, since circumcision was in that part of his person. But Christian writers conceive that the hand was placed under the thigh in honour of the blessed seed.[1] Yet it may be that these earliest fathers had something different in view ; and there are those among the Jews who assert that it was a token of subjection, when the servant was sworn on the thigh of his master. The more plausible opinion is, that the ancients in this manner swore by Christ ; but because I do not willingly follow uncertain conjectures, I leave the question undecided. Nevertheless the latter supposition appears to me the more simple ; namely, that servants, when they swore fidelity to

---

[1] *Under my thigh.* " A sign which Jacob also required of his son Joseph, (Gen. xlvii. 29,) either to signify subjection, or for a further mystery of the covenant of circumcision, or rather of Christ the promised seed, who was to come out of Abraham's loins or thigh."—*Ainsworth.*

their lords, were accustomed to testify their subjection by
this ceremony, especially since they say that this practice is
still observed in certain parts of the East. That it was no
profane rite, which would detract anything from the glory of
God, we infer from the fact that the name of God is interposed. It is true that the servant placed his hand under
the thigh of Abraham, but he is adjured by God, the Creator
of heaven and earth ; and this is the sacred method of ad-
juration, whereby God is invoked as the witness and the
judge ; for this honour cannot be transferred to another without casting a reproach upon God. Moreover, we are taught,
by the example of Abraham, that they do not sin who demand an oath for a lawful cause ; for this is not recited
among the faults of Abraham, but is recorded to his peculiar
praise. It has already been shown that the affair was of the
utmost importance, since it was undertaken in order that
the covenant of God might be ratified among his posterity.
He was therefore impelled, by just reasons, most anxiously
to provide for the accomplishment of his object, by taking
an oath of his servant : and beyond doubt, the disposition,
and even the virtue of Isaac, were so conspicuous, that in
addition to his riches, he had such endowments of mind and
person, that many would earnestly desire affinity with him.
His father, therefore, fears lest, after his own death, the inhabitants of the land should captivate Isaac by their allurements. Now, though Isaac has hitherto steadfastly resisted
those allurements, the snares of which few young men escape,
Abraham still fears lest, by shame and the dread of giving
offence, he may be overcome. The holy man wished to anticipate these and similar dangers, when he bound his servant
to fidelity, by interposing an oath ; and it may be that some
secret necessity also impelled him to take this course.

3. *That thou shalt not take a wife.* The kind of discipline
which prevailed in Abraham's house is here apparent. Although this man was but a servant, yet, because he was put
in authority by the master of the family, his servile condition did not prevent him from being next in authority to
his lord ; so that Isaac himself, the heir and successor of
Abraham, submitted to his direction. To such an extent

did the authority of Abraham and reverence for him prevail, that when he substituted a servant in his place, he caused this servant, by his mere will or word, to exercise a power which other masters of families find it difficult to retain for themselves. The modesty also of Isaac, who suffered himself to be governed by a servant, is obvious; for it would have been in vain for Abraham to enter into engagements with his servant, had he not been persuaded that his son would prove submissive and tractable. It here appears what great veneration he cherished towards his father; because Abraham, relying on Isaac's obedience, confidently calls his servant to him. Now this example should be taken by us as a common rule, to show that it is not lawful for the children of a family to contract marriage, except with the consent of parents; and certainly natural equity dictates that, in a matter of such importance, children should depend upon the will of their parents. How detestable, therefore, is the barbarity of the Pope, who has dared to burst this sacred bond asunder! Wherefore the wantonness of youths is to be restrained, that they may not rashly contract nuptials without consulting their fathers.

4. *But thou shalt go unto my country and to my kindred.* It seems that, in the choice of the place, Abraham was influenced by the thought, that a wife would more willingly come from thence to be married to his son, when she knew that she was to marry one of her own race and country. But because it afterwards follows that the servant came to Padan Aram, some hence infer that Mesopotamia was Abraham's country. The solution, however, of this difficulty is easy. We know that Mesopotamia was not only the region contained between the Tigris and the Euphrates, but that a part also of Chaldea was comprehended in it; for Babylon is often placed there by profane writers. The Hebrew name simply means, " Syria of the rivers." They give the name " Aram" to that part of Syria which, beginning near Judea, embraces Armenia and other extensive regions, and reaches almost to the Euxine Sea. But when they especially designate those lands which are washed or traversed by the Tigris and Euphrates, they add the name " Padan : "

for we know that Moses did not speak scientifically, but in a popular style. Since, however, he afterwards relates that Laban, the son of Nahor, dwelt at Charran, (chap. xxix. 4,) it seems to me probable that Nahor, who had remained in Chaldea, because it would be troublesome to leave his native soil, in process of time changed his mind; either because filial piety constrained him to attend to his decrepit and declining father, or because he had learned that he might have there a home as commodious as in his own country. It certainly appears from the eleventh chapter that he had not migrated at the same time with his father.[1]

5. *And the servant said unto him.* Since he raises no objection respecting Isaac, we may conjecture that he was so fully persuaded of his integrity as to have no doubt of his acquiescence in his father's will. We must also admire the religious scrupulosity of the man, seeing he does not rashly take an oath. What pertained to the faithful and diligent discharge of his own duty he might lawfully promise, under the sanction of an oath; but since the completion of the affair depended on the will of others, he properly and wisely adduces this exception, "Peradventure the woman will not be willing to follow me."

6. *Beware that thou bring not my son thither again.* If the woman should not be found willing, Abraham, commending the event to God, firmly adheres to the principal point, that his son Isaac should not return to his country, because in this manner he would have deprived himself of the promised inheritance. He therefore chooses rather to live by hope, as a stranger, in the land of Canaan, than to rest among his relatives in his native soil: and thus we see that, in perplexed and confused affairs, the mind of the holy man was not drawn aside from the command of God by any agitating cares; and we are taught, by his example, to follow God through every obstacle. However, he afterwards declares that he looks for better things. By such words he confirms the confidence of his servant, so that he, anticipating with greater alacrity a prosperous issue, might prepare for the journey.

[1] See Gen. xi. 31.

7. *The Lord God of heaven.* By a twofold argument Abraham infers, that what he is deliberating respecting the marriage of his son will, by the grace of God, have a prosperous issue. First, because God had not led him forth in vain from his own country into a foreign land; and secondly, because God had not falsely promised to give the land, in which he was dwelling as a stranger, to his seed. He might also with propriety be confident that his design should succeed, because he had undertaken it only by the authority, and, as it were, under the auspices of God; for it was his exclusive regard for God which turned away his mind from the daughters of Canaan. He may, however, be thought to have inferred without reason that God would give his son a wife from that country and kindred to which he himself had bidden farewell. But whereas he had left his relatives only at the divine command, he hopes that God will incline their minds to be propitious and favourable to him. Meanwhile he concludes, from the past kindnesses of God, that his hand would not fail him in the present business; as if he would say, " I, who at the command of God left my country, and have experienced his continued help in my pilgrimage, do not doubt that he will also be the guide of thy journey, because it is in reliance on his promise that I lay upon thee this injunction." He then describes the mode in which assistance would be granted; namely, that God would send his angel, for he knew that God helps his servants by the ministration of angels, of which he had already received many proofs. By calling God " the God of heaven," he celebrates that divine power which was the ground of his confidence.

10. *And the servant took ten camels.* He takes the camels with him, to prove that Abraham is a man of great wealth, in order that he may the more easily obtain what he desires. For even an open-hearted girl would not easily suffer herself to be drawn away to a distant region, unless on the proposed condition of being supplied with the conveniences of life. Exile itself is sad enough, without poverty as its attendant. Therefore, that the maid might not be deterred by the apprehension of want, but rather invited by the prospect of affluence, he ladens ten camels with presents, to give suffi-

cient proof to the inhabitants of Chaldea of the domestic opulence of Abraham. What follows, namely, " that all the substance of Abraham was in the hand of his servant," some of the Hebrews improperly explain as meaning that the servant took with him an account of all Abraham's wealth, described and attested in written documents. It is rather the assigning of the reason of the fact, which might appear improbable, that the servant assumed so much power to himself. Therefore Moses, having said that a man who was but a servant set out on a journey with such a sumptuous and splendid equipage, immediately adds, that he did this of his own accord, because he had all the substance of Abraham in his hand. In saying that he came to the city of Nahor, he neither mentions the name of the city nor the part of Chaldea, or of any other region, where he dwelt, but only says, in general terms, that he came to " Syria of the rivers," concerning which term I have said something above.

12. *O Lord God of my master Abraham.* The servant, being destitute of counsel, betakes himself to prayers. Yet he does not simply ask counsel of the Lord ; but he also prays that the maid appointed to be the wife of Isaac should be brought to him with a certain sign, from which he might gather that she was divinely presented to him. It is an evidence of his piety and faith, that in a matter of such perplexity he is not bewildered, as one astonished ; but breaks forth into prayer with a collected mind. But the method which he uses[1] seems scarcely consistent with the true rule of prayer. For, first, we know that no one prays aright unless he subjects his own wishes to God. Wherefore there is nothing more unsuitable than to prescribe anything, at our own will, to God. Where, then, it

[1] " Divinatio quâ utitur." The word *divinatio* seems to be too strong for the occasion. The servant certainly sought a sign from heaven ; and may seem improperly to have prescribed to God in what way his prayer should be answered. He might, however, be acting under a divine impulse; and the context would lead to such an inference. But if it was a weakness in this good man to be thus minute in his stipulations, it was one which God neither reproved nor condemned ; and therefore it seems harsh to give it the name of *divination*. Calvin's object, however, is, in thus strongly stating the case, to meet it as an objection, by a conclusive answer. A method which, the reader will have observed, he frequently adopts.—*Ed.*

may be asked, is the religion of the servant, who, according to his own pleasure, imposes a law upon God? Secondly, there ought to be nothing ambiguous in our prayers; and absolute certainty is to be sought for only in the Word of God. Now, since the servant prescribes to God what answer shall be given, he appears culpably to depart from the suitable modesty of prayer; for although no promise had been given him, he nevertheless desires to be made fully certain respecting the whole affair. God, however,[1] in hearkening to his wish, proves, by the event, that it was acceptable to himself. Therefore we must know, that although a special promise had not been made at the moment, yet the servant was not praying rashly, nor according to the lust of the flesh, but by the secret impulse of the Spirit. Moreover, the general law, by which all the pious are bound, does not prevent the Lord, when he determines to give something extraordinary, from directing the minds of his servants towards it; not that he would lead them away from his word, but only that he makes some peculiar concession to them in their mode of praying. The sum of the prayer before us is this: " O Lord, if a damsel shall present herself who, being asked to give me drink, shall also kindly and courteously offer it to my camels, I will seek after her as a wife for my master Isaac, just as if she were delivered into my hand by thee." He seems, indeed, to be laying hold on some dubious conjecture; but since he reposes on the Providence of God, he is certainly persuaded that this token shall be to him equivalent to an oracle; because God, who is the guardian of his enterprise, will not suffer him to err. Meanwhile this is worthy of remark, that he does not fetch the sign of recognition from afar, but takes it from something present; for she who shall be thus humane to an unknown guest, will, by that very act, give proof of an excellent disposition. This observation may be of use to prevent inquisitive men from adducing this example as a precedent for vain prognostications. In the words themselves the following particulars are to be noticed: first, that he addresses himself to the God of his master Abraham; not as being himself a stranger

---

[1] Calvin's answer to the objection above stated begins here.—*Ed.*

to the worship of God, but because the affair in question depends upon the promise given to Abraham. And truly he had no confidence in prayer, from any other source than from the covenant into which God had entered with the house of Abraham. The expression " cause to meet me this day,"[1] Jerome renders, " meet me, I pray, this day." But the verb is transitive, and the servant of Abraham intimates by the use of it, that the affairs of men were so ordered by the counsel and the hand of God, that the issue of them was not fortuitous ; as if he would say, " O Lord, in vain shall I look on this side and on that; in vain shall I catch at success by my own labour, industry and various contrivances, unless thou direct the work." And when he immediately afterwards subjoins, " show kindness to my master," he implies that in this undertaking he rests upon nothing but the grace which God had promised to Abraham.

15. *Before he had done speaking.* The sequel sufficiently demonstrates that his wish had not been foolishly conceived. For the quickness of the answer manifests the extraordinary indulgence of God, who does not suffer the man to be long harassed with anxiety. Rebekah had, indeed, left her house before he began to pray ; but it must be maintained that the Lord, at whose disposal are both the moments of time and the ways of men, had so ordered it on both sides as to give clear manifestation of his Providence. For sometimes he keeps us the longer in suspense, till, wearied with praying, we may seem to have lost our labour ; but in this affair, in order that his blessing might not seem doubtful, he suddenly interposed. The same thing also happened to Daniel, unto whom the angel appeared, before the conclusion of his prayer. (Dan. ix. 21.) Now, although it frequently happens

[1] " Et dixit Iehova Deus domini mei Abraham, occurrere fac nunc coram me hodie, et fac misericordiam cum domino meo Abraham." Dathe seems to have taken the same view of the passage with Calvin. " O Iova Deus domini mei Abrahami, fac pro tuo erga dominum meum Abrahamum amore, ut mihi jam *quam quæro*, occurrat." " O Lord God of my master Abraham, cause, according to thy love towards my master Abraham, that she whom I seek may meet me." The English version is simply, " I pray thee, send me good speed this day." But probably the more specific meaning attached by Calvin and Dathe to the passage is the true one. Calvin properly objects against the translation of the Vulgate as being *intransitive*, whereas הקרה (*hakreh*) is transitive.—*Ed.*

that, on account of our sloth, the Lord delays to grant our
requests, it is, at such times, expedient for us, that what we
ask should be delayed. In the meantime, he has openly
and conspicuously proved, by unquestionable examples, that
although the event may not immediately respond to our
wishes, the prayers of his people are never in vain : yea, his
own declaration, that before they cry he is mindful of their
wants, is invariably fulfilled. (Is. lxv. 24.)

21. *And the man, wondering at her, held his peace.* This
wondering of Abraham's servant, shows that he had some
doubt in his mind. He is silently inquiring within himself,
whether God would render his journey prosperous. Has he,
then, no confidence concerning that divine direction, of
which he had received the sign or pledge ? I answer, that
faith is never so absolutely perfect in the saints as to prevent the occurrence of many doubts. There is, therefore, no
absurdity in supposing that the servant of Abraham, though
committing himself generally to the providence of God, yet
wavers, and is agitated, amidst a multiplicity of conflicting
thoughts. Again, faith, although it pacifies and calms the
minds of the pious, so that they patiently wait for God, still
does not exonerate them from all care ; because it is necessary that patience itself should be exercised, by anxious
expectation, until the Lord fulfil what he has promised.
But though this hesitation of Abraham's servant was not
free from fault, inasmuch as it flowed from infirmity of faith ;
it is yet, on this account, excusable, because he did not turn
his eyes in another direction, but only sought from the event
a confirmation of his faith, that he might perceive God to be
present with him.

22. *The man took a golden ear-ring.* His adorning the
damsel with precious ornaments is a token of his confidence.
For since it is evident by many proofs that he was an honest
and careful servant, he would not throw away without discretion the treasures of his master. He knows, therefore,
that these gifts will not be ill-bestowed; or, at least, relying
on the goodness of God, he gives them, in faith, as an earnest of future marriage. But it may be asked, Whether
God approves ornaments of this kind, which pertain not so

much to neatness as to pomp? I answer, that the things
related in Scripture are not always proper to be imitated.
Whatever the Lord commands in general terms is to be
accounted as an inflexible rule of conduct; but to rely on
particular examples is not only dangerous, but even foolish
and absurd. Now we know how highly displeasing to God
is not only pomp and ambition in adorning the body, but all
kind of luxury. In order to free the heart from inward cupidity, he condemns that immoderate and superfluous splendour, which contains within itself many allurements to vice.
Where, indeed, is pure sincerity of heart found under splendid ornaments? Certainly all acknowledge this virtue to be
rare. It is' not, however, for us expressly to forbid every
kind of ornament; yet because whatever exceeds the frugal
use of such things is tarnished with some degree of vanity;
and more especially, because the cupidity of women is, on
this point, insatiable; not only must moderation, but even
abstinence, be cultivated as far as possible. Further, ambition silently creeps in, so that the somewhat excessive adorning of the person soon breaks out into disorder. With
respect to the ear-rings and bracelets of Rebekah, as I do
not doubt that they were those in use among the rich, so
the uprightness of the age allowed them to be sparingly and
frugally used; and yet I do not excuse the fault. This
example, however, neither helps us, nor alleviates our guilt,
if, by such means, we excite and continually inflame those
depraved lusts which, even when all incentives are removed,
it is excessively difficult to restrain. The women who desire to shine in gold, seek in Rebekah a pretext for their
corruption. Why, therefore, do they not, in like manner,
conform to the same austere kind of life and rustic labour
to which she applied herself? But, as I have just said,
they are deceived who imagine that the examples of the
saints can sanction them in opposition to the common law
of God. Should any one object that it is abhorrent to the
modesty of a virtuous and chaste maiden to receive ear-rings
and bracelets from a man who was a stranger, and whom
she had never before seen. In the first place, it may be,
that Moses passes over much conversation held on both

sides, by which it is probable she was induced to venture on
the reception of them.   It may also be, that he relates first
what was last in order.   For it follows soon afterwards in
the context, that the servant of Abraham inquired whose
daughter she was.   We must also take into account the
simplicity of that age.   Whence does it arise that it was not
disreputable for a maid to go alone out of the city, unless
that then the morals of mankind did not require so severe a
guard for the preservation of modesty ?   Indeed, it appears
from the context, that the ornaments were not given her for
a dishonourable purpose ;[1] but a portion is offered to the
parents to facilitate the contract for marriage.   Interpreters
are not agreed respecting the value of the presents.   Moses
estimates the ear-rings at half a shekel, and the bracelets at
ten shekels.   Jerome, instead of half a shekel, reads two
shekels.   I conceive the genuine sense to be, that the bracelets were worth ten shekels, and the frontal ornament or
ear-rings worth half that sum, or five shekels.   For since
nothing is added after the word בקע, (bekah,) it has reference
to the greater number.[2]   Otherwise there is no suitable proportion between the bracelets and the ornaments for the
head.   Moreover, if we take the shekel for four Attic
drachms, the value is trifling ; therefore I think the weight
of gold is indicated, which makes the sum much greater
than the piece of money called a shekel.

26. *And the man bowed down his head.*   When the servant
of Abraham hears that he had alighted upon the daughter
of Bethuel, he is more and more elated with hope.   Yet he

[1] " Non turpis lenocinii causâ datum esse."

[2] Some suppose that by the ear-rings is meant an ornament for the face
or forehead, as appears in the margin of our version, and as Calvin here
seems to intimate.   But the increased knowledge of Eastern customs which
recent times have furnished, has given weight to the opinion of older
commentators, that a nose-jewel is here intended.   This ornament was
not suspended from the central cartilaginous substance of the nose, but
from one side, which was bored for the purpose.   Calvin's interpretation,
that the weight of this ornament was the half of ten shekels, instead of
half a shekel, cannot be admitted.   Though, according to its weight, it
might not be worth more than ten or twelve shillings ; yet its workmanship might be costly ; and if it contained some precious stone, which is not
improbable, it might be of very great value.   There can be no doubt that
the presents generally were exceedingly valuable.—*Ed.*

does not exult, as profane men are wont to do, as if the occurrence were fortuitous ; but he gives thanks to God, regarding it, as the result of Providence, that he had been thus
opportunely led straight to the place he had wished.   He
does not, therefore, boast of his good fortune ; but he declares that God had dealt kindly and faithfully with Abraham ; or, in other words, that, for his own mercy's sake, God
had been faithful in fulfilling his promises.   It is true that
the same form of speech is applied to the persons present ;
just as it follows soon after in the same chapter, (ver. 49,)
" *If ye will deal kindly and truly with my master, tell me.*"
The language is, however, peculiarly suitable to the character of God, both because he gratuitously confers favours upon
men, and is specially inclined to beneficence : and also, by
never frustrating their hope, he proves himself to be faithful and true.   This thanksgiving, therefore, teaches us
always to have the providence of God before our eyes, in
order that we may ascribe to him whatever happens prosperously to us.

28. *And the damsel ran and told them of her mother's
house.*   It is possible, that the mother of Rebekah occupied
a separate house ; not that she had a family divided from
that of her husband, but for the purpose of keeping her
daughters and maidens under her own custody.   The expression may, however, be more simply explained to mean,
that she came directly to her mother's chamber ; because
she could more easily relate the matter to her than to her
father.   It is also probable, that when Bethuel was informed
of the fact, by the relation of his wife, their son Laban was
sent by both of them to introduce the stranger.   Other explanations are needless.

33. *I will not eat until I have told my errand.*[1]   Moses
begins to show by what means the parents of Rebekah were

---

[1] It was the custom of the ancients on occasions of this kind first to
take their meal together, and when the wants of nature had been supplied,
and the spirit had been exhilarated, to open the subject of communication ;
but Abraham's servant purposely reverses this order, to show his earnestness in attending to his master's business ; and perhaps also his confidence
of success, in consequence of the favourable indications which God had
given in answer to his prayers.   See *Dathe* and *Le Clerc.—Ed.*

induced to give her in marriage to their nephew. That the servant, when food was set before him, should refuse to eat till he had completed his work is a proof of his diligence and fidelity; and it may with propriety be regarded as one of the benefits which God had vouchsafed to Abraham, that he should have a servant so faithful, and so intent upon his duty. Since, however, this was the reward of the holy discipline which Abraham maintained, we cannot wonder that very few such servants are to be found, seeing that everywhere they are so ill-governed.

Moreover, although the servant seems to weave a superfluous story, yet there is nothing in it which is not available to his immediate purpose. He knew that it was a feeling naturally inherent in parents, not willingly to send away their children to a distance. He therefore first commemorates Abraham's riches, that they might not hesitate to connect their daughter with a husband so wealthy. He secondly explains that Isaac was born of his mother in her old age; not merely for the purpose of informing them that he had been miraculously given to his father, whence they might infer that he had been divinely appointed to this greatness and eminence; but that an additional commendation might be given on account of Isaac's age. In the third place, he affirms that Isaac would be the sole heir of his father. Fourthly, he relates that he had been bound by an oath to seek a wife for his master Isaac, from among his own kindred; which special choice on the part of Abraham was very effectual in moving them to compliance. Fifthly, he states that Abraham, in full confidence that God would be the leader of his journey, had committed the whole business to him. Sixthly, he declares, that whatever he had asked in prayer he had obtained from the Lord; whence it appeared that the marriage of which he was about to treat was according to the will of God. We now see the design of his narration: First, to persuade the parents of Rebekah that he had not been sent for the purpose of deceiving them, that he had not in anything acted craftily, or by oblique methods, but in the fear of the Lord, as the religious obligation of marriage requires. Secondly, that he was desiring nothing which would not be

profitable and honourable for them.   And lastly, that God
had been the director of the whole affair.

Moreover, since the servant of Abraham, though persuaded
that the angel of God would be the guide of his journey, yet
neither directs his prayers nor his thanksgivings to him, we
may hence learn that angels are not, in such a sense, constituted the ministers of God to us, as that they should be invoked by us, or should transfer to themselves the worship
due to God ; a superstition which prevails nearly over the
whole world to such a degree, that men turn aside a portion
of their faith from the only fountain of all good to the rivu-
lets which flow from it.   The clause, *the Lord, before whom
I walk*, (ver. 40,) which some refer to the probity and good
conscience of Abraham, I rather explain as applying to the
faith, by which he set God before him, as the governor of
his life, being confident that he was the object of God's care,
and dependent upon his grace.

If ye will deal kindly.[1]   I have lately related the force of
this expression ; namely, to act with humanity and good faith.
He thus modestly and suppliantly asks them to consent to the
marriage of Isaac and Rebekah : should he meet with a repulse from them, he says, he will go either to the right hand
or to the left ; that is, he will look around elsewhere.   For
he places the right hand and the left in contrast with the
straight way in which he had been led to them.   It is, however,
with fertile ingenuity that some of the Hebrews explain the
words as meaning, that he would go to Lot, or to Ishmael.

50.   *The thing proceedeth from the Lord.*   Whereas they
are convinced by the discourse of the man, that God was the
Author of this marriage, they avow that it would be unlawful for them to offer anything in the way of contradiction.
They declare that the thing proceedeth from the Lord ; because he had, by the clearest signs, made his will manifest.
Hence we perceive, that although the true religion was
in part observed among them, and in part infected with
vicious errors, yet the fear of God was never so utterly extinguished, but this axiom remained firmly fixed in all their
minds, that God must be obeyed.   If, then, wretched idola-

[1] " Si facitis misericordiam."

ters, who had almost fallen away from religion, nevertheless
so subjected themselves to God, as to acknowledge it to be
unlawful for them to swerve from his will, how much more
prompt ought our obedience to be ? Therefore, as soon as
the will of God is made known to us, not only let our
tongues be silent, but let all our senses be still ; because it
is an audacious profanation to admit any thought which is
opposed to that will.

52. *He worshipped.* Moses again repeats that Abraham's
servant gave thanks to God ; and it is not without reason
that he so often inculcates this religious duty ; because, since
God requires nothing greater from us, the neglect of it betrays the most shameful indolence. The acknowledgment
of God's kindness is a sacrifice of sweet-smelling savour ;
yea, it is a more acceptable service than all sacrifices. God
is continually heaping innumerable benefits upon men. Their
ingratitude, therefore, is intolerable, if they fail to exercise
themselves in celebrating those benefits.

54. *And they rose up in the morning.* On this point
Moses insists the more particularly ; partly, for the purpose
of commending the faithful industry of the servant in fulfilling his master's commands ; partly, for that of teaching,
that his mind was inflamed by the Spirit of God, for he is so
ardent as to allow no truce to others, and no relaxation to
himself. Thus, although he conducted himself as became
an honest and prudent servant, it is still not to be doubted
that the Lord impelled him, for Isaac's sake, to act as he did.
So the Lord watches over his own people while they sleep,
expedites and accomplishes their affairs in their absence,
and influences the dispositions of all, so far as is expedient,
to render them assistance. It is by a forced interpretation,
that some would explain the ten days, during which Laban
and his mother desire the departure of Rebekah to be deferred, as meaning years or months. For it was merely the
tender wish of the mother, who could ill bear that her
daughter should thus suddenly be torn away from her bosom.

57. *We will call the damsel.* Bethuel, who had before
unreservedly given his daughter in marriage, now seems to
adhere, with but little constancy, to his purpose. When, how-

ever, he had previously offered his daughter, without making
any exception, he is to be understood as having done it, only
so far as he was able.   But now, Moses declares that he did
not exercise tyranny over his daughter, so as to thrust her
out reluctantly, or to compel her to marry against her will,
but left her to her own free choice.   Truly, in this matter, the
authority of parents ought to be sacred : but a middle course
is to be pursued, so that the parties concerned may make
their contract spontaneously, and with mutual consent.   It
is not right to understand that Rebekah in answering so explicitly, showed contempt for the paternal roof, or too anxiously desired a husband ;[1] but since she saw that the affair
was transacted by the authority of her father, and with the
consent of her mother, she also herself acquiesced in it.

59. *And they sent away Rebekah.*   Moses first relates, that
Rebekah was honourably dismissed ; because her nurse was
given unto her.   Moreover, I doubt not that they had domestic nurses, who were their handmaidens ; not that mothers
entirely neglected that duty, but that they committed the care
of education to one particular maid.   They therefore who
assisted mothers with subsidiary service were called nurses.
Moses afterwards adds, that Rebekah's relatives " blessed
her," (verse 60,) by which expression he means, that they
prayed that her condition might be a happy one.   We know
that it was a solemn custom, in all ages, and among all
people, to accompany marriages with all good wishes.   And
although posterity has greatly degenerated from the pure
and genuine method of celebrating marriages used by the
fathers ; yet it is God's will that some public testimony
should stand forth, by which men may be admonished, that
no nuptials are lawful, except those which are rightly consecrated.   Now, the particular form of benediction which is
here related, was probably in common use, because nature
dictates that the propagation of offspring is the special end
of marriage.   Under the notion of victory (ver. 60) is comprehended a prosperous state of life.   The Lord, however,
directed their tongues to utter a prophecy of which they
themselves were ignorant.   " To possess the gates of ene-

---

[1] " Vel procax juvencula maritum nimis cupide appeteret."

mies," means to obtain dominion over them ; because judgment was administered in the gates, and the bulwarks of the
city were placed there.

63. *And Isaac went out.* It appears that Isaac dwelt
apart from his father; either because the family was too
large, or because such was the custom. And perhaps Abraham had already married another wife ; so that, for the sake
of avoiding contentions, it would seem more convenient for
him to have a house of his own. Thus great wealth has its
attendant troubles. Doubtless, of all earthly blessings granted by God, none would have been sweeter to Abraham than
that of living with his son. However, I by no means think
that he was deprived of his society and assistance. For such
was the piety of Isaac, that he undoubtedly studied to discharge every duty towards his father: this alone was wanting, that they did not live in the same house. Moses also
relates how it happened that Isaac met with his wife before
she reached his home. For he says, that Isaac went out in
the evening to *meditate* or to *pray.* For the Hebrew word
שׂוּחַ (*soach*) may mean either. It is probable that he did
this according to his custom, and that he sought a place of
retirement for prayer, in order that his mind, being released
from all avocations, might be the more at liberty to serve
God. Whether, however, he was giving his mind to meditation or to prayer, the Lord granted him a token of his own
presence in that joyful meeting.

64. *And Rebekah lifted up her eyes.* We may easily conjecture that Isaac, when he saw the camels, turned his steps
towards them, from the desire of seeing his bride ; this gave
occasion to the inquiry of Rebekah. Having received the
answer, she immediately, for the sake of doing honour to
her husband, dismounted her camel to salute him. For that
she fell, struck with fear, as some suppose, in no way agrees
with the narrative. She had performed too long a journey,
under the protection of many attendants, to be so greatly
afraid at the sight of one man. But these interpreters are
deceived, because they do not perceive, that in the words of
Moses, the reason is afterwards given to this effect, that
when Rebekah saw Isaac, she alighted from her camel ;

because she had inquired of the servant who he was, and had been told that he was the son of his master Abraham. It would not have entered into her mind to make such inquiry respecting any person whom she might accidentally meet: but seeing she had been informed that Abraham's house was not far distant, she supposes him at least to be one of the domestics. Moses also says that she took a veil: which was a token of shame and modesty. For hence also, the Latin word which signifies " to marry,"[1] is derived, because it was the custom to give brides veiled to their husbands. That the same rite was also observed by the fathers, I have no doubt.[2] So much the more shameful, and the less capable of excuse, is the licentiousness of our own age; in which the apparel of brides seems to be purposely contrived for the subversion of all modesty.

67. *And Isaac brought her into his mother Sarah's tent.* He first brought her into the tent, then took her as his wife. By the very arrangement of his words, Moses distinguishes between the legitimate mode of marriage and barbarism. And certainly the sanctity of marriage demands that man and woman should not live together like cattle; but that, having pledged their mutual faith, and invoked the name of God, they might dwell with each other. Besides, it is to be observed, that Isaac was not compelled, by the tyrannical command of his father, to marry; but after he had given his mind to her he took her freely, and cordially gave her the assurance of conjugal fidelity.

And Isaac was comforted after his mother's death. Since his grief for the death of his mother was now first assuaged, we infer how great had been its vehemence; for a period sufficiently long had already elapsed.[3] We may also hence infer, that the affection of Isaac was tender and gentle: and that his love to his mother was of no common kind, seeing

---

[1] " Verbum nubendi." The original meaning of the word *nubere* is to *veil*, or *cover*.

[2] " Isaac was walking, and it would therefore have been the highest breach of Oriental good manners, to have remained on the camel when presented to him. No doubt they all alighted and walked to meet him, conducting Rebekah as a bride to meet the bridegroom."—*Bush.*—*Ed.*

[3] The time from the death of Sarah to Isaac's marriage was three years. —*Ed.*

he had so long lamented her death. And the knowledge of this fact is useful to prevent us from imagining that the holy patriarchs were men of savage manners and of iron hardness of heart, and from becoming like those who conceive fortitude to consist in brutality. Only care must be taken that grief should be duly mitigated ; lest it burst forth in impious murmurings, or subvert the hope of a future resurrection. I do not however entirely excuse the sorrow of Isaac ; I only advise, that what belongs to humanity, ought not to be altogether condemned. And although it was culpable not to be able to efface grief from the mind, until the opposite joy of marriage prevailed over it ; Moses still reckons it among the benefits conferred by God, that he applies a remedy of any kind to his servant.

CHAPTER XXV.

1. Then again Abraham took a wife, and her name *was* Keturah.

2. And she bare him Zimran, and Jokshan, and Medan, and Midian, and Ishbak, and Shuah.

3. And Jokshan begat Sheba and Dedan. And the sons of Dedan were Asshurim, and Letushim, and Leummim.

4. And the sons of Midian; Ephah, and Epher, and Hanoch, and Abidah, and Eldaah. All these *were* the children of Keturah.

5. And Abraham gave all that he had unto Isaac.

6. But unto the sons of the concubines, which Abraham had, Abraham gave gifts, and sent them away from Isaac his son, (while he yet lived,) eastward, unto the east country.

7. And these *are* the days of the years of Abraham's life which he lived, an hundred threescore and fifteen years.

8. Then Abraham gave up the ghost, and died in a good old age, an old man, and full *of years;* and was gathered to his people.

9. And his sons Isaac and Ishmael

1. Et addidit Abraham, et accepit uxorem, cujus nomen erat Cetura.

2. Et peperit ei Zimram, et Iocsan, et Medan, et Midian, et Isbah, et Suah.

3. Et Iocsan genuit Seba, et Dedan. Filii autem Dedan fuerunt Assurim, et Letusim, et Leummin.

4. Filii vero Midian, Hephah, et Hepher, et Hanoch, et Abidah, et Eldaah : omnes isti, filii Ceturæ.

5. Porro dedit Abraham omnia, quæ sua erant, ipsi Ishac.

6. Et filiis concubinarum quas habebat Abraham, dedit Abraham dona ; et emisit eos ab Ishac filio suo, quum adhuc viveret, ad Orientem, ad terram Orientalem.

7. Porro isti sunt dies annorum vitæ Abraham quos vixit, centum anni et septuaginta anni et quinque anni.

8. Et obiit, et mortuus est Abraham in senectute bona, senex et satur : et congregatus est ad populos suos.

9. Et sepelierunt eum Ishac et

buried him in the cave of Machpelah, in the field of Ephron the son of Zohar the Hittite, which *is* before Mamre;

10. The field which Abraham purchased of the sons of Heth: there was Abraham buried, and Sarah his wife.

11. And it came to pass after the death of Abraham, that God blessed his son Isaac: and Isaac dwelt by the well Lahai-roi.

12. Now these *are* the generations of Ishmael, Abraham's son, whom Hagar the Egyptian, Sarah's handmaid, bare unto Abraham.

13. And these *are* the names of the sons of Ishmael, by their names, according to their generations: The first-born of Ishmael, Nebajoth; and Kedar, and Adbeel, and Mibsam,

14. And Mishma, and Dumah, and Maasa,

15. Hadar, and Tema, Jetur, Naphish, and Kedemah.

16. These *are* the sons of Ishmael, and these *are* their names, by their towns, and by their castles; twelve princes according to their nations.

17. And these *are* the years of the life of Ishmael, an hundred and thirty and seven years: and he gave up the ghost, and died, and was gathered unto his people.

18. And they dwelt from Havilah unto Shur, that *is* before Egypt, as thou goest toward Assyria: *and* he died in the presence of all his brethren.

19. And these *are* the generations of Isaac, Abraham's son: Abraham begat Isaac.

20. And Isaac was forty years old when he took Rebekah to wife, the daughter of Bethuel the Syrian of Padan-aram, the sister to Laban the Syrian.

21. And Isaac entreated the Lord for his wife, because she *was* barren: and the Lord was entreated of him, and Rebekah his wife conceived.

22. And the children struggled together within her: and she said, If *it be* so, why *am* I thus? And she went to enquire of the Lord.

Ismael filii ejus in spelunca duplici, in agro Ephron filii Sohar Hittæi, quæ est ante Mamre,

10. In agro quem emit Abraham a filiis Heth: ibi sepultus est Abraham et Sarah uxor ejus.

11. Et fuit, postquam mortuus est Abraham, benedixit Deus Ishac filio ejus; et habitavit Ishac apud Puteum viventis videntis me.

12. Istæ autem generationes Ismael filii Abraham, quem peperit Hagar Ægyptia ancilla Sarah ipsi Abraham.

13. Et hæc nomina filiorum Ismael per nomina sua, per generationes suas: primogenitus Ismael, Nebajoth, et Cedar, et Abdeel, et Mibsam,

14. Et Mismah, et Dumah, et Masa,

15. Hadar, et Thema, Jetur, Naphis, et Cedmah.

16. Isti sunt filii Ismael, et ista nomina eorum per villas suas, et per castella sua, duodecim principes per familias suas.

17. Et isti sunt anni vitæ Ismael, centum anni, et triginta anni, et septem anni: et obiit, et mortuus est, et congregatus est ad populos suos.

18. Et habitaverunt ab Havilah usque ad Sur, quæ est ante Ægyptum, dum pergis in Assur: coram omnibus fratribus suis habitavit.

19. Istæ vero sunt generationes Ishac filii Abraham: Abraham genuit Ishac.

20. Et erat Ishac quadragenarius, quando accepit Ribcam filiam Bethuel Aramæi de Padan Aram, sororem Laban Aramæi, sibi in uxorem.

21. Et oravit Ishac Iehovam respectu uxoris suæ, quia sterilis erat: et exoratus est ab ipso Iehova, et concepit Ribca uxor ejus.

22. Et collidebant se filii in utero ejus, et dixit, Si ita, ut quid ego? et ivit ad interrogandum Iehovam.

23. And the Lord said unto her, Two nations *are* in thy womb, and two manner of people shall be separated from thy bowels; and *the one* people shall be stronger than *the other* people; and the elder shall serve the younger.

24. And when her days to be delivered were fulfilled, behold, *there were* twins in her womb.

25. And the first came out red, all over like an hairy garment; and they called his name Esau.

26. And after that came his brother out, and his hand took hold on Esau's heel; and his name was called Jacob: and Isaac *was* threescore years old when she bare them.

27. And the boys grew: and Esau was a cunning hunter, a man of the field; and Jacob *was* a plain man, dwelling in tents.

28. And Isaac loved Esau, because he did eat of *his* venison; but Rebekah loved Jacob.

29. And Jacob sod pottage: and Esau came from the field, and he *was* faint.

30. And Esau said to Jacob, Feed me, I pray thee, with that same red *pottage;* for I *am* faint: therefore was his name called Edom.

31. And Jacob said, Sell me this day thy birthright.

32. And Esau said, Behold, I *am* at the point to die; and what profit shall this birthright do to me?

33. And Jacob said, Swear to me this day; and he sware unto him: and he sold his birthright unto Jacob.

34. Then Jacob gave Esau bread and pottage of lentiles; and he did eat and drink, and rose up, and went his way. Thus Esau despised *his* birthright.

23. Tunc dixit Iehova ad eam, Duæ gentes sunt in utero tuo, et duo populi a visceribus tuis separabunt se: et populus populo robustior erit, et major serviet minori.

24. Et impleti sunt dies ejus ut pareret, et ecce gemini *erant* in utero ejus.

25. Egressus est autem prior rufus, totus ipse sicut pallium pilosum: et vocaverunt nomen ejus Esau.

26. Et postea egressus est frater ejus, et manus ejus tenebat calcaneum Esau, et vocarunt nomen Iahacob. Ishac autem erat sexagenarius, quando peperit eos.

27. Et creverunt pueri: et fuit Esau vir peritus venationis, vir agricola: sed Iahacob erat vir integer, manens in tabernaculis.

28. Et dilexit Ishac Esau, quia venatio *erat* in ore ejus, et Ribca diligebat Iahacob.

29. Coxit autem Iahacob coctionem: et venit Esau ex agro, et erat lassus.

30. Et dixit Esau ad Iahacob, Fac me comedere nunc de rufo, rufo isto: quia lassus sum: idcirco vocarunt nomen ejus Edom.

31. Tunc dixit Iahacob, Vende hoc tempore primogenituram tuam mihi.

32. Et dixit Esau, Ecce ego vado ut moriar, et utquid mihi primogenitura?

33. Dixit itaque Iahacob, Iura mihi hoc tempore. Et juravit ei: et vendidit primogenituram suam ipsi Iahacob.

34. Et Iahacob dedit Esau panem et coctionem lenticularum, et comedit, atque bibit: et surrexit, et abiit, contempsitque Esau primogenituram.

1. *Then again Abraham took a wife.*[1] It seems very ab-

---

[1] " Et addidit Abraham et accepit uxorem." The Geneva version of our own Bible has it : " Now Abraham had taken him another wife called Keturah;" and adds in the margin, " while Sarah was yet alive," which agrees, as will appear in what follows, with the opinion of Calvin, expressed in this Commentary.—*Ed.*

surd that Abraham, who is said to have been dead in his own body thirty-eight years before the decease of Sarah, should, after her death, marry another wife. Such an act was, certainly, unworthy of his gravity. Besides, when Paul commends his faith, (Rom. iv. 19,) he not only asserts that the womb of Sarah was dead, when Isaac was about to be born, but also that the body of the father himself was dead. Therefore Abraham acted most foolishly, if, after the loss of his wife, he, in the decrepitude of old age, contracted another marriage. Further, it is at variance with the language of Paul, that he, who in his hundredth year was cold and impotent,[1] should, forty years afterwards, have many sons. Many commentators, to avoid this absurdity, suppose Keturah to have been the same person as Hagar. But their conjecture is immediately refuted in the context; where Moses says, Abraham gave gifts to the sons of his concubines. The same point is clearly established from 1 Chron. i. 32. Others conjecture that, while Sarah was yet living, he took another wife. This, although worthy of grave censure, is however not altogether incredible. We know it to be not uncommon for men to be rendered bold by excessive license. Thus Abraham having once transgressed the law of marriage, perhaps, after the dispute respecting Hagar, did not desist from the practice of polygamy. It is also probable that his mind had been wounded, by the divorce which Sarah had compelled him to make with Hagar. Such conduct indeed was disgraceful, or, at least, unbecoming in the holy patriarch. Nevertheless no other, of all the conjectures which have been made, seems to me more probable. If it be admitted, the narrative belongs to another place; but Moses is frequently accustomed to place those things which have precedence in time, in a different order. And though this reason should not be deemed conclusive, yet the fact itself shows an inverted order in the history.[2] Sarah had passed

---

[1] " Frigidus, et ad generandum impotens."

[2] " Atque ut hæc ratio non urgeat, res tamen ipsa ostendit esse in hac historia, ὕστερον πρότερον." " Et encore que ceste raison ne presse point, toutefois le faict monstre, qu'en ceste histoire il y a des choses mises devant derriere."—*French Tr.* The old English translator has it: " And though this reason serve not; yet nevertheless the matter itself declareth, that

her ninetieth year, when she brought forth her son Isaac;
she died in the hundred and twenty-seventh year of her
age; and Isaac married when he was forty years old. Therefore, nearly four years intervened between the death of his
mother and his nuptials. If Abraham took a wife after this,
what was he thinking of, seeing that he had been during so
many years accustomed to a single life? It is therefore lawful to conjecture that Moses, in writing the life of Abraham,
when he approached the closing scene, inserted what he had
before omitted. The difficulty, however, is not yet solved.
For whence proceeded Abraham's renovated vigour,[1] since
Paul testifies that his body had long ago been withered by
age? Augustine supposes not only that strength was imparted to him for a short space of time, which might suffice
for Isaac's birth; but that by a divine restoration, it flourished again during the remaining term of his life. Which
opinion, both because it amplifies the glory of the miracle,
and for other reasons, I willingly embrace.[2] And what I
have before said, namely, that Isaac was miraculously born,
as being a spiritual seed, is not opposed to this view; for it
was especially on his account that the failing body of Abraham was restored to vigour. That others were afterwards
born was, so to speak, adventitious. Thus the blessing of

there is in this history a *Hysteron proteron*, that is, a setting of the cart
before the horse."—*Ed.*

[1] " Unde enim novus illi ad muliebrem concubitum vigor."

[2] On the question, whether Abraham married Keturah during Sarah's
life, or not till after her death, authorities are much divided. Whichever
side is taken the difficulties are great, yet perhaps on neither side insuperable. So far as merely human probabilities are concerned, the evidence
would turn in favour of Calvin's hypothesis, which is supported by Dr. A.
Clarke and Professor Bush; the arguments of the latter writer, which
seem to be mainly drawn from Calvin, are very forcibly put. On the
other hand, great consideration is due to the authority of such men as
Patrick, Le Clerc, Kidder, and Scott, who would preserve the present
order of the sacred narrative; and would account for the events related on
the ground of a miraculous renewal and continuance of strength, which
Calvin himself allows to have taken place. It is in favour of this latter
mode of interpretation, that it certainly better accords with the general
character of Abraham, and is more consistent with the testimony which
the Scriptures bear to his faith, than the other hypothesis; besides which
the order of the narrative remains undisturbed. See this question treated
at length in *Exercitationes Andreæ Riveti in Genesin*, p. 548. Lugd.
1633.—*Ed.*

God pronounced in the words, " Increase and multiply," which was annexed expressly to marriage, is also extended to unlawful connexions. Certainly, if Abraham married a wife while Sarah was yet alive, (as I think most probable,) his adulterous connexion was unworthy of the divine bene- diction. But although we know not why this addition was made to the just measure of favour granted to Abraham, yet the wonderful providence of God appears in this, that while many nations of considerable importance descended from his other sons, the spiritual covenant, of which the rest also bore the sign in their flesh, remained in the exclusive possession of Isaac.

6. *But unto the sons of the concubines.* Moses relates, that when Abraham was about to die, he formed the design of removing all cause of strife among his sons after his death, by constituting Isaac his sole heir, and dismissing the rest with suitable gifts. This dismissal was, indeed, apparently harsh and cruel; but it was agreeable to the ap- pointment and decree of God, in order that the entire pos- session of the land might remain for the posterity of Isaac. For it was not lawful for Abraham to divide, at his own pleasure, that inheritance which had been granted entire to Isaac. Wherefore, no course was left to him but to provide for the rest of his sons in the manner here described. If any person should now select one of his sons as his heir, to the exclusion of the others, he would do them an injury; and, by applying the torch of injustice, in disinheriting a part of his children, he would light up the flame of perni- cious strifes in his family. Wherefore, we must note the special reason by which Abraham was not only induced, but compelled, to deprive his sons of the inheritance, and to re- move them to a distance; namely, lest by their intervention, the grant which had been divinely made to Isaac should, of necessity, be disturbed. We have elsewhere said that, among the Hebrews, she who is a partaker of the bed, but not of all the goods, is styled a concubine. The same distinction has been adopted into the customs, and sanctioned by the laws of all nations. So, we shall afterwards see, that Leah and Rachel were principal wives, but that Bilhah and Zil-

pah were in the second rank; so that their condition remained servile, although they were admitted to the conjugal
bed. Since Abraham had made Hagar and Keturah his
wives on this condition, it seems that he might lawfully
bestow on their sons, only a small portion of his goods; to
have transferred, however, from his only heir to them, equal
portions of his property, would have been neither just nor
right. It is probable that no subsequent strife or contention
took place respecting the succession; but by sending the sons
of the concubines far away, he provides against the danger
of which I have spoken, lest they should occupy a part of the
land which God had assigned to the posterity of Isaac alone.

7. *And these are the days.* Moses now brings us down to
the death of Abraham; and the first thing to be noticed
concerning his age is the number of years during which he
lived as a pilgrim; for he deserves the praise of wonderful
and incomparable patience, for having wandered through
the space of a hundred years, while God led him about in
various directions, contented, both in life and death, with
the bare promise of God. Let those be ashamed who find it
difficult to bear the disquietude of one, or of a few years,
since Abraham, the father of the faithful, was not merely
a stranger during a hundred years, but was also often cast
forth into exile. Meanwhile, however, Moses expressly shows
that the Lord had fulfilled his promise, "Thou shalt die in
a good old age:" for although he fought a hard and severe
battle, yet his consolation was neither light nor small; because he knew that, amidst so many sufferings, his life was
the object of Divine care. But if this sole looking unto God
sustained him through his whole life, amidst the most bois-
terous waves, amidst many bitter griefs, amidst tormenting
cares, and in short an accumulated mass of evils; let us also
learn—that we may not become weary in our course—to
rely on this support, that the Lord has promised us a happy
issue of life, and one truly far more glorious than that of
our father Abraham.

8. *Then Abraham gave up the ghost.*[1] They are mistaken

---

[1] "Et obiit Abraham." And Abraham died. The expression "gave up
the ghost" is not a literal rendering of the original.—*Ed.*

who suppose that this expression denotes sudden death, as
intimating that he had not been worn out by long disease,
but expired without pain. Moses rather means to say that
the father of the faithful was not exempt from the common
lot of men, in order that our minds may not languish when
the outward man is perishing ; but that, by meditating on
that renovation which is laid up as the object of our hope,
we may, with tranquil minds, suffer this frail tabernacle to be
dissolved. There is therefore no reason why a feeble, emaciat-
ed body, failing eyes, tremulous hands, and the lost use of all
our members, should so dishearten us, that we should not
hasten, after the example of our father, with joy and alacrity
to our death. But although Abraham had this in common
with the human race, that he grew old and died ; yet Moses,
shortly afterwards, puts a difference between him and the promiscuous multitude of men as to manner of dying ; namely,
that he should " die in a good old age, and satisfied with life."
Unbelievers, indeed, often seem to participate in the same
blessing ; yea, David complains that they excelled in this kind
of privilege ; and a similar complaint occurs in the book of Job,
namely, that they fill up their time happily, till in a moment
they descend into the grave.[1] But what I said before must
be remembered, that the chief part of a good old age consists in a good conscience and in a serene and tranquil mind.
Whence it follows, that what God promises to Abraham, can
only apply to those who truly cultivate righteousness : for
Plato says, with equal truth and wisdom, that a good hope
is the nutriment of old age ; and therefore old men who have
a guilty conscience are miserably tormented, and are inwardly
racked as by a perpetual torture. But to this we must add,
what Plato knew not, that it is godliness which causes a
good old age to attend us even to the grave, because faith is
the preserver of a tranquil mind. To the same point belongs
what is immediately added, " he was full of days," so that
he did not desire a prolongation of life. We see how many
are in bondage to the desire of life ; yea, nearly the whole

---

[1] See Psalm lxxiii. 4. " There are no bands in their death ; but their
strength is firm ;" and Job xxi. 13, " They spend their days in wealth,
and in a moment go down to the grave."—*Ed.*

world languishes between a weariness of the present life and an inexplicable desire for its continuance. That satiety of life, therefore, which shall cause us to be ready to leave it, is a singular favour from God.

And was gathered to his people. I gladly embrace the opinion of those who believe the state of our future life to be pointed out in this form of expression; provided we do not restrict it, as these expositors do, to the faithful only; but understand by it that mankind are associated together in *death* as well as in life.[1] It may seem absurd to profane men, for David to say, that the reprobate are gathered together like sheep into the grave; but if we examine the expression more closely, this gathering together will have no existence if their souls are annihilated.[2] The mention of Abraham's burial will presently follow. Now he is said to be gathered to his fathers, which would be inconsistent with fact if human life vanished, and men were reduced to annihilation: wherefore the Scripture, in speaking thus, shows that another state of life remains after death, so that a departure out of the world is not the destruction of the whole man.

9. *And his sons Isaac and Ishmael buried him.* Hence it appears, that although Ishmael had long ago been dismissed, he was not utterly alienated from his father, because he performed the office of a son in celebrating the obsequies of his deceased parent. Ishmael, rather than the other sons, did this, as being nearer.

12. *Now these are the generations of Ishmael.* This narration is not superfluous. In the commencement of the chapter, Moses alludes to what was done for the sons of Keturah. Here he speaks designedly more at large, for the purpose of showing that the promise of God, given in the seventeenth chapter, was confirmed by its manifest accom-

---

[1] Rivetus speaks in similar language on this clause. "This is never said concerning beasts when they die; and, therefore, from this form of speech, it is to be observed, that men by death are not reduced to nothing, nor does the whole of man die. . . . . The Scripture, in speaking thus, points out some other state; so that departure out of the world is not the destruction of the whole man."—*Exercitatio* cxiii. p. 553.

[2] See Psalm xlix.

plishment. In the first place, it was no common gift of God that Ishmael should have twelve sons who should possess rank and authority over as many tribes; but inasmuch as the event corresponded with the promise, we must chiefly consider the veracity of God, as well as the singular benevolence and honour which he manifested towards his servant Abraham, when, even in those benefits which were merely adventitious, he dealt so kindly and liberally with him; for that may rightly be regarded as adventitious which was superadded to the spiritual covenant: therefore Moses, after he has enumerated the towns in which the posterity of Ishmael was distributed, buries that whole race in oblivion, that substantial perpetuity may remain only in the Church, according to the declaration in Psalm cxxii. 28, "The sons of sons shall inhabit."[1] Further, Moses, as with his finger, shows the wonderful counsel of God, because, in assigning a region distinct from the land of Canaan to the sons of Ishmael, he has both provided for them in future, and kept the inheritance vacant for the sons of Isaac.

18. *He died in the presence of all his brethren.*[2] The major part of commentators understand this of his *death;* as if Moses had said that the life of Ishmael was shorter than that of his brethren, who long survived him: but because the word נָפַל (*naphal*) is applied to a *violent* death, and Moses testifies that Ishmael died a *natural* death, this exposition cannot be approved. The Chaldean Paraphrast supposes the word "*lot*" to be understood, and elicits this sense, that the *lot fell* to him, so as to assign him a habitation not far from his brethren. Although I do not greatly differ in this matter, I yet think that the words are not to be thus distorted.[3] The word נָפַל sometimes signifies to

---

[1] "Filii filiorum habitabunt." In the English it is, "The children of thy servants shall continue."—*Ed.*

[2] "Coram omnibus fratribus suis habitavit." He *dwelt* in the presence of all his brethren.

[3] This is the interpretation of Vatablus, favoured by Professor Bush, who says, "As Ishmael's death has already been mentioned, and as the term 'fall' is seldom used in the Scriptures in reference to 'dying,' except in cases of sudden and violent death, as when one 'falls' in battle, the probability is, that it here signifies that his territory or possessions 'fell' to him in the presence of his brethren, or immediately contiguous to their borders."—*Bush.*

lie down, or to rest, and also to dwell. The simple assertion therefore of Moses is, that a habitation was given to Ishmael opposite his brethren, so that he should indeed be a neighbour to them, and yet should have his distinct boundaries : [1] for I do not doubt that he referred to the oracle contained in the sixteenth chapter, where, among other things, the angel said to his mother Hagar, " He shall remain, or pitch his tents *in the presence of his brethren.*" Why does he rather speak thus of Ishmael than of the others, except for this reason, that whereas they migrated towards the eastern region, Ishmael, although the head of a nation, separated from the sons of Abraham, yet retained his dwelling in their neighbourhood? Meanwhile the intention of God is also to be observed, namely, that Ishmael, though living near his brethren, was yet placed apart in an abode of his own, that he might not become mingled with them, but might dwell in their presence, or opposite to them. Moreover, it is sufficiently obvious that the prediction is not to be restricted *personally* to Ishmael.

19. *These are the generations of Isaac.* Because what Moses has said concerning the Ishmaelites was incidental, he now returns to the principal subject of the history, for the purpose of describing the progress of the Church. And in the first place, he repeats that Isaac's wife was taken from Mesopotamia. He expressly calls her the sister of Laban the Syrian, who was hereafter to become the father-in-law of Jacob, and concerning whom he had many things to relate. But it is chiefly worthy of observation that he declares Rebekah to have been barren during the early years of her marriage. And we shall afterwards see that her barrenness continued, not for three or four, but for twenty years, in order that her very despair of offspring might give greater lustre to the sudden granting of the blessing. But nothing seems less accordant with reason, than that the propagation of the Church should be thus small and slow. Abraham, in his extreme old age, received (as it seems) a

---

[1] Calvin's interpretation, though opposed to the Vulgate and to our own version, is supported by the Septuagint, the Targum Onkelos, the Syriac, and the Arabic versions. See *Walton's Polyglott.—Ed.*

slender solace for his long privation of offspring, in having all his hope centred in one individual. Isaac also, already advanced in years, and bordering on old age, was not yet a father. Where, then, was the seed which should equal the stars of heaven in number? Who would not suppose that God was dealing deceitfully in leaving those houses empty and solitary, which, according to his own word, ought to be replenished with teeming population? But that which is recorded in the psalm must be accomplished in reference to the Church, that " he maketh her who had been barren to keep house, and to be a joyful mother of many children." (Psalm cxiii. 9.) For this small and contemptible origin, these slow and feeble advances, render more illustrious that increase, which afterwards follows, beyond all hope and expectation, to teach us that the Church was produced and increased by divine power and grace, and not by merely natural means. It is indeed possible, that God designed to correct or moderate any excess of attachment in Isaac. But this is to be observed as the chief reason for God's conduct, that as the holy seed was given from heaven, it must not be produced according to the common order of nature, to the end, that we learn that the Church did not originate in the industry of man, but flowed from the grace of God alone.

21. *And Isaac entreated the Lord for his wife.* Some translate the passage, " Isaac entreated the Lord *in the presence* of his wife ;" and understand this to have been done, that she also might add her prayers, and they might jointly supplicate God. But the version here given is more simple. Moreover, this resort to prayer testifies that Isaac knew that he was deprived of children, because God had not blessed him. He also knew that fruitfulness was a special gift of God. For although the favour of obtaining offspring was widely diffused over the whole human race, when God uttered the words " increase and multiply ;" yet to show that men are not born fortuitously, he distributes this power of production in various degrees. Isaac, therefore, acknowledges, that the blessing, which was not at man's disposal, must be sought for by prayer from God. It now truly appears, that he was endued with no ordinary constancy of

faith. Forasmuch as the covenant of God was known to
him, he earnestly (if ever any did) desired seed. It, therefore, had not now, for the first time, entered into his mind to
pray, seeing that for more than twenty years he had been
disappointed of his hope. Hence, although Moses, only in
a single word, says that he had obtained offspring by his
prayers to God ; yet reason dictates that these prayers had
continued through many years. The patience of the holy
man is herein conspicuous, that while he seems in vain to
pour forth his wishes into the air, he still does not remit the
ardour of his devotion. And as Isaac teaches us, by his example, to persevere in prayer ; so God also shows that he
never turns a deaf ear to the wishes of his faithful people,
although he may long defer the answer.

22. *And the children struggled together.* Here a new
temptation suddenly arises, namely, that the infants struggle
together in their mother's womb. This conflict occasions
the mother such grief that she wishes for death. And no
wonder ; for she thinks that it would be a hundred times
better for her to die, than that she have within her the horrible prodigy of twin-brothers, shut up in her womb, carrying
on intestine war. They, therefore, are mistaken, who attribute this complaint to female impatience, since it was not
so much extorted by pain or torture, as by abhorrence of the
prodigy. For she doubtless perceived that this conflict did
not arise from natural causes, but was a prodigy portending
some dreadful and tragic end. She also necessarily felt
some fear of the divine anger stealing over her : as it is
usual with the faithful not to confine their thoughts to the
evil immediately present with them, but to trace it to its
cause ; and hence they tremble through the apprehension of
divine judgment. But though in the beginning she was
more grievously disturbed than she ought to have been, and,
breaking out into murmurings, preserved neither moderation
nor temper ; yet she soon afterwards receives a remedy and
solace to her grief. We are thus taught by her example to
take care that we do not give excessive indulgence to sorrow
in affairs of perplexity, nor inflame our minds by inwardly
cherishing secret causes of distress. It is, indeed, difficult

to restrain the first emotions of our minds ; but before they become ungovernable, we must bridle them, and bring them into subjection. And chiefly we must pray to the Lord for moderation ; as Moses here relates that Rebekah went to ask counsel from the Lord ; because, indeed, she perceived that nothing would be more effectual in tranquillizing her mind, than to aim at obedience to the will of God, under the conviction that she was directed by him. For although the response given might be adverse, or, at least, not such as she would desire, she yet hoped for some alleviation from a gracious God, with which she might be satisfied. A question here arises respecting the way in which Rebekah asked counsel of God. It is the commonly received opinion that she inquired of some prophet what was the nature of this prodigy : and Moses seems to intimate that she had gone to some place to hear the oracle. But since that conjecture has no probability, I rather incline to a different interpretation ; namely, that she, having sought retirement, prayed more earnestly that she might receive a revelation from heaven. For, at that time, what prophets, except her husband and her father-in-law, could she have found in the world, still less in that neighbourhood ? Moreover, I perceive that God then commonly made known his will by oracles. Once more, if we consider the magnitude of the affair, it was more fitting that the secret should be revealed by the mouth of God, than manifested by the testimony of man. In our times a different method prevails. For God does not, at this day, reveal things future by such miracles ; and the teaching of the Law, the Prophets, and the Gospel, which comprises the perfection of wisdom, is abundantly sufficient for the regulation of our course of life.

23. *Two nations.* In the first place, God answers that the contention between the twin-brothers had reference to something far beyond their own persons ; for in this way he shows that there would be discord between their posterities. When he says, " there are two nations," the expression is emphatical ; for since they were brothers and twins, and therefore of one blood, the mother did not suppose that they would be so far disjoined as to become the heads of distinct

nations; yet God declares that dissension should take place between those who were by nature joined together. Secondly, he describes their different conditions, namely, that victory would belong to one of these nations, forasmuch as this was the cause of the contest, that they could not be equal, but one was chosen and the other rejected. For since the reprobate give way reluctantly, it follows of necessity that the children of God have to undergo many troubles and contests on account of their adoption. Thirdly, the Lord affirms that the order of nature being inverted, the younger, who was inferior, should be the victor.

We must now see what this victory implies. They who restrict it to earthly riches and wealth coldly trifle. Undoubtedly by this oracle Isaac and Rebekah were taught that the covenant of salvation would not be common to the two people, but would be reserved only for the posterity of Jacob. In the beginning, the promise was apparently general, as comprehending the whole seed : now, it is restricted to one part of the seed. This is the reason of the conflict, that God divides the seed of Jacob (of which the condition appeared to be one and the same) in such a manner that he adopts one part and rejects the other : that one part obtains the name and privilege of the Church, the rest are reckoned strangers ; with one part resides the blessing of which the other is deprived ; as it afterwards actually occurred : for we know that the Idumæans were cut off from the body of the Church ; but the covenant of grace was deposited in the family of Jacob. If we seek the cause of this distinction, it will not be found in nature ; for the origin of both nations was the same. It will not be found in merit ; because the heads of both nations were yet enclosed in their mother's womb when the contention began. Moreover God, in order to humble the pride of the flesh, determined to take away from men all occasion of confidence and of boasting. He might have brought forth Jacob first from the womb ; but he made the other the first-born, who, at length, was to become the inferior. Why does he thus, designedly, invert the order appointed by himself, except to teach us that, without regard to dignity, Jacob, who was to be the heir of the pro-

mised benediction, was gratuitously elected ? The sum of
the whole, then, is, that the preference which God gave to
Jacob over his brother Esau, by making him the father of
the Church, was not granted as a reward for his merits,
neither was obtained by his own industry, but proceeded
from the mere grace of God himself. But when an entire
people is the subject of discourse, reference is made not to
the secret election, which is confirmed to few, but the common adoption, which spreads as widely as the external
preaching of the word. Since this subject, thus briefly
stated, may be somewhat obscure, the readers may recall to
memory what I have said above in expounding the seventeenth chapter, namely, that God embraced, by the grace of
his adoption, all the sons of Abraham, because he made a
covenant with all ; and that it was not in vain that he appointed the promise of salvation to be offered promiscuously
to all, and to be attested by the sign of circumcision in their
flesh ; but that there was a special chosen seed from the
whole people, and these should at length be accounted the
legitimate sons of Abraham, who by the secret counsel of
God are ordained unto salvation. Faith, indeed, is that
which distinguishes the spiritual from the carnal seed ; but
the question now under consideration is the *principle* on
which the distinction is made, not the symbol or mark by
which it is attested. God, therefore, chose the whole seed
of Jacob without exception, as the Scripture in many places
testifies ; because he has conferred on all alike the same
testimonies of his grace, namely, in the word and sacraments.
But another and peculiar election has always flourished,
which comprehended a certain definite number of men, in
order that, in the common destruction, God might save
those whom he would.

A question is here suggested for our consideration. Whereas Moses here treats of the former kind of election,[1] Paul
turns his words to the latter.[2] For while he attempts to
prove, that not all who are Jews by natural descent are
heirs of life ; and not all who are descended from Jacob

[1] Namely, that which is general or national.—*Ed.*
[2] Namely, that which is particular or individual.—*Ed.*

according to the flesh are to be accounted true Israelites ; but
that God chooses whom he will, according to his own good
pleasure, he adduces this testimony, " the elder shall serve
the younger." (Rom. ix. 7, 8, 12.) They who endeavour to
extinguish the doctrine of gratuitous election, desire to persuade their readers that the words of Paul also are to be
understood only of external vocation ; but his whole discourse is manifestly repugnant to their interpretation ; and
they prove themselves to be not only infatuated, but impudent in their attempt to bring darkness or smoke over this
light which shines so clearly. They allege that the dignity
of Esau is transferred to his younger brother, lest he should
glory in the flesh ; inasmuch as a new promise is here given
to the latter. I confess there is some force in what they
say ; but I contend that they omit the principal point in the
case, by explaining the difference here stated, of the external vocation. But unless they intend to make the covenant
of God of none effect, they must concede that Esau and
Jacob were alike partakers of the external calling ; whence
it appears, that they to whom a common vocation had been
granted, were separated by the secret counsel of God. The
nature and object of Paul's argument is well known. For
when the Jews, inflated with the title of the Church, rejected the Gospel, the faith of the simple was shaken, by the
consideration that it was improbable that Christ, and the
salvation promised through him, could possibly be rejected
by an elect people, a holy nation, and the genuine sons of
God. Here, therefore, Paul contends that not all who descend from Jacob, according to the flesh, are true Israelites,
because God, of his own good pleasure, may choose whom he
will, as heirs of eternal salvation. Who does not see that
Paul descends from a general to a particular adoption, in
order to teach us, that not all who occupy a place in the
Church are to be accounted as true members of the Church ?
It is certain that he openly excludes from the rank of children those to whom (he elsewhere says) " pertaineth the adoption ;" whence it is assuredly gathered, that in proof of this
position, he adduces the testimony of Moses, who declares
that God chose certain from among the sons of Abraham to

himself, in whom he might render the grace of adoption firm and efficacious. How, therefore, shall we reconcile Paul with Moses? I answer, although the Lord separates the whole seed of Jacob from the race of Esau, it was done with a view to the Church, which was included in the posterity of Jacob. And, doubtless, the general election of the people had reference to this end, that God might have a Church separated from the rest of the world. What absurdity, then, is there in supposing that Paul applies to special election the words of Moses, by which it is predicted that the Church shall spring from the seed of Jacob? And an instance in point was exhibited in the condition of the heads themselves of these two nations. For Jacob was not only called by the external voice of the Lord, but, while his brother was passed by, he was chosen an heir of life. That good pleasure of God, which Moses commends in the person of Jacob alone, Paul properly extends further: and lest any one should suppose, that after the two nations had been rendered distinct by this oracle, the election should pertain indiscriminately to all the sons of Jacob, Paul brings, on the opposite side, another oracle, " I will have mercy on whom I will have mercy ;" where we see a certain number severed from the promiscuous race of Jacob's sons, in the salvation of whom the special election of God might triumph. Whence it appears that Paul wisely considered the counsel of God, which was, in truth, that he had transferred the honour of primogeniture from the elder to the younger, in order that he might choose to himself a Church, according to his own will, out of the seed of Jacob ; not on account of the merits of men, but as a matter of mere grace. And although God designed that the means by which the Church was to be collected should be common to the whole people, yet the end which Paul had in view is chiefly to be regarded ; namely, that there might always be a body of men in the world which should call upon God with a pure faith, and should be kept even to the end. Let it therefore remain as a settled point of doctrine, that among men some perish, some obtain salvation ; but the cause of this depends on the secret will of God. For whence does it arise that they who are born of

Abraham are not all possessed of the same privilege? The disparity of condition certainly cannot be ascribed either to the virtue of the one, or to the vice of the other, seeing they were not yet born. Since the common feeling of mankind rejects this doctrine, there have been found, in all ages, acute men, who have fiercely disputed against the election of God. It is not my present purpose to refute or to weaken their calumnies: let it suffice us to hold fast what we gather from Paul's interpretation; that whereas the whole human race deserves the same destruction, and is bound under the same sentence of condemnation, some are delivered by gratuitous mercy, others are justly left in their own destruction: and that those whom God has chosen are not preferred to others, because God foresaw they *would be* holy, but in order that they *might be* holy. But if the first origin of holiness is the election of God, we seek in vain for that difference in men, which rests solely in the will of God. If any one desires a mystical interpretation of the subject,[1] we may give the following:[2] whereas many hypocrites, who are for a time enclosed in the womb of the Church, pride themselves upon an empty title, and, with insolent boastings, exult over the true sons of God; internal conflicts will hence arise, which will grievously torment the mother herself.

24. *And when her days to be delivered were fulfilled.* Moses shows that the intestine strife in her womb continued to the time of bringing forth; for it was not by mere accident that Jacob seized his brother by the heel and attempted to get out before him. The Lord testified by this sign that the effect of his election does not immediately appear; but rather that the intervening path was strewed with troubles and conflicts. Therefore Esau's name was allotted to him on account of his asperity; which even from earliest infancy assumed a manly form; but the name Jacob signifies that this giant, vainly striving in his boasted strength, had still been vanquished.[3]

---

[1] Si quis anagogen desideret.

[2] Nous pourrons dire.—*French Tr.* The original has no corresponding expression; but one to the same effect is obviously understood.—*Ed.*

[3] The names of the two brothers was significant of their character. Esau is called Edom, which signifies *red*, because he was of sanguinary

27. *And the boys grew.* Moses now briefly describes the manners of them both. He does not, indeed, commend Jacob on account of those rare and excellent qualities, which are especially worthy of praise and of remembrance, but only says that he was *simple.* The word םת, *(tam,)* although generally taken for *upright* and *sincere,* is here put antithetically. After the sacred writer has stated that Esau was robust, and addicted to hunting, he places on the opposite side the mild disposition of Jacob, who loved the quiet of home so much, that he might seem to be indolent ; just as the Greeks call those persons οἰκόσιτους, who, dwelling at home, give no evidence of their industry. In short, the comparison implies that Moses praises Esau on account of his vigour, but speaks of Jacob as being addicted to domestic leisure ; and that he describes the disposition of the former as giving promise that he would be a courageous man, while the disposition of the latter had nothing worthy of commendation. Seeing that, by a decree of heaven, the honour of primogeniture would be transferred to Jacob, why did God suffer him to lie down in his tent, and to slumber among ashes; unless it be, that he sometimes intends his election to be concealed for a time, lest men should attribute something to their own preparatory acts ?

28. *And Isaac loved Esau.* That God might more clearly show his own election to be sufficiently firm, to need no assistance elsewhere, and even powerful enough to overcome any obstacle whatever, he permitted Esau to be so preferred to his brother, in the affection and good opinion of his father, that Jacob appeared in the light of a rejected person. Since, therefore, Moses clearly demonstrates, by so many circumstances, that the adoption of Jacob was founded on the sole good pleasure of God, it is an intolerable presumption to suppose it to depend upon the will of man ; or to ascribe it, in part, to means, (as they are called,) and to human preparations.[1] But how was it possible for the father, who was

temperament. He is said to have been hairy or shaggy, שער, from which word the mountainous country he inhabited was called *Seir.* The name Jacob, יעקב, means to supplant, or trip up the heels.— *Ed.*

[1] Cest une outrecuidance insupportable de la vouloir faire dependre de la volonté de l'homme, ou transporter une partie d'icelle aux moyens et preparatifs humain.—*French Tr.*

not ignorant of the oracle, to be thus pre-disposed in favour
of the first-born, whom he knew to be divinely rejected ?. It
would rather have been the part of piety and of modesty to
subdue his own private affection, that he might yield obedience to God.   The first-born prefers a natural claim to the
chief place in the parent's affection ; but the father was not
at liberty to exalt *him* above his brother, who had been
placed in subjection by the oracle of God.   That also is still
more shameful and more unworthy of the holy patriarch,
which Moses adds ; namely, that he had been induced to
give this preference to Esau, by the taste of his venison.
Was he so enslaved to the indulgence of the palate, that,
forgetting the oracle, he despised the grace of God in Jacob,
while he preposterously set his affection on him whom God
had rejected ?   Let the Jews now go and glory in the flesh ;
since Isaac, preferring food to the inheritance destined for
his son, would pervert (as far as he had the power) the gratuitous covenant of God !   For there is no room here for
excuse ; since with a blind, or, at least, a most inconsiderate
love to his first-born, he undervalued the younger.   It is uncertain whether the mother was chargeable with a fault of
the opposite kind.   For we commonly find the affections of
parents so divided, that if the wife sees any one of the sons
preferred by her husband, she inclines, by a contrary spirit
of emulation, more towards another.   Rebekah loved her
son Jacob more than Esau.   If, in so doing, she was obeying
the oracle, she acted rightly ; but it is possible that her love
was ill regulated.   And on this point the corruption of nature too much betrays itself.   There is no bond of mutual
concord more sacred than that of marriage : children form
still further links of connection ; and yet they often prove
the occasion of dissension.   But since we soon after see Rebekah chiefly in earnest respecting the blessing of God, the
conjecture is probable, that she had been induced, by divine
authority, to prefer the younger to the first-born.   Meanwhile, the foolish affection of the father only the more fully
illustrates the grace of the divine adoption.

29. *And Jacob sod pottage.*   This narration differs little
from the sport of children.   Jacob is cooking pottage ; his

brother returns from hunting weary and famishing, and barters his birthright for food.   What kind of bargain, I pray,
was this ?   Jacob ought of his own accord to have satisfied
the hunger of his brother.   When being asked, he refuses to
do so : who would not condemn him for his inhumanity ?
In compelling Esau to surrender his right of primogeniture,
he seems to make an illicit and frivolous compact.   God,
however, put the disposition of Esau to the proof in a matter of small moment ; and still farther, designed to present
an instance of Jacob's piety, or, (to speak more properly,) he
brought to light what lay hid in both.   Many indeed are
mistaken in suspending the cause of Jacob's election on the
fact, that God foresaw some worthiness in him ; and in
thinking that Esau was reprobated, because his future impiety had rendered him unworthy of the divine adoption
before he was born.   Paul, however, having declared election to be gratuitous, denies that the distinction is to be
looked for in the persons of men ; and, indeed, first assumes
it as an axiom, that since mankind is ruined from its origin,
and devoted to destruction, whosoever are saved are in no
other way freed from destruction than by the mere grace of
God.   And, therefore, that some are preferred to others, is
not on account of their own merits ; but seeing that all are
alike unworthy of grace, they are saved whom God, of his
own good pleasure, has chosen.   He then ascends still higher,
and reasons thus : " Since God is the Creator of the world,
he is, by his own right, in such a sense, the arbiter of life
and death, that he cannot be called to account ; but his own
will is (so to speak) the *cause of causes.*   And yet Paul does
not, by thus reasoning, impute tyranny to God, as the sophists triflingly allege in speaking of his absolute power.
But whereas He dwells in inaccessible light, and his judgments are deeper than the lowest abyss, Paul prudently
enjoins acquiescence in God's sole purpose; lest, if men seek
to be too inquisitive, this immense chaos should absorb all
their senses.   It is therefore foolishly inferred by some, from
this place, that whereas God chose one of the two brothers,
and passed by the other, the merits of both had been foreseen.   For it was necessary that God should have decreed

that Jacob should differ from Esau, otherwise he would not have been unlike his brother. And we must always remember the doctrine of Paul, that no one excels another by means of his own industry or virtue, but by the grace of God alone. Although, however, both the brothers were by nature equal, yet Moses represents to us, in the person of Esau, as in a mirror, what kind of men all the reprobate are, who, being left to their own disposition, are not governed by the Spirit of God. While, in the person of Jacob, he shows that the grace of adoption is not idle in the elect, because the Lord effectually attests it by his vocation. Whence then does it arise that Esau sets his birthright to sale, but from this cause, that he, being deprived of the Spirit of God, relishes only the things of the earth? And whence does it happen that his brother Jacob, denying himself his own food, patiently endures hunger, except that under the guidance of the Holy Spirit, he raises himself above the world and aspires to a heavenly life? Hence, let us learn, that they to whom God does not vouchsafe the grace of his Spirit, are carnal and brutal; and are so addicted to this fading life, that they think not of the spiritual kingdom of God; but they whom God has undertaken to govern, are not so far entangled in the snares of the flesh as to prevent them from being intent upon their high vocation. Whence it follows, that all the reprobate remain immersed in the corruptions of the flesh; but that the elect are renewed by the Holy Spirit, that they may be the workmanship of God, created unto good works. If any one should raise the objection, that part of the blame may be ascribed to God, because he does not correct the stupor and the depraved desires inherent in the reprobate, the solution is ready, that God is exonerated by the testimony of their own conscience, which compels them to condemn themselves. Wherefore, nothing remains but that all flesh should keep silence before God, and that the whole world, confessing itself to be obnoxious to his judgment, should rather be humbled than proudly contend.

30. *Feed me, I pray thee, with that same red pottage.*[1]

---

[1] Literally the passage would run, " Feed me, I pray thee, with that *red*, that red," the word pottage being understood. " The repetition of

Although Esau declares in these words that he by no means desires delicacies, but is content with food of any kind, (seeing that he contemptuously designates the pottage from its colour only, without regard to its taste,) we may yet lawfully conjecture that the affair was viewed in a serious light by his parents; for his own name had not been given him on account of any ludicrous matter.   In desiring and asking food he commits nothing worthy of reprehension; but when he says, " Behold I am at the point to die, and what profit shall this birthright do to me?" he betrays a profane desire entirely addicted to the earth and to the flesh.   It is not, indeed, to be doubted that he spake sincerely, when he declared that he was impelled by a sense of the approach of death.   For they are under a misapprehension who understand him to use the words, " Behold I die," as if he meant merely to say, that his life would not be long, because, by hunting daily among wild beasts, his life was in constant danger.   Therefore, in order to escape immediate death, he exchanges his birthright for food; notwithstanding, he grievously sins in so doing, because he regards his birthright as of no value, unless it may be made profitable in the present life.   For, hence it happens, that he barters a spiritual for an earthly and fading good.   On this account the Apostle calls him a " profane person," (Heb. xii. 16,) as one who settles in the present life, and will not aspire higher.   But it would have been his true wisdom rather to undergo a thousand deaths than to renounce his birthright; which, so far from being confined within the narrow limits of one age alone, was capable of transmitting the perpetuity of a heavenly life to his posterity also.[1]   Now, let each of us look well to himself; for since the disposition of us all is earthly,

the epithet, and the omission of the substantive, indicated the extreme haste and eagerness of the asker.   His eye was caught by the colour of the dish; and being faint with hunger and fatigue, he gave way to the solicitations of appetite, regardless of consequences."—*Bush.*

[1] It is to be remembered that the birthright included not merely earthly advantages, but those also which were spiritual.   Till the tribe of Levi was accepted by God, in lieu of all the first-born of Israel, the eldest son was the *priest* of the family as well as its natural head.   And this was probably the part of the birthright which Esau treated with peculiar contempt, and for which the Apostle Paul styles him a " profane person."—*Ed.*

if we follow nature as our leader, we shall easily renounce
the celestial inheritance. Therefore, we should frequently
recall to mind the Apostle's exhortation, " Let us not be
profane persons as Esau was."

33. *And Jacob said, Swear to me.* Jacob did not act
cruelly towards his brother, for he took nothing from him,
but only desired a confirmation of that right which had been
divinely granted to him ; and he does this with a pious intention, that he may hereby the more fully establish the
certainty of his own election. Meanwhile the infatuation
of Esau is to be observed, who, in the name and presence of
God, does not hesitate to set his birthright to sale. Although
he had before rushed inconsiderately upon the food under
the maddening impulse of hunger; now, at least, when an
oath is exacted from him, some sense of religion should have
stolen over him to correct his brutal cupidity. But he is
so addicted to gluttony that he makes God himself a witness
of his ingratitude.

34. *Then Jacob gave.* Although, at first sight, this statement seems to be cold and superfluous, it is nevertheless of
great weight. For, in the first place, Moses commends the
piety of holy Jacob, who in aspiring to a heavenly life, was
able to bridle the appetite for food. Certainly he was not a
log of wood; in preparing the food for the satisfying of his
hunger, he would the more sharpen his appetite. Wherefore he must of necessity do violence to himself in order to
bear his hunger. But he would never have been able in this
manner to subdue his flesh, unless a spiritual desire of a
better life had flourished within him. On the other side, the
remarkable indifference of his brother Esau is emphatically
described in few words, " he did eat and drink, and rose up
and went his way." For what reason are these four things
stated ? Truly, that we may know what is declared immediately after, that he accounted the incomparable benefit of
which he was deprived as nothing. The complaint of the
Lacedemonian captive is celebrated by the historians. The
army, which had long sustained a siege, surrendered to the
enemy for want of water. After they had drunk out of the
river, O comrades, (he exclaimed,) for what a little pleasure

have we lost an incomparable good! He, miserable man, having quenched his thirst, returned to his senses, and mourned over his lost liberty. But Esau having satisfied his appetite, did not consider that he had sacrificed a blessing far more valuable than a hundred lives, to purchase a repast which would be ended in half an hour. Thus are all profane persons accustomed to act: alienated from the celestial life, they do not perceive that they have lost anything, till God thunders upon them out of heaven. As long as they enjoy their carnal wishes, they cast the anger of God behind them; and hence it happens that they go stupidly forward to their own destruction. Wherefore let us learn, if, at any time, we, being deceived by the allurements of the world, swerve from the right way, quickly to rouse ourselves from our slumber.

CHAPTER XXVI.

1. AND there was a famine in the land, besides the first famine that was in the days of Abraham. And Isaac went unto Abimelech king of the Philistines unto Gerar.

2. And the Lord appeared unto him, and said, Go not down into Egypt; dwell in the land which I shall tell thee of.

3. Sojourn in this land, and I will be with thee, and will bless thee: for unto thee, and unto thy seed, I will give all these countries; and I will perform the oath which I sware unto Abraham thy father:

4. And I will make thy seed to multiply as the stars of heaven, and will give unto thy seed all these countries: and in thy seed shall all the nations of the earth be blessed;

5. Because that Abraham obeyed my voice, and kept my charge, my commandments, my statutes, and my laws.

6. And Isaac dwelt in Gerar.

7. And the men of the place asked *him* of his wife; and he said, She *is* my sister: for he feared to say, *She is* my wife; lest, *said he*, the men of

1. Deinde fuit fames in terra præter famem superiorem, quæ fuerat in diebus Abraham: et profectus est Ishac ad Abimelech regem Pelisthim in Gerar.

2. Nam visus est ei Iehova, et dixit, Ne descendas in Ægyptum: habita in terra quam dicam tibi.

3. Inhabita terram hanc, et ero tecum, et benedicam tibi: quia tibi et semini tuo dabo omnes terras istas: et statuam juramentum quod juravi ad Abraham patrem tuum.

4. Et multiplicare faciam semen tuum sicut stellas cœli, et dabo semini tuo omnes terras istas: benedicenturque in semine tuo omnes gentes terræ:

5. Eo quod obedierit Abraham voci meæ, et custodierit custodiam meam, præcepta mea, statuta mea, et leges meas.

6. Et habitavit Ishac in Gerar.

7. Et interrogaverunt incolæ regionis de uxore ejus; et dixit, Soror mea est: quia timuit dicere, uxor mea est: ne forte occiderent me in-

the place should kill me for Rebekah; because she *was* fair to look
upon.

8. And it came to pass, when he
had been there a long time, that
Abimelech king of the Philistines
looked out at a window, and saw,
and, behold, Isaac *was* sporting with
Rebekah his wife.

9. And Abimelech called Isaac,
and said, Behold, of a surety she *is*
thy wife ; and how saidst thou, She
is my sister ?   And Isaac said unto
him, Because I said, Lest I die for
her.

10. And Abimelech said, What *is*
this thou hast done unto us ? one of
the people might lightly have lien
with thy wife, and thou shouldest
have brought guiltiness upon us.

11. And Abimelech charged all
his people, saying, He that toucheth
this man, or his wife, shall surely be
put to death.

12. Then Isaac sowed in that
land, and received in the same year
an hundred-fold; and the Lord
blessed him.

13. And the man waxed great,
and went forward, and grew, until
he became very great:

14. For he had possession of flocks,
and possession of herds, and great
store of servants : and the Philistines envied him.

15. For all the wells which his
father's servants had digged in the
days of Abraham his father, the
Philistines had stopped them, and
filled them with earth.

16. And Abimelech said unto
Isaac, Go from us; for thou art
much mightier than we.

17. And Isaac departed thence,
and pitched his tent in the valley of
Gerar, and dwelt there.

18. And Isaac digged again the
wells of water which they had digged
in the days of Abraham his father;
for the Philistines had stopped them
after the death of Abraham : and he
called their names after the names
by which his father had called them.

19. And Isaac's servants digged

colæ regionis propter Ribcam, quia
pulchra aspectu erat.

8. Verum fuit, quum protracti
essent ei ibi dies, aspexit Abimelech
rex Pelisthim per fenestram, et vidit,
et ecce Ishac ludebat cum Ribca
uxore sua.

9. Tunc vocavit Abimelech Ishac,
et dixit, Vere ecce uxor tua est; et
quomodo dixisti, Soror mea est?
Et dixit ad eum Ishac, Quia dixi,
Ne forte moriar propter eam.

10. Et dixit Abimelech, Quid hoc
fecisti nobis? paulum abfuit quin
dormierit unus e populo cum uxore
tua, et venire fecisses super nos delictum.

11. Præcepit itaque Abimelech
omni populo, dicendo, Qui tetigerit
virum hunc, et uxorem ejus, moriendo morietur.

12. Et sevit Ishac in terra ipsa,
et reperit in anno ipso centum mo-
dios : et benedixit ei Iehova.

13. Et crevit vir, et perrexit per-
gendo et crescendo, donec cresceret
valde.

14. Et fuit ei possessio pecudum,
et possessio boum, et proventus mul-
tus : et inviderunt ei Pelisthim.

15. Itaque omnes puteos, quos
foderant servi patris sui in diebus
Abraham patris sui, obturaverunt
Pelisthim, et impleverunt eos terra.

16. Et dixit Abimelech ad Ishac,
Abi a nobis : quia longe fortior es
nobis.

17. Abiit ergo inde Ishac, et mansit in valle Gerar, et habitavit ibi.

18. Postquam reversus est Ishac,
fodit puteos aquæ, quos foderant in
diebus Abraham patris sui : quia
obturaverant eos Pelisthim mortuo
Abraham : et vocavit eos nominibus
secundum nomina, quibus vocaverat
eos pater suus.

19. Et foderunt servi Ishac in

in the valley, and found there a well of springing water.

20. And the herdmen of Gerar did strive with Isaac's herdmen, saying, The water *is* ours: and he called the name of the well Esek; because they strove with him.

21. And they digged another well, and strove for that also: and he called the name of it Sitnah.

22. And he removed from thence, and digged another well; and for that they strove not: and he called the name of it Rehoboth; and he said, For now the Lord hath made room for us, and we shall be fruitful in the land.

23. And he went up from thence to Beer-sheba.

24. And the Lord appeared unto him the same night, and said, I *am* the God of Abraham thy father: fear not, for I *am* with thee, and will bless thee, and multiply thy seed, for my servant Abraham's sake.

25. And he builded an altar there, and called upon the name of the Lord, and pitched his tent there: and there Isaac's servants digged a well.

26. Then Abimelech went to him from Gerar, and Ahuzzath one of his friends, and Phichol the chief captain of his army.

27. And Isaac said unto them, Wherefore come ye to me, seeing ye hate me, and have sent me away from you?

28. And they said, We saw certainly that the Lord was with thee: and we said, Let there be now an oath betwixt us, *even* betwixt us and thee, and let us make a covenant with thee;

29. That thou wilt do us no hurt, as we have not touched thee, and as we have done unto thee nothing but good, and have sent thee away in peace: thou *art* now the blessed of the Lord.

30. And he made them a feast, and they did eat and drink.

31. And they rose up betimes in the morning, and sware one to another: and Isaac sent them away, and they departed from him in peace.

valle, et invenerunt ibi puteum aquæ vivæ.

20. Sed litigaverunt pastores Gerar cum pastoribus Ishac, dicendo, Nostra est aqua: et vocavit nomen putei Hesech, quia litigaverunt cum eo.

21. Et foderunt puteum alium, et litigaverunt etiam super eo: et vocavit nomen ejus Sitnah.

22. Et transtulit se inde, et fodit puteum alium, et non litigaverunt super eo: ideo vocavit nomen ejus Rehoboth: et dixit, Quia nunc dilatationem fecit Iehova nobis, et crevimus in terra.

23. Et ascendit inde in Beersebah.

24. Et visus est ei Iehova nocte ipsa, et dixit, Ego sum Deus Abraham patris tui: ne timeas, quia tecum sum, et benedicam tibi, et multiplicare faciam semen tuum propter Abraham servum meum.

25. Tunc ædificavit ibi altare, et invocavit nomen Iehovæ, et tetendit ibi tabernaculum suum: et foderunt ibi servi Ishac puteum.

26. Porro Abimelech profectus est ad eum ex Gerar, et Ahuzath *qui erat* ex amicis ejus, et Phichol princeps exercitus ejus.

27. Et dixit ad eos Ishac, Cur venistis ad me, et vos odio habuistis me, et emisistis me ne essem vobiscum?

28. Et dixerunt, Videndo vidimus quod esset Iehova tecum, et diximus, Sit nunc juramentum inter nos, inter nos et inter te, et percutiamus fœdus tecum.

29. Si feceris nobiscum malum: quemadmodum non tetigimus te, et quemadmodum fecimus tecum duntaxat bonum, et dimisimus te in pace: tu nunc es benedictus Iehovæ.

30. Instruxit autem eis convivium, et ederunt, atque biberunt.

31. Et surrexerunt mane: et juraverunt alter alteri: et deduxit eos Ishac, et abierunt ab eo in pace.

32. And it came to pass the same day, that Isaac's servants came, and told him concerning the well which they had digged, and said unto him, We have found water.

33. And he called it Shebah: therefore the name of the city is Beer-sheba unto this day.

34. And Esau was forty years old when he took to wife Judith the daughter of Beeri the Hittite, and Bashemath the daughter of Elon the Hittite;

35. Which were a grief of mind unto Isaac and to Rebekah.

32. Adhæc fuit, in die ipsa venerunt servi Ishac, et nuntiaverunt ei de puteo quem foderant, et dixerunt ei, Invenimus aquam.

33. Et vocavit eum Sibhah: idcirco nomen urbis est Beer-sebah usque ad diem hanc.

34. Erat autem Esau quadragenarius, et accepit uxorem Iehudith filiam Beeri Hittæi, et Bosmath filiam Elon Hittæi.

35. Et irritabant spiritum Ishac et Ribcæ.

1. *And there was a famine.* Moses relates that Isaac was tried by nearly the same kind of temptation as that through which his father Abraham had twice passed. I have before explained how severe and violent was this assault. The condition in which it was the will of God to place his servants, as strangers and pilgrims in the land which he had promised to give them, seemed sufficiently troublesome and hard ; but it appears still more intolerable, that he scarcely suffered them to exist (if we may so speak) in this wandering, uncertain, and changeable kind of life, but almost consumed them with hunger. Who would not say that God had forgotten himself, when he did not even supply his own children,—whom he had received into his especial care and trust,—however sparingly and scantily, with food ? But God thus tried the holy fathers, that we might be taught, by their example, not to be effeminate and cowardly under temptations. Respecting the terms here used, we may observe, that though there were two seasons of dearth in the time of Abraham, Moses alludes only to the one, of which the remembrance was most recent.[1]

2. *And the Lord appeared unto him.* I do not doubt but a reason is here given why Isaac rather went to the country of Gerar than to Egypt, which perhaps would have been

[1] Abimelech, king of the Philistines, mentioned in this verse, was not he who is spoken of in Gen. xxi., but perhaps his descendant. "It is probable the name was common to the kings of Gerar, as Pharaoh was to the kings of Egypt. The meaning of the word אבימלך is, *My father the king.* Kings ought to be the fathers of their country."—*Menochius in Poli Syn.*

more convenient for him ; but Moses teaches that he was
withheld by a heavenly oracle, so that a free choice was not
left him. It may here be asked, why does the Lord prohibit
Isaac from going to Egypt, whither he had suffered his father
to go ?   Although Moses does not give the reason, yet we
may be allowed to conjecture that the journey would have
been more dangerous to the son. The Lord could indeed
have endued the son also with the power of his Spirit, as he
had done his father Abraham, so that the abundance and
delicacies of Egypt should not have corrupted him by their
allurements ; but since he governs his faithful people with
such moderation, that he does not correct all their faults at
once, and render them entirely pure, he assists their infir-
mities, and anticipates, with suitable remedies, those evils by
which they might be ensnared.   Because, therefore, he knew
that there was more infirmity in Isaac than there had been
in Abraham, he was unwilling to expose him to danger ;
for he is faithful, and will not suffer his own people to be
tempted beyond what they are able to bear.   (1 Cor. x. 13.)
Now, as we must be persuaded, that however arduous and
burdensome may be the temptations which alight upon us,
the Divine help will never fail to renew our strength ; so, on
the other hand, we must beware lest we rashly rush into
dangers ; but each should be admonished by his own infirmity to proceed cautiously and with fear.

Dwell in the land. God commands him to settle in the
promised land, yet with the understanding that he should
dwell there as a stranger. The intimation was thus given,
that the time had not yet arrived in which he should exercise dominion over it. God sustains indeed his mind with
the hope of the promised inheritance, but requires this honour
to be given to his word, that Isaac should remain inwardly
at rest, in the midst of outward agitations ; and truly we
never lean upon a better support than when, disregarding
the appearance of things present, we depend entirely upon
the word of the Lord, and apprehend by faith that blessing
which is not yet apparent. Moreover, he again inculcates
the promise previously made, in order to render Isaac more
prompt to obey ; for so is the Lord wont to awaken his ser-

vants from their indolence, that they may fight valiantly for
him, while he constantly affirms that their labour shall not
be in vain ; for although he requires from us a free and un-
reserved obedience, as a father does from his children, he
yet so condescends to the weakness of our capacity, that he
invites and encourages us by the prospect of reward.

5. *Because that Abraham obeyed my voice.* Moses does
not mean that Abraham's obedience was the reason why the
promise of God was confirmed and ratified to him ; but from
what has been said before, (chap. xxii. 18,) where we have a
similar expression, we learn, that what God freely bestows
upon the faithful is sometimes, beyond their desert, ascribed
to themselves; that they, knowing their intention to be approved by the Lord, may the more ardently addict and devote themselves entirely to his service : so he now commends
the obedience of Abraham, in order that Isaac may be stimulated to an imitation of his example. And although laws,
statutes, rites, precepts, and ceremonies, had not yet been
written, Moses used these terms, that he might the more
clearly show how sedulously Abraham regulated his life according to the will of God alone—how carefully he abstained
from all the impurities of the heathen—and how exactly he
pursued the straight course of holiness, without turning aside
to the right hand or to the left : for the Lord often honours
his own law with these titles for the sake of restraining our
excesses ; as if he should say that it wanted nothing to constitute it a perfect rule, but embraced everything pertaining
to absolute holiness. The meaning therefore is, that Abraham, having formed his life in entire accordance with the
will of God, walked in his pure service.

7. *And the men of the place asked him.* Moses relates
that Isaac was tempted in the same manner as his father
Abraham, in having his wife taken from him ; and without
doubt he was so led by the example of his father, that he,
being instructed by the similarity of the circumstances,
might become associated with him in his faith. Nevertheless, on this point he ought rather to have avoided
than imitated his father's fault ; for no doubt he well
remembered that the chastity of his mother had twice been

put in great danger; and although she had been wonderfully rescued by the hand of God, yet both she and her husband paid the penalty of their distrust: therefore the negligence of Isaac is inexcusable, in that he now strikes against the same stone. He does not in express terms deny his wife; but he is to be blamed, first, because, for the sake of preserving his life, he resorts to an evasion not far removed from a lie; and secondly, because, in absolving his wife from conjugal fidelity, he exposes her to prostitution: but he aggravates his fault, principally (as I have said) in not taking warning from domestic examples, but voluntarily casting his wife into manifest danger. Whence it appears how great is the propensity of our nature to distrust, and how easy it is to be devoid of wisdom in affairs of perplexity. Since, therefore, we are surrounded on all sides with so many dangers, we must ask the Lord to confirm us by his Spirit, lest our minds should faint, and be dissolved in fear and trembling; otherwise we shall be frequently engaged in vain enterprises, of which we shall repent soon, and yet too late to remedy the evil.

8. *Abimelech, king of the Philistines, looked out at a window.* Truly admirable is the kind forbearance of God, in not only condescending to pardon the twofold fault of his servant, but in stretching forth his hand, and in wonderfully averting, by the application of a speedy remedy, the evil which he would have brought upon himself. God did not suffer— what twice had occurred to Abraham—that his wife should be torn from his bosom; but stirred up a heathen king, mildly, and without occasioning him any trouble, to correct his folly. But although God sets before us such an example of his kindness, that the faithful, if at any time they may have fallen, may confidently hope to find him gentle and propitious; yet we must beware of self-security, when we observe, that the holy woman who was, at that time, the only mother of the Church on earth, was exempted from dishonour, by a special privilege. Meanwhile, we may conjecture, from the judgment of Abimelech, how holy and pure had been the conduct of Isaac, on whom not even a suspicion of evil could fall; and further, how much greater integrity

flourished in that age than in our own. For why does he
not condemn Isaac as one guilty of fornication, since it was
probable that some crime was concealed, when he disingenu-
ously obtruded the name of sister, and tacitly denied her to
be his wife? and therefore I have no doubt that his religion,
and the integrity of his life, availed to defend his character.
By this example we are taught so to cultivate righteousness
in our whole life, that men may not be able to suspect anything wicked or dishonourable respecting us; for there is
nothing which will more completely vindicate us from every
mark of infamy than a life passed in modesty and temperance. We must, however, add, what I have also before
alluded to, that lusts were not, at that time, so commonly
and so profusely indulged, as to cause an unfavourable suspicion to enter into the mind of the king concerning a
sojourner of honest character. Wherefore, he easily persuades himself that Rebekah was a wife and not a harlot.
The chastity of that age is further proved from this, that
Abimelech takes the familiar sporting of Isaac with Rebekah
as an evidence of their marriage.[1] But now licentiousness
has so broken through all bounds, that husbands are compelled to hear in silence of the dissolute conduct of their
wives with strangers.

10. *What is this thou hast done unto us?* The Lord does
not chastise Isaac as he deserved, perhaps because he was
not so fully endued with patience as his father was; and,
therefore, lest the seizing of his wife should dishearten him,
God mercifully prevents it. Yet, that the censure may produce the deeper shame, God constitutes a heathen his master
and his reprover. We may add, that Abimelech chides his
folly, not so much with the design of injuring him, as of up-
braiding him. It ought, however, deeply to have wounded
the mind of the holy man, when he perceived that his offence
was obnoxious to the judgment even of the blind. Wherefore, let us remember that we must walk in the light which
God has kindled for us, lest even unbelievers, who are

---

[1] The following passage is here omitted in the translation :—" Non enim
de coitu loquitur Moses, sed de aliquo liberiore gestu, qui vel dissolutæ
lasciviæ, vel conjugalis amoris testis esset."

wrapped in the darkness of ignorance, should reprove our stupor. And certainly when we neglect to obey the voice of God, we deserve to be sent to oxen and asses for instruction.[1] Abimelech, truly, does not investigate nor prosecute the whole offence of Isaac, but only alludes to one part of it. Yet Isaac, when thus gently admonished by a single word, ought to have condemned himself, seeing that, instead of committing himself and his wife to God, who had promised to be the guardian of them both, he had resorted, through his own unbelief, to an illicit remedy. For faith has this property, that it confines us within divinely prescribed bounds, so that we attempt nothing except with God's authority or permission. Whence it follows that Isaac's faith wavered when he swerved from his duty as a husband. We gather, besides, from the words of Abimelech, that all nations have the sentiment impressed upon their minds, that the violation of holy wedlock is a crime worthy of divine vengeance, and have consequently a dread of the judgment of God. For although the minds of men are darkened with dense clouds, so that they are frequently deceived; yet God has caused some power of discrimination between right and wrong to remain, so that each should bear about with him his own condemnation, and that all should be without excuse. If, then, God cites even unbelievers to his tribunal, and does not suffer them to escape just condemnation, how horrible is that punishment which awaits us, if we endeavour to obliterate, by our own wickedness, that knowledge which God has engraven on our consciences?

11. *And Abimelech charged all his people.* In denouncing capital punishment against any who should do injury to this stranger, we may suppose him to have issued this edict as a special privilege ; for it is not customary thus rigidly to avenge every kind of injury. Whence, then, arose this disposition on the part of the king to prefer Isaac to all the native inhabitants of the country, and almost to treat him as an equal, except that some portion of the divine majesty

---

[1] The allusion is obviously to Isaiah i. 3 : " The ox knoweth his owner, and the ass his master's crib ; but Israel doth not know, my people doth not consider."—*Ed.*

shone forth in him, which secured to him this degree of
reverence? God, also, to assist the infirmity of his servant,
inclined the mind of the heathen king, in every way, to
show him favour. And there is no doubt that his general
modesty induced the king thus carefully to protect him ;
for he, perceiving him to be a timid man, who had been on
the point of purchasing his own life by the ruin of his wife,
was the more disposed to assist him in his dangers, in
order that he might live in security under his own government.

12. *Then Isaac sowed.* Here Moses proceeds to relate in
what manner Isaac reaped the manifest fruit of the blessing
promised to him by God ; for he says, that when he had
sowed, the increase was a hundredfold : which was an extraordinary fertility, even in that land. He also adds, that he
was rich in cattle, and had a very great household. Moreover, he ascribes the praise of all these things to the blessing
of God ; as it is also declared in the psalm, that the Lord
abundantly supplies what will satisfy his people while they
sleep. (Ps. cxxvii. 2.) It may, however, be asked, how
could Isaac sow when God had commanded him to be a
stranger all his life ? Some suppose that he had bought a
field, and so translate the word קנה *(kanah)* a possession ;
but the context corrects their error: for we find soon afterwards, that the holy man was not delayed, by having land to
sell, from removing his effects elsewhere : besides, since
the purchasing of land was contrary to his peculiar vocation
and to the command of God, Moses undoubtedly would not
have passed over such a notable offence. To this may be
added, that since express mention is immediately made of a
tent, we may hence infer, that wherever he might come, he
would have to dwell in the precarious condition of a stranger.
We must, therefore, maintain, that he sowed in a hired field.
For although he had not a foot of land in his own possession,
yet, that he might discharge the duty of a good householder,
it behoved him to prepare food for his family ; and perhaps
hunger quickened his care and industry, that he might with
the greater diligence make provision for himself against the
future. Nevertheless, it is right to keep in mind, what I

have lately alluded to, that he received as a divine favour
the abundance which he had acquired by his own labour.

14. *And the Philistines envied him.* We are taught by
this history that the blessings of God which pertain to
the present earthly life are never pure and perfect, but
are mixed with some troubles, lest quiet and indulgence
should render us negligent. Wherefore, let us all learn
not too ardently to desire great wealth. If the rich are
harassed by any cause of disquietude, let them know that
they are roused by the Lord, lest they should fall fast
asleep in the midst of their pleasures; and let the poor
enjoy this consolation, that their poverty is not without its
advantages. For it is no light good to live free from envy,
tumults, and strifes. Should any one raise the objection,
that it can by no means be regarded as a favour, that God,
in causing Isaac to abound in wealth, exposed him to envy,
to contentions, and to many troubles; there is a ready
answer, that not all the troubles with which God exercises
his people, in any degree prevent the benefits which he bestows upon them from retaining the taste of his paternal
love. Finally, he so attempers the favour which he manifests towards his children in this world, that he stirs them
up, as with sharp goads, to the consideration of a celestial
life. It was not, however, a slight trial, that the simple
element of water, which is the common property of all
animals, was denied to the holy patriarch; with how much
greater patience ought we to bear our less grievous sufferings! If, however, at any time we are angry at being unworthily injured; let us remember that, at least, we are not
so cruelly treated as holy Isaac was, when he had to contend
for water. Besides, not only was he deprived of the element
of water, but the wells which his father Abraham had dug
for himself and his posterity were filled up. This, therefore,
was the extreme of cruelty, not only to defraud a stranger
of every service due to him, but even to take from him what
had been obtained by the labour of his own father, and what
he possessed without inconvenience to any one.

16. *And Abimelech said unto Isaac.* It is uncertain
whether the king of Gerar expelled Isaac of his own accord

from his kingdom, or whether he commanded him to settle elsewhere, because he perceived him to be envied by the people. He possibly might, in this manner, advise him as a friend; although it is more probable that his mind had become alienated from Isaac; for at the close of the chapter Moses relates, that the holy man complains strongly of the king as well as of others. But since we can assert nothing with certainty respecting the real feelings of the king, let it suffice to maintain, what is of more importance, that in consequence of the common wickedness of mankind, they who are the most eminent fall under the suspicion of the common people. Satiety, indeed, produces ferocity. Wherefore there is nothing to which the rich are more prone than proudly to boast, to carry themselves more insolently than they ought, and to stretch every nerve of their power to oppress others. No such suspicion, indeed, could fall upon Isaac; but he had to bear that envy which was the attendant on a common vice. Whence we infer, how much more useful and desirable it often is, for us to be placed in a moderate condition; which is, at least, more peaceful, and which is neither exposed to the storms of envy, nor obnoxious to unjust suspicions. Moreover, how rare and unwonted was the blessing of God in rendering Isaac prosperous, may be inferred from the fact, that his wealth had become formidable both to the king and to the people. A large inheritance truly had descended to him from his father; but Moses shows, that from his first entrance into the land, he had so greatly prospered in a very short time, that it seemed no longer possible for the inhabitants to endure him.

18. *And Isaac digged again the wells of water.* First, we see that the holy man was so hated by his neighbours, as to be under the necessity of seeking a retreat for himself which was destitute of water; and no habitation is so troublesome and inconvenient for the ordinary purposes of life as that which suffers from scarcity of water. Besides, the abundance of his cattle and the multitude of his servants—who were like a little army—rendered a supply of water very necessary; whence we learn that he was brought into severe straits. But that this last necessity did not instigate him to seek

revenge, is a proof of singular forbearance; for we know that
lighter injuries will often rack the patience even of humane
and moderate men.   If any one should object to this view,
that he was deficient in strength; I grant, indeed, that
he was not able to undertake a regular war; but as his
father Abraham had armed four hundred servants, he also
certainly had a large troop of domestics, who could easily
have repelled any force brought against him by his neighbours.   But the hope which he had entertained when he
settled in the valley of Gerar, was again suddenly cut off.
He knew that his father Abraham had there used wells
which were his own, and which he had himself discovered;
and although they had been stopped up, yet they were
well known to have sufficient springs of water to prevent
the labour of digging them again from being mispent.   Moreover, the fact that the wells had been obstructed ever
since the departure of Abraham, shows how little respect
the inhabitants had for their guest; for although their own
country would have been benefited by these wells, they chose
rather to deprive themselves of this advantage than to have
Abraham for a neighbour; for, in order that such a convenience might not attract him to the place, they, by stopping
up the wells, did, in a certain sense, intercept his way.   It
was a custom among the ancients, if they wished to involve
any one in ruin, and to cut him off from the society of men,
to interdict him from water, and from fire : thus the Philistines, for the purpose of removing Abraham from their vicinity, deprive him of the element of water.

He called their names.   He did not give new names to
the wells, but restored those which had been assigned them
by his father Abraham, that, by this memorial, the ancient
possession of them might be renewed.   But subsequent violence compelled him to change their names, that at least he
might, by some monument, make manifest the injury which
had been done by the Philistines, and reprove them on account of it : for whereas he calls one well *strife*, or *contention*, another *hostility*, he denies that the inhabitants possessed that by right, or by any honest title, which they had
seized upon as enemies or robbers.   Meanwhile, it is right to

consider, that in the midst of these strifes he had a contest not less severe with thirst and deficiency of water, whereby the Philistines attempted to destroy him ; such is the scope of the history. First, Moses, according to his manner, briefly runs through the summary of the affair : namely, that Isaac intended to apply again to his own purpose the wells which his father had previously found, and to acquire, in the way of recovery, the lost possession of them. He then prosecutes the subject more diffusely, stating that, when he attempted the work, he was unjustly defrauded of his labour ; and whereas, in digging the third well, he gives thanks to God, and calls it *Room*,[1] because, by the favour of God, a more copious supply is now afforded him, he furnishes an example of invincible patience. Therefore, however severely he may have been harassed, yet when, after he had been freed from these troubles, he so placidly returns thanks to God, and celebrates his goodness, he shows that in the midst of trials he has retained a composed and tranquil mind.

23. *And he went up from thence to Beer-sheba.* Next follows a more abundant consolation, and one affording effectual refreshment to the mind of the holy man. In the tranquil enjoyment of the well, he acknowledges the favour which God had showed him : but forasmuch as one word of God weighs more with the faithful than the accumulated mass of all good things, we cannot doubt that Isaac received this oracle more joyfully than if a thousand rivers of nectar had flowed unto him : and truly Moses designedly commemorates in lofty terms this act of favour, that the Lord encouraged him by his own word, (verse 24 ;) whence we may learn, in ascribing proper honour to each of the other gifts of God, still always to give the palm to that proof of his paternal love which he grants us in his word. Food, clothing, health, peace, and other advantages, afford us a taste of the Divine goodness ; but when he addresses us familiarly, and expressly declares himself to be our Father, then indeed it is that he thoroughly refreshes us to satiety. Moses does not explain

---

[1] Latitudines, a literal Latin translation of the Hebrew word רהבת, (*Rehoboth,*) a plural form, expressing the notion of abundant enlargement and room.— *Ed.*

what had been the cause of Isaac's removal to Beer-sheba,
the ancient dwelling-place of his fathers. It might be that
the Philistines ceased not occasionally to annoy him ; and
thus the holy man, worn out with their implacable malice,
removed to a greater distance. It is indeed probable, taking
the circumstance of the time into account, that he was sorrowful and anxious ; for as soon as he had arrived at that
place, God appeared unto him on the very first night. Here,
then, something very opportune is noticed. Moreover, as
often as Moses before related that God had appeared unto
Abraham, he, at the same time, showed that the holy man
was either tormented with grievous cares, or was held in
suspense under some apprehension, or was plunged in sadness, or, after many distresses, was nearly borne down by
fatigue, so as to render it apparent that the hand of God
was seasonably stretched out to him as his necessity required,
lest he should sink under the evils which surrounded him.
So now, as I explain it, he came to Isaac, for the purpose of
restoring him, already wearied and broken down by various
miseries.

24. *And the Lord appeared unto him.* This vision (as I
have elsewhere said) was to prepare him to listen more attentively to God, and to convince him that it was God with
whom he had to deal; for a voice *alone* would have had less
energy. Therefore God *appears,* in order to produce confidence in and reverence towards his word. In short, visions
were a kind of symbols of ·the Divine presence, designed to
remove all doubt from the minds of the holy fathers respecting him who was about to speak. Should it be objected,
that such evidence was not sufficiently sure, since Satan
often deceives men by similar manifestations, being, as it
were, the ape of God ;—we must keep in mind what has been
said before, that a clear and unambiguous mark was engraven
on the visions of God, by which the faithful might certainly
distinguish them from those which were fallacious, so that
their faith should not be kept in suspense : and certainly,
since Satan can only delude us in the dark, God exempts his
children from this danger, by illuminating their eyes with
the brightness of his countenance. Yet God did not fully

manifest his glory to the holy fathers, but assumed a form by means of which they might apprehend him according to the measure of their capacities ; for, as the majesty of God is infinite, it cannot be comprehended by the human mind, and by its magnitude it absorbs the whole world. Besides, it follows of necessity that men, on account of their infirmity, must not only faint, but be altogether annihilated in the presence of God. Wherefore, Moses does not mean that God was seen in his true nature and greatness, but in such a manner as Isaac was able to bear the sight. But what we have said, namely, that the vision was a testimony of Deity, for the purpose of giving credibility to the oracle, will more fully appear from the context ; for this appearance was not a mute spectre ; but the word immediately followed, which confirmed, in the mind of Isaac, faith in gratuitous adoption and salvation.

I am the God of Abraham. This preface is intended to renew the memory of all the promises before given, and to direct the mind of Isaac to the perpetual covenant which had been made with Abraham, and which was to be transmitted, as by tradition, to his posterity. The Lord therefore begins by declaring himself to be the God who had spoken at the first to Abraham, in order that Isaac might not sever the present from the former oracles : for as often as he repeated the testimony of his grace to the faithful, he sustained their faith with fresh supports. Yet he would have that very faith to remain based upon the first covenant by which he had adopted them to himself : and we must always keep this method in mind, in order that we may learn to gather together the promises of God, as they are combined in an inseparable bond. Let this also ever occur to us, as a first principle, that God thus kindly promises us his grace because he has freely adopted us.

Fear not. Since these words are elsewhere expounded, I shall now be the more brief. In the first place, we must observe, that God thus addresses the faithful for the purpose of tranquillizing their minds ; for, if his word be withdrawn, they necessarily become torpid through stupidity, or are tormented with disquietude. Whence it follows, that we can

receive peace from no other source than from the mouth of
the Lord, when he declares himself the author of our salvation ; not that we are then free from all fear, but because the
confidence of faith is sufficiently efficacious to assuage our
perturbations.   Afterwards the Lord gives proofs of his love,
by its effect, when he promises that he will bless Isaac.

   25. *And he builded an altar there.*   From other passages
we are well aware that Moses here speaks of public worship ;
for inward invocation of God neither requires an altar, nor
has any special choice of place ; and it is certain that the
saints, wherever they lived, worshipped.   But because religion ought to maintain a testimony before men, Isaac, having erected and consecrated an altar, professes himself a
worshipper of the true and only God, and by this method
separates himself from the polluted rites of heathens.   He
also built the altar, not for himself alone, but for his whole
family ; that there, with all his household, he might offer
sacrifices.   Moreover, since the altar was built for the external exercises of faith, the expression, he called upon God,
implies as much as if Moses had said that Isaac celebrated
the name of God, and gave testimony of his own faith.   The
visible worship of God had also another use ; namely, that
men, according to their infirmity, may stimulate and exercise
themselves in the fear of God.   Besides, since we know that
sacrifices were then commanded, we must observe that Isaac
did not rashly trifle in worshipping God, but adhered to the
rule of faith, that he might undertake nothing without the
word of God.   Whence also we infer how preposterous and
erroneous a thing it is to imitate the fathers, unless the Lord
join us with them by means of a similar command.   Meanwhile, the words of Moses clearly signify, that whatever exercises of piety the faithful undertake are to be directed to
this end, namely, that God may be worshipped and invoked.
To this point, therefore, all rites and ceremonies ought to
have reference.   But although it was the custom of the holy
fathers to build an altar in whatever place they pitched their
tent, we yet gather, from the connexion of the words, that
after God appeared to his servant Isaac, this altar was built
by him in token of his gratitude.

And there Isaac's servants digged a well. It is remarkable that whereas this place had already received its name
from the well which had been dug in it, Isaac should there
again have to seek water, especially since Abraham had purchased, for himself and his posterity, the right to the well
from the king. Moreover, the digging itself was difficult
and laborious; for Moses had a design in saying, that afterwards the servants came and said to him, "We have found
water." I have, therefore, no doubt, that throughout the whole
of that region a conspiracy had been entered into by the inhabitants, for the purpose of expelling the holy man, through
want of water; so that this well of Sheba also had been fraudulently stopped up. The context also shows, that the first
care of the holy patriarch concerned the worship of God, because Moses relates that an altar was erected, before he speaks
of the well. Now it is of importance to observe with what
great troubles these holy fathers continually had to contend;
which they never would have been able to overcome or to
endure, unless they had been far removed from our delicate
course of living. For how severely should we feel the loss
of water, seeing that we often rage against God if we have
not abundance of wine? Therefore, by such examples, let
the faithful learn to accustom themselves to patient endurance : and if at any time food and other necessaries of life
fail them, let them turn their eyes to Isaac, who wandered,
parched with thirst, in the inheritance which had been
divinely promised him.[1]

26. *Then Abimelech went to him.* We have had an exactly
similar narrative in the twenty-first chapter and the twenty-
second verse. The Lord, therefore, followed Isaac with the
same favour which he had before shown to his father Abraham. For it was no common blessing, that Abimelech
should voluntarily seek his friendship. Besides, he would be
relieved from no little care and anxiety, when his neighbours, who had harassed him in so many ways, being now
themselves afraid of him, desire to secure his friendship.

---

[1] Qui siticulosus in hæreditate sibi divinitus promissa erravit.   Qui est
errant en l'heritage qui Dieu lui avoit promis, et tarrissant de soif.—
Fr. Tr.

Therefore the Lord both confers signal honour upon his servant, and provides at the same time for his tranquillity. There is not the least doubt that the king was led to this measure, by a secret divine impulse. For, if he was afraid, why did he not resort to some other remedy? why did he humble himself to supplicate a private man? why, at least, did he not rather send for him, or command him with authority to do what he wished?   But God had so forcibly impressed his mind, that he, forgetting his regal pride, sought for peace and alliance with a man who was neither covetous, nor warlike, nor furnished with a great army. Thus we may learn, that the minds of men are in the hand of God, so that he not only can incline those to gentleness who before were swelling with fury, but can humble them by terror, as often as he pleases.

27. *And Isaac said unto them, Wherefore come ye to me?* Isaac not only expostulates concerning injuries received, but protests that in future he can have no confidence in them, since he had found in them a disposition so hostile to himself. This passage teaches us, that it is lawful for the faithful to complain of their enemies, in order, if possible, to recall them from their purpose of doing injury, and to restrain their force, frauds, and acts of injustice. For liberty is not inconsistent with patience : nor does God require of his own people, that they should silently digest every injury which may be inflicted upon them, but only that they should restrain their minds and hands from revenge.[1] Now, if their minds are pure and well regulated, their tongues will not be virulent in reproaching the faults of others; but their sole purpose will be to restrain the wicked by a sense of shame from iniquity. For where there is no hope of profiting by complaints, it is better to cherish peace by silence ; unless, perhaps, for the purpose of rendering those who delight themselves in wickedness inexcusable.   We must, indeed, always beware, lest, from a desire of vengeance, our tongues

[1] Neque hoc à suis requirit Deus, ut quicquid noxæ illatum fuerit, taciti devorent; sed tantum ut animos et manus contineant à vindicta.

Dieu ne requiert point des siens, qu'ils avallent sans mot dire toutes les nuisances qu'on leur fera, mais seulement qu'ils gardent leurs cœurs et leur mains de vengence.—*Fr. Tr.*

break out in reproaches ; and, as Solomon says, " hatred stirreth up strifes." (Prov. x. 12.)

28. *We saw certainly that the Lord was with thee.* By this argument they prove that they desired a compact with Isaac, not insidiously, but in good faith, because they acknowledge the favour of God towards him. For it was necessary to purge themselves from this suspicion, seeing that they now presented themselves so courteously to one against whom they had before been unreasonably opposed. This confession of theirs, however, contains very useful instruction. Profane men in calling one, whose affairs all succeed well and prosperously, the blessed of the Lord, bear testimony that God is the author of all good things, and that from him alone flows all prosperity. Exceedingly base, therefore, is our ingratitude, if, when God acts kindly towards us, we pass by his benefits with closed eyes. Again, profane men regard the friendship of one whom God favours, as desirable for themselves ; considering that there is no better or holier commendation than the love of God. Perversely blind, therefore, are they, who not only neglect those whom God declares to be dear unto him, but also iniquitously vex them. The Lord proclaims himself ready to execute vengeance on any one who may injure those whom he takes under his protection ; but the greater part, unmoved by this most terrible denunciation, still wickedly afflict the good and the simple. We here, however, see that the sense of nature dictated to unbelievers, what we scarcely credit when spoken by the mouth of God himself. Still it is surprising that they should be afraid of an inoffensive man ; and should require from him an oath that he would do them no injury. They ought to have concluded, from the favour which God had showed him, that he was a just man, and therefore there could be no danger from him ; yet because they form their estimate of him from their own disposition and conduct, they also distrust his probity. Such perturbation commonly agitates unbelievers, so that they are inconsistent with themselves; or at least waver and are tossed between conflicting sentiments, and have nothing fixed and equable. For those principles of right judgment, which

spring up in their breasts, are soon smothered by depraved
affections.   Hence it happens, that what is justly conceived
by them vanishes ; or is at least corrupted, and does not
bring forth good fruit.

29. *As we have not touched thee.*   An accusing conscience
urges them to desire to hold him closely bound unto them ;
and therefore they require an oath from him that he will not
hurt them.   For they knew that he might rightfully avenge
himself on them for the sufferings he had endured : but they
dissemble on this point, and even make a wonderful boast
of their own acts of kindness.   At first, indeed, the humanity
of the king was remarkable, for he not only entertained
Isaac with hospitality, but treated him with peculiar honour ;
yet he by no means continued to act thus to the end.   It
accords, however, with the common custom of men, to disguise their own faults by whatever artifice or colour they
can invent.   But if we have committed any offence, it rather
becomes us ingenuously to confess our fault, than by denying
it, to wound still more deeply the minds of those whom we
have injured.   Nevertheless Isaac, since he had already sufficiently pierced their consciences, does not press them any
further.   For strangers are not to be treated by us as domestics ; but if they do not receive profit, they are to be left to
the judgment of God.   Therefore, although Isaac does not
extort from them a just confession ; yet, that he may not be
thought inwardly to cherish any hostility towards them, he
does not refuse to strike a covenant with them.   Thus we
learn from his example, that if any have estranged themselves from us, they are not to be repelled when they again
offer themselves to us.   For if we are commanded to follow
after peace, even when it seems to fly from us, it behoves us
far less to be repulsive, when our enemies voluntarily seek
reconciliation ; especially if there be any hope of amendment
in future, although true repentance may not yet appear.
And he receives them to a feast, not only for the sake of
promoting peace, but also for the sake of showing that he,
having laid aside all offence, has become their friend.

Thou art now the blessed of the Lord.   This is commonly
explained to mean that they court his favour by flatteries,

just as persons are accustomed to flatter when they ask a
favour; but I rather think this expression to have been added
in a different sense. Isaac had complained of their injuries
in having expelled him through envy: they answer, that there
was no reason why any particle of grief should remain in his
mind, since the Lord had treated him so kindly and so exactly
according to his own wish; as if they had said, What dost thou
want? Art thou not content with thy present success? Let
us grant that we have not discharged the duty of hospitality
towards thee; yet the blessing of God abundantly suffices to
obliterate the memory of that time. Perhaps, however, by
these words, they again assert that they are acting towards
him with good faith, because he is under the guardianship
of God.

31. *And sware one to another.* Isaac does not hesitate to
swear; partly, that the Philistines may be the more easily
appeased; partly, that he may not be suspected by them.
And this is the legitimate method of swearing, when men
mutually bind themselves to the cultivation of peace. A
simple promise, indeed, ought to have sufficed; but since
dissimulation or inconstancy causes men to be distrustful of
each other, the Lord grants them the use of his name, that
this more holy confirmation may be added to our covenants;
and he does not only permit, he even commands us to swear
as often as necessity requires it. (Deut. vi. 13.) Meanwhile we must beware, lest his name be profaned by rashly
swearing.

32. *And it came to pass the same day.* Hence it appears,
(as I have said a little before,) that the waters were not found
in a moment of time. If it be asked, whence a supply of
water had been obtained for his cattle and his household
during the intervening days, I doubt not, indeed, that he
either bought it, or was compelled to go to a distance to see
if any one would be found from whom he might obtain it by
entreaty. With respect to the name, [Sheba,] they are mistaken, in my judgment, who deem it to be any other than
that which Abraham had first given to the well. For since
the Hebrew word is ambiguous, Abraham alluded to the
covenant which he had struck with the king of Gerar; but

now Isaac recalling this ancient memorial to mind, joins with it the covenant in which he had himself engaged.

34. *And Esau was forty years old.* For many reasons Moses relates the marriages of Esau. Inasmuch as he mingled himself with the inhabitants of the land, from whom the holy race of Abraham was separated,˙ and contracted affinities by which he became entangled; this was a kind of prelude of his rejection. It happened also, by the wonderful counsel of God, that these daughters-in-law were grievous and troublesome to the holy patriarch (Isaac) and his wife, in order that they might not by degrees become favourable to that reprobate people. If the manners of the people had been pleasing, and they had had good and obedient daughters, perhaps also, with their consent, Isaac might have taken a wife from among them. But it was not lawful for those to be bound together in marriage, whom God designed to be perpetual enemies. For how would the inheritance of the land be secured to the posterity of Abraham, but by the destruction of those among whom he sojourned for a time? Therefore God cuts off all inducements to these inauspicious marriages, that the disunion which he had established might remain. It appears hence, with what perpetual affection Esau was loved by Isaac; for although the holy man justly regarded his son's wives with aversion, and his mind was exasperated against them, he never failed to act with the greatest kindness towards his son, as we shall afterwards see. We have elsewhere spoken concerning polygamy. This corruption had so far prevailed in every direction among many people, that the custom, though vicious, had acquired the force of law. It is not, therefore, surprising that a man addicted to the flesh indulged his appetite by taking two wives.

CHAPTER XXVII.

1. AND it came to pass, that when Isaac was old, and his eyes were dim, so that he could not see, he called Esau his eldest son, and said

1. Fuit autem quum senuisset Ishac, et caligassent oculi ejus ita ut non videret, vocavit Esau filium suum majorem, et dixit ad eum,

unto him, My son. And he said
unto him, Behold, *here am* I.

2. And he said, Behold now, I am
old, I know not the day of my death.

3. Now therefore take, I pray
thee, thy weapons, thy quiver and
thy bow, and go out to the field,
and take me *some* venison;

4. And make me savoury meat,
such as I love, and bring *it* to me,
that I may eat; that my soul may
bless thee before I die.

5. And Rebekah heard when Isaac
spake to Esau his son. And Esau
went to the field to hunt *for* venison,
and to bring *it.*

6. And Rebekah spake unto Jacob
her son, saying, Behold, I heard thy
father speak unto Esau thy brother,
saying,

7. Bring me venison, and make me
savoury meat, that I may eat, and
bless thee before the Lord before
my death.

8. Now therefore, my son, obey
my voice, according to that which I
command thee.

9. Go now to the flock, and fetch
me from thence two good kids of the
goats; and I will make them savoury meat for thy father, such as
he loveth.

10. And thou shalt bring *it* to thy
father, that he may eat, and that he
may bless thee before his death.

11. And Jacob said to Rebekah
his mother, Behold, Esau my brother
is a hairy man, and I *am* a smooth
man:

12. My father peradventure will
feel me, and I shall seem to him as
a deceiver; and I shall bring a curse
upon me, and not a blessing.

13. And his mother said unto him,
Upon me *be* thy curse, my son; only
obey my voice, and go fetch me
them.

14. And he went, and fetched, and
brought *them* to his mother: and his
mother made savoury meat, such as
his father loved.

15. And Rebekah took goodly
raiment of her eldest son Esau,
which *were* with her in the house,

Fili mi.   Et dixit ad eum, Ecce
adsum.

2. Et dixit, Ecce nunc senui :
non novi diem quo moriar.

3. Nunc igitur cape quæso instru-
menta tua, pharetram tuam, et arcum tuum, et egredere in agrum, et
venare mihi venationem.

4. Et fac mihi cibos sapidos, quemadmodum diligo, et affer mihi, et
comedam : ut benedicat tibi anima
mea antequam moriar.

5. Ribca autem audiebat, dum
loqueretur Ishac ad Esau filium
suum : et perrexit Esau in agrum,
ut venaretur venationem, ut afferret.

6. Tunc Ribca dixit ad Iahacob
filium suum, dicendo, Ecce, audivi
patrem tuum loquentem ad Esau
fratrem tuum, dicendo,

7. Affer mihi venationem, et fac
mihi cibos, et comedam, et benedicam tibi coram Domino antequam
moriar.

8. Nunc igitur, fili mi, obedi voci
meæ in eo quod præcipio tibi.

9. Vade nunc ad pecudes, et cape
mihi inde duos hœdos caprarum
bonos, et faciam ex eis escas sapidas
patri tuo, quemadmodum diligit.

10. Et afferes patri tuo, et comedet, ut benedicat tibi antequam
moriatur.

11. Et dixit Iahacob ad Ribcam
matrem suam, Ecce Esau frater
meus est vir pilosus, et ego vir lævis :

12. Si forte palpaverit me pater
meus, ero in oculis ejus tanquam
illusor : et venire faciam super me
maledictionem et non benedictionem.

13. Tunc dixit ei mater ejus,
Super me *sit* maledictio tua, fili mi :
veruntamen obedi voci meæ et vade,
cape mihi.

14. Profectus est itaque, et accepit, et attulit matri suæ, et fecit
mater ejus cibos sapidos, quemadmodum diligebat pater ejus.

15. Et accepit Ribca vestes Esau
filii sui majoris delectabiles, quæ
erant apud se in domo, et induit

and put them upon Jacob her younger son.

16. And she put the skins of the kids of the goats upon his hands, and upon the smooth of his neck.

17. And she gave the savoury meat and the bread, which she had prepared, into the hand of her son Jacob.

18. And he came unto his father, and said, My father. And he said, Here *am* I; who *art* thou, my son?

19. And Jacob said unto his father, I *am* Esau thy first-born; I have done according as thou badest me: arise, I pray thee, sit and eat of my venison, that thy soul may bless me.

20. And Isaac said unto his son, How *is it* that thou hast found *it* so quickly, my son? And he said, Because the Lord thy God brought *it* to me.

21. And Isaac said unto Jacob, Come near, I pray thee, that I may feel thee, my son, whether thou *be* my very son Esau or not.

22. And Jacob went near unto Isaac his father; and he felt him, and said, The voice *is* Jacob's voice, but the hands *are* the hands of Esau.

23. And he discerned him not, because his hands were hairy, as his brother Esau's hands. So he blessed him.

24. And he said, *Art* thou my very son Esau? And he said, I *am*.

25. And he said, Bring *it* near to me, and I will eat of my son's venison, that my soul may bless thee. And he brought *it* near to him, and he did eat: and he brought him wine, and he drank.

26. And his father Isaac said unto him, Come near now, and kiss me, my son.

27. And he came near, and kissed him: and he smelled the smell of his raiment, and blessed him, and said, See, the smell of my son *is* as the smell of a field which the Lord hath blessed:

28. Therefore God give thee of the dew of heaven, and the fatness

Iahacob filium suum minorem.

16. Et pelles hœdorum caprarum circumdedit manibus ejus, et lævitati colli ejus.

17. Deditque cibos sapidos et panem, quos paraverat, in manu Iahacob filii sui.

18. Venit ergo ad patrem suum, et dixit, Pater mi. Ille autem respondit, Ecce adsum: qui es, fili mi?

19. Et dixit Iahacob ad patrem suum, Ego sum Esau primogenitus tuus, feci quemadmodum loquutus es ad me: surge nunc, sede, et comede de venatione mea, ut benedicat mihi anima tua.

20. Et dixit Ishac ad filium suum, Quid hoc *quod* festinasti ad inveniendum, fili mi? Cui respondit, Quia occurrere fecit Iehova Deus tuus coram me.

21. Tunc dixit Ishac ad Iacob, Appropinqua nunc, et palpabo te, fili mi, utrum sis ipse filius meus Esau, an non.

22. Et appropinquavit Iahacob Ishac patri suo: qui palpavit eum, et dixit, Vox vox Iahacob est: at manus, manus Esau.

23. Et non agnovit eum: quia erant manus ejus sicut manus Esau fratris sui pilosæ: et benedixit ei:

24. Et dixit, Tu es ipse filius meus Esau? Respondit, Sum.

25. Tunc dixit, Admove mihi, et comedam de venatione filii mei, ut benedicat tibi anima mea. Et admovit ei, et comedit: attulitque ei vinum, et bibit.

26. Et dixit ad eum Ishac pater ejus, Appropinqua nunc, et osculare me, fili mi.

27. Et appropinquavit, et osculatus est eum: et odoratus est odorem vestimentorum ejus: et benedixit ei, et dixit, Vide, odorem filii mei sicut odorem agri, cui benedixit Iehova.

28. Et det tibi Deus de rore cœli, et *de* pinguedinibus terræ, et

of the earth, and plenty of corn and wine:

29. Let people serve thee, and nations bow down to thee: be lord over thy brethren, and let thy mother's sons bow down to thee: cursed *be* every one that curseth thee, and blessed *be* he that blesseth thee.

30. And it came to pass, as soon as Isaac had made an end of blessing Jacob, and Jacob was yet scarce gone out from the presence of Isaac his father, that Esau his brother came in from his hunting.

31. And he also had made savoury meat, and brought it unto his father, and said unto his father, Let my father arise, and eat of his son's venison, that thy soul may bless me.

32. And Isaac his father said unto him, Who *art* thou? And he said, I *am* thy son, thy first-born, Esau.

33. And Isaac trembled very exceedingly, and said, Who? where *is* he that hath taken venison, and brought *it* me, and I have eaten of all before thou camest, and have blessed him? yea, *and* he shall be blessed.

34. And when Esau heard the words of his father, he cried with a great and exceeding bitter cry, and said unto his father, Bless me, *even* me also, O my father!

35. And he said, Thy brother came with subtilty, and hath taken away thy blessing.

36. And he said, Is not he rightly named Jacob? for he hath supplanted me these two times: he took away my birthright; and, behold, now he hath taken away my blessing. And he said, Hast thou not reserved a blessing for me?

37. And Isaac answered and said unto Esau, Behold, I have made him thy lord, and all his brethren have I given to him for servants; and with corn and wine have I sustained him: and what shall I do now unto thee, my son?

38. And Esau said unto his father, Hast thou but one blessing, my

multitudinem frumenti et musti novi.

29. Serviant tibi populi, et incurvent se tibi populi: esto dominus fratribus tuis, et incurvent se tibi filii matris tuæ: maledicentes tibi, maledicti erunt, et benedicentes tibi, benedicti.

30. Et fuit, quando complevit Ishac benedicere Iahacob: fuit, inquam, tantum egrediendo egressus erat Iahacob a facie Ishac patris sui, tunc Esau frater ejus venit a venatione sua.

31. Et fecit etiam ipse cibos sapidos, et attulit patri suo: dixitque patri suo, Surgat pater meus, et comedat de venatione filii sui, ut benedicat mihi anima tua.

32. Et dixit ei Ishac pater ejus, Quis es? Ille respondit, Ego sum filius tuus, primogenitus tuus Esau.

33. Et expavit Ishac pavore magno vehementissime, et dixit, Quis *est*, et ubi est qui venatus est venationem, et attulit mihi, et comedi ex omnibus antequam venires? et benedixi ei, etiam benedictus erit.

34. Quum audisset Esau verba patris sui, clamavit clamore magno, et amaro valde, dixitque patri suo, Benedic mihi: etiam ego *filius tuus sum*, pater mi.

35. Et dixit, Venit frater tuus dolose et accepit benedictionem tuam.

36. Dixit ergo, Vere vocatum est nomen ejus Iahacob, quia supplantavit me jam duabus vicibus: primogenituram meam accepit, et ecce nunc accepit benedictionem meam. Et dixit, Annon reservasti mihi *apud te* benedictionem?

37. Et respondit Ishac, et dixit ad Esau, Ecce, dominum posui eum tibi, et omnes fratres ejus dedi ei in servos, frumentumque et vinum addixi ei: et tibi nunc quid faciam, fili mi?

38. Tunc dixit Esau ad patrem suum, Numquid benedictio una est

father? bless me, *even* me also, O my father! And Esau lifted up his voice, and wept.

39. And Isaac his father answered and said unto him, Behold, thy dwelling shall be the fatness of the earth, and of the dew of heaven from above;

40. And by thy sword shalt thou live, and shalt serve thy brother: and it shall come to pass, when thou shalt have the dominion, that thou shalt break his yoke from off thy neck.

41. And Esau hated Jacob, because of the blessing wherewith his father blessed him: and Esau said in his heart, The days of mourning for my father are at hand; then will I slay my brother Jacob.

42. And these words of Esau her elder son were told to Rebekah. And she sent and called Jacob her younger son, and said unto him, Behold, thy brother Esau, as touching thee, doth comfort himself, *purposing* to kill thee.

43. Now therefore, my son, obey my voice; and arise, flee thou to Laban my brother, to Haran;

44. And tarry with him a few days, until thy brother's fury turn away;

45. Until thy brother's anger turn away from thee, and he forget *that* which thou hast done to him: then I will send and fetch thee from thence: why should I be deprived also of you both in one day?

46. And Rebekah said to Isaac, I am weary of my life because of the daughters of Heth: if Jacob take a wife of the daughters of Heth, such as these *which are* of the daughters of the land, what good shall my life do me?

tibi, pater mi? benedic mihi, et etiam ego *filius tuus*, pater mi: et elevavit Esau vocem suam et flevit.

39. Tunc respondit Ishac pater ejus, et dixit ad eum, Ecce, de pinguedinibus terræ erit habitatio tua et de rore cœli desuper.

40. Et in gladio tuo vives, et fratri tuo servies: et erit, quando dominaberis, franges jugum ejus a collo tuo.

41. Itaque odio habuit Esau Iahacob propter benedictionem, qua benedixerat ei pater ejus: et cogitavit Esau in corde suo, Appropinquabunt dies luctus patris mei, et occidam Iahacob fratrem meum.

42. Et nuntiata sunt Ribcæ verba Esau filii sui majoris: et misit, et vocavit Iahacob filium suum minorem, et dixit ad eum, Ecce, Esau frater tuus consolatur se super te, ut occidat te.

43. Et nunc fili mi, obedi voci meæ, et surge, et fuge ad Laban fratrem meum in Charan.

44. Et habita cum eo dies aliquot, donec avertatur furor fratris tui a te.

45. Donec avertatur ira fratris tui a te, et obliviscatur eorum quæ fecisti ei: et mittam, et accipiam te inde: utquid orbabor etiam ambobus vobis die una?

46. Et dixit Ribca ad Ishac, Angustiis affecta sum in vita mea propter filias Heth: si acceperit Iahacob uxorem de filiabus Heth, sicut istas de filiabus terræ, utquid est mihi vita?

1. *And it came to pass that when Isaac was old.* In this chapter Moses prosecutes, in many words, a history which does not appear to be of great utility. It amounts to this; Esau having gone out, at his father's command, to hunt; Jacob, in his brother's clothing, was, by the artifice of his mother, induced to obtain by stealth the blessing due by the right of nature to the first-born. It seems even like child's

play to present to his father a kid instead of venison, to feign himself to be hairy by putting on skins, and, under the name of his brother, to get the blessing by a lie. But in order to learn that Moses does not in vain pause over this narrative as a most serious matter, we must first observe, that when Jacob received the blessing from his father, this token confirmed to him the oracle by which the Lord had preferred him to his brother. For the benediction here spoken of was not a mere prayer but a legitimate sanction, divinely interposed, to make manifest the grace of election. God had promised to the holy fathers that he would be a God to their seed for ever. They, when at the point of death, in order that the succession might be secured to their posterity, put them in possession, as if they would deliver, from hand to hand, the favour which they had received from God. So Abraham, in blessing his son Isaac, constituted him the heir of spiritual life with a solemn rite. With the same design, Isaac now, being worn down with age, imagines himself to be shortly about to depart this life, and wishes to bless his first-born son, in order that the everlasting covenant of God may remain in his own family. The Patriarchs did not take this upon themselves rashly, or on their own private account, but were public and divinely ordained witnesses. To this point belongs the declaration of the Apostle, " the less is blessed of the better." (Heb. vii. 7.) For even the faithful were accustomed to bless each other by mutual offices of charity; but the Lord enjoined this peculiar service upon the patriarchs, that they should transmit, as a deposit to posterity, the covenant which he had struck with them, and which they kept during the whole course of their life. The same command was afterwards given to the priests, as appears in Num. vi. 24, and other similar places. Therefore Isaac, in blessing his son, sustained another character than that of a father or of a private person, for he was a prophet and an interpreter of God, who constituted his son an heir of the same grace which he had received. Hence appears what I have already said, that Moses, in treating of this matter, is not without reason thus prolix. But let us weigh each of the circumstances of the case in its proper order ; of

which this is the first, that God transferred the blessing of
Esau to Jacob, by a mistake on the part of the father ; whose
eyes, Moses tells us, were dim.   The vision also of Jacob was
dull when he blessed his grandchildren Ephraim and Manasseh ; yet his want of sight did not prevent him from
cautiously placing his hands in a transverse direction.   But
God suffered Isaac to be deceived, in order to show that it
was not by the will of man that Jacob was raised, contrary
to the course of nature, to the right and honour of primogeniture.

2. *Behold, now I am old, I know not the day of my death.*
There is not the least doubt that Isaac implored daily blessings on his sons all his life: this, therefore, appears to have
been an extraordinary kind of benediction.   Moreover, the
declaration that he knew not the day of his death, is as much
as if he had said, that death was every moment pressing so
closely upon him, a decrepid and failing man, that he dared
not promise himself any longer life.   Just as a woman with
child when the time of parturition draws near, might say,
that she had now no day certain.   Every one, even in the
full vigour of age, carries with him a thousand deaths.
Death claims as its own the fœtus in the mother's womb,
and accompanies it through every stage of life.   But as it
urges the old more closely, so they ought to place it more
constantly before their eyes, and should pass as pilgrims
through the world, or as those who have already one foot
in the grave.   In short, Isaac, as one near death, wishes
to leave the Church surviving him in the person of his son.

4. *That my soul may bless thee.*   Wonderfully was the
faith of the holy man blended with a foolish and inconsiderate carnal affection.   The general principle of faith flourishes in his mind, when, in blessing his son, he consigns
to him, under the direction of the Holy Spirit, the right
of the inheritance which had been divinely promised to
himself.   Meanwhile, he is blindly carried away by the love
of his first-born son, to prefer him to the other ; and in
this way he contends against the oracle of God.   For he
could not be ignorant of that which God had pronounced
before the children were born.   If any one would excuse

him, inasmuch as he had received no command from God to change the accustomed order of nature by preferring the younger to the elder; this is easily refuted: because when he knew that the first-born was rejected, he still persisted in his excessive attachment. Again, in neglecting to inquire respecting his duty, when he had been informed of the heavenly oracle by his wife, his indolence was by no means excusable. For he was not altogether ignorant of his calling; therefore, his obstinate attachment to his son was a kind of blindness, which proved a greater obstacle to him than the external dimness of his eyes. Yet this fault, although deserving of reprehension, did not deprive the holy man of the right of pronouncing a blessing; but plenary authority remained with him, and the force and efficacy of his testimony stood entire, just as if God himself had spoken from heaven; to which subject I shall soon again allude.

5. *And Rebekah heard.* Moses now explains more fully the artifice by which Jacob attained the blessing. It truly appears ridiculous, that an old man, deceived by the cunning of his wife, should, through ignorance and error, have given utterance to what was contrary to his wish. And surely the stratagem of Rebekah was not without fault; for although she could not guide her husband by salutary counsel, yet it was not a legitimate method of acting, to circumvent him by such deceit. For, as a lie is in itself culpable, she sinned more grievously still in this, that she desired to sport in a sacred matter with such wiles. She knew that the decree by which Jacob had been elected and adopted was immutable; why then does she not patiently wait till God shall confirm it in fact, and shall show that what he had once pronounced from heaven is certain? Therefore, she darkens the celestial oracle by her lie, and abolishes, as far as she was able, the grace promised to her son. Now, if we consider farther, whence arose this great desire to bestir herself; her extraordinary faith will on the other hand appear. For, as she did not hesitate to provoke her husband against herself, to light up implacable enmity between the brothers, to expose her beloved son Jacob to the danger of immediate death, and to disturb the whole family; this cer-

tainly flowed from no other source than her faith.[1]   The inheritance promised by God was firmly fixed in her mind; she knew that it was decreed to her son Jacob.   And therefore, relying upon the covenant of God, and keeping in mind the oracle received, she forgets the world.   Thus, we see, that her faith was mixed with an unjust and immoderate zeal.   This is to be carefully observed, in order that we may understand that a pure and distinct knowledge does not always so illuminate the minds of the pious as to cause them to be governed, in all their actions, by the Holy Spirit, but that the little light which shows them their path is enveloped in various clouds of ignorance and error; so that while they hold a right course, and are tending towards the goal, they yet occasionally slide.   Finally, both in Isaac and in his wife the principle of faith was pre-eminent.   But each, by ignorance in certain particulars, and by other faults, either diverged a little from the way, or, at least, stumbled in the way.   But seeing that, nevertheless, the election of God stood firm; nay, that he even executed his design through the deceit of a woman, he vindicates, in this manner, the whole praise of his benediction to his own gratuitous goodness.

11. *And Jacob said to Rebekah.* That Jacob does not voluntarily present himself to his father, but rather fears lest, his imposture being detected, he should bring a curse upon himself, is very contrary to faith.[2]   For when the Apostle teaches, that " whatsoever is not of faith is sin," (Rom. xiv. 23,) he trains the sons of God to this sobriety, that they may not permit themselves to undertake anything

[1] This is a dangerous position, however it may be modified or explained. True faith never leads to sin.   It was the mixture, not to say the predominance of unbelief, which caused Rebekah, instead of waiting for the fulfilment of God's promises in his own way, to plot and to execute a scheme of imposture, which involved herself and her family in perpetual disquietude.   What Calvin calls zeal, he ought to have called rashness and something worse.—*Ed*.

[2] There is a great want of Calvin's accustomed caution and soundness in all this reasoning.   It certainly was right that Jacob should feel and express the fear, lest the deception which his mother required him to practise should be detected, and should bring a curse upon him and not a blessing.   It would indeed have been a still higher proof of integrity, and a still stronger exercise of faith, had he repelled the importunities of his mother, saying. " How shall I do this wickedness, and sin against God ?" —*Ed*.

with a doubtful and perplexed conscience. This firm persuasion is the only rule of right conduct, when we, relying on the command of God, go intrepidly wheresoever he calls us. Jacob, therefore, by debating with himself, shows that he was deficient in faith ; and certainly, although he was not entirely without it, yet, in this point, he is convicted of failure. But by this example we are again taught, that faith is not always extinguished by a given fault ; yet, if God sometimes bears with his servants thus far, that he turns, what they have done perversely, to their salvation, we must not hence take a license to sin. It happened by the wonderful mercy of God, that Jacob was not cut off from the grace of adoption. Who would not rather fear than become presumptuous ? And whereas we see that his faith was obscured by doubting, let us learn to ask of the Lord the spirit of prudence to govern all our steps. There was added another error of no light kind : for why does he not rather reverence God than dread his father's anger ? why does it not rather occur to his mind, that a foul blot would stain the hallowed adoption of God, when it seemed to owe its accomplishment to a lie ? For although it tended to a right end, it was not lawful to attain that end, through this oblique course. Meanwhile, there is no doubt that faith prevailed over these impediments. For what was the cause why he preferred the bare and apparently empty benediction of his father,[1] to the quiet which he then enjoyed, to the conveniences of home, and finally to life itself ? According to the flesh, the father's benediction, of which he was so desirous, that he knowingly and willingly plunged himself into great difficulties, was but an imaginary thing. Why did he act thus, but because in the exercise of simple faith in the

---

[1] Quid enim fuit causæ cur nuda et in speciem inania patris *vota* . . . præferret? Tymme translates *vota* " wishes," and either for the sake of making sense of the passage, or because the edition from which he made his version had a different reading, he puts the word " mother" in the place of " father." But as the Amsterdam and Berlin editions both have the word *patris* and not *matris*, the translation above given seems to be required. It agrees substantially with the French version, which is as follows : Car qui a este cause qu'il a preferé la benediction de son pere, laquelle sembloit nue et vaine en apparence, au repos duquel il jouissoit lors, &c.—*Ed.*

word of God, he more highly valued the hope which was
hidden from him, than the desirable condition which he actually enjoyed?   Besides, his fear of his father's anger had
its origin in the true fear of God.   He says that he feared
lest he should bring upon himself a curse.   But he would
not so greatly have dreaded a verbal censure, if he had not
deemed the grace deposited in the hands of his father worth
more than a thousand lives.   It was therefore under an impulse of God that he feared his father, who was really God's
minister.   For when the Lord sees us creeping on the earth,
he draws us to himself by the hand of man.[1]

13. *Upon me be thy curse, my son.*   Here Rebekah sins
again, because she burns with such hasty zeal that she
does not consider how highly God disapproves of her evil
course.   She presumptuously subjects herself to the curse.
But whence this unheeding confidence?   Being unfurnished
with any divine command, she took her own counsel.   Yet
no one will deny that this zeal, although preposterous,
proceeds from special reverence for the word of God.   For
since she was informed by the oracle of God, that Jacob was
preferred in the sight of God, she disregarded whatever was
visible in the world, and whatever the sense of nature dictated, in comparison with God's secret election.   Therefore
we are taught by this example, that every one should walk
modestly and cautiously according to the rule of his vocation; and should not dare to proceed beyond what the Lord
allows in his word.

14. *And he went and fetched.*   Although it is probable
that Jacob was not only influenced by a desire to yield obedience to the authority of his mother, but was also persuaded
by her reasonings, he yet sinned by overstepping the bounds
of his vocation.   When Rebekah had taken the blame upon
herself, she told him, doubtless, that injury was done to no
one: because Jacob was not stealing away another's right,

---

[1] It is much more probable that Jacob was influenced by a precipitate
and ambitious desire to snatch the blessing from the hand of his brother;
and though he paused for a moment at the apprehension of consequences,
should his mother's scheme fail, yet he too readily acquiesced, and exposed
himself to subsequent dangers, not from a supreme regard to the will of
God, but from that self-love which so often overshoots its mark.—*Ed.*

but only seeking the blessing which was decreed to him by the celestial oracle. It seemed a fair and probable excuse for the fraud, that Isaac, unless he should be imposed upon, was prepared to invalidate the election of God. Therefore Jacob, instead of simply declining from what was right in submission to his mother, was rather obeying the word of God. In the meantime (as I have said) this particular error was not free from blame: because the truth of God was not to be aided by such falsehoods. The paternal benediction was a seal of God's grace, I confess it; but she ought rather to have waited till God should bring relief from heaven, by changing the mind and guiding the tongue of Isaac, than have attempted what was unlawful. For if Balaam, who prostituted his venal tongue, was constrained by the Spirit, contrary to his own wish, to bless the elect people, whom he would rather have devoted to destruction, (Num. xxii. 12,) how much more powerfully would the same spirit have influenced the tongue of holy Isaac, who was not a mercenary man, but one who desired faithfully to obey God, and was only hurried by an error in a contrary direction? Therefore, although in the main, faith shone pre-eminently in holy Jacob, yet in this respect he bears the blame of rashness, in that he was distrustful of the providence of God, and fraudulently gained possession of his father's blessing.

19. *And Jacob said unto his father, I am Esau.*[1] At first Jacob was timid and anxious; now, having dismissed his fear, he confidently and audaciously lies. By which example we are taught, that when any one has transgressed the proper bounds of duty, he soon allows himself unmeasured license. Wherefore there is nothing better than for each to keep himself within the limits divinely prescribed to him, lest by attempting more than is lawful, he should open the door to Satan. I have before shown how far his seeking the blessing by fraud, and insinuating himself into the possession of it by falsehood, was contrary to faith. Yet this par-

---

[1] " In this speech of Jacob's there are three direct falsehoods. 1st, ' I am *Esau;*' 2d, ' I have done according as thou *badest* me ;' 3d, ' Eat of my *venison.*' We ought not to be extremely solicitous to find excuses for all the actions of holy men."—*Cornelius a Lapide in Poli Syn.*

ticular fault and divergence from the right path, did not prevent the faith which had been produced by the oracle from holding on, in some way, its course. In excusing the quickness of his return by saying that the venison was brought to him by God, he speaks in accordance with the rule of piety: he sins, however, in mixing the sacred name of God with his own falsehoods. Thus, when there is a departure from truth, the reverence which is apparently shown to God is nothing else than a profanation of his glory. It was right that the prosperous issue of his hunting should be ascribed to the providence of God, lest we should imagine that any good thing was the result of chance; but when Jacob pretended that God was the author of a benefit which had not been granted to himself, and that, too, as a cloak for his deception, his fault was not free from perjury.

21. *Come near, I pray thee, that I may feel thee.* It hence appears that the holy man was suspicious of fraud, and therefore hesitated. Whence it may seem that the benediction was vain, seeing it had no support of faith. But it thus pleased God so to perform his work by the hand of Isaac, as not to make him, who was the instrument, a willing furtherer of his design. Nor is it absurd that Isaac, like a blind man, should ignorantly transfer the blessing to a different person from him whom he intended. The ordinary function of pastors has something of a similar kind; for since by the command of God, they reconcile men to him, yet they do not discern to whom this reconciliation comes; thus they cast abroad the seed, but are uncertain respecting the fruit. Wherefore God does not place the office and power with which he has invested them, under the control of their own judgment. In this way the ignorance of Isaac does not nullify the heavenly oracles; and God himself, although the senses of his servant fail, does not desist from the accomplishment of his purpose. Here we have a clear refutation of the figment of the Papists, that the whole force of the sacrament depends upon the intention of the man who consecrates; as if, truly, it were left to the will of man to frustrate the design of God. Nevertheless, what I have already so often said must be remembered, that however Isaac

might be deceived in the person of his son, he yet did not
pronounce the blessing in vain : because a general faith remained in his mind, and in part governed his conduct.   In
forming his judgment from the touch, disregarding the voice,
he did not act according to the nature of faith.   And, therefore, with respect to the person, he was plainly in error.
This, however, did not happen in consequence of negligence ;
since he diligently and even anxiously turned every way,
that he might not deprive the first-born of his right.   But
it pleased the Lord thus to render his senses dull, partly for
the purpose of showing how vain it is for men to strive to
change what he has once decreed, (because it is impossible
but that his counsel should remain firm and stable though
the whole world should oppose it,) and partly, for the purpose of correcting, by this kind of chastisement, the absurd
attachment by which Isaac was too closely bound to his
first-born.   For whence arose this minute investigation, except from the fact that an inordinate love of Esau, which
had taken entire possession of his mind, turned him aside
from the divine oracle ?   Therefore, since he yielded an excessive indulgence to natural feeling, he deserved in every
way to be blinded.   So much the greater care ought we to
take that, in carrying on God's work, we should not give the
reins to our human affections.

26. *Come near now, and kiss me.*   We know that the
practice of kissing was then in use, which many nations retain to this day.   Profane men, however, may say, that it is
ludicrous for an old man, whose mind was already obtuse,
and who moreover had eaten and drunk heartily, should pour
forth his benedictions upon a person who was only acting a
part.[1]   But whereas Moses has previously recorded the oracle
of God, by which the adoption was destined for the younger
son, it behoves us reverently to contemplate the secret providence of God, towards which profane men pay no respect.
Truly Isaac was not so in bondage to the attractions of
meat and drink as to be unable, with sobriety of mind, to

---

[1] Vota sua in comicam personam effundit.   Espande ses vœus et benedictions sur une personne disguisee et masquee.   Should bestow his vows
and benedictions upon a person masked and disguised.—*Fr. Tr.*

reflect upon the divine command given unto him, and to undertake in seriousness, and with a certain faith in his own vocation, the very work in which, on account of the infirmity of his flesh, he vacillated and halted.   Therefore, we must not form our estimate of this blessing from the external appearance, but from the celestial decree ; even as it appeared at length, by the issue, that God neither vainly sported, nor that man rashly proceeded in this affair : and, truly, if the same religion dwells in us which flourished in the patriarch's heart, nothing will hinder the divine power from shining forth the more clearly in the weakness of man.

27. *See, the smell of my son is as the smell of a field.*   The allegory of Ambrose on this passage is not displeasing to me.   Jacob, the younger brother, is blessed under the person of the elder; the garments which were borrowed from his brother breathe an odour grateful and pleasant to his father. In the same manner we are blessed, as Ambrose teaches, when, in the name of Christ, we enter the presence of our Heavenly Father : we receive from him the robe of righteousness, which, by its odour, procures his favour ; in short, we are thus blessed when we are put in his place.   But Isaac seems here to desire and implore nothing for his son but what is earthly ; for this is the substance of his words, that it might be well with his son in the world, that he might gather together the abundant produce of the earth, that he might enjoy great peace, and shine in honour above others.   There is no mention of the heavenly kingdom ; and hence it has arisen, that men without learning, and but little exercised in true piety, have imagined that these holy fathers were blessed by the Lord only in respect to this frail and transitory life.   But it appears from many passages to have been far otherwise : and as to the fact that Isaac here confines himself to the earthly favours of God, the explanation is easy ; for the Lord did not formerly set the hope of the future inheritance plainly before the eyes of the fathers, (as he now calls and raises us directly towards heaven,) but he led them as by a circuitous course.   Thus he appointed the land of Canaan as a mirror and pledge to them of the celestial inheritance.   In all his acts of kindness he gave them tokens

of his paternal favour, not indeed for the purpose of making
them content with present good, so that they should neglect
heaven, or should follow a merely empty shadow, as some foolishly suppose ; but that, being aided by such helps, according
to the time in which they lived, they might by degrees rise
towards heaven ; for since Christ, the first-fruits of those
who rise again, and the author of the eternal and incorruptible life, had not yet been manifested, his spiritual
kingdom was, in this way, shadowed forth under figures only,
until the fulness of the time should come ; and as all the
promises of God were involved, and in a sense clothed in
these symbols, so the faith of the holy fathers observed the
same measure, and made its advances heavenward by means
of these earthly rudiments. Therefore, although Isaac makes
the temporal favours of God prominent, nothing is further
from his mind than to confine the hope of his son to this
world ; he would raise him to the same elevation to which
he himself aspired. Some proof of this may be drawn from
his own words ; for this is the principal point, that he assigns
him the dominion over the nations. But whence the hope
of such a dignity, unless he had been persuaded that his
race had been elected by the Lord, and, indeed, with this stipulation, that the right of the kingdom should remain with
one son only ? Meanwhile, let it suffice to adhere to this
principle, that the holy man, when he implores a prosperous
course of life for his son, wishes that God, in whose paternal
favour stands our solid and eternal happiness, may be propitious to him.

29. *Cursed be every one that curseth thee.* What I have
before said must be remembered, namely, that these are not
bare wishes, such as fathers are wont to utter on behalf of
their children, but that promises of God are included in
them ; for Isaac is the authorized interpreter of God, and
the instrument employed by the Holy Spirit ; and therefore,
as in the person of God, he efficaciously pronounces those
accursed who shall oppose the welfare of his son. This then
is the confirmation of the promise, by which God, when he
receives the faithful under his protection, declares that he
will be an enemy to their enemies. The whole force of the

benediction turns to this point, that God will prove himself to be a kind father to his servant Jacob in all things, so that he will constitute him the chief and the head of a holy and elect people, will preserve and defend him by his power, and will secure his salvation in the face of enemies of every kind.

30. *Jacob was yet scarce gone out.* Here is added the manner in which Esau was repulsed, which circumstance availed not a little to confirm the benediction to Jacob : for if Esau had not been rejected, it might seem that he was not deprived of that honour which nature had given him: but now Isaac declares, that what he had done, in virtue of his patriarchal office, could not but be ratified. Here, truly, it again appears, that the primogeniture which Jacob obtained, at the expense of his brother, was made his by a free gift ; for if we compare the works of both together, Esau obeys his father, brings him the produce of his hunting, prepares for his father the food obtained by his own labour, and speaks nothing but the truth : in short, we find nothing in him which is not worthy of praise. Jacob never leaves his home, substitutes a kid for venison, insinuates himself by many lies, brings nothing which would properly commend him, but in many things deserves reprehension. Hence it must be acknowledged, that the cause of this event is not to be traced to works, but that it lies hid in the eternal counsel of God. Yet Esau is not unjustly reprobated, because they who are not governed by the Spirit of God can receive nothing with a right mind ; only let it be firmly maintained, that since the condition of all is equal, if any one is preferred to another, it is not because of his own merit, but because the Lord hath gratuitously elected him.

33. *And Isaac trembled very exceedingly.*[1] Here now again the faith which had been smothered in the breast of the holy man shines forth and emits fresh sparks ; for there is no doubt that his fear springs from faith. Besides, it is no common fear which Moses describes, but that which utterly

---

[1] The original is very forcible, and cannot be fully expressed in a translation. " Isaac trembled with a great trembling exceedingly." The Septuagint represents him as in an ecstasy of astonishment.—*Ed.*

confounds the holy man : for, whereas he was perfectly conscious of his own vocation, and therefore was persuaded that
the duty of naming the heir with whom he should deposit the
covenant of eternal life was divinely enjoined upon him, he
no sooner discovered his error than he was filled with fear,
that in an affair so great and so serious God had suffered him
to err ; for unless he had thought that God was the director
of this act, what should have hindered him from alleging his
ignorance as an excuse, and from becoming enraged against
Jacob, who had stolen in upon him by fraud and by unjus-
tifiable arts ?   But although covered with shame on account
of the error he had committed, he nevertheless, with a collected mind, ratifies the benediction which he had pronounced ; and I do not doubt that he then, as one awaking,
began to recall to memory the oracle to which he had not been
sufficiently attentive.   Wherefore, the holy man was not impelled by ambition to be thus tenacious of his purpose, as
obstinate men are wont to be, who prosecute to the last what
they have once, though foolishly, begun ; but the declaration, " I have blessed him, yea, and he shall be blessed," was
the effect of a rare and precious faith ; for he, renouncing
the affections of the flesh, now yields himself entirely to God,
and, acknowledging God as the Author of the benediction
which he had uttered, ascribes due glory to him in not
daring to retract it.   The benefit of this doctrine pertains to
the whole Church, in order that we may certainly know,
that whatever the heralds of the gospel promise to us by the
command of God, will be efficacious and stable, because they
do not speak as private men, but as by the command of God
himself ; and the infirmity of the minister does not destroy
the faithfulness, power, and efficacy of God's word.   He who
presents himself to us charged with the offer of eternal happiness and life, is subject to our common miseries and to
death ; yet, notwithstanding, the promise is efficacious.   He
who absolves us from sins is himself a sinner ; but because
his office is divinely assigned him, the stability of this grace,
having its foundation in God, shall never fail.

34. *He cried with a great and exceeding bitter cry.*   Though
Esau persists in imploring the blessing, he yet gives a sign

of desperation, which is the reason why he obtains no benefit, because he enters not by the gate of faith. True piety, indeed, draws forth tears and great cries from the children of God ; but Esau, trembling and full of fears, breaks out in wailings ; afterwards he casts, at a venture, his wish into the air, that he also may receive a blessing. But his blind incredulity is reproved by his own words ; for whereas one blessing only had been deposited with his father, he asks that another should be given to him, as if it were in his father's power indiscriminately to breathe out blessings, independently of the command of God. Here the admonition of the Apostle may suggest itself to our minds, " that Esau, when he sought again the forfeited blessing with tears and loud lamentations, found no place for repentance," (Heb. xii. 17 ;) for they who neglect to follow God when he calls on them, afterwards call upon him in vain, when he has turned his back. So long as God addresses and invites us, the gate of the kingdom of heaven is in a certain sense open : this opportunity we must use, if we desire to enter, according to the instruction of the Prophet, " Seek ye the Lord while he may be found ; call ye upon him while he is near." (Isa. lv. 6.) Of which passage Paul is the interpreter, in defining that to be the acceptable time of the day of salvation in which grace is brought unto us by the gospel. (2 Cor. v. 17.) They who suffer that time to pass by, may, at length, knock too late, and without profit, because God avenges himself of their idleness. We must therefore fear lest if, with deafened ears, we suffer the voice of God now to pass unheeded by, he should, in turn, become deaf to our cry. But it may be asked, how is this repulse consistent with the promise, " If the wicked will turn from all his sins that he hath committed, and keep all my statutes, and do that which is lawful and right, he shall surely live ?" (Ezekiel xxiii. 21.) Moreover, it may seem at variance with the clemency of God to reject the sighings of those who, being crushed by misery, fly for refuge to his mercy. I answer, that repentance, if it be true and sincere, will never be too late ; and the sinner who, from his soul, is displeased with himself, will obtain pardon : but God in this manner punishes the contempt of

his grace, because they who obstinately reject it, do not seriously purpose in their mind to return to him. Thus it is
that they who are given up to a reprobate mind are never
touched with genuine penitence. Hypocrites truly break
out into tears, like Esau, but their heart within them will
remain closed as with iron bars. Therefore, since Esau
rushes forward, destitute of faith and repentance, to ask a
blessing, there is no wonder that he should be rejected.

36. *Is he not rightly named Jacob?* That the mind of
Esau was affected with no sense of penitence appears hence ;
he accused his brother and took no blame to himself. But
the very beginning of repentance is grief felt on account of
sin, together with self-condemnation. Esau ought to have
descended into himself, and to have become his own judge.
Having sold his birthright, he had darted, like a famished
dog, upon the meat and the pottage ; and now, as if he had
done no wrong, he vents all his anger on his brother. Further, if the blessing is deemed of any value, why does he
not consider that he had been repelled from it, not simply
by the fraud of man, but by the providence of God? We
see, therefore, that like a blind man feeling in the dark, he
cannot find his way.

37. *Behold, I have made him thy Lord.* Isaac now more
openly confirms what I have before said, that since God was
the author of the blessing, it could neither be vain nor
evanescent. For he does not here magnificently boast of his
dignity, but keeps himself within the bounds and measure
of a servant, and denies that he is at liberty to alter anything. For he always considers, (which is the truth,) that
when he sustains the character of God's representative, it is
not lawful for him to proceed further than the command will
bear him. Hence, indeed, Esau ought to have learned from
whence he had fallen by his own fault, in order that he
might have humbled himself, and might rather have joined
himself with his brother, in order to become a partaker of his
blessing, as his inferior, than have desired anything separately for himself. But a depraved cupidity carries him
away, so that he, forgetful of the kingdom of God, pursues
and cares for nothing except his own private advantage.

Again, we must notice Isaac's manner of speaking, by which he claims a certain force and efficacy for his benediction, as if his word carried with it dominion, abundance of corn and wine, and whatever else God had promised to Abraham. For God, in requiring the faithful to depend on himself alone, would nevertheless have them to rest securely upon the word, which, at his command, is declared to them by the tongue of men. In this way *they* are said to remit sins, who are only the messengers and interpreters of free forgiveness.

38. *Hast thou but one blessing?* Esau seems to take courage; but he neglects the care of his soul, and turns, like a swine, to the pampering of his flesh. He had heard that his father had nothing left to grant; because, truly, the full and entire grace of God so rested upon Jacob, that out of his family there was no happiness. Wherefore, if Esau sought his own welfare, he ought to have drawn from that fountain, and rather to have subjected himself to his brother, than to have cut himself off from a happy connexion with him. He chose, however, rather to be deprived of spiritual grace, provided he might but possess something of his own, and apart from his brother, than to be his inferior at home. He could not be ignorant, that there was one sole benediction by which his brother Jacob had been constituted the heir of the divine covenant : for Isaac would be daily discoursing with them concerning the singular privilege which God had vouchsafed to Abraham and his seed. Esau would not previously have complained so bitterly, unless he had felt that he had been deprived of an incomparable benefit. Therefore, by departing from this one source of blessing, he indirectly renounces God, and cuts himself off from the body of the Church, caring for nothing but this transitory life. But it would have been better for him, miserably to perish through the want of all things in this world, and with difficulty to draw his languishing breath, than to slumber amidst temporal delights. What afterwards follows ;—namely, that he wept with loud lamentations,—is a sign of fierce and proud indignation, rather than of penitence ; for he remitted nothing of his ferocity, but raged like a cruel beast of prey.

So the wicked, when punishment overtakes them, bewail the salvation they have lost; but, meanwhile, do not cease to delight themselves in their vices; and instead of heartily seeking after the righteousness of God, they rather desire that his deity should be extinct. Of a similar character is that gnashing of teeth and weeping in hell which, instead of stimulating the reprobate to seek after God, only consumes them with unknown torments.

39. *Behold, thy dwelling shall be the fatness of the earth.* At length Esau obtains what he had asked. For, perceiving himself to be cast down from the rank and honour of primogeniture, he chooses rather to have prosperity in the world, separated from the holy people, than to submit to the yoke of his younger brother. But it may be thought that Isaac contradicts himself, in offering a new benediction, when he had before declared, that he had given to his son Jacob all that was placed at his disposal. I answer, that what has been before said concerning Ishmael must be noted in this place. For God, though he hearkened to Abraham's prayer for Ishmael, so far as concerned the present life, yet immediately restricts his promise, by adding the exception implied in the declaration, that in Isaac only should the seed be called. I do not, however, doubt, that the holy man, when he perceived that his younger son Jacob was the divinely ordained heir of a happy life, would endeavour to retain his first-born, Esau, in the bond of fraternal connection, in order that he might not depart from the holy and élect flock of the Church. But now, when he sees him obstinately tending in another direction, he declares what will be his future condition. Meanwhile the spiritual blessing remains in its integrity with Jacob alone, to whom Esau refusing to attach himself, voluntarily becomes an exile from the kingdom of God. The prophecy uttered by Malachi, (i. 3,) may seem to be contradictory to this statement. For, comparing the two brothers, Esau and Jacob, with each other, he teaches that Esau was hated, inasmuch as a possession was given to him in the deserts; and yet Isaac promises him a fertile land. There is a twofold solution: either that the Prophet, speaking comparatively, may with truth call Idumea a desert in com-

parison with the land of Canaan, which was far more fruitful ; or else that he was referring to his own times. For
although the devastation of both lands had been terrible,
yet the land of Canaan in a short time flourished again,
while the territory of Edom was condemned to perpetual
sterility, and given up to dragons. Therefore, although God,
with respect to his own people, banished Esau to desert
mountains, he yet gave to him a land sufficiently fertile in
itself to render the promise by no means nugatory. For
that mountainous region both had its own natural fruitfulness, and was so watered by the dew of heaven, that it
would yield sustenance to its inhabitants.

40. *By thy sword shalt thou live, and shalt serve thy
brother.* It is to be observed that events are here predicted
which were never fulfilled in the person of Esau ; and therefore, that the prophecy is concerning things at that time far
distant. For Jacob was so far from having obtained dominion over his brother, that on his return from Padan-aram, he
suppliantly tendered him his obedience ; and the breaking
off of the yoke which Isaac here mentions, is referred to a
very remote period. He is therefore relating the future condition of Esau's posterity. And he says first, that they shall
live by their sword : which words admit a twofold sense,
either that, being surrounded by enemies, they shall pass a
warlike and unquiet life; or that they shall be free, and their
own masters. For there is no power to use the sword where
there is no liberty. The former meaning seems the more
suitable ; namely, that God would limit his promise, lest
Esau should be too much exalted : for nothing is more desirable than peace. The holy people also are warned that
there will always be some enemies to infest them. This,
however, is a very different thing from living by his own
sword ; which is as if he had said, that the sons of Esau, like
robbers, should maintain their security by arms and violence,
rather than by legitimate authority. A second limitation of
the promise is, that though armed with the sword, he should
still not escape subjection to his brother. For the Idumeans
were, at length, made tributary to the chosen people ;[1] but

[1] That is, under King David.—*Ed.*

the servitude was not long continued; because when the kingdoms were divided, the power by which they had held all their neighbours in subjection and fear, was cut off; yet the Lord would have the Idumeans brought into subjection for a short time, that he might furnish a visible demonstration of this prophecy. As to the rest of the time, the restless and unbridled liberty of Esau was more-wretched than any state of subjection.

41. *And Esau hated Jacob.* It hence appears more clearly, that the tears of Esau were so far from being the effect of true repentance, that they were rather evidences of furious anger. For he is not content with secretly cherishing enmity against his brother, but openly breaks out in wicked threats. And it is evident how deeply malice had struck its roots, when he could indulge himself in the desperate purpose of murdering his brother. Even a profane and sacrilegious contumacy betrays itself in him, seeing that he prepares himself to abolish the decree of God by the sword. I will take care, he says, that Jacob shall not enjoy the inheritance promised to him. What is this but to annihilate the force of the benediction, of which he knew that his father was the herald and the minister? Moreover, a lively picture of a hypocrite is here set before us. He pretends that the death of his father would be to him a mournful event: and doubtless it is a religious duty to mourn over a deceased father. But it was a mere pretence on his part, to speak of the day of mourning, when in his haste to execute the impious murder of his brother, the death of his father seemed to come too slowly, and he rejoiced at the prospect of its approach.[1] With what face could he ever pretend to any human affection, when he gasps for his brother's death, and at the same time attempts to subvert all the laws of nature? It is even possible, that an impulse of nature itself, extorted from him the avowal, by which he would the more grievously condemn himself; as God often censures the wicked out of their

---

[1] " The Greek translateth, ' Let the days of my father's mourning be nigh, that I may kill Jacob my brother;' so making it a wish for his father's speedy death; and the Hebrew also will bear that translation."— *Ainsworth.*

own mouth, and renders them more inexcusable. But if a sense of shame alone restrains a cruel mind, this is not to be deemed worthy of great praise; nay, it even betrays a stupid and brutal contempt of God. Sometimes, indeed, the fear of man influences even the pious, as we have seen, in the preceding chapter, respecting Jacob: but they soon rise above it, so that with them the fear of God predominates; while forgetfulness of God so pervades the hearts of the wicked, that they rest their hopes in men alone. Therefore, he who abstains from wickedness merely through the fear of man, and from a sense of shame, has hitherto made but little progress. Yet the confession of the Papists is chiefly honoured by them with this praise, that it deters many from sin, through the fear lest they should be compelled to proclaim their own disgrace. But the rule of piety is altogether different, since it teaches our conscience to set God before us as our witness and our judge.

42. *And these words of Esau . . . . were told to Rebekah.* Moses now makes a transition to a new subject of history, showing how Jacob, as a wanderer from his father's house, went into Mesopotamia. Without doubt, it was an exceedingly troublesome and severe temptation to the holy matron, to see that, by her own deed, her son was placed in imminent danger of death. But by faith she wrestled to retain the possession of the grace once received. For, if she had been impelled by a merely womanly attachment to her younger son, it certainly would have been her best and shortest method, to cause the birthright to be restored to Esau: for thus the cause of emulation would have been removed; and he who was burning with grief at the loss of his right, would have had his fury appeased. It is therefore an evidence of extraordinary faith, that Rebekah does not come to any agreement, but persuades her son to become a voluntary exile, and chooses rather to be deprived of his presence, than that he should give up the blessing he had once received. The benediction of the father might now seem illusory; so as to make it appear wonderful that so much should be made of it by Rebekah and Jacob: nevertheless, they were so far from repenting of what they had done, that they do not re-

fuse the bitter punishment of exile, if only Jacob may carry
with him the benediction uttered by his father. Moreover,
we are taught by this example, that we must bear it patiently,
if the cross attends the hope of a better life, as its companion;
or even if the Lord adopts us into his family, with this condition, that we should wander as pilgrims without any certain
dwelling-place in the world. For, on this account, Jacob is
thrust out from his paternal home, where he might quietly
have passed his life, and is compelled to migrate to a strange
land; because the blessing of God is promised unto him.
And as he did not attempt to purchase temporal peace with
his brother by the loss of the grace received; so must we
beware lest any carnal advantage or any allurements of the
world should draw us aside from the course of our vocation:
let us rather bear with magnanimity losses of all kinds, so
that the anchor of our hope may remain fixed in heaven.
When Rebekah says that Esau consoled himself with the
thought, that he would slay his brother; the meaning is,
that he could not be pacified by any other means, than by
this wicked murder.

44. *And tarry with him a few days.* This circumstance
mitigates the severity of banishment. For the shortness of
the time of suffering avails not a little to support us in adversity. And it was probable that the enmity of Esau would
not prove so obstinate as to be unassuaged by his brother's
absence. In the Hebrew expression which is translated " a
few days," the word few is literally " one " put in the plural
number.[1] Rebekah means, that as soon as Jacob should have
gone away of his own accord, the memory of the offence
would be obliterated from the mind of Esau; as if she had
said, Only depart hence for a little while, and we shall soon
assuage his anger.

45. *Why should I be deprived of you both in one day?* Why
does Rebekah fear a double privation? for there was no danger
that Jacob, endued with a disposition so mild and placid,
should rise up against his brother. We see, therefore, that

---

[1] Hebraice ad verbum habetur, Unis diebus. ימים אחדים (*yamim ache-
dim*).   There is no mode of giving a literal rendering of the expression in
the English language.—*Ed.*

Rebekah concluded that God would be the avenger of the iniquitous murder. Moreover, although God, for a time, might seem to overlook the deed, and to suspend his judgment, it would yet be necessary for him to withdraw from the parricide. Therefore, by this law of nature, Rebekah declares that she should be entirely bereaved ; because she would be compelled to dread and to detest him who survived But if Rebekah anticipated in her mind what the judgment of God would be, and devoted the murderer to destruction, because she was persuaded that wickedness so great would not be unpunished ; much less ought we to close our eyes against the manifest chastisements of God.[1]

46. *And Rebekah said to Isaac.* When Jacob might have fled secretly, his mother, nevertheless, obtains leave for his departure from his father; for so a well-ordered domestic government and discipline required. In giving another cause than the true one to her husband, she may be excused from the charge of falsehood ; inasmuch as she neither said the whole truth nor left the whole unsaid. No doubt, she truly affirms that she was tormented, even to weariness of life, on account of her Hittite daughters-in-law : but she prudently conceals the more inward evil, lest she should inflict a mortal wound on her husband : and also, lest she should the more influence the rage of Esau ; for the wicked, often, when their crime is detected, are the more carried away with desperation. Now, although in consequence of the evil manners of her daughters-in-law, affinity with the whole race became hateful to Rebekah, yet in this again the wonderful providence of God is conspicuous, that Jacob neither blended, nor entangled himself, with the future enemies of the Church.

[1] The French is more diffuse : "Tant plus nous faut-il appercevoir les fleaux de Dieu qui sont manifestes, et ne faut point ciller les yeux en ne faisant semblant de les voir." So much the more ought we to perceive the scourges of God, which are manifest; and we ought not to wink as pretending not to see them.—*Fr. Tr.*

CHAPTER XXVIII.

1. AND Isaac called Jacob, and blessed him, and charged him, and said unto him, Thou shalt not take a wife of the daughters of Canaan.

2. Arise, go to Padan-aram, to the house of Bethuel thy mother's father, and take thee a wife from thence of the daughters of Laban thy mother's brother.

3. And God Almighty bless thee, and make thee fruitful, and multiply thee, that thou mayest be a multitude of people;

4. And give thee the blessing of Abraham, to thee, and to thy seed with thee; that thou mayest inherit the land wherein thou art a stranger, which God gave unto Abraham.

5. And Isaac sent away Jacob: and he went to Padan-aram unto Laban, son of Bethuel the Syrian, the brother of Rebekah, Jacob's and Esau's mother.

6. When Esau saw that Isaac had blessed Jacob, and sent him away to Padan-aram, to take him a wife from thence; and that, as he blessed him, he gave him a charge, saying, Thou shalt not take a wife of the daughters of Canaan;

7. And that Jacob obeyed his father and his mother, and was gone to Padan-aram;

8. And Esau seeing that the daughters of Canaan pleased not Isaac his father;

9. Then went Esau unto Ishmael, and took unto the wives which he had Mahalath the daughter of Ishmael, Abraham's son, the sister of Nebajoth, to be his wife.

10. And Jacob went out from Beer-sheba, and went toward Haran.

11. And he lighted upon a certain place, and tarried there all night, because the sun was set; and he took of the stones of that place, and put *them for* his pillows, and lay down in that place to sleep.

12. And he dreamed, and behold

1. Vocavit ergo Ishac Iahacob, et benedixit ei: præcepitque, et dixit ei, Non capies uxorem de filiabus Chenaan.

2. Surge, vade in Padan Aram, ad domum Bethuel patris matris tuæ, et cape tibi inde uxorem de filiabus Laban fratris matris tuæ.

3. Deus autem omnipotens benedicat tibi, et crescere faciat te, et multiplicare faciat te, et sis in cœtum populorum.

4. Et det tibi benedictionem Abraham, tibi et semini tuo tecum, ut hæreditate accipias terram peregrinationum tuarum, quam dedit Deus ipsi Abraham.

5. Et misit Ishac Iahacob, et profectus est in Padan Aram ad Laban filium Bethuel Aramæi fratris Ribcæ, matris Iahacob et Esau.

6. Et vidit Esau quod benedixisset Ishac Iahacob, et misisset eum in Padan Aram, ut caperet sibi inde uxorem: et benedicendo ei, præcepisset ei, dicendo, Non accipies uxorem de filiabus Chenaan:

7. Et obedivisset Iahacob patri suo et matri suæ, et ivisset in Padan Aram.

8. Videns præterea Esau quod malæ filiæ Chenaan in oculis Ishac patris sui:

9. Tunc abiit Esau ad Ismael, et accepit Mahalath filiam Ismael filii Abraham sororem Nebajoth, super uxores suas, sibi in uxorem.

10. Iahacob vero egressus est e Beer-sebah, et perrexit in Aram:

11. Et occurrit in locum, et pernoctavit ibi, quia occubuerat sol: et tulit de lapidibus loci, et posuit sub capite suo, et dormivit in loco eodem.

12. Et somniavit, et ecce scala

a ladder set up on the earth, and the top of it reached to heaven; and behold the angels of God ascending and descending on it.

13. And, behold, the Lord stood above it, and said, I *am* the Lord God of Abraham thy father, and the God of Isaac: the land whereon thou liest, to thee will I give it, and to thy seed;

14. And thy seed shall be as the dust of the earth; and thou shalt spread abroad to the west, and to the east, and to the north, and to the south: and in thee, and in thy seed, shall all the families of the earth be blessed.

15. And, behold, I *am* with thee, and will keep thee in all *places* whither thou goest, and will bring thee again into this land; for I will not leave thee, until I have done *that* which I have spoken to thee of.

16. And Jacob awaked out of his sleep, and he said, Surely the Lord is in this place, and I knew *it* not.

17. And he was afraid, and said, How dreadful *is* this place! this *is* none other but the house of God, and this *is* the gate of heaven.

18. And Jacob rose up early in the morning, and took the stone that he had put *for* his pillows, and set it up *for* a pillar, and poured oil upon the top of it.

19. And he called the name of that place Beth-el: but the name of that city *was called* Luz at the first.

20. And Jacob vowed a vow, saying, If God will be with me, and will keep me in this way that I go, and will give me bread to eat, and raiment to put on,

21. So that I come again to my father's house in peace, then shall the Lord be my God:

22. And this stone, which I have set *for* a pillar, shall be God's house: and of all that thou shalt give me, I will surely give the tenth unto thee.

erecta erat super terram, et caput ejus tangebat cœlum; et ecce, Angeli Dei ascendebant et descendebant per eam.

13. Et ecce, Iehova stabat super eam, et dixit, Ego Iehova Deus Abraham patris tui, et Deus Ishac: terram, super quam tu dormis, tibi dabo et semini tuo.

14. Et erit semen tuum sicut pulvis terræ, et multiplicaberis ad Occidentem, et ad Orientem, et ad Aquilonem, et ad Meridiem: et benedicentur in te omnes familiæ terræ, et in semine tuo.

15. Et ecce sum tecum, et custodiam te quocunque profectus fueris, et redire faciam te ad terram hanc: quia non derelinquam te, donec faciam quod loquutus sum tibi.

16. Deinde expergefactus est Iahacob a somno suo, et dixit, Vere est Iehova in loco isto, et ego nesciebam.

17. Timuit ergo, et dixit, Quam terribilis est locus iste! non est hic nisi domus Dei, et hic est porta cœli.

18. Surrexit autem Iahacob mane, et tulit lapidem, quem posuerat sub capite suo, et posuit eum in statuam, et effudit oleum supra summitatem ejus.

19. Et vocavit nomen loci ipsius Beth-el, et quidem Luz erat nomen urbis prius.

20. Adhæc vovit Iahacob votum, dicendo, Si fuerit Iehova Deus mecum, et custodierit me in via ista, quam ego ingredior, et dederit mihi panem ad vescendum, et vestimentum ad operiendum:

21. Et reversus fuero in pace ad domum patris mei, erit Iehova mihi in Deum.

22. Et lapis iste, quem posui in statuam, erit domus Dei: et omne quod dederis mihi, decimando decimabo illud tibi.

1. *And Isaac called Jacob, and blessed him.* It may be asked, whether the reason why Isaac repeats anew the bene-

diction which he had before pronounced, was that the former one had been of no force ; whereas, if he was a prophet and interpreter of the will of God, what had once proceeded from his mouth ought to have been firm and perpetual. I answer, although the benediction was in itself efficacious, yet the faith of Jacob required support of this kind : just as the Lord, in reiterating frequently the same promises, derogates nothing either from himself or from his word, but rather confirms the certainty of that word to his servants, lest, at any time, their confidence should be shaken through the infirmity of the flesh. What I have said must also be kept in mind, that Isaac prayed, not as a private person, but as one furnished with a special command of God, to transmit the covenant deposited with himself to his son Jacob. It was also of the greatest importance that now, at length, Jacob should be blessed by his father, knowingly and willingly ; lest at a future time a doubt, arising from the recollection of his father's mistake and of his own fraud, might steal over his mind. Therefore Isaac, now purposely directing his words to his son Jacob, pronounces the blessing to be due to him by right, lest it should be thought that, having been before deceived, he had uttered words in vain, under a false character.

2. *Arise, go to Padan-aram.* In the first place, he commands him to take a wife from his maternal race. He might have sent for her by some one of his servants, as Rebekah had been brought to him ; but perhaps he took this course to avoid the envy of Esau, who might regard it as a reproach if more solicitude were manifested about his brother's marriage than about his own.

3. *And God Almighty bless thee.* Here follows the form of benediction, which slightly differs in words from the former, but nevertheless tends to the same end. First, he desires that Jacob should be blessed by God ; that is, that he should be so increased and amplified in his own offspring, as to grow into a multitude of nations ; or, in other words, that he should produce many people who might combine into one body under the same head ; as if he had said, " Let there arise from thee many tribes, who shall constitute one people." And this truly was, in some measure, fulfilled when

Moses distributed the people into thirteen divisions. Nevertheless, Isaac looked for a further result, namely, that many were at length to be gathered together out of various nations, to the family of his son, that, in this manner, from a vast and previously scattered multitude, might be formed one assembly. For it is not to be doubted, that he wished to hand down what he had received ; seeing that he immediately afterwards celebrates the memory of the original covenant, deriving his present benediction from thence as its source : as if he had said, that he transferred whatever right he had from his father, to his son Jacob, in order that the inheritance of life might remain with him, according to the covenant of God made with Abraham. They who expound this as being said in the way of comparison, as if Isaac[1] wished those benefits which God had before conferred on Abraham to be in the same manner granted to his son, attenuate the meaning of the words. For since God, in making his covenant with Abraham, had annexed this condition, that it should descend to his posterity, it was necessary to trace its commencement to his person as its root. Therefore, Isaac constitutes his son Jacob the heir of Abraham, as successor to the benediction deposited with him, and promised to his seed. This also appears more clearly from the context following, where he assigns to him the dominion over the land, because it had been given to Abraham. Moreover, we perceive, in this member of the sentence, with what consistency of faith the holy fathers rested on the word of the Lord ; for otherwise, they would have found it no small temptation to be driven about as strangers and pilgrims in the very land, the possession of which had been divinely assigned them a hundred years before. But we see, that in their wanderings and their unsettled mode of life, they no less highly estimated what God had promised them, than if they had already been in the full enjoyment of it. And this is the true trial of faith ; when relying on the word of God alone, although tossed on the waves of the world, we stand as firmly as if

---

[1] In the editions of Amsterdam and Berlin, the name *Jacob* is here inserted ; and the old English version has it too. The mistake is obvious, and stands corrected in the French translation.—*Ed.*

our abode were already fixed in heaven. Isaac expressly fortifies his son against this temptation, when he calls the land of which he constitutes him lord, "the land of his wanderings." For by these words he teaches him that it was possible he might be a wanderer all the days of his life: but this did not hinder the promise of God from being so ratified, that he, contented with that alone, might patiently wait for the time of revelation. Even the plural number[1] seems to express something significant, namely, that Jacob would be a wanderer not once only, but in various ways and perpetually. Since, however, the Hebrew plural has not always such emphasis, I do not insist on this interpretation. It is more worthy of notice, that the faith of Jacob was proved by a severe and rigid trial, seeing, that for this very reason, the land is promised to him in *word* only, while in *fact*, he is cast far away from it. For he seems to be the object of ridicule, when he is commanded to possess the dominion of the land, and yet to leave it and to bid it farewell, and to depart into distant exile.

6. *When Esau saw.* A brief narration concerning Esau is here inserted, which it is useful to know; because we learn from it that the wicked, though they exalt themselves against God, and though, in contempt of his grace, they please themselves in obtaining their desires, are yet not able to despise that grace altogether. So now, Esau is penetrated with a desire of the blessing; not that he aspires to it sincerely and from his heart; but perceiving it to be something valuable, he is impelled to seek after it, though with reluctance. A further fault is, that he does not seek it as he ought: for he devises a new and strange method of reconciling God and his father to himself; and therefore all his diligence is without profit. At the same time he does not seem to be careful about pleasing God, so that he may but propitiate his father. Before all things, it was his duty to cast aside his profane disposition, his perverse manners, and his corrupt affections of the flesh, and then to bear with meekness the chastisement inflicted upon him: for genuine repentance would have dictated to him this sentiment, "Seeing I have hitherto ren-

[1] Terram peregrinationum—the land of *wanderings*.

dered myself unworthy of the birthright, my brother is deservedly preferred before me. Nothing, therefore, remains
for me but to humble myself; and since I am deprived of
the honour of being the head, let it suffice me to be at least
one of the members of the Church." And, certainly, it
would have been more desirable for him to remain in some
obscure corner of the Church, than, as one cut off and torn
away from the elect people, to shine with a proud pre-eminence on earth. He aims, however, at nothing of this kind,
but attempts, by I know not what prevarications, to appease
his father in whatever way he may be able. Moses, in this
example, depicts all hypocrites to the life. Eor as often as
the judgment of God urges them, though they are wounded
with the pain of their punishment, they yet do not seek a true
remedy ; for having aimed at offering one kind of satisfaction
only, they entirely neglect a simple and real conversion : and
even in the satisfaction offered, they only make a pretence.
Whereas Esau ought thoroughly to have repented, he only
tried to correct the single fault of his marriage ; and this too
in a most absurd manner. Yet another defect follows: for
while he retains the wives who were so hateful to his parents,
he supposes he has discharged his duty by marrying a third.
But by this method, neither was the trouble of his parents
alleviated, nor his house cleansed from guilt. And now truly,
whence does he marry his third wife ? From the race of
Ishmael, whom we know to have been himself degenerate,
and whose posterity had departed from the pure worship of
God. A remarkable proof of this is discernible at the present day, in the pretended and perfidious intermeddlers, who
imagine they can admirably adjust religious differences by
simply adorning their too gross corruptions with attractive
colours.[1] The actual state of things compels them to confess
that the vile errors and abuses of Popery have so far pre-

[1] The Council of Trent is here obviously referred to, which held its ses-
sions from the year 1545 to the year 1563.   This council was the Romanist
reaction upon the Protestant reformation.   Father Paul gives a singular
and graphic description of the persons, the characters, and the arguments,
by which this last council of the Church of Rome was distinguished.   It
will be remembered that Calvin's Commentary on Genesis was published
about the middle of this protracted period.—*Ed.*

vailed as to render a Reformation absolutely necessary : but they are unwilling that the filth of this Camarine marsh be stirred ;[1] they only desire to conceal its impurities, and even that they do by compulsion. For they had previously called their abominations the sacred worship of God ; but since these are now dragged to light by the word of God, they therefore descend to novel artifices. They flatter themselves, however, in vain, seeing they are here condemned by Moses, in the person of Esau. Away, then, with their impure pretended reformation, which has nothing simple nor sincere. Moreover, since it is a disease inherent in the human race, willingly to attempt to deceive God by some fictitious pretext, let us know that we do nothing effectually, until we tear up our sins by the roots, and thoroughly devote ourselves to God.

10. *And Jacob went out.* In the course of this history we must especially observe, how the Lord preserved his own Church in the person of one man. For Isaac, on account of his age, lay like a dry trunk ; and although the living root of piety was concealed within his breast, yet no hope of further offspring remained in his exhausted and barren old age. Esau, like a green and flourishing branch, had much of show and splendour, but his vigour was only momentary. Jacob, as a severed twig, was removed into a far distant land ; not that, being ingrafted or planted there, he should acquire strength and greatness, but that, being moistened with the dew of heaven, he might put forth his shoots as into the air itself. For the Lord wonderfully nourishes him, and supplies him with strength, until he shall bring him back again to his father's house. Meanwhile, let the reader diligently observe, that while he who was blessed by God is cast into exile ; occasion of glorying was given to the reprobate Esau, who was left in the possession of

---

[1] Camarina was a city on the south of Sicily, placed near the mouths of two rivers, close to which was a marsh or lake, called the Camarine lake, injurious to health, and often producing pestilence. It is reported that the inhabitants consulted Apollo whether or not they should drain it. The answer was, that it would be better undrained. This answer they disregarded, and in consequence the enemy found it easy to attack and plunder the city. Hence the proverb, " Ne moveas Camarinam ;" that is, " Do not get rid of one evil to bring on you a greater."—*Ed.*

everything, so that he might securely reign without a rival. Let us not, then, be disturbed, if at any time the wicked sound their triumphs, as having gained their wishes, while we are oppressed. Moses mentions the name of Beersheba, because, as it formed one of the boundaries of the land of Canaan, and lay towards the great desert and the south, it was the more remote from the eastern region towards which Jacob was going. He afterwards adds Charran, (chap. xxix.,) where Abraham, when he left his own country, dwelt for some time. Now, it appears that not only the pious old man Terah, when he followed his son, or accompanied him on his journey, came to Charran where he died; but that his other son Nahor, with his family, also came to the same place. For we read in the eleventh chapter, that Terah took his son Abraham, and Lot his grandson, and Sarai his daughter-in-law. Whence we infer that Nahor, at that time, remained in Chaldea, his native country. But now, since Moses says, that Laban dwelt at Charran, we may hence conjecture, that Nahor, in order that he might not appear guilty of the inhumanity of deserting his father, afterwards gathered together his goods and came to him.

Moses here, in a few words, declares what a severe and arduous journey the holy man (Jacob) had, on account of its great length: to which also another circumstance is added; namely, that he lay on the ground, under the open sky, without a companion, and without a habitation. But as Moses only briefly alludes to these facts, so will I also avoid prolixity, as the thing speaks for itself. Wherefore, if, at any time, we think ourselves to be roughly treated, let us remember the example of the holy man, as a reproof to our fastidiousness.

12. *And he dreamed.* Moses here teaches how opportunely, and (as we may say) in the critical moment, the Lord succoured his servant. For who would not have said that holy Jacob was neglected by God, since he was exposed to the incursion of wild beasts, and obnoxious to every kind of injury from earth and heaven, and found nowhere any help or solace? But when he was thus reduced to the last necessity, the Lord suddenly stretches out his

hand to him, and wonderfully alleviates his trouble by a re-markable oracle. As, therefore, Jacob's invincible perseve-rance had before shone forth, so now the Lord gives a memorable example of his paternal care towards the faithful. Three things are here to be noticed in their order ; first, that the Lord appeared unto Jacob in a dream ; secondly, the nature of the vision as described by Moses ; thirdly, the words of the oracle. When mention is made of a dream, no doubt that mode of revelation is signified, which the Lord formerly was wont to adopt towards his servants. (Numb. xii. 6.) Jacob, therefore, knew that this dream was divinely sent to him, as one differing from common dreams ; and this is intimated in the words of Moses, when he says that God appeared to him in a dream. For Jacob could not see God, nor perceive him present, unless his majesty had been dis-tinguishable by certain marks.

And behold a ladder. Here the *form* of the vision is related, which is very pertinent to the subject of it ; namely, that God manifested himself as seated upon a ladder, the extreme parts of which touched heaven and earth, and which was the vehicle of angels, who descended from heaven upon earth. The interpretation of some of the Hebrews, that the ladder is a figure of the Divine Providence, cannot be admitted : for the Lord has given another sign more suit-able.[1] But to us, who hold to this principle, that the cove-nant of God was founded in Christ, and that Christ himself was the eternal image of the Father, in which he manifested himself to the holy patriarchs, there is nothing in this vision intricate or ambiguous. For since men are alienated from God by sin, though he fills and sustains all things by his

[1] Whatever force and truth, as well as beauty, there may be in the ex-position of Calvin which follows, he appears to have dismissed too hastily the opinion of the Jews, that the vision was symbolical of *Divine Provi-dence.* The circumstances of Jacob seemed to require some such intima-tions of Divine protection and care during his journey, as this interpretation of the vision presents. And in every way the passage thus understood is both useful and encouraging. There is, however, no need to question, that the higher mystical interpretation, on which Calvin exclusively in-sists, is legitimately applicable, as conveying the ultimate and, in short, the most important meaning of the vision. The reader may consult the 123d Exercitation of Rivetus on this subject.—*Rivetus in Gen.,* p. 602.

power, yet that communication by which he would draw us to himself is not perceived by us ; but, on the other hand, so greatly are we at variance with him, that, regarding him as adverse to us, we, in our turn, flee from his presence Moreover the angels, to whom is committed the guardian-ship of the human race, while strenuously applying them-selves to their office, yet do not communicate with us in such a way that we become conscious of their presence.   It is Christ alone, therefore, who connects heaven and earth : he is the only Mediator who reaches from heaven down to earth : he is the medium through which the fulness of all celestial blessings flows down to us, and through which we, in turn, ascend to God.   He it is who, being the head over angels, causes them to minister to his earthly members. Therefore, (as we read in John i. 51,) he properly claims for himself this honour, that after he shall have been manifested in the world, angels shall ascend and descend.   If, then, we say that the ladder is a figure of Christ, the exposition will not be forced.   For the similitude of a ladder well suits the Mediator, through whom ministering angels, righteousness and life, with all the graces of the Holy Spirit, descend to us step by step.   We also, who were not only fixed to the earth, but plunged into the depths of the curse, and into hell itself, ascend even unto God.   Also, the God of hosts is seated on the ladder ; because the fulness of the Deity dwells in Christ ; and hence also it is, that it reaches unto heaven.   For although all power is committed even to his human nature by the Father, he still would not truly sus-tain our faith, unless he were God manifested in the flesh. And the fact that the body of Christ is finite, does not pre-vent him from filling heaven and earth, because his grace and power are everywhere diffused.   Whence also, Paul being witness, he ascended into heaven that he might fill all things. They who translate the particle עַל by the word " near," entirely destroy the sense of the passage.   For Moses wishes to state that the fulness of the Godhead dwelt in the per-son of the Mediator.   Christ not only approached unto us, but clothed himself in our nature, that he might make us one with himself.   That the ladder was a symbol of Christ,

is also confirmed by this consideration, that nothing was
more suitable than that God should ratify his covenant of
eternal salvation in his Son to his servant Jacob. And hence
we feel unspeakable joy, when we hear that Christ, who so
far excels all creatures, is nevertheless joined with us. The
majesty, indeed, of God, which here presents itself conspicuously to view, ought to inspire terror; so that every knee
should bow to Christ, that all creatures should look up to
him and adore him, and that all flesh should keep silence in
his presence. But his friendly and lovely image is at the
same time depicted; that we may know by his descent, that
heaven is opened to us, and the angels of God are rendered
familiar to us. For hence we have fraternal society with
them, since the common Head both of them and us has his
station on earth.

13. *I am the Lord God of Abraham.* This is the third
point which, I said, was to be noticed: for mute visions are
cold; therefore the word of the Lord is as the soul which
quickens them. The figure, therefore, of the ladder was the
inferior appendage of this promise; just as God illustrates
and adorns his word by external symbols, that both greater
clearness and authority may be added to it. Whence also
we prove that sacraments in the Papacy are frivolous, because no voice is heard in them which may edify the soul.
We may therefore observe, that whenever God manifested
himself to the fathers, he also *spoke,* lest a mute vision should
have held them in suspense. Under the name יהוה (*Jehovah*)
God teaches that he is the only Creator of the world, that
Jacob might not seek after other gods. But since his
majesty is in itself incomprehensible, he accommodates himself to the capacity of his servant, by immediately adding,
that he is the God of Abraham and Isaac. For though it is
necessary to maintain that the God whom we worship is the
only God; yet because when our senses would aspire to the
comprehension of his greatness, they fail at the first attempt;
we must diligently cultivate that sobriety which teaches us
not to desire to know more concerning him than he reveals
unto us; and then he, accommodating himself to our weakness, according to his infinite goodness, will omit nothing

which tends to promote our salvation. And whereas he made a special covenant with Abraham and Isaac, proclaiming himself their God, he recalls his servant Jacob to the true source of faith, and retains him also in his perpetual covenant. This is the sacred bond of religion, by which all the sons of God are united among themselves, when from the first to the last they hear the same promise of salvation, and agree together in one common hope. And this is the effect of that benediction which Jacob had lately received from his father; because God with his own mouth pronounces him to be the heir of the covenant, lest the mere testimony of man should be thought illusive.

The land whereon thou liest. We read that the land was given to his posterity; yet he himself was not only a stranger in it to the last, but was not permitted even to die there. Whence we infer, that under the pledge or earnest of the land, something better and more excellent was given, seeing that Abraham was a spiritual possessor of the land, and contented with the mere beholding of it, fixed his chief regard on heaven. We may observe, however, that the seed of Jacob is here placed in opposition to the other sons of Abraham, who, according to the flesh, traced their origin to him, but were cut off from the holy people: yet, from the time when the sons of Jacob entered the land of Canaan, they had the perpetual inheritance unto the coming of Christ, by whose advent the world was renewed.

14. *And thy seed shall be as the dust of the earth.* The sum of the whole is this, Whatever the Lord had promised to Abraham, Jacob transmitted to his sons. Meanwhile it behoved the holy man, in reliance on this divine testimony, to hope against hope; for though the promise was vast and magnificent, yet, wherever Jacob turned himself, no ray of good hope shone upon him. He saw himself a solitary man; no condition better than that of exile presented itself; his return was uncertain and full of danger; but it was profitable for him to be thus left destitute of all means of help, that he might learn to depend on the word of God alone. Thus, at the present time, if God freely promises to give us all things, and yet seems to approach us empty-handed, it is still

proper that we should pay such honour and reverence to his word, that we may be enriched and filled with faith. At length, indeed, after the death of Jacob, the event declared how efficacious had been this promise : by which example we are taught that the Lord by no means disappoints his people, even when he defers the granting of those good things which he has promised, till after their death.

And in thee, and in thy seed, shall all the families of the earth be blessed.[1] This clause has the greater weight, because in Jacob and in his seed the blessing is to be restored from which the whole human race had been cut off in their first parent. But what this expression means, I have explained above ; namely, that Jacob will not only be an exemplar, or *formula* of blessing, but its fountain, cause, or foundation ; for though a certain exquisite degree of happiness is often signified by an expression of this kind ; yet, in many passages of Scripture, it means the same as to desire from any one his blessing, and to acknowledge it as his gift. Thus men are said to bless themselves in God, when they acknowledge him as the author of all good. So here God promises that in Jacob and his seed all nations shall bless themselves, because no happiness will ever be found except what proceeds from this source. That, however, which is peculiar to Christ, is without impropriety transferred to Jacob, in whose loins Christ then was. Therefore, inasmuch as Jacob, at that time, represented the person of Christ, it is said that all nations are to be blessed in him ; but, seeing that the manifestation of a benefit so great depended on another, the expression *in thy seed* is immediately added in the way of explanation. That the word seed is a collective noun, forms no objection to this interpretation, (as I have elsewhere said,) for since all unbelievers deprive themselves of honour and of grace, and are thus accounted strangers ; it is necessary to refer to the Head, in order that the unity of the seed may appear. Whoever will reverently ponder this, will easily

---

[1] Et benedicent se in te omnes fines terræ. "And all the ends of the earth shall bless themselves in thee." The reader will perceive that Calvin's remarks turn chiefly on the expression "bless themselves," which does not appear in our version.—*Ed.*

see that, in this interpretation, which is that of Paul, there is nothing tortuous or constrained.

15. *I am with thee, and will keep thee.* God now promptly anticipates the temptation which might steal over the mind of holy Jacob ; for though he is, for a time, thrust out into a foreign land, God declares that he will be his keeper until he shall have brought him back again. He then extends his promise still further ; saying, that he will never desert him till all things are fulfilled. There was a twofold use of this promise : first, it retained his mind in the faith of the divine covenant ; and, secondly, it taught him that it could not be well with him unless he were a partaker of the promised inheritance.

16. *And Jacob awaked.* Moses again affirms that this was no common dream ; for when any one awakes he immediately perceives that he had been under a delusion in dreaming. But God impressed a sign on the mind of his servant, by which, when he awoke, he might recognise the heavenly oracle which he had heard in his sleep. Moreover, Jacob, in express terms, accuses himself, and extols the goodness of God, who deigned to present himself to one who sought him not ; for Jacob thought that he was there alone : but now, after the Lord appeared, he wonders, and exclaims that he had obtained more than he could have dared to hope for. It is not, however, to be doubted that Jacob had called upon God, and had trusted that he would be the guide of his journey ; but, because his faith had not availed to persuade him that God was thus near unto him, he justly extols this act of grace. So, whenever God anticipates our wishes, and grants us more than our minds have conceived ; let us learn, after the example of this patriarch, to wonder that God should have been present with us. Now, if each of us would reflect how feeble his faith is, this mode of speaking would appear always proper for us all ; for who can comprehend, in his scanty measure, the immense multitude of gifts which God is perpetually heaping upon us ?

17. *And he was afraid, and said.* It seems surprising that Jacob should fear, when God spoke so graciously to him ; or that he should call that place " dreadful," where he had been

filled with incredible joy. I answer, although God exhilarates his servants, he at the same time inspires them with fear, in order that they may learn, with true humility and self-denial, to embrace his mercy. We are not therefore to understand that Jacob was struck with terror, as reprobates are, as soon as God shows himself; but he was inspired with a fear which produces pious submission. He also properly calls that place the *gate of heaven*, on account of the manifestation of God: for, because God is placed in heaven as on his royal throne, Jacob truly declares that, in seeing God, he had penetrated into heaven. In this sense the preaching of the gospel is called the kingdom of heaven, and the sacraments may be called the gate of heaven, because they admit us into the presence of God. The Papists, however, foolishly misapply this passage to their temples, as if God dwelt in filthy places.[1] But if we concede, that the places which they designate by this title, are not polluted with impious superstitions, yet this honour belongs to no peculiar place, since Christ has filled the whole world with the presence of his Deity. Those helps to faith only, (as I have before taught,) by which God raises us to himself, can be called the gates of heaven.

18. *And Jacob rose up early.* Moses relates that the holy father was not satisfied with merely giving thanks at the time, but would also transmit a memorial of his gratitude to posterity. Therefore he raised a monument, and gave a name to the place, which implied that he thought such a signal benefit of God worthy to be celebrated in all ages. For this reason, the Scripture not only commands the faithful to sing the praises of God among their brethren; but also enjoins them to train their children to religious duties, and to propagate the worship of God among their descendants.

And set it up for a pillar. Moses does not mean that the stone was made an idol, but that it should be a special memorial. God indeed uses this word מצבה, (*matsbah*,) when he forbids statues to be erected to himself, (Lev. xxvi. 1,) because almost all statues were objects of veneration, as if they were likenesses of God. But the design of

---

[1] In fœtidis lupanaribus.

Jacob was different ; namely, that he might leave a testimony
of the vision which had appeared unto him, not that he
might represent God by that symbol or figure.   Therefore
the stone was not there placed by him, for the purpose of
depressing the minds of men into any gross superstition, but
rather of raising them upward.   He used oil as a sign of
consecration, and not without reason ; for as, in the world,
everything is profane which is destitute of the Spirit of God,
so there is no pure religion except that which the heavenly
unction sanctifies.   And to this point the solemn right of consecration, which God commanded in his law, tends, in order
that the faithful may learn to bring in nothing of their own,
lest they should pollute the temple and worship of God.
And though, in the times of Jacob, no teaching had yet been
committed to writing ; it is, nevertheless, certain that he had
been imbued with that principle of piety which God from
the beginning had infused into the hearts of the devout :
wherefore, it is not to be ascribed to superstition that he
poured oil upon the stone ; but he rather testified, as I have
said, that no worship can be acceptable to God, or pure,
without the sanctification of the Spirit.   Other commentators argue, with more subtlety, that the stone was a symbol
of Christ, on whom all the graces of the Spirit were poured
out, that all might draw out of his fulness ; but I do not
know that any such thing entered the mind of Moses or of
Jacob.   I am satisfied with what I have before stated, that
a stone was erected to be a witness or a memorial (so to
speak) of a vision, the benefit of which reaches to all ages.
It may be asked, Whence did the holy man obtain oil in the
desert ?   They who answer that it had been brought from a
neighbouring city are, in my opinion, greatly deceived ; for
this place was then void of inhabitants, as I shall soon show.
I therefore rather conjecture, that on account of the necessity of the times, seeing that suitable accommodations could
not always be had, he had taken some portion of food for his
journey along with him ; and as we know that great use was
made of oil in those parts, it is no wonder if he carried a
flaggon of oil with his bread.

19. *And he called the name of that place Beth-el.*   It may

appear absurd that Moses should speak of that place as a city, respecting which he had a little while before said that Jacob had slept there in the open air ; for why did not he seek an abode, or hide himself in some corner of a house ? But the difficulty is easily solved, because the city was not yet built ; neither did the place immediately take the name which Jacob had assigned, but lay long concealed. Even when a town was afterwards built on the spot, no mention is made of Beth-el, as if Jacob had never passed that way ; for the inhabitants did not know what had been done there, and therefore they called the city Luz,[1] according to their own imagination ; which name it retained until the Israelites, having taken possession of the land, recalled into common use, as by an act of restoration, the former name which had been abolished. And it is to be observed, that when posterity, by a foolish emulation, worshipped God in Beth-el, seeing that it was done without a divine command, the prophets severely inveighed against that worship, calling the name of the place Bethaven, that is, the house of iniquity : whence we infer how unsafe it is to rely upon the examples of the fathers without the word of God. The greatest care, therefore, must be taken, in treating of the worship of God, that what has been once done by men, should not be drawn into a precedent ; but that what God himself has prescribed in his word should remain an inflexible rule.

20. *And Jacob vowed a vow.* The design of this vow was, that Jacob would manifest his gratitude, if God should prove favourable unto him. Thus they offered peace-offerings under the law, to testify their gratitude ; and since thanksgiving is a sacrifice of a sweet odour, the Lord declares vows of this nature to be acceptable to him ; and therefore we must also have respect to this point, when we are asked *what* and *how* it is lawful to vow to God ;

---

[1] The word לוז (*Luz*) signifies an almond-tree, and the town may have derived this name from the fact that almond-trees abounded in the neighbourhood. Yet the verb from which it is taken means " to turn away, to depart, to go back ;" also " to be perverse, or wicked ;" and it is not impossible that this name may have been assigned to it on account of the wickedness of its inhabitants. See the Lexicons of Schindler, Gesenius, &c.—*Ed.*

for some are too fastidious, who would utterly condemn all vows rather than open the door to superstitions. But if the rashness of those persons is perverse, who indiscriminately pour forth their vows, we must also beware lest we become like those on the opposite side, who disallow all vows without exception. Now, in order that a vow may be lawful and pleasing to God, it is first necessary that it should tend to a right end ; and next, that men should devote nothing by a vow but what is in itself approved by God, and what he has placed within their own power. When the separate parts of this vow are examined, we shall see holy Jacob so regulating his conduct as to omit none of these things which I have mentioned. In the first place, he has nothing else in his mind than to testify his gratitude. Secondly, he confines whatever he is about to do, to the lawful worship of God. In the third place, he does not proudly promise what he had not the power to perform, but devotes the tithe of his goods as a sacred oblation. Wherefore, the folly of the Papists is easily refuted ; who, in order to justify their own confused farrago of vows, catch at one or another vow, soberly conceived, as a precedent, when in the meantime their own license exceeds all bounds. Whatever comes uppermost they are not ashamed to obtrude upon God. One man makes his worship to consist in abstinence from flesh, another in pilgrimages, a third in sanctifying certain days by the use of sackcloth, or by other things of the same kind ; and not to God only do they make their vows, but also admit any dead person they please into a participation of this honour. They arrogate to themselves the choice of perpetual celibacy. What do they find in the example of Jacob which has any similitude or affinity to such rashness, that they should hence catch at such a covering for themselves? But, for the purpose of bringing all these things clearly to light, we must first enter upon an explanation of the words. It may seem absurd that Jacob here makes a covenant with God, to be his worshipper, if he will give him what he desires ; as if truly he did not intend to worship God for nothing. I answer, that, by interposing this condition, Jacob did not by any means act from distrust, as if he doubted of

God's continual protection ; but that in this manner he made provision against his own infirmity, in preparing himself to celebrate the divine goodness by a vow previously made.[1] The superstitious deal with God just as they do with mortal man ; they try to soothe him with their allurements. The design of Jacob was far different ; namely, that he might the more effectually stimulate himself to the duties of religion. He had often heard from the mouth of God, " I will be always with thee ;" and he annexes his vow as an appendage to that promise. He seems indeed, at first sight, like a mercenary, acting in a servile manner ; but since he depends entirely upon the promises given unto him, and forms both his language and his affections in accordance with them, he aims at nothing but the confirmation of his faith, and gathers together those aids which he knows to be suitable to his infirmity. When, therefore, he speaks of food and clothing, we must not, on that account, accuse him of solicitude respecting this earthly life alone ; whereas he rather contends, like a valiant champion, against violent temptations. He found himself in want of all things ; hunger and nakedness were continually threatening him with death, not to mention his other innumerable dangers : therefore he arms himself with confidence, that he might proceed through all difficulties and obstacles, being fully assured that every kind of assistance was laid up for him in the grace of God: for he confesses himself to be in extreme destitution, when he says, " If the Lord will supply me with food and raiment." It may nevertheless be asked, since his grandfather Abraham had sent his servant with a splendid retinue, with camels and precious ornaments ; why does Isaac now send away his son without a single companion, and almost without provisions ? It is possible that he was thus dismissed, that the mind of cruel Esau might be moved to tenderness by a spectacle so miserable. Yet, in my judgment, another reason was of greater weight ; for Abraham, fearing lest his son Isaac should remain with his relatives, took an oath from his

---

[1] Se desposant à celebrer la bonté de Dieu, en se vouant expressement à luy. Preparing himself to celebrate the goodness of God, in devoting himself expressly to him.—*Fr. Tr.*

servant that he would not suffer his son to go into Mesopotamia. But now, since necessity compels holy Isaac to determine differently for his son Jacob ; he, at least, takes care
not to do anything which might retard his return. He
therefore supplies him with no wealth, and with no delicacies
which might ensnare his mind, but purposely sends him
away poor and empty, that he might be the more ready to
return. Thus we see that Jacob preferred his father's house
to all kingdoms, and had no desire of settled repose elsewhere.

21. *Then shall the Lord be my God.* In these words Jacob
binds himself never to apostatize from the pure worship of
the One God ; for there is no doubt that he here comprises
the sum of piety. But he may seem to promise what far
exceeds his strength ; for newness of life, spiritual righteousness, integrity of heart, and a holy regulation of the whole
life, were not in his own power. I answer, when holy men
vow those things which God requires of them, and which are
due from them as acts of piety ; they, at the same time,
embrace what God promises concerning the remission of
sins by the help of his Holy Spirit. Hence it follows that
they ascribe nothing to their own strength ; and also, that
whatever falls short of entire perfection does not vitiate their
worship, because God, mercifully and with paternal indulgence, pardons them.

22. *And this stone which I have set for a pillar.* This
ceremony was an appendage to divine worship ; for external
rites do not make men true worshippers of God, but are only
aids to piety. But because the holy fathers were then at
liberty to erect altars wherever they pleased, Jacob poured
a libation upon the stone, because he had then no other
sacrifice to offer ; not that he worshipped God according to
his own will, (for the direction of the Spirit was instead of
the written law,) but he erected in that place a stone—as he
was permitted to do by the kindness and permission of God—
which should be a testimony of the vision. Moreover, this
form of speech, that " the stone shall be Beth-el," is *metony-
mical ;* as we are sanctioned, by common usage, to transfer to
external signs what properly belongs to the things represented. I have lately shown how ignorantly posterity has

abused this holy exercise of piety. What next follows respecting the offering of tithes, is not a simple ceremony, but has a duty of charity annexed ; for Jacob enumerates, in a threefold order, first, the spiritual worship of God ; then the external rite, by which he both assists his own piety, and makes profession of it before men ; in the third place, an oblation, by which he exercises himself in giving friendly aid to his brethren ; for there is no doubt that tithes were applied to that use.

CHAPTER XXIX.

1. THEN Jacob went on his journey, and came into the land of the people of the east.

2. And he looked, and behold a well in the field, and, lo, there *were* three flocks of sheep lying by it ; for out of that well they watered the flocks : and a great stone *was* upon the well's mouth.

3. And thither were all the flocks gathered : and they rolled the stone from the well's mouth, and watered the sheep, and put the stone again upon the well's mouth in his place.

4. And Jacob said unto them, My brethren, whence *be* ye? And they said, Of Haran *are* we.

5. And he said unto them, Know ye Laban the son of Nahor? And they said, We know *him.*

6. And he said unto them, *Is* he well? And they said, *He is* well ; and, behold, Rachel his daughter cometh with the sheep.

7. And he said, Lo, *it is* yet high day, neither *is it* time that the cattle should be gathered together : water ye the sheep, and go *and* feed *them.*

8. And they said, We cannot, until all the flocks be gathered together, and *till* they roll the stone from the well's mouth ; then we water the sheep.

9. And while he yet spake with them, Rachel came with her father's sheep ; for she kept them.

10. And it came to pass, when Jacob saw Rachel, the daughter of

1. Et levavit Iahacob pedes suos, et perrexit ad terram filiorum Orientalium.

2. Et vidit, et ecce puteus erat in agro, ecce quoque ibi tres greges pecudum, qui cubabant juxta illum : quia e puteo ipso potum dabant gregibus, et lapis magnus erat super os putei.

3. Et congregabant se illuc omnes greges, et revolvebant lapidem ab ore putei potumque dabant pecudibus : et restituebant lapidem super os putei in locum suum.

4. Dixit ergo ad eos Iahacob, Fratres mei unde estis? Et dixerunt, De Charan sumus.

5. Tunc dixit ad eos, Numquid nostis Laban filium Nachor? Et dixerunt, Novimus.

6. Et dixit ad eos, Numquid est pax ei? Et dixerunt, Pax : et ecce Rachel filia ejus veniens cum pecudibus.

7. Tunc dixit, Ecce, adhuc dies magnus : non est tempus ut congregetur pecus : potum date pecudibus, et ite, pascite.

8. Qui dixerunt, Non possumus, donec congregentur omnes greges, et revolvant lapidem ab ore putei, et potum demus pecudibus.

9. Adhuc eo loquente cum eis, Rachel venit cum pecudibus quæ erant patris sui : quia ipsa pascebat.

10. Fuit autem quando vidit Iahacob Rachel filiam Laban fratris

Laban his mother's brother, and the sheep of Laban his mother's brother, that Jacob went near, and rolled the stone from the well's mouth, and watered the flock of Laban his mother's brother.

11. And Jacob kissed Rachel, and lifted up his voice, and wept.

12. And Jacob told Rachel that he *was* her father's brother, and that he *was* Rebekah's son: and she ran and told her father.

13. And it came to pass, when Laban heard the tidings of Jacob his sister's son, that he ran to meet him, and embraced him, and kissed him, and brought him to his house. And he told Laban all these things.

14. And Laban said to him, Surely thou *art* my bone and my flesh. And he abode with him the space of a month.

15. And Laban said unto Jacob, Because thou *art* my brother, shouldest thou therefore serve me for nought? tell me, what *shall* thy wages *be?*

16. And Laban had two daughters: the name of the elder *was* Leah, and the name of the younger *was* Rachel.

17. Leah *was* tender-eyed; but Rachel was beautiful and well-favoured.

18. And Jacob loved Rachel; and said, I will serve thee seven years for Rachel thy younger daughter.

19. And Laban said, *It is* better that I give her to thee, than that I should give her to another man: abide with me.

20. And Jacob served seven years for Rachel; and they seemed unto him *but* a few days, for the love he had to her.

21. And Jacob said unto Laban, Give *me* my wife, for my days are fulfilled, that I may go in unto her.

22. And Laban gathered together all the men of the place, and made a feast.

23. And it came to pass in the

matris suæ, et pecudes Laban fratris matris suæ, accessit Iahacob, et revolvit lapidem ab ore putei, et potum dedit pecudibus Laban fratris matris suæ.

11. Et osculatus est Iahacob Rachel, qui elevavit vocem suam, et flevit.

12. Et nuntiavit Iahacob ipsi Rachel quod frater patris sui esset, et quod filius Ribcæ esset: cucurrit itaque, et nuntiavit patri suo.

13. Et fuit, quum audisset Laban sermonem (*vel, nuntium*) Iahacob filii sororis suæ, cucurrit in occursum ejus, et amplexatus est eum, osculatusque est eum, et deduxit eum ad domum suam, et narravit ipsi Laban omnia hæc.

14. Tunc dixit ei Laban, Profecto os meum et caro mea es. Et habitavit cum eo mensem integrum.

15. Dixit autem Laban ad Iahacob, Num quoniam frater meus es, servies mihi gratis? indica mihi quæ sit merces tua.

16. Et Laban *erant* duæ filiæ: nomen majoris, Leah, et nomen minoris Rachel.

17. Oculi autem Leah erant teneri: at Rachel erat pulchra forma, et pulchra aspectu.

18. Dilexit itaque Iahacob Rachel: et dixit, Serviam tibi septem annos pro Rachel filia tua minore.

19. Tunc dixit Laban, Melius est ut dem eam tibi, quam dem eam viro alteri: mane mecum.

20. Servivit itaque Iahacob pro Rachel septem annos; et fuerunt in oculis ejus sicut dies pauci, eo quod diligeret eam.

21. Postea dixit Iahacob ad Laban, Da uxorem meam: quia completi sunt dies mei, ut ingrediar ad eam.

22. Et congregavit Laban omnes viros loci, et fecit convivium.

23. Fuit autem vesperi, in vespera

evening, that he took Leah his daughter, and brought her to him; and he went in unto her.

24. And Laban gave unto his daughter Leah Zilpah his maid *for* an handmaid.

25. And it came to pass, that, in the morning, behold, it *was* Leah: and he said to Laban, What *is* this thou hast done unto me? did not I serve with thee for Rachel? wherefore then hast thou beguiled me?

26. And Laban said, It must not be so done in our country, to give the younger before the first-born.

27. Fulfil her week, and we will give thee this also, for the service which thou shalt serve with me yet seven other years.

28. And Jacob did so, and fulfilled her week; and he gave him Rachel his daughter to wife also.

29. And Laban gave to Rachel his daughter Bilhah his handmaid to be her maid.

30. And he went in also unto Rachel, and he loved also Rachel more than Leah, and served with him yet seven other years.

31. And when the Lord saw that Leah *was* hated, he opened her womb; but Rachel *was* barren.

32. And Leah conceived, and bare a son; and she called his name Reuben: for she said, Surely the Lord hath looked upon my affliction; now therefore my husband will love me.

33. And she conceived again, and bare a son; and said, Because the Lord hath heard that I *was* hated, he hath therefore given me this *son* also: and she called his name Simeon.

34. And she conceived again, and bare a son; and said, Now this time will my husband be joined unto me, because I have born him three sons: therefore was his name called Levi.

35. And she conceived again, and bare a son; and she said, Now will I praise the Lord: therefore she called his name Judah; and left bearing.

accepit Leah filiam suam, et adduxit eam ad illum, et ingressus est ad eam.

24. Et dedit Laban ei Zilpah ancillam suam, Leah filiæ suæ ancillam.

25. Et fuit mane, et ecce erat Leah, et dixit ad Laban, Quid hoc fecisti mihi? numquid non pro Rachel servivi tibi? et utquid decepisti me?

26. Tunc dixit Laban, Non fit ita in loco nostro, ut detur minor ante primogenitam.

27. Comple hebdomadem hujus, et dabimus tibi etiam hanc pro servitute, quam servies mihi adhuc septem annos alios.

28. Fecit ergo Iahacob sic, et complevit hebdomadem illius, et dedit ei Rachel filiam suam in uxorem.

29. Et dedit Laban Rachel filiæ suæ Bilhah ancillam suam in ancillam.

30. Et ingressus est etiam ad Rachel: et dilexit etiam Rachel magis quam Leah: servivitque ei adhuc septem annos alios.

31. Vidit autem Iehova quod exosa esset Leah, et aperuit vulvam ejus, et Rachel erat sterilis.

32. Et concepit Leah, et peperit filium, vocavitque nomen ejus Reuben: quia dixit, Nempe vidit Iehova afflictionem meam: nunc enim diliget me vir meus.

33. Et concepit adhuc, et peperit filium, et dixit, Quia audivit Iehova quod exosa essem, dedit mihi etiam hunc. Et vocavit nomen ejus Simeon.

34. Et concepit adhuc, et peperit filium, et dixit, Nunc vice hac copulabitur vir meus mihi, quia peperi ei tres filios. Idcirco vocavit nomen ejus Levi.

35. Et concepit adhuc, et peperit filium, et dixit, Vice hac confitebor Iehovæ. Idcirco vocavit nomen ejus Iehudah: et destitit a pariendo.

1. *Then Jacob went on his journey.*[1] Moses now relates
the arrival of Jacob in Mesopotamia, and the manner in
which he was received by his uncle; and although the narration may seem superfluous, it yet contains nothing but
what is useful to be known; for he commends the extraordinary strength of Jacob's faith, when he says, that "he lifted
up his feet" to come into an unknown land. Again, he
would have us to consider the providence of God, which
caused Jacob to fall in with the shepherds, by whom he was
conducted to the home he sought; for this did not happen
accidentally, but he was guided by the hidden hand of God
to that place; and the shepherds, who were to instruct and
confirm him respecting all things, were brought thither at
the same time. Therefore, whenever we may wander in uncertainty through intricate windings, we must contemplate,
with eyes of faith, the secret providence of God which governs us and our affairs, and leads us to unexpected results.

4. *My brethren, whence be ye?* The great frankness of
that age appears in this manner of meeting together; for,
though the fraternal name is often abused by dishonest and
wicked men, it is yet not to be doubted that friendly intercourse was then more faithfully cultivated than it is now.
This was the reason why Jacob salutes unknown men as
brethren, undoubtedly according to received custom. Frugality also is apparent, in that Rachel sometimes pays attention to the flock; for, since Laban abounds with servants,
how does it happen that he employs his own daughter in a
vile and sordid service, except that it was deemed disgraceful
to educate children in idleness, softness, and indulgence?
Whereas, on the contrary, at this day, since ambition, pride,
and refinement, have rendered manners effeminate, the care
of domestic concerns is held in such contempt, that women, for
the most part, are ashamed of their proper office. It followed,
from the same purity of manners which has been mentioned,

---

[1] Et levavit Iahacob pedes suos. And Jacob lifted up his feet. See
margin of English Bible. This is a correct translation of the Hebrew
רגליו ישא, (*yissa reglav.*) " The phrase is emphatic, and implies that he
travelled on briskly and cheerfully, notwithstanding his age, being refreshed in his spirit by the recent manifestation of the Divine favour:"—
Bush.—*Ed.*

that Jacob ventured so unceremoniously to kiss his cousin ;
for much greater liberty was allowed in their chaste and
modest mode of living.[1] In our times, impurity and ungovernable lusts are the cause why not only kisses are suspected,
but even looks are dreaded ; and not unjustly, since the world
is filled with every kind of corruption, and such perfidy prevails, that the intercourse between men and women is seldom
conducted with modesty : [2]wherefore, that ancient simplicity
ought to cause us deeply to mourn ; so that this vile corruption into which the world has fallen may be distasteful to us,
and that the contagion of it may not affect us and our families.
The order of events, however, is inverted in the narration of
Moses ; for Jacob did not kiss Rachel till he had informed
her that he was her relative. Hence also his weeping; for,
partly through joy, partly through the memory of his father's
house, and through natural affection, he burst into tears.

13. *And he told Laban all these things.* Since Laban had
previously seen one of Abraham's servants replenished with
great wealth, an unfavourable opinion of his nephew might
instantly enter into his mind : it was therefore necessary for
holy Jacob to explain the causes of his own departure, and
the reason why he had been sent away so contemptibly
clothed. It is also probable that he had been instructed by
his mother respecting the signs and marks by which he
might convince them of his relationship : therefore Laban
exclaims, " Surely thou art my bone and my flesh ;" intimating that he was fully satisfied, and that he was induced by
indubitable tokens to acknowledge Jacob as his nephew.
This knowledge inclines him to humanity ; for the sense of
nature dictates that they who are united by ties of blood
should endeavour to assist each other ; but though the bond
between relatives is closer, yet our kindness ought to extend more widely, so that it may diffuse itself through the

---

[1] Nam in vita casta et modesta multo major erat libertas. Car la
liberté estoit beaucoup plus grande en leur facon de vivre, chaste et mo-
deste.—*Fr. Tr.*

[2] It is scarcely to be doubted that, notwithstanding Calvin's sweeping
charge, there were many exceptions to this general dissoluteness of manners in his days, as we must thankfully acknowledge there are in our own
times, however extensively the evil he reprobates may have prevailed.— *Ed.*

whole human race. If, however, all the sons of Adam are thus
joined together, that spiritual relationship which God produces
between the faithful, and than which there is no holier bond
of mutual benevolence, ought to be much more effectual.

14. *And he abode with him the space of a month.* Though
Laban did not doubt that Jacob was his nephew by his sister,
he nevertheless puts his character to trial during a month,
and then treats with him respecting wages. Hence may be
inferred the uprightness of the holy man; because he was
not idle while with his uncle, but employed himself in honest
labours, that he might not in idleness eat another's bread
for nothing; hence Laban is compelled to acknowledge that
some reward beyond his mere food was due to him. When
he says, " Because thou art my brother, shouldest thou
therefore serve me for nought ?" his meaning may be twofold; either that it would be excessively absurd and unjust
to defraud a relation of his due reward, for whom he ought
to have greater consideration than for any stranger; or that
he was unwilling to exact gratuitous service under the colour
of relationship. This second exposition is the more suitable,
and is received nearly by the consent of all. For they read
in one connected sentence, " Because thou art my brother,
shalt thou therefore serve me for nought ?" Moreover, we
must note the end for which Moses relates these things. In
the first place, a great principle of equity is set before us in
Laban; inasmuch as this sentiment is inherent in almost all
minds, " that justice ought to be mutually cultivated," till
blind cupidity draws them away in another direction. And
God has engraven in man's nature a law of equity; so that
whoever declines from that rule, through an immoderate desire of private advantage, is left utterly without excuse. But
a little while after, when it came to a matter of practice,
Laban, forgetful of this equity, thinks only of what may be
profitable to himself. Such an example is certainly worthy of
notice, for men seldom err in general principles, and therefore, with one mouth, confess that every man ought to receive what is his due : but as soon as they descend to their
own affairs, perverse self-love blinds them, or at least enve-
lopes them in such clouds that they are carried in an oppo-

site course. Wherefore, let us learn to restrain ourselves, that a desire of our own advantage may not prevail to the sacrifice of justice. And hence has arisen the proverb, that no one is a fit judge in his own cause, because each, being unduly favourable to himself, becomes forgetful of what is right. Wherefore, we must ask God to govern and restrain our affections by a spirit of sound judgment. Laban, in wishing to enter into a covenant, does what tends to avoid contentions and complaints. The ancient saying is known, " We should deal lawfully with our friends, that we may not afterwards be obliged to go to law with them." For, whence arise so many legal broils, except that every one is more liberal towards himself, and more niggardly towards others than he ought to be? Therefore, for the purpose of cherishing concord, firm compacts are necessary, which may prevent injustice on one side or the other.

18. *I will serve thee seven years.* The iniquity of Laban betrays itself in a moment; for it is a shameful barbarity to give his daughter, by way of reward, in exchange for Jacob's services, making her the subject of a kind of barter. He ought, on the other hand, not only to have assigned a portion to his daughter, but also to have acted more liberally towards his future son-in-law. But under the pretext of affinity, he defrauds him of the reward of his labour, the very thing which he had before acknowledged to be unjust.[1] We therefore perceive still more clearly what I have previously alluded to, that although from their mother's womb men have a general notion of justice, yet as soon as their own advantage presents itself to view, they become actually unjust, unless the Lord reforms them by his Spirit. Moses does not

---

[1] Perhaps undue severity of language is here used respecting Laban; for we find it not unusual for the father to demand something for his daughter, instead of giving a dowry with her. See the history of Shechem, who says concerning Dinah, " Ask me never so much dowry and gift, and I will give it." Chap. xxxiv. 12. David also had to purchase Saul's daughter by the slaughter of the Philistines. The Prophet Hosea bought his wife " for fifteen pieces of silver and a homer and a half of barley." Still it was by no means generous on the part of Laban to make such terms with a near relative; and, at all events, he ought to have given to his daughters and their children any profit that he might have obtained by his hard bargain with Jacob.—*Ed.*

here relate something rare or unusual, but what is of most common occurrence. For though men do not set their daughters to sale, yet the desire of gain hurries the greater part so far away, that they prostitute their honour and sell their souls. Further, it is not altogether to be deemed a fault that Jacob was rather inclined to love Rachel; whether it was that Leah, on account of her tender eyes, was less beautiful, or that she was pleasing only by the comeliness of her eyes,[1] while Rachel excelled her altogether in elegance of form. For we see how naturally a secret kind of affection produces mutual love. Only excess is to be guarded against, and so much the more diligently, because it is difficult so to restrain affections of this kind, that they do not prevail to the stifling of reason. Therefore he who shall be induced to choose a wife, because of the elegance of her form, will not necessarily sin, provided reason always maintains the ascendency, and holds the wantonness of passion in subjection. Yet perhaps Jacob sinned in being too self-indulgent, when he desired Rachel the younger sister to be given to him, to the injury of the elder; and also, while yielding to the desire of his own eyes, he undervalued the virtues of Leah: for this is a very culpable want of self-government, when any one chooses a wife only for the sake of her beauty, whereas excellence of disposition ought to be deemed of the first importance. But the strength and ardour of his attachment manifests itself in this, that he felt no weariness in the labour of seven years: but chastity was also joined with it, so that he persevered, during this long period, with a patient and quiet mind in the midst of so many labours. And here again the integrity and continence of that age is apparent, because, though dwelling under the same roof, and accustomed to familiar intercourse, Jacob yet conducted himself with modesty, and abstained from all impropriety. Therefore, at the close of the appointed time he said, " Give me my wife, that I may go in unto her," by which he implies that she had been hitherto a pure virgin.

[1] This latter opinion is adopted by Dr. A. Clarke, who says, " The chief recommendation of Leah was her *soft* and *beautiful* eyes; but Rachel was beautiful in her *shape, person, mien,* and *gait,* and beautiful in her countenance." The greater part of commentators, however, take the same view of the case as our translators.— *Ed.*

22. *And Laban gathered together.* Moses does not mean that a supper was prepared for the whole people, but that many guests were invited, as is customary in splendid nuptials ; and there is no doubt that he applied himself with the greater earnestness to adorn that feast, for the purpose of holding Jacob bound by a sense of shame, so that he should not dare to depreciate the marriage into which he had been deceived. We hence gather what, at that time, was the religious observance connected with the marriage bed. For this was the occasion of Jacob's deception, that, out of regard for the modesty of brides, they were led veiled into the chamber; but now, the ancient discipline being rejected, men become almost brutal.

25. *And he said to Laban.* Jacob rightly expostulates respecting the fraud practised upon him. And the answer of Laban, though it is not without a pretext, yet forms no excuse for the fraud. It was not the custom to give the younger daughters in marriage before the elder : and injustice would have been done to the first-born by disturbing this accustomed order. But he ought not, on that account, craftily to have betrothed Rachel to Jacob, and then to have substituted Leah in her place. He should rather have cautioned Jacob himself, in time, to turn his thoughts to Leah, or else to refrain from marriage with either of them. But we may learn from this, that wicked and deceitful men, when once they have turned aside from truth, make no end of transgressing : meanwhile, they always put forward some pretext for the purpose of freeing themselves from blame. He had before acted unjustly toward his nephew in demanding seven years' labour for his daughter; he had also unjustly set his daughter to sale, without dowry, for the sake of gain ; but the most unworthy deed of all was perfidiously to deprive his nephew of his betrothed wife, to pervert the sacred laws of marriage, and to leave nothing safe or sound. Yet we see him pretending that he has an honourable defence for his conduct, because it was not the custom of the country to prefer the younger to the elder.

27. *Fulfil her week.* Laban now is become callous in wickedness, for he extorts other seven years from his nephew to allow him to marry his other daughter. If he had

had ten more daughters, he would have been ready thus
to dispose of them all: yea, of his own accord, he obtrudes
his daughter as an object of merchandise, thinking nothing
of the disgrace of this illicit sale, if only he may make it a
source of gain.   In this truly he grievously sins, that he not
only involves his nephew in polygamy, but pollutes both him
and his own daughters by incestuous nuptials.   If by any
means a wife is not loved by her husband, it is better to re-
pudiate her than that she should be retained as a captive,
and consumed with grief by the introduction of a second
wife.   Therefore the Lord, by Malachi, pronounces divorce
to be more tolerable than polygamy. (Mal. ii. 14.)   Laban,
blinded by avarice, so sets his daughters together, that they
spend their whole lives in mutual hostility.   He also perverts all the laws of nature by casting two sisters into one
marriage-bed.[1]   Since Moses sets these crimes before the Israelites in the very commencement of their history, it is not
for them to be inflated by the sense of their nobility, so that
they should boast of their descent from holy fathers.   For,
however excellent Jacob might be, he had no other offspring
than that which sprung from an impure source; since, contrary to nature, two sisters are mixed together in one bed;[2]
and two concubines are afterwards added to the mass.   We
have seen indeed, above, that this license was too common
among oriental nations; but it was not allowable for men,
at their own pleasure, to subvert, by a depraved custom, the
law of marriage divinely sanctioned from the beginning.
Therefore, Laban is, in every way, inexcusable.   And although
necessity may, in some degree, excuse the fault of Jacob, it
cannot altogether absolve him from blame.   For he might
have dismissed Leah, because she had not been his lawful
wife: because the mutual consent of the man and the woman,
respecting which mistake is impossible, constitutes marriage.
But Jacob reluctantly retains her as his wife, from whom
he was released and free, and thus doubles his fault by polygamy, and trebles it by an incestuous marriage.   Thus we
see that the inordinate love of Rachel, which had been once

[1] It is here added, " ut altera sit alterius pellex."
[2] Quasi belluino more.

excited in his mind, was inflamed to such a degree, that he possessed neither moderation nor judgment. With respect to the words made use of, interpreters ascribe to them different meanings. Some refer the demonstrative pronoun to the week ;[1] others to Leah, as if it had been said, that he should not have Rachel until he had lived with her sister one week. But I rather explain it of Rachel, that he should purchase a marriage with her by another seven years' service; not that Laban deferred the nuptials to the end of that time, but that Jacob was compelled to engage himself in a new servitude.

30. *And he loved also Rachel more than Leah.*   No doubt Moses intended to exhibit the sins of Jacob, that we might learn to fear, and to conform all our actions to the sole rule of God's word.   For if the holy patriarch fell so grievously, who among us is secure from a similar fall, unless kept by the guardian care of God?   At the same time, it appears how dangerous it is to imitate the fathers while we neglect the law of the Lord.   And yet the foolish Papists so greatly delight themselves in this imitation, that they do not scruple to observe, as a law, whatever they find to have been practised by the fathers.   Besides which, they own as fathers those who are worthy of such sons, so that any raving monk is of more account with them than all the patriarchs.   It was not without fault on Leah's part that she was despised by her husband ; and the Lord justly chastised her, because she, being aware of her father's fraud, dishonourably obtained possession of her sister's husband ; but her fault forms no excuse for Jacob's lust.

31. *And when the Lord saw.*   Moses here shows that Jacob's extravagant love was corrected by the Lord ; as the affections of the faithful, when they become inordinate, are wont to be tamed by the rod.   Rachel is loved, not without wrong to her sister, to whom due honour is not given.   The

---

[1] מלא שבע זאת, (*Malai shebuah zot.*) The demonstrative pronoun זאת, if applied to *week*, would require the translation to be, " Fulfil *this* week;" that is, the week of Leah ; meaning the festive week in which the marriage was commemorated, and, as soon as that week was over, he would also give Jacob his remaining daughter to wife. This opinion is supported by eminent critics.—*Ed.*

Lord, therefore, interposes as her vindicator, and, by a suitable remedy, turns the mind of Jacob into that direction, to which it had been most averse. This passage teaches us, that offspring is a special gift of God; since the power of rendering one fertile, and of cursing the womb of the other with barrenness, is expressly ascribed to him. We must observe further, that the bringing forth of offspring tends to conciliate husbands to their wives. Whence also the ancients have called children by the name of *pledges ;* because they avail, in no slight degree, to increase and to cherish mutual love. When Moses asserts that Leah was hated, his meaning is, that she was not loved so much as she ought to have been. For she was not intolerable to Jacob, neither did he pursue her with hatred ; but Moses, by the use of this word, amplifies his fault, in not having discharged the duty of a husband, and in not having treated her who was his first wife with adequate kindness and honour. It is of importance carefully to notice this, because many think they fulfil their duty if they do not break out into mortal hatred. But we see that the Holy Spirit pronounces those as hated who are not sufficiently loved ; and we know, that men were created for this end, that they should love one another. Therefore, none will be counted guiltless of the crime of hatred before God, but he who embraces his neighbours with love. For not only will a secret displeasure be accounted as hatred, but even that neglect of brethren, and that cold charity which ever reigns in the world. But in proportion as any one is more closely connected with another, must be the endeavour to adhere to each other in a more sacred bond of affection. Moreover, with respect to married persons, though they may not openly disagree, yet if they are cold in their affection towards each other, this disgust is not far removed from hatred.

32. *She called his name Reuben.* Moses relates that Leah was not ungrateful to God. And truly, I do not doubt, that the benefits of God were then commonly more appreciated than they are now. For a profane stupor so occupies the mind of nearly all men, that, like cattle, they swallow up whatever benefits God, in his kindness, bestows upon them.

Further, Leah not only acknowledges God as the author of
her fruitfulness; but also assigns as a reason, that her affliction had been looked upon by the Lord, and a son had been
given her who should draw the affection of her husband
to herself.   Whence it appears probable, that when she saw
herself despised, she had recourse to prayer, in order that
she might receive more succour from heaven.   For thanksgiving is a proof that persons have previously exercised themselves in prayer; since they who hope for nothing from God
do, by their indolence, bury in oblivion all the favours he
has conferred upon them.   Therefore, Leah inscribed on the
person of her son[1] a memorial whereby she might stir herself
up to offer praise to God.   This passage also teaches, that
they who are unjustly despised by men are regarded by the
Lord.   Hence it affords a singularly profitable consolation
to the faithful; who, as experience shows, are for the most
part despised in the world.   Whenever, therefore, they are
treated harshly and contumeliously by men, let them take
refuge in this thought, that God will be the more propitious
to them.   Leah followed the same course in reference to her
second son; for she gave him a name which is derived from
" hearing,"[2] to recall to her memory that her sighs had been
heard by the Lord.   Whence we conjecture (as I have just before said) that when affliction was pressing upon her, she
cast her griefs into the bosom of God.   Her third son she
names from " joining;"[3] as if she would say, now a new
link is interposed, so that she should be more loved by her
husband.   In her fourth son, she again declares her piety
towards God, for she gives to him the name of " praise,"[4] as
having been granted to her by the special kindness of God.
She had, indeed, previously given thanks to the Lord; but

---

[1] ראובן.   " See a son."
[2] שמעון, from שמע, (shamah,) to hear.
[3] לוי, from לוה, (lavah,) to join.
[4] יהודה, from ידה, (yadah,) to praise.   There is something, as Calvin
intimates, in the series of names given by Leah to her children, which
seems to show the pious feelings of her heart.   In her first-born, *Reuben*,
she acknowledged that God had *looked* upon her affliction; in *Simeon*,
that he had *heard* her prayer; in *Levi*, that he had *joined* her husband
to her; and in *Judah*, she commemorates all these mercies with gratitude
and *praise.—Ed.*

whereas more abundant material for praise is supplied, she acknowledges not once only, nor by one single method, but frequently, that she has been assisted by the favour of God.

CHAPTER XXX.

1. AND when Rachel saw that she bare Jacob no children, Rachel envied her sister; and said unto Jacob, Give me children, or else I die.

2. And Jacob's anger was kindled against Rachel; and he said, *Am* I in God's stead, who hath withheld from thee the fruit of the womb?

3. And she said, Behold my maid Bilhah, go in unto her; and she shall bear upon my knees, that I may also have children by her.

4. And she gave him Bilhah her handmaid to wife; and Jacob went in unto her.

5. And Bilhah conceived, and bare Jacob a son.

6. And Rachel said, God hath judged me, and hath also heard my voice, and hath given me a son: therefore called she his name Dan.

7. And Bilhah, Rachel's maid, conceived again, and bare Jacob a second son.

8. And Rachel said, With great wrestlings have I wrestled with my sister, and I have prevailed: and she called his name Naphtali.

9. When Leah saw that she had left bearing, she took Zilpah her maid, and gave her Jacob to wife.

10. And Zilpah, Leah's maid, bare Jacob a son.

11. And Leah said, A troop cometh: and she called his name Gad.

12. And Zilpah, Leah's maid, bare Jacob a second son.

13. And Leah said, Happy am I, for the daughters will call me blessed: and she called his name Asher.

14. And Reuben went, in the days of wheat-harvest, and found man-

1. Porro vidit Rachel, quod non pareret ipsi Iahacob: et invidit Rachel sorori suæ, et dixit ad Iahacob, Da mihi filios: sin minus, mortua sum.

2. Et iratus est furor Iahacob in Rachel, et dixit, Numquid pro Deo sum, qui prohibuit a te fructum ventris?

3. Et dixit, Ecce ancilla mea Bilhah, ingredere ad eam, et pariet super genua mea: et erit etiam mihi filius ex ea.

4. Dedit ergo ei Bilhah ancillam suam in uxorem, et ingressus est ad eam Iahacob.

5. Et concepit Bilhah, et peperit ipsi Iahacob filium.

6. Et dixit Rachel, Iudicavit me Deus, et etiam audivit vocem meam, et dedit mihi filium. Idcirco vocavit nomen ejus Dan.

7. Et concepit adhuc, et peperit Bilhah ancilla Rachel filium secundum ipsi Iahacob.

8. Tunc dixit Rachel, Luctationibus divinis luctata sum cum sorore mea, etiam prævalui. Et vocavit nomen ejus Nephthali.

9. Vidit autem Leah, quod cessasset parere, et accepit Zilpah ancillam suam, et dedit eam Iahacob in uxorem.

10. Et peperit Zilpah ancilla Leah ipsi Iahacob filium.

11. Et dixit Leah, Venit turba: et vocavit nomen ejus Gad.

12. Et peperit Zilpah ancilla Leah filium secundum ipsi Iahacob.

13. Et dixit Leah, Ut beata dicar, quia beatam me dicent filiæ. Et vocavit nomen illius Aser.

14. Ivit autem Reuben in diebus messis triticeæ, et reperit mandra-

drakes in the field, and brought them unto his mother Leah. Then Rachel said to Leah, Give me, I pray thee, of thy son's mandrakes.

15. And she said unto her, *Is it* a small matter that thou hast taken my husband? and wouldest thou take away my son's mandrakes also? And Rachel said, Therefore he shall lie with thee to-night for thy son's mandrakes.

16. And Jacob came out of the field in the evening, and Leah went out to meet him, and said, Thou must come in unto me; for surely I have hired thee with my son's mandrakes. And he lay with her that night.

17. And God hearkened unto Leah, and she conceived, and bare Jacob the fifth son.

18. And Leah said, God hath given me my hire, because I have given my maiden to my husband: and she called his name Issachar.

19. And Leah conceived again, and bare Jacob the sixth son.

20. And Leah said, God hath endued me *with* a good dowry; now will my husband dwell with me, because I have born him six sons: and she called his name Zebulun.

21. And afterwards she bare a daughter, and called her name Dinah.

22. And God remembered Rachel, and God hearkened to her, and opened her womb.

23. And she conceived, and bare a son; and said, God hath taken away my reproach:

24. And she called his name Joseph; and said, The Lord shall add to me another son.

25. And it came to pass, when Rachel had born Joseph, that Jacob said unto Laban, Send me away, that I may go unto mine own place, and to my country.

26. Give *me* my wives and my children, for whom I have served thee, and let me go · for thou knowest my service which I have done thee.

goras in agro, et attulit eas Leah matri suæ. Et dixit Rachel ad Leah, Da quæso mihi de mandragoris filii tui.

15. Et dixit ei, Numquid parum est quod abstuleris virum meum, ut auferas etiam mandragoras filii mei? Et dixit Rachel, Idcirco dormiat tecum hac nocte pro mandragoris filii tui.

16. Venit autem Iahacob ex agro vesperi, et egressa est Leah in occursum ejus, et dixit, Ad me ingredieris: quia mercando mercata sum te mandragoris filii mei. Et dormivit cum ea nocte illa.

17. Exaudivit Deus Leah, et concepit, et peperit ipsi Iahacob filium quintum.

18. Tunc dixit Leah, Dedit Deus mercedem meam: quia dedi ancillam meum viro meo. Et vocavit nomen ejus Issachar.

19. Et concepit adhuc Leah, et peperit filium sextum ipsi Iahacob.

20. Dixit ergo Leah, Dotavit me Deus dote bona: vice hac habitavit mecum vir meus: quia peperi ei sex filios. Et vocavit nomen ejus Zebulon.

21. Et postea peperit filiam: et vocavit nomen ejus Dinah.

22. Porro recordatus est Deus Rachel, et exaudivit eam Deus, et aperuit vulvam illius.

23. Et concepit, et peperit filium, et dixit, Amovit Deus probrum meum.

24. Et vocavit nomen ejus Ioseph, dicendo, Addat Iehova mihi filium alium.

25. Fuit autem quum peperisset Rachel Ioseph, dixit Iahacob ab Laban, Dimitte me, et ibo ad locum meum, et ad terram meam.

26. Da uxores meas, et liberos meos, propter quas servivi tibi, et ibo: tu enim nosti servitium meum, quo servivi tibi.

27. And Laban said unto him, I pray thee, if I have found favour in thine eyes, *tarry: for* I have learned by experience that the Lord hath blessed me for thy sake.

28. And he said, Appoint me thy wages, and I will give *it.*

29. And he said unto him, Thou knowest how I have served thee, and how thy cattle was with me.

30. For *it was* little which thou hadst before I *came*, and it is *now* increased unto a multitude; and the Lord hath blessed thee since my coming: and now, when shall I provide for mine own house also?

31. And he said, What shall I give thee? And Jacob said, Thou shalt not give me any thing. If thou wilt do this thing for me, I will again feed *and* keep thy flock.

32. I will pass through all thy flock to-day, removing from thence all the speckled and spotted cattle, and all the brown cattle among the sheep, and the spotted and speckled among the goats; and *of such* shall be my hire.

33. So shall my righteousness answer for me in time to come, when it shall come for my hire before thy face: every one that *is* not speckled and spotted among the goats, and brown among the sheep, that shall be counted stolen with me.

34. And Laban said, Behold, I would it might be according to thy word.

35. And he removed that day the he-goats that were ring-straked and spotted, and all the she-goats that were speckled and spotted, *and* every one that had *some* white in it, and all the brown among the sheep, and gave *them* into the hand of his sons.

36. And he set three days' journey betwixt himself and Jacob: and Jacob fed the rest of Laban's flocks.

37. And Jacob took him rods of green poplar, and of the hazel and chestnut-tree, and pilled white strakes in them, and made the white appear which *was* in the rods.

27. Et dixit ad eum Laban, Si, quæso, inveni gratiam in oculis tui, (expertus sum quod benedixit mihi Iehova propter te.)

28. Dixit ergo, Indica mercedem tuam mihi, et dabo.

29. Et dixit ad eum, Tu nosti qualiter servierim tibi, et quale fuit pecus tuum mecum:

30. Quia pusillum, quod fuit tibi ante me, crevit in multitudinem, et benedixit Dominus tibi ad *ingressum* pedis mei: et nunc quando faciam etiam ego domui meæ?

31. Et dixit, Quid dabo tibi? Respondit Iahacob, Non dabis mihi quicquam, si feceris mihi hoc, revertar, pascam, pecudes tuas custodiam.

32. Transibo per omnes pecudes tuas hodie, removendo inde omne pecus parvum punctis parvis respersum, et respersum maculis latis: et omnem agnum rufum in ovibus et respersum maculis latis, et respersum punctis parvis in capris: et erit merces mea.

33. Et testificabitur mihi justitia mea die crastino, quum venerit ad mercedem meam coram te: quicquid non erit punctis parvis respersum, et maculis latis respersum in capris, et rufum in ovibus, furto ablatum erat a me.

34. Tunc dixit Laban, Ecce utinam sit secundum verbum tuum.

35. Removit itaque in die illa hircos minores variegatos, et maculis respersos, et omnes capras punctis parvis respersas, et maculis latis respersas, omne in quo erat candor, et omne rufum in ovibus, et dedit in manus filiorum suorum.

36. Et posuit viam trium dierum inter se et inter Iahacob: et Iahacob pascebat pecudes Laban residuas.

37. Tulit autem sibi Iahacob virgam populeam viridem, et amygdalinam, et castaneam, et decorticavit in eis cortices albos, denudationem candoris, qui erat in virgis.

38. And he set the rods which he had pilled before the flocks in the gutters in the watering-troughs, when the flocks came to drink, that they should conceive when they came to drink.

39. And the flocks conceived before the rods, and brought forth cattle ring-straked, speckled, and spotted.

40. And Jacob did separate the lambs, and set the faces of the flocks toward the ring-straked and all the brown in the flock of Laban; and he put his own flocks by themselves, and put them not unto Laban's cattle.

41. And it came to pass, whensoever the stronger cattle did conceive, that Jacob laid the rods before the eyes of the cattle in the gutters, that they might conceive among the rods.

42. But when the cattle were feeble, he put *them* not in: so the feebler were Laban's, and the stronger Jacob's.

43. And the man increased exceedingly, and had much cattle, and maid-servants, and men-servants, and camels, and asses.

38. Et statuit virgas, quas decorticavit, in fluentis, in canalibus aquarum (ad quos veniebant pecudes ad bibendum) e regione pecudum, ut coirent dum venirent ad bibendum.

39. Et coibant pecudes prope virgas, et pariebant pecudes *fœtus* lineis distinctos, et punctis parvis respersos, et maculis latis respersos.

40. Et oves separavit Iahacob, et posuit facies pecudum ad *fœtus* lineis distinctos: et omne rufum in pecudibus *erat* Laban: et posuit sibi greges seorsum, et non posuit eos juxta pecudes Laban.

41. Fuit autem, in omni coitu pecudum primitivarum, ponebat Iahacob virgas in oculis pecudum in canalibus, ut coirent ad virgas.

42. Ad serotinos vero coitus pecudum non ponebat: et erant serotina ipsius Laban: primitiva autem ipsius Iahacob.

43. Crevit vir ergo supra modum: fueruntque ei pecudes multæ, et ancillæ, et servi, et cameli, et asini.

1. *And when Rachel saw.* Here Moses begins to relate that Jacob was distracted with domestic strifes. But although the Lord was punishing him, because he had been guilty of no light sin in marrying two wives, and especially sisters; yet the chastisement was paternal; and God himself, seeing that he is wont mercifully to pardon his own people, restrained in some degree his hand. Whence also it happened, that Jacob did not immediately repent, but added new offences to the former. But first we must speak of Rachel. Whereas she rejoiced to see her sister subjected to contempt and grief, the Lord represses this sinful joy, by giving his blessing to Leah, in order to make the condition of both of them equal. She hears the grateful acknowledgment of her sister, and learns from the names given to the four sons, that God had pitied, and had sustained by his favour, her who had been unjustly despised by man. Nevertheless envy inflames her, and will not suffer anything of the

dignity becoming a wife to appear in her. We see what ambition can do. For Rachel, in seeking pre-eminence, does not spare even her own sister; and scarcely refrains from venting her anger against God, for having honoured that sister with the gift of fruitfulness. Her emulation did not proceed from any injuries that she had received, but because she could not bear to have a partner and an equal, though she herself was really the younger. What would she have done had she been provoked, seeing that she envies her sister who was contented with her lot ? Now Moses, by exhibiting this evil in Rachel, would teach us that it is inherent in all; in order that each of us, tearing it up by the roots, may vigilantly purify himself from it. That we may be cured of envy, it behoves us to put away pride and self-love ; as Paul prescribes this single remedy against contentions, " Let nothing be done through vain-glory." (Phil. ii. 3.)

2. *And Jacob's anger was kindled.* The tenderness of Jacob's affection rendered him unwilling to offend his wife ; yet her unworthy conduct compelled him to do so, when he saw her petulantly exalt herself, not only against her sister, who piously, holily, and thankfully was enjoying the gifts of God ; but even against God himself, of whom it is said that " the fruit of the womb is his reward."   (Ps. cxxvii. 3.)   On this account, therefore, Jacob is angry, because his wife ascribes nothing to the providence of God, and, by imagining that children are the offspring of chance, would deprive God of the care and government of mankind. It is probable that Jacob had been already sorrowful on account of his wife's barrenness. He now, therefore, fears lest her folly should still farther provoke God's anger to inflict more severe strokes. This was a holy indignation, by which Jacob maintained the honour due to God, while he corrected his wife, and taught her that it was not without sufficient cause that she had been hitherto barren. For when he affirms that the Lord had shut her womb, he obliquely intimates that she ought the more deeply to humble herself.

3. *Behold my maid Bilhah.* Here the vanity of the female disposition appears. For Rachel is not induced to flee unto the Lord, but strives to gain a triumph by illicit arts.

Therefore she hurries Jacob into a third marriage. Whence
we infer, that there is no end of sinning, when once the
Divine institution is treated with neglect. And this is what
I have said, that Jacob was not immediately brought back
to a right state of mind by Divine chastisements. He acts,
indeed, in this instance, at the instigation of his wife: but
is his wife in the place of God, from whom alone the law of
marriage proceeds? But to please his wife, or to yield to
her importunity, he does not scruple to depart from the
command of God. *To bear upon the knees*, is nothing more
than to commit the child when born to another to be brought
up. Bilhah was a maid-servant; and therefore did not bear
for herself but for her mistress, who, claiming the child as
her own, thus procured the honour of a mother. Therefore
it is added, in the way of explanation, *I shall have children*,
or *I shall be built up by her*. For the word which Moses
here uses, is derived from בֵּן, *a son :* because children are as
the support and stay of a house. But Rachel acted sinfully,
because she attempted, by an unlawful method, and in
opposition to the will of God, to become a mother.

5. *And Bilhah conceived.* It is wonderful that God should
have deigned to honour an adulterous connexion with offspring: but he does sometimes thus strive to overcome by
kindness the wickedness of men, and pursues the unworthy
with his favour. Moreover, he does not always make the
punishment equal to the offences of his people, nor does he
always rouse them, alike quickly, from their torpor, but waits
for the matured season of correction. Therefore it was his
will that they who were born from this faulty connexion,
should yet be reckoned among the legitimate children ; just
as Moses shortly before called Bilhah a wife, who yet might
more properly have been called a harlot. And the common
rule does not hold, that what had no force from the beginning
can never acquire validity by succession of time ; for although the compact, into which the husband and wife sinfully
entered against the Divine command and the sacred order
of nature, was void; it came to pass nevertheless, by special
privilege, that the conjunction, which in itself was adulterous,
obtained the honour of wedlock. At length Rachel begins

to ascribe to God what is his own ; but this confession of hers is so mixed up with ambition, that it breathes nothing of sincerity or rectitude. She pompously announces, that her cause has been undertaken by the Lord. As if truly, she had been so injured by her sister, that she deserved to be raised by the favour of God ; and as if she had not attempted to deprive herself of his help. We see, then, that under the pretext of praising God, she rather does him wrong, by rendering him subservient to her desires. Add to this, that she imitates hypocrites, who, while in adversity, rush against God with closed eyes ; yet when more prosperous fortune favours them, indulge in vain boastings, as if God smiled upon all their deeds and sayings. Rachel, therefore, does not so much celebrate the goodness of God, as she applauds herself. Wherefore let the faithful, instructed by her example, abstain from polluting the sacred name of God by hypocrisy.

8. *With great wrestlings.*[1] Others translate it, " I am joined with the joinings of God ;"[2] as if she exulted in having recovered what she had lost ; or, certainly, in having obtained an equal degree of honour with her sister. Others render it, " I am doubled with the duplications of God." But both derive the noun and the verb from the root פתל, (*patal,*) which signifies a twisted thread. The former of these senses comes to this ; that since Rachel has attained a condition equal to that of her sister, there is no reason why her sister should claim any superiority over her. But the latter sense expresses more confident boasting, since she proclaims herself a conqueror, and doubly superior. But a more simple meaning is (in my opinion) adduced by others, namely, that she " wrestled with divine or excellent wrestlings." For the Hebrews indicate all excellence by adding the name of God ; because the more excellent anything is, the more does the glory of God shine in it. But perverse is that boasting with which she glories over her sister, when she ought rather suppliantly to have implored forgiveness. In

[1] Luctationibus divinis. Margin of English Bible, " with wrestlings of God."

[2] Conjunctionibus Dei conjuncta sum.

Rachel the pride of the human mind is depicted ; because they whom God has endowed with his benefits, for the most part are so elated, that they rage contumeliously against their neighbours. Besides, she foolishly prefers herself to her sister in fruitfulness, in which she is still manifestly inferior. But they who are puffed up with pride have also the habit of malignantly depreciating those gifts which the Lord has bestowed on others, in comparison with their own smaller gifts. Perhaps, also, she expected a numerous progeny, as if God were under obligation to her. She did not, as pious persons are wont to do, conceive hope from benefits received ; but, by a confident presumption of the flesh, made herself sure of everything she wished. Hitherto, then, she gave no sign of pious modesty. Whence is this, but because her temporary barrenness had not yet thoroughly subdued her ? Therefore we ought the more to beware, lest if God relaxes our punishments, we, being inflated by his kindness, should perish.

9. *When Leah saw that she had left bearing.* Moses returns to Leah, who, not content with four sons, devised a method whereby she might always retain her superior rank : and therefore she also, in turn, substitutes her maid in her place. And truly Rachel deserved such a reward of her perverse design ; since she, desiring to snatch the palm from her sister, does not consider that the same contrivance to which she had resorted, might speedily be employed against herself. Yet Leah sins still more grievously, by using wicked and unjust arts in the contest. Within a short period, she had experienced the wonderful blessing of God ; and now, because she ceased from bearing, for a little while, she despairs concerning the future, as if she had never participated in the Divine favour. What, if her desire was strong ; why did she not resort to the fountain of blessing ? In obtruding, therefore, her maid, she gave proof not only of impatience, but also of distrust ; because with the remembrance of Divine mercy, faith also is extinguished in her heart. And we know that all who rely upon the Lord are so tranquil and sedate in their mind, that they patiently wait for what he is about to give. And it is the just punishment of

unbelief when any one stumbles through excessive haste.
So much the more ought we to beware of the assaults of the
flesh, if we desire to maintain a right course.

As to the name *Gad*, this passage is variously expounded
by commentators. In this point they agree, that בגד (*Ba-
gad*) means the same as if Leah had said "the time of
bearing is come."[1] But some suppose גד (*Gad*) to be the
prosperous star of Jupiter; others, Mercury; others, *good
fortune*. They adduce Isaiah lxv. 11, where it is written,
"they offer a libation to Gad."[2] But the context of the
Prophet shows that this ought rather to be understood of the
host of heaven, or of the number of false gods ; because it
immediately follows that they offer sacrifices to the stars,
and furnish tables for a multitude of gods : the punishment
is then added, that as they had fabricated an immense number of deities, so God will "number" them "to the sword." As
it respects the present passage, nothing is less probable than
that Leah should extol the planet Jupiter instead of God,
seeing that she, at least, maintained the principle that the
propagation of the human race flows from God alone. I wonder
also that interpreters understand this of prosperous fortune,
when Moses afterwards, chap. xlix. 19, leads us to an opposite
meaning. For the allusion he there makes would be inappropriate, " Gad, a troop shall overcome him," &c., unless it
had been the design of Leah to congratulate herself on the
troop of her children. For since she had so far surpassed
her sister,[3] she declares that she has children in great abundance. When she proclaims herself *happy*[4] in her sixth son,

[1] Venit felicitas. In the French translation, " Mon heur est venu."
My hour is come. The word בגד is explained in the margin of the He-
brew Bible by בא גד. Venit turma, ceu *exercitus*—a troop or army cometh.
See Schindler.—*Ed.*

[2] " Ye are they that forsake the Lord, that forget my holy mountain,
that prepare a table for that *troop* (margin, Gad), and that furnish a
drink-offering to that number" (margin, Meni).—English Translation.
Calvin has quoted from memory, and not accurately, having put libation
instead of table.—*Ed.*

[3] Nam quum sesquialtera parte superior esset, prædicat se habere in
magna copia liberos.

[4] " And Leah said, Happy am I, for the daughters shall call me blessed ;
and she called his name Asher."—English Translation.

It may be observed that the names given to these children of the hand-

it again appears in what great esteem fecundity was then
held.   And certainly it is a great honour, when God confers
on mortals the sacred title of parents, and through them propagates the human race formed after his own image.

14. *And Reuben went in the days of wheat harvest.*   This
narration of the fact that a boy brought home I know not
what kind of fruit out of the fields, and presented it to his
mother, by which she purchased of her sister one night with
her husband, has the appearance of being light and puerile.
Yet it contains a useful instruction.   For we know how
foolishly the Jews glory in extolling the origin of their own
nation: for they scarcely deign to acknowledge that they
have sprung from Adam and Noah, with the rest of mankind.   And certainly they do excel in the dignity of their
ancestors, as Paul testifies, (Rom. ix. 5,) but they do not
acknowledge this as coming from God.   Wherefore the Spirit
purposely aimed at beating down this arrogance, when he
described their race as sprung from a beginning so mean and
abject.   For he does not here erect a splendid stage on which
they may exhibit themselves ; but he humbles them and
exalts the grace of God, seeing that he had brought forth his
Church out of nothing.   Respecting the kind of fruit mentioned, I have nothing certain to adduce.[1]   That it was
fragrant is gathered from Canticles vii. 13.[2]   And whereas
all translate it *mandrakes,* I do not contend on that point.

15. *Is it a small matter that thou hast taken my husband ?*
Moses leaves more for his readers to reflect upon than he ex-

maidens were far less indicative of a pious state of mind, than those which
Leah had previously given to her own sons.   A fact which confirms the
remarks of Calvin on the impiety of the course pursued by the rival wives.
Rachel seems to make no reference to God in the names of the children
of her handmaid ; Leah, in imitating the example of her sister, seems to
lose her own previous devotional feeling ; and both sink in our esteem, as
they proceed in their unseemly contentions.—*Ed.*

[1] Mandrakes—Heb. דוּדָאִים, (*dudaim,*) from דּוּד, (*dud,*) beloved ; supposed to be a species of melon with purple flowers.   It grows abundantly
in Palestine, and is held in high respect for its prolific virtues.   Gesenius
describes mandrakes as "Love apples (Liebes äpfel), the apples of the Man-
dragora, an herb resembling the belladonna, with a root like a carrot, having
white and reddish blossoms of a sweet smell, and with yellow odoriferous
apples."—*Ed.*

[2] "The mandrakes give a smell, and at our gates are all manner of
pleasant fruits."

presses in words ; namely, that Jacob's house had been filled with contentions and strifes. For Leah speaks haughtily, because her mind had been long so exasperated that she could not address herself mildly and courteously to her sister. Perhaps the sisters were not thus contentious by nature ; but God suffered them to contend with each other, that the punishment of polygamy might be exhibited to posterity. And it is not to be doubted that this domestic private quarrel, yea, hostile dissension, brought great grief and torment to the holy man. But the reason why he found himself thus distracted by opposite parties was, that against all right, he had broken the unity of the conjugal bond.

17. *And God hearkened unto Leah.* Moses expressly declares this, in order that we may know how indulgently God dealt with that family. For who would have thought, that, while Leah was hatefully denying to her sister the fruits gathered by her boy, and was purchasing, by the price of those fruits, a night with her husband, there would be any place for prayers ? Moses, therefore, teaches us, that pardon was granted for these faults, to prove that the Lord would not fail to complete his work notwithstanding such great infirmity. But Leah ignorantly boasts that her son was given to her as a reward of her sin ; for she had violated the fidelity of holy wedlock, when she introduced a fresh concubine to oppose her sister. Truly, she is so far from the confession of her fault, that she proclaims her own merit. I grant there was some excuse for her conduct ; for she intimates that she was not so much excited by lust, as by modest love, because she desired to increase her family and to fulfil the duty of an honourable mother of a family. But though this pretext is specious in the eyes of men, yet the profanation of holy marriage cannot be pleasing to God. She errs, therefore, in taking what was *no cause* for *the cause.* And this is the more to be observed ; because it is a fault which too much prevails in the world, for men to reckon the free gifts of God as their own reward ; yea, even to boast of their deserts, when they are condemned by the word of God. In her sixth son, she more purely and rightly estimates the divine goodness, when she gives thanks to God, that, by his kind-

ness, her husband would hereafter be more closely united to her, (ver. 20). For although he had lived with her before, yet, being too much attached to Rachel, he was almost entirely alienated from Leah. It has before been said, that children born in lawful wedlock are bonds to unite the minds of their parents.

21. *And afterward she bare a daughter.* It is not known whether Jacob had any other daughter ; for it is not uncommon in Scripture, when genealogies are recorded, to omit the women, since they do not bear their own name, but lie concealed under the shadow of their husbands. Meanwhile, if anything worthy of commemoration occurs to any women, especial mention is then made of them. This was the case with Dinah, on account of the violence done to her ; of which more will be said hereafter. But whereas the sons of Jacob subsequently regarded it as an indignity that their sister should marry one of another nation ; and as Moses records nothing of any other daughters, either as being settled in the land of Canaan, or married in Egypt, it is probable that Dinah was the only one born to him.

22. *And God remembered Rachel.* Since with God nothing is either *before* or *after*, but all things are present, he is subject to no forgetfulness, so that, in the lapse of time, he should need to be reminded of what is past. But the Scripture describes the presence and memory of God from the effect produced upon ourselves, because we conceive him to be such as he appears to be by his acts. Moreover, whether Rachel's child was born the last of all, cannot with certainty be gathered from the words of Moses. They who, in this place, affirm that the figure *hysteron proteron*, which puts the last first, is used, are moved by the consideration, that if Joseph had been born after the last of his brethren, the age which Moses records in chapter xli. 46, would not accord with the fact. But they are deceived in this, that they reckon the nuptials of Rachel from the end of the second seven years; whereas it is certainly proved from the context, that although Jacob agreed to give his service for Rachel, yet he obtained her immediately ; because from the beginning, the strife between the two sisters broke forth. Moses clearly intimates, in this

place, that the blessing of God was bestowed late, when
Rachel had despaired of issue, and had long been subject to
reproach because of her barrenness.   On account of this
prosperous omen she gave the name Joseph[1] to her son, deriving the hope of two sons from the prospect of *one*.[2]

25. *Send me away, that I may go.*   Seeing that Jacob had
been retained by a proposed reward for his services, it might
appear that he was acting craftily in desiring his dismissal
from his father-in-law.   I cannot, however, doubt that the
desire to return had already entered his mind, and that he
ingenuously avowed his intention.   First; having experienced,
in many ways, how unjust, how perfidious, and even cruel,
Laban had been, there is no wonder that he should wish to
depart from him, as soon as ever the opportunity was afforded.
Secondly ; since, from the long space of time which had
elapsed, he hoped that his brother's mind would be appeased,
he could not but earnestly wish to return to his parents ;
especially as he had been oppressed by so many troubles,
that he could scarcely fear a worse condition in any other
place.   But the promise of God was the most powerful stimulant of all to excite his desire to return.   For he had not
rejected the benediction which was dearer to him than his
own life.   To this point his declaration refers, " I will go to
my own place and to my country ;" for he does not use this
language concerning Canaan, only because he was born there,
but because he knew that it had been divinely granted to
him.   For if he had said that he desired to return, merely
because it was his native soil, he might have been exposed
to ridicule ; since his father had passed a wandering and unsettled life, continually changing his abode.   I therefore
conclude, that although he might have dwelt commodiously
elsewhere, the oracle of God, by which the land of Canaan had
been destined for him, was ever fresh in his memory.   And although, for a time, he submits to detention, this does not alter
his purpose to depart : for necessity, in part, extorted it from

---

[1] יוסף, (*Yoseph*,) he will add.
" The Lord shall add to me another son."   This may be regarded
either as a prophecy respecting Benjamin, or as a prayer which was fulfilled when Benjamin was born.—*Ed.*

him, since he was unable to extricate himself from the snares
of his uncle; in part also, he voluntarily gave way, in order
that he might acquire something for himself and his family,
lest he should return poor and naked to his own country.
But here the insane wickedness of Laban is discovered.
After he had almost worn out his nephew and son-in-law, by
hard and constant toil for fourteen years, he yet offers him
no wages for the future. The equity, of which at first he
had made such pretensions, had already vanished. For the
greater had been the forbearance of Jacob, the more tyrannical license did he usurp over him. So the world abuses
the gentleness of the pious; and the more meekly they conduct themselves, the more ferociously does the world assail
them. But though, like sheep, we are exposed, in this world,
to the violence and injuries of wolves; we must not fear lest
they should hurt or devour us, since the Heavenly Shepherd
keeps us under his protection.

27. *I pray thee, if I have found favour in thine eyes.* We
perceive hence, that Jacob had not been a burdensome guest,
seeing that Laban soothes him with bland address, in order
to procure from him a longer continuance in his service.
For, sordid and grasping as he was, he would not have suffered Jacob to remain a moment in his house, unless he had
found his presence to be a certain source of gain. Inasmuch
therefore, as he not only did not thrust him out, but anxiously
sought to retain him, we hence infer that the holy man had
undergone incredible labours, which had not only sufficed for
the sustenance of a large family, but had also brought great
profit to his father-in-law. Wherefore, he complains afterwards, not unjustly, that he had endured the heat of the
day, and the cold of the night. Nevertheless, there is no
doubt, that the blessing of God availed more than any labours
whatever, so that Laban perceived Jacob to be a kind of
horn of plenty, as he himself confesses. For he not only
commends his fidelity and diligence, but expressly declares
that he himself had been blessed by the Lord, for Jacob's
sake. It appears, then, that the wealth of Laban had so
increased, from the time of Jacob's coming, that it was as if
his gains had visibly distilled from heaven. Moreover, as

the word ‫נחש‬ (*nachash*), among the Hebrews, means to know
by auguries or by divination, some interpreters imagine that
Laban, having been instructed in magic arts, found that the
presence of Jacob was useful and profitable to him.   Others,
however, expound the words more simply, as meaning that
he had proved it to be so by experiment.   To me the true
interpretation seems to be, as if he had said, that the blessing of God was as perceptible to him, as if it had been attested
by prophecy, or found out by augury.

29. *Thou knowest how I have served thee.*   This answer of
Jacob is not intended to increase the amount of his wages ;
but he would expostulate with Laban, and would charge him
with acting unjustly and unkindly in requiring a prolongation of the time of service.   There is also no doubt that he
is carried forth, with every desire of his mind, towards the
land of Canaan.   Therefore a return thither was, in his view,
preferable to any kind of riches whatever.   Yet, in the meantime, he indirectly accuses his father-in-law, both of cunning
and of inhumanity, in order that he may extort something
from him, if he must remain longer.   For he could not hope
that the perfidious old fox would, of himself, perform an act
of justice ; neither does Jacob simply commend his own industry, but shows that he had to deal with an unjust and
cruel man.   Meanwhile, it is to be observed, that although he
had laboured strenuously, he yet ascribes nothing to his own
labour, but imputes it entirely to the blessing of God that
Laban had been enriched.   For though when men faithfully
devote themselves to their duty, they do not lose their labour;
yet their success depends entirely upon the favour of God.
What Paul asserts concerning the efficacy of teaching, extends still further, " that he who plants and he who waters
is nothing," (1 Cor. iii. 7,) for the similitude is taken from
general experience.   The use of this doctrine is twofold.
First, whatever I attempt, or to whatever work I apply my
hands, it is my duty to desire God to bless my labour, that
it may not be vain and fruitless.   Then, if I have obtained
anything, my second duty is to ascribe the praise to God ;
without whose blessing, men in vain rise up early, fatigue
themselves the whole day, late take rest, eat the bread of

carefulness, and taste even a little water with sorrow. With respect to the meaning of the *words*, when Jacob says, "It was little that thou hadst *in my sight*,"[1] Jerome has well and skilfully translated them "before I came." For Moses puts the *face* of Jacob for his actual *coming* and dwelling with Laban.

30. *And now, when shall I provide for mine own house also?* He reasons, that when he had so long expended his labours for another, it would be unjust that his own family should be neglected. For nature prescribes this order, that every one should take care of the family committed to him. To which point the saying of Solomon is applicable, "Drink water from thy own fountains, and let rivers flow to thy neighbours."[2] Had Jacob been alone, he might have devoted himself more freely to the interests of another; but now, since he is the husband of four wives, and the father of a numerous offspring, he ought not to be forgetful of those whom he has received at the hand of God to bring up.

31. *Thou shalt not give me anything.* The antithesis between this and the preceding clause is to be noticed. For Jacob does not demand for himself certain and definite wages; but he treats with Laban, on this condition, that he shall receive whatever offspring may be brought forth by the sheep and goats of a pure and uniform colour, which shall prove to be party-coloured and spotted. There is indeed some obscurity in the words. For, at first, Jacob seems to require for himself the spotted sheep as a present reward. But from the thirty-third verse another sense may be gathered: namely, that Jacob would suffer whatever was variegated in the flock to be separated and delivered to the sons of Laban to be fed; but that he himself would retain the unspotted sheep and goats. And certainly it would be absurd that Jacob should now claim part of the flock for himself, when he had just confessed, that hitherto he had made no gain. Moreover, the gain thus acquired would have been more than was just; and there was no hope that this could be obtained from Laban.

---

[1] In conspectu meo. לפני. Ver. 30.

[2] Et defluant rivi ad vicinos. The English version is different: "Drink waters out of thine own cistern; and running waters out of thine own well."

A question however arises, by what hope, or by what counsel had Jacob been induced to propose this condition? A little afterwards, Moses will relate that he had used cunning, in order that party-coloured and spotted lambs might be brought forth by the pure flock; but in the following chapter he more fully declares that Jacob had been divinely instructed thus to act. Therefore, although it was improbable in itself that this agreement should prove useful to the holy man, he yet obeys the celestial oracle, and wishes to be enriched in no other manner than according to the will of God. But Laban was dealt with according to his own disposition; for he eagerly caught at what seemed advantageous to himself, but God disappointed his shameful cupidity.

33. *So shall my righteousness answer for me.* Literally it is, " My righteousness shall answer in me." But the particle בִּ *(bi)* signifies *to me* or *for me.*[1] The sense, however, is clear, that Jacob does not expect success, except through his faith and integrity.[2] Respecting the next clause, interpreters differ. For some read, " When thou shalt come to my reward."[3] But others, translating in the third person, explain it of righteousness, which shall come to the reward, or to the remunerating of Jacob. Although either sense will suit the passage, I rather refer it to righteousness; because it is immediately added, " before thee."[4] For it would be an improper form of expression, " Thou wilt come before thine own eyes to my reward." It now sufficiently appears what Jacob meant. For he declares that he hoped for a testimony of his faith and uprightness from the Lord, in the happy result of his labours, as if he had said, " The Lord who is the best judge and vindicator of my righteousness, will indeed

[1] In the Amsterdam edition the particle is כִּ, evidently the printer's mistake. In Hengstenberg's edition, it is לִ, which looks as if the editor, instead of turning to the original, had, at a venture, translated Calvin's Latin words *mihi*, or *pro me*, into Hebrew.—*Ed.*

[2] *Vide* Vatablus in Poli Syn.

[3] That is, to see that I receive my reward or wages, at the time when the flock is divided according to our compact.—*Ed.*

[4] This seems to be the sense in which the English translators understood the passage. " So shall my righteousness answer for me in time to come, when it (my righteousness) shall come for my hire (or reward) before thy face." *Coram te.*—*Ed.*

show with what sincerity and faithfulness I have hitherto conducted myself." And though the Lord often permits sinners to be enriched by wicked arts, and suffers them to acquire abundant gain by seizing the goods of others as their own : this proves no exception to the rule, that his blessing is the ordinary attendant on good faith and equity. Wherefore, Jacob justly gave this token of his fidelity, that he committed the success of his labours to the Lord, in order that his integrity might hence be made manifest. The sense of the words is now clear, " My righteousness shall openly testify for me, because it will voluntarily come to remunerate me ; and that so obviously, that it shall not be hidden even from thee." A tacit reproof is couched in this language, intimating that Laban should feel how unjustly he had withheld the wages of the holy man, and that God would shortly show, by the result, how wickedly he had dissembled respecting his own obligation to him. For there is an antithesis to be understood between the future and the past time, when he says, " *To-morrow* [or in time to come] it will answer for me," since indeed, *yesterday* and the *day before*, he could extort no justice from Laban.

Every one that is not speckled and spotted. Jacob binds himself to the crime and punishment of theft, if he should take away any unspotted sheep from the flock : as if he would say, " Shouldst thou find with me anything unspotted, I am willing to be charged as a thief; because I require nothing to be given to me but the spotted lambs." Some expound the words otherwise, " Whatsoever thou shalt find deficient in thy flock, require of me, as if I had stolen it;" but this appears to me a forced interpretation.

35. *And he removed that day.* From this verse the form of the compact is more certainly known. Laban separates the sheep and goats marked with spots from the pure flock, that is, from the white or black, and commits these to his sons to be fed ; interposing a three days' journey between them and the rest ; lest, by promiscuous intercourse, a party-coloured offspring should be produced. It follows, therefore, that, in the flock which Jacob fed, nothing remained but cattle of one colour : thus but faint hope of gain remained

to the holy man, while every provision was made for Laban's advantage. It also appears, from the distance of the places, in which Laban kept his flocks apart, that he was not less suspicious than covetous ; for dishonest men are wont to measure others by their own standard ; whence it happens that they are always distrustful and alarmed.

37. *And Jacob took him rods of green poplar.* The narration of Moses, at first sight, may seem absurd : for he either intends to censure holy Jacob as guilty of fraud, or to praise his indůstry. But from the context it will appear that this adroitness was not culpable. Let us then see how it is to be excused. Should any one contend that he was impelled to act as he did, by the numerous injuries of his father-in-law, and that he sought nothing but the reparation of former losses ; the defence would perhaps be plausible : yet in the sight of God it is neither firm nor probable ; for although we may be unjustly treated, we must not enter the contest with equal injustice. And were it permitted to avenge our own injuries, or to repair our own wrongs, there would be no place for legal judgments, and thence would arise horrible confusion. Therefore Jacob ought not to have resorted to this stratagem, for the purpose of producing degenerate cattle, but rather to have followed the rule which the Lord delivers by the mouth of Paul, that the faithful should study to overcome evil with good, (Rom. xii. 21.) This simplicity, I confess, ought to have been cultivated by Jacob, unless the Lord from heaven had commanded otherwise. But in this narrative there is a *hysteron proteron,* (a putting of the last first,) for Moses first relates the fact, and then subjoins that Jacob had attempted nothing but by the command of God. Wherefore, it is not for those persons to claim him as their advocate, who oppose malignant and fraudulent men with fallacies like their own ; because Jacob did not, of his own will, take license craftily to circumvent his father-in-law, by whom he 'had been unworthily deceived ; but, pursuing the course prescribed to him by the Lord, kept himself within due bounds. In vain, also, according to my judgment, do some dispute whence Jacob learnt this ; whether by long practice or by the teaching of his fathers ; for it is possible, that he had been suddenly

instructed respecting a matter previously unknown. If any one object, the absurdity of supposing, that this act of deceit was suggested by God ; the answer is easy, that God is the author of no fraud, when he stretches out his hand to protect his servant. Nothing is more appropriate to him, and more in accordance with his justice, than that he should interpose as an avenger, when any injury is inflicted. But it is not our part to prescribe to him his method of acting. He suffered Laban to retain what he unjustly possessed ; but in six years he withdrew his blessing from Laban, and transferred it to his servant Jacob. If an earthly judge condemns a thief to restore twofold or fourfold, no one complains : and why should we concede less to God, than to a mortal and perishing man ? He had other methods in his power ; but he purposed to connect his grace with the labour and diligence of Jacob, that he might openly repay to him those wages of which he had been long defrauded. For Laban was constrained to open his eyes, which being before shut, he had been accustomed to consume the sweat and even the blood of another. Moreover, as it respects physical causes, it is well known, that the sight of objects by the female has great effect on the form of the fœtus.[1] Now Jacob did three things. For first, he stripped the bark from twigs that he might make bare some white places by the incisions in the bark, and thus a varying and manifold colour was produced. Secondly, he chose the times when the males and females were assembled. Thirdly, he put the twigs in the waters.[2] By the *stronger* cattle Moses may be understood to speak of those who bore in spring—by the feeble, those who bore in autumn.

43. *And the man increased exceedingly.* Moses added this for the purpose of showing that he was not made thus sud-

---

[1] The whole passage is this :—Porro quantum ad physicam rationem spectat, satis notum est, aspectum in coitu ad formam fœtus multum valere. Id quum mulieribus accidat, præcipue in brutis pecudibus locum habet, ubi nulla viget ratio, sed violentus libidinis impetus grassatur.

[2] Tertio, posuit in aquis virgas: quia sicut potus animalia vegetat, sic incitat etiam ad coitum. Hoc modo accidit ut virgæ in conspectu essent, quum incalescebant. Quod de robustis ac debilibus dicit Moses, sic intellige, in priore admissura, quæ sit sub initium veris, Jacob posuisse virgas in canalibus, ut sibi vernos fœtus acquireret, qui meliores erant: in serotina vero admissura circa autumnum, tali artificio usum non esse.

denly rich without a miracle. We shall see hereafter how great his wealth was. For being entirely destitute, he yet gathered out of nothing, greater riches than any man of moderate wealth could do in twenty or thirty years. And that no one may deem this fabulous, as not being in accordance with the usual method, Moses meets the objection by saying, that the holy man was enriched in an extraordinary manner.

CHAPTER XXXI.

1. And he heard the words of Laban's sons, saying, Jacob hath taken away all that *was* our father's; and of *that* which *was* our father's hath he gotten all this glory.

2. And Jacob beheld the countenance of Laban, and, behold, it *was* not toward him as before.

3. And the Lord said unto Jacob, Return unto the land of thy fathers, and to thy kindred; and I will be with thee.

4. And Jacob sent and called Rachel and Leah to the field unto his flock,

5. And said unto them, I see your father's countenance, that it *is* not toward me as before; but the God of my father hath been with me.

6. And ye know, that with all my power I have served your father.

7. And your father hath deceived me, and changed my wages ten times: but God suffered him not to hurt me.

8. If he said thus, The speckled shall be thy wages; then all the cattle bare speckled: and if he said thus, The ring-straked shall be thy hire; then bare all the cattle ring-straked.

9. Thus God hath taken away the cattle of your father, and given *them* to me.

10. And it came to pass at the time that the cattle conceived, that I lifted up mine eyes, and saw in a dream, and, behold, the rams which

1. Postea audivit verba filiorum Laban dicentium, Tulit Iahacob omnia quæ erant patris nostri: et de his quæ erant patris nostri, acquisivit omnem gloriam hanc.

2. Et vidit Iahacob faciem Laban, et ecce non erat cum eo sicut heri et nudiustertius.

3. Dixit autem Iehova ad Iahacob, Revertere ad terram patrum tuorum, et ad cognationem tuam, et ero tecum.

4. Et misit Iahacob, et vocavit Rachel et Leah in agrum ad pecudes suas.

5. Qui dixit ad eas, Video faciem patris vestri, quod non sit erga me sicut heri et nudiustertius: Deus autem patris mei fuit mecum.

6. Et vos nostis, quod omnibus viribus meis servierim patri vestro:

7. At pater vester mentitus est mihi, et mutavit mercedem meam decem vicibus: sed non permisit ei Deus, ut malefaceret mihi.

8. Si ita dicebat, Punctis parvis respersa erunt merces tua: pariebant omnes pecudes punctis parvis respersa: et si ita dicebat, Lineis distincta erunt merces tua: tunc pariebant omnes pecudes lineis distincta.

9. Et abstulit Deus pecus patris vestri, et dedit mihi.

10. Et fuit, in tempore quo coibant pecudes, levavi oculos meos, et vidi in somnio, et ecce hirci majores ascendebant super capras variegatas,

leaped upon the cattle *were* ring-straked, speckled, and grisled.

11. And the angel of God spake unto me in a dream, *saying,* Jacob. And I said, Here *am* I.

12. And he said, Lift up now thine eyes and see, all the rams which leap upon the cattle *are* ring-straked, speckled, and grisled: for I have seen all that Laban doeth unto thee.

13. I *am* the God of Beth-el, where thou anointedst the pillar, *and* where thou vowedst a vow unto me: now arise, get thee out from this land, and return unto the land of thy kindred.

14. And Rachel and Leah answered and said unto him, *Is there* yet any portion or inheritance for us in our father's house?

15. Are we not counted of him strangers? for he hath sold us, and hath quite devoured also our money.

16. For all the riches which God hath taken from our father, that *is* ours, and our children's: now then, whatsoever God hath said unto thee, do.

17. Then Jacob rose up, and set his sons and his wives upon camels:

18. And he carried away all his cattle, and all his goods which he had gotten, the cattle of his getting, which he had gotten in Padan-aram, for to go to Isaac his father in the land of Canaan.

19. And Laban went to shear his sheep: and Rachel had stolen the images that *were* her father's.

20. And Jacob stole away unawares to Laban the Syrian, in that he told him not that he fled.

21. So he fled with all that he had; and he rose up, and passed over the river, and set his face *toward* the mount Gilead.

22. And it was told Laban on the third day, that Jacob was fled.

23. And he took his brethren with him, and pursued after him seven days' journey; and they overtook him in the mount Gilead.

punctis parvis respersas, et maculis latis respersas.

11. Et dixit ad me Angelus Dei in somnio, Iahacob. Et dixi, Ecce adsum.

12. Et dixit, Leva nunc oculos tuos, et vide omnes hircos majores ascendentes super capras lineis distinctas, punctis parvis respersas, et maculis latis respersas: vidi enim omnia, quæ Laban facit tibi.

13. Ego Deus Bethel, ubi unxisti statuam, ubi vovisti mihi votum: nunc surge, egredere de terra hac, et revertere ad terram cognationis tuæ.

14. Et respondit Rachel et Leah, et dixerunt ei, Numquid adhuc est nobis pars et hæreditas in domo patris nostri?

15. Nonne extraneæ reputatæ sumus ab eo, quod vendidit nos, et consumpsit etiam consumendo argentum nostrum?

16. Quia omnes divitiæ, quas abstulit Deus a patre nostro, nostræ sunt, ac filiorum nostrorum: nunc igitur omnia, quæ dixit Deus ad te, fac.

17. Et surrexit Iahacob, et sustulit filios suos et uxores suas super camelos.

18. Et abduxit omnes pecudes suas, et omnem substantiam suam, quam acquisierat, pecudes acquisitionis suæ, quas acquisierat in Padan Aram, ut veniret ad Ishac patrem suum in terram Chenaan.

19. Laban autem profectus erat ad tondendum oves suas, et furata est Rachel idola, quæ erant patri suo.

20. Furatus itaque est Iahacob cor Laban Aramæi, quia non indicavit ei quod fugeret.

21. Et fugit ipse, et omnia quæ erant ei: et surrexit, et transivit flumen, posuitque faciem suam ad montem Gilhad.

22. Et nuntiatum fuit ipsi Laban die tertia, quod fugeret Iahacob.

23. Tunc sumpsit fratres suos secum, secutusque est eum itinere septem dierum, et assecutus est eum in monte Gilhad.

24. And God came to Laban the Syrian in a dream by night, and said unto him, Take heed that thou speak not to Jacob either good or bad.

25. Then Laban overtook Jacob. Now Jacob had pitched his tent in the mount: and Laban with his brethren pitched in the mount of Gilead.

26. And Laban said to Jacob, What hast thou done, that thou hast stolen away unawares to me, and carried away my daughters, as captives *taken* with the sword?

27. Wherefore didst thou flee away secretly, and steal away from me, and didst not tell me, that I might have sent thee away with mirth, and with songs, with tabret, and with harp?

28. And hast not suffered me to kiss my sons and my daughters? Thou hast now done foolishly in *so* doing.

29. It is in the power of my hand to do you hurt: but the God of your father spake unto me yesternight, saying, Take thou heed that thou speak not to Jacob either good or bad.

30. And now, *though* thou wouldest needs be gone, because thou sore longedst after thy father's house, *yet* wherefore hast thou stolen my gods?

31. And Jacob answered and said to Laban, Because I was afraid: for I said, Peradventure thou wouldest take by force thy daughters from me.

32. With whomsoever thou findest thy gods, let him not live: before our brethren discern thou what *is* thine with me, and take *it* to thee. For Jacob knew not that Rachel had stolen them.

33. And Laban went into Jacob's tent, and into Leah's tent, and into the two maid-servants' tents; but he found *them* not. Then went he out of Leah's tent, and entered into Rachel's tent.

34. Now Rachel had taken the images, and put them in the camel's furniture, and sat upon them. And Laban searched all the tent, but found *them* not.

35. And she said to her father,

24. Porro venit Deus ad Laban Aramæum in somnio noctis, et dixit ei, Cave tibi ne forte loquaris cum Iahacob a bono usque ad malum.

25. Assecutus autem est Laban ipsum Iahacob: et Iahacob fixerat tabernaculum suum in monte, et Laban fixit cum fratribus suis in monte Gilhad.

26. Et dixit Laban ad Iahacob, Quid fecisti, et furatus es cor meum, et abduxisti filias meas sicut captivas gladio?

27. Utquid abscondisti te ut fugeres? et furatus es me, et non indicasti mihi, et dimisissem te cum lætitia et canticis, cum tympano et cithara.

28. Et non permisisti mihi, ut oscularer filios meos et filias meas: nunc stulte egisti *sic* faciendo.

29. Est fortitudo in manu mea ad inferendum vobis malum: sed Deus patris vestri nocte præterita dixit ad me, dicendo, Cave tibi ne loquaris cum Iahacob a bono usque ad malum.

30. Et nunc eundo ivisti: si desiderando desirabas ire ad domum patris tui, utquid furatus es deos meos?

31. Et respondit Iahacob, et dixit ad Laban, Quia timui, si dixissem, ne forte raperes filias tuas a me.

32. Is, cum quo inveneris deos tuos non vivat . coram fratribus nostris, agnosce si quid est apud me *de tuo*, et cape tibi: nesciebat autem Iahacob, quod Rachel furata esset eos.

33. Et venit Laban in tabernaculum Iahacob, et in tabernaculum Leah, et in tabernaculum ambarum ancillarum, et non invenit: et egressus de tabernaculo Lea, venit in tabernaculum Rachel.

34. Rachel autem acceperat idola, et posuerat ea in clitellis cameli, et sedebat super ea: et contrectavit Laban totum tabernaculum, et non invenit.

35. Et dixit ad patrem suum, Ne

Let it not displease my lord that I cannot rise up before thee; for the custom of women *is* upon me. And he searched, but found not the images.

36. And Jacob was wroth, and chode with Laban: and Jacob answered and said to Laban, What *is* my trespass? what *is* my sin, that thou hast so hotly pursued after me?

37. Whereas thou hast searched all my stuff, what hast thou found of all thy household stuff? set *it* here before my brethren and thy brethren, that they may judge betwixt us both.

38. This twenty years *have* I *been* with thee; thy ewes and thy she-goats have not cast their young, and the rams of thy flock have I not eaten.

39. That which was torn *of beasts* I brought not unto thee; I bare the loss of it: of my hand didst thou require it, *whether* stolen by day, or stolen by night.

40. *Thus* I was; in the day the drought consumed me, and the frost by night; and my sleep departed from mine eyes.

41. Thus have I been twenty years in thy house: I served thee fourteen years for thy two daughters, and six years for thy cattle; and thou hast changed my wages ten times.

42. Except the God of my father, the God of Abraham, and the Fear of Isaac, had been with me, surely thou hadst sent me away now empty. God hath seen mine affliction, and the labour of my hands, and rebuked *thee* yesternight.

43. And Laban answered and said unto Jacob, *These* daughters *are* my daughters, and *these* children *are* my children, and *these* cattle *are* my cattle, and all that thou seest *is* mine: and what can I do this day unto these my daughters, or unto their children which they have born?

44. Now therefore come thou, let us make a covenant, I and thou; and let it be for a witness between me and thee.

45. And Jacob took a stone, and set it up *for* a pillar.

sit ira in oculis domini mei, quod non possim surgere a facie tua: quia consuetudo mulierum est mihi: et scrutatus est, et non invenit idola.

36. Tunc iratus est Iahacob, et jurgatus est cum Laban: et respondit Iahacob, et dixit ad Laban, Quæ est prævaricatio mea, quod peccatum meum, quod persecutus es me?

37. Quando contrectasti omnem supellectilem meam, quid invenisti ex omni supellectili domus tuæ? pone hic coram fratribus meis et fratribus tuis, et declarent inter nos ambos.

38. Iam viginti annos *fui* tecum; oves tuæ et capræ non abortiverunt: et arietes pecudum tuarum non comedi.

39. Raptum non attuli tibi, ego pœnas luebam pro eo: de manu mea requirebas illud, quod furto ablatum erat tam die quam nocte.

40. *Ita* fui ut interdiu consumeret me æstus, et gelu in nocte, et recedebat somnus meus ab oculis meis.

41. Iam mihi *sunt* viginti anni in domo tua: servivi tibi quatuordecim annos pro duabus filiabus tuis, et sex annos pro pecudibus tuis, et mutasti mercedem meam decem vicibus.

42. Nisi Deus patris mei, Deus Abraham, et pavor Ishac fuisset pro me, certe nunc vacuum dimisisses me: afflictionem meam et laborem manuum mearum vidit Deus, et increpavit *te* nocte præterita.

43. Tunc respondit Laban, et dixit ad Iahacob, Filiæ, filiæ meæ sunt: et filii, filii mei sunt: et pecudes meæ sunt: et quicquid vides, meum est: et filiabus meis quid faciam istis hodie, vel filiis earum quos pepererunt?

44. Et nunc, veni, percutiamus fœdus ego et tu, et erit in testimonium inter me et inter te.

45. Tulit itaque Iahacob lapidem, et erexit illum in statuam.

46. And Jacob said unto his brethren, Gather stones; and they took stones, and made an heap: and they did eat there upon the heap.

47. And Laban called it Jegar-sahadutha: but Jacob called it Galeed.

48. And Laban said, This heap *is* a witness between me and thee this day. Therefore was the name of it called Galeed;

49. And Mizpah: for he said, The Lord watch between me and thee, when we are absent one from another.

50. If thou shalt afflict my daughters, or if thou shalt take *other* wives besides my daughters, no man *is* with us; see, God *is* witness betwixt me and thee.

51. And Laban said to Jacob, Behold this heap, and behold *this* pillar, which I have cast betwixt me and thee;

52. This heap *be* witness, and *this* pillar *be* witness, that I will not pass over this heap to thee, and that thou shalt not pass over this heap and this pillar unto me, for harm.

53. The God of Abraham, and the God of Nahor, the God of their father, judge betwixt us. And Jacob sware by the fear of his father Isaac.

54. Then Jacob offered sacrifice upon the mount, and called his brethren to eat bread: and they did eat bread, and tarried all night in the mount.

55. And early in the morning Laban rose up, and kissed his sons and his daughters, and blessed them: and Laban departed, and returned unto his place.

46. Et dixit Iahacob fratribus suis, Colligite lapides: et tulerunt lapides, et fecerunt cumulum, et comederunt ibi super cumulum.

47. Et vocavit eum Laban Jegar Sahadutha: Iahacob autem vocavit eum Galhed.

48. Et dixit Laban, Cumulus iste sit testis inter me et te hodie. Idcirco vocavit nomen ejus Galhed,

49. Et Mispah: quia dixit, Speculetur Iehova inter me et te, quando latebimus alter alterum.

50. Si afflixeris filias meas, et si acceperis uxores super filias meas, non est quisquam nobiscum, vide, Deus est testis inter me et te.

51. Dixit ergo Laban ad Iahacob, Ecce, cumulus iste, et ecce statua, quam jeci inter me et te.

52. Testis cumulus iste, et testis statua, quod ego non transibo *veniens* ad te cumulum istum, et quod tu non transibis *veniens* ad me cumulum istum, et statuam istam, ad malum.

53. Deus Abraham et Deus Nachor judicet inter nos, Deus patris eorum: et juravit Iahacob per pavorem patris sui Ishac.

54. Et mactavit Iahacob victimam in monte, et vocavit fratres suos, ut comederent panem: et comederunt panem, et pernoctaverunt in monte.

55. Et surrexit Laban mane, et osculatus est filios suos ac filias suas, benedixitque eis, et abiit: et reversus est Laban ad locum suum.

1. *And he heard the words.* Although Jacob ardently desired his own country, and was continually thinking of his return to it; yet his admirable patience appears in this, that he suspends his purpose till a new occasion presents itself. I do not, however, deny, that some imperfection was mixed with this virtue, in that he did not make more haste to return; but that the promise of God was always retained in his mind will shortly appear. In this respect, however, he

showed something of human nature, that for the sake of obtaining wealth he postponed his return for six years : for when Laban was perpetually changing his terms, he might justly have bidden him farewell.   But that he was detained by force and fear together, we infer from his clandestine flight.   Now, at least, he had a sufficient cause for asking his dismissal ; because his riches had become grievous and hateful to the sons of Laban : nevertheless he does not dare openly to withdraw himself from their enmity, but is compelled to flee secretly. Yet though his tardiness is in some degree excusable, it was probably connected with indolence ; even as the faithful, when they direct their course towards God, often do not pursue it with becoming fervour.   Wherefore, whenever the indolence of the flesh retards us, let us learn to fan the ardour of our spirits into a flame.   There is no doubt that the Lord corrected the infirmity of his servant, and gently spurred him on as he proceeded in his course.   For if Laban had treated him kindly and pleasantly, his mind would have been lulled to sleep ; but now he is driven away by adverse looks.   So the Lord often better secures the salvation of his people, by subjecting them to the hatred, the envy, and the malevolence of the wicked, than by suffering them to be soothed with bland address.   It was far more useful to holy Jacob to have his father-in-law and his sons opposed, than to have them courteously obsequious to his wishes ; because their favour might have deprived him of the blessing of God.   We also have more than sufficient experience of the power of earthly attractions, and of the ease with which, when they abound, the oblivion of celestial blessings steals over us.   Wherefore let us not think it hard to be awakened by the Lord, when we fall into adversity, or receive but little favour from the world ; for hatred, threats, disgrace, and slanders, are often more advantageous to us than the applause of all men on every side.   Moreover, we must notice the inhumanity of Laban's sons, who complain throughout as if they had been plundered by Jacob.   But sordid and avaricious men labour under the disease of thinking that they are robbed of everything with which they do not gorge themselves.   For since their avarice is insatiable, it follows of necessity that the prosperity of others torments them, as if they themselves would be thereby reduced to want. They do not consider whether Jacob acquired this great wealth justly or unjustly; but they are enraged and envious, because they conceive that so much has been abstracted from them. Laban had before confessed, that he had been enriched by the coming of Jacob, and even that he had been blessed by the Lord for Jacob's sake ; but now his sons murmur, and he himself is tortured with grief, to find that Jacob also is made a partaker of the same blessing. Hence we perceive the blindness of avarice which can never be satisfied. Whence also it is called by Paul " the root of all evil ;" because they who desire to swallow up everything must be perfidious, and cruel, and ungrateful, and in every way unjust. Besides, it is to be observed that the sons of Laban, in the impetuosity of their younger years, give vent to their vexation ; but the father, like a cunning old fox, is silent, yet betrays his wickedness by his countenance.

3. *And the Lord said unto Jacob.* The timidity of the holy man is here more plainly seen ; for he, perceiving that evil was designed against him by his father-in-law, still dared not to move a foot, unless encouraged by a new oracle. But the Lord, who, by facts, had shown him already that no longer delay was to be made, now also urges him by words. Let us learn from this example, that although the Lord may incite us to duty by adversity, yet we shall thereby profit little, unless the stimulus of the word be added. And we see what will happen to the reprobate ; for either they become stupified in their wickedness, or they break out into fury. Wherefore, that the instruction conveyed by outward things may profit us, we must ask the Lord to shine upon us in his own word. The design, however, of Moses chiefly refers to this point, that we may know that Jacob returned to his own country, under the special guidance of God. Now the land of Canaan is called the land of Abraham and Isaac, not because they had sprung from it; but because it had been divinely promised to them as their inheritance. Wherefore, by this voice the holy man was admonished, that although Isaac had been a stranger, yet,

in the sight of God, he was the heir and lord of that land, in which he possessed nothing but a sepulchre.

4. *And Jacob sent.* He sends for his wives, in order to explain to them his intention, and to exhort them to accompany him in his flight; for it was his duty as a good husband to take them away with him; and therefore it was necessary to inform them of his design. And he was not so blind as to be unmindful of the many dangers of his plan. It was difficult to convey women, who had never left their father's house, to a remote region, by an unknown journey. Moreover, there was ground to fear lest they, in seeking protection for themselves, might betray their husband to his enemies. The courage of many would so far have failed them, in such a state of perturbation, that they would have disregarded conjugal fidelity, to provide for their own safety. Jacob, therefore, acted with great constancy in choosing rather to expose himself to danger than to fail in the duty of a good husband and master of a family. If his wives had refused to accompany him, the call of God would have compelled him to depart. But God granted him what was far more desirable, that his whole family, with one consent, were prepared to follow him: moreover, his wives, with whose mutual strifes his house before had rung, now freely consent to go with him into exile. So the Lord, when in good faith we discharge our duty, and shun nothing which he commands, enables us to succeed, even in the most doubtful affairs. Further, from the fact that Jacob calls his wives to him into the field, we infer what an anxious life he led. Certainly it would have been a primary convenience of his life, to dwell at home with his wives. He was already advanced in age, and worn down with many toils; and therefore he had the greater need of their service. Yet satisfied with a cottage in which he might watch over his flock, he lived apart from them. If, then, there had been a particle of equity in Laban and his sons, they would have found no cause for envy.

5. *I see your father's countenance.* This address consists of two parts. For first, he speaks of his own integrity, and expostulates concerning the perfidy of his father-in-law. He

next testifies that God is the author of his prosperity, in
order that Rachel and Leah may the more willingly accompany him.   And whereas he had become very rich in a
short space of time, he purges himself from all suspicion ;
and even appeals to them as witnesses of his diligence.
And though Moses does not minutely relate everything ; yet
there is no doubt that the honesty of their husband had
been made clear to them by many proofs, and that, on the
other hand, the injuries, frauds, and rapacity of their father,
were well known.   When he complains that his wages had
been changed ten times, it is probable that the number *ten*
is simply put for *many* times.   Nevertheless it may be, that
within six years Laban might thus frequently have broken
his agreements ; since there would be twice as many seasons
of breeding lambs, namely, at spring and autumn, as we have
said.   But this narration of the dream, although it follows
in a subsequent part of the history, shows that holy Jacob
had undertaken nothing but by the Divine command.   Moses
had before related the transaction simply, saying nothing respecting the counsel from which it had proceeded ; but now,
in the person of Jacob himself, he removes all doubt respecting it ; for he does not intimate that Jacob was lying, in
order, by this artifice, to deceive his wives ; but he introduces the holy servant of God, avowing truly, and without
pretence, the case as it really was.   For otherwise he would
have abused the name of God, not without abominable impiety, by connecting this vision with that former one, in
which we see that the gate of heaven was opened unto him.

13. *I am the God of Beth-el.*   It is not wonderful that the
angel should assume the person of God : either because God
the Father appeared to the holy patriarchs in his own Word,
as in a lively mirror, and that under the form of an angel ; or
because angels, speaking by the command of God, rightly
utter their words, as from his mouth.   For the prophets are
accustomed to this form of speaking ; not that they may
exalt themselves into the place of God ; but only that the
majesty of God, whose ministers they are, may shine forth
in his message.   Now, it is proper that we should more carefully consider the force of this form of expression.   He does

not call himself the God of Beth-el, because he is confined
within the limits of a given place, but for the purpose of re-
newing to his servant the remembrance of his own promise ;
for holy Jacob had not yet attained to that degree of perfection which rendered the more simple rudiments unnecessary
for him.   But little light of true doctrine at that time prevailed ; and even that was wrapped in many shadows.
Nearly the whole world had apostatized to false gods ; and
that region, nay, even the house of his father-in-law, was
filled with unholy superstitions.   Therefore, amid so many
hinderances, nothing was more difficult for him than to hold
his faith in the one true God firm and invincible.   Wherefore, in the first place, pure religion is commended to him,
in order that, among the various errors of the world, he may
adhere to the obedience and worship of that God whom he
had once known.   Secondly ; the promise which he had before received is anew confirmed to him, in order that he may
always keep his mind fixed on the special covenant which
God had made with Abraham and his posterity.   Thus he is
directed to the land of Canaan, which was his own inheritance ; lest the temporal blessing of God, which he was soon
to enjoy, should detain his heart in Mesopotamia.   For since
this oracle was only an appendix of the previous one, whatever benefits God afterwards bestowed ought to be referred
to that first design.   We may also conjecture from this passage, that Jacob had before preached to his household concerning the true God and the true religion, as became a
pious father of his family.   For he would have acted absurdly
in uttering this discourse, unless his wives had been previously instructed respecting that wonderful vision.   To
the same point belongs what he had said before, " that the
God of his father had brought him assistance."   For it is
just as if he would openly distinguish the God whom he
worshipped from the god of Laban.   And now, because he
holds familiar discourse with his wives, as on subjects which
they know, the conjecture is probable, that it was not Jacob's
fault if they were not imbued with the knowledge of the one
God, and with sincere piety.   Further, by this oracle the
Lord declared that he is always mindful of the godly, even

when they seem to be cast down and deserted. For who
would not have said that the outcast Jacob was now deprived
of all celestial help? And truly the Lord appears to him
late; but beyond all expectation shows, that he had never
been forgetful of him. Let the faithful, also, at this day,
feel that he is the same towards them; and if, in any way,
the wicked tyrannically oppress them by unjust violence, let
them bear it patiently, until at length, in due time, he shall
avenge them.

14. *And Rachel and Leah answered.* Here we perceive
that to be fulfilled which Paul teaches, that all things work
together for good to the children of God. (Rom. viii. 28.)
For since the wives of Jacob had been unjustly treated by
their father, they so far act in opposition to the natural tenderness of their sex, that at the desire of their husband,
they become willing to follow him into a distant and unknown region. Therefore, if Jacob is compelled to take
many and very bitter draughts of grief, he is now cheered
by the most satisfying compensation, that his wives are not
separated from him by their attachment to their father's
house: but rather, being overcome by the irksome nature of
their sufferings, they earnestly undertake to join him in his
flight. " There is nothing," they say, " which should cause
us to remain with our father; for daughters adhere to their
fathers, because they are esteemed members of his family;
but what a cruel rejection is this, not only that he has passed
us off[1] without dowry, but that he has set us to sale, and
has devoured the price for which he sold us?" By the word
money (ver. 15), I understand the price of sale. For they
complain that, at least, they had not received, instead of
dowry, the profit which had been unjustly extorted from
their husband, but this gain also had been unjustly suppressed by their covetous father. Therefore the particle גַּם
(*gam*) is inserted, which is used for the purpose of amplification among the Hebrews. For this increased not a little the
meanness of Laban, that, as an insatiable whirlpool, he had
absorbed the gain acquired by this most dishonourable traffic.
And it is to be noted, that they were then devoted to their

---

[1] The word in the original is harsh, " prostituit."

husband, and were therefore free to depart from their father ; especially since they knew that the hand of God was stretch- ed out to them. There is also no doubt, seeing they were persuaded that Jacob was a faithful prophet of God, but that they freely embraced the heavenly oracle from his mouth ; for at the close of their reply, they show that they did not so much yield to his wish as to the command of God.

16. *For all the riches which God hath taken from our father.* Rachel and Leah confirm the speech of Jacob ; but yet in a profane and common manner, not with a lively and pure sense of religion. For they only make a passing allusion to the fact, that God, in pity to his servant, had deigned to honour him with peculiar favour ; and in the meantime, in- sist upon a reason of little solidity, that what they were carrying away was justly their due, because a part of the inheritance pertained to them. They do not argue that the riches they possessed were theirs, because they had been justly acquired by the labour of their husband ; but because they themselves ought not to have been defrauded of their dowry, and now deprived of their lawful inheritance. For this reason they mention also their children with themselves, as having sprung from the blood of Laban. By this method they not only obscure the blessing of God, but indulge them- selves in greater license than is right. They also form a mean estimate of their husband's labours, in boasting that the fruit of those labours proceeded from themselves. Where- fore we are, by no means, to seek hence a precedent for the way in which each is to defend his own right, or to attempt the recovery of it, when it has been unjustly wrested from him.

17. *Then Jacob rose up.* The departure of Jacob Moses afterwards more fully relates, he now only briefly says that " he rose up ;" by which he means, that as soon as he could obtain the consent of his wives to go with him, he yielded to no other obstacles. Herein appears the manly strength and constancy of his mind. For Moses leaves many things to be reflected upon by his readers ; and especially that intermediate period, during which the holy man was doubtless agitated with a multiplicity of cares. He had believed that his exile from home would be only for a short time : but, deprived of

the sight of his parents and of his native soil during twenty
years, he suffered many things so severe and bitter, that the
endurance of them might have rendered him callous, or, at
least, might have so oppressed him as to have consumed the
remnant of his life.   He was now verging towards old age,
and the coldness of old age produces tardiness.   Yet the
flight for which he was preparing was not free from danger.
Therefore it was necessary that he should be armed with the
spirit of fortitude, in order that the vigour and alacrity of
which Moses speaks, might cause him to hasten his steps.
And since we read that the departure of the holy man was
effected by stealth, and was attended with discredit ; let us
learn, whenever God abases us, to turn our minds to such
examples as this.

19. *And Rachel had stolen.*   Although the Hebrews sometimes call those images תרפים, *(teraphim,)* which are not
set forth as objects of worship : yet since this term is commonly used in an ill sense, I do not doubt that they were
the household gods of Laban.[1]   Even he himself, shortly
afterwards, expressly calls them his gods.   It appears hence
how great is the propensity of the human mind to idolatry :
since in all ages this evil has prevailed ; namely, that men
seek out for themselves visible representations of God.   From
the death of Noah not yet two hundred years had elapsed ;
Shem had departed but a little while before ; his teaching,
handed down by tradition, ought most of all to have flourished among the posterity of Terah ; because the Lord had
chosen this family to himself, as the only sanctuary on earth
in which he was to be worshipped in purity.   The voice of
Shem himself was sounding in their ears until the death of
Abraham ; yet now, from Terah himself, the common filth
of superstition inundated this place, while the patriarch
Shem was still living and speaking.   And though there is
no doubt that he endeavoured, with all his power, to bring
back his descendants to a right mind, we see what was his
success.   It is not indeed to be believed, that Bethuel had

---

[1] See the subject of Teraphim discussed at length in Rivetus, who confirms the opinion of Calvin by arguments and illustrations drawn from
learned writers.   Exercitatio cxxxii.—*Ed.*

been entirely ignorant of the call of Abraham ; yet neither he, with his family, was, on that account, withdrawn from this vanity. Holy Jacob also had not been silent during twenty years, but had endeavoured, by counsel and admonition, to correct these gross vices, but in vain ; because superstition, in its violent course, prevailed. Therefore, that idolatry is almost innate in the human mind, the very antiquity of its origin bears witness. And that it is so firmly fixed there as scarcely to be capable of being uprooted, shows its obstinacy. But it is still more absurd, that not even Rachel could be healed of this contagion, in so great a length of time. She had often heard her husband speaking of the true and genuine worship of God : yet she is so addicted to the corruptions which she had imbibed from her childhood, that she is ready to infect the land chosen by God with them. She imagines that, with her husband, she is following God as her leader, and at the same time takes with her the idols by which she would subvert his worship. It is even possible that by the excessive indulgence of his beloved wife, Jacob might give too much encouragement to such superstitions. Wherefore, let pious fathers of families learn to use their utmost diligence that no stain of evil may remain in their wives or children. Some inconsiderately excuse Rachel, on the ground that, by a pious theft, she wished to purge her father's house from idols. But if this had been her design, why, in crossing the Euphrates, did she not cast away these abominations ? why did she not, after her departure, explain to her husband what she had done ? But there is no need of conjecture, since, from the sequel of the history, it is manifest that the house of Jacob was polluted with idols, even to the time of the violation of Dinah. It was not, then, the piety of Rachel, but her insane hankering after superstition which impelled her to the theft : because she thought that God could not be worshipped but through idols ; for this is the source of the disease, that since men are carnal, they imagine God to be carnal too.

20. *And Jacob stole away unawares to Laban.*[1] By the

---

[1] Et furatus est Jahacob cor Laban. The margin of the English translation renders the passage in the same way, " And Jacob stole away the

Hebrew form of expression, " stole away the heart of Laban,"
Moses shows that Jacob departed privately, or by stealth,
unknown to his father-in-law.   Meanwhile, he wishes to
point out to what straits Jacob was reduced, so that he had
no hope of deliverance but in flight.   For Laban had determined to hold him all his life as a captive, as if he had been
a slave bound to the soil, or sentenced to the mines.   Therefore let us also learn, by his example, when the Lord calls
us, courageously to strive against every kind of obstacle,
and not to be surprised if many arduous difficulties oppose
themselves against us.

22. *And it was told Laban.*   The Lord gave to his servant
the interval of a three days' journey, so that having passed
the Euphrates, he might enter the boundaries of the promised land.   And perhaps, in the mean time, he cooled the
rage of Laban, the assault of which, in its first heat, might
have been intolerably severe.[1]   By afterwards permitting
Jacob to be intercepted in the midst of his journey, God intended to render his own interposition the more illustrious.
It seemed desirable that Jacob's course should not be interrupted, and that he should not be filled with alarm by the
hostile approach of his father-in-law ; but when Laban, like
a savage wild beast, breathing nothing but slaughter, is suddenly restrained by the Lord, this was far more likely to confirm the faith of the holy man, and therefore far more useful
to him.   For, as in the very act of giving assistance, the
power of God shone forth more clearly ; so, relying on Divine
help, he passed more courageously through remaining trials.
Whence we learn, that those perturbations which, at the time,
are troublesome to us, yet tend to our salvation, if only we
obediently submit to the will of God ; who purposely thus
tries us, that he may indeed show more fully the care which
he takes of us.   It was a sad and miserable sight, that

heart of Laban."   To this translation the remarks of Calvin apply.   He
understands the passage, however, in the sense which the English version
of the text gives.—*Ed.*

    [1] " Doubtless this pursuit, undertaken with such vehemence by Laban,
was for the purpose of bringing back Jacob with all his family and all his
wealth, and under the pretext that he had taken flight and had been guilty
of theft, to retain him henceforth as a captive, and to subject him to perpetual slavery."—*Rivetus in Gen.*, p. 635.

Jacob, taking so large a family with him, should flee as if his conscience had accused him of evil : but it was far more bitter and more formidable, that Laban, intent on his destruction, should threaten his life. Yet the method of his deliverance, which is described by Moses, was more illustrious than any victory. For God, descending from heaven to bring assistance to his servant, places himself between the parties, and in a moment assuages the indomitable fury with which Laban was inflamed.

23. *And pursued him seven days' journey.* Since the cruelty of Laban was now appeased, or at least bridled, he did not dare severely to threaten ; but laying aside his ferocity, he descended to feigned and hypocritical blandishments He complains that injury had been done him, because he had been kept in ignorance of Jacob's departure, whom he would rather have sent forth with customary tokens of joy, in token of his paternal affection. Thus hypocrites, when the power of inflicting injury is taken away from them, heap false complaints upon the good and simple, as if the blame rested with them. Wherefore, if at any time wicked and perfidious men, when they have unjustly harassed us, put forward some pretext of equity on their own part, we must bear with the iniquity ; not because a just defence is to be entirely omitted ; but because we find it inevitable that perverse men, ever ready to speak evil, will shamelessly cast upon us the blame of crimes of which we are innocent. Meanwhile, we must prudently guard against giving them the occasion against us which they seek.

29. *It is in the power of my hand.* The Hebrew phrase is different, " my hand is to power ;" yet the meaning is clear, that Laban declares he is ready to take vengeance. Some expound the words thus : " my hand is to God ;" but from other places it appears that the word אֵל is taken for *power.* But Laban, inflated with foolish boasting, contradicts himself ; for whereas he had been forbidden by God to attempt anything against Jacob, where was the *power* of which he boasted ? We see, therefore, he precipitates himself by a blind impulse, as if, at his own pleasure, he could do anything against the purpose of God. For when he per-

ceives that God is opposed to him, he yet does not hesitate
to glory in his own strength ; and why is this, unless he
aimed at being superior to God ?　Finally; pride is always
the companion of unbelief; so that unbelievers, although
vanquished, yet cease not impetuously to rise up against
God.　To this they add another sin, that they complain of
being unjustly oppressed by God.

But the God of your father.　Why does he not also acknowledge God as his own God, unless because Satan had
so fascinated his mind already, that he chose rather to wander
in darkness than to turn to the light presented before him ?
Willingly or unwillingly, he is compelled to yield to the God
of Abraham ; and yet he defrauds him of the glory which is
due, by retaining those fictitious deities by which he had
been deceived.　We see then that the ungodly, even when
they have had proof of the power of God, yet do not entirely
submit themselves to his authority.　Wherefore, when God
manifests himself to us, we must also seek from heaven the
spirit of meekness, which shall bend and subdue us to obedience unto himself.

30. *Wherefore hast thou stolen my gods ?*[1]　The second
head of accusation which is alleged against Jacob is, that he
had not departed through love to his country, nor for any
just and probable cause ; but that, in fact, he was implicated in an act of robbery.　Heavy and disgraceful charge,
of which Jacob was far from being guilty !　But we learn
hence, that no one can live so innocently in the world, but
he must sometimes bear undeserved reproach and marks of
infamy.　Whenever this may happen to us, let that precious
promise sustain us, that the Lord, in his own time, will
bring forth our innocence as the morning light. (Ps. xxxvii. 6.)
For by this artifice Satan attempts to seduce us from the
practice of well-doing, when, without any fault of ours, we
are traduced by false calumnies.　And since the world is
ungrateful, it often makes the very worst return for acts of

[1] " Wonderful is the madness of idolatry.　He confesses that those whom
he calls his *gods*, might yet be carried off by theft.　It was the part of
impiety that he worshipped idols ; but it was the part of folly that he
declared those to be gods, who were unable to preserve themselves from
being stolen."—*Rivetus in Gen.*, p. 656.

kindness. Some, indeed, are found, who, with heroic magnanimity, despise unfavourable reports, because they esteem the testimony of a good conscience more highly than depraved popular opinion. But it behoves the faithful to look to God, that their conscience may never fail them. We see that Laban calls his gods תרפים, (*teraphim*,) not because he thought the Deity was enclosed within them; but because he worshipped these images in honour of the gods. Or rather, because, when he was about to pay homage to God, he turned himself to those images. At this day, by the sole difference of a word, the Papists think they skilfully effect their escape, because they do not attribute to idols the name of gods. But the subterfuge is frivolous, since in reality they are altogether alike; for they pour forth before pictures or statues whatever honour they acknowledge to be due to the one God. To the ancient idolaters the pretext was not wanting, that by a metonymy they styled those images gods, which were formed for the sake of representing God.

31. *And Jacob answered.* He briefly refutes each head of the accusation: with respect to his secret departure, he modestly excuses himself, as having been afraid that he might be deprived of his wives. And in this way he takes part of the blame to himself, deeming it sufficient to exonerate himself from the malice of which he was thought to be guilty. He does not dispute, as a casuist, whether it was lawful to depart by stealth; but leaves it undetermined whether or not his fear was culpable. Let all the children of God learn to imitate this modesty, lest through an immoderate desire to vindicate their own reputation, they should rush into contentions: just as we have seen many raise tragic scenes out of nothing, because they will not endure that any censure, however trifling, should be cast upon them. Jacob, therefore, was content with this excuse, that he had done nothing wickedly. His defence on the other charge follows, in which Jacob shows his confidence, by adjudicating the person to death, with whom the things stolen should be found.[1] He speaks, indeed, from his heart;

---

[1] " Jacob might cover himself with the shield of his own innocence; but

but if the truth had then been discovered, he must, of necessity, have been ashamed of his rashness. Therefore, though
he was not conscious of guilt, he yet sinned through excessive haste, in not having diligently inquired before he pronounced concerning a doubtful matter. He ought to have
called both his wives and his children, and to have inquired
of each how the affair stood. He was, indeed, persuaded,
that his family was so well conducted, that no suspicion of
the theft had ever entered into his mind ; but he ought not
so to have relied upon his own discipline, as to be free from
fear when a crime is alleged against his family. Wherefore,
let us learn to suspend our judgment in matters of which we
are ignorant, lest we should repent too late of our temerity.
We may add, that hence it happened, that the pollution
which he might have exterminated immediately, continued
still longer in the family of Jacob.

32. *That Rachel had stolen them.* Moses relates the manner in which Rachel had concealed her theft ; namely, by
sitting on the idols, and pretending the custom of women as
her excuse. It is a question, whether she did this through
shame or pertinacity. It was disgraceful to be caught in
the act of theft ; she also dreaded the severe sentence of her
husband. Yet to me it appears probable, that fear did not
so much influence her as the obstinate love of idolatry. For
we know how greatly superstition infatuates the mind.
Therefore, as if she had obtained an incomparable treasure,
she' thinks that she must attempt anything rather than
allow herself to be deprived of it. Moreover, she chooses
rather to incur the displeasure of her father and her husband, than to relinquish the object of her superstition.
To her stratagem she also adds lying words, so that she
deserves manifold censure.

36. *And Jacob was wroth, and chode with Laban.* Jacob
again acts amiss, in contending with Laban about a matter
not sufficiently known, and in wrongfully fastening on him
the charge of calumny. For although he supposed all his

it was not large enough to cover all others, not even his most beloved wife,
whom he, in ignorance, adjudicates to death, and incautiously gives sentence against her."—*Rivetus in Gen.*, p. 657.

family to be free from blame, yet he was deceived by his
own negligence. He acts, indeed, with moderation, because
in expostulating with Laban he does not use reproaches;
but in this he is not to be excused, that he undertakes the
cause of his whole family, when they were not exempt from
blame. If any one should make the objection to this statement, that Jacob was constrained by fear, because Laban
had brought with him a great band of companions: the circumstances themselves show, that his mind was thus influenced
by moderation rather than by fear. For he boldly resists,
and shows no sign of fear ; only he abstains from the insolence of evil speaking. He then adds that he had just cause
of accusation against Laban ; not because he wished to rise
in a spirit of recrimination against his father-in-law ; but because it was right that the kindred and associates of Laban
should be made witnesses of all that had passed, in order
that, by the protracted patient endurance of Jacob, his integrity might be the more manifest. Jacob also calls to
mind, not only that he had been a faithful keeper of the
flock, but also that his labour had been rendered prosperous
by the blessing of God ; he adds, besides, that he had been
held accountable for all losses. In this he insinuates against
Laban the charge of great injustice : for it was not the duty
of Jacob voluntarily to inflame the avarice and rapacity of
his father-in-law, by attempting to soothe him; but he yielded,
by constraint, to his injuries. When he says that "sleep
departed from his eyes," he not only intimates that he passed
sleepless nights, but that he had so contended against nature
itself, as to defraud himself of necessary repose.

42. *Except the God of my father.* Jacob here ascribes it
to the favour of God, that he was not about to return home
entirely empty ; whereby he not only aggravates the sin of
Laban, but meets an objection which might seem at variance
with his complaints. He therefore denies that he has been
made rich by the kindness of his father-in-law ; but testifies
that he has been favourably regarded by the Lord : as if he
had said, " I owe it not to thee, that thou hast not further
injured me ; but God, who is propitious to me, has withstood
thee." Now, since God is not the defender of unfaithfulness,

nor is wont to help the wicked, the integrity of Jacob may be ascertained from the fact that God interposed as his vindicator. It is also to be observed, that by expressly distinguishing the God of Abraham from all fictitious gods, he declares that there is no other true God : by which he, at the same time, proves himself to be a truly pious worshipper. The expression " the fear of Isaac," is to be taken passively for the God whom Isaac revered ; just as, on account of the reverence due to him, he is called " the fear and the dread" of his people.[1] A similar expression occurs immediately after, in the same chapter. Now the pious, while they fear God, are by no means horror-struck at his presence, like the reprobates ; but trembling at his judgment, they walk circumspectly before him.

God hath seen my affliction, and the labour of my hands. This was spoken from a pious feeling that God would bring help to him when afflicted, if he should conduct himself with fidelity and honesty. Therefore, in order that the Lord may sustain us with his favour, let us learn to discharge our duty rightly ; let us not flee from our proper work ; and let us not refuse to purchase peace by submitting to many inconveniences. Further, if they from whom we have deserved well treat us severely and unjustly, let us bear our cross in hope and in silence, until the Lord shall succour us : for he will never forsake us, as the whole Scripture testifies. But Jacob distinctly presses his father-in-law with his own confession. For why had God rebuked him, unless because he was persecuting an innocent man in defiance of justice and equity ; for as I have lately intimated, it is abhorrent to the nature of God to favour evil and unjust causes.

43. *These daughters are my daughters.* Laban begins now to speak in a manner very different from before : he sees that he has no farther ground of contention. Therefore, being convinced, he buries all strife, and glides into placid and amicable discourse. " Why," he asks, " should I be hostile to thee, when all things between us are common ? Shall I rage against my own bowels ? for both thy wives

---

[1] Isaiah viii. 13. " Sanctify the Lord of hosts himself; and let him be your fear, and let him be your dread."

and thy children are my own blood ; wherefore I ought to be affected towards you, as if you all were part of myself."[1] He now answers like an honourable man.   Whence, then, has this humanity so suddenly sprung up in the breast of him who lately had been hurried onward, without any respect to right or wrong, to ruin Jacob ; unless it were, that he knew Jacob to have acted towards him with fidelity, and to have been at length compelled by necessity to adopt the design of departing by stealth ?   And this was an indication that he was not absolutely desperate : for we may find many persons of such abandoned impudence, that though overcome and silenced by arguments, they yet do not cease to rush headlong in insane rebellion.   From this passage we infer, that although avarice and other sinful affections take away judgment and soundness of mind ; there yet remains a know-ledge of truth engraven on the souls of men, which being stirred up emits scintillations, to prevent the universal triumph of depravity.   If any one before had said, " What doest thou, Laban ? what brutality is this to rage against thine own bowels ?" the remonstrance would not have been heard, for he burned with headstrong fury.   But now he voluntarily suggests this to himself, and proclaims what he would have been unwilling to hear from another.   It appears, then, that the light of justice which now breaks forth, had been smothered in his mind.   In short, it is self-love alone which blinds us ; because we all judge aright where personal interests are not concerned.   If, however, it should so happen that we are for a time in perplexity, we must still seek to obey the dictates of reason and justice.   But if any one har-dens himself in wickedness, the interior and hidden know-ledge, of which I have spoken, will yet remain engraven in his mind, and will suffice for his condemnation.

44. *Let us make a covenant, I and thou.*   Laban here acts as men conscious of guilt are wont to do, when they wish to guard themselves against revenge : and this kind of trepida-

---

[1] Acsi gererem omnium personam.   " As if I bore the person or char-acter of all," perhaps, " as your representative—the one who personates you."   Yet, in the translation, the sense is given which will, perhaps, on the whole, be most intelligible to the reader.—*Ed.*

tion and anxiety is the just reward of evil deeds. Besides, wicked men always judge of others from their own disposition : whence it happens that they have fears on all sides. Moses before relates a somewhat similar example, when Abimelech made a covenant with Isaac. Wherefore we must take the greater care, if we desire to possess tranquil minds, that we act sincerely and without injury towards our neighbours. Meanwhile Moses shows how placable Jacob was, and how easily he permitted himself to be conciliated. He had endured very many and grievous wrongs; but now, forgetting all, he freely stretches out the hand of kindness : and so far is he from being pertinacious in defending his own right, that he, in a manner, anticipates Laban himself, being the first to take a stone, and set it up for a pillar. And truly it becomes the children of God, not only with alacrity to embrace peace, but even ardently to search for it, as we are commanded in Psalm xxxiv. 14.[1] As to the heap of stones, it was always the practice to use some ceremony which might confirm the compact on both sides ; on this occasion a heap of stones is raised, in order that the memory of the covenant might be transmitted to posterity. That Jacob took part in this was a proof, as we have said, of a mind disposed to peace. He freely complained, indeed, when it was right to do so; but when the season of pacification arrived, he showed that he cherished no rancour. Moses, in relating afterwards that " they did eat there, upon the heap," does not observe the order of the history. For, on both sides, the conditions of the covenant were agreed upon and declared, before the feast was celebrated : but this figure of speech (as we have before seen) was sufficiently in use.

47. *And Laban called it.* Each, in his own language, gives a name, of the same signification, to the heap. Whence it appears, that Laban used the Syrian tongue, though born of the race of Heber. But it is not wonderful that he, dwelling among Syrians, should have accustomed himself to the language as well as to the manners of the Syrians. And a little before, he is twice called a Syrian ; as if Moses would describe him as degenerate, and alienated from the Hebrews.

---

[1] " Depart from evil and do good; seek peace and pursue it."

But this seems by no means accordant with the previous history, where we read that the daughters of Laban gave Hebrew names to their sons. Yet the solution is not difficult ; for since the affinity between these languages was great, the inflection of one word into another was easy : besides, if the wives of Jacob were tractable, it is not surprising that they should have learned his language. And beyond doubt, he would himself make a point of this matter : seeing he knew that his family was separated from the rest of the nations. Moses, in using the name of Galeed, does it proleptically ; for since he was writing for his own times, he does not scruple to give it the generally received name. Moreover we hence infer, that ceremonies and rites ought to refer to that which those who use them mutually agree upon. Which rule also ought to be applied to the sacraments ; because if the word by which God enters into covenant with us be taken away, useless and dead figures will alone remain.

49. *The Lord watch between me and thee.* Laban commits to the judgment of God, for vengeance, whatever offence either of them should be guilty of against the other in his absence ; as if he would say, " Though the knowledge of the injury should not reach me, because I shall be far distant, yet the Lord, who is everywhere present, will behold it." Which sentiment he more clearly expresses afterwards, when he says, " No one is with us ; God will be witness between me and thee." By which words he means, that God will be a severe avenger of every wickedness, though there should be no judge upon earth to decide the cause. And certainly if there were any religion flourishing within us, the presence of God would influence us far more than the observation of men. But it arises from the brutal stupidity of our flesh, that we reverence men only ; as if we might mock God with impunity, when we are not convicted by the testimony of men. If, then, this common feeling of nature dictated to Laban, that the frauds which were hidden from men would come into judgment before God ; we who enjoy the light of the gospel should indeed be ashamed to seek a covert for our fallacies. Hence also, we gather the legitimate use of an oath,

which the Apostle declares in his epistle to the Hebrews; namely, that men, in order to put an end to their controversies, resort to the judgment of God.

50. *If thou shalt take other wives besides my daughters.* Laban declares that it would be a species of perfidy, if Jacob should take to himself any other wives. But he had himself compelled Jacob to the act of polygamy: for whence was it that the holy man had more wives than one, except that Leah had been craftily substituted in the place of Rachel? But he now, from a pure sentiment of nature, condemns the fault, of which, blinded by avarice, he had wickedly been the author. And certainly, when the bond of marriage is broken, than which none among men is more sacred, the whole of human society sinks into decay. Wherefore, those fanatical men, who, at this day, delight to defend polygamy, have no need of any other judge than Laban.

53. *The God of Abraham.* It is indeed rightly and properly done, that Laban should adjure Jacob by the name of God. For this is the confirmation of covenants; to appeal to God on both sides, that he may not suffer perfidy to pass unpunished. But he sinfully blends idols with the true God, between whom there is nothing in common. Thus, truly, men involved in superstitions, are accustomed to confound promiscuously sacred things with profane, and the figments of men with the true God. He is compelled to give some honour to the God of Abraham, yet he lies plunged in his own idolatrous pollution; and, that his religion may not appear the worse, he gives it the colour of antiquity. For in calling him the God of his father, he boasts that this God was handed down to him from his ancestors. Meanwhile Jacob does not swear superstitiously. For Moses expressly declares, that he sware only by the " fear of Isaac ;" whence we learn that he did not assent to the preposterous form of oath dictated by his father-in-law; as too many do, who, in order to gain the favour of the wicked, pretend to be of the same religion with them. But when once the only God is made known to us, we wickedly suppress his truth, unless by its light all the clouds of error are dispersed.

54. *And called his brethren to eat bread.* In courteously

receiving his kindred, by whom he had been ill-treated, as his guests, Jacob showed his kindness. Moses also intimates that it was by the special favour of God that, after the most dreadful storm which threatened the holy man with destruction, a placid serenity suddenly shone forth. To the same cause is to be assigned what immediately follows, that Laban departed in a friendly manner: for by this method the Lord openly manifested himself as the guardian of his servant, seeing that he wonderfully delivered him as a lost sheep out of the jaws of the wolf. And truly, not only was the fury of Laban appeased ; but he put on paternal affection, as if he had been changed into a new man.

55. *And blessed them.* The character of the person is here to be noticed, because Laban, who had lapsed from true piety, and was a man of unholy and wicked manners, yet retained the habit of giving his blessing. For we are hereby taught, that certain principles of divine knowledge remain in the hearts of the wicked, so that no excuse may be left to them on the ground of ignorance ; for the custom of pronouncing a blessing arises hence, that men are certainly persuaded that God alone is the author of all good things. For although they may proudly arrogate what they please to themselves ; yet when they return to their right mind, they are compelled, whether they will or no, to acknowledge that all good proceeds from God alone.

CHAPTER XXXII.

1. AND Jacob went on his way, and the angels of God met him.

2. And when Jacob saw them, he said, This *is* God's host: and he called the name of that place Mahanaim.

3. And Jacob sent messengers before him to Esau his brother, unto the land of Seir, the country of Edom.

4. And he commanded them, saying, Thus shall ye speak unto my lord Esau ; Thy servant Jacob saith thus, I have sojourned with Laban, and stayed there until now :

1. Postea Iahacob abiit in viam suam, et occurrerunt ei Angeli Dei.

2. Et dixit Iahacob, quando vidit eos, Castra Dei sunt hæc : et vocavit nomen loci illius Mahanaim.

3. Misit autem Iahacob nuntios ante se ad Esau fratrem suum ad terram Sehir in regionem Edom.

4. Et præcepit eis dicendo, Sic dicetis domino meo Esau, Sic dixit servus tuus Iahacob, Cum Laban habitavi et moratus sum huc usque.

5. And I have oxen, and asses, flocks, and men-servants, and women-servants : and I have sent to tell my lord, that I may find grace in thy sight.

6. And the messengers returned to Jacob, saying, We came to thy brother Esau, and also he cometh to meet thee, and four hundred men with him.

7. Then Jacob was greatly afraid and distressed : and he divided the people that *was* with him, and the flocks, and herds, and the camels, into two bands ;

8. And said, If Esau come to the one company, and smite it, then the other company which is left shall escape.

9. And Jacob said, O God of my father Abraham, and God of my father Isaac, the Lord which saidst unto me, Return unto thy country, and to thy kindred, and I will deal well with thee :

10. I am not worthy of the least of all the mercies, and of all the truth, which thou hast showed unto thy servant ; for with my staff I passed over this Jordan, and now I am become two bands.

11. Deliver me, I pray thee, from the hand of my brother, from the hand of Esau : for I fear him, lest he will come and smite me, *and* the mother with the children.

12. And thou saidst, I will surely do thee good, and make thy seed as the sand of the sea, which cannot be numbered for multitude.

13. And he lodged there that same night ; and took of that which came to his hand a present for Esau his brother ;

14. Two hundred she-goats and twenty he-goats, two hundred ewes and twenty rams,

15. Thirty milch camels with their colts, forty kine and ten bulls, twenty she-asses and ten foals.

16. And he delivered *them* into the hand of his servants, every drove by themselves ; and said unto his ser-

5. Et sunt mihi boves et asini, pecudes et servi, et ancillæ, et misi ut nuntiarem domino meo, ut invenirem gratiam in oculis tuis.

6. Reversi autem sunt nuntii ad Iahacob, dicendo, Venimus ad fratrem tuum, ad Esau, et etiam pergit in occursum tuum, et quadringenti viri cum eo.

7. Et timuit Iahacob valde, et angustiis affectus est ; et divisit populum, qui erat secum, et pecudes, et boves, et camelos in duas turmas.

8. Dixit enim, Si veniret Esau ad turmam unam, et percusserit eam, turma, quæ remanserit, evadet.

9. Et dixit Iahacob, Deus patris mei Abraham, et Deus patris mei Ishac, Domine, qui dixisti ad me, Revertere ad terram tuam et cognationem tuam, et benefaciam tibi.

10. Minor sum cunctis misericordiis, et omni veritate, quam fecisti cum servo tuo : quia in baculo meo transivi Iordanem hunc, et nunc factus sum in duas turmas.

11. Erue me nunc de manu fratris mei, de manu Esau : timeo enim eum, ne forte veniat, et percutiat me, matremque cum filiis.

12. Et tu dixisti, Benefaciendo benefaciam tibi, et ponam semen tuum sicut arenam maris, quæ non numeratur præ multitudine.

13. Et pernoctavit ibi nocte ipsa, et accepit ex iis, quæ occurrebant ad manum suam, munus *mittendum* ad Esau fratrem suum.

14. Capras ducentas et hircos viginti, oves ducentas et arietes viginti :

15. Camelos lactantes, et pullos earum triginta : vaccas quadraginta, et juvencos decem : asinas viginti, et pullos decem.

16. Et dedit in manum servorum suorum, singulos greges seorsum : dixitque ad servos suos, Transite

vants, Pass over before me, and put
a space betwixt drove and drove.

17. And he commanded the foremost, saying, When Esau my brother
meeteth thee, and asketh thee, saying, Whose *art* thou? and whither
goest thou? and whose *are* these
before thee?

18. Then thou shalt say, *They be*
thy servant Jacob's; it *is* a present
sent unto my lord Esau: and, behold, also he *is* behind us.

19. And so commanded he the
second, and the third, and all that
followed the droves, saying, On this
manner shall ye speak unto Esau,
when ye find him.

20. And say ye moreover, Behold,
thy servant Jacob *is* behind us. For
he said, I will appease him with the
present that goeth before me, and
afterward I will see his face; peradventure he will accept of me.

21. So went the present over before him; and himself lodged that
night in the company.

22. And he rose up that night,
and took his two wives, and his two
women-servants, and his eleven sons,
and passed over the ford Jabbok.

23. And he took them, and sent
them over the brook, and sent over
that he had.

24. And Jacob was left alone; and
there wrestled a man with him until
the breaking of the day.

25. And when he saw that he prevailed not against him, he touched
the hollow of his thigh; and the
hollow of Jacob's thigh was out of
joint as he wrestled with him.

26. And he said, Let me go, for
the day breaketh. And he said, I
will not let thee go, except thou
bless me.

27. And he said unto him, What
is thy name? And he said, Jacob.

28. And he said, Thy name shall
be called no more Jacob, but Israel:
for as a prince hast thou power with
God and with men, and hast prevailed.

29. And Jacob asked *him*, and
said, Tell *me*, I pray thee, thy name.

ante me, et interstitium ponetis inter
gregem et gregem.

17. Et præcepit primo, dicendo,
Si occurrerit tibi Esau frater meus,
et interrogaverit te, dicendo, Cujus
es, et quo pergis, et cujus sunt ista
ante te?

18. Dices, Servi tui Iahacob munus est, missum ad dominum meum
Esau: et ecce etiam ipse est post
nos.

19. Præcepit etiam secundo, etiam
tertio, etiam cunctis pergentibus
post greges, dicendo, Secundum verbum hoc loquemini ad Esau, quando
invenietis eum.

20. Et dicetis etiam, Ecce servus
tuus Iahacob est post nos: dixit
enim, Placabo faciem ejus munere,
quod vadit ante me, et postea videbo
faciem ejus, si forte suscipiat faciem
meam.

21. Transivit itaque munus ante
eum: et ipse pernoctavit nocte ipsa
cum turma.

22. Et surrexit nocte ipsa, et accepit duas uxores suas, et duas ancillas suas, et undecim liberos suos,
et transivit vadum Jaboc.

23. Et accepit eos, et transire fecit eos torrentem, transire, inquam,
fecit *omnia* quæ erant sibi.

24. Porro remansit Iahacob solus
ipse: et luctatus est vir cum eo,
donec ascendit aurora.

25. Et vidit quod non prævaleret
ei, et tetigit palam femoris ejus, et
movit se pala femoris Iahacob, luc-
tante illo cum eo.

26. Tunc dixit, Dimitte me, quia
ascendit aurora. Cui respondit, Non
dimittam te, nisi benedixeris mihi.

27. Et dixit ad eum, Quod est
nomen tuum? Et ait, Iahacob.

28. Tunc dixit, Non Iahacob dicetur ultra nomen tuum, sed Israel:
quia princeps fuisti cum Deo, et hominibus prævalebis.

29. Et interrogavit Iahacob, et
dixit, Indica, quæso, nomen tuum.

And he said. Wherefore *is* it *that* thou dost ask after my name ? And he blessed him there.

30. And Jacob called the name of the place Peniel: for I have seen God face to face, and my life is preserved.

31. And as he passed over Penuel, the sun rose upon him, and he halted upon his thigh.

32. Therefore the children of Israel eat not *of* the sinew which shrank, which *is* upon the hollow of the thigh, unto this day: because he touched the hollow of Jacob's thigh in the sinew that shrank.

Et dixit. Utquid interrogas de nomine meo ? et benedixit ei illic.

30. Vocavit ergo Iahacob nomen loci, Peniel: quia vidi Deum facie ad faciem, et evasit anima mea.

31. Et ortus est ei sol, quando transivit Penuel, et claudicabat in femore suo.

32. Idcirco non comedunt filii Israel nervum contractionis, qui est in pala femoris, usque ad diem hanc: quia tetigit palam femoris Iahacob in nervo contractionis.

1. *And Jacob went on his way.* After Jacob has escaped from the hands of his father-in-law, that is, from present death, he meets with his brother, whose cruelty was as much, or still more, to be dreaded ; for by the threats of this brother he had been driven from his country ; and now no better prospect lies before him. He therefore proceeds with trepidation, as one who goes to the slaughter. Seeing, however, it was scarcely possible but that he should sink oppressed by grief, the Lord affords him timely succour ; and prepares him for this conflict, as well as for others, in such a manner that he should stand forth a brave and invincible champion in them all. Therefore, that he may know himself to be defended by the guardianship of God, angels go forth to meet him, arranged in ranks on both sides. Hebrew interpreters think that the camp of the enemy had been placed on one side ; and that the angels, or rather God, stood on the other. But it is much more probable, that angels were distributed in two camps on different sides of Jacob, that he might perceive himself to be everywhere surrounded and fortified by celestial troops; as in Psalm xxxiv. 7, it is declared that angels, to preserve the worshippers of God, pitch their tents around them. Yet I am not dissatisfied with the opinion of those who take the dual number simply for the plural; understanding that Jacob was entirely surrounded with an army of angels. Now the use of this vision was twofold ; for, first, since the holy man was very anxious about the future, the Lord designed early to

remove this cause of terror from him; or, at least, to afford him some alleviation, lest he should sink under temptation. Secondly, God designed, when Jacob should have been delivered from his brother, so to fix the memory of the past benefit in his mind, that it should never be lost. We know how prone men are to forget the benefits of God. Even while God is stretching out his hand to help them, scarcely one out of a hundred raises his eyes towards heaven. Therefore it was necessary that the visible protection of God should be placed before the eyes of the holy man ; so that, as in a splendid theatre, he might perceive that he had been lately delivered, not by chance, out of the hand of Laban ; but that he had the angels of God fighting for him ; and might certainly hope, that their help would be ready for him against the attempts of his brother; and finally, that, when the danger was surmounted, he might remember the protection he had received from them. This doctrine is of use to us all, that we may learn to mark the invisible presence of God in his manifested favours. Chiefly, however, it was necessary that the holy man should be furnished with new weapons to endure the approaching contest. He did not know whether his brother Esau had been changed for the better or the worse. But he would rather incline to the suspicion that the sanguinary man would devise nothing but what was hostile. Therefore the angels appear for the purpose of confirming his faith in future, not less than for that of calling past favours to his remembrance. The number of these angels also encourages him not a little : for although a single angel would suffice as a guardian for us, yet the Lord acts more liberally towards us. Therefore they who think that each of us is defended by one angel only, wickedly depreciate the kindness of God. And there is no doubt that the devil, by this crafty device, has endeavoured, in some measure, to diminish our faith. The gratitude of the holy man is noted by Moses, in the fact that he assigns to the place a name, (Galeed,) as a token of perpetual remembrance.

3. *And Jacob sent messengers.* It now happened, by the providence of God, that Esau, having left his father, had gone to Mount Seir of his own accord ; and had thus de-

parted from the land of promise, by which means the possession of it would remain void for the posterity of Jacob,
without slaughter among brethren.   For it was not to be
believed that he had changed his habitation, either because
he was compelled by his father's command, or because he
was willing to be accounted inferior to his brother.   I rather
conjecture that he had become greatly enriched, and that
this induced him to leave his father's house.   For we know
that profane persons and men of this world so vehemently
pant for present advantages, that when anything offers itself
in accordance with their desire, they are hurried towards it
with a brutish impetuosity.   Esau was imperious and ferocious ; he was incensed against his mother ; had shaken off all
reverence for his father, and knew that he was himself also
obnoxious to them both : his wives were engaged in incessant
contentions; it seemed to him hard and troublesome, to be in
the condition of a child in the family, when he was now advancing to old age ; for proud men do not regard themselves
as free, so long as any one has the pre-eminence over them.
Therefore, in order to pass his life free from the authority of
others, he chose to live in a state of separation from his
father ; and, allured by this attraction, he disregarded the
promised inheritance, and left the place for his brother.   I
have said that this was done by the divine will : for God
himself declares by Malachi, that it was by a species of
banishment that Esau was led to Mount Seir. (Mal. i. 3.)[1]   For
although he departed voluntarily ; yet, by the secret counsel
of God was he deprived of that land which he had earnestly
desired.   But, attracted by the present lust of dominion, he
was blinded in his choice ; since the land of Seir was mountainous and rugged, destitute of fertility and pleasantness.
Moreover, he would appear to himself a great man, in giving
his own name to the country.   Nevertheless, it is probable
that Moses called that country the land of Edom by the
figure *prolepsis*, because it afterwards began to be so called.
The question now occurs, Whence did Jacob know that his
brother dwelt in that region ?   Though I assert nothing as

---

[1] " I hated Esau, and laid his mountains and his heritage waste for the
dragons of the wilderness."— *English Translation.*

certain ; yet the conjecture is probable, that he had been informed of it by his mother ; for, in the great number of her servants, a faithful messenger would not be wanting. And it is easily gathered from the words of Moses, that Jacob, before he had entered the land, knew the fact respecting the new residence of his brother. And we know that many things of this kind were omitted by Moses, which may easily suggest themselves to the mind of the reader.

4. *Thus shall ye speak unto my lord Esau.* Moses here relates the anxiety of Jacob to appease his brother. For this suppliant deprecation was extorted only by great and severe torture of mind. It seems, however, to be an absurd submission, whereby he cedes to his brother that dominion for which he had contended at the hazard of his life. For if Esau has the primogeniture, what does Jacob reserve for himself ? For what end did he bring upon himself such hatred, expose himself to such dangers, and at length endure twenty years of banishment, if he does not refuse to be in subjection to his brother ? I answer, that though he gives up the temporal dominion, he yields nothing of his right to the secret benediction. He knows that the effect of the divine promise is still suspended: and therefore, being content with the hope of the future inheritance, he does not hesitate, at present, to prefer his brother in honour to himself, and to profess himself his brother's servant. Nor was there anything feigned in these words ; because he was willing to bear his brother on his shoulders ; so that he might not lose his own future right, which was as yet concealed.

5. *I have oxen.* Jacob does not proclaim his riches for the sake of boasting, but that by this method Esau might be inclined to humanity. For it would have been exceedingly disgraceful, cruelly to drive away one who had been enriched, by the favour of God, in a distant land. Besides, he cuts off occasion of future emulation: for if he had come empty and famishing, Esau might conceive fresh indignation against him,· through fear of the expense which might be entailed on himself. Therefore Jacob declares, that he does not come for the purpose of consuming his father's substance, nor of being made rich by his brother's ruin : as

if he had said, " Let thy earthly inheritance be secure ; thy
claim shall not be injured by me ; only suffer me to live."
By this example we are taught in what way we are to cultivate peace with the wicked.   The Lord does not indeed
forbid us to defend our own right, so far as our adversaries
allow ; but we must rather recede from that right, than
originate contention by our own fault.

6. *And the messengers returned.*   Esau advances to meet
his brother with a feeling of benevolence : but Jacob, reflecting on his cruel ferocity, inflated spirits, and savage threats,
expects no humanity from him.   And the Lord willed that the
mind of his servant should be oppressed by this anxiety for a
time, although without any real cause, in order the more to
excite the fervour of his prayer.   For we know what coldness, on this point, security engenders.   Therefore, lest our
faith, being stirred up by no stimulants, should become torpid, God often suffers us to fear things which are not terrible
in themselves.   For although he anticipates our wishes, and
opposes our evils, he yet conceals his remedies until he has
exercised our faith.   Meanwhile it is to be noted, that the
sons of God are never endued with a constancy so steadfast,
that the infirmity of the flesh does not betray itself in them.
For they who fancy that faith is exempt from all fear, have
had no experience of the true nature of faith.   For God
does not promise that he will be present with us, for the
purpose of removing the sense of our dangers, but in order
that fear may not prevail, and overwhelm us in despair.
Moreover our faith is never so firm at every point, as to repel wicked doubts and sinful fears, in the way that might
be wished.

7. *And he divided the people.*   Moses relates that Jacob
formed his plans according to the existing state of affairs.   He divides his family into two parts,[1] and puts his
maids in the foremost place, that they may bear the first
assault, if necessary ; but he places his free wives further

---

[1] " Into two bands," more literally, " into two camps or encampments ;"
לִשְׁנֵי מַחֲנוֹת, (*leshenai machanoth*).   The word here used is the same in
which the host of God is described in the second verse, and from which the
name of the city Mahanaim is derived.—*Ed.*

from the danger. Hence indeed we gather, that Jacob was not so overcome with fear as to be unable to arrange his plans. We know that when a panic seizes the mind, it is deprived of discretion ; and they who ought to look after their own concerns, become stupid and inanimate. Therefore it proceeded from the spirit of faith that Jacob interposed a certain space between the two parts of his family, in order that if any destruction approached, the whole seed of the Church might not perish. For by this scheme, he offered the half of his family to the slaughter, that, at length, the promised inheritance might come to the remainder who survived.

9. *O God of my father Abraham.* Having arranged his affairs as the necessity of the occasion suggested, he now betakes himself to prayer. And this prayer is evidence that the holy man was not so oppressed with fear as to prevent faith from proving victorious. For he does not, in a hesitating manner, commend himself and his family to God ; but trusting both to God's promises and to the benefits already received, he casts his cares and his troubles into his heavenly Father's bosom. We have declared before, what is the point aimed at in assigning these titles to God ; in calling God the God of his fathers Abraham and Isaac, and what the terms mean ; namely, that since men are so far removed from God, that they cannot, by their own power, ascend to his throne, he himself comes down to the faithful. God in thus calling himself the God of Abraham and Isaac, graciously invites their son Jacob to himself: for, access to the God of his fathers was not difficult to the holy man. Again, since the whole world had sunk under superstition, God would have himself to be distinguished from all idols, in order that he might retain an elect people in his own covenant. Jacob, therefore, in expressly addressing God as the God of his fathers, places fully before himself the promises given to him in their person, that he may not pray with a doubtful mind, but may securely rely on this stay, that the heir of the promised blessing will have God propitious towards him. And indeed we must seek the true rule of prayer in the word of God, that we may not rashly break

through to Him, but may approach him in the manner in which he has revealed himself to us. This appears more clearly from the adjoining context, where Jacob, recalling the command and promise of God to memory, is supported as by two pillars. Certainly the legitimate method of praying is, that the faithful should answer to God who calls them ; and thus there is such a mutual agreement between his word and their vows, that no sweeter and more harmonious symphony can be imagined. " O Lord," he says, " I return at thy command : thou also didst promise protection to me returning ; it is therefore right that thou shouldest become the guide of my journey." This is a holy boldness, when, having discharged our duty according to God's calling, we familiarly ask of him whatsoever he has promised ; since he, by binding himself gratuitously to us, becomes in a sense voluntarily our debtor. But whoever, relying on no command or promise of God, offers his prayers, does nothing but cast vain and empty words into the air. This passage gives stronger confirmation to what has been said before, that Jacob did not falsely pretend to his wives, that God had commanded him to return. For if he had then spoken falsely, no ground of hope would now be left to him. But he does not scruple to approach the heavenly tribunal with this confidence, that he shall be protected by the hand of God, under whose auspices he had ventured to return to the land of Canaan.

10. *I am not worthy of the least of all the mercies.*[1] Although this expression sounds harsh to Latin ears, the sense is not obscure. Jacob confesses, that greater mercies of God had been heaped upon him than he had dared to hope for : and therefore, far be it from him that he should plead anything of dignity or merit, for the purpose of obtaining what he asks. He therefore says, that he is less than God's favours ; because he felt himself to be unworthy of those excellent gifts which the Lord had so liberally bestowed upon him. Moreover, that the design of the holy patriarch may more clearly appear, the craft of Satan is to be observed :

[1] Minor sum cunctis misericordiis : " I am less than all the mercies."— *Margin of English Translation.*

for, in order to deter us from praying, through a sense of our unworthiness, he would suggest to us this thought, "Who art thou that thou shouldst dare to enter into the presence of God ?" Jacob early anticipates this objection, in declaring beforehand that he is unworthy of God's former gifts, and at the same time acknowledges that God is not like men, in ever becoming weary to continue and increase his acts of kindness. Meanwhile, Jacob collects materials for confidence from the fact, that he has so often found God benignant towards him. Therefore, he had a double end in view ; first, because he wished to counteract the distrust which might steal upon him in consequence of the magnitude of God's gifts ; and then, he turns those gifts to a different purpose, to assure himself that God would be the same to him that he had hitherto been. He uses two words, *mercies* and *truth*, to show that God is inclined by his mere goodness to benefit us ; and in this way proves his own faithfulness. This combination of mercy with truth frequently occurs in the Scriptures, to teach us that all good things flow to us through the gratuitous favour of God ; but that we are made capable of receiving them, when by faith we embrace his promises.

For with my staff.[1] Jacob does not enumerate separately the mercies of God, but under one species comprises the rest ; namely, that whereas he had passed over Jordan, a poor and solitary traveller, he now returns rich, and replenished with abundance. The antithesis between a *staff* and *two troops* is to be noticed ; in which he compares his former solitude and poverty with his present affluence.

11. *Deliver me.* After he has declared himself to be bound by so many of God's benefits that he cannot boast of his own merits, and thus raised his mind to higher expectation, he now mentions his own necessity, as if he would say, " O Lord, unless thou choosest to reduce so many excellent gifts to nothing, now is the time for thee to succour me, and to avert the destruction which, through my brother, is suspended over me." But having thus expressed his fear, he adds a clause concerning the blessing promised him,

---

[1] That is, " *poor, naked,* and *weak.*"—*Rivet. in Gen.*, p. 676.

that he may confirm himself in the promises made to him. *To slay the mother with the children,* I suppose to have been a proverbial saying among the Jews, which means to leave nothing remaining. It is a metaphor taken from birds, when hawks seize the young with their dams, and empty the whole nest.[1]

13. *And took of that which came to his hand.* In endeavouring to appease his brother by presents, he does not act distrustfully, as if he doubted whether he should be safe under the protection of God. This, indeed, is a fault too common among men, that when they have prayed to God, they turn themselves hither and thither, and contrive vain subterfuges for themselves: whereas the principal advantage of prayer is, to wait for the Lord in silence and quietness. But the design of the holy man was not to busy and to vex himself, as one discontented with the sole help of God. For although he was certainly persuaded that to have God propitious to him would alone be sufficient, yet he did not omit the use of the means which were in his power, while leaving success in the hand of God. For though by prayer we cast our cares upon God, that we may have peaceful and tranquil minds; yet this security ought not to render us indolent. For the Lord will have all the aids which he affords us applied to use. But the diligence of the pious differs greatly from the restless activity of the world; because the world, relying on its own industry, independently of the blessing of God, does not consider what is right or lawful; moreover it is always in trepidation, and by its bustling, increases more and more its own disquietude. The pious, however, hoping for the success of their labour, only from the mercy of God, apply their minds in seeking out means, for this sole reason, that they may not bury the gifts of God by their own torpor. When they have discharged their duty, they still depend on the same grace of God; and when nothing remains which they can attempt, they nevertheless are at rest.

[1] Perhaps Calvin's interpretation would appear more striking, had the original been more literally rendered, " the mother *upon* the children," (על בנים,) which would represent the hawk as pouncing upon the parent bird when seated on her young, or protecting them beneath her feathers. —*Ed.*

14. *Two hundred she-goats.* Hence we perceive the value which Jacob set upon the promise given to him, seeing he does not refuse to make so great a sacrifice of his property. We know that those things which are obtained with great toil and trouble are the more highly esteemed. So that generally they who are enriched by their own labour are proportionably sparing and tenacious. It was, however, no trivial diminution even of great wealth, to give forty cows, thirty camels with their young, twenty bulls, and as many asses with their foals, two hundred she-goats, and as many sheep, with twenty rams, and the same number of he-goats. But Jacob freely lays upon himself this tax, that he may obtain a safe return to his own country. Certainly it would not have been difficult to find some nook where he might live with his property entire : and an equally commodious habitation might have been found elsewhere. But, that he might not lose the benefit of the promise, he purchases, at so great a price, from his brother, a peaceable abode in the land of Canaan. Therefore should we be ashamed of our effeminacy and tardiness, who wickedly turn aside from the duty of our calling, as soon as any loss is to be sustained. With a clear and loud voice the Lord commands us to do what he pleases ; but some, because they find it troublesome to take up their burdens, lie in idleness ; pleasures also keep back some ; riches or honours impede others ; finally, few follow God, because scarcely one in a hundred will bear to be losers. In putting a space between the messengers, and in sending them at different times from each other, he does it to mitigate by degrees the ferocity of his brother : whence we infer again, that he was not so seized with fear, as to be unable prudently to order his affairs.

22. *And he rose up that night.* After he has prayed to the Lord, and arranged his plans, he now takes confidence and meets the danger. By which example the faithful are taught, that whenever any danger approaches, this order of proceeding is to be observed ; first, to resort directly to the Lord ; secondly, to apply to immediate use whatever means of help may offer themselves ; and thirdly, as persons prepared for any event, to proceed with intrepidity whitherso-

ever the Lord commands. So Jacob, that he might not fail in this particular, does not dread the passage which he perceives to be full of hazard, but, as with closed eyes, pursues his course. Therefore, after his example, we must overcome anxiety in intricate affairs, lest we should be hindered or retarded in our duty. He remains alone,—having sent forward his wives and children,[1]—not that he might himself escape if he heard of their destruction, but because solitude was more suitable for prayer. And there is no doubt that, fearing the extremity of his peril, he was completely carried away with the ardour of supplication to God.

24. *There wrestled a man with him.*[2] Although this vision was particularly useful to Jacob himself, to teach him beforehand that many conflicts awaited him, and that he might certainly conclude that he should be the conqueror in them all; there is yet not the least doubt that the Lord exhibited, in his person, a specimen of the temptations—common to all his people—which await them, and must be constantly submitted to, in this transitory life. Wherefore it is right to keep in view this design of the vision, which is to represent all the servants of God in this world as wrestlers; because the Lord exercises them with various kinds of conflicts. Moreover, it is not said that Satan, or any mortal man, wrestled with Jacob, but God himself: to teach us that our faith is tried by him; and whenever we are tempted, our business is truly with him, not only because we fight under his auspices, but because he, as an antagonist, descends into the arena to try our strength. This, though at first sight it seems absurd, experience and reason teaches us to be true. For as all prosperity flows from his goodness, so adversity is either the rod with which he corrects our sins, or the test of our faith and patience. And since there is no kind of temptation by which God does not try his faithful people,

---

[1] " Over the brook Jabbok." יבק is the proper name of a stream near Mount Gilead, on the northern border of the Ammonites, flowing into Jordan on the east, now called *Wady Zurka, i.e.*, blue river. The name is alluded to in verse 25, as if it were from the root אבק, (*Abak*,) which in Niphal means *to wrestle.*—See *Gesenius' Lexicon.* The name is, therefore, here given proleptically.—*Ed.*

[2] יאבק, *yebek,* from אבק, *dust,* because in wrestling the dust is raised.— *Gesenius.*

the similitude is very suitable, which represents him as coming, hand to hand, to combat with them. Therefore, what was once exhibited under a visible form to our father Jacob, is daily fulfilled in the individual members of the Church ; namely, that, in their temptations, it is necessary for them to wrestle with God. He is said, indeed, to tempt us in a different manner from Satan ; but because he alone is the Author of our crosses and afflictions, and he alone creates light and darkness, (as is declared in Isaiah,) he is said to tempt us when he makes a trial of our faith. But the question now occurs, Who is able to stand against an Antagonist, at whose breath alone all flesh perishes and vanishes away, at whose look the mountains melt, at whose word or beck the whole world is shaken to pieces, and therefore to attempt the least contest with him would be insane temerity ? But it is easy to untie the knot. For we do not fight against him, except by his own power, and with his own weapons ; for he, having challenged us to this contest, at the same time furnishes us with means of resistance, so that he both fights *against* us and *for* us. In short, such is his apportioning of this conflict, that, while he assails us with one hand, he defends us with the other ; yea, inasmuch as he supplies us with more strength to resist than he employs in opposing us, we may truly and properly say, that he fights *against* us with his *left* hand, and *for* us with his *right* hand. For while he lightly opposes us, he supplies invincible strength whereby we overcome. It is true he remains at perfect unity with himself : but the double method in which he deals with us cannot be otherwise expressed, than that in striking us with a human rod, he does not put forth his full strength in the temptation ; but that in granting the victory to our faith, he becomes in us stronger than the power by which he opposes us. And although these forms of expression are harsh, yet their harshness will be easily mitigated in practice. For if temptations are contests, (and we know that they are not accidental, but are divinely appointed for us,) it follows hence, that God acts in the character of an antagonist, and on this the rest depends ; namely, that in the temptation itself he appears to be weak *against* us, that he may conquer *in* us.

Some restrict this to one kind of temptation only, where God openly and avowedly manifests himself as our adversary, as if armed for our destruction.   And truly, I confess, that this differs from common conflicts, and requires, beyond all others, a rare, and even heroic strength.   Yet I include willingly every kind of conflict in which God exercises the faithful : since in all they have God for an antagonist, although he may not openly proclaim himself hostile unto them.   That Moses here calls *him* a man whom a little after he declares to have been God, is a sufficiently usual form of speech.   For since God appeared under the form of a man, the name is thence assumed ; just as, because of the visible symbol, the Spirit is called a dove ; and, in turn, the name of the Spirit is transferred to the dove.   That this disclosure was not sooner made to the holy man, I understand to be for this reason, because God had resolved to call him, as a soldier, robust and skilful in war, to more severe contests. For as raw recruits are spared, and young oxen are not immediately yoked to the plough ; so the Lord more gently exercises his own people, until, having gathered strength, they become more inured to toil.   Jacob, therefore, having been accustomed to bear sufferings, is now led forth to real war.   Perhaps also, the Lord had reference to the conflict which was then approaching.   But I think Jacob was admonished, at his very entrance on the promised land, that he was not there to expect a tranquil life for himself. For his return to his own country might seem to be a kind of release ; and thus Jacob, like a soldier who had kept his term of service, would have given himself up to repose. Wherefore it was highly necessary for him to be taught what his future condition should be.   We, also, are to learn from him, that we must fight during the whole course of our life ; lest any one, promising himself rest, should wilfully deceive himself.   And this admonition is very needful for us ; for we see how prone we are to sloth.   Whence it arises, that we shall not only be thinking of a truce in perpetual war ; but also of peace in the heat of the conflict, unless the Lord rouse us.

25. *And when he saw that he prevailed not against him.* Here is described to us the victory of Jacob, which, however,

was not gained without a wound.   In saying that the wrestling angel, or God, wished to retire from the contest, because
he saw he should not prevail, Moses speaks after the manner
of men.   For we know that God, when he descends from
his majesty to us, is wont to transfer the properties of human
nature to himself.   The Lord knew with certainty the event
of the contest, before he came down to engage in it; he had
even already determined what he would do: but his knowledge is here put for the experience of the thing itself.

He touched the hollow of his thigh.   Though Jacob gains
the victory; yet the angel strikes him on the thigh, from
which cause he was lame even to the end of his life.   And
although the vision was by night, yet the Lord designed
this mark of it to continue through all his days, that it
might thence appear not to have been a vain dream.   Moreover, by this sign it is made manifest to all the faithful,
that they can come forth conquerors in their temptations,
only by being injured and wounded in the conflict.   For we
know that the strength of God is made perfect in our weakness, in order that our exaltation may be joined with humility; for if our own strength remained entire, and there were
no injury or dislocation produced, immediately the flesh would
become haughty, and we should forget that we had conquered
by the help of God.   But the wound received, and the weakness which follows it, compel us to be modest.

26. *Let me go.*   God concedes the praise of victory to his
servant, and is ready to depart, as if unequal to him in
strength: not because a truce was needed by him, to whom
it belongs to grant a truce or 'peace whenever he pleases;
but that Jacob might rejoice over the grace afforded to him.
A wonderful method of triumphing; where the Lord, to
whose power all praise is entirely due, yet chooses that
feeble man shall excel as a conqueror, and thus raises him
on high with special eulogy.   At the same time he commends
the invincible perseverance of Jacob, who, having endured a
long and severe conflict, still strenuously maintains his ground.
And certainly we adopt a proper mode of contending, when we
never grow weary, till the Lord recedes of his own accord.
We are, indeed, permitted to ask him to consider our infir-

mity, and, according to his paternal indulgence, to spare the
tender and the weak : we may even groan under our burden, and desire the termination of our contests ; nevertheless,
in the meantime, we must beware lest our minds should become relaxed or faint ; and rather endeavour, with collected
mind and strength, to persist unwearied in the conflict.
The reason which the angel assigns, namely, that *the day
breaketh*, is to this effect, that Jacob may know that he has
been divinely taught by the nocturnal vision.[1]

I will not let thee go, except. Hence it appears, that at
length the holy man knew his antagonist ; for this prayer,
in which he asks to be blessed, is no common prayer. The
inferior is blessed by the greater ; and therefore it is the property of God alone to bless us. Truly the father of Jacob did
not otherwise bless him, than by divine command, as one who
represented the person of God. A similar office also was imposed on the priests under the law, that, as ministers and
expositors of divine grace, they might bless the people.
Jacob knew, then, that the combatant with whom he had
wrestled was God ; because he desires a blessing from him,
which it was not lawful simply to ask from mortal man. So,
in my judgment, ought the place in Hosea (chap. xii. 3) to
be understood, " Jacob prevailed over the angel, and was
strengthened ; he wept, and made supplication to him." For
the Prophet means, that after Jacob had come off conqueror,
he was yet a suppliant before God, and prayed with tears.
Moreover, this passage teaches us always to expect the blessing of God, although we may have experienced his presence
to be harsh and grievous, even to the disjointing of our members. For it is far better for the sons of God to be blessed,
though mutilated and half destroyed, than to desire that
peace in which they shall fall asleep, or than they should
withdraw themselves from the presence of God, so as to

---

[1] There might be other reasons why the angel should say, " Let me go,
for the day breaketh." The vision was intended for Jacob *alone;* had the
struggle been continued till daylight, others would have witnessed it, and
a vain curiosity would have been excited, which God did not design to
gratify. The break of day, also, would be the time when Jacob himself
must set about the work of conducting his family ; and, therefore, on his
account, it was important that no farther delay should take place.—*Ed.*

turn away from his command, that they may riot with the
wicked.

28. *Thy name shall be called no more Jacob.* Jacob, as
we have seen, received his name from his mother's womb,
because he had seized the heel of his brother's foot, and
had attempted to hold him back. God now gives him a new
and more honourable name ; not that he may entirely abolish
the other, which was a token of memorable grace, but that
he may testify a still higher progress of his grace. Therefore, of the two names the second is preferred to the former,
as being more honourable. The name is derived from שׂרה,
or שׂור, which signifies to rule, as if he were called a Prince
of God : for I have said, a little before, that God had transferred the praise of his own strength to Jacob, for the purpose
of triumphing in his person. The explanation of the name
which is immediately annexed, is thus given literally by Moses,
" Because thou hast ruled with, or, towards God and towards
man, and shalt prevail." Yet the sense seems to be faithfully
rendered by Jerome :[1] but if Jacob acted thus heroically with
God, much more should he prove superior to men ; for certainly it was the purpose of God to send forth his servant to
various combats, inspired with the confidence resulting from
so great a victory, lest he should afterwards become vacillating. For he does not merely impose a name, as men are accustomed to do, but with the name he gives the thing itself
which the name implies, that the event may correspond with it.

29. *Tell me, I pray thee, thy name.* This seems opposed
to what is declared above ; for I have lately said, that when
Jacob sought a blessing, it was a token of his submission.
Why, therefore, as if he were of doubtful mind, does he now
inquire the name of him whom he had before acknowledged
to be God ? But the solution of the question is easy; for,
though Jacob does acknowledge God, yet, not content with
an obscure and slight knowledge, he wishes to ascend higher.
And it is not to be wondered at, that the holy man, to whom
God had manifested himself under so many veils and cover-
ings, that he had not yet obtained any clear knowledge

---

[1] Quoniam si contra Deum fortis fuisti, quanto magis contra homines
prævalebis ? If thou hast been so strong against God, how much more
shalt thou prevail against men ?—*Vulgate.*

of him, should break forth in this wish; nay, it is certain
that all the saints, under the law, were inflamed with this
desire.   Such a prayer also of Manoah, is read in the book
of Judges, (xiii. 18,) to which the answer from God is added,
except that there, the Lord pronounces his name to be wonderful and secret, in order that Manoah may not proceed
further.   The sum therefore is this, that though Jacob's wish
was pious, the Lord does not grant it, because the time of
full revelation was not yet completed : for the fathers, in
the beginning, were required to walk in the twilight of
morning ; and the Lord manifested himself to them, by degrees, until, at length, Christ the Sun of Righteousness arose, in
whom perfect brightness shines forth.   This is the reason why
he rendered himself more conspicuous to Moses, who nevertheless was only permitted to behold his glory from behind :
yet because he occupied an intermediate place between patriarchs and apostles, he is said, in comparison with them,
to have seen, face to face, the God who had been hidden from
the fathers.   But now, since God has approached more nearly
unto us, our ingratitude is most impious and detestable, if
we do not run to meet him with ardent desire to obtain such
great grace; as also Peter admonishes us in the first chapter
of his first epistle. (Ver. 12, 13.)   It is to be observed, that
although Jacob piously desires to know God more fully, yet,
because he is carried beyond the bounds prescribed to the
age in which he lived, he suffers a repulse : for the Lord, cutting short his wish, commands him to rest contented with
his own blessing.   But if that measure of illumination which
we have received, was denied to the holy man, how intolerable
will be our curiosity, if it breaks forth beyond the extended
limit now prescribed by God.

30. *And Jacob called the name of the place.*[1]   The gratitude of our father Jacob is again commended, because he
took diligent care that the memory of God's grace should
never perish.   He therefore leaves a monument to posterity,
from which they might know that God had appeared there ;
for this was not a private vision, but had reference to the
whole Church.   Moreover, Jacob not only declares that he

---

[1] פְּנִיאֵל, (*Peniel,*) the face of God.

has seen the face of God, but also gives thanks that he has been snatched from death. This language frequently occurs in the Scriptures, and was common among the ancient people; and not without reason; for, if the earth trembles at the presence of God, if the mountains melt, if darkness overspreads the heavens, what must happen to miserable men! Nay, since the immense majesty of God cannot be comprehended even by angels, but rather absorbs them; were his glory to shine on us it would destroy us, and reduce us to nothing, unless he sustained and protected us. So long as we do not perceive God to be present, we proudly please ourselves; and this is the imaginary life which the flesh foolishly arrogates to itself when it inclines towards the earth. But the faithful, when God reveals himself to them, feel themselves to be more evanescent than any smoke. Finally; would we bring down the pride of the flesh, we must draw near to God. So Jacob confesses that, by the special indulgence of God, he had been rescued from destruction when he saw God. It may however be asked, "Why, when he had obtained so slight a taste only of God's glory, he should boast that he had seen him, face to face?" I answer, it is in no way absurd that Jacob highly celebrates this vision above all others, in which the Lord had not so plainly appeared unto him; and yet, if it be compared with the splendour of the gospel, or even of the law, it will appear like sparks, or obscure rays. The simple meaning then is, that he saw God in an unwonted and extraordinary manner. Now, if Jacob so greatly exults and congratulates himself in that slender measure of knowledge; what ought we to do at this day, to whom Christ, the living image of God, is evidently set before our eyes in the mirror of the gospel! Let us therefore learn to open our eyes, lest we be blind at noonday, as Paul exhorts us in the second epistle to the Corinthians, the third and fourth chapters.

31. *And he halted upon his thigh.* It is probable, and it may be gathered even from the words of Moses, that this halting was without the sense of pain, in order that the miracle might be the more evident. For God, in the flesh of his servant, has exhibited a spectacle to all ages, from

which the faithful may perceive that no one is such a powerful combatant as not to carry away some wound after a spiritual conflict, for infirmity ever cleaves to all, that no one may be pleased with himself above measure. Whereas Moses relates that the Jews abstained from the shrunken sinew, or that part of the thigh in which it was placed: this was not done out of superstition.[1] For that age, as we know, was the infancy of the Church; wherefore the Lord retained the faithful, who then lived, under the teaching of the schoolmaster. And now, though, since the coming of Christ, our condition is more free; the memory of the fact ought to be retained among us, that God disciplined his people of old by external ceremonies.

CHAPTER XXXIII.

1. And Jacob lifted up his eyes, and looked, and, behold, Esau came, and with him four hundred men. And he divided the children unto Leah, and unto Rachel, and unto the two handmaids.

2. And he put the handmaids and their children foremost, and Leah and her children after, and Rachel and Joseph hindermost.

3. And he passed over before them, and bowed himself to the ground seven times, until he came near to his brother.

4. And Esau ran to meet him, and embraced him, and fell on his neck, and kissed him: and they wept.

5. And he lifted up his eyes, and saw the women and the children, and said, Who *are* those with thee? And he said, The children which God hath graciously given thy servant.

1. Levavit autem Iahacob oculos suos, et vidit, et ecce Esau veniebat, et cum eo erant quadringenti viri: et divisit liberos cum Leah et cum Rachel, et cum ambabus ancillis.

2. Tunc posuit ancillas et liberos earum prius, et Leah et liberos ejus posteriores, Rachel autem et Ioseph postremos.

3. Et ipse transivit ante eos, et incurvavit se super terram septem vicibus, donec appropinquaret fratri suo.

4. Cucurrit vero Esau in occursum ejus, et complexus est eum, et jactavit se super collum ejus, et osculatus est eum; et fleverunt.

5. Postea levavit oculos suos, et vidit uxores et liberos, et dixit, Qui isti tibi? Et dixit, Liberi *sunt*, quos donavit Deus servo tuo.

[1] The sinew which shrank; "that sinew or tendon which fastens the hip-bone in its socket, which comprehends the flesh of that muscle which is connected to it. He that ate of this was to be beaten, as the Jewish masters tell us."—*Patrick.* See also Ainsworth on this passage. Professor Bush says, "At present the Jews do not know what sinew this was, nor even which thigh it was in; and the effect of this uncertainty is, that they judge it necessary to abstain from both the hind quarters, lest they should inadvertently eat the interdicted sinew. They sell those parts to Christians."—*Ed.*

6. Then the handmaidens came near, they and their children, and they bowed themselves:

7. And Leah also with her children came near, and bowed themselves : and after came Joseph near and Rachel, and they bowed themselves.

8. And he said, What *meanest* thou by all this drove which I met? And he said, *These are* to find grace in the sight of my lord.

9. And Esau said, I have enough, my brother; keep that thou hast unto thyself.

10. And Jacob said, Nay, I pray thee, if now I have found grace in thy sight, then receive my present at my hand; for therefore I have seen thy face, as though I had seen the face of God, and thou wast pleased with me.

11. Take, I pray thee, my blessing that is brought to thee; because God hath dealt graciously with me, and because I have enough. And he urged him, and he took *it*.

12. And he said, Let us take our journey, and let us go, and I will go before thee.

13. And he said unto him, My lord knoweth that the children *are* tender, and the flocks and herds with young *are* with me; and if men should overdrive them one day, all the flock will die.

14. Let my lord, I pray thee, pass over before his servant; and I will lead on softly, according as the cattle that goeth before me and the children be able to endure, until I come unto my lord unto Seir.

15. And Esau said, Let me now leave with thee *some* of the folk that *are* with me. And he said, What needeth it? let me find grace in the sight of my lord.

16. So Esau returned that day on his way unto Seir.

17. And Jacob journeyed to Succoth, and built him an house, and made booths for his cattle: therefore the name of the place is called Succoth.

18. And Jacob came to Shalem, a

6. Et appropinquaverunt ancillæ ipsæ, et liberi earum, et incurvaverunt se.

7. Et appropinquavit etiam Leah, et liberi ejus, et incurvaverunt se : et subinde appropinquavit Ioseph et Rachel, et incurvaverunt se.

8. Et dixit, Qui isti? tuane omnis turma illa, quam obviam habui? Et dixit, Ut invenirem gratiam in oculis domini mei.

9. Et dixit Esau, Est mihi multum, frater mi, sit tuum quod tuum est.

10. Ait autem Iahacob, Ne quæso: si nunc inveni gratiam in oculis tuis; accipe munus meum e manu mea : quia idcirco vidi faciem tuam, acsi viderem faciem Angeli : et propitius eris erga me.

11. Cape quæso benedictionem meam, quæ allata est tibi : quia donavit mihi Deus, et quia sunt mihi omnia. Et coegit eum, et accepit.

12. Tunc dixit, Proficiscamur, et ambulemus, et ambulabo ante te.

13. Sed dixit ad eum, Dominus meus scit, quod pueri teneri sunt : et pecudes, et boves fœtæ sunt mihi : et *si* pulsaverint eas die una, morientur omnes pecudes.

14. Transeat quæso dominus meus ante servum suum, et ego ducam me pedetentim ad pedem gregis, qui est ante me, et ad pedem puerorum, donec veniam ad dominum meum in Sehir.

15. Et dixit Esau, Stare faciam nunc tecum de populo, qui est mecum. Et dixit, Utquid hoc? inveniam gratiam in oculis domini mei.

16. Reversus est itaque in die ipsa Esau per viam suam in Sehir.

17. Iahacob autem profectus est in Suchoth, et ædificavit sibi domum, et pecudibus suis fecit tabernacula : idcirco vocavit nomen loci Suchoth.

18. Et venit Iahacob incolumis in

city of Shechem, which *is* in the land of Canaan, when he came from Padan-aram, and pitched his tent before the city.

19. And he bought a parcel of a field, where he had spread his tent, at the hand of the children of Hamor, Shechem's father, for an hundred pieces of money.

20. And he erected there an altar, and called it El-elohe-Israel.

civitatem Sechem, quæ erat in terra Chenaan, quando venit ipse de Padan Aram, et mansit ante urbem.

19. Et emit partem agri, in quo tetendit tabernaculum suum, de manu filiorum Hamor patris Sechem, centum nummis.

20. Et statuit ibi altare: et vocavit illud, Fortis Deus Israel.

1. *And Jacob lifted up his eyes.* We have said how greatly Jacob feared for himself from his brother; but now when Esau himself approaches, his terror is not only renewed, but increased. For although he goes forth like a courageous and spirited combatant to this contest, he is still not exempt from a sense of danger; whence it follows, that he is not free, either from anxiety or fear. For his cruel brother had still the same cause of hatred against him as before. And it was not probable, that, after he had left his father's house, and had been living as he pleased, he had become more mild. Therefore, as in a doubtful affair, and one of great danger, Jacob placed his wives and children in the order described; that, if Esau should attempt anything hostile, the whole seed might not perish, but part might have time for flight. The only thing which appears to be done by him out of order is, that he prefers Rachel and her son Joseph to all the rest; whereas the substance of the benediction is really in Judah. But his excuse in reference to Judah is, that the oracle had not yet been revealed; nor, in fact, was made known till shortly before his death, in order that he might become at once its witness and its herald. Meanwhile, it is not to be denied, that he was excessively indulgent to Rachel. It is, indeed, a proof of distinguished courage, that, from a desire to preserve a part of his seed, he precedes his companies, and offers himself as a victim, if necessity demanded it. For there is no doubt that the promise of God was his authority and his guide in this design; nor would he have been able, unless sustained by the confident expectation of celestial life, thus bravely to meet death. It happens, indeed, sometimes, that a father, regardless of himself, will expose his life to danger for his

children : but holy Jacob's reason was different ; for the promise of God was so deeply fixed in his mind, that he, disregarding the earth, looked up towards heaven.   But while
he follows the word of God, yet by the affection of the flesh,
he is slightly drawn aside from the right way. For the faith of
the holy fathers was not so pure, in all respects, but that they
were liable to swerve to one side or the other.   Nevertheless,
the Spirit always so far prevailed, that the infirmity of the
flesh might not divert them from their aim, but that they
might hold on their course.   So much the more ought every
one of us to be suspicious of himself, lest he should deem
himself perfectly pure, because he intends to act rightly ;
for the flesh ever mingles itself with our holy purpose, and
many faults and corruptions steal in upon us.   But God
deals kindly with us, and does not impute faults of this kind
to us.

3. *And bowed himself to the ground seven times.*   This, indeed, he might do for the sake of giving honour : for we
know that the people of the east are addicted to far more
ceremonies than are in use with us.   To me, however, it
seems more probable, that Jacob did not pay this honour
simply to his brother, but that he worshipped God, partly to
give him thanks, and partly to implore him to render his brother propitious ; for he is said to have bowed down seven times
before he approached his brother.   Therefore, before he came
in sight of his brother, he had already given the token of
reverence or worship.   Hence we may conjecture, as I have
said, that this homage was paid to God and not to man : yet
this is not at variance with the fact, that he also approached
as a suppliant, for the purpose of assuaging his brother's
ferocity by his humiliation.[1]   If any one object, that in this

---

[1] Rivetus judiciously observes on this passage: " There are those who
think that by this ceremony Jacob worshipped God ; but by what argument they prove this I do not see ; for whatever precedes or follows indicates that he wished to show reverence to his brother ; and for this reason,
he went before his family ; so also the handmaidens and their sons bowed
themselves ; likewise Leah and her sons, and lastly, Rachel with Joseph ;
in each case the same word is used, which the Vulgate renders ' adored.'
This verse also proves the same thing ; for after he saw his brother approaching, he bowed seven times, till his brother drew near. . . . . This,
therefore, was civil reverence, (reverentia civilis,) which did not derogate

manner he depreciated his right of primogeniture; the answer is easy, that the holy man, by the eyes of faith, was looking higher; for he knew that the effect of the benediction was deferred to its proper season, and was, therefore, now like the decaying seed under the earth. Therefore, although he was despoiled of his patrimony, and lay contemptible at his brother's feet; yet since he knew that his birthright was secured to him, he was contented with this latent right, counted honours and riches as nothing, and did not shrink from being regarded as an inferior in the presence of his brother.

4. *And Esau ran to meet him.* That Esau meets his brother with unexpected benevolence and kindness, is the effect of the special favour of God. Therefore, by this method, God proved that he has the hearts of men in his hand, to soften their hardness, and to mitigate their cruelty as often as he pleases: in short, that he tames them as wild beasts are wont to be tamed; and then, that he hearkened to the prayers of his servant Jacob. Wherefore, if at any time the threats of enemies alarm us, let us learn to resort to this sacred anchor. God, indeed, works in various ways, and does not always incline cruel minds to humanity; but, while they rage, he restrains them from doing harm by his own power: but if it is right, he can as easily render them placable towards us; and we here see that Esau became so towards his brother Jacob. It is also possible, that even while cruelty was pent up within, the feeling of humanity may have had a temporary ascendency. And as we see that the Egyptians were constrained, for a moment, to the exercise of humanity, although they were rendered nothing better than before, as their madness, which soon afterwards broke out, bears witness: so it is credible that the malice of Esau was now under constraint; and not only so, but that his mind was divinely moved to put on fraternal affection. For even in the reprobate, God's established order of nature prevails, not indeed in an even tenor, but as far as he restrains them, to the end that they may not mingle all

from the spiritual right and prerogative of the covenant entered into with Jehovah." This account seems much more probable than that given by Calvin.—*Ed.*

things in one common slaughter. And this is most necessary for the preservation of the human race. For few are so governed by the spirit of adoption, as sincerely to cultivate mutual charity among themselves, as brethren. Therefore, that men spare each other, and do not furiously rush on each other's destruction, arises from no other cause than the secret providence of God, which watches for the protection of mankind. But to God the life of his own faithful people is still more precious, so that he vouchsafes to them peculiar care. Wherefore it is no wonder, that for the sake of his servant Jacob, he should have composed the fierce mind of Esau to gentleness.

5. *And he lifted up his eyes.* Moses relates the conversation held between the brothers. And as Esau had testified his fraternal affection by tears and embraces, there is no doubt that he inquires after the children in a spirit of congratulation. The answer of Jacob breathes piety as well as modesty; for when he replies, that his numerous seed had been given him by God, he acknowledges and confesses that children are not so produced by nature as to subvert the truth of the declaration, that "the fruit of the womb is a reward and gift of God." And truly, since the fecundity of brute animals is the gift of God, how much more is this the case with men, who are created after his own image. Let parents then learn to consider, and to celebrate the singular kindness of God, in their offspring. It is the language of modesty, when Jacob calls himself the servant of his brother. Here again it is proper to recall to memory what I have lately touched upon, that the holy man caught at nothing either of earthly advantage or honour in the birthright; because the hidden grace of God was abundantly sufficient for him, until the appointed time of manifestation. And it becomes us also, according to his example, while we sojourn in this world, to depend upon the word of the Lord ; that we may not deem it wearisome, to be held wrapped in the shadow of death, until our real life be manifested. For although apparently our condition is miserable and accursed, yet the Lord blesses us with his word; and, on this account only, pronounces us happy, because he owns us as sons.

6. *Then the handmaidens came near.*   The wives of Jacob, having left their country, had come as exiles into a distant land.   Now, at their first entrance, the terror of death meets them ; and when they prostrate themselves in the presence of Esau, they do not know whether they are not doing homage to their executioner.   This trial was very severe to them, and grievously tormented the mind of the holy man : but it was right that his obedience should be thus tried, that he might become an example to us all.   Moreover, the Holy Spirit here places a mirror before us, in which we may contemplate the state of the Church as it appears in the world. For though many tokens of the divine favour are manifest in the family of Jacob ; nevertheless we perceive no dignity in him while lying with unmerited contempt in the presence of a profane man.   Jacob also himself thinks that he is well treated, if he may be permitted by his brother, as a matter of favour, to dwell in the land of which he was the heir and lord.   Therefore let us bear it patiently, if, at this day also, the glory of the Church, being covered with a sordid veil, is an object of derision to the wicked.

8. *What meanest thou by all this drove ?*   He does not inquire as if he were altogether ignorant ; seeing he had heard from the servants, that oxen and camels and asses and other cattle were sent him as a present ; but for the purpose of refusing the gift offered to him : for when anything does not please us, we are wont to make inquiry as concerning a thing unknown to us.   Jacob, however, is urgent ; nor does he cease to ask, till he induces his brother to receive the gift : for this was as a pledge of reconciliation.   Besides, for the purpose of persuading his brother, he declares, that it would be taken as a great kindness not to refuse what was given.   For we do not willingly receive anything but what we certainly know to be offered to us freely and with a ready mind.   And because it is not possible that we should willingly honour any but those we love, Jacob says that he rejoiced in the sight of his brother as if he had seen God or an angel : by which words he means, not only that he truly loved his brother, but also that he held him in esteem.   But it may seem, that he does wrong to God, in comparing Him with a reprobate man ; and

that he speaks falsely, because had the choice been given him, he would have desired nothing more earnestly than to avoid this meeting with his brother. Both these knots are easily untied. It is an accustomed form of speaking among the Hebrews, to call whatever is excellent, divine. And certainly Esau being thus changed, was no obscure figure of the favour of God: so that Jacob might properly say, that he had been exhilarated by that friendly and fraternal reception, as if he had seen God or an angel; that is, as if God had given some sign of his presence. And, indeed, he does not speak feignedly, nor pretend something different from what he has in his mind. For, being himself perfectly free from all hatred, it was his chief wish, to discharge whatever duty he could towards his brother; provided that Esau, in return, would show himself a brother to him.

10. *Receive my present at my hand.* This noun may be taken passively as well as actively. If understood actively, the sense will be, " Accept the present by which I desire to testify my goodwill towards thee." If understood passively, it may be referred to God, as if Jacob had said, " Those things which the Lord has bestowed upon me by his grace, I liberally impart to thee, that thou mayest be, in some measure, a partaker with me of that divine blessing which I have received." But not to insist upon a word, Jacob immediately afterwards clearly avows that whatever he possesses, is not the fruit of his labour or industry, but has been received by him through the grace of God, and by this reasoning he attempts to induce his brother to accept the gift; as if he had said, " The Lord has poured upon me an abundance, of which some part, without any loss to me, may overflow to thee." And though Jacob thus speaks under the impulse of present circumstances, he yet makes an ingenuous confession by which he celebrates the grace of God. Nearly the same words are on the tongues of all; but there are few who truly ascribe to God what they possess: the greater part sacrifice to their own industry. Scarcely one in a hundred is convinced, that whatever is good flows from the gratuitous favour of God ; and yet by nature this sense is engraven upon our minds, but we obliterate it by our ingratitude. It has appeared

already, how laborious was the life of Jacob: nevertheless, though he had suffered the greatest annoyances, he celebrates only the mercy of God.

12. *Let us take our journey.* Although Esau was inclined to benevolence, Jacob still distrusts him: not that he fears to be ensnared, or that he suspects perfidy to lie hidden under the garb of friendship; but that he cautiously avoids new occasions of offence: for a proud and ferocious man might easily be exasperated again by light causes. Now, though just reason for fear was not wanting to the holy man, yet I dare not deny that his anxiety was excessive. He suspected the liberality of Esau; but did he not know that a God was standing between them, who, as he was convinced by clear and undoubted experience, watched for his salvation? For, whence such an incredible change of mind in Esau, unless he had been divinely transformed from a wolf into a lamb? Let us then learn, from this example, to restrain our anxieties, lest when God has provided for us, we tremble, as in an affair of doubt.

13. *My lord knoweth.* The things which Jacob alleges, as grounds of excuse, are true; nevertheless he introduces them under false pretexts; except, perhaps, as regards the statement, that he was unwilling to be burdensome and troublesome to his brother. But since he afterwards turns his journey in another direction, it appears that he feigned something foreign to what was really in his mind. He says that he brings with him many encumbrances, and therefore requests his brother to precede him. " *I will follow* (he says) *at the feet of the children;* that is, I will proceed gently as the pace of the children will bear; and thus I will follow at my leisure, until I come to thee in Mount Seir." In these words he promises what he was not intending to do; for, leaving his brother, he journeyed to a different place.[1] But

---

[1] Peter Martyr inclines to the opinion of Calvin, though he expresses himself with greater caution. There appears no reason to doubt that Jacob said what he meant. It is true he might have other reasons besides those he gave, for not accompanying his brother; reasons sufficient to deter a pious mind from too close and frequent intercourse with persons uninfluenced by true religion. But it is by no means certain that Jacob did not go to Seir; though he would probably go unaccompanied by his wives and children, his flocks and herds. The omission of the sacred writers to mention it, affords no proof that he did not take the journey.

truth is so precious to God, that he will not allow us to lie or deceive, even when no injury follows. Wherefore, we must take care, when any fear of danger occupies our minds, that we do not turn aside to these subterfuges.

17. *And Jacob journeyed to Succoth.* In the word Succoth, as Moses shortly afterwards shows, there is a *prolepsis.* It is probable that Jacob rested there for some days, that he might refresh his family and his flock after the toil of a long journey; for he had found no quiet resting-place till he came thither. And therefore he gave to that place the name of Succoth, or "Tents," because he had not dared firmly to plant his foot elsewhere. For though he had pitched tents in many other places; yet on this alone he fixes the memorial of divine grace, because now at length it was granted to him that he might remain in some abode. But since it was not commodious as a dwelling-place, Jacob proceeded farther till he came t❋ ichem. Now, whereas the city has its recent name from the son of Hamor, its former name is also mentioned, (ver. 18;) for I agree with the interpreters who think Salem to be a proper name. Although I do not contend, if any one prefers a different interpretation; namely, that Jacob came *in safety* to Sichem.[1] But though this city may have been called Salem, we must nevertheless observe, that it was different from the city afterwards called Jerusalem; as there were also two cities which bore the name of Succoth. As respects the subject in hand, the purchase of land which Moses records in the nineteenth verse, may seem to have been absurd. For Abraham would buy nothing all his life but a sepulchre; and Isaac his son, waiving all immediate possession of lands, was contented with that paternal inheritance; for God had constituted them lords and heirs of the land, with this condition, that they should be strangers in it unto death. Jacob therefore

Still less, is there any proof that he did not *intend* to take it; which is all that a regard to truth and sincerity required of him.—*Ed.*

[1] To understand the above passage the English reader will require to be informed that the word דֹּשׁ, (*Shalem,*) which our translators, with Calvin, regarded as a *proper name,* means also "peace," or "safety;" and therefore the 18th verse may be read "Jacob came in safety to the city of Sichem." And this is the translation given in Calvin's own version, *Et venit Iahacob incolumis in civitatem Sechem.* Thus his own text is, singularly enough, at variance with his Commentary.—*Ed.*

may seem to have done wrong in buying a field for himself
with money, instead of waiting the proper time.   I answer,
that Moses has not expressed all that ought to come freely
into the mind of the reader.   Certainly from the price we may
readily gather that the holy man was not covetous.   He pays
a hundred pieces of money ; could he acquire for himself large
estates at so small a price, or anything more than some nook
in which he might live without molestation ?   Besides, Moses
expressly relates that he bought that part on which he had
pitched his tent opposite the city.   Therefore he possessed
neither meadows, nor vineyards, nor arable land.   But since
the inhabitants did not grant him an abode near the city,
he made an agreement with them, and purchased peace at a
small price.[1]   This necessity was his excuse ; so that no one
might say, that he had bought from man what he ought to
have expected as the free gift of God : or that, when he
ought to have embraced, by hope, the dominion of the promised land, he had been in too great haste to enjoy it.

20. *And he erected there an altar.*   Jacob having obtained
a place in which he might provide for his family, set up the
solemn service of God ; as Moses before testified concerning
Abraham and Isaac.   For although, in every place, they gave
themselves up to the pure worship of God in prayers and
other acts of devotion ; nevertheless they did not neglect the
external confession of piety, whenever the Lord granted
them any fixed place in which they might remain.   For (as
I have elsewhere stated) whenever we read that an altar was
built by them, we must consider its design and use : namely, that they might offer victims, and might invoke the
name of God with a pure rite ; so that, by this method, their
religion and faith might be made known.   I say this, lest any
one should think that they rashly trifled with the worship
of God ; for it was their care to direct their actions accord-

---

[1] " For a hundred pieces of money."   The word rendered pieces of
money, קְשִׂיטָה, (*Kisitah*,) means also *lambs ;* and the price given might
have been one hundred lambs ; the probability, however, is, that the coin
itself was called a *lamb*, as we have a coin called a *sovereign*.   It is supposed that the coin bore the image of a *lamb*, perhaps because it was the
conventional price at which lambs were generally valued.   The testimony
of St. Stephen (Acts vii. 16) is decisive as to the fact that money was in
use.—*Ed.*

ing to the divinely prescribed rule which was handed down to them from Noah and Shem. Wherefore, under the word " altar," let the reader understand, by *synecdoche*, the external testimony of piety. Moreover, it may hence be clearly perceived how greatly the love of divine worship prevailed in the holy man; because though broken down by various troubles, he nevertheless was not forgetful of the altar. And not only does he privately worship God in the secret feeling of his mind; but he exercises himself in ceremonies which are useful and commanded by God. For he knew that men want helps, as long as they are in the flesh, and that sacrifices were not instituted without reason. He had also another purpose; namely, that his whole family should worship God with the same sense of piety. For it behoves a pious father of a family diligently to take care that he has no profane house, but rather that God should reign there as in a sanctuary. Besides, since the inhabitants of that region had fallen into many superstitions, and had corrupted the true worship of God, Jacob wished to make a distinction between himself and them. The Shechemites and other neighbouring nations had certainly altars of their own. Therefore Jacob, by establishing a different method of worship for his household, thus declares that he has a God peculiar to himself, and has not degenerated from the holy fathers, from whom the perfect and genuine religion had proceeded. This course could not but subject him to reproach, because the Shechemites and other inhabitants would feel that they were despised : but the holy man deemed anything preferable to mixing himself with idolaters.

21. *And he called it El-elohe-Israel.*[1] This name appears little suitable to the altar; for it sounds as if a heap of stones or turf formed a visible statue of God. But the meaning of the holy man was different. For, because the altar was a memorial and pledge of all the visions and promises of God, he honours it with this title, to the end that, as often as he beheld the altar, he should call God to

---

[1] Et vocavit illud, Fortis Deus Israel; " the strong God of Israel." The margin of the English translation is more literal, " God, the God of Israel."—*Ed.*

remembrance. That inscription of Moses, " The Lord is my
help," has the same signification; and also that which Ezekiel inscribes on the New Jerusalem, " the Lord is there."
And truly in these forms of speaking there is a want of
strict propriety of metaphor; yet this is not without reason.
For as superstitious men foolishly and wickedly attach God
to symbols, and, as it were, draw him down from his heavenly
throne to render him subject to their gross inventions: so
the faithful, piously and rightly, ascend from earthly signs
to heaven. The conclusion is this: Jacob wished to testify
that he worshipped no other God than him who had been
manifested by certain oracles, in order that he might distinguish Him from all idols. And we must observe it as a rule
of modesty, not to speak carelessly concerning the mysteries
and the glory of the Lord, but from a sense of faith, so far,
indeed, as he is made known to us in his word. Moreover
Jacob had respect to his posterity; for since the Lord had appeared to him, on the express condition, that he would make
with him the covenant of salvation, Jacob leaves this monument, from which, after his death, his descendants might
ascertain that his religion had not flowed from a dark or obscure well, or from a turbid pool, but from a clear and pure
fountain; as if he had engraved the oracles and visions, by
which he had been taught, upon the altar.

CHAPTER XXXIV.

1. AND Dinah the daughter of Leah, which she bare unto Jacob, went out to see the daughters of the land.
2. And when Shechem the son of Hamor the Hivite, prince of the country, saw her, he took her, and lay with her, and defiled her.
3. And his soul clave unto Dinah the daughter of Jacob; and he loved the damsel, and spake kindly unto the damsel.
4. And Shechem spake unto his father Hamor, saying, Get me this damsel to wife.

1. Et egressa est Dinah filia Leah, quam pepererat ipsi Iahacob, ut viderat filias regionis.
2. Et vidit eam Sechem filius Hamor Hivvæi principis terræ, et tulit eam, et concubuit cum ea, et humiliavit eam.
3. Et adhæsit anima ejus ipsi Dinah filiæ Iahacob, et dilexit puellam: et loquutus est ad cor puellæ.
4. Et dixit Sechem ad Hamor patrem suum, dicendo, Cape mihi puellam hanc in uxorem.

5. And Jacob heard that he had defiled Dinah his daughter ; (now his sons were with his cattle in the field ;) and Jacob held his peace until they were come.

6. And Hamor the father of Shechem went out unto Jacob to commune with him.

7. And the sons of Jacob came out of the field when they heard *it ;* and the men were grieved ; and they were very wroth, because he had wrought folly in Israel, in lying with Jacob's daughter ; which thing ought not to be done.

8. And Hamor communed with them, saying, The soul of my son Shechem longeth for your daughter : I pray you give her him to wife.

9. And make ye marriages with us, *and* give your daughters unto us, and take our daughters unto you.

10. And ye shall dwell with us : and the land shall be before you ; dwell and trade ye therein, and get you possessions therein.

11. And Shechem said unto her father, and unto her brethren, Let me find grace in your eyes, and what ye shall say unto me I will give.

12. Ask me never so much dowry and gift, and I will give according as ye shall say unto me : but give me the damsel to wife.

13. And the sons of Jacob answered Shechem and Hamor his father deceitfully, and said, (because he had defiled Dinah their sister :)

14. And they said unto them, We cannot do this thing, to give our sister to one that is uncircumcised ; for that *were* a reproach unto us :

15. But in this will we consent unto you : If ye will be as we *be,* that every male of you be circumcised ;

16. Then will we give our daughters unto you, and we will take your daughters to us, and we will dwell with you, and we will become one people.

17. But if ye will not hearken unto us, to be circumcised ; then will we take our daughter, and we will be gone.

5. Audivit autem Iahacob, quod violasset Dinah filiam suam : et filii ejus erant cum pecudibus ejus in agro, et siluit Iahacob, donec venirent ipsi.

6. Egressus est autem Hamor pater Sechem ad Iahacob, ut loqueretur cum eo.

7. Porro filii Iahacob venerunt de agro : *qui* quum audierunt ipsi, dolore affecti sunt viri, iratique sunt valde : quia flagitium designasset in Israel, ut coiret cum filia Iahacob : et sic non fiet.

8. Et loquutus est Hamor cum eis, dicendo, Sechem filii mei complacuit anima in filia vestra : date quæso eam illi in uxorem.

9. Et affinitatem contrahite nobiscum : filias vestras dabitis nobis, et filias nostras accipietis vobis.

10. Et nobiscum habitabitis, et terra erit coram vobis, habitate, et negotiamini in ea, et possessiones acquirite in ea.

11. Adhæc dixit Sechem ad patrem ejus, et ad fratres ejus, Inveniam gratiam in oculis vestris : et quod dixeritis mihi, dabo.

12. Augete mihi valde dotem, et donum : et dabo quemadmodum dixeritis mihi, et date mihi puellam in uxorem.

13. Et responderunt filii Iahacob ad Sechem et Hamor patrem ejus in dolo, et loquuti sunt, (quia violaverat Dinah sororem suam,)

14. Et dixerunt ad eos, Non possumus facere hoc, ut demus sororem nostram viro, cui est præputium : quia opprobrium esset nobis.

15. Veruntamen in hoc acquiescemus vobis, si fueritis sicut nos, ut circumcidatur in vobis omnis masculus.

16. Et dabimus filias nostras vobis, et filias vestras capiemus nobis : et habitabimus vobiscum, et erimus in populum unum.

17. Quodsi non obedieritis nobis, ut circumcidamini : capiemus filiam nostram et recedemus.

18. And their words pleased Hamor, and Shechem, Hamor's son.

19. And the young man deferred not to do the thing, because he had delight in Jacob's daughter ; and he *was* more honourable than all the house of his father.

20. And Hamor and Shechem his son came unto the gate of their city, and communed with the men of their city, saying,

21. These men *are* peaceable with us ; therefore let them dwell in the land, and trade therein ; for the land, behold, *it is* large enough for them ; let us take their daughters to us for wives, and let us give them our daughters.

22. Only herein will the men consent unto us for to dwell with us, to be one people, if every male among us be circumcised, as they *are* circumcised.

23. *Shall* not their cattle, and their substance, and every beast of theirs, *be* ours? only let us consent unto them, and they will dwell with us.

24. And unto Hamor, and unto Shechem his son, hearkened all that went out of the gate of his city ; and every male was circumcised, all that went out of the gate of his city.

25. And it came to pass on the third day, when they were sore, that two of the sons of Jacob, Simeon and Levi, Dinah's brethren, took each man his sword, and came upon the city boldly, and slew all the males.

26. And they slew Hamor and Shechem his son with the edge of the sword, and took Dinah out of Shechem's house, and went out.

27. The sons of Jacob came upon the slain, and spoiled the city, because they had defiled their sister.

28. They took their sheep, and their oxen, and their asses, and that which *was* in the city, and that which *was* in the field,

18. Et placuerunt verba eorum in oculis Hamor, et in oculis Sechem filii Hamor.

19. Nec tardavit juvenis ad perficiendum negotium, quia complacuerat ei in filia Iahacob : et ipse erat honorabilis præ tota domo patris sui.

20. Et venit Hamor et Sechem filius ejus ad portam civitatis suæ, et loquuti sunt ad viros civitatis suæ, dicendo,

21. Viri isti pacati sunt nobiscum, et habitabunt in terra, et negotiabuntur in ea (et terra ecce, lata est spatiis ante eos) filias eorum accipiemus nobis in uxores, et filias nostras dabimus eis.

22. Veruntamen in hoc acquiescent nobis viri, ut habitent nobiscum, ut sint populus unus, quando circumcisus erit in nobis omnis masculus, quemadmodum ipsi sunt circumcisi.

23. Greges eorum, et substantia eorum et omnia jumenta eorum, nonne nostra erunt? tantum acquiescamus eis, et habitabunt nobiscum.

24. Et assensi sunt Hamor et Sechem filio ejus, omnes qui egrediebantur per portam civitatis ejus : et circumciderunt se omnis masculus, omnes egredientes per portam civitatis ejus.

25. Et fuit in die tertia, quum essent ipsi dolore affecti, acceperunt duo filii Iahacob Simhon et Levi fratres Dinah, quisque gladium suum, et venerunt ad civitatem confidenter, et occiderunt omnem masculum.

26. Et Hamor et Sechem filium ejus occiderunt acie gladii, et tulerunt Dinah e domo Sechem et egressi sunt.

27. Filii Iahacob progressi sunt super occisos, et prædati sunt urbem, quia violaverant sororem suam.

28. Pecudes eorum, et boves eorum, et asinos eorum, et quæ erant in urbe, et quæ in agro, acceperunt.

29. And all their wealth, and all their little ones, and their wives took they captive, and spoiled even all that *was* in the house.

30. And Jacob said to Simeon and Levi, Ye have troubled me, to make me to stink among the inhabitants of the land, among the Canaanites and the Perizzites: and I *being* few in number, they shall gather themselves together against me, and slay me; and I shall be destroyed, I and my house.

31. And they said, Should he deal with our sister as with an harlot?

29. Et omnem substantiam eorum, et omnes parvulos eorum, et uxores eorum captivas duxerunt, et prædati sunt omnia, quæ erant in domo.

30. Et dixit Iahacob ad Simhon et ad Levi, Turbastis me, ut fœtere feceritis me habitatoribus terræ, Chenanæo, et Perizæo: et ego paucos mecum habeo, et congregabunt se adversum me, et percutient me, et disperdar ego, et domus mea.

31. At dixerunt, Numquid ut cum meretrice aget cum sorore nostra?

1. *And Dinah . . . . went out.* This chapter records a severe contest, with which God again exercised his servant. How precious the chastity of his daughter would be to him, we may readily conjecture from the probity of his whole life. When therefore he heard that she was violated, this disgrace would inflict the deepest wound of grief upon his mind: yet soon his grief is trebled, when he hears that his sons, from the desire of revenge, have committed a most dreadful crime. But let us examine everything in order. Dinah is ravished, because, having left her father's house, she wandered about more freely than was proper. She ought to have remained quietly at home, as both the Apostle teaches and nature itself dictates; for to girls the virtue is suitable, which the proverb applies to women, that they should be οἰκουροὶ, or keepers of the house. Therefore fathers of families are taught to keep their daughters under strict discipline, if they desire to preserve them free from all dishonour; for if a vain curiosity was so heavily punished in the daughter of holy Jacob, not less danger hangs over weak virgins at this day, if they go too boldly and eagerly into public assemblies, and excite the passions of youth towards themselves. For it is not to be doubted that Moses in part casts the blame of the offence upon Dinah herself, when he says, " she went out to see the daughters of the land ;" whereas she ought to have remained under her mother's eyes in the tent.

3. *And his soul clave unto Dinah.* Moses intimates that she was not so forcibly violated, that Shechem having once

abused her, treated her with contempt, as is usual with harlots; for he loved her as a wife; and did not even object to
be circumcised that he might have her; but the fervour of
lust had so prevailed, that he first subjected her to disgrace.
And therefore although he embraced Dinah with real and
sincere attachment, yet, in this want of self-government, he
grievously sinned. Shechem "spoke to the heart" of the
maid, that is, he addressed her courteously, to allure her to
himself by his bland speeches: whence it follows, that when
she was unwilling and resisted, he used violence towards her.

4. *And Shechem said to his father Hamor.* In this place
it is more clearly expressed, that Shechem desired to have
Dinah for his wife; for his lust was not so unbridled, that
when he had defiled, he despised her. Besides, a laudable
modesty is shown, since he pays deference to the will of his
father; for he does not attempt to form a contract of marriage of his own mind, but leaves this to his father's authority. For though he had basely fallen through the precipitate ardour of lust; yet now returning to himself, he follows
the guidance of nature. So much the more ought young
men to take heed to themselves, lest in the slippery period
of their age, the lusts of the flesh should impel them to many
crimes. For, at this day, greater license everywhere prevails, so that no moderation restrains youths from shameful
conduct. Since, however, Shechem, under the rule and
direction of nature, desired his father to be the procurer of
his marriage, we hence infer that the right which parents
have over their children is inviolable; so that they who attempt to overthrow it, confound heaven and earth. Wherefore, since the Pope, in honour of marriage, has dared to
break this sacred bond of nature; this fornicator Shechem
alone, will prove a judge sufficient, and more than sufficient,
to condemn that barbarous conduct.

5. *And Jacob heard.* Moses inserts a single verse concerning the silent sorrow of Jacob. We know that they who
have not been accustomed to reproaches, are the more grievously affected when any dishonour happens to them. Therefore the more this prudent man had endeavoured to keep his
family pure from every stain, chaste and well-ordered, the

more deeply is he wounded. But since he is at home alone, he dissembles, and keeps his grief to himself, till his sons return from the field. Moreover, by this word, Moses does not mean that Jacob deferred vengeance till their return ; but that, being alone and devoid of counsel and of consolation, he lay prostrate as one disheartened. The sense then is, that he was so oppressed with insupportable grief, that he held his peace.[1] By using the word " defiled," Moses teaches us what is the true purity of man ; namely, when chastity is religiously cultivated, and every one possesses his vessel in honour. But whoever prostitutes his body to fornication, filthily defiles himself. If then Dinah is said to have been polluted, whom Shechem had forcibly violated, what must be said of voluntary adulterers and fornicators ?

7. *And the sons of Jacob came out of the field.* Moses begins to relate the tragic issue of this history. Shechem, indeed, had acted wickedly and impiously; but it was far more atrocious and wicked that the sons of Jacob should murder a whole people, to avenge themselves of the private fault of one man. It was by no means fitting to seek a cruel compensation for the levity and rashness of one youth, by the slaughter of so many men. Again, who had constituted them judges, that they should dare, with their own hands, to execute vengeance for an injury inflicted upon them ? Perfidy was also superadded, because they proceeded, under the pretext of a covenant, to perpetrate this enormous crime. In Jacob, moreover, we have an admirable example of patient endurance ; who, though afflicted with so many evils, yet did not faint under them. But chiefly we must consider the mercy of God, by which it came to pass, that the covenant of grace remained with the posterity of Jacob. For what seemed less suitable, than that a few men in whom such furious rage and such implacable malice reigned, should be reckoned among the people and the sons of God, to the ex-

---

[1] Or, he might be restrained by prudence from imparting his feelings to others, lest by making them public, he should expose himself to danger, before he was prepared to meet it. At all events, it was wise to restrain the expression of his indignation, till he was surrounded by those who might help him with their counsel, or attempt the rescue of his daughter from the hands of her violator.—*Ed.*

clusion of all the world besides ? We see certainly that it
was not through any power of their own that they had not
altogether declined from the kingdom of God. Whence it appears that the favour which God had vouchsafed unto them
was gratuitous, and not founded upon their merits. We also
require to be treated by Him with the same indulgence, seeing that we should utterly fall away, if God did not pardon our
sins. The sons of Jacob have, indeed, a just cause of offence,
because not only are they affected with their own private
ignominy, but they are tormented with the indignity of the
crime, because their sister had been dragged forth from the
house of Jacob, as from a sanctuary, to be violated. For
this they chiefly urge, that it would have been wickedness
to allow such disgrace in the elect and holy people:[1] but
they themselves, through the hatred of one sin, rush furiously forward to greater and more intolerable crimes. Therefore we must beware, lest, after we have become severe judges
in condemning the faults of others, we hasten inconsiderately
into evil. But chiefly we must abstain from violent remedies which surpass the evil we desire to correct.

Which thing ought not to be done.[2] Interpreters commonly
explain the passage as meaning, " it is not becoming that
such .. thing should be done ;" but, in my judgment, it applies more properly to the sons of Jacob, who had determined
with themselves that the injury was not to be borne. Yet
they wrongfully appropriate to themselves the right of taking revenge : why do they not rather reflect thus ; " God,
who has received us under his care and protection, will not
suffer this injury to pass unavenged ; in the meantime, it is
our part to be silent, and to leave the act of punishing, which

---

[1] " He had wrought folly in Israel." Ainsworth says, " Or against Israel." " Israel being put for the posterity of Israel." Professor Bush
says, " Rather, ' Because folly had been wrought in Israel,' (the active
for the passive)." But perhaps Ainsworth's translation is to be preferred.
" This is the first instance on record where the family of Jacob is designated by the distinguished patronymic title of ' Israel,' which afterwards
became the dominant appellation of his posterity."—*Bush in loc.—Ed.*
[2] Et sic non fiet. " And so it may not, or shall not be done." The
sense given in the English translation is that which Calvin rejects, though
he allows it to be the common meaning attached by commentators to the
expression.—*Ed.*

is not placed in our hands, entirely to his sovereign will."
Hence we may learn, when we are angry at the sins of other
men, not to attempt anything which is beyond our own duty.

8. *And Hamor communed with them.* Though the sons
of Jacob were justly incensed, yet their indignation ought
to have been appeased, or at least somewhat mitigated, by
the great courteousness of Hamor.   And if the humanity of
Hamor could not reconcile the sons of Jacob to Shechem,
the old man himself was indeed worthy of a benignant reception.   We see what equitable conditions he offers; he
himself was the prince of the city, the sons of Jacob were
strangers.   Therefore their minds must have been savage
beyond measure, not to be inclined to lenity.   Besides, the
suppliant entreaty of Shechem himself deserved this, that
they should have granted forgiveness to his fervent love.
Therefore, that they remained implacable, is a sign of most
cruel pride.   What would they have done to enemies who
had purposely injured them, when they are not moved by
the prayers of him, who, being deceived by blind love, and
by the error of incontinency, has injured them without any
malicious intention?

13. *And the sons of Jacob answered.*   The commencement
of their perfidious course is here related: for they, being outrageous rather than simply angry, wish to overthrow the whole
city, and not being sufficiently strong to contend against so
great a number of people, they contrive a new fraud, in order
that they may suddenly rise upon the inhabitants weakened
by wounds.   Therefore, since the Shechemites had no strength
to resist, it became a cruel butchery rather than a conquest,
which increased the atrocity of wickedness in Jacob's sons,
who cared for nothing so that they might but gratify their
rage.   They allege in excuse, that, whereas they were separated from other nations, it was not lawful for them to give
wives of their own family to the uncircumcised.   Which indeed was true if they said it sincerely; but they falsely use
the sacred name of God as a pretext; yea, their double profanation of that name proves them to be doubly sacrilegious;
for they cared nothing about circumcision, but were intent
on this one thing, how they might crush the miserable men

in a state of weakness. Besides, they wickedly sever the
sign from the truth which it represents ; as if any one, by
laying aside his uncircumcision, might suddenly pass over
into the Church of God. And in this mode they pollute the
spiritual symbol of life, by admitting foreigners, promiscuously and without discrimination, into its society. But since
their pretence has some colour of probability, we must observe what they say, that it would be disgraceful to them to
give their sister to a man uncircumcised. This also is true,
if they who used the words were sincere ; for since they bore
the mark of God in their flesh, it was wicked in them to
contract marriages with unbelievers. So also, at the present
time, our baptism separates us from the profane, so that
whoever mixes himself with them, fixes a mark of infamy
upon himself.

18. *And their words pleased Hamor.* Moses prosecutes
the history until he comes to the slaughter of the Shechemites. Hamor had, no doubt, been induced by the entreaties
of his son, to show himself thus tractable. Whence appears
the excessive indulgence of the kind old man. He ought,
in the beginning, severely to have corrected the fault of his
son ; but he not only covers it as much as possible, but yields
to all his wishes. This moderation and equity would have
been commendable, if what his son had required was just ;
but that the old man, for the sake of his son, should adopt a
new religion, and suffer a wound to be inflicted on his own
flesh, cannot be deemed free from folly. The youth is said
not to have delayed, because he vehemently loved the maid,
and excelled in dignity among his own citizens ; and on
account of the honour of his rank he easily obtained what
he wished : for the fervour of his love would have availed
nothing, unless he had possessed the power of accomplishing
his object.

21. *These men are peaceable.* Moses describes the mode
of acting, whereby they persuaded the Shechemites to accept the conditions which the sons of Jacob had imposed.
It was difficult to induce a whole people to submit in an
affair of such magnitude to a few foreigners. For we know
what displeasure a change of religion produces : but Hamor

and Shechem reason from utility ; and this is natural rhetoric. For although honour has a more plausible appearance, it is yet for the most part cold in persuasion. But
among the vulgar, utility carries almost every point ; because
the major part eagerly pursues what it deems expedient for
itself. With this design, Hamor and Shechem extol the
family of Jacob for their honesty and tranquil habits, in order
that the Shechemites may deem it useful to themselves to
receive such guests. They add that the land is sufficiently
large, so that no loss is to be feared on the part of the original
inhabitants. They then enumerate other advantages ; meanwhile, they cunningly conceal the private and real cause of
their request. Whence it follows that all these pretexts
were fallacious. But it is a very common disease, that men
of rank who have great authority, while making all things
subservient to their own private ends, feign themselves to be
considerate for the common good, and pretend to a desire
for the public advantage. And, truly, it may be believed,
that the persons here spoken of were the best among all the
people, and were endowed with singular superiority ; for the
Shechemites had chosen Hamor for their prince, as one who
was pre-eminent in excellent gifts. Yet we see how he and
his son lie and deceive, under the appearance of rectitude.
Whence also we perceive hypocrisy to be so deeply rooted in
human minds, that it is a miracle to find any one entirely
free from it ; especially where private advantage is concerned.
From this example let all who govern, learn to cultivate sincerity in public designs, without any sinister regard to their
own interests. On the other hand ; let the people exercise
self-government, lest they too earnestly seek their own advantage ; because it will often happen that they are caught
by a specious appearance of good, as fishes by the hook. For
as self-love is blind, we are drawn without judgment to
the hope of gain. And the Lord also justly chastises this
cupidity, to which he sees us to be unduly prone, when he
suffers us to be deceived by it. Moses says that this discourse took place in the gate of the city, where public assemblies were then wont to be held and judgment administered.

24. *And unto Hamor and unto Shechem his son hearkened,*
&c. Apparently this consent may be ascribed to modesty
and humanity ; for, by readily obeying their princes, and
kindly admitting the strangers to an equality of rights in
the city, they show themselves, in both respects, modest and
humane. But if we reflect on the true import of circumcision,
it will easily appear that they were too much addicted to their
own selfish interests. They knew that, by a new sacrament,
they would be committed to a different worship of God. They
had not yet been taught that the ablutions and sacrifices, to
which they had been all their life accustomed, were unprofitable trifles. Therefore, to change their religion so carelessly betrays, on their part, a gross contempt of God; for never
do they who seriously worship God, so suddenly cast aside
their superstitions, unless they are convinced by sound doctrine and arguments. But the Shechemites, blinded by an
evil conscience, and by the hope of gain, pass over, like men
half brutalized, to an unknown God. " Search the isles,
(saith the Prophet,) is there any nation which deserts its
gods, who yet are not gods ?"[1] Yet this was done at Shechem,
when no defect had been shown to exist in the received superstitions ; wherefore none ought to wonder that a sad result
followed this levity of mind. Nevertheless, Simeon and Levi
were not, on that account, excusable for the indulgence of
their own cruelty: yea, their impiety appears the more detestable, because they not only rush impetuously upon men,
but, in a sense, trample upon the sacred covenant of God, of
which alone they make their boast. Certainly, if they had
no feeling for the men themselves, yet reverence for God ought
to have restrained their ferocity, when they reflected from
what cause the weakness of the Shechemites proceeded.

25. *Simeon and Levi, Dinah's brethren.* Because Moses
says that the slaughter took place on the third day, the Hebrews think that, at that time, the pain of the wound was
most severe. The proof, however, is not valid ; nor is it of
much moment. Although Moses names only two authors of
the slaughter, it does not appear to me probable that they
came alone, but that they were the leaders of the troop : for

[1] Jer. ii. 10, 11.

Jacob had a large family, and it might be that they called some of their brothers to join them; yet, because the affair was conducted by their counsel and direction, it is ascribed to them, as Carthage is said to have been destroyed by Scipio. Moses also calls them the brothers of Dinah, because they were by the same mother. We have seen that Dinah was the daughter of Leah; for which reason Simeon and Levi, whose own sister she was by both parents, were the more enraged at the violation of her chastity : they were therefore impelled, not so much by the common reproach brought upon the holy and elect race, (according to their recent boast,) as by a sense of the infamy brought upon themselves. However, there is no reader who does not readily perceive how dreadful and execrable was this crime. One man only had sinned, and he endeavoured to compensate for the injury, by many acts of kindness; but the cruelty of Simeon and Levi could only be satiated by the destruction of the whole city ; and, under the pretext of a covenant, they form a design against friends and hospitable persons, in a time of peace, which would have been deemed intolerable against enemies in open war. Hence we perceive how mercifully God dealt with that people; seeing that, from the posterity of a sanguinary man, and even of a wicked robber, he raised up a priesthood for himself. Let the Jews now go and be proud of their noble origin. But the Lord declared his gratuitous mercy by too many proofs for the ingratitude of man to be able to obscure it. Moreover, we hence learn that Moses did not speak from carnal sense; but was the instrument of the Holy Spirit, and the herald of the celestial Judge ; for though he was a Levite, he yet is so far from sparing his own race, that he does not hesitate to brand the father of his tribe with perpetual infamy. And it is not to be doubted that the Lord purposely intended to stop the mouths of impure and profane men, such as the Lucianists, who confess that Moses was a very great man, and of rare excellence ; but that he procured for himself, by craft and subtlety, authority over a great people, as if, indeed, an acute and intelligent man would not have known that, by this single act of wickedness, the honour of his race would be greatly tarnished. He had, however, no other design than to extol the goodness of God towards his people; and truly there was nothing which he less desired than to exercise dominion, as appears clearly from the fact, that he transferred the office of priesthood to another family, and commanded his sons to be only ministers. With respect to the Shechemites, although in the sight of God they were not innocent; seeing they preferred their own advantage to a religion which they thought lawful, yet it was not the Lord's will that they should be so grievously punished for their fault; but he suffered this signal punishment to follow the violation of one maid, that he might testify to all ages his great abhorrence of lust. Besides, seeing that the iniquity had arisen from a prince of the city, the punishment is rightly extended to the whole body of the people: for since God never commits the government to evil and vicious princes, except in righteous judgment, there is no wonder that, when they sin, they involve their subjects with them in the same condemnation. Moreover, from this example let us learn, that if, at any time, fornications prevail with impunity, God will, at length, exact punishments so much the more severe: for if the violation of one maid was avenged by the horrible massacre of a whole city; he will not sleep nor be quiet, if a whole people indulge in a common license of fornication, and, on all sides, connive at each other's iniquity. The sons of Jacob acted indeed wickedly; but we must observe 'that fornication was, in this manner, divinely condemned.

27. *The sons of Jacob came.* Moses shows that, not content with simple revenge, they fly together to the spoil. As it respects the words, they are said to have " come upon the slain," either because they made themselves a way over the slaughtered bodies; or because, in addition to the slaughter, they rushed to the plunder. In whichever way it is taken, Moses teaches that, not satisfied with their former wickedness, they made this addition to it. Be it, that they were blinded with anger in shedding blood; yet by what right do they sack the city? This certainly cannot be ascribed to anger. But these are the ordinary fruits of human in-

temperance, that he who gives himself the rein in perpetrating one wickedness, soon breaks out into another. Thus
the sons of Jacob, from being murderers, become also robbers,
and the guilt of avarice is added to that of cruelty. The
more anxious then should be our endeavours to bridle our
desires; lest they should mutually fan each other, so that at
length, by their combined action, a dreadful conflagration
should arise ; but especially, we must beware of using force
of arms, which brings with it many perverse and brutal assaults. Moses says that the sons of Jacob did this, because
the Shechemites had defiled their sister ; but the whole city
was not guilty. Moses, however, only states in what way
the authors of the slaughter are affected: for although they
wish to appear just avengers of the injury, yet they pay no
respect to what it was lawful for them to do, and make no
attempt to control their depraved affections, and consequently
set no bounds to their wickedness. Should any one prefer
taking the expression in a higher sense, it may be referred
to the judgment of God, by which the whole city was involved in guilt, because no one had opposed the lust of the
prince : perhaps many had consented to it, as not being very
much concerned about the unjust dishonour done to their
guests; but the former sense is what I most approve.

30. *And Jacob said.* Moses declares that the crime was
condemned by the holy man, lest any one should think that
he had participated in their counsel. He also expostulates
with his sons, because they had caused him to stink among
the inhabitants of the land; that is, they had rendered him
so odious, that no one would be able to bear him. If then
the neighbouring nations should conspire among themselves,
he would be unable to resist them, seeing he had so small a
band, in comparison with their great number. He also expressly names the Canaanites and Perizzites, who, though
they had received no wrong, were yet by nature exceedingly
prone to inflict injury. But Jacob may seem to act preposterously, in overlooking the offence committed against God,
and in considering only his own danger. Why is he not rather
angry at their cruelty ? why is he not offended at their perfidy? why does he not reprove their rapaciousness ? It is how-

ever probable, that when he saw them terror-stricken at their recent crime, he suited his words to their state of mind. For he acts as if he were complaining that he, rather than the She-chemites, was slain by them. We know that men are seldom if ever drawn to repentance, except by the fear of punishment: especially when they have any specious pretext as a covering for their fault. Besides, we know not whether Moses may not have selected this as a part out of a long expostulation, to cause his readers to understand that the fury of Simeon and Levi was so outrageous, that they were more insensible than brute beasts to their own destruction and that of their whole family. This is clear from their own answer, which not only breathes a barbarous ferocity, but shows that they had no feeling. It was barbarous, first, because they excuse themselves for having destroyed a whole people and plun-dered their city, on account of the injury done by one man; secondly, because they answer their father so shortly and contumaciously; thirdly, because they obstinately defend the revenge which they had rashly taken. Moreover, their insensibility was prodigious, because they were not affected by the thought of their own death, and that of their parents, wives, and children, which seemed just at hand. Thus we are taught, how intemperate anger deprives men of their senses. We are also admonished, that it is not enough for us to be able to lay blame on our opponents; but we must always see how far it is lawful for us to proceed.

CHAPTER XXXV.

1. AND God said unto Jacob, Arise, go up to Beth-el, and dwell there; and make there an altar unto God, that appeared unto thee when thou fleddest from the face of Esau thy brother.

2. Then Jacob said unto his house-hold, and to all that *were* with him, Put away the strange gods that *are* among you, and be clean, and change your garments:

3. And let us arise, and go up to Beth-el; and I will make there an

1. Dixit autem Deus ad Iahacob, Surge, ascende in Beth-el, et mane ibi: et fac ibi altare Deo, qui visus est tibi, dum fugeres a facie Esau fratris tui.

2. Et dixit Iahacob familiæ suæ, et omnibus qui erant secum, Remo-vete deos alienos, qui sunt in medio vestri, et mundate vos, vestimentaque vestra mundate.

3. Et surgamus, et ascendamus in Beth-el, et faciam illic altare Deo,

altar unto God, who answered me in the day of my distress, and was with me in the way which I went.

4. And they gave unto Jacob all the strange gods which *were* in their hand, and *all their* ear-rings which *were* in their ears; and Jacob hid them under the oak which *was* by Shechem.

5. And they journeyed: and the terror of God was upon the cities that *were* round about them, and they did not pursue after the sons of Jacob.

6. So Jacob came to Luz, which *is* in the land of Canaan, that *is*, Beth-el, he, and all the people that *were* with him.

7. And he built there an altar, and called the place El-beth-el; because there God appeared unto him, when he fled from the face of his brother.

8. But Deborah, Rebekah's nurse, died, and she was buried beneath Beth-el under an oak : and the name of it was called Allon-bachuth.

9. And God appeared unto Jacob again, when he came out of Padan-aram, and blessed him.

10. And God said unto him, Thy name *is* Jacob: thy name shall not be called any more Jacob, but Israel shall be thy name; and he called his name Israel.

11. And God said unto him, I *am* God Almighty; be fruitful and multiply: a nation, and a company of nations, shall be of thee, and kings shall come out of thy loins;

12. And the land which I gave Abraham and Isaac, to thee I will give it, and to thy seed after thee will I give the land.

13. And God went up from him in the place where he talked with him.

14. And Jacob set up a pillar in the place where he talked with him, *even* a pillar of stone; and he poured a drink-offering thereon, and he poured oil thereon.

15. And Jacob called the name of the place where God spake with him, Beth-el.

qui exaudivit me in die angustiæ meæ, et fuit mecum in via, qua ambulavi.

4. Dederunt ergo ipsi Iahacob omnes deos alienos, qui erant in manu sua, et inaures quæ erant in auribus suis, et abscondit eos Iahacob subter quercum, quæ erat apud Sechem.

5. Tunc profecti sunt, et fuit terror Dei super urbes, quæ erant in circuitibus eorum, et non persequuti sunt filios Iahacob.

6. Et venit Iahacob in Luz, quæ est in terra Chenaan, hæc est Beth-el, ipse et omnis populus qui erat cum eo.

7. Et ædificavit ibi altare, et vocavit locum El Beth-el: quia apparuerant ei Angeli, dum fugeret a facie fratris sui.

8. Mortua est autem Deborah nutrix Ribcah, et sepulta est subter Beth-el sub quercu: et vocavit nomen ejus Allon Bachuth.

9. Porro visus fuerat Deus ipsi Iahacob adhuc, dum veniret de Padan Aram, et benedixerat ei.

10. Atque dixerat ei ipse Deus, Nomen tuum est Iahacob: non vocabitur nomen tuum ultra Iahacob, sed Israel erit nomen tuum, et vocavit nomen ejus Israel.

11. Et dixit ei Deus, Ego sum Deus omnipotens, cresce, et multiplicare: gens, et cœtus Gentium erit ex te, et reges e lumbis tuis egredientur.

12. Et terram, quam dedi Abraham et Isaac, tibi dabo, et semini tuo post te dabo terram *istam*.

13. Et ascendit ab eo Deus e loco, in quo loquutus est cum eo.

14. Tunc statuit Iahacob statuam in loco, in quo loquutus est cum eo, statuam lapideam: et libavit super illam libamen, et effudit super illam oleum.

15. Et vocavit Iahacob nomen loci, in quo loquutus est cum ipso Deus, Beth-el.

16. And they journeyed from Beth-el; and there was but a little way to come to Ephrath: and Rachel travailed, and she had hard labour.

17. And it came to pass, when she was in hard labour, that the midwife said unto her, Fear not; thou shalt have this son also.

18. And it came to pass, as her soul was in departing, (for she died,) that she called his name Ben-oni: but his father called him Benjamin.

19. And Rachel died, and was buried in the way to Ephrath, which is Beth-lehem.

20. And Jacob set a pillar upon her grave: that is the pillar of Rachel's grave unto this day.

21. And Israel journeyed, and spread his tent beyond the tower of Edar.

22. And it came to pass, when Israel dwelt in that land, that Reuben went and lay with Bilhah his father's concubine: and Israel heard it. Now the sons of Jacob were twelve.

23. The sons of Leah; Reuben, Jacob's first-born, and Simeon, and Levi, and Judah, and Issachar, and Zebulun.

24. The sons of Rachel; Joseph and Benjamin.

25. And the sons of Bilhah, Rachel's handmaid; Dan and Naphtali.

26. And the sons of Zilpah, Leah's handmaid; Gad and Asher. These are the sons of Jacob, which were born to him in Padan-aram.

27. And Jacob came unto Isaac his father unto Mamre, unto the city of Arbah, which is Hebron, where Abraham and Isaac sojourned.

28. And the days of Isaac were an hundred and fourscore years.

29. And Isaac gave up the ghost, and died, and was gathered unto his people, being old and full of days: and his sons Esau and Jacob buried him.

16. Profecti vero sunt de Beth-el: erat autem adhuc ferme milliare terræ ad veniendum in Ephrath, et peperit Rachel, et difficultatem passa est, dum pareret.

17. Fuit autem, ea difficultatem patiente dum pareret, dixit ei obstetrix, Ne timeas, quia etiam iste tibi filius.

18. Et fuit, egrediente anima ejus dum moreretur, vocavit nomen ejus Benoni: at pater ejus vocavit eum Benjamin.

19. Mortua est itaque Rachel, et sepulta est in via Ephrath, hæc est Bethlehem.

20. Et statuit Iahacob titulum super sepulcrum ejus: hic est titulus sepulcri Rachel usque ad diem hanc.

21. Et profectus est Israel, et tetendit tabernaculum suum trans turrim Eder.

22. Et fuit quum habitaret Israel in terra ipsa, profectus est Reuben, et concubuit cum Bilhah concubina patris sui: et audivit Israel. Fuerunt autem filii Iahacob duodecim.

23. Filii Leah, primogenitus Iahacob, Reuben, et Simhon, et Levi, et Iehudah, et Issachar, et Zebulun.

24. Filii Rachel, Ioseph et Benjamin.

25. Et filii Bilhah ancillæ Rachel, Dan et Nephthali.

26. Et filii Zilpah ancillæ Leah, Gad et Aser. Isti sunt filii Iahacob, qui nati sunt in Padan Aram.

27. Et venit Iahacob ad Ishac patrem suum in Mamre civitatem Arbah: hæc est Hebron, in qua habitavit Abraham et Ishac.

28. Et fuerunt dies Ishac, centum anni et octoginta anni.

29. Et obiit Ishac, et mortuus est, et collectus est ad populos suos, senex et satur dierum: et sepelierunt eum Esau et Iahacob filii ejus.

1. *And God said unto Jacob.* Moses relates that when Jacob had been reduced to the last extremity, God came to

his help in the right time, and as at the critical juncture.
And thus he shows, in the person of one man, that God
never deserts his Church which he has once embraced,
but will procure its salvation.   We must, however, observe
the order of his procedure; for God did not immediately
appear to his servant, but suffered him first to be tormented
by grief and excessive cares, that he might learn patience,
deferring his consolation to the time of extreme necessity.
Certainly the condition of Jacob was then most miserable.
For all, on every side, might be so incensed against him
that he would be surrounded with as many deaths as
there were neighbouring nations : and he was not so stupid
as to be insensible of his danger.   God suffered the holy
man to be thus tossed with cares and tormented with
troubles, until, by a kind of resurrection, he restored him,
as one half-dead.   Whenever we read this and similar
passages, let us reflect that the providence of God watches
for our salvation, even when it most seems to sleep.   Moses
does not say how long Jacob was kept in anxiety, but we
may infer from the context, that he had been very greatly
perplexed, when the Lord thus revived him.   Moreover, we
must observe that the principal medicine by which he was
restored, was contained in the expression, " The Lord spake."
Why did not God by a miracle translate him to some other
place, and thus immediately remove him from all danger?
Why did he not even, without a word, stretch out the hand
over him, and repress the ferocity of all, so that no one should
attempt to hurt him ?   But Moses does not insist upon this
point in vain.   For hereby we are taught whence our greatest consolation in our afflictions is to be sought ; and also,
that it is the principal business of our life, to depend upon
the word of God, as those who are certainly persuaded that,
when he has promised salvation, he will deal well with us,
so that we need not hesitate to walk through the midst of
deaths.   Another reason· for the vision was, that Jacob
might not only truly perceive that God was his deliverer ;
but, being forewarned by his word, might learn to ascribe to
God whatever afterwards followed.   For seeing that we are
slow and dull, bare experience by no means suffices to attest

the favour of God towards us, unless faith arising from the
word be added.

Go up to Beth-el. Though it is God's design to raise his
servant from death to life, he may yet have appeared to hold
him up to derision; for the objection was ready, " Thou indeed, O Lord, commandest me to go up, but all the ways are
closed; for my sons have raised such a flame against me,
that I cannot remain safe in any hiding-place. I dare
scarcely move a finger : what therefore will become of me, if
with a great multitude, I now begin to move my camp ? shall
I not provoke new enmities against me by my movements ?"
But by this mode the faith of Jacob was most fully proved ;
because, knowing God to be the leader and guardian of his
journey, he girded himself to it, relying on the divine
favour. Moreover, the Lord does not simply command what
it is his will to have done, but he encourages his servant, by
adding the promise. For, in reminding him that he is the
same God who had before appeared unto him as he was
fleeing in alarm from his brother, a promise is included in
these words. The altar also refers to the same point ; for
since it is the divinely appointed token of thanksgiving, it
follows that Jacob would come thither in safety, in order that
he might duly celebrate the grace of God. God chooses and
assigns Beth-el, rather than any other place, for his sanctuary ; because the very sight of it would greatly avail to take
away terror, when he should remember that there the glory
of the Lord had been seen by him. Further, since God exhorts his servant to gratitude, he shows that he is kind to
the faithful, in order that they, in return, may own themselves to be indebted for everything to his grace, and may
exercise themselves in the celebration of it.

2. *Then Jacob said unto his household.* The prompt obedience of Jacob is here described. For when he heard the
voice of God, he neither doubted nor disputed with himself
respecting what was necessary to be done: but, as he was
commanded, he quickly prepared himself for his journey.
But to show that he obeyed God, he not only collected his
goods, but also purified his house from idols. For if we desire that God should be propitious to us, all hinderances are

to be removed, which in any way separate him from us. Hence also we perceive to what point the theft of Rachel tended. For, (as we have said,) she neither wished to draw her father away from superstition, but rather followed him in his fault ; nor did she keep this poison to herself, but spread it through the whole family. Thus was that sacred house infected with the worst contagion. Whence also it appears, how great is the propensity of mankind to impious and vicious worship; since the domestics of Jacob, to whom the pure religion had been handed down, thus eagerly laid hold on the idols offered to them. And Jacob was not entirely ignorant of the evil : but it is probable that he was so far under the influence of his wife, that, by connivance, he silently cherished this plague of his family. And truly, in one word, he convicts and condemns both himself and the rest, by calling idols " strange gods." For whence arose the distinction here made, unless from his knowing that he ought to be devoted to one God only ? For there is a tacit comparison between the God of Abraham and all other gods which the world had wickedly invented for itself : not because it was in the power of Abraham to determine who should be the true God : but because God had manifested himself to Abraham, he also wished to assume His name. Jacob therefore confesses his own negligence, in having admitted to his house idols, against which the door had been closed by God. For wherever the knowledge of the true God shines, it is necessary to drive far away whatever men fabricate to themselves which is contrary to the true knowledge of him. But whereas Jacob had been lulled to sleep either by the blandishments of his wife, or had neglected to do his duty, through the carelessness of the flesh, he is now aroused by the fear of danger, to become more earnest in the pure worship of God. If this happened to the holy patriarch, how much more ought carnal security to be dreaded by us, in the season of prosperity ? If, however, at any time such torpor and neglect shall have stolen upon us, may the paternal chastisement of God excite and stimulate us diligently to purge ourselves from whatever faults we, by our negligence, may have contracted. The infinite goodness of God is here conspicuous;

seeing that he still deigned to regard the house of Jacob, though polluted with idols, as his sanctuary. For although Jacob mingled with idolaters, and even his wife,—a patroness of idolatry,—slept in his bosom, his sacrifices were always acceptable to God. Yet this great benignity of God in granting pardon, neither lessens the fault of the holy man, nor ought to be used by us as an occasion for negligence. For though Jacob did not approve of these superstitions, yet it was not owing to him that the pure worship of God was not gradually subverted. For the corruption which originated with Rachel was now beginning to spread more widely. And the example of all ages teaches the same thing. For scarcely ever does the truth of God so prevail among men, however strenuously pious teachers may labour in maintaining it, but that some superstitions will remain among the common people. If dissimulation be added to them, the mischief soon creeps onward, until it takes possession of the whole body. By being thus cherished, the mass of superstitions which at this day pervades the Papacy, has gained its influence. Wherefore we must boldly resist those beginnings of evil, lest the true religion should be injured by the sloth and silence of the pastors.

And be clean, and change your garments. This is an exhortation to the external profession of penitence. For Jacob wishes that his domestics, who before had polluted themselves, should testify their renewed purification by a change of garments. With the same design and end, the people, after they had made the golden calves, were commanded by Moses to put off their ornaments. Only in that instance a different method was observed; namely, that the people having laid aside their ornaments, simply confessed their guilt by mournful and mean apparel: but in the house of Jacob the garments were changed, in order that they who had been defiled might come forth as new men: yet the end (as I have said) was the same, that by this external rite, idolaters might learn how great was the atrocity of their wickedness. For although repentance is an inward virtue, and has its seat in the heart, yet this ceremony was by no means superfluous; for we know how little disposed men are to be displeased with themselves on account of their sins, unless they are pierced with many goads. Again, the glory of God is also concerned in this, that men should not only inwardly reflect upon their guilt, but at the same time openly declare it. This then is the sum; although God had given no express command concerning the purifying of his house, yet because he had commanded an altar to be raised, Jacob, in order that he might yield pure obedience to God, took care that all impediments should be removed; and he did this when necessity compelled him to seek help from God.

4. *And they gave unto Jacob.* Though the holy man had his house in suitable subordination; yet as all yielded such prompt obedience to his command by casting away their idols, I doubt not that they were influenced by the fear of danger. Whence also we infer how important it is for us to be aroused from slumber by suffering. For we know how pertinacious and rebellious is superstition. If, in a peaceful and joyous state of affairs, Jacob had given any such command, the greater part of his family would have fraudulently concealed their idols: some, perhaps, would have obstinately refused to surrender them; but now the hand of God urges them, and with ready minds they quickly repent. It is also probable, that, according to the circumstances of the time, Jacob preached to them concerning the righteous judgment of God, to inspire them with fear. When he commands them to " cleanse themselves," it is as if he had said, " Hitherto ye have been defiled before the Lord ; now, seeing that he has regarded us so mercifully, wash out this filth, lest he should again avert his face from us." It seems, however, absurd, that Jacob should have buried the idols under an oak, and not rather have broken them in pieces and consumed them in the fire, as we read that Moses did with the golden calves, (Exod. xxxii. 20,) and Hezekiah with the brazen serpent, (2 Kings xviii. 4.) The fact is not thus related without reason : but the infirmity of Jacob is touched upon, because he had not been sufficiently provident against the future. And perhaps the Lord punished his previous excessive connivance and want of firmness, by depriving him of prudence or courage. Yet God accepted his obedience,

although it had some remainder of defect, knowing that it was the design of the holy man to remove idols from his family, and, in token of his detestation, to bury them in the earth. The ear-rings were doubtless badges of superstition; as at this day innumerable trifles are seen in the Papacy, by which impiety displays itself.

5. *And the terror of God was upon the cities.* It now manifestly appears that deliverance was not in vain promised to the holy man by God; since, amidst so many hostile swords, he goes forth not only in safety but undisturbed. By the destruction of the Shechemites all the neighbouring people were inflamed with enmity against a single family; yet no one moves to take vengeance. The reason is explained by Moses, that the terror of God had fallen upon them, which repressed their violent assaults. Hence we may learn that the hearts of men are in the hands of God; that he can inspire those with fortitude who in themselves are weak; and, on the other hand, soften their iron-hardness whenever he pleases. Sometimes, indeed, he suffers many to cast up the foam of their pride, against whom he afterwards opposes his power: but he often weakens those with fear who were naturally bold as lions: thus we find these giants, who were able to devour Jacob a hundred times, so struck with terror that they faint away. Wherefore, whenever we see the wicked furiously bent on our destruction, lest our hearts should fail with fear and be broken by desperation, let us call to mind this terror of God, by which the rage, however furious, of the whole world may be easily subdued.

7. *And he built there an altar.* It has been already stated why it behoved the holy fathers, wherever they came, to have an altar of their own, distinct from those of other nations; namely, to make it manifest that they did not worship gods of various kinds, a practice to which the world was then everywhere addicted, but that they had a God peculiar to themselves. For although God is worshipped with the mind, yet an external confession is the inseparable companion of faith. Besides, all acknowledge how very useful it is to us to be stirred up by outward helps to the worship of God. If any one object that these altars differed nothing from other altars in

appearance ; I answer, that whereas others rashly, and with inconsiderate zeal, built altars to unknown gods, Jacob always adhered to the word of God. And there is no lawful altar but that which is consecrated by the word ; nor indeed did the worship of Jacob excel by any other mark than this, that he attempted nothing beyond the command of God. In calling the name of the place " The God of Beth-el,"[1] he is thought to be too familiar ; and yet this very title commends the faith of the holy man, and that rightly, since he confines himself within the divinely prescribed bounds. The Papists act foolishly in affecting the praise of humility by a modesty which is most degrading. But the humility of faith is praiseworthy, seeing it does not desire to know more than God permits. And as when God descends to us, he, in a certain sense, abases himself, and stammers with us, so he allows us to stammer with him. And this is to be truly wise, when we embrace God in the manner in which he accommodates himself to our capacity. For in this way, Jacob does not keenly dispute concerning the essence of God, but renders God familiar to himself by the oracle which he has received. And because he applies his senses to the revelation, this stammering and simplicity (as I have said) is acceptable to God. Now, though at this day, the knowledge of God has shined more clearly, yet since God, in the gospel, takes upon him the character of a nursing father, let us learn to subject our minds to him ; only let us remember that he descends to us in order to raise us up to himself. For he does not speak to us in this earthly manner, to keep us at a distance from heaven, but rather by this vehicle, to draw us up thither. Meanwhile this rule must be observed, that since the name of the altar was given by a celestial oracle, the building of it was a proof of faith. For where the living voice of God does not sound, whatever pomps may be introduced will be like shadowy spectres ; as in the Papacy nothing can be seen except bladders filled with wind. It may be added that Jacob shows the constant tenor

---

[1] As the word *Beth-el* means the House of God, the farther addition of *El*, the name of God, seems to be a tautology ; and this is made by Calvin the basis of an objection which he proceeds to answer.—*Ed.*

of his faith, from the time that God began to manifest himself to him; because he keeps in view the fact, that the angels had appeared unto him.[1] For since the word is in the plural number, I willingly interpret it of angels ; and this is not contrary to the former doctrine; for although the majesty of God was then conspicuous, so far as he could comprehend it, yet Moses does not without reason mention the angels whom Jacob saw ascending and descending on the steps of the ladder. For he then beheld the glory of God in the angels, as we see the splendour of the sun flowing to us through his rays.

8. *But Deborah, Rebekah's nurse, died.* Here is inserted a short narration of the death of Deborah, whom we may conclude to have been a holy matron, and whom the family of Jacob venerated as a mother ; for the name given in perpetuity to the place, testifies that she was buried with peculiar honour, and with no common mourning. Shortly afterwards the death and burial of Rachel are to be recorded : yet Moses does not say that any sign of mourning for Deborah was transmitted to posterity ;[2] therefore it is probable that she was held by all in the place of a grandmother. But it may be asked, how she then happened to be in Jacob's company, seeing that he had not yet come to his father ; and the age of a decrepid old woman rendered her unfit for so long a journey.[3] Some interpreters imagine that she had

---

[1] Quia apparuerunt ei Angeli dum fugeret a facie fratris sui. In the English translation the name of God is put instead of angels, and no doubt rightly. The reason given for Calvin's translation of the word אלהים, (*Elohim,*) by *angels* is, that, contrary to the usual custom, when the word means God, it is accompanied by a verb in the plural number. But this is not conclusive. See note 2, vol. i., p. 531, on chap. xx. ver. 13.

Yet there is some difficulty in the passage, arising from the apparent harshness of the repetition of *El*, the name of God, in this title. Bush thinks that the first El does not belong to the name of the place. Rivetus reads the first *El* as the genitive, supposing the word *place* to be understood. " And he called the place, ' the place of the God of Beth-el.' This Dathé thinks harsh, and he follows Michaelis in connecting למקום with the first אל. And he called the place of God, Beth-el."—*Ed.*

[2] 'The meaning, perhaps, is, that no monumental pillar was raised to Deborah, as was done to Rachel; the probable reason given for the fact, namely, that she was regarded as a grandmother, does not seem very intelligible.—*Ed.*

[3] It appears, from a calculation of the ages of Rebekah, of Jacob, and

been sent by Rebekah to meet her son Jacob; but I do not
see what probability there is in the conjecture; nor yet have
I anything certain to affirm, except that, perhaps, she had
loved Jacob from a boy, because she had nursed him; and
when she knew the cause of his exile, she followed him from
her regard for religion. Certainly Moses does not in vain
celebrate her death with an eulogy so remarkable.

9. *And God appeared unto Jacob.* Moses, having introduced
a few words on the death of Deborah, recites a second vision,
by which Jacob was confirmed, after his return to Beth-el.
Once, in this place, God had appeared unto him, when he was
on his way into Mesopotamia. In the meantime God had
testified in various methods, as need required, that he would
be present with him everywhere through his whole journey;
but now he is brought back again to that very place where
a more illustrious and memorable oracle had been given
him, in order that he may receive again a new confirmation
of his faith. The blessing of God here means nothing else
than his promise; for though men pray for blessings on
each other; God declares himself to be the sole Dispenser
of perfect happiness. Now Jacob heard at this time nothing new; but the same promise is repeated to him, that
he, as one who had returned from captivity to his own
country, and had gathered new strength to his faith, might
accomplish with greater courage the remaining course of
his life.

10. *Thy name shall not be called any more Jacob.* We
have before given the meaning of these words. The former
name is not abolished, but the dignity of the other, which
was afterwards put upon him, is preferred: for he was called
Jacob from the womb, because he had strongly wrestled with

of Rachel, that Deborah must, at this time, have lived far beyond the common term of human life. "Jacob was then about one hundred and seven
years of age. Isaac had been sixty years old when Jacob was born; he
married Rebekah when he was at the age of forty, and she could not be
less than twenty at the time of her marriage; it will follow that she bore
twins in, or after, the fortieth year of her age. If these forty years be added to the one hundred and seven of Jacob's life, this will make one
hundred and forty-seven. Supposing Deborah to have been twenty-five
when she was given as a nurse to Rebekah, she could not now be less than
one hundred and seventy years old."—See *Rivetus*, p. 701.—*Ed.*

his brother ; but he was afterwards called Israel, because he entered into contest with God, and obtained the victory ; not that he had prevailed by his own power, (for he had borrowed courage and strength and arms from God alone,) but because it was the Lord's will freely to confer upon him this honour.   He therefore speaks comparatively, showing that the name Jacob is obscure and ignoble when compared with the name Israel.   Some understand it thus, " Not only shalt thou be called Jacob, but the surname of Israel shall be added ;" yet the former exposition seems to me the more simple ; namely, that the old name, having in it less of splendour, should give place to the second.   What Augustine adduces is specious rather than solid ; namely, that he was called Jacob in reference to his present life, but Israel in reference to his future life.   Let this, however, be regarded as settled, that a double name was given to the holy man, of which one was by far the most excellent ; for we see that the prophets often combine them both, thus marking the constancy of God's grace from the beginning to the end.

11. *I am God Almighty.*   God here, as elsewhere, proclaims his own might, in order that Jacob may the more certainly rely on his faithfulness.   He then promises that he will cause Jacob to increase and multiply, not only into one nation, but into a multitude of nations.   When he speaks of " a nation," he no doubt means that the offspring of Jacob should become sufficiently numerous to acquire the body and the name of one great people.   But what follows concerning " nations" may appear absurd ; for if we wish it to refer to the nations which, by gratuitous adoption, are inserted into the race of Abraham, the form of expression is improper : but if it be understood of sons by natural descent, then it would be a curse rather than a blessing, that the Church, the safety of which depends on its unity, should be divided into many distinct nations.   But to me it appears that the Lord, in these words, comprehended both these benefits ; for when, under Joshua, the people was apportioned into tribes, as if the seed of Abraham was propagated into so many distinct nations ; yet the body was not thereby divided ; it is called an assembly of nations, for this reason, because in

connection with that distinction a sacred unity yet flourished.
The language also is not improperly extended to the Gentiles,
who, having been before dispersed, are collected into one
congregation by the bond of faith ; and although they were
not born of Jacob according to the flesh ; yet, because faith
was to them the commencement of a new birth, and the
covenant of salvation, which is the seed of spiritual birth,
flowed from Jacob, all believers are rightly reckoned among
his sons, according to the declaration, " I have constituted
thee a father of many nations."

And kings shall come out of thy loins.   This, in my judgment, ought properly to be referred to David and his posterity ; for God did not approve of the kingdom of Saul, and
therefore it was not established ; and the kingdom of Israel
was but a corruption of the legitimate kingdom.   I acknowledge truly that, sometimes, those things which have sprung
from evil sources are numbered among God's benefits ; but
because here the simple and pure benediction of God is
spoken of, I willingly understand it of David's successors
only.   Finally ; Jacob is constituted the lord of the land, as
the sole heir of his grandfather Abraham, and of his father
Isaac ; for the Lord manifestly excludes Esau from the holy
family, when he transfers the dominion of the land, by hereditary right, to the posterity of Jacob alone.

13. *And God went up from him.*   This ascent of God is
analogous to his descent ; for God, who fills heaven and earth,
is yet said to descend to us, though he changes not his place,
whenever he gives us any token of his presence ; a mode
of expression adopted in accommodation to our littleness.
He went up, therefore, from Jacob, when he disappeared
from his sight, or when the vision ended.   By the use of
such language, God shows us the value of his word, because,
indeed, he is near to us in the testimony of his grace ; for,
seeing that there is a great distance between us and his
heavenly glory, he descends to us by his word.   This, at
length, was fully accomplished in the person of Christ ; who
while, by his own ascension to heaven, he raised our faith
thither ; nevertheless dwells always with us by the power of
his Spirit.

14. *And Jacob set up a pillar.* Though it is possible that he may again have erected a sacred monument, in memory of the second vision ; yet I readily subscribe to the opinion of those who think that reference is made to what had been done before ; as if Moses should say, that was the ancient temple of God, in which Jacob had poured forth his libation : for he had not been commanded to come thither for the sake of dwelling there ; but in order that a fresh view of the place might renew his faith in the ancient oracle, and more fully confirm it. We read elsewhere that altars were built by the holy fathers, where they intended to remain longer ; but their reason for doing so was different : for whereas Jacob had made a solemn vow in Beth-el, on condition that he should be brought back by the Lord in safety ; thanksgiving is now required of him, after he has become bound by his vow,[1] that, being strengthened, he may pass onward on his journey.

16. *And they journeyed from Beth-el.* We have seen how severe a wound the defilement of his daughter inflicted on holy Jacob, and with what terror the cruel deed of his two sons had inspired him. Various trials are now blended together, by which he is heavily afflicted throughout his old age ; until, on his departure into Egypt, he receives new joy at the sight of his son Joseph. But even this was a most grievous temptation, to be exiled from the promised land even to his death. The death of his beloved wife is next related ; and soon after follows the incestuous intercourse of his firstborn with his wife Bilhah. A little later, Isaac his father dies ; then his son Joseph is snatched away, whom he supposes to have been torn in pieces by wild beasts. While he is almost consumed with perpetual mourning, a famine arises, so that he is compelled to seek food from Egypt. There another of his sons is kept in chains ; and, at length, he is deprived of his own most beloved Benjamin, whom he sends

---

[1] Nunc gratiarum actio ab eo exigitur, postquam reus voti factus est, ut confirmatus alio transeat. The French translation of " postquam reus voti factus est " is, " apres qu'il a eu jouissance de son souhait," " after he had obtained the enjoyment of his wish;" and this would read more smoothly than the translation given above ; but is " reus voti " capable of such a version ?— *Vide Lexicon Facciolati, sub voce reus.—Ed.*

away as if his own bowels were torn from him. We see, therefore, by what a severe conflict, and by what a continued succession of evils, he was trained to the hope of a better life. And whereas Rachel died in childbirth, through the fatigue of the journey, before they reached a resting-place ; this would prove no small accession to his grief. But, as to his being bereaved of his most beloved wife, this was probably the cause, that the Lord intended to correct the exorbitance of his affection for her. The Holy Spirit fixes no mark of infamy upon Leah, seeing that she was a holy woman, and endowed with greater virtue ; but Jacob more highly appreciated Rachel's beauty. This fault in the holy man was cured by a bitter medicine, when his wife was taken away from him: and the Lord often deprives the faithful of his own gifts, to correct their perverse abuse of them. The wicked, indeed, more audaciously profane the gifts of God ; but if God connives longer at their misconduct, a more severe condemnation remains to them on account of his forbearance. But in taking away from his own people the occasion of sinning, he promotes their salvation. Whoever, therefore, desires the continued use of God's gifts, let him learn not to abuse them, but to enjoy them with purity and sobriety.

17. *The midwife said unto her.* We know that the ancients were very desirous of offspring, especially of male offspring. Since Rachel therefore does not accept this kind of consolation when offered, we infer that she was completely oppressed with pain. She therefore died in agonies, thinking of nothing but her sad childbirth and her own sorrows : from the feeling of which she gave a name to her son ; but Jacob afterwards corrected the error. For the change of the name sufficiently shows, that, in his judgment, the excess of sorrow in his wife was wrong ; seeing that she had branded his son with a sinister and opprobrious name ;[1] for that sadness is not free from ingratitude, which so occupies our

---

[1] Rachel, in the act of dying, called her son Benoni, the son of my sorrow ; Jacob called him Benjamin, the son of my right hand. It is worthy of remark that Benjamin was the only son of Jacob born in the land of Canaan.— *Ed.*

minds in adversity that the kindness of God does not exhi-
larate them ; or, at least, does not infuse some portion of
sweetness to mitigate our grief. Then her burial is mentioned ; to which the holy fathers could not have attended
with such religious care, except on account of their hope
of the future resurrection. Whenever, therefore, we read concerning their burying the dead, as if they were anxious about
the performance of some extraordinary duty, let us think
of that end of which I have spoken ; for it was no foolish
ceremony, but a lively symbol of the future resurrection.
I acknowledge, indeed, that profane and degenerate men at
that time, in various places, vainly incurred much expense
and toil in burying their dead, only as an empty solace of
their grief. But although they had declined from the original institution into gross errors, yet the Lord caused that
this rite should remain entire among his own people. Moreover, he designed that a testimony should exist among unbelievers, by which they might be rendered inexcusable.
For since, independently of instruction, this sentiment was
innate in all men, that to bury the dead was one of the
offices of piety, nature has clearly dictated to them that the
human body is formed for immortality ; and, therefore, that,
by sinking into death, it does not utterly perish. The statue or monument, erected by him, signifies the same thing.
He reared no citadel which might stand as a token of his
glory among his posterity : but he took care to raise the
memorial of a sepulchre, which might be a witness to all
ages that he was more devoted to the life to come ; and, by
the providence of God, this memorial remained standing,
till the people returned out of Egypt.

22. *Reuben went and lay with Bilhah.* A sad and even
tragic history is now related concerning the incestuous intercourse of Reuben with his mother-in-law. Moses, indeed,
calls Bilhah Jacob's concubine : but though she had not
come into the hands of her husband, as the mistress of the
family and a partaker of his goods ; yet, as it respected the
bed, she was his lawful wife, as we have before seen. If even
a stranger had defiled the wife of the holy man, it would
have been a great disgrace ; it was, however, far more atrocious

that he should suffer such an indignity from his own son.
But how great and how detestable was the dishonour, that
the mother of two tribes should not only contaminate herself
with adultery, but even with incest ; which crime is so abhorrent to nature, that, not even among the Gentiles, has it
ever been held tolerable ? And truly, by the wonderful artifice of Satan, this great obscenity penetrated into the holy
house, in order that the election of God might seem to be of
no effect. Satan endeavours, by whatever means he can, to
pervert the grace of God in the elect ; and since he cannot
effect that, he either covers it with infamy, or at least obscures
it. Hence it happens that disgraceful examples often steal
into the Church. And the Lord, in this manner, suffers his
own people to be humbled, that they may be more attentively
careful of themselves, that they may more earnestly watch
unto prayer, and may learn entirely to depend on his mercy.
Moses only relates that Jacob was informed of this crime ;
but he conceals his grief, not because he was unfeeling, (for
he was not so stupid as to be insensible to sorrow,) but
because his grief was too great to be expressed. For here
Moses seems to have acted as the painter did who, in representing the sacrifice of Iphigenia, put a veil over her father's
face, because he could not sufficiently express the grief of
his countenance. In addition to this eternal disgrace of the
family, there were other causes of anxiety which transfixed
the breast of the holy man. The sum of his happiness was
in his offspring, from which the salvation of the whole world
was to proceed. Whereas, already, two of his sons had been
perfidious and sanguinary robbers; the first-born, now, exceeds
them both in wickedness. But here the gratuitous election of
God has appeared the more illustrious, because it was not on
account of their worthiness that he preferred the sons of Jacob
to all the world ; and also because, when they had fallen so
basely, this election nevertheless remained firm and efficacious.
Warned by such examples, let us learn to fortify ourselves
against those dreadful scandals by which Satan strives to
disturb us. Let every one also privately apply this to the
strengthening of his own faith. For sometimes even good
men slide, as if they had fallen from grace. Desperation

would necessarily be the consequence of such ruin, unless the Lord, on the other hand, held out the hope of pardon. A remarkable instance of this is set before us in Reuben ; who, after this extreme act of iniquity, yet retained his rank of a patriarch in the Church. We must, however, remain under the custody of fear and watchfulness, lest temptation should seize upon us unawares, and thus the snares of Satan should envelop us. For the Holy Spirit did not design to set before us an example of vile lust, in order that every one might rush into incestuous connexions ; but would rather expose to infamy the baseness of this crime, in an honourable person, that all, on that account, might more vehemently abhor it. This passage also refutes the error of Novatus. Reuben had been properly instructed ; he bore in his flesh, from early infancy, the symbol of the divine covenant ; he was even born again by the Spirit of God ; we see, therefore, what was the deep abyss from which he was raised by the incredible mercy of God. The Novatians, therefore, and similar fanatics, have no right to cut off the hope of pardon from the lapsed : for it is no slight injury to Christ, if we suppose the grace of God to be more restricted by his advent.

Now the sons of Jacob were twelve. Moses again recounts the sons of Jacob in a regular series. Reuben is put the first among them, not for the sake of honour, but that he may be loaded with the greater opprobrium : for the greater the honour which any one receives from the Lord, the more severely is he to be blamed, if he afterwards makes himself the slave of Satan, and deserts his post. Moses seems to insert this catalogue before the account of the death of Isaac, for the purpose of discriminating between the progeny of Jacob and the Idumeans, of whom he is about to make mention in the following chapter. For on the death of Isaac the fountain of the holy race became divided, as into two streams ; but since the adoption of God restrained itself to one branch only, it was necessary to distinguish it from the other.

28. *And the days of Isaac.* The death of Isaac is not related in its proper order, as will soon appear from the connection of the history : but, as we have elsewhere seen, the

figure *hysteron proteron* was familiar to Moses.[1] When it is said, *that he died old, and full of days,* the meaning is, that, having fulfilled the course of his life, he departed by a mature death ; this, therefore, is ascribed to the blessing of God. Nevertheless, I refer these words not merely to the duration of his life, but also to the state of his feelings ; implying that Isaac, being satisfied with life, willingly and placidly departed out of the world. For we may see certain decrepid old men, who are not less desirous of life than they were in the flower of their age ; and with one foot in the grave, they still have a horror of death. Therefore, though long life is reckoned among the blessings of God ; yet it is not enough for men to be able to count up a great number of years ; unless they feel that they have lived long, and, being satisfied with the favour of God and with their own age, prepare themselves for their departure. Now, in order that old men may have their minds formed to this kind of moderation, it behoves them to have a good conscience, to the end, that they may not flee from the presence of God ; for an evil conscience pursues and agitates the wicked with terror. Moses adds, that Isaac was buried by his two sons. For since, at that time, the resurrection was not clearly revealed, and its first fruits had not yet appeared, it behoved the holy fathers to be so much the more diligently trained in significant ceremonies, in order that they might correct the impression produced by the semblance of destruction which is presented in death. By the fact that Esau is put first, we are taught again, that the fruit of the paternal benediction was not received by Jacob in this life ; for he who was the first-born by right, is still subjected to the other, after his father's death.

---

[1] The death of Isaac is mentioned here, out of place, to prevent the subsequent interruption of the history. The events of the thirty-seventh and thirty-eighth chapters preceded it ; for Isaac lived about fifteen years after the removal of Joseph into Egypt.— *Ed.*

CHAPTER XXXVI.

1. Now these *are* the generations of Esau, who *is* Edom.

2. Esau took his wives of the daughters of Canaan; Adah the daughter of Elon the Hittite, and Aholibamah the daughter of Anah, the daughter of Zibeon the Hivite:

3. And Bashemath, Ishmael's daughter, sister of Nebajoth.

4. And Adah bare to Esau Eliphaz; and Bashemath bare Reuel;

5. And Aholibamah bare Jeush, and Jaalam, and Korah. These *are* the sons of Esau, which were born unto him in the land of Canaan.

6. And Esau took his wives, and his sons, and his daughters, and all the persons of his house, and his cattle, and all his beasts, and all his substance, which he had got in the land of Canaan, and went into the country from the face of his brother Jacob.

7. For their riches were more than that they might dwell together; and the land wherein they were strangers could not bear them because of their cattle.

8. Thus dwelt Esau in Mount Seir. Esau *is* Edom.

9. And these *are* the generations of Esau, the father of the Edomites, in Mount Seir.

10. These *are* the names of Esau's sons; Eliphaz the son of Adah the wife of Esau; Reuel the son of Bashemath the wife of Esau.

11. And the sons of Eliphaz were Teman, Omar, Zepho, and Gatam, and Kenaz.

12. And Timna was concubine to Eliphaz, Esau's son: and she bare to Eliphaz Amalek: these *were* the sons of Adah, Esau's wife.

13. And these *are* the sons of Reuel; Nahath, and Zerah, Shammah, and Mizzah: these were the sons of Bashemath, Esau's wife.

14. And these were the sons of

1. Istæ vero sunt generationes Esau, hic est Edom.

2. Esau accepit uxores suas e filiabus Chenaan, Hadah filiam Elon Hittæi, et Aholibamah filiam Anah, filiam Sibhon Hivvæi,

3. Et Bosmath filiam Ismael sororem Nebajoth.

4. Et peperit Adah ipsi Esau Eliphaz: et Bosmath peperit Rehuel.

5. Et Aholibamah peperit Jehus, et Jahalam, et Corah: isti filii Esau, qui nati sunt ei in terra Chenaan.

6. Et accepit Esau uxores suas, et filios suos, et filias suas, et omnes animas domus suæ, et pecudes suas, et omnia jumenta sua, et omnem acquisitionem suam, quam acquisierat in terra Chenaan: et profectus est ad *aliam* terram a facie Iahacob fratris sui.

7. Erat enim substantia eorum multa, ita ut nequirent habitare pariter: nec poterat terra peregrinationum eorum ferre eos propter substantiam eorum.

8. Habitavit itaque Esau in monte Sehir: Esau est Edom.

9. Ac istæ sunt generationes Esau patris Edom in monte Sehir.

10. Ista sunt nomina filiorum Esau: Eliphaz filius Hadah uxoris Esau, Rehuel filius Bosmath uxoris Esau.

11. Et fuerunt filii Eliphaz, Theman, Omar, Sepho, et Gahatham, et Cenaz.

12. Timnah autem fuit concubina Eliphaz filii Esau, et peperit ipsi Eliphaz Hamalec. Isti sunt filii Hadah uxoris Esau.

13. Isti vero sunt filii Rehuel: Nahath, et Zerach, Sammah, et Mizza: isti sunt filii Bosmath uxoris Esau.

14. Et isti fuerunt filii Aholiba-

Aholibamah, the daughter of Anah, the daughter of Zibeon, Esau's wife; and she bare to Esau Jeush, and Jaalam, and Korah.

15. These *were* dukes of the sons of Esau: the sons of Eliphaz, the first-born *son* of Esau ; duke Teman, duke Omar, duke Zepho, duke Kenaz,

16. Duke Korah, duke Gatam, *and* duke Amalek. These *are* the dukes *that came* of Eliphaz in the land of Edom : these *were* the sons of Adah.

17. And these *are* the sons of Reuel, Esau's son; duke Nahath, duke Zerah, duke Shammah, duke Mizzah. These *are* the dukes *that came* of Reuel in the land of Edom ; these *are* the sons of Bashemath, Esau's wife.

18. And these *are* the sons of Aholibamah, Esau's wife ; duke Jeush, duke Jaalam, duke Korah : these *were* the dukes *that came* of Aholibamah, the daughter of Anah, Esau's wife.

19. These *are* the sons of Esau, who *is* Edom, and these *are* their dukes.

20. These *are* the sons of Seir the Horite, who inhabited the land; Lotan, and Shobal, and Zibeon, and Anah,

21. And Dishon, and Ezer, and Dishan. These *are* the dukes of the Horites, the children of Seir in the land of Edom.

22. And the children of Lotan were Hori, and Heman : and Lotan's sister *was* Timna.

23. And the children of Shobal *were* these; Alvan, and Manahath, and Ebal, Shepho, and Onam.

24. And these *are* the children of Zibeon; both Ajah and Anah: this *was that* Anah that found the mules in the wilderness, as he fed the asses of Zibeon his father.

25. And the children of Anah *were* these; Dishon, and Aholibamah the daughter of Anah.

26. And these *are* the children of Dishon; Hemdan, and Eshban, and Ithran, and Cheran.

mah filiæ Hanah filiæ Sibhon uxoris Esau, quos peperit ipsi Esau: Jehu, et Jahalam, et Corah.

15. Isti duces filiorum Esau. Filii Eliphaz primogeniti Esau, dux Theman, dux Omar, dux Sepho, dux Chenaz,

16. Dux Corah, dux Gahatham, dux Hamalec : isti sunt duces Eliphaz in terra Edom: isti sunt filii Hadah.

17. Et isti sunt filii Rehuel filii Esau: dux Nahath, dux Zerach, dux Sammah, dux Mizzah : isti sunt duces Rehuel in terra Edom: isti sunt filii Bosmath uxoris Esau.

18. Isti autem sunt filii Aholibamah uxoris Esau, dux Jehus, dux Jahalam, dux Corah: isti sunt duces Aholibamah filiæ Hanah uxoris Esau.

19. Isti sunt filii Esau, et isti duces eorum: ipse est Edom.

20. Isti sunt filii Sehir Horæi, habitatores terræ: Lotan, et Sobal, et Sibhon, et Hanah,

21. Et Dison, et Eser, et Disan. Isti duces Horæorum filiorum Sehir in terra Edom.

22. Et fuerunt filii, Lotan, Hori, et Heman : et soror Lotan, Thimnah.

23. Isti sunt filii Sobal: Halvan, et Manahath, et Hebal, Sepho, et Onam.

24. Et isti sunt filii Sibhon: Ajah et Hanah: hic est Hanah, qui invenit mulos in deserto, quum pasceret asinos Sibhon patris sui.

25. Et isti sunt filii Hanah: Disan, et Aholibamah filia Hanah.

26. Et isti sunt filii Dison: Hemdan, et Esban, et Ithran, et Cheran.

27. The children of Ezer *are* these; Bilhan, and Zaavan, and Akan.

28. The children of Dishan *are* these; Uz, and Aran.

29. These *are* the dukes *that came* of the Horites; duke Lotan, duke Shobal, duke Zibeon, duke Anah,

30. Duke Dishon, duke Ezer, duke Dishan. These *are* the dukes *that came* of Hori, among their dukes in the land of Seir.

31. And these *are* the kings that reigned in the land of Edom, before there reigned any king over the children of Israel.

32. And Bela the son of Beor reigned in Edom: and the name of his city *was* Dinhabah.

33. And Bela died; and Jobab the son of Zerah of Bozrah reigned in his stead.

34. And Jobab died; and Husham of the land of Temani reigned in his stead.

35. And Husham died; and Hadad the son of Bedad, who smote Midian in the field of Moab, reigned in his stead: and the name of his city *was* Avith.

36. And Hadad died; and Samlah of Masrekah reigned in his stead.

37. And Samlah died; and Saul of Rehoboth *by* the river reigned in his stead.

38. And Saul died; and Baal-hanan the son of Achbor reigned in his stead.

39. And Baal-hanan the son of Achbor died; and Hadar reigned in his stead: and the name of his city *was* Pau; and his wife's name *was* Mehetabel, the daughter of Matred, the daughter of Mezahab.

40. And these *are* the names of the dukes *that came* of Esau, according to their families, after their places, by their names; duke Timnah, duke Alvah, duke Jetheth,

41. Duke Aholibamah, duke Elah, duke Pinon,

42. Duke Kenaz, duke Teman, duke Mibzar,

43. Duke Magdiel, duke Iram. These *be* the dukes of Edom, according to their habitations in the land

27. Isti sunt filii Eser: Bilhan, et Zaavan, et Acan.

28. Isti sunt filii Disan: Us et Aran.

29. Isti sunt duces Horæorum: dux Lotan, dux Sobal, dux Sibhon, dux Hanah.

30. Dux Dison, dux Eser, dux Disan: isti sunt duces Horæorum, in ducibus eorum, in terra Sehir.

31. Et isti sunt reges, qui regnaverunt in terra Edom, antequam regnaret rex super filios Israel.

32. Nempe regnavit in Edom, Belah filius Behor: et nomen urbis ejus Dinhabah.

33. Et mortuus est Belah, et regnavit pro eo Jobab, filius Zerah de Bosrah.

34. Et mortuus est Jobab, et regnavit pro eo Hussam e terra Australi.

35. Et mortuus est Hussam, et regnavit pro eo Hadad filius Bedad, qui percussit Midian in agro Moab: et nomen urbis ejus Avith.

36. Et mortuus est Hadad, et regnavit pro eo Samlah de Masrecah.

37. Et mortuus est Samlah, et regnavit pro eo Saul de Rehoboth fluminis.

38. Et mortuus est Saul et regnavit pro eo Bahal-hanan filius Hachbor.

39. Et mortuus est Bahal-hanan filius Hachbor, et regnavit pro eo Hadar: et nomen civitatis ejus Pahu: nomen autem uxoris ejus Mehetabel filia Matred filiæ Me-zahab.

40. Ista ergo sunt nomina ducum Esau, per familias suas, per loca sua, secundum nomina sua: dux Thimnah, dux Haluah, dux Jetheth,

41. Dux Aholibamah, dux Elah, dux Pinon,

42. Dux Cenaz, dux Theman, dux Mibsar,

43. Dux Magdiel, dux Hiram: isti sunt duces Edom per habitationes suas, in terra hæreditatis

of their possession : he *is* Esau, the   ipsorum : ipse est Esau pater E-
father of the Edomites.   dom.

1. *Now these are the generations of Esau.* Though Esau
was an alien from the Church in the sight of God ; yet since
he also, as a son of Isaac, was favoured with a temporal
blessing, Moses celebrates his race, and inscribes a sufficiently lengthened catalogue of the people born from him.
This commemoration, however, resembles an honourable
sepulture. For although Esau, with his posterity, took the
precedence ; yet this dignity was like a bubble, which is
comprised under the figure of the world, and which quickly
perishes. As, therefore, it has been before said of other
profane nations, so now Esau is exalted as on a lofty theatre.
But since there is no permanent condition out of the kingdom of God, the splendour attributed to him is evanescent,
and the whole of his pomp departs like the passing scene of
the stage. The Holy Spirit designed, indeed, to testify that
the prophecy which Isaac uttered concerning Esau was not
vain ; but he has no sooner shown its effect, than he turns
away our eyes, as if he had cast a veil over it, that we
may confine our attention to the race of Jacob. Now,
though Esau had children by three wives, in whom afterwards the blessing of God shone forth, yet polygamy is not,
on that account, approved, nor the impure lust of man excused : but in this the goodness of God is rather to be
admired, which, contrary to the order of nature, gave a good
issue to evil beginnings.

6. *And went into the country from the face of his brother
Jacob.* Moses does not mean that Esau departed purposely
to give place to his brother ; for he was so proud and ferocious, that he never would have allowed himself to seem his
brother's inferior. But Moses, without regard to Esau's design, commends the secret providence of God, by which he
was driven into exile, that the possession of the land might
remain free for Jacob alone. Esau removed to Mount Seir,
through the desire of present advantage, as is elsewhere
stated. Nothing was less in his mind than to provide for
his brother's welfare ; but God directed the blind man by
his own hand, that he might not occupy that place in the

land which he had appointed for his own servant.   Thus it
often happens that the wicked do good to the elect children
of God, contrary to their own intention ; and while their
hasty cupidity pants for present advantages, they promote
the eternal salvation of those whose destruction they have
sometimes desired.   Let us, then, learn from the passage
before us, to see, by the eyes of faith, both in accidental
circumstances (as they are called) and in the evil designs of
men, that secret providence of God, which directs all events
to a result predetermined by himself.   For when Esau went
forth, that he might live more commodiously apart from his
father's family, he is said to have departed from the face of
his brother, because the Lord had so determined it.   It is
stated indefinitely, that he departed " into the country ;"
because, being in uncertainty respecting his plan, he sought
a home in various places, until Mount Seir presented itself ;
and as we say, he went out at a venture.[1]

9. *And these are the generations of Esau, the father of the
Edomites.*[2]   Though Esau had two names, yet in this place
the second name refers to his posterity, who are called
Idumeans.   For, to make it appear what God had bestowed
upon him for the sake of his father Isaac, Moses expressly
calls him the father of a celebrated and famous people.
And certainly, it served this purpose not a little, to trace the
effect and fulfilment of the prophecy in the progeny of Esau.
For if the promise of God so mightily flourished towards a
stranger, how much more powerfully would it put itself forth
towards the children, to whom pertaineth the adoption, and
consequently the inheritance of grace ?   Esau was an obscure man, and a sojourner in that country : whence therefore is it, that suddenly rulers should spring from him, and
a great body of people should flourish, unless because the
benediction which proceeded from the mouth of Isaac, was
confirmed by the result ?   For Esau did not reign in this
desert without opposition ; since a people of no ignoble
name previously inhabited Mount Seir.   On this account
Moses relates that the men who had before inhabited that

---

[1] Quemadmodum Gallice dicitur, *Il s'en est allé à son aventure.*
[2] Patris Edom.

land were mighty: so that it would not have been easy for a stranger to acquire such power as Esau possessed, if he had not been divinely assisted.

24. *This was that Anah that found the mules.* Mules are the adulterous offspring of the horse and the ass. Moses says that Anah was the author of this connection.[1] But I do not consider this as said in praise of his industry ; for the Lord has not in vain distinguished the different kinds of animals from the beginning. But since the vanity of the flesh often solicits the children of this world, so that they apply their minds to superfluous matters, Moses marks this unnatural pursuit in Anah, who did not think it sufficient to have a great number of animals; but he must add to them a degenerate race produced by unnatural intercourse. Moreover, we learn hence, that there is more moderation among brute animals in following the law of nature, than in men, who invent vicious admixtures.

31. *These are the kings that reigned, &c.* We must keep in memory what we have said a little before, that reprobates are suddenly exalted, that they may immediately fall, like the herb upon the roofs, which is destitute of root, and has a hasty growth, but withers the more quickly. To the two sons of Isaac had been promised the honour that kings should spring from them. The Idumeans first began to reign, and thus the condition of Israel seemed to be inferior. But at length, lapse of time taught how much better it is, by creeping on the ground, to strike the roots deep, than to acquire an extravagant pre-eminence for a moment, which speedily vanishes away. There is, therefore, no reason why the faithful, who slowly pursue their way, should envy the quick children of this world, their rapid succession of delights; since the felicity which the Lord promises them is far more stable, as it is expressed in the psalm, " The children's children shall dwell there, and their inheritance shall be perpetual." (Psalm cii. 28.)

---

[1] The word ימים, rendered mules by our translators, and by Calvin, is of doubtful signification; it occurs in this place only. It is by many commentators translated " waters," or " warm springs;" and probably this interpretation is to be preferred. The reader may see the question discussed in Professor Bush's note on this verse.—*Ed.*

CHAPTER XXXVII.

1. AND Jacob dwelt in the land wherein his father was a stranger, in the land of Canaan.

2. These *are* the generations of Jacob. Joseph, *being* seventeen years old, was feeding the flock with his brethren; and the lad *was* with the sons of Bilhah, and with the sons of Zilpah, his father's wives: and Joseph brought unto his father their evil report.

3. Now Israel loved Joseph more than all his children, because he *was* the son of his old age: and he made him a coat of *many* colours.

4. And when his brethren saw that their father loved him more than all his brethren, they hated him, and could not speak peaceably unto him.

5. And Joseph dreamed a dream, and he told *it* his brethren: and they hated him yet the more.

6. And he said unto them, Hear, I pray you, this dream which I have dreamed:

7. For, behold, we *were* binding sheaves in the field, and, lo, my sheaf arose, and also stood upright; and, behold, your sheaves stood round about, and made obeisance to my sheaf.

8. And his brethren said to him, Shalt thou indeed reign over us? or shalt thou indeed have dominion over us? And they hated him yet the more for his dreams, and for his words.

9. And he dreamed yet another dream, and told it his brethren, and said, Behold, I have dreamed a dream more; and, behold, the sun, and the moon, and the eleven stars, made obeisance to me.

10. And he told *it* to his father, and to his brethren: and his father rebuked him, and said unto him, What *is* this dream that thou hast dreamed? Shall I, and thy mother,

---

1. Habitavit itaque Iahacob in terra peregrinationum patris sui, in terra Chenaan.

2. Istæ sunt generationes Iahacob. Joseph filius septendecim annorum pascebat cum fratribus suis pecudes, et erat puer cum filiis Bilhah et cum filiis Zilpah uxorum patris sui: et retulit Ioseph obloquutionem eorum malam patri eorum.

3. Porro Israel diligebat Joseph præ cunctis filiis suis, quia filius senectutis erat ei: et fecerat ei tunicam multicolorem.

4. Et viderunt fratres ejus, quod eum diligeret patèr eorum præ cunctis fratribus ejus, et odio habebant eum, et non poterant alloqui eum pacifice.

5. Somniavit autem Joseph somnium, et nuntiavit fratribus suis: et addiderunt amplius odio habere eum.

6. Dixit enim ad eos, Audite quæso somnium hoc quod somniavi.

7. Ecce enim ligabamus manipulos in medio agri: et ecce surrexit manipulus meus, ac etiam stabat: et ecce circumdabant manipuli vestri, et incurvabant se manipulo meo.

8. Et dixerunt ei fratres ejus, Num regnando regnabis super nos? num dominando dominaberis nobis? Addiderunt ergo adhuc odio habere eum propter somnium ejus, et propter verba ejus.

9. Et somniavit adhuc somnium alterum, et narravit illud fratribus suis, et dixit, Ecce, somniavi somnium adhuc: et ecce, sol et luna et undecim stellæ incurvabant se mihi.

10. Et narravit patri suo et fratribus suis: et increpavit eum pater ejus, et dixit ei, Quid est hoc somnium quod somniasti? num veniendo veniemus ego et mater tua, et fra-

and thy brethren, indeed come to bow down ourselves to thee to the earth?

11. And his brethren envied him; but his father observed the saying.

12. And his brethren went to feed their father's flock in Shechem.

13. And Israel said unto Joseph, Do not thy brethren feed *the flock* in Shechem? come, and I will send thee unto them. And he said to him, Here *am I*.

14. And he said to him, Go, I pray thee, see whether it be well with thy brethren, and well with the flocks; and bring me word again. So he sent him out of the vale of Hebron, and he came to Shechem.

15. And a certain man found him, and, behold, *he was* wandering in the field: and the man asked him, saying, What seekest thou?

16. And he said, I seek my brethren: tell me, I pray thee, where they feed *their flocks*.

17. And the man said, They are departed hence; for I heard them say, Let us go to Dothan. And Joseph went after his brethren, and found them in Dothan.

18. And when they saw him afar off, even before he came near unto them, they conspired against him to slay him.

19. And they said one to another, Behold, this dreamer cometh.

20. Come now therefore, and let us slay him, and cast him into some pit; and we will say, Some evil beast hath devoured him: and we shall see what will become of his dreams.

21. And Reuben heard *it*, and he delivered him out of their hands; and said, Let us not kill him.

22. And Reuben said unto them, Shed no blood, *but* cast him into this pit that *is* in the wilderness, and lay no hand upon him; that he might rid him out of their hands, to deliver him to his father again.

23. And it came to pass, when Joseph was come unto his brethren,

tres tui, ut incurvemus nos tibi ad terram?

11. Et inviderunt ei fratres ejus: sed pater ejus observabat rem.

12. Profecti autem sunt fratres ejus, ut pascerent pecudes patris sui in Sechem.

13. Et dixit Israel ad Joseph, Nonne fratres tui pascunt in Sechem? veni, et mittam te ad eos. Et dixit ei, Ecce adsum.

14. Et ait ei, Vade nunc, vide incolumitatem fratrum tuorum, et incolumitatem pecorum, et refer mihi rem: et misit eum ex valle Hebron: et venit in Sechem.

15. Porro invenit eum vir, et ecce errabat in agro: interrogavit autem eum vir ille, dicendo, Quid quæris?

16. Et dixit, Fratres meos ego quæro, nuntia, obsecro, mihi, ubi ipsi pascant.

17. Et dixit vir ille, Profecti sunt hinc: audivi enim eos dicentes, Eamus in Dothan. Et perrexit Joseph post fratres suos, et invenit eos in Dothan.

18. Et viderunt eum e longinquo: et antequam appropinquaret eis, machinati sunt contra eum ut interimerent eum.

19. Ac dicebat alter alteri, Ecce, magister ille somniorum venit.

20. Nunc igitur venite, et occidamus illum, et projiciamus eum in unam e cisternis: et dicemus, Bestia mala devoravit eum: et videbimus quid erunt somnia ejus.

21. Et audivit Reuben, et eripuit eum e manu eorum, et dixit, Ne percutiamus eum *in* anima.

22. Dixit ergo ad eos Reuben, Ne effundatis sanguinem: projicite eum in cisternam hanc, quæ est in deserto, et manum ne mittatis in eum: ut erueret eum e manu eorum, ut reduceret eum ad patrem suum.

23. Et fuit, ut venit Joseph ad fratres suos, exuerunt Joseph tunica

that they stripped Joseph out of his coat, *his* coat of *many* colours, that *was* on him;

24. And they took him, and cast him into a pit: and the pit *was* empty, *there was* no water in it.

25. And they sat down to eat bread: and they lifted up their eyes, and looked, and, behold, a company of Ishmeelites came from Gilead, with their camels bearing spicery, and balm, and myrrh, going to carry *it* down to Egypt.

26. And Judah said unto his brethren, What profit *is it* if we slay our brother, and conceal his blood?

27. Come, and let us sell him to the Ishmeelites, and let not our hand be upon him; for he *is* our brother, *and* our flesh: and his brethren were content.

28. Then there passed by Midianites, merchant-men; and they drew and lifted up Joseph out of the pit, and sold Joseph to the Ishmeelites for twenty *pieces* of silver: and they brought Joseph into Egypt.

29. And Reuben returned unto the pit; and, behold, Joseph *was* not in the pit: and he rent his clothes.

30. And he returned unto his brethren, and said, The child *is* not; and I, whither shall I go?

31. And they took Joseph's coat, and killed a kid of the goats, and dipped the coat in the blood:

32. And they sent the coat of *many* colours, and they brought *it* to their father; and said, This have we found: know now whether it *be* thy son's coat or no.

33. And he knew it, and said, *It is* my son's coat; an evil beast hath devoured him: Joseph is without doubt rent in pieces.

34. And Jacob rent his clothes, and put sackcloth upon his loins, and mourned for his son many days.

35. And all his sons, and all his daughters, rose up to comfort him; but he refused to be comforted: and

sua, tunica multicolore, quæ erat super eum.

24. Et tulerunt eum, et projecerunt eum in cisternam: et cisterna erat vacua, non erat in ea aqua.

25. Postea sederunt ut comederent panem, et levaverunt oculos suos, et viderunt, et ecce turba Ismaelitarum veniebat de Gilhad, et cameli eorum portabant aromata, et resinam, et stacten, iter facientes ut deferrent in Ægyptum.

26. Et dixit Jehudah fratribus suis, Quæ utilitas si occiderimus fratrem nostrum, et celaverimus sanguinem ejus?

27. Venite, et vendamus eum Ismaelitis, et manus nostra ne sit in eum, quia frater noster, caro nostra est: et paruerunt ei fratres ejus.

28. Et transierunt viri Madianitæ mercatores, et extraxerunt et sustulerunt Joseph e cisterna: et vendiderunt Joseph Ismaelitis viginti argenteis, qui abduxerunt Ioseph in Ægyptum.

29. Deinde reversus est Reuben ad cisternam, et ecce non erat Joseph in cisterna, et scidit vestimenta sua.

30. Et reversus est ad fratres suos, et dixit, Puer non est, et ego quo, ego *quo* ibo?

31. Et tulerunt tunicam Joseph, et jugulaverunt hircum caprarum, et tinxerunt tunicam in sanguine.

32. Et miserunt tunicam multicolorem, et deferri fecerunt ad patrem suum, et dixerunt, Hanc invenimus, agnosce nunc utrum tunica filii tui sit, annon.

33. Et agnovit eam, et dixit, Tunica filii mei est: bestia mala devoravit eum, rapiendo raptus est Ioseph.

34. Et scidit Iahacob vestimenta sua, et posuit saccum in lumbis suis, et luxit super filio suo diebus multis.

35. Et surrexerunt omnes filii ejus, et omnes filiæ ejus, ut consolarentur eum, sed noluit consolationem

he said, For I will go down into the grave unto my son mourning. Thus his father wept for him.

36. And the Midianites sold him into Egypt unto Potiphar, an officer of Pharaoh's, *and* captain of the guard.

admittere: et dixit, Certe descendam ad filium meum lugens ad sepulcrum: et luxit eum pater ejus.

36. Madianitæ autem vendiderunt eum in Ægypto Potiphar satrapæ Pharaonis, principi satellitum.

1. *And Jacob dwelt.* Moses confirms what he had before declared, that, by the departure of Esau, the land was left to holy Jacob as its sole possessor. Although in appearance he did not obtain a single clod ; yet, contented with the bare sight of the land, he exercised his faith ; and Moses expressly compares him with his father, who had been a stranger in that land all his life. Therefore, though by the removal of his brother to another abode, Jacob was no little gainer; yet it was the Lord's will that this advantage should be hidden from his eyes, in order that he might depend entirely upon the promise.

2. *These are the generations of Jacob.* By the word תולדות (*toledoth*) we are not so much to understand a genealogy, as a record of events, which appears more clearly from the context. For Moses having thus commenced, does not enumerate sons and grandsons, but explains the cause of the envy of Joseph's brethren, who formed a wicked conspiracy against him, and sold him as a slave : as if he had said, " Having briefly summed up the genealogy of Esau, I now revert to the series of my history, as to what happened to the family of Jacob."[1] Moreover, Moses being about to speak

[1] The second verse is rendered by Professor Bush in a manner different from that of any other commentator whom the Editor has had the opportunity of consulting. His view of the passage is, at least, worthy of consideration. " The correct translation," he says, " is doubtless the following : ' Joseph, being seventeen years old, was tending his brethren among the flocks, and he a (mere) lad, (even) the sons of Bilhah, &c.' The mention of his youth is brought in parenthetically, as something peculiarly worthy of notice ; while the clause, ' the sons of Bilhah, &c.,' is designed to limit and specify the term ' brethren ' going before." This interpretation he proceeds to vindicate by reference to passages of similar construction, which we have not room to quote. The point which it would establish is, that Jacob assigned to his boy, of seventeen years of age, the superintendence or oversight of the sons of Bilhah among the flocks; so that he was rather an overlooker of the *shepherds* than of the *sheep*. This would show more clearly the propriety of Joseph's conduct, in carrying an ill report of his brethren to their father ; and would also account for the hostility they

of the abominable wickedness of Jacob's sons, begins with
the statement, that Joseph was dear beyond the rest to his
father, because he had begotten him in his old age : and as
a token of tender love, had clothed him with a coat woven
of many colours.   But it was not surprising that the boy
should be a great favourite with his aged father, for so it is
wont to happen : and no just ground is here given for envy ;
seeing that sons of a more robust age, by the dictate of nature,
might well concede such a point.   Moses, however, states this
as the cause of odium, that the mind of his father was more
inclined to him than to the rest.   The brethren conceive enmity against the boy, whom they see to be more tenderly loved
by their father, as having been born in his old age.[1]   If they
did not choose to join in this love to their brother, why did
they not excuse it in their father ?   Hence, then, we perceive
their malignant and perverse disposition.   But, that a many-
coloured coat and similar trifles inflamed them to devise a
scheme of slaughter, is a proof of their detestable cruelty.
Moses also says that their hatred increased, because Joseph
conveyed the evil speeches of his brethren to their father.
Some expound the word *evil* as meaning some intolerable
crime ; but others more correctly suppose, that it was a complaint of the boy that his brothers vexed him with their
reproaches ; for, what follows in Moses, I take to have been
added in explanation, that we may know the cause for which
he had been treated so ill and with such hostility.   It may
be asked, why Moses here accuses only the sons of Bilhah
and Zilpah, when, afterwards, he does not exempt the sons
of Leah from the same charge ?   One, indeed, of her sons,
Reuben, was milder than any of the rest ; next to him was
Judah, who was his uterine brother.   But what is to be said
of Simeon ? what of Levi ?   Certainly since they were older,
it is probable that they were leaders in the affair.   The suspicion may, however, be entertained, that because these were

felt towards him.   But it may be doubted whether this interpretation can
stand.—*Ed.*
   [1] "Son of his old age."   The Chaldee renders it, "a wise son ;" as if he
were a man in intellect, while a boy in years.   This would avoid a difficulty : for Benjamin was far more properly the son of Jacob's old age than
Joseph.—*Ed.*

the sons of concubines and not of true wives, their minds would be more quickly moved with envy ; as if their servile extraction, on the mother's side, subjected them to contempt.

6. *And Joseph dreamed a dream.* Moses having stated what were the first seeds of this enmity, now ascends higher, and shows that Joseph had been elected, by the wonderful purpose of God, to great things ; that this had been declared to him in a dream ; and that, therefore, the hatred of his brethren broke forth into madness. God, however, revealed in dreams what he would do, that afterwards it might be known that nothing had happened fortuitously : but that what had been fixed by a celestial decree, was at length, in its proper time, carried forward through circuitous windings to its completion. It had been predicted to Abraham that his seed should be wanderers from the land of Canaan. In order, then, that Jacob might pass over into Egypt, this method was divinely appointed; namely, that Joseph, being president over Egypt in a time of famine, might bring his father thither with his whole family, and supply them with food. Now, from the facts first related, no one could have conjectured such a result. The sons of Jacob conspire to put the very person to death, without whom they cannot be preserved ; yea, he who was ordained to be the minister of salvation to them, is thrown into a well, and with difficulty rescued from the jaws of death. Driven about by various misfortunes, he seems to be an alien from his father's house. Afterwards, he is cast into prison, as into another sepulchre, where, for a long time, he languishes. Nothing, therefore, was less probable than that the family of Jacob should be preserved by his means, when he was cut off from it, and carried far away, and not even reckoned among the living. Nor did any hope of his liberation remain, especially from the time in which he was neglected by the chief butler ; but being condemned to perpetual imprisonment, he was left there to rot. God, however, by such complicated methods, accomplishes what he had purposed. Wherefore, in this history, we have not only a most beautiful example of Divine Providence, but also two other points are added especially worthy of notice : first, that the Lord

performs his work by wonderful and unusual modes; and, secondly, that he brings forth the salvation of his Church, not from magnificent splendour, but from death and the grave. Besides, in the person of Joseph, a lively image of Christ is presented, as will more fully appear from the context. But since these subjects will be often repeated, let us follow the thread of Moses' discourse. God, of his mere grace, conferred peculiar honour on the boy, who was the last but one among twelve, in giving him the priority among his brethren. For, by what merit or virtue shall we say that he attained the lordship over his brethren? Afterwards he seemed, indeed, to acquire this by his own great benefi- cence: but from the dream we learn, that it was the free gift of God, which in no way depended upon Joseph's bene- ficence. Rather, he was ordained to be chief, by the mere good pleasure of God, in order that he might show kindness to his brethren. Now, since the Lord was, at that time, wont to reveal his secrets by two methods—by visions and by dreams—one of these kinds is here noted. For no doubt Joseph had often dreamed in the common manner: but Moses shows that a dream was now divinely sent to him, which might have the force and weight of an oracle. We know that dreams are often produced by our daily thoughts: sometimes they are indications of an unhealthy state of the body: but whenever God intends to make known his counsel by dreams, he engraves on them certain marks, which distinguish them from passing and frivolous imaginations, in order that their credibility and authority may stand firm. Thus Joseph, be- ing certainly persuaded that he had not been deluded by an empty spectre, fearlessly announced his dream as a celestial oracle. Now, although the dominion is promised to him under a rural symbol, it is one which does not seem suitable for instruction to the sons of Jacob; for we know that they were herdsmen, not ploughmen. Since they had no harvest which they could gather in, it seems hardly congruous that homage should be paid to his *sheaf.* But perhaps God de- signedly chose this similitude, to show that this prophecy was not founded upon the present fortunes of Joseph, and that the material of his dominion would not consist in those things which were at hand, but that it should be a future benefit, the cause of which was to be sought for elsewhere than at home.

8. *Shalt thou indeed reign over us ?* Here it is plainly shown to us that the paternal favour of God towards the elect, is like a fan to excite against them the enmity of the world. When the sons of Jacob heard that they were fighting in vain against God, their unjust hatred ought, by such means, to have been corrected. For it was as if God, setting himself in the midst, would repress their fury by these words, " Your impious conspiring will be fruitless ; for although you boast, I have constituted as your chief, the man whose ruin your wicked envy hurries you to seek." Perhaps, also, by this consolatory dream, he intended to alleviate the trouble of the holy youth. Yet their obstinacy caused it to be the more increased. Let us then learn not to be grieved if, at any time, the shining of the grace of God upon us should cause us to be envied. The sons of Jacob, however, were but too acute interpreters of the dream: yet they deride it as a fable, because it was repugnant to their wishes. Thus it often happens that they who are ill-disposed, quickly perceive what is the will of God: but, because they feel no reverence, they despise it. To this contumacy, however, succeeds a stupor which destroys their former quick-sightedness.

9. *And he dreamed yet another dream.* The scope of this dream is the same. The only difference is, that God, to inspire greater confidence in the oracle, presents him with a figure from heaven. The brethren of Joseph had despised what was said concerning the sheaves ; the Lord now calls upon them to look towards heaven, where his august Majesty shines forth. It may, however, be asked, how it can be reconciled with fact, that his mother, who was now dead, could come and bow down to him. The interpretation of certain Hebrews, who refer it to Bilhah, is frigid, and the sense appears plain without such subterfuges : for the sun and moon designate the head of the family on each side : thus, in this figure, Joseph sees himself reverenced by the whole house of his father.

10. *And his father rebuked him.* If Jacob suspected that the dream originated in vain ambition, he rightly rebuked

his son ; but if he knew that God was the author of the dream,
he ought not to have expostulated with him.　But that he
did know it, may be hence inferred, because he is afterwards
said seriously to have considered it.　For Moses, making a distinction between him and his sons, says that *they* breathed
nothing but the *virus* of envy ; while *he* revolved in-his own
mind what this might mean ; which could not have happened,
unless he had been affected with reverence.　But seeing that
a certain religious impression on the subject rested on his
mind, how was it that he rebuked his son ?　This truly was
not giving honour to God and to his word.　For it ought to
have occurred to the mind of Jacob that, although Joseph
was under his authority, he yet sustained a prophetic character.　It is probable, when he saw his sons so malevolent,
that he wished to meet the danger by feigning what he did
not feel : for he was not offended at the dream, but he was
unwilling to exasperate the minds of those who, on account
of their pride, would not bear to be in subjection.　Therefore
I do not doubt that he feignedly reproved his son, from a
desire to appease contention.　Nevertheless, this method of
pretending to be adverse to the truth, when we are endeavouring to appease the anger of those who rage against it,
is by no means approved by God.　He ought rather ingenuously to have exhorted his sons not to " kick against the
pricks."　Or at least he should have used this moderate
address, " If this is a common dream, let it be treated with
ridicule rather than with anger ; but if it has proceeded from
God, it is wicked to speak against it."　It is even possible that
the unsuitableness of the dream had struck the mind of the
old man.　For we know how difficult it is entirely to throw off
all sense of superiority.　Certainly, though Jacob declines
slightly from the right course, yet his piety appears to be of
no common order ; because his reverence for the oracle so
easily prevailed over every other feeling.　But the most
wicked obstinacy betrays itself in his sons, seeing they break
out into greater enmity.　For though they despise the dream,
yet they are not made angry about nothing.　Gladly would
they have had their brother as a laughing-stock ; but a certain secret sense of the Deity constrains them, so that, with

or against their will, they are compelled to feel that there is something authentic in the dream. Meanwhile, a blind ferocity impels them to an unintentional resistance against God. Therefore, that we may be held in obedience to God, let us learn to bring down our high spirits; because the beginning of docility is for men to submit to be brought into order. This obstinacy in the sons of Jacob was most censurable, because they not only rejected the oracle of God through their hatred of subjection, but were hostile to his messenger and herald. How much less excusable, then, will be our hardness, if we do not meekly submit our necks to the yoke of God; since the doctrine of humility, which subdues and even mortifies us, is not only more clearly revealed, but also confirmed by the precious blood of Christ? If, however, we see many refractory persons at this day, who refuse to embrace the gospel, and who perversely rise up against it, let us not be disturbed as by some new thing, seeing that the whole human race is infected with the disease of pride; for by the gospel all the glory of the flesh is reduced to nothing; rather let us know that all remain obstinate, except those who are rendered meek by the subduing influence of the Spirit.

12. *And his brethren went.* Before Moses treats of the horrible design of fratricide, he describes the journey of Joseph, and amplifies, by many circumstances, the atrocity of the crime. Their brother approaches them in the discharge of a duty, to make a fraternal inquiry after their state. He comes by the command of his father; and obeys it without reluctance, as appears from his answer. He searches them out anxiously; and though they had changed their place, he spares neither labour nor trouble till he finds them. Therefore their cruelty was something more than madness, seeing they did not shrink with horror from contriving the death of a brother so pious and humane. We now see that Moses does not relate, without a purpose, that a man met Joseph in his wanderings, and told him that his brethren had departed to Dothan. For the greater was his diligence in his indefatigable pursuit, so much the less excusable were they by whom such an unworthy recompense was repaid.

18. *And when they saw him afar off.*   Here again Moses,
so far from sparing the fame of his own family by adulation,
brands its chiefs with a mark of eternal infamy, and exposes
them to the hatred and execration of all nations.   If, at any
time, among heathens, a brother murdered his brother, such
impiety was treated with the utmost severity in tragedies,
that it might not pass into an example for imitation.   But
in profane history no such thing is found, as that nine
brethren should conspire together for the destruction of an
innocent youth, and, like wild beasts, should pounce upon
him with bloody hands.   Therefore a horrible, and even
diabolical fury, took possession of the sons of Jacob, when,
having cast aside the sense of nature, they were thus prepared cruelly to rage against their own blood.

But, in addition to this wickedness, Moses condemns their
impious contempt of God, *Behold this master of dreams.*
For why do they insult the unhappy youth, except because
he had been called by the celestial oracle to an unexpected
dignity ?   Besides, in this manner, they themselves proclaim
their own baseness more publicly than any one could do,
who should purposely undertake severely to chastise them.
They confess that the cause why they persecuted their
brother was his having dreamed ; as if truly this was an
inexpiable offence ; but if they are indignant at his dreams,
why do they not rather wage war with God ?   For Joseph
deemed it necessary to receive, as a precious deposit, what
had been divinely revealed unto him.   But because they
did not dare directly to assail God, they wrap themselves in
clouds, that, losing sight of God, they may vent their fury
against their brother.   If such blindness seized upon the
patriarchs, what shall become of the reprobates, whom obstinate malice drives along, so that they do not hesitate to resist
God even to the last ?   And we see that they willingly disturb and excite themselves, as often as they are offended
with the threatenings and chastisements of God, and rise up
against his ministers for the sake of taking vengeance.   The
same thing, indeed, would at times happen to us all, unless
God should put on his bridle to render us submissive.   With
respect to Joseph, the special favour of God was manifested

to him, and he was raised to the highest dignity; but only in a dream, which is ridiculed by the wicked scorn of his brethren. To this is also added a conspiracy, so that he narrowly escaped death. Thus the promise of God, which had exalted him to honour, almost plunges him into the grave. We, also, who have received the gratuitous adoption of God amidst many sorrows, experience the same thing. For, from the time that Christ gathers us into his flock, God permits us to be cast down in various ways, so that we seem nearer hell than heaven. Therefore, let the example of Joseph be fixed in our minds, that we be not disquieted when many crosses spring forth to us from the root of God's favour. For I have before showed, and the thing itself clearly testifies, that in Joseph was adumbrated, what was afterwards more fully exhibited in Christ, the Head of the Church, in order that each member may form itself to the imitation of his example.

20. *And cast him into some pit.* Before they perpetrate the murder, they seek a pretext whereby they may conceal their crime from men. Meanwhile, it never enters into their mind, that what is hidden from men cannot escape the eyes of God. But so stupid is hypocrisy, that while it flees from the disgrace of the world, it is careless about the judgment of God. But it is a disease deeply rooted in the human mind, to put some specious colour on every extreme act of iniquity. For although an inward judge convicts the guilty, they yet confirm themselves in impudence, that their disgrace may not appear unto others.

And we shall see what will become of his dreams. As if the truth of God could be subverted by the death of one man, they boast that they shall have attained their wish when they have killed their brother; namely, that his dreams will come to nothing. This is not, indeed, their avowed purpose, but turbulent envy drives them headlong to fight against God. But whatever they design in thus contending with God in the dark, their attempts will, at length, prove vain. For God will always find a way through the most profound abyss, to the accomplishment of what he has decreed. If, then, unbelievers provoke us by their reproaches,

and proudly boast that our faith will profit us nothing; let
not their insolence discourage or weaken us, but let us confidently proceed.

21. *And Reuben heard it.* It may be well to observe,
while others were hastening to shed his blood, by whose
care Joseph was preserved.   Reuben doubtless, in one affair,
was the most wicked of them all, when he defiled his father's
couch ; and that unbridled lust, involving other vices, was
the sign of a depraved nature : now suddenly, he alone, having a regard to piety, and being mindful of fraternal duty,
dissolves the impious conspiracy.   It is uncertain whether he
was now seeking the means of making some compensation,
for the sake of which he might be restored to his father's
favour.   Moses declares that it was his intention to restore
the boy in safety to his father : whence the conjecture which
I have stated is probable, that he thought the life of his
brother would be a sufficient price by which he might reconcile his father's mind to himself.   However this may be, yet
the humanity which he showed in attempting to liberate his
brother, is a proof that he was not abandoned to every kind
of wickedness.   And perhaps God, by this testimony of his
penitence, designed in some degree to lessen his former disgrace.   Whence we are taught that the characters of men are
not to be estimated by a single act, however atrocious, so as
to cause us to despair of their salvation.

22. *Cast him into this pit.* The pious fallacy to which
Reuben descended, sufficiently proves with what vehemence
the rage of his brethren was burning.   For he neither dares
openly to oppose them, nor to dissuade them from their
crime ; because he saw that no reasons would avail to soften
them.   Nor does it extenuate their cruelty, that they consent
to his proposal, as if they were disposed to clemency ; for if
either one course or the other were necessary, it would have
been better for him immediately to die by their hands, than
to perish by slow hunger in the pit, which is the most cruel
kind of punishment.   Their gross hypocrisy is rather to be
noticed ; because they think that they shall be free from
crime, if only they do not stain their hands with their brother's blood.   As if, indeed, it made any difference, whether

they ran their brother through with a sword, or put him to death by suffocation. For the Lord, when he accuses the Jews by Isaiah, of having hands full of blood, does not mean that they were assassins, but he calls them bloody, because they did not spare their suffering brethren. Therefore, the sons of Jacob are nothing better, in casting their brother alive under ground, that, as one buried, he might in vain contend with death, and perish after protracted torments; and in choosing a pit in the desert, from which no mortal could hear his dying cry, though his sighing would ascend even to heaven. It was a barbarous thought, that they should not touch his life, if they did not embrue their hands in his blood; since it was a kind of death, not less violent, which they wished to inflict by hunger. Reuben, however, accommodating his language to their brutal conceptions, deemed it sufficient to repress, by any kind of artifice, their impetuosity for the present.

23. *They stripped Joseph out of his coat.*[1] We see that these men are full of fictions and lies. They carelessly strip their brother; they feel no dread at casting him with their own hands into the pit, where hunger worse than ten swords might consume him; because they hope their crime will be concealed; and in taking home his clothes, no suspicion of his murder would be excited; because, truly, their father would believe that he had been torn by a wild beast. Thus Satan infatuates wicked minds, so that they entangle themselves by frivolous evasions. Conscience is indeed the fountain of modesty; but Satan so soothes by his allurements those whom he has entangled in his snares, that conscience itself, which ought to have cited them as guilty before the bar of God, only hardens them the more. For, having found out

---

[1] The coat of many colours was supposed by some to be the garment belonging of right to the first-born; consequently, Reuben would be entitled to it, till he forfeited it by his misconduct. Jacob, therefore, is understood to have transferred this coat, together with the rank of primogeniture, from Reuben to the eldest son of Rachel, his most beloved wife. If this were so, it would make the conduct of Reuben, on this occasion, still more generous than it appears on the ordinary supposition. There is, however, this objection to such an interpretation, that Jacob is said to have *made it* for Joseph, (see ver. 3,) and not merely to have *given it* to him.— *Ed.*

subterfuges, they break forth far more audaciously into sin, as if they might commit with impunity whatever escapes the eyes of men.   Surely it is a reprobate sense, a spirit of frenzy and of stupor, which is withheld from any daring attempt, only by a fear of the shame of men ; while the fear of divine judgment is trodden under foot.   And although all are not carried thus far, yet the fault of paying more honour to men than to God, is too common.   The repetition of the word *coat* in the sentence of Moses is emphatical, showing that this mark of the father's love could not mollify their minds.

25. *And they sat down to eat bread.*   This was an astonishing barbarity, that they could quietly feast, while, in intention, they were guilty of their brother's death : for, had there been one drop of humanity in their souls, they would at least have felt some inward compunctions ; yea, commonly, the very worst men are afraid after the commission of a crime. Since the patriarchs fell into such a state of insensibility, let us learn, from their example, to fear lest, by the righteous anger of God, the same lethargy should seize upon our senses. Meanwhile, it is proper to consider the admirable progress of God's counsel.   Joseph had already passed through a double death : and now, as if by a third death, he is, beyond all expectation, rescued from the grave.   For what was it less than death, to be sold as a slave to foreigners ?   Indeed his condition was rendered worse by the change ; because Reuben, secretly drawing him out of the pit, would have brought him back to his father : whereas now he is dragged to a distant part of the earth, without hope of return.   But this was a secret turn, by which God had determined to raise him on high.   And at length, he shows by the event, how much better it was that Joseph should be led far away from his own family, than that he should remain in safety at home. Moreover, the speech of Judah, by which he persuades his brethren *to sell* Joseph, has somewhat more reason.   For he ingenuously confesses that they would be guilty of homicide, if they suffered him to perish in the pit.   What gain shall we make, he says, if his blood be covered ; for our hands will nevertheless be polluted with blood.   By this time their fury was in some degree abated, so that they listened to

more humane counsel ; for though it was outrageous perfidy to sell their brother to strangers ; yet it was something to send him away alive, that, at least, he might be nourished as a slave. We see, therefore, that the diabolical flame of madness, with which they had all burned, was abating, when they acknowledged that they could profit nothing by hiding their crime from the eyes of men ; because homicide must of necessity come into view before God. For at first, they absolved themselves from guilt, as if no Judge sat in heaven. But now the sense of nature, which the cruelty of hatred had before benumbed, begins to exert its power. And certainly, even in the reprobate, who seem entirely to have cast off humanity, time shows that some residue of it remains. When wicked and violent affections rage, their tumultuous fervour hinders nature from acting its part. But no minds are so stupid, that a consideration of their own wickedness will not sometimes fill them with remorse : for, in order that men may come inexcusable to the judgment-seat of God, it is necessary that they should first be condemned by themselves. They who are capable of cure, and whom the Lord leads to repentance, differ from the reprobates in this, that while the latter obstinately conceal the knowledge of their crimes, the former gradually return from the indulgence of sin, to obey the voice of reason. Moreover, what Judah here declares concerning his brother, the Lord, by the prophet, extends to the whole human race. Whenever, therefore, depraved lust impels to unjust violence, or any other injury, let us remember this sacred bond by which the whole of society is bound together, in order that it may restrain us from evil doings. For man cannot injure man, but he becomes an enemy to his own flesh, and violates and perverts the whole order of nature.

28. *Then there passed by Midianites.* Some think that Joseph was twice sold in the same place. For it is certain, since Midian was the son of Abraham and Keturah, that his sons were distinct from the sons of Ishmael : and Moses has not thoughtlessly put down these different names.[1]

---

[1] Perhaps, however, the passage may be better explained by supposing the caravan which was passing, to be made up of Ishmaelites and Midianites. The Ishmaelites might form the larger and more conspicuous part of the

But I thus interpret the passage: that Joseph was exposed for sale to any one who chose, and seeing the purchase of him was declined by the Midianites, he was sold to the Ishmaelites. Moreover, though they might justly suspect the sellers of having stolen him, yet the desire of gain prevents them from making inquiry. We may also add, what is probable, that, on the journey, they inquired who Joseph was. But they did not set such a value on their common origin as to prevent them from eagerly making gain. This passage, however, teaches us how far the sons of Abraham, after the flesh, were preferred to the elect offspring, in which, nevertheless, the hope of the future Church was included. We see that, of the two sons of Abraham, a posterity so great was propagated, that from both proceeded merchants in various places : while that part of his seed which the Lord had chosen to himself was yet small. But so the children of this world, like premature fruit, quickly arrive at the greatest wealth and at the summit of happiness ; whereas the Church, slowly creeping through the greatest difficulties, scarcely attains, during a long period, to the condition of mediocrity.

30. *And he returned.* We may hence gather that Reuben, under pretence of some other business, stole away from his brethren, that, unknown to them all, he might restore his brother, drawn out of the pit, to his father; and that therefore he was absent at the time when Joseph was sold. And there is no wonder that he was anticipated, when he had taken his course in a different direction from theirs, intending to reach the pit by a circuitous path. But now at length Reuben having lost all hope, unfolds to his brethren the intention which before he dared not confess, lest the boy should be immediately murdered.

31. *And they took Joseph's coat.* They now return to their first scheme. In order that their father may have no suspicion of their crime, they send the bloody coat, from which he might conjecture that Joseph had been torn by some wild beast. Although Moses alludes to this briefly, I yet think that they rather sent some of their servants, who

company, and thus give the name to the whole ; but the actual purchasers of Joseph might be the Midianitish merchants among them.—*Ed.*

were not accessary to the crime, than any of their number. For he says soon afterwards, that his sons and daughters came to offer some consolation to him in his grief. And although in the words they use, there lurks some appearance of insult, it seems to me more probable that they gave this command to avert suspicion from themselves. For they feign themselves to be of confused mind, as is usual in affairs of perplexity. Yet whatever they intend, their wickedness drives them to this point, that they inflict a deadly wound upon the mind of their father. This is the profit which hypocrites gain by their disguises, that in wishing to escape the consequences of one fault, they add sin to sin. With respect to Jacob, it is a wonder that after he had been tried in so many ways, and always come forth a conqueror, he should now sink under grief. Certainly it was very absurd that the death of his son should occasion him greater sorrow than the incestuous pollution of his wife, the slaughter of the Shechemites, and the defilement of his daughter. Where was that invincible strength, by which he had even prevailed over the angel? Where the many lessons of patience with which God had exercised him, in order that he might never fail? This disposition to mourn, teaches us that no one is endued with such heroic virtues, as to be exempt from that infirmity of the flesh, which betrays itself sometimes even in little things; whence also it happens, that they who have long been accustomed to the cross, and who like veteran soldiers ought bravely to bear up against every kind of attack, fall like young recruits in some slight skirmish. Who then among us may not fear for himself, when we see holy Jacob faint, after having given so many proofs of patience?

35. *And all his sons and daughters rose up.* The burden of his grief is more clearly expressed by the circumstance that all his sons and daughters meet together to comfort him. For by the term " rose up," is implied a common deliberation, they having agreed to come together, because necessity urged them. But hence it appears how vast is the innate dissimulation of men. The sons of Jacob assume a character by no means suitable to them; and perform an office of piety, from which their minds are most alien. If they had

had respect unto God, they would have acknowledged their fault, and though no remedy might have been found for their evil, yet repentance would have brought forth some fruit; but now they are satisfied with a vanity as empty as the wind. By this example we are taught how carefully we ought to avoid dissimulation, which continually implicates men in new snares.

But he refused to be comforted. It may be asked, whether Jacob had entirely cast off the virtue of patience : for so much the language seems to mean. Besides, he sins more grievously, because he, knowingly and voluntarily, indulges in grief : for this is as if he would purposely augment his sorrow, which is to rebel against God. But I suppose his refusal to be restricted to that alleviation of grief which man might offer. For nothing is more unreasonable than that a holy man, who, all his life had borne the yoke of God with such meekness of disposition, should now, like an unbroken horse, bite his bridle ; in order that, by nourishing his grief, he might confirm himself in unsubdued impetuosity. I therefore do not doubt that he was willing now to submit himself unto the Lord, though he rejects human consolations. He seems also angrily to chide his sons, whose envy and malevolence towards Joseph he knew, as if he would upbraid them by declaring that he esteemed this one son more than all the rest : since he rather desires to be with him, dead in the grave, than to enjoy the society of ten living sons whom he had yet remaining ; for I except little Benjamin. I do not, however, here excuse that excess of grief which I have lately condemned. And certainly he proves himself to be overwhelmed with sadness, in speaking of the grave, as if the sons of God did not pass through death to a better life. And hence we learn the blindness of immoderate grief, which almost quenches the light of faith in the saints ; so much the more diligent, then, ought we to be in our endeavour to restrain it. Job greatly excelled in piety ; yet we see, after he had been oppressed by the magnitude of his grief, in what a profane manner he mixes men with beasts in death. If the angelic minds of holy men were thus darkened by sadness, how much deeper gloom will rest upon us, unless God, by the shining of his word and Spirit, should scatter it, and we also, with suitable anxiety, meet the temptation, before it overwhelms us? The principal mitigation of sorrow is the consolation of the future life; to which whosoever applies himself, need not fear lest he should be absorbed by excess of grief. Now though the immoderate sorrow of Jacob is not to be approved; yet the special design of Moses was, to set a mark of infamy on that iron hardness which cruelly reigned in the hearts of his sons. They saw that, if their father should miserably perish, consumed with grief, they would be the cause of it; in short, they saw that he was already dying through their wickedness. If they are not able to heal the wound, why, at least, do they not attempt to alleviate his pain? Therefore they are exceedingly cruel, seeing that they have not sufficient care of their father's life, to cause them to drop a single word in mitigation of his sorrow, when it was in their power to do so.

36. *And the Midianites sold him into Egypt.* It was a sad spectacle, that Joseph should be thus driven from one hand to another. For it added no small indignity to his former suffering, that he is set to sale as a slave. The Lord, however, ceased not to care for him. He even suffered him to be transferred from hand to hand, in order that, at length, it might indeed appear, that he had come, by celestial guidance, to that very dominion which had been promised him in his dreams. Potiphar is called a eunuch, not because he was one really; but because, among the Orientals, it was usual to denote the satraps and princes of the court by that name. The Hebrews are not agreed respecting the dignity which Moses ascribes to him; for some explain it as the " chief of the slaughterers,"[1] whom the Greek interpreters follow. But I rather agree with others, who say that he was " the prefect of the soldiers;" not that he had the command of the whole army, but because he had the royal troops under his hand and authority: such are now the captains of the guard, if

---

[1] The term applies primarily to butchers, who slaughter animals for *food;* then to persons who slaughter animals for *sacrifice;* and then to executioners who put men to the slaughter under the authority of the monarch or the state.— *Ed.*

you join with it another office which the prefects of the prison exercise. For this may be gathered from the thirty-ninth chapter.[1]

CHAPTER XXXVIII.

1. AND it came to pass at that time, that Judah went down from his brethren, and turned in to a certain Adullamite, whose name *was* Hirah.

2. And Judah saw there a daughter of a certain Canaanite, whose name *was* Shuah; and he took her, and went in unto her.

3. And she conceived, and bare a son; and he called his name Er.

4. And she conceived again, and bare a son; and she called his name Onan.

5. And she yet again conceived, and bare a son; and called his name Shelah: and he was at Chezib when she bare him.

6. And Judah took a wife for Er his first-born, whose name *was* Tamar.

7. And Er, Judah's first-born, was wicked in the sight of the Lord; and the Lord slew him.

8. And Judah said unto Onan, Go in unto thy brother's wife, and marry her, and raise up seed to thy brother.

9. And Onan knew that the seed should not be his: and it came to pass, when he went in unto his brother's wife, that he spilled *it* on the ground, lest that he should give seed to his brother.

10. And the thing which he did displeased the Lord; wherefore he slew him also.

11. Then said Judah to Tamar his daughter-in-law, Remain a widow

1. Fuit autem tempore illo descendit Jehudah a fratribus suis, et declinavit ad virum Hadullamitem, et nomen ejus Hirah.

2. Et vidit ibi Jehudah filiam viri Chenaanaei: et nomen ejus Suah: qui accepit eam, et ingressus est ad eam.

3. Quæ concepit, et peperit filium, et vocavit nomen ejus Her.

4. Et concepit adhuc, et peperit filium, et vocavit nomen ejus Onan.

5. Et addidit adhuc, et peperit filium, et vocavit nomen ejus Selah: erat autem in Chezib, quando hunc ipsa peperit

6. Et accepit Jehudah uxorem ipsi Her primogenito suo, et nomen ejus Thamar.

7. Verum erat Her primogenitus Jehudah malus in oculis Jehovæ, ideo interemit eum Jehova.

8. Et dixit Jehudah ad Onan, Ingredere ad uxorem fratris tui, et affinitatem contrahe cum ea, et suscita semen fratri tuo.

9. Et cognovit Onan, quod non sibi futurum esset semen: et erat quando ingrediebatur ad uxorem fratris sui, corrumpebat *semen* super terram, ne poneret semen fratri suo.

10. Displicuit autem in oculis Jehovæ quod fecit, ideoque mori fecit etiam eum.

11. Et dixit Jehudah ad Thamar nurum suam, Mane vidua in domo

---

[1] See ver. 20.   The words rendered " prefects of the prison," are præfecti hospitii—and in the French, Prevosts de l'hostel—perhaps, prefects of the town-house, or town-hall, would have been more correct.   The expression in the original, שר־הטבחים, *sar-hatabachim*, means the captain of the executioners; that is, of the king's body guard, whose office it was to inflict capital punishments; as in the Turkish court at present.—*See Gesenius' Lexicon.*—*Ed.*

at thy father's house, till Shelah my son be grown : for he said, Lest peradventure he die also, as his brethren *did*. And Tamar went and dwelt in her father's house.

12. And, in process of time, the daughter of Shuah, Judah's wife, died : and Judah was comforted, and went up unto his sheep-shearers to Timnath, he and his friend Hirah the Adullamite.

13. And it was told Tamar, saying, Behold, thy father-in-law goeth up to Timnath to shear his sheep.

14. And she put her widow's garments off from her, and covered her with a vail, and wrapped herself, and sat in an open place, which *is* by the way to Timnath : for she saw that Shelah was grown, and she was not given unto him to wife.

15. When Judah saw her, he thought her *to be* an harlot ; because she had covered her face.

16. And he turned unto her by the way, and said, Go to, I pray thee, let me come in unto thee ; (for he knew not that she *was* his daughter-in-law.) And she said, What wilt thou give me, that thou mayest come in unto me ?

17. And he said, I will send *thee* a kid from the flock. And she said, Wilt thou give *me* a pledge till thou send *it ?*

18. And he said, What pledge shall I give thee ? And she said, Thy signet, and thy bracelets, and thy staff that *is* in thine hand : and he gave *it* her, and came in unto her ; and she conceived by him.

19. And she arose, and went away, and laid by her vail from her, and put on the garments of her widowhood.

20. And Judah sent the kid by the hand of his friend the Adullamite, to receive *his* pledge from the woman's hand ; but he found her not.

21. Then he asked the men of that place, saying, Where *is* the harlot that *was* openly by the way-side ? And they said, There was no harlot in this *place*.

patris tui, donec crescat Selah filius meus : dicebat enim, Ne forte moriatur etiam ipse, sicut et fratres ejus, et abiit Thamar, et mansit in domo patris sui.

12. Et multiplicati sunt dies, et mortua est filia Suah uxor Jehudah : et consolatus est se Jehudah, et ascendit ad tonsores ovium suarum, ipse, et Hirah amicus ejus, Hadullamita in Thimnath.

13. Et nuntiatum fuit ipsi Thamar, dicendo, Ecce, socer tuus ascendit in Thimnath ad tondendum oves suas.

14. Tunc removit vestes viduitatis suæ a se, et operuit *se* velamine, et celavit se, mansitque in ostio Henaim, quod erat juxta viam Thimnath : viderat enim quod creverat Selah, ipsa vero non fuerat data ei in uxorem.

15. Et vidit eam Jehudah, et putavit eam esse meretricem : operuerat enim faciem suam.

16. Et declinavit ad eam e via : et dixit, Age quæso, ingrediar ad te (non enim noverat quod nurus sua esset). Illa dixit, Quid dabis mihi, si ingrediaris ad me ?

17. Et ait, Ego mittam hœdum caprarum de pecudibus. Et dixit, Num dabis pignus donec miseris ?

18. Et dixit, Quod pignus vis ut dem tibi ? Et dixit, Sigillum tuum, et pallium tuum, et virgam tuam, quæ est in manu tua. Et dedit ei : et ingressus est ad eam, et concepit ex eo.

19. Illa surrexit, et abiit, et removit velamen suum a se, et induit se vestibus viduitatis suæ.

20. Et misit Jehudah hœdum caprarum per manum amici sui Hadullamitæ, ut caperet pignus e manu mulieris ; qui non invenit eam.

21. Et interrogavit viros loci illius, dicendo, Ubi est meretrix illa in Henaim juxta viam ? Et dixerunt, Non fuit hic meretrix.

22. And he returned to Judah, and said, I cannot find her; and also the men of the place said, *that* there was no harlot in this *place*.

23. And Judah said, Let her take *it* to her, lest we be shamed: behold, I sent this kid, and thou hast not found her.

24. And it came to pass, about three months after, that it was told Judah, saying, Tamar thy daughter-in-law hath played the harlot; and also, behold, she *is* with child by whoredom. And Judah said, Bring her forth, and let her be burnt.

25. When *she* was brought forth, she sent to her father-in-law, saying, By the man whose these *are am* I with child: and she said, Discern, I pray thee, whose *are* these, the signet, and bracelets, and staff.

26. And Judah acknowledged *them*, and said, She hath been more righteous than I; because that I gave her not to Shelah my son: and he knew her again no more.

27. And it came to pass, in the time of her travail, that, behold, twins *were* in her womb.

28. And it came to pass, when she travailed, that *the one* put out *his* hand; and the midwife took and bound upon his hand a scarlet thread, saying, This came out first.

29. And it came to pass, as he drew back his hand, that, behold, his brother came out; and she said, How hast thou broken forth? *this* breach *be* upon thee: therefore his name was called Pharez.

30. And afterward came out his brother, that had the scarlet thread upon his hand; and his name was called Zarah.

22. Reversus est ergo ad Jehudah, et dixit, Non inveni eam: et etiam viri illius loci dixerunt, Non fuit hic meretrix.

23. Et dixit Jehudah, Capiat sibi, ne forte simus in probrum: ecce, misi hœdum hunc, et tu non invenisti eam.

24. Et fuit, circiter post tres menses, nuntiatum fuit ipsi Jehudah, dicendo, Fornicata est Thamar nurus tua, et etiam ecce, est gravida ex fornicationibus. Et dixit Jehudah, Educite eam, et comburatur.

25. Ipsa, quum educeretur, misit ad socerum suum, dicendo, De viro cujus hæc sunt, sum gravida. Et dixit, Agnosce quæso, cujus sint sigillum, et pallium, et virga isthæc.

26. Et agnovit Jehudah, et dixit, Justior me est: idcirco enim *hœc fecit*, quod non dedi eam Selah filio meo. Verum non addidit adhuc cognoscere eam.

27. Et fuit, in tempore quo parturiebat ipsa, ecce, gemini erant in utero ejus.

28. Fuit autem, ea pariente, *unus* dedit manum, et accepit obstetrix, et ligavit ad manum ejus coccinum, dicendo, Iste egressus est prior.

29. Et fuit, quum retraheret manum suam, ecce, egressus est frater ejus, et dixit, Cur rupisti super te interstitium? et vocavit nomen ejus Peres.

30. Et postea egressus est frater ejus, ad cujus manum erat coccinum: et vocavit nomen ejus Zerah.

1. *And it came to pass at that time, that Judah.* Before Moses proceeds in relating the history of Joseph, he inserts the genealogy of Judah, to which he devotes more labour, because the Redeemer was thence to derive his origin; for the continuous history of that tribe, from which salvation was to be sought, could not remain unknown, without loss. And yet its glorious nobility is not here celebrated, but the

greatest disgrace of the family is exposed. What is here
related, so far from inflating the minds of the sons of Judah,
ought rather to cover them with shame. Now although, at
first sight, the dignity of Christ seems to be somewhat tarnished by such dishonour : yet since here also is seen that
" emptying" of which St. Paul speaks,[1] it rather redounds
to his glory, than, in the least degree, detracts from it. First,
we wrong Christ, unless we deem him alone sufficient to blot
out any ignominy arising from the misconduct of his progenitors, which offer to unbelievers occasion of offence. Secondly,
we know that the riches of God's grace shines chiefly in this,
that Christ clothed himself in our flesh, with the design of
making himself of no reputation. Lastly, it was fitting
that the race from which he sprang should be dishonoured
by reproaches, that we, being content with him alone, might
seek nothing besides him ; yea, that we might not seek
earthly splendour in him, seeing that carnal ambition is
always too much inclined to such a course. These two things,
then, we may notice ; first, that peculiar honour was given
to the tribe of Judah, which had been divinely elected as the
source whence the salvation of the world should flow ; and
secondly, that the narration of Moses is by no means honourable to the persons of whom he speaks ; so that the Jews
have no right to arrogate anything to themselves or to their
fathers. Meanwhile, let us remember that Christ derives no
glory from his ancestors ; and even, that he himself has no
glory in the flesh, but that his chief and most illustrious
triumph was on the cross. Moreover, that we may not be
offended at the stains with which his ancestry was defiled,
let us know that, by his infinite purity, they were all cleansed ;
just as the sun, by absorbing whatever impurities are in the
earth and air, purges the world.

2. *And Judah saw there a daughter of a certain Canaanite.*
I am not satisfied with the interpretation which some give
of " merchant" to the word Canaanite. For Moses charges
Judah with perverse lust, because he took a wife out of that
nation with which the children of Abraham were divinely

---

[1] Phil. ii. 7. " But made himself of no reputation," literally, " emptied
himself, *ἑαυτὸν ἐκένωσι.*"— *Ed.*

commanded to be at perpetual strife. For neither he nor his other brethren were ignorant that they sojourned in the land of Canaan, under the stipulation, that afterwards their enemies were to be cut off and destroyed, in order that they might possess the promised dominion over it. Moses, therefore, justly regards it as a fault, that Judah should entangle himself in a forbidden alliance; and the Lord, at length, cursed the offspring thus accruing to Judah, that the prince and head of the tribe of Judah might not be born, nor Christ himself descend, from this connexion. This also ought to be numbered among the exercises of Jacob's patience, that a wicked grandson was born to him through Judah, of whose sin he was not ignorant. Moses says, that the youth was cut off by the vengeance of God. The same thing is not said of others whom a sudden death has swept away in the flower of their age. I doubt not, therefore, that the wickedness, of which death was the immediate punishment, was extraordinary, and known to all men. And although this trial was in itself severe to the holy patriarch; yet nothing tormented his mind more than the thought, that he could scarcely hope for the promise of God to be so ratified that the inheritance of grace should remain in the possession of wicked and abandoned men. It is true that a large family of children is regarded as a source of human happiness. But this was the peculiar condition of the holy patriarch, that, though God had promised him an elect and blessed seed, he now sees an accursed progeny increase and shoot forth together with his offspring, which might destroy the expected grace. It is said, that *Er was wicked in the sight of the Lord,* (verse 7.) Notwithstanding, his iniquity was not hidden from men. Moses, however, means that he was not merely infected with common vices, but rather was so addicted to crimes, that he was intolerable in the sight of God.

7. *And the Lord slew him.* We know that long life is reckoned among the gifts of God; and justly: for since it is by no means a despicable honour that we are created after the image of God, the longer any one lives in the world, and daily experiences God's care over him, it is certain that he is the more bountifully dealt with by the Lord. Even

amidst the many miseries with which life is filled, this
divine goodness still shines forth, that God invites us to
himself, and exercises us in the knowledge of himself; while
at the same time he adorns us with such dignity, that he
subjects to our authority whatever is in the world.   Wherefore it is no wonder that God, as an act of kindness,
prolongs the life of man.   Whence it follows, that when the
wicked are taken away by a premature death, a punishment
for their wickedness is inflicted upon them: for it is as if
the Lord should pronounce judgment from heaven, that they
are unworthy to be sustained by the earth, unworthy to
enjoy the common light of heaven.   Let us therefore learn,
as long as God keeps us in the world, to meditate on his
benefits, to the end that every one may the more cheerfully
endeavour to give praise to God for the life received from
him.   And although, at the present day also, sudden death
is to be reckoned among the scourges of God ; since that
doctrine is always true, " Bloody and deceitful men shall
not live out half their days," (Ps. lv. 23 ;) yet God executed
this judgment more fully under the law, when the knowledge of a future life was comparatively obscure ; for now,
since the resurrection is clearly manifested to us in Christ,
it is not right that death should be so greatly dreaded.
And this difference between us and the ancient people of
God is elsewhere noted.   Nevertheless, it can never be laid
down as a general rule, that they who had a long life were
thereby proved to be pleasing and acceptable to the Lord,
whereas God has sometimes lengthened the life of reprobates,
in aggravation of their punishment.   We know that Cain
survived his brother Abel many centuries.   But as God does
not always, and to all persons, cause his temporal benefits
manifestly to flow in a perpetual and equable course ; so
neither, on the other hand, does he always execute temporal
punishments by the same rule.   It is enough that, as far
as the present life is concerned, certain examples of punishments and rewards are set before us.   Moreover, as the
miseries of the present life, which spring from the corruption of nature, do not extinguish the first and special grace
of God ; so, on the other hand, death, which is in itself the

curse of God, is so far from doing any injury, that it tends, by a supernatural remedy, to the salvation of the elect. Especially now, from the time that the first-fruits of the resurrection in Christ have been offered, the condition of those who are quickly taken out of life is in no way deteriorated ; because Christ himself is gain both for life and death. But the vengeance of God was so clear and remarkable in the death of Er, that the earth might plainly appear to have been purged as from its filthiness.

8. *Go in unto thy brother's wife.* Although no law had hitherto been prescribed concerning brother's marriages, that the surviving brother should raise up seed to one who was dead ; it is, nevertheless, not wonderful that, by the mere instinct of nature, men should have been inclined to this course. For since each man is born for the preservation of the whole race, if any one dies without children, there seems to be here some defect of nature. It was deemed therefore an act of humanity to acquire some name for the dead, from which it might appear that they had lived. Now, the only reason why the children born to the surviving brother, should be reckoned to him who had died, was, that there might be no dry branch in the family ; and in this manner they took away the reproach of barrenness. Besides, since the woman is given as a help to the man, when any woman married into a family, she was, in a certain sense, given up to the name of that family. According to this reasoning, Tamar was not altogether free, but was held under an obligation to the house of Judah, to procreate some seed. Now, though this does not proceed from any rule of piety, yet the Lord had impressed it upon the hearts of man as a duty of humanity ; as he afterwards commanded it to the Jews in their polity. Hence we infer the malignity of Onan, who envied his brother this honour, and would not allow him, when dead, to obtain the title of father ; and this redounds to the dishonour of the whole family. We see that many grant their own sons to their friends for adoption : it was, therefore, an outrageous act of barbarity to deny to his own brother what is given even to strangers. . . . .[1]

[1] A line or two is here omitted, as well as the comment on the tenth verse.—*Ed.*

11. *Then said Judah to Tamar.* Moses intimates that Tamar was not at liberty to marry into another family, so long as Judah wished to retain her under his own authority. It is possible that she voluntarily submitted herself to the will of her father-in-law, when she might have refused : but the language seems to mean, that it was according to a received practice, that Tamar should not pass over to another family, except at the will of her father-in-law, as long as there was a successor who might raise up seed by her. However this may be, Judah acted very unjustly in keeping one bound, whom he intended to defraud. For truly there was no cause why he should be unwilling to allow her to depart free from his house, unless he dreaded the charge of inconstancy. But he should not have allowed this ambitious sense of shame to render him perfidious and cruel to his daughter-in-law. Besides, this injury sprung from a wrong judgment : because, without considering the causes of the death of his sons, he falsely and unjustly transfers the blame to an innocent woman. He believes the marriage with Tamar to have been an unhappy one ; why therefore does he not, for his own sake, permit her to seek a husband elsewhere ? But in this also he does wrong, that whereas the cause of his sons' destruction was their own wickedness, he judges unfavourably of Tamar herself, to whom no evil could be imputed. Let us then learn from this example, whenever anything adverse happens to us, not to transfer the blame to another, nor to gather from all quarters doubtful suspicions, but to shake off our own sins. We must also beware lest a foolish shame should so prevail over us, that while we endeavour to preserve our reputation uninjured among men, we should not be equally careful to maintain a good conscience before God.

13. *And it was told Tamar.* Moses relates how Tamar avenged herself for the injury done her. She did not at first perceive the fraud, but discovered it after a long course of time. When Shelah had grown up, finding herself deceived, she turned her thoughts to revenge. And it is not to be doubted that she had long meditated, and, as it were, hatched this design. For the message respecting Judah's departure was not brought to her accidentally ; but, because she

was intent upon her purpose, she had set spies who should bring her an account of all his doings.   Now, although she formed a plan which was base, and unworthy of a modest woman, yet this circumstance is some alleviation of her crime, that she did not desire a connexion with Judah, except while in a state of celibacy.   In the meantime, she is hurried, by a blind error of mind, into another crime, not less detestable than adultery.   For, by adultery, conjugal fidelity would have been violated ; but, by this incestuous intercourse, the whole dignity of nature is subverted.   This ought carefully to be observed, that they who are injured should not hastily rush to unlawful remedies.   It was not lust which impelled Tamar to prostitute herself.   She grieved, indeed, that she had been forbidden to marry, that she might remain barren at home : but she had no other purpose than to reproach her father-in-law with the fraud by which he had deceived her : at the same time, we see that she committed an atrocious crime.   This is wont to happen, even in good causes, when any one indulges his carnal affections more than is right.   What Moses alludes to respecting garments of widowhood, pertains to the law of modesty.   For elegant clothing which may attract the eyes of men, does not become widows.   And therefore, Paul concedes more to wives than to them ; as having husbands whom they should wish to please.

14. *And sat in an open place.*[1]   Interpreters expound this passage variously.   Literally, it is " in the door of fountains, or of eyes."   Some suppose there was a fountain which branched into two streams ; others think that a broad place is indicated, in which the eyes may look around in all directions.   But a third exposition is more worthy of reception ; namely, that by this expression is meant a way which is forked and divided into two ; because then, as it were, a door is opened before the eyes, that they which are really in one way may diverge in two directions.   Probably it was a place whence Tamar might be seen, to which some by-way was near, where Judah might turn, so that he should not be guilty of fornication, in a public way, under

[1] Mansitque in ostio Henaim, " in the door of eyes, or Enajim."—*Margin of English Version.—Ed.*

the eyes of all. When it is said she veiled her face, we hence infer that the license of fornication was not so un- bridled as that which, at this day, prevails in many places. For she dressed herself after the manner of harlots, that Judah might suspect nothing. And the Lord has caused this sense of shame to remain engraven on the hearts of those who live wickedly, that they may be witnesses to themselves of their own vileness. For if men could wash out the stains from their sins, we know that they would do so most wil- lingly. Whence it follows, that while they flee from the light, they are affected with horror against their will, that their conscience may anticipate the judgment of God. By degrees, indeed, the greater part have so far exceeded all measure in stupor and impudence, that they are less careful to hide their faults; yet God has never suffered the sense of nature to be so entirely extinguished, by the brutal intem- perance of those who desire to sin with impunity, but that their own obscenity shall compel even the most wicked to be ashamed.[1] In short, the veil of Tamar shows that forni- cation was not only a base and filthy thing in the sight of God and the angels; but that it has always been condemned, even by those who have practised it.

15. *When Judah saw her.* It was a great disgrace to Ju- dah that he hastily desired intercourse with an unknown woman. He was now old; and therefore age alone, even in a lascivious man, ought to have restrained the fervour of in- temperance. He sees the woman at a distance, and it is not possible that he should have been captivated by her beauty.[2] . . . Hence we gather, that the fear of God, or a regard to justice and prosperity, cannot have flourished greatly in the heart of one who thus eagerly breaks forth to the indulgence of his passions. He is therefore set before us as an example, that we may learn how easily the lust of the flesh would break forth, unless the Lord should restrain it; and thus, conscious of our infirmity, let us desire from the Lord, a spirit

---

[1] The following sentence is omitted in the translation. " Putida igitur fuit Cynici illius protervia, qui in flagitio deprehensus, sine rubore jactavit se plantare hominem."

[2] The original here adds, " Pruritus tamen non secus in eo accenditur quam in equo, qui ad equarum odorem adhinnit."

8

of continence and moderation. But lest the same security should steal over us, which caused Judah to precipitate himself into fornication ; let us mark, that the dishonour which Judah sustained in consequence of his incest, was a punishment divinely inflicted upon him. Who then will indulge in a crime which he sees, by this dreadful kind of vengeance, to be so very hateful to God ?

16. *What wilt thou give me*, &c.   Tamar did not wish to make a gain by the prostitution of her person, but to have a certain pledge, in order that she might boast of the revenge taken for the injury she had received : and indeed there is no doubt that God blinded Judah, as he deserved ; for how did it happen that he did not know the voice of his daughter-in-law, with which he had been long familiar? Besides, if a pledge must be given for the promised kid, what folly to deliver up his ring to a harlot ? I pass over the absurdity of his giving a double pledge. It appears, therefore, that he was then bereft of all judgment ; and for no other cause are these things written by Moses, than to teach us that his miserable mind was darkened by the just judgment of God, because, by heaping sin upon sin, he had quenched the light of the Spirit.

20 *And Judah sent the kid.*   He sends by the hand of a friend, that he may not reveal his ignominy to a stranger. This is also the reason why he does not dare to complain of the lost pledges, lest he should expose himself to ridicule. For I do not approve the sense given, by some, to the words, *Let her take it to her, lest we be shamed,* as if Judah would excuse himself, as having fulfilled the promise he had given. Another meaning is far more suitable ; namely, that Judah would rather lose the ring, than, by spreading the matter further, give occasion to the speeches of the vulgar ; because lighter is the loss of money than of character. He might also fear being exposed to ridicule for having been so credulous. But he was chiefly afraid of the disgrace arising from his fornication. Here we see that men who are not governed by the Spirit of God are always more solicitous about the opinion of the world than about the judgment of God. For why, when the lust of the flesh excited him, did

it not come into his mind, "Behold now I shall become vile in the sight of God and of angels?" Why, at least, after his lust has cooled, does he not blush at the secret knowledge of his sin? But he is secure, if only he can protect himself from public infamy. This passage, however, teaches, what I have said before, that fornication is condemned by the common sense of men, lest any one should seek to excuse himself on the ground of ignorance.

24. *And it came to pass about three months after.* Tamar might sooner have exposed the crime; but she waited till she should be demanded for capital punishment; for then she would have stronger ground for expostulation. The reason why Judah subjects his daughter-in-law to a punishment so severe, was, that he deemed her guilty of adultery: for what the Lord afterwards confirmed by his law, appears then to have prevailed by custom among men, that a maid, from the time of her espousals, should be strictly faithful to her husband. Tamar had married into the family of Judah; she was then espoused to his third son. It was not therefore simple and common fornication which was the question for judgment; but the crime of adultery, which Judah prosecuted in his own right, because he had been injured in the person of his son. Now this kind of punishment is a proof that adultery has been greatly abhorred in all ages. The law of God commands adulterers to be stoned. Before punishment was sanctioned by a written law, the adulterous woman was, by the consent of all, committed to the flames. This seems to have been done by a divine instinct, that, under the direction and authority of nature, the sanctity of marriage might be fortified, as by a firm guard: and although man is not the lord of his own body, but there is a mutual obligation between himself and his wife, yet husbands who have had illicit intercourse with unmarried women have not been subject to capital punishment; because that punishment was awarded to women, not only on account of their immodesty, but also, of the disgrace which the woman brings upon her husband, and of the confusion caused by the clandestine admixture of seeds. For what else will remain safe in human society, if license be given to bring in by stealth the off-

spring of a stranger? to steal a name which may be given to spurious offspring? and to transfer to them property taken away from the lawful heirs? It is no wonder, then, that formerly the fidelity of marriage was so sternly asserted on this point. How much more vile, and how much less excusable, is our negligence at this day, which cherishes adulteries, by allowing them to pass with impunity. Capital punishment, indeed, is deemed too severe for the measure of the offence. Why then do we punish lighter faults with greater rigour? Truly, the world was beguiled by the wiles of Satan, when it suffered the law, engraven on all by nature, to become obsolete. Meanwhile, a pretext has been found for this gross madness, in that Christ dismissed the adulteress in safety, (John viii. 11,) as if, truly, he had undertaken to inflict punishment upon thieves, homicides, liars, and sorcerers. In vain, therefore, is a rule sought to be established by an act of Christ, who purposely abstained from the office of an earthly judge. It may however be asked, since Judah, who thus boldly usurps the right of the sword, was a private person, and even a stranger in the land; whence had he this great liberty to be the arbiter of life and death? I answer, that the words ought not to be taken as if he would command, on his own authority, his daughter-in-law to be put to death, or as if executioners were ready at his nod; but because the offence was verified and made known, he, as her accuser, freely pronounces concerning the punishment, as if the sentence had already been passed by the judges. Indeed I do not doubt that assemblies were then wont to be held, in which judgments were passed; and therefore I simply explain, that Judah commanded Tamar to be brought forward in public; in order that, the cause being tried, she might be punished according to custom. But the specification of the punishment is to this effect, that the case is one which does not admit of dispute; because Tamar is convicted of the crime before she is cited to judgment.

26. *And Judah acknowledged them.* The open reproach of Tamar proceeded from the desire of revenge. She does not seek an interview with her father-in-law, for the purpose of appeasing his mind; but, with a deliberate contempt of

death, she demands him as the companion of her doom. That Judah immediately acknowledges his fault, is a proof of his honesty; for we see with how many fallacies nearly all are wont to cover their sins, until they are dragged to the light, and all means of denying their guilt have failed. Here, though no one is present who could extort a confession, by force or threats, Judah voluntarily stoops to make one, and takes the greater share of the blame to himself. Yet, seeing that, in confessing his fault, he is now silent respecting punishment; we hence infer, that they who are rigid in censuring others, are much more pliant in forgiving themselves. In this, therefore, we ought to imitate him; that, without rack or torture, truth should so far prevail with us, that we should not be ashamed to confess, before the whole world, those sins with which God charges us. But we must avoid his partiality; lest, while we are harsh towards others, we should spare ourselves. This narrative also teaches us the importance of not condemning any one unheard; not only because it is better that the innocent should be absolved than that a guilty person should perish, but also, because a defence brings many things to light, which sometimes render a change in the form of judgment necessary.

She hath been more righteous than I. The expression is not strictly proper; for he does not simply approve of Tamar's conduct; but speaks comparatively, as if he would say, that he had been, unjustly and without cause, angry against a woman, by whom he himself might rather have been accused. Moreover, by the result, it appears how tardily the world proceeds in exacting punishment for crimes, where no private person stands forward to avenge his own injury. An atrocious and horrible crime had been committed; as long as Judah thought himself aggrieved, he pressed on with vehemence, and the door of judgment was opened. But now, when the accusation is withdrawn, both escape; though certainly it was the duty of all to rise up against them. Moses however intimates that Judah was sincerely penitent; because " he knew" his daughter-in-law " again no more." He also confirms what I have said before, that by nature men are imbued with a great horror of such a crime. For whence did it arise, that he abstained from intercourse with Tamar, unless he judged naturally, that it was infamous for a father-in-law to be connected with his daughter-in-law ? Whoever attempts to destroy the distinction which nature dictates, between what is base and what is honourable, engages, like the giants, in open war with God.

27. *Behold twins were in her womb.* Although both Judah obtained pardon for his error, and Tamar for her wicked contrivance ; yet the Lord, in order to humble them, caused a prodigy to take place in the birth. Something similar had before happened in the case of Jacob and Esau, but for a different reason : as we know that prodigies sometimes portend good, sometimes evil. Here, however, there is no doubt that the twins, in their very birth, bring with them marks of their parents' infamy. For it was both profitable to themselves that the memory of their shame should be renewed, and it served as a public example, that such a crime should be branded with eternal disgrace. There is an ambiguity in the meaning of the midwife's words. Some suppose the " breaking forth" to apply to the membrane of the womb,[1] which is broken when the fœtus comes forth. Others more correctly suppose, that the midwife wondered how Pharez, having broken through the barrier interposed, should have come out first ; for his brother, who had preceded him, was, as an intervening wall, opposed to him. To some the expression appears to be an imprecation ; as if it had been said, " Let the blame of the rupture be upon thee." But Moses, so far as I can judge, intends to point out nothing more, than that a prodigy took place at the birth.

CHAPTER XXXIX.

1. AND Joseph was brought down to Egypt ; and Potiphar, an officer of Pharaoh, captain of the guard, an Egyptian, bought him of the hands of the Ishmeelites, which had brought him down thither.

1. Joseph autem ductus est in Ægyptum, et emit eum Potiphar princeps Pharaonis, princeps satellitum, vir Ægyptius, e manu Ismaelitarum, qui deduxerant eum illuc.

[1] " Secundinis,"—secundina is the membrane which incloses the fœtus during the period of gestation ; and which, being rent at the protrusion of the child, comes away as part of the after-birth. The whole is called *secundine* in English, and in French " *arrière faix.*"—*Ed.*

2. And the Lord was with Joseph, and he was a prosperous man; and he was in the house of his master the Egyptian.

3. And his master saw that the Lord *was* with him, and that the Lord made all that he did to prosper in his hand.

4. And Joseph found grace in his sight, and he served him: and he made him overseer over his house, and all *that* he had he put into his hand.

5. And it came to pass, from the time *that* he had made him overseer in his house, and over all that he had, that the Lord blessed the Egyptian's house for Joseph's sake; and the blessing of the Lord was upon all that he had in the house, and in the field.

6. And he left all that he had in Joseph's hand; and he knew not ought he had, save the bread which he did eat: and Joseph was *a* goodly *person*, and well-favoured.

7. And it came to pass after these things, that his master's wife cast her eyes upon Joseph; and she said, Lie with me.

8. But he refused; and said unto his master's wife, Behold, my master wotteth not what *is* with me in the house, and he hath committed all that he hath to my hand:

9. *There is* none greater in this house than I; neither hath he kept back anything from me but thee, because thou *art* his wife: how then can I do this great wickedness, and sin against God?

10. And it came to pass, as she spake to Joseph day by day, that he hearkened not unto her, to lie by her, *or* to be with her.

11. And it came to pass about this time, that *Joseph* went into the house to do his business; and *there was* none of the men of the house there within.

12. And she caught him by his garment, saying, Lie with me: and he left his garment in her hand, and fled, and got him out.

2. Et fuit Iehova cum Joseph: itaque fuit vir prospere agens, fuit-que in domo domini sui Ægyptii.

3. Et vidit dominus ejus, quod Iehova esset cum eo: et omnia quæ ipse faciebat, Iehova prosperabat in manu ejus.

4. Et invenit Joseph gratiam in oculis ejus, et ministrabat ei: et præposuit eum domui suæ: et omnia quæ erant ei, dedit in manum ejus.

5. Fuit autem ex eo tempore, quo præposuit eum domui suæ, et omnibus quæ erant ei, benedixit Iehova domui Ægyptii propter Joseph: et fuit benedictio Iehovæ in omnibus, quæ erant ei in domo et in agro.

6. Reliquit ergo omnia sua in manu Joseph, et non cognovit cum eo quicquam, nisi panem quem ipse comedebat: erat autem Joseph pulcher forma, et pulcher aspectu.

7. Et fuit, post hæc levavit uxor domini ejus, oculos suos super Joseph, et dixit, Concumbe mecum.

8. Et renuit, et dixit ad uxorem domini sui, Ecce, dominus meus non cognovit mecum, quid sit in domo: et omnia quæ erant ei, dedit in manum meam.

9. Non est major me in domo hac: et non prohibuit a me quicquam nisi te, eo quod tu sis uxor ejus: et quomodo faciam malum grande hoc, ut peccem contra Deum?

10. Et fuit, quum loqueretur ipsa ad Joseph quotidie, nec ei morem gereret, ut cum ea concumberet, et ut esset cum ea.

11. Fuit inquam, secundum diem hanc ingressus est domum, ut faceret opus suum: et non erat quisquam ex viris domus illic in domo:

12. Tunc apprehendit eum per vestimentum ejus, dicendo, Concumbe mecum. Ergo reliquit vestimentum suum in manu ejus, et fugit, egressusque est foras.

13. And it came to pass, when she saw that he had left his garment in her hand, and was fled forth,

14. That she called unto the men of her house, and spake unto them, saying, See, he hath brought in an Hebrew unto us to mock us; he came in unto me to lie with me, and I cried with a loud voice :

15. And it came to pass, when he heard that I lifted up my voice and cried, that he left his garment with me, and fled, and got him out.

16. And she laid up his garment by her, until his lord came home.

17. And she spake unto him according to these words, saying, The Hebrew servant, which thou hast brought unto us, came in unto me to mock me :

18. And it came to pass, as I lifted up my voice and cried, that he left his garment with me, and fled out.

19. And it came to pass, when his master heard the words of his wife, which she spake unto him, saying, After this manner did thy servant to me; that his wrath was kindled.

20. And Joseph's master took him, and put him into the prison, a place where the king's prisoners *were* bound : and he was there in the prison.

21. But the Lord was with Joseph, and showed him mercy, and gave him favour in the sight of the keeper of the prison.

22. And the keeper of the prison committed to Joseph's hand all the prisoners that *were* in the prison; and whatsoever they did there, he was the doer *of it.*

23. The keeper of the prison looked not to any thing *that was* under his hand; because the Lord was with him, and *that* which he did, the Lord made *it* to prosper.

13. Et fuit, quum vidisset ipsa, quod reliquisset vestimentum suum in manu sua, et fugisset foras :

14. Vocavit viros domus suæ, et dixit ad eos, dicendo, Videte, adduxit nobis virum Hebræum, ut illuderet nobis : ingressus est ad me ut concumberet mecum, et clamavi voce magna.

15. Et fuit, quum audisset ipse, quod elevassem vocem meam et clamassem, reliquit vestimentum suum apud me, et fugit, egressusque est foras.

16. Retinuit autem vestimentum ejus apud se, donec veniret dominus ejus ad domum suam.

17. Et loquuta est ad eum secundum verba ista, dicendo, Ingressus est ad me servus Hebræus, ut illuderet mihi.

18. Et fuit, quum elevassem vocem meam, et clamassem, reliquit vestimentum suum apud me, et fugit foras.

19. Fuit autem, quum audisset dominus ejus verba uxoris suæ, quæ loquuta est ad eum, dicendo, Secundum hæc fecit mihi servus tuus : iratus est furor ejus.

20. Et accepit dominus ipsius Joseph eum, et posuit eum in domo carceris, in loco in quo vincti regis vinciebantur, fuitque illic in domo carceris.

21. Fuit vero Iehova cum Joseph, et inclinavit ad eum misericordiam, et dedit gratiam ejus in oculis principis domus carceris.

22. Et dedit princeps domus carceris in manu Joseph omnes vinctos, qui erant in domo carceris : et omnia quæ faciebant illic, ipse faciebat.

23. Neque princeps domus carceris videbat quicquam *ex iis quæ erant* in manu ejus, eo quod Iehova erat cum eo : et quod ipse faciebat, Iehova secundabat.

1. *And Joseph was brought down.* For the purpose of connecting it with the remaining part of the history, Moses

repeats what he had briefly touched upon, that Joseph had
been sold to Potiphar the Egyptian: he then subjoins that
God was with Joseph, so that he prospered in all things.
For although it often happens that all things proceed with
wicked men according to their wish, whom God nevertheless does not bless with his favour; still the sentiment is
true and the expression of it proper, that it is never well
with men, except so far as the Lord shows himself to be
gracious to them. For he vouchsafes his blessing, for a time,
even to reprobates, with whom he is justly angry, in order
that he may gently invite and even allure them to repentance; and may render them more inexcusable, if they remain obstinate ; meanwhile, he curses their felicity. Therefore, while they think they have reached the height of
fortune, their prosperity, in which they delighted themselves, is turned into ruin. Now whensoever God deprives
men of his blessing, whether they be strangers or of his own
household, they must necessarily decline ; because no good
flows except from Him as the fountain. The world indeed
forms for itself a goddess of fortune, who whirls round the
affairs of men ; or each man adores his own industry ; but
Scripture draws us away from this depraved imagination, and
declares that adversity is a sign of God's absence, but prosperity, a sign of his presence. However, there is not the least
doubt that the peculiar and extraordinary favour of God appeared towards Joseph, so that he was plainly known to be
blessed by God. Moses immediately afterwards adds, that
Joseph *was in the house of his master*, to teach us that he
was not at once elevated to an honourable condition. There
was nothing more desirable than liberty ; but he is reckoned
among the slaves, and lives precariously, holding his life
itself subject to the will of his master. Let us then learn,
even amidst our sufferings, to perceive the grace of God ;
and let it suffice us, when anything severe is to be endured,
to have our cup mingled with some portion of sweetness, lest
we should be ungrateful to God, who, in this manner, declares that he is present with us.

3. *And his master saw.* Here that which has been lately
alluded to more clearly appears, that the grace of God shone

forth in Joseph, in no common or usual manner; since it became thus manifest to a man who was a heathen, and, in this respect, blind. How much more base is our ingratitude, if we do not refer all our prosperous events to God as their author; seeing that Scripture often teaches us, that nothing proceeding from men, whether counsels, or labours, or any means which they can devise, will profit them, except so far as God gives his blessing. And whereas Potiphar, on this account, conceived so much greater regard for Joseph, as to set him over his house; we hence gather, that heathens may be so affected by religion, as to be constrained to ascribe glory to God. However, his ingratitude again betrays itself, when he despises that God whose gifts he estimates so highly in the person of Joseph. He ought at least to have inquired who that God was, that he might conform himself to the worship due to him: but he deems it enough, insomuch as he thinks it will be for his private advantage, to acknowledge that Joseph was divinely directed, in order that he may use his labour with greater profit.

The Lord made all that he did to prosper in his hand. This was a wonderful method of procedure, that the entire blessing by which the Lord was pleased to testify his paternal love towards Joseph, should turn to the gain of the Egyptians. For since Joseph neither sowed nor reaped for himself, he was not at all enriched by his labour. But in this way it was brought about that a proud man, who otherwise might have abused him as a vile and sordid slave, should treat him humanely and liberally. And the Lord often soothes the wicked by such favours, lest when they have suffered any injury, they should turn the fury of their indignation against the pious. We here see how abundantly the grace of God is poured out upon the faithful, since a portion of his kindness flows from them even to the reprobate. We are also taught what an advantage it is to receive the elect children of God to our hospitality, or to join ourselves to those whom the divine favour thus accompanies, that it may diffuse its fragrance to those who are near them. But since it would not greatly profit us to be saturated with those temporal benefits of God, which suffocate and ruin the reprobate; we ought to centre all our wishes on this one point, that God may be propitious to us. Far better was it for Joseph that Potiphar's wealth should be increased for his sake ; than it was for Potiphar to make great gain by Joseph.

6. *And he left all that he had.*[1] Joseph reaped this fruit of the divine love and kindness towards him, that he was cheered by some alleviation of his servitude, at least, for a short time. But a new temptation soon assailed him. For the favour which he had obtained was not only annihilated, but became the cause and origin of a harsher fortune. Joseph was governor over the whole house of Potiphar. From that post of honour he is hurried into prison, in order that he may be soon brought forth to the punishment of death. What then could enter into his mind, but that he was forsaken and abandoned by God, and was continually exposed to new dangers ? He might even imagine that God had declared himself his enemy. This history, therefore, teaches us that the pious have need of peculiar discernment to enable them, with the eyes of faith, to consider those benefits of God by which he mitigates the severity of their crosses. For when he seems to stretch out his hand to them, for the sake of bringing them assistance, the light which had shone forth often vanishes in a moment, and denser darkness follows in its place. But here it is evident, that the Lord, though he often plunges his own people into the waves of adversity, yet does not deceive them ; seeing that, by sometimes moderating their sufferings, he grants them time to breathe. So Joseph, though fallen from his office as governor of the house, was yet never deserted ; nor had that relaxation of his sufferings proved in vain, by which his mind was raised, not to pride, but to the

---

[1] " Potiphar placed Joseph over his house and over all his substance, and the Lord blessed him for the sake of Joseph, in all which he had, in the house and in the field. Joseph had also, after his exaltation, a man who was over his house. A peculiar and characteristic Egyptian trait ! ' Among the objects of tillage and husbandry,' says *Rosellini*, ' which are pourtrayed on the Egyptian tombs, we often see a steward who takes account and makes a registry of the harvest, before it is deposited in the storehouse.' "—*Hengstenberg's Egypt and the Books of Moses*, p. 24. Such incidental testimony to the truth of the sacred narrative, is invaluable, especially at a time when men, wise above what is written, are endeavouring to bring the sacred volume into contempt, by casting a doubt upon the veracity of Moses.—*Ed.*

patient endurance of a new cross.   And truly for this end, God meets with us in our difficulties, that then, with collected strength, as men refreshed, we may be the better prepared for other conflicts.

And Joseph was a goodly person, and well-favoured. Whereas elegance of form was the occasion of great calamity to holy Joseph, let us learn not greatly to desire those graces of person which may conciliate the favour of the world ; but rather let each be content with his own lot.   We see to how many dangers they are exposed, who excel in beauty ; for it is very difficult for such to restrain themselves from all lascivious desires.   Although in Joseph religion so prevailed that he abhorred all impurity ; yet Satan contrived a means of destruction for him, from another quarter, just as he is accustomed to turn the gifts of God into snares whereby to catch souls.   Wherefore we must earnestly ask of God, that amid so many dangers, he would govern us by his Spirit, and preserve those gifts with which he has adorned us, pure from every stain.   When it is said that Potiphar's wife " cast her eyes upon Joseph," the Holy Spirit, by this form of speech, ad-monishes all women, that if they have chastity in their heart, they must guard it by modesty of demeanour.   For, on this account also, they bear a veil upon their heads, that they may restrain themselves from every sinful allurement : not that it is wrong for a woman to look at men; but Moses here describes an impure and dissolute look.   She had often before looked upon Joseph without sin : but now, for the first time, she casts her eyes upon him, and contemplates his beauty more boldly and wantonly than became a modest woman.   Thus we see that the eyes were as torches to inflame the heart to lust.   By which example we are taught that nothing is more easy, than for all our senses to infect our minds with depraved desires, unless we are very earnestly on our guard.   For Satan never ceases diligently to suggest those things which may incite us to sin.   The senses both readily embrace the occasion of sin which is presented to them, and also eagerly and quickly convey it to the mind.   Wherefore let every one endeavour sedulously to govern his eyes, and his ears, and the other members of his body, unless he wishes to open so many doors to Satan, into the innermost affections of his heart : and especially as the sense of the eyes is the most tender, no common care must be used in putting them under restraint.

7. *Lie with me.*[1] Moses only briefly touches upon the chief points, and the sum of the things he relates. For there is no doubt that this impure woman endeavoured, by various arts, to allure the pious youth, and that she insinuated herself by indirect blandishments, before she broke forth to such a shameless kind of license. But Moses, omitting other things, shows that she had been pushed so far by base lust, as not to shrink from openly soliciting a connection with Joseph. Now as this filthiness is a signal proof that carnal lust acts from blind and furious impulses ; so, in the person of Joseph, an admirable example of fidelity and continence is set before us. His fidelity and integrity appear in this, that he acknowledges himself to be the more strictly bound, the greater the power with which he is entrusted. Ingenuous and courageous men have this property, that the more is confided to them, the less they can bear to deceive : but it is a rare virtue for those who have the power of doing injury to cultivate honesty gratuitously. Wherefore Joseph is not undeservedly commended by Moses, for regarding the authority with which he was invested by his master, as a bridle to restrain him from transgressing the bounds of duty. Besides, he gives also a proof of his gratitude, in bringing forward the benefits received from his master, as a reason why he should not subject him to any disgrace. And truly hence arises at this day such confusion everywhere, that men are half brutal, because this sacred bond of mutual society is broken. All, indeed, confess, that

---

[1] " How great the corruption of manners with reference to the marriage relation was among the Egyptians, appears from *Herodotus*, whose account *Larcher* has compared with the one under consideration. The wife of one of the oldest kings was untrue to him. It was long before a woman could be found who was faithful to her husband ; and when one was, at last, found, the king took her without hesitation to himself. From such a state of morals the Biblical narrative can easily be conceived to be natural. The evidence of the monuments is also not very favourable to the Egyptian women. Thus they are represented as addicted to excess in drinking wine, as even becoming so much intoxicated, as to be unable to stand or walk alone, or to carry their liquor discreetly."—*Egypt and the Books of Moses*, p. 25.—*Ed.*

if they have received any benefit from another, they are under obligation to him : one even reproaches another for his ingratitude; but there are few who sincerely follow the example of Joseph. Lest, however, he should seem to be restrained only by a regard to man, he also declares that the act would be offensive to God. And, indeed, nothing is more powerful to overcome temptation than the fear of God. But he designedly commends the generosity of his master, in order that the wicked woman may desist from her abandoned purpose. To the same point is the objection which he mentions, *Neither hath he kept anything back from me but thee, because thou art his wife.* Why does he say this, except that, by recalling the religious obligation of marriage, he may wound the corrupt mind of the woman, and may cure her of her insane passion ? Therefore he not only strenuously strives to liberate himself from her wicked allurements ; but, lest her lusts should prove indomitable, he proposes to her the best remedy. And we may know that the sanctity of marriage is here commended to us in the history of Joseph, whereby the Lord would declare himself to be the maintainer of matrimonial fidelity, so that none who violate another's bed should escape his vengeance. For he is a surety between the man and his wife, and requires mutual chastity from each. Whence it follows that, besides the injury inflicted upon man, God himself is grievously wronged.

10. *As she spake to Joseph day by day.* The constancy of Joseph is commended ; from which it appears that a real fear of God reigned in his mind. Whence it came to pass that he not only repelled one attack, but stood forth, to the last, the conqueror of all temptations. We know how easy it is to fall when Satan tempts us through another: because we seem exempt from blame, if he who induces us to commit the crime, bears a part of it.[1] Holy Joseph, therefore,

[1] Scimus quam lubricus sit lapsus, dum aliunde nobis flabella suscitat Satan: quia videmur culpâ exempti, si ejus partem sustinet qui nos ad flagitium inducit. The French translation is, Nous savons combien il est aisé de tomber, quand Satan nous suscite des soufflets d'ailleurs : car il nous semble que nous sommes exempts de la faute, si celuy qui nous a induit à mal en soustient une partie. The sentiment of the passage seems loosely expressed, and certainly required some limitation. The old English translator omits it, as he does many others, entirely.—*Ed.*

must have been endowed with the extraordinary power of
the Spirit, seeing that he stood invincible to the last,
against all the allurements of the impious woman. So
much the more detestable is the wickedness of her, who is
neither corrected by time, nor restrained by many repulses.
When she sees a stranger, and one who had been sold as a
slave, so discreet and so faithful to his master, when she is
also sacredly admonished by him not to provoke the anger
of God, how indomitable is that lust which gives no place to
shame. Now, because we here see into what evils persons
will rush, when regard to propriety is extinguished by carnal
intemperance, we must entreat the Lord that he will not
suffer the light of his Spirit to be quenched within us.

11. *And it came to pass about this time.* That is, in the
process of time, seeing she will not desist from soliciting holy
Joseph, it happens at length, that she adds force to blandishments. Now, Moses here describes the crisis[1] of the
combat. Joseph had already exhibited a noble and memorable example of constancy; because, as a youth, so often
tempted, through a constant succession of many days, he
had preserved the even tenor of his way; and at that age,
to which pardon is wont to be granted, if it break forth into
intemperance, he was more moderate than almost any old
man. But now when the woman openly raves, and her love
is turned into fury, the more arduous the contest has become, the more worthy of praise is his magnanimity, which
remains inflexible against this assault. Joseph saw that he
must incur the danger of losing both his character and his
life : he chose to sacrifice his character, and was prepared
to relinquish life itself, rather than to be guilty of such
wickedness before God. Seeing the Spirit of God proposes
to us such an example in a youth, what excuse does he
leave for men and women of mature age, if they voluntarily
precipitate themselves into crime, or fall into it by a light
temptation? To this, therefore, we must bend all our efforts,
that regard for God alone, may prevail to subdue all carnal
affections, and even that we may more highly value a good
and upright conscience than the plaudits of the whole world.

[1] *Epitasis,* Greek ἐπίτασις, the point in a play wherein the plot thickens.—*Ed.*

For no one will prove that he heartily loves virtue, but he who, being content with God as his only witness, does not hesitate to submit to any disgrace, rather than decline from the path of duty. And truly, since even among heathens such proverbs as these are current, "that conscience is a thousand witnesses," and that it is "a most beautiful theatre," we should be greatly ashamed of our stupor, unless the tribunal of God stands so conspicuously in our view, as to cast all the perverse judgments of the world into the shade. Therefore, away with those vain pretexts, " I wish to avoid offence," " I am afraid lest men should interpret amiss what I have done aright;" because God does not regard himself as being duly honoured, unless we, ceasing to be anxious about our own reputation, follow wheresoever he alone calls us; not that he wishes us simply to be indifferent to our own reputation, but because it is an indignity, as well as an absurdity, that he should not be preferred to men. Let, then, the faithful, as much as in them lies, endeavour to edify their neighbours by the example of an upright life; and for this end, let them prudently guard against every mark of evil; but if it be necessary to endure the infamy of the world, let them through this temptation also, proceed in the direction of their divine vocation.

He hath brought in an Hebrew unto us. Here we see what desperation can effect. For the wicked woman breaks forth from love into fury. Whence it clearly appears what brutal impulses lust brings with it, when its reins are loosened. Certainly when Satan has once gained the dominion over miserable men, he never ceases to hurry them hither and thither, until he drives them headlong by the spirit of giddiness and madness. We see, also, how he hardens to obstinacy the reprobate, whom he holds fast bound under his power. God, indeed, often inspires the wicked with terror, so that they commit their crimes with trembling. And it is possible that the signs of a guilty conscience appeared in the countenance and in the words of this impure woman: nevertheless, Satan confirms her in that degree of hardness, that she boldly adopts the design to ruin the holy youth; and, at the moment, contrives the fraud by which she may oppress him, though innocent, just as if she had long meditated, at leisure, on his destruction. She had before sought secrecy, that no witness might be present; now she calls her domestics, that, by this kind of prejudging of the case, she may condemn the youth before her husband. Besides, she involves her husband in the accusation, that she may compel him, by a sense of shame, to punish the guiltless. " It is by thy fault, (she says,) that this stranger has been mocking me." What other course does she leave open to her husband, than that he should hasten, with closed eyes, to avenge her, for the sake of purging himself from this charge? Therefore, though all wicked persons are fearful, yet they contract such hardness from their stupor, that no fear hinders them from rushing obstinately forward into every abyss of iniquity, and insolently trampling upon the good and simple. And we must observe this trial of the holy man, in order that we may take care to be clothed with that spirit of fortitude, which not even the iron-hardness of the wicked shall be able to break. Even this other trial was not a light one, that he receives so unworthy a reward of his humanity. He had covered the disgrace of the woman in silence, in order that she might have had opportunity to repent, if she had been curable; he now sees that, by his modesty, he has brought himself into danger of death. We learn, by his not sinking under the trial, that it was his sincere determination to yield himself freely to the service of God. And we must do the same, in order that the ingratitude of men may, by no means, cause us to swerve from our duty.

19. *When his master heard the words of his wife.* Seeing that a colour so probable was given to the transaction, there is no wonder that jealousy, the motions of which are exceedingly vehement and ardent, should so far have prevailed with Potiphar, as to cause him to credit the calumnies of his wife. Yet the levity with which he instantly thrust a servant, whom he had found prudent and honest, into prison, without examining the cause, cannot be excused. He ought certainly to have been less under the influence of his wife. And, therefore, he received the just reward of his too easy folly, by cherishing with honour, a harlot in the place of a wife, and

by almost performing the office of a pander.   This example
is useful to all ; yet husbands especially are taught that they
must use prudence, lest they should be carried rashly hither
and thither, at the will of their wives.   And, truly, since we
everywhere see that they who are too obsequious to their
wives are held up to ridicule ; let us know that the folly of
these men is condemned by the just judgment of God, so
that we may learn to pray for the spirit of gravity and moderation.   There is no doubt that Moses expressly condemns
the rashness of Potiphar, in becoming inflamed against Joseph, as soon as he had heard his wife, and in giving the reins
to his indignation, just as if the guilt of Joseph had been
proved ; for thus all equity is excluded, no just defence is allowed, and finally, the true and accurate investigation of the
cause is utterly rejected.   But it may be asked, How could
the jealousy of Potiphar be excited, since Moses before has
said that he was an eunuch ?[1]   The solution of the question
is easy ; they were accustomed to be called eunuchs in the
East, not only who were so really, but who were satraps and
nobles.   Wherefore, this name is of the same force as if Moses
had said that he was one of the chief men of the court.[2]

20. *And put him into the prison.*   Though Moses does not
state with what degree of severity Joseph was afflicted at the
beginning of his imprisonment, yet we readily gather that he
was not allowed any liberty, but was thrust into some obscure
dungeon.   The authority of Potiphar was paramount ; he
had the keeper of the prison under his power, and at his disposal.   What clemency could be hoped for from a man who
was jealous and carried away with the vehemence of his
anger ?   There is no doubt that what is related of Joseph in

[1] See the comment on chap. xxxvii. 36.
[2] To the whole of this account the sceptical writers of the continent
imagine that they have found an insuperable objection.   *Tuch* remarks,
" The narrator abandons the representation of a distinguished Egyptian,
in whose house *the women live separately,*" &c.   " The error," observes
Hengstenberg, " however, lies here, not on the side of the author, but on
that of his critics.   They are guilty of inadvertently transferring that
which universally prevails in the East to Egypt, which the author avoids,
and thereby exhibits his knowledge of the condition of the Egyptians.
According to the monuments, the women in Egypt lived under far less restraint than in the East, or even in *Greece.*"—*Egypt and the Books of
Moses,* p. 26.—*Ed.*

Psalm cv. 18, " His feet were made fast in fetters, and the iron entered into his soul," had been handed down by tradition from the fathers.   What a reward of innocence! for, according to the flesh, he might ascribe whatever he was suffering to his integrity.   Truly, in this temptation he must have mourned in great perplexity and anxiety before God. And though Moses does not record his prayers, yet, since it is certain that he was not crushed beneath the cross, and did not murmur against it, it is also probable that he was reposing on the hope of Divine help.   And to flee unto God is the only stay which can support us in our afflictions, the only armour which renders us invincible.

21. *But the Lord was with Joseph.*   It appears, from the testimony of the Psalmist just cited, that Joseph's extreme sufferings were not immediately alleviated.   The Lord purposely suffered him to be reduced to extremity, that he might bring him back as from the grave.   We know that as the light of the sun is most clearly seen when we are looking from a dark place; so, in the darkness of our miseries, the grace of God shines more brightly when, beyond expectation, he succours us.   Moreover, Moses says, *the Lord was with Joseph,* because he extended this grace or mercy towards him; whence we may learn, that God, even when he delivers us from unjust violence, or when he assists us in a good cause, is yet induced to do so by his own goodness. For since we are unworthy that he should grant us his help, the cause of its communication must be in himself; seeing that he is merciful.   Certainly if merits, which should lay God under obligation, are to be sought for in men, they would have been found in Joseph; yet Moses declares that he was assisted by the gratuitous favour of God.   This, however, is no obstacle to his having received the reward of his piety, which is perfectly consistent with the gratuitous kindness of God. The manner of exercising this kindness is also added; namely, that the Lord gave him favour with the keeper of the prison. There is, indeed, no doubt that Joseph was acceptable to the keeper for many reasons: for even virtue conciliates favour to itself; and Moses has before shown that the holy man was amiable in many ways; but because it often hap-

pens that the children of God are treated with as great inhumanity as if they were the worst of all men, Moses expressly states that the keeper of the prison, at length, became humane; because his mind, which was not spontaneously disposed to equity, had been divinely inclined to it. Therefore, that the keeper of the prison, having laid aside his cruelty, acted with kindness and gentleness, was a change which proceeded from God, who governs the hearts of men according to his own will. But it is a wonder that the keeper of the prison did not fear lest he should incur the displeasure of Potiphar: and even that Potiphar himself, who without difficulty could have interfered, should yet have suffered a man whom he mortally hated to be thus kindly and liberally treated. It may be answered with truth, that his cruelty had been divinely restrained: but it is also probable that he had suspected, and at length, been made acquainted with the subtle scheme of his wife. Although, however, he might be appeased towards holy Joseph, he was unwilling to acquit him to his own dishonour. Meanwhile the remarkable integrity of Joseph manifests itself in this, that when he is made the guard of the prison, and has the free administration of it, he nevertheless does not attempt to escape, but waits for the proper season of his liberation.

CHAPTER XL.

1. AND it came to pass after these things, *that* the butler of the king of Egypt and *his* baker had offended their lord the king of Egypt.

2. And Pharaoh was wroth against two *of* his officers, against the chief of the butlers, and against the chief of the bakers.

3. And he put them in ward in the house of the captain of the guard, into the prison, the place where Joseph *was* bound.

4. And the captain of the guard charged Joseph with them, and he served them; and they continued a season in ward.

5. And they dreamed a dream both of them, each man his dream in

1. Fuit autem, posthæc peccaverunt pincerna regis Ægypti, et pistor contra dominum suum regem Ægypti.

2. Itaque iratus est Pharao contra utrumque satrapam suum, contra principem pincernarum et contra principem pistorum.

3. Et posuit illos in custodia domus principis satellitum, in domo carceris, in loco in quo Joseph vinctus erat.

4. Et præposuit princeps satellitum ipsum Joseph eis, et ministrabat eis: fuerunt autem per annum in custodia.

5. Porro somniaverunt somnium uterque ipsorum, quisque somnium

one night, each man according to the interpretation of his dream, the butler and the baker of the king of Egypt, which *were* bound in the prison.

6. And Joseph came in unto them in the morning, and looked upon them, and, behold, they *were* sad.

7. And he asked Pharaoh's officers, that *were* with him in the ward of his lord's house, saying, Wherefore look ye *so* sadly to-day?

8. And they said unto him, We have dreamed a dream, and *there is* no interpreter of it. And Joseph said unto them, *Do* not interpretations *belong* to God? tell me *them*, I pray you.

9. And the chief butler told his dream to Joseph, and said to him, In my dream, behold, a vine *was* before me;

10. And in the vine *were* three branches: and it *was* as though it budded, *and* her blossoms shot forth; and the clusters thereof brought forth ripe grapes:

11. And Pharaoh's cup *was* in my hand: and I took the grapes, and pressed them into Pharaoh's cup, and I gave the cup into Pharaoh's hand.

12. And Joseph said unto him, This *is* the interpretation of it : The three branches *are* three days.

13. Yet within three days shall Pharaoh lift up thine head, and restore thee unto thy place; and thou shalt deliver Pharaoh's cup into his hand, after the former manner when thou wast his butler.

14. But think on me when it shall be well with thee, and shew kindness, I pray thee, unto me; and make mention of me unto Pharaoh, and bring me out of this house :

15. For indeed I was stolen away out of the land of the Hebrews; and here also have I done nothing that they should put me into the dungeon.

16. When the chief baker saw that the interpretation was good, he said unto Joseph, I also *was* in my dream, and, behold, *I had* three white baskets on my head.

suum nocte eadem : singuli secundum interpretationem somnii sui, pincerna et pistor qui fuerant regi Ægypti, qui erant vincti in domo carceris.

6. Et venit ad eos Joseph mane, et vidit eos, et ecce, erant tristitia affecti.

7. Tunc interrogavit principes Pharaonis, qui erant secum in custodia domus domini sui, dicendo, Cur facies vestræ sunt afflictæ hodie ?

8. Et dixerunt ad eum, Somnium somniavimus, et qui interpretetur illud, non est. Et dixit ad eos Joseph, Nonne Dei sunt interpretationes ? narrate quæso mihi.

9. Et narravit princeps pincernarum somnium suum ipsi Joseph, et dixit ei, Me somniante, ecce, vitis *erat* coram me.

10. Et in vite erant tres rami, et dum floreret, ascendit flos ejus, et maturuerunt botri ejus in uvas.

11. Et calix Pharaonis erat in manu mea, et accipiebam uvas, et exprimebam eas in calicem Pharaonis, et dabam calicem in manu Pharaonis.

12. Et dixit ei Joseph, Hæc est interpretatio ejus, Tres rami, tres dies sunt.

13. In fine trium dierum elevabit Pharao caput tuum, et redire faciet te ad locum tuum, et dabis calicem Pharaoni in manu ejus secundum consuetudinem primam, quando eras pincerna ejus.

14. Sed memento mihi tecum, quum bene fuerit tibi : et fac quæso mecum misericordiam, et mentionem mei fac Pharaoni, et educere fac me e domo hac:

15. Quia furto auferendo, furto ablatus sum e terra Hebræorum : et etiam hic non feci quicquam, ut ponerent me in carcerem.

16. Et vidit princeps pistorum, quod bene interpretatus esset, et dixit ad Joseph, Etiam me somniante, ecce, tria canistra alba super caput meum.

17. And in the uppermost basket *there was* of all manner of bakemeats for Pharaoh; and the birds did eat them out of the basket upon my head.

18. And Joseph answered and said, This *is* the interpretation thereof: The three baskets *are* three days.

19. Yet within three days shall Pharaoh lift up thy head from off thee, and shall hang thee on a tree; and the birds shall eat thy flesh from off thee.

20. And it came to pass the third day, *which was* Pharaoh's birthday, that he made a feast unto all his servants: and he lifted up the head of the chief butler and of the chief baker among his servants.

21. And he restored the chief butler unto his butlership again; and he gave the cup into Pharaoh's hand:

22. But he hanged the chief baker, as Joseph had interpreted to them.

23. Yet did not the chief butler remember Joseph, but forgat him.

17. Et in canistro superiori erat ex omni cibo Pharaonis, opere pistorio: et aves comedebant illud e canistro, quod erat super caput meum.

18. Et respondit Joseph, et dixit, Hæc est interpretatio ejus, Tria canistra, tres dies sunt.

19. In fine trium dierum auferet Pharao caput tuum a te, et suspendet te in ligno, et comedent aves carnem tuam a te.

20. Et fuit in die tertia, die qua natus fuerat Pharao, fecit convivium omnibus servis suis, et elevavit caput principis pincernarum et caput principis pistorum in medio servorum suorum.

21. Ac redire fecit principem pincernarum ad propinationem suam, et dedit calicem in manu Pharaoni:

22. Principem autem pistorum suspendit, quemadmodum interpretatus fuerat eis Joseph.

23. Et non est recordatus princeps pincernarum ipsius Joseph, sed oblitus est ejus.

1. *And it came to pass after these things.* We have already seen, that when Joseph was in bonds, God cared for him. For whence arose the relaxation afforded him, but from the divine favour? Therefore, God, before he opened the door for his servant's deliverance, entered into the very prison to sustain him with his strength. But a far more illustrious benefit follows; for he is not only liberated from prison, but exalted to the highest degree of honour. In the meantime, the providence of God led the holy man through wonderful and most intricate paths. The butler and baker of the king are cast into the prison; Joseph expounds to them their dreams. Restoration to his office having been promised to the butler, some light of hope beams upon the holy captive; for the butler agreed, after he should have returned to his post, to become the advocate for Joseph's pardon. But, again, that hope was speedily cut off, when the butler failed to speak a word to the king on behalf of the miserable captive. Joseph, therefore, seemed to himself to be buried in perpetual

oblivion, until the Lord again suddenly rekindles the light which had been smothered, and almost extinguished. Thus, when he might have delivered the holy man directly from prison, he chose to lead him around by circuitous paths, the better to prove his patience, and to manifest, by the mode of his deliverance, that he has wonderful methods of working, hidden from our view. He does this that we may learn not to measure, by our own sense, the salvation which he has promised us; but that we may suffer ourselves to be turned hither or thither by his hand, until he shall have performed his work. By the butler and the baker we are not to understand any common person of each rank, but those who presided over the rest; for, soon afterwards, they are called eunuchs or nobles. Ridiculous is the fiction of the trifler Gerundensis, who, according to his manner, asserts that they were made eunuchs for the sake of infamy, because Pharaoh had been enraged against them. They were, in short, two of the chief men of the court. Moses now more clearly declares that the prison was under the authority of Potiphar. Whence we learn what I have before said, that his anger had been mitigated, since without his consent, the jailor could not have acted with such clemency towards Joseph. Even Moses ascribes such a measure of humanity to Potiphar, that he committed the butler and baker to the charge of Joseph. Unless, perhaps, a new successor had been then appointed in Potiphar's place; which, however, is easily refuted from the context, because a little afterwards Moses says that the master of Joseph was the captain of the guard, (ver. 3.) When Moses says they were kept in prison *a season*, some understand by the word, *a whole year;* but in my judgment they are mistaken; it rather denotes a long but uncertain time, as appears from other places.

5. *And they dreamed a dream.* What I have before alluded to respecting dreams must be recalled to memory; namely, that many frivolous things are presented to us, which pass away and are forgotten;[1] some, however, have the force

---

[1] Calvin's words are: " Quæ transeunt per portam corneam."—*Vide Virgil. Æneid. VI. in finem.* This is an obviously mistaken allusion, arising probably from a lapse of memory in Calvin, or in the transcriber

and significance of prophecy. Of this kind were these two dreams, by which God made known the hidden result of a future matter. For unless the mark of a celestial oracle had been engraven upon them, the butler and the baker would not have been in such consternation of mind. I acknowledge, indeed, that men are sometimes vehemently agitated by vain and rashly conceived dreams ; yet their terror and anxiety gradually subsides ; but God had fixed an arrow in the minds of the butler and the baker, which would not suffer them to rest ; and by this means, each was rendered more attentive to the interpretation of his dream. Moses, therefore, expressly declares that it was a presage of something certain.

6. *And Joseph came in unto them in the morning.* As I have lately said, we ought here to behold, with the eyes of faith, the wonderful providence of God. For, although the butler and baker are certainly informed of their own fate ; yet this was not done so much out of regard to them, as in favour of Joseph ; whom God designed, by this method, to make known to the king. Therefore, by a secret instinct he had rendered them sad and astonished, as if he would lead them by the hand to his servant Joseph. It is, however, to be observed, that by a new inspiration of the Spirit, the gift of prophecy, which he had not before possessed, was imparted to him in the prison. When he had previously dreamed himself, he remained, for a while, in suspense and doubt respecting the divine revelation ; but now he is a certain interpreter to others. And though, when he was inquiring into the cause of their sadness, he perhaps did not think of dreams ; yet, from the next verse it appears that he was conscious to himself of having received the gift of the Spirit ; and, in this confidence, he exhorts them to relate the dreams, of which he was about to be the interpreter. *Do not interpretations* (he says) *belong to God ?* Certainly he does not arrogantly transfer to himself what he acknowledges to be peculiar to God ; but according to the means which his vocation

---

of his works. He should have said "portam eburnam." The ancient mythologists distinguished true dreams from false, by representing the former as passing through the "horny gate," (porta cornea,) the latter through the "ivory gate," (porta eburna.)—*Ed.*

supplied, he offers them his service. This must be noted, in order that no one may undesignedly usurp more to himself than he knows that God has granted him. For, on this account, Paul so diligently teaches that the gifts of the Spirit are variously distributed, (1 Cor. xii. 4,) and that God has assigned to each a certain post, in order that no one may act ambitiously, or intrude himself into another's office; but rather that each should keep himself within the bounds of his own calling. Unless this degree of moderation shall prevail, all things will necessarily be thrown into confusion; because the truth of God will be distorted by the foolish temerity of many; peace and concord will be disturbed, and, in short, no good order will be maintained. Let us learn, therefore, that Joseph confidently promised an interpretation of the dreams, because he knew that he was furnished and adorned with this gift by God. The same remark applies to his interrogation respecting the dreams. For he does not attempt to proceed beyond what his own power authorized him to do: he does not, therefore, divine what they had dreamed, but confesses it was hidden from him. The method pursued by Daniel was different, for he was enabled, by a direct revelation, to state and interpret the dream which had entirely escaped the memory of the king of Babylon. (Dan. ii. 28.) He, therefore, relying upon a larger measure of the Spirit, does not hesitate to profess that he can both divine and interpret dreams. But Joseph, to whom the half only of these gifts was imparted, keeps himself within legitimate bounds. Besides, he not only guards himself against presumption; but, by declaring that whatever he has received is from God, he ingenuously testifies that he has nothing from himself. He does not, therefore, boast of his own quickness or clear-sightedness, but wishes only to be known as the servant of God. Let those who excel, follow this rule; lest, by ascribing too much to themselves, (which commonly happens,) they obscure the grace of God. Moreover, this vanity is to be restrained, not only that God alone may be glorified, and may not be robbed of his right; but that prophets, and teachers, and all others who are indued with heavenly grace, may humbly submit themselves to the direction of the Spirit. What

Moses says is also to be observed, that Joseph was concerned at the sadness of those who were with him in prison.   For thus men become softened by their own afflictions, so that they do not despise others who are in misery ; and, in this way, common sufferings generate sympathy.   Wherefore it is not wonderful that God should exercise us with various sorrows ; since nothing is more becoming than humanity towards our brethren, who, being weighed down with trials, lie under contempt.   This humanity, however, must be learned by experience ; because our innate ferocity is more and more inflated by prosperity.

12. *The three branches are three days.*   Joseph does not here offer what he thought to be probable, like some ambiguous conjecturer ; but asserts, by the revelation of the Spirit, the meaning of the dream.   For why does he say, that by the three branches, three *days* rather than *years* are signified, unless because the Spirit of God had suggested it ? Joseph, therefore, proceeds, by a special impulse above nature, to expound the dream ; and by immediately commending himself to the butler, as if he was already restored, shows how certain and indubitable was the truth of his interpretation : as if he had said, " Be convinced that what thou hast heard of me has come from God."   Where also he shows how honourably he thinks of the oracles of God, seeing that he pronounces concerning the future effect with as much confidence as if it had already taken place.   But it may be deemed absurd, that Joseph asks for a reward of his prophecy.   I answer, that he did not speak as one who would set the gift of God to sale : but it came into his mind, that a method of deliverance was now set before him by God, which it was not lawful for him to reject.   Indeed, I do not doubt that a hope of better fortune had been divinely imparted to him.   For God, who, even from his childhood, had twice promised him dominion, did not leave him, amidst so many straits, entirely destitute of all consolation.   Now this opportunity of seeking deliverance was offered to him by none but God.   Wherefore, it is not surprising that Joseph should thus make use of it. With respect to the expression, *Lift up thine head ;* it signifies to raise any one from a low and contemptible condition,

to one of some reputation. Therefore, *"Pharaoh will lift up thine head,"* means, he will bring thee forth from the darkness of the prison, or he will raise thee who art fallen, and restore thee to thy former rank. For I take the word to mean simply *place* or *rank*, and not *basis*.[1]

14. *Show kindness I pray thee unto me.*[2] Although the expression "show kindness" is used among the Hebrews to describe the common exercise of humanity; there is yet no doubt that Joseph spoke simply as his own sad and afflicted condition suggested, for the purpose of inclining the mind of the butler to procure him help. He insists, however, chiefly on this, that he had been thrust into prison for no crime, in order that the butler might not refuse his assistance to an innocent man. For although they who are most wicked find patrons; yet commendation elicited by importunity, which rescues a wicked man from deserved punishment, is in itself an odious and infamous thing. It is, however, probable that Joseph explained his whole cause, so that he fully convinced the butler of his innocence.

16. *When the chief baker saw.*[3] He does not care respecting the skill and fidelity of Joseph as an interpreter; but because Joseph had brought good and useful tidings to his companion, he also desires an interpretation, which he hopes will prove according to his mind. So, many, with ardour and alacrity, desire the word of God, not because they simply wish to be governed by the Lord, and to know what is right, but because they dream of mere enjoyment. When, however, the

---

[1] Pro loco et ordine simpliciter accipio, non autem pro basi. The passage needs explanation. The word רֹאשֶׁ֫ךָ, rendered "thy head," might be rendered "thy *nail*," and some writers have supposed that it should be so translated in this place. The reason given for such a rendering arises from a supposed custom among eastern monarchs of having a large white tablet, on which the name of each officer of state was inscribed, and a *nail* was placed in a hole opposite the name. When the officer offended, the nail was removed from its place, that is, from its *basis* or foundation, and the man's distinction and character were lost.—*Junius in Poli Synopsin.—Ed.*

[2] Fac quæso mecum misericordiam.

[3] "The chief baker, in his dream, carries the wicker baskets with various choice baker's commodities on his head. Similar woven baskets, flat and open, for carrying grapes and other fruits, are found represented on the monuments. The art of baking was carried to a high degree of perfection among the Egyptians."—*Egypt and the Books of Moses,* p. 27.—*Ed.*

doctrine does not correspond with their wishes, they depart sorrowful and wounded. Now, although the explanation of the dream was about to prove unpleasant and severe; yet Joseph, by declaring, without ambiguity, what had been revealed unto him, executed with fidelity the office divinely committed to him. This freedom must be maintained by prophets and teachers, that they may not hesitate, by their teaching, to inflict a wound on those whom God has sentenced to death. All love to be flattered. Hence the majority of teachers, in desiring to yield to the corrupt wishes of the world, adulterate the word of God. Wherefore, no one is a sincere minister of God's word, but he, who despising reproach, and being ready, as often as it may be necessary, to attack various offences, will frame his method of teaching according to the command of God. Joseph would, indeed, have preferred to augur well concerning both; but since it is not in his power to give a prosperous fortune to any one, nothing remains for him but frankly to pronounce whatever he has received from the Lord. So, formerly, although the people chose for themselves prophets who would promise them abundance of wine and oil and corn, while they exclaimed loudly against the holy prophets, because they let fall nothing but threatenings, (for these complaints are related in Micah,) yet it was the duty of the servants of the Lord, who had been sent to denounce vengeance, to proceed with severity, although they brought upon themselves hatred and danger.

19. *Pharaoh shall lift up thy head from off thee.* This phrase (in the original) is ambiguous without some addition; and may be taken in a good or a bad sense; just as we say, " With *regard* to any one," or " With *respect* to him;" here the expression is added " from thee." Yet there seems to be an allusion of this kind, as if Joseph had said, " Pharaoh will lift up thy head, that he may take it off." Now, when Moses relates, that what Joseph had predicted happened to both of them, he proves by this sign that Joseph was a true prophet of God, as it is written in Jeremiah. (xxviii. 9.) For that the prophets sometimes threatened punishments, which God abstained from inflicting, was done for this reason, because to such prophecies a condition was annexed. But when

the Lord speaks positively by his servants, it is necessary
that whatever he predicts should be confirmed by the result.
Therefore, Moses expressly commends in Joseph, his confidence in the heavenly oracle. With regard to what Moses
records, that Pharaoh celebrated his birth-day by a great
feast, we know that this custom has always been in use, not
only among kings, but also among plebeian men. Nor is the
custom to be condemned, if only men would keep the right
end in view ; namely, that of giving thanks unto God by
whom they were created and brought up, and whom they
have found, in innumerable ways, to be a beneficent Father.
But such is the depravity of the world, that it greatly dis-
torts those things which formerly were honestly instituted
by their fathers, into contrary corruptions. Thus, by a vicious
practice, it has become common for nearly all to abandon
themselves to luxury and wantonness on their birth-day. In
short, they keep up the memory of God, as the Author of
their life, in such a manner as if it were their set purpose to
forget Him.

23. *Yet did not the chief butler remember.* This was the
most severe trial of Joseph's patience, as we have before intimated. For since he had obtained an advocate who, without trouble, was able to extricate him from prison, especially
as the opportunity of doing so had been granted to him by
God, he felt a certain assurance of deliverance, and earnestly waited for it every hour. But when he had remained
to the end of the second year in suspense, not only did this
hope vanish, but greater despair than ever rested upon his
mind. Therefore, we are all taught, in his person, that nothing is more improper, than to prescribe the time in which
God shall help us ; since he purposely, for a long season,
keeps his own people in anxious suspense, that, by this very
experiment, they may truly know what it is to trust in Him.
Besides, in this manner he designed openly to claim for himself the glory of Joseph's liberation. For, if liberty had been
granted to him through the entreaty of the butler, it would
have been generally believed that this benefit was from man
and not from God. Moreover, when Moses says, that the
butler was forgetful of Joseph, let it be so understood, that

he did not dare to make any mention of him, lest he should be subjected to reproach, or should be troublesome to the king himself. For it is common with courtiers perfidiously to betray the innocent, and to deliver them to be slain, rather than to offend those of whom they themselves are afraid.

CHAPTER XLI.

1. AND it came to pass at the end of two full years, that Pharaoh dreamed ; and, behold, he stood by the river.

2. And, behold, there came up out of the river seven well-favoured kine, and fat-fleshed ; and they fed in a meadow.

3. And, behold, seven other kine came up after them out of the river, ill-favoured, and lean-fleshed ; and stood by the *other* kine upon the brink of the river.

4. And the ill-favoured and lean-fleshed kine did eat up the seven well-favoured and fat kine. So Pharaoh awoke.

5. And he slept, and dreamed the second time : and, behold, seven ears of corn came up upon one stalk, rank and good.

6. And, behold, seven thin ears, and blasted with the east wind, sprung up after them.

7. And the seven thin ears devoured the seven rank and full ears. And Pharaoh awoke, and, behold, *it was* a dream.

8. And it came to pass in the morning, that his spirit was troubled ; and he sent and called for all the magicians of Egypt, and all the wise men thereof : and Pharaoh told them his dreams ; but *there was* none that could interpret them unto Pharaoh.

9. Then spake the chief butler unto Pharaoh, saying, I do remember my faults this day.

10. Pharaoh was wroth with his servants, and put me in ward in the

1. Verum fuit in fine duorum annorum dierum, Pharao somniavit, et ecce, stabat juxta flumen.

2. Ecce autem e flumine ascendebant septem vaccæ pulchræ aspectu, et pingues carne, et pascebant in carecto.

3. Et ecce, septem vaccæ aliæ ascendebant post eas e flumine, turpes aspectu, et tenues carne, et stabant juxta vaccas, *quæ erant* juxta ripam fluminis.

4. Et comederunt vaccæ turpes aspectu, et tenues carne, septem vaccas pulchras aspectu et pingues : et expergefactus est Pharao.

5. Deinde dormivit, et somniavit secundo, et ecce, septem spicæ ascendebant in culmo uno pingues et pulchræ.

6. Et ecce, septem spicæ tenues, et arefactæ Euro, oriebantur post eas.

7. Et deglutiverunt spicæ tenues, septem spicas pingues et plenas : et expergefactus est Pharao, et ecce somnium.

8. Et fuit, mane consternatus est spiritus ejus : misit igitur, et vocavit omnes magos Ægypti, et omnes sapientes ejus, et narravit Pharao eis somnium suum, et non erat ex eis qui interpretaretur ipsi Pharaoni.

9. Et loquutus est princeps pincernarum ad Pharaonem, dicendo, Peccata mea ego reduco in memoriam hodie.

10. Pharao iratus est contra servos suos, et posuit me in custodiam

captain of the guard's house, *both* me and the chief baker :

11. And we dreamed a dream in one night, I and he: we dreamed each man according to the interpretation of his dream.

12. And *there was* there with us a young man, an Hebrew, servant to the captain of the guard; and we told him, and he interpreted to us our dreams : to each man according to his dream he did interpret.

13. And it came to pass, as he interpreted to us, so it was; me he restored unto mine office, and him he hanged.

14. Then Pharaoh sent and called Joseph, and they brought him hastily out of the dungeon: and he shaved *himself,* and changed his raiment, and came in unto Pharaoh.

15. And Pharaoh said unto Joseph, I have dreamed a dream, and *there is* none that can interpret it: and I have heard say of thee, *that* thou canst understand a dream to interpret it.

16. And Joseph answered Pharaoh, saying, *It is* not in me: God shall give Pharaoh an answer of peace.

17. And Pharaoh said unto Joseph, In my dream, behold, I stood upon the bank of the river :

18. And, behold, there came up out of the river seven kine, fat-fleshed, and well-favoured; and they fed in a meadow.

19. And, behold, seven other kine came up after them, poor, and very ill-favoured, and lean-fleshed, such as I never saw in all the land of Egypt for badness :

20. And the lean and the ill-favoured kine did eat up the first seven fat kine.

21. And when they had eaten them up, it could not be known that they had eaten them ; but they *were* still ill-favoured, as at the beginning. So I awoke.

22. And I saw in my dream, and, behold, seven ears came up in one stalk, full and good :

23. And, behold, seven ears, with-

domus principis satellitum, me et principem pistorum.

11. Et somniavimus somnium nocte eadem, ego et ipse: uterque secundum interpretationem somnii sui somniavimus.

12. Ibi autem erat nobiscum puer Hebræus, servus principis satellitum, et narravimus ei, et interpretatus est nobis somnia nostra, utrique secundum somnium suum interpretatus est.

13. Et fuit, quemadmodum interpretatus est nobis, sic fuit : me redire fecit ad locum meum, et ipsum suspendit.

14. Tunc misit Pharao, et arcessivit Joseph, et celeriter eduxerunt eum e carcere, et totondit *se*, et mutavit vestes suas, et venit ad Pharaonem.

15. Et dixit Pharao ad Joseph, Somnium somniavi, et qui illud interpretetur non est: ego autem audivi de te dici, quod audias somnium ad interpretandum illud.

16. Et respondit Joseph ad Pharaonem, dicendo, Præter me, Deus respondebit in pacem Pharaonis.

17. Tunc loquutus est Pharao ad Joseph, Me somniante ecce, stabam juxta ripam fluminis.

18. Et ecce, e flumine ascendebant septem vaccæ pingues carne, et pulchræ forma, et pascebant in carecto.

19. Ecce vero septem vaccæ aliæ ascendebant post eas tenues, et turpes forma valde, et tenues carne : non vidi similes illis in tota terra Ægypti in turpitudine.

20. Et comederunt vaccæ tenues et turpes, septem vaccas priores pingues.

21. Et venerunt ad interiora earum, et non est cognitum quod venissent ad interiora earum : et aspectus earum turpis, quemadmodum in principio : et expergefactus sum.

22. Vidi præterea dum somniarem, et ecce, septem spicæ ascendebant in culmo uno plenæ et pulchræ.

23. Et ecce item septem spicæ

ered, thin, *and* blasted with the east wind, sprung up after them:

24. And the thin ears devoured the seven good ears. And I told *this* unto the magicians; but *there was* none that could declare *it* to me.

25. And Joseph said unto Pharaoh, The dream of Pharaoh *is* one: God hath shewed Pharaoh what he *is* about to do.

26. The seven good kine *are* seven years; and the seven good ears *are* seven years: the dream *is* one.

27. And the seven thin and ill-favoured kine that came up after them, *are* seven years: and the seven empty ears, blasted with the east wind, shall be seven years of famine.

28. This *is* the thing which I have spoken unto Pharaoh: What God *is* about to do he sheweth unto Pharaoh.

29. Behold, there come seven years of great plenty throughout all the land of Egypt:

30. And there shall arise after them seven years of famine; and all the plenty shall be forgotten in the land of Egypt; and the famine shall consume the land:

31. And the plenty shall not be known in the land by reason of that famine following; for it *shall be* very grievous.

32. And for that the dream was doubled unto Pharaoh twice; *it is* because the thing *is* established by God, and God will shortly bring it to pass.

33. Now therefore let Pharaoh look out a man discreet and wise, and set him over the land of Egypt.

34. Let Pharaoh do *this*, and let him appoint officers over the land, and take up the fifth part of the land of Egypt in the seven plenteous years.

35. And let them gather all the food of those good years that come, and lay up corn under the hand of Pharaoh, and let them keep food in the cities.

36. And that food shall be for store to the land against the seven

parvæ et tenues, percussæ Euro germinabant post eas.

24. Et deglutiverunt spicæ tenues, septem spicas pulchras. Et dixi ad magos, et non fuit qui indicaret mihi.

25. Et dixit Joseph ad Pharaonem, Somnium Pharaonis unum est: quæ Deus facit, indicavit Pharaoni.

26. Septem vaccæ pulchræ, septem anni sunt, et septem spicæ pulchræ, septem anni sunt: somnium idem est.

27. Et septem vaccæ vacuæ et turpes, ascendentes post eas, septem anni sunt: et septem spicæ vacuæ arefactæ Euro, erunt septem anni famis.

28. Hoc est verbum quod loquutus sum ad Pharaonem, quod Deus facit, videre fecit Pharaonem.

29. Ecce, septem anni veniunt abundantiæ magnæ in omni terra Ægypti.

30. Et surgent septem anni famis post eos: et erit in oblivione omnis abundantia in terra Ægypti, et consumet fames terram.

31. Nec cognoscetur abundantia in terra, propter famem ipsam sequentem, quia gravis erit valde.

32. Propterea vero iteratum est somnium ipsi Pharaoni duabus vicibus, quia firma est res a Deo, et festinat Deus facere eam.

33. Nunc igitur provideat Pharao virum prudentem, et sapientem, et constituat illum super terram Ægypti.

34. Faciat Pharao, et præficiat præfectos super terram, et quintam partem sumat a terra Ægypti in septem annis abundantiæ.

35. Et congregent totam annonam horum annorum bonorum qui venient, congregent, inquam, frumentum sub manu Pharaonis, cibum in urbibus, et servent.

36. Et erit cibus in deposito pro terra, pro septem annis famis qui

years of famine, which shall be in the land of Egypt; that the land perish not through the famine.

37. And the thing was good in the eyes of Pharaoh, and in the eyes of all his servants.

38. And Pharaoh said unto his servants, Can we find *such a one* as this *is*, a man in whom the Spirit of God *is?*

39. And Pharaoh said unto Joseph, Forasmuch as God hath shewed thee all this, *there is* none so discreet and wise as thou *art:*

40. Thou shalt be over my house, and according unto thy word shall all my people be ruled: only in the throne will I be greater than thou.

41. And Pharaoh said unto Joseph, See, I have set thee over all the land of Egypt.

42. And Pharaoh took off his ring from his hand, and put it upon Joseph's hand, and arrayed him in vestures of fine linen, and put a gold chain about his neck:

43. And he made him to ride in the second chariot which he had; and they cried before him, Bow the knee: and he made him *ruler* over all the land of Egypt.

44. And Pharaoh said unto Joseph, I *am* Pharaoh, and without thee shall no man lift up his hand or foot in all the land of Egypt.

45. And Pharaoh called Joseph's name Zaphnath-paaneah; and he gave him to wife Asenath, the daughter of Poti-pherah priest of On. And Joseph went out over *all* the land of Egypt.

46. And Joseph *was* thirty years old when he stood before Pharaoh king of Egypt. And Joseph went out from the presence of Pharaoh, and went throughout all the land of Egypt.

47. And in the seven plenteous years the earth brought forth by handfuls.

48. And he gathered up all the food of the seven years, which were in the land of Egypt, and laid up

erunt in terra Ægypti: ita non succidetur terra propter famem.

37. Placuit sermo in oculis Pharaonis, et in oculis omnium servorum ejus.

38. Et dixit Pharao ad servos suos, Num inveniemus talem virum, in quo Spiritus Dei?

39. Dixit ergo Pharao ad Joseph, Postquam cognoscere fecit Deus te totum hoc, non est intelligens et sapiens sicut tu.

40. Tu eris super domum meam, et ad os tuum osculabitur omnis populus meus: tantum solio major ero te.

41. Itaque dixit Pharao ad Joseph, Vide, posui te super totam terram Ægypti.

42. Et removit Pharao annulum suum e manu sua, posuitque illum in manu Joseph: et indui fecit eum vestibus byssinis, et posuit torquem aureum in collo ejus.

43. Et equitare fecit eum in curru secundi, qui erat apud se, clamabantque ante eum, Abrech, (*id est, pater tener,*) et constituit eum super universam terram Ægypti.

44. Dixit ergo Pharao ad Joseph, Ego Pharao, et sine te non levabit quisquam manum suam et pedem suum in tota terra Ægypti.

45. Et vocavit Pharao nomen Joseph, Saphenath-Paneah, (*id est, vir cui abscondita revelata sunt, vel, absconditorum expositor,*) et dedit ei Asenath filiam Poti-pherah principis On in uxorem, et egressus est Joseph super terram Ægypti.

46. Joseph vero erat vir triginta annorum, quando stetit coram Pharaone rege Ægypti: et egressus est Joseph a facie Pharaonis, et transivit per totam terram Ægypti.

47. Et protulit terra septem annis saturitatis ad collectiones.

48. Et congregavit de universis cibis septem annorum, qui fuerunt in terra Ægypti, et posuit cibum in

the food in the cities : the food of the field, which *was* round about every city, laid he up in the same.

49. And Joseph gathered corn as the sand of the sea, very much, until he left numbering : for *it was* without number.

50. And unto Joseph were born two sons before the years of famine came, which Asenath, the daughter of Poti-pherah priest of On, bare unto him.

51. And Joseph called the name of the first-born Manasseh : For God, *said he*, hath made me forget all my toil, and all my father's house.

52. And the name of the second called he Ephraim : For God hath caused me to be fruitful in the land of my affliction.

53. And the seven years of plenteousness that was in the land of Egypt were ended.

54. And the seven years of dearth began to come, according as Joseph had said : and the dearth was in all lands ; but in all the land of Egypt there was bread.

55. And when all the land of Egypt was famished, the people cried to Pharaoh for bread : and Pharaoh said unto all the Egyptians, Go unto Joseph ; what he saith to you, do.

56. And the famine was over all the face of the earth. And Joseph opened all the storehouses, and sold unto the Egyptians ; and the famine waxed sore in the land of Egypt.

57. And all countries came into Egypt to Joseph for to buy *corn ;* because that the famine was *so* sore in all lands.

urbibus : cibum agri civitatis, qui erat in circuitu ejus, posuit in medio ejus.

49. Congregavit itaque Joseph frumentum, tanquam arenam maris multum valde, adeo ut cessaverit numerari, quia non erat numerus.

50. Porro ipsi Joseph nati sunt duo filii antequam veniret annus famis, quos peperit ei Asenath filia Poti-pherah principis On.

51. Et vocavit Joseph nomen primogeniti, Menasseh : quia *dixit*, Oblivisci fecit me Deus omnis laboris mei, et omnis domus patris mei.

52. Nomen autem secundi vocavit Ephraim : quia *dixit*, Crescere fecit me Deus in terra afflictionis meæ.

53. Et finiti sunt septem anni saturitatis, quæ fuit in terra Ægypti.

54. Inceperunt vero septem anni famis venire, quemadmodum dixerat Joseph, fuitque fames in omnibus terris : at in tota terra Ægypti erat panis.

55. Postea esuriit tota terra Ægypti, et clamavit populus ad Pharaonem pro pane : et dixit Pharao omnibus Ægyptiis, Ite ad Joseph, quod dixerit vobis, facietis.

56. Et fames erat in omni superficie terræ : et aperuit Joseph omnia horrea, in quibus erant *frumenta*, et vendidit Ægyptiis : et invaluit fames in terra Ægypti.

57. Et omnes habitatores terræ venerunt in Ægyptum, ut emerent a Joseph : quia invaluerat fames in omni terra.

1. *At the end of two full years.*[1] What anxiety oppressed

---

[1] In fine duorum annorum dierum. " In the account of Pharaoh's dream, we are first struck with the use of the word אָחוּ, (*Achu*,) Nile grass, an Egyptian word for an Egyptian thing." A note on this passage adds, " Our translators have inaccurately rendered it *meadow*, (ver. 2,) the aquatic plants of the Nile, particularly those of the *litus* kind, were so valuable in Egypt, that they were reaped in as regular a harvest as the flax and corn." The writer proceeds, " In the next place, the seven poor and the seven fat kine attract our attention. The symbol of the cow is very peculiar and

the mind of the holy man during this time, each of us may
conjecture from his own feeling ; for we are so tender and
effeminate, that we can scarcely bear to be put off for a short
time.   The Lord exercised his servant not only by a delay of
long continuance, but also by another kind of temptation,
because he took all human grounds of hope away from him :
therefore Moses puts " years of days " for complete and full
years.   That we may better understand the invincible nature of
his fortitude, we must also notice that winding course of divine
providence, of which I have spoken, and by which Joseph was
led about, till he rose into notice with the king.   In the king's
dream, this is worthy to be observed in the first place, that God
sometimes deigns to present his oracles even to unbelieving
and profane men.   It was certainly a singular honour to be
instructed concerning an event yet fourteen years future :
for truly the will of God was manifested to Pharaoh, just as
if he had been taught by the word, except that the interpretation of it was to be sought elsewhere.   And although
God designs his word especially for the Church, yet it ought
not to be deemed absurd that he sometimes admits even
aliens into his school, though for an inferior end.   The doctrine which leads to the hope of eternal life belongs to the
Church ; while the children of this world are only taught,
incidentally, concerning the state of the present life.   If
we observe this distinction, we shall not wonder that some
oracles are common to profane and heathen men, though
the Church possesses the spiritual doctrine of life, as the
treasure of its own inheritance.   That another dream succeeded to the former, arose from two causes ; for God both
designed to rouse the mind of Pharaoh to more diligent
inquiry, and to add more light to a vision which was obscure.   In short, he follows the same course in this dream
which he does in his daily method of procedure ; for he
repeats a second time what he has before delivered, and

exclusively Egyptian. . . . . It is scarcely conceivable that a foreign inventor should have confined himself so closely to the peculiar Egyptian
symbols.   The circumstance that the kine come up out of the Nile, the
fat and also the lean, has reference to the fact that Egypt owes all its
fertility to this stream, and that famine succeeds as soon as it fails."—
Egypt and the Books of Moses, p. 28.—*Ed.*

sometimes inculcates still more frequently, not only that the doctrine may penetrate more deeply into men's hearts, and thus affect them the more ; but also that he may render it more familiar to their minds. That by the second dream God designed to illustrate more fully what was obscure in the first, appears from this, that the figure used was more appropriate to the subject revealed. At first, Pharaoh saw fat cows devoured by lean ones. This did not so clearly prefigure the seven years' abundance, and as many years of want in corn and other seeds, as the vision of the ears of corn did : for the similitude, in the latter case, better agrees with the thing represented.

8. *In the morning his spirit was troubled.* A sting was left in Pharaoh's heart, that he might know that he had to deal with God ; for this anxiety was as an inward seal of the Spirit of God, to give authenticity to the dream ; although Pharaoh deserved to be deprived of the advantage of this revelation, when he resorted to magicians and soothsayers, who were wont to turn the truth of God into a lie.[1] He was convinced by a secret impulse that the dream sent by God portended something important ; but he seeks out imposters, who would darken, by their fallacies, the light which was divinely kindled ; and it is the folly of the human mind to gather to itself leaders and teachers of error. No doubt he believed them to be true prophets ; but because he voluntarily closes his eyes, and hastens into the snare, his false opinion forms no sufficient excuse for him ; otherwise men, by merely shutting their eyes, might have some plausible pretext for mocking God with impunity : and we see that many seek protection for themselves in that gross ignorance

[1] "Pharaoh calls ' all the magicians of Egypt, and all the wise men thereof,' that they might interpret the dream by which he is troubled. . . . . Now, we find in Egyptian antiquity an order of persons, to whom this is entirely appropriate, which is here ascribed to the magicians. The priests had a double office, the practical worship of the gods, and the pursuit of that which in Egypt was accounted as wisdom. The first belonged to the so-called prophets, the second to the holy scribes. These last were the learned men of the nation ; as in the *Pentateuch* they are called *wise men*, so the classical writers named them *sages*. . . . . The interpretation of dreams and also divination belonged to the order of the holy scribes."— *Egypt and the Books of Moses*, p. 29.—*Ed.*

in which they knowingly and purposely involve themselves. Pharaoh, therefore, as far as he was able, deprived himself of the benefit of the prophecy, by seeking for magicians as the interpreters of it. So we see it daily happens that many lose hold of the truth, because they either bring a cloud over themselves by their own indolence, or too eagerly catch at false and spurious inventions. But because the Lord would, at that time, succour the kingdom of Egypt, he drew Pharaoh back, as by main force, from his error.

There was none that could interpret. By this remedy God provided that the dream should not fail. We know what an inflated and impudent race of men these soothsayers were, and how extravagantly they boasted. How did it then happen that they gave the king no answer, seeing they might have trifled in any way whatever with a credulous man, who willingly suffered himself to be deluded? Therefore, that he might desist from inquiry, he is not allowed to find what he had expected in his magicians: and the Lord so strikes dumb the wicked workers of deceit, that they cannot even find a specious explanation of the dreams. Moreover, by this method, the anxiety of the king is sharpened; because he considers that what has escaped the sagacity of the magicians must be something very serious and secret. By which example we are taught, that the Lord provides the best for us, when he removes the incitements of error from those of us who wish to be deceived; and we must regard it as a singular favour, when either false prophets are silenced, or their fatuity is, in any manner, discovered to us. As for the rest, the king might hence easily gather how frivolous and nugatory was the profession of wisdom, in which the Egyptians gloried above all others; for they boasted that they were possessed of the science of divination which ascended above the very heavens. But now, as far as they are concerned, the king is without counsel, and, being disappointed of his hope, is filled with anguish; nevertheless he does not so awake as to shake off his superstition. Thus we see that men, though admonished, remain still in their torpor. Whence we plainly perceive how inexcusable is the obstinacy of the world, which does not desist from following those delusions which are openly condemned as foolishness, from heaven.

9. *Then spake the chief butler.* Although the Lord took pity on Egypt, yet he did it not for the sake of the king, or of the country, but that Joseph might, at length, be brought out of prison; and further, that, in the time of famine, food might be supplied to the Church: for although the produce was stored with no design beyond that of providing for the kingdom of Egypt; yet God chiefly cared for his Church, which he esteemed more highly than ten worlds. Therefore the butler, who had resolved to be silent respecting Joseph, is constrained to speak for the liberation of the holy man. In saying, *I do remember my faults this day,* he is understood by some as confessing the fault of ingratitude, because he had not kept the promise he had given. But the meaning is different; for he could not speak concerning his imprisonment, without interposing a preface of this kind, through fear, lest suspicion should enter into the mind of the king, that his servant thought himself injured; or, should take offence, as if the butler had not been sensible of the benefit conferred upon him. We know how sensitive are the minds of kings; and the courtier had found this out by long experience: therefore he begins by acknowledging that he had been justly cast into prison. Whence it follows that he was indebted to the clemency of the king for restoration to his former state.

14. *Then Pharaoh sent and called Joseph.* We see in the person of a proud king, as in a glass, what necessity can effect. They whose circumstances are happy and prosperous will scarcely condescend to hear those whom they esteem true prophets, still less will they listen to strangers. Wherefore it was necessary that the obstinacy of Pharaoh should be first subdued, in order that he might send for Joseph, and accept him as his master and instructor. The same kind of preparation is also necessary even for the elect; because they never become docile until the pride of the flesh is laid low. Whenever, therefore, we are cast into grievous troubles, which keep us in perplexity and anxiety, let us know that God, in this manner, is accomplishing his design of render-

ing us obedient to himself. When Moses relates that Joseph, before he came into the presence of the king, changed his garments, we may hence conjecture that his clothing was mean. To the same point, what is added respecting his "shaving himself," ought, in my opinion, to be referred: for since Egypt was a nation of effeminate delicacy, it is probable that they, being studious of neatness and elegance, rather nourished their hair than otherwise.[1] But as Joseph put off his squalid raiment, so, that he might have no remaining cause of shame, he is shaved. Let us know, then, that the servant of God lay in filth even to the day of his deliverance.

15. *And Pharaoh said unto Joseph.* We see that Pharaoh offers himself as a disciple to Joseph, being persuaded, by the statement of the butler, that he is a prophet of God. This is, indeed, a constrained humility; but it is expressly recorded, in order that, when the opportunity of learning[2] is afforded us, we may not refuse reverently to honour the gifts of the Spirit. Now, though Joseph, in referring Pharaoh to God, seems to deny that he himself is about to interpret the dream, yet his answer bears on a different point: for, because he knew that he was conversing with a heathen addicted to superstitions, he wishes, above all things, to ascribe to God the glory due to him; as if he had said, I am able to do nothing in this matter, nor will I offer anything as from myself; but God alone shall be the interpreter of his own secret.[3] Should any one object, that

---

[1] This conjecture of Calvin's is erroneous. "*Herodotus* mentions it among the distinguishing peculiarities of the Egyptians, that they commonly were shaved, but in mourning they allowed the beard to grow. The sculptures also agree with this representation. 'So particular,' says *Wilkinson*, 'were they on this point, that to have neglected it was a subject of reproach and ridicule; and whenever they intended to convey the idea of a man of low condition, or a slovenly person, the artists represented him with a beard.'"—*Egypt and the Books of Moses*, p. 30.—*Ed.*

[2] In the Amsterdam edition, it is "facultas dicendi," but in Hengstenberg's it is "facultas discendi;" and as the French version has it "le moyen d'apprendre," there can be no doubt that the later Latin edition is right. —*Ed.*

[3] The force of Joseph's language is remarkable: "Without me, God will answer to the peace of Pharaoh." He thus entirely renounces, in a single word, all the personal honour which the heathen monarch was dis-

whenever God uses the agency of men, their office ought to be referred to in connection with his command: that indeed I acknowledge, but yet so that the whole glory may remain with God; according to the saying of St. Paul, " Neither is he that planteth anything, neither he that watereth." (1 Cor. iii. 7.) Moreover, Joseph not only desires to embue the mind of Pharaoh with some relish for piety, but, by ascribing the gift of interpreting dreams to God alone, confesses that he is destitute of it, until he obtains it from God. Wherefore, let us also learn, from the example of holy Joseph, to honour the grace of God even among unbelievers; and if they shut the door against the entire and full doctrine of piety; we must, at least, endeavour to instil some drops of it into their minds. Let us also reflect on this, that nothing is less toler-able than for men to arrogate to themselves anything as their own; for this is the first step of wisdom, to ascribe nothing to ourselves; but modestly to confess, that whatever in us is worthy of praise, flows only from the fountain of God's grace. It is especially worthy of notice, that as the Spirit of understanding is given to any one from heaven, he will become a proper and faithful interpreter of God.

16. *God shall give Pharaoh an answer of peace.* Joseph added this from the kindly feeling of his heart; for he did not yet comprehend what the nature of the oracle would be. Therefore he could not, in his character as a prophet, pro-mise a successful and desirable issue; but, as it was his duty sincerely to deliver what he received from the Lord, however sad and severe it might prove; so, on the other hand, this liberty presented no obstacle to his wishing a joy-ful issue to the king. Therefore, what is here said to the king concerning peace, is a prayer rather than a prophecy.

17. *In my dream.* This whole narration does not need to be explained, for Pharaoh only repeats what we have be-fore considered, with the addition, that the lean cows, having devoured the fat ones, were rendered nothing better. Where-by God designed to testify, that the dearth would be so great, that the people, instead of being nourished by the

posed to pay him, that God alone may have the glory due unto his name. —*Ed.*

abundance of food gathered together, would be famished, and drag on a miserable existence. Joseph, in answering that the two dreams were one, simply means, that one and the same thing was showed unto Pharaoh by two figures. But before he introduces his interpretation, he maintains that this is not a merely vanishing dream, but a divine oracle: for unless the vision had proceeded from God, it would have been foolish to inquire anxiously what it portended. Pharaoh, therefore, does not here labour in vain in inquiring into the counsel of God. The form of speaking, however, requires to be noticed; because Joseph does not barely say that God will declare beforehand what may happen from some other quarter, but what he himself is about to do. We hence infer, that God does not indolently contemplate the fortuitous issue of things, as most philosophers vainly talk; but that he determines, at his own will, what shall happen. Wherefore, in predicting events, he does not give a response from the tables of fate, as the poets feign concerning their Apollo, whom they regard as a prophet of events which are not in his own power, but declares that whatever shall happen will be his own work. So Isaiah, that he may ascribe to God alone the glory due to him, attributes to him, both the revealing of things future, and the government of all his events, by his own authority. (Is. xlv. 7.) For he cries aloud that God is neither deceived, nor deceives, like the idols; and he declares that God alone is the author of good and evil; understanding by *evil*, adversity. Wherefore, unless we would cast God down from his throne, we must leave to him his power of action, as well as his foreknowledge. And this passage is the more worthy of observation; because, in all ages, many foolish persons have endeavoured to rob God of half his glory, and now (as I have said) the same figment pleases many philosophers; because they think it absurd to ascribe to God whatever is done in the world: as if truly the Scripture had in vain declared, that his "judgments are a great deep." (Ps. xxxvi. 7.) But while they would subject the works of God to the judgment of their own brain, having rejected his word, they prefer giving credit to Plato respecting celestial mysteries. "That God," they say, " has foreknowledge of all

things, does not involve the necessity of their occurrence:"
as if, indeed, we asserted, that bare prescience was the cause
of things, instead of maintaining the connection established
by Moses, that God foreknows things that are future, because he had determined to do them; but they ignorantly
and perversely separate the providence of God from his eternal counsel, and his continual operation.   Above all things,
it is right to be fully persuaded that, whenever the earth
is barren, whether frost, or drought, or hail, or any other
thing, may be the cause of it, the whole result is directed by
the counsel of God.

32. *And for that the dream was doubled.*   Joseph does
not mean to say, that what God may have declared but once,
is mutable: but he would prevent Pharaoh's confidence respecting the event revealed, from being shaken. For since God pronounces nothing but from his own fixed and steadfast purpose, it is enough that he should have spoken once.   But
our dulness and inconstancy cause him to repeat the same
thing the more frequently, in order that what he has certainly decreed, may be fixed in our hearts; otherwise, as
our disposition is variable, so, what we have once heard from
his mouth, is tossed up and down by us, until it entirely
escapes our memory.   Moreover, Joseph not only commemorates the stability of the heavenly decree, but also declares
that what God has determined to do, is near at hand, lest
Pharaoh himself should slumber in the confident expectation
of longer delay.   For though we confess that the judgments
of God are always hanging over our heads, yet unless we
are stimulated by the thought of their speedy approach, we
are but slightly affected with anxiety and fear respecting
them.

33. *Now therefore let Pharaoh look out a man.*   Joseph
does more than he had been asked to do; for he is not
merely the interpreter of the dream; but, as fulfilling the
office of a prophet, he adds instruction and counsel. For
we know that the true and lawful prophets of God do not
barely predict what will happen in future; but propose remedies for impending evils.   Therefore Joseph, after he
had uttered a prophecy of the changes which would take

place in fourteen years, now teaches what ought to be done ; and exhorts Pharaoh to be vigilant in the discharge of his duty. And one of the marks by which God always distinguished his own prophets from false prognosticators, was to endue them with the power of teaching and exhorting, that they might not uselessly predict future events. Let us grant that the predictions of Apollo, and of all the magicians were true, and were not entangled with ambiguous expressions ; yet whither did they tend, but either to drive men headlong in perverse confidence, or to plunge them into despair ? A very different method of prophesying was divinely prescribed, which would form men to piety, would lead them to repentance, and would excite them to prayer when oppressed with fear. Moreover, because the prophecy of which mention is here made, was published only for the temporal advantage of this fleeting life, Joseph proceeds no further than to show the king for what purpose the dream had been sent to him ; as if he had said, " Be not sorry on account of this revelation; accept this advantage from it, that thou mayest succour the poverty of thy kingdom." However, there is no doubt that God guided his tongue, in order that Pharaoh might entrust him with this office. For he does not craftily insinuate himself into the king's favour, nor abuse the gift of revelation to his private gain: but, what had been divinely ordained was brought to its proper issue without his knowledge ; namely, that the famishing house of Jacob should find unexpected sustenance.

35. *Under the hand of Pharaoh.* Whereas prosperity so intoxicates men, that the greater part make no provision for themselves against the future, but absorb the present abundance by intemperance ; Joseph advises the king to take care that the country may have its produce laid up in store. Besides, the common people would also form themselves to habits of frugality, when they understood that this great quantity of corn was not collected in vain by the king, but that a remedy was hereby sought for some unwonted calamity. In short, because luxury generally prevails in prosperity, and wastes the blessings of God, the bridle of authority was necessary. This is the reason why Joseph directed that

garners should be established under the power of the king,
and that corn should be gathered into them. He concludes
at length, that the dream was useful, although at first sight,
it would seem sad and inauspicious: because, immediately
after the wound had been shown, the means of cure were
suggested.

38. *Can we find such a one as this?* We see that necessity is an excellent teacher. If prefects or judges are to be
created, some one is advanced to the honour because he is a
favourite, without consideration of his desert; whence it
happens that they who are most unworthy frequently creep
into office. And although we see political order disturbed
and mankind involved in many inconveniences, because they
who are least suitable, rashly push themselves, by wicked
contrivances, into affairs for which they are not able to manage;
nevertheless, ambition triumphs, and subverts equity. But
necessity extorts a sober judgment. Pharaoh says nothing
but what is naturally engraven on the hearts of all men, that
honours ought to be conferred on none but competent persons,
and such as God has furnished with the necessary qualifications. Experience, however, abundantly teaches, that this
law of nature slips from the memory, whenever men are free
to offend against it with impunity. Therefore the pride of
Pharaoh was wisely so subdued, that he, setting aside ambition, preferred a foreigner just brought out of prison, to all
his courtiers, because he excelled them in virtue. The same
necessity restrained the nobles of the kingdom, so that they
did not each contend, according to their custom, to obtain
the priority of rank for themselves. And although it was
but a compulsory modesty, inasmuch as they were ashamed
to resist the public good; yet there is no doubt, that God
inspired them with fear, so that, by the common consent
of all, Joseph was made president of the whole kingdom. It
is also to be observed that Pharaoh, though he had been infatuated by his soothsayers, nevertheless honours the gifts
of the Spirit in Joseph: because God, indeed, never suffers
man to become so brutalized, as not to feel his power, even
in their darkness. And therefore whatever impious defection may hurry them away, there still abides with them a

remaining sense of Deity. Meanwhile, that knowledge is of little worth, which does not correct a man's former madness; for he despises the God whom with his mouth he proclaims: and has no conception of any other than I know not what confused divinity. This kind of knowledge often enlightens profane men, yet not so as to cause them to repent. Whereby we are admonished to regard any particular principle as of small value, till solid piety springs from it and flourishes.

40. *Thou shalt be over my house.* Not only is Joseph made governor of Egypt, but is adorned also with the insignia of royalty, that all may reverence him, and may obey his command. The royal signet is put upon his finger for the confirmation of decrees. He is clothed in robes of fine linen, which were then a luxury, and were not to be had at any common price. He is placed in the most honourable chariot.[1] It may, however, be asked, whether it was lawful for the holy man to appear with so great pomp? I answer, although such splendour can scarcely ever be free from blame, and therefore frugality in external ornaments is best; yet all kind of splendour in kings and other princes of the world is not to be condemned, provided they neither too earnestly desire it, nor make an ostentatious display of it. Moderation is, indeed, always to be cultivated; but since it was not in Joseph's power to prescribe the mode of investiture, and the royal authority would not have been granted to him without the accustomed pomp of state, he was at liberty to accept more than seemed in itself desirable. If the option be given to the servants of God, nothing is safer for them, than to cut off whatever they can of outward splendour. And where

---

[1] Of the marks of distinction conferred by Pharaoh upon Joseph, mentioned in verses 42 and 43 of this chapter; the first is the signet-ring which was common to the nations of the East as well as to Egypt. The next is the " vesture of fine linen," or *byssus,* which was a peculiarly Egyptian token of honour. The third is the gold chain, or the necklace of gold, " of which the Egyptian monuments afford abundant explanation." Modern objectors to the Mosaic account pretend that all the ornaments here mentioned belong to a later date. But such remarks, as Hengstenberg observes, " have interest only as they show how far the investigations of the rationalists, in reference to the Pentateuch, fall short of the present advanced state of knowledge respecting Egyptian antiquity."—*Ed.*

it is necessary for them to accommodate themselves to public custom, they must beware of all ostentation and vanity.
With respect to the explanation of the words; whereas we
render them, " At thy mouth all the people shall *kiss*,"[1] others
prefer to read, " shall be *armed ;*" others, " shall be fed at thy
will or commandment ;" but as the proper signification of the
verb נשק (*nashak*) is to kiss, I do not see why interpreters
should twist it to another sense.   Yet I do not think that
here any special token of reverence is intended; but the
phrase rather seems to be metaphorical, to the effect that
the people should cordially receive and obediently embrace
whatever might proceed from the mouth of Joseph : as if
Pharaoh had said, " Whatever he may command, it is my
will that the people shall receive with one consent, as if all
should kiss him."   " The second chariot," is read by the
Hebrews in construction, for the chariot of the viceroy, who
holds the second place from the king.   The sense, however,
is clear, that Joseph has the precedence of all the nobles of
Egypt.

There are various opinions about the meaning of the
word אברך, (*abraik.*)   They who explain it by " tender
father," because Joseph, being yet in tender years, was endowed with the prudence and gravity of old age, seem to me
to bring something from afar to correspond with their own
fancy.   They who render it " the father of the king," as if the
word were compounded of the Hebrew noun אב, (*ab,*) and the
Arabic רך, (*rak,*) have little more colour for their interpretation.   If, indeed, the word be Hebrew, the meaning preferred by others, " Bow the knee," seems to me more probable.
But because I rather suppose that Egyptian terms are referred to by Moses, both in this place and shortly afterwards, I
advise the readers not to distort them in vain.   And truly
those interpreters are ridiculously subtle, who suppose that
a Hebrew name was given him by an Egyptian king, which
they render either " the Redeemer of the world," or " the Ex-

---

[1] Osculabitur totus populus ad os tuum.   The English version is, " According unto thy word shall all my people be ruled :" which is a free
translation, bearing, according to Calvin's explanation, the true sense of
the original.   The margin of our Bible gives " be armed," or, " kiss," instead of the words " be ruled."—*Ed.*

pounder of mysteries."[1] I prefer following the Greek interpreters, who, by leaving both words untouched, sufficiently prove that they thought them to be of a foreign language. That the father-in-law of Joseph was, as is commonly believed, a *priest*, is what I cannot refute, though I can scarcely be induced to believe it. Therefore, since כהן (*cohen*) signifies a *prince* as well as a *priest*, it seems to me probable that he was one of the nobles of the court, who might also be the satrap or prefect of the city of On.[2]

46. *And Joseph was thirty years old.* For two reasons Moses records the age at which Joseph was advanced to the government of the kingdom. First, because it is seldom that old men give themselves up to be governed by the young: whence it may be inferred that it was by the singular providence of God that Joseph governed without being envied, and that reverence and majesty were given him beyond his years. For if there was danger lest Timothy's youth should render him contemptible, Joseph would have been equally exposed to contempt, unless authority had been divinely procured for him. And although he could not have obtained this authority by his own industry, yet it is probable that the extraordinary virtues with which God had endowed him,

---

[1] This is the rendering given of the name *Zaphnath-paneah* by Jerome, and by the Chaldee Paraphrast respectively. The reader may consult Rivetus in his Exercitation clviii., Gesenius's Lexicon, and the Commentaries of Bush and Dr. A. Clarke.—*Ed.*

[2] That the word כהן (*cohen*) generally signifies *priest*, is not to be disputed. Gesenius earnestly contends that this is its *invariable* meaning; but to establish his point, he is obliged to regard some as priests who were not of the tribe of Levi. This seems conclusive against him; for there is no room for doubt that none were, or could be, priests who sprang from any other tribe. Yet so much, perhaps, ought to be conceded to the primary meaning of the word, that it should be translated priest, wherever the sense of the passage does not require another interpretation. Such a rule would determine its meaning in this passage. The following remarks of Hengstenberg deserve attention. " According to chapter xli. 45, Pharaoh gives to Joseph, Asenath, the daughter of Potiphera, the priest of On, in marriage. This name (which means he who belongs to the sun) is very common on the Egyptian monuments, and is especially appropriate for the Priest of On, or Heliopolis (the city of the sun). Since Pharaoh evidently intended, by this act, to establish the power bestowed on Joseph upon a firm basis, it is implied in this account; first, that Egyptian High Priests occupied a very important position; and, secondly, that among them the High Priest of On was the most distinguished. Both these points are confirmed by history."—*See Egypt and the Books of Moses*, p. 32.—*Ed.*

availed not a little to increase and confirm it. A second reason for noting his age is, that the reader may reflect on the long duration of the sufferings with which he had been, in various ways, afflicted. And however humane his treatment might have been ; still, thirteen years of exile, which had prevented his return to his father's house, not merely by the bond of servitude, but also by imprisonment, would prove a most grievous trial. Therefore, it was only after he had been proved by long endurance, that he was advanced to a better state. Moses then subjoins, that he discharged his duties with diligence and with most punctual fidelity ; for the circuit taken by him, which is here mentioned, was a proof of no common industry. He might, indeed, have appointed messengers, on whose shoulders he could have laid the greater part of the labour and trouble ; but because he knew himself to be divinely called to the work, as one who had to render an account to the divine tribunal, he refused no part of the burden. And Moses, in a few words, praises his incredible prudence, in having quickly found out the best method of preserving the corn. For it was an arduous task to erect storehouses in every city, which should contain the entire produce of one year, and a fifth part more.[1] This arrangement was also not less a proof of sagacity, in providing that the inhabitants of any given region should not have to seek food at a distance. Immediately afterwards his integrity is mentioned, which was equally deserving of praise ; because in the immense accumulation which was made, he abstained from all self-indulgence, just as if some humble office only, had been assigned to him. But it is to the praise of both these virtues that, after he has collected immense heaps, he remits nothing of his wonted diligence, until he has accomplished all the duties of the office which he had undertaken. The ancient proverb

[1] " The labours of Joseph in building storehouses are placed vividly before us in the paintings upon the monuments, which show how common the storehouse was in ancient Egypt. In a tomb at *Elethya*, a man is represented whose business it evidently was to take account of the number of bushels which another man, acting under him, measures. . . . Then follows the transportation of the grain. From the measurer, others take it and carry it into the storehouses."—*Egypt and the Books of Moses*, p. 36. —*Ed.*

says, " Satiety produces disgust," and in the same manner
abundance is commonly the mother of idleness. Whence,
therefore, is it, that the diligence of Joseph holds on its even
course, and does not become remiss at the sight of present
abundance, except because he prudently considers, that, however great the plenty might be, seven years of famine would
swallow it all up ? He manifested also his fidelity, and his
extraordinary care for the public safety, in this, that he did
not become weary by the assiduous labour of seven years,
nor did he ever rest till he had made provision for the seven
years which still remained.

50. *And unto Joseph were born two sons.* Although the
names which Joseph gave his sons in consequence of the
issue of his affairs, breathe somewhat of piety, because in them
he celebrates the kindness of God : yet the oblivion of his
father's house, which, he says, had been brought upon him,
can scarcely be altogether excused. It was a pious and holy
motive to gratitude, that God had caused him to " forget"
all his former miseries ; but no honour ought to have been
so highly valued, as to displace from his mind the desire and
the remembrance of his father's house. Granted that he is
Viceroy of Egypt, yet his condition is unhappy, as long as he
is an exile from the Church. Some, in order to exculpate
the holy man, explain the passage as meaning that he so
rejoiced in the present favour of God, as to make him afterwards forgetful of the injuries inflicted upon him by his brethren ; but this (in my judgment) is far too forced. And
truly, we must not anxiously labour to excuse the sin of
Joseph ; but rather, I think, we are admonished how greatly
we ought to be on our guard against the attractions of the
world, lest our minds should be unduly gratified by them.
Behold Joseph, although he purely worships God, is yet so
captivated by the sweetness of honour, and has his mind so
clouded, that he becomes indifferent to his father's house,
and pleases himself in Egypt. But this was almost to wander from the fold of God. It was, indeed, a becoming
modesty, that from a desire of proclaiming the Divine goodness towards him, he was not ashamed to perpetuate a memorial of his depressed condition in the names of his sons.

They who are raised on high, from an obscure and ignoble position, desire to extinguish the knowledge of their origin, because they deem it disgraceful to themselves. Joseph, however, regarded the commendation of Divine grace more highly than an ostentatious future nobility.

53. *And the seven years....were ended.* Already the former unwonted fertility, which showed Joseph to have been a true prophet, had procured for him a name and reputation; and in this way the Egyptians had been restrained from raising any tumult against him. Nevertheless, it is wonderful that a people so proud should have borne, in the time of prosperity, the rule of a foreigner. But the famine which followed proved a more sharp and severe curb for the subjugation of their lofty and ferocious spirits, in order that they might be brought into subjection to authority. When, however, Moses says that there was corn in all the land of Egypt, while the neighbouring regions were suffering from hunger, he seems to intimate that wheat had also been laid up by private persons. And, indeed, (as we have said elsewhere,) it was impossible but the rumour of the approaching famine would be spread abroad, and would everywhere infuse fears and solicitude, so that each person would make some provision for himself. Nevertheless, however provident each might be, what they had preserved would, in a short time, be consumed. Whence it appeared with what skill and prudence Joseph had perceived from the beginning, that Egypt would not be safe, unless provisions were publicly gathered together under the hand of the king.

55. *Go unto Joseph.* It is by no means unusual for kings, while their subjects are oppressed by extreme sufferings, to give themselves up to pleasures. But Moses here means something else; for Pharaoh does not exonerate himself from the trouble of distributing corn, because he wishes to enjoy a repose free from all inconvenience; but because he has such confidence in holy Joseph, that he willingly leaves all things to him, and does not allow him to be disturbed in the discharge of the office which he had undertaken.

CHAPTER XLII.

1. Now when Jacob saw that there was corn in Egypt, Jacob said unto his sons, Why do ye look one upon another?

2. And he said, Behold, I have heard that there is corn in Egypt: get you down thither, and buy for us from thence; that we may live, and not die.

3. And Joseph's ten brethren went down to buy corn in Egypt.

4. But Benjamin, Joseph's brother, Jacob sent not with his brethren: for he said, Lest peradventure mischief befall him.

5. And the sons of Israel came to buy *corn* among those that came: for the famine was in the land of Canaan.

6. And Joseph *was* the governor over the land, *and* he *it was* that sold to all the people of the land: and Joseph's brethren came, and bowed down themselves before him *with* their faces to the earth.

7. And Joseph saw his brethren, and he knew them, but made himself strange unto them, and spake roughly unto them; and he said unto them, Whence come ye? And they said, From the land of Canaan to buy food.

8. And Joseph knew his brethren, but they knew not him.

9. And Joseph remembered the dreams which he dreamed of them, and said unto them, Ye *are* spies; to see the nakedness of the land ye are come.

10. And they said unto him, Nay, my lord; but to buy food are thy servants come.

11. We *are* all one man's sons: we *are* true *men*, thy servants are no spies.

12. And he said unto them, Nay, but to see the nakedness of the land ye are come.

13. And they said, Thy servants

1. Quum autem videret Jahacob quod esset frumentum in Ægypto, dixit Jahacob filiis suis, Utquid aspicitis vos?

2. Et dixit, Ecce, audivi quod est frumentum in Ægypto : descendite illuc, et emite nobis inde, et vivemus, nec moriemur.

3. Descenderunt ergo fratres Joseph decem, ut emerent frumentum in Ægypto.

4. (Nam Benjamin fratrem Joseph non misit Jahacob cum fratribus suis : quia dixit, Ne forte accidat ei mors.)

5. Et venerunt filii Israel, ut emerent in medio venientium : erat enim fames in terra Chenaan.

6. Joseph autem erat dominus super terram : ipse vendebat toti populo terræ : venerunt, inquam, fratres Joseph, et incurvaverunt se ei in faciem super terram.

7. Et vidit Joseph fratres suos, et agnovit eos, et alienum se ostendit eis : locutusque est cum eis dura, et dixit eis, Unde venistis? Et dixerunt, De terra Chenaan ad emendum cibum.

8. Agnovit Joseph fratres suos : ipsi autem non agnoverunt eum.

9. Et recordatus est Joseph somniorum, quæ somniaverat de eis, dixitque, Exploratores estis, ad videndum nuditatem terræ venistis.

10. Et dixerunt ad eum, Nequaquam, domine mi : sed servi tui venerunt ad emendum cibum.

11. Omnes nos filii ejusdem viri sumus : veraces sumus, non sunt servi tui exploratores.

12. Et dixit illis, Nequaquam : sed nuditatem terræ venistis ad videndum.

13. Et dixerunt, Duodecim servi

are twelve brethren, the sons of one man in the land of Canaan; and, behold, the youngest *is* this day with our father, and one *is* not.

14. And Joseph said unto them, That *is it* that I spake unto you, saying, Ye *are* spies.

15. Hereby ye shall be proved: By the life of Pharaoh ye shall not go forth hence, except your youngest brother come hither.

16. Send one of you, and let him fetch your brother, and ye shall be kept in prison, that your words may be proved, whether *there be any* truth in you: or else, by the life of Pharaoh, surely ye *are* spies.

17. And he put them all together into ward three days.

18. And Joseph said unto them the third day, This do, and live; *for* I fear God.

19. If ye *be* true *men*, let one of your brethren be bound in the house of your prison: go ye, carry corn for the famine of your houses:

20. But bring your youngest brother unto me; so shall your words be verified, and ye shall not die. And they did so.

21. And they said one to another, We *are* verily guilty concerning our brother, in that we saw the anguish of his soul, when he besought us, and we would not hear; therefore is this distress come upon us.

22. And Reuben answered them, saying, Spake I not unto you, saying, Do not sin against the child? and ye would not hear; therefore, behold, also his blood is required.

23. And they knew not that Joseph understood *them;* for he spake unto them by an interpreter.

24. And he turned himself about from them, and wept; and returned to them again, and communed with them, and took from them Simeon, and bound him before their eyes.

25. Then Joseph commanded to fill their sacks with corn, and to restore every man's money into his

tui fratres sumus, filii viri ejusdem in terra Chenaan: et ecce, minimus est cum patre nostro hodie, et unus non est.

14. Tunc dixit ad eos Joseph, Hoc est quod locutus sum ad vos, dicendo, Exploratores estis.

15. In hoc probabimini: per vitam Pharaonis, si egressi fueritis hinc, nisi quum venerit frater vester minimus huc.

16. Mittite ex vobis unum, et accipiat fratrem vestrum, vos autem vincti eritis, et probabuntur verba vestra, an veritas sit penes vos: sin minus, per vitam Pharaonis certe exploratores estis.

17. Et congregavit eos in custodiam tribus diebus.

18. Dixit autem eis Joseph die tertio, Hoc facite, et vivetis: Déum ego timeo.

19. Si veraces estis, frater vester unus ligetur in domo custodiæ vestræ: vos autem ite, auferte alimentum ad abigendam famem e domibus vestris.

20. Tunc fratrem vestrum minimum adducetis ad me, et vera cognoscentur (*Heb. verificabuntur*) verba vestra, et non moriemini: et fecerunt ita.

21. Dicebat autem alter alteri, Vere deliquimus contra fratrem nostrum: quia vidimus angustiam animæ ejus dum deprecaretur nos, et non audivimus: idcirco venit super nos angustia hæc.

22. Et respondit Reuben ad eos, dicendo, Nonne dixi vobis, dicendo, Ne peccetis in puerum, et non audistis? et etiam sanguis ejus, ecce, requiritur.

23. Ipsi autem ignorabant, quod audiret Joseph: quia interpres erat inter eos.

24. Et vertit se ab eis, et flevit: postea reversus est ad eos, loquutusque est eis: et accepit ab eis Simhon, ligavitque eum in oculis eorum.

25. Tunc præcepit Joseph, et impleverunt vasa eorum frumento: *præcepit* etiam ut restituerent ar-

sack, and to give them provision for the way: and thus did he unto them.

26. And they laded their asses with the corn, and departed thence.

27. And as one of them opened his sack, to give his ass provender in the inn, he espied his money; for, behold, it *was* in his sack's mouth.

28. And he said unto his brethren, My money is restored; and, lo, *it is* even in my sack: and their heart failed *them*, and they were afraid, saying one to another, What *is* this *that* God hath done unto us?

29. And they came unto Jacob their father ùnto the land of Canaan, and told him all that befell unto them; saying,

30. The man, *who is* the lord of the land, spake roughly to us, and took us for spies of the country.

31. And we said unto him, We *are* true *men;* we are no spies.

32. We *be* twelve brethren, sons of our father: one *is* not, and the youngest *is* this day with our father in the land of Canaan.

33. And the man, the lord of the country, said unto us, Hereby shall I know that ye *are* true *men;* leave one of your brethren *here* with me, and take *food for* the famine of your households, and be gone;

34. And bring your youngest brother unto me: then shall I know that ye *are* no spies, but *that* ye *are* true *men: so* will I deliver you your brother, and ye shall traffick in the land.

35. And it came to pass, as they emptied their sacks, that, behold, every man's bundle of money *was* in his sack: and when *both* they and their father saw the bundles of money, they were afraid.

36. And Jacob their father said unto them, Me have ye bereaved *of my children:* Joseph *is* not, and Simeon *is* not, and ye will take Benjamin *away.* All these things are against me.

37. And Reuben spake unto his

gentum eorum, uniuscujusque in sacco suo, et darent eis escam ad iter : et fecit eis sic.

26. Et tulerunt frumentum suum super asinos suos, et abierunt inde.

27. Aperuit autem unus saccum suum, ut daret pabulum asino suo, in hospitio : et vidit pecuniam suam, et ecce, erat in ore sacci sui.

28. Et dixit fratribus suis, Reddita est pecunia mea, et etiam ecce, est in sacco meo.   Et egressum est cor eorum, et obstupuerunt alter ad alterum, dicendo, Utquid hoc fecit Deus nobis ?

29. Et venerunt ad Jahacob patrem suum in terram Chenaan, et annuntiaverunt ei omnia quæ acciderant eis, dicendo,

30. Loquutus est vir dominus terræ nobiscum dura, et constituit nos tanquam exploratores terræ.

31. Nos vero diximus ad eum, Veraces sumus, non sumus exploratores.

32. Duodecim sumus fratres filii patris nostri : unus non est, et minimus hodie est cum patre nostro in terra Chenaan.

33. Tunc dixit nobis vir dominus terræ, In hoc cognoscam quod veraces estis, Fratrem vestrum unum relinquite mecum, et *ad expellendam* famem domorum vestrarum capite, et ite :

34. Et adducite fratrem vestrum minimum ad me, tunc cognoscam quod non estis exploratores, sed veraces : fratrem vestrum dabo vobis, et in terra negotiabimini.

35. Porro fuit, ipsis evacuantibus saccos suos, ecce, uniuscujusque ligatura pecuniæ suæ erat in sacco suo : et viderunt ligaturas pecuniarum suarum, ipsi, et pater eorum, et timuerunt.

36. Et dixit ad eos Jahacob pater eorum, Me orbastis, Joseph non est, et Simhon non est, et Benjamin capietis : adversum me sunt omnia hæc.

37. Tunc dixit Reuben ad pa-

father, saying, Slay my two sons, if I bring him not to thee: deliver him into my hand, and I will bring him to thee again.

38. And he said, My son shall not go down with you; for his brother is dead, and he is left alone: if mischief befall him by the way in the which ye go, then shall ye bring down my gray hairs with sorrow to the grave.

trem suum, dicendo, Duos filios meos mori facias, nisi reduxero eum ad te: da eum in manum meam, et ego reducam eum ad te.

38. Et dixit, Non descendet filius meus vobiscum, quia frater ejus mortuus est, et ipse solus remansit : et accidet ei mors in via per quam ibitis : et descendere facietis canitiem meam cum mœrore ad sepulcrum.

1. *Now when Jacob saw.* Moses begins, in this chapter, to treat of the occasion which drew Jacob with his whole family into Egypt ; and thus leaves it to us to consider by what hidden and unexpected methods God may perform whatever he has decreed. Though, therefore, the providence of God is in itself a labyrinth ; yet when we connect the issue of things with their beginnings, that admirable method of operation shines clearly in our view, which is not generally acknowledged, only because it is far removed from our observation. Also our own indolence hinders us from perceiving God, with the eyes of faith, as holding the government of the world ; because we either imagine fortune to be the mistress of events, or else, adhering to near and natural causes, we weave them together, and spread them as veils before our eyes. Whereas, therefore, scarcely any more illustrious representation of Divine Providence is to be found than this history furnishes ; let pious readers carefully exercise themselves in meditation upon it, in order that they may acknowledge those things which, in appearance, are fortuitous, to be directed by the hand of God.

Why do ye look one upon another ? Men are said to look one upon another, when each is waiting for the other, and, for want of counsel, no one dares to attempt anything. Jacob, therefore, censures this inactivity of his sons, because none of them endeavours to provide for the present necessity. Moses also says that they went into Egypt at the command of their father, and even without Benjamin ; by which he intimates that filial reverence at that time was great ; because envy of their brother did not prevent them from leaving their wives and children, and undertaking a long journey. He also adds, that they came in the midst of a great crowd of people; which enhances the fame of Joseph; who, while supplying food for all Egypt, and dispensing it by measure, till the end of the drought, could also afford assistance to neighbouring nations.

6. *And Joseph was the governor*[1] *over the land.* Moses connects the honour of Joseph with his fidelity and diligence. For although he was possessed of supreme authority, he nevertheless submitted to every possible laborious service, just as if he had been a hired servant. From which example we must learn, that as any one excels in honour, he is bound to be the more fully occupied in business; but that they who desire to combine leisure with dignity, utterly pervert the sacred order of God. Let it be, moreover, understood, that the corn was sold by Joseph, not as if he measured it out with his own hands, or himself received the money for it, seeing that it was set to sale in many parts of the kingdom, and he could scarcely have attended to one single store-house: but that the whole of the stores were under his power.

7. *He made himself strange unto them.* It may be asked for what purpose Joseph thus tormented his brethren with threats and with terror. For if he was actuated by a sense of the injury received from them, he cannot be acquitted of the desire of revenge. It is, however, probable, that he was impelled neither by anger nor a thirst of vengeance, but that he was induced by two just causes to act as he did. For he both desired to regain his brother Benjamin, and wished to ascertain,—as if by putting them to the torture,—what was in their mind, whether they repented or not; and, in short, what had been their course of life since he had seen them last. For, had he made himself known at the first interview, it was to be feared lest they, keeping their father out of sight, and wishing to cast a vail over the detestable wickedness which they had committed, should only increase it by a new crime. There lurked, also, a not unreasonable suspicion concerning his brother Benjamin, lest they should attempt something perfidious and cruel against him. It

---

[1] השליט (*Hashalit*) " Of the Hebrew Shallet and Shilton, is made in Arabic the name *Sultan*, a title whereby the chief rulers of Egypt and Babylon are still called."—*Ainsworth.*—*Ed.*

was therefore important that they should be more thoroughly
sifted ; so that Joseph, being fully informed of the state
of his father's house, might take his measures according to
circumstances ; and also, that previous to pardon, some
punishment might be inflicted which would lead them more
carefully to reflect upon the atrocity of their crime.   For
whereas he afterwards showed himself to be placable and
humane ; this did not arise from the fact, that his anger
being assuaged, he became, by degrees, inclined to compassion ; but rather, as Moses elsewhere subjoins, that he
sought retirement, because he could " no longer refrain himself;" herein intimating at the same time, that Joseph had *forcibly* repressed his tears so long as he retained a severe aspect;
and, therefore, that he had felt throughout the same affection
of pity towards them.   And it appears that a special impulse
moved him to this whole course of action.   For it was no
common thing, that Joseph, beholding so many authors of
his calamities, was neither angry nor changed in his manner, nor broke out into reproaches ; but was composed both
in his countenance and his speech, as if he had long meditated at leisure, respecting the course he would pursue.   But
it may be inquired again, whether his dissimulation, which
was joined with a falsehood, is not to be blamed ; for we
know how pleasing integrity is to God, and how strictly he
prohibits his own people from deceit and falsehoods.   Whether God governed his servant by some special movement,
to depart without fault, from the common rule of action, I
know not ; seeing that the faithful may sometimes piously
do things which cannot lawfully be drawn into a precedent.
Of this, however, in considering the acts of the holy fathers,
we must always beware ; lest they should lead us away from
that law which the Lord prescribes to all in common.   By
the general command of God, we must all cultivate sincerity.
That Joseph feigned something different from the truth,
affords no pretext to excuse us if we attempt anything of
the same kind.   For, though a liberty granted by privilege
would be pardoned, yet if any one, relying on a private example, does not scruple to subvert the law of God, so as to
give himself license to do what is therein forbidden, he shall

justly suffer the punishment of his audacity. And yet I do not think that we ought to be very anxious to excuse Joseph, because it is probable that he suffered something from human infirmity, which God forgave him ; for by Divine mercy alone could that dissimulation, which in itself was not without fault, escape condemnation.

9. *And Joseph remembered the dreams.* When the boy Joseph had spoken of receiving obeisance, the absurdity of the thing impelled his brethren wickedly to devise his death. Now, although they bow down to him without knowing him, there is yet nothing better for them. Indeed, their only means of safety, is to prostrate themselves at his feet, and to be received by him as suppliants. Meanwhile, their conspiracy, by which they attempted to subvert the celestial decree, lest they should have to bear the yoke, was rendered fruitless. So the Lord forcibly restrains the obstinate, just as wild and refractory horses are wont to be more severely treated, the more they kick and are restive. Wherefore, there is nothing better than meekly to compose the mind to gentleness, that each may take his own lot contentedly, though it be not very splendid. It may, however, seem absurd, that Joseph should, at this time, have recalled his dream to mind, as if it had been forgotten through the lapse of years ; which, indeed, could not be, unless he had lost sight of the promises of God. I answer, nothing is here recorded but what frequently happens to ourselves: for although the word of God may be dwelling in our hearts, yet it does not continually occur to us, but rather is sometimes so smothered that it may seem to be extinct, especially when faith is oppressed by the darkness of affliction. Besides, it is nothing wonderful, if a long series of evils should have buried, in a kind of oblivion, his dreams which indicated prosperity. God had exalted him, by these dreams, to the hope of great and distinguished authority. He is, however, cast into a well not unlike a grave. He is taken hence to be sold as a slave ; he is carried to a distant land ; and, as if slavery would not prove sufficiently severe, he is shut up in prison. And though his misery is in some degree mitigated, when he is released from his iron fetters, yet there was little, if any, pro-

spect of deliverance. I do not, however, think that the hope
entertained by him was entirely destroyed, but that a cloud
passed over it, which deprived him of the light of comfort.
A different kind of temptation followed ; because nothing is
more common than for great and unexpected felicity to in-
toxicate its possessors. And thus it happened, as we have recently read, that a forgetfulness of his father's house stole
over the mind of the holy man. He was not, therefore, so
mindful of his dreams as he ought to have been. Another
excuse may probably be alleged ; that he, at the moment,
compared his dreams with the event. And truly it was no
common virtue to apply what was passing, thus Immediately
for the confirmation of the Divine oracle. For we readily
perceive, that those dreams which so quickly recur to the
memory, had not been obliterated through length of time. So
the disciples remembered the words of the Lord after he had
risen from the dead ; because, by the sight of the fact predicted, their knowledge became more clear; whereas, before,
nothing but transient sparks of it had shined in their hearts.

15. *By the life of Pharaoh.* From this formula of swearing a new question is raised ; for that which is commanded
in the law, that we should swear only by the name of God,
had already been engraven on the hearts of the pious; since
nature dictates that this honour is to be given to God alone,
that men should defer to his judgment, and should make
him the supreme arbiter and vindicator of faith and truth.
If we should say that this was not simply an oath, but a
kind of obtestation, the holy man will be, in some degree,
excusable. He who swears by God wishes him to interpose
in order to inflict punishment on perjury. They who swear
by their life or by their hand, deposit, as it were, what they
deem most valuable, as a pledge of their faithfulness. By
this method the majesty of God is not transferred to mortal
man ; because it is a very different thing to cite him as witness who has the right of taking vengeance, and to assert
by something most dear to us, that what we say is true. So
Moses, when he calls heaven and earth to witness, does not
ascribe deity to them, and thus fabricate a new idol ; but, in
order that higher authority may be given to the law, he de-

clares that there is no part of the world which will not cry out before the tribunal of God, against the ingratitude of the people, if they reject the doctrine of salvation. Notwithstanding, there is, I confess, in this form of swearing which Joseph uses, something deserving of censure; for it was a profane adulation, among the Egyptians, to swear by the life of the king. Just as the Romans swore by the genius of their prince, after they had been reduced to such bondage that they made their Cæsars equal to gods. Certainly this mode of swearing is abhorrent to true piety. Whence it may be perceived that nothing is more difficult to the holy servants of God than to keep themselves so pure, while conversant with the filth of the world, as to contract no spots of defilement from it. Joseph, indeed, was never so infected with the corruptions of the court, but that he remained a pure worshipper of God: nevertheless we see, that in accommodating himself to this depraved custom of speaking, he had received some stain. His repetition of the expression shows, that when any one has once become accustomed to evil, he becomes exceedingly prone to sin again and again. We observe, that they who have once rashly assumed the license of swearing, pour forth an oath every third word, even when speaking of the most frivolous things. So much the greater caution ought we to use, lest any such indulgence should harden us in this wicked custom.

17. *And he put them altogether into ward.* Here, not by words only, as before, but by the act itself, Joseph shows himself severe towards his brethren, when he shuts them all up in prison, as if about to bring them to punishment: and during three days torments them with fear. We said a little while ago, that from this fact no rule for acting severely and rigidly is to be drawn; because it is doubtful whether he acted rightly or otherwise. Again, it is to be feared lest they who plead his example should be far removed from his mildness, and that they should prove to be rather his apes than his true imitators. Meanwhile, it plainly appears what he was aiming at; for he does not mitigate their punishment, as if at the end of three days he was appeased; but he renders them more anxious about the redemption of their

brother, whom he retains as a hostage. Lest, however, immoderate fear should deter them from returning, he promises to act with good faith towards them : and to convince them of that, he declares that he fears God, which expression is worthy of observation. Doubtless he speaks from the inward feeling of his heart, when he declares that he will deal well and truly with them, because he fears God. Therefore the commencement and the fountain of that good and honest conscience, whereby we cultivate fidelity and justice towards men, is the fear of God. There appears indeed some probity in the despisers of God ; but it soon goes off in smoke, unless the depraved affections of the flesh are restrained as with a bridle, by the thought that God is to be feared, because he will be the Judge of the world. For whoever does not think that he must render an account, will never so cultivate integrity as to refrain from pursuing what he supposes will be useful to himself. Wherefore, if we wish to be free from perfidy, craft, cruelty, and all wicked desire of doing injury, we must labour earnestly that religion may flourish among us. For whenever we act with want of sincerity or humanity towards each other, impiety openly betrays itself. For whatever there is of rectitude or justice in the world, Joseph comprised in this short sentence, when he said, that he feared God.

21. *And they said one to another.* This is a remarkable passage, showing that the sons of Jacob, when reduced to the greatest straits, recall to memory a fratricide committed thirteen years previously. Before affliction pressed upon them, they were in a state of torpor. Moses relates that, even lately, they had spoken without agitation of Joseph's death, as if conscious to themselves of no evil. But now they are compelled (so to speak) to enter into their own consciences. We see then, how in adversity, God searches and tries men ; and how, while dissipating all their flattering illusions, he not only pierces their minds with secret fear, but extorts a confession which they would gladly avoid. And this kind of examination is very necessary for us. Wonderful is the hypocrisy of men in covering their evils; and if impunity be allowed, their negligence will be increased two-

fold. Wherefore no remedy remains, except that they who
give themselves up to slumber when the Lord deals gently
with them, should be awakened by afflictions and punishments. Joseph therefore produced some good effect, when
he extorted from his brethren the acknowledgment of their
sin, in which they had securely pleased themselves. And
the Lord had compassion on them, in taking away the
covering with which they had been too long deceived. In
the same manner, while he daily chastises us by the hand of
man, he draws us, as guilty, to his tribunal. Nevertheless
it would profit but little to be tried by adversity, unless he
inwardly touched the heart; for we see how few reflect on
their sins, although admonished by most severe punishments;
certainly no one comes to this state of mind but with reluctance. Wherefore, there is no doubt that God, in order to
lead the sons of Jacob to repentance, impelled them, as well
by the secret instinct of his Spirit as by outward chastisement, to become sensible of that sin which had been too long
concealed. Let the reader also observe, that the sons of
Jacob did not only fix their minds on something which was
close at hand, but considered that divine punishments were
inflicted in various ways upon sinners. And doubtless, in
order to apprehend the divine judgments, we must extend
our views afar. Sometimes indeed God, by inflicting present
punishment on sinners, holds them up for observation as on a
theatre; but often, as if aiming at another object, he takes vengeance on our sins unexpectedly, and from an unseen quarter.
If the sons of Jacob had merely looked for some *present* cause
of their sufferings, they could have done nothing but loudly
complain that they had been injured; and at length despair
would have followed. But while considering how far and
wide the providence of God extends, looking beyond the occasion immediately before their eyes, they ascend to a remote
cause. It is, however, doubtful, whether they say that they
shall be *held guilty* on account of their brother, or for their
brother's sake, or that they will themselves *confess* that they
have sinned: for the Hebrew noun, אשמים, (*ashaimim*,) is
ambiguous, because it sometimes refers to the crime committed, and sometimes to the punishment, as in Latin,

piaculum signifies both the crime and the expiation.   On the whole, it is of little consequence which meaning is preferred, for they acknowledge their sin either in its guilt or its punishment.   But the latter sense appears to me the more simple and genuine, that they are deservedly punished because they had been so cruel to their brother.

In that we saw the anguish of his soul.   They acknowledge that it is by the just judgment of God, that they obtained nothing by their suppliant entreaties, because they themselves had acted so cruelly towards their brother.   Christ had not yet uttered the sentence, " With what measure ye mete, it shall be measured unto you again," (Matt. vii. 2,) but it was a dictate of nature, that they who had been cruel to others, were unworthy of commiseration.   The more heed ought we to take, that we prove not deaf to so many threatenings of Scripture.   Dreadful is that denunciation, " Whoso stoppeth his ears at the cry of the poor, he also shall cry himself, and shall not be heard." (Prov. xxi. 13.)   Therefore while we have time, let us learn to exercise humanity, to sympathize with the miserable, and to stretch out our hand for the sake of giving assistance.   But if at any time it happens that we are treated roughly by men, and our prayers are proudly rejected; then, at least, let the question occur to us, whether we ourselves have in anything acted unkindly towards others; for although it were better to be wise beforehand; it is, nevertheless, some advantage, whenever others proudly despise us, to reflect whether they with whom we have had to deal, have not experienced similar hardships from us.   " Our brother," they say, " entreated us when he was in the last extremity: we rejected his prayers : therefore it is by divine retribution that we can obtain nothing."   By these words they bear witness that the hearts of men are so under Divine government, that they can be inclined to equity, or hardened in inflexible rigour.   Moreover, their cruelty was hateful to God, because, since his goodness is diffused through heaven and earth, and his beneficence is extended not only to men, but even to brute animals, nothing is more contrary to his nature, than that we should cruelly reject those who implore our protection.

22. *And Reuben answered them.* Because he had attempted to deliver Joseph out of the hands of his brethren, in order to restore him in safety to his father, he magnifies their fault, in not having, at that time, listened to any prudent counsel : and I understand his words as conveying a reproof for their too late repentance. Whereas Joseph was not yet satisfied with this confession, but retained Simeon in bonds,[1] and dismissed the rest in suspense and perplexity, this was not done from malevolence, but because he was not certain about the safety of his brother Benjamin, and the state of his father's house. For he might justly fear lest, when they found that their wicked contrivance of putting their brother to death, was discovered, they might again attempt some horrible crime, as desperate men are wont to do ; or, at least, might desert their father, and flee to some other country. Nevertheless the act of Joseph is not to be drawn into a precedent : because it is not always right to be thus austere. We ought also to beware lest the offender be swallowed up by grief, if we are not mild, and disposed to forgiveness. Therefore we must seek the spirit of discretion from heaven, which shall so govern us that we may do nothing by rash impetuosity, or immoderate severity. This, indeed, is to be remembered, that under the stern countenance of Joseph was concealed not only a mild and placid disposition, but the most tender affection.

27. *And as one of them opened his sack.* With what intention Joseph had commanded the price paid for the corn to be secretly deposited in the sacks of his brethren, may easily be conjectured ; for he feared lest his father being already impoverished, would not be able again to buy provisions. The brethren, having found their money, knew not where to seek the cause ; except that, being terrified, they perceived that the hand of God was against them. That they were greatly astonished appears from their not voluntarily return-

---

[1] Ainsworth says of Simeon, " He seemeth by this, to have been the chief procurer of Joseph's trouble. He was by nature bold and fierce, as his fact against the Shechemites doth manifest." If so, this act of Joseph would appear to him, and perhaps to the rest of the brethren, as a special Divine retribution for his cruelty towards Joseph.—*Ed.*

ing to Joseph, in order to prove their own innocence : for the remedy of the evil was at hand, if they had not been utterly blinded.   Wherefore we must ask God to supply us, in doubtful and troubled affairs, not only with fortitude, but also with prudence.   We see also how little can be effected even by a great multitude, unless the Lord preside among them.   The sons of Jacob ought mutually to have exhorted each other, and to have consulted together what was necessary to be done : but there is an end to all deliberation ; no solace nor remedy is suggested.   Even while each sees the rest agitated, they mutually increase each other's trepidation.   Therefore, the society and countenance of men will profit us nothing, unless the Lord strengthen us from heaven.

28. *What is this that God hath done unto us ?*   They do not expostulate with God, as if they thought this danger had come upon them without cause : but, perceiving that God was angry with them in many ways, they deplore their wretchedness.   But why do they not rather turn their thoughts to Joseph ?   For the suspicion was natural, that this had been done by fraud, because he wished to lay new snares for them.   How does it happen, then, that losing sight of man, they set God as an avenger directly before them ?   Truly, because this single thought possessed their minds, that a just reward, and such as their sins deserved, would be given them ; and, from that time, they referred whatever evils happened to the same cause.   Before (as we have said) they were asleep : but from the time that they began to be affected by the lively fear of God's judgment, his providence always presented itself to their view.   So David, when, by the inward suggestion of the Spirit, he has learned that the rod with which he was chastised had been sent from heaven, is not distracted or perplexed, though he sees plainly that the evils have proceeded from another quarter ; but prays to God to heal the wounds which *He* had made. It is no common act of prudence, and is at the same time profitable, whenever any adversity overtakes us, to accustom ourselves to the consideration of the judgments of God.   We see how unbelievers, while they imagine their misfortunes to be accidental, or while they are bent on accusing their enemies,

only exasperate their grief by fretting and raging, and thus cause the anger of God to burn the more against them. But he who, in his affliction, exercises himself in reflecting on his own sins, and sets God before him as his Judge, will humble himself in the divine presence, and will compose his mind to patience by the hope of pardon. Let us, however, remember that the providence of God is not truly acknowledged, except in connection with his justice. For, though the men by whose hand he chastises us are often unjust, yet, in an incomprehensible manner, he executes his judgments through them, against which judgments it is not lawful for us either to reply or to murmur. For sometimes even the reprobate, though they acknowledge themselves to be stricken by the hand of God, yet do not cease to complain against him, as Moses teaches us by the example of Cain. I do not, however, understand that this complaint was made by the sons of Jacob, for the purpose of charging God with tyrannical violence ; but because they, being overcome with fear, inferred from this double punishment that God was highly displeased with them.

29. *And they came unto Jacob their father.* Here is a long repetition of the former history, but it is not superfluous; because Moses wished to show how anxiously they made their excuse to their father for having left Simeon in chains, and how strenuously they pleaded with him, that, for the sake of obtaining Simeon's liberty, he should allow them to take their brother Benjamin : for this was greatly to the purpose. We know what a sharp dart is hunger: and yet, though the only method of relieving their want was to fetch corn out of Egypt, Jacob would rather that he and his family should perish, than allow Benjamin to accompany the rest. What can he mean by thus peremptorily refusing what his sons were compelled by necessity to ask, except to show that he was suspicious of them ? This also more clearly appears from his own words, when he imputes his bereavement to them. For, though their declaration, that Joseph had been torn by a wild beast, had some colour of probability, there still remained in the heart of the holy patriarch a secret wound, arising from suspicion ; because he was fully aware of

their fierce and cruel hatred of the innocent youth. Moreover, it is useful for us to know this; for it appears hence how miserable was the condition of the holy man, whose mind, during thirteen successive years, had been tortured with dire anxiety. Besides, his very silence added greatly to his torment, because he was compelled to conceal the grief he felt. But the chief burden of the evil was the temptation which oppressed him, that the promise of God might prove illusory and vain. For he had no hope except from the promised seed; but he seemed to be bringing up devils at home, from whom a blessing was no more to be expected than life from death. He thought Joseph to be dead, Benjamin alone remained to him uncorrupted: how could the salvation of the world proceed from such a vicious offspring? He must, therefore, have been endowed with great constancy, seeing he did not cease to rely upon God; and being certainly persuaded that he cherished in his house the Church, of which scarcely any appearance was left, he bore with his sons till they should repent. Let the faithful now apply this example to themselves, lest their minds should give way at the horrible devastation which is almost everywhere perceived.

35. *As they emptied their sacks.* Here, again, it appears how greatly they had been alarmed in their journey, seeing that each had not at least examined his sack, after money had been found in one. But these things are written to show that, as soon as men are smitten with fear, they have no particle of wisdom and of soundness of mind, until God tranquillizes them. Moreover, Joseph did not act with sufficient consideration, in that he occasioned very great grief to his father, whose poverty he really intended to relieve. Whence we learn that even the most prudent are not always so careful, but that something may flow from their acts which they do not wish.

36. *Me have ye bereaved.* Jacob does not, indeed, openly accuse his sons of the crime of their brother's murder; yet he is angry as if, two of his sons being already taken away, they were hastening to destroy the third. For he says that all these evils were falling on himself alone; because he does not think that they were affected as they ought to be, nor

shared his grief with him, but were carelessly making light of the destruction of their brethren, as if they had no interest in their lives. It seems, however, exceedingly barbarous that Reuben should offer his two sons to his father to be slain, if he did not bring Benjamin back. Jacob might, indeed, slay his own grandchildren : what comfort, then, could he take in acting cruelly to his own bowels ? But this is what I before alluded to, that they were suspected of having dealt perfidiously towards Joseph ; for which reason Reuben deemed it necessary to assuage his father's fear, by such a vehement protestation ; and to give this pledge, that he and his brethren were designing nothing wicked against Benjamin.

38. *My son shall not go down with you.* Again we see, as in a lively picture, with what sorrow holy Jacob had been oppressed. He sees his whole family famishing : he would rather be torn away from life than from his son: whence we gather that he was not iron-hearted: but his patience is the more deserving of praise, because he contended with the infirmity of the flesh, and did not sink under it. And although Moses does not give a rhetorical amplification to his language, we nevertheless easily perceive that he was overcome with excessive grief, when he thus complained to his sons, " You are too cruel to your father, in taking away from me a third son, after I have been plundered of first one and then another."

CHAPTER XLIII.

1. AND the famine *was* sore in the land.

2. And it came to pass, when they had eaten up the corn which they had brought out of Egypt, their father said unto them, Go again, buy us a little food.

3. And Judah spake unto him, saying, The man did solemnly protest unto us, saying, Ye shall not see my face, except your brother *be* with you.

4. If thou wilt send our brother with us, we will go down and buy thee food :

1. Porro fames gravis erat in terra.

2. Itaque quum finissent edere alimentum, quod attulerant ex Ægypto, dixit ad eos pater eorum, Revertimini, emite nobis pusillum cibi.

3. Et dixit ad eum Jehudah, dicendo, Contestando contestatus est nos vir, dicendo, Non videbitis faciem meam, nisi fuerit frater vester vobiscum.

4. Si miseris fratrem nostrum nobiscum, descendemus, et ememus tibi cibum.

5. But if thou wilt not send *him*, we will not go down: for the man said unto us, Ye shall not see my face, except your brother *be* with you.

6. And Israel said, Wherefore dealt ye *so* ill with me, *as* to tell the man whether ye had yet a brother?

7. And they said, The man asked us straitly of our state, and of our kindred, saying, *Is* your father yet alive? have ye *another* brother? and we told him according to the tenor of these words. Could we certainly know that he would say, Bring your brother down?

8. And Judah said unto Israel his father, Send the lad with me, and we will arise and go; that we may live, and not die, both we, and thou, *and* also our little ones.

9. I will be surety for him; of my hand shalt thou require him: if I bring him not unto thee, and set him before thee, then let me bear the blame for ever:

10. For except we had lingered, surely now we had returned this second time.

11. And their father Israel said unto them, If *it must be* so now, do this; Take of the best fruits in the land in your vessels, and carry down the man a present, a little balm, and a little honey, spices and myrrh, nuts and almonds.

12. And take double money in your hand: and the money that was brought again in the mouth of your sacks, carry *it* again in your hand; peradventure it *was* an oversight.

13. Take also your brother, and arise, go again unto the man:

14. And God Almighty give you mercy before the man, that he may send away your other brother, and Benjamin. If I be bereaved *of my children*, I am bereaved.

15. And the men took that present, and they took double money in their hand, and Benjamin; and rose up, and went down to Egypt, and stood before Joseph.

16. And when Joseph saw Ben-

5. Quod si non miseris, non descendemus: vir enim ille dixit nobis, Non videbitis faciem meam, nisi fuerit frater vester vobiscum.

6. At dixit Israel, Utquid malefecistis mihi, ut nuntiaretis viro, quod adhuc frater esset vobis.

7. Et dixerunt, Interrogando interrogavit vir ille de nobis et cognatione nostra, dicendo, Num adhuc pater vester vivit? num est vobis frater? et nuntiavimus ei secundum verba ista: numquid sciendo sciebamus, quod dicturus esset, Descendere faciatis fratrem vestrum?

8. Et dixit Jehudah ad Israel patrem suum, Mitte puerum mecum, et surgemus, et proficiscemur, et vivemus, et non moriemur etiam nos, etiam tu, etiam parvuli nostri.

9. Ergo fidejubeo pro illo, de manu mea requiras eum: nisi reduxero eum ad te, et statuero eum ante te, poenæ obnoxius ero tibi omnibus diebus.

10. Quia nisi tardavissemus, certe nunc reversi fuissemus jam bis.

11. Et dixit illis Israel pater eorum, Si ita nunc *oportet*, hoc facite: tollite de optimis fructibus terræ in vasis vestris, et deferte ad virum munus, pusillum resinæ et pusillum mellis, aromata, et stacten, pineas, et amygdalas.

12. Et pecuniam duplicem capite in manibus vestris: et pecuniam repositam in ore saccorum vestrorum reponetis in manu vestra, si forte error esset.

13. Et fratrem vestrum capite, et surgite, revertemini ad virum.

14. Deus autem omnipotens det vobis misericordias ante virum, et dimittat vobis fratrem vestrum alium, et Benjamin: et ego quemadmodum orbatus sum, orbatus sum.

15. Et ceperunt viri munus hoc, et duplicem pecuniam ceperunt in manu sua, et Benjamin: et surrexerunt, et descenderunt in Ægyptum, et steterunt coram Joseph.

16. Et vidit Joseph cum eis Ben-

jamin with them, he said to the ruler of his house, Bring *these* men home, and slay, and make ready : for *these* men shall dine with me at noon.

17. And the man did as Joseph bade : and the man brought the men into Joseph's house.

18. And the men were afraid, because they were brought into Joseph's house ; and they said, Because of the money that was returned in our sacks at the first time are we brought in ; that he may seek occasion against us, and fall upon us, and take us for bond-men, and our asses.

19. And they came near to the steward of Joseph's house, and they communed with him at the door of the house,

20. And said, O sir, we came indeed down at the first time to buy food :

21. And it came to pass, when we came to the inn, that we opened our sacks, and, behold, *every* man's money *was* in the mouth of his sack, our money in full weight ; and we have brought it again in our hand.

22. And other money have we brought down in our hands to buy food : we cannot tell who put our money in our sacks.

23. And he said, Peace *be* to you, fear not ; your God, and the God of your father, hath given you treasure in your sacks : I had your money. And he brought Simeon out unto them.

24. And the man brought the men into Joseph's house, and gave *them* water, and they washed their feet ; and he gave their asses provender.

25. And they made ready the present against Joseph came at noon : for they heard that they should eat bread there.

26. And when Joseph came home, they brought him the present which *was* in their hand into the house, and bowed themselves to him to the earth.

27. And he asked them of *their* welfare, and said, *Is* your father

jamin, et dixit præfecto domus suæ, Adduc viros in domum, et macta, et præpara : quia mecum comedent viri in meridie.

17. Et fecit vir, quemadmodum dixit Joseph : et venire fecit vir homines in domum Joseph.

18. Et timuerunt viri, quod adducti essent in domum Joseph, et dixerunt, Propter pecuniam, quæ reddita est in saccis nostris in principio, sumus adducti, ut volvat se contra nos, et jactet se super nos, et capiat nos in servos, et asinos nostros.

19. Et accesserunt ad virum, qui erat super domum Joseph, et loquuti sunt ad eum in ostio domus :

20. Et dixerunt, Quæsumus, domine mi : descendendo descendimus in principio ad emendum escam.

21. Et fuit quum venissemus ad hospitium, et aperuissemus saccos nostros, ecce, pecunia uniuscujusque erat in ore sacci sui : pecunia nostra secundum pondus suum : et retulimus eam in manu nostra.

22. Et pecuniam aliam detulimus in manu nostra ad emendum escam : nescimus, quis posuerit pecuniam nostram in saccis nostris.

23. Et dixit, Pax vobis, ne timeatis, Deus vester, et Deus patris vestri dedit vobis thesaurum in saccis vestris, pecunia vestra venit ad me : et adduxit ad eos Simhon.

24. Et venire fecit vir ille homines in domum Joseph : et dedit aquam, et laverunt pedes suos, et dedit pabulum asinis eorum.

25. Paraverunt autem munus, dum veniret Joseph in meridie : audierunt enim, quod ibi comesturi essent panem.

26. Et venit Joseph ad domum, et attulerunt ei munus, quod erat in manu eorum, in domum : et incurvaverunt se ei super terram.

27. Et interrogavit eos de prosperitate, et dixit, Num sanus est

well, the old man of whom ye spake?
Is he yet alive?

28. And they answered, Thy servant our father *is* in good health, he *is* yet alive: and they bowed down their heads, and made obeisance.

29. And he lifted up his eyes, and saw his brother Benjamin, his mother's son, and said, *Is* this your younger brother, of whom ye spake unto me? And he said, God be gracious unto thee, my son.

30. And Joseph made haste; for his bowels did yearn upon his brother: and he sought *where* to weep; and he entered into *his* chamber, and wept there.

31. And he washed his face, and went out, and refrained himself, and said, Set on bread.

32. And they set on for him by himself, and for them by themselves, and for the Egyptians, which did eat with him, by themselves: because the Egyptians might not eat bread with the Hebrews; for that *is* an abomination unto the Egyptians.

33. And they sat before him, the first-born according to his birthright, and the youngest according to his youth: and the men marvelled one at another.

34. And he took *and sent* messes unto them from before him: but Benjamin's mess was five times so much as any of theirs. And they drank, and were merry with him.

pater vester senex, quem dixeratis? Num adhuc vivit?

28. Et dixerunt, Prospere est servo tuo patri nostro, adhuc vivit: et prociderunt, et incurvaverunt se.

29. Et levavit oculos suos, et vidit Benjamin fratrem suum, filium matris suæ, et dixit, Num iste est frater vester minimus, quem dixeratis mihi? Et dixit, Deus misereatur tui, fili mi.

30. Et festinavit Joseph, quia incaluerant miserationes ejus super fratrem suum, et quæsivit ut fleret: ingressus est itaque cubiculum, et flevit ibi.

31. Et lavit faciem suam, et egressus est, et vim fecit sibi, et dixit, Apponite panem.

32. Et apposuerunt ei seorsum, illisque seorsum: et Ægyptiis, qui comedebant cum eo, seorsum: non enim poterant Ægyptii comedere cum Hebræis panem: quia abominatio erat Ægyptiis.

33. Et sederunt coram eo primogenitus secundum primogenituram suam, et parvus juxta parvitatem suam: et admirati sunt viri unusquisque ad proximum suum.

34. Et accepit partes a facie sua ad illos, et multiplicavit partem Benjamin plus quam partes omnium illorum, quinque partibus: et biberunt, et inebriaverunt se cum eo.

1. *And the famine was sore in the land.* In this chapter is recorded the second journey of the sons of Jacob into Egypt, when the former supply of provision had been exhausted. It may, however, here be asked, how Jacob could have supported his family, even for a few days, with so small a quantity of corn: for, suppose it to be granted that several asses were conducted by each of the brethren, what was this to sustain three hundred persons?[1] For, since Abraham had a much larger number of servants, and mention has been made above of the servants of Isaac; it is incredible that

---

[1] Dr. A. Clarke supposes the asses to have amounted to several *scores*, if not *hundreds*. The latter supposition seems improbable.—*Ed.*

Jacob was so entirely destitute, as to have no servants left. If we say, that he, being a stranger, had been compelled to sell them all, it is but an uncertain guess. It seems to me more probable that they lived on acorns, herbs, and roots. For we know that the orientals, especially when any necessity urges, are content with slender and dry food, and we shall see presently, that, in this scarcity of wheat, there was a supply of other food. I suppose, therefore, that no more corn had been bought than would suffice to furnish a frugal and restricted measure of food for Jacob himself, and for his children and grandchildren : and that the food of the servants was otherwise provided for. There is, indeed, no doubt that the whole region had been compelled to resort to acorns, and fruits of this kind, for food for the servants, and that wheaten bread was a luxury belonging to the rich. This was, indeed, a severe trial, that holy Jacob, of whom God had engaged to take care, should almost perish, with his family, through hunger, and that the land of which he was constituted the lord, in order that he might there happily enjoy the abundance of all things, should even deny him bread as a stranger. For he might seriously doubt what was the meaning of that remarkable promise, " I am God Almighty, grow and multiply : I will bless thee." It is profitable for us to know these conflicts of the holy fathers, that, fighting with the same arms with which they conquered, we also may stand invincible, although God should withhold present help.

3. *And Judah spake unto him, saying.* Judah seems to feign something, for the purpose of extorting from his father what he knew he would not freely grant ; but it is probable that many discourses had been held on both sides, which Moses, according to his custom, has not related. And since Joseph so ardently desired the sight of his brother Benjamin, it is not surprising that he should have laboured, in every possible way, to obtain it. It may also have happened that he had caused some notification or legal summons to be served, by which his brother was cited to make his appearance, as in judicial causes. This however deserves to be noticed, that Moses relates the long disputation which Jacob had with his sons, in order that we may know with what difficulty he

allowed his son Benjamin to be torn away from him.   For, though hunger was pressing, he nevertheless contended for retaining him, just as if he were striving for the salvation of his whole family.   Whence, again, we may conjecture, that he suspected his sons of a wicked conspiracy ; and on this account Judah offers himself as a surety.   For he does not promise anything respecting the event, but only, for the sake of clearing himself and his brethren, he takes Benjamin under his care, with this condition, that if any injury should be done to Benjamin, he would bear the punishment and the blame. From the example of Jacob let us learn patient endurance, should the Lord often compel us, by pressure of circumstances, to do many things contrary to the inclination of our own minds ; for Jacob sends away his son, as if he were delivering him over unto death.

11. *Take of the best fruits.*[1]   Though the fruits which Moses enumerates were, for the most part, not very precious, because the condition of holy Jacob was not such that he could send any royal present ; yet, according to his slender ability, he wished to appease Joseph.   Besides we know that fruits are not always estimated according to their cost.   And now, having commanded his sons to do what he thought necessary, he has recourse to prayer, that God would give them favour with the governor of Egypt.   We must attend to both these points whenever we are perplexed in any business ; for we must not omit any of those things which are expedient, or which may seem to be of use ; and yet we must place our reliance upon God.   For the tranquillity of faith has no affinity with indolence : but he who expects a prosperous issue of his affairs from the Lord, will, at the same time, look closely to the means which are in his power, and will apply them to present use.   Meanwhile, let the faithful observe this moderation, that when they have tried all means, they still ascribe nothing to their own industry.   At the same time, let them be certainly convinced that all their endeavours will be in vain, unless the Lord bless them.   It is to be observed, also, in the form of his supplication, that Jacob regards the hearts of men

[1] Literally, "Fruits of the song;" alluding to the songs which were sung over the ingathering of harvest.—*Ed.*

as subject to the will of God. When we have to deal with men, we too often neglect to look unto the Lord, because we do not sufficiently acknowledge him as the secret Governor of their hearts. But to whatever extent unruly men may be carried away by violence, it is yet certain that their passions are turned by God in whatever direction he pleases, so that he can mitigate their ferocity as often as he sees good ; or can permit those to become cruel, who before were disposed to mildness. So Jacob, although his sons had found an austere severity in Joseph, yet trusts that his heart will be so in the hand of God, that it shall be suddenly moulded to humanity. Therefore, as we must hope in the Lord, when men deal unjustly with us, and must pray that they may be changed for the better ; so, on the other hand, we must remember that, when they act with severity towards us, it is not done without the counsel of God.

14. *If I be bereaved.* Jacob may seem here to be hardly consistent with himself ; for, if the prayer which Moses has just related, was the effect of faith, he ought to have been more calm ; and, at least, to have given occasion to the manifestation of the grace of God. But he appears to cut himself off from every ground of confidence, when he supposes that nothing is left for him but bereavement. It is like the speech of a man in despair, " I shall remain bereaved as I am." As if truly he had prayed in vain ; or had feignedly professed that the remedy was in the hand of God. If, however, we observe to whom his speech was directed, the solution is easy. It is by no means doubtful that he stood firmly on the promise which had been given to him, and therefore he would hope for some fruit of his prayers ; yet he wished deeply to affect his sons, in order that they might take greater care of their brother. For, it was in no common manner that Benjamin was intrusted to their protection, when they saw their father altogether overcome and almost lifeless with grief, until he should receive his son again in safety. Interpreters, however, expound these words variously. Some think that he complained, because now he was about to be entirely bereaved. To others, the meaning seems to be, that nothing worse could happen ; since he had lost Joseph, whom he had

preferred to all the rest. Others are disposed to mark a double bereavement, as if he had said, " I have lost two sons, and now a third follows them." But what, if we should thus interpret the words, " I see what is my condition ; I am a most wretched old man ; my house, which lately was filled with people, I find almost deserted." So that, in general terms, he is deploring the loss of all his sons, and is not speaking of a part only. Moreover, it was his design to inspire his sons with a degree of solicitude which should cause them to attend to their duty with greater fidelity and diligence.[1]

16. *And he said to the ruler of his house.* Here we perceive the fraternal disposition of Joseph ; though it is uncertain whether he was perfectly reconciled, as I will shortly show, in its proper place. If, however, remembering the injury, he loved his brethren less than before, he was still far from having vindictive feelings towards them. But because it was something suspicious that foreigners and men of ignoble rank should be received in a friendly manner, like known guests, to a banquet, by the chief governor of the kingdom, the sons of Jacob would conceive a new fear ; namely, that he wished to cast them all into chains ; and that their money had been craftily concealed in their sacks, in order that it might prove the occasion of accusation against them. It is however probable, that the crime which they had committed against Joseph, occurred to their minds, and that this fear had proceeded from a guilty conscience. For, unless the judgment of God had tormented them, there was no cause why they should apprehend such an act of perfidy. It may seem absurd, that unknown men should be received to a feast by a

---

[1] There is, however, another interpretation of the passage which is worthy of attention. In our version, the words are, " If I am bereaved of my children, I am bereaved ;" but the expression, *of my children*, is not in the original. The close translation is simply, " If I be bereaved, I am bereaved." And this may be the language of entire resignation to the will of God. Jacob had had a severe struggle in his mind, before he could give up his beloved Benjamin ; but having at length succeeded, he seems now freely to surrender himself and his family to the divine will. " If I am bereaved, I am bereaved." I know the worst, and I am prepared to meet it. Ainsworth says, " A like phrase is in Esther iv. 16, ' If I perish, I perish.' Both of them seem to be a committing of themselves, and of the event of their actions, unto God in faith ; which, if it fell out otherwise than they wished, they would patiently bear."—*Ed.*

prince of the highest dignity.   But why not rather incline to
a different conjecture ; namely, that the governor of Egypt
has done this for the purpose of exhibiting to his friends the
new and unwonted spectacle of eleven brethren sitting at
one table ?   It will, indeed, sometimes happen that similar
anxiety to that felt by Joseph's brethren, may invade even
the best of men ; but I would rather ascribe it to the judgment of God, that the sons of Jacob, whose conscience accused
them of having inhumanly treated their brother, suspected
that they would be dealt with in the same manner.   However, they take an early opportunity of vindicating themselves, before inquiry is made respecting the theft.   Now,
freely to declare that the money had been found in their
sacks, and that they had brought it from home to repay it
immediately, was a strong mark of their innocence.   Moreover,
they do this in the very porch of the house, because they
suspected that, as soon as they entered, the question would
be put to them.

23. *Peace be to you.*   Because שלום, (*shalom,*) among the
Hebrews, signifies not only peace, but any prosperous and
desirable condition, as well as any joyful event, this passage may be expounded in two ways : either that the ruler
of Joseph's house commands them to be of a peaceful and
secure mind ; or that he pronounces it to be well and happy
with them.   The sum of his answer, however, amounts to
this, that there was no reason for fear, because their affairs
were in a prosperous state.   And since, after the manner of
men, it was not possible that they should have paid the money for the corn which was found in their sacks, he ascribes
this to the favour of God.   For though true religion was then
almost extinct in the world, God nevertheless caused some
knowledge of his goodness always to remain in the hearts of
men, which should render them responsible.   Hence it has
happened that, following nature as their guide, unbelievers
have called every peculiarly excellent gift *Divine.*   Moreover,
because corruption was so prevalent, that each nation deemed
it lawful to worship different gods, the ruler of Joseph's house
distinguishes the God worshipped by the sons of Jacob from
Egyptian idols.   The conjecture, however, is probable, that

this man had been imbued with some sense of religion. We know how great was the arrogance of that nation, and that it supposed the whole world besides, to be deceived in the worship of gods. Therefore, unless he had learned something better, he never would have assigned so great an honour to any other gods than those of his own country. Moreover, he does not ascribe the miracle to the God of the land of Canaan, but to the peculiar God of their father. I, therefore, do not doubt that Joseph, though not permitted openly to correct anything in the received superstitions, endeavoured, at least in his own house, to establish the true worship of the one God, and always held fast the covenant, concerning which, as a boy, he had heard his father speak. This is the more to be observed, because the holy man could not swerve, even in the least degree, from the common practice, without incurring the odium of a nation so proud. Therefore, the excellency of Joseph is commended in the person of his steward; because without fear of public envy, he gives honour, within his own walls, to the true God. If any one should ask, whence he knew that Jacob was a worshipper of the true God; the answer is ready; that Joseph, notwithstanding his assumed severity, had commanded that Simeon should be gently treated in prison. Though he had been left as a hostage, yet, if he had been regarded as a spy, the keeper of the prison would have dealt more harshly with him. There must, therefore, have been some command given respecting the humane or moderate treatment of him. Whence the probable conjecture is elicited, that Joseph had explained the affair to his steward, who was admitted to his secret counsels.

25. *Against Joseph came at noon-day.* It is doubtful whether this was the ordinary hour of dining among the Egyptians, or whether Joseph, on that day, sat down earlier than he was accustomed to do, on account of his guests. It is, however, most likely that the usual custom of dining was observed. Although, among the people of the East, there might be a different manner of living, dinners were in use, not only among the Egyptians, but also in Judea, and in other neighbouring regions. Yet it is probable that this was to them, also, in the place of a supper, both because

they would sit long at table, and our quick method of eating would not have been tolerable to people in those heated climes; especially when they received guests with greater luxury than usual, as it will presently appear, was done at this time. The washing of the feet, (as we have seen before,) was a part of hospitality, and intended to relieve weariness; because, in those parts, the feet might easily become inflamed whenever they journeyed on foot. It was also more honourable, according to ancient custom, that a portion of food should be sent to each from Joseph, rather than that it should be distributed by the cook. But because these things are trivial, and are not conducive to piety, I only slightly touch upon them; and would even omit them entirely, except that, to remove a scruple from the minds of the unskilful, is sometimes useful, if it be but done sparingly and with brevity.

32. *Because the Egyptians might not eat,* &c.[1] Moses says they might not eat with the Hebrews, because they abhorred it, as being unlawful. For seeing that their religion forbade it, they were so bound, that they *could* not do what they did not *dare* to do. This passage teaches us how great was the pride of that nation; for, whence did it arise that they so utterly detested the Hebrews, unless because they thought themselves alone to be pure and holy in the world, and acceptable to God? God, indeed, commands his worshippers to abstain from all the pollutions of the Gentiles. But it behoves any one who separates himself from others, to be himself pure and upright. Therefore superstitious persons vainly attempt to claim this privilege for themselves, seeing they carry their impurity within, and are destitute of sincerity. Superstition, also, is affected with

---

[1] " At the entertainment to which Joseph invited his brethren, they sat apart from the Egyptians, while Joseph was again separated from both. The author [Moses] shows the reason of this in the remark, ‘ Because the Egyptians might not eat bread with the Hebrews, for that is an abomination to the Egyptians.’ *Herodotus* also remarks, that the Egyptians abstained from all familiar intercourse with foreigners, since these were unclean to them, especially because they slew and ate the animals which were sacred among the Egyptians. The circumstance that Joseph eats separately from the other Egyptians is strictly in accordance with the great difference of rank, and the spirit of caste, which prevailed among the Egyptians."— *Egypt and the Books of Moses,* p. 39.—*Ed.*

another disease; namely, that it is full of pride, so that it despises all men, under the pretext that they are vicious. It is asked, however, whether the Egyptians were separated from Joseph, because they regarded him as polluted: for this the words of Moses seem to intimate. If this interpretation is received, then they esteemed their false religion so highly, that they did not scruple to load their governor with reproaches. I rather conjecture, that Joseph sat apart from them, for the sake of honour; since it would be absurd that they, who disdained to sit at the same table with him, should be invited as his guests. Therefore it is probable that this distinct order was made by Joseph himself, that he might maintain his own dignity; and yet that the sons of Jacob were not mixed with the Egyptians, because the former were an abomination to the latter. For though the origin of Joseph was known, yet he had so passed over to the Egyptians, that he had become as one of their body. For which reason, also, the king had given him a name, when he adorned him with the insignia of his office as chief governor. Now, when we see that the church of God was, at that time, so proudly despised by profane men, we need not wonder that we also, at the present day, are subjected to similar reproach. Meanwhile, we must endeavour to keep ourselves pure from the filth of the world, for the Lord's sake; and yet this desire must be so attempered, that we may be alienated from the vices, rather than from the persons of men. For on this account does God sanctify his children, that they may beware of the vices of the unbelievers among whom they are conversant; and nevertheless may allure, as many as are curable, to a participation of their piety. Two things are here to be attended to; first, that we may be fully persuaded of the genuineness of our faith; secondly, that our excessive and fruitless fastidiousness may not entirely alienate many from the Lord, who otherwise might have been won. For we are not expressly commanded so to abhor the wicked, as not eat with them; but to avoid such association as may subject us to the same yoke. Besides, this passage confirms what I have before said, that the Hebrews had derived their name, not from their passing over

the river, (as some falsely imagine,) but from their ancestor
Heber. Nor was the fame of a single small and distantly
situated family, sufficiently celebrated in Egypt, to become
the cause of public dissension.

33. *The first-born according to his birthright.*[1] Although
of the sons of Jacob four were born of bond-women ; yet,
since they were the elder, they had precedence of their
younger brethren, who had descended from free-born mothers ;
whence it appears that they had been accustomed by their
father to keep this order. What, then, some one may say,
becomes of the declaration, " the son of the bond-woman
shall not be heir with the son of the free-woman ?" Truly,
I think, since Ishmael was rejected, by the divine oracle
proceeding from the mouth of Sarah, as Esau was afterwards,
Jacob was fully taught that he had as many heirs as he had
sons. Hence arose that equality which caused each to keep
his place, first, middle, or last, according to his age. But
the design of Moses was to show, that although Benjamin
was the youngest, yet he was preferred to all the rest in
honour ; because Joseph could not refrain from giving him
the principal token of his love. It was, indeed, his intention to remain unknown ; but affection so far prevails, that,
beyond the purpose of his mind, he suddenly breaks out into
a declaration of his affection. From the concluding portion
of the chapter we gather, what I recently intimated, that
the feast was unusually luxurious, and that they were received to it, in a liberal and joyful manner, beyond the
daily custom. For the word שׁכר, (*shakar,*) they " were
merry," signifies, either that they were not always accustomed to drink wine, or that there was more than ordinary
indulgence at the sumptuous tables spread for them. Here,
however, no intemperance is implied, (so that drunkards may
not plead the example of the holy fathers as a pretext for
their crime,) but an honourable and moderate liberality. I
acknowledge, indeed, that the word has a double meaning,

[1] " It appears that the brothers of Joseph *sat* before him at the table,
while, according to patriarchal practice, they were accustomed to recline.
It appears from the sculptures, that the Egyptians also were in the habit
of sitting at table, although they had couches."—*Egypt and the Books of
Moses,* p. 39.—*Ed.*

and is often taken in an ill sense ; as in chap. ix., ver. 21, and in similar places : but in the present instance the design of Moses is clear. Should any one object, that a frugal use of food and drink is simply that which suffices for the nourishing of the body : I answer, although food is properly for the supply of our necessities, yet the legitimate use of it may proceed further. For it is not in vain, that our food has savour as well as vital nutriment ; but thus our heavenly Father sweetly delights us with his delicacies. And his benignity is not in vain commended in Psalm civ. 15, where he is said to create " wine that maketh glad the heart of man." Nevertheless, the more kindly he indulges us, the more solicitously ought we to restrict ourselves to a frugal use of his gifts. For we know how unbridled are the appetites of the flesh. Whence it happens that, in abundance, it is almost always lascivious, and in penury, impatient. We must, however, adhere to St. Paul's method, that we know how to abound and to suffer need ; that is, we must take great care if we have unusual plenty, that it does not hurry us into luxury ; and, on the other hand, we must see to it, that we bear poverty with an equal mind. Some one, perhaps, will say, that the flesh is more than sufficiently ingenious in giving a specious colour to its excesses ; and, therefore, nothing more should be allowed to it than necessity demands. And, truly, I confess, we must diligently attend to what Paul prescribes, (Rom. xiii. 14,) " Make not provision for the flesh to fulfil the lusts thereof." But because it greatly concerns all pious people to receive their food from the hand of God, with quiet consciences, it is necessary for them to know to what extent the use of food and wine is lawful.

CHAPTER XLIV.

1. AND he commanded the steward of his house, saying, Fill the men's sacks *with* food, as much as they can carry, and put every man's money in his sack's mouth.

2. And put my cup, the silver cup, in the sack's mouth of the youngest,

1. Et præcepit præfecto domus suæ, dicendo, Imple saccos virorum esca, quantum potuerint ferre, et pone pecuniam uniuscujusque in ore sacci sui,

2. Et scyphum meum, scyphum argenteum, pone in ore sacci junioris,

and his corn-money. And he did according to the word that Joseph had spoken.

3. As soon as the morning was light, the men were sent away, they and their asses.

4. *And* when they were gone out of the city, *and* not *yet* far off, Joseph said unto his steward, Up, follow after the men; and when thou dost overtake them, say unto them, Wherefore have ye rewarded evil for good?

5. *Is* not this *it* in which my lord drinketh, and whereby indeed he divineth? Ye have done evil in so doing.

6. And he overtook them, and he spake unto them these same words.

7. And they said unto him, Wherefore saith my lord these words? God forbid that thy servants should do according to this thing.

8. Behold, the money which we found in our sacks' mouth we brought again unto thee out of the land of Canaan: how then should we steal out of thy lord's house silver or gold?

9. With whomsoever of thy servants it be found, both let him die, and we also will be my lord's bondmen.

10. And he said, Now also *let* it *be* according unto your words: he with whom it is found shall be my servant; and ye shall be blameless.

11. Then they speedily took down every man his sack to the ground, and opened every man his sack.

12. And he searched, *and* began at the eldest, and left at the youngest; and the cup was found in Benjamin's sack.

13. Then they rent their clothes, and laded every man his ass, and returned to the city.

14. And Judah and his brethren came to Joseph's house; for he *was* yet there; and they fell before him on the ground.

15. And Joseph said unto them, What deed *is* this that ye have done? wot ye not that such a man as I can certainly divine?

et pecuniam alimenti ejus: et fecit secundum verbum Joseph, quod loquutus fuerat.

3. Mane illuxit, et viri dimissi sunt, ipsi et asini eorum.

4. Ipsi egressi erant urbem, nec longe abierant, quum Joseph dixit præfecto domus suæ, Surge, persequere viros, et apprehende eos, et dices eis, Utquid reddidistis malum pro bono?

5. Nonne hic est, in quo bibit dominus meus: et ipse augurando auguratur in eo? male fecistis quod fecistis.

6. Et apprehendit eos, et loquutus est ad eos verba ista.

7. Et dixerunt ad eum, Utquid loquitur dominus meus secundum verba ista? absit a servis tuis, ut faciant secundum verbum hoc.

8. Ecce: pecuniam, quam invenimus in ore saccorum nostrorum, retulimus ad te e terra Chenaan: et quomodo furati essemus e domo domini tui argentum vel aurum.

9. Is penes quem inventus fuerit e servis tuis, moriatur: et etiam nos erimus domino meo servi.

10. Et dixit, Etiam nunc secundum verba vestra ita sit: is penes quem inventus fuerit, erit mihi servus, et vos eritis innocentes.

11. Et festinaverunt, et deposuerunt unusquisque saccum suum super terram: et aperuerunt singuli saccum suum.

12. Scrutatus est autem: a maximo incepit, et in minimo finivit: et inventus est scyphus in sacco Benjamin.

13. Et sciderunt vestimenta sua, et oneravit unusquisque asinum suum, et reversi sunt in urbem.

14. Veneruntque Jehudah et fratres ejus ad domum Joseph, et erat adhuc ipse ibi: et prostraverunt se coram eo super terram.

15. Et dixit ad eos Joseph, Quod facinus est hoc quod fecistis? nonne nostis quod augurando auguratur vir, qui est sicut ego?

16. And Judah said, What shall we say unto my lord? what shall we speak? or how shall we clear ourselves? God hath found out the iniquity of thy servants: behold, we *are* my lord's servants, both we, and *he* also with whom the cup is found.

17. And he said, God forbid that I should do so: *but* the man in whose hand the cup is found, he shall be my servant; and as for you, get you up in peace unto your father.

18. Then Judah came near unto him, and said, Oh my lord, let thy servant, I pray thee, speak a word in my lord's ears, and let not thine anger burn against thy servant: for thou *art* even as Pharaoh.

19. My lord asked his servants, saying, Have ye a father, or a brother?

20. And we said unto my lord, We have a father, an old man, and a child of his old age, a little one; and his brother is dead, and he alone is left of his mother, and his father loveth him.

21. And thou saidst unto thy servants, Bring him down unto me, that I may set mine eyes upon him.

22. And we said unto my lord, The lad cannot leave his father: for *if* he should leave his father, *his father* would die.

23. And thou saidst unto thy servants, Except your youngest brother come down with you, ye shall see my face no more.

24. And it came to pass, when we came up unto thy servant my father, we told him the words of my lord.

25. And our father said, Go again, *and* buy us a little food.

26. And we said, We cannot go down: if our youngest brother be with us, then will we go down: for we may not see the man's face, except our youngest brother *be* with us.

27. And thy servant my father said unto us, Ye know that my wife bare me two *sons:*

28. And the one went out from

16. Respondit Jehudah, Quid dicemus domino meo? quid loquemur, et in quo justificabimus nos? Deus invenit iniquitatem servorum tuorum: ecce, sumus servi domini mei, etiam nos, etiam ille in cujus manu inventus est scyphus.

17. Ille autem dixit, Absit a me ut faciam hoc: vir in cujus manu inventus est scyphus, ipse erit mihi servus: et vos ascendite in pace ad patrem vestrum.

18. Et accessit ad eum Jehudah, et dixit, Quæso, domine mi: loquatur quæso servus tuus verbum in auribus domini mei, et ne irascatur furor tuus in servum tuum: quia tu sicut Pharao.

19. Dominus meus interrogavit servos suos, dicendo, Numquid est vobis pater vel frater?

20. Et diximus domino meo, Est nobis pater senex, et puer senectutum parvus, frater autem ejus mortuus est: et remansit ipse tantum matri suæ, itaque pater ejus diligit eum.

21. Et dixisti servis tuis, Descendere facite eum ad me, et ponam oculum meum super eum.

22. Respondimus vero domino meo, Non potest puer relinquere patrem suum, et si reliquerit patrem suum, morietur.

23. Tu autem dixisti servis tuis, Nisi descendat frater vester minimus vobiscum, ne addatis ut videatis faciem meam.

24. Fuit igitur, quando ascendimus ad servum tuum patrem meum, et narravimus ei verba domini mei,

25. Dixit pater noster, Revertimini, emite nobis pusillum escæ.

26. Et diximus, non possumus descendere: si fuerit frater noster minimus nobiscum, descendemus: quia non possumus videre faciem viri illius, fratre nostro minimo non existente nobiscum.

27. Tunc dixit servus tuus pater meus nobis, Vos nostis quod duos peperit mihi uxor mea.

28. Egressus est unus a me, et

me, and I said, Surely he is torn in pieces; and I saw him not since:

29. And if ye take this also from me, and mischief befall him, ye shall bring down my gray hairs with sorrow to the grave.

30. Now therefore, when I come to thy servant my father, and the lad be not with us; seeing that his life is bound up in the lad's life;

31. It shall come to pass, when he seeth that the lad is not with us, that he will die: and thy servants shall bring down the gray hairs of thy servant our father with sorrow to the grave.

32. For thy servant became surety for the lad unto my father, saying, If I bring him not unto thee, then I shall bear the blame to my father for ever.

33. Now therefore, I pray thee, let thy servant abide instead of the lad a bondman to my lord; and let the lad go up with his brethren.

34. For how shall I go up to my father, and the lad be not with me? lest peradventure I see the evil that shall come on my father.

dixi, Certe rapiendo raptus est: et non vidi eum hactenus.

29. Et capietis etiam hunc a facie mea, et accidet ei mors, descendereque facietis canitiem meam in malo ad sepulcrum.

30. Nunc ergo quum venero ad servum tuum patrem meum, et puer non fuerit nobiscum, (et anima ejus ligata est cum anima ipsius):

31. Erit sane, quum viderit ipse quod non sit puer, morietur, et descendere facient servi tui canitiem servi tui patris nostri cum dolore ad sepulcrum.

32. Servus enim tuus fidejussit pro puero patri meo, dicendo, Si non reduxero eum ad te, obnoxius ero pœnæ patri meo omnibus diebus.

33. Et nunc maneat quæso servus tuus pro puero servus domino meo, puer autem ascendat cum fratribus suis.

34. Quomodo enim ascendam ad patrem meum, si puer non fuerit mecum? ne forte videam malum quod inveniet patrem meum.

1. *And he commanded the steward of his house.* Here Moses relates how skilfully Joseph had contrived to try the dispositions of his brethren. We have said elsewhere that, whereas God has commanded us to cultivate simplicity, we are not to take this, and similar examples, as affording license to turn aside to indirect and crafty arts. For it may have been that Joseph was impelled by a special influence of the Spirit to this course. He had also a reason, of no common kind, for inquiring very strictly in what manner his brethren were affected. Charity is not suspicious. Why, then, does he so distrust his brethren ; and why cannot he suppose that they have anything good, unless he shall first have subjected them to the most rigid examination ? Truly, since he had found them to be exceedingly cruel and perfidious, it is but an excusable suspicion, if he does not believe them to be changed for the better, until he has obtained a thorough perception and conviction of their penitence. But since, in this respect, it is a rare and very difficult virtue to

observe a proper medium, we must beware of imitating the example of Joseph, in an austere course of acting, unless we have laid all vindictive feelings aside, and are pure and free from all enmity. For love, when it is pure, and exempt from all turbid influence, will best decide how far it is right to proceed. It may, however, be asked, " If the sons of Jacob had been easily induced to betray the safety of Benjamin, what would Joseph himself have done?" We may readily conjecture, that he examined their fidelity, in order that, if he should find them dishonest, he might retain Benjamin, and drive them with shame from his presence. But, by pursuing this method, his father would have been deserted, and the Church of God ruined. And certainly, it is not without hazard to himself that he thus terrifies them: because he could scarcely have avoided the necessity of denouncing some more grievous and severe punishment against them, if they had again relapsed. It was, therefore, due to the special favour of God, that they proved themselves different from what he had feared. In the meantime, the advantage of his examination was twofold; first, because the clearly ascertained integrity of his brethren rendered his mind more placable towards them ; and secondly, because it lightened, at least in some degree, the former infamy, which they had contracted by their wickedness.

2. *And put my cup, the silver cup.* It may seem wonderful that, considering his great opulence, Joseph had not rather drunk out of a golden cup. Doubtless, either the moderation of that age was still greater than has since prevailed, and the splendour of it less sumptuous ; or else this conduct must be attributed to the moderation of the man, who, in the midst of universal license, yet was contented with a plain and decent, rather than with a magnificent style of living. Unless, perhaps, on account of the excellence of the workmanship, the silver was more valuable than gold : as it is manifest from secular history, that the workmanship has often been more expensive than the material itself. It is, however, probable, that Joseph was sparing in domestic splendour, for the sake of avoiding envy. For unless he had been prudently on his guard, a contention would

have arisen between him and the courtiers, resulting from a spirit of emulation. Moreover, he commands the cup to be enclosed in Benjamin's sack, in order that he might claim him as his own, when convicted of the theft, and might send the rest away: however, he accuses all alike, as if he knew not who among them had committed the crime. And first, he reproves their ingratitude, because, when they had been so kindly received, they made the worst possible return; next, he contends that the crime was inexpiable, because they had stolen what was most valuable to him; namely, the cup in which he was accustomed both to drink and to divine. And he does this through his steward, whom he had not trained to acts of tyranny and violence. Whence I infer, that the steward was not altogether ignorant of his master's design.

5. *Whereby, indeed, he divineth.*[1] This clause is variously expounded. For some take it as if Joseph pretended that he consulted soothsayers in order to find out the thief. Others translate it, " by which he hath tried you, or searched you out;" others, that the stolen cup had given Joseph an unfavourable omen. The genuine sense seems to me to be this: that he had used the cup for divinations and for magical arts; which, however, we have said, he feigned, for the sake of aggravating the charge brought against them. But the question arises, how does Joseph allow himself to resort to such an expedient? For besides that it was sinful for him to profess augury; he vainly and unworthily transfers to imaginary deities the honour due only to divine grace. On a former occasion, he had declared that he

---

[1] " *Jamblichus*, in his book on Egyptian mysteries, mentions the practice of divining by cups. That this superstition, as well as many others, has continued even to modern times, is shown by a remarkable passage in Norden's Travels. When the author, with his companions, had arrived at Dorri, the most remote extremity of Egypt, or rather in Nubia, where they were able to deliver themselves from a perilous condition, only through great presence of mind, they sent one of their company to a malicious and powerful Arab, to threaten him. He answered them, ' I know what sort of people you are. I have consulted my cup, and found in it, that you are from a people of whom one of our prophets has said, There will come Franks under every kind of pretence to spy out the land. They will bring with them a great multitude of their countrymen, to conquer the country and to destroy all the people.'"—*Egypt and the Books of Moses,* p. 40.—*Ed.*

was unable to interpret dreams, except so far as God should suggest the truth to him ; now he obscures this entire ascription of praise to divine grace ; and what is worse, by boasting that he is a magician rather than proclaiming himself a prophet of God, he impiously profanes the gift of the Holy Spirit.   Doubtless, in this dissimulation, it is not to be denied, that he sinned grievously.   Yet I think that, at the first, he had endeavoured, by all means in his power, to give unto God his due honour ; and it was not his fault that the whole kingdom of Egypt was ignorant of the fact that he excelled in skill, not by magical arts, but by a celestial gift. But since the Egyptians were accustomed to the illusions of the magicians, this ancient error so prevailed, that they believed Joseph to be one of them ; and I do not doubt that this rumour was spread abroad among the people, although contrary to his desire and intention.   Now Joseph, in feigning himself to be a stranger to his brethren, combines many falsehoods in one, and takes advantage of the prevailing vulgar opinion that he used auguries.   Whence we gather, that when any one swerves from the right line, he is prone to fall into various sins.   Wherefore, being warned by this example, let us learn to allow ourselves in nothing except what we know is approved by God.   But especially must we avoid all dissimulation, which either produces or confirms mischievous impostures.   Besides, we are warned, that it is not sufficient for any one to oppose a prevailing vice for a time ; unless he add constancy of resistance, even though the evil may become excessive.   For he discharges his duty very defectively, who, having once testified that he is displeased with what is evil, afterwards, by his silence or connivance, gives it a kind of assent.

7. *And they said unto him.* The sons of Jacob boldly excuse themselves, because a good conscience gives them confidence. They also argue from the greater to the less : for they contend, that their having voluntarily brought back the money, which they might with impunity have applied to their own use, was such a proof of their honesty, as to make it incredible that they should have been so blinded by a little gain, as to bring upon themselves the greatest disgrace,

together with immediate danger of their lives.   They, therefore, declared themselves ready to submit to any punishment,
if they were found guilty of the theft.   When the cup was
discovered in Benjamin's sack, Moses does not relate any of
their complaints ; but only declares, that they testified the
most bitter grief by rending their garments.   I do not doubt
that they were struck dumb by the unexpected result ; for
they were confounded, not only by the magnitude of their
grief, but by perceiving themselves to be obnoxious to punishment, for that of which their conscience did not accuse them.
Therefore, when they come into the presence of Joseph, they
confess the injury, not because they acknowledge that the
crime has been committed by them, but because excuse
would be of no avail ; as if they would say, " It is of no
use to deny a thing which is manifest in itself."   In this
sense, they say that their iniquity has been found out by
God ; because, although they had some secret suspicion of
fraud, thinking that this had been a contrivance for the
purpose of bringing an unjust charge against them, they
choose rather to trace the cause of their punishment to the
secret judgment of God.[1]   Some interpreters believe that
they here confessed their crime committed against Joseph ;
but that opinion is easily refuted, because they constantly
affirm that he had been torn by a wild beast, or had perished
by some accident.   Therefore, the more simple meaning is
that which I have adduced ; that although the truth of the
fact is not apparent, yet they are punished by God as guilty
persons.   They do not, however, speak hypocritically ; but
being troubled and astonished in their perplexed affairs, there
is nothing left for them but the consciousness that this punishment is inflicted by the secret judgment of God.   And I
wish that they who, when smitten by the rod of God, do not
immediately perceive the cause, would adopt the same course ;
and when they find that men are unjustly incensed against
them, would recall to mind the secret judgments of God, by
which it becomes us to be humbled.   Moreover, whereas Judah
speaks in the name of them all, we may hence infer, that he
had already obtained precedence among his brethren.   And

[1] See verse 16.

Moses exhibits him as their head and chief, when he expressly states that *he* and the rest came. For though the dignity of primogeniture had not yet been conferred upon him, by the solemn judgment of his father, yet it was intended for him. Certainly, in taking the post of speaker for the rest, his authority appears in his language. Again, it is necessary to recall to memory, in reference to the language of Joseph, what I have before said, that although at first he had endeavoured to ascribe the glory to God, he now sins in pretending that he is a soothsayer or diviner. Some, to extenuate the fault, say that the allusion is, not to the art of augury, but to his skill in judging; there is, however, no need to resort to forced expositions for the sake of excusing the man; for he speaks according to the common understanding of the multitude, and thus foolishly countenances the received opinion.

16. *Behold, we are my lord's servants.* They had before called themselves servants through modesty; now they consign themselves over to him as slaves. But in the case of Benjamin they plead for a mitigation of the severity of the punishment; and this is a kind of entreaty, that he might not be capitally punished, as they had agreed to, at the first.[1]

17. *God forbid that I should do so.*[2] If Joseph intended to retain Benjamin alone, and to dismiss the others, he would have done his utmost, to rend the Church of God by the worst possible dissension. But I have previously shown (what may also be elicited from the context) that his design was nothing else than to pierce their hearts more deeply. He must have anticipated great mischief, if he had perceived that they did not care for their brother: but the Lord provided against this danger, by causing the earnest

---

[1] On the whole of this verse, Dr. A. Clarke remarks, " No words can more strongly mark *confusion* and *perturbation* of mind. They no doubt all thought that Benjamin had actually stolen the cup." He also thinks it probable that this very cup had been used by Benjamin at the dinner. —*Ed.*

[2] " God forbid" is an expression frequently used by our translators, both in the Old and New Testament, where the name of God does not occur in the original. The term here used has the same meaning as *Absit* in Latin, and Μὴ γένοιτο in Greek. Literally this passage would read, " Far be it from me to do so." See also verse 7.—*Ed.*

apology of Judah not only to soften his mind, but even to draw forth tears and weeping in profusion.

18. *Let thy servant, I pray thee, speak a word.* Judah suppliantly asks that leave may be given him to speak, because his narrative was about to be prolix. And whereas nobles are offended, and take it angrily, if any address them with too great familiarity, Judah begins by declaring that he is not ignorant of the great honour which Joseph had received in Egypt, for the purpose of showing that he was becoming bold, not through impertinence, but through necessity. Afterwards he recites in what manner he and his brethren had departed from their father. There are two principal heads of his discourse; first, that they should be the means of bringing a sorrow upon their father which would prove fatal; and secondly, that he had bound himself individually, by covenant, to bring the youth back. With respect to the grief of his father, it is a sign of no common filial piety, that he wished himself to be put in Benjamin's place, and to undergo perpetual exile and servitude, rather than convey to the miserable old man tidings which would be the cause of his destruction. He proves his sincerity by offering himself as a surety, in order that he may liberate his brother. Because חָטָא (*chatah*) among the Hebrews, sometimes signifies to be in fault, and sometimes to be under penalty; some translate the passage, "I shall have sinned against my father;" or, "I shall be accused of sin;" while others render it, "I shall be deemed guilty, because he will complain of having been deceived by my promise." The latter sense is the more appropriate, because, truly, he would not escape disgrace and censure from his father, as having cruelly betrayed a youth committed to his care.

CHAPTER XLV.

1. THEN Joseph could not refrain himself before all them that stood by him; and he cried, Cause every man to go out from me. And there stood no man with him, while Joseph

1. Tunc non potuit Joseph se comprimere coram omnibus, qui stabant juxta se, et clamavit, Educite omnem virum a me: et non stetit quisquam cum eo, quan-

made himself known unto his brethren.

2. And he wept aloud: and the Egyptians and the house of Pharaoh heard.

3. And Joseph said unto his brethren, I *am* Joseph: doth my father yet live? And his brethren could not answer him; for they were troubled at his presence.

4. And Joseph said unto his brethren, Come near to me, I pray you. And they came near. And he said, I *am* Joseph your brother, whom ye sold into Egypt.

5. Now therefore be not grieved nor angry with yourselves that ye sold me hither; for God did send me before you to preserve life.

6. For these two years *hath* the famine *been* in the land: and yet *there are* five years, in the which *there shall* neither *be* earing nor harvest.

7. And God sent me before you to preserve you a posterity in the earth, and to save your lives by a great deliverance.

8. So now, *it was* not you *that* sent me hither, but God: and he hath made me a father to Pharaoh, and lord of all his house, and a ruler throughout all the land of Egypt.

9. Haste ye, and go up to my father, and say unto him, Thus saith thy son Joseph, God hath made me lord of all Egypt; come down unto me, tarry not:

10. And thou shalt dwell in the land of Goshen, and thou shalt be near unto me, thou, and thy children, and thy children's children, and thy flocks, and thy herds, and all that thou hast:

11. And there will I nourish thee, for yet *there are* five years of famine; lest thou, and thy household, and all that thou hast, come to poverty.

12. And, behold, your eyes see, and the eyes of my brother Benjamin, that *it is* my mouth that speaketh unto you.

do patefecit se Joseph fratribus suis.

2. Et emisit vocem suam cum fletu: et audierunt Ægyptii, audivit et domus Pharaonis.

3. Dixit autem Joseph fratribus suis, Ego sum Joseph, num adhuc vivit pater meus? et non potuerunt fratres ejus respondere ei: quia territi erant a facie ejus.

4. Et dixit Joseph fratribus suis, Accedite quæso ad me. Et accesserunt. Et dixit, Ego sum Joseph frater vester, quem vendidistis in Ægyptum.

5. Et nunc ne dolore afficiamini, et ne sit ira in oculis vestris quod vendideritis me huc: nam propter vitam misit me Deus ante vos.

6. Jam enim duo anni famis fuerunt in medio terræ, et adhuc quinque anni sunt, in quibus non erit aratio et messis.

7. Et misit me Deus ante vos, ut ponam vobis reliquias in terra: et ut vivificem vos evasione magna.

8. Nunc itaque non vos misistis me huc, sed Deus: et posuit me in patrem Pharaoni, et in dominum toti domui ejus, et dominatorem in tota terra Ægypti.

9. Festinate, et ascendite ad patrem meum, et dicite ei, Sic dicit filius tuus Joseph, Posuit me Deus in dominum toti Ægypto, descende ad me, ne stes.

10. Et habitabis in terra Gosen, et eris propinquus mihi, tu et filii tui, et filii filiorum tuorum, et pecudes tuæ, et boves tui, et omnia quæ sunt tibi.

11. Et alam te ibi, quia adhuc quinque anni famis sunt: ne forte inopia vel egestate conficiaris tu et domus tua, et omne quod est tibi.

12. Et ecce, oculi vestri vident et oculi fratris mei Benjamin, quod os meum loquitur ad vos.

13. And ye shall tell my father
of all my glory in Egypt, and of all
that ye have seen; and ye shall
haste and bring down my father
hither.

14. And he fell upon his brother
Benjamin's neck, and wept; and
Benjamin wept upon his neck.

15. Moreover, he kissed all his
brethren, and wept upon them: and
after that his brethren talked with
him.

16. And the fame thereof was
heard in Pharaoh's house, saying,
Joseph's brethren are come. And
it pleased Pharaoh well, and his servants.

17. And Pharaoh said unto Joseph, Say unto thy brethren, This do
ye; lade your beasts, and go, get
you unto the land of Canaan;

18. And take your father, and
your households, and come unto me:
and I will give you the good of the
land of Egypt, and ye shall eat the
fat of the land.

19. Now thou art commanded,
this do ye; Take you waggons out
of the land of Egypt for your little
ones, and for your wives, and bring
your father, and come.

20. Also regard not your stuff:
for the good of all the land of Egypt
is yours.

21. And the children of Israel
did so, and Joseph gave them waggons, according to the commandment
of Pharaoh, and gave them provision
for the way.

22. To all of them he gave each
man changes of raiment; but to
Benjamin he gave three hundred
pieces of silver, and five changes of
raiment.

23. And to his father he sent after this *manner:* ten asses laden
with the good things of Egypt, and
ten she-asses laden with corn and
bread and meat for his father by the
way.

24. So he sent his brethren away,
and they departed: and he said unto
them, See that ye fall not out by the
way.

13. Nuntiate autem patri meo
omnem gloriam meam in Ægypto,
et omnia quæ vidistis: et festinate,
et descendere facite patrem meum
huc.

14. Et jactavit se super collum
Benjamin fratris sui, et flevit: Benjamin quoque flevit super collum ejus.

15. Et osculatus est omnes fratres
suos, et flevit super eos, et postea
loquuti sunt fratres ejus cum eo.

16. Et vox audita est in domo
Pharaonis, dicendo, Venerunt fratres
Joseph, et placuit in oculis Pharao-
nis, et in oculis servorum ejus.

17. Et dixit Pharao ad Joseph,
Dic fratribus tuis, Hoc facite, one-
rate jumenta vestra, et ite, ingredi-
mini terram Chenaan.

18. Et capite patrem vestrum, et
familias vestras, et venite ad me: et
dabo vobis bonum terræ Ægypti, et
comedetis pinguedinem terræ.

19. Et tu jussus es, Hoc facite,
capite vobis de terra Ægypti currus
pro parvulis vestris, et pro uxoribus
vestris: et tollite patrem vestrum,
et venite.

20. Et oculus vester ne parcat supellectili vestræ: quia bonum omnis
terræ Ægypti vestrum erit.

21. Fecerunt ergo sic filii Israel,
et dedit eis Joseph currus juxta sermonem Pharaonis, et dedit eis escam
pro itinere.

22. Omnibus ipsis dedit unicuique
mutatorias vestes, et ipsi Benjamin
dedit trecentos argenteos, et quinque mutatorias vestes.

23. Patri autem suo misit secundum hoc, decem asinos ferentes de
bono Ægypti, et decem asinas ferentes frumentum, et panem, et escam
patri suo pro itinere.

24. Et dimisit fratres suos, et
abierunt, et dixit ad eos, Ne tumul-
tuemini in via.

25. And they went up out of Egypt, and came into the land of Canaan unto Jacob their father,

26. And told him, saying, Joseph *is* yet alive, and he *is* governor over all the land of Egypt.   And Jacob's heart fainted, for he believed them not.

27. And they told him all the words of Joseph, which he had said unto them: and when he saw the waggons, which Joseph had sent to carry him, the spirit of Jacob their father revived.

28. And Israel said, *It is* enough; Joseph my son *is* yet alive : I will go and see him before I die.

25. At ascenderunt ex Ægypto, et venerunt in terram Chenaan, ad Jahacob patrem suum.

26. Et nuntiaverunt ei, dicendo, Adhuc Joseph vivit: et quod ipse dominaretur in omni terra Ægypti: et dissolutum est cor ejus, quia non credebat eis.

27. Et retulerunt ei omnia verba Joseph, quæ loquutus fuerat ad eos : et vidit currus, quos miserat Joseph ut ferrent eum, et revixit spiritus Jahacob patris eorum.

28. Et dixit Israel, Sufficit, adhuc Joseph filius meus vivit : ibo, et videbo eum, antequam moriar.

1. *Then Joseph could not refrain himself.*[1]   Moses relates in this chapter the manner in which Joseph made himself known to his brethren.   In the first place, he declares, that Joseph had done violence to his feelings, as long as he presented to them an austere and harsh countenance.   At length the strong fraternal affection, which he had suppressed during the time that he was breathing severe threatenings, poured itself forth with more abundant force : whence it appears that nothing severe or cruel had before been harboured in his mind.   And whereas it thus bursts forth in tears, this softness or tenderness is more deserving of praise than if he had maintained an equable temper.   Therefore the stoics speak foolishly when they say, that it is an heroic virtue not to be touched with compassion.   Had Joseph stood inflexible, who would not have pronounced him to be a stupid, or iron-hearted man ?   But now, by the vehemence of his feelings, he manifests a noble magnanimity, as well as a divine moderation ; because he was so superior both to anger and to hatred, that he ardently loved those who had wickedly conspired to effect his ruin, though they had received no

[1] The division of chapters in this place is singularly unhappy.   It interrupts one of the most touching scenes recorded in the sacred volume, just in the middle.   It separates the irresistible appeal of Judah to the feelings of Joseph from its immediate and happy effect.   In the Hebrew Bible, the section commences with Judah's address, and no break is made where this chapter commences ; so that the whole is given as one continuous narrative. —*Ed.*

injury from him.   He commands all men to depart, not because he was ashamed of his kindred, (for he does not afterwards dissemble the fact that they were his brethren, and
he freely permits the report of it to be carried to the king's
palace,) but because he is considerate for their feelings, that
he might not make known their detestable crime to many
witnesses.   And it was not the smallest part of his clemency,
to desire that their disgrace should be wholly buried in
oblivion.   We see, therefore, that witnesses were removed,
for no other reason than that he might more freely comfort
his brethren ; for he not only spared them, by not exposing
their crime; but when shut up alone with them, he abstained
from all bitterness of language, and gladly administered to
them friendly consolation.

3. *I am Joseph.* Although he had given them the clearest
token of his mildness and his love, yet, when he told them
his name, they were terrified, as if he had thundered against
them : for while they revolve in their minds what they
have deserved, the power of Joseph seems so formidable to
them, that they anticipate nothing for themselves but death.
When, however, he sees them overcome with fear, he utters
no reproach, but only labours to calm their perturbation.
Nay, he continues gently to soothe them, until he has rendered them composed and cheerful.   By this example we
are taught to take heed lest sadness should overwhelm those
who are truly and seriously humbled under a sense of shame.
So long as the offender is deaf to reproofs, or securely flatters
himself, or wickedly and obstinately repels admonitions, or
excuses himself by hypocrisy, greater severity is to be used
towards him.   But rigour should have its bounds, and as soon
as the offender lies prostrate, and trembles under the sense
of his sin, let that moderation immediately follow which may
raise him who is cast down, by the hope of pardon.   Therefore, in order that our severity may be rightly and duly attempered, we must cultivate this inward affection of Joseph,
which will show itself at the proper time.

4. *Come near to me, I pray you.* This is more efficacious
than any mere words, that he kindly invites them to his embrace.   Yet he also tries to remove their care and fear by

the most courteous language he can use.   He so attempers
his speech, indeed, that he mildly accuses, and again consoles
them; nevertheless, the consolation greatly predominates,
because he sees that they are on the point of desperation,
unless he affords them timely relief.   Moreover, in relating
that he had been sold, he does not renew the memory of their
guilt, with the intention of expostulating with them; but only
because it is always profitable that the sense of sin should
remain, provided that immoderate terror does not absorb the
unhappy man, after he has acknowledged his fault.   And
whereas the brethren of Joseph were more than sufficiently
terrified, he insists the more fully on the second part of his
purpose; namely, that he may heal the wound.   This is the
reason why he repeats, that God had sent him for their preservation; that by the counsel of God himself he had been
sent beforehand into Egypt to preserve them alive; and that,
in short, he had not been sent into Egypt by them, but had
been led thither by the hand of God.[1]

8. *So now, it was not you that sent me hither.*   This is a
remarkable passage, in which we are taught that the right
course of events is never so disturbed by the depravity and
wickedness of men, but that God can direct them to a good
end.   We are also instructed in what manner and for what
purpose we must consider the providence of God.   When
men of inquisitive minds dispute concerning it, they not only
mingle and pervert all things without regard to the end designed, but invent every absurdity in their power, in order
to sully the justice of God.   And this rashness causes some
pious and moderate men to wish this portion of doctrine to
be concealed from view; for as soon as it is publicly declared
that God holds the government of the whole world, and that
nothing is done but by his will and authority, they who
think with little reverence of the mysteries of God, break

---

[1] Only two years of the famine had now elapsed, and there were yet five
years in which there should be " neither earing nor harvest," so that this
was indeed but the commencement of the grievous suffering to which
Jacob's family would have been exposed, but for the extraordinary interposition of Divine providence in their favour.   The word *earing* is an obsolete Saxon term by which our translators have rendered the Hebrew word
חריש, (*charish,*) which means *ploughing,* or preparing the ground for seed.
—*Ed.*

forth into various questions, not only frivolous but injurious. But, as this profane intemperance of mind is to be restrained, so a just measure is to be observed on the other hand, lest we should encourage a gross ignorance of those things which are not only made plain in the word of God, but are exceedingly useful to be known. Good men are ashamed to confess, that what men undertake cannot be accomplished except by the will of God ; fearing lest unbridled tongues should cry out immediately, either that God is the author of sin, or that wicked men are not to be accused of crime, seeing they fulfil the counsel of God. But although this sacrilegious fury cannot be effectually rebutted, it may suffice that we hold it in detestation. Meanwhile, it is right to maintain, what is declared by the clear testimonies of Scripture, that whatever men may contrive, yet, amidst all their tumult, God from heaven overrules their counsels and attempts ; and, in short, does, by their hands, what he has himself decreed. Good men, who fear to expose the justice of God to the calumnies of the impious, resort to this distinction, that God *wills* some things, but *permits* others to be done. As if, truly, any degree of liberty of action, were he to cease from governing, would be left to men. If he had only *permitted* Joseph to be carried into Egypt, he had not *ordained* him to be the minister of deliverance to his father Jacob and his sons ; which he is now expressly declared to have done. Away, then, with that vain figment, that, by the *permission* of God only, and not by his *counsel* or *will*, those evils are committed which he afterwards turns to a good account. I speak of evils with respect to men, who propose nothing else to themselves but to act perversely. And as the vice dwells in them, so ought the whole blame also to be laid upon them. But God works wonderfully through their means, in order that, from their impurity, he may bring forth his perfect righteousness. This method of acting is secret, and far above our understanding. Therefore it is not wonderful that the licentiousness of our flesh should rise against it. But so much the more diligently must we be on our guard, that we do not attempt to reduce this lofty standard to the measure of our own littleness. Let this sentiment remain fixed with us, that while

the lust of men exults, and intemperately hurries them
hither and thither, God is the ruler, and, by his secret rein,
directs their motions whithersoever he pleases. At the same
time, however, it must also be maintained, that God acts so
far distinctly from them, that no vice can attach itself to his
providence, and that his decrees have no affinity with the
crimes of men. Of which mode of procedure a most illustrious example is placed before our eyes in this history.
Joseph was sold by his brethren; for what reason, but because they wished, by any means whatever, to ruin and annihilate him? The same work is ascribed to God, but for a
very different end; namely, that in a time of famine the
family of Jacob might have an unexpected supply of food.
Therefore he willed that Joseph should be as one dead, for
a short time, in order that he might suddenly bring him forth
from the grave, as the preserver of life. Whence it appears,
that although he seems, at the commencement, to do the
same thing as the wicked; yet there is a wide distance between their wickedness and his admirable judgment. Let
us now examine the words of Joseph. For the consolation
of his brethren he seems to draw the veil of oblivion over
their fault. But we know that men are not exempt from
guilt, although God may, beyond expectation, bring what
they wickedly attempt, to a good and happy issue. For
what advantage was it to Judas that the redemption of the
world proceeded from his wicked treachery? Joseph, however, though he withdraws, in some degree, the minds of his
brethren from a consideration of their own guilt, until they
can breathe again after their immoderate terror, neither traces
their fault to God as its cause, nor really absolves them from
it; as we shall see more clearly in the last chapter. And
doubtless, it must be maintained, that the deeds of men are
not to be estimated according to the event, but according to
the measure in which they may have failed in their duty, or
may have attempted something contrary to the Divine command, and may have gone beyond the bounds of their calling.
Some one, for instance, has neglected his wife or children, and
has not diligently attended to their necessities; and though
they do not die, unless God wills it, yet the inhumanity of

the father, who wickedly deserted them when he ought to
have relieved them, is not screened or excused by this pretext. Therefore, they whose consciences accuse them of evil,
derive no advantage from the pretence that the providence
of God exonerates them from blame. But on the other hand,
whenever the Lord interposes to prevent the evil of those who
desire to injure us, and not that only, but turns even their
wicked designs to our good; he subdues, by this method,
our carnal affections, and renders us more just and placable.
Thus we see that Joseph was a skilful interpreter of the providence of God, when he borrowed from it an argument for
granting forgiveness to his brethren. The magnitude of the
crime committed against him might so have incensed him
as to cause him to burn with the desire of revenge: but
when he reflects that their wickedness had been overruled
by the wonderful and unwonted goodness of God, forgetting
the injury received, he kindly embraces the men whose dishonour God had covered with his grace. And truly charity
is ingenious in hiding the faults of brethren, and therefore
she freely applies to this use anything which may tend to appease anger, and to set enmities at rest. Joseph also is carried
forward to another view of the case; namely, that he had
been divinely chosen to help his brethren. Whence it happens, that he not only remits their offence, but that, from
an earnest desire to discharge the duty enjoined upon him,
he delivers them from fear and anxiety as well as from want.
This is the reason why he asserts that he was ordained to
" put for them a remnant,"[1] that is, to preserve a remaining
seed, or rather to preserve them alive, and that by an excellent and wonderful deliverance. In saying that he is a
father to Pharaoh, he is not carried away with empty boasting as vain men are wont to be ; nor does he make an ostentatious display of his wealth ; but he proves, from an event so
great and incredible, that he had not obtained the post he
occupied by accident, nor by human means ; but rather
that, by the wonderful counsel of God, a lofty throne had

---

[1] Ver. 7. Ut ponam vobis reliquias in terrâ. " To preserve you a posterity," (or, as in the margin,) " to put for you a remnant" in the earth.—
English translation.—Ed.

been raised for him, from which he might succour his father and his whole family.

9. *Thus saith thy son Joseph.* In giving this command, he shows that he spoke of his power in order to inspire his father with stronger confidence. We know how dilatory old men are; and, besides, it was difficult to tear holy Jacob away from the inheritance which was divinely promised to him. Therefore Joseph, having pointed out the necessity for the step, declares what a desirable relief the Lord had offered. It may, however, be asked, why the oracle did not occur to their minds, concerning which they had been instructed by their fathers, namely, that they should be strangers and servants in a strange land. (Gen. xv. 13.) For it seems that Joseph here promises nothing but mere pleasures, as if no future adversity was to be apprehended. But though nothing is expressly declared on this point by Moses, yet I am induced, by a probable conjecture, to believe that Jacob was not forgetful of the oracle. For, unless he had been retained by some celestial chain, he never could have remained in Egypt after the expiration of the time of scarcity. For by remaining there voluntarily, he would have appeared to cast away the hope of the inheritance promised him by God. Seeing, then, that he does not provide for his return into the land of Canaan, but only commands his corpse to be carried thither; nor yet exhorts his sons to a speedy return, but suffers them to settle in Egypt; he does this, not from indolence, or because he is allured by the attractions of Egypt, or has become weary of the land of Canaan; but because he is preparing himself and his offspring to bear that tyranny, concerning which he had been forewarned by his father Isaac. Therefore he regards it as an advantage that, at his first coming, he is hospitably received; but, in the meantime, he revolves in his mind what had been spoken to Abraham.

16. *And the fame thereof was heard in Pharaoh's house.* What Moses now relates, was prior in the order of events. For before Joseph sent for his father, the report of the coming of his brethren had reached the palace. And Joseph would not have promised so confidently a home to his brethren in Egypt, except by the king's permission. What,

therefore, Moses had before briefly alluded to, he now more fully explains; namely, that the king, with a ready and cheerful mind, declared his high esteem for Joseph, in freely offering to his father and brethren, the most fertile part of Egypt for their dwelling. And from another statement of Moses it appears that, as long as he lived, the Israelites were treated with clemency and kindness. For, in the first chapter of Exodus, and the eighth verse, the commencement of the tyranny and cruelty is said to have been made by his successor, to whom Joseph was unknown.

22. *And to all of them he gave each man changes of raiment.* That he furnishes his brethren with supplies for their journey is not wonderful : but to what purpose was it that he loaded them with money and garments, seeing they would so soon return ? I, indeed, do not doubt that he did it on account of his father and the wives of his brethren, in order that they might have less reluctance to leave the land of Canaan. For he knew that his message would scarcely be believed, unless some manifest tokens of its truth were presented. It might also be, that he not only endeavoured to allure those who were absent, but that he also wished to testify, more and more, his love towards his brethren. But the former consideration has more weight with me, because he took greater care in furnishing Benjamin than the rest. Jerome has translated the expression, " changes of raiment," by " two robes," and other interpreters, following him, expound it as meaning " different kinds of garments." I know not whether this be solid. I rather suppose they were elegant garments, such as were used at nuptials and on festal days ; for I think that constant custom was silently opposed to this variety of dress.

24. *See that ye fall not out by the way.* Some explain the passage as meaning, that Joseph asks his brethren to be of tranquil mind, and not to disturb themselves with needless fear ; he rather exhorts them, however, to mutual peace. For, since the word רגז, (*ragaz,*) sometimes signifies to tremble or be afraid, and sometimes, to make a tumult, the latter sense is the more appropriate : for we know that the children of God are not only easily appeased, if any one has

injured them, but that they also desire others should live together in concord. Joseph was pacified towards his brethren; but at the same time he admonishes them not to stir up any strife among themselves. For there was reason to fear lest each, in attempting to excuse himself, should try to lay the blame on others, and thus contention would arise. We ought to imitate this kindness of Joseph; that we may prevent, as much as possible, quarrels and strifes of words; for Christ requires of his disciples, not only that they should be lovers of peace, but also that they should be peace-makers. Wherefore, it is our duty to remove, in time, all matter and occasion of strife. Besides, we must know, that what Joseph taught his brethren, is the command of the Spirit of God to us all; namely, that we should not be angry with each other. And because it generally happens that, in faults common to different parties, one maliciously accuses another; let each of us learn to acknowledge and confess his own fault, lest altercations should end in combats.

26. *And Jacob's heart fainted.* We know that some persons have fainted with sudden and unexpected joy. Therefore, certain interpreters suppose that the heart of Jacob was, in a sense, suffocated, as if seized by a kind of ecstatic stupor. But Moses assigns a different cause; namely, that not having confidence in his sons, he was agitated between hope and fear. And we know, that they who are held in suspense, by hearing some incredible message, are struck with torpor, as if they were lifeless. It was not, therefore, a simple affection of joy, but a certain mingled perturbation which shook the mind of Jacob. Therefore, Moses shortly after says, that his spirit revived; when he, having returned to himself, and being composed in mind, believed that which he had heard to be true. And he shows that his love towards Joseph had not languished through length of time, inasmuch as he set no value upon his own life, except so far as it would permit him to enjoy a sight of Joseph. He had before assigned to himself continual sorrow, even to the grave; but now he declares that he shall have a joyful death.

CHAPTER XLVI.

1. AND Israel took his journey with all that he had, and came to Beer-sheba, and offered sacrifices unto the God of his father Isaac.

2. And God spake unto Israel in the visions of the night, and said, Jacob, Jacob. And he said, Here am I.

3. And he said, I am God, the God of thy father : fear not to go down into Egypt; for I will there make of thee a great nation.

4. I will go down with thee into Egypt; and I will also surely bring thee up again : and Joseph shall put his hand upon thine eyes.

5. And Jacob rose up from Beer-sheba: and the sons of Israel carried Jacob their father, and their little ones, and their wives, in the waggons which Pharaoh had sent to carry him.

6. And they took their cattle, and their goods, which they had gotten in the land of Canaan, and came into Egypt, Jacob, and all his seed with him :

7. His sons, and his sons' sons with him, his daughters, and his sons' daughters, and all his seed, brought he with him into Egypt.

8. And these are the names of the children of Israel which came into Egypt, Jacob and his sons : Reuben, Jacob's first-born.

9. And the sons of Reuben; Hanoch, and Phallu, and Hezron, and Carmi.

10. And the sons of Simeon ; Jemuel, and Jamin, and Ohad, and Jachin, and Zohar, and Shaul the son of a Canaanitish woman.

11. And the sons of Levi ; Gershon, Kohath, and Merari.

12. And the sons of Judah ; Er, and Onan, and Shelah, and Pharez, and Zarah : but Er and Onan died in the land of Canaan. And the sons of Pharez were Hezron and Hamul.

1. Itaque profectus est Israel, et quæcunque habebat, et venit in Beersebah, et sacrificavit sacrificia Deo patris sui Ishac.

2. Et dixit Deus ad Israel in visionibus noctis, dixit inquam, Jahacob, Jahacob. Ille respondit, Ecce, adsum.

3. Et dixit, Ego sum Deus, Deus patris tui : ne timeas descendere in Ægyptum : quia in gentem magnam ponam te ibi.

4. Ego descendam tecum in Ægyptum, et ego ascendere etiam te faciam ascendendo : Joseph quoque ponet manum suam super oculos tuos.

5. Postea surrexit Jahacob de Beersebah, et sustulerunt filii Israel Jahacob patrem suum, et parvulos suos, et uxores super currus, quos miserat Pharao ad ferendum eum.

6. Et ceperunt pecudes suas, et substantiam quam acquisierant in terra Chenaan : veneruntque in Ægyptum Jahacob, et omne semen ejus cum ipso :

7. Filii ejus, et filii filiorum ejus cum eo, filiæ ejus, et filiæ filiorum ejus : et omne semen suum deduxit secum in Ægyptum.

8. Hæc sunt autem nomina filiorum Israel, qui ingressi sunt in Ægyptum, Jahacob et filii ejus : primogenitus Jahacob, Reuben.

9. Et filii Reuben, Hanoch, et Phallu, et Hesron, et Charmi.

10. Filii vero Simhon, Jemuel, et Jamin, et Ohad, et Jachin, et Sohar, et Saul filius Chenaanitidis.

11. Filii Levi, Gerson, Cehath, et Merari.

12. Filii Jehudah, Her, et Onam, et Selah, et Peres, et Zerah : et mortuus est Her et Onam in terra Chenaan. Fuerunt autem filii Peres, Hesron, et Hamul.

13. And the sons of Issachar; Tola, and Phuvah, and Job, and Shimron.

14. And the sons of Zebulun ; Sered, and Elon, and Jahleel.

15. These *be* the sons of Leah, which she bare unto Jacob in Padan-aram, with his daughter Dinah : all the souls of his sons and his daughters *were* thirty and three.

16. And the sons of Gad ; Ziphion, and Haggi, Shuni, and Ezbon, Eri, and Arodi, and Areli.

17. And the sons of Asher; Jimnah, and Ishuah, and Isui, and Beriah, and Serah their sister. And the sons of Beriah ; Heber, and Malchiel.

18. These *are* the sons of Zilpah, whom Laban gave to Leah his daughter; and these she bare unto Jacob, *even* sixteen souls.

19. The sons of Rachel, Jacob's wife; Joseph, and Benjamin.

20. And unto Joseph, in the land of Egypt, were born Manasseh and Ephraim, which Asenath, the daughter of Poti-pherah priest of On, bare unto him.

21. And the sons of Benjamin *were* Belah, and Becher, and Ashbel, Gera, and Naaman, Ehi, and Rosh, Muppim, and Huppim, and Ard.

22. These *are* the sons of Rachel, which were born to Jacob: all the souls *were* fourteen.

23. And the sons of Dan; Hushim.

24. And the sons of Naphtali ; Jahzeel, and Guni, and Jezer, and Shillem.

25. These *are* the sons of Bilhah, which Laban gave unto Rachel his daughter; and she bare these unto Jacob: all the souls *were* seven.

26. All the souls that came with Jacob into Egypt, which came out of his loins, besides Jacob's sons' wives, all the souls *were* threescore and six.

27. And the sons of Joseph, which were born him in Egypt, *were* two souls: all the souls of the house of Jacob, which came into Egypt, *were* threescore and ten.

13. Et filii Issachar, Tholah, et Puvah, et Job, et Simron.

14. Filii vero Zebulon, Sered, et Elon, et Jahleel.

15. Isti sunt filii Leah, quos peperit ipsi Jahacob in Padan Aram, et Dinah filiam ejus : omnes animæ filiorum ejus, et filiarum ejus fuerunt triginta et tres.

16. Filii autem Gad, Siphion et Hagghi, Suni et Esbon, Heri et Arodi, et Areli.

17. Et filii Aser, Imnah, et Isvah, et Isvi, et Berihah, et Serah soror eorum. Filii vero Berihah, Heber et Malchiel.

18. Isti sunt filii Zilpah, quam dedit Laban Leah filiæ suæ, et peperit istos ipsi Jahacob, sedecim animas.

19. Filii Rachel uxoris Jahacob, Joseph et Benjamin.

20. Nati sunt autem ipsi Joseph in terra Ægypti, quos peperit ei Asenath filia Poti-pherah principis On, Menasseh et Ephraim.

21. Filii vero Benjamin, fuerunt Belah, et Becher, et Asbel, Gera et Naaman, Ehi et Ros, Muppim, et Huppim, et Arde.

22. Isti sunt filii Rachel qui nati sunt ipsi Jahacob : omnes animæ, quatuordecim.

23. Et filii Dan, Hussim.

24. Filii Nephthali, Jahsecl, et Guni, et Jeser, et Sillem.

25. Isti sunt filii Bilhah, quam dedit Laban Rachel filiæ suæ, et peperit istos ipsi Jahacob : omnes animæ septem.

26. Omnes animæ, quæ venerunt cum Jahacob in Ægyptum, quæ egressæ sunt de femore ejus, præter uxores filiorum Jahacob, omnes, inquam, animæ fuerunt sexaginta et sex.

27. Et filii Joseph, qui nati sunt ei in Ægypto, animæ duæ. Omnes animæ domus Jahacob, quæ ingressæ sunt in Ægyptum, fuerunt septuaginta.

28. And he sent Judah before him unto Joseph, to direct his face unto Goshen ; and they came into the land of Goshen.

29. And Joseph made ready his chariot, and went up to meet Israel his father, to Goshen, and presented himself unto him ; and he fell on his neck, and wept on his neck a good while.

30. And Israel said unto Joseph, Now let me die, since I have seen thy face, because thou *art* yet alive.

31. And Joseph said unto his brethren, and unto his father's house, I will go up, and shew Pharaoh, and say unto him, My brethren, and my father's house, which *were* in the land of Canaan, are come unto me :

32. And the men *are* shepherds, for their trade hath been to feed cattle ; and they have brought their flocks, and their herds, and all that they have.

33. And it shall come to pass, when Pharaoh shall call you, and shall say, What *is* your occupation ?

34. That ye shall say, Thy servants' trade hath been about cattle from our youth even until now, both we *and* also our fathers ; that ye may dwell in the land of Goshen : for every shepherd *is* an abomination unto the Egyptians.

28. Porro Jehudah misit ante se ad Joseph ad præparandum locum ante se in Gosen, et venerunt in terram Gosen.

29. Et ligavit Joseph currum suum, et ascendit in occursum Israel patris sui in Gosen : et conspectus est ei, et jactavit se ad collum ejus, flevitque super collum ejus adhuc.

30. Et dixit Israel ad Joseph, Moriar hac vice, postquam vidi faciem tuam : adhuc enim tu vivis.

31. Et dixit Joseph fratribus suis, et domui patris sui, Ascendam, et nuntiabo Pharaoni : et dicam ei. Fratres mei, et domus patris mei, qui erant in terram Chenaan, venerunt ad me.

32. Atque viri pastores pecudum sunt, quia viri pecuarii sunt : et pecudes eorum, et boves eorum, et omnia quæ erant eis, adduxerunt.

33. Erit ergo quum vocaverit vos Pharao, et dixerit, Quod est opus vestrum ?

34. Dicetis, Viri pecuarii fuerunt servi tui a pueritia nostra et usque nunc, etiam nos, etiam patres nostri : ut habitetis in terra Gosen, quia abominatio Ægyptiis est omnis pastor pecudum.

1. *And Israel took his journey.* Because the holy man is compelled to leave the land of Canaan and to go elsewhere, he offers, on his departure, a sacrifice to the Lord, for the purpose of testifying that the covenant which God had made with his fathers was confirmed and ratified to himself. For, though he was accustomed to exercise himself in the external worship of God, there was yet a special reason for this sacrifice. And, doubtless, he had then peculiar need of support, lest his faith should fail : for he was about to be deprived of the inheritance promised to him, and of the sight of that land which was the type and the pledge of the heavenly country. Might it not come into his mind that he had hitherto been deluded with a vain hope ? Therefore, by re-

newing the memory of the divine covenant, he applies a suitable remedy against falling from the faith.   For this reason,
he offers a sacrifice on the very boundaries of that land, as I
have just said ; that we might know it to be something more
than usual.   And he presents this worship to the God of
his fathers, to testify that, although he is departing from
that land, into which Abraham had been called ; yet he
does not thereby cut himself off from the God in whose worship he had been educated.   It was truly a remarkable proof
of constancy, that when cast out by famine into another
region, so that he might not even be permitted to sojourn
in the land of which he was the lawful lord ; he yet retains,
deeply impressed on his mind, the hope of his hidden right.
It was not without subjecting himself to odium that he differed openly from other nations, by worshipping the God of
his fathers.   But what profit was there in having a religion
different from all others ?   Seeing, then, that he does not repent of having worshipped the God of his fathers, and that
he now also perseveres in fear and reverence towards Him ;
we hence infer how deeply he was rooted in true piety.   By
offering a sacrifice, he both increases his own strength, and
makes profession of his faith ; because, although piety is not
bound to external symbols, yet he will not neglect those helps,
the use of which he has found to be, by no means, superfluous.

2. *And God spake unto Israel.*   In this manner, God
proves that the sacrifice of Jacob was acceptable to him, and
again stretches out his hand to ratify anew his covenant.
The vision by night availed for the purpose of giving greater
dignity to the oracle.   Jacob indeed, inasmuch as he was
docile and ready to yield obedience to God, did not need
to be impelled by force and terror ; yet, because he was a
man encompassed with flesh, it was profitable for him that
he should be affected as with the glory of a present God, in
order that the word might penetrate more effectually into
his heart.   It is, however, proper to recall to memory what I
have said before, that the *word* was joined with it ; because
a silent vision would have profited little or nothing.   We
know that superstition eagerly snatches at mere spectres ;
by which means it presents God in a form of its own.   But

since no living image of God can exist without the word, whenever God has *appeared* to his servants, he has also *spoken* to them. Wherefore, in all outward signs, let us be ever attentive to his voice, if we would not be deluded by the wiles of Satan. But if those visions, in which the majesty of God shines, require to be animated by the word, then they who obtrude signs, invented at the will of men, upon the Church, exhibit nothing else than the empty pomps of a profane theatre. Just as in the Papacy, those things which are called sacraments, are lifeless phantoms which draw away deluded souls from the true God. Let this mutual connexion, then, be observed, that the vision which gives greater dignity to the word, precedes it; and that the word follows immediately, as if it were the soul of the vision. And there is no question that this was an appearance of the visible glory of God, which did not leave Jacob in suspense and hesitation; but which, by removing his doubt, firmly sustained him, so that he confidently embraced the oracle.

3. *Jacob, Jacob.* The design of the repetition was to render him more attentive. For, by thus familiarly addressing him, God more gently insinuates himself into his mind: as, in the Scripture, he kindly allures us, that he may prepare us to become his disciples. The docility of the holy man appears hence, that as soon as he is persuaded that God speaks, he replies that he is ready to receive with reverence whatever may be spoken, to follow wheresoever he may be called, and to undertake whatever may be commanded. Afterwards, a promise is added, by which God confirms and revives the faith of his servant. Whereas, the descent into Egypt was to him a sad event, he is bidden to be of good and cheerful mind; inasmuch as the Lord would always be his keeper, and after having increased him there to a great nation, would bring him back again to the place, whence he now compelled him to depart. And, indeed, Jacob's chief consolation turned on this point; that he should not perpetually wander up and down as an exile, but should, at length, enjoy the expected inheritance. For, since the possession of the land of Canaan was the token of the Divine favour, of spiritual blessings, and of eternal felicity; if holy Jacob was

defrauded of this, it would have availed him little or nothing to have riches, and all kinds of wealth and power heaped upon him, in Egypt. The return promised him is not, however, to be understood of his own person, but refers to his posterity. Now, as Jacob, relying on the promise, is commanded boldly to go down into Egypt; so it is the duty of all the pious, after his example, to derive such strength from the grace of God, that they may gird themselves to obey his commands. The title by which God here distinguishes himself, is attached to the former oracles which Jacob had received by tradition from his fathers. For why does he not rather call himself the Creator of heaven and earth, than the God of Isaac or of Abraham, except for this reason, that the dominion over the land of Canaan depends on the previous covenant, which he now ratifies anew ? At the same time also, he encourages his servant by examples drawn from his own family, lest he should cease to proceed with constancy in his calling. For, when he had seen that his father Isaac, and had heard that his grandfather Abraham, though long surrounded by great troubles, never gave way to any temptations, it ill became him to be overcome by weariness in the same course; especially since, in the act of dying, they handed their lamp to their posterity, and took diligent care to leave the light of their faith to survive them in their family. In short, Jacob is taught that he must not seek, in crooked and diverse paths, that God whom he had learned, from his childhood, to regard as the Ruler of the family of Abraham ; provided it did not degenerate from his piety. Moreover, we have elsewhere stated how far, in this respect, the authority of the Fathers ought to prevail. For it was not the design of God, either that Jacob should subject himself to men, or should approve, without discrimination, whatever was handed down from his ancestors,—seeing that he so often condemns in the Jews, a foolish imitation of their fathers,—but his design was to keep Jacob in the true knowledge of himself.

4. *And Joseph shall put his hand upon thine eyes.* This clause was added for the sake of showing greater indulgence. For though Jacob, in desiring that, when he died, his eyes

should be closed by the hand of Joseph, showed that some infirmity of the flesh was involved in the wish; yet God is willing to comply with it, for the sake of moderating the grief of a fresh banishment.   Moreover, we know that the custom of closing the eyes was of the greatest antiquity; and that this office was discharged by one most closely connected with the deceased either by blood or affection.

5. *And Jacob rose up.*   By using the words " rose up," Moses seems to denote that Jacob received new vigour from the vision.   For although the former promises were not forgotten, yet the addition of the recent memorial came most opportunely, in order that he, bearing the land of Canaan in his heart, might endure his absence from it with equanimity.   When it is said that he took with him all that he had acquired, or possessed in the land of Canaan, it is probable that his servants and handmaids came together with his cattle.[1]   But, on his departure, no mention is made of them: nay, a little afterwards, when Moses enumerates the separate heads of each tribe, he says that only seventy souls came with him.   Should any one say that Jacob had been compelled to liberate his slaves, on account of the famine, or that he lost them through some misfortune to us unknown, the conjecture is unsatisfactory; for it is most incredible that he, who had been an industrious master of a family, and had abounded in the earthly blessings of God, should have become so entirely destitute, that not even one little servant remained to him.   It is more probable that, when the children of Israel

---

[1] " A remarkable parallel to the description of the arrival of Jacob's family in Egypt, is furnished by a scene in a tomb at Beni Hassan, representing strangers who arrive in Egypt.   They carry their goods with them upon asses.   The first figure is an Egyptian scribe, who presents an account of their arrival to a person in a sitting posture, one of the principal officers of the reigning Pharaoh—(compare the phrase, princes of Pharaoh, ver. 15.)   The next, likewise an Egyptian, ushers them into his presence, and two of the strangers advance, bringing presents, the wild goat and the gazelle, probably as productions of their country.   Four men with bows and clubs follow, leading an ass, on which are two children in panniers, accompanied by a boy and four women.   Last, another ass laden and two men, one of whom carries a bow and club, and the other a lyre, on which he plays with the plectrum.   All the men have beards, contrary to the custom of the Egyptians," &c.—*Egypt and the Books of Moses*, p. 40.   It is supposed by some that this sculpture was intended to represent the arrival of Jacob and his family, recorded in this chapter.—*Ed.*

were themselves employed in servile works, they were then
deprived of their servants in Egypt; or, at least, a sufficient
number was not left them, to inspire them with confidence
in any enterprise.   And although, in the account of their
deliverance, Moses is silent respecting their servants, yet it
may be easily gathered from other passages, that they did
not depart without servants.

8. *These are the names of the children of Israel.*   He recounts the sons and grandsons of Jacob, till he arrives at
their full number.   The statement that there were but
seventy souls, while Stephen (Acts vii. 14) adds five more,
is made, I doubt not, by an error of the transcribers.   For the
solution of Augustine is weak, that Stephen, by a prolepsis,
enumerates also three who afterwards were born in Egypt;
for he must then have formed a far longer catalogue.
Again, this interpretation is repugnant to the design of the
Holy Spirit, as we shall hereafter see: because the subject
here treated of, is not respecting the number of children
Jacob left behind him at his death, but respecting the number of his family on the day when he went down into Egypt.
He is said to have brought with him, or to have found there,
seventy souls born unto him, in order that the comparison of
this very small number, with that immense multitude which
the Lord afterwards led forth, might the more fully illustrate
His wonderful benediction.   But that the error is to be imputed
to the transcribers, is hence apparent, that with the Greek interpreters, it has crept only into one passage, while, elsewhere,
they agree with the Hebrew reckoning.   And it was easy
when numerals were signified by marks, for one passage to be
corrupted.   I suspect also that this happened from the following cause, that those who had to deal with the Scripture
were generally ignorant of the Hebrew language; so that,
conceiving the passage in the Acts to be vitiated, they rashly
changed the true number.   If any one, however, chooses
rather to suppose that Luke in this instance accommodated
himself to the rude and illiterate, who were accustomed to
the Greek version, I do not contend with them.[1]   In the

Various methods have been resorted to, for the purpose of accounting
for the difference of numbers given in this chapter and in Acts vii. 14.
It is true that Luke, after the Septuagint, says there were seventy-five

words of Moses there is, indeed, no ambiguity, nor is there
any reason why so small a matter, in which there is no absurdity, should give us any trouble; for it is not wonderful,
that, in this mode of notation, one letter should have been
put in the place of another. It is more to the purpose, to examine wherefore this small number of persons is recorded
by Moses. For, the more improbable it appears, that seventy
men, in no. lengthened space of time, should have grown to
such a multitude; so much the more clearly does the grace
of God shine forth. And this is also the reason why he so
frequently mentions this number. For it was, by no means,
according to human apprehension, a likely method of propa-
gating the Church, that Abraham should live childless even
to old age; that, after the death of Isaac, Jacob alone
should remain; that he, being increased with a moderate
family, should be shut up in a corner of Egypt, and that
there an incredible number of people should spring up from
this dry fountain.[1] When Moses declares that Shaul, one of
the sons of Simeon, was born of a Canaanitish woman, while
he does not even mention the mothers of the other sons, his
intention, I doubt not, is to fix a mark of dishonour on his
race. For the holy Fathers were on their guard, not to mix
in marriage with that nation, from which they were separated by the decree of heaven. When Moses, having put
down the names of Leah's sons, says there were thirty-three
souls, whereas he has only mentioned thirty-two; I understand that Jacob himself is to be reckoned the first in order.
The statement that he had so many sons or daughters by
Leah does not oppose this conclusion. For although, strictly
speaking, his discourse is concerning sons, yet he commences

souls, whereas the Hebrew mentions only seventy. The reading of the
Septuagint is, " The sons of Joseph, who were with him in Egypt, were
nine souls; all the souls of the house of Jacob which came with Jacob into
Egypt, were seventy-five souls." Add then *nine* to the sixty-six, mentioned
in verse 26, and the number is made up. There is, however, some difficulty to make out the *nine.*—*See Patrick, Poole, Bush,* &c. *in loc.*—*Ed.*

[1] From the date of God's promise of a holy seed to Abraham, unto the
birth of Isaac was twenty-five years. · Isaac lived sixty years before Jacob
was born. Jacob had nearly reached the age of eighty at the time of his
marriage. So that about two hundred and forty years elapsed before more
than two persons were born of a family which was to be as the stars of heaven, and as the sand on the sea-shore, for multitude!—*See Bush in loc.*—*Ed.*

with the head of the family. I reject the interpretation of
the Hebrews, who suppose Jochebed the mother of Moses to
be included, as being overstrained. A question suggests
itself concerning the daughters, whether there were more
than two. If Dinah alone were named, it might be said
that express mention was made of her, because of the
notorious fact which had happened to her. But since Moses
enumerates another female in the progeny of Aser, I rather
conjecture that these had remained unmarried, or single ;
for no mention is made of those who were wives.

28. *And he sent Judah before him unto Joseph.* Because
Goshen[1] had been selected by Joseph as the abode of his
father and his brethren, Jacob now desires, that, on his
coming, he may find the place prepared for him : for the expression which Moses uses, implies, not that he requires a
house to be built and furnished for him, but only that he
may be permitted there to pitch his tent without molestation. For it was necessary that some unoccupied place
should be assigned him ; lest, by taking possession of the
pastures or fields of the inhabitants, he might give them an
occasion for exciting a tumult.

In the meeting of Jacob with his son Joseph, Moses describes their vehement feeling of joy, to show that the holy
Fathers were not destitute of natural affection. It must, how-

[1] Though Moses does not describe in express terms the position of the
land of Goshen ; yet the incidental allusions contained in the narrative,
are sufficient to fix its locality ; and the fact that those allusions are such
as could only be made by a writer conversant with its peculiarities, affords
decisive evidence of the veracity of Moses as a writer of history.
1. The land of Goshen appears as the eastern border-land of Egypt;
for on this side Jacob's family entered, see ver. 28.
2. It appears as lying near the chief city of Egypt, (see xlv. 10.) What
that city was, may be inferred from Numbers xiii. 22, which points to Zoan
or Tanis. This implies, that Zoan was one of the oldest cities of Egypt,
and that it held the first rank. God is said to have performed his "wonders in the field of Zoan," (Ps. lxxviii. 12, 43,) alluding to the plagues of
Egypt.
3. The land of Goshen is described as *pasture land*, and,
4. As one of the most *fruitful* regions of Egypt.
" All these circumstances harmonize, and the different points, discrepant
as they may seem, find their application, when we fix upon the land of
Goshen as the region east of the Tanitic arm of the Nile, as far as the
isthmus of Suez, or the border of the Arabian desert."—*See Egypt and the
Books of Moses*, pp. 43-45.—*Ed.*

ever, be remembered that, although the affections spring from
good principles, yet they always contract some evil, from the
corrupt propensity of the flesh ; and have chiefly this fault,
that they always exceed their bounds : whence it follows,
that they do not need to be eradicated, but to be kept within
due bounds.

31. *I will go up and show Pharaoh.*   After Joseph had
gone forth to meet his father for the purpose of doing him
honour, he also provides what will be useful for him.   On
this account, he advises Jacob to declare that he and all his
family were keepers of cattle, to the end that he might obtain, from the king, a dwelling-place for them, in the land of
Goshen.   Now although his moderation deserves commendation on the ground, that he usurps no authority to himself,
but that, as one of the common people, he waits the pleasure
of the king : he yet may be thought craftily to have devised
a pretext, by which he might circumvent the king.   We see
what he desired.   Seeing that the land of Goshen was fertile, and celebrated for its rich pastures ; this advantage so
allured his mind, that he wished to fix his father there :
but then, keeping out of Pharaoh's sight the richness of the
land, he puts forth another reason ; namely, that Jacob with
his sons, were men held in abomination, and that, therefore, he was seeking a place of seclusion, in which they might
dwell apart from the Egyptians.   It is not, however, very
difficult to untie this knot.   The fertility of the land of
Goshen was so fully known to the king, that no room was
left for fraud or cunning, (though kings are often too profuse, and foolishly waste much, because they know not what
they grant,) yea, Pharaoh, of his own accord, had offered
them, unsolicited, the best and choicest place in the kingdom.
Therefore this bounty of his was not elicited from him by
stratagem ; because he was free to form his own judgment
respecting what he would give.   And truly Joseph, in order
that he might act modestly, felt it necessary to seek a habitation in Goshen, on this pretext.   For it would have been
absurd, or at least inconsiderate, for men who were obscure
and strangers, to desire an abode in the best and most convenient place for themselves, as if they possessed a right to

choose for themselves. Joseph, therefore, having regard to his
own modesty and that of his father, adduces another cause,
which was yet a true one. For seeing that the Egyptians held
the occupation of shepherds in abhorrence,[1] he explains to
the king that this would be a suitable retreat for his brethren.
Herein was no dissimulation, because, in no other place, was
a quiet habitation accessible to them. Nevertheless, though
it was hard for the holy Fathers to be thus opprobriously rejected, and, as it were, to be loathed by a whole nation ; yet
this ignominy with which they were branded, was most profitable to themselves. For, had they been mingled with the
Egyptians, they might have been scattered far and wide ; but
now, seeing that they are objects of detestation, and are thought
unworthy to be admitted to common society, they learn, in
this state of separation from others, to cherish more fervently
mutual union between themselves ; and thus the body of the
Church, which God had set apart from the whole world, is
not dispersed. So the Lord often permits us to be despised
or rejected by the world, that being liberated and cleansed
from its pollution, we may cultivate holiness. Finally, he
does not suffer us to be bound by chains to the earth, in order
that we may be borne upward to heaven.

CHAPTER XLVII.

1. THEN Joseph came and told
Pharaoh, and said, My father, and
my brethren, and their flocks, and
their herds, and all that they have,
are come out of the land of Canaan ;
and, behold, they *are* in the land of
Goshen.

1. Et venit Joseph, et nuntiavit
Pharaoni, et dixit, Pater meus, et
fratres mei, et pecudes eorum, et
boves eorum, et omnia quæ erant eis,
venerunt e terra Chenaan : et ecce,
sunt in terra Gosen.

2. And he took some of his brethren, *even* five men, and presented
them unto Pharaoh.

2. Et de extremis fratribus suis
cepit quinque viros, et statuit eos
ante Pharaonem.

3. And Pharaoh said unto his

3. Tunc dixit Pharao ad fratres

[1] " The monuments even now furnish abundant evidence of this hatred
of the Egyptians to shepherds. The artists of Upper and Lower Egypt
vie with each other in caricaturing them. In proportion as the cultivation of the land was the more unconditionally the foundation of the
Egyptian state, the idea of coarseness and barbarism was united with the
idea of a shepherd among the Egyptians."—*Egypt and the Books of Moses*,
p. 42.—*Ed.*

brethren, What *is* your occupation?
And they said unto Pharaoh, Thy
servants *are* shepherds, both we, *and*
also our fathers.

4. They said, moreover, unto
Pharaoh, For to sojourn in the land
are we come ; for thy servants have
no pasture for their flocks ; for the
famine *is* sore in the land of Canaan ; now therefore, we pray thee,
let thy servants dwell in the land of
Goshen.

5. And Pharaoh spake unto Joseph, saying, Thy father and thy
brethren are come unto thee :

6. The land of Egypt *is* before
thee : in the best of the land make
thy father and brethren to dwell ; in
the land of Goshen let them dwell :
and if thou knowest *any* men of activity among them, then make them
rulers over my cattle.

7. And Joseph brought in Jacob
his father, and set him before Pharaoh : and Jacob blessed Pharaoh.

8. And Pharaoh said unto Jacob,
How old *art* thou ?

9. And Jacob said unto Pharaoh,
The days of the years of my pilgrimage *are* an hundred and thirty
years : few and evil have the days of
the years of my life been, and have
not attained unto the days of the
years of the life of my fathers in the
days of their pilgrimage.

10. And Jacob blessed Pharaoh,
and went out from before Pharaoh.

11. And Joseph placed his father
and his brethren, and gave them a
possession in the land of Egypt, in
the best of the land, in the land of Ra-
meses, as Pharaoh had commanded.

12. And Joseph nourished his father, and his brethren, and all his
father's household, with bread, according to *their* families.

13. And *there was* no bread in all
the land : for the famine *was* very
sore, so that the land of Egypt, and
all the land of Canaan, fainted by
reason of the famine.

14. And Joseph gathered up all

ejus, Quæ sunt opera vestra? Et
dixerunt ad Pharaonem, Pastores
ovium sunt servi tui, etiam nos, etiam
patres nostri.

4. Et dixerunt ad Pharaonem, Ut
peregrinaremur in hac terra, venimus, quia non est pascuum pecudibus, quæ sunt servis tuis : *gravis*
enim fames est in terra Chenaan :
nunc igitur habitent quæso servi tui
in terra Gosen.

5. Et dixit Pharao ad Joseph,
dicendo, Pater tuus et fratres tui
venerunt ad te.

6. Terra Ægypti coram te est, in
optimo terræ hujus habitare fac patrem tuum, et fratres tuos, habitent
in terra Gosen. Et si cognoveris
quod sint inter eos viri robusti, pones
eos præfectos pecorum super ea quæ
sunt mihi.

7. Postea adduxit Joseph ipsum
Jahacob patrem suum, et statuit
eum coram Pharaone, et salutavit
Jahacob ipsum Pharaonem.

8. Et dixit Pharao ad Jahacob,
Quot sunt dies annorum vitæ tuæ ?

9. Et dixit Jahacob ad Pharaonem, Dies annorum peregrinationum
mearum sunt triginta et centum anni : pauci et mali fuerunt dies annorum vitæ meæ, et non attigerunt
dies annorum vitæ patrum meorum
in diebus peregrinationum suarum.

10. Et salutavit Jahacob ipsum
Pharaonem, et egressus est a facie
Pharaonis.

11. Et habitare fecit Joseph patrem suum et fratres suos, et dedit
eis possessionem in terra Ægypti, in
optimo terræ, in terra Rahameses,
quemadmodum præceperat Pharao.

12. Et aluit Joseph patrem suum,
et fratres suos, et omnem domum
patris sui pane, usque ad os parvuli.

13. At panis non erat in omni
terra : gravis enim fames erat valde,
et elanguit terra Ægypti et terra
Chenaan propter famem.

14. Et collegit Joseph omnem pe-

the money that was found in the land of Egypt, and in the land of Canaan, for the corn which they bought: and Joseph brought the money into Pharaoh's house.

15. And when money failed in the land of Egypt, and in the land of Canaan, all the Egyptians came unto Joseph, and said, Give us bread: for why should we die in thy presence? for the money faileth.

16. And Joseph said, Give your cattle; and I will give you for your cattle, if money fail.

17. And they brought their cattle unto Joseph: and Joseph gave them bread *in exchange* for horses, and for the flocks, and for the cattle of the herds, and for the asses; and he fed them with bread for all their cattle for that year.

18. When that year was ended, they came unto him the second year, and said unto him, We will not hide *it* from my lord, how that our money is spent; my lord also hath our herds of cattle: there is not ought left in the sight of my lord, but our bodies and our lands:

19. Wherefore shall we die before thine eyes, both we and our land? buy us and our land for bread, and we and our land will be servants unto Pharaoh; and give *us* seed, that we may live, and not die, that the land be not desolate.

20. And Joseph bought all the land of Egypt for Pharaoh; for the Egyptians sold every man his field, because the famine prevailed over them: so the land became Pharaoh's.

21. And as for the people, he removed them to cities from *one* end of the borders of Egypt even to the *other* end thereof.

22. Only the land of the priests bought he not: for the priests had a portion *assigned them* of Pharaoh, and did eat their portion which Pharaoh gave them; wherefore they sold not their lands.

23. Then Joseph said unto the people, Behold, I have bought you

cuniam, quæ inventa est in terra Chenaan pro alimento quod ipsi emebant; et intulit Joseph pecuniam in domum Pharaonis.

15. Et consumpta est pecunia e terra Ægypti, et e terra Chenaan: et venit omnis Ægyptus ad Joseph, dicendo, Da nobis panem: et utquid moriemur coram te? defecit enim pecunia.

16. Tunc dixit Joseph, Date pecudes vestras, et dabo vobis pro pecudibus vestris, si defecit pecunia.

17. Et adduxerunt pecudes suas ad Joseph, et dedit eis Joseph panem pro equis, et pro grege pecudum, et pro armento boum, et pro asinis: et sustentavit eos pane pro omnibus gregibus illorum anno ipso.

18. Finitus vero est annus ipse, et venerunt ad eum anno secundo, et dixerunt ei, Non abscondemus a domino meo, quod integra pecunia, et grex jumentorum apud dominum meum: non remansit coram domino meo præterquam corpus nostrum, et terra nostra.

19. Utquid moriemur in oculis tuis, etiam nos, etiam terra nostra? eme nos, et terram nostram pro pane, et vivemus nos et terra nostra servi Pharaonis: da semen, et vivemus, et non moriemur, et terra non desolabitur.

20. Et emit Joseph omnem terram Ægypti pro Pharaone: vendiderunt enim Ægyptii unusquisque agrum suum, quia invaluerat super eos fames: et fuit terra ipsi Pharaoni.

21. Et populum transire fecit ad urbes ab extremitate termini Ægypti usque ad extremitatem ejus.

22. Tantummodo terram sacerdotum non emit, quia pars sacerdotibus erat a Pharaone, et comedebant partem suam, quam dederat eis Pharao: idcirco non vendiderunt terram suam.

23. Tunc dixit Joseph ad populum, Ecce, emi vos hodie, et terram

this day, and your land, for Pharaoh: lo, *here is* seed for you, and ye shall sow the land.

24. And it shall come to pass, in the increase, that ye shall give the fifth *part* unto Pharaoh; and four parts shall be your own, for seed of the field, and for your food, and for them of your households, and for food for your little ones.

25. And they said, Thou hast saved our lives: let us find grace in the sight of my lord, and we will be Pharaoh's servants.

26. And Joseph made it a law over the land of Egypt unto this day, *that* Pharaoh should have the fifth *part;* except the land of the priests only, *which* became not Pharaoh's.

27. And Israel dwelt in the land of Egypt, in the country of Goshen; and they had possessions therein, and grew, and multiplied exceedingly.

28. And Jacob lived in the land of Egypt seventeen years: so the whole age of Jacob was an hundred forty and seven years.

29. And the time drew nigh that Israel must die: and he called his son Joseph, and said unto him, If now I have found grace in thy sight, put, I pray thee, thy hand under my thigh, and deal kindly and truly with me: bury me not. I pray thee, in Egypt:

30. But I will lie with my fathers; and thou shalt carry me out of Egypt, and bury me in their burying-place. And he said, I will do as thou hast said.

31. And he said, Swear unto me. And he sware unto him. And Israel bowed himself upon the bed's head.

vestram Pharaoni: ecce, vobis semen, et seretis terram.

24. Et erit, e frugibus dabitis quintam partem Pharaoni, et quatuor partes erunt vobis pro semine agri, et pro cibo vestro, et eorum qui sunt in domibus vestris, et ad comedendum pro parvulis vestris.

25. Et dixerunt, Vivificasti nos: inveniamus gratiam in oculis domini mei, et erimus servi Pharaonis.

26. Et posuit illud Joseph in statutum usque ad diem hanc super terram Ægypti Pharaoni pro quinta *parte:* terra tamen sacerdotum duntaxat non fuit Pharaoni.

27. Et habitavit Israel in terra Ægypti, in terra Gosen: et stationem habuerunt in ea, et creverunt, et multiplicati sunt valde.

28. Et vixit Jahacob in terra Ægypti septendecim annos: et fuerunt dies Jahacob anni vitæ ejus, septem anni et quadraginta et centum anni.

29. Appropinquaverunt autem dies Israel ut moreretur, et vocavit filium suum Joseph, et dixit ei, Si quæso inveni gratiam in oculis tuis, pone quæso manum tuam sub femore meo, et facies mecum misericordiam et veritatem, Ne quæso sepelias me in Ægypto.

30. Et dormiam cum patribus meis; et tolles me ex Ægypto, et sepelies me in sepulcro eorum. Et dixit, Ego faciam secundum verbum tuum.

31. Et dixit, Jura mihi et juravit ei, et incurvavit se Israel ad caput lecti.

1. *Then Joseph came.* Joseph indirectly intimates to the king, his desire to obtain a habitation for his brethren in the land of Goshen. Yet this modesty was (as we have said) free from cunning. For Pharaoh both immediately recognises his wish, and liberally grants it to him; declaring beforehand that the land of Goshen was most

excellent. Whence we gather, that what he gave, he gave
in the exercise of his own judgment, not in ignorance; and
that he was not unacquainted with the wish of Joseph, who
yet did not dare to ask for what was the best. Joseph
may be easily excused for having commanded his father,
with the greater part of his brethren, to remain in that region. For neither was it possible for them to bring their
cattle along with them, nor yet to leave their cattle in order
to come and salute the king; until some settled abode was
assigned them, where, having pitched their tents, they might
arrange their affairs. For it would have shown a want of
respect, to take possession of a place, as if it had been granted
to them; when they had not yet received the permission of
the king. They, therefore, remain in that district, in a state
of suspense, until, having ascertained the will of the king,
they may, with greater certainty, fix their abode there. That
Joseph " brought five from the extreme limits of his brethren,"[1] is commonly thus explained, that they who were of
least stature were brought into the presence of the king:
because it was to be feared lest he might take the stronger
into his army. But since the Hebrew word קָצֶה signifies
the two extremities, the beginning and the end; I think
they were chosen from the first and the last, in order that
the king, by looking at them might form his judgment concerning the age of the whole.

3. *Thy servants are shepherds.* This confession was hu-
miliating to the sons of Jacob, and especially to Joseph himself, whose high, and almost regal dignity, was thus marked
with a spot of disgrace: for among the Egyptians (as we
have said) this kind of life was disgraceful and infamous.
Why, then, did not Joseph adopt the course, which he might
easily have done, of describing his brethren as persons engaged in agriculture, or any other honest and creditable

[1] Quod Joseph *quinque ex fratrum extremitate adduxit.* In the text
Calvin has it, " Et de extremis fratribus suis cepit quinque viros." The
English version renders the passage, " *some* of his brethren." Other interpreters, a " definite part." Gesenius, however, translates the term
מִקְצֵה, " from the whole;" which perhaps gives the best sense. " And he
took from the whole number of his brethren, five men, and presented them
unto Pharaoh."—*Ed.*

method of living ? They were not so addicted to the feeding
of cattle as to be altogether ignorant of agriculture, or incapable of accustoming themselves to other modes of gaining a
livelihood : and although they would not immediately have
found it productive, we see how ready the liberality of the
king was to help them.   Indeed it would not have been difficult for them to become invested with offices at court. How
then does it happen that Joseph, knowingly and purposely,
exposes his brethren to an ignominy, which must bring
dishonour also on himself, except because he was not very
anxious to escape from worldly contempt ?   To live in splendour among the Egyptians would have had, at first, a plausible appearance ; but his family would have been placed in
a dangerous position.   Now, however, their mean and contemptible mode of life proves a wall of separation between
them and the Egyptians : yea, Joseph seems purposely to labour to cast off, in a moment, the nobility he had acquired, that
his own posterity might not be swallowed up in the population
of Egypt, but might rather merge in the body of his ancestral
family.   If, however, this consideration did not enter their
minds, there is no doubt that the Lord directed their tongues,
so as to prevent the noxious admixture, and to keep the body
of the Church pure and distinct.   This passage also teaches
us, how much better it is to possess a remote corner in the
courts of the Lord, than to dwell in the midst of palaces, beyond the precincts of the Church.   Therefore, let us not think
it grievous to secure a sacred union with the sons of God, by
enduring the contempt and reproaches of the world ; even as
Joseph preferred this union to all the luxuries of Egypt. But
if any one thinks that he cannot otherwise serve God in purity, than by rendering himself disgusting to the world; away
with all this folly !   The design of God was this, to keep
the sons of Jacob in a degraded position, until he should restore them to the land of Canaan : for the purpose, then, of
preserving themselves in unity till the promised deliverance
should take place, they did not conceal the fact that they
were shepherds.   We must beware, therefore, lest the desire
of empty honour should elate us : whereas the Lord reveals
no other way of salvation, than that of bringing us under

discipline. Wherefore let us willingly be without honour, for a time, that, hereafter, angels may receive us to a participation of their eternal glory. By this example also, they who are brought up in humble employments, are taught that they have no need to be ashamed of their lot. It ought to be enough, and more than enough, for them, that the mode of living which they pursue is lawful, and acceptable to God. The remaining confession of the brethren (verse 4) was not unattended with a sense of shame; in which they say, that they had come to sojourn there, compelled by hunger; but hence arose advantage not to be despised. For as they came down few, and perishing with hunger, and so branded with infamy that scarcely any one would deign to speak with them; the glory of God afterwards shone so much the more illustriously out of this darkness, when, in the third century from that time, he wonderfully led them forth, a mighty nation.

5. *And Pharaoh spake unto Joseph.* It is to be ascribed to the favour of God that Pharaoh was not offended when they desired that a separate dwelling-place might be granted to them; for we know that nothing is more indignantly borne by kings, than that their favours should be rejected. Pharaoh offers them a perpetual home, but they rather wish to depart from him. Should any one ascribe this to modesty, on the ground that it would have been proud to ask for the right of citizenship, in order that they might enjoy the same privilege as natives; the suggestion is indeed plausible. It is, however, fallacious, for in asking to be admitted as guests and strangers, they took timely precaution that Pharaoh should not hold them bound in the chains of servitude. The passage of Sophocles is known:—

Ὅς τις δὲ πρὸς τύραννον ἐμπορεύεται,
Κείνου 'στὶ δοῦλος, κἂν ἐλεύθερος μόλῃ.[1]

[1] The passage does not occur in any of the tragedies of Sophocles extant; but it is found among the fragments of lost plays, selected from different authors of antiquity by whom they had been quoted. The words here introduced are taken from Plutarch's Life of Pompey. It may be observed, that the word τύραννος is not necessarily to be understood in a bad sense. It sometimes merely means a king; but the idea of *arbitrary* power, whe-

> " Who refuge seeks within a tyrant's door,
> When once he enters there, is free no more."
>
> *Langhorne's Plutarch.*

It was therefore of importance to the sons of Jacob to declare, *in limine*, on what condition they wished to live in Egypt. And so much the more inexcusable was the cruelty exercised towards them, when, in violation of this compact, they were most severely oppressed, and were denied that opportunity of departure, for which they had stipulated. Isaiah indeed says that the king of Egypt had some pretext for his conduct, because the sons of Jacob had voluntarily placed themselves under his authority, (Is. lii. 4;) but he is speaking comparatively, in order that he may the more grievously accuse the Assyrians, who had invaded the posterity of Jacob, when they were quiet in their own country, and expelled them thence by unjust violence. Therefore the law of hospitality was wickedly violated when the Israelites were oppressed as slaves, and when the return into their own country, for which they had silently covenanted, was denied them; though they had professed that they had come thither as guests; for fidelity and humanity ought to have been exercised towards them, by the king, when once they were received under his protection. It appears, therefore, that the children of Israel so guarded themselves, as in the presence of God, that they had just ground of complaint against the Egyptians. But seeing that the pledge given them by the king proved of no advantage to them according to the flesh; let the faithful learn, from their example, to train themselves to patience. For it commonly happens, that he who enters the court of a tyrant, is under the necessity of laying down his liberty at the door.

6. *The land of Egypt.* This is recorded not only to show that Jacob was courteously received, but also, that nothing was given him by Joseph but at the command of the king. For the greater was his power, the more strictly was he bound to take care, lest, being liberal with the king's property, he might defraud both him and his people. And I

ther well or ill used, is always involved in it. For the passage itself, see " Sophoclis Tragædiæ Septem." Tom. ii. Fragmenta, p. 95. *Oxon.*, 1826.—*Ed.*

would that this moderation so prevailed among the nobles of the world, that they would conduct themselves, in their private affairs, no otherwise than if they were plebeians : but now, they seem to themselves to have no power, unless they may prove it by their license to sin. And although Joseph, by the king's permission, places his family amidst the best pastures; yet he does not avail himself of the other portion of the royal beneficence, to make his brethren keepers of the king's cattle; not only because this privilege would have excited the envy of many against them, but because he was unwilling to be entangled in such a snare.

7. *And Joseph brought in Jacob his father.* Although Moses relates, in a continuous narrative, that Jacob was brought to the king, yet I do not doubt that some time had intervened ; at least, till he had obtained a place wherein he might dwell; and where he might leave his family more safely, and with a more tranquil mind ; and also, where he might refresh himself, for a little while, after the fatigue of his journey. And whereas he is said to have blessed Pharaoh, by this term Moses does not mean a common and profane salutation, but the pious and holy prayer of a servant of God. For the children of this world salute kings and princes for the sake of honour, but, by no means, raise their thoughts to God. Jacob acts otherwise ; for he adjoins to civil reverence that pious affection which causes him to commend the safety of the king to God. And Jeremiah prescribes this rule to the Jews, that they should pray for the peace of Babylon as long as they were to live in exile ; because in the peace of that land and empire their own peace would be involved. (Jer. xxix. 7.) If this duty was enjoined on miserable captives, forcibly deprived of their liberty, and torn from their own country ; how much more did Jacob owe it to a king so humane and beneficent? But of whatever character they may be who rule over us, we are commanded to offer up public prayers for them. (1 Tim. ii. 1.) Therefore the same subjection to authority is required severally from each of us.

8. *How old art thou ?* This familiar question proves that Jacob was received courteously and without ceremony. But the answer is of far greater moment, in which Jacob declares

that the time of his pilgrimage was a hundred and thirty years. For the Apostle, in his epistle to the Hebrews, (xi. 13-16,) gathers hence the memorable doctrine, that God was not ashamed to be called the God of the patriarchs, because they had confessed themselves to be strangers and pilgrims on the earth. Of one man only this is mentioned ; but because he had been instructed by his forefathers, and had handed down the same instruction to his son, the Apostle honours them all with the same eulogy. Therefore, as they were not ashamed to wander during the whole course of their life, and to be opprobriously called foreigners and strangers wherever they came ; so God vouchsafed to them the incomparable dignity, that they should be heirs of heaven. But (as it has been said before) no persons ever had a more peculiar and hereditary possession in the world, than the holy fathers had in the land of Canaan. The Lord is said to have cast his line, in order that he might assign to each nation its bounds : but an eternal possession, through a continual succession of ages, was never promised to any nation, as it was to the posterity of Abraham. In what spirit, then, ought we to dwell in a world, where no certain repose, or fixed abode is promised us ? Moreover, this is described by Paul as the common condition of all pious persons under the reign of Christ, that they should " have no certain dwelling-place ;" (1 Cor. iv. 11 ;) not that all should be alike cast out as exiles, but because the Lord calls all his people, as by the sound of the trumpet, to be wanderers, lest they should become fixed in their nests on earth. Therefore, whether any one remains in his own country, or is compelled continually to change his place, let him diligently exercise himself in the meditation, that he is sojourning, for a short time, upon earth, till, having completed his course, he shall depart to the heavenly country.

9. *Few and evil have the days of the years of my life been.* Jacob may here seem to complain that he had lived but a little while, and that, in this short space of time, he had endured many and grievous afflictions. Why does he not rather recount the great and manifold favours of God which formed an abundant compensation for every kind of evil ? Besides, his complaint respecting the shortness of life seems unworthy

of him; for why did he not deem a whole century and a
third part of another sufficient for him? But if any one will
rightly weigh his words, he rather expresses his own gratitude, in celebrating the goodness of God towards his fathers.
For he does not so much deplore his own decrepitude, as he
extols the vigour divinely afforded to his fathers. Certainly
it was no new and unwonted thing to see a man, at his age,
broken down and failing, and already near to the grave.
Wherefore, this comparison (as I have said) was only intended
to ascribe glory to God, whose blessing towards Abraham and
Isaac had been greater than to himself. But he does not compare himself with his fathers in sufferings, as if they had been
treated with greater indulgence; for we know that they had
been tried to the utmost with all kinds of temptations: he
merely states that he had not attained their age; as if he had
said, "I, indeed, have arrived at those years which, by others, is
deemed a mature old age, and which complete the proper term
of life; but the Lord so prolonged the life of my fathers, that
they far exceeded this limit." He makes mention of *evil*
days, in order to show that he was not so much broken down
and consumed by years, as by labours and troubles; as if he
had said, "My senses might yet have flourished in their
vigour, if my strength had not been exhausted by continual
labours, by excessive cares, and by most grievous sufferings."
We now see that nothing was less in the mind of the holy
man than to expostulate with God. Yet it may seem absurd that he speaks of his life as being shorter than that of
his fathers. For, whence does he conjecture that so little time
should still remain for him, as to prevent him from attaining
their age? Should any one answer, that he formed this conjecture from the weakness of his body, which was half dead;
the solution will not prove satisfactory. For Isaac had dimness of sight and trembling limbs thirty years before his death.
But it is not absurd to suppose that Jacob was every moment
giving himself over to death, as if the sepulchre were before
his eyes. He was, however, uncertain what length of time was
decreed for him in the secret counsel of God. Wherefore,
being unconcerned about the remainder of his life, he speaks
just as if he were about to die on the next day.

12. *And Joseph nourished his father*, &c., *according to their families.*[1] Some explain the expression, " the mouth of the little one," as if Joseph nourished his father and his whole family, in the manner in which food is conveyed to the mouths of children. These interpreters regard the form of speech as emphatical, because, during the famine, Jacob and his family had no more anxiety about the providing of food than children, who cannot even stretch out their hand to receive it. Others translate it "youth," but I know not with what meaning.[2] Others take it, simply, according to the proportion and number of the little children. To me the genuine sense seems to be that he fed all, from the greatest to the least. Therefore, there was sufficient bread for the whole family of Jacob, because, by the care of Joseph, provision was made to supply nourishment even to the little ones. In this manner Moses commemorates both the clemency of God, and the piety of Joseph; for it was an instance of uncommon attention, that these hungry husbandmen, who had not a grain of corn, were entirely fed at his expense.

13. *And all the land of Canaan fainted.* It was a memorable judgment of God, that the most fertile regions, which were accustomed to supply provisions for distant and transmarine nations, were reduced to such poverty that they were almost consumed. The word להה, (*lahah,*) which Moses uses, is explained in two ways. Some say that they were driven to madness on account of the famine; others, that they were so destitute of food that they fainted; but whichever method of interpretation be approved, we see that they who had been accustomed to supply others with food, were themselves famishing. Therefore it is not for those who cultivate fertile lands to trust in their abundance; rather let them acknowledge that a large supply of provision does not so much spring from the bowels of the earth, as it distils, or rather flows down from heaven, by the secret blessing of God. For there is no luxuriance so great, that it is not soon exchanged for barrenness, when God sprinkles it with

---

[1] Usque ad os parvuli. Even to the mouth of the little one. לפי חטף, (*Lephi chataph.*)
[2] Alii vertunt pubem; sed nescio quo sensu.

salt instead of rain.   Meanwhile, it is right to turn our eyes
to that special kindness of God by which he nourishes his
own people in the midst of famine, as it is said in the thirty-
seventh Psalm and the nineteenth verse.   If, however, God
is pleased to try us with famine, we must pray that he
would prepare us to endure hunger with a meek and equal
mind, lest we should rage, like fierce, and even ravenous wild
beasts.   And although it is possible that grievous commo-
tions were raised during the protracted scarcity, (as it is said
in the old proverb that the belly has no ears,) yet the more
simple sense of the passage seems to me to be, that the
Egyptians and Canaanites had sunk under the famine, and
were lying prostrate, as if at the point of death.   Moreover,
Moses pursues the history of the famine, with the intention
of showing that the prediction of Joseph was verified by the
event ; and that, by his skill and industry, the greatest dangers were so well and dexterously provided against, that
Egypt ought justly to acknowledge him as the author of its
deliverance.

14. *And Joseph gathered up all the money.*   Moses first
declares that the Egyptian king had acted well and wisely,
in committing the work of providing corn to the sole care
and authority of Joseph.   He then commends the sincere
and faithful administration of Joseph himself.   We know
how few persons can touch the money of kings without defiling themselves by peculation.   Amid such vast heaps of
money, the opportunity of plundering was not less than the
difficulty of self-restraint.   But Moses says, that whatever
money Joseph collected, he brought into the house of the
king.   It was a rare and unparalleled integrity, to keep the
hands pure amidst such heaps of gold.   And he would not
have been able to conduct himself with such moderation,
unless his divine calling had proved as a bridle to hold him
in ; for they who are restrained from thefts and rapaciousness
by worldly motives alone, would immediately put forth their
hand to the prey, unless they feared the eyes and the judgments of men.   But inasmuch as Joseph might have sinned
without a witness of his fault ; it follows that the true fear
of God flourished in his breast.   Plausible and well coloured

pretexts, in excuse of the theft, would doubtless present themselves. " When you are serving a tyrant, why may it not be
lawful for you to apply some part of the gain to your own
advantage ?" So much the more does it appear that he was
fortified by downright honesty ; since he repelled all temptations, lest he should desire fraudulently to enrich himself
at the expense of another.

15. *And when money failed.* Moses does not mean that
all the money in Egypt had been brought into the royal
treasury ; for there were many of the nobles of the court free
from the effects of the famine ; but the simple meaning of
the expression is that nearly all had been exhausted ; that
now the common people had not money enough to buy corn ;
and that, at length, extreme necessity had driven the Egyptians to the second remedy of which he is about to speak.
Moreover, although, like persons driven to desperation,
they might seem arrogantly to rise up against Joseph ;
yet the context shows that nothing was farther from their
minds than to terrify, by their boldness, the man whose
compassion they suppliantly implore. Wherefore the question, *Why should we die in thy presence?* has no other signification than that they felt themselves ruined, unless his clemency should afford them relief. But it may be asked how
the Canaanites supported their lives. There is indeed no
doubt that a grievous pestilence, the attendant on famine,
would carry off many, unless they received assistance from
other regions, or were miserably fed on herbs and roots. And
perhaps the barrenness was not there so great, but that they
might gather half, or a third part of their food, from the
fields.

16. *Give your cattle.* It was a miserable spectacle, and
one which might have softened hearts of iron, to see rich
farmers, who previously had kept provision stored in their
granaries for others, now begging food. Therefore, Joseph
might be deemed cruel, because he does not give bread gratuitously to those who are poor and exhausted, but robs them
of all their cattle, sheep, and asses. Seeing, however, that
Joseph is transacting the business of another, I dare not
charge his strictness with cruelty. If, during the seven

fruitful years, he had extorted corn by force from an unwilling people, he would now have acted tyrannically in seizing their flocks and herds. But seeing that they had been at liberty to lay up, in their private stores, what they had sold to the king, they now pay the just penalty of their negligence. Joseph also perceived that they were deprived of their possessions by a divine interposition, in order that the king alone might be enriched by the spoils of all. Besides, since it was lawful for him to offer corn for sale, it was also lawful for him to exchange it for cattle. Truly, the corn belonged to the king; why then should he not demand a price from the purchasers? But they were poor, and therefore it was but just to succour them in their want. Were this rule to prevail, the greater part of sales would be unlawful. For no one freely parts with what he possesses. Wherefore, if his valuation of the cattle was fair, I do not see what was deserving of reprehension in the conduct of Joseph; especially as he was not dealing with his own property, but had been appointed prefect over the corn, with this condition, that he should acquire gain, not for himself, but for the king. If any one should object that he ought at least to have exhorted the king to content himself with the abundant pecuniary wealth which he had obtained; I answer, that Moses relates, by the way, but a few things out of many. Any one, therefore, may easily conjecture, that a business of such great consequence, was not transacted by Joseph, without the cognizance and judgment of the king. But what, if it appeared to the king's counsellors, an equitable arrangement, that the farmers should receive, in return for their cattle, food for the whole year? Lastly, seeing that we stand or fall by the judgment of God alone, it is not for us to condemn what his law has left undecided.

18. *They came to him the second year.* Moses does not reckon the second year from the date of the famine, but from the time when the money had failed. But since they knew, from the oracle, that the termination of the dearth was drawing near, they desired not only that corn should be given them for food, but also for seed. Whence it appears that they had become wise too late, and had neglected

the useful admonition of God, at the time when they ought to have made provision for the future. Moreover, when they declare that their money and cattle had failed, they do it, not for the purpose of expostulating with Joseph, as if they had been unjustly deprived of these things by him; but for the purpose of showing that the only thing remaining for them was to purchase food and seed at the price of their lands, and that they could not otherwise be preserved, unless Joseph would enter into this compact. For it would have been the part of impudence to offer no price or compensation. They begin by saying, that they had nothing at hand, and that, therefore, their lives would be lost, unless Joseph were willing to buy their lands; and in order to excite his compassion, they ask again, why he would suffer them to die, and their very land to perish? For this is the death of the earth, when the cultivation of it is neglected, and when, being reduced to a desert, it can bring forth nothing more.

20. *And Joseph bought all the land.* Any one might suppose it to be the height of cruel and inexplicable avarice, that Joseph should take away from the miserable husbandmen, the very fields, by the produce of which they nourished the kingdom. But I have before showed, that unless every kind of purchase is to be condemned, there is no reason why Joseph should be blamed. If any one should say that he abused their penury; this alone would suffice for his excuse, that no wiles of his, no circumvention, no force, no threats, had reduced the Egyptians to this necessity. He transacted the king's business with equal fidelity and industry; and fulfilled the duties of his office, without resorting to violent edicts. When the famine became urgent, it was lawful to expose wheat to sale, as well to the rich as to the poor: afterwards it was not less lawful to buy the cattle; and now, at last, why should it not be lawful to acquire the land for the king, at a just price? To this may be added, that he extorted nothing, but entered into treaty with them, at their own request. I confess, indeed, that it is not right to take whatever may be offered without discrimination: for if severe necessity presses, then he who wishes, by all means,

to escape it, will submit to hard conditions. Therefore, when any one thus invites us, to defraud him, we are not, by his necessities, rendered excusable. But I do not defend Joseph, on this sole ground, that the Egyptians voluntarily offered him their lands, as men who were ready to purchase life, at any price; but I say, this ought also to be considered, that he acted with equity, even though he left them nothing. The terms would have been more severe, if they themselves had been consigned to perpetual slavery; but he now concedes to them personal liberty, and only covenants for their fields, which, perhaps, the greater part of the people had bought from the poor. If he had stripped of their clothing those whom he was feeding with corn, this would have been to put them indirectly and slowly to death. For what difference does it make, whether I compel a man to die by hunger or by cold? But Joseph so succours the Egyptians, that in future they should be free, and should be able to obtain a moderate subsistence by their labour. For though they might have to change their abode, yet they are all made stewards of the king: and Joseph restores to them, not only the lands, but the implements which he had bought. Whence it appears that he had used what clemency he was able, in order to relieve them. Meanwhile, let those who are too intent on wealth beware lest they should falsely employ Joseph's example as a pretext: because it is certain that all contracts, which are not formed according to the rule of charity, are vicious in the sight of God; and that we ought, according to that equity which is inwardly dictated to us by a secret instinct of nature, so to act towards others, as we wish to be dealt with ourselves.

21. *And as for the people, he removed them to cities.* This removal was, indeed, severe; but if we reflect how much better it was to depart to another place; in order that they might be free cultivators of the land, than to be attached to the soil, and employed as slaves in servile work; no one will deny that this was a tolerable, and even a humane exercise of authority. Had each person cultivated his field, as he had been accustomed to do, the exaction of tribute would have seemed to be grievous. Joseph, there-

fore, contrived a middle course, which might mitigate the new and unwonted burden, by assigning new lands to each, with a tribute attached to them. The passage may, however, be differently expounded; namely, that Joseph caused all the farmers to go to the cities to receive the provisions, and to settle their public accounts. If this sense is approved, the fact that Egypt was divided into provinces, afterwards called *nomes*, (νομοὶ,) may probably hence have received its origin. This removing from place to place would, however, have been alike injurious to the king and to the people at large, because they would not be able to make their skill and practice applicable to new situations. Yet, since the matter is not of great moment, and the signification of the word is ambiguous, I leave the question undecided.

22. *Only the land of the priests.* The priests were exempted from the common law, because the king granted them a maintenance. It is, indeed, doubtful, whether this was a supply for their present necessity, or whether he was accustomed to nourish them at his own expense. But seeing that Moses makes mention of their lands, I rather incline to the conjecture, that, whereas they had before been rich, and this dearth had deprived them of their income, the king conferred this privilege upon them; and hence it arose that their lands remained unto them free.[1] The ancient historians, however, injudiciously invent many fables concerning the state of that land. I know not whether the statement that the farmers, content with small wages, sow and reap for the king and the priests, is to be traced to this regulation of Joseph or not. But, passing by these things, it is more to the purpose to observe, what

---

[1] The following passage from Sir J. G. Wilkinson's Manners and Customs of the Ancient Egyptians, will be read with interest. The priests " enjoyed important privileges, which extended to their whole family. They were exempt from taxes; they consumed no part of their own income in any of their necessary expenses; and they had one of the three portions into which the land of Egypt was divided, free from all duties. They were provided for, from the public stores, out of which they received a stated allowance of corn, and all the other necessaries of life; and we find that when Pharaoh, by the advice of Joseph, took all the land of the Egyptians in lieu of corn, the priests were not obliged to make the same sacrifice of their landed property, nor was the tax of the fifth part entailed upon it, as on that of other people."—Vol. i. p. 262.—*Ed.*

Moses wished distinctly to testify; namely, that a heathen
king paid particular attention to Divine worship, in supporting the priests gratuitously, for the purpose of sparing their
lands and their property.   Truly this is placed before our
eyes, as a mirror, in which we may discern that a sentiment
of piety which they cannot wholly efface, is implanted in
the minds of men.   It was the part of foolish, as well as of
wicked superstition, that Pharaoh nourished such priests as
these, who infatuated the people by their impostures: yet
this was, in itself, a design worthy of commendation, that
he did not suffer the worship of God to fall into decay;
which, in a short time, must have happened, if the priests
had perished in the famine.   Whence we infer how sedulously we ought to be on our guard, that we undertake nothing with an indiscreet zeal; because nothing is more easy,
in so great a corruption of human nature, than for religion
to degenerate into frivolous trifles.   Nevertheless, because
this inconsiderate devotion (as it may be called) flowed from
a right principle, what should be the conduct of our princes,
who desire to be deemed Christians?   If Pharaoh was so
solicitous about his priests, that he nourished them to his
own destruction, and that of his whole kingdom, in order
that he might not be guilty of impiety against false gods;
what sacrilege is it, in Christian princes, that the lawful
and sincere ministers of holy things should be neglected,
whose work they know to be approved by God, and salutary to themselves?   But it may be asked, whether it was
lawful for holy Joseph to undertake this office, for by so
doing, he employed his labour in cherishing impious superstitions?   But though I can readily grant that in such great,
and arduous, and manifold offices of trust, it was easy for
him to slide into various faults; yet I dare not absolutely
condemn this act; nor can I, however, deny that he may
have erred, in not resisting these superstitions with sufficient
boldness.   But since he was required by no law, to destroy
the priests by hunger, and was not altogether allowed to
dispense the king's corn at his own pleasure; if the king
wished that food should be gratuitously supplied to the
priests, he was no more at liberty to deny it to them than

to the nobles at court. Therefore, though he did not willingly take charge of such dependents, yet when the king imposed the duty upon him, he could not refuse it, though he knew them to be unworthy to be fed on the dirt of oxen.

23. *Then Joseph said unto the people.* Here Moses describes the singular humanity of Joseph, which, as it then repressed all complaints, so, at this time, it justly dispels and refutes the calumnies with which he is assailed. The men, who were entirely destitute, and, in a sense, exiles, he reinstates in their possessions, on the most equitable condition, that they should pay a fifth part of the produce to the king. It is well known that formerly, in various places, kings have demanded by law the payment of tenths; but that, in the time of war, they doubled this tax. Therefore, what injury, can we say, was done to the Egyptians, when Joseph burdened the land, bought for the king, with a fifth part of its income; especially seeing that country is so much richer than others, that with less labour than elsewhere, it brings forth fruit for the maintenance of its cultivators? Should any one object that the king would have acted more frankly had he taken the fifth part of the land; the answer is obvious, that this was useful not only as an example, but also, for the purpose of quieting the people, by shutting the mouths of the captious. And certainly this indirect method, by which Joseph introduced the tax of a fifth part, had no other object than that of inducing the Egyptians to cultivate their lands with more alacrity, when they were convinced that, by such a compact, they were treated with clemency. And to this effect was their confession, which is recorded by Moses, expressed. For, first, they acknowledge that they owe their lives to him; secondly, they do not refuse to be the servants of the king. Whence we gather, that the holy man so conducted himself between the two parties, as greatly to enrich the king, without oppressing the people by tyranny. And I wish that all governors would practise this moderation, that they would only so far study the advantage of kings, as could be done without injury to the people. There is a celebrated saying of Tiberius Cæsar, which savoured little of tyranny, though

he appears to have been a sanguinary and insatiable tyrant, that it is the part of a shepherd to shear the flock, but not to tear off the skin. At this day, however, kings do not believe that they rule freely, unless they not only flay their subjects, but entirely devour them. For they do not generally invest any with authority, except those who are sworn to the practice of slaughter. So much the more does the clemency of Joseph deserve praise, who so administered the affairs of Egypt, as to render the immense gains of the king compatible with a tolerable condition of the people.

27. *And Israel dwelt in the land.* Moses does not mean that Jacob and his sons were proprietors of that land which Pharaoh had granted them as a dwelling-place, in the same manner in which the other parts of Egypt were given to the inhabitants for a perpetual possession : but that they dwelt there commodiously for a time, and thus were in possession by favour, provided they continued to be peaceable. Hence the cause that they so greatly increased, in a very short space of time. Therefore, what is here related by Moses belongs to the history of the following period ; and he now returns to the proper thread of his narrative, in which he purposed to show how God protected his Church from many deaths ; and not that only, but wonderfully exalted it by his own secret power.

28. *And Jacob lived.* It was no common source of temptation to the holy old man, to be an exile from the land of Canaan, for so many years. Be it so, that on account of the famine, he was compelled to go to Egypt ; why could he not return when the fifth year was passed ? For he did not stupidly lie there in a state of torpor, but he remained quiet, because free egress was not allowed him. Wherefore, also, in this respect, God did not lightly exercise his patience. For, however sweet might be the delights of Egypt, yet he was more than miserable to be deprived of the sight of that land which was the lively figure of his celestial country. With the men of this world, indeed, earthly advantage would have prevailed : but such was the piety of the holy man, that the profit of the flesh weighed nothing against the loss of spiritual good. But he was more deeply wounded, when he saw his death approaching : because, not only was

he himself deprived of the inheritance promised to him, but he was leaving his sons, of doubtful, or at least of feeble, faith, buried in Egypt as in a sepulchre. Moreover, his example is proposed to us, that our minds may not languish or become enfeebled by the weariness of a protracted warfare : yea, the more Satan attempts to depress them to the earth, the more fervently let them look and soar towards heaven.

29. *And he called his son Joseph.* Hence we infer, not only the anxiety of Jacob, but his invincible magnanimity. It is a proof of great courage, that none of the wealth or the pleasures of Egypt could so allure him, as to prevent him from sighing for the land of Canaan, in which he had always passed a painful and laborious life. But the constancy of his faith appeared still more excellent, when he, commanding his dead body to be carried back to Canaan, encouraged his sons to hope for deliverance. Thus it happened that he, being dead, animated those who were alive and remained, as with the sound of a trumpet. For, to what purpose was this great care respecting his sepulture, except that the promise of God might be confirmed to his posterity ? Therefore, though his faith was tossed as upon the waves, yet it was so far from suffering shipwreck, that it conducted others into the haven. Moreover, he demands an oath from his son Joseph, not so much on account of distrust, as to show that a matter of the greatest consequence was in hand. Certainly he would not, by lightly swearing, profane the name of God : but the more sacred and solemn the promise was, the more ought all his sons to remember, that it was of great importance that his body should be carried to the sepulchre of his fathers. It is also probable that he prudently thought of alleviating any enmity which might be excited against his son Joseph. For he knew that this choice of his sepulchre would be, by no means, gratifying to the Egyptians ; seeing it seemed like casting a reproach on their whole kingdom. This stranger, forsooth, as if he could find no fit place for his body in this splendid and noble country, wishes to be buried in the land of Canaan. Therefore, in order that Joseph might more freely dare to ask, and might more easily obtain, this favour from the king, Jacob binds him by an oath. And

certainly Joseph afterwards makes use of this pretext, to avoid giving offence. This also was the reason why he required Joseph to do for him that last office, which was a duty devolving on the brothers in common ; for such a favour would scarcely have been granted to the rest ; and they would not have ventured on the act, unless permission had been obtained. But, as strangers and mean men, they had neither favour nor authority. Besides, it was especially necessary for Joseph to be on his guard, lest becoming ensnared by the allurements of Egypt, he should gradually forsake his own kindred. It must, however, be known, that the solemnity of an oath was designedly interposed by Jacob, to show that he did not, in vain, desire for himself, a sepulchre in the land where he had met with an unfavourable reception ; where he had endured many sufferings ; and from which, at length, being expelled by hunger, he had become an exile. As to his commanding the hand to be put under his thigh, we have explained what this symbol means in chapter xxiv. ver. 2.

30. *But I will lie with my fathers.*[1] It appears from this passage, that the word "sleep," whenever it is put for "die," does not refer to the soul, but to the body. For, what did it concern him, to be buried with his fathers in the double cave,[2] unless to testify that he was associated with them after death ? And by what bond were he and they joined together, except this, that not even death itself could extinguish the power of their faith ; which would seem to utter this voice from the same sepulchre, "Now also we have a common inheritance."

31. *And Israel bowed himself upon the bed's head.* By this expression, Moses again affirms that Jacob esteemed it a singular kindness, that his son should have promised to do what he had required respecting his burial. For he exerts his weak body as much as he is able, in order to give thanks unto God, as if he had obtained something most desirable. He is said to have worshipped towards the head of his bed : because, seeing he was quite unable to rise from the bed on which he lay, he yet composed himself with a solemn air

---

[1] Dormiam, "I will sleep."
[2] The cave of Machpelah. See above, on Gen. xxiii. 9.—*Ed.*

in the attitude of one who was praying. The same is recorded of David (1 Kings i. 47) when, having obtained his last
wish, he celebrates the grace of God. The Greeks have
translated it, " at the top of his staff:" which the Apostle
has followed in the Epistle to the Hebrews, (xi. 21.) And
though the interpreters seem to have been deceived by the
similitude of words ; because, with the Hebrews, מִטָּה signifies "bed," מוֹטָה, "a staff;" yet the Apostle allows himself
to cite the passage as it was then commonly used, lest he
might offend unskilful readers, without necessity.[1] Moreover, they who expound the words to mean that Jacob worshipped the sceptre of his son, absurdly trifle. The exposition of others, that he bowed his head, leaning on the top of
his staff, is, to say the least, tolerable. But since there is
no ambiguity in the words of Moses, let it suffice to keep in
memory what I have said, that, by this ceremony, he openly
manifested the greatness of his joy.

CHAPTER XLVIII.

1. AND it came to pass after these things, that one told Joseph, Behold, thy father is sick : and he took with him his two sons, Manasseh and Ephraim.

2. And one told Jacob, and said, Behold, thy son Joseph cometh unto thee: and Israel strengthened him-self, and sat upon the bed.

3. And Jacob said unto Joseph,

1. Et fuit post hæc dictum fuit ipsi Joseph, Ecce, pater tuus ægro-tat : tunc accepit duos filios suos se-cum, Menasseh et Ephraim.

2. Et nuntiavit ipsi Jahacob, et dixit, Ecce, filius tuus Joseph venit ad te. Et roboravit se Israel, et sedit super lectum.

3. Et dixit Jahacob ipsi Joseph,

[1] The reasoning of Calvin, besides being in every respect unsatisfactory, is founded on a misquotation of the original. He appears to have put down the words from memory, or else his transcriber has made the mistake for him. The only difference between the words rendered "a bed" and a "staff" lies in the Masoretic punctuation ; of which, it is well known, the authority is disputed. Perhaps one of the strongest arguments on the side of those opposed to the *points*, is derived from this passage and the Apostle's interpretation of it. If the word is not pointed, then it may mean either a bed or a staff; if, on the other hand, the present points are of equal authority with the text, the Apostle has quoted it wrong. The latter sup-position is not to be endured. It seems to follow, then, that the original was either not pointed, or the copy used by St. Paul was pointed differently from the present text, or he knew that the points were not to be relied upon, for giving the precise meaning of the Holy Spirit in the word.—*Ed.*

God Almighty appeared unto me at Luz in the land of Canaan, and blessed me,

4. And said unto me, Behold, I will make thee fruitful, and multiply thee, and I will make of thee a multitude of people; and will give this land to thy seed after hee *for* an everlasting possession.

5. And now thy two sons, Ephraim and Manasseh, which were born unto thee in the land of Egypt, before I came unto thee into Egypt, *are* mine; as Reuben and Simeon, they shall be mine.

6. And thy issue, which thou begettest after them, shall be thine, *and* shall be called after the name of their brethren in their inheritance.

7. And as for me, when I came from Padan, Rachel died by me in the land of Canaan in the way, when yet *there was* but a little way to come unto Ephrath: and I buried her there in the way of Ephrath; the same *is* Beth-lehem.

8. And Israel beheld Joseph's sons, and said, Who *are* these?

9. And Joseph said unto his father, They *are* my sons, whom God hath given me in this *place*. And he said, Bring them, I pray thee, unto me, and I will bless them.

10. Now the eyes of Israel were dim for age, *so that* he could not see. And he brought them near unto him; and he kissed them, and embraced them.

11. And Israel said unto Joseph, I had not thought to see thy face; and, lo, God hath shewed me also thy seed.

. 12. And Joseph brought them out from between his knees, and he bowed himself with his face to the earth.

13. And Joseph took them both, Ephraim in his right hand toward Israel's left hand, and Manasseh in his left hand toward Israel's right hand, and brought *them* near unto him.

14. And Israel stretched out his right hand, and laid *it* upon Ephraim's head, who *was* the younger, and his

Deus omnipotens apparuit mihi in Luz in terra Chenaan, et benedixit mihi.

4. Et dixit ad me, Ecce, ego crescere facio te, et multiplicabo te, et ponam te in cœtum populorum, et dabo terram hanc semini tuo post te in hæreditatem perpetuam.

5. Et nunc duo filii tui, qui nati sunt tibi in terra Ægypti, antequam venirem ad te in Ægyptum, mei sunt, Ephraim et Menasseh, sicut Reuben et Simhon erunt mei.

6. Verum liberi tui, quos generabis post eos, tui erunt : secundum nomen fratrum suorum vocabuntur in hæreditate sua.

7. Porro me veniente e Padan, mortua est mihi Rachel in terra Chenaan in via, quum adhuc esset milliare terræ ad veniendum in E-phrath : et sepelivi eam in via Ephrath, ipsa est Bethlehem.

8. Et vidit Israel filios Joseph, et dixit, Cujus sunt isti?

9. Et dixit Joseph patri suo, Filii mei sunt quos dedit mihi Deus hic. Et dixit, Duc eos quæso ad me, et benedicam eis.

10. (Oculi enim Israel graves erant propter senectutem, nec poterat videre) et accedere fecit eos ad illum, et osculatus est eos, et amplexatus est eos.

11. Et dixit Israel ad Joseph, Videre faciem tuam non putabam, et ecce, videre fecit me Deus etiam semen tuum.

12. Eduxit itaque Joseph eos a genibus suis, et incurvavit se in faciem suam super terram.

13. Et tulit Joseph ambos ipsos, Ephraim ad dexteram suam, a sinistra Israel, et Menasseh ad sinistram suam, a dextra Israel : accedere inquam fecit ad eum.

14. Et extendit Israel dexteram suam, et posuit super caput Ephraim, qui erat minor : et sinistram

left hand upon Manasseh's head, guiding his hands wittingly ; for Manasseh *was* the first-born.

15. And he blessed Joseph, and said, God, before whom my fathers Abraham and Isaac did walk, the God which fed me all my life long unto this day,

16. The Angel which redeemed me from all evil, bless the lads ; and let my name be named on them, and the name of my fathers Abraham and Isaac ; and let them grow into a multitude in the midst of the earth.

17. And when Joseph saw that his father laid his right hand upon the head of Ephraim, it displeased him : and he held up his father's hand, to remove it from Ephraim's head unto Manasseh's head.

18. And Joseph said unto his father, Not so, my father : for this *is* the first-born ; put thy right hand upon his head.

19. And his father refused, and said, I know *it*, my son, I know *it* : he also shall become a people, and he also shall be great ; but truly his younger brother shall be greater than he, and his seed shall become a multitude of nations.

20. And he blessed them that day, saying, In thee shall Israel bless, saying, God make thee as Ephraim, and as Manasseh. And he set Ephraim before Manasseh.

21. And Israel said unto Joseph, Behold, I die ; but God shall be with you, and bring you again unto the land of your fathers.

22. Moreover, I have given to thee one portion above thy brethren, which I took out of the hand of the Amorite with my sword and with my bow.

suam super caput Menasseh : consulto dirigens manus suas, quum Menasseh esset primogenitus.

15. Et benedixit ipsi Joseph. et dixit, Deus, in cujus conspectu ambulaverunt patres mei Abraham et Ishac, Deus qui pascit me ab ætate mea usque ad diem hanc,

16. Angelus qui redemit me ab omni malo, benedicat pueris : et vocetur in eis nomen meum, et nomen patrum meorum Abraham et Ishac, et instar piscium sint in multitudinem in medio terræ.

17. Vidit autem Joseph, quod poneret pater suus manum dexteram suam super caput Ephraim, et displicuit in oculis ejus, et sustentavit manum patris sui, ut removeret eam a capite Ephraim, super caput Menasseh.

18. Et dixit Joseph patri suo, Non sic, pater mi : quia iste est primogenitus, pone dexteram tuam super caput ejus.

19. Verum renuit pater ejus, et dixit, Novi, fili mi, novi, etiam ipse erit in populum, et etiam ipse crescet : et tamen frater ejus minor crescet magis quam ipse, et semen ejus erit plenitudo Gentium.

20. Et benedixit eis in die ipsa, dicendo, In te benedicet Israel, dicendo, Ponat te Deus sicut Ephraim et Menasseh : et posuit Ephraim ante Menasseh.

21. Et dixit Israel ad Joseph, Ecce, ego morior : et erit Deus vobiscum, et redire faciet vos ad terram patrum vestrorum.

22. Ego autem dedi tibi partem unam super fratres tuos, quam cepi e manu Emoræi gladio meo, et arcu meo.

1. *After these things.* Moses now passes to the last act of Jacob's life, which, as we shall see, was especially worthy of remembrance. For, since he knew that he was invested by God with no common character, in being made the father of the fathers of the Church, he fulfilled, in the immediate

prospect of death, the prophetic office, respecting the future state of the Church, which had been enjoined upon him. Private persons arrange their domestic affairs by their last wills; but very different was the method pursued by this holy man, with whom God had established his covenant, with this annexed condition, that the succession of grace should flow down to his posterity. But before I enter fully on the consideration of this subject, these two things are to be observed, to which Moses briefly alludes: first, that Joseph, being informed of his father's sickness, immediately went to see him; and, secondly, that Jacob, having heard of his arrival, attempted to raise his feeble and trembling body, for the sake of doing him honour. Certainly, the reason why Joseph was so desirous of seeing his father, and so prompt to discharge all the other duties of filial piety, was, that he regarded it as a greater privilege to be a son of Jacob, than to preside over a hundred kingdoms. For, in bringing his sons with him, he acted as if he would emancipate them from the country in which they had been born, and restore them to their own stock. For they could not be reckoned among the progeny of Abraham, without rendering themselves detested by the Egyptians. Nevertheless, Joseph prefers that reproach for them, to every kind of wealth and glory, if they may but become one with the sacred body of the Church. His father, however, rising before him, pays him becoming honour, for the kindness received at his hand. Meanwhile, by so doing, he fulfils his part in the prediction, which before had inflamed his sons with rage; lest his constituting Ephraim and Manasseh the heads of two tribes, should seem grievous and offensive to his sons.

3. *And Jacob said unto Joseph.* The design of the holy man was to withdraw his son from the wealth and honours of Egypt, and to reunite him to the holy race, from which he had been, for a little while, separated. Moreover, he neither proudly boasts of his own excellence, nor of his present riches, nor of his power, for the sake of inducing his son to comply with his wishes; but simply sets before him the covenant of God. So also it is right, that the grace of adoption, as soon as it is offered to us, should, by filling our thoughts, extinguish

our desire for everything splendid and costly in the world. This passage is, doubtless, remarkable. Joseph was possessed of the most exalted dignity; he foresees that the most excellent nobility would pass, through the memory of his name, to his posterity: he is able to leave them an ample patrimony: nor would it be difficult so to advance them in royal favour, that they might obtain rank among the nobles of the kingdom. Too many examples show how easy it is not only to be caught, but altogether fascinated, by such allurements. Yea, the greater part know, by their own experience, that, as soon as the least ray of hope beams upon us, from the world, we are torn away from the Lord, and alienated from the pursuit of the heavenly life. If a very few drops thus inebriate our flesh, how dangerous is it to drink from the full bowl? But to all the riches and honours of Egypt, Jacob opposes the vision in which God had adopted himself and his race, as his own people. Whenever, therefore, Satan shall try to entangle us with the allurements of the world, that he may draw us away from heaven, let us remember for what end we are called; in order that, in comparison with the inestimable treasure of eternal life, all that the flesh would otherwise prefer, may become loathsome. For, if holy Joseph formerly held an obscure vision in such esteem, that, for this sole object, forgetting Egypt, he gladly passed over to the de- spised flock of the Church; how shameful, at this day, is our folly, how vile our stupor, how detestable our ingratitude, if, at least, we are not equally affected, when our heavenly Father, having opened the gate of his kingdom, with unut- terable sweetness invites us to himself? At the same time, however, we must observe, that holy Jacob does not obtrude vain imaginations, for the purpose of alluring his son; but places before him the sure promise of God, on which he may safely rely. Whence we are taught, that our faith is not rightly founded on anything except the sole word of God; and also, that this is a sufficiently firm support of faith, to prevent it from ever being shaken or overthrown by any devices whatever. Wherefore, whenever Satan attempts to draw us hither and thither by his enticements, let us learn to turn our minds to the word of God, and so firmly to rely upon its hidden blessings, that, with a lofty spirit, we may spurn those things which the flesh now sees and touches. Jacob says that God appeared to him in the land of Canaan, in order that Joseph, aspiring after that land, might become alienated in the affection of his heart from the kingdom of Egypt.

And blessed me. In this place the word " blessed" does not signify the present effect or manifestation of a happy life, in the way in which the Lord is sometimes said to bless his people, when he indeed declares, by the favour with which he follows them, that he openly makes them happy, because they are received under his protection. But Jacob regards himself as blessed, because he, having embraced the grace promised to him, does not doubt of its effect. And, therefore, I take what immediately follows ; namely, *I will make thee fruitful,* &c., as explanatory of what precedes. Now the Lord promised that he would cause an assembly of nations to descend from him : because thirteen tribes, of which the whole body of the nation consisted, were, in a sense, so many nations. But since this was nothing more than a prelude to that greatness which should afterwards follow, when God, having scattered seed over the whole world, should gather together a church for himself, out of all nations ; we may, while we recognise the accomplishment of the benediction under the old dispensation, yet allow that it refers to something greater. When therefore the people increased to so great a multitude, and thirteen populous tribes flowed from the twelve patriarchs, Jacob began already to grow to an assembly of nations. But from the time that the spiritual Israel was diffused through all quarters of the world, and various nations were congregated into one Church, this multiplication tended towards its completion. Wherefore, it is no wonder that holy Jacob should so highly estimate this most distinguished mark of divine favour, though, indeed, it was deeply hidden from carnal perception. But inasmuch as the Lord had held him long in suspense, profane men have said, that the old man was in his dotage. Few indeed are to be found, in this age, like Joseph, who disregarding the enjoyment of pleasures which are at hand, yield entire submission to the plain declaration of God's word. But as Jacob,

relying in confidence on invisible grace, had overcome every
kind of temptation : so now his son, and the true heir of his
faith, regards with reverence the oracles of the Lord ; esteem-
ing more highly the promise which he was persuaded had
come down from heaven, though it was in the form of a
dream, than all the riches of Egypt which he enjoyed.

For an everlasting possession. We have elsewhere shown
the meaning of this expression : namely, that the Israelites
should be perpetual heirs of the land until the coming of
Christ, by which the world was renewed. The Hebrew word
עוֹלָם (*olam*) is by some taken merely for *a long time*, by
others for *eternity :* but seeing that Christ prolongs, to the
end of time, the grace which was previously shadowed forth
to the patriarchs ; the phrase, in my judgment, refers to
eternity. For that portion of land was promised to the
ancient people of God, until the renovation introduced by
Christ : and now, ever since the Lord has assigned the whole
world to his people, a fuller fruition of the inheritance belongs to us.

5. *And now thy two sons.* Jacob confers on his son the
special privilege, that he, being one, should constitute two
chiefs ; that is, that his two sons should succeed to an equal
right with their uncles, as if they had been heirs in the first
degree. But what is this ! that a decrepid old man assigns
to his grandchildren, as a royal patrimony, a sixth part of
the land in which he had wandered as a stranger, and from
which now again he is an exile ! Who would not have said
that he was dealing in fables ? It is a common proverb,
that no one can give what he has not. What, therefore, did
it profit Joseph to be constituted, by an imaginary title, lord
of that land, in which the donor of it was scarcely permitted
to drink the very water he had dug for with great labour, and
from which, at length, famine expelled him ? But it hence
appears with what firm faith the holy fathers relied upon the
word of the Lord, seeing they chose rather to depend upon
his lips, than to possess a fixed habitation in the land. Jacob
is dying an exile in Egypt ; and meanwhile, calls away the
governor of Egypt from his dignity into exile, that he may
be well and happy. Joseph, because he acknowledges his

father as a prophet of God, who utters no inventions of his own, esteems as highly the dominion offered to him, which has never yet become apparent, as if it were already in his possession. Moreover, that Jacob commands the other sons of Joseph, (if there should be any,) to be reckoned in the families of these two brothers, is as if he directed them to be adopted by the two whom he adopts to himself.

7. *And as for me, when I came from Padan.* He mentions the death and burial of his wife Rachel, in order that the name of his mother might prove a stimulus to the mind of Joseph. For since all the sons of Jacob had sprung from Syria, it was not a little to the purpose, that they should be thoroughly acquainted with the history which we have before considered ; namely, that their father, returning into the land of Canaan, by the command and under the protection of God, brought his wives with him. For if it was not grievous to women, to leave their father, and to journey into a distant land, their example ought to be no slight inducement to their sons to bid farewell to Egypt ; and at the command of the same God, strenuously prepare themselves for taking possession of the land of Canaan.

8. *And Israel beheld Joseph's sons.* I have no doubt that he had inquired concerning the youths, before he called them his heirs. But in the narration of Moses there is a *hysteron proteron.* And in the answer of Joseph we observe, what we have elsewhere alluded to, that the fruit of the womb is not born by chance, but is to be reckoned among the precious gifts of God. This confession indeed finds a ready utterance from the tongues of all ; but there are few who heartily acknowledge that their seed has been given them by God. And hence a large proportion of man's offspring becomes continually more and more degenerate : because the ingratitude of the world renders it unable to perceive the effect of the blessings of God. We must now briefly consider the design of Moses : which was to show that a solemn symbol was interposed, by which the adoption might be ratified. Jacob puts his hands upon his grandsons ; for what end ? Truly to prove that he gave them a place among his sons : and thus constitutes Joseph who was *one,* into two *chiefs.* For

this was not his wish as a private person ; according to the
manner in which fathers and grandfathers are wont to pray
for prosperity to their descendents : but a divine authority
suggested it, as was afterwards proved by the event.   Therefore he commands them to be brought near to him, that he
might confer on them a new honour, as if he had been appointed the dispenser of it by the Lord ; and Joseph, on the
other hand, begins with adoration, giving thanks to God.

12. *And Joseph brought them out.*   Moses explains more
fully what he had touched upon in a single word.   Joseph
brings forth his sons from his own lap to his father's knees,
not only for the sake of honour, but that he may present
them to receive a blessing from the prophet of God ; for
he was certainly persuaded, that holy Jacob did not desire
to embrace his grandsons after the common manner of men ;
but inasmuch as he was the interpreter of God, he wished to
impart to them the blessing deposited with himself.   And
although, in dividing the land of Canaan, he assigned them
equal portions with his sons, yet the imposition of his hands
had respect to something higher ; namely, that they should
be two of the patriarchs of the Church, and should hold an
honourable pre-eminence in the spiritual kingdom of God.

14. *And Israel stretched out his right hand.*   Seeing his
eyes were dim with age, so that he could not, by looking,
discern which was the elder, he yet intentionally placed his
hands across.   And therefore Moses says that he *guided his
hands wittingly*, because he did not rashly put them forth,
nor transfer them from one youth to the other for the sake
of feeling them : but using judgment, he purposely directed
his right hand to Ephraim who was the younger : but placed
his left hand on the first-born.   Whence we gather that the
Holy Spirit was the director of this act, who irradiated the
mind of the holy man, and caused him to see more correctly,
than those who were the most clear-sighted, into the nature
of this symbolical act.   I shall avoid saying more, because
we shall be able to inquire into it from other passages.

15. *God before whom.*   Although Jacob knew that a dispensation of the grace of God was committed to him, in order
that he might effectually bless his grandchildren ; yet he arro-

gates nothing to himself, but suppliantly resorts to prayer,
lest he should, in the least degree, detract from the glory of
God.   For as he was the legitimate administrator of the
blessing, so it behoved him to acknowledge God as its sole
Author.   And hence a common rule is to be deduced for all
the ministers and pastors of the Church.   For though they
are not only called witnesses of celestial grace, but are also
entrusted with the dispensation of spiritual gifts ; yet when
they are compared with God, they are nothing ; because he
alone contains all things within himself.   Wherefore let them
learn willingly to keep their own place, lest they should obscure the name of God.   And truly, since the Lord, by no
means, appoints his ministers, with the intention of derogating
from his own power ; therefore, mortal man cannot, without
sacrilege, desire to seem anything separate from God.   In the
words of Jacob we must note, first, that he invokes God, in
whose sight his fathers Abraham and Isaac had walked : for
since the blessing depended upon the covenant entered into
with them, it was necessary that their faith should be an intervening link between them and their descendants.   God
had chosen them and their posterity for a people unto himself : but the promise was efficacious for this reason, because,
being apprehended by faith, it had taken a lively root.   And
thus it came to pass, that they transmitted the right of succession to Jacob himself.   We now see that he does not bring
forward, in vain, or unseasonably, that faith of the fathers,
without which he would not have been a legitimate successor
of grace, by the covenant of God : not that Abraham and
Isaac had acquired so great an honour for themselves, and
their posterity ; or were, in themselves, so excellent ; but
because the Lord seals and sanctions by faith, those benefits
which he promises us, so that they shall not fail.

The God which fed me.   Jacob now descends to his own
feelings, and states that from his youth he had constantly
experienced, in various ways, the divine favour towards him.
He had before made the knowledge of God received through
his word, and the faith of his fathers, the basis of the blessing he pronounces ; he now adds another confirmation from
experience itself ; as if he would say, that he was not pro-

nouncing a blessing which consisted in an empty sound of
words, but one of which he had himself enjoyed the fruit, all
his life long.   Now though God causes his sun to shine indiscriminately on the good and evil, and feeds unbelievers as
well as believers : yet because he affords, only to the latter,
the peculiar sense of his paternal love in the use of his gifts,
Jacob rightly uses this as a reason for the confirmation of his
faith, that he had always been protected by the help of God.
Unbelievers are fed, even to the full, by the liberality of God :
but they gorge themselves, like swine, which, while acorns are
falling for them from the trees, yet have their snouts fixed to
the earth.   But in God's benefits this is the principal thing,
that they are pledges or tokens of his paternal love towards
us.   Jacob, therefore, from the sense of piety, with which the
children of God are endued, rightly adduces, as proof of the
promised grace, whatever good things God had bestowed upon
him ; as if he would say, that he himself was a decisive example to show how truly and faithfully the Lord had engaged
by covenant to be a father to the children of Abraham.   Let
us also learn hence, carefully to consider and meditate upon
whatever benefits we receive from the hand of God, that they
may prove so many supports for the confirmation of our faith.
The best method of seeking God is to begin at his word ; after
this, (if I may so speak,) experimental knowledge is added.
Now whereas, in this place, the singular gratitude of the holy
man is conspicuous; yet this circumstance adds to his honour,
that, while involved in manifold sufferings, by which he was
almost borne down, he celebrates the continual goodness of
God.   For although, by the rare and wonderful power of
God, he had been, in an extraordinary manner, delivered
from many dangers ; yet it was a mark of an exalted and
courageous mind, to be able to surmount so many and so
great obstacles, to fly on the wings of faith to the goodness
of God, and instead of being overwhelmed by a mass of evils,
to perceive the same goodness in the thickest darkness.

16. *The Angel which redeemed me.* He so joins the Angel
to God as to make him his equal. Truly he offers him
divine worship, and asks the same things from him as from
God. If this be understood indifferently of any angel what-

ever, the sentence is absurd. Nay, rather, as Jacob himself
sustains the name and character of God, in blessing his son,[1]
he is superior, in this respect, to the angels. Wherefore it is
necessary that Christ should be here meant, who does not
bear in vain the title of Angel, because he had become the
perpetual Mediator. And Paul testifies that he was the
Leader and Guide of the journey of his ancient people.
(1 Cor. x. 4.) He had not yet indeed been sent by the Father, to approach more nearly to us by taking our flesh, but
because he was always the bond of connection between God
and man, and because God formally manifested himself in
no other way than through him, he is properly called the
Angel. To which may be added, that the faith of the fathers was always fixed on his future mission. He was therefore the Angel, because even then he poured forth his rays,
that the saints might approach God, through him, as Mediator. For there was always so wide a distance between God
and men, that, without a mediator, there could be no communication. Nevertheless though Christ appeared in the form
of an angel, we must remember what the Apostle says to
the Hebrews, (ii. 16,) that " he took not on him the nature
of angels," so as to become one of *them*, in the manner in
which he truly became *man ;* for even when angels put on
human bodies, they did not, on that account, become men.
Now since we are taught, in these words, that the peculiar
office of Christ is to defend us and to deliver us from all evil,
let us take heed not to bury this grace in impious oblivion:
yea, seeing that now it is more clearly exhibited to us, than
formerly to the saints under the law, since Christ openly declares that the faithful are committed to his care, that not
one of them might perish, (John xvii. 12,) so much the more
ought it to flourish in our hearts, both that it may be highly
celebrated by us with suitable praise, and that it may stir us
up to seek this guardianship of our best Protector. And this
is exceedingly necessary for us ; for if we reflect how many
dangers surround us, that we scarcely pass a day without
being delivered from a thousand deaths ; whence does this

---

[1] In benedicendo filio.   It appears that though the singular number is
used, yet reference is made to the two grandsons of Jacob.—*Ed.*

arise, except from that care which is taken of us, by the Son of God, who has received us under his protection, from the hand of his Father.

And let my name be named on them. This is a mark of the adoption before mentioned: for he puts his name upon them, that they may obtain a place among the patriarchs. Indeed the Hebrew phrase signifies nothing else than to be reckoned among the family of Jacob. Thus the name of the husband is said to be called upon the wife, (Is. iv. 1,) because the wife borrows the name from the head to which she is subject. So much the more ridiculous is the ignorance of the Papists, who would prove hence that the dead are to be invoked in prayers. Jacob, say they, desired after his death to be invoked by his posterity. What! that being prayed to, he might bring them succour; and not—according to the plain intention of the speaker—that Ephraim and Manasseh might be added to the society of the patriarchs, to constitute two tribes of the holy people! Moreover it is wonderful, that the Papists, having under this pretext framed for themselves innumerable patrons, should have passed over Abraham, Isaac, and Jacob, as unworthy of the office. But the Lord, by this brutish stupor, has avenged their impious profanation of his name. What Jacob adds in the next clause, namely, that they should *grow into a multitude,*[1] refers also to the same promise. The sum amounts to this, that the Lord would complete in them, what he had promised to the patriarchs.

17. *And when Joseph saw.* Because by crossing his arms, Jacob had so placed his hands as to put his left hand upon the head of the first-born, Joseph wished to correct this proceeding, as if it had been a mistake. He thought that the error arose from dimness of vision; but his father followed the Spirit of God as his secret guide, in order that he might transfer the title of honour, which nature had conferred upon

---

[1] ירדגו, (*yedegu,*) Ainsworth translates the passage, " let them increase like fish into a multitude." The Hebrew word for fish is from the above root, because of their prolific property; and consequently the use of such a term naturally suggests the notion of an extraordinary increase. Thus the Chaldee paraphrase adds, " like the fishes of the sea." Hence, in the time of Moses there were 85,200 men of war descended from Joseph, a greater number than from any other of Jacob's sons. *See Ainsworth.—Ed.*

the elder to the younger.   For, as he did not rashly assume to himself the office of conveying the blessing ; so was it not lawful for him to attempt anything according to his own will. And at length it was evident by the event, that whatever he had done had been dictated to him from heaven.   Whereas Joseph took it amiss, that Manasseh, who by the right of nature was first, should be cast down to the second place, this feeling arose from faith and from holy reverence for the prophetic office.   For he would easily have borne to see him make a mistake in the order of embracing the youths ; if he had not known that his father, as a minister of divine grace, so far from acting a futile part, was but pronouncing on earth what God would ratify in heaven.   Yet he errs in binding the grace of God to the accustomed order of nature : as if the Lord did not often purposely change the law of nature, to teach us that what he freely confers upon us, is entirely the result of his own will.   If God were rendering to every one his due, a certain rule might properly be applied to the distribution of his favours ; but since he owes no one anything, he is free to confer gifts at his own pleasure.   More especially, lest any one should glory in the flesh, he designedly illustrates his own free mercy, in choosing those who had no worthiness of their own.   What shall we say was the cause, why he raised Ephraim above his own brother, to whom, according to usage, he was inferior ?   If any one should suppose that Ephraim had some hidden seed of excellence, he not only vainly trifles, but impiously perverts the counsel of God. For since God derives from himself and from his own liberality, the cause, why he prefers one of the two to the other : he confers the honour upon the younger, for the purpose of showing that he is bound by no claims of human merit ; but that he distributes his gifts freely, as it seems good unto him.   And while this liberty of God is extended to every kind of good, it yet shines the most clearly in the first adoption, whereby he predestinates to himself, those whom he sees fit, out of the ruined mass.   Wherefore, be it our part to leave to God his whole power untouched, and if at any time, our carnal sense rebels, let us know that none are more truly wise than they who are willing to account themselves blind,

when contemplating the wonderful dealings of God, in order
that they may trace the cause of any difference he makes, to
himself alone.   We have seen above, that the eyes of Jacob
were dim: but in crossing his arms, with apparent negligence,
in order to comply with God's purpose of election, he is more
clear-sighted than his son Joseph, who, according to the sense
of the flesh, inquires with too much acuteness.   They who
insanely imagine that this judgment was formed from a view
of their works, sufficiently declare, by this one thing, that
they do not hold the first rudiments of faith.   For either the
adoption common both to Manasseh and to Ephraim, was a
free gift, or a reward of debt.   Concerning this second supposition all ambiguity is removed, by many passages of
Scripture, in which the Lord makes known his goodness, in
having freely loved and chosen his people.   Now no one is so
ignorant, as not to perceive that the first place is not assigned
to one or the other, according to merit ; but is given gratuitously, since it so pleases the Lord.   With regard to the
posture of the hands, the subtlety of certain persons, who
conjecture that the mystery of the cross was included in it,
is absurd ; for the Lord intended nothing more than that
the crossing of the right hand and the left should indicate a
change in the accustomed order of nature.

19. *He also shall become a people.*   Jacob does not dispute which of the youths shall be the more worthy; but only
pronounces what God had decreed with himself, concerning
each, and, what would take place after a long succession of
time.   He seeks, therefore, no causes elsewhere ; but contents
himself with this one statement, that Ephraim will be more
greatly multiplied than Manasseh.   And truly our dignity is
hidden in the counsel of God alone, until, by his vocation, he
makes it manifest what he wills to do with us.   Meanwhile,
sinful emulation is forbidden, when he commands Manasseh
to be contented with his lot.   They are therefore altogether
insane, who hew out dry and perforated cisterns, in seeking
causes of divine adoption ; whereas, everywhere, the Scripture
defines in one word, that they are called to salvation whom
God has chosen, (Rom. viii. 29,) and that the primary source of
election is his free good pleasure.   The form of the benediction,

which is shortly afterwards related, more fully confirms what I have alluded to, that the grace of God towards both is commended, in order that Manasseh, considering that more was given to him than he deserved, might not envy his brother. Moreover, this blessing pronounced on Ephraim and Manasseh is not to be taken in the same sense as the former, in which it is said, *In thy seed shall all nations be blessed :* but the simple meaning is, that the grace of God should be so conspicuous towards the two sons of Joseph, as to furnish the people of Israel with a form by which to express their good wishes.

21. *And Israel said unto Joseph.* Jacob repeats what he had said. And truly all his sons, and especially Joseph and his sons, required something more than one simple confirmation, in order that they might not fix their abode in Egypt, but might dwell, in their minds, in the land of Canaan. He mentions his own death, for the purpose of teaching them that the eternal truth of God by no means depended on the life of men : as if he had said, my life, seeing it is short and fading, passes away ; but the promise of God, which has no limit, will flourish when I also am dead. No vision had appeared unto his sons, but God had ordained the holy old man as the intermediate sponsor of his covenant. He therefore sedulously fulfils the office enjoined upon him, taking timely precaution that their faith should not be shaken by his death. So when the Lord delivers his word to the world by mortal men, although they die, having finished their course of life according to the flesh ; yet the voice of God is not extinguished with them, but quickens us even at the present day. Therefore Peter writes, that he will endeavour, that after his decease, the Church may be mindful of the doctrine committed unto him. (2 Pet. i. 15.)

Unto the land of your fathers. It is not without reason that he claims for himself and his fathers, the dominion over that land in which they had always wandered as strangers ; for whereas it might seem that the promise of God had failed, he excites his sons to a good hope, and pronounces, with a courageous spirit, that land to be his own, in which, at length, he scarcely obtained a sepulchre, and that only by

favour. Whence then was this great confidence, except that
he would accustom his sons, by his example, to have faith in
the word of God ? Now this doctrine is also common to us ;
because we never rely with sufficient firmness on the word of
God, so long as we are led by our own feelings. Nay, until
our faith rises to lay hold on those things which are removed
afar off, we know not what it is to set our seal to the word of
God.

22. *I have given to thee one portion.* In order to increase
the confidence of his son Joseph, Jacob here assigns him a
portion beyond his proper lot. Some expound the passage
otherwise ; as if he called him a double heir in his two sons,
thus honouring him with one portion more than the rest.
But there is no doubt that he means a certain territory.
And John, (chap. iv. 5,) removes all controversy ; for, speaking of the field adjoining Sychar, which before was called
Shechem, says, it was that which Jacob gave to his son
Joseph. And, in the last chapter of Joshua, (ver. 32,) it is
said to have come into the possession of the sons of Joseph.
But in the word שׁכם, (*shechem,*) which among the Hebrews
signifies a *part*, allusion is made to the proper name of the
place. But here a question arises ; how can he say that he
had obtained the field by his sword and by his bow, which
he had purchased with money, as is stated before, (chap.
xxxiii. 19,) and is again recorded in the above mentioned
chapter of Joshua ? Seeing, however, that only a small portion
of the field, where he might pitch his tents, was bought, I do
not doubt that here he comprised a much greater space.
For we may easily calculate, from the price, how small a portion of land he possessed, before the destruction of the city.
He gives, therefore, now to his son Joseph, not only the place
of his tent, which had cost a hundred pieces of silver, but
the field which had been the common of the city of Sychar.
But it remains to inquire how he may be said to have obtained
it by his sword, whereas the inhabitants had been wickedly
and cruelly slain by Simeon and Levi. How then could it be
acquired by the right of conquest, from those against whom
war had been unjustly brought ; or rather, against whom,
without any war, the most cruel perfidy had been practised ?

Jerome resorts to allegory, saying that the field was obtained by money, which is called strength, or justice. Others suppose a prolepsis, as if Jacob was speaking of a future acquisition of the land : a meaning which, though I do not reject, seems yet somewhat forced. I rather incline to this interpretation : first, that he wished to testify that he had taken nothing by means of his two sons Simeon and Levi ; who, having raged like robbers, were not lawful conquerors, and had never obtained a single foot of land, after the perpetration of the slaughter. For, so far were they from gaining anything, that they compelled their father to fly ; nor would escape have been possible, unless they had been delivered by miracle. When, however, Jacob strips them of their empty title, he transfers the right of victory to himself, as being divinely granted to him. For though he always held their wickedness in abhorrence, and will show his detestation of it in the next chapter ; yet, because they had armed his whole household, they fought as under his auspices. Gladly would he have preserved the citizens of Shechem, a design which he was not able to accomplish ; yet he appropriates to himself the land left empty and deserted by their destruction, because, for his sake, God had spared the murderers.[1]

CHAPTER XLIX.

1. AND Jacob called unto his sons, and said, Gather yourselves together, that I may tell you *that* which shall befall you in the last days.

2. Gather yourselves together, and hear, ye sons of Jacob ; and hearken unto Israel your father.

1. Postea vocavit Jahacob filios suos, et dixit, Congregate vos, et annuntiabo vobis quod eventurum est vobis in novissimo dierum.

2. Congregate vos, et audite filii Jahacob, audite inquam Israel patrem vestrum.

[1] Perhaps this interpretation of a confessedly obscure passage, will be deemed rather ingenious than solid. It is supposed by many, that Jacob refers to some transaction of which no record is preserved. He may, like Abraham, on some occasion, have armed his household to recover from the hands of the Amorites the field of Shechem, which he had previously purchased. But the whole must be left in hopeless obscurity. Ainsworth thinks that Jacob is speaking proleptically, and representing the future conduct of his children under Joshua, whose sword and bow he here calls his own. But this seems far-fetched. The Chaldee interpretation, that the sword and bow are figuratively used for *prayer* and *supplication,* is still more improbable.—*Ed.*

3. Reuben, thou *art* my first-born, my might, and the beginning of my strength, the excellency of dignity, and the excellency of power:

4. Unstable as water, thou shalt not excel; because thou wentest up to thy father's bed; then defiledst thou *it :* he went up to my couch.

5. Simeon and Levi *are* brethren; instruments of cruelty *are in* their habitations.

6. O my soul, come not thou into their secret; unto their assembly, mine honour, be not thou united! for in their anger they slew a man, and in their self-will they digged down a wall.

7. Cursed *be* their anger, for *it was* fierce; and their wrath, for it was cruel: I will divide them in Jacob, and scatter them in Israel.

8. Judah, thou *art he* whom thy brethren shall praise: thy hand *shall be* in the neck of thine enemies; thy father's children shall bow down before thee.

9. Judah *is* a lion's whelp: from the prey, my son, thou art gone up: he stooped down, he couched as a lion, and as an old lion: who shall rouse him up ?

10. The sceptre shall not depart from Judah, nor a lawgiver from between his feet, until Shiloh come; and unto him *shall* the gathering of the people *be :*

11. Binding his fole unto the vine, and his ass's colt unto the choice vine; he washed his garments in wine, and his clothes in the blood of grapes:

12. His eyes *shall be* red with wine, and his teeth white with milk.

13. Zebulun shall dwell at the haven of the sea; and he *shall be* for an haven of ships: and his border *shall be* unto Zidon.

14. Issachar *is* a strong ass couching down between two burdens:

15. And he saw that rest *was* good, and the land that *it was* pleasant; and bowed his shoulder to bear, and became a servant unto tribute.

3. Reuben primogenitus meus, tu fortitudo mea, et principium roboris mei: excellentia dignitatis et excellentia roboris.

4. Velocitas *fuit tibi* instar aquæ, non excelles: quia ascendisti cubile patris tui, tunc polluisti stratum meum, evanuit.

5. Simhon et Levi fratres, arma iniquitatis in habitationibus eorum.

6. In secretum eorum non veniat anima mea, in cœtu eorum non uniaris lingua mea: quia in furore suo occiderunt virum, et voluntate sua eradicaverunt murum.

7. Maledictus furor eorum, quia robustus, et ira eorum, quia dura est: dividam eos in Jahacob et dispergam eos in Israel.

8. Jehudah *es* tu, laudabunt te fratres tui: manus tua erit in cervice inimicorum tuorum, incurvabunt se tibi filii patris tui.

9. Ut catulus leonis Jehudah: e præda, fili mi, ascendisti: incurvavit se, cubuit sicut leo, sicut leo major, quis suscitabit eum ?

10. Non recedet sceptrum ex Jehudah, et Legislator e medio pedum ejus, donec veniat Messias: et ei erit aggregatio populorum.

11. Ligans ad vitem pullum suum, et ad ramum filium asinæ suæ: lavit in vino vestimentum suum, et in sanguine uvarum operimentum suum..

12. Rubicundus oculis a vino, et candidus dentibus a lacte.

13. Zebulon in portu marium habitabit, et erit in portum navium, et terminus ejus usque ad Sidon.

14. Issachar *ut* asinus osseus, cubans inter duas sarcinas.

15. Et vidit requiem, quod esset bonum: et terram quod esset pulchra, et inclinavit humerum suum ad portandum, et fuit tributo serviens.

16. Dan shall judge his people, as one of the tribes of Israel.

17. Dan shall be a serpent by the way, an adder in the path, that biteth the horse heels, so that his rider shall fall backward.

18. I have waited for thy salvation, O Lord.

19. Gad, a troop shall overcome him: but he shall overcome at the last.

20. Out of Asher his bread *shall be* fat, and he shall yield royal dainties.

21. Naphtali *is* a hind let loose: he giveth goodly words.

22. Joseph *is* a fruitful bough, *even* a fruitful bough by a well, *whose* branches run over the wall.

23. The archers have sorely grieved him, and shot *at him*, and hated him:

24. But his bow abode in strength, and the arms of his hands were made strong by the hands of the mighty *God* of Jacob: (from thence *is* the Shepherd, the stone of Israel :)

25. *Even* by the God of thy father, who shall help thee; and by the Almighty, who shall bless thee with blessings of heaven above, blessings of the deep that lieth under, blessings of the breasts, and of the womb:

26. The blessings of thy father have prevailed above the blessings of thy progenitors unto the utmost bound of the everlasting hills: they shall be on the head of Joseph, and on the crown of the head of him that was separate from his brethren.

27. Benjamin shall ravin *as* a wolf: in the morning he shall devour the prey, and at night he shall divide the spoil.

28. All these *are* the twelve tribes of Israel: and this *is it* that their father spake unto them, and blessed them; every one according to his blessing he blessed them.

29. And he charged them, and said unto them, I am to be gathered unto my people: bury me with my

16. Dan judicabit populum suum sicut unus e tribubus Israel.

17. Erit Dan *ut* serpens juxta viam, *ut* cerastes juxta semitam, mordens calcaneos equi, et cecidit equitans retrorsum.

18. Salutem tuam exspectavi Jehova.

19. Gad, exercitus succidet eum, et ipse succidet ad extremum.

20. Aser, erit pinguis panis ejus, et ipse dabit delicias regis.

21. Naphthali *ut* cerva dimissa, dans eloquia pulchritudinis.

22. *Ut* arbor fructificans Joseph, ut ramus crescens juxta fontem, rami incedent super murum.

23. Et amaritudine affecerunt eum, et jaculati sunt, et odio habuerunt eum sagittarii.

24. Et mansit in fortitudine arcus ejus, et roboraverunt se brachia manuum ejus a manibus potentis Jahacob, inde pastor lapidis Israel.

25. A Deo patris tui, et adjuvabit te: et ab Omnipotente, et benedicet tibi benedictionibus cœli sursum, benedictionibus abyssi cubantis deorsum, benedictionibus uberum et vulvæ.

26. Benedictiones patris tui fortiores fuerunt benedictionibus genitorum meorum, usque ad terminum collium perpetuorum erunt super caput Joseph, et super verticem Nazaræi inter fratres suos.

27. Benjamin *ut* lupus rapiet, mane comedet prædam, et vesperi dividet spolia.

28. Omnes istæ tribus Israel duodecim. Et hoc est quod loquutus est eis pater eorum, et benedixit eis, unicuique secundum benedictionem suam, benedixit eis.

29. Et præcepit eis, et dixit ad eos, Ego congregor ad populum meum: sepelite me cum patribus

fathers in the cave that *is* in the field of Ephron the Hittite,

30. In the cave that *is* in the field of Machpelah, which *is* before Mamre, in the land of Canaan, which Abraham bought with the field of Ephron the Hittite, for a possession of a burying place.

31. There they buried Abraham and Sarah his wife ; there they buried Isaac and Rebekah his wife; and there I buried Leah.

32. The purchase of the field, and of the cave that *is* therein, *was* from the children of Heth.

33. And when Jacob had made an end of commanding his sons, he gathered up his feet into the bed, and yielded up the ghost, and was gathered unto his people.

meis in spelunca, quæ est in agro Hephron Hittæi.

30. In spelunca, quæ est in agro duplici, quæ est ante Mamre: in terra Chenaan, quam emit Abraham cum agro ab Hephron Hittæo in possessionem sepulcri.

31. Ibi sepelierunt Abraham et Sarah uxorem ejus : ibi sepelierunt Ishac et Ribcah uxorem ejus, et ibi sepelivi Leah.

32. Emptio agri et speluncæ, quæ est in eo, *fuit* a filiis Heth.

33. Et finem fecit Iahacob præcipiendi filiis suis : et collegit pedes suos in lecto et obiit, et aggregatus est ad populos suos.

1. *And Jacob called.* In the former chapter, the blessing on Ephraim and Manasseh was related, because, before Jacob should treat of the state of the whole nation about to spring from him, it was right that these two grandsons should be inserted into the body of his sons. Now, as if carried above the heavens, he announces, not in the character of a man, but as from the mouth of God, what shall be the condition of them all, for a long time to come. And it will be proper first to remark, that as he had then thirteen sons, he sets before his view, in each of their persons, the same number of nations or tribes : in which act the admirable lustre of his faith is conspicuous. For since he had often heard from the Lord, that his seed should be increased to a multitude of people, this oracle is to him like a sublime mirror, in which he may perceive things deeply hidden from human sense. Moreover, this is not a simple confession of faith, by which Jacob testifies that he hopes for whatever had been promised him by the Lord ; but he rises superior to men, as the interpreter and ambassador of God, to regulate the future state of the Church. Now, since some interpreters perceived this prophecy to be noble and magnificent, they have thought that it would not be adorned with its proper dignity, unless they should extract from it certain new mysteries. Thus it has happened, that in striving earnestly to elicit profound alle-

gories, they have departed from the genuine sense of the
words, and have corrupted, by their own inventions, what
is here delivered for the solid edification of the pious.
But lest we should depreciate the literal sense, as if it did
not contain speculations sufficiently profound, let us mark
the design of the Holy Spirit.   In the first place, the sons
of Jacob are informed beforehand, of their future fortune,
that they may know themselves to be objects of the special
care of God; and that, although the whole world is governed
by his providence, they, notwithstanding, are preferred to
other nations, as members of his own household.   It seems
apparently a mean and contemptible thing, that a region
productive of vines, which should yield abundance of choice
wine, and one rich in pastures, which should supply milk, is
promised to the tribe of Judah.   But if any one will consider that the Lord is hereby giving an illustrious proof
of his own election, in descending, like the father of a
family, to the care of food, and also showing, in minute
things, that he is united by the sacred bond of a covenant
to the children of Abraham, he will look for no deeper mystery.   In the second place; the hope of the promised inheritance is again renewed unto them.   And, therefore, Jacob,
as if he would put them in possession of the land by his
own hand, expounds familiarly, and as in an affair actually
present, what kind of habitation should belong to each of
them.   Can the confirmation of a matter so serious, appear
contemptible to sane and prudent readers?   It is, however, the principal design of Jacob more correctly to point
out from whence a king should arise among them, who
should bring them complete felicity.   And in this manner
he explains what had been promised obscurely, concerning
the blessed seed.   In these things there is so great weight,
that the simple treating of them, if only we were skilful interpreters, ought justly to transport us with admiration.
But (omitting all things else) an advantage of no common
kind consists in this single point, that the mouth of impure
and profane men, who freely detract from the credibility of
Moses, is shut, so that they no longer dare to contend that
he did not speak by a celestial impulse.   Let us imagine

that Moses does not relate what Jacob had before prophesied, but speaks in his own person; whence, then, could he
divine what did not happen till many ages afterwards?
Such, for instance, is the prophecy concerning the kingdom
of David. And there is no doubt that God commanded the
land to be divided by lot, lest any suspicion should arise
that Joshua had divided it among the tribes, by compact,
and as he had been instructed by his master. After the
Israelites had obtained possession of the land, the division
of it was not made by the will of men. Whence was it that
a dwelling near the sea-shore was given to the tribe of
Zebulun; a fruitful plain to the tribe of Asher; and to the
others, by lot, what is here recorded; except that the Lord
would ratify his oracles by the result, and would show openly,
that nothing then occurred which he had not, a long time
before, declared should take place? I now return to the
words of Moses, in which holy Jacob is introduced, relating
what he had been taught by the Holy Spirit concerning
events still very remote. But some, with canine rage, demand,[1]
Whence did Moses derive his knowledge of a conversation,
held in an obscure hut, two hundred years before his time? I
ask in return, before I give an answer, Whence had he his
knowledge of the places in the land of Canaan, which he assigns, like a skilful surveyor, to each tribe? If this was a
knowledge derived from heaven, (which must be granted,)
why will these impious babblers deny that the things which
Jacob had predicted, were divinely revealed to Moses? Besides,
among many other things which the holy fathers had handed
down by tradition, this prediction might then be generally
known. Whence was it that the people, when tyrannically
oppressed, implored the assistance of God as their deliverer?
Whence was it, that at the simple hearing of a promise formerly given, they raised their minds to a good hope, unless
that some remembrance of the divine adoption still flourished
among them? If there was a general acquaintance with the
covenant of the Lord among the people; what impudence
will it be to deny that the heavenly servants of God more
accurately investigated whatever was important to be known

---

[1] Sed oblatrant quidam protervi canes.

respecting the promised inheritance ?   For the Lord did not
utter oracles by the mouth of Jacob which, after his death,
a sudden oblivion should destroy ; as if he had breathed, I
know not what sounds, into the air.   But rather he delivered
instruction common to many ages ; that his posterity might
know from what source their redemption, as well as the
hereditary title of the land, flowed down to them.   We know
how tardily, and even timidly, Moses undertook the province
assigned him, when he was called to deliver his own people:
because he was aware that he should have to deal with an
intractable and perverse nation.   It was, therefore, necessary, that he should come prepared with certain credentials
which might give proof of his vocation.   And, hence, he
put forth these predictions, as public documents from the
sacred archives of God, that no one might suppose him to
have intruded rashly into his office.

Gather yourselves together.[1]   Jacob begins with inviting
their attention.   For he gravely enters on his subject, and
claims for himself the authority of a prophet, in order to
teach his sons that he is by no means making a private tes-
tamentary disposition of his domestic affairs ; but that he is
expressing in words, those oracles which are deposited with
him, until the event shall follow in due time.   For he does
not command them simply to listen to his wishes, but gathers
them into an assembly by a solemn rite, that they may
hear what shall occur to them in the succession of time.
Moreover, I do not doubt, that he places this future period
of which he speaks, in opposition to their exile in Egypt,
that, when their minds were in suspense, they might look
forward to that promised state.   Now, from the above re-

---

[1] The reader will observe, that the entire structure of these predictions
is poetical.   The prophecies of the Old Testament are generally delivered
in this form ; and God has thus chosen the most natural method of conveying prophetic intelligence, through the medium of that elevated strain
of diction, which suggests itself to imaginative minds, which is peculiarly
fitted to deal with sublime and invisible realities, and which best serves to
stir up animated feelings, and to fix important truths in the memory of
the reader.   They who wish to examine more minutely the poetical character of the chapter, are referred to Dr. Adam Clarke's Commentary,
and to Caunter's Poetry of the Pentateuch.   A few observations, in passing, will be made in the notes to such passages as derive elucidation
from their poetical structure.—*Ed.*

marks, it may be easily inferred, that, in this prophecy is comprised the whole period from the departure out of Egypt to the reign of Christ: not that Jacob enumerates every event, but that, in the summary of things on which he briefly touches, he arranges a settled order and course, until Christ should appear.

3. *Reuben, thou art my first-born.* He begins with the first-born, not for the sake of honour, to confirm him in his rank; but that he may the more completely cover him with shame, and humble him by just reproaches. For Reuben is here cast down from his primogeniture; because he had polluted his father's bed by incestuous intercourse with his mother-in-law. The meaning of his words is this: " Thou, indeed, by nature the first-born, oughtest to have excelled, seeing thou art my strength, and the beginning of my manly vigour; but since thou hast flowed away like water, there is no more any ground for arrogating anything to thyself. For, from the day of thy incest, that dignity which thou receivedst on thy birth-day, from thy mother's womb, is gone and vanished away. The noun אוֹן, some translate *seed*, others *grief;* and turn the passage thus: " Thou, my strength, and the beginning of my grief or seed." They who prefer the word *grief*, assign as a reason, that children bring care and anxiety to their parents. But if this were the true meaning, there would rather have been an antithesis between strength and sorrow. Since, however, Jacob is reciting, in continuity, the declaration of the dignity which belongs to the first-born, I doubt not that he here mentions the beginning of his manhood. For as men, in a certain sense, live again in their children, the first-born is properly called the " beginning of strength." To the same point belongs what immediately follows, that he had been the excellency of dignity and of strength, until he had deservedly deprived himself of both. For Jacob places before the eyes of his son Reuben his former honour, because it was for his profit to be made thoroughly conscious whence he had fallen. So Paul says, that he set before the Corinthians the sins by which they were defiled, in order to make them ashamed. (1 Cor. vi. 5.) For whereas we are disposed

to flatter ourselves in our vices, scarcely any one of us is brought back to a sane mind, after he has fallen, unless he is touched with a sense of his vileness. Moreover, nothing is better adapted to wound us, than when a comparison is made between those favours which God bestows upon us, and the punishments we bring upon ourselves by our own fault. After Adam had been stripped of all good things, God reproaches him sharply, and not without ridicule, " Behold Adam is as one of us." What end is this designed to answer, except that Adam, reflecting with himself how far he is changed from that man, who had lately been created according to the image of God, and had been endowed with so many excellent gifts, might be confounded and fall prostrate, deploring his present misery ? We see, then, that reproofs are necessary for us, in order that we may be touched to the quick by the anger of the Lord. For so it happens, not only that we become displeased with the sins of which we are now bearing the punishment, but also, that we take greater care diligently to guard those gifts of God which dwell within us, lest they perish through our negligence. They who refer the " excellency of dignity" to the priesthood, and the " excellency of power" to the kingly office, are, in my judgment, too subtle interpreters. I take the more simple meaning of the passage to be ; that if Reuben had stood firmly in his own rank, the chief place of all excellency would have belonged to him.

4. *Unstable as water.* He shows that the honour which had not a good conscience for its keeper, was not firm but evanescent ; and thus he rejects Reuben from the primogeniture. He declares the cause, lest Reuben should complain that he was punished when innocent: for it was also of great consequence, in this affair, that he should be convinced of his fault, lest his punishment should not be attended with profit. We now see Jacob, having laid carnal affection aside, executing the office of a prophet with vigour and magnanimity. For this judgment is not to be ascribed to anger, as if the father desired to take private vengeance of his son : but it proceeded from the Spirit of God ; because Jacob kept fully in mind the burden imposed upon

him. The word עלה (*alach*) at the close of the sentence
signifies to depart, or to be blown away like the ascending
smoke, which is dispersed.[1] Therefore the sense is, that the
excellency of Reuben, from the time that he had defiled his
father's bed, had flowed away and become extinct. For to
expound the expression concerning the bed, to mean that it
ceased to be Jacob's conjugal bed, because Bilhah had been
divorced, is too frigid.

5. *Simeon and Levi are brethren.* He condemns the massacre of the city of Shechem by his two sons Simeon and
Levi, and denounces the punishment of so great a crime.
Whence we learn how hateful cruelty is to God, seeing that
the blood of man is precious in his sight. For it is as if he
would cite to his own tribunal those two men, and would demand vengeance on them, when they thought they had
already escaped. It may, however, be asked, whether pardon had not been granted to them long ago; and if God had
already forgiven them, why does he recall them again to
punishment? I answer, it was both privately useful to
themselves, and was also necessary as an example, that this
slaughter should not remain unpunished, although they
might have obtained previous forgiveness. For we have
seen before, when they were admonished by their father,
how far they were from that sorrow which is the commencement of true repentance; and it may be believed that afterwards they became stupified more and more, with a kind of
brutish torpor, in their wickedness; or at least, that they

---

[1] The literal translation of Calvin's version is, " Thy velocity was like
that of water, thou shalt not excel: because thou wentest up into thy father's couch, then thou pollutedst my bed, he has *vanished*." This gives the
patriarch's expression a different turn from that supposed by our translators; who understand the last word in the sentence to be a repetition of
what had been said before, only putting it in the third person, as expressive of indignation; as if he had turned round from Reuben to his other
children and said—" Yes, I declare he went up into my bed!" Another
view is given in the margin of our Bible, " My couch is gone;" which
means that, by this defilement, the marriage bond was broken. To this
version Calvin objects at the close of the paragraph. But both these con-
structions seem forced. Calvin's appears the most natural. He represents Reuben as having lost all, by his criminal conduct. Honour, excellence, priority, virtue, and consequently character and influence, had all
gone up as the dew from the face of the earth, and had *vanished away.*
—*Ed.*

had not been seriously affected with bitter grief for their sin. It was also to be feared lest their posterity might become addicted to the same brutality, unless divinely impressed with horror at the deed. Therefore the Lord, partly for the purpose of humbling them, partly for that of making them an example to all ages, inflicted on them the punishment of perpetual ignominy. Moreover, by thus acting, he did not retain the punishment while remitting the guilt, as the Papists foolishly dream : but though truly and perfectly appeased, he administered a correction suitable for future times. The Papists imagine that sins are only half remitted by God ; because he is not willing to absolve sinners gratuitously. But Scripture speaks far otherwise. It teaches us that God does not exact punishments which shall compensate for offences ; but such as shall purge hearts from hypocrisy, and shall invite the elect—the allurements of the world being gradually shaken off—to repentance, shall stir them up to vigilant solicitude, and shall keep them under restraint by the bridle of fear and reverence. Whence it follows that nothing is more preposterous, than that the punishments which we have deserved, should be redeemed by satisfactions, as if God, after the manner of men, would have what was owing paid to him ; nay, rather there is the best possible agreement between the gratuitous remission of punishments and those chastenings of the rod, which rather prevent future evils, than follow such as have been already committed.

To return to Simeon and Levi. How is it that God, by inflicting a punishment which had been long deferred, should drag them back as guilty fugitives to judgment ; unless because impunity would have been hurtful to them ? And yet he fulfils the office of a physician rather than of a judge, who refuses to *spare*, because he intends to *heal ;* and who not only heals two who are sick, but, by an antidote, anticipates the diseases of others, in order that they may beware of cruelty. This also is highly worthy to be remembered, that Moses, in publishing the infamy of his own people, acts as the herald of God: and not only does he proclaim a disgrace common to the whole nation, but brands with infamy, the special tribe from which he sprung. Whence it plainly appears, that he paid no respect to his own flesh and blood ; nor was he to be induced, by favour or hatred, to give a false colour to anything, or to decline from historical fidelity : but, as a chosen minister and witness of the Lord, he was mindful of his calling, which was that he should declare the truth of God sincerely and confidently. A comparison is here made not only between the sons of Jacob personally ; but also between the tribes which descended from them. This certainly was a specially opportune occasion for Moses to defend the nobility of his own people. But so far is he from heaping encomiums upon them, that he frankly stamps the progenitor of his own tribe with an everlasting dishonour, which should redound to his whole family. Those Lucianist dogs, who carp at the doctrine of Moses, pretend that he was a vain man who wished to acquire for himself the command over the rude common people. But had this been his project, why did he not also make provision for his own family ? Those sons whom ambition would have persuaded him to endeavour to place in the highest rank, he puts aside from the honour of the priesthood, and consigns them to a lowly and common service. Who does not see that these impious calumnies have been anticipated by a divine counsel rather than by merely human prudence, and that the heirs of this great and extraordinary man were deprived of honour, for this reason, that no sinister suspicion might adhere to him ? But to say nothing of his children and grandchildren, we may perceive that, by censuring his whole tribe in the person of Levi, he acted not as a man, but as an angel speaking under the impulse of the Holy Spirit, and free from all carnal affection. Moreover, in the former clause, he announces the crime : afterwards, he subjoins the punishment. The crime is, that the arms of violence are in their tabernacles ; and therefore he declares, both by his tongue and in his heart, that he holds their counsel in abhorrence,[1] because, in their desire of revenge, they cut off a city with its inhabitants. Respecting the meaning of the words commentators differ. For some take the

---

[1] If this interpretation were admitted, the passage would read thus: "Simeon and Levi are brethren, instruments of cruelty are their swords."

word מכרות (*makroth*) to mean *swords ;* as if Jacob had said,
that their *swords* had been wickedly polluted with innocent
blood.   But they think more correctly, who translate the
word *habitations ;* as if he had said, that unjust violence
dwelt among them, because they had been so sanguinary.   I
do not doubt that the word כבד (*chabod*) is put for the
tongue, as in other places ;[1] and thus the sense is clear, that
Jacob, from his heart, so detests the crime perpetrated by
his sons, that his tongue shall not give any assent to it
whatever.   Which he does, for this end, that they may begin
to be dissatisfied with themselves, and that all others may
learn to abhor perfidy combined with cruelty.   *Fury,* beyond
doubt, signifies a perverse and blind impulse of anger :[2] and
lust is opposed to rational moderation ;[3] because they are
governed by no law.   Interpreters also differ respecting the
meaning of the word שור (*shor*).[4]   Some translate it " bul-
lock," and think that the Shechemites are allegorically denoted by it, seeing they were sufficiently robust and powerful
to defend their lives, had not Simeon and Levi enervated
them by fraud and perfidy.   But a different exposition is far
preferable, namely, that they " overturned a wall."   For
Jacob magnifies the atrociousness of their crime, from the
fact, that they did not even spare *buildings* in their rage.

[1] In cœtu eorum non uniaris lingua mea.   This is Calvin's version ; and
it may perhaps be vindicated by the use made of the word כבד in other
passages, where the tongue is metaphorically called the *glory* of man.
Yet the passage plainly admits of another and perhaps a more simple signification.—*Ed.*
[2] Quia in furore suâ, &c.   Because in their fury they killed a man.—*Ed.*
[3] *Libido* is not the word used in Calvin's version, though his commentary proceeds on that supposition.   His words are " voluntate suâ eradicaverunt murum."   In their will, or pleasure, they uprooted a wall.—*Ed.*
[4] The marginal reading of our Bible for " they digged down a wall," is
" they houghed oxen."   Some translators who think that the word ought
to be rendered " ox," and not " wall," regard the word *ox* as a metaphorical term for a brave and powerful man.   Thus Herder, in Caunter's
Poetry of the Pentateuch, gives the following version :—

> " My heart was not joined in their company,
>   When in anger they slew a hero,
>   And in revenge destroyed a noble ox."

Dr. A. Clarke suggests an alteration in the word, which gives the passage another sense :

> " In their anger they slew a man,
>   And in their pleasure they murdered a *prince.*"—*Ed.*

7. *Cursed be their anger.* What I have said must be kept in mind; namely, that we are divinely admonished by the mouth of the holy prophet, to keep at a distance from all wicked counsels. Jacob pronounces a woe upon their fury. Why is this, unless that others may learn to put a restraint upon themselves, and to be on their guard against such cruelty? However, (as I have already observed,) it will not suffice to preserve our hands pure, unless we are far removed from all association with crime. For though it may not always be in our power to repress unjust violence; yet that concealment of it is culpable, which approaches to the appearance of consent. Here even the ties of kindred, and whatever else would bias a sound judgment, must be dismissed from the mind: since we see a holy father, at the command of God, so severely thundering against his own sons. He pronounces the anger of Simeon and Levi to be so much the more hateful, because, in its commencement, it was violent, and even to the end, it was implacable.

I will divide them in Jacob. It may seem a strange method of proceeding, that Jacob, while designating his sons patriarchs of the Church, and calling them heirs of the divine covenant, should pronounce a malediction upon them instead of a blessing. Nevertheless it was necessary for him to begin with the chastisement, which should prepare the way for the manifestation of God's grace, as will be made to appear at the close of the chapter: but God mitigates the punishment, by giving them an honourable name in the Church, and leaving them their right unimpaired: yea, his incredible goodness unexpectedly shone forth, when that which was the punishment of Levi, became changed into the reward of the priesthood. The dispersion of the Levitical tribe had its origin in the crime of their father, lest he should congratulate himself on account of his perverse and lawless spirit of revenge. But God, who in the beginning had produced light out of darkness, found another reason why the Levites should be dispersed abroad among the people,—a reason not only free from disgrace, but highly honourable,—namely, that no corner of the land might be destitute of competent instructors. Lastly, he constituted them overseers and governors, in his name, over every part of the land, as if he would scatter everywhere the seed of eternal salvation, or would send forth ministers of his grace. Whence we conclude, how much better it was for Levi to be chastised at the time, for his own good, than to be left to perish, in consequence of present impunity in sin. And it is not to be deemed strange, that, when the land was distributed, and cities were given to the Levites, far apart from each other, this reason was suppressed,[1] and one entirely different was adduced ; namely, that the Lord was their inheritance. For this, as I have lately said, is one of the miracles of God, to bring light out of darkness. Had Levi been sentenced to distant exile, he would have been most worthy of the punishment : but now, God in a measure spares him, by assigning him a wandering life in his paternal inheritance. Afterwards, the mark of infamy being removed, God sends his posterity into different parts, under the title of a distinguished embassy. In Simeon there remained a certain, though obscure trace of the curse : because a distinct territory did not fall to his sons by lot ; but they were mixed with the tribe of Judah, as is stated in Joshua xix. 1. Afterwards they went to Mount Seir, having expelled the Amalekites and taken possession of their land, as it is written, 1 Chron. iv. 40-43. Here, also, we perceive the manly fortitude of holy Jacob's breast, who, though a decrepit old man and an exile, lying on his private and lowly couch, nevertheless assigns provinces to his sons, as from the lofty throne of a great king. He also does this in his own right, knowing that the covenant of God was deposited with him, by which he had been called the heir and lord of the land : and at the same time he claims for himself authority as sustaining the character of a prophet of God. For it greatly concerns us, when the word of God sounds in our ears, to apprehend by faith the thing proclaimed, as if his ministers had been commanded to carry into effect what they pronounce. Therefore it was said to Jeremiah, " See I have this day set

---

[1] As being no longer applicable to the case, because it was purely personal and belonged to Levi, only as an individual, and not to his descendents.—*Ed.*

thee over the nations and over the kingdoms, to root out, and to pull down, and to destroy, and to throw down, and to build, and to plant." (Jer. i. 10.) And the prophets are generally commanded to set their faces against the countries which they threaten, as if they were furnished with a large army to make the attack.

8. *Judah, thou art he whom thy brethren shall praise.* In the word *praise* there is an allusion to the name of Judah ; for so he had been called by his mother, because his birth had given occasion for praising God. The father adduces a new etymology, because his name shall be so celebrated and illustrious among his brethren, that he should be honoured by them all equally with the first-born.[1] The *double portion,* indeed, which he recently assigned to his son Joseph, depended on the right of primogeniture : but because the *kingdom* was transferred to the tribe of Judah, Jacob properly pronounces that his name should be held worthy of praise. For the honour of Joseph was temporary ; but here a stable and durable kingdom is treated of, which should be under the authority of the sons of Judah. Hence we gather, that when God would institute a perfect state of government among his people, the monarchical form was chosen by him. And whereas the appointment of a king under the law, was partly to be attributed to the will of man, and partly to the divine decree ; this combination of human with divine agency must be referred to the commencement of the monarchy, which was inauspicious, because the people had tumultuously desired a king to be given them, before the proper time had arrived. Hence their unseemly haste was the cause why the kingdom was not immediately set up in the tribe of Judah, but was brought forth, as an abortive offspring, in the person of Saul. Yet at length, by the favour and in the legitimate order of God, the pre-eminence of the tribe of Judah was established in the person of David.

Thy hand shall be in the neck of thine enemies. In these

---

[1] The original privilege of the birthright, taken from Reuben, was divided between Joseph and Judah; Joseph receiving the *double portion* belonging to the eldest son; Judah the regal distinction.—*Ed.*

words he shows that Judah should not be free from enemies ;
but although many would give him trouble, and would endeavour to deprive him of his right, Jacob promises him
victory ; not that the sons of David should always prevail
against their enemies, (for their ingratitude interfered with
the constant and equable course of the grace of God,) but
in this respect, at least, Judah had the superiority, that
in his tribe stood the royal throne which God approved, and
which was founded on his word. For though the kingdom
of Israel was more flourishing in wealth and in number of
inhabitants, yet because it was spurious, it was not the object
of God's favour : nor indeed was it right, that, by its tinselled
splendour, it should eclipse the glory of the Divine election
which was engraven upon the tribe of Judah.   In David,
therefore, the force and effect of this prophecy plainly appeared ; then again in Solomon ; afterwards, although the
kingdom was mutilated, yet was it wonderfully preserved by
the hand of God ; otherwise, in a short space, it would have
perished a hundred times. Thus it came to pass, that the
children of Judah imposed their yoke upon their enemies.
Whereas defection carried away ten tribes, which would not
bow their knees to the sons of David ; the legitimate government was in this way disturbed, and lawless confusion
introduced ; yet nothing could violate the decree of God,
by which the right to govern remained with the tribe of
Judah.

9. *Judah is a lion's whelp.* This similitude confirms the
preceding sentence, that Judah would be formidable to his
enemies. Yet Jacob seems to allude to that diminution
which took place, when the greater part of the people revolted to Jeroboam. For then the king of Judah began to
be like a sleeping lion, for he did not shake his mane to diffuse his terror far and wide, but, as it were, laid him down in
his den. Yet a certain secret power of God lay hidden under
that torpor, and they who most desired his destruction, and
who were most able to do him injury, did not dare to disturb him. Therefore, after Jacob has transferred the supreme
authority over his brethren to Judah alone ; he now adds,
by way of correction, that, though his power should happen

to be diminished, he would nevertheless remain terrible to his enemies, like a lion who lies down in his lair.[1]

10. *The sceptre shall not depart.* Though this passage is obscure, it would not have been very difficult to elicit its genuine sense, if the Jews, with their accustomed malignity, had not endeavoured to envelop it in clouds. It is certain that the Messiah, who was to spring from the tribe of Judah, is here promised. But whereas they ought willingly to run to embrace him, they purposely catch at every possible subterfuge, by which they may lead themselves and others far astray in tortuous by-paths. It is no wonder, then, if the spirit of bitterness and obstinacy, and the lust of contention have so blinded them, that, in the clearest light, they should have perpetually stumbled. Christians, also, with a pious diligence to set forth the glory of Christ, have, nevertheless, betrayed some excess of fervour. For while they lay too much stress on certain words, they produce no other effect than that of giving an occasion of ridicule to the Jews, whom it is necessary to surround with firm and powerful barriers, from which they shall be unable to escape. Admonished, therefore, by such examples, let us seek, without contention, the true meaning of the passage. In the first place, we must keep in mind the true design of the Holy Spirit, which, hitherto, has not been sufficiently considered or expounded with sufficient distinctness. After he has invested the tribe of Judah with supreme authority, he immediately declares that God would show his care for the people, by preserving the state of the kingdom, till the promised felicity should attain its highest point. For the dignity of Judah is so maintained as to show that its proposed end was the common salvation of the whole people. The bless-

---

[1] Bishop Lowth's translation is this :—

"Judah is a lion's whelp.
From the prey, my son, thou art gone up—
He stoopeth down, he coucheth as a lion,
And as a lioness; who shall rouse him?"

It is to be observed that three different words are here used in the original to express the metaphor, which illustrates the character of the tribe of Judah. First, גּוּר, (*gur,*) the lion's cub ; secondly, אַרְיֵה, (*aryah,*) the full-grown lion ; and, thirdly, לָבִיא, (*labi,*) the old lioness. These different terms are supposed to represent the tribe of Judah in its earliest period, in the age of David, and in subsequent times.

ing promised to the seed of Abraham (as we have before
seen) could not be firm, unless it flowed from one head.
Jacob now testifies the same thing, namely, that a King
should come, under whom that promised happiness should
be complete in all its parts.   Even the Jews will not deny,
that while a lower blessing rested on the tribe of Judah, the
hope of a better and more excellent condition was herein held
forth.   They also freely grant another point, that the Messiah is the sole Author of full and solid happiness and glory.
We now add a third point, which we may also do, without
any opposition from them ; namely, that the kingdom which
began from David, was a kind of prelude, and shadowy representation of that greater grace which was delayed, and
held in suspense, until the advent of the Messiah.   They have
indeed no relish for a spiritual kingdom ; and therefore they
rather imagine for themselves wealth and power, and propose to themselves sweet repose and earthly pleasures, than
righteousness, and newness of life, with free forgiveness of
sins.   They acknowledge, nevertheless, that the felicity which
was to be expected under the Messiah, was adumbrated by
their ancient kingdom.   I now return to the words of Jacob.

Until Shiloh come, he says, the sceptre, or the dominion,
shall remain in Judah.   We must first see what the word
שׁילוֹה (*shiloh*) signifies.   Because Jerome interprets it,
" He who is to be sent," some think that the place has been
fraudulently corrupted, by the letter ה substituted for the
letter ח ; which objection, though not firm, is plausible.
That which some of the Jews suppose, namely, that it
denotes the place (Shiloh) where the ark of the covenant
had been long deposited, because, a little before the commencement of David's reign, it had been laid waste, is
entirely destitute of reason.   For Jacob does not here predict the time when David was to be appointed king ; but
declares that the kingdom should be established in his
family, until God should fulfil what he had promised concerning the special benediction of the seed of Abraham.   Besides the form of speech, "until Shiloh come," for "until Shiloh
come to an end," would be harsh and constrained.   Far more
correctly and consistently do other interpreters take this ex-

pression to mean " his son," for among the Hebrews a son is called שׁיל, (*shil.*) They say also that ה is put in the place of the relative ו; and the greater part assent to this signification.[1] But again, the Jews dissent entirely from the meaning of the patriarch, by referring this to David. For (as I have just hinted) the origin of the kingdom in David is not here promised, but its absolute perfection in the Messiah. And truly an absurdity so gross, does not require a lengthened refutation. For what can this mean, that the kingdom should not come to an end in the tribe of Judah, till it should have been erected? Certainly the word *depart* means nothing else than to *cease.* Further, Jacob points to a continued series, when he says the scribe[2] shall not depart from between his feet. For it behoves a king so to be placed upon his throne that a lawgiver may sit between his feet. A kingdom is therefore described to us, which after it has been constituted, will not cease to exist till a more perfect state shall succeed; or, which comes to the same point; Jacob honours the future kingdom of David with this title, because it was to be the token and pledge of that happy glory which had been before ordained for the race of Abraham. In short, the kingdom which he transfers to the tribe of Judah, he declares shall be no common kingdom, because from it, at length, shall proceed the fulness of the promised benediction. But here the Jews haughtily object, that the event convicts us of error. For it appears that the kingdom by no means endured until the coming of Christ; but rather that the sceptre was broken, from the time

[1] Calvin seems to assent to this interpretation, which is by no means generally accepted. Gesenius renders שׁילה, *tranquillity*—" until tranquillity shall come;" but the more approved rendering is " the Peaceable One," or " the Pacifier." He who made peace for us, by the sacrifice of Himself.—*Ed.*

[2] Scribam recessurum negat ex pedibus. But in the text, Calvin uses the word *Legislator;* the French version translates it *Legislateur;* and the English translation is lawgiver. It is evident that Calvin had a reason for using the term *Scribe;* for the original מחקק, (*mechokaik,*) rather means a scribe or lawyer, than a *lawgiver;* and rather describes one who aids in the administration of laws, than one who frames them. In this sense, he supposes, and probably with truth, that the term is here applied. The expression " from between his feet," has been the subject of much criticism; but perhaps no view of it is so satisfactory as that maintained by Calvin.—*Ed.*

that the people were carried into captivity. But if they give
credit to the prophecies, I wish, before I solve their objection, that they would tell me in what manner Jacob here
assigns the kingdom to his son Judah. For we know, that
when it had scarcely become his fixed possession, it was
suddenly rent asunder, and nearly its whole power was possessed by the tribe of Ephraim. Has God, according to these
men, here promised, by the mouth of Jacob, some evanescent
kingdom? If they reply, the sceptre was not then broken,
though Rehoboam was deprived of a great part of his people;
they can by no means escape by this cavil; because the
authority of Judah is expressly extended over all the tribes,
by these words, " Thy mother's sons shall bow their knee
before thee." They bring, therefore, nothing against *us*, which
we cannot immediately, in turn, retort upon *themselves*.

Yet I confess the question is not yet solved; but I wished
to premise this, in order that the Jews, laying aside their
disposition to calumniate, may learn calmly to examine the
matter itself, with us. Christians are commonly wont to
connect perpetual government with the tribe of Judah, in
the following manner. When the people returned from
banishment, they say, that, in the place of the royal sceptre,
was the government which lasted to the time of the Macca-
bees. That afterwards, a third mode of government succeeded, because the chief power of judging rested with the
SEVENTY, who, it appears by history, were chosen out of the
regal race. Now, so far was this authority of the royal race
from having fallen into decay, that Herod, having been cited
before it, with difficulty escaped capital punishment, because
he contumaciously withdrew from it. Our commentators,
therefore, conclude that, although the royal majesty did not
shine brightly from David until Christ, yet some pre-eminence remained in the tribe of Judah, and thus the oracle
was fulfilled. Although these things are true, still more
skill must be used in rightly discussing this passage. And,
in the first place, it must be kept in mind, that the tribe of
Judah was already constituted chief among the rest, as pre-
eminent in dignity, though it had not yet obtained the
dominion. And, truly, Moses elsewhere testifies, that supre-

macy was voluntarily conceded to it by the remaining tribes, from the time that the people were redeemed out of Egypt. In the second place, we must remember, that a more illustrious example of this dignity was set forth in that kingdom which God had commenced in David. And although defection followed soon after, so that but a small portion of authority remained in the tribe of Judah ; yet the right divinely conferred upon it, could by no means be taken away. Therefore, at the time when the kingdom of Israel was replenished with abundant opulence, and was swelling with lofty pride, it was said, that the lamp of the Lord was lighted in Jerusalem. Let us proceed further : when Ezekiel predicts the destruction of the kingdom, (chap. xxi. 26,) he clearly shows how the sceptre was to be preserved by the Lord, until it should come into the hands of Christ : " Remove the diadem, and take off the crown ; this shall not be the same : I will overturn, overturn, overturn it, until he come whose right it is." It may seem at first sight that the prophecy of Jacob had failed when the tribe of Judah was stripped of its royal ornament. But we conclude hence, that God was not bound always to exhibit the visible glory of the kingdom on high. Otherwise, those other promises which predict the restoration of the throne, which was cast down and broken, were false. Behold the days come in which I will " raise up the tabernacle of David that is fallen, and close up the breaches thereof, and I will raise up his ruins." (Amos ix. 11.) It would be absurd, however, to cite more passages, seeing this doctrine occurs frequently in the prophets. Whence we infer, that the kingdom was not so confirmed as always to shine with equal brightness ; but that, though, for a time, it might lie fallen and defaced, it should afterwards recover its lost splendour. The prophets, indeed, seem to make the return from the Babylonian exile the termination of that ruin ; but since they predict the restoration of the kingdom no otherwise than they do that of the temple and the priesthood, it is necessary that the whole period, from that liberation to the advent of Christ, should be comprehended. The crown, therefore, was cast down, not for one day only, or from one single head, but for a long time, and in various methods, until God placed it on Christ, his own lawful king. And truly Isaiah describes the origin of Christ, as being very remote from all regal splendour: " There shall come forth a rod out of the stem of Jesse, and a branch shall grow out of his roots." (Isaiah xi. 1.) Why does he mention Jesse rather than David, except because Messiah was about to proceed from the rustic hut of a private man, rather than from a splendid palace ? Why from a tree cut down, having nothing left but the root and the trunk, except because the majesty of the kingdom was to be almost trodden under foot till the manifestation of Christ ? If any one object, that the words of Jacob seem to have a different signification; I answer, that whatever God has promised at any time concerning the external condition of the Church, was so to be restricted, that, in the mean time, he might execute his judgments in punishing men, and might try the faith of his own people. It was, indeed, no light trial, that the tribe of Judah, in its third successor to the throne, should be deprived of the greater portion of the kingdom. Even a still more severe trial followed, when the sons of the king were put to death in the sight of their father, when he, with his eyes thrust out, was dragged to Babylon, and the whole royal family was at length given over to slavery and captivity. But this was the most grievous trial of all; that when the people returned to their own land, they could in no way perceive the accomplishment of their hope, but were compelled to lie in sorrowful dejection. Nevertheless, even then, the saints, contemplating, with the eyes of faith, the sceptre hidden under the earth, did not fail, or become broken in spirit, so as to desist from their course. I shall, perhaps, seem to grant too much to the Jews, because I do not assign what they call a real dominion, in uninterrupted succession, to the tribe of Judah. For our interpreters, to prove that the Jews are still kept bound by a foolish expectation of the Messiah, insist on this point, that the dominion of which Jacob had prophesied, ceased from the time of Herod; as if, indeed, they had not been tributaries five hundred years previously; as if, also, the dignity of the royal race had not been extinct as long as the tyranny of Antiochus prevailed; as if, lastly, the Asmonean race had not usurped to itself both the rank and power of princes, until the Jews became subject to the Romans. And that is not a sufficient solution which is proposed; namely, that either the regal dominion, or some lower kind of government, are disjunctively promised; and that from the time when the kingdom was destroyed, the scribes remained in authority. For I, in order to mark the distinction between a lawful government and tyranny, acknowledge that counsellors were joined with the king, who should administer public affairs rightly and in order. Whereas some of the Jews explain, that the *right* of government was given to the tribe of Judah, because it was unlawful for it to be transferred elsewhere, but that it was not necessary that the *glory* of the crown once given should be perpetuated, I deem it right to subscribe in part to this opinion. I say, in part, because the Jews gain nothing by this cavil, who, in order to support their fiction of a Messiah yet to come, postpone that subversion of the regal dignity which, in fact, long ago occurred.[1] For we must keep in memory what I have said before, that while Jacob wished to sustain the minds of his descendents until the coming of the Messiah; lest they should faint through the weariness of long delay, he set before them an example in their temporal kingdom: as if he had said, that there was no reason why the Israelites, when the kingdom of David fell, should allow their hope to waver; seeing that no other change should follow, which could answer to the blessing promised by God, until the Redeemer should appear. That the nation was grievously harassed, and was under servile oppression some years before the coming of Christ happened, through the wonderful

---

[1] Quia nihil hoc cavilla proficiunt Judæi, ad figmentum venturi sui Messiæ trahentes vetustum regni excidium. Literally translated, the sense of the passage would not be obvious to the English reader. It is hoped that the true meaning of the passage is given above. The original, however, is given, that the learned reader may form his own judgment. It is well known that modern Jews regard their present depression as a proof that the Messiah has not yet come, and therefore they draw out (trahentes) or postpone the execution of God's threatened judgments, which we regard as having taken place under Titus and the Romans, to a period still future. This seems to be Calvin's meaning.—*Ed.*

counsel of God, in order that they might be urged by continual chastisements to wish for redemption.   Meanwhile, it was necessary that some collective body of the nation should remain, in which the promise might receive its fulfilment. But now, when, through nearly fifteen centuries, they have been scattered and banished from their country, having no polity, by what pretext can they fancy, from the prophecy of Jacob, that a Redeemer will come to them ?   Truly, as I would not willingly glory over their calamity ; so, unless they, being subdued by it, open their eyes, I freely pronounce that they are worthy to perish a thousand times without remedy.   It was also a most suitable method for retaining them in the faith, that the Lord would have the sons of Jacob turn their eyes upon one particular tribe, that they might not seek salvation elsewhere ; and that no vague imagination might mislead them.   For which end, also, the election of this family is celebrated, when it is frequently compared with, and preferred to Ephraim and the rest, in the Psalms.   To us, also, it is not less useful, for the confirmation of our faith, to know that Christ had been not only promised, but that his origin had been pointed out, as with a finger, two thousand years before he appeared.[1]

And unto him shall the gathering of the people be.   Here truly he declares that Christ should be a king, not over one people only, but that under his authority various nations shall be gathered, that they might coalesce together.   I know, indeed, that the word rendered " gathering" is differently expounded by different commentators ; but they who derive it from the root קהה, to make it signify the *weakening* of the people, rashly and absurdly misapply what is said of the

[1] On this passage, which has given so much trouble to commentators, and which Calvin has considered at such length, it may be observed, that the term rendered *sceptre* means also *rod*, and sometimes is translated *tribe;* perhaps because each of the twelve tribes had its *rod* laid up in the tabernacle and temple.   Hence it may be inferred that the expression, " The sceptre shall not depart from Judah," means that Judah alone should continue in its integrity, as a tribe, till the coming of the Messiah.   This renders it unnecessary to attempt any proof of the retention of regal power and authority in the tribe.   See Ainsworth and Bush *in loc.*   The reader may also refer to an elaborate investigation of the subject in Rivetus, Exercitations 178 and 179.—*Ed.*

saving dominion of Christ, to the sanguinary pride with which they puffed up. If the word *obedience* is preferred, (as it is by others,) the sense will remain the same with that which I have followed. For this is the mode in which the gathering together will be effected; namely, that they who before were carried away to different objects of pursuit, will consent together in obedience to one common Head. Now, although Jacob had previously called the tribes about to spring from him by the name of *peoples*, for the sake of amplification, yet this gathering is of still wider extent. For, whereas he had included the whole body of the nation by their families, when he spoke of the ordinary dominion of Judah, he now extends the boundaries of a new king : as if he would say, " There shall be kings of the tribe of Judah, who shall be pre-eminent among their brethren, and to whom the sons of the same mother shall bow down : but at length He shall follow in succession, who shall subject other *peoples* unto himself." But this, we know, is fulfilled in Christ; to whom was promised the inheritance of the world ; under whose yoke the nations are brought; and at whose will they, who before were scattered, are gathered together. Moreover, a memorable testimony is here borne to the vocation of the Gentiles, because they were to be introduced into the joint participation of the covenant, in order that they might become one people with the natural descendents of Abraham, under one Head.

11. *Binding his fole unto the vine, and his ass's colt,* &c. He now speaks of the situation of the territory which fell by lot to the sons of Judah ; and intimates, that so great would be the abundance of vines there, that they would everywhere present themselves as readily as brambles, or unfruitful shrubs, in other places. For since asses are wont to be bound to the hedges, he here reduces vines to this contemptible use. The hyperbolical forms of speech which follow are to be applied to the same purpose ; namely, that Judah shall wash his garments in wine, and his eyes be red therewith. He means that the abundance of wine shall be so great, that it may be poured out to wash with, like water, at no great expense ; but that, by constant copious drinking, the eyes would contract redness. But it seems by no means

proper, that a profuse intemperance or extravagance should
be accounted a blessing. I answer, although fertility and
affluence are here described, still the abuse of them is not
sanctioned. If the Lord deals very bountifully with us, yet
he frequently prescribes the rule of using his gifts with
purity and frugality, lest they should stimulate the incon-
tinence of the flesh. But in this place Jacob, omitting to
state what is lawful, extols that abundance which would
suffice for luxury, and even for vicious and perverse excesses,
unless the sons of Judah should voluntarily use self-government. I abstain from those allegories which to some appear
plausible ; because, as I said at the beginning of the chapter,
I do not choose to sport with such great mysteries of God.
To these lofty speculators the partition of the land which
God prescribed, for the purpose of accrediting his servant
Moses, seems a mean and abject thing. But unless our
ingratitude has attained a senseless stupor, we ought to be
wholly transported with admiration at the thought, that
Moses, who had never seen the land of Canaan, should treat
of its separate parts as correctly as he could have done, of a
few acres cultivated by his own hand. Now, supposing he
had heard a general report of the existence of vines in the
land ; yet he could not have assigned to Judah abundant
vineyards, nor could he have assigned to him rich pastures,
by saying that his teeth should be white with drinking milk,
unless he had been guided by the Spirit.

13. *Zebulun shall dwell at the haven of the sea.* Although
this blessing contains nothing rare or precious, (as neither do
some of those which follow,) yet we ought to deem this fact
as sufficiently worthy of notice, that it was just as if God was
stretching out his hand from heaven, for the deliverance of the
children of Israel, and for the purpose of distributing to each
his own dwelling-place. Before mention is made of the lot
itself, a maritime region is given to the tribe of Zebulun,
which it obtained by lot two hundred years afterwards. And
we know of how great importance that hereditary gift was,
which, like an earnest, rendered the adoption of the ancient
people secure. Therefore, by this prophecy, not only one
tribe, but the whole people, ought to have been encouraged

to lay hold, with alacrity, of the offered blessing which was
certainly in store for them.   But it is said that the portion
of Zebulun should not only be on the sea-shore, but should
also have havens ; for Jacob joins its boundary with the
country of Zidon ; in which tract, we know, there were commodious and noble havens. For God, by this prophecy, would
not only excite the sons of Zebulun more strenuously to
prepare themselves to enter upon the land ; but would also
assure them, when they obtained possession of the desired
portion, that it was the home which had been distinctly proposed and ordained for them by the will of God.

14. *Issachar.* Here mention is partly made of the inheritance, and an indication is partly given of the future condition of this tribe. Although he is called a *bony* ass on account
of his strength,[1] which would enable him to endure labours,
especially such as were rustic, yet at the same time his sloth
is indicated : for it is added a little afterwards, that he should
be of servile disposition. Wherefore the meaning is, that the
sons of Issachar, though possessed of strength, were yet quiet
rather than courageous, and were as ready to bear the burden
of servitude as mules are to submit their backs to the pack-
saddle and the load. The reason given is, that, being content
with their fertile and pleasant country, they do not refuse to
pay tribute to their neighbours, provided they may enjoy
repose.   And although this submissiveness is not publicly
mentioned either to their praise or their condemnation, it
is yet probable that their indolence is censured, because their
want of energy hindered them from remaining in possession
of that liberty which had been divinely granted unto them.

16. *Dan shall judge his people.* In the word *judge* there
is an allusion to his name: for since, among the Hebrews, דּוּן
signifies to judge, Rachel, when she returned thanks to God,
gave this name to the son born to her by her handmaid, as
if God had been the vindicator of her cause and right.
Jacob now gives a new turn to the meaning of the name ;
namely, that the sons of Dan shall have no mean part in the
government of the people. For the Jews foolishly restrict
it to Samson, because he alone presided over the whole

[1] Asinus osseus.

people, whereas the language rather applies to the perpetual
condition of the tribe.   Jacob therefore means, that though
Dan was born from a concubine, he shall still be one of the
judges of Israel : because not only shall his offspring possess
a share of the government and command, in the common
polity, so that this tribe may constitute one head ; but it
shall be appointed the bearer of a standard to lead the fourth
division of the camp of Israel.[1]   In the second place, his
subtle disposition is described.   For Jacob compares this
people to serpents, who rise out of their lurking-places, by
stealth, against the unwary whom they wish to injure.   The
sense then is, that he shall not be so courageous as earnestly
and boldly to engage in open conflict ; but that he will fight
with cunning, and will make use of snares.   Yet, in the
meantime, he shows that he will be superior to his enemies,
whom he does not dare to approach with collected forces, just
as serpents who, by their secret bite, cast down the horse
and his rider.   In this place also no judgment is expressly
passed, whether this subtlety of Dan is to be deemed worthy
of praise or of censure : but conjecture rather inclines us to
place it among his faults, or at least his disadvantages, that
instead of opposing himself in open conflict with his enemies, he will fight them only with secret frauds.[2]

18. *I have waited for thy salvation, O Lord.*   It may be
asked, in the first place, what occasion induced the holy man
to break the connection of his discourse, and suddenly to
burst forth in this expression ; for whereas he had recently
predicted the coming of the Messiah, the mention of salvation would have been more appropriate in that place.   I
think, indeed, that when he perceived, as from a lofty watch-

[1] See Numbers ii., where the order of the tribes in their encampment is
given.   Judah had the standard for the three tribes on the east, Reuben for
the three tribes on the south, Ephraim for the three tribes on the west, and
Dan for the remaining three tribes on the north of the tabernacle.—*Ed.*

[2] The word שְׁפִיפֹן, (*sheppiphon*,) translated " adder," occurs only in this
place.   It is supposed by Bochart to be the *cerastes*, " a serpent so called,"
says Calmet, " because it has horns on its forehead."   Dr. A. Clarke gives
this translation :—
> " Dan shall be a serpent on the way,
> A cerastes upon the track,
> Biting the heels of the horse,
> And his rider shall fall backwards."—*Ed.*

tower, the condition of his offspring continually exposed to various changes, and even to be tossed by storms which would almost overwhelm them, he was moved with solicitude and fear; for he had not so put off all paternal affection, as to be entirely without care for those who were of his own blood. He, therefore, foreseeing many troubles, many dangers, many assaults, and even many slaughters, which threatened his seed with as many destructions, could not but condole with them, and, as a man, be troubled at the sight. But in order that he might rise against every kind of temptation with victorious constancy of mind, he commits himself unto the Lord, who had promised that he would be the guardian of his people. Unless this circumstance be observed, I do not see why Jacob exclaims here, rather than at the beginning or the end of his discourse, that he waited for the salvation of the Lord. But when this sad confusion of things presented itself to him, which was not only sufficiently violent to shake his faith, but was more than sufficiently burdensome entirely to overwhelm his mind, his best remedy was to oppose to it this shield. I doubt not also, that he would advise his sons to rise with him to the exercise of the same confidence. Moreover, because he could not be the author of his own salvation, it was necessary for him to repose upon the promise of God. In the same manner, also, must we, at this day, hope for the salvation of the Church: for although it seems to be tossed on a turbulent sea, and almost sunk in the waves, and though still greater storms are to be feared in future; yet amidst manifold destructions, salvation is to be hoped for, in that deliverance which the Lord has promised. It is even possible that Jacob, foreseeing by the Spirit, how great would be the ingratitude, perfidy, and wickedness of his posterity, by which the grace of God might be smothered, was contending against these temptations. But although he expected salvation not for himself alone, but for all his posterity, this, however, deserves to be specially noted, that he exhibits the life-giving covenant of God to many generations, so as to prove his own confidence that, after his death, God would be faithful to his promise. Whence also it follows, that, with his last breath, and as if in the midst of death, he laid hold on

eternal life. But if he, amidst obscure shadows, relying on
a redemption seen afar off, boldly went forth to meet death;
what ought we to do, on whom the clear day has shined; or
what excuse remains for us, if our minds fail amidst similar
agitations ?[1]

19. *Gad, a troop.* Jacob also makes allusion to the name
of Gad. He had been so called, because Jacob had obtained
a numerous offspring by his mother Leah. His father now
admonishes him, that though his name implied a *multitude,*
he should yet have to do with a great number of enemies,
by whom, for a time, he would be oppressed: and he predicts this event, not that his posterity might confide in their
own strength, and become proud; but that they might prepare
themselves to endure the suffering by which the Lord intended, and now decreed to humble them. Yet, as he here
exhorts them to patient endurance, so he presently raises
and animates them by the superadded consolation, that, at
length, they should emerge from oppression, and should triumph over those enemies by whom they had been vanquished
and routed; but this only at the last. Moreover, this prophecy may be applied to the whole Church, which is assailed
not for one day only, but is perpetually crushed by fresh
attacks, until at length God shall exalt it to honour.

20. *Out of Asher.* The inheritance of Asher is but just
alluded to, which he declares shall be fruitful in the best
and finest wheat, so that it shall need no foreign supply of
food, having abundance at home. By *royal dainties,* he means
such as are exquisite. Should any one object, that it is no
great thing to be fed with nutritious and pleasant bread; I
answer; we must consider the end designed; namely, that they

[1] Jewish commentators suppose the patriarch's exclamation to have
been suggested in this place, by a prospective view of the temporal deliver-
ances wrought for Israel, by warriors of the tribe of Dan. So the Chaldee
Paraphrast represents him as saying, " I look not for the salvation of
Gideon, because it is a temporal salvation ; nor for the salvation of Samp-
son the son of Manoah, because it is transitory; but I look for the redemption of Christ the Son of David, who is to come to call to himself the
children, whose salvation my soul desireth." *See Bush and Dr. A. Clarke.*
Yet there is something affecting in the thought, that the exclamation might
be a sudden burst of holy desire for the immediate fruition of the glory
which the dying patriarch now saw so near at hand.— *Ed.*

might hereby know that they were fed by the paternal care of God.

21. *Naphtali*. Some think that in the tribe of Naphtali fleetness is commended; I rather approve another meaning, namely, that it will guard and defend itself by eloquence and suavity of words, rather than by force of arms. It is, however, no despicable virtue to soothe ferocious minds, and to appease excited anger, by bland and gentle discourse; or if any offence has been stirred up, to allay it by a similar artifice. He therefore assigns this praise to the sons of Naphtali, that they shall rather study to fortify themselves by humanity, by sweet words, and by the arts of peace, than by the defence of arms. He compares them to a hind let loose, which having been taken in hunting, is not put to death, but is rather cherished with delicacies.[1]

22. *Joseph is a fruitful bough.* Others translate it, " a son of honour,"[2] and both are suitable; but I rather incline to the former sense, because it seems to me that it refers to the name Joseph, by which *addition* or *increase* is signified; although I have no objection to the similitude taken from a tree, which, being planted near a fountain, draws from the watered earth the moisture and sap by which it grows the faster. The sum of the figure is, that he is born to grow like a tree situated near a fountain, so that, by its beauty and lofty stature, it may surmount the obstacles around it. For I do not interpret the words which follow to mean that there will be an assemblage of *virgins* upon the walls, whom

---

[1] As the word אילה, rendered *hind*, sometimes means a tree, it is supposed by some, that it should be so translated here. Bochart suggests this translation :—

" Naphtali is a spreading oak,
    Producing beautiful branches."

Dr. A. Clarke strenuously defends this version, and says, " perhaps no man who understands the genius of the Hebrew language will attempt to dispute its propriety." Yet perhaps the received translation is not to be so easily disposed of. It may be granted that Bochart's figure is more beautiful; but it will be difficult to show that his translation is equally literal and correct. Caunter suggests another rendering :—

" Naphtali is a deer roaming at liberty,
    He shooteth forth noble branches,"—or antlers.—*Ed.*

[2] " Filium decoris." The original is בנ פרת, (*Ben porath*,) literally, " the son of fruitfulness." The name of Joseph's son, Ephraim, is derived from this word.—*Ed.*

the sight of the tree shall have attracted ; but, by a continued
metaphor, I suppose the tender and smaller branches to be
called daughters.[1]   And they are said "to run over the wall"
when they spread themselves far and wide. Besides, Jacob's
discourse does not relate simply to the whole tribe, nor is it
a mere prophecy of future times ; but the personal history
of Joseph is blended with that of his descendents. Thus
some things are peculiar to himself, and others belong to the
two tribes of Ephraim and Manasseh. So when Joseph is
said to have been " grieved," this is wont to be referred
especially to himself. And whereas Jacob has compared him
to a tree; so he calls both his brethren and Potiphar, with
his wife, " archers."[2]   Afterwards, however, he changes the
figure by making Joseph himself like a strenuous archer,
whose bow abides in strength, and whose arms are not relaxed, nor have lost, in any degree, their vigour ; by which
expressions he predicts the invincible fortitude of Joseph,
because he has yielded to no blows however hard and severe.
At the same time we are taught that he stood, not by the
power of his own arm, but as being strengthened by the hand
of God, whom he distinguishes by the peculiar title of " the
mighty God of Jacob," because he designed his power to be
chiefly conspicuous, and to shine most brightly in the Church.
Meanwhile, he declares that the help by which Joseph was
assisted, arose from hence, that God had chosen that family
for himself. For the holy fathers were extremely solicitous
that the gratuitous covenant of God should be remembered
by themselves and by their children, whenever any benefit
was granted unto them. And truly it is a mark of shameful negligence, not to inquire from what fountain we drink
water. In the mean time he tacitly censures the impious and
ungodly fury of his ten sons ; because, by attempting the
murder of their brother, they, like the giants, had carried on

---

[1] בנות, (*Banoth,*) literally, " the *daughters* went over the wall." But
Calvin, with our translators, wisely interprets the expression as a poetical
one, meaning the branches, (which are the daughters of the tree,) according to a very usual phraseology of the Hebrew Scriptures.—*Ed.*
[2] Archers, literally, " Lords of the arrows."
    " The archers shot at him with poisoned arrows,
      They have pursued him with hatred."
Waterland in Caunter's Poetry of the Pentateuch, vol. i., p. 223.—*Ed.*

war against God. He also admonishes them for the future, that they should rather choose to be protected by the guardianship of God, than to make him their enemy, seeing that he is alike willing to give help to all. And hence arises a consideration consolatory to all the pious, when they hear that the power of God resides in the midst of the Church, if they do but glory in him alone ; as the Psalm teaches, " Some trust in chariots, and some in horses ; but we will invoke the name of the Lord our God." (Psal. xx. 7.) The sons of Jacob, therefore, must take care lest they, by confiding in their own strength, precipitate themselves into ruin ; but must rather bear themselves nobly and triumphantly in the Lord.

What follows admits of various interpretations. Some translate it, " From thence is the shepherd, the stone of Israel ;" as if Jacob would say, that Joseph had been the nourisher and rock, or stay of his house. Others read, "the shepherd of the stone," in the genitive case, which I approve, except that they mistake the sense, by taking " stone" to mean family. I refer it to God, who assigned the office of shepherd to his servant Joseph, in the manner in which any one uses the service of a hireling to feed his flock. For whence did it arise that he nourished his own people, except that he was the dispenser of the Divine beneficence ? Moreover, under this type, the image of Christ is depicted to us, who, before he should come forth as the conqueror of death and the author of life, was set as a mark of contradiction, (Heb. xii. 3,) against whom all cast their darts ; as now also, after his example, the Church also must be transfixed with many arrows, that she may be kept by the wonderful help of God. Moreover, lest the brethren should maliciously envy Joseph, Jacob sets his victory in an amiable point of view to them, by saying that he had been liberated in order that he might become their nourisher or shepherd.

25. *Even by the God of thy father.* Again, he more fully affirms that Joseph had been delivered from death, and exalted to such great dignity, not by his own industry, but by the favour of God : and there is not the least doubt that he commends to all the pious, the mere goodness of God, lest

they should arrogate anything to themselves, whether they may have escaped from dangers, or whether they may have risen to any rank of honour. *By the God of thy father.* In designating God by this title, he again traces whatever good Joseph has received, to the covenant, and to the fountain of gratuitous adoption; as if he had said, " Whereas thou hast proved the paternal care of God in helping thee, I desire that thou wouldst ascribe this to the covenant which God has made with me." Meanwhile, (as we have said before,) he separates from all fictitious idols the God whom he transmits to his descendents to worship.

After he has declared, that Joseph should be blessed in every way, both as it respects his own life, and the number and preservation of his posterity; he affirms that the effect of this benediction is near and almost present, by saying, that he blessed Joseph more efficaciously than he himself had been blessed by his fathers. For although, from the beginning, God had been true to his promises, yet he frequently postponed the effect of them, as if he had been feeding Abraham, Isaac, and Jacob with nothing but words. For, to what extent were the patriarchs multiplied in Egypt? Where was that immense seed which should equal the sands of the sea shore and the stars of heaven? Therefore, not without reason, Jacob declares that the full time had arrived in which the result of his benediction, which had lain concealed, should emerge as from the deep. Now, this comparison ought to inspire us with much greater alacrity at the present time; for the abundant riches of the grace of God which have flowed to us in Christ, exceeds a hundredfold, any blessings which Joseph received and felt.

What is added respecting *the utmost bound of the everlasting hills,* some wish to refer to distance of place, some to perpetuity of time. Both senses suit very well; either that the felicity of Joseph should diffuse itself far and wide to the farthest mountains of the world; or that it should endure as long as the everlasting hills, which are the firmest portions of the earth, shall stand. The more certain and genuine sense, however, is to be gathered from the other passage, where Moses repeats this benediction; namely, that the fertility of the land would extend to the tops of the mountains; and these mountains are called perpetual, because they are most celebrated. He also declares that this blessing should be *upon his head*, lest Joseph might think that his good wishes were scattered to the winds; for by this word he intends to show, if I may so speak, that the blessing was substantial. At length he calls Joseph נזיר, (*nazir,*) among his brethren, either because he was their *crown*, on account of the common glory which redounds from him to them all, or because, on account of the dignity by which he excels, he was *separated* from them all.[1] It may be understood in both senses. Yet we must know that this excellency was temporal, because Joseph, together with the others, was required to take his proper place, and to submit himself to the sceptre of Judah.

27. *Benjamin shall ravin as a wolf.* Some of the Jews think the Benjamites are here condemned; because, when they had suffered lusts to prevail, like lawless robbers, among them, they were at length cut down and almost destroyed by a terrible slaughter, for having defiled the Levite's wife. Others regard it as an honourable encomium, by which Saul, or Mordecai was adorned, who were both of the tribe of Benjamin. The interpreters of our own age most inaptly apply it to the apostle Paul, who was changed from a wolf into a preacher of the Gospel. Nothing seems to me more probable than that the disposition and habits of the whole tribe is here delineated; namely, that they would live by plunder. *In the morning they would seize and devour the prey, in the evening they would divide the spoil;* by which words he describes their diligence in plundering.

28. *All these are the twelve tribes of Israel.* Moses would teach us by these words, that his predictions did not apply only to the sons of Jacob, but extended to their whole race. We have, indeed, shown already, with sufficient clearness,

---

[1] " The blessings of thy father have prevailed over the blessings of the
    eternal mountains,
And the desirable things of the everlasting hills.
These shall be on the head of Joseph,
And on his crown who was separated from his brethren."
                                                    Dr. A. Clarke.

that the expressions relate not to their persons only; but this verse was to be added, in order that the readers might more clearly perceive the celestial majesty of the Spirit. Jacob beholds his twelve sons. Let us grant that, at that time, the number of his offspring, down to his great grandchildren, had increased a hundredfold. He does not, however, merely declare what is to be the condition of six hundred or a thousand men, but subjects regions and nations to his sentence; nor does he put himself rashly forward, since it is found afterwards, by the event, that God had certainly made known to him, what he had himself decreed to execute. Moreover, seeing that Jacob beheld, with the eyes of faith, things which were not only very remote, but altogether hidden from human sense; woe be unto our depravity, if we shut our eyes against the very accomplishment of the prediction in which the truth conspicuously appears.

But it may seem little consonant to reason, that Jacob is said to have blessed his posterity. For, in deposing Reuben from the primogeniture, he pronounced nothing joyous or prosperous respecting him; he also declared his abhorrence of Simeon and Levi. It cannot be alleged that there is an *antiphrasis* in the word of benediction, as if it were used in a sense contrary to what is usual; because it plainly appears to be applied by Moses in a *good*, and not an *evil* sense. I therefore reconcile these things with each other thus; that the temporal punishments with which Jacob mildly and paternally corrected his sons, would not subvert the covenant of grace on which the benediction was founded; but rather, by obliterating their stains, would restore them to the original degree of honour from which they had fallen, so that, at least, they should be patriarchs among the people of God. And the Lord daily proves, in his own people, that the punishments he lays upon them, although they occasion shame and disgrace, are so far from opposing their happiness, that they rather promote it. Unless they were purified in this manner, it were to be feared lest they should become more and more hardened in their vices, and lest the hidden *virus* should produce corruption, which at length would penetrate to the vitals. We see how freely the flesh indulges itself, even when God rouses us by the tokens of his anger. What then do we suppose would take place if he should always connive at transgression? But when we, after having been reproved for our sins, repent, this result not only absorbs the curse which was felt at the beginning, but also proves that the Lord blesses us more by punishing us, than he would have done by sparing us. Hence it follows, that diseases, poverty, famine, nakedness, and even death itself, so far as they promote our salvation, may deservedly be reckoned blessings, as if their very nature were changed; just as the letting of blood may be not less conducive to health than food. When it is added at the close, *every one according to his blessing*, Moses again affirms, that Jacob not only implored a blessing on his sons, from a paternal desire for their welfare, but that he pronounced what God had put into his mouth; because at length the event proved that the prophecies were efficacious.

29. *And he charged them.* We have seen before, that Jacob especially commanded his son Joseph to take care that his body should be buried in the land of Canaan. Moses now repeats that the same command was given to all his sons, in order that they might go to that country with one consent; and might mutually assist each other in performing this office. We have stated elsewhere why he made such a point of conscience of his sepulture; which we must always remember, lest the example of the holy man should be drawn injudiciously into a precedent for superstition. Truly he did not wish to be carried into the land of Canaan, as if he would be the nearer heaven for being buried there: but that, being dead, he might claim possession of a land which he had held during his life, only by a precarious tenure. Not that any advantage would hence accrue to him privately, seeing he had already fulfilled his course; but because it was profitable that the memory of the promise should be renewed, by this symbol, among his surviving sons, in order that they might aspire to it. Meanwhile, we gather that his mind did not cleave to the earth; because, unless he had been an heir of heaven, he would never have hoped that God, for the sake of one who was dead, would

prove so bountiful towards his children. Now, to give the greater weight to his command, Jacob declares that this thing had not come first into his own mind, but that he had been thus taught by his forefathers. " Abraham," he says, " bought that sepulchre for himself and his family : hitherto, we have sacredly kept the law delivered to us by him. You must therefore take care not to violate it, in order that after my death also, some token of the favour of God may continue with us."

33. *He gathered up his feet.* The expression is not superfluous : because Moses wished thereby to describe the placid death of the holy man : as if he had said, that the aged saint gave directions respecting the disposal of his body, as easily as healthy and vigorous men are wont to compose themselves to sleep. And truly a wonderful vigour and presence of mind was necessary for him, when, while death was in his countenance, he thus courageously fulfilled the prophetic office enjoined upon him. And it is not to be doubted that such efficacy of the Holy Spirit manifested itself in him, as served to produce, in his sons, confidence in, and reverence for his prophecies. At the same time, however, it is proper to observe, that it is the effect of a good conscience, to be able to depart out of the world without terror. For since death is by nature formidable, wonderful torments agitate the wicked, when they perceive that they are summoned to the tribunal of God. Moreover, in order that a good conscience may lead us peacefully and quietly to the grave, it is necessary to rely upon the resurrection of Christ ; for we then go willingly to God, when we have confidence respecting a better life. We shall not deem it grievous to leave this failing tabernacle, when we reflect on the everlasting abode which is prepared for us.

CHAPTER L.

1. AND Joseph fell upon his father's face, and wept upon him, and kissed him.

2. And Joseph commanded his servants the physicians to embalm

1. Et jactavit se Joseph super faciem patris sui, et flevit super eum, et osculatus est eum.

2. Et præcepit Joseph servis suis medicis, ut aromatibus condirent

his father: and the physicians embalmed Israel.

3. And forty days were fulfilled for him; for so are fulfilled the days of those which are embalmed: and the Egyptians mourned for him threescore and ten days.

4. And when the days of his mourning were past, Joseph spake unto the house of Pharaoh, saying, If now I have found grace in your eyes, speak, I pray you, in the ears of Pharaoh, saying,

5. My father made me swear, saying, Lo, I die: in my grave which I have digged for me in the land of Canaan, there shalt thou bury me. Now therefore let me go up, I pray thee, and bury my father, and I will come again.

6. And Pharaoh said, Go up and bury thy father, according as he made thee swear.

7. And Joseph went up to bury his father: and with him went up all the servants of Pharaoh, the elders of his house, and all the elders of the land of Egypt,

8. And all the house of Joseph, and his brethren, and his father's house: only their little ones, and their flocks, and their herds, they left in the land of Goshen.

9. And there went up with him both chariots and horsemen: and it was a very great company.

10. And they came to the threshing-floor of Atad, which is beyond Jordan; and there they mourned with a great and very sore lamentation: and he made a mourning for his father seven days.

11. And when the inhabitants of the land, the Canaanites, saw the mourning in the floor of Atad, they said, This is a grievous mourning to the Egyptians: wherefore the name of it was called Abel-mizraim, which is beyond Jordan.

12. And his sons did unto him according as he commanded them:

13. For his sons carried him into the land of Canaan, and buried him in the cave of the field of Machpelah,

patrem suum, et aromatibus condiverunt medici ipsum Israel.

3. Completi autem sunt ei quadraginta dies: sic enim complentur dies *eorum* qui condiuntur aromatibus: et fleverunt eum Ægyptii septuaginta diebus.

4. Transierunt itaque dies luctus ejus: et loquutus est Joseph ad domum Pharaonis dicendo, Si quæso inveni gratiam in oculis vestris, loquimini quæso in auribus Pharaonis, dicendo,

5. Pater meus adjuravit me, dicendo, Ecce, ego morior: in sepulcro meo, quod fodi mihi in terra Chenaan, sepelies me: nunc igitur ascendam, obsecro, et sepeliam patrem meum, et revertar.

6. Et dixit Pharao, Ascende, et sepeli patrem tuum, quemadmodum adjuravit te.

7. Ascendit ergo Joseph ut sepeliret patrem suum: ascenderuntque cum eo omnes servi Pharaonis seniores domus ejus, et omnes seniores terræ Ægypti,

8. Et omnis domus Joseph, et fratres ejus, et domus patris ejus: tantummodo parvulos suos, et pecudes suas, et boves suos reliquerent in terra Gosen.

9. Et ascenderunt cum eo etiam currus, etiam equites: et fuit turma gravis valde.

10. Porro venerunt usque ad aream Atad, quæ est trans Jordanem: et planxerunt ibi planctu magno et gravi valde: et fecit patri suo luctum septem diebus.

11. Et viderunt habitatores terræ Chenaanæi luctum in area Atad, et dixerunt, Luctus gravis est iste Ægyptiis: idcirco vocatum fuit nomen ejus Abel-Misraim, (*id est luctus Ægyptiorum,*) qui est trans Jordanem.

12. Fecerunt ergo filii ejus ei sic, quemadmodum præceperat eis.

13. Quia tulerunt eum filii ejus in terra Chenaan, sepelieruntque eum in spelunca agri duplici, quam

which Abraham bought with the field, for a possession of a burying-place of Ephron the Hittite, before Mamre.

14. And Joseph returned into Egypt, he, and his brethren, and all that went up with him to bury his father, after he had buried his father.

15. And when Joseph's brethren saw that their father was dead, they said, Joseph will peradventure hate us, and will certainly requite us all the evil which we did unto him.

16. And they sent a messenger unto Joseph, saying, Thy father did command before he died, saying,

17. So shall ye say unto Joseph, Forgive, I pray thee now, the trespass of thy brethren, and their sin; for they did unto thee evil: and now, we pray thee, forgive the trespass of the servants of the God of thy father. And Joseph wept when they spake unto him.

18. And his brethren also went and fell down before his face; and they said, Behold, we *be* thy servants.

19. And Joseph said unto them, Fear not; for *am* I in the place of God?

20. But as for you, ye thought evil against me; *but* God meant it unto good, to bring to pass, as *it is* this day, to save much people alive.

21. Now therefore fear ye not: I will nourish you, and your little ones. And he comforted them, and spake kindly unto them.

22. And Joseph dwelt in Egypt, he and his father's house: and Joseph lived an hundred and ten years.

23. And Joseph saw Ephraim's children of the third *generation*: the children also of Machir, the son of Manasseh, were brought up upon Joseph's knees.

24. And Joseph said unto his brethren, I die: and God will surely visit you, and bring you out of this land unto the land which he sware to Abraham, to Isaac, and to Jacob.

25. And Joseph took an oath of the children of Israel, saying, God

emit Abraham cum agro in possessionem sepulcri, ab Hephron Hittæo, ante Mamre.

14. Et reversus est Joseph in Ægyptum, ipse et fratres ejus, et omnes qui ascenderant cum eo ad sepeliendum patrem ejus, postquam sepelivit patrem suum.

15. Videntes autem fratres Joseph, quod mortuus esset pater eorum, dixerunt, Fortasse odio habebit nos Joseph, et reddendo reddet nobis omne malum, quo affecimus eum.

16. Propterea mandarunt ad Joseph, dicendo, Pater tuus præcepit, antequam moreretur, dicendo,

17. Sic dicetis Joseph, Obsecro, parce nunc sceleri fratrum tuorum, et peccato eorum: quia malum intulerunt tibi, nunc igitur parce quæso sceleri servorum Dei patris tui. Flevit autem Joseph, dum illi loquerentur cum eo.

18. Nam profecti sunt etiam fratres ejus, et prostraverunt se coram eo, et dixerunt, Ecce, sumus tibi servi.

19. Et dixit ad eos Joseph, Ne timeatis: numquid enim loco Dei sum?

20. Vos quidem cogitastis adversum me malum: Deus *autem* cogitavit illud in bonum, ut faceret secundum diem hanc, ut vivificaret populum multum.

21. Nunc itaque ne timeatis, ego alam vos, et parvulos vestros. Et consolatus est eos, et loquutus est ad cor eorum.

22. Et habitavit Joseph in Ægypto, ipse et domus patris ejus: et vixit Joseph centum et decem annos.

23. Et vidit Joseph ipsi Ephraim filios tertiæ generationis: etiam filii Machir filii Menasseh educati sunt super genua Joseph.

24. Et dixit Joseph fratribus suis, Ego morior, et Deus visitando visitabit vos, et ascendere faciet vos e terra hac ad terram, quam juravit Abraham, Ishac et Jahacob.

25. Et adjuravit Joseph filios Israel, dicendo, Visitando visitabit

will surely visit you, and ye shall carry up my bones from hence.

26. So Joseph died, *being* an hundred and ten years old: and they embalmed him, and he was put in a coffin in Egypt.

Deus vos, et tolletis ossa mea hinc.

26. Itaque mortuus est Joseph filius centum et decem annorum: et aromatibus condierunt eum, et positus est in arca in Ægypto.

1. *And Joseph fell upon his father's face.* In this chapter, what happened after the death of Jacob, is briefly related. Moses, however, states that Jacob's death was honoured with a double mourning—natural (so to speak) and ceremonial. That Joseph falls upon his father's face and sheds tears, flows from true and pure affection; that the Egyptians mourn for him seventy days, since it is done for the sake of honour, and in compliance with custom, is more from ostentation and vain pomp, than from true grief: and yet the dead are generally mourned over in this manner, that the last debt due to them may be discharged. Whence also the proverb has originated, that the mourning of the heir is laughter under a mask. And although sometimes minds are penetrated with real grief; yet something is added to it, by the affectation of making a show of pious sorrow, so that they indulge largely in tears in the presence of others, who would weep more sparingly if there were no witnesses of their grief. Hence those friends who meet together, under the pretext of administering consolation, often pursue a course so different, that they call forth more abundant weeping. And although the ceremony of mourning over the dead arose from a good principle; namely, that the living should meditate on the curse entailed by sin upon the human race, yet it has always been tarnished by many evils; because it has been neither directed to its true end, nor regulated by due moderation. With respect to the genuine grief which is not unnaturally excited, but which breaks forth from the depth of our hearts, it is not, in itself, to be censured, if it be kept within due bounds. For Joseph is not here reproved because he manifests his grief by weeping; but his filial piety is rather commended. We have, however, need of the rein, and of self-government, lest, through intemperate grief, we are hurried, by a blind impulse, to murmur against God:

for excessive grief always precipitates us into rebellion. More-over, the mitigation of sorrow is chiefly to be sought for, in the hope of a future life, according to the doctrine of Paul.

2. *And Joseph commanded his servants.* Although for-merly more labour was expended on funerals, and that even without superstition, than has been deemed right subse-quently to the proof given of the resurrection exhibited by Christ :[1] yet we know that among the Egyptians there was greater expense and pomp than among the Jews. Even the ancient historians record this among the most memorable customs of that nation. Indeed it is not to be doubted (as we have said elsewhere) that the sacred rite of burial de-scended from the holy fathers, to be a kind of mirror of the future resurrection : but as hypocrites are always more dili-gent in the performance of ceremonies, than they are, who possess the solid substance of things ; it happens that they who have declined from the true faith, assume a far more ostentatious appearance than the faithful, to whom pertain the truth and the right use of the symbol. If we compare the Jews with ourselves, these shadowy ceremonies, in which God required them to be occupied, would, at this time, ap-pear intolerable ; though compared with those of other nations, they were moderate and easily to be borne. But the heathen scarcely knew why they incurred so much labour and expense. Hence we infer how empty and trivial a mat-ter it is, to attend only to external signs, when the pure doctrine which exhibits their true origin and their legitimate end, does not flourish. It is an act of piety to bury the dead. To embalm corpses with aromatic spices, was, in former times, no fault; inasmuch as it was done as a public symbol of future incorruption. For it is not possible but that the sight of a dead man should grievously affect us ; as if one common end, without distinction, awaited both us and the beasts that perish. At this day the resurrection of Christ is a sufficient support for us against yielding to this temptation. But the an-

---

[1] Que depuis que Jesus Christ nous a baillé claire demonstrance de la resurrection des morts—than since the time that Jesus Christ has given us a clear demonstration of the resurrection of the dead.—*French Trans-lation.*

cients, on whom the full light of day had not yet shone, were aided by figures : they, however, whose minds were not raised to the hope of a better life, did nothing else than trifle, and foolishly imitate the holy fathers.   Finally, where faith has not so breathed its odour, as to make men know that something remains for them after death, all embalming will be vapid.   Yea, if death is to them the eternal destruction of the body, it would be an impious profanation of a sacred and useful ceremony, to attempt to place what had perished under such costly custody.   It is probable that Joseph, in conforming himself to the Egyptians, whose superfluous care was not free from absurdity; acted rather from fear than from judgment, or from approval of their method.   Perhaps he improperly imitated the Egyptians, lest the condition of his father might be worse than that of other men.   But it would have been better, had he confined himself to the frugal practice of his fathers.   Nevertheless though *he* might be excusable, the same practice is not now lawful for *us.* For unless we wish to subvert the glory of Christ, we must cultivate greater sobriety.

3. *And forty days were fulfilled for him.*   We have shown already that Moses is speaking of a ceremonial mourning ; and therefore he does not prescribe it as a law, or produce it as an example which it is right for us to follow.   For, by the laws, certain days were appointed, in order that time might be given for the moderating of grief in some degree ; yet something also was conceded to ambition.   Another rule, however, for restraining grief is given to us by the Lord. And Joseph stooped, more than he ought, to the perverted manners of the Egyptians ; for the world affects to believe that whatever is customary is lawful ; so that what generally prevails, carries along everything it meets, like a violent inundation.   The seventy days which Moses sets apart to solemn mourning, Herodotus, in his second book, assigns to the embalming.   But Diodorus writes that the seasoning of the body was completed in thirty days.   Both authors diligently describe the method of embalming.   And though I will not deny that, in the course of time, the skill and industry in practising this art increased, yet it appears to me

probable that this method of proceeding was handed down
from the fathers.[1]

4. *Joseph spake unto the house of Pharaoh.* A brief narration is here inserted of the permission obtained for Joseph, that, with the goodwill and leave of the king, he might
convey his father's remains to the sepulchre of "the double
cave." Now, though he himself enjoyed no common degree
of favour, he yet makes use of the courtiers as his interces-
sors. Why did he act thus, unless on the ground that the
affair was in itself odious to the people? For nothing (as
we have said before) was less tolerable to the Egyptians, than
that their land, of the sanctity of which they made their especial boast, should be despised. Therefore Joseph, in order to
transfer the offence from himself to another, pleads necessity:
as if he would say, that the burying of his father was not
left to his own choice, because Jacob had laid him under
obligation as to the mode of doing it, by the imposition of an
oath. Wherefore, we see that he was oppressed by servile
fear, so that he did not dare frankly and boldly to profess
his own faith; since he is compelled to act a part, in order
to transfer to the deceased whatever odium might attend
the transaction. Now, whereas a more simple and upright
confession of faith is required of the sons of God, let none
of us seek refuge under such pretexts: but rather let us
learn to ask of the Lord the spirit of fortitude and constancy which shall direct us to bear our testimony to true
religion. Yet if men allow us the free profession of religion,
let us give thanks for it. Now, seeing that Joseph did not
dare to move his foot, except by permission of the king, we
infer hence, that he was bound by his splendid fortune, as
by golden fetters. And truly, such is the condition of all
who are advanced to honour and favour in royal courts; so
that there is nothing better for men of sane mind, than to be
content with a private condition. Joseph also mitigates the
offence which he feared he was giving, by another circum-

[1] It would appear that the mourning for Jacob was a kind of royal
mourning. "On the death of every Egyptian king, a general mourning
was instituted throughout the country for seventy-two days."—*Manners
and Customs of the Ancient Egyptians, by Sir J. G. Wilkinson,* vol. i.
p. 255.—*Ed.*

stance, when he says, that the desire to be buried in the
land of Canaan was not one which had recently entered into
his father's mind, because he had dug his grave there long
before ; whence it follows that he had not been induced to
do so by any disgust taken against the land of Egypt.

5. *And Pharaoh said.*   We have seen that Joseph adopts
a middle course.   For he was not willing utterly to fail in
his duty ; yet, by catching at a pretext founded on the command of his father, he did not conduct himself with sufficient
firmness.   It is possible that Pharaoh was inclined, by the
modesty of his manner, more easily to assent to his requests.
Yet this cowardice is not, on that account, so sanctioned that
the sons of God are at liberty to indulge themselves in it:
for if they intrepidly follow where duty calls, the Lord will
give the issue which is desired, beyond all expectation.   For,
although, humanly speaking, Joseph's bland submission succeeded prosperously, it is nevertheless certain that the proud
mind of the king was influenced by God to concede thus
benignantly what had been desired.   It is also to be observed, what great respect for an oath prevailed among blind
unbelievers.   For, though Pharaoh himself had not sworn,
he still deemed it unlawful for him to violate, by his own
authority, the pledge given by another.   But at this day, reverence for God has become so far extinct, that men commonly
regard it as a mere trifle to deceive, on one side or another,
under the name of God.   But such unbridled license, which
even Pharaoh himself denounces, shall not escape the judgment of God with impunity.

7. *And Joseph went up.*   Moses gives a full account of
the burial.   What he relates concerning the renewed mourning of Joseph and his brethren, as well as of the Egyptians, ought by no means to be established as a rule among
ourselves.   For we know, that since our flesh has no self-
government, men commonly exceed bounds both in sorrowing and in rejoicing.   The tumultuous clamour, which the
inhabitants of the place admired, cannot be excused.   And
although Joseph had a right end in view, when he fixed the
mourning to last through seven successive days, yet this
excess was not free from blame.   Nevertheless, it was not

without reason that the Lord caused this funeral to be thus honourably celebrated : for it was of great consequence that a kind of sublime trophy should be raised, which might transmit to posterity the memory of Jacob's faith. If he had been buried privately, and in a common manner, his fame would soon have been extinguished ; but now, unless men wilfully blind themselves, they have continually before their eyes a noble example, which may cherish the hope of the promised inheritance : they perceive, as it were, the standard of that deliverance erected, which shall take place in the fulness of time. Wherefore, we are not here to consider the honour of the deceased so much as the benefit of the living. Even the Egyptians, not knowing what they do, bear a torch before the Israelites, to teach them to keep the course of their divine calling : the Canaanites do the same, when they distinguish the place by a new name ; for hence it came to pass that the knowledge of the covenant of the Lord flourished afresh.[1]

14. *And Joseph returned.* Although Joseph and the rest had left so many pledges in Egypt, that it would be necessary for them to return ; it is yet probable that they were rather drawn back thither by the oracle of God. For God never permitted them to choose an abode at their own will ; but as he had before led Abraham, Isaac, and Jacob in their journeyings, so he held their sons shut up in the land of Goshen, as within barriers. And there is no doubt that the holy fathers left that oracle which we have in the fifteenth chapter and the thirteenth verse, to their sons, to be kept in faithful custody as a precious treasure.[2] They return, therefore, into Egypt, not only because they were compelled by present necessity, but because it was not lawful for them to

[1] Calvin, in his criticism on Joseph's conduct with reference to his father's funeral, seems to bear hard upon the motives of the patriarch. As there is nothing in Joseph's previous history which is derogatory either to his moral courage or his integrity, it is scarcely justifiable to impute a want of firmness and of straightforwardness to him on this occasion. Is not the concluding portion of Calvin's remarks a sufficient answer to all that has gone before? And may we not conclude, that the whole of the circumstances of Jacob's funeral were divinely ordered to perpetuate his memory?—*Ed.*

[2] " And he said unto Abram, Know of a surety that thy seed shall be a stranger in a land that is not theirs, and shall serve them; and they shall afflict them four hundred years."

shake off with the hand, the yoke which God had put upon
their necks. But if the Lord does not hold all men bound by
voluntary obedience to himself, he nevertheless holds their
minds by his secret rein, that they may not withdraw themselves from his government ; nor can we form any other conjecture than that they were restrained by his fear, so that
even when admonished of the tyrannical oppression which
was coming upon them, they did not attempt to make their
escape. We know that their disposition was not so mild as
to prevent them from rebelling against lighter burdens.
Wherefore, on this point, a special sense of religious obligation subdued them, so that they prepared themselves quietly
and silently to endure the hardest servitude.

15. *And when Joseph's brethren saw that their father was
dead.* Moses here relates, that the sons of Jacob, after the
death of their father, were apprehensive lest Joseph should
take vengeance for the injury they had done him. And
whence this fear, but because they form their judgment of
him according to their own disposition ? That they had found
him so placable they do not attribute to true piety towards
God, nor do they account it a special gift of the Spirit : but
rather, they imagine that, out of respect to his father alone,
he had hitherto been so far restrained, as barely to postpone
his revenge. But, by such perverse judgment, they do a great
injury to one who, by the liberality of his treatment, had borne
them witness that his mind was free from all hatred and ma-
levoience. Part of the injurious surmise reflected even upon
God, whose special grace had shone forth in the moderation
of Joseph. Hence, however, we gather, that guilty consciences
are so disturbed by blind and unreasonable fears, that they
stumble in broad day-light. Joseph had absolved his brethren from the crime they had committed against him ; but
they are so agitated by guilty compunctions, that they voluntarily become their own tormentors. And they have not
themselves to thank, that they did not bring down upon
themselves the very punishment which had been remitted ;
because the mind of Josep'. might well have been wounded
by their distrust. For, what could they mean by still malignantly suspecting him to whose compassion they had again

and again owed their lives ?   Yet I do not doubt, that long
ago they had repented of their wickedness ; but, perhaps,
because they had not yet been sufficiently purified, the Lord
suffered them to be tortured with anxiety and trouble : first,
to make them a proof to others, that an evil conscience
is its own tormentor, and, then, to humble them under a renewed sense of their own guilt ; for, when they regard themselves as obnoxious to their brother's judgment, they cannot
forget, unless they are worse than senseless, the celestial
tribunal of God.   What Solomon says, we see daily fulfilled,
that " the wicked flee when no man pursueth ;" (Prov. xxviii.
1 ;) but, in this way, God compels the fugitives to give up
their account.   They would desire, in their supine torpor, to
deceive both God and men ; and they bring upon their
minds, as far as they arc able, the callousness of obstinacy :
in the mean time, whether they will or no, they are made to
tremble at the sound of a falling leaf, lest their carnal security should obliterate their sense of the judgment of God.
(Lev. xxvi. 36.)   Nothing is more desirable than a tranquil mind.   While God deprives the wicked of this singular
benefit, which is desired by all, he invites us to cultivate integrity.   But especially, seeing that the patriarchs, who were
already affected with penitence for their wickedness, are yet
thus severely awakened, a long time afterwards, let none of
us yield to self-indulgence ; but let each diligently examine
himself, lest hypocrisy should inwardly cherish the secret
stings of the wrath of God ; and may that happy peace,
which can find no place in a double heart, shine within our
thoroughly purified breasts.   For this due reward of their
neglect remains for all those who do not draw nigh to God
sincerely and with all their heart, that they are compelled
to stand before the judgment-seat of mortal man.   Wherefore, there is no other method which can free us from disquietude, but that of returning into favour with God.   Whosoever shall despise this remedy, shall be afraid not only of
man, but also of a shadow, or a breath of wind.

16. *And they sent a messenger.*   Because they are ashamed themselves to speak, they engage messengers of peace, in
whom Joseph might have greater confidence.   But here also

we perceive that they who have an accusing conscience are
destitute of counsel and of reason. For if Jacob had been
solicitous on this point, why did he not effect reconciliation
between the son who was so obedient unto himself, and his
brethren ? Besides, for what reason should they attempt to
do that through mediators, which they could do so much
better in their own persons ? The Lord, therefore, suffers
them to act like children ; that we, being instructed by their
example, may look for no advantage from the use of frivolous inventions. But it may be asked, where the sons of
Jacob found men to whom they could venture to commit
such a message ; for it was no light thing to make known
their execrable crime to strangers ? And it would have been
folly to subject themselves to this infamy among the Egyptians. The most probable conjecture is, that some domestic
witnesses were chosen from the number of their own servants ;
for though Moses makes no mention of such, when he relates
that Jacob departed into Egypt ; yet that some were brought
with him, may easily be gathered from certain considerations.

17. *Forgive, I pray thee now.* They do not dissemble the
fact that they had grievously sinned ; and they are so far
from extenuating their fault, that they freely heap up
words in charging themselves with guilt. They do not,
therefore, ask that pardon should be granted them as if the
offence were light : but they place in opposition to the atrocity of their crime, first, the authority of their father, and
then the sacred name of God. Their confession would have
been worthy of commendation, had they proceeded directly,
and without tortuous contrivances, to appease their brother.
Now, since they have drawn from the fountain of piety the
instruction that it is right for sin to be remitted to the servants of God ; we may receive it as a common exhortation,
that if we have been injured by the members of the Church,
we must not be too rigid and immoveable in pardoning the
offence. This humanity indeed is generally enjoined upon
us towards all men : but when the bond of religion is superadded, we are harder than iron, if we are not inclined to the
exercise of compassion. And we must observe, that they

expressly mention the God of Jacob: because the peculiar faith and worship by which they were distinguished from the rest of the nations, ought to unite them with each other in a closer bond: as if God, who had adopted that family, stood forth in the midst of them as engaged to produce reconciliation.

And Joseph wept when they spake unto him. It cannot be ascertained with certainty from the words of Moses, whether the brethren of Joseph were present, and were speaking, at the time he wept. Some interpreters imagine that a part was here acted designedly; so that when the mind of Joseph had been sounded by others, the brethren, soon afterwards, came in, during the discourse. I rather incline to a different opinion; namely, that, when he knew, from the messengers, that their minds were tormented, and they were troubling themselves in vain, he was moved with sympathy towards them. Then, having sent for them, he set them free from all care and fear; and their speech, when they themselves were deprecating his anger, drew forth his tears. Moreover, by thus affectionately weeping over the sorrow and anxiety of his brethren, he affords us a remarkable example of compassion. But if we have an arduous conflict with the impetuosity of an angry temper, or the obstinacy of a disposition to hatred, we must pray to the Lord for a spirit of meekness, the force of which manifests itself not less effectually, at this day, in the members of Christ, than formerly in Joseph.

19. *Am I in the place of God ?* Some think that, in these words, he was rejecting the honour paid him: as if he would say, that it was unjustly offered to him, because it was due to God alone. But this interpretation is destitute of probability, since he often permitted himself to be addressed in this manner, and knew that the minds of his brethren were utterly averse to transfer the worship of God to mortal man. And I equally disapprove another meaning given to the passage, which makes Joseph refuse to exact punishment, because he is not God: for he does not restrain himself from retaliating the injury, in the hope that God will prove his avenger. Others adduce a third signification; namely, that the whole affair was conducted by the counsel of God, and

not by his own : which though I do not entirely reject, because it approaches the truth, yet I do not embrace the interpretation as true.   For the word תחת (*tachat*) sometimes signifies *instead of*, sometimes it means *subjection*.   Therefore if the note of interrogation were not in the way, it might well be rendered, " Because I am *under* God ;" and then the sense would be, " Fear not, for I am under God ;" so that Joseph would teach them, that because he is subject to the authority of God, it is not his business to lead the way, but to follow.   But, whereas ה, the note of interrogation, is prefixed to the word, it cannot be otherwise expounded than to mean that it would be wrong for him, a mortal man, to presume to thwart the counsel of God.   But as to the sum of the matter, there is no ambiguity.   For seeing that Joseph considers the design of divine providence, he restrains his feelings as with a bridle, lest they should carry him to excess. He was indeed of a mild and humane disposition; but nothing is better or more suitable to assuage his anger, than to submit himself to be governed by God.   When, therefore, the desire of revenge urges us, let all our feelings be subjected to the same authority.   Moreover, since he desires his brethren to be tranquil and secure, from the consideration, that he, ascribing due honour to God, willingly submits to obey the Divine command ; let us learn, hence, that it is most to our advantage to deal with men of moderation, who set God before them as their leader, and who not only submit to his will, but also cheerfully obey him.   For if any one is impotently carried away by the lust of the flesh, we must fear a thousand deaths from him, unless God should forcibly break his fury. Now as it is the one remedy for assuaging our anger, to acknowledge what we ourselves are, and what right God has over us ; so, on the other hand, when this thought has taken full possession of our minds, there is no ardour, however furious, which it will not suffice to mitigate.

20. *Ye thought evil against me.*   Joseph well considers (as we have said) the providence of God ; so that he imposes it on himself as a compulsory law, not only to grant pardon, but also to exercise beneficence.   And although we have treated at large on this subject, in the forty-fifth chapter,

yet it will be useful also to repeat something on it now. In the first place, we must notice this difference in his language: for whereas, in the former passage, Joseph, desiring to soothe the grief, and to alleviate the fear of his brethren, would cover their wickedness by every means which ingenuity could suggest; he now corrects them a little more openly and freely; perhaps because he is offended with their disingenuousness. Yet he holds to the same principle as before. Seeing that, by the secret counsel of God, he was led into Egypt, for the purpose of preserving the life of his brethren, he must devote himself to this object, lest he should resist God. He says, in fact, by his action, " Since God has deposited your life with me, I should be engaged in war against him, if I were not to be the faithful dispenser of the grace which he had committed to my hands." Meanwhile, he skilfully distinguishes between the wicked counsels of men, and the admirable justice of God, by so ascribing the government of all things to God, as to preserve the divine administration free from contracting any stain from the vices of men. The selling of Joseph was a crime detestable for its cruelty and perfidy; yet he was not sold except by the decree of heaven. For neither did God merely remain at rest, and by conniving for a time, let loose the reins of human malice, in order that afterwards he might make use of this occasion; but, at his own will, he appointed the order of acting which he intended to be fixed and certain. Thus we may say with truth and propriety, that Joseph was sold by the wicked consent of his brethren, and by the secret providence of God. Yet it was not a work common to both, in such a sense that God sanctioned anything connected with or relating to their wicked cupidity: because while they are contriving the destruction of their brother, God is effecting their deliverance from on high. Whence also we conclude, that there are various methods of governing the world. This truly must be generally agreed, that nothing is done without his will; because he both governs the counsels of men, and sways their wills and turns their efforts at his pleasure, and regulates all events: but if men undertake anything right and just, he so actuates and moves them inwardly by his Spirit, that whatever is good in them, may justly be said to be received from him : but if Satan and ungodly men rage, he acts by their hands in such an inexpressible manner, that the wickedness of the deed belongs to them, and the blame of it is imputed to them. For they are not induced to sin, as the faithful are to act aright, by the impulse of the Spirit, but they are the authors of their own evil, and follow Satan as their leader. Thus we see that the justice of God shines brightly in the midst of the darkness of our iniquity. For as God is never without a just cause for his actions, so men are held in the chains of guilt by their own perverse will. When we hear that God frustrates the wicked expectations, and the injurious desires of men, we derive hence no common consolation. Let the impious busy themselves as they please, let them rage, let them mingle heaven and earth ; yet they shall gain nothing by their ardour; and not only shall their impetuosity prove ineffectual, but shall be turned to an issue the reverse of that which they intended, so that they shall promote our salvation, though they do it reluctantly. So that whatever poison Satan produces, God turns it into medicine for his elect. And although in this place God is said to have " meant it unto good," because contrary to expectation, he had educed a joyful issue out of beginnings fraught with death : yet, with perfect rectitude and justice, he turns the food of reprobates into poison, their light into darkness, their table into a snare, and, in short, their life into death. If human minds cannot reach these depths, let them rather suppliantly adore the mysteries they do not comprehend, than, as vessels of clay, proudly exalt themselves against their Maker.

To save much people alive. Joseph renders his office subservient to the design of God's providence ; and this sobriety is always to be cultivated, that every one may behold, by faith, God from on high holding the helm of the government of the world, and may keep himself within the bounds of his vocation ; and even, being admonished by the secret judgments of God, may descend into himself, and exhort himself to the discharge of his duty : and if the reason of this does not immediately appear, we must still take care that we do not fly in confused and erratic circuits, as fanatical men are wont to do. What Joseph says respecting his being divinely chosen "to save much people alive," some extend to the Egyptians. Without condemning such an extension, I would rather restrict the application of the words to the family of Jacob ; for Joseph amplifies the goodness of God by this circumstance, that the seed of the Church would be rescued from destruction by his labour. And truly, from these few men, whose seed would otherwise have been extinct before their descendents had been multiplied, that vast multitude sprang into being, which God soon afterwards raised up.

21. *I will nourish you.* It was a token of a solid and not a feigned reconciliation, not only to abstain from malice and injury, but also to "overcome evil with good," as Paul teaches, (Rom. xii. 21:) and truly, he who fails in his duty, when he possesses the power of giving help, and when the occasion demands his assistance, shows, by this very course, that he is not forgetful of injury. This requires to be the more diligently observed, because, commonly, the greater part weakly conclude that they forgive offences if they do not retaliate them ; as if indeed we were not taking revenge when we withdraw our hands from giving help. You would assist your brother if you thought him worthy : he implores your aid in necessity ; you desert him because he has done you some unkindness ; what hinders you from helping him but hatred ? Therefore, we shall then only prove our minds to be free from malevolence, when we follow with kindness those enemies by whom we have been ill treated. Joseph is said to have spoken "to the heart of his brethren," because, by addressing them with suavity and kindness, he removed all their scruples ; as we have before seen, that Shechem spoke to the heart of Dinah, when he attempted to console her with allurements, in order that, forgetting the dishonour he had done her, she might consent to marry him.

22. *And Joseph dwelt in Egypt.* It is not without reason that Moses relates how long Joseph lived, because the length of the time shows the more clearly his unfailing constancy : for although he is raised to great honour and power among the Egyptians, he still is closely united with his father's

house. Hence it is easy to conjecture, that he gradually took his leave of the treasures of the court, because he thought there was nothing better for him to do than to hold them in contempt, lest earthly dignity should separate him from the kingdom of God. He had before spurned all the allurements which might have occupied his mind in Egypt: he now counts it necessary to proceed further, that, laying aside his honour, he may descend to an ignoble condition, and wean his own sons from the hope of succeeding to his worldly rank. We know how anxiously others labour, both that they themselves may not be reduced in circumstances, and that they may leave their fortune entire to their posterity: but Joseph, during sixty years, employed all his efforts to bring himself and his children into a state of submission, lest his earthly greatness should alienate them from the little flock of the Lord. In short, he imitated the serpents, who cast off their *exuviæ*, that, being stripped of their old age, they may gather new strength. He sees the children of his own grandchildren; why does not his solicitude to provide for them increase, as his children increase? Yet he has so little regard for worldly rank or opulence, that he would rather see them devoted to a pastoral life, and be despised by the Egyptians, if only they might be reckoned in the family of Israel. Besides, in a numerous offspring during his own life, the Lord afforded him some taste of his benediction, from which he might conceive the hope of future deliverance: for, among so many temptations, it was necessary for him to be encouraged and sustained, lest he should sink under them.

24. *And Joseph said unto his brethren.* It is uncertain whether Joseph died the first or the last of the brethren, or whether a part of them survived him. Here indeed Moses includes, under the name of brethren, not only those who were really so, but other relations. I think, however, that certain of the chiefs of each family were called at his command, from whom the whole of the people might receive information: and although it is probable that the other patriarchs also gave the same command respecting themselves, since the bones of them all were, in like manner, conveyed

into the land of Canaan; yet special mention is made of
Joseph alone, for two reasons. First, since the eyes of them
all were fixed upon him, on account of his high authority, it
was his duty to lead their way, and cautiously to beware lest
the splendour of his dignity should cast a stumblingblock
before any of them.   Secondly, it was of great consequence,
as an example, that it should be known to all the people,
that he who held the second place in the kingdom of Egypt,
regardless of so great an honour, was contented with his own
condition, which was only that of the heir of a bare promise.

I die. This expression has the force of a command to
his brethren to be of good courage after his death, because
the truth of God is immortal; for he does not wish them to
depend upon his life or that of another man, so as to cause
them to prescribe a limit to the power of God; but he would
have them patiently to rest till the suitable time should
arrive.   But whence had he this great certainty, that he
should be a witness and a surety of future redemption, except from his having been so taught by his father?   For we
do not read that God had appeared unto him, or that an
oracle had been brought to him by an angel from heaven;
but because he was certainly persuaded that Jacob was a
divinely appointed teacher and prophet, who should transmit
to his sons the covenant of salvation deposited with him;
Joseph relies upon his testimony not less securely than if
some vision had been presented to him, or he had seen angels
descending to him from heaven: for unless the hearing of
the word is sufficient for our faith, we deserve not that
God, whom we then defraud of his honour, should condescend to deal with us: not that faith relies on human authority, but because it hears God speaking through the mouth
of men, and by their external voice is drawn upwards;
for what God pronounces through men, he seals on our
hearts by his Spirit. Thus faith is built on no other foundation than God himself; and yet the preaching of men
is not wanting in its claim of authority and reverence.
This restraint is put upon the rash curiosity of those men,
who, eagerly desiring visions, despise the ordinary ministry
of the Church; as if it were absurd that God, who for-

merly showed himself to the fathers out of heaven, should send forth his voice out of the earth. But if they would reflect how gloriously he once descended to us in the person of his only-begotten Son, they would not so importunately desire that heaven should daily be opened unto them. But, not to insist upon these things; when the brethren saw that Joseph,—who in this respect was inferior to his fathers, as having been partaker of no oracle,—had been imbued by them with the doctrine of piety, so that he contended with a faith similar to theirs; they would at once be most ungrateful and malignant, if they rejected the participation of his grace.

25. *God will surely visit you.* By these words he intimates that they would be buried as in oblivion, so long as they remained in Egypt: and truly that exile was as if God had turned his back on them for a season. Nevertheless, Joseph does not cease to fix the eyes of his mind on God; as it is written in the Prophet, "I will wait upon the Lord that hideth his face from the house of Jacob." (Is. viii. 17.) This passage also clearly teaches what was the design of this anxious choice of his sepulchre, namely, that it might be a seal of redemption: for after he has asserted that God was faithful, and would, in his own time, grant what he had promised, he immediately adjures his brethren to carry away his bones. These were useful relics, the sight of which plainly signified that, by the death of men, the eternal covenant in which Joseph commands his posterity safely to rest, had by no means become extinct; for he deems it sufficient to adduce the oath of God, to remove all their doubts respecting their deliverance.

INDEX

OF HEBREW WORDS EXPLAINED.

INDEX

OF PASSAGES OF HOLY SCRIPTURE QUOTED OR REFERRED TO IN THE COMMENTARY AND NOTES ON THE BOOK OF GENESIS.

GENERAL INDEX.

A

ABEL, was probably Cain's twin brother, i. 189, 191; his profession a keeper of sheep, 192; respect which God had to him and to his sacrifice, 194-196; is murdered by Cain, 204, 205.

Abimelech, king of Gerar, in the time of Abraham, takes Sarah, Abraham's wife, to his house, i. 522; is warned by God in a dream not to injure her, 523; asserts his innocence, 524; is compassionated by God, 525; is commanded to restore Sarah to Abraham, 525, 526; obeys the command, 527; his kindness to Abraham, 532; Abraham's prayer in his behalf, 533; covenant between him and Abraham, 551-556.

Abimelech, king of the Philistines in the time of Isaac, reproves Isaac for having given out that Rebekah was his sister, ii. 58, 61, 62; denounces capital punishment against such as should injure Isaac, 63, 65, 66, 72; desires to enter into covenant with Isaac, 72-75; the covenant between them, 76.

Abram, or Abraham, son of Terah, means of determining the period between the deluge and the calling of, i. 332; his calling to be accounted the renovation of the Church, 333; his father and grandfather apostates from the true worship of God, 333, 334; was not his father's eldest son, 335; his wife Sarah's sterility, 338; leaves his native soil and proceeds to Canaan in obedience to the command of God, 338, 340-346; was, previous to this, plunged in idolatry, 343, 387; the divine promises made to him, 346-349, 410, 411, 414-420, 444-459, 571, 572; the strength of his faith,

346, 350, 352, 353, 357, 358, 376, 386, 411, 412, 459, 460, 464, 547, 560, 561, 563, 564, 567, 568; builds an altar to God in token of his gratitude, 353, 356, 368, 377; his faith directed to the blood of Christ, 355; his continual wanderings, 356, 357; goes down to Egypt, 358; persuades his wife to use dissimulation, 359; his sin in this, 360, 362, 365; his departure from Egypt, 367; his wealth, ib.; strife between his herdsmen and those of Lot, 370, 371; his endeavours to restore peace, 371, 372; is treated unjustly by Lot, 372, 373; this loss made up to him by God, 374, 375; rescues Lot from the four kings, 383; entered into covenants of friendship with the princes of Canaan, 384; is called an Hebrew from his ancestor Eber, ib.; undertakes war by the direction of God's Spirit, 383-386; is entertained and blessed by Melchizedek, 386, 387, 391, 392; gives tithes to Melchizedek, 392; his freedom from avarice, 394, 395; his complaint of being childless, 401, 402; his faith of having a numerous seed strengthened by the sight of the stars, 403, 404; was justified by faith alone, 404-406; the time when he was thus justified, 408, 409; offers sacrifice at the command of God, 412, 413; is promised a placid and quiet death, 418; the nations enumerated whose land was to be given to his offspring, 421; is prevailed upon by Sarah to take Hagar as a concubine, 424; long believed Ishmael to be the promised seed, 442; his name changed from Abram to Abraham, 447; the covenant made with him a spiritual one, 450; is promised a legitimate seed by Sarah, 459; his prayer in behalf of Ishmael, 461;

ated the world in a moment refuted, 78, 103; the history of the
creation the book of the unlearned,
80; philosophical accuracy of language not studied by Moses in his
history of it, 85-87; was distributed
over six days for our sake, 92;
after its completion the work approved of God, 100.

Crime and fault, great difference between, i. 524.

Crimes, celebrity of name gained by,
evils of, i. 246.

Cross, the, to be borne patiently, ii.
102.

Cruelty, its hatefulness to God, ii. 444.

Cupidity condemned, ii. 509.

Cups, divining by, prevalent among the
Egyptians, ii. 368.

Curse pronounced on the serpent, i.
166-168; and on Adam, after his
apostasy, 172-180; and on the earth
for his sin, 173, 174.

Curtius, Quintus quoted, i. 123.

D

DAN, character and future condition of
the tribe of, predicted by Jacob on
his death-bed, ii. 462, 463.

Day of salvation to be improved without delay, ii. 95.

Dead, the, mourning for, if duly moderated, lawful, i. 578; closing their
eyes an ancient custom, ii. 390;
principle in which the embalming
of them originated, 477. See *Burial.*

Dead Sea, or the lake Asphaltites, i.
381.

D'Albret, Jeanne, Queen of Navarre,
Calvin's encomium on her as a
friend of the Reformation, i. xlvi,
xlvii.

Death, the effect of sin, i. 127, 179,
180; is fitted to correct the pride
of man, 328; peace in, the great
distinction between the reprobate
and the children of God, 417; is
not the destruction of the whole
man, ii. 38; peace in, the effect of
a good conscience, 473.

Deborah, Rebekah's nurse, her great
age and death, ii. 239.

Decrees of God, in vain for men to
strive to defeat them, ii. 90; have
no affinity with the crimes of men,
379.

Deluge, the, reasons unknown to us
why the Spirit of God has left so
imperfect an account of the state

of the world between it and the
creation, i. 227; was caused by the
wickedness of man, 240, 247, 253,
255; the divine forbearance previously long exercised toward mankind, 241, 247, 249; why it involved
the inferior animals in destruction,
250; its approach foretold to Noah,
254; probably commenced in spring,
264, 280; was brought on gradually,
270, 271; is not to be ascribed to
chance, 272, 273, 278; Noah's deliverance from it a figure of baptism, 273; its waters abated by
the instrumentality of the winds,
277, 278; is never again to be
repeated, 283; complete restoration of the world subsequent to it,
286; fabulous account of it by the
heathen poets, 313; rapid multiplication of mankind after it, 314,
380, 381.

Depravity of man, is total and universal, i. 248, 284, 285; manifested in
the early and rapid corruption of
the descendents of Shem, 333, 334.
See *Corruption of human nature.*

Devils, their enmity against God, i.
212; are his executioners, 505.

Diligence commended, ii. 24, 338.

Dinah, probably the only daughter of
Jacob, ii. 148, 170; her vain curiosity, 218; her chastity violated by
Shechem, 218; is desired by Shechem in marriage, 219, 393.

Dinners in use among the Egyptians,
ii. 359.

Dionysius impiously boasted that the
gods favour the sacrilegious, i. 222.

Dissimulation, to be guarded against,
ii. 273, 369.

Distinction between the godly and ungodly, i. 411, 417, 418; ii. 347, 348.

Distinction between the true and hypocritical Church, i. 547.

Distinctions of rank advantageous, i.
246.

Divining by cups, prevalent among the
Egyptians, ii. 368.

Divorce, not to be rashly allowed, i.
136; more tolerable than polygamy, ii. 133.

Dominion, the lust of, prevalent among
men in all ages, i. 380.

Dove, sent forth by Noah from the
ark after the water of the deluge
began to abate, i. 279.

Dreams, a means by which God was
wont to reveal his secrets, i. 414,
526; ii. 112, 261, 306, 307, 387.

109 ; is blessed by his father, 98, 99 ; becomes an exile from the kingdom of God, 98, 99 ; purposes to murder Jacob, 100; attempts reconciliation with his father, but not careful about pleasing God, 108 ; marries a third wife, 109 ; his impious and ferocious character, 187 ; meets Jacob with unexpected benevolence and kindness, 207 ; interview between him and Jacob, 208 ; his descendents, 252. See *Judas*.

Eternity of the world maintained by Aristotle, i. xlix.

Eucherius held the tree of life to be a figure of Christ, i. 117.

Eunuch, a term applied to satraps and princes of the courts of oriental kings, ii. 274, 301, 306.

Euphrates, the, i. 118, 119, 121, 122.

Europeans, Japheth, the progenitor of, i. 313.

Eve, her formation, i. 128, 129, 131, 132, 135 ; objection against the manner of her formation answered, 133 ; is tempted and overcome by Satan, 146-151 ; prevails on Adam to eat the forbidden fruit, 151, 152; in what her first sin consisted, 152-154 ; her sense of shame after her fall, 158, 159 ; her attempt at self-defence before God, 164, 165 ; sentence pronounced upon her, 171 ; her name given her by Adam, 181; was a true worshipper of God, 224. See *Adam. Cain. Abel.*

Events, future, not now revealed by God, ii. 43.

Evils, sin the cause of all, i. 177.

Example of the saints not to be imitated, unless agreeable to the word of God, i. 253, 412 ; ii. 21, 71, 120, 134, 339, 389.

Examples, evil, the worst contagion, i. 230, 252.

Eye, the, an inlet to sin, ii. 295.

Eyes of the dead, closing them an ancient custom, ii. 390.

F

FABLES, Jewish, i. 337, 495, 540, 570, 576.

Face of God, what is meant by one's being hidden from, i. 212.

Fair complexion, anciently deemed a recommendation in Egypt, i. 360.

Faith, our knowledge that the worlds were created by the word of God

to be traced to, i. 63 ; how it produces purity, 195 ; is an active principle, 258, 346, 353 ; is supported by external symbols, 298, 412, 451 ; ii. 387 ; should remain unshaken, amidst the greatest outward distresses, i. 358, 376 ; ii. 107 ; in what sense it justifies, i. 407 ; good men not justified first by faith and afterwards by works, 408, 409 ; cannot be disjoined from a pure conscience, 445; its only foundation the word of God, 446 ; ii. 422 ; springs from election, i. 449 ; its property to take encouragement for the future from the experience of the past, 510 ; secures victory over temptations, 562 ; is often mixed with anxious care, ii. 20 ; distinguishes the spiritual from the carnal seed of Abraham, 45 ; is not exempt from all fear, 189.

Faith of Abraham. See *Abraham.*

Faith of Isaac. See *Isaac.*

Faith of Lot. See *Lot.*

Faith of Noah. See *Noah.*

Faithful, the, are justified by faith alone, like Abraham, i. 407; are liable to be assailed on every side, 414 ; their prayers are heard by God, 434, 516, 526 ; ii. 19, 42 ; are useful to others, 106; are the true Israelites, 242. See *People of God.*

Faithfulness of God, i. 538 ; ii. 23.

Fall of man. See *Adam. Eve. Satan. Serpent.*

Falling on the face, the ancient rite of adoration, i. 445.

Falsehood, God's truth not to be aided by, ii. 88.

Fathers, the patriarchal, were animated by the hope of a better life, i. 576; are not to be imitated in opposition to the law of God, 253, 412 ; ii. 21, 71, 120, 134, 339, 389.

Fault and crime, great difference between, i. 524.

Faults of good men, the, why many studiously pry into, i. 303.

Fear, the fruit of iniquity, i. 216.

Fear of God, may, from the corruption of our nature, degenerate into a fault, i. 476; is not inconsistent with faith, 481, 482; ii. 117, 118 ; the want of it leads to all kinds of wickedness and cruelty, i. 529; ii. 180 ; actuates all the pious, 177; is the source of integrity, 343.

Feasts, convivial, not forbidden, i. 542.

Feet, washing of the, a custom in the East, i. 471.

Felicity, God the source of, to his people, i. 400.

First-born, why called " the beginning of strength," ii. 442; advantages of primogeniture, ii. 53, 208, 248.

Fishes and birds, created on the fifth day of the creation, i. 88.

Flatterers of kings, i. 362.

Flesh, a name applied by God to man as a mark of ignominy, i. 242 ; and also without any mark of censure, 253; "all flesh," a name given to animals of every kind, 259.

Forbearance of God, i. 329, 374, 418, 419, 484, 485, 526.

Forgiveness, duty of, ii. 376, 484, 489; men more ready to forgive themselves than others, 288.

Fortune, the Deluge not to be ascribed to, i. 272, 273, 278.

Fratricide, abhorrence of the crime of, among the heathen, ii. 265.

Fraud of Laban. See Laban.

French Protestant Bible, the first, Calvin's share in it, i. xvi.

Frugality commended, i. 491.

Funerals, pride displayed in, i. 328; were conducted with greater expense and pomp among the Egyptians than among the Jews, ii. 477. See Burial.

Future events, not now revealed by God, ii. 43.

Future life, a, known to the patriarchs, ii. 38, 91, 92, 115, 417, 477 ; consolation of, the chief mitigation of sorrow, 274.

G

Gad, son of Jacob, his birth, ii. 145 ; future condition of the tribe of, predicted by Jacob on his death-bed, 465.

Ganges, the river, incorrectly supposed to be Pison, i. 119. 123.

Garden of Eden. See Eden.

Genesis, the great object of the book of, i. 64, 65.

Geneva version of the Bible, its author, i. xvii.

Gentiles, their calling to the faith of the gospel predicted, i. 309, 446, 447, 449, 450; ii. 460.

Gerundensis, ii. 306.

Giants, the antediluvian, why so called, i. 244 ; were proud and ferocious

tyrants, 246 ; were the first nobility, ib. ; fables invented by the heathen poets concerning, 246, 324.

Gihon, incorrectly thought by many to be the Nile, i. 119, 124.

God, curious inquiries into his *essence* condemned, i. 60; nature of his rest on the seventh day after the creation of the world, 103 ; works constantly in the government of the world, 103 ; is not the author of evil, 142, 144 ; his care of his own people, 208, 276, 400, 416, 430, 517, 523, 550; ii. 26, 61, 136, 150, 171, 208, 233 ; what is implied in one's being hidden from his face, i. 212; human affections ascribed to him, 247, 249 ; has no need of new counsel, after the manner of men, 250, 478 ; uses the language of irony, 330 : his authority should regulate us in everything, 350, 351; is the source of his people's felicity, 400; allows them to question him, 411; two ways in which he looks down upon men for the purpose of helping them, 433; what is meant by living before him, 461 ; stretches forth his hand to save his people at the critical moment, 502 ; different ways in which he is said to be present with men, 551 ; in what sense he is said to tempt men, 561 ; ii. 196 ; sometimes speedily answers prayer and sometimes delays the answer, ii. 19, 80 ; how the name " man" is applied to him, 197 ; what is meant by seeing him face to face, 202; he restrains the cruelty of the wicked, 207 ; sense in which ascending and descending are ascribed to him, 242; distinction between his *willing* and *permitting* certain things condemned, 378, 487; makes use of the wickedness of men for accomplishing his purposes, 379, 488; his sovereignty in distributing his gifts, 431. See *Faithfulness of God. Forbearance of God. Grace of God. Judge of the World. Power of God. Providence of God. Truth of God.*

Godly and ungodly, distinction between them, i. 411, 417, 418 ; ii. 347, 348.

Gomorrah, wickedness of its inhabitants, i. 483, 484, 491; is destroyed by fire and brimstone from heaven, 512; why infants were involved in that destruction, 513. See *Sodom.*

Good, the. See *People of God.*
Goshen, position of the land of, ii. 393, 394, 398.
Gospel, impediments to the preaching of it through the whole world, i. 465; is to be offered indiscriminately to all, 503; the preaching of it called "the kingdom of heaven," ii. 118; the pride of man opposed to it, 264.
Government of God. See *Providence of God.*
Government, civil, is not to be violated, i. 431.
Government, monarchical, chosen by God for his ancient people as the most perfect form, ii. 450.
Grace of God, is not bound to the accustomed order of nature, i. 431; is what makes one man excel another, ii. 52.
Grass, the earth on the third day of the creation commanded to bring it forth, i. 82.
Gratitude to God. See *Thanksgiving.*
Gratitude to man, duty of, i. 386, 393.
Greek interpreters or Septuagint. See *Septuagint.*
Greek translations of the Pentateuch, were procured by Ptolemy, king of Egypt, i. xlviii.
Gregory I., Pope, argument by which he defends statues and pictures in churches, i. 80.
Grief at the wickedness of men, in what sense it is ascribed to God, i. 249.
Grief, immoderate, on the death of friends to be restrained, ii. 273; if duly moderated is not to be censured, 476; the consolation of a future life the chief mitigation of, 274.

H

HAGAR, Sarah's handmaid, i. 425, 426; begins to hold her mistress in contempt, 427; is met in the wilderness in her flight from the house of her mistress by an angel, 430; is reproved by him for her flight, 432; is encouraged by him, 432-434; betakes herself to prayer, 435; her previous character, 435, 438; her penitential spirit, 437, 438; is ejected with her son Ishmael from the family of Abraham, 541, 547, 548; her distress after her ejection, 549; is met by an angel, 550; ii. 36.
Ham, the youngest son of Noah, i. 235; mocks his father, 301; his

wicked character, 302; why the judgment of God for his mockery of his father is pronounced on his son Canaan and not on himself, 305-307; was the progenitor of the Africans, 313.
Hamor, the father of Shechem, endeavours to obtain Dinah, Jacob's daughter, for his son in marriage, ii. 222; perfidy and cruelty of Jacob's sons towards, 222-228.
Haran, son of Terah, and brother of Abraham, his death, i. 337.
Harp and organ invented by Jubal, i. 218.
Harvest and seed time secured so long as the earth endures, i. 286; songs sung at the ingathering of harvest, ii. 355.
Havila, the land of, i. 123.
Head, to lift up one's head, what it denotes, ii. 309; to lift up the head from off one, its meaning, 311.
Heart, integrity of, proceeds from God, ii. 343.
Hearts of men are in the hand of God, ii. 73, 207, 237, 345, 355.
Heathen, the, were the first cultivators of astronomy and medicine, i. 218.
Heathen philosophers, their ignorance of the creation and origin of the world and of the human race, i. xlviii, xlix.
Heathen poets, their fables concerning the antediluvian giants, i. 246, 324; their fabulous account of the deluge, 313; and of the rapid multiplication of men after it, 381, 513.
Heathen sacrifices, their origin, i. 193.
Heavens and earth, God exhibited in, i. 59; our eyes not sufficiently clear-sighted to discern what they represent, 62; the knowledge to be thence derived not sufficient for salvation, ib.
Hebrews, the, derived their name from Eber, a descendent of Shem, i. 320; ii. 361; the Egyptians forbidden by their religion to eat with, ii. 360. See *Israelites. Jews.*
Hebrew Doctors. See *Jewish Writers.*
Hebrew language has no neuter gender, i. 533.
Hebrew points, i. 189; ii. 418.
Hebron, was anciently called Kirjath-arba, i. 576.
Hengstenberg, Dr., his explanation of the word Elohim, i. 72, 108, 110.
Henry IV. of France, Calvin's Commentary on Genesis dedicated to

him when a boy, i. xlv ; Calvin's advices to him, liii, liv.

Herbs and trees, why created before the sun and moon, i. 82.

Hiddekel, a name applied to the Tigris, i. 118, 121-123.

History, advantages of the study of, i. 480.

Historians, heathen, are fabulous in treating of a remote antiquity, i. xlix.

Holy life, a, is inseparable from true faith, i. 445.

Homicide, frivolous distinction of, into four kinds by the Jews, i. 249.

Honour due to parents, i. 302 ; ii. 14, 264.

Honours to be conferred only on the deserving, ii. 327.

Horace quoted, i. 177, 327.

Hospitality, is practised by Abraham, i. 468 ; the duty of, 469 ; Lot distinguished for, 495, 496, 498 ; the oppression of the Israelites in Egypt a violation of the law of, ii. 402.

Human nature, corruption of, the consequence of Adam's fall, i. 154, 248, 284 ; its transmission from Adam, 156. See *Adam*.

Human race, why God willed that they should proceed from one source, i. 97.

Humanity commended and enjoined, i. 294, 348, 428, 469 ; ii. 128, 345 ; humanity of Reuben, ii. 267.

Husbands, duty of wives to obey their, i. 474, 533 ; brides in the East given veiled to their, ii. 29 ; are not to be too obsequious to their wives, 301.

Hypocrisy, God's hatred of, i. 196 ; is to be guarded against, 443 ; ii. 143 ; is deeply rooted in the human mind, 224, 266, 343 ; hypocrisy of Jacob's sons, 267.

Hypocrites, nothing sincere in their religious worship, i. 196, 197 ; their pretended friendship to be dreaded, 204 ; distinguished from the genuine worshippers of God, 354 ; always seek excuses, 476 ; mingle in the Church with the people of God, and despise them, 546, 547 ; ii. 48 ; a lively picture of them exhibited in Esau, ii. 100, 109 ; never truly repent, 109 ; ascribe their prosperity to God's favour for them, 143, 172 ; heap false complaints upon the good, 172 ; disguise one sin by another, 272.

Hypotyposis, a rhetorical figure, its meaning, i. 330.

I

Idleness condemned, i. 125 ; ii. 238, 332.

Idolatry, propensity of the human mind to, ii. 169, 170, 358 ; madness of, 173, 174, 234, 235.

Idumeans, the, are descended from Abraham, i. 446 ; were cut off from the body of the Church, ii. 44, 98, 99 ; Isaac's prediction concerning, 99, 253, 254.

Image of God in which man was created, Augustine's refined speculations concerning, i. 93 ; is erroneously referred by Anthropomorphites to the human body, 94 ; in what it consists, 94, 95 ; image of God and likeness of God phrases of synonymous import, 93, 94 ; why Paul denies the woman to be the image of God, 96 ; Christ the living image of God, ii. 202.

Images, popish, worship of, ii. 174.

Immortality, not to be sought on earth, i. 327.

Impatience, to be guarded against, i. 427.

Impunity of the wicked is sometimes an occasion of alluring even the good to sin, i. 254.

Incest, is abhorrent to nature, ii. 246, 288.

Infants, error of the Anabaptists in denying that God's covenant is common to, i. 297, 298 ; cruel superstition of consigning them to perdition when a sudden death has prevented their being baptized, 458 ; why involved in the destruction of Sodom and Gomorrah, 513 ; unnatural for mothers not to nurse their own, 540.

Ingratitude, entered into the first sin of Adam and Eve, i. 153 ; is to be guarded against, 438, 521, 549 ; ii. 26, 54, 74, 201.

Inheritance, or felicity, reward put for, i. 400.

Iniquity, fear, the fruit of, i. 216.

Injuries, duty in reference to, ii. 172, 177, 489.

Insects, noxious, are to be traced to the sin of man, i. 104.

Integrity of heart particularly required by God, i. 443; integrity of life proceeds from the fear of God, ii. 343.

surreptitiously obtains his father's
blessing, 84, 86, 87, 88 ; his death
resolved on by Esau, 100 ; is forced
in consequence to become a wanderer from his father's house, 101,
102 ; has pronounced on him anew,
previous to his departure, the blessing by his father, 105, 106 ; trial
of his faith, 108 ; the arduousness
of his journey, 111 ; his vision of
the ladder, 112, 114-116 ; how he
was the fountain of blessedness to
all nations, 116 ; extols the goodness of God, 117 ; erects a stone as
a memorial of gratitude for the vision, 118 ; his vows to God, 120-
123 ; pours a libation on the stone
he had erected, 123 ; arrives in
Mesopotamia at the house of his
uncle Laban, 127 ; informs his
uncle of his circumstances, 128 ;
employs himself in honest labours,
129 ; is hardly dealt with by his
uncle, 130, 150, 151, 154, 165, 176;
his affection for Rachel, his uncle's
daughter, 131 ; is deceived by Laban, and marries Leah, 132 ; also
marries Rachel, 134; fails in kindness to Leah, 135 ; his polygamy
punished by domestic strife, 140,
147 ; is hurried by Rachel into a
third marriage, 142 ; desires to
leave Laban and return to his parents, 149 ; his treaty with Laban,
by which he was to receive the
spotted offspring of the sheep and
goats, 152 ; his device for making
the sheep and goats bring forth a
spotted offspring, 155, 156 ; is
treated inhumanely by Laban's
sons, 162, 163 ; returns to his own
country under the special guidance
of God, 163 ; his wives consent to
go with him, 164, 165, 167, 168 ;
dream in which an angel of the
Lord appeared to him, 165 ; is
pursued by Laban, who accuses
him of robbery, 171-173 ; his defence, 174-178 ; his placable character, 179; covenant between him
and Laban, 178-180; his alarm at
the prospect of meeting his brother
Esau, 185, 205 ; the means he
adopts for appeasing his brother,
188 ; betakes himself to prayer,
190 ; acknowledges his own want
of merit, 191, 192; his rich present
to his brother, 194 ; wrestles with
God, who appeared to him in the
form of a man, 195-197 ; prevails,

198, 199 ; his name changed from
Jacob to Israel, 200, 240; his reverence towards his brother, 206 ;
is met by Esau with unexpected
kindness, 207, 211 ; interview between the two brothers, 208, 210;
his suspicion of Esau, 211 ; erects an
altar, 213 ; his grief on hearing of
the violation of his daughter Dinah's
chastity, 220 ; the perfidy and cruelty of his sons to the Shechemites,
222-228; expostulates with them,
228 ; is commanded by God to go
up to Bethel, 233 ; purifies his house
from idols, ib. ; his infirmity in
burying the idols under an oak and
not rather destroying them, 236 ;
builds an altar at Bethel, 237; his
numerous trials, 243 ; loses Rachel
by death, 244; his grief for Joseph,
when sold by his brethren, 272,273;
his ten sons go down to Egypt to
buy corn, 337, 346; his suspicion of
his sons, 348 ; their second journey
into Egypt, 353 ; allows with difficulty his son Benjamin to go down
with them, 355-357; his feelings on
hearing that Joseph was alive and
governor of Egypt, 383; his deep
rooted piety, 387; his vision in which
God ratifies his former covenant
with him, 387-389 ; goes down to
Egypt with his family, 390; Goshen
selected as an abode for him and
his sons by Joseph, 393, 394, 398;
his descendants providentially kept
from intermarrying with the Egyptians, 395, 400; condition on which
his sons wished to live in Egypt,
402; is introduced to Pharaoh by
Joseph, 403; binds Joseph by an
oath to bury him in Canaan, 416,
417; his address to his sons on his
death-bed, and his predictions concerning the future fortunes of their
families, 420-472; charges his sons
to bury him in Canaan, 472 ; his
placid death, 473; mourning for
him by his sons and the Egyptians,
476; is buried in Canaan, 480; his
funeral honourably celebrated, 481.
Japheth, the eldest son of Noah, i. 235,
320 ; his filial piety and modesty,
302, 303; the benediction his father
pronounces on him, 308; was the
progenitor of the Europeans, 313.
Jehovah, a name of God, place where
it first occurs in Scripture, and its
meaning, i. 109.
Jerome, i. 113; his petulant reproaches

against the married state, 128 ;
quoted, 131, 160, 200, 245, 278, 280,
294, 317, 388, 437, 473, 485, 566,
583, 584; ii. 19, 22, 435, 453.

Jerusalem was anciently called Salem,
i. 388.

Jews, the, began the day with the
evening, i. 77; divide their year
into six parts, 286; their forming
one church with the Gentiles predicted, 309, 446, 447; their error
in holding circumcision to be still
in force, 456; their foolish gloria-
tion in the origin of their nation,
ii. 50, 146, 226; their superstition,
203. See *Hebrews. Israelites.*

Jewish Calendar, i. 264, 286.

Jewish Writers, their ridiculous opinion respecting God's holding communication with the earth and angels at the creation of man, i. 92,
107; imagine Abel's sacrifice was
consumed by fire from heaven, 196,
200, 213; their fable respecting
Lamech, 219, 228; and concerning
Abraham, 337, 349, 436; and concerning the angels who appeared
to Lot, 495; and concerning Sarah's
giving milk, 540; and concerning
the ram which appeared on Mount
Moriah when Abraham was about
to sacrifice his son, 570; and concerning Sarah's beauty in her old
age, 576; their frivolous distinction
of four kinds of homicide, 294.

Job, his unbecoming language under
the pressure of affliction, ii. 273.

Joseph, son of Jacob by Rachel, his
birth, ii. 149; is wickedly conspired against by his brethren, 253;
the cause of this his father's partiality for him, 259; his future eminence revealed to him in dreams,
260-262, 340; was a type of Christ,
261, 266; his brethren's envy and
hatred of him increased by their
knowledge of his dreams, 262, 263;
his death cruelly contrived by them,
264-266; his murder prevented by
the humanity of Reuben, 267, 268;
is sold by them to a company of
Midianites, 270, 271; his brethren's
false report to his father that he
had been torn in pieces by wild
beasts, 271-273; is sold by the Midianites to Potiphar, the Egyptian,
274; gains the favour of Potiphar,
293; is placed by Potiphar over his
house and over all his substance,
294; was distinguished for the graces

of his person, 295; is tempted by
the wife of Potiphar, 296; his fidelity and integrity, 296-298; is falsely accused by her, 300; is cast into
prison by Potiphar, 300, 301; conciliates the goodwill of the keeper
of the prison, 302, 303; interprets
the dream of Pharaoh's chief butler,
and chief baker, 307-310; is forgotten by the chief butler after his restoration to office, 312; interprets
Pharaoh's dreams, 324, 325; is
made governor of Egypt, 328; and
has the precedence of all its nobles,
329; his marriage to the daughter
of the Prefect of the city On, 330;
his labours in erecting storehouses,
331; his ten brethren come down
to Egypt to buy corn, 337; his apparent harshness towards them,
338; his swearing by the life of
Pharaoh censurable, 341, 342; shuts
his brethren up in prison, 342; endeavoured to establish the worship
of the true God in his own family,
359; his affection for Benjamin,
362; entertains his brethren, 359-
362; was sparing in domestic splendour, 367; his dissimulation towards
his brethren, 368, 369; makes himself known to them, 375, 376; borrows from the providence of God
an argument for exercising forgiveness towards them, 380, 382; selects Goshen as an abode for them
and his father, 393, 394, 398; his
faithful administration, 407, 410;
his singular humanity, 414; his father binds him by an oath to bury
him in Canaan, 416, 417; his faith,
422; his two sons Ephraim and Manasseh are blessed by Jacob, 426,
430-432; his grief on his father's
death, 476; buries his father in Canaan, 480; his affection for his brethren, 485, 486, 488; his death-bed
scene, ii. 490-492.

Josephus quoted, i. 278, 583.

Jovinian, Jerome's book against, i. 128.

Jubal, a descendent of Cain, the inventor of the harp and organ, i. 218.

Judas, character of his repentance, i.
211. See *Esau.*

Judah, son of Jacob, his sin in marrying a Canaanitish woman, ii. 278,
279; his perfidy and cruelty to
Tamar, his daughter-in-law, 282-
286; his incest with her, 283, his
purpose of bringing her to punishment, 286, 287; acknowledges his

preciousness in the sight of God, 523; are tried according to the measure of their faith, 564; have no reason for languishing when their outward man is perishing, ii. 37; may lawfully complain of their enemies, 73; are not always governed in their actions by the Spirit of God, 85; are for the most part despised by the world, 136; in what sense God wrestles with them, 196; their deliverance delayed for the trial of their faith, 312; are strangers and pilgrims in this world, 404; difference in the way in which temporal benefits are bestowed on them and on unbelievers, 428; are purified by the divine chastisements, 471, 472. See *Faithful.*

Perfection, angelical, erroneously placed in poverty, i. 367.

Pharaoh, king of Egypt when Abraham sojourned in that country, i. 362-365.

Pharaoh, king of Egypt in Joseph's time, casts his chief butler and chief baker into prison, ii. 305; restores the chief butler to his office, 310; beheads the chief baker, 311; celebrates his birth-day, 312; his dreams, 318, 319; and their interpretation by Joseph, 324, 325; makes Joseph governor of Egypt, 328; gratuitously maintains the Egyptian priests during the famine, ii. 412.

Philistines, the, their cruelty, ii. 65.

Philosophers condemned, who in studying the works of creation are forgetful of the Creator, i. 60. See *Heathen philosophers.*

Piety, how its genuineness is proved, i. 482; a sense of, implanted in the minds of men, ii. 413.

Pious, the. See *People of God.*

Pison, the, incorrectly thought by many to be the Ganges, i. 119, 123.

Plato, character of his writings, i. xlix; ascribes reason and intelligence to the stars, 87; defends the sacredness of the marriage tie, 128, 388; his remarks on the hope of the virtuous in old age, 417; ii. 37, 324.

Pliny quoted, i. 121-123.

Plurality of persons in the Godhead, proved from the Mosaic account of the creation of man, i. 92, 183; farther proof of, 331; is not proved from the history of the destruction of Sodom and Gomorrah, 513, 531.

Poets, heathen. See *Heathen poets.*

Polygamy condemned, i. 97; inconsistent with the original divine institution of marriage, 136, 137, 424, 573; ii. 33, 142; was introduced by Lamech, a descendant of Cain, i. 217; began at an early period to prevail in every direction, ii. 77, 181, 252.

Pomponius Mela quoted, i. 121.

Poor, the, admonished, i. 369.

Pope, the, i. 307; his barbarity in imposing celibacy on the clergy, i. 551; ii. 14, 219.

Popish religion, its character, i. 446. See *Papists.*

Porphyry, his cavil in reference to the ark refuted, i. 257.

Posterity of Adam. See *Adam. Corruption of Human nature. Man. Mankind.*

Potiphar, an officer of the court of Pharaoh, king of Egypt, buys Joseph from the Midianites, ii. 274; his favour for him, 293; places him over his house and over all his substance, 294; his wife tempts Joseph, 296-298; and falsely accuses him, 300; he casts Joseph into prison, 300, 301; his anger towards Joseph is mitigated, 306.

Poverty, angelical perfection erroneously placed in, i. 367; does not want its advantages, ii. 65.

Power of God, the, is not to be estimated by human reason, i. 475; by doubting the divine promises, we sinfully detract from, 476; is not limited because he is unable to destroy the reprobate without saving the elect, 511.

Prayer, ought to be regulated by the will of God, i. 509; ii. 17, 190, 191; its answer sometimes speedily granted, and at other times delayed, ii. 19, 20; manner in which it ought to be performed, 17, 190, 191; encouragement to perseverance in, 42; ought to be accompanied with the use of means, 193; is the armour which renders us invincible in affliction, 302.

Prayers of the faithful, are heard by God, i. 434, 516, 526; ii. 19, 42; are useful to others, ii. 106.

Pride, betrayed itself in the first sin of Adam and Eve, i. 153; is with difficulty corrected, 328; its punishment, 548; is natural to the human heart, ii. 144; is the companion of unbelief, 173 ; is opposed to the Gospel, 264.

Pride of the Egyptians, ii. 360, 361.

Pride of the Sodomites, i. 501.

Priesthood, Levitical, subordinate to the priesthood of Christ, i. 303.

Priests, Egyptian, were gratuitously maintained by Pharaoh during the famine, ii. 412.

Priests, Levitical, were to bless the people, i. 391; ii. 199.

Primogeniture, or birthright, advantages of, ii. 53, 208, 248.

Profession of religion. See *Religion.*

Prolepsis, a rhetorical figure, its meaning, i. 344, 356, 553; ii. 180, 187, 212, 391, 435.

Promises of God, the faith of his people established by their being repeated, i. 265; by doubting them we sinfully detract from God's power, 476; the fulfilment of them sometimes long deferred, ii. 116.

Prophecies of Scripture, are nearly all written in verse, i. 305 ; ii. 441.

Prophets, the ancient, excited hatred by uttering the divine threatenings, ii. 311 ; the true distinguished from the false, 326.

Prosperity, is to be ascribed to God, ii. 74, 151, 193, 211, 293; intoxicates men, ii. 326, 341.

Proud, the, fight against God, i. 327, 328, 331. See *Pride.*

Providence of God, is to be reposed on when God seems to be most forgetful of us, i. 276; human affairs under, 436 ; success in our affairs to be ascribed to, ii. 23, 112, 127; its secret influence keeps men from destroying each other, 208 ; watches for the salvation of the righteous when it most seems to sleep, 232 ; Joseph's history a beautiful example of, 260, 307, 330, 378-380; is inseparable from God's eternal counsel, 325 ; admirable method of the operation of, 337, 376.

Ptolemy, king of Egypt, procured the translation of the books of Moses into Greek, i. xlviii.

Punishment, a dread of, not true repentance, i. 211 ; its inefficacy to bring the wicked to true repentance, ii. 98 ; while remitting the guilt of sin, God does not retain the punishment, 445.

Purity, how it is the effect of faith, i. 195.

R

Rabbins, Jewish, referred to, i. 85, 130.

Race, a, resemblance of human life to, i. 402.

Rachel, daughter of Laban, ii. 127; is greatly beloved by Jacob, 131, 205; becomes his wife, 134 ; envies her sister Leah, 141 ; hurries Jacob into a third marriage, 142 ; her pride, 144; contention between her and her sister Leah, 140, 147, 148; birth of her son Joseph, 149; is willing to leave her father's house, and accompany Jacob to his own country, 167, 168; carries off her father's household gods, 169 ; her superstition, 170; manner in which she concealed her theft, 175; her death, 244 ; her burial, 245, 425, 462.

Rain, is in the hand of God, i. 80, 11f, 512.

Rainbow, the, existed before the deluge, i. 299; was consecrated into a sign or pledge giving security against a second deluge, 290.

Rank, distinctions of, advantageous, i. 246.

Raven sent forth by Noah from the ark, i. 279.

Rebekah, is providentially selected by Abraham's servant as a wife for Isaac, ii. 20-23; her parents are induced to give her to Isaac in marriage, 24, 25; her departure from her father's house, 27; she meets Isaac, 29; is married to him, ib. ; her sterility during the first twenty years of her married state, 40; asks counsel of God, 43 ; loves Jacob more than Esau, 50; her sinful stratagem to procure for Jacob his father's blessing, 84, 85, 87 ; her trial from Esau's purpose to murder Jacob, 101-103.

Reclining at table, a patriarchal custom, ii. 362.

Reformation. See *Calvin. Erasmus.*

Religion, a, is not to be rashly changed, ii. 225.

Religion, Popish, its character, i. 446. See *Papists.*

Religion, an external profession of, requisite, i. 354; ii. 71, 213, 214, 238; a sense of religion is engraven on the hearts of all men, 358.

Remission of the *fault* and of the *punishment*, a distinction unfounded, i. 178.

of the human family, 146; his artifice in tempting the woman, 146-151; overcomes her, 151; sentence pronounced on him, 168-171; has set himself from the beginning to corrupt the worship of God, 223; is an ingenious contriver of falsehoods, 246, 569; is a wonderful adept at deceiving, 401; his wiles to be guarded against, 425; is God's executioner, 504; is the ape of God, ii. 69; in what way he tempts, i. 169; ii. 191, 192, 196, 246, 295.

Satiety produces ferocity, ii. 66; and disgust, 332.

Saturn, the planet, reference to, 86, 87.

Schismatics denounced, i. lii.

Scriptures, the, are not to be tortured to an allegorical sense, i. 257, 279, 545; ii. 438, 439, 461.

Scripture, the prophecies of, are nearly all written in verse, i. 305; ii. 441.

Security of the wicked, i. 505; ii. 54, 111; carnal, to be guarded against, ii. 234.

Seed of the woman, means her posterity generally, i. 170.

Seed of Abraham, meaning of the words, i. 171.

Seed-time and harvest secured as long as the earth endures, i. 28.

Seeking God, best method of, ii. 428.

Self-love blinds us in judging of what is right, ii. 129, 178, 224.

Self-renunciation enjoined, ii. 351.

Semiramis, i. 121; is said to have founded Babylon, i. 318.

Senses, the, inlets to sin, ii. 295.

Septuagint, the, greatly neglected by the heathen, i. xlviii; quoted, 131, 136, 160, 199, 242, 279, 498; ii. 330, 391, 418.

Sepulchre purchased by Abraham, i. 583; ii. 417.

Serpent, made use of by Satan for seducing our first parents, i. 140, 145; how it is called subtle, 140; is to be understood literally and not allegorically, 142; is said to have done what Satan did by its instrumentality, 166; the sentence pronounced upon it, 166-168.

Servants, male and female, termed "souls," i. 351; their duty when harshly treated by their masters, 431.

Servetus, maintained that Christ was the son of God, only as to his human nature, i. 75.

Seth, his birth and the piety of himself and his family, i. 223, 224; the offspring of Adam traced only in the Mosaic narrative through the line of Seth, because the Church was confined to his family, 227, 228, 234; was born, like others of Adam's children, in sin, 228, 229; the corruption of his descendants by intermarrying with the daughters of Cain, 237-240, 245; why his descendants are called "the sons of God," 238, 239.

Seven, the number, designates in Scripture a multitude, i. 222.

Shechem, or Sichem, i. 352; ii. 212, 434.

Shechem, violates the chastity of Dinah, Jacob's daughter, ii. 218; desires to obtain her in marriage, 219, 222; perfidy and cruelty of the sons of Jacob towards, 222-228.

Shechemites, the, their idolatry, ii. 214; facility with which they submit to be circumcised, 225; the perfidy and cruelty of Jacob's sons towards, 222-228, 447.

Shekel of the sanctuary, its value, i. 583.

Shem, the second son of Noah, i. 235; his filial piety and modesty, 302, 303; blessing pronounced on him by his father, 308; was the progenitor of the Asiatics, 313; the Mosaic history principally relates to his race, 314; the benediction pronounced on him did not descend to all his offspring indiscriminately, but only to the sons of Eber, 320; a great part of his posterity apostatized from the true worship of God, 333.

Shepherds, the occupation of, held in abomination by the Egyptians, ii. 395, 399.

Shield, God ascribes to himself the office and property of, i. 400.

Shiloh, meaning and reference of the term, ii. 453.

Sichem. See Shechem.

Siddim, battle fought in the vale of, i. 381.

Signs, their use, i. 298, 453; are not to be severed from God's word, 298; 420, 451; ii. 388; the faithful ascend from them to heaven, 215.

Simeon, son of Jacob, his cruelty to the Shechemites, ii. 226, 229; is retained in prison by his brother Joseph, 346, 348, 359; his cruelty

Way of the Lord, what it denotes, i. 482.

Wealth. See *Riches.*

Wealthy, the. See *Rich.*

Whittingham, William, brother-in-law to Calvin, was the author of the Geneva version of the Bible, i. xvii.

Wicked, the, character of their repentance, i. 211; ii. 95, 108, 109; make the offences of others a pretext for indulgence in sin, i. 302; their trouble in death, 418; their obstinacy in sin, 552; ii. 299; despise God's threatenings, i. 505; their security, ib.; ii. 54, 111; are forgetful of God, 101; are not able altogether to despise his grace, 108; their terror of God, 118, 177; judge of others by their own dispositions, 179; their cruelty restrained by God, 207; often do good to the faithful contrary to their intention, 253; are devoted to destruction, 305. See *Reprobate.*

Wickedness of man is not excused because God may overrule it for good, ii. 379.

Will of God, why manifested to us, i. 481; nothing done without it, ii. 378, 487.

Winds, the, are governed by God, i. 277.

Wine, introduction of its use, i. 300; may be used in moderation, ii. 362, 363.

Wisdom, first step of, to ascribe nothing to ourselves, ii. 323.

Wives, their duty to obey their husbands, i. 474, 533; ii. 300, 301.

Woman, a contraction for womb-man, i. 135.

Woman, the, why denied by Paul to be the image of God, i. 96; was created to be the help-meet of man, 128, 129; was necessary to man even in a state of innocency, 130, 131; her subjection to her husband, 172; effects of Eve's first transgression upon her, ib.

Woman, seed of the, meaning of, i. 171.

Women, rarely mentioned in Scripture genealogies, i. 573; ii. 148.

Word, or promise of God, to be trusted in, 267, 276; is better than external signs, 299; is conjoined with symbols, 421, 451; ought not to be separated from his power, 476; tranquillizes the mind, ii. 70; is sometimes forgotten in affliction, 340; faith founded upon, 422.

Word of God, or the Scriptures, the most certain rule of our life, i. 539; ii. 87, 134; ought not to be adulterated, 311. See *Scriptures.*

Works, good, what is necessary to their being so, i. 194, 195, 409; do not justify, 265, 407, 572; the grace of Christ alone gives them worth, 266; the rewards of them are the rewards of grace, 265, 572; ii. 302.

World, the, its eternity maintained by Aristotle, i. xlix; not eternal, 70, 109; the error that God created it in a moment refuted, 78, 103; why God took the space of six days in creating it, 78; its continual preservation to be ascribed to him, 103, 104; the physical disorders in it the fruit of sin, 104, 177. See *Creation,* &c.

World, the allurements of, to be guarded against, ii. 332.

Worldly advantages are not to be suffered to draw us aside from the path of duty, ii. 112.

Worship of God, faith necessary in order to its being acceptable, i. 282; use of, ii. 71; early and extensive apostasy of mankind from it after the deluge, 166-170, 237.

Worshippers of God, the true, distinguished from hypocrites, i. 344.

Y

Year, the, began, according to the Jewish calendar, in March, i. 264; was divided by the Jews into six parts, 286.

Z

Zeal, preposterous, ii. 87.

Zebulon, character of the tribe of, predicted by Jacob on his death-bed, ii. 461.

Geneva